## MATTHEW

# THE NIV
# APPLICATION
# COMMENTARY

*From biblical text . . . to contemporary life*

# THE NIV APPLICATION COMMENTARY SERIES

MATTHEW

# THE NIV APPLICATION COMMENTARY

*From biblical text . . . to contemporary life*

## MICHAEL J. WILKINS

ZONDERVAN™

GRAND RAPIDS, MICHIGAN 49530 USA

*For*

*Barbara and Stuart Campbell*

*Margaret and John Melia*

*Leon and Mary Wilkins*

*Parental figures in our lives who have modeled discipleship to Jesus for us*

# ZONDERVAN™

*The NIV Application Commentary: Matthew*
Copyright © 2004 by Michael J. Wilkins

Requests for information should be addressed to:

Zondervan, *Grand Rapids, Michigan 49530*

---

**Library of Congress Cataloging-in-Publication Data**

Wilkins, Michael J.
　　Matthew / Michael J. Wilkins—1st ed.
　　　　p. cm.—(NIV application commentary)
　　Includes bibliographical references and indexes.
　　ISBN: 0-310-49310-2
　　1. Bible. N.T. Matthew—Commentaries. I. Title. II. Series.
BS2575.53 .W55 2004
226.2'077—dc22　　　　　　　　　　　　　　　2003022094
　　　　　　　　　　　　　　　　　　　　　　　CIP

---

*Printed in the United States of America*

---

04 05 06 07 08 09 10 /❖ DC/ 10 9 8 7 6 5 4 3 2 1

# Contents

7
**Series Introduction**

11
**General Editor's Preface**

13
**Author's Preface**

15
**Abbreviations**

19
**Introduction**

37
**Outline of Matthew's Gospel**

47
**Bibliography**

53
**Text and Commentary on Matthew**

973
**Scripture Index**

1000
**Subject Index**

# The NIV Application Commentary Series

When complete, the NIV Application Commentary
will include the following volumes:

## Old Testament Volumes

*Genesis*, John H. Walton

*Exodus*, Peter Enns

*Leviticus/Numbers*, Roy Gane

*Deuteronomy*, Daniel I. Block

*Joshua*, L. Daniel Hawk

*Judges/Ruth*, K. Lawson Younger

*1-2 Samuel*, Bill T. Arnold

*1-2 Kings*, Gus Konkel

*1-2 Chronicles*, Andrew E. Hill

*Ezra/Nehemiah*, Douglas J. Green

*Esther*, Karen H. Jobes

*Job*, Dennis R. Magary

*Psalms Volume 1*, Gerald H. Wilson

*Psalms Volume 2*, Gerald H. Wilson

*Proverbs*, Paul Koptak

*Ecclesiastes/Song of Songs*, Iain Provan

*Isaiah*, John N. Oswalt

*Jeremiah/Lamentations*, J. Andrew Dearman

*Ezekiel*, Iain M. Duguid

*Daniel*, Tremper Longman III

*Hosea/Amos/Micah*, Gary V. Smith

*Jonah/Nahum/Habakkuk/Zephaniah*,
　　James Bruckner

*Joel/Obadiah/Malachi*, David W. Baker

*Haggai/Zechariah*, Mark J. Boda

## New Testament Volumes

*Matthew*, Michael J. Wilkins

*Mark*, David E. Garland

*Luke*, Darrell L. Bock

*John*, Gary M. Burge

*Acts*, Ajith Fernando

*Romans*, Douglas J. Moo

*1 Corinthians*, Craig Blomberg

*2 Corinthians*, Scott Hafemann

*Galatians*, Scot McKnight

*Ephesians*, Klyne Snodgrass

*Philippians*, Frank Thielman

*Colossians/Philemon*, David E. Garland

*1-2 Thessalonians*, Michael W. Holmes

*1-2 Timothy/Titus*, Walter L. Liefeld

*Hebrews*, George H. Guthrie

*James*, David P. Nystrom

*1 Peter*, Scot McKnight

*2 Peter/Jude*, Douglas J. Moo

*Letters of John*, Gary M. Burge

*Revelation*, Craig S. Keener

To see which titles are available,
visit our web site at www.zondervan.com

# NIV Application Commentary
# **Series Introduction**

THE NIV APPLICATION COMMENTARY SERIES is unique. Most commentaries help us make the journey from our world back to the world of the Bible. They enable us to cross the barriers of time, culture, language, and geography that separate us from the biblical world. Yet they only offer a one-way ticket to the past and assume that we can somehow make the return journey on our own. Once they have explained the *original meaning* of a book or passage, these commentaries give us little or no help in exploring its *contemporary significance*. The information they offer is valuable, but the job is only half done.

Recently, a few commentaries have included some contemporary application as *one* of their goals. Yet that application is often sketchy or moralistic, and some volumes sound more like printed sermons than commentaries.

The primary goal of the NIV Application Commentary Series is to help you with the difficult but vital task of bringing an ancient message into a modern context. The series not only focuses on application as a finished product but also helps you think through the *process* of moving from the original meaning of a passage to its contemporary significance. These are commentaries, not popular expositions. They are works of reference, not devotional literature.

The format of the series is designed to achieve the goals of the series. Each passage is treated in three sections: *Original Meaning, Bridging Contexts*, and *Contemporary Significance*.

THIS SECTION HELPS you understand the meaning of the biblical text in its original context. All of the elements of traditional exegesis—in concise form—are discussed here. These include the historical, literary, and cultural context of the passage. The authors discuss matters related to grammar and syntax and the meaning of biblical words.[1] They also seek to explore the main ideas of the passage and how the biblical author develops those ideas.

---

1. Please note that in general, when the authors discuss words in the original biblical languages, the series uses a general rather than a scholarly method of transliteration.

After reading this section, you will understand the problems, questions, and concerns of the *original audience* and how the biblical author addressed those issues. This understanding is foundational to any legitimate application of the text today.

THIS SECTION BUILDS a bridge between the world of the Bible and the world of today, between the original context and the contemporary context, by focusing on both the timely and timeless aspects of the text.

God's Word is *timely*. The authors of Scripture spoke to specific situations, problems, and questions. The author of Joshua encouraged the faith of his original readers by narrating the destruction of Jericho, a seemingly impregnable city, at the hands of an angry warrior God (Josh. 6). Paul warned the Galatians about the consequences of circumcision and the dangers of trying to be justified by law (Gal. 5:2–5). The author of Hebrews tried to convince his readers that Christ is superior to Moses, the Aaronic priests, and the Old Testament sacrifices. John urged his readers to "test the spirits" of those who taught a form of incipient Gnosticism (1 John 4:1–6). In each of these cases, the timely nature of Scripture enables us to hear God's Word in situations that were *concrete* rather than abstract.

Yet the timely nature of Scripture also creates problems. Our situations, difficulties, and questions are not always directly related to those faced by the people in the Bible. Therefore, God's word to them does not always seem relevant to us. For example, when was the last time someone urged you to be circumcised, claiming that it was a necessary part of justification? How many people today care whether Christ is superior to the Aaronic priests? And how can a "test" designed to expose incipient Gnosticism be of any value in a modern culture?

Fortunately, Scripture is not only timely but *timeless*. Just as God spoke to the original audience, so he still speaks to us through the pages of Scripture. Because we share a common humanity with the people of the Bible, we discover a *universal dimension* in the problems they faced and the solutions God gave them. The timeless nature of Scripture enables it to speak with power in every time and in every culture.

Those who fail to recognize that Scripture is both timely and timeless run into a host of problems. For example, those who are intimidated by timely books such as Hebrews, Galatians, or Deuteronomy might avoid reading them because they seem meaningless today. At the other extreme, those who are convinced of the timeless nature of Scripture, but who fail to discern its timely element, may "wax eloquent" about the Melchizedekian priest-hood to a sleeping congregation, or worse still, try to apply the holy wars of the Old Testament in a physical way to God's enemies today.

The purpose of this section, therefore, is to help you discern what is timeless in the timely pages of the Bible—and what is not. For example, how do the holy wars of the Old Testament relate to the spiritual warfare of the New? If Paul's primary concern is not circumcision (as he tells us in Gal. 5:6), what *is* he concerned about? If discussions about the Aaronic priesthood or Melchizedek seem irrelevant today, what is of abiding value in these passages? If people try to "test the spirits" today with a test designed for a specific first-century heresy, what other biblical test might be more appropriate?

Yet this section does not merely uncover that which is timeless in a pas-sage but also helps you to see *how* it is uncovered. The authors of the com-mentaries seek to take what is implicit in the text and make it explicit, to take a process that normally is intuitive and explain it in a logical, orderly fash-ion. How do we know that circumcision is not Paul's primary concern? What clues in the text or its context help us realize that Paul's real concern is at a deeper level?

Of course, those passages in which the historical distance between us and the original readers is greatest require a longer treatment. Conversely, those passages in which the historical distance is smaller or seemingly nonex-istent require less attention.

One final clarification. Because this section prepares the way for dis-cussing the contemporary significance of the passage, there is not always a sharp distinction or a clear break between this section and the one that fol-lows. Yet when both sections are read together, you should have a strong sense of moving from the world of the Bible to the world of today.

THIS SECTION ALLOWS the biblical message to speak with as much power today as it did when it was first written. How can you apply what you learned about Jerusalem, Ephesus, or Corinth to our present-day needs in Chicago, Los Angeles, or London? How can you take a message originally spoken in Greek, Hebrew, and Aramaic and com-municate it clearly in our own language? How can you take the eternal truths originally spoken in a different time and culture and apply them to the sim-ilar-yet-different needs of our culture?

In order to achieve these goals, this section gives you help in several key areas.

(1) It helps you identify contemporary situations, problems, or questions that are truly comparable to those faced by the original audience. Because contemporary situations are seldom identical to those faced by the original audience, you must seek situations that are analogous if your applications are to be relevant.

(2) This section explores a variety of contexts in which the passage might be applied today. You will look at personal applications, but you will also be encouraged to think beyond private concerns to the society and culture at large.

(3) This section will alert you to any problems or difficulties you might encounter in seeking to apply the passage. And if there are several legitimate ways to apply a passage (areas in which Christians disagree), the author will bring these to your attention and help you think through the issues involved.

In seeking to achieve these goals, the contributors to this series attempt to avoid two extremes. They avoid making such specific applications that the commentary might quickly become dated. They also avoid discussing the significance of the passage in such a general way that it fails to engage contemporary life and culture.

Above all, contributors to this series have made a diligent effort not to sound moralistic or preachy. The NIV Application Commentary Series does not seek to provide ready-made sermon materials but rather tools, ideas, and insights that will help you communicate God's Word with power. If we help you to achieve that goal, then we have fulfilled the purpose for this series.

The Editors

# General Editor's Preface

IT IS PROBABLY SAFE to say that the most-often read part of the Gospel of Matthew in our day is the Sermon on the Mount (chs. 5–7). The Sermon on the Mount may even be the most read portion of the whole New Testament today. It is easy to imagine why. We live in a moralistic, legalistic, individualistic age. The Sermon on the Mount can be read as a guidebook for ethical living, to be followed regardless of what you think of God, the Jewish community, or the Christian church. Indeed, one of the best thinkers of our age, one of the twentieth-century's finest human beings, Albert Schweitzer, read it this way and said that the Sermon on the Mount captured the essence of Christianity. Unfortunately, this is the wrong way to read the Sermon on the Mount and the Gospel of Matthew as a whole.

Why? Because reading it this way assumes that the way we choose to behave determines who we are and determines our identity. And that's not true at all. What the Gospel of Matthew teaches us in general and what the Sermon on the Mount teaches us in particular is that who we are (or more precisely, whose we are, i.e., whom we choose to follow or identify with) determines how we behave. If we choose to follow Jesus as Messiah, Matthew tells us, then the Sermon on the Mount is a description of how we will behave.

Does this sound like too fine a distinction to make? Does it sound like splitting hairs, like making a mountain out of a molehill? Perhaps it is overstating it just a bit. But the point is worth making simply because viewing the Sermon on the Mount this way changes it from a sermon to an ethical treatise, and it takes the essence of Christianity as a gift of grace and turns it into a modern philosophy. Three important things happen, all of them bad, when we read the Sermon on the Mount incorrectly.

(1) We overestimate our goodness. It is tempting to think of our characters as something we carefully craft, using a brick of honesty here, a two-by-four of generosity there, built on a cement foundation of discipline and energy. In such a scenario we choose the goal and we choose the building methods and materials we need to achieve the goal. And it is up to us to make the grade. Matthew says we are not that good.

(2) We underestimate our capacity for evil. The reason we cannot let our innate, God-created goodness dominate our personalities is because we have been infected with a pervasive force that has radically impaired our ability

to let our lights of goodness shine. We all feel this force and perhaps wish it weren't true. Matthew says we choose to identify with the Messiah because when it comes right down to it, we have no other choice. "Unless you change and become like little children, you will never enter the kingdom of heaven."

(3) We rely less on God than we should. Because we are tempted not to choose first of all to identify with the Messiah and let our characters emerge as a result of that choice rather than vice versa, we decide to do a little remedial work to make ourselves a little more acceptable to God before we submit. When we make that choice, however, we make it impossible to rely on God as we should. We reserve a bit, usually quite a bit, of what we think is self-creative energy to make ourselves acceptable in God's sight. In that reserve, we change the message of the gospel.

The Sermon on the Mount is an impossible ideal if read as an ethical treatise to which we need to measure up. It is a wonderful description of what we can become if we identify ourselves with Christ and allow his love to express itself through us. Read that way, it is a glorious promise of what we are and what we will become: the hope of Christian living that Matthew saw so clearly.

Terry C. Muck

# Author's Preface

MATTHEW'S GOSPEL HAS HELD a special place in my life for over twenty-five years. The last five years in particular have been the most rewarding. Writing a commentary of this nature, with the three sections—Original Meaning, Bridging Contexts, and Contemporary Significance—has been like writing three commentaries at once. But that is the brilliance of this commentary series and the impact that writing the commentary has had on me personally. As I have walked with Jesus in his first-century historical setting through Matthew's meticulous written reflections, as I have been instructed through Matthew's theological intentions for his community, and as I have opened myself to allow Matthew's insights to Jesus' identity and mission to penetrate to my heart, soul, mind, and strength, I have been changed.

The experience of writing this commentary has been one of the most deeply enriching spiritual experiences of my life. Hearing Jesus' teaching in his discourses, especially the Sermon on the Mount, has molded my worldview, my theology, and my ethical life as I try to follow the principles of the kingdom of heaven. Watching Jesus' ministry unfold among his closest followers, to the distantly interested, and toward the intensely antagonistic has shaped the way I deal with people. In particular, entering into Jesus' passion experience of his final days on earth and into those final hours on the cross has impacted me intensely. Matthew took me to Jesus' heart on the cross, and my own heart broke, and yet was uniquely mended, as Jesus expended his atoning sacrifice for humanity's sin.

I also thank a host of people who have made this possible. I thank executive editor Jack Kuhatschek at Zondervan for the invitation to write this commentary and for his patience as the years stretched out for me to finish it. You are a gracious, gentle, yet highly motivated leader, Jack; thank you. I thank you, Terry Muck, for your supervision, and Scot McKnight, for your careful reading of the manuscript. Verlyn Verbrugge, hands-on senior editor who so diligently expends his vast New Testament expertise and technical knowledge, thank you for your support, encouragement, and desire to help authors bring to fruition their years of labor. I appreciate my association with Zondervan. I thank especially Stan Gundry for providing the diligent top leadership as editor-in-chief, Joyce Ondersma for the loving care of the authors, and Jack Kragt for advancing our life's work. Together you all have made Zondervan, in my view, the premier evangelical publishing house. It is an honor to be associated with you.

I also thank my colleagues—the faculty, administration, staff, and students—at Talbot School of Theology, Biola University, for your gracious support. You have heard me teach, preach, and reflect on Matthew for many years. Thank you for believing in me and supporting my writing. To name any would leave some out, so I can only say thank you collectively to all of you. If there is one exception, it is to Dennis Dirks, my fellow dean, who has sacrificed the most personally to support me so that I can carry out my own calling. You are the epitome of what many today blather about—servant leadership. Thank you, dear friend.

My research assistants over the years have provided substantial support in gathering bibliography, tracking down resources, and assisting me in exploring technical themes in Matthew's Gospel. I especially acknowledge Todd Wendorff, Gary Manning, Ray Bonesteele, Mark Fender, Steve Earle, Marcus Choi, Betty Talbert-Wetler, and Aaron Devine. Esther Sunukjian compiled the Scripture index. To those I have overlooked, please excuse me, but know that you have contributed significantly.

My final and most climactic thanks go to my family. Of all of the Gospels, Matthew's extends the most significant place to the family—both ecclesial and biological. For most of the years I wrote this commentary, I was honored to be on the adult pastoral staff part-time at San Clemente Presbyterian Church, San Clemente, California. You heard me teach and preach on Matthew's Gospel many, *many* times. You always supported and encouraged me to be rigorous academically and radical practically. Thank you.

And for all of these years, I was privileged to have a wife, children, parental figures, and a host of extended family who helped me to understand and apply what Matthew teaches. Thank you all—especially to our daughter Wendy, daughter Michelle and her husband, Dan, and their baby, Melia Noël, born just this week—thank you for allowing me to grow as a father and now grandfather. And to my wife, Lynne—we have grown together in Jesus as we have tried to raise our family for him, and we continue to walk together even more intimately as Jesus leads us into this next wonderful phase of our lives together. Thank you, my dear wife and friend, for the support that you always give in helping me to balance life and for the incredible joy that you bring to my life daily.

Michael J. Wilkins
Talbot School of Theology,
Biola University

# Abbreviations

| | |
|---|---|
| *ABD* | David N. Freedman, ed., *Anchor Bible Dictionary*, 6 vols. (New York: Doubleday, 1992) |
| *ABR* | *Australian Biblical Review* |
| ABRL | Anchor Bible Reference Library |
| ACCSNT | Ancient Christian Commentary on Scripture: New Testament |
| *b.* | Babylonian Talmud |
| *BAR* | *Biblical Archaeology Review* |
| *BBR* | *Bulletin for Biblical Research* |
| BDAG | Walter Bauer, *A Greek-English Lexicon of the New Testament and Other Early Christian Literature*, trans. W. Arndt and W. Gingrich; 3d ed., rev. Frederick W. Danker (Chicago: Univ. of Chicago Press, 2000) |
| BDF | Blass, Debrunner, *A Grammar of the Greek New Testament and Other Early Christian Literature*, trans. and ed. Robert Funk (Chicago: Univ. of Chicago Press, 1961) |
| *Bib* | *Biblica* |
| *BibSac* | *Bibliotheca sacra* |
| BNTC | Black's New Testament Commentaries |
| BST | The Bible Speaks Today |
| *BT* | *The Bible Translator* |
| *BTDB* | Walter A. Elwell, ed., *Baker Theological Dictionary of the Bible* (Grand Rapids: Baker, 1994) |
| *BZ* | *Biblische Zeitschrift* |
| BZNW | Beihefte zur Zeitschrift für die neutestamentliche Wissenschaft |
| *CBQ* | *Catholic Biblical Quarterly* |
| CBQMS | Catholic Biblical Quarterly Monograph Series |
| CGTC | Cambridge Greek Testament Commentary |
| CNT | Commentaire du Nouveau Testament |
| *CurBS* | *Currents in Research: Biblical Studies* |
| *DBI* | Leland Ryken, James Wilhoit, and Tremper Longman III, eds., *Dictionary of Biblical Imagery* (Downers Grove, Ill.: InterVarsity Press, 1998) |
| *DJBP* | Jacob Neusner and William Green, eds., *Dictionary of Judaism in the Biblical Period* (Peabody, Mass.: Hendrickson, 1099) |

## Abbreviations

| | |
|---|---|
| *DJG* | Joel Green, Scot McKnight, and I. Howard Marshall, eds., *Dictionary of Jesus and the Gospels* (Downers Grove, Ill.: InterVarsity Press, 1992) |
| *DLNTD* | C. A. Evans and S. E. Porter, eds., *Dictionary of Later New Testament and Its Development* (Downers Grove, Ill.: InterVarsity Press, 2000) |
| DSB | Daily Study Bible Commentary Series |
| *DSD* | *Dead Sea Discoveries* |
| *EBC* | *Expositor's Bible Commentary* |
| *EJR* | *Encyclopedia of the Jewish Religion* |
| *ExpTim* | *Expository Times* |
| GNC | Good News Commentary |
| HTKNT | Herders theologischer Kommentar zum Neuen Testament |
| *IBD* | J. D. Douglas, ed., *The Illustrated Bible Dictionary*, 3 vols. (Downers Grove, Ill.: InterVarsity Press, 1986) |
| ICC | International Critical Commentary |
| IVPNTC | InterVarsity Press New Testament Commentary |
| *ISBE* | G. Bromiley, ed., *International Standard Bible Encyclopedia*, 4 vols., rev. ed. (Grand Rapids: Eerdmans, 1979–1988) |
| *JBL* | *Journal of Biblical Literature* |
| *JETS* | *Journal of the Evangelical Theological Society* |
| *JSNT* | *Journal for the Study of the New Testament* |
| JSNTSup | Journal for the Study of the New Testament Supplement Series |
| JSPSup | Journal for the Study of the Pseudepigrapha: Supplement Series |
| LEC | Library of Early Christianity |
| Louw-Nida | Johannes Louw and Eugene Nida, *Greek-English Lexicon of the New Testament: Based on Semantic Domains*, 2d ed., 2 vols. (New York: United Bible Society, 1989) |
| *m.* | Mishnah |
| NCB | New Century Bible |
| *NDBT* | Desmond Alexander, Brian Rosner, D. A. Carson, and Graeme Goldsworth, eds., *New Dictionary of Biblical Theology* (Downers Grove, Ill.: InterVarsity Press, 2000) |
| *NIB* | Leander Keck, gen. ed., *New Interpreter's Bible: A Commentary in 12 Volumes* (Nashville: Abingdon, 1995) |
| *NIDNTT* | Colin Brown, ed., *New International Dictionary of New Testament Theology*, 4 vols. (Grand Rapids: Zondervan, 1967–1971) |
| NIGTC | New International Greek Testament Commentary |

| | |
|---|---|
| NIV | New International Version |
| *NovT* | *Novum Testamentum* |
| NovTSup | Novum Testamentum Supplements |
| NSBT | New Studies in Biblical Theology |
| NTM | New Testament Message |
| *NTS* | *New Testament Studies* |
| NTTS | New Testament Tools and Studies |
| PNTC | Pillar New Testament Commentary |
| *RB* | *Revue biblique* |
| SBC | Student's Bible Commentary |
| *SBLSP* | *Society of Biblical Literature Seminar Papers* |
| SBT | Studies in Biblical Theology |
| *SJT* | *Scottish Journal of Theology* |
| SM | Sermon on the Mount |
| SNTSMS | Society for New Testament Studies Monograph Series |
| Str.-B. | Strack-Billerbeck |
| *t.* | Tosefta |
| *TBT* | *The Bible Today* |
| *TCGNT* | Bruce Metzger, *The Textual Commentary on the Greek New Testament*, 2d ed. (New York: American Bible Society, 1994) |
| *TLZ* | *Theologische Literaturzeitung* |
| TNTC | Tyndale New Testament Commentary |
| *TrinJ* | *Trinity Journal* |
| *TT* | *Theology Today* |
| *TynBul* | *Tyndale Bulletin* |
| WBC | Word Biblical Commentary |
| *WTJ* | *Westminster Theological Journal* |
| *y.* | Jerusalem Talmud |
| *ZIBBC* | *Zondervan Illustrated Bible Backgrounds Commentary* |
| *ZPEB* | Merrill C. Tenney, gen. ed., *Zondervan Pictorial Encyclopedia of the Bible* (Grand Rapids: Zondervan, 1975–1976) |

# Introduction

WE ARE ABOUT TO EMBARK on a journey through one of the most treasured writings of the Christian faith. The Gospel according to Matthew, according to citations found in early Christian writers, was the most widely read and frequently used Gospel in the formative years of the church. Manlio Simonetti, a renowned expert in patristic literature, states of Matthew's Gospel: "It is no exaggeration to state that the faithful who lived between the end of the first and the end of the second centuries came to know the words and deeds of Christ on the basis of this text."[1] It has retained its appeal throughout the centuries and exerted a powerful influence on the church.[2] Many contend that this Gospel was the most important one for much of church history.[3] One of the main reasons why this Gospel is so important is because of its verification that Jesus was the long-awaited Messiah of Israel, who had brought salvation not just to the Jews but to all nations.

By the time of the writing of this Gospel, Jesus Messiah had arrived with little fanfare in Israel some thirty years prior. He was associated with the fiery prophet John the Baptist, but that became a dangerous association, since John was beheaded by the Roman puppet ruler of Galilee, Herod Antipas. Like John, Jesus Messiah soon became popular with the people, attracting thousands to hear his message, experience his healing miracles, and be challenged by his preaching about the arrival of the kingdom of heaven. But also like John, Jesus Messiah became the target of opposition from the religious and political powers in Israel. That opposition escalated dramatically until sadly, in the third year of his ministry during the Passover season, he was arrested, tried by both the Jewish religious establishment and the Roman occupying government, and executed by crucifixion.

At first this seemed to put an end to the messianic movement surrounding Jesus. But soon rumors began circulating that Jesus Messiah had been

---

1. Manlio Simonetti, ed., *Matthew 1–13* (ACCSNT; Downers Grove, Ill.: InterVarsity Press, 2001), 1A:xxxvii.

2. For a brief historical survey, see Simonetti, *Matthew 1–13*, 1A:xxxvii–xli. A study that is still valuable for establishing this thesis is Édouard Massaux, *The Influence of the Gospel of Saint Matthew on Christian Literature before Saint Irenaeus*, Book 1: *The First Ecclesiastical Writers*, trans. Norman J. Belval and Suzanne Hecht, ed. Arthur J. Bellinzoni (New Gospel Studies 5/1; 1950; Macon, Ga.: Mercer Univ. Press, 1990).

3. E.g., Ulrich Luz, *Matthew 1–7: A Commentary*, trans. Wilhelm C. Linss (1985; Minneapolis: Augsburg, 1989), 81.

---

resurrected, that he had appeared to his followers, and that all he had preached about the arrival of the kingdom of heaven was true. He really was the Messiah of Israel and the Savior of humanity. His followers began to spread his message throughout the Mediterranean world. But as happened in his own earthly ministry, Jesus' message created divisions among those who heard it. Pockets of Jews became followers of Jesus Messiah in Palestine, in the increasingly important gathering of Judaism in Syria Antioch, and even in Rome, the hated center of Roman imperialism. Wherever Diaspora Judaism had settled, it was impacted by the persistent, and even pervasive, incursions of Jewish Christians.

Emperor Claudius had been troubled by the fast-spreading Christian movement, which Suetonius apparently records as a result of the dispute over one "Chrestus" in Rome in the 40s.[4] This may well have been a dispute between Jews and Christians over the preaching about Jesus Messiah.[5] Christians claimed that Jesus was raised from the dead and pointed to an empty tomb. Jews countered with the story of a stolen body. Frustrated with both sides, Claudius expelled all the Jews from Rome (Christianity was seen as a sect of Judaism; Acts 18:2).

Caesar (Claudius?) then did one other thing. He had a local governor set up the famous "Nazareth Decree" in approximately A.D. 50 in Nazareth, the birthplace of the object of the furor. This is a stone slab with an imperial decree warning of capital punishment for those violating tombs, and points to the seriousness with which disturbing graves and moving dead bodies was held in the ancient world. It may also give some insight to the events in Matthew's narrative, if it was erected (as some propose) in response to the controversy between Jews and Christians about Jesus' empty tomb.[6] This would be consistent with Matthew's statement that the Jews continued to circulate a story about Jesus' body being stolen by his disciples (see comments on 28:11–15).

It is into these kinds of controversies that the first Gospel was written. The very first verse gives the direction to the author's purpose for writing: to establish Jesus' identity as the Messiah, heir to the promises of Israel's throne through King David and heir to the promises of the blessing to all the nations through the patriarch Abraham. So this first Gospel serves as an evangelistic tool to Jews, contending that they should turn to Jesus as their long-

---

4. Suetonius, *Claudius* 25.4.

5. Cf. F. F. Bruce, *The Acts of the Apostles: Greek Text with Introduction and Commentary*, 3d ed. (Grand Rapids: Eerdmans, 1990), 391.

6. The slab is said to have been found in Nazareth in 1878, but dated to the first century B.C. through the Greek script-type. It is in the possession of the Bibliothèque Nationale in Paris (see the photo in E. M. Blaiklock, "Nazareth Decree," *ZPEB*, 4:391–92).

awaited Messiah, but also to Gentiles, emphasizing that salvation through Jesus Messiah is available to them. It also serves as an apologetic tool to Jewish-Christians, encouraging them to stand firm in the face of opposition from their Jewish compatriots and from Gentile pagans, knowing that Jesus Messiah has fulfilled the promised arrival of the kingdom of heaven.

Against the backdrop of a world increasingly hostile to Christianity, the author solidifies his church's identity as the true people of God, who transcend ethnic, economic, and religious barriers to find oneness in their adherence to Jesus Messiah. His Gospel becomes a manual on discipleship, as Jew and Gentile are made disciples of Jesus Messiah and learn to obey all that he commanded his original disciples.

# The Author of the First Gospel

IT APPEARS OBVIOUS that the person responsible for penning this Gospel has Jewish concerns in view, which leads us to the question of his identity. As we open to this book in our modern translations, we usually find the title "Matthew," or "The Gospel According to Matthew." But many longtime readers are surprised to discover that all of the four Gospels are technically anonymous. The titles that are now assigned to each one were likely not headings to the original manuscript. They were added later to distinguish the four Gospels from one another.

Additionally, none of the Gospel writers states his name explicitly within the text as the author. This is actually what we should expect, because they were not writing letters to far off church communities to which were attached the names of the addressees and senders, such as we find in the New Testament letters. Rather, they were compiling gospel stories for churches of which they were active participants and leaders. They likely stood among the assembly and first read their Gospel account themselves. To attach their names as authors would have been unnecessary, for their audiences knew their identity. It may have even been seen as inappropriate to attach their names to their accounts, since they did not intend to assert their own authority but to record for their audiences the matchless story of Jesus' life and ministry.

## Ancient Records of Authorship

THEREFORE, WE MUST look to the records of church history to find evidence for the authorship of the Gospels. The earliest church tradition unanimously ascribes the first Gospel to Matthew, the tax collector who was called to be one of the original twelve disciples of Jesus. Written toward the end of the first century, the *Didache* demonstrates direct knowledge of the first Gospel, quoting it more than any of the other three (e.g., quoting the Lord's Prayer: cf. *Did.* 8:2; Matt. 6:9–11). A few years later, a letter of Pseudo-Barnabas cites the first Gospel as divinely inspired Scripture (*Barnabas* 4.14 [Matt. 22:14]). The first explicit mention of this Gospel dates to the third decade of the second century, by Papias, bishop of Hierapolis in Asia Minor (c. 135), and then somewhat later in the second century by Irenaeus, bishop of Lyons in Gaul (c. 175).

Papias (c. 60–130) claimed that he was a hearer of the apostle John, and he was later a companion of Polycarp (Irenaeus, *Against Heresies* 5.33.4). He was quoted and endorsed by the church historian Eusebius (c. 325, as saying, "Matthew for his part compiled/collected the oracles in the Hebrew [Aramaic] dialect and every person translated/interpreted them as he was able" (Eusebius, *Eccl. Hist.* 3.39.16).

Irenaeus was born in Asia Minor in approximately 135, studied under Polycarp, bishop of Smyrna, and according to tradition died as a martyr around 200. In one of his five monumental books against the gnostic heresies (c. 175), Irenaeus states, "Matthew also issued a written Gospel among the Hebrews in their own dialect, while Peter and Paul were preaching at Rome, and laying the foundations of the Church" (*Against Heresies* 3.1.1).

These church leaders either knew the apostolic community directly or were taught by those associated with the apostles; thus, they were directly aware of the origins of the Gospels. While the full meaning of their statements is still open to discussion, no competing tradition assigning the first Gospel to any other author has survived, if any ever existed. Subsequent authors (e.g., Hippolytus, Tertullian, Cyprian, Novatian) cite the Gospel of Matthew regularly as inspired Scripture on the same level as the Old Testament.[7]

The testimony of the early church fathers to the apostolic authorship of the Synoptic Gospels (Matthew, Mark, and Luke) cannot be lightly overlooked.[8] All of the evidence uniformly supports the belief that Matthew (the tax collector turned disciple), Mark (the companion of Peter and Paul), and Luke (Paul's "beloved physician") were the authors of the Gospels attributed to them. It is difficult to conceive why Christians as early as the second century would ascribe these otherwise anonymous Gospels to three such unlikely candidates if they did not in fact write them. Mark and Luke were not among Jesus' twelve apostles. Mark is best known for abandoning Paul (Acts 13:13; cf. 15:37–40), and Luke is particularly obscure, being mentioned by name only once in the New Testament (Col. 4:14). Matthew, although an apostle,

---

7. Simonetti, *Matthew 1–13*, xxxvii.

8. John and his Gospel likewise, but we treat here only the Synoptics, which deal with similar issues.

is also best known for a negative characteristic—his unconscionable past as a tax collector (Matt. 9:9–13). Tax collectors were considered traitorous to their nation.

By contrast, the apocryphal gospels consistently picked better-known and exemplary figures—such as Philip, Peter, James, Bartholomew, or Mary—for their fictitious authors.[9] Even Thomas, despite his famous doubts about Jesus' resurrection (John 20:25), seems a more likely person to whom to attribute a Gospel than Matthew, Mark, or Luke, because he ultimately made such a profound declaration of faith in the risen Jesus (cf. John 20:28). This is consistent with the gnostic *Gospel of Thomas* purporting to be written by the apostle Thomas. False ascription of the first Gospel to a relatively obscure apostle such as Matthew seems unlikely until a later date, when canonization of apostles was common.

Some modern scholars deny the Matthean authorship of the first Gospel on the basis that they subscribe to the priority of Mark and cannot imagine how an apostle (Matthew) would borrow from a nonapostle (Mark). But even if Matthew did have access to Mark's Gospel, Mark represented Peter's authoritative account and would certainly only give an even greater apostolic weight to the account.

## Matthew, the Person

THE LIST OF the twelve disciples in Matthew's Gospel refers to him as "Matthew the tax collector" (10:3), which harks back to the incident when Jesus called Matthew while he was sitting in the tax office (cf. 9:9; 10:3). When recounting the call, the first Gospel refers to him as "Matthew" (9:9), while Mark's Gospel refers to him as "Levi, son of Alphaeus" (Mark 2:14), and Luke's Gospel refers to him simply as "Levi" (Luke 5:27). Speculation surrounds the reason for the variation, but most scholars suggest that this tax collector had two names, Matthew Levi, either from birth or from the time of his conversion.[10] Some have attempted to show that Levi was not one of the Twelve and therefore different from Matthew, but this is unwarranted speculation, since the circumstances of the calling is the same in Matthew and in Mark and Luke.[11]

---

9. For the complete collection of apocryphal gospels, see Wilhelm Schneemelcher, ed., *New Testament Apocrypha*, rev. ed. vol. 1 (Louisville: Westminster John Knox, 1990).

10. For example, D. A. Carson leans toward "Matthew Levi" being a double name given to him from birth ("Matthew," *EBC* [Grand Rapids: Zondervan, 1984], 8:224), while Donald Hagner suggests that the name "Matthew" was given to Levi after his conversion (*Matthew 1–13* [WBC 33A; Dallas: Word, 1993], 237–38).

11. For a treatment of the evidence equating Matthew and Levi as one person, see R. T. France, *Matthew: Evangelist and Teacher* (Grand Rapids: Zondervan, 1989), 66–70.

The name Levi may indicate that he was from the tribe of Levi and therefore familiar with Levitical practices.[12] Mark's record of the calling refers to him as "the son of Alphaeus" (Mark 2:14), which some have understood to mean that he was the brother of the apostle "James son of Alphaeus" (cf. Mark 3:18). But since the other pairs of brothers are specified to be brothers and are linked as such, it is unlikely that Matthew-Levi and James were brothers.

Matthew Levi was called to follow Jesus while he was sitting in the tax collector's booth. This booth was probably located on one of the main trade highways near Capernaum, collecting tolls for Herod Antipas from the commercial traffic traveling through this area. Matthew immediately followed Jesus and arranged a banquet for him at his home, to which were invited a large crowd of tax collectors and sinners (Matt. 9:10–11; Luke 5:29–30). Since tax collectors generally were fairly wealthy and were despised by the local populace (cf. Zacchaeus, Luke 19:1–10), Matthew's calling and response were completely out of the ordinary and required nothing short of a miraculous turnaround in this tax collector's life.

Little else is known of Matthew Levi except for the widely attested tradition that he is the author of the Gospel that now bears his name. As a tax collector he would have been trained in secular scribal techniques, and as a Galilean Jewish Christian he would have been able to interpret the life of Jesus from the perspective of the Old Testament expectations.[13] Eusebius said that Matthew first preached to "Hebrews" and then to "others," including places such as Persia, Parthia, and Syria (*Eccl. Hist.* 3:24.6). The traditions are mixed regarding Matthew's death, with some saying that he died a martyr's death and others a natural death.

# Date and Destination

NO PRECISE DATE for the writing of Matthew is known, although Jesus' prophecy of the overthrow of Jerusalem (24:1–28) has been used to indicate that the Gospel may have been written after A.D. 70. However, such a conclusion is necessary only if one denies Jesus the ability to predict the future. Since the early church father Irenaeus (c. 175) indicates that Matthew wrote his Gospel while Paul and Peter were still alive (Irenaeus, *Against Heresies* 3.1.1), the traditional dating has usually settled on the late 50s or early 60s. Matthew tells us that as of the time he was writing, the "field of blood" in

---

12. W. F. Albright and C. S. Mann, *Matthew* (AB 26; Garden City, N.Y.: Doubleday, 1971), clxxvii–clxxviii, clxxxiii–clxxxiv.

13. Cf. France, *Matthew*, 70–74.

---

Jerusalem continued to be called by that name (27:8), showing his continual connection with conditions in Palestine and hinting that this is prior to the devastation in Jerusalem in 70.[14]

The highly influential church at Antioch in Syria, with its large Jewish-Christian and Gentile contingents (cf. Acts 11:19–26; 13:1–3), has often been recognized as the original recipients of the Gospel. This is confirmed in part because of its influence on Ignatius the bishop of Antioch and on the *Didache*. But Matthew's message was equally relevant for the fledgling church throughout the ancient world and appears to have been disseminated fairly quickly.

## Matthew's Distinctive Perspectives

MATTHEW'S GOSPEL RETAINED its appeal throughout the centuries and exerted a powerful influence on the church through much of history. Its popularity is explained at least in part because of the following distinctives that are found throughout this Gospel.

**Christology.** The church has consistently drawn on this Gospel as the foundational clarification of the identity of Jesus Christ, who is the Son of God, the King of Israel, and the Lord of the church. From the announcement of Jesus' conception (1:18–25), to the divinely superintended protection of the child (2:15), to the Father's heavenly announcements at the baptism and transfiguration (3:17; 17:5), to Jesus' anguished prayers in the Garden (26:39, 42), Matthew focuses on Jesus' identity as the incarnate Son of God the Father.

Matthew also gives focused perspective on Jesus as the promised King of Israel (1:1–16; 2:1–6), who came to inaugurate the kingdom of heaven (4:12–17), even though life in this kingdom would be of a different sort from what many expected (cf. ch. 13). That life in the kingdom of heaven is especially centered on an intimate, ongoing relationship of Jesus with his disciples throughout the ages (28:20), which alone in Matthew's Gospel is designated to become "the church" that Jesus himself will build and superintend (16:18; 18:17). The portrait that Matthew paints of Jesus to clarify his identity and mission is often colored most clearly by the various titles associated with him.

Matthew opens his Gospel with the name "Jesus Christ" (1:1). *Jesus* is explained as his given name, which is the common designation throughout

---

14. For a more complete defense of the early dating of Matthew prior to A.D. 70, perhaps as early as the late 50s to early 60s, see Craig L. Blomberg, *Matthew* (NAC 22; Nashville: Broadman, 1992), 41–42; or perhaps in response to Neronian persecution in A.D. 65–67, see Robert H. Gundry, *Matthew: A Commentary on His Handbook for a Mixed Church Under Persecution*, 2d ed. (Grand Rapids: Eerdmans, 1994), 599–609; or more generally in the 60s, see Carson, "Matthew," 19–21.

his life and denotes his role as Savior (cf. 1:21). *Christ,* which in Hebrew is *mašiaḥ* or Messiah, is a title meaning "anointed one." It occurs thirty-nine times to describe kings (2 Sam. 1:14, 16; cf. 1QSa 2:14, 20), priests (Ex. 28:41; cf. 1QS 9:11), and prophets (Ps. 105:15; cf. CD 2:12; 5:21–6:1; 1QM 11:7–8). It came to be an expression linked in the Jewish mind to David as the anointed king of Israel and to the promise of the "anointed one" who would be the light of hope for the people of Israel. Matthew points to this title as rightly belonging to Jesus because of his lineage as a descendant of David (see comments on 1:16–18).

The name "Christ" has provided the church with its most widely used title. The fact that the believers in Jesus were at an early stage described as "Christians" is eloquent testimony to the importance of this concept in their minds. Jesus accepted the designation and in so doing was claiming to be God's "Anointed" agent in establishing the kingdom (26:63–64). He was the Christ, the messianic king in its fullest sense. His hesitation or reservation in using the title to refer to himself had only to do with the popular use of the term in the first century, which carried political overtones. Jesus was careful to define or restrict the use of the term to designate the kind of messianic deliver he was to be (see 4:12–17).

*Son of David* is an important expression in this Gospel.[15] Matthew uses the name of the great king seventeen times, more than any other book of the New Testament. Like the title "Messiah," "son of David" expresses a promised figure who would perpetuate David's throne, thereby pointing to Messiah's lineage and royal expectation of an eternal throne (see 2 Sam. 7:11b–16). But it also evoked images of a Messiah as a mighty warrior like David, who would destroy Israel's enemies and reestablish the throne in Jerusalem and the kingdom of Israel as in the golden days of David. The hope of a restored kingdom was seen to be a fulfillment of the divine promise to David (see comments on 9:27).

The title *Son of God* is a powerful designation in this Gospel to reveal Jesus Messiah's true identity. The expression bears witness to a relationship between Jesus and God throughout Matthew's narrative. Jesus is uniquely God's Son by way of conception (1:21–23), as is fulfilled in Jesus' return from Egypt (2:15), reiterated by the Father at Jesus' baptism (3:17), challenged by the devil at the temptations (4:2, 5), and acknowledged by demons who are about to be exorcised (8:29). Throughout Matthew's narrative Jesus continually lays claim to a unique relationship to his heavenly Father.[16] This also

---

15. See 1:1; 9:27; 12:23; 15:22; 20:30–31; 21:9, 15; 22:42, 45.

16. See 7:21; 10:32–33; 11:25–27; 12:50; 15:13; 18:35; 20:23; 24:36; 25:34; 26:39, 42; 26:53; 28:19.

points back to the profound prophecy about David's line, "I will be his father, and he will be my son" (2 Sam. 7:14), which spoke immediately of Solomon but also of the future messianic line.

The importance of "Son of God" in this Gospel is seen not only in its explicit use (e.g., 8:29; 14:33; 16:16; cf. 3:17; 17:5), but also where it is implied.[17] Jesus refers to God as his Father some twenty-three times in Matthew, fifteen of which are unique to this Gospel (see comments on 5:16). Peter confesses Jesus as "the Christ, the Son of the living God" (16:16), the most exalted title in Matthew. The confession is made only by believers (except where it is blasphemy; cf. 4:3, 6) and only by revelation (16:7; 11:27; cf. 13:11). The Fourth Gospel makes explicit the ontological Sonship of Jesus, while Matthew assumes it as the foundation of the relationship (see comments on 1:20–23). Jesus is the divine Son of the heavenly Father.[18]

The title *Son of Man* may be the most significant to get at Jesus' clarification of his self-identity (see comments on 8:18–22). During his earthly ministry the expression would have struck a relatively ambiguous chord. Those who heard the expression would recall its use in Ezekiel, where God refers to the prophet with the expression "son of man" over ninety times (e.g., Ezek. 2:1, 3, 6, 8, etc.; cf. Dan. 8:17), pointing to Ezekiel's frailty as a human before the mighty God revealed in the vision.[19] But they also would recall how the expression "Son of Man" was used in Daniel's prophecy to refer to a glorified sovereign ruler, the apocalyptic messianic figure who rules forever with the Ancient of Days (Dan. 7:13–14).

With such a general ambiguity, "Son of Man" is for Jesus a convenient vehicle to convey his messianic identity. It did not have popular associations attached to it, such as were attached to titles like "Messiah," "Son of David," or even "Son of God." Instead, he could teach the meaning of his true identity by referring to himself as "Son of Man."[20] With a general threefold progression, Jesus uses the expression to clarify exactly who he is and what is his ministry.

---

17. E.g., 1:23—'The virgin . . . will give birth to a son . . . Immanuel . . . God with us.

18. In the rich associations connected with "Son of God," it is important to understand the intended contextual force. Carson notes, "As it is wrong to see ontological Sonship in every use, so is it wrong to exclude it prematurely" ("Matthew," 109).

19. Leslie C. Allen, *Ezekiel 1–19* (WBC 29; Dallas: Word, 1994), 38.

20. No one else uses the expression to refer to Jesus, and in the rest of the New Testament the title is used of Jesus only once (Acts 7:56), except for three Old Testament references or quotations (Heb. 2:6 = Ps. 8:5; Rev. 1:13 and 14:14 = Dan. 7:13). In every instance except two the title is found only on the lips of Jesus, but even in these it should be noted that the audience used this title because Jesus had previously used it as a self-designation (John 12:23), and the angel is simply repeating Jesus' own words (Luke 24:7).

- The Son of Man is the humble Servant, who has come to forgive sins of common sinners in his earthly ministry (8:20; 9:6; 11:19; 12:8; 12:32; 12:40).
- The Son of Man is the Suffering Servant, whose atoning death and resurrection will redeem his people (16:13, 27–28; 17:9, 12, 22; 20:18, 28; 26:2, 24, 45).
- The Son of Man is the glorious King and Judge, who will return to bring the kingdom of heaven to earth (10:23; 13:37, 41; 19:28; 24:27, 30, 37, 39, 44; 25:31; 26:64).

Jesus' mission was not always understood because of the misperceptions and faulty expectations of the people, the religious leaders, and even his own disciples. But at the end, after he used the sufficiently ambiguous title "Son of Man" to clarify his identity and ministry, when he used it for the last time at his trial before Caiaphas and the Sanhedrin, it was perfectly clear that he was claiming to be the divine Messiah of Israel (cf. 26:63–68).

*Lord* is also a title that increasingly reveals Jesus' identity and mission. Sometimes during his ministry, the term is used by people simply as a title of respect (e.g., 8:21; 18:21; 26:22). But the use of the title in Matthew's Gospel also has much more significance. We find that "Lord" is the title that is regularly used by people who approach Jesus in search of divine aid (e.g., 8:2, 5; 9:28; 15:22, 25; 17:15; 20:30, 31, 33), including his own disciples when they need divine assistance (e.g., 8:25; 14:30). As Jesus' ministry unfolds, his disciples use the title with increasing deference, because he is turning out to be more than they had originally understood him to be. He is connected with God's power and has a relationship with God as the Son who can only be addressed with a title normally reserved for God, "Lord" (e.g., 14:28; 16:25; 17:4).

This is particularly momentous when people see his miraculous deeds, call on him as Lord, and then worship him (14:33), an activity reserved solely for deity. "Lord" is also one of the titles, like "Son of Man," that Jesus uses to refer to himself in a way that increasingly reveals his divine identity.[21] As the only One who refers to God in heaven as "my Father" (e.g., 7:21) and the One who has authority to banish false prophets to eternal judgment (7:22–23), Jesus is more than any mere respected master; he is the Lord, who is worshiped as having all authority in heaven and earth (28:16–20).

**Salvation-historical particularism and universalism.** The terms *particularism* and *universalism* indicate that Matthew's Gospel places striking emphasis on both the fulfillment of the promises of salvation to a particular people, Israel, and the fulfillment of the universal promise of salvation to all the peoples of

---

21. See 9:38; 21:3; 22:43–45; 23:38; 24:42; 25:37, 44. France, *Matthew*, 287–88.

the earth. The church, made up of every nationality, has cherished this Gospel because Matthew aims to record the continuation of the history of salvation to all nations. His introductory statement that Jesus Christ is both the "son of David" and the "son of Abraham" (1:1) is the preliminary indication that salvation promises made both through David to God's chosen people, Israel (e.g., 2 Sam. 7:8–17), and through Abraham to all peoples (Gen. 12:1–3; 22:18), have been fulfilled through the life and ministry of Jesus Christ, the promised Savior of all nations.

Matthew's Gospel alone points explicitly to Jesus' intention to go first to "the lost sheep of Israel" (10:5–6; 15:24), showing historically how God's promise of salvation to Israel was indeed fulfilled. Yet the promises made to Abraham that he would be a blessing to all the nations are also fulfilled as Jesus extends salvation to the Gentiles (cf. 21:44; 28:19). The church throughout the ages has found assurance in Matthew's Gospel that God truly keeps his promises to his people.

**The bridge between Old and New Testaments.** Matthew's Gospel has been a pivotal book throughout church history to help the church understand the relationship between Old and New Testaments. Placed first in the earliest collections of the New Testament canon, this Gospel is a natural bridge between the Old Testament and the New Testament. Matthew demonstrates repeatedly that Old Testament hopes, prophecies, and promises have now been fulfilled in the person and ministry of Jesus. Matthew begins with the "fulfillment" of the messianic genealogy in the birth of Jesus (1:1–17), and then goes on to demonstrate the fulfillment in Jesus' life and ministry of various Old Testament prophecies and themes (e.g., 1:22–23; 2:4–5, 15, 17, 23) and the fulfillment of the Old Testament law (5:17–48). The early church likely placed Matthew first in the New Testament canon precisely because of its value as a bridge between the Testaments.

**A "great commission" for evangelism and mission.** This first Gospel has held special status in the missionary and evangelistic outreach of the church because of the prominent placement of the Great Commission, which climactically concludes the story of Jesus' ministry (28:18–20). The form of Jesus' commission to "make disciples of all the nations" (28:19) is unique to Matthew's Gospel, providing continuity between Jesus' ministry of making disciples in his earthly ministry and the ministry of making disciples to which the church has been called. This is Jesus' final command, and it uniquely charges his followers with an imperative that has impelled Christians throughout church history to look outward to all the peoples of the earth who have not yet heard and obeyed the gospel of the kingdom of heaven. This Great Commission has been at the heart of evangelistic and missionary endeavor throughout the history of the church.

**The new community of faith**. Facing the threat of gathering Roman persecution within a pagan world, Matthew addresses a church that is representative of the emerging community of faith. The community apparently has a large membership of Jewish Christians, who are familiar with temple activities and the Jewish religious system. But it also has a large contingent of Gentile Christians, who are discovering their heritage of faith in God's universal promise of salvation. The church has consistently found in Matthew a call to a new community that transcends ethnic and religious barriers to find oneness in its adherence to Jesus Messiah. The church has continually been challenged by Matthew's message that former barriers to discipleship have now been abolished.

The offer of discipleship found in the Great Commission broke down the same barriers that Jesus broke down all through his earthly ministry. Restrictions on the basis of gender, ethnicity, social status, and religious practice were abolished so that now women and men, Jew and Gentile, rich and poor, clean and unclean are all called to be Jesus' disciples. With Matthew's clear understanding of the Old Testament and Jewish practices, his Gospel has held a radical position in sustaining Jesus' call to "all . . . who are weary and burdened" (11:28).

Matthew alone among the evangelists uses the term *ekklesia*, which later became the term that designates the church. He emphasizes explicitly that God's program of salvation history will find its continuation in the present age as Jesus builds his church and maintains his presence within its assembly (16:18; 18:15–20; cf. 28:20). Whoever responds to his invitation (22:10) is brought within the church to enjoy his fellowship and demonstrate the true community of faith.

**The disciples, crowds, and Jewish leaders.**[22] These three groups provide a background for Matthew's story of Jesus. The "Jewish leaders" are the antagonists, the one's responsible for Jesus' crucifixion. The "crowds" are a basically neutral group; they are the object of Jesus' ministry of preaching, teaching, and healing, but as a group they do not exercise faith in him. The "disciples" are Jesus' true followers, true believers.

The "crowd" is not attached in any serious way to Jesus and are at various times either positively or negatively oriented toward him.[23] The crowds are the mass of people who are the objects of Jesus' saving ministry. His objective is to make them disciples. As Jesus teaches and preaches, the sign of faith is when one comes out of the crowd and calls Jesus "Lord" (cf. 8:18,

---

22. See Michael J. Wilkins, *The Concept of Disciple in Matthew's Gospel: As Reflected in the Use of the Term Μαθητής* (NovTSup 29; Leiden: Brill, 1988).

23. J. R. C. Cousland, *The Crowds in the Gospel of Matthew* (NovTSup 102; Leiden: Brill, 2002).

21; 17:14–15). When an individual comes out of the crowd, he or she chooses either to exercise faith and become a believer or to remain an unbeliever (cf. 19:16–22).

**The role of Peter.** Peter plays an important role as a leader and spokesman for the disciples in the several incidents in this Gospel. Matthew narrates five incidents about Peter in five central chapters found nowhere else in the Gospels (14:28–31; 15:15; 16:17–19; 17:24–27; 18:21). He emphasizes Peter's leadership role but also shows how Peter is an imperfect leader in process of development, as Jesus prepares him for the early days of the church ahead.[24]

For example, in 14:28–31, Peter demonstrates tremendous courage when he requests to walk to Jesus on the water, something no Old Testament figures ever did. Yet at the same time, Peter's courage to walk to Jesus on the water becomes the occasion for failure when he begins to sink. The following graph of events clearly demonstrates how Peter is up and down in his discipleship to Jesus, yet how he is continually led forward to be a leader among the Twelve.

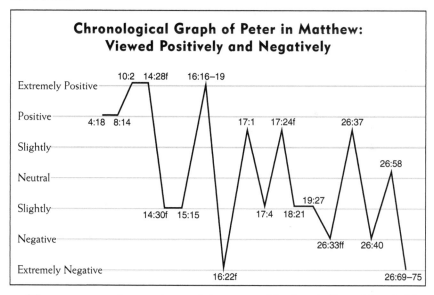

**Chronological Graph of Peter in Matthew: Viewed Positively and Negatively**

**The structure of narrative and discourse.** Matthew's Gospel has held a favored place in the history of the church because of its extended collection of Jesus' teaching ministry, especially the Sermon on the Mount.[25] Matthew

24. For Matthew's portrait of Peter and his developing leadership role, see Michael J. Wilkins, *Discipleship in the Ancient World and Matthew's Gospel*, 2d ed. (Grand Rapids: Baker, 1995), 173–216, 264.

25. Donald Guthrie, *New Testament Introduction*, 3d ed. (Downers Grove, Ill.: InterVarsity Press, 1970), 21.

has collected the most complete compilation of Jesus' teachings, exhortations, prophecies, and parables found anywhere in Scripture.

The concluding element of the Great Commission, in which Jesus states that new disciples are to be taught "to obey everything I have commanded you" (28:20), gives a hint to one overall purpose for this Gospel. Matthew records five of Jesus' major discourses, all of which are addressed primarily to Jesus' disciples (chs. 5–7; 10; 13; 18; 24–25), and signals the conclusion of each with the recurring identical formula: "When Jesus had finished . . ." (7:28; 11:1; 13:53; 19:1; 26:1). These discourses provide a wholistic presentation on the kind of discipleship that was to be taught to disciples as the basis for full-orbed obedience to Christ and became the basis for Christian instruction within the church. These discourses reveal that Jesus' disciples will be characterized by what they are taught to follow in these directives.

*Kingdom-life disciples* (chs. 5–7). The Kingdom-Life Proclamation, popularly called the Sermon on the Mount, develops what it means to be "kingdom-life disciples." Jesus expounds the reality of a radical everyday discipleship lived in the presence and power of the kingdom of God within the disciples' everyday world. This kind of discipleship involves an inside-out transformation into the righteousness of the kingdom (5:20). The ultimate example of this righteousness is Jesus himself, who has come to fulfill the Old Testament revelation of God's will for his people (5:17, 21–47), so that Jesus' disciples can pursue clearly the goal to be perfect as their heavenly Father is perfect (5:48). Kingdom life, therefore, addresses all aspects of what discipleship to Jesus means during this age, including ethical, religious, marital, emotional, and economic dimensions.

*Mission-driven disciples* (ch. 10). The Mission Mandate develops what it means to be "mission-driven disciples." Jesus commissions all his disciples to go out to share and live the gospel of the kingdom of God to an alien and often hostile world until his return. Mission in this age is a responsibility of all believers (10:24–25, 40–42), not just a special category of persons. It occurs in both public confession to the world (10:32–33) and in private commitments to one's family (10:34–39). Like Jesus, his disciples can expect opposition and persecution (10:24–25) from Jews and Gentiles, from the religious and political world, as well as from one's own closest family and companions (10:17–21). Yet they need not fear because the Spirit will provide power and guidance (10:19–20), and the Father will exercise sovereign care and control (10:28–33). The centrality of the presence of Jesus in the disciples' life is the most vital characteristic of the mission, so that the disciples increasingly grow to be like the Master (10:24).

*Clandestine-kingdom disciples* (ch. 13). The Parabolic Disclosure develops what it means to be "clandestine-kingdom disciples." Through his parables

Jesus tests the hearts of the crowd to reveal whether the message of the kingdom of heaven has taken root and is producing fruit, or whether it has been unproductive (13:18–23). Through parables Jesus also reveals to his disciples the secrets of the kingdom of God, making known that, during this age, the kingdom will exist in a hidden form. It will be an undercover kingdom, not the overpowering political, militaristic, and dominant cultural manifestation of God's rule that many expected (13:31–33). So the Parabolic Discourse reveals what it means for Jesus' disciples to live as kingdom subjects in a world that has not yet experienced the fully consummated kingdom of God.

However, Jesus' disciples will act demonstrably different from others in this world through an inside-out transformation. Only at the end of this age will a final separation be made fully known between those who belong to the kingdom of heaven and those who do not (13:41–43, 49–50). The incongruity of its hiddenness and inconspicuousness causes many to overlook the kingdom of God; yet to those who discover its presence, it is the most precious reality of this age (13:44–46). Therefore, Jesus' disciples are to give closest attention to the priority of the kingdom in their lives, so that they will continue to be the treasure of revelation to a watching world (13:51–52). The Parabolic Discourse clarifies what discipleship to Jesus is like in the inaugurated but not consummated kingdom of God.

*Community-based disciples* (ch. 18). In the Community Prescription, Jesus declares how kingdom life is to be expressed through the church that he will establish on earth through his disciples. This discourse clarifies how discipleship to Jesus is expressed through a church that is characterized by humility, responsibility, purity, accountability, discipline, forgiveness, reconciliation, and restoration. This fourth discourse is addressed to insiders. The first and third discourses were primarily addressed to Jesus' disciples, but the crowds were included for other particular purposes (see comments on 5:1–2; 7:28–29; 13:1–2, 10–17), and the religious leaders were an implied object of rebuke (5:20; 6:1–18; 12:24–32, 46–50). But like the second and fifth discourses, the fourth is directed exclusively to Jesus' disciples.

The collection and organization of the Community Prescription is unique to Matthew's Gospel, as is much of the content. The uniqueness accentuates Jesus' urgency to prepare his disciples for the time that is soon coming when a new community of faith will replace Israel during this age as Jesus' body functioning as his witness to the reality of the kingdom's presence. The uniqueness of this passage also accentuates the way that the presence of the kingdom of heaven turns upside down the values of this world and how the new community, the church, will be a living witness to this overturn.

*Expectant-sojourner disciples* (chs. 24–25). In the Olivet Discourse (or Eschatological Forecast), Jesus looks down the long corridor of time and prophesies to his disciples of his return, the end of the age, and the establishment of his messianic throne. This discourse culminates Jesus' teaching on discipleship by describing how his disciples are to live each day in this age of the already–not yet consummation of the kingdom of God in expectant preparation for his return with power. They are to expect that Jesus could return at any time, yet responsibly plan as though he is not returning for an extended period of time.

*Leaders.* We can find in Matthew other significant themes scattered throughout the Gospel that supplement what is found in the discourses. Particularly relevant are extended messages directed to the religious leadership of Israel. These are messages to which leaders today should pay strict attention, because they contain principles and warnings we also must heed.[26]

# Three Horizons

WITH THESE VARIOUS characteristics before us, it is no wonder that Matthew's Gospel has been a favorite of Christians for more than two millennia. The full impact of this magnificent Gospel is best appreciated through the well-known practice of reading the Gospels on three horizons.[27]

(1) The first horizon is the level of Jesus' historical ministry. In this commentary we will explore this horizon in the Original Meaning sections. Here we view the unfolding mission of Jesus Messiah to his people Israel, with the universal implications that will result for all the nations. We will try to place ourselves in the first-century historical setting to see and hear Jesus as those who followed him around. History is of vital importance in understanding the Gospels, because they record what actually took place in space and time. The Gospel writers were either witnesses or recorders of the heart of the Christian message that God had acted in history. They were "reporting solid history, and the chief actor in their drama was a flesh-and-blood character, living a human life under Palestinian skies."[28] This historical record was the basis of the Gospel writer's faith, who wished to impart historical truth (e.g., Luke 1:1–4).

(2) We must try to understand Matthew's unique perspective in which he instructs his community with regard to their own particular issues. For this, we try to understand Matthew's own background and emphases and those of his community. Matthew did not create historical data to substantiate Jesus'

---

26. Esp. relevant here are chs. 9; 12; 15; 17; 19; 20–22; culminating in ch. 23.

27. E.g., Sidney Greidanus, *The Modern Preacher and the Ancient Text: Interpreting and Preaching Biblical Literature* (Grand Rapids: Eerdmans, 1988), 300–306. Greidanus emphasizes two horizons, but also includes the reader's own horizon, to which I refer as the third horizon.

28. Ralph P. Martin, *New Testament Foundations: A Guide for Christian Students.* Volume 1: *The Four Gospels* (Grand Rapids: Eerdmans, 1975), 43.

messianic identity or satisfy his audience's needs, but he did view Jesus' life from his own unique perspective. The Gospel writers wished to present the facts of history so as to convince their readers that Jesus was indeed the Christ, the Savior, so that people would believe and find eternal life in his name (e.g., John 20:30–31). When we look at Matthew's Gospel, we discover that it is presented in such a way that he challenges us to ask, "What manner of man is this, and what will we do with him?" We will especially explore this horizon in the Bridging Contexts sections of the commentary.

(3) The third horizon is that of the contemporary reader. We are really not much different as humans from those explored in the first two horizons, but there are contemporary issues and circumstances we must address to make the reading of Matthew immediately relevant. These issues we will explore in the Contemporary Significance sections of the commentary. Matthew begins by referring to Jesus as Immanuel, "God with us" (1:23), and concludes with Jesus' declaration, "I am with you always, to the very end of the age" (28:20). There is not a more radical claim than understanding that Jesus is God incarnate, who came to be with his people and who, although he has now ascended to be with the Father, still remains with his people. That was the essence of discipleship to Jesus in the first century, and it remains the privilege of Christians today as we walk with Jesus in the world of the twenty-first century.

# Outline of Matthew's Gospel

I. The Arrival in History of Jesus Messiah (1:1–2:23)
    A. Jesus Messiah Brings a New Beginning for Humanity (1:1)
    B. Jesus Messiah's Genealogy (1:2–17)
        1. From Abraham to King David (1:2–6)
        2. From King David to the Babylonian Exile (1:6–11)
        3. From the Babylonian Exile to Jesus Messiah (1:12–16)
        4. The Culmination of Matthew's Genealogy in Jesus Messiah (1:16–17)
    C. The Angelic Announcement of the Conception of Jesus Messiah (1:18–25)
    D. Magi Report the Star-Sign of the Birth of "the King of the Jews" (2:1–12)
        1. The Magi's Journey (2:1–2)
        2. Herod's Cunning Duplicity (2:3–8)
        3. The Magi Worship the Child (2:9–12)
    E. Old Testament Prophecies Fulfilled in Jesus Messiah (2:13–23)
        1. The Escape to Egypt (2:13–15)
        2. The Massacre of Bethlehem's Boys (2:16–18)
        3. The Return to Nazareth (2:19–23)

II. John the Baptist Prepares for the Appearance of the Messianic Kingdom (3:1–17)
    A. John the Baptist Appears (3:1–6)
    B. John the Baptist Prophesies of the Impact of the Coming One (3:7–12)
    C. The Appearance of Jesus Messiah for Baptism by John the Baptist (3:13–17)

III. Jesus Messiah Begins to Advance the Messianic Kingdom (4:1–25)
    A. Temptations of the Messiah (4:1–11)
        1. The Setting of the Temptations (4:1–2)
        2. The First Temptation—Personal: Turning Stones into Bread (4:3–4)
        3. The Second Temptation—National: Jumping off the Temple Pinnacle (4:5–7)

4. The Third Temptation—Universal: Worshiping
   Satan (4:8–10)
5. The Outcome of the Temptations (4:11)
B. Jesus Messiah Begins His Galilean Ministry (4:12–17)
C. Jesus Messiah Calls Fishers of Men (4:18–22)
D. Jesus Messiah Displays the Gospel of the Kingdom
   (4:23–25)

IV. **First Discourse—The Sermon on the Mount—
Kingdom-Life Proclamation (5:1–7:29)**
A. The Setting of the Sermon (5:1–2)
B. The Beatitudes and Witness of the Kingdom of Heaven
   (5:3–16)
   1. The Beatitudes (5:3–12)
   2. Salt and Light: True Disciples Witness to the
      Kingdom of Heaven (5:13–16)
C. Jesus Messiah Fulfills the Law: The Messianic Kingdom
   in Relation to the Law (5:17–48)
   1. Jesus and the Kingdom Fulfill the Law (5:17–20)
   2. The Antitheses: Jesus Messiah's Declarative
      Fulfillment of the Law (5:21–48)
      a. Murder—Nurturing Relationships (5:21–26)
      b. Adultery—Marital Oneness (5:27–30)
      c. Divorce—Marriage Sanctity Inviolate (5:31–32)
      d. Oaths—Transparent Honesty (5:33–37)
      e. Eye for an Eye—Servanthood (5:38–42)
      f. Love and Hatred—Unconditional Commitment
         (5:43–47)
   3. Conclusion: The Pursuit of Perfection (5:48)
D. The Development of Kingdom Life in the Real World
   (6:1–7:12)
   1. Public Kingdom Spirituality in Religious Life
      (6:1–18)
      a. The Principle (6:1)
      b. Alms (6:2–4)
      c. Prayer (6:5–15)
      d. Fasting (6:16–18)
   2. Personal Kingdom Spirituality in the Everyday World
      (6:19–34)
      a. Choose Your Master: God or Wealth (6:19–24)
      b. Choose Your Provider: God or Worry (6:25–34)

    3. Interpersonal Kingdom Spirituality in Community
      Relationships (7:1–12)
      a. Judging Others Inappropriately (7:1–5)
      b. Evaluating Others Appropriately (7:6)
      c. God's Guidance in Relationship to Others (7:7–12)
  E. Warning! With Jesus or Against Him (7:13–29)
    1. Narrow and Broad Gates and Roads (7:13–14)
    2. True and False Prophets (7:15–20)
    3. True and False Disciples (7:21–23)
    4. Wise and Foolish Builders (7:24–27)
    5. The Reaction of the Crowds (7:28–29)

**V. The Authoritative Power of Messiah: Kingdom Power Demonstrated (8:1–9:38)**
  A. Healing the Marginalized (8:1–17)
    1. Cleansing the Leper: Purity Boundaries (8:1–4)
    2. Healing the Centurion's Servant: Ethnic Boundaries (8:5–13)
    3. Healing Peter's Mother-in-Law: Gender Boundaries (8:14–15)
    4. The Many: The Demon-Possessed: All Boundaries (8:16–17)
  B. Expected Discipleship Disappointed (8:18–22)
  C. Overpowering Satan's Strongholds (8:23–9:8)
    1. Calming a Storm: Authority over Nature (8:23–27)
    2. Exorcising the Demoniacs: Authority over the Spirit World (8:28–34)
    3. Healing the Paralytic: Authority over Sin (9:1–8)
  D. Unexpected Discipleship Revealed (9:9–17)
    1. Calling Matthew and Other Sinners (9:9–13)
    2. Discipleship and Religious Traditions (9:14–17)
  E. Unexpected Miracles Demonstrate Extraordinary Compassion (9:18–34)
    1. The Dead Have Life (9:18–26)
    2. The Blind Have Sight (9:27–31)
    3. The Mute Have Voice (9:32–34)
  F. The Messiah at Work Enlists Workers (9:35–38)

**VI. Second Discourse—Mission Mandate—Authoritative Mission of Messiah's Messengers (10:1–42)**
  A. Commissioning the Twelve for Mission (10:1–4)
  B. Instructions for the Short-Term Mission to Israel (10:5–15)

C. Instructions for the Long-Term Mission to the World
(10:16–23)
D. Characteristics of Missionary Disciples (10:24–42)
1. Disciples and the Master in Mission (10:24–25)
2. Fearless Followers (10:26–31)
3. Acknowledging Jesus' Supremacy in Public (10:32–33)
4. Allegiance to Jesus' Supremacy at Home (10:34–39)
5. Reward for Receiving Jesus' Mission-Disciples
(10:40–42)

VII. **Opposition to the Messiah Emerges (11:1–12:50)**
A. John the Baptist Questions Jesus (11:2–6)
B. Jesus' Tribute to John the Baptist (11:7–15)
C. The Discontented Generation (11:16–19)
D. The Privileged Unrepentant Cities (11:20–24)
E. An Invitation to a Relationship with the Father and
the Son (11:25–30)
F. Confrontations with the Pharisees over the Sabbath
(12:1–14)
1. Working on the Sabbath (12:1–8)
2. Healing on the Sabbath (12:9–14)
G. God's Spirit-Anointed Servant (12:15–21)
H. Confrontations with the Pharisees over the Source of
Jesus' Miraculous Power (12:22–37)
1. The Pharisees Accuse Jesus of Demonism (12:22–24)
2. Jesus' Defense (12:25–29)
3. Jesus' Offense (12:30–37)
I. Confrontations with the Pharisees over Their Demand
for a "Sign" (12:38–42)
J. The Wicked Generation and the Return of the Evil Spirit
(12:43–45)
K. Jesus' Disciples Are His True Family (12:46–50)

VIII. **Third Discourse—Parabolic Disclosure—Mysteries of the
Messianic Kingdom (13:1–58)**
A. The Opening of the Parabolic Discourse (13:1–23)
1. The Parable of the Sower and Soils (13:3b–9)
2. Jesus' Purpose for Speaking in Parables (13:10–17)
3. Interpretation of the Parable of the Sower and Soils
(13:18–23)
B. Further Parables Told to the Crowds (13:24–33)
1. The Parable of the Wheat and the Weeds (13:24–30)

2. The Parable of the Mustard Seed (13:31–32)
3. The Parable of the Leaven (13:33)
4. Parables that Reveal Hidden Things (13:34–35)
C. Explanations and Parables Told to the Disciples (13:36–50)
   1. Interpretation of the Parable of the Wheat and Weeds (13:36–43)
   2. The Parable of the Hidden Treasure (13:44)
   3. The Parable of the Costly Pearl (13:45–46)
   4. The Parable of the Dragnet (13:47–50)
D. The Parable of the Householder's Treasure (13:51–52)
E. Transition To a Clarification of the Messiah's Identity and Mission (13:53)

IX. **The Identity of the Messiah Revealed (13:54–16:20)**
A. Prophet(s) Without Honor (13:53–14:12)
   1. Jesus Rejected at Nazareth (13:54–58)
   2. John the Baptist Beheaded by Herod Antipas (14:1–12)
B. Compassionate Healer and Supplier for Israel (14:13–21)
C. The Son of God Is Worshiped (14:22–36)
   1. Walking on the Water (14:22–33)
   2. The Son of God Heals at Gennesaret (14:34–36)
D. The True Teacher of the Word of God (15:1–20)
   1. The Traditions of the Jewish Elders (15:1–9)
   2. Purity and Impurity from the Heart (15:10–20)
E. Compassionate Healer and Provider for Gentiles (15:21–39)
   1. Jesus Withdraws to Gentile Regions (15:21)
   2. A Gentile Woman Acknowledges Jesus as the Son of David (15:21–28)
   3. Many Gentiles Glorify the God of Israel (15:29–31)
   4. Feeding the Four Thousand (15:32–38)
   5. A Brief Return to Jewish Territory (15:39)
F. Peter Confesses Jesus As the Christ, the Son of the Living God (16:1–20)
   1. Jesus to Give No More Signs (16:1–4)
   2. Spiritual Leaven of the Pharisees and Sadducees (16:5–12)
   3. Who Is the Son of Man? (16:13–14)
   4. Peter's Confession of Jesus' Identity (16:15–16)
   5. Jesus' Pronouncements about Peter (16:17–19)

X. **The Suffering of the Messiah Revealed (16:21–17:27)**
   A. The Suffering Sacrifice (16:21–28)
      1. The Suffering and Risen Messiah (16:21)
      2. Peter's Presumption (16:22–23)
      3. The Cost of Discipleship (16:24–27)
      4. The Son of Man Coming in His Kingdom (16:27–28)
   B. The Beloved, Transfigured Son (17:1–13)
      1. The Transfiguration of Jesus (17:1–8)
      2. John the Baptist and the Coming of Elijah (17:9–13)
   C. Sons of the Kingdom (17:14–27)
      1. The Healing and Exorcism of an Epileptic Boy (17:14–20)
      2. The Second Passion Prediction (17:22–23)
      3. Paying the Temple Tax (17:24–27)

XI. **The Community of the Messiah Revealed (18:1–20:34)**
   A. Fourth Discourse—Community Prescription— Characteristics of Life in the Kingdom Community (18:1–35)
      1. The Greatness of Humility (18:1–4)
      2. Shelter for the Humble (18:5–9)
      3. Angelic Protection of the Little Ones (18:10)
      4. The Divine Search for Lost Sheep (18:12–14)
      5. Disciplining Wayward Disciples (18:15–17)
      6. Consensus on Community Discipline and Life (18:18–20)
      7. Forgiveness in the Community Toward Sinning Disciples (18:21–35)
   B. The Sanctity of Marriage in the Community (19:1–12)
      1. Journeying Through Judea to Jerusalem (19:1–2)
      2. The Question of Divorce in the Community (19:3–9)
      3. The Question of Singleness in the Community (19:10–12)
   C. Valuing the Kingdom Community (19:13–20:34)
      1. The Kingdom Community Belongs to Little Ones (19:13–15)
      2. The Tragedy of the Rich Young Man (19:16–22)
      3. The Gracious Reward for Those Who Follow Jesus (19:23–30)
      4. The Parable of the Vineyard Workers (20:1–16)
      5. Jesus' Third Passion Prediction (20:17–19)

6. The Example of Jesus for Community Sacrifice, Suffering and Service (20:20–28)
7. Merciful Healing of Two Blind Men in Jericho (20:29–34)

XII. **The Messiah Asserts His Authority over Jerusalem (21–23)**
A. The Climactic Entry into Jerusalem: Jesus' Authority as Messiah (21:1–11)
B. The Temple Actions: Jesus' Pronouncement on the Temple Establishment (21:12–17)
C. Cursing the Fig Tree: Jesus' Judgment of the Nation (21:18–22)
D. Controversies in the Temple Court over Jesus' Authority (21:23–22:46)
   1. Three Parables of Condemnation of Religious Leadership of Israel (21:28–22:14).
      a. The Parable of the Two Sons (21:28–32)
      b. The Parable of the Wicked Tenants (21:33–46)
      c. The Parable of the Wedding Banquet (22:1–14)
   2. Four Debates with the Religious Leaders Concerning Jesus' Authority and Identity (22:15–46)
      a. Tribute in the Kingdoms (22:15–22)
      b. Marriage at the Resurrection (22:23–33)
      c. The Greatest Commandment (22:34–40)
      d. The Son of David (22:41–46)
E. Warnings and Woes of Judgment Against the Teachers of the Law and the Pharisees (23:1–36)
   1. Warning the Crowds and the Disciples (23:1–12)
   2. Woes on the Teachers of the Law and the Pharisees (23:13–32)
   3. Final Invective: Murderers of the Righteous (23:33–36)
   4. Lament over Jerusalem (23:37–39)

XIII. **Fifth Discourse—Olivet Discourse—The Delay, Return, and Judgment of Messiah (24:1–25:46)**
A. The Setting of the Discourse (24:1–3)
B. The Beginning of Birth Pains (24:4–14)
   1. Sufferings Throughout the World (24:4–8)
   2. Sufferings of Jesus' Disciples (24:9–13)
   3. Preaching the Gospel to All Nations (24:14)
C. Description of "Great Tribulation" (24:15–28)
   1. The Abomination That Causes Desolation (24:15)

2. Flight of Believers (24:16–20)
3. "Great Tribulation" (24:21)
4. The Days Cut Short (24:22)
5. Warnings About False Messiahs (24:23–28)
D. Description of the Coming of the Son of Man (24:29–31)
E. The Lesson of the Fig Tree (24:32–35)
F. The "Time" of Jesus' Coming (24:36–41)
G. Parabolic Exhortations to Watch and Be Prepared for the Coming of the Son of Man (24:42–25:30)
1. The Parable of the Homeowner and the Thief (24:42–44)
2. The Parable of Two Kinds of Servants (24:45–51)
3. The Parable of the Ten Virgins (25:1–13)
4. The Parable of the Talents (25:14–30)
H. Judgment at the End (25:31–46)
1. Sheep Separated from Goats (25:31–33)
2. The Reward of the Sheep (25:34–40)
3. The Punishment of the Goats (25:41–46)

XIV. **The Crucified Messiah (26:1–27:66)**
A. Jesus' Prediction and the Plot of the Religious Leaders (26:1–5)
B. Jesus Anointed at Bethany (26:6–13)
C. Judas Arranges the Betrayal (26:14–16)
D. The Passover and the Lord's Supper (26:17–30)
E. Peter's Denial Predicted (26:31–35)
F. Gethsemane: Jesus' Agonizing Prayers (26:36–46)
G. Jesus' Arrest (26:47–56)
H. The Jewish Trial of Jesus (26:57–27:10)
1. Jesus Before the Sanhedrin (26:57–68)
2. Peter's Denials of Jesus (26:69–75)
3. Jesus Condemned by the Sanhedrin and Delivered to Pilate (27:1–2)
4. Judas's Remorse and Suicide (27:3–10)
I. The Roman Trial of Jesus (27:11–26)
1. Jesus Before Pilate (27:11–14)
2. The Crowd, Barabbas, and Jesus (27:15–18)
3. The Dream of Pilate's Wife (27:19)
4. The Religious Leaders, the Crowd, and Jesus' Blood (27:20–26)

J.  Jesus Messiah Is Crucified (27:27–44)
    1. The Soldiers Flog and Mock Jesus (27:27–31)
    2. The Journey to Golgotha (27:32–34)
    3. Jesus Is Crucified (27:35–38)
    4. The Mocking of Messiah (27:39–44)
K. The Death of Jesus Messiah (27:45–50)
L. Testimonies to Jesus' death (27:51–54)
    1. Testimony from the Temple (27:51)
    2. Testimony from the Dead (27:51b–53)
    3. Testimony from Gentiles (27:54)
M. The Women Followers of Jesus (27:55–56)
N. The Burial of Jesus Messiah (27:57–61)
O. The Guard at the Tomb (27:62–66)

**XV. The Resurrection and Commission of the Messiah (28:1–20)**
    A. The Women Disciples of Jesus Discover an Empty Tomb
       (28:1–7)
    B. The Risen Jesus Appears to the Women Disciples (28:8–10)
    C. The Conspiracy to Deny the Truth of Jesus' Resurrection
       (28:11–15)
    D. The Risen Jesus' Great Commission (28:16–20)

# Bibliography

## Commentaries

Albright, W. F., and C. S. Mann. *Matthew.* AB 26. Garden City, N.Y.: Doubleday, 1971.

Allen, Willoughby C. *A Critical and Exegetical Commentary on the Gospel According to St. Matthew.* ICC. 3d ed. Edinburgh: T. & T. Clark, 1912.

Augsburger, Myron S. *Matthew.* The Communicator's Commentary. Waco, Tex.: Word, 1982.

Barclay, William. *The Gospel of Matthew.* 2 vols. DSB. Rev. ed. Philadelphia: Westminster, 1975.

Barton, Bruce B., Mark Fackler, Linda K. Taylor, and David R. Veerman. *Matthew.* Life Application Bible Commentary. Wheaton: Tyndale, 1996.

Beare, Francis Wright. *The Gospel According to Matthew: Translation, Introduction and Commentary.* San Francisco: Harper & Row, 1981.

Betz, Hans Dieter. *The Sermon on the Mount: A Commentary on the Sermon on the Mount, Including the Sermon on the Plain (Matthew 5:3–7:27 and Luke 6:20–49).* Hermeneia. Minneapolis: Fortress, 1995.

Blomberg, Craig L. *Matthew.* NAC 22. Nashville: Broadman, 1992.

Boring, M. Eugene. "The Gospel of Matthew: Introduction, Commentary, and Reflections." *The New Interpreter's Bible.* Vol. 8. Nashville: Abingdon, 1995.

Broadus, John. *Matthew.* An American Commentary. Valley Forge, Pa.: Judson, 1886.

Brown, Raymond E. *The Birth of the Messiah: A Commentary on the Infancy Narratives in the Gospels of Matthew and Luke.* ABRL. Rev. ed. New York: Doubleday, 1993.

_____. *The Death of the Messiah: From Gethsemane to the Grave. A Commentary on the Passion Narratives in the Four Gospels.* 2 vols. ABRL. New York: Doubleday, 1994.

Bruce, A. B. "The Gospel According to Matthew." *The Expositor's Greek Testament.* Vol. 1. Grand Rapids: Eerdmans, 1976.

Bruner, Frederick Dale. *Matthew.* 2 vols. *The ChristBook (Matthew 1–12)* and *The Churchbook (Matthew 13–28).* Dallas: Word, 1987, 1990.

Buchanan, George Wesley. *The Gospel of Matthew.* 2 vols. Mellen Biblical Commentary. Lewiston, N.Y.: Mellen Biblical Press, 1996.

Carson, D. A. "Matthew." *The Expositor's Bible Commentary.* Vol. 8. Grand Rapids: Zondervan, 1984.

47

# Bibliography

Davies, Margaret. *Matthew*. Readings: A New Biblical Commentary. Sheffield: JSOT Press, 1993.

Davies, W. D., and Dale C. Allison Jr. *A Critical and Exegetical Commentary on the Gospel According to Saint Matthew*. 3 vols. ICC. Edinburgh: T. & T. Clark, 1988, 1991, 1997.

Hare, Douglas R. A. *Matthew*. Interpretation. Louisville: John Knox, 1993.

Fenton, J. C. *Saint Matthew*. Westminster Pelican Commentaries. Philadelphia: Westminster, 1963.

Filson, Floyd V. *The Gospel According to St. Matthew*. BNTC. 2d ed. London: Adam & Charles Black, 1971.

France, R. T. *The Gospel According to Matthew*. TNTC. Grand Rapids: Eerdmans, 1985.

Gardner, Richard B. *Matthew*. Believers Church Bible Commentary. Scottdale, Pa.: Herald, 1991.

Garland, David E. *Reading Matthew*. New York: Crossroad, 1993.

Glasscock, Ed. *Matthew*. Moody Gospel Commentary. Chicago: Moody Press, 1997.

Gnilka, J. *Das Matthäusevangelium*. 2 vols. HTKNT. Freiburg: Herder, 1986, 1988.

Green, H. Benedict. *The Gospel According to Matthew: Introduction and Commentary*. The New Clarendon Bible (New Testament). Oxford: Oxford Univ. Press, 1975.

Green, Michael. *The Message of Matthew: The Kingdom of Heaven*. BST. Downers Grove, Ill.: InterVarsity Press, 2000.

Guelich, Robert A. *The Sermon on the Mount: A Foundation for Understanding*. Waco, Tex.: Word, 1982.

Gundry, Robert H. *Matthew: A Commentary on His Handbook for a Mixed Church Under Persecution*. 2d ed. Grand Rapids: Eerdmans, 1994.

Hagner, Donald. *Matthew 1–13*. WBC 33A. Dallas: Word, 1993.

_____. *Matthew 14–28*. WBC 33B. Dallas: Word, 1995.

Harrington, Daniel J. *The Gospel of Matthew*. Sacra Pagina. Collegeville, Minn.: Michael Glazier, 1991.

Hendriksen, William. *Exposition of the Gospel According to Matthew*. Grand Rapids: Baker, 1973.

Hill, David. *The Gospel of Matthew*. NCB. Grand Rapids: Eerdmans, 1972.

Keener, Craig S. *A Commentary on the Gospel of Matthew*. Grand Rapids: Eerdmans, 1999.

_____. *Matthew*. IVPNTC. Downers Grove, Ill.: InterVarsity Press, 1997.

Leiva-Merikakis, Erasmo. *Fire of Mercy, Heart of the Word: Meditations on the Gospel According to St. Matthew*. Vol. 1. San Francisco: Ignatius, 1996.

Levine, Amy-Jill. *A Feminist Companion to Matthew*. Feminist Companion to the New Testament and Early Christian Writings. Vol. 1. Sheffield: Sheffield Academic Press, 2001.

Long, Thomas G. *Matthew*. Westminster Bible Companion. Louisville: Westminster John Knox, 1997.

Luz, Ulrich. *Matthew 1–7: A Commentary*. 1985. Trans. Wilhelm C. Linss. Hermeneia. Minneapolis: Augsburg, 1989.

_____. *Matthew 8–20: A Commentary*. Hermeneia. Trans. James E. Crouch. Minneapolis: Fortress, 2001.

MacArthur, John. *Matthew 1–7; Matthew 8–15; Matthew 16–23; Matthew 24–28*. MacArthur New Testament Commentary. Chicago: Moody Press, 1985, 1987, 1989.

McNeile, Alan Hugh. *The Gospel According to Matthew: The Greek Text with Introduction, Notes, and Indices*. Grand Rapids: Baker, 1980.

Meier, John P. *Matthew*. NTM 3. Wilmington, Del.: Michael Glazier, 1980.

Morgan, G. Campbell. *The Gospel According to Matthew*. Old Tappan, N.J.: Revell, n.d.

Morris, Leon. *The Gospel According to Matthew*. PNTC. Grand Rapids: Eerdmans, 1992.

Mounce, Robert H. *Matthew*. GNC. San Francisco: Harper & Row, 1985.

Overman, J. Andrew. *Church and Community in Crisis: The Gospel According to Matthew*. The New Testament in Context. Valley Forge, Pa.: Trinity Press International, 1996.

Perlewitz, M. *The Gospel of Matthew*. Message of Biblical Spirituality 8. Wilmington, Del.: Michael Glazier, 1988.

Plummer, Alfred. *An Exegetical Commentary on the Gospel According to St. Matthew*. Grand Rapids: Baker, 1982.

Ridderbos, H. N. *Matthew*. BSC. Grand Rapids: Zondervan, 1987.

Robertson, Archibald Thomas. "The Gospel According to Matthew." *Word Pictures in the New Testament*. Vol. 1. Nashville: Broadman, 1930.

Ryle, J. C. *Matthew: Expository Thoughts on the Gospels*. Reprinted in The Crossway Classic Commentaries. Wheaton: Crossway, 1993.

Sand, Alexander. *Das Evangelium nach Matthäus*. Regensburger Neues Testament. Regensburg: Friedrich Pustet, 1986.

Schnackenburg, Rudolf. *The Gospel of Matthew*. Trans. Robert R. Barr. Grand Rapids: Eerdmans, 2002.

Schweizer, Eduard. *The Good News According to Matthew*. Atlanta: John Knox, 1975.

Senior, Donald. *Matthew*. Abingdon New Testament Commentaries. Nashville: Abingdon, 1998.

Simonetti, Manlio, ed. *Matthew 1–13*. ACCSNT 1a. Downers Grove, Ill.: InterVarsity Press, 2001.

_____. *Matthew 14–28*. ACCSNT 1b. Downers Grove, Ill.: InterVarsity Press, 2002.

Smith, R. H. *Matthew.* Augsburg Commentary on the New Testament. Minneapolis: Augsburg, 1989.

Tasker, R. V. G. *The Gospel According to St. Matthew: An Introduction and Commentary.* TNTC. Grand Rapids: Eerdmans, 1961.

Toussaint, Stanley D. *Behold the King: A Study of Matthew.* Portland, Ore.: Multnomah, 1981.

Trilling, Wolfgang. *The Gospel According to St. Matthew.* 2 vols. New York: Crossroad, 1981.

Walvoord, John F. *Matthew: Thy Kingdom Come.* Chicago: Moody Press, 1974.

Weber, Stuart K. *Matthew.* Holman New Testament Commentary. Nashville: Holman, 2000.

Wilkins, Michael. "Matthew." *ZIBBC.* Grand Rapids: Zondervan, 2002.

Zanchettin, Leo, ed. *Matthew: A Devotional Commentary.* Mahwah, N.J.: Paulist, 1997.

## Special Studies

This is only a sampling of the vast literature on Matthew. Shorter studies, such as journal articles and chapters in books, are found in the footnotes.

Aune, David E., ed. *The Gospel of Matthew in Current Study: Studies in Memory of William G. Thompson, S.J.* Grand Rapids: Eerdmans, 2001.

Bauckham, Richard. *Gospel Women: Studies of the Named Women in the Gospels.* Grand Rapids: Eerdmans, 2002.

Bornkamm, Günther, Gerhard Barth, and Heinz Joachim Held. *Tradition and Interpretation in Matthew.* Trans. Percy Scott. Philadelphia: Westminster, 1963.

Brown, Jeannine K. *The Disciples in Narrative Perspective: The Portrayal and Function of the Matthean Disciples.* SBL Academia Biblica 9. Atlanta: Society of Biblical Literature, 2002.

Burkett, Delbert. *The Son of Man Debate: A History and Evaluation.* SNTSMS 107. Cambridge: Cambridge Univ. Press, 1999.

Caragounis, Chrys. *Peter and the Rock.* BZNW 58. Berlin/New York: de Gruyter, 1990.

Carter, Warren. *Households and Discipleship: A Study of Matthew 19–20.* JSNTSup 103. Sheffield: JSOT Press, 1994.

_____. *Matthew: Storyteller, Interpreter, Evangelist.* Peabody, Mass.: Hendrickson, 1996.

_____, and John Paul Heil, *Matthew's Parables: Audience-Oriented Perspectives.* CBQMS 30. Washington, D.C.: Catholic Biblical Association of America, 1998.

Cousland, J. R. C. *The Crowds in the Gospel of Matthew.* NovTSup 102. Leiden: Brill, 2002.

Davis, Stephen, Daniel Kendall, and Gerald O'Collins, eds. *The Resurrection: An Interdisciplinary Symposium on the Resurrection of Jesus*. Oxford: Oxford Univ. Press, 1997.

Donaldson, Terence L. *Jesus on the Mountain: A Study in Matthean Theology*. JSNTSup 8. Sheffield: JSOT Press, 1985.

Edwards, Richard A. *Matthew's Story of Jesus*. Philadelphia: Fortress, 1985.

_____. *Matthew's Narrative Portrait of Disciples: How the Text-Connoted Reader Is Informed*. Harrisburg, Pa.: Trinity Press International, 1997.

France, R. T. *Matthew: Evangelist and Teacher*. Grand Rapids: Zondervan, 1989.

Gerhardsson, Birger. *The Testing of God's Son (Matt 4:1–11 and Par.)*. ConBNT 2.1. Lund: Gleerup, 1996.

Goodacre, Mark. *The Case Against Q: Studies in Markan Priority and the Synoptic Problem*. Harrisburg, Pa.: Trinity Press International, 2002.

Green, H. Benedict. *Matthew, Poet of the Beatitudes*. JSNTSup 203. Sheffield: Sheffield Academic Press, 2001.

Howell, David B. *Matthew's Inclusive Story: A Study in the Narrative Rhetoric of the First Gospel*. JSNTSup 42. Sheffield: JSOT Press, 1990.

Ilan, Tal. *Jewish Women in Greco-Roman Palestine: An Inquiry into Image and Status*. Tübingen: J. C. B. Mohr (Paul Siebeck), 1995.

Kingsbury, Jack Dean. *Matthew As Story*. 2d ed. Philadelphia: Fortress, 1988.

_____. *Matthew: Structure, Christology, Kingdom*. 2d ed. Minneapolis: Fortress, 1989.

Knowles, Michael. *Jeremiah in Matthew's Gospel: The Rejected-Prophet Motif in Matthean Redaction*. JSNTSup 68. Sheffield: Sheffield Academic Press, 1993.

Köstenberger, Andreas J., and Peter T. O'Brien. *Salvation to the Ends of the Earth: A Biblical Theology of Mission*. NSBT 11. Downers Grove, Ill.: InterVarsity Press, 2001.

Kupp, David D. *Matthew's Emmanuel: Divine Presence and God's People in the First Gospel*. SNTSMS. Cambridge: Cambridge Univ. Press, 1997.

LaGrand, James. *The Earliest Christian Mission to "All Nations" in the Light of Matthew's Gospel*. International Studies in Formative Christianity and Judaism. Atlanta: Scholars Press, 1995.

Levine, Amy-Jill. *The Social and Ethnic Dimensions of Matthean Salvation History*. Studies in the Bible and Early Christianity 14. Lewiston, N.Y.: Mellen, 1988.

McKnight, Scot. *A Light Among the Gentiles: Jewish Missionary Activity in the Second Temple Period*. Minneapolis: Fortress, 1990.

Orton, David E. *The Understanding Scribe: Matthew and the Apocalyptic Ideal*. JSNTSup 25. Sheffield: Sheffield Academic Press, 1989.

Powell, Mark Allan, and David R. Bauer, eds. *Who Do You Say That I Am? Essays on Christology. In Honor of Jack Dean Kingsbury*. Louisville: Westminster John Knox, 1999.

Robinson, James M., Paul Hoffmann, and John S. Kloppenborg, eds. *The Critical Edition of Q: Synopsis Including the Gospels of Matthew and Luke, Mark and Thomas, with English, German and French Translations of Q and Thomas.* Hermeneia. Minneapolis: Fortress, 2000.

Rousseau, John J., and Rami Arav. *Jesus and His World: An Archaeological and Cultural Dictionary.* Minneapolis: Fortress, 1995.

Saldarini, Anthony J. *Matthew's Christian-Jewish Community.* Chicago: Univ. of Chicago Press, 1994.

Sim, David C. *Apocalyptic Eschatology in the Gospel of Matthew.* SNTSMS 88. Cambridge: Cambridge Univ. Press, 1996.

_____. *The Gospel of Matthew and Christian Judaism: The History and Social Setting of the Matthean Community.* Studies of the New Testament and Its World. Edinburgh: T. & T. Clark, 1998.

Stanton, Graham N. *A Gospel for a New People: Studies in Matthew.* Edinburgh: T. & T. Clark, 1992.

Tan, Kim Huat. *The Zion Traditions and the Aims of Jesus.* SNTSMS. Cambridge: Cambridge Univ. Press, 1997.

Twelftree, Graham H. *Jesus the Miracle Worker: A Historical and Theological Study.* Downers Grove, Ill.: InterVarsity Press, 1999.

Vledder, Evert-Jan. *Conflict in the Miracle Stories: A Socio-Exegetical Study of Matthew 8 and 9.* JSNTSup 152. Sheffield: Sheffield Academic Press, 1997.

Webb, Robert L. *John the Baptizer and Prophet: A Socio-Historical Study.* JSNTSup 62. Sheffield: JSOT Press, 1991.

Wenham, David. *The Rediscovery of Jesus' Eschatological Discourse.* Gospel Perspectives 4. Sheffield: JSOT Press, 1984.

Wilkins, Michael J. *The Concept of Disciple in Matthew's Gospel As Reflected in the Use of the Term μαθητής.* NovTSup 59. Leiden: Brill, 1988.

_____. *Following the Master: A Biblical Theology of Discipleship.* Grand Rapids: Zondervan, 1992.

_____. *Discipleship in the Ancient World and Matthew's Gospel.* 2d ed. Grand Rapids: Baker, 1995.

Yamasaki, Gary. *John the Baptist in Life and Death: Audience-Oriented Criticism of Matthew's Narrative.* JSNTSup 167. Sheffield: Sheffield Academic Press, 1998.

Yang, Yong-Eui. *Jesus and the Sabbath in Matthew's Gospel.* JSNTSup 139. Sheffield: Sheffield Academic Press, 1997.

# Matthew 1:1–17

A RECORD OF the genealogy of Jesus Christ the son of David, the son of Abraham:

² Abraham was the father of Isaac,
   Isaac the father of Jacob,
   Jacob the father of Judah and his brothers,
   ³ Judah the father of Perez and Zerah, whose mother
      was Tamar,
   Perez the father of Hezron,
   Hezron the father of Ram,
   ⁴ Ram the father of Amminadab,
   Amminadab the father of Nahshon,
   Nahshon the father of Salmon,
   ⁵ Salmon the father of Boaz, whose mother was Rahab,
   Boaz the father of Obed, whose mother was Ruth,
   Obed the father of Jesse,
   ⁶ and Jesse the father of King David.

David was the father of Solomon, whose mother had been
      Uriah's wife,
   ⁷ Solomon the father of Rehoboam,
   Rehoboam the father of Abijah,
   Abijah the father of Asa,
   ⁸ Asa the father of Jehoshaphat,
   Jehoshaphat the father of Jehoram,
   Jehoram the father of Uzziah,
   ⁹ Uzziah the father of Jotham,
   Jotham the father of Ahaz,
   Ahaz the father of Hezekiah,
   ¹⁰ Hezekiah the father of Manasseh,
   Manasseh the father of Amon,
   Amon the father of Josiah,
   ¹¹ and Josiah the father of Jeconiah and his brothers at the
      time of the exile to Babylon.

¹² After the exile to Babylon:
   Jeconiah was the father of Shealtiel,
   Shealtiel the father of Zerubbabel,

<sup>13</sup>Zerubbabel the father of Abiud,
Abiud the father of Eliakim,
Eliakim the father of Azor,
<sup>14</sup>Azor the father of Zadok,
Zadok the father of Akim,
Akim the father of Eliud,
<sup>15</sup>Eliud the father of Eleazar,
Eleazar the father of Matthan,
Matthan the father of Jacob,
<sup>16</sup>and Jacob the father of Joseph, the husband of Mary, of
whom was born Jesus, who is called Christ.

<sup>17</sup>Thus there were fourteen generations in all from Abraham to David, fourteen from David to the exile to Babylon, and fourteen from the exile to the Christ.

DURING THIS TIME the Mediterranean world experienced the famed *pax Romana* (Lat., "Roman peace"), a condition of comparative calm that originated with the reign of Caesar Augustus (27 B.C.–A.D. 14) and lasted at least to the reign of Marcus Aurelius (A.D. 161–180). The Roman historian Tacitus attributes the beginnings of this period of peace almost single-handedly to the immense powers of Augustus. But as Tacitus observes, the concord that Augustus inaugurated did not bring with it freedom for all of his subjects. Many throughout the Roman world hoped for change. He writes:

> Nobody had any immediate worries as long as Augustus retained his physical powers, and kept himself going, and his House, and the peace of the empire. But when old age incapacitated him, his approaching end brought hopes of change. A few people started idly talking of the blessings of freedom. Some, more numerous, feared civil war; others wanted it.[1]

Tides of revolution continually swirled just below the surface and periodically rose to disturb the *pax Romana*.

In one of the remote regions of the empire, where a variety of disturbances repeatedly surfaced, the hoped-for freedom finally arrived in a most unexpected way. A rival to Augustus was born in Israel. But this rival did not

---

1. Cornelius Tacitus, *The Annals of Imperial Rome* 1.4; trans. Michael Grant (rev. ed.; New York: Penguin, 1976).

appear with fanfare, nor would he challenge directly the military and political might of Rome. Even many of his own people eventually became disappointed with the revolution that he would bring, ~~because it was a revolution of the heart, not one of swords or chariots.~~

This was the revolution brought by Jesus, the long-awaited Messiah of Israel. Matthew's Gospel harks back upon a long history of anticipation within Israel. His recounting elucidates how Jesus' life and ministry fulfilled the promises of the Old Testament prophets, but also shows how Jesus disappointed many of the misplaced expectations of the people.

## Jesus Messiah Brings a New Beginning for Humanity (1:1)

MATTHEW INTRODUCES HIS Gospel with language reminiscent of Genesis. The Greek word that the NIV renders "genealogy" in 1:1 is *genesis*[2] ("beginnings"), which is also the title of the first book of the Old Testament in the Septuagint (the LXX, the Greek translation of the Old Testament). In fact, an almost identical expression to Matthew 1:1 occurs in the LXX of Genesis 2:4 and 5:1 to narrate both the beginning record of God's creation and the first genealogy of God's human creatures. Moreover, in Matthew the expression functions not only as a heading for the genealogy in 1:2–17,[3] but also for the beginning narrative of Jesus' infancy in 1:18–2:23.[4] A case can also be made that the expression functions as a title for the entire book about Jesus that follows.[5] Just as Genesis gave the story of one beginning—God's creation and covenant relations with Israel—so the Gospel of Matthew gives the story of a new beginning—the arrival of Jesus the Messiah and the kingdom of God (cf. also Mark 1:1).

Matthew's opening words ("Jesus Christ the son of David, the son of Abraham") had special importance to a Jewish audience, which traced its ancestry through the covenants God made with Israel. The heading, with Jesus' names and his ancestry, is packed with meaning.[6]

---

2. According to BDAG, 192, this word means "origin, source, productive cause, beginning," which in this context indicates "an account of someone's life."

3. Gundry, *Matthew*, 13.

4. Carson, "Matthew," *EBC*, 8:61, emphasizes that the recurrence of the noun *genesis* in 1:18 indicates that with the phrase Matthew focuses not just on the genealogy but on the more expansive "origin of Jesus Christ" in chs. 1–2.

5. W. D. Davies and Dale C. Allison Jr., *A Critical and Exegetical Commentary on the Gospel According to Saint Matthew*, Vol. 1: *Introduction and Commentary on Matthew I–VII* (ICC; Edinburgh: T. & T. Clark, 1988), 149–54, argue convincingly that the expression *biblos geneseos* is a title for the entire book. See also Leon Morris, *The Gospel According to Matthew* (PNTC; Grand Rapids: Eerdmans, 1992), 19.

6. The expressions "son of David" and "son of Abraham" stand in apposition to "Jesus Christ," indicating that the titles are a further explanation of Jesus' identity.

In common practice a person had a single personal name, which often carried some religious significance. This book is about "Jesus" (*Iesous*), which is his historical, everyday name, the name normally used in the narrative of the Gospels. This name is Yeshua in Hebrew (meaning "Yahweh saves," cf. Neh. 7:7), which is a shortened form of Joshua (*yehošuaᶜ*), "Yahweh is salvation" (Ex. 24:13); this name will come to have profound notions of salvation associated with it in Jesus' life and ministry (cf. 1:21).[7]

"Christ" (*Christos*) is a title, derived from the Hebrew *mašiaḥ* ("anointed"), that harks back to David as the anointed king of Israel. The term came to be associated with the promise of an "anointed one" who would be the light of hope for the people of Israel. God had promised David through Nathan the prophet that his house and throne would be established forever (2 Sam. 7:11b–16)—a promise now seen as having been fulfilled in Jesus as the Messiah. The full name using the transliterated form (i.e., "Jesus Christ") is accurate and traditional, but in common usage it can be misunderstood to be something like a first and last name.

"Son of David" is an important expression in Matthew's Gospel (9:27; 12:23; 15:22; 20:30–31; 21:9, 15; 22:42, 45). Matthew uses the name of this great king seventeen times, more than any other book of the New Testament. King David was the revered, conquering warrior of Israel's history. The wording "son of David" expresses a promised figure who would perpetuate David's throne, thereby pointing to the Messiah's lineage and royal expectation (see 2 Sam. 7:11b–16). But it also evoked images of a Messiah who would come conquering—a mighty warrior like David who would destroy Israel's enemies and reestablish the throne in Jerusalem and the kingdom of Israel as in the golden days of David.

But Jesus is also "the son of Abraham." In tracing the ancestry not only to David but also to Abraham, Matthew holds a light of hope to the entire world. The covenant God made with Abraham established Israel as a chosen people, but it was also a promise that his line would be a blessing to all the nations (Gen. 12:1–3; 22:18).[8]

Consequently, the introduction of this Gospel with its ancestry of Jesus offers an important key to interpreting Matthew's message. Jesus' ministry brought fulfillment of God's covenant to the particular people of Israel (e.g., 10:6; 15:24), but it also brought fulfillment of God's promise to bring universal

---

7. Cf. Birger Gerhardsson, "The Christology of Matthew," in *Who Do You Say That I Am? Essays on Christology in Honor of Jack Dean Kingsbury*, ed. Mark Allan Powell and David R. Bauer (Louisville: Westminster John Knox, 1999), 16–17.

8. See, e.g., M. Daniel Carroll R., "Blessing the Nations: Toward a Biblical Theology of Mission from Genesis," *BBR* 10 (2000): 17–34; Richard J. Erickson, "Joseph and the Birth of Isaac in Matthew 1," *BBR* 10 (2000): 35–51.

hope to all the nations (cf. 21:43; 28:19). This latter theme becomes increasingly pronounced in the Gospel and rises to a climax in the concluding commission (cf. 28:18–20).

## Jesus Messiah's Genealogy (1:2–17)

GENEALOGIES WERE IMPORTANT in the ancient world and played an especially significant role for the Jews. According to the Old Testament (e.g., 1 Chron. 1–9), God's people kept extensive genealogies, which served as a record of a family's descendants but were also used for practical and legal purposes to establish a person's heritage, inheritance, legitimacy, and rights. Knowledge of one's descent was especially necessary, if a dispute occurred, to ensure that property went to the right person.[9]

Matthew most likely draws on some of the genealogies found in the Old Testament[10] and uses similar wording. For the list of individuals after Zerubbabel, when the Old Testament ceases, Matthew probably uses other records that have since been lost. Sources indicate that extensive genealogical records were extant during the first century,[11] with some of the more important records of political and priestly families kept in the temple. Later rabbinic tradition, for example, tried to establish the descent from David of a near contemporary to Jesus, Rabbi Hillel, through a genealogical scroll that was purportedly located in Jerusalem.[12] The official extrabiblical genealogies were lost with the destruction of the temple and Jerusalem in A.D. 70, though private genealogies were retained elsewhere.

Luke gives a genealogy of Jesus as well (see Luke 3:23–38).[13] There are several basic differences between Matthew's (1:2–17) and Luke's list. (1) Matthew gives a descending genealogy, beginning with the earliest ancestor, Abraham, placed at the head and citing later generations in forward lines of descent (i.e., moving from father to son), culminating with the birth of Jesus. This is the more common form of Jewish genealogy in the Old

---

9. Cf. Marshall D. Johnson, *The Purpose of Biblical Genealogies with Special Reference to the Setting of the Genealogies of Jesus*, 2d ed. (SNTSMS 8; Cambridge: Cambridge Univ. Press, 1988).

10. E.g., Gen. 4:17–18; 5:3–32; 10:1–32; 46:8–27; 1 Chron.1:34; 2:1–15; 3:1–24; Ruth 4:12–22. See John Nolland, "Genealogical Annotation in Genesis as Background for the Matthean Genealogy of Jesus," *TynBul* 47 (May 1996): 115–22, who suggests that Matthew studied the Genesis genealogies and patterned his own after them.

11. E.g., Josephus, *Life* 6; *Contra Apion* 1.28–56.

12. *Genesis Rabbah* 98:8; *j. Ta'anit* 4:2; see Anthony J. Saldarini, *Pharisees, Scribes and Sadducees in Palestinian Society: A Sociological Approach* (Wilmington, Del.: Michael Glazier, 1988), 204–6.

13. For discussion, see Raymond E. Brown, *The Birth of the Messiah: A Commentary on the Infancy Narratives in the Gospels of Matthew and Luke*, rev. ed. (ABRL; New York: Doubleday, 1993), 84–95.

Testament (e.g., Gen. 5:1–32). Luke gives an ascending form of genealogy that reverses the order (moving from son to father), starting with Jesus and tracing it backward to Adam (Luke 3:23–38; cf. Ezra 7:1–5). This reverse order is more commonly found in some Greco-Roman genealogies.

(2) Matthew places special emphasis on the covenants made with Israel, in line with the opening verse of his Gospel, by tracing Jesus' lineage to David (1:6) and Abraham (1:2). Luke places special emphasis on Jesus' relation to all of humanity and to God himself by tracing his lineage to "Adam, the son of God" (Luke 3:38)—Jesus is the son of Adam and the son of God.

(3) The names of several persons after the Babylonian deportation differ between the two genealogies. For example, Matthew follows the line through Jeconiah, Shealtiel, and Zerubbabel, while Luke follows the line through Neri, Shealtiel, and Zerubbabel.

(4) Matthew omits several names that are found in the genealogy of Luke, most likely for the purpose of literary symmetry for memorization (see comments on 1:17, below). The verb *gennao* ("give birth to, father") is used in each link of Matthew's genealogy and is often used to indicate a more remote ancestor (e.g., grandfather or great-grandfather).

(5) One of the most significant features of Matthew's record is his emphasis on Jesus' kingly lineage. David is not simply the son of Jesse (Luke 3:31–32) but he is "King David" (Matt. 1:6). Further, Matthew traces Jesus' genealogy through David's son Solomon, who had succeeded his father as king of Israel, while Luke traces the line through David's son Nathan, who never reigned as king (cf. 1:6; Luke 3:32; cf. 2 Sam. 5:14).

What accounts for the differences in the genealogies of Jesus given in Matthew and Luke? Two basic explanations are often cited, although the variations are numerous. (1) The first view emphasizes generally that Matthew gives Jesus' line through his father Joseph while Luke gives Jesus' line through his mother Mary. (2) The second basic view emphasizes that Matthew and Luke focus on Joseph in both genealogies but for different purposes. While fully accounting for the differences remains unsolvable with the information we now possess, it does seem clear that Matthew intends to demonstrate Jesus' legal claim to the throne of David. David's greater Son, the anticipated Davidic messianic king, has arrived with the birth of Jesus.[14]

**From Abraham to King David (1:2–6a).** Matthew's emphases in his genealogy give clues to his understanding of Jesus' identity and ministry.[15] The basic pattern of the genealogy is established in the first listing: "Abraham was the father of Isaac" (lit., "Abraham fathered Isaac"). This is in line

---

14. Cf. 22:41–46; 2 Sam. 7:12–16; Ps. 89:19–29, 35–37; 110:1–7; 132:11–12.

15. Matthew's emphases, when seen as a whole, give important clues to Jesus' identity and future ministry.

with the typical Old Testament wording, such as the LXX rendering of 1 Chronicles 1:34: "Abraham fathered Isaac." This same pattern occurs forty times, using the active voice of the verb *gennao* (cf. the KJV expression, "begat"). This expression emphasizes the human descent of each generation, which paves the way for a dramatic change of construction in 1:16, where a passive voice occurs, by which Matthew points to the divine origin of Jesus.

Matthew states that Jacob fathered "Judah and his brothers," probably to point to the inclusiveness of the covenant family of Israel from which Messiah would come. Judah was the son of Jacob who would carry the scepter, the ruling staff (Gen. 49:8–12). The Messiah would come from the royal line of Judah (Gen. 49:10), but he lived within the covenant people that came from the lines of the other brothers. Through Tamar, Judah fathered two brothers, Zerah and Perez (Matt. 1:2), who are probably mentioned because they were twins (Gen. 38:27–30).

Approximately 450 years are enclosed within the four generations of the families from Perez to Amminadab, who was connected with the first census taken of the Israelite nation by Moses during the desert wanderings (Num. 1:7).[16] Approximately 400 more years elapse during the span of time of the six generations listed from Nahshon, who led the tribe of Judah in the desert, to the rise of the monarchy with David's birth.[17] This is a direct indication that Matthew omits names from the genealogy in 1 Chronicles 2:5, 9–15. Such omission was common in the ancient world, primarily to make a genealogy easy to memorize (see comment on 1:17).

Boaz (cf. 1 Chron. 2:11–12) is the first person in the genealogy since Judah who is well known in the Old Testament narratives. He is one of the leading characters in the book of Ruth, where he marries Ruth the Moabitess and fathers Obed (Matt. 1:5; cf. Ruth 4:17, 21; 1 Chron. 2:12). Little else is known of Obed except that he fathers Jesse (Matt. 1:5; cf. Ruth 4:17, 21), who in turn fathers David. Jesse figures prominently in the Old Testament narrative, primarily during the anointing of David by Samuel, the early rise of David to power in the court of Saul, and David's initiation to military life with the slaying of Goliath (1 Sam. 16–17).

The inclusion of five women in Jesus' genealogy—Tamar, Rahab, Ruth, Bathsheba, and Mary—is often recognized as a clue to Matthew's emphasis.[18]

---

16. Cf. Gen. 15:13; Ex. 12:40, approximately 1898–1445 B.C.

17. Cf. Num. 2:3; 7:12; 2 Sam. 5:4, approximately 1445–1040 B.C. For extended discussion of the chronologies see J. Barton Payne, "Chronology of the Old Testament," *ZPEB*, 1:834–36.

18. For discussion, see Johnson, *The Purpose of Biblical Genealogies*, 152–79; Hagner, *Matthew 1–13*, 10; Beverly Roberts Gaventa, *Mary: Glimpses of the Mother of Jesus* (Columbia: Univ. of South Carolina, 1995), 33–39.

Women were not usually included in Old Testament genealogies, for descent was normally traced through men as the head of the family. When women were included, there was usually some particular reason.[19] Similarly, Matthew seems to have several reasons for including these women in Jesus' genealogy (see Bridging Contexts).

Tamar (cf. Gen. 38), Judah's daughter-in-law, gave birth to Perez and Zerah after she tricked Judah into thinking that she was a temple prostitute and had intercourse. Judah had not fulfilled his vow of giving her to his youngest son, so she took the situation into her own hands. Her lineage is not made clear—some suggest that she was a Canaanite,[20] while others insist she was not.[21] Tamar is also listed in the genealogy found in 1 Chronicles 2:4: "Tamar, Judah's daughter-in-law, bore him Perez and Zerah." Since Matthew's phraseology is so similar to that of 1 Chronicles, Matthew may have brought over her name simply because it was listed there, or he may have intended to include a woman whose rights were abused by men.

Rahab (cf. Josh. 2) was a Gentile and a prostitute of Jericho, who protected the two spies sent by Joshua to reconnoiter the land promised to the people of Israel (Josh. 2:1–21). Only here do we find Rahab featured in David's ancestry, a fact not recorded elsewhere in Scripture nor anywhere else in Jewish writings.[22]

Ruth (cf. Ruth 3) is a Moabitess (e.g., Ruth 1:4; 2:1, 6). To the tenth generation a Moabite was not to be admitted to the congregation (Deut. 23:3), but here Matthew makes clear that Gentile women, Rahab and Ruth, were in the royal line of Jesus.

As noted above, one of the most significant features of Matthew's record is the emphasis on Jesus' kingly lineage. David is not simply the son of Jesse (as is stated in Luke's genealogy, Luke 3:31–32) but is "King David" (Matt. 1:6), an explicit emphasis on royalty in the genealogy of Jesus. From here Matthew maintains an emphasis on kingship, using the word "king" twenty-two times, more than any other book in the New Testament. Throughout his Gospel, Matthew maintains a focus on Jesus as "the King of the Jews."[23]

---

19. E.g., 1 Chron. 1:39; 2:3–4, 16, 18, 24, 26, 29, 48–49; 3:9.

20. E.g., Gordon Wenham, *Genesis 16–50* (WBC 2; Waco, Tex.: Word, 1987), 366; Richard Bauckham, "Tamar's Ancestry and Rahab's Marriage: Two Problems in the Matthean Genealogy," *NovT* 37 (1995): 313–329.

21. John Sailhamer, "Genesis," *EBC*, 2:232.

22. See Johnson, *The Purpose of Biblical Genealogies*, 162–65.

23. See 2:2; 27:11, 29, 37, 42. This is likewise emphasized by the contrast with King Herod and his son Archelaus (2:1–23), the mention of the king in the parable (22:1–13), and the Son of Man seated as king on the throne on Judgment Day (25:31–46).

**From King David to the Babylonian exile (1:6b–11).** Next Matthew traces the genealogy of Jesus during the monarchy that lasted in the southern kingdom of Judah from King David to the Babylonian exile. It was a time of intense strife in both the northern and southern kingdoms. Strife came from within as various factions contended for power and from outside as conquest loomed from Assyria and Babylon. Matthew may have patterned this section after 1 Chronicles 3:10–14, because the genealogies in both Chronicles and Matthew omit several kings found in the narrative of the books of Kings and Chronicles. As in the listing from Abraham to David, names were omitted to make it uniform for ease of memorization (see comment on 1:17).

"Uriah's wife," whom we know as Bathsheba (cf. 2 Sam 11:1–27), is the fourth woman named in the line of Jesus. She was a person of questionable ethical and moral character, like Tamar and Rahab before her.

As noted above, Matthew traces Jesus' genealogy through David's son Solomon. That lineage culminates in the birth of Jesus as the ruling royal pedigree. The striking characteristic of this section is the alternating series of godly and wicked kings that ruled Israel. The genuineness, and unlikeliness, of this genealogy must have stunned Matthew's readers. Jesus' ancestors were humans with all of the foibles, yet potentials, of everyday people. God worked through them to bring about his salvation.

There is, in other words, no pattern of righteousness in the lineage of Jesus. Adulterers, prostitutes, heroes, and Gentiles are all found in the genealogy from Abraham to David. We see that wicked kings fathered good kings, and good kings fathered wicked kings. Wicked Rehoboam (cf. 1 Kings 14:21–31) and his wicked son Abijah (cf. 15:1–7) had offspring who were good kings—Asa (cf. 15:10–11) and Jehoshaphat cf. 22:41–44). Their offspring was the wicked king Joram (cf. 2 Kings 8:16–19). As Carson notes, "Good or evil, they were part of Messiah's line; for though grace does not run in the blood, God's providence cannot be deceived or outmaneuvered."[24]

Matthew moves directly from Jehoram to Uzziah, omitting reference to Ahaziah (2 Kings 8:25–26), Joash (also called Jehoash, 2 Kings 12:1–3), and Amaziah (2 Kings 14:1–4), who was the immediate biological father of Uzziah or Azariah (2 Kings 14:21–22). The alternating sequence of good and evil kings then continues through Josiah, who fathered the wicked king Jeconiah or Coniah (Matt. 1:11; cf. Jer. 22:24, 28; 24:1), also called Jehoiachin (2 Chron. 36:9).

According to the Old Testament record (2 Kings 23:31–24:20), several ungodly kings ruled briefly after Josiah just before the Exile: his sons Jehoahaz, Jehoiakim, and Zedekiah and his grandson Jehoiachin/Jeconiah (cf.

---

24. Carson, "Matthew," 67.

2 Kings 24:18–25:7; 2 Chron. 36:10). What then does Matthew mean when he states that Josiah was "the father of Jeconiah and his brothers at the time of the exile to Babylon"? A way of resolving the difficulty is to recognize that the LXX at times uses the Greek name *Ioakim* for both Jehoiakim and his son Jehoiachin/Jeconiah.[25] Thus, Matthew's reference to "Jeconiah and his brothers" may well have a double entendre, intending the readers to think of the end of the Davidic rule in Jerusalem with Jehoiakim and the ongoing history of David's lineage with his son Jehoiachin[26] (cf. the expression Judah "and his brothers" in 1:2). The nation then goes into exile and returns without a ruling king, which must await the arrival of the heir to the throne, Jesus Messiah.

**From the Babylonian exile to Jesus Messiah (1:12–16).** After the return of Israel from the Exile, the Davidic line continues through Jeconiah. Apparently Jehoiachin/Jeconiah died in Babylon during the Exile (cf. Jer. 52:34). He was a wicked king (2 Kings 24:8–9; 2 Chron. 36:9), and his evil was so great that Jeremiah's blistering prophecy declared that "none of his offspring will prosper, none will sit on the throne of David or rule anymore in Judah" (Jer. 23:30).

With such a stunning prophetic curse on Jeconiah and his offspring, we might assume this also invalidates Jesus' claim to the throne. However, as suggested above, if Matthew follows Joseph's legal claim to the throne and Luke follows Mary's biological claim to the throne (which includes Joseph's legal claim as the adoptive heir of Heli), it helps explain how Matthew recognizes that the curse against Jeconiah does not invalidate the legal line. The curse would have prevented a natural, biological son from ascending to the throne, although the legal claim to the throne could apparently still come through Jeconiah's line.

Jeconiah fathered Shealtiel (1 Chron. 3:17), who in turn fathered Zerubbabel, the leader of the first group allowed to return to Israel from the Exile. Zerubbabel was the governor of Judah under the Persian king Darius I (Ezra 3:2; 5:2) and is held in high esteem as a man of renown in Jewish tradition (Sir. 49:11). The nine names from Abiud to Jacob are known to us only from Matthew's genealogy, not from elsewhere in the Old Testament or any other Jewish literature. Matthew may have had access to genealogical records stored in the temple that were destroyed with the sacking of Jerusalem by the Romans in A.D. 70.

---

25. See in the LXX 4 Kings 24:6, 8, 12, 15; 25:27; Jer. 52:31.

26. See John Nolland, "Jeconiah and His Brothers (Matthew 1:11)," *BBR* 7 (1997): 169–77. See also Hagner, *Matthew 1–13*, 5–6, for a similar conclusion using a somewhat different approach. The major difficulty with this view is that there is no conclusive evidence that the name Jeconiah, unlike the name Jehoiakim, evoked images of both persons.

**The culmination of Matthew's genealogy in Jesus Messiah (1:16–17).**
Matthew now arrives at the culmination of the genealogy. Jesus is the true
son of David, a rightful legal heir to the covenant promises linked to the
Davidic throne. He is likewise the true son of Abraham, a rightful legal heir
to the covenant promises linked to the Abrahamic seed and land. But there
is much more about Jesus than anyone may have anticipated. His birth was
not like any other in the line of David.

Matthew displays intentional precision in his account of Jesus' earthly
life and ministry in order to accentuate truths that are important for devotion and doctrine. In the genealogy, he writes, "... and Jacob the father of
Joseph, the husband of Mary, of whom was born Jesus, who is called Christ"
(1:16).[27] The English obscures two important points that Matthew makes
about Jesus in the Greek text.

(1) Behind the English words "of whom" stands the Greek relative pronoun
*hes*. The feminine gender of the relative pronoun points specifically to Mary
as the one from whom Jesus Christ was born. This genealogy has regularly
emphasized the male who fathers a child, but here Matthew delivers a precise statement of the relationship of Jesus Christ to Joseph and Mary. While
the genealogy establishes Joseph as the legal father of Jesus, Matthew emphasizes that Mary is the biological parent "of whom" Jesus was born, preparing
the reader for the virgin birth by shifting attention from Joseph to Mary.

(2) The expression "was born" translates the verb *gennao* in a passive voice
and gives further clarification of the origin of Jesus. As we noted earlier, in
1:2–16 there are forty occurrences of this same verb. All the others are in the
active voice (e.g., 1:2: "Abraham was the father of"; lit., " fathered, gave birth
to" Isaac), emphasizing the human action in giving birth to a child. But in 1:16
the verb is in the passive voice, where the subject, Mary, receives the action
or is acted upon. Matthew specifies that it was not the sole action of Mary
who gave birth, preparing the reader for the angelic announcement of divine
action in the conception and birth of Jesus (1:18–25). This is a common
construction in the New Testament, which many grammarians call a "divine
passive," where God is the assumed agent of the action.[28] By way of contrast,
Matthew uses the verb *tikto* in the active voice where Mary is the *subject* who
gives birth to Jesus (1:25).

By the use of the feminine form of the relative pronoun "of whom" and
the passive form of the verb "was born," Matthew intentionally stresses that

---

27. There are complex textual critical problems behind the text of 1:16, but the best reading is that found in all major Greek texts today, which also lies behind the NIV; see John
Nolland, "A Text-Critical Discussion of Matthew 1:16," *CBQ* 58 (October 1996): 665–73.

28. BDF, 72 (§130.1); Daniel B. Wallace, *Greek Grammar Beyond the Basics: An Exegetical
Syntax of the New Testament* (Grand Rapids: Zondervan, 1996), 437.

Mary is the mother of Jesus, but that she was "acted upon" to give birth to the child. Later Matthew will clarify that the conception is miraculous, brought about by the Spirit of God coming upon her (1:18–25). Jesus is indeed the Christ, the Messiah, the son of David, the son of Abraham (1:1), but he is also the Son of God, Immanuel, "God with us" (1:23). This is no ordinary king in the line of David.

Matthew further reveals that even the structure of the genealogy intends to culminate in Jesus Messiah. Genealogies were often organized for ease of memorization. Matthew structures the genealogy to count fourteen generations from the covenant made with Abraham to the covenant made with David, fourteen generations from the end of David's reign to the deportation to Babylon, and fourteen generations from the Babylonian deportation down to Jesus.

There are forty-one names in the genealogy, which creates a difficulty, because fourteen generations multiplied by the three groups of generations equals forty-two names. This probably indicates that one name needs to be counted twice. On this reckoning, the fourteen names in the first group of fourteen generations begin with Abraham and end with David. The second group of fourteen generations runs from David to the deportation to Babylon, and the fourteen names to be counted in this group begin with Solomon and end with Jeconiah. The third group of fourteen generations, from the deportation to Jesus, begins again by counting Jeconiah and ends with Jesus' name. As we suggested above, the name "Jeconiah" may serve as a double entendre to indicate both Jehoiakim and the end of the second group of generations, and also to indicate Jehoiachin and the beginning of the third group of generations after the deportation. On this supposition, the name "Jeconiah" is counted twice to indicate the two different rulers and eras in Matthew's genealogy. Thus, the breakdown is as follows:

> Abraham to David
> Solomon to Jeconiah/Jehoiakim
> Jeconiah/Jehoiachin to Jesus

Some generations in the family tree were skipped so that the structure could be made uniform for memorization, while other members were given certain kinds of prominence to make a particular point. David is mentioned twice, although only counted once, to emphasize for Jewish readers that Jesus is the Davidic Messiah. The number fourteen may even be a subtle reference to David, because the numerical value of the Hebrew consonants of his name is fourteen (d w d = 4+6+4). The Jewish practice of counting the numerical value for letters is called *gematria*.[29] Alluding to the number of the

---

29. R. J. Werblowsky and G. Wigoder, eds., *EJR* (New York: Holt, Rhinehart, Winston, 1965), 154 (sub "Gematria").

consonants for David's name would have been significant for an audience that was intimately familiar with this Hebrew background and practice.

 **PURPOSE OF A GOSPEL.** When the Gospels are compared with other writings of antiquity, it becomes clear that the authors wrote on two levels: to present the historical Jesus and to offer a perspective on Jesus that addressed the needs and concerns of the Gospel writer's own audience. On both levels the authors intended either to awaken or to strengthen the faith of their readers.[30] The unique viewpoint of each author on both levels is apparent by simply reading the first verse(s) of each Gospel. Notice how strikingly different each one begins:

Matthew 1:1: "A record of the genealogy of Jesus Christ the son of David, the son of Abraham."

Mark 1:1: "The beginning of the gospel about Jesus Christ, the Son of God."

Luke 1:1—4: "Many have undertaken to draw up an account of the things that have been fulfilled among us, just as they were handed down to us by those who from the first were eyewitnesses and servants of the word. Therefore, since I myself have carefully investigated everything from the beginning, it seemed good also to me to write an orderly account for you, most excellent Theophilus, so that you may know the certainty of the things you have been taught."

John 1:1: "In the beginning was the Word, and the Word was with God, and the Word was God."

As discussed in the introduction, each of the Gospels gives an accurate recounting of the historical details of Jesus' life and ministry, yet each offers a unique perspective on that life and ministry for the particular needs of the audience being addressed.[31] For example, Mark's Gospel appears to be focused on a basic proclamation of the gospel for those who may have needed a

---

30. See, e.g., David E. Aune, *The New Testament in Its Literary Environment*, ed. Wayne A. Meeks (LEC; Philadelphia: Westminster, 1987), 59–63.

31. Although each Gospel most likely had an original audience to which it was addressed, the Gospels were not intended exclusively for any one particular community but were written with an eye on the broader audience that would be reached as each of the Gospels was circulated. See Richard Bauckham, ed., *The Gospels for All Christians: Rethinking the Gospel Audiences* (Grand Rapids: Eerdmans, 1998), and generally, Martin Hengel, *The Four Gospels and the One Gospel of Jesus Christ: An Investigation of the Collection and Origin of the Canonical Gospels* (Harrisburg, Pa.: Trinity Press International, 2000).

primer on Jesus' life and ministry. Luke states explicitly that he is giving a historical recounting to convince Theophilus of the factuality of the life and ministry of Jesus. And John gives a theological reflection about Jesus as the eternal Logos, a reflection that may have been needed not so much for the first generation of the church but for later believers.

What about Matthew? Matthew's opening verse gives an important clue to his overall purpose and perspective. It had special meaning for those with a Jewish background, attempting both to awaken the faith of Jews and to strengthen the faith of Jewish Christians, insofar as Jesus is the "Messiah," the "son of David," the heir to the promises of Israel's throne through King David. But this Gospel is also intended to awaken and strengthen the faith of those from a Gentile background. Gentiles and Gentile Christians would find tremendous hope in seeing that as the "son of Abraham," Jesus' lineage brings fulfillment to the promises to all the nations of the world, because he is the heir to the universal covenantal blessing established through the patriarch.

This is an important clue to one of Matthew's purposes for writing his Gospel. He directs his story to those with a Jewish background, detailing how Jesus is the fulfillment of the promises made to the people of Israel. Yet he will weave into the story a message to those from all nations, detailing how Jesus brought fulfillment to the universal hope of salvation for all people.

**The faithfulness of God.** As the heading flows directly into the genealogy, Matthew unfolds the lineage of Jesus, the One whom he has identified as the Messiah. However, the genuineness—and the unlikeliness—of this genealogy must have stunned Matthew's readers. Jesus' descendants were humans with all of the foibles, yet potentials, of everyday people. But God worked through people such as these to bring about his plan of salvation.

There is no pattern of righteousness in the lineage of Jesus. We find adulterers, prostitutes, heroes, and Gentiles. Wicked Rehoboam was the father of wicked Abijah, who was the father of good king Asa. Asa was the father of good king Jehoshaphat (1:8), who was the father of wicked king Joram. While this does not excuse Matthew's readers of their responsibility to pursue godliness, because ultimately even the privileged who pursued wickedness were judged, it surely caused them, as it should us, to stand in awe of the God who sovereignly works his will through everyday people.

Thus, at the very start of his Gospel, Matthew points his readers beyond the personal qualifications of individuals who belong to the line of the Messiah. He focuses instead on the faithfulness of God to bring about his plan of salvation. As will be made clear throughout Matthew's story of Jesus' life and ministry, it was God's overwhelming love for his people that energized his faithfulness. After noting the juxtaposition of sinners with righteous people in the genealogy, Michael Green exclaims, "At the very beginning of the Gospel the all-embracing love of God is emphasized. Nothing can stand in its path. There is nobody who does not need it."[32] This becomes the explicit message of Matthew's story about Jesus Messiah.

**Men and women.** Most scholars see the inclusion of the five women in Jesus' genealogy as another clue to Matthew's emphases. As noted above, women were not always included in Old Testament genealogies. When they were included, there was usually some particular reason. Speculation about Matthew's purpose has a long history,[33] but he seems to have a variety of reasons for including these women in Jesus' genealogy. Something positive can be said for each of the following, although it may be difficult to narrow Matthew's purpose to any one alone.

(1) Women had experienced increasing marginalization and even abuse within Jewish society. Jesus' line includes Tamar, a woman wrongfully denied motherhood by the deceitfulness of men. The women in the genealogy represent the gender equality that had been denied them within much of Jewish culture.[34] From the beginning Jesus came to restore the personal equality and dignity of women with men.

(2) Tamar, Rahab, and Bathsheba had reputations for morally indiscreet behavior and character. They are examples of women sinners Jesus came to save, a powerful statement about the offer of salvation to those of either gender.[35]

(3) The first four women may have been Gentiles, although the ethnicity of Tamar and Bathsheba is unclear.[36] It is clear, however, that Ruth was a Moabitess, and to the tenth generation a Moabite was not to be admitted to the congregation (Deut. 23:3). Rahab was undoubtedly a Canaanite. Matthew may thus be indicating that salvation is a possibility for every ethnic group, which is a strong motif in this Gospel (Matt. 8:5–13; 28:18–20). Jesus Messiah, who could not have male Gentiles in his ancestry, nonetheless had

---

32. Michael Green, *The Message of Matthew: The Kingdom of Heaven* (BST; Downers Grove, Ill.: InterVarsity Press, 2000), 59.

33. For recent summaries with evaluations of the various views, see Johnson, *The Purpose of Biblical Genealogies*, 152–79; Brown, *The Birth of the Messiah*, 71–74; Davies and Allison, *Matthew I-VII*, 170–72; John C. Hutchison, "Women, Gentiles, and the Messianic Mission in Matthew's Genealogy," *BibSac* 158 (April–June 2001): 152–64.

34. Gaventa, *Mary*, 33–39; Wim J. Weren, "The Five Women in Matthew's Genealogy," *CBQ* 59 (April 1997): 288–305.

35. Morris, *Matthew*, 23.

36. The ethnicity of Bathsheba is uncertain because she is mentioned only by her first husband's name, Uriah the Hittite; cf. John Nolland, "The Four (Five) Women and other Annotations in Matthew's Genealogy," *NTS* 43 (1997): 527–39.

Gentile ancestors in these women, suggesting his suitability as the Messiah for Gentiles as well as for Jews.[37]

(4) The women mentioned had unusual marriages, sexual scandals, or suspicions of having had illegitimate children. Matthew may be disarming prejudice against Mary's circumstances by those Jews who might forget their own history, even as he refutes charges of illegitimacy against Mary (1:18–25).[38]

(5) These women each represent a crucial period in Israel's history when a Gentile displayed extraordinary faith in contrast to Jews who lacked courage and faith: Tamar versus Judah's disloyalty, Rahab versus the desert generation's faithlessness, Ruth versus the unfaithful Israelites at the time of the judges, and Uriah versus David's sinfulness with Bathsheba. The messianic line was preserved, even through Gentiles, when Israel was unfaithful.[39]

The overriding importance of Matthew's opening verses is to understand that God is faithful to his covenant promises to Israel and to all the nations. With the birth of Jesus Messiah, the dawning of salvation has arrived for all people regardless of ethnicity, gender, or status. Indeed, by including these unexpected names in the messianic genealogy, Matthew shows that God can use anyone—however marginalized or despised—to bring about his purposes. Against the backdrop of a world increasingly hostile to Christianity, Matthew solidifies his church's identity as the true people of God, who transcend ethnic, economic, and religious barriers to find oneness in their adherence to Jesus Messiah.

AS PEOPLE BEGIN a study Matthew's Gospel for the first time, a glazed look almost invariably comes over their faces as they turn to chapter 1 and read the opening verses. It's nothing but a list of names! What could possibly be the contemporary significance of such a dry list? We may even, to our own tragic loss, turn away from this magnificent Gospel if we don't see the value of Matthew's heading and genealogy.

---

37. Ulrich Luz, *Matthew 1–7*, 109–10; Bauckham, "Tamar's Ancestry and Rahab's Marriage," 313; Craig S. Keener, *A Commentary on the Gospel of Matthew* (Grand Rapids: Eerdmans, 1999), 78–81.

38. Brown, *The Birth of the Messiah*, 71–74; Edwin D. Freed, "The Women in Matthew's Genealogy," *JSNT* 29 (1987): 3–19; Craig L. Blomberg, "The Liberation of Illegitimacy: Women and Rulers in Matthew 1–2," *BTB* 21 (1991): 145–50; Hagner, *Matthew 1–13*, 10; Davies and Allison, *Matthew I-VII*, 170–72.

39. Hutchison, "Women, Gentiles, and the Messianic Mission in Matthew's Genealogy," 152–64. In this view the intention is not primarily to draw attention to the four women, but four Old Testament stories that illustrate how God remained faithful to his covenants, even though Israel was unfaithful. Cf. also John Paul Heil, "The Narrative Roles of the Women in Matthew's Genealogy," *Bib* 72 (1991): 538–45.

**The apologetic value.** Jewish readers would immediately recognize the significance of Matthew's opening verses for establishing Jesus' claim to the Davidic throne and clarifying his messianic identity. For those stirred to believe in Jesus as Messiah, the fulfillment of their hopes is realized as they begin their new life with him. This was at least part of Matthew's purpose for writing his Gospel, and even today it has immediate relevance to Jews and Christians alike.

This was the experience of the prolific scholar of the eighteenth century, Alfred Edersheim. Born into a Jewish family in Vienna, Austria in 1825, young Alfred became a Christian in his early twenties under the influence of Scottish Presbyterian chaplains serving in Europe. He went to Scotland and England, where he entered pastoral ministry and then studied and later lectured at Cambridge and Oxford. He spent the bulk of his adult life writing on the life of Christ, culminating with what is probably his most influential work, *The Life and Times of Jesus the Messiah*, which he designated as his *apologia pro vita mea* ("a defense for my life").[40] Like the apostle Matthew, Alfred Edersheim found in Jesus' life and ministry what the genealogy attested, that Jesus was indeed the Messiah of his people Israel. In commenting on Jesus' nativity, Edersheim gives a stirring testimony to his Messiah:

> He was the One perfect Man—the ideal of humanity, His doctrine the one absolute teaching. The world has known none other, none equal. And the world has owned it, if not by the testimony of words, yet by the evidence of facts. . . . If He be not the Messiah, He has at least thus far done the Messiah's work. If He be not the Messiah, there has at least been none other, before or after Him. If He be not the Messiah, the world has not, and never can have, a Messiah.[41]

Edersheim found in the record of another Jew before him, the evangelist Matthew, a convincing record of the factuality of Jesus as the hope of Israel, the Messiah, the Son of David. Thus, as we begin our study of Matthew's Gospel, we find in it a message that is of vast, immediate value to any Jewish reader, and also of value for Christians to help Jews understand more fully the true identity of Jesus Messiah.

One objective, therefore, will be for us to truly understand how this Gospel can speak directly to the needs of our Jewish friends and neighbors, offering them a clear understanding of how Jesus can indeed fulfill their hopes and dreams.

---

40. Alfred Edersheim, *The Life and Times of Jesus the Messiah* (1899; repr.; Grand Rapids: Eerdmans, 1971), xix.

41. Ibid., 180–81.

**Roots.** Matthew's opening verses also have striking relevance for readers of any background. As he traces Jesus' lineage back to Abraham, he clarifies that the covenantal promise includes all humanity. We all can find our roots in the salvation history traced in Jesus' genealogy.

Try asking people if they can trace back their own lineage. On occasion I will call two or three people up to the front of my class and ask them to write on the board the names of their parents, grandparents, great-grandparents, and so on, as far back as they can remember. Almost without exception students can only go back to their grandparents, or at most their great-grandparents. On one occasion three young men at the seminary came up at the same time—one from a Japanese-Hawaiian background, one from a Mexican-American background, and one from a Chinese-American background. In spite of their cultural differences, they each could go back only three generations.

Much of this may be attributable to the fact that we are no longer an oral culture, in which young people used to be steeped in their heritage by memorizing their family tree. Another factor may be that we are a much more mobile world, with many young people growing up removed from their extended family. Moreover, in our modern self-importance, we often ignore the past.

But despite our lack of knowledge of our family heritage, Matthew shows us that we have another set of roots—roots of faith. Once a person becomes a Christian, she or he is immediately adopted into a family of faith that has a long and well-documented genealogy. Through church history we can trace back through nearly two thousand years to the family of faith initiated by Jesus, and through him to the covenantal roots God had established through the patriarch Abraham. The apostle John tells us:

> He came to that which was his own, but his own did not receive him. Yet to all who received him, to those who believed in his name, he gave the right to become children of God—children born not of natural descent, nor of human decision or a husband's will, but born of God. (John 1:11–13)

Contrasting his earthly family and his family of faith, Jesus asked, "'Who is my mother, and who are my brothers?' Pointing to his disciples, he said, 'Here are my mother and my brothers. For whoever does the will of my Father in heaven is my brother and sister and mother'" (12:49–50). Jesus' fulfillment of the covenantal promises made to Abraham enables all who have heard his call to salvation to join his spiritual family. No matter what may be our pedigree, or lack of pedigree, we all now have roots in the Messiah's line, which unites all Christians of whatever background, race, color, culture, or nationality in the promises of God.

**History.** Christians are historians. Since we now have roots in the salvation-historical family of God, we must become diligent in the discovery and solidification of that history. The crucifixion, resurrection, and ascension of Jesus were the core of the preaching of the early church. The early Christians had seen these mighty events occur, and they were profoundly struck with the uniqueness of Jesus as the atoning sacrifice for the sins of humanity. Therefore, they had to carefully document the events of Jesus' life and ministry and to give credible answers to the challenges against Jesus in their day. As such they were diligent historians, with the theological foundation of their faith firmly embedded in the facts of history.

We must be no less diligent today. The challenges to the person and work of Jesus are as ferocious today as they were during the first century. Pluralism, secularism, and relativism pose direct challenges to the uniqueness of Jesus in our day and require that we rest our beliefs on the firm foundation of the facts of history, not wishful thinking, emotional subjectivity, or historical speculation. By implication, this becomes the responsibility of church leaders and members alike. Each of us must be well schooled and trained in the uniqueness of Jesus among the religions of the world, among the philosophical schools, and among political ideologies.

This requires a thorough understanding of who Jesus is, what he came to do, and how he carried it out. As N. T. Wright muses, "I long for the day when seminarians will again take delight in the detailed and fascinated study of the first century. If that century was not the moment when history reached its great climax, the church is simply wasting its time."[42]

All of us as Christians are called to solidify our faith in a careful and credible understanding of the earthly ministry of our Lord Jesus Messiah. This is one of the primary purposes for our study of Matthew's Gospel.

---

42. N. T. Wright, *The Challenge of Jesus: Rediscovering Who Jesus Was and Is* (Downers Grove, Ill.: InterVarsity Press, 1999), 31.

# Matthew 1:18–25

THIS IS HOW the birth of Jesus Christ came about: His mother Mary was pledged to be married to Joseph, but before they came together, she was found to be with child through the Holy Spirit. [19]Because Joseph her husband was a righteous man and did not want to expose her to public disgrace, he had in mind to divorce her quietly.

[20]But after he had considered this, an angel of the Lord appeared to him in a dream and said, "Joseph son of David, do not be afraid to take Mary home as your wife, because what is conceived in her is from the Holy Spirit. [21]She will give birth to a son, and you are to give him the name Jesus, because he will save his people from their sins."

[22]All this took place to fulfill what the Lord had said through the prophet: [23]"The virgin will be with child and will give birth to a son, and they will call him Immanuel"—which means, "God with us."

[24]When Joseph woke up, he did what the angel of the Lord had commanded him and took Mary home as his wife. [25]But he had no union with her until she gave birth to a son. And he gave him the name Jesus.

AT THE START of this crucial narrative section, Matthew signals with a mild adversative[1] that he has come to the central focus and purpose for listing the preceding genealogy—the conception and birth of the Messiah. Jesus is both son of David and son of Abraham (1:1), but also is now revealed to be the Son of God.[2] The beginning[3] of a new era in Israel's history occurs with the story of Jesus' conception in

1. The conjunction *de* (not translated in the NIV) focuses the reader's attention on the birth of Jesus as the culmination of the lineage; "the birth of Jesus comes into a class of its own" (Carson, "Matthew," 81 n.18).

2. The emphasis in this important pericope continues to be on Jesus' genealogical links, but Matthew introduces also the Son of God motif, which will become explicit later in the narrative (e.g., 3:17; see Jack Dean Kingsbury, *Matthew As Story*, 2d ed. (Philadelphia: Fortress, 1988), 49–58; Gerhardsson, "The Christology of Matthew," 21–23.

3. The same word for "beginning" (*genesis*) that occurred in 1:1 reoccurs here (NIV, "birth"). This is not only the narrative of the birth of Jesus but the beginning of a new era.

the little town of Nazareth in Galilee (cf. Luke 2:4–5). Joseph and Mary are both at this time in Nazareth because it is their hometown (Luke 2:39) and the place where they will eventually raise their son (see comments on Matt. 2:23; Luke 2:39–40).

### The Angelic Announcement of the Conception of Jesus Messiah (1:18–21)

As WAS THE custom for young people anticipating marriage, Joseph and Mary were pledged to each other in a period of "betrothal" or "engagement," a more weighty undertaking than is found in many current cultures. The marriage customs of Jewish culture at that time usually included two basic stages of the relationship, the betrothal and the wedding.[4]

(1) The betrothal stage involved the choosing of a spouse. The family in ancient Near Eastern culture usually initiated the arrangements. A text from the Laws of Eshnunna from Babylonia (ca. 2000 B.C.) states: "If a man takes a(nother) man's daughter without asking the permission of her father and her mother and concludes no formal marriage contract with her father and her mother, even though she may live in his house for a year, she is not a housewife."[5] The Old Testament nowhere gave such a binding legislation, recognizing that a good wife is from the Lord, not one's parents (Prov. 19:14), and we find examples of young men and women making their preferences known (Ruth 2–4). Yet customarily the parents of a young man chose a young woman to be engaged to their son (e.g., Gen. 21:21; 38:6). Young men and women were often pledged between twelve and thirteen years of age, although later rabbinic texts suggest that men in Jesus' day often married around the age of eighteen (m. ʾAbot 5:21; b. Qidd. 29b–30a).

A second stage of betrothal involved official arrangements. In a formal prenuptial agreement before witnesses, the young man and woman entered into the official state of betrothal. This was a legally binding contract, which gave the man legal rights over the young woman, and it could only be broken by a formal process of divorce (cf. m. Ketub. 1:2; 4:2). Three types of gifts could be exchanged during this period. (a) The bride price (cf. Gen. 34:12) was a compensation gift from the family of the bridegroom to the family of the bride, sealing the covenant and binding the two families. (b) The dowry (cf. Gen. 24:59) was a gift to the bride or the groom from her father, enabling

---

4. See Joachim Jeremias, *Jerusalem in the Time of Jesus: An Investigation into Economic and Social Conditions During the New Testament Period*, trans. (Philadelphia: Fortress, 1969), 363–68; J. S. Wright and J. A. Thompson, "Marriage," *IBD*, 2:955–56; Victor P. Hamilton, "Marriage (OT and ANE)," *ABD*, 4:559–69.

5. J. B. Pritchard, ed., *Ancient Near Eastern Texts Relating to the Old Testament*, 3d. ed. (Princeton: Princeton Univ. Press, 1969), no. 27.

---

them economically to start a new family. (c) The bridegroom's gift to the bride was a symbol of commitment to their relationship (cf. Gen. 23:53).

Apparently the terminology "husband" and "wife" were used during this stage to refer to the betrothed partners (see 1:16, 19, 20, 24). While there is some evidence in Judea of the betrothed couple being alone during this interval at the man's father's home (*m. Ketub.* 1:5; *b. Ketub.* 9b, 12a), in Galilee sexual relations between the betrothed partners were not tolerated, and the girl did not leave her own family to live with the man. Sexual unfaithfulness with another person during this stage was considered adultery, the penalty for which was death by stoning (cf. Lev. 20:10; Deut. 22:23–24), although by New Testament times stoning was rare. If one of the partners died during the betrothal period, the one remaining alive was a "widow" or "widower." Therefore, Joseph was considered Mary's "husband" (1:19) even though Matthew specifies that this was "before they came together," a euphemism for sexual relations (cf. 1 Cor. 7:5).

(2) In a formal ceremony about a year after the betrothal, the marriage proper took place (*m. Ketub.* 5:2; *m. Ned.* 10:5). Dressed in special wedding garments, the bridegroom and companions went in procession to the bride's home and escorted the bride and bridesmaids back to the groom's home, where a wedding supper was held (Matt. 22:1–14; cf. Ps. 45:14–15). Parents and friends blessed the couple (Gen. 24:60; Tobit 7:13), and the father of the bride drew up a written marriage contract. Soon afterward in a specially prepared nuptial chamber (cf. Ps. 19:5; Tobit 7:16), the couple prayed and then sexually consummated the marriage, after which a bloodstained cloth was exhibited as proof of the bride's virginity (Deut. 22:13–21). The wedding festivities continued sometimes for a week or more (Gen. 29:27; Tobit 8:20). Afterward the couple established their own household, although they usually lived with the extended family.

By the time of the narrative in Matthew, Mary is approximately four months pregnant. She has spent three months with Elizabeth, her "relative"[6] (Luke 1:36, 56), but now returns to Nazareth, where she "was found" to be pregnant. This does not imply that Mary has attempted to conceal the pregnancy (i.e., she is "found out"), but rather that it becomes known to others, including Joseph. This is not yet *public* knowledge, because Joseph can still divorce her privately (1:19).

Matthew states simply that the child was conceived through[7] the Holy Spirit. Without knowing of the supernatural origin of the conception, Joseph

---

6. *Syngenis* is a general term, which could refer to an aunt or a cousin.

7. Matthew uses the preposition *ek* in 1:18, echoing its use in 1:3, 5 (2x), 6, and 16 in the genealogical context (cf. 1:20). This preposition can be rendered "by the Holy Spirit,"

naturally thinks that Mary has committed adultery.[8] As a righteous man it was appropriate for him to obtain a certificate of divorce. This is the normal sense of "righteous" in the Old Testament—right behavior according to the law. The same adjective is used of Zechariah and Elizabeth (Luke 1:6) and Simeon (2:25).

But at this point Joseph experiences a personal dilemma. He cannot follow through and marry her, because that would condone what he thinks is Mary's sin of adultery. Divorce for adultery was not optional but mandatory among many groups in ancient Judaism, because adultery produced a state of impurity that, as a matter of legal fact, dissolved the marriage.[9] Yet, his concern for her long-term reputation compels him to avoid exposing Mary to public disgrace.[10]

Therefore, Joseph has only two options open to him. On the one hand, he could seek a public divorce, where her condition will become known overtly. But then she will be subject to community disgrace as an adulteress, and it could make her liable to be stoned according to the law. On the other hand, he could divorce her privately. The law did not require the deed to be made public, making allowance for a relatively private divorce (two or three witnesses). The latter was the only option that would allow Joseph to maintain his personal righteousness according to the law and yet save Mary from public disgrace and from possible death.[11]

The character and compassion of Joseph is revealed in this dilemma. Matthew distinguishes between Joseph's purpose (*thelo*; NIV "did not want") and desire (*boulomai*; NIV "he had in mind"). Joseph intends to maintain his personal righteousness, yet his desire is also to have compassion for the woman to whom he is engaged, even though he considers her an adulteress.

Into this dilemma comes the stunning appearance of the angel of the Lord (1:20), who announces in a dream to Joseph the miraculous conception of the child (1:20). Sometimes in the Old Testament God himself is represented by

---

indicating agency or means (Hagner, *Matthew 1–13*, 17; R. T. France, *The Gospel According to Matthew* [TNTC; Grand Rapids: Eerdmans, 1985], 77; see Wallace, *Greek Grammar*, 125–27, 371, 741). On the other hand, in Koine Greek the preposition is used increasingly with the genitive to express the sense of source (Wallace, *Greek Grammar*, 77, 109 n. 102). In that case, the child's source of origin is "*from* the Holy Spirit." However, that is not too far from saying agency, which is admirably reflected in the NIV "through the Holy Spirit" (but see comments on 1:20).

8. See Dale C. Allison Jr., "Divorce, Celibacy and Joseph (Matthew 1.18–25 and 19.1–12)," *JSNT* 49 (1993): 3–10.

9. Markus Bockmuehl, "Matthew 5.32; 19.9 in the Light of Pre-Rabbinic Halakah," *NTS* 35 (1989): 291–95.

10. The clauses should be rendered, "being righteous, *and yet* not willing to stigmatize her" (Brown, *Birth of the Messiah*, 127–28).

11. The law did not require her to be stoned (see esp. Deut. 22:13–21, since the girl may have been raped).

the phrase "the angel of the LORD,"[12] but here the angel is one of God's created spirit beings.[13] The word "angel" (*angelos*, "messenger") speaks of one of the primary roles of angels as messengers from God to humanity.[14] Nothing is said of this angel's appearance, but angels sometimes took the form of humans in the Old Testament (Gen. 18).

Angels are not normally named in Scripture, except for Michael (Dan. 10:13; Rev. 12:7, 8) and Gabriel (Dan. 8:15–26; 9:20–27; Luke 1:26). Gabriel is "the angel of the Lord" who announces both the conception of John the Baptist to Zechariah and the conception of Jesus to Mary (Luke 1:11–20, 26–38). It is plausible that the unnamed "angel of the Lord" who announces the birth of Jesus to the shepherds (Luke 2:9) and the conception of Jesus to Joseph here in Matthew's narrative (Matt. 1:20–23) is also Gabriel, who seems to have a special role in announcements.[15] In Matthew's narrative, angels specifically appear only in the infancy accounts (Matt. 1:20, 24; 2:13, 19), at Jesus' temptation (4:11), and in the resurrection scene (28:2, 5), fitting testimony to these significant events in Jesus' ministry. Angels are also mentioned in Jesus' teaching, indicating either their present or future roles in human history (4:6; 13:39, 41, 49; 16:27; 18:10; 22:30; 24:31, 36; 25:31, 41; 26:53).

Dreams were commonly believed in the ancient world not only to be of natural origin but also to be a medium of divine communication.[16] In the Old Testament, dreams were believed to derive from natural (Eccl. 5:3), divine (Gen. 28:12; Dan. 2:19), and evil (Deut. 13:1, 2; Jer. 23:32) sources. The primary use of the dream in the Old Testament is to point to a message from God about present activities (Num. 12:6; Job 33:15–17) or future events (Gen. 37:5–11; Dan. 7:1–28). In the New Testament, the expression "in a dream" (*kat' onar*) is found only in Matthew's Gospel. In each case the dream is in some way related to Jesus and involves some kind of supernatural guidance (cf. Matt. 1:20; 2:12, 13, 19, 22; 27:19).

The angelic appearance in a dream provides the guidance Joseph needs. The angel addresses Joseph as "son of David," the only time in Matthew's Gospel that the expression is used of anyone other than Jesus. The title ties Joseph and these incidents to the preceding genealogy (1:1). The regal line will now be tested as Joseph is called to play a significant role in the arrival

---

12. Gen. 21:17; 22:15–18; Ex. 3:2–6; Judg. 6:11–24.

13. Cf. Zech. 1:8–17; Luke 1:26; *1 En.* 6:7; 8:3–4; 69:1.

14. Lawrence Osborn, "Entertaining Angels: Their Place in Contemporary Theology," *TynBul* 45 (1994): 273–96.

15. See Larry W. Hurtado, *One God, One Lord: Early Christian Devotion and Ancient Jewish Monotheism* (Philadelphia: Fortress, 1988), 71–92; Carol A. Newsom, "Gabriel," *ABD*, 2:863; Carol A. Newsom and Duane F. Watson, "Angel," *ABD*, 1:248–55.

16. Ovid, *Metamorphoses* 9.685–701; Tacitus, *Annals* 2.14.

of the Davidic Messiah. The command "do not be afraid" (1:20) does not imply that fear figures into Joseph's dilemma about his pregnant betrothed Mary. Rather, he is not to fear the consequences and stigma that will be attached to him when he completes the wedding stage of the marital relationship. Who will believe the staggering story of the angel's next words?

The angel dramatically announces to Joseph that the conception of the child is from the Holy Spirit,[17] not from Joseph (which Joseph knows personally) or any other man (which he has suspected). Here at the beginning of the New Testament age, the Holy Spirit plays a crucial role. Old Testament writers repeatedly refer to the Spirit of God as the agency of God's power (e.g., Gen. 1:2; Judg. 3:10), but not until the Incarnation is the Spirit clearly understood as a person distinct from the Father and Son. Matthew pays special attention to this distinction (cf. Matt. 3:16–17; 10:20; 12:18, 28; 28:19), preparing the way for understanding that in the present age, the Holy Spirit has been sent to carry out the work of God on the stage of human history. Jesus Messiah is God incarnate, whose miraculous conception and origin are only explained through the work of God the Holy Spirit.

The name "Jesus" was popular in Judaism of the first century (see comments on 1:1), given to sons as a symbolic hope for Yahweh's anticipated sending of salvation. A widely held expression of this hope was the expectation of a Messiah who would save Israel from Roman oppression and purify his people (e.g., *Pss. Sol.* 17). But the angel draws on a less popular, although perhaps more important theme: salvation from sin as the basic need of Israel (cf. Ps. 130:8; *Pss. Sol.* 18:3–5). This salvation is now at hand, so Matthew points his readers to the central purpose of Jesus' earthly life and ministry: He himself "will save his people from their sins" by giving his life a ransom for many (cf. 20:28).

The term for people here is *laos*, which normally indicates the people of Israel in Matthew's narrative (e.g., 4:16; 27:25). The expression draws the reader back to the genealogy and the established royal status of Jesus as the Davidic Messiah, heir to David's throne over the people of Israel (1:6, 16). But here "his people" goes beyond only Israel and ultimately points to the salvation that Messiah offers to the entire world as the son of Abraham (1:1; cf. 2:6; 3:9; 8:11; 16:18). This salvation brought by Jesus will be the basis of the righteousness of the kingdom of heaven that he inaugurates as the One who fulfills the law (cf. 4:12–17; 5:17–20).[18]

---

17. This is the same prepositional phrase with *ek* that was found in 1:18. Matthew seems to be indicating both agency and source, which may explain why the NIV renders the phrase *"through* the Holy Spirit" in 1:18, but *"from* the Holy Spirit" here in 1:20.

18. David R. Bauer, "The Kingship of Jesus in the Matthean Infancy Narrative: A Literary Analysis," *CBQ* 57 (1995): 306–23.

## The Prophesied Immanuel (1:22–23)

THE NARRATIVE CONTINUES with the reader being informed that the events of Jesus' miraculous conception fulfill a prophecy from the Lord through the prophet Isaiah. The words spoken here may be a continuation of the angel's message in the dream to Joseph, the only time in Scripture an angel quotes Scripture to clarify how these events fulfill an ancient prophecy.[19] Or, more likely, these words are an interpretive aside by Matthew, clarifying for his readers how the preceding events relate to Old Testament prophecy.[20] The events of the supernatural conception of Jesus Messiah take place "to fulfill what the Lord had said through the prophet." Matthew emphasizes that the prophecy is ultimately from the Lord, but the prophet is the intermediate agent through whom God spoke to his people.[21]

This introduces the first instance of Matthew's "fulfillment formula." Similar expressions occur prominently in chapter 2, but also throughout the Gospel (see 2:5–6, 15, 17–18, 23; 4:14–16; 8:17; 11:10; 12:17–21; 13:14–15, 35; 21:4–5; 26:31, 56; 27:9–10). This formula occurs only in Matthew among the Synoptic Gospels in such a regular fashion (cf. also John 12:38–39; 13:18; 19:24, 28, 36–37). The precise construction of the fulfillment formula varies somewhat,[22] but regularly involves an introduction wherein Matthew points to an event or teaching of Jesus that "fulfills" (*pleroo*) an Old Testament passage, which is then normally cited.

As discussed in the introduction, "fulfill" can indicate a direct prediction-fulfillment, in which an event of Jesus' earthly life and ministry brings to actualization predictive prophecy (e.g., 1:22–23). Or "fulfill" can indicate the way in which Jesus' life and teaching bring to full meaning the entire Old Testament Scripture (e.g., 5:17–20). Or "fulfill" can indicate the way in which Jesus' earthly life and ministry is a divinely orchestrated analogical or typological correspondence or recapitulation of the nation of Israel's history (e.g., 2:15, 17–18).

Here, Matthew declares that the events surrounding the conception of Jesus fulfills directly the prophet Isaiah's sublime prophecy made during the

---

19. Carson, "Matthew," 76–77, emphasizes that the precise fulfillment formula used here with *gegonen*, "took place," is found only three times in Matthew (1:22; 21:4; 26:56); the final one is most likely not an aside by Matthew but is Jesus' interpretation.

20. Hagner, *Matthew 1–13*, 20; Davies and Allison, *Matthew,* 1:211. Most English versions, including the NIV, place a closed quotation mark with a period after 1:22, ending the angel's direct quotation.

21. Matthew consistently uses *hypo* for God's ultimate agency ("by the Lord," cf. 2:15; 22:31) and *dia* for the prophet's intermediate agency ("through the prophet," e.g., 2:5, 15, 17, 23; 4:14; 8:17; 13:35; 24:15; 27:9).

22. See the variations and discussion in the introduction; see also Hagner, *Matthew 1–13*, liv–lvii.

dark days of national threat under the reign of Ahaz, king of Judah. In 734 B.C. Ahaz feared his reign would soon end because of the threat of attack from the north. Pekah king of Israel and Rezin king of Aram (Syria) had formed an unholy alliance and were threatening to invade Judah and replace Ahaz with a puppet king, the son of Tabeel (Isa. 7:6). The prophet Isaiah declared that God would not allow this to happen, reassuring Ahaz that God would maintain the promise that a descendent of David would sit on his throne forever (2 Sam. 7:11–17). In order to confirm that these two kings would not conquer Judah, Isaiah prophesied that the Lord would give to Ahaz a sign: A virgin would give birth.

There are two primary words for "virgin" in Hebrew. The term ʿalmah, which occurs in the prophecy of Isaiah 7:14, means "maiden" or "young girl," and many scholars contend that it almost always refers to an unmarried, virgin woman (e.g., Gen. 24:43; Ex. 2:8; Ps. 68:25).[23] The other primary term is betulah, which can indicate a "virgin" (Gen. 24:16; Lev. 21:3) but also an "old widow" (Joel 1:8). The Greek translators of Isaiah 7:14 rendered the Hebrew term ʿalmah with the Greek word parthenos, which almost without exception specifies a sexually mature, unmarried woman who is a virgin.[24]

The history of interpretation of Isaiah 7:14 and its relationship to Matthew 1:22–23 is extensive,[25] but three basic views emerge. (1) Some suggest that the original sign was intended solely for the historical circumstances of Ahaz and Judah, but Matthew takes it typologically to refer to Jesus.[26] In this view, Isaiah had in mind a young woman who was a virgin at the time but who would later become married and have a child she would name Immanuel. Isaiah may have been referring to the royal son Hezekiah, born heir to the throne of King Ahaz, or Maher-Shalal-Hash-Baz (cf. Isa. 8:4, 8), or some anonymous child named Immanuel born to a woman Ahaz knew. When this child was born and named Immanuel, Ahaz would know that Isaiah's prophecies were correct and

---

23. The debated passage is Prov. 30:19; see Allen P. Ross, "Proverbs," *EBC*, 5:1124.

24. The exception is Gen. 34:4, where the term *parthenos* is used of Dinah, even though she had already been violated (cf. 34:3).

25. For older studies, see J. G. Machen, *The Virgin Birth of Christ* (Grand Rapids: Baker, 1971), and Charles Lee Feinberg, *Is the Virgin Birth in the Old Testament?* (Whittier: Emeth, 1967). For more recent studies see Gerard Van Groningen, *Messianic Revelation in the Old Testament* (Grand Rapids: Baker, 1990), esp. 521–37; Daniel Schibler, "Messianism and Messianic Prophecy in Isaiah 1–12 and 28–33," in *The Lord's Anointed: Interpretation of Old Testament Messianic Texts*, ed. P. E. Satterthwaite, R. S. Hess, and G. J. Wenham (Grand Rapids: Baker, 1995), 87–104.

26. E.g., J. D. W. Watts, *Isaiah 1–33* (WBC 24; Waco, Tex.: Word, 1985), 98–104; Davies and Allison, *Matthew*, 1:213; Warren Carter, "Evoking Isaiah: Matthean Soteriology and an Intertextual Reading of Isaiah 7–9 and Matthew 1:23 and 4:15–16," *JBL* 119 (Fall 2000): 503–20.

that deliverance was near. In this view, Matthew's use of the text goes beyond the original intentions of the prophecy.

(2) Others suggest that there was no real fulfillment in the birth of any child at the time of Ahaz but that it was intended as a messianic prophecy that was only fulfilled in the birth of Jesus. The term ʿalmah must be taken as referring to a "virgin," which means that the prophecy was not fulfilled by a miraculous birth at the time of Isaiah but could only point ahead to the fulfillment in the conception and birth of Jesus.[27]

(3) The most satisfactory interpretation takes the best of these views and recognizes that God was giving through Isaiah a sign that had historical significance and fulfillment in the days of Ahaz, but that God was also giving through Isaiah a prophecy of a future messianic deliverer that was fulfilled in the conception and birth of Jesus.[28] The Jewish translators of the LXX, hundreds of years before Christ's birth, seem to indicate by the use of *parthenos* that something deeper was meant by the prophet than was completely fulfilled in the events of Isaiah's day. And later Jewish scribes saw a deeper meaning in the context when they interpreted Immanuel, meaning "God with us," to be a promise of the golden age (cf. Isa. 2:2–4; 9:2–7; 11:1–16) when the messianic son of David would bring judgment on the wicked and blessing on the righteous. This was to be the ultimate time of God's presence manifested in Israel.

Isaiah prophesied that a woman who was a virgin at the time of Ahaz (734 B.C.) would bear a son named Immanuel. Since neither the queen nor Isaiah's wife was a virgin, this was most likely some unmarried young woman within the royal house with whom Ahaz was familiar. The woman would marry, conceive a child, and, when he was born, give him the name Immanuel, perhaps as a symbolic hope of God's presence in the dark times of national difficulty. Before the child was old enough to know the difference between right and wrong, Judah would be delivered from the threat of invasion from the two northern kings (Isa. 7:14–17). The northern alliance was broken in 732 B.C., when Tiglath-Pileser III of Assyria destroyed Damascus, conquered Aram, and put Rezin to death.

All this happened within the time frame miraculously predicted as the sign to Ahaz. Thus, there was immediate fulfillment of a miraculous prediction.

---

27. E.g., Carson, "Matthew," 78–80, esp. citing an earlier work by J. A. Motyer, "Context and Content in the Interpretation of Isaiah 7:14," *TynBul* 21 (1970): 118–25.

28. E.g., Geoffrey W. Grogan, "Isaiah," *EBC*, 6:62–65; Hagner, *Matthew 1–13*, 20–21; Blomberg, *Matthew*, 58–59. For a significant study that emphasizes the importance of maintaining that a messianic New Testament interpretation of an Old Testament text is in fact the meaning intended by the Old Testament author, see John H. Sailhamer, "The Messiah and the Hebrew Bible," *JETS* 44 (March 2001): 5–23.

While no record is given of Ahaz's reaction as he saw the unfolding of these predicted events, he would have been rebuked for his lack of faith and his manipulative attempts to achieve the security of Judah and the line of David through his pro-Assyrian policy.

Matthew looks back to the Old Testament and declares that the birth of the child Jesus, who would save his people from their sins, ultimately fulfills the prophecy of Isaiah 7:14. The sign given to Ahaz and the house of Judah ("you" in Isa. 7:14 is plural) was God's miraculous prediction of military salvation from the attack of Pekah and Rezin, but it was also a prediction of a future messianic figure who would provide spiritual salvation from sin. Isaiah's sign, in other words, demonstrates both that Immanuel's birth will signal deliverance from invasion for Ahaz and the house of David and that there would be a future messianic deliverer named Immanuel, truly God with us.

This interpretation takes seriously both the immediate context of the prediction to Ahaz in 7:14 and the broader context of Isaiah's prophecy, in which a future messianic age would honor "Galilee of the Gentiles" (Isa. 9:1–2) with a child born who would be called "Wonderful Counselor, Mighty God, Everlasting Father, Prince of Peace" (9:6). Of this one to whom Isaiah points, only Jesus could be the true fulfillment: "Of the increase of his government and peace there will be no end. He will reign on David's throne and over his kingdom, establishing and upholding it with justice and righteousness from that time on and forever" (9:7).

The angel instructs Joseph to name the child "Jesus," which is what he is called throughout his earthly life and in the early church. We have no record of Jesus ever being called "Immanuel" by his family or followers. Instead, as Matthew translates it for us, we see that the name is intended as a title to indicate Jesus' messianic identity: "God with us." Both his common name and his titular name indicate profound truths: *Jesus* specifies what he does ("God saves"), and *Immanuel* specifies who he is ("God with us"). These are highly charged names that speak of a profound Christological orientation by Matthew. Note how he concludes his Gospel with the same theme, where Jesus promises his disciples, "I will be with you always" (28:20). In Jesus Messiah, God is with us indeed.[29]

## Joseph's Immediate Obedience (1:24–25)

WHEN JOSEPH AWAKES from his sleep, he is obedient to the angel's directive and carries out the second phase of the marital process by engaging in the

---

29. The angel Gabriel used a similar expression when he said to Mary, "The Lord is with you" (Luke 1:28), indicating that God would be with her through the conception and birth of the Son of the Most High.

formal wedding ceremony. At the conclusion of the rites, Joseph takes Mary home to live with him (and perhaps with his extended family) as a fully married couple, except that "he had no union with her until she gave birth to a son" (1:25). The delicate way Matthew phrases this expression (lit., "he was not knowing her") was a common way of referring to abstaining from sexual intercourse in both Hebrew and Greek. Sexual abstinence during pregnancy was widely observed in Judaism of the first century.[30] Abstinence maintained Joseph and Mary's ritual purification during the pregnancy as well as ensured that Jesus was virgin-born. But this is not a hint of continued celibacy after Jesus' birth. The word "until" most naturally means that Mary and Joseph had normal marital sexual relations after Jesus' birth, from which other children were born (see 12:46; 13:55).[31]

While Luke focuses on Mary's obedience and submission to the angelic announcement of these stupendous events (e.g., Luke 1:38), Matthew emphasizes Joseph's likewise remarkable character. In the situation of finding his betrothed wife pregnant, he knows he is not the father. Once the angelic announcement is made, Joseph is immediately obedient, as he will be throughout the infancy account. Not only is Mary seen as a godly woman, but Joseph takes the lead in carrying out the angel's instructions. Matthew specifies that "he [Joseph] gave him the name Jesus" (1:25). Joseph conducts himself as an obedient leader in his marriage and family and as a godly man throughout, an emphasis surely not lost on a Jewish-Christian audience.

THE VIRGIN BIRTH. Among the Gospel writers, both Matthew and Luke not only give attention to Jesus' genealogy, but both also give accounts of his miraculous conception and infancy. In Luke's account, the essential features of the announcement of the conception to Mary by the angel Gabriel combine the remarkable facts of both human and divine natures. The child has a human lineage descended from Adam (Luke 3:23–38), a human name, "Jesus" (1:31), and experiences a human birth (2:6–7). But the child also has a divine relationship as "Son of God" (1:35), a divine description, "the Son of the Most High" (1:32), and experiences a miraculous conception through the Holy Spirit by a virgin mother (1:35).

30. See *Pseudo-Phocylides* 186 (c. 100 B.C.–100 A.D.); Josephus, *Against Apion* 2:202–3.

31. Dale C. Allison Jr., "Divorce, Celibacy and Joseph (Matthew 1.18–25 and 19.1–12)," 6 n.16. See the interesting discussion of this passage by Roman Catholic scholar Raymond Brown in the light of the doctrine of the "perpetual virginity" of Mary, which he says is not Matthew's emphasis in this passage (*The Birth of the Messiah*, 132).

Matthew's presentation supports with equal firmness the fact of the virgin birth as announced to Joseph by the angel of the Lord. Matthew also attests to both human and divine natures in the remarkable conception of Jesus. The child has a human lineage through King David and the patriarch Abraham (1:1–17), a human name, "Jesus," by which he identifies with "his people" (1:21), and a human birth (1:25). But the child also has a divine relationship through the Holy Spirit (1:23), a divine description, "Immanuel—which means, 'God with us'" (1:22), and a divine origin through the Holy Spirit in his conception by his virgin mother (1:18, 20).

Without giving details, the angelic announcement makes clear that the mode of conception is not by any ordinary human means but by a totally unparalleled action of the Holy Spirit. Matthew does not theorize how such a conception could take place but merely presents it as historically authentic. Matthew understands that there is something both natural and supernatural about Jesus in his conception, birth, and development. He presents the virgin conception and birth of Jesus as an accepted fact, thus accounting for the astounding truth that God has taken on human nature and is now with his people. It is only this God-man who, as Matthew's story unfolds, can save his people from their sins, which should cause them to pause in unending gratitude and to worship him as Jesus, "God saves," and Immanuel, "God with us."

By identifying Jesus as "God with us," Matthew continues a theme that permeated the Old Testament concept of God with his people. When giving the law to Israel in the desert, God stressed his covenantal intent: "I will walk among you and be your God, and you will be my people" (Lev. 26:12). The nation was called to a relationship in which God was with his people. No other person or god was to take a place of preeminence and so usurp his place. Even when God called men and women to leadership roles (e.g., Moses, Joshua, the judges, prophets), they were only intermediate leaders. God alone was to have the place of preeminence.

In fact, no human king ruled over Israel, at first, in the covenantal relationship. God was their sovereign. But having an invisible sovereign was difficult for the people of Israel. Since the surrounding nations had kings whom they could see and follow, the people of Israel wanted a king too. To God this was equivalent to rejecting him as king (1 Sam. 8:7). He considered this an evil thing (12:17). He did allow a human king to rule for him, even establishing Saul and calling David's line, but God intended to be their king himself. The promise of a coming Davidic Messiah is intertwined with the promise that God himself would be with his people (e.g., Ezek. 37:24–28).[32]

---

32. For discussion of the "I am with you" theme in the Old Testament tradition, see David D. Kupp, *Matthew's Emmanuel: Divine Presence and God's People in the First Gospel* (SNTSMS 90; Cambridge: Cambridge Univ. Press, 1996), 138–56.

The significance of Matthew's interpretation of Jesus' name as Immanuel, therefore, cannot be overstated. God has come to be with his people to fulfill the deepest meaning of the covenant. In Jesus, God is now with his people personally as their Savior. This theme forms the heart of a personal relationship of Jesus with his followers that comes to characterize his unique form of discipleship (see comment on 4:18–22).[33]

**Learning from other figures in the story.** Can the characters other than Jesus teach us something as well? Yes, but to learn from them accurately and appropriately, we must always understand them first in relation to Jesus. If we stay focused on Jesus as the center-stage person of Matthew's narrative, we can more accurately understand the role that other figures play in relationship to him as they come on and off the stage. But if we rush to other figures first without understanding how they play a role in relationship to Jesus' historical ministry and Matthew's intended story line, we may fall prey to "moralizing." This means that we draw moral inferences of what it means "to do" or "to become" as Christians from identifying with characters in the story, but often our inferences are at the expense of the actual point and intention of the text.[34]

Nevertheless, ancient authors, including the biblical authors, did teach moral and ethical lessons through other lesser characters they described in their stories.[35] The principal point is to understand the role of each.

MATTHEW'S OPENING NARRATIVE is a strong reminder that the Gospels are first and foremost a story about Jesus. Jesus is always center stage. Other characters will move on and off the stage and will receive focused attention for specific purposes. But the question we must continually ask throughout every pericope of the story is: "What is this passage telling us about Jesus?" By focusing our attention on Jesus' earthly ministry, we are much more likely to hear clearly what Matthew intended to tell us in his story about Jesus Christ, the son of David, the son of Abraham (1:1). Then we can make appropriate contemporary application to our own lives.

---

33. For this Old Testament theme in relationship to the appearance of Jesus, see Michael J. Wilkins, *Following the Master: A Biblical Theology of Discipleship* (Grand Rapids: Zondervan, 1992), 51–69, esp. 57 and 66. Also drawing this relationship in Matt. 1 with the birth of the "God-With-Us" Messiah, but more critically, is Kupp, *Matthew's Emmanuel*, 157–75.

34. Greidanus, *The Modern Preacher and the Ancient Text*, 163–66. For helpful instruction to avoid this phenomenon and other improper ways of bridging the gap from the text to modern application, see pp. 157–87.

35. Aune, *The New Testament in Its Literary Environment*, 35–43.

**The picture of Jesus.** Two things especially stand out in this passage. (1) Matthew records in straightforward fashion the most incredible miracle of history, the conception and birth of Jesus to a virgin mother through the Holy Spirit. He does not embellish the story to try to convince his readers of the truthfulness of his account; rather, he assumes it. Apparently the miracle is so well known in the community that he only has to state it. We may not be able to understand completely the depth of the miraculous incarnation, but Matthew impels us at the very start of his story to deal with it.

(2) Jesus the Messiah came to be Savior for the sins of his people. Many within Israel were looking for physical salvation from the hardships they had suffered under various conquering forces, including the current iron fist of Rome. They hoped for a conquering son of David. However, there was a consistent thread of hope of salvation from sin at the heart of Old Testament prophetic messages. Matthew points to Jesus as the redemptive Son of David, who came to those hoping for the fulfillment of the words of the psalmist in Psalm 130:7–8:

> O Israel, put your hope in the LORD,
>     for with the LORD is unfailing love
>     and with him is full redemption.
> He himself will redeem Israel
>     from all their sins.

This is the fundamental purpose behind Jesus' ministry. The message we proclaim must just as clearly be centered in the offer of salvation from sin.

In these two emphases we see that Matthew's story of Jesus is unlike any other. It is a unique story of a unique person with a unique conception and a unique message and ministry.

**The virgin birth.** With both Matthew and Luke giving special attention to the narrative of the divine conception, we can conclude that Jesus' virgin birth has profound significance for our Christian faith and life.

(1) To begin with, the virgin birth points to the divine nature of Jesus. Taken together with his ability to forgive sins (9:6), the confirmatory nature of his miraculous ministry (14:33), the uniqueness of his death on the cross (27:46, 54), and the marvel of the resurrection (28:9), the virgin birth points to an absolute uniqueness about Jesus Christ. His conception, ministry, and resurrection are nothing short of declarations of his divine nature, which impels us to regard his claims upon our lives as second to none.

(2) The account of the virgin birth speaks of one person in whom is united full deity and full humanity. It was through the virgin birth that God chose to send his Son to become both perfect man and God. Donald Guthrie concludes, "It cannot be said that the incarnation demands the virgin birth, for God

could have accomplished it another way. But it can and must be said that the virgin birth of Jesus is entirely appropriate to the nature of the one who became flesh although He was equal with God (Phil. 2:6)."[36] This supremely points to how the sacrifice of the human on the cross could atone for the sins of humanity. Jesus is enabled to carry the sins of the world to the cross only because his divine nature is infinitely capable to sustain his humanity.

(3) The virgin birth signals Jesus' true humanity without inherited sin. Through the powerful work of the Holy Spirit overshadowing Mary in the conception of Jesus, the unbroken line of the descent of sin was interrupted, so that Jesus was born holy (cf. Luke 1:35).[37] As a true human, Jesus can empathize deeply with our human experiences and temptations (Heb. 4:15–16) and can provide an example of how to overcome temptation (see comments on Matt. 4:1–11). The sinlessness of Jesus throughout his life is centered in the fact that his divine nature is so powerful in its determination to do good that it cannot be overcome by any temptation to his human nature. Thus, he is enabled to be the unique, human, sinless sacrifice for our sin.

(4) The virgin birth of Jesus denotes the beginning stage of the redemption of humanity that had been created in the image of God but had been distorted by the effects of sin. The process of redemption will involve our becoming alive through the sacrifice he will provide for our sin (2 Cor. 5:17–21), but then it will also involve patterning our lives after Jesus (2 Cor. 3:18; 1 Peter 2:21). Jesus is the full image of God (Col. 1:15–20); he is the one person whose humanity was never spoiled by sin (Heb. 4:15). Since the outworking of the image of God is seen most fully in Jesus, the Christian life means to pattern ourselves after him.

Therefore, Matthew's record of the virgin conception and birth narrates a unique, miraculous event by which Jesus, the sinless Savior, came into the world to save his people from their sins. This is the beginning of the primary story line of this Gospel. Yet the narrative of the virgin birth is also the beginning stage by which the Immanuel, God with us, becomes the pattern for the kind of transforming life that he will produce in all who believe in him (Rom. 8:29).

As Matthew's Gospel unfolds, watch for some of the following ways that Jesus sets a perfect example for the kind of life that will be produced in us as we follow him as his disciples.

- Jesus had perfect fellowship with the Father (11:25–30; cf. John 17).
- Jesus obeyed the Father's will perfectly (26:42; cf. John 4:34; 5:30; 6:38).

---

36. Donald Guthrie, *New Testament Theology* (Downers Grove, Ill.: InterVarsity Press, 1981), 374.

37. For discussion see Wayne Grudem, *Systematic Theology: An Introduction to Biblical Doctrine* (Grand Rapids: Zondervan, 1994), 529–31.

- Jesus always displayed a strong love for humans, regardless how much they were lost, sick, sorrowing, or sinful (9:36; 10:6; cf. Mark 1:41; Luke 7:13).
- Jesus' love was demonstrated by freely giving up his life for us (20:28; cf. John 15:13).

In a holistic way, Jesus' process of development in his human life becomes a complete example of the way in which we can focus our development as persons redeemed by him and transformed by his Spirit. This is the earliest indication of what it will mean to be Jesus' disciples. Jesus' early years are an example of the way in which all of us can now develop as whole persons, including all aspects of human growth (see Luke 2:52). He experienced human development as we do, yet perfectly, so that we have the perfect example of what it means for us to be fully human.

We will discuss this more fully as Matthew's story goes along, but as foreign as this may seem to us at first, discipleship means living a fully human life in this world in union with Jesus Christ and growing in conformity to his image.[38]

**Learning from Joseph.** Joseph is an important person in Matthew 1, as are the angel of the Lord, the Holy Spirit, and Mary. Nonetheless, the central message of this narrative is not about Joseph or any other figure but about Jesus, even though he appears only in the final verse (1:25). The entire narrative concerns Jesus: who he is, how he came into history, and what his role and identity will be. Each of the other figures have much to teach us, but to learn from them accurately and appropriately we must keep the message about Jesus central (see comments in Bridging Contexts).

When compared to Luke's Gospel, which emphasizes the role of Mary throughout his infancy narrative (cf. Luke 1:26–56; 2:19, 34–35), Matthew gives special attention to Joseph. We may see from this that Matthew has given awareness to Joseph to accentuate aspects of his role that have significance for our own lives.[39]

(1) In the first place, Joseph is an example for us in the way he establishes his priorities. His purpose for his life and relationships stays focused on maintaining his righteous standing before the Lord by his obedience to the law. His commitment to righteousness is striking, because it is displayed in his sexual restraint and his abhorrence of what he considers infidelity. This

---

38. For a more complete discussion, see Michael J. Wilkins, *In His Image: Reflecting Christ in Everyday Life* (Colorado Springs: NavPress, 1997), 111–24.

39. For an attempt to connect Joseph's example with the development of discipleship later in Matthew's Gospel, see Carolyn Thomas, "The Nativity Scene: A Challenge to Discipleship," *TBT* 28 (1990): 26–33.

is especially important to emphasize when we remember that Joseph is most likely a relatively young man, perhaps in his late teens. Young men are notorious for their struggle with sexual purity. As a young man still in the passions of his youth, Joseph provides us an example of a godly young man who attempts to establish the values of God's will for his life. This is a realistic kind of picture that we may want to emphasize to our own young people in order that they may identify more closely with Joseph's commitment to righteousness.

(2) Joseph's obedience to the law is not legalistic. He is concerned not only about his own obedience to the law but also about showing compassion for Mary and having regard for her well-being. He does not abandon his faithfulness to the law in order to care for Mary, nor does he abandon Mary when her condition presents him with a dilemma about his own righteousness. Rather, he attempts to balance his obedience with compassion. Jesus will condemn time and again the scribes and Pharisees for their nitpicking legalism that overrules compassion and mercy (e.g., 9:10–13)—a sad commentary on some of the religious leadership of his day. However, Matthew demonstrates to us in Joseph's balanced example that the people of Israel at that time did not wholesale adopt a rigid legalism of do's and don'ts.

Joseph is in the line of other Old Testament figures whose pursuit of righteousness was guided by the values and goals of the law, which included compassion and mercy, as an expression of God's will. In the broadest sense, a righteous person is one whose life is bounded by the reality of God, meaning both purity of life and compassion of heart. Joseph, not of the religious elite, exemplifies the pursuit of that daily reality. In our own day we can point to many examples of men and women whose lives exemplify that balanced pursuit of righteousness. Those who come to mind are often well-known Christian leaders who have dedicated their lives to being an example for their flocks. But the ones who often impress me the most are laymen and laywomen whose lives and hearts are made pure in the obscurity of everyday life—homemakers, police officers, business leaders, nurses, teachers, and so on. Young Joseph is one of them.

(3) Joseph's obedience to the message of the angel of the Lord overrules his own suspicions of Mary's faithlessness as well as fear for the ruin of his own reputation and honor. Joseph's emotional state at the time the angel appears to him must have been intensely conflicted. But this special revelation of God, at this paramount crossroad of history, gives him the guidance and stability that enables him to help carry out God's program of salvation, even when he will become subject to ridicule and false accusations of moral failure.

We may never experience such a dramatic appearance from God, but each of us will encounter unexpected circumstances and risks as we attempt to carry out God's will for our lives. A young man engaged to be married recently told me that Joseph's obedience in these circumstances had profoundly impacted him. He had been struggling with trusting his fiancée, because in an earlier relationship a young lady he had loved had been unfaithful to him. He didn't know how he could ever really trust a woman again. His fear had begun to paralyze him in his relationship with his fiancée—fear of being hurt again and of being ridiculed for having an unfaithful wife. But he told me that he learned from this incident two important lessons. First, "trust" is not 100 percent knowledge; rather, it means to believe what he has seen and heard in his fiancée's life, and then on the basis of what he knows as best as he can to be true, believe her. That was scary for him, because he could be made a fool again. But the second thing he learned was that once he came to the point where he believed her, he then had to put their relationship in God's hands and believe in God to keep them both faithful to the relationship. So his real trust is in God. I think that he has learned a key lesson about a Christian marriage, which is founded on mutual trust but energized and maintained by the power of God.

**The role of the Holy Spirit.** The explicit nature of the role of the Holy Spirit in this passage enables us to begin to see the unfolding revelation of God throughout the Scripture. In the Old Testament, Yahweh is revealed as the one true God in distinction from the many gods of the people around Israel (Deut. 6:4, 14). In the stage of history depicted in the Gospels, as we have already noted, Jesus, God the Son, is the central figure, sustaining an intimate relationship to God the Father (cf. 3:17; 17:5). But as will become increasingly clear, when the earthly ministry of Jesus is accomplished with the cross and resurrection, God the Holy Spirit takes over a primary role on the stage of history. This activity of the Spirit is more explicit in the expansion of the church in the book of Acts and in the teaching of later New Testament authors, but we begin to see it come into play with the conception and birth of Jesus Messiah.

Today we live in that third stage of human history. Once Jesus ascended to heaven, he sent the Holy Spirit to provide the power, the guidance, the comfort, and the presence of God for carrying out the work of building the church, fulfilling the Great Commission, and transforming Jesus' disciples into the image of Christ.

That is what I emphasized to the engaged young man I mentioned earlier. He and his future wife have the privilege to be indwelt by the Holy Spirit of God, who will make their own marriage rise to the level that God has designed for it. Suspicion, self-protection, taking and not giving, bitterness, and anger—these are all too often cancers that can eat away at a marriage, as they could have in the relationship of young Joseph and Mary. But in this age, marriage, like any relationship among believers, can be transformed by the power of the Spirit.

The apostle Paul speaks of the transformation of relationships touched by the Holy Spirit. He encourages young pastor Titus to remind the churches "to be obedient, to be ready to do whatever is good, to slander no one, to be peaceable and considerate, and to show true humility toward all men" (Titus 3:1–2). Because relationships weren't always that way, Paul continues, practically as his own confession, "At one time we too were foolish, disobedient, deceived and enslaved by all kinds of passions and pleasures. We lived in malice and envy, being hated and hating one another" (Titus 3:3). I have had the unfortunate experience of seeing many marriages and other relationships typified by those descriptions. But then Paul gives one of the most glowing testimonies of the way that relationships can be transformed through the work of the Spirit:

> But when the kindness and love of God our Savior appeared, he saved us, not because of righteous things we had done, but because of his mercy. He saved us through the washing of rebirth and renewal by the Holy Spirit, whom he poured out on us generously through Jesus Christ our Savior. (Titus 3:4–6)

What a privilege and responsibility we now have to live at this stage of history. In their obedience to the work of the Spirit, young Joseph and Mary, at the very beginning of this age, give us a precursor of how godly relationships can be pure and characterized by serving one another. Today, that is the real basis on which we can pursue a godly marriage and family and, indeed, see the transformation of any of our relationships, both within and outside of the church, through the transforming work of God's Spirit.

# Matthew 2:1-12

AFTER JESUS WAS born in Bethlehem in Judea, during the time of King Herod, Magi from the east came to Jerusalem ²and asked, "Where is the one who has been born king of the Jews? We saw his star in the east and have come to worship him."

³When King Herod heard this he was disturbed, and all Jerusalem with him. ⁴When he had called together all the people's chief priests and teachers of the law, he asked them where the Christ was to be born. ⁵"In Bethlehem in Judea," they replied, "for this is what the prophet has written:

⁶"'But you, Bethlehem, in the land of Judah,
    are by no means least among the rulers of Judah;
for out of you will come a ruler
    who will be the shepherd of my people Israel.'"

⁷Then Herod called the Magi secretly and found out from them the exact time the star had appeared. ⁸He sent them to Bethlehem and said, "Go and make a careful search for the child. As soon as you find him, report to me, so that I too may go and worship him."

⁹After they had heard the king, they went on their way, and the star they had seen in the east went ahead of them until it stopped over the place where the child was. ¹⁰When they saw the star, they were overjoyed. ¹¹On coming to the house, they saw the child with his mother Mary, and they bowed down and worshiped him. Then they opened their treasures and presented him with gifts of gold and of incense and of myrrh. ¹²And having been warned in a dream not to go back to Herod, they returned to their country by another route.

As CHAPTER 2 opens, the narrative time frame has jumped ahead upwards of two years (see comments on 2:16). Matthew ended chapter 1 with Jesus being born and named (1:25). Now this baby is a "child" (2:8, 10), and the family is living "in Bethlehem in Judea" (2:1).[1] Bethlehem is located six miles south/southwest of Jerusalem.[2]

Luke informs us that before the birth of Jesus, Joseph and Mary traveled from Nazareth in Galilee to Bethlehem in Judea for the mandated census ordered by Caesar Augustus (Luke 2:1–7). They most likely performed a wedding ceremony in Nazareth, after which they traveled to Bethlehem for the census, where the child was born.[3] Luke does not mention any of the events found in Matthew 2 except to say that after the presentation of the child in the temple, "when Joseph and Mary had done everything required by the Law of the Lord, they returned to Galilee to their own town of Nazareth" (Luke 2:39).

Most who try to harmonize the infancy accounts suggest that the events of Matthew 2 occur after the temple visit but before the permanent return to Nazareth to raise the child.[4] Others suggest the trip to Nazareth in Luke 2:39 took place prior to the events of Matthew 2, proposing that after the family left the temple, they went to Nazareth for their personal belongings (Luke 2:29) since they had decided to raise the child in Bethlehem. Then, after taking up residence in Bethlehem, the events of Matthew 2:1–22 unfold. When they return from Egypt and discover the danger of continuing to live in Bethlehem, they return permanently to Nazareth.[5] It is somewhat difficult to posit an intermediary visit to Nazareth based on the surface reading of Luke 2:39–

1. "In Judea" distinguishes this town from Bethlehem of Zebulun (Josh. 19:10, 15), located near Nazareth.

2. Henri Cazelles, "Bethlehem," *ABD*, 1:712.

3. Matthew suggests that the couple performed the official wedding ceremony prior to the birth of Jesus (1:24–25), so Luke's expression that the couple were still "betrothed" while on their way to Bethlehem indicates that the marriage was not yet sexually consummated, implying a virgin birth (cf. Darrell Bock, *Luke 1:1–9:50* [Grand Rapids: Baker, 1994], 205–6).

4. E.g., A. T. Robertson, *A Harmony of the Gospels for Students of the Life of Christ: Based on the Broadus Harmony in the Revised Version* (New York: Harper & Row, 1922), 13; Robert H. Stein, *Luke* (NAC; Nashville: Broadman, 1992), 118. In this view, Luke 2:39a occurs before the events of Matthew 2:1–22, and Luke 2:39b occurs after these events and parallels Matt. 2:23, when the family returns from Egypt and goes to Nazareth to avoid Archelaus. This is possible, although Luke 2:39 seems to imply that the trip to Nazareth occurs immediately after the temple presentation.

5. Robert L. Thomas and Stanley N. Gundry, eds., *The NIV Harmony of the Gospels* (Harper & Row, 1978), 38 note o.

40. In any case, after Jesus' birth and his presentation in the temple, Joseph and Mary decide to raise the child in Bethlehem, Joseph's ancestral city.

## The Magi's Journey to Jerusalem (2:1–2)

THE EVENTS MATTHEW is about to narrate take place "during the time of King Herod." Palestine, the region of land comprising the biblical Israel and Judah, was one of the many regions that fell to the ever-expanding Roman Empire. A series of problems within the Hasmonean dynasty had left it fair game for the voracious appetite of Roman military expansion. In 63 B.C., the renowned general Pompey advanced on Jerusalem and captured the city as well as the rest of Palestine. The Romans installed local figures to rule for them, and eventually Herod, an Idumean/Nabatean by bloodline, gained prominence and ruled under Rome from 37 to 4 B.C. Herod, called "king of the Jews," ruled firmly and at times ruthlessly. He most likely died in March, 4 B.C. (see discussion below). Since Herod is still alive when the Magi arrive in Jerusalem as much as two years after Jesus was born, the dating of Jesus' birth is placed by most scholars at between 6 and 4 B.C. (see comments on 2:16).

The universal significance of the birth of the child Jesus is heralded immediately because Magi from the east arrive in Jerusalem seeking to worship the one born "king of the Jews" (1:1–2). The term "Magi" (*magos*, "magician") originally referred to a priestly caste in ancient Persia, perhaps followers of Zoroaster (c. 630?–550? B.C.), a Persian teacher and prophet. Babylonian elements were subsequently introduced, including astrology, demonology, wisdom, and magic. Magi were usually leading figures in the religious court life of their country of origin, employing a variety of scientific (astrology), diplomatic (wisdom), and religious (magical incantations) elements in their work. These practices were distinct from a more common type of "magician" found elsewhere (e.g., *magos* in Acts 13:6, 8).

These Magi came from "the east" and were looking for the one born "king of the Jews." They apparently had been exposed to Old Testament prophecies from Jewish colonies situated in the east. Although many Jews returned to Palestine after the Exile, many remained in the east, especially in Babylon, in Parthia to the north, and in Arabia to the southwest. Pagan leaders, both political and religious, were well aware of Jewish religious distinctives, such as Sabbath observance and marital restrictions,[6] and there were significant Jewish centers of learning in Babylon at the time of the Magi.[7] Gentile religious leaders in the east were regularly exposed to Hebrew Scriptures, prophecy, and teachers.

---

6. Josephus, *Ant.* 18:318–19, 340, 449–52.
7. *b. Pesaḥ* 6:1; cf. *y. Pesaḥ* 6:1, 33a.

If the Magi came from the environs of Babylon,[8] they would have traveled approximately nine hundred miles. The trade route from Babylon followed the Euphrates River north, then south through the Orontes River valley of Syria into Palestine. Since they would have had to make arrangements for the journey and gather a traveling party, it would have taken several months from the time they first saw the star until they arrived in Jerusalem.[9]

In spite of the well-known Christmas carol "We Three Kings of Orient Are," there is little historical certainty behind the wording of the stanza. As early as the third century A.D., the Magi were considered kings, fulfilling Psalm 72:11, "All kings will bow down to him." But the Magi were probably more along the lines of religious advisers to their court. Their actual number is uncertain. Eastern tradition sets their number at twelve, but Western tradition sets it at three, based on the three gifts of gold, incense, and myrrh.[10] Likely the Magi, whatever their number, traveled with a much larger number of attendants and guards for the long journey.

The Magi's goal is to find "the one who has been born king of the Jews." Matthew has traced the lineage through King David (1:6), preparing for Jesus Messiah to be called "king of the Jews." The people of Israel had long waited for the rightful heir to the throne, but God announces his arrival first through these Gentile Magi. An expectation had circulated in the world of the first century that a ruler would arise from Judea. Suetonius writes, "Throughout the whole of the East there had spread an old and persistent belief: destiny had decreed that at that time men coming forth from Judea would seize power [and rule the world]."[11] Israel's prophets had long spoken of a period of world peace and prosperity that would be instituted by a future Davidic deliverer (e.g., Ezek. 34:23–31). This belief had penetrated beyond the borders of Israel, so that others were looking for a ruler(s) to arise from the land of Judea.[12]

---

8. Tony T. Maalouf argues that the Magi came from the Arabian Desert communities, much closer to Jerusalem; see "Were the Magi from Persia or Arabia?" *BibSac* 156 (1999): 399–442.

9. Note that Ezra took four months with a group of four to five thousand people to go that route (Ezra 7:9). The Magi may have been able to travel more quickly, but still slowly compared to modern rates of travel.

10. The traditional names of the Magi—Balthasar, Melchior, and Gaspar (or Caspar)—first appear in a mosaic in a sixth-century church in Ravenna, Italy, but there is no historical support for these designations.

11. Suetonius, *Vespasian* 5.

12. Josephus (*J.W.* 3:399–408; 6:310–15) and Tacitus (*History* 5:13) both note this widespread expectation. They contend that the Jews were wrong and that the expectation was actually fulfilled with the ascension of Vespasian to the throne after his victories in Palestine. But the Jews themselves (obviously not Josephus, a Jew) certainly did not find the fulfillment of their Old Testament prophetic hope in Vespasian.

The Magi announce of the king whom they seek, "We saw his star in the east and have come to worship him." The word "east" (*anatole*) can mean either the "rising" of the sun and stars (cf. Luke 1:78) or the locale called "the east" (Rev. 21:13).[13] The phrase "from the east" in 2:1 appears to be the latter, but the expression "in the east" in 2:2 implies the former, indicating that they saw the star rise. That is, they didn't see the star rise in the eastern part of the sky, otherwise it would have caused them to travel east. Rather, while they were to the east of Jerusalem, the star rose, perhaps to the west of them, causing them to travel west to Jerusalem.

Through the Jewish community in their homeland, the Magi would have become familiar with Balaam's prophecy, "A star will come out of Jacob; a scepter will rise out of Israel" (Num. 24:17). In many quarters within Judaism this prophecy was understood to point to a messianic deliverer (e.g., CD 7:18—26; 4QTest. 9—13). In Revelation, Jesus refers to himself in similar language: "I am the Root and the Offspring of David, and the bright Morning Star" (Rev. 22:16; cf. 2:28; 2 Peter 1:19).

There are several proposals as to the nature of this star.[14] (1) Many suggest that it was a natural phenomenon that can be traced back to some known astronomical event, whether a comet,[15] a supernova, or a conjunction of planets. One widely discussed possibility is that the attention of the Magi was attracted by an unusual conjunction of planets that occurred on May 27, 7 B.C.[16] In ancient Babylonian astrology, Jupiter represented the primary deity. When Jupiter came close to Saturn (which represented the Jews), in the constellation Pisces (which represented Palestine), the Magi referred to Jupiter as the star of the king they were seeking, and the association with Saturn and Pisces showed them in which nation (the Jews) and where (Palestine) to look for him. A related suggestion draws on this conjunction but links the specific star to a supernova that Chinese and Korean astronomers recorded in March to April 5 B.C.[17]

---

13. See BDAG, 74.

14. For brief discussion of the predominant views, see Brown, *Birth of the Messiah*, 170—74, and W. P. Armstrong and J. Finegan, "Chronology of the NT," *ISBE*, 1:687—88. For more diverse views, see E. Jerry Vardaman and Edwin M. Yamauchi, eds., *Chronos, Kairos, Christos: Nativity and Chronological Studies Presented to Jack Finegan* (Winona Lake: Eisenbrauns, 1989). The varied hypotheses become more speculative in the second volume, E. Jerry Vardaman, ed., *Chronos, Kairos, Christos II: Chronological, Nativity, and Religious Studies in Memory of Ray Summers* (Macon, Ga: Mercer Univ. Press, 1998).

15. E.g., Halley's Comet, visible in 12 and 11 B.C.

16. See the work of the astronomer David Hughes, *The Star of Bethlehem: An Astronomer's Confirmation* (New York: Walker, 1979).

17. Mark Kidger, *The Star of Bethlehem: An Astronomer's View* (Princeton, N.J.: Princeton Univ. Press, 1999), argues that the conjunction alerted the Magi to some special event and the supernova triggered their journey.

(2) Others suggest that the "star" was a supernatural astral phenomenon that God used to herald Jesus' birth. This is suggested in the text by the description of the star, which appears and reappears and moves and directs the Magi to the precise house that Jesus and his family occupied. Some suggest that perhaps only the Magi saw this starlike phenomenon.

(3) Another plausible suggestion is that the supernatural phenomenon was actually an angel sent to the Magi to announce the birth of Messiah and to guide them to Jesus so that they would be a witness to his birth through their worship. Good angels are commonly referred to as stars (e.g., Job 38:7; Dan. 8:10; Rev. 1:16, 20; 2:1; 3:1), as are fallen angels (Rev. 8:10, 11; 9:1; perhaps Isa. 14:12–13). Angels guided and protected Israel to the Promised Land (Ex. 14:19; 23:20), and they often appear in Jewish and Christian literature as guides.[18] New Testament scholar Dale Allison cites the apocryphal Arabic *Gospel of the Infancy* 7, which expands Matthew's account of the Magi to say, "In the same hour there appeared to them an angel in the form of that star which had before guided them on their journey."[19]

This last view is consistent with the prominent place of the angel of the Lord in the overall infancy narrative: announcing to Joseph the virginal conception of Jesus (1:20), warning the Magi not to return to Herod (2:12), warning Joseph to flee with the family to Egypt (2:13), telling them to go back to Israel (2:19), and guiding them in a dream to Nazareth (2:22).

In any case, with their mixture of influence from paganism, astrology, and Jewish Scriptures, it is doubtful that the Magi knowingly come to worship Jesus in recognition of his incarnate nature as the God-man. They most likely desire to worship the "king of the Jews" in a way similar to how leading figures from a subservient country paid homage to the king of a ruling country. The Magi are giving rightful homage to Jesus as the promised ruler to arise in Israel, but their worship is far more than even they intended.[20]

## Herod's Cunning Duplicity (2:3–8)

APPARENTLY HEROD IS familiar with the star symbolism that was to announce the arrival of the Messiah, so he does not challenge the Magi. His first reaction at first seems surprising: "He was disturbed, and all Jerusalem with him." Herod knows he is not the rightful heir to the Davidic kingdom; he has

---

18. E.g., *1 En.* 1:2 and passim; *T. Levi* 2–5; *History of the Rechabites* 1:3 and passim.

19. See Dale C. Allison, "What Was the Star That Guided the Magi?" *BibRev* 9 (November–December 1993): 24.

20. See David Peterson, *Engaging with God: A Biblical Theology of Worship* (Downers Grove, Ill.: InterVarsity Press, 1992), 85; Albright and Mann, *Matthew: Introduction, Translation, and Notes*, 13–14.

usurped the throne by aligning himself with Rome. So with the Magi's announcement that they are seeking the one born king of the Jews, he probably perceives that invading forces from the east may perhaps join forces within Israel to oust him and place a king on the throne who is from the true line of the expected Messiah.

Herod has no fear of attack from the west, because that is where the Roman Empire lies, and he is the Rome-sanctioned ruler of Judea. However, he develops a profound fear of attacks from the east. During the Hasmonean struggle for supremacy between Antigonus and Hyrcanus II, Antigonus joined forces with the Parthians, an empire to the northeast of Israel, who invaded Judea and besieged Jerusalem. Herod fled to Rome, where he appealed for help to oust the Parthians and claim the throne. After recapturing Jerusalem in 37 B.C., Herod built a series of fortress-palaces all along the eastern border to ensure safety from invading forces.[21] Herod also dedicated his reign and resources to a number of magnificent architectural projects. These projects often benefited his Jewish subjects, such as the rebuilding of the temple in Jerusalem, begun in 20/19 B.C. and completed in A.D. 63.

The final years of Herod's reign were characterized by constant domestic problems. His ten wives had produced offspring who contended against each other for his throne. As he became older, he grew increasingly paranoid, and he had a number of his own family members imprisoned and executed—for example, his wife Miramne I and later her two sons, Alexander and Aristobulus. After several incidents of this sort, Caesar Augustus supposedly made the famous pun that he would rather be Herod's pig (*hys*) than his son (*huios*).[22]

Not only is Herod disturbed at the arrival of the Magi, but so also is "all Jerusalem with him." The word "Jerusalem" is the designation for the holy city (4:5; 27:53), but it also represents the religious and political leadership of Israel. The leadership may be disturbed along with Herod because they know the consequences they might suffer if he were to fly into a rage at the perceived threat of the arriving forces with the Magi. But more likely, their reaction gives a clue to the spiritual health of Israel's leadership. They have aligned themselves politically with Herod, and if his power base is threatened, so is theirs. One would expect the religious leadership to celebrate at the report of the birth of the king of Israel, but the arrival of the true king of the Jews presents a threat to Israel's corrupt religious and political power. From

---

21. See Josephus, *Ant.* 14:335–69; 17:23.

22. Macrobius, *Saturnalia* 2.f.11. The saying is given in Latin, but it depends on the Greek spelling and pronunciation for the pun; note too the Jewish antipathy for swine.

the outset of Matthew's story, Jerusalem is potentially negative toward Jesus and joins forces with those who will soon attempt to kill him (2:16, 20).[23]

The central leadership of the Jews was lodged in the "chief priests" and the "teachers of the law" (*grammateus*). The chief priests were members of the Sanhedrin (cf. 26:57; Mark 14:53), joining the high priest in giving oversight to the temple activities, treasury, and priestly orders. The term *grammateus* (also trans. "scribe") was once most closely associated with reading, writing, and making copies of the Scriptures. But by New Testament times it came to signify an expert in relation to the interpretation of law and is used interchangeably with the term "lawyer" or "expert in the law" (*nomikos;* cf. Matt. 23:4; Luke 11:45—46). These were the official interpreters of the Old Testament (see comments on 8:19).

Herod's inquiry as to "where the Christ was to be born" demonstrates that the concept of "king of the Jews" (2:2) had become linked with "the Christ," the Messiah. The religious leaders cite the prophet Micah, who centuries earlier referred to Bethlehem as not least among "the clans of Judah," because it would be the birthplace of the future ruler, the Messiah (Micah 5:2). Their quotation also has an allusion to a famous shepherding theme cited at David's installation as king over Israel, "You will shepherd my people Israel, and you will become their ruler" (2 Sam. 5:2).[24] The prophetic expectation of the Davidic Messiah being born in Bethlehem had become widespread in Israel (cf. John 7:42). This village is twice honored, because the birthplace of David the king is now also the birthplace of Jesus the Christ, the king and shepherd of Israel.

Herod's duplicity takes over as he secretly brings in the Magi and attempts to find out when the star had appeared to them (2:7). The need for secrecy may have been to keep the Jews who were hoping for the arrival of Messiah from warning the Magi of Herod's treachery.[25] Or perhaps if the child the

---

23. Peter W. L. Walker, *Jesus and the Holy City: New Testament Perspectives on Jerusalem* (Grand Rapids: Eerdmans, 1996), 33—34. For a helpful literary analysis that contrasts Herod and the religious leadership with Jesus as the rightful "king of the Jews," see Bauer, "The Kingship of Jesus," 306—23. Bauer suggests that the expression "all Jerusalem" is intended by Matthew to set the stage for the emphasis on the religious leaders of Israel being blamed for leading the people of Israel to reject Jesus and to take his blood on their heads (cf. 27:20, 25).

24. The shepherd motif associated with Jesus Messiah is pronounced in the New Testament: Jesus refers to himself as "the good shepherd" (John 10:11); the writer of the book of Hebrews calls Jesus "that great Shepherd of the sheep" (Heb. 13:20); the apostle Peter emphasizes that leaders in the church are to "shepherd" the flock (1 Peter 5:2; cf. John 21:16) for Jesus, "the Chief Shepherd" (1 Peter 5:4); and concerning the martyrs who come out of the great tribulation, "the Lamb at the center of the throne will be their shepherd" (Rev. 7:17).

25. Hagner, *Matthew 1—13*, 30.

Magi are seeking really is the coming Messiah, and if Herod were to eliminate the child, it would not sit well with the Jewish people. So he goes about his plans secretly so that he can be rid of the threat to his throne without the people knowing of it. It seems inconceivable that he would try to get rid of the Messiah for the sake of his own throne, but Herod was an Idumean, and any thought of a Jewish deliverer taking over his power would be ruthlessly resisted. Note too that Herod considered himself "King of the Jews."

The distance of the Magi's homeland from Palestine likely prevented them from knowing about Herod's ruthless reputation, so they think that Herod sincerely wants to acknowledge the arrival of the Messiah. Herod is confident he has deceived the Magi, because he does not send an escort with them to Bethlehem, and he has no reason to doubt that they will follow through and return to tell him the child's whereabouts. It is divine intervention that will spoil his plans.

### The Magi Worship the Child (2:9–12)

THE STAR THAT led them to Palestine now apparently reappears and leads the Magi the six miles to the child in Bethlehem. The description of the activity of the star implies a supernatural phenomenon, since it is difficult to reconstruct how any form of star could go ahead of them and stop or remain over the place where the child was. Since the Magi have already been informed that the Messiah was to be born in Bethlehem, the star doesn't so much guide them to the town but to the place in the town where the child and family are now located. This is consistent with some kind of supernatural angelic guidance (see comments on 2:2).

Jesus, with Mary and Joseph, is now in a "house" in Bethlehem. Recently excavated houses for common people from the first century era display regular features. Houses built on level ground often formed a series of rooms built around a courtyard. Included in these rooms were living spaces, which doubled as sleeping quarters, cooking area, stables, and storage rooms. Houses built in hilly areas might be two stories high. The lower floor had a courtyard surrounded by stables while the upper floor had the living/sleeping rooms. In rocky cavernous areas, the lower floor might incorporate caves or grottos into the structure as underground stables.[26]

The term for Jesus in 2:8, 9, 11 (also 2:13, 14, 20, 21) is "child" (*paidion*), which normally designates an infant or toddler.[27] Since Herod will later attempt to have

---

26. John S. Holladay Jr., "House, Israelite," *ABD*, 3:313; Rousseau and Arav, "House," *Jesus and His World*, 128–31.

27. Luke uses the same term to refer to Jesus at his birth and presentation in the temple when he was only a few days old (Luke 2:17, 27).

all boys under two years old killed, the child is now perhaps nearly two. Whether the house in which they live is the same one connected to the stable in which Jesus was born is unknown, but since the young family has stayed in Bethlehem instead of returning to Nazareth to raise their son, it implies that Joseph has arranged for permanent living quarters in a family house.

The purpose of the Magi's pilgrimage to see the child is accomplished as they "bowed down and worshiped him" (2:11). Although they see both the child and Mary, his mother, they worship the child only. Joseph is not mentioned, even though he has, and will continue to have, a substantial role in the narrative. The true center of their attention is the infant Jesus.

The word used to describe the Magi's "worship" is one normally reserved for the veneration of deity.[28] It is a clear principle in Scripture that God alone is to receive worship, never an intermediary, not even an angel (e.g., Acts 14:11–15; Rev. 19:10). But it is doubtful that at this time these quasi-pagan religious figures understand Jesus' divine nature. Since it took even Jesus' closest followers some time to comprehend the nature of the Incarnation, it is doubtful that the Magi are knowingly worshiping Jesus as the God-man. Yet in spite of their blend of pagan religious background with Jewish influence, their worship is probably far more than even they understand.[29] At the least they understand that this is God's Messiah, and they worship the God of Israel through him. At the same time, their worship is a clear indictment of the Herodian leadership in Jerusalem, who will soon attempt to kill, not worship, the infant king of the Jews.

When approaching royalty or persons of high religious, political, or social status, gifts were often brought to demonstrate obeisance (Gen. 43:11–15; 1 Sam. 9:7–8; 1 Kings 10:1–2). The word "treasures" is used of the treasury of a nation (1 Macc. 3:29) or, as here, some kind of receptacle or "treasure-box,"[30] used by the Magi for carrying valuables—gold, incense, and myrrh—that they present to the newborn king. This act of worship recalls Old Testament passages where leaders of Gentile nations presented gifts to the king of Israel, and it looks forward prophetically to the nations honoring the coming Messiah.[31]

---

28. The verb is *proskyneo*, "worship," with the dative direct object *auto*, "him." This dative is the case of personal interest, which normally lends itself to emphasize the worship of deity (cf. 14:33; Wallace, *Greek Grammar*, 172–73).

29. Peterson, *Engaging with God*, 85.

30. Josephus (*Ant.* 9:163; cf. 2 Kings 12:9–11) uses the term to designate the wooden chest that the high priest Jehoiada placed beside the altar to collect the people's offerings for renovating the temple. Matthew uses the word for a personal "storehouse" (Matt. 13:52) as well as to indicate the things laid up in store: treasure in heaven (6:20; cf. treasures in Christ, Col. 2:3).

31. Cf. Ps. 72:10–11; Isa. 60:5–6, 11; 66:20; Zeph. 3:10; Hag. 2:7–8.

---

"Gold" is the most-often mentioned valued metal in Scripture; as in modern times, it was prized throughout the ancient world as a medium of exchange as well as for making jewelry, ornaments, and dining instruments for royalty. "Incense" (or "frankincense"; cf. Lev. 2:1; 14:7; Neh. 13:9) is derived from the gummy resin of the tree *Boswellia*.[32] The gum produced a sweet odor when burned. Frankincense was used for secular purposes as a perfume (Song 3:6; 4:6, 14), but in Israel it was used ceremonially as part of a recipe for the only incense permitted on the altar (Ex. 30:9, 34–38).[33] "Myrrh" is the sap that exudes from a small tree found in Arabia, Abyssinia, and India. It consists of a mixture of resin, gum, and the oil myrrhol, which produces its characteristic odor. Sold in either liquid or solid form, myrrh was used in incense (Ex. 30:23), as a perfume for garments (Ps. 45:8; Song 3:6) or for a lover's couch (Est. 2:13; Prov. 7:17), and as a stimulant tonic (cf. Mark 15:23). The Jews did not practice full embalming of corpses, but a dead body was prepared for burial by washing, dressing it in special garments, and packing it with fragrant myrrh and other spices to stifle the smell of a body as it decayed (John 19:39).[34]

There is a long history of interpretation that finds symbolic significance in these gifts in accord with Jesus' life and ministry: e.g., gold represents his kingship, incense his deity, myrrh his sacrificial death and burial.[35] But this reads too much into the Magi's understanding of who Jesus is. Rather, these three gifts indicate the esteem with which the Magi revere the child and represent giving him the honor due him as king of the Jews. More than the Magi know or intend, these gifts are likely used to providentially support the family in their flight to and stay in Egypt.

But the danger from Herod's paranoid jealousy of the infant king comes to the forefront as the Magi are warned in a dream not to return to him with their report (2:12). Dreams were commonly understood in the ancient world to be means of divine communication to humans (see comments on 1:20). Joseph is the primary recipient of dreams: announcing the virginal conception of Jesus (1:20), warning the family to go to Egypt (2:13), telling them to go back to Israel (2:19), and guiding them to Nazareth (2:22). In most of these an angel is specificallly mentioned as the one who engages Joseph. Therefore, it seems plausible that the angel appears also in this dream to the

---

32. The tree is found in South Arabia, Ethiopia, Somalia, and India. During the summer the bark of the tree was peeled back and deep incisions were made in the tree. An amber gum secreted, which turned to a whitish color on the surface of the resin.

33. See W. E. Shewell-Cooper, "Frankincense," *ZPEB*, 2:606–7.

34. See Kjeld Nielsen, "Incense," *ABD*, 3:404–9; Victor H. Matthews, "Perfumes and Spices," *ABD*, 5:226–28; Joel Green, "Burial of Jesus," *DJG*, 88–92.

35. E.g., Irenaeus, *Against Heresies* 3.9.2; Origen, *Contra Celsum* 1:60.

Magi, warning them of Herod's duplicity. If so, the warning in a dream is consistent with the view that the star guiding them was an angel, who now directs them back to their homeland.

Instead of retracing their steps through Jerusalem, where Herod awaits them, "they returned to their country by another route" (2:12). Behind the expression "they returned" is a word (*anachoreo*) that highlights a thematic pattern of hostility, withdrawal, and prophetic fulfillment that recurs in the narrative.[36] Matthew emphasizes that in spite of recurring hostile circumstances, God's sovereign care surrounds Jesus Messiah's earthly life. Under the threatening cloud of hostility, the Magi avoid Herod in Jerusalem, necessitating a long detour back to their homeland.

They may have traveled south around the lower extremity of the Dead Sea to link up with the trade route north through Nabatea and Decapolis east of the Jordan River. Or they may have traveled south to Hebron and then west to the Mediterranean coast to link up with the trade route traveling north on the coastal plain. Herod's long arm of military security covered most of even these circuitous routes, so the Magi and entourage must have traveled swiftly and as secretly as possible. Their sacrifice and endurance is profound testimony to the impact of having seen and worshiped the infant Jesus, the true king of the Jews, and the hope even of Gentile seekers.

GOD'S SOVEREIGN CARE. Ambition, strength, and strategy are characteristics that we expect to find in those successful in politics, the military, entertainment, sports, or business. God can, and has, used those characteristics in his people throughout history as he has brought about his will on earth. Joshua's ambition to bring the people of Israel to the Promised Land was exemplary to all the people as he followed God's lead without wavering (Josh. 1:6–9; 23:6–11). The strength that Moses demonstrated in the face of resistant Pharaoh and over the forces of nature has stood for centuries as one of the most spectacular displays of God's own strength (e.g., Ps. 105:23–45). The strategy that King David displayed when conquering the giant Goliath and vanquishing God's enemies is legendary among military leaders (e.g., 1 Sam. 17:50–54; 2 Sam. 8:11–15). God can, and does, use ambition, strength, and strategy to carry out his will.

---

36. Cf. also 2:13, "when they had gone"; 2:14, "left for Egypt"; 2:22–23; 4:12–18; 12:15–21; 14:12–14; 15:21–28; 27:5–10; see Deirdre Good, "The Verb ἀναχωρέω in Matthew's Gospel," *NovT* 32 (1990): 1–12.

However, the unexpectedness of the infancy account signals to us that God will turn those characteristics upside down as he initiates this crucial stage of salvation history. The picture that Matthew paints of the arrival of Jesus is breathtaking in its potential but alarming in its vulnerability. Jesus is King of the Jews (2:1), Messiah (2:4), and Ruler (2:6), who will "shepherd" his people Israel (2:6). In him are localized the prophetic hopes of the people of Israel as they strain under the yoke of Rome. This is no ordinary child, but he is the ruler who will once again bring safety to the beleaguered people of God.

Yet Jesus is just a little child. He has no royal courtiers to care for him, no military guard to defend him. He has no palace or army. In fact, an ominous note is sounded. This vulnerable, humble little claimant to Israel's throne will be threatened by the conniving tyrant, Herod. Who will care for the little future king? Who will protect him? How can he possibly survive to bring about those roles prophesied for him?

This is what makes the unexpectedness of Matthew's story so striking. The ambition, strength, and strategy of Herod and the religious leadership of Jerusalem are contrasted with the vulnerability of the child. Herod's entire career was marked by ruthless ambition as he deposed all the Hasmonean aspirants to the throne. He orchestrated alliances with whomever was in power in Rome so that he had the strength of the Roman military and political machines behind him. He had a callous brilliance behind his strategy, keeping at bay the competing forces in Israel through grudging gratitude for his building accomplishments, yet fear of his cruelty and hatred of his religious and political treachery. No aspirant to the throne could hope to compete with Herod—especially one so vulnerable as the infant Jesus lying helplessly in the arms of a young, peasant mother and protected only by a lowly, unproven father from the insignificant town of Nazareth.

Yet throughout the narrative, the theme that underlies all of these events is that God is in control. As he begins his redemption of humanity, his hand is on every event that transpires. The miraculous appearance of the star to Gentile Magi signaled that God was initiating messianic deliverance for Israel—and for all humanity. The child and parents are sovereignly routed to Bethlehem, his prophesied birthplace, despite living in faraway Nazareth. With a significance that they could not possibly fully comprehend, pagan Magi prostrate themselves in worship of the only One who is divinely worthy of their veneration. The humble child and parents are providentially supplied with gifts that will enable them to escape the increasingly murderous ravages of a paranoid slaughterer. And the devious plan of one of the most powerful figures in the ancient world is stymied by innocent Magi as they heed a miraculous warning in a dream. In spite of recurring hostile circumstances, God's sovereign care is exercised in Jesus Messiah's earthly life.

Human ambition, power, and strategy often cannot see the hand of God and unwittingly attempt to thwart his purposes. Herod and the religious leadership in Jerusalem were blinded to God's plan of redemption because of the lust for their own plans and purposes. Their blindness then caused them to attempt to hinder God's design. Only eyes of faith are open to see God's activities, because he often performs behind the scenes of human history in unexpected ways to bring about his purposes.

Matthew accentuates this elegant theme at the beginning of his story so that his readers will open their eyes of faith to see the working of God in the life of Jesus Messiah. The theme of God's sovereignty displayed in the infancy narrative sets a trajectory for Matthew's recounting of Jesus' entire ministry. Jesus does not operate according to typical human expectations and ambitions, he does not come with typical human power, fanfare, or fame, and he will often run counter to typical human strategies. He comes, remarkably, as a humble servant, bringing justice to both Jew and Gentile alike, offering healing and hope and a message of good news to the hurting and marginalized (cf. 12:15–21).

The unexpectedness of this kind of Messiah will potentially cause offense to even his own renowned herald, John the Baptist, who must learn to look for God's activity in redeeming Israel and not force his own understanding on God's Messiah (11:2–6).[37] The unexpectedness of this kind of Messiah will infuriate the religious establishment of Israel, leading to their own hard-hearted sin (12:22–32) and their condemnation and execution of the only One for whom they should have been looking (26:1–2). And the unexpectedness of Jesus' redemptive, sacrificial, messianic ministry will baffle even his own disciples, for they have in mind the ways of humans, not the ways of God (16:21–23; 20:20–28).

Ambition, strength, and strategy—these characteristics are exhibited in God's plan of salvation that is worked out in the entrance of Jesus Messiah to history. But those characteristics are displayed with divine expression, not human. Matthew focuses our attention on the fact that God is in control, even as the events surrounding his work unfold in unexpected ways.

---

37. The difficulty of comprehending the unexpectedness of Jesus' messianic ministry continues even to this day. Jewish scholars often have the same difficulty with Jesus' messianic ministry as did many in the Jewish establishment of the first century. They suggest that Jesus was a "failure" as the Messiah because he did not bring the final and complete redemption of the world in the sociopolitical realm; e.g., Byron L. Sherwin, "Who Do You Say That I Am?" in *Jesus Through Jewish Eyes: Rabbis and Scholars Engage an Ancient Brother in a New Conversation*, ed. Beatrice Bruteau (Maryknoll, N.Y.: Orbis, 2001), 36–38. See comments below on 11:2–6.

**GOD'S LOVE—AND OURS.** "She had a habit of saying little silent prayers about the simplest everyday things, and now she whispered: 'Please God, make him think I am still pretty.'" What heart-wrenching words! Della's knee-length, cascading, beautiful brown hair was her most prized possession, but she has just cut it off to sell to a wigmaker. She does it so she will have money to buy her beloved husband, Jim, a Christmas present. With the money from the sale of her hair she will be able to buy a gold watch chain on which Jim can hang his most prized possession, the gold watch that had been his father's and grandfather's.

Della and Jim are a newly wed young couple who subsist in near poverty. They have little money for finery in their hovel of an apartment, let alone for extravagant Christmas gifts. Without knowing what she has done, Jim will be coming home on Christmas Eve to find Della shorn of her beautiful hair, all to buy the gold chain for him that he cannot possibly afford to buy for himself. Will he still think her to be pretty?

But in a tear-jerking twist in this classic story told by O. Henry, we learn that Jim has sold his cherished watch to buy a set of tortoise shell combs with jeweled rims for his beloved young wife's beautiful hair—the very set she has yearned over for so long but can never hope to buy for herself.

Della now has cropped hair, but with the finest gift her young husband could sacrifice to buy. And Jim, now has no watch, but with the most precious gift his young bride could sacrifice to bring to him for Christmas. O. Henry muses at the end of the story:

> Here I have lamely related to you the uneventful chronicle of two foolish children in a flat who most unwisely sacrificed for each other the greatest treasures of their house. But in a last word to the wise of these days let it be said that of all who give gifts these are the wisest. Of all who give and receive gifts, such as they are wisest. Everywhere they are wisest. They are the magi.[38]

I just reminded my wife of this story, which she had last read in college nearly thirty years ago, and immediately tears filled her eyes. That tells you as much about my wife's tender spirit as it does about the poignancy of the story! Henry may have added a bit of an allegorical twist to his story, but he certainly touches a basic element in all of us. The very act of sacrificial giving defines what it means to love each other. The Magi in Matthew's story

---

38. O. Henry, "The Gift of the Magi," *The Complete Works of O. Henry* (Garden City, N.Y.: Doubleday, Doran, 1936), 10.

may have been impelled by that kind of love in their worship and gift-giving at the arrival of the King of the Jews. It's hard to get inside their head and heart historically to know for sure. But I think that Henry is right to extrapolate from their actions what the Magi themselves may not even have guessed fully—our sacrificial worship and love of Jesus will produce true, sacrificial love for each other.

**Personal response to Jesus.** Matthew is not putting down on record just another religious story. He is telling what has been famously entitled for the film screen *The Greatest Story Ever Told*. God has entered history in the person of Jesus Messiah, and the world has never been the same. Henry rightly recognized that all of our sacrifice is but a faint reflection of what lies behind the Christmas story. We rightfully focus on the Magi, but we certainly must focus on the sacrificial love of God, of which the apostle Paul tells us, "God demonstrates his own love for us in this: While we were still sinners, Christ died for us" (Rom. 5:8).

Sometimes we get caught up in sentimental images of the Christmas story: a haloed baby Jesus resting peacefully in a hay-filled trough in a quaint stall in a field near Bethlehem on a midwinter starry night with the beatific mother Mary and antiquated father Joseph, camels arriving with three Magi, all surrounded by donkeys and sheep with shepherds from the fields and an angelic host. Our purpose here is not to disrupt sentimentally held traditions but to understand clearly Matthew's emphasis so that we can more carefully align our lives with the immense significance of the arrival of Jesus Messiah.

The purpose of the Magi's visit was to worship the one born "king of the Jews." True, their worship was probably homage given to Jesus as a human king, but their actions point to a deeper tribute than even they knew. Matthew has informed his readers that Jesus was divinely conceived (1:18–25), so to honor him truly is to worship the only One who is worthy of worship, God himself. Jesus is not only the "king of the Jews," but he is also One who provides the hope of salvation for the entire world. If these Gentile Magi have recognized Jesus as Israel's king, then the Jews should certainly acknowledge him as the Messiah.[39] But will they? As Matthew turns to the response of the Jewish leadership to the Magi's astounding announcement, he tragically records only duplicity and treachery. It is sobering to recognize that those who had the greatest opportunity to worship the true king of the Jews became pawns of the usurper, Herod.

As we reflect on our own religious and political agendas, we should also take a sober look at our own response to Jesus. It isn't always in the accom-

---

39. Steve Willis, "Matthew's Birth Stories: Prophecy and the Magi," *ExpTim* 105 (1993): 43–45.

plishments of our lives that our relationship with Jesus is measured most accurately. Every pastor or youth worker or Sunday school teacher knows how busy we can become with marking out our own activities and priorities. In the busyness of our service it is possible to lose sight of the work of God in us and around us. Are we ready to acknowledge Jesus' presence in all the details of our lives, or do our own desires and ambitions cause us to overlook his influence?

At this most fundamental level, Matthew teaches us that Jesus' arrival in history to initiate the salvation of his people from their sins surely requires that we give ourselves to him. When we do so, his life becomes the pattern for our own lives. The mutual self-sacrificial giving of Della and Jim is indeed a profound example for our own lives, but it is most importantly derived from the implication of the sacrifice of the Incarnation. I am awestruck when I consider that God's giving in Jesus' incarnation and crucifixion is the foundation and example for my own giving. The apostle Paul strikes that note when he declares, "Husbands, love your wives, just as Christ loved the church and gave himself up for her" (Eph. 5:25).

Many marriages experience what I call the "tug-of-war" syndrome, where each partner tugs to have his or her needs met by their spouse. A state of equilibrium can be attained when each has tugged hard enough so that they are relatively satisfied. But if you have ever been in a tug-of-war at a picnic, you'll remember that the equilibrium is tenuous, because it is maintained only through the tension of an unending expenditure of energy. Many couples grow so tired of this kind of continual struggle in a relational tug-of-war that they give up.

However, instead of tugging, couples can be taught how to give. In premarital counseling I ask couples to perform an experiment. They must commit themselves for two months never to ask to have their own personal needs met but only to ask how each can meet the other's needs. What they will discover is that the equilibrium that they attain is not one of tension but of grace. They both give to the other without being asked, and their own needs are met by receiving, not demanding. The experiment ends up in most cases as the basis of a new kind of marital relationship, in which giving is the operating guideline, not taking.

The couples usually react incredulously when I first propose the experiment. One young woman said, quite honestly, "I'm so used to nagging him I'll never get him to help me with the wedding plans or take me out to dinner. He just doesn't think about my needs many times." But when they both began to understand that they were going to attempt to follow God's pattern of grace toward us, they were both amazed at their responses to each other. He developed a whole new set of daily priorities, where he consistently asked, "What does she need today that I can supply?" And in turn, she was free to make sure that he got what he felt he needed, like the regular Saturday afternoon to play basketball with his buddies. Remarkably, he often volunteered even to give that time up if he saw that she needed him! They both found their responsibility in giving what the other needed, not demanding what they themselves needed. Instead of tugging, they learned an entirely new pattern of giving. But that kind of graceful equilibrium is made possible only by a fundamental transformation in our lives when we experience God's giving, displayed so graphically in the little infant in Bethlehem.[40]

Such is the story that Matthew tells, quite in line with the verse that we know too well from the apostle John, who said, "For God so loved the world that he gave his one and only Son" (John 3:16).

40. I have developed this theme more fully in a popular article: Michael J. Wilkins, "Because God Is Generous," *Moody Magazine* (March–April 2001), 15–17.

# Matthew 2:13–23

WHEN THEY HAD gone, an angel of the Lord appeared to Joseph in a dream. "Get up," he said, "take the child and his mother and escape to Egypt. Stay there until I tell you, for Herod is going to search for the child to kill him."

¹⁴So he got up, took the child and his mother during the night and left for Egypt, ¹⁵where he stayed until the death of Herod. And so was fulfilled what the Lord had said through the prophet: "Out of Egypt I called my son."

¹⁶When Herod realized that he had been outwitted by the Magi, he was furious, and he gave orders to kill all the boys in Bethlehem and its vicinity who were two years old and under, in accordance with the time he had learned from the Magi. ¹⁷Then what was said through the prophet Jeremiah was fulfilled:

¹⁸"A voice is heard in Ramah,
        weeping and great mourning,
    Rachel weeping for her children
        and refusing to be comforted,
    because they are no more."

¹⁹After Herod died, an angel of the Lord appeared in a dream to Joseph in Egypt ²⁰and said, "Get up, take the child and his mother and go to the land of Israel, for those who were trying to take the child's life are dead."

²¹So he got up, took the child and his mother and went to the land of Israel. ²²But when he heard that Archelaus was reigning in Judea in place of his father Herod, he was afraid to go there. Having been warned in a dream, he withdrew to the district of Galilee, ²³and he went and lived in a town called Nazareth. So was fulfilled what was said through the prophets: "He will be called a Nazarene."

IN THE NARRATIVE in this chapter, Jesus' personal history repeats certain aspects of the national history of Israel, such as going to Egypt and coming back under divine protection (Hos. 11:1), the sorrowing of mothers over slaughtered infants in Bethlehem and the sorrowing over exiled children at the time of the Babylonian captivity (Jer. 31:15), and the hoped-for redemptive Branch (Isa. 11:1).

## The Family's Escape to Egypt (2:13–15)

ONCE THE MAGI escaped safely, the angel of the Lord again appears in a dream to warn Joseph about Herod's scheme to murder the child (cf. 2:16). This is his third dream (cf. 1:20; 2:12) and the second communication from the angel of the Lord to Joseph. Joseph again becomes the intermediary who provides for the safety and security of the child and mother. Although he is not the biological father, Joseph is a central figure in Matthew's narration (Luke focuses on Mary, the mother). Matthew may be continuing the legal aspect of Joseph's fatherhood from the genealogy, but he is also chronicling the leadership role that the father played in the typical Jewish family.

The angel makes explicit what has been implicit in the narrative to this point—Herod's paranoiac grasp of the throne drives him to attempt to kill the infant king of the Jews.[1] The angel instructs Joseph how he is to care for the child and mother, and Joseph is again immediately obedient, escaping to Egypt by night with the child and his mother.

The Egyptian border lay approximately eighty miles from Bethlehem. At the border began the most arduous journey, perhaps leading to the main Jewish community in Alexandria, Egypt, a city that lay on the Mediterranean Sea at the western edge of the Nile Delta. In this large metropolis lived about one million Jews. Almost anywhere in Egypt the family would have been immediately safe from Herod, since it was a Roman province outside of his jurisdiction. Joseph, Mary, and Jesus stayed there until after Herod's death (March/April 4 B.C.), when the angel tells them to return to Israel (2:20).

As in the narrative of the conception and birth of Jesus, Matthew points to the flight and later return from Egypt as a "fulfillment of Scripture." It is difficult to see how Hosea's reference back to the Exodus can imply for

---

1. In the expression "Herod is going to search for the child *to kill* him," Matthew uses the same word as in the passion narrative, where the chief priests and elders seek "to kill" Jesus (27:20; NIV: "to have Jesus executed"). This initial persecution of Jesus by Herod and the religious leadership parallels Jesus' last days in Jerusalem, where the political and religious leadership seek to eliminate Jesus' perceived threat to their power (cf. Hagner, *Matthew 1–13*, 35; Davies and Allison, *Matthew*, 1:260).

Matthew that Jesus' life fulfills what the prophet had said. This allows us to see that Matthew has a multifaceted perspective on the way that Jesus "fulfills" the Old Testament Scriptures. (1) In some cases, "fulfill" indicates the way in which the events of Jesus' earthly life and ministry bring to actualization predictive prophecy. Such fulfillment may be a specific prediction, as in 1:22–23 (the virgin birth), or it may be a collective predictive theme, as in 3:15, where Jesus' life ministry brings to actualization the collective Old Testament prophecy of salvation-historical righteousness.

(2) In other cases, "fulfill" can indicate the way in which Jesus brings to its intended full meaning the entire Old Testament Scripture, such as his dramatic declaration in the Sermon on the Mount, "Do not think that I have come to abolish the Law or the Prophets; I have not come to abolish them but to fulfill them" (see comments on 5:17–20).

(3) In still other cases, Matthew's use of "fulfill" can indicate the way in which Jesus' earthly life and ministry corresponded analogically or typologically (some say recapitulated or repeated) to certain aspects of the national history of Israel. This is apparently what Matthew has in view when he cites the prophet Hosea to say, "Out of Egypt I called my son" (2:15; see also 2:17–18).[2] In the context of his prophecy, Hosea recounts how God had faithfully brought Israel out of Egypt in the Exodus.[3] Matthew's point of comparison is the corporate solidarity between the nation Israel as God's son being rescued and delivered by God, and Jesus as the One who will be revealed to be God's "Son" par excellence.[4] Jesus Messiah is not only "son of David, son of Abraham" (1:1), but he is God's Son, which points ahead to the unique manner in which the voice from heaven will specify Jesus as the beloved Son (3:17; 17:5), and the way in which Jesus will address God as his Father (26:39–42).

Further, Old Testament authors consistently reminded the nation of Israel to look back to their redemption by God when he brought them out of Egypt.[5] The annual Passover was a reminder, as well as a promise, that God had provided a sacrificial lamb for his people Israel. As Matthew harks back

---

2. See Tracy L. Howard, "The Use of Hosea 11:1 in Matthew 2:15: An Alternative Solution," *BibSac* 143 (October–December 1986): 314–28, who describes Matthew's use of Hos. 11:1 as "analogical correspondence"; that is, Matthew saw an analogy between the events of the nation described in Hos. 11:1–2 and the events of Messiah in Matt. 2:13–15. Jesus is the One who *actualizes* and *completes* all that God intended for the nation (p. 322).

3. Matthew gives both the ultimate origin and agency of the prophecy expressed by *hypo* ("*by* the Lord") and the immediate agent of prophecy expressed by *dia* ("*through* the prophet"), as in 1:22.

4. Kaiser, *The Messiah in the Old Testament* (Grand Rapids: Zondervan, 1995), 35.

5. E.g., Ps. 78; 81; 105–6; Jer. 2:6; 7:22–25; Ezek. 20:1–20; Mic. 6:1–4.

to Hosea's recounting of God's faithfully bringing Israel out of Egypt under divine protection, he points out how Jesus' infancy corresponds analogically to Israel's history. The life of Jesus is the historical completion of the process of redemption. No threat from any public official can thwart the process. Jesus here recapitulates the promise to Israel that redemption is at hand. As Craig Blomberg emphasizes,

> Matthew sees striking parallels in the patterns of God's activities in history in ways he cannot attribute to coincidence. Just as God brought the nation of Israel out of Egypt to inaugurate his original covenant with them, so again God is bringing the Messiah, who fulfills the hopes of Israel, out of Egypt as he is about to inaugurate his new covenant.[6]

Matthew is not trying to emphasize that Jesus is a new Moses but that he actualizes the promise to the nation Israel of redemption that was initiated with the Exodus and Passover.

## The Massacre of Bethlehem's Boys (2:16–18)

MATTHEW RETURNS TO narrating the historical incidents surrounding the hideous murder of the infants at Bethlehem by Herod. When Herod realized that the Magi somehow had gotten wind of his true intentions and fled, he decided to take the situation into his own hands by putting to death any potential challenger to his throne. His earlier query of the Magi about the time of the appearing of the star gave him a fairly good estimate of the birth of the child (2:7). So he ordered all the boys in the Bethlehem vicinity who were born within the two-year time period to be killed. This would reckon to approximately ten to thirty boys of that age, given the size of the town.[7] Although this is not as large a number as is often graphically portrayed in reenactments in modern movies, it is still a heart-rending loss for the village.

No other historical records exist of this incident, which is not surprising, since Bethlehem was a somewhat small, rural town at this time. The number of infant boys massacred was a huge loss for Bethlehem, but it was not an incident to stand out significantly when seen in the light of other horrific events in Herod's infamous career.

---

6. Blomberg, *Matthew*, 67 ; see also Hagner, *Matthew 1–13*, 36; John H. Sailhamer, "Hosea 11:1 and Matthew 2:15," *WTJ* 63 (2001): 83–92.

7. Only 123 men had returned to Bethlehem from the Babylonian exile (Ezra 2:21), and it appears not to have grown beyond a small village of perhaps 1,000 people at the birth of Jesus.

Matthew speaks of Bethlehem's grief as a tragic reminder of the heartache experienced earlier in Israel's history, fulfilling what was said "through the prophet Jeremiah":[8]

> A voice is heard in Ramah,
>> weeping and great mourning,
> Rachel weeping for her children
>> and refusing to be comforted,
> because they are no more. (Matt. 2:18; cf. Jer. 31:15)

Centuries earlier, Nebuchadnezzar's army had gathered the captives from Judah in the town of Ramah before they were taken into exile to Babylon (Jer. 40:1−2). Jeremiah depicts Rachel, who is the personification of the mothers of Israel, mourning for her children as they are being carried away. She has no comfort as they are removed from the land, because they are "no more"—that is, no longer a nation and considered as dead. But even as Jeremiah pictures this dreadful mourning for exiled Israel, he offers from God a word of comfort: There is hope for their future because God will restore Rachel's children to their own land (31:16−17), and messianic joy will come in the future establishment of the new covenant with Israel (31:31−34).

Matthew's use of the Jeremiah narrative is similar to the way that he earlier cited the prophet Micah (cf. 2:15). This is not fulfillment in the sense of prediction-accomplishment (see comments on 1:23; 2:6, 13−15); rather, it is a case of analogical correspondence. As Herod attempts to eliminate the newborn king of the Jews, the events of Jesus' earthly life correspond analogically to an earlier attempt by a foreign power to wipe out God's chosen people. But the advent of Jesus' life also marks the arrival of the comfort promised to the Jews sent into exile.

In Bethlehem, once again the nation of Israel experiences suffering and anguish, but the earlier promise will now be actualized. Rachel had died and was buried in Zelzah near Ramah, while traveling to Bethlehem.[9] Matthew links the site of the deportation and the site of the massacre, where in both cases foreign forces attempt to wipe out God's plan of salvation through the

---

8. Since Matthew gives only the immediate agent of prophecy ("*through* the prophet") and not also the ultimate agency ("*by* the Lord"), as in 1:22 and 2:15, perhaps he is attempting to avoid any misunderstanding by his readers that God is responsible for this great evil; rather, the blame for the horrific deed is directly Herod's; see Michael Knowles, *Jeremiah in Matthew's Gospel: The Rejected-Prophet Motif in Matthean Redaction* (JSNTSup 68; Sheffield: Sheffield Academic Press, 1993), 15, 33−52.

9. Gen. 35:19; 48:7; cf. 1 Sam. 10:2. Later tradition confused these references to imply that Bethlehem was the site of Rachel's tomb; see Gordon J. Wenham, *Genesis 16−50*, 327.

chosen people of Israel and through the Messiah. But "God's power is greater than the power of sorrow-bringing forces,"[10] so with God's sovereign protection of the infant Messiah, he brings to completion the experience of the weeping at both the Exile and Bethlehem. The promised messianic deliverer has arrived to inaugurate the new covenant promised by Jeremiah (Jer. 31:31–35).[11]

## Herod's Death (2:19)

NOT LONG AFTER ordering the grisly murder of the infant boys at Bethlehem, Herod became deathly ill with a painful terminal disease (see Bridging Contexts section). He died at the age of sixty-nine at his palace in Jericho in March, 4 B.C.[12] He had commanded that many influential Jews should be executed when he died so that people would mourn at the time of his death instead of rejoicing, but the order was countermanded by his sister Salome.[13] An extensive burial procession of national dignitaries and military units marched with Herod's body on a golden bier studded with precious stones to where he was buried (near the Herodium).

After remaking his will at least seven times, Herod had finally settled on dividing the kingdom between three of his remaining sons, Archelaus, Herod Antipas, and Herod Philip.[14] Archelaus, a nineteen-year-old son by Malthace, succeeded to his throne over Judea, Samaria, and Idumea (cf. 2:22). He reigned from 4 B.C. to A.D. 6 and quickly displayed the same kind of cruelty that had marked his father's reign. He overreacted to an uprising in the temple at Passover after his father's death by sending in troops and cavalry, who killed about three thousand pilgrims.[15] Because of his cruelty, Augustus Caesar feared a revolution from the people, so he deposed Archelaus and banished him to Gaul in A.D. 6. The rule over Judea was thereafter passed to Roman rulers called prefects, one of whom was Pontius Pilate (A.D. 26–36; Luke 3:1; 23:1).

Herod Antipas, the seventeen-year-old younger brother of Archelaus by Malthace, became tetrarch of Galilee and Perea; he reigned from 4 B.C. to A.D. 39 (cf. Matt. 14:1–12; Luke 23:6–12). He is the most prominent of Herod's sons in the New Testament because he ruled the region of Jesus' primary

---

10. Bob Becking, "'A Voice Was Heard in Ramah.' Some Remarks on Structure and Meaning of Jeremiah 31,15–17," *BZ* 38 (1994): 242.

11. See ibid., 229–42; also see Willis, "Matthew's Birth Stories," 43–45.

12. For extensive discussion on the date of Herod's death, see Harold W. Hoehner, *Chronological Aspects of the Life of Christ* (Grand Rapids: Zondervan 1977), 11–27.

13. See Josephus, *Ant.* 17:174–79, 193.

14. See ibid., 17:188–89.

15. Ibid., 17:213–18; idem, *J.W.* 2.6.2 §§88–90.

ministry. His chief infamy comes from his execution of John the Baptist for criticizing his scandalous marriage to his half-brother's wife (see comments on Matt. 14:1–12) and from his interview of Jesus prior to his crucifixion (cf. Luke 23:6–12).

### The Family's Return to Nazareth (2:19–23)

WHEN HEROD THE GREAT dies, the angel appears once again to Joseph in a dream. This is the fourth of five dreams in the narrative of the first two chapters and the third of four interchanges between Joseph and an angel. The angel instructs Joseph to bring the child and mother back to Israel, because the threat from Herod is over. The plural "those who were trying to take the child's life are dead" is probably another reference to the culpability of the Jewish leadership in Jerusalem, whose power base would be threatened along with Herod's if a new king was to rule the Jews (cf. 2:3).[16]

The family probably stayed in Egypt no more than a year. When they discover that Herod's son Archelaus is ruling over the region of Judea in his father's place, Joseph is warned in another dream not to return to Bethlehem. Therefore, the family takes a detour to Nazareth in the region of Galilee, a region governed by Herod Antipas. In Nazareth the parents raise Jesus, away from the political machinations of Jerusalem.

Nazareth was located in the hills in lower Galilee at an elevation of 1,300 feet, midway between the Mediterranean Sea and the Sea of Galilee. It was not a strategic town politically, militarily, or religiously in Jesus' day. At this time, it probably had a small population of around five hundred people.[17] A ten-minute walk up to the ridge north of Nazareth provided villagers with a magnificent view of the trade routes a thousand feet below on the valley floor as well as of Herod Antipas's capital city, Sepphoris.

Being miraculously protected and guided, Jesus will grow up in Nazareth, and "he will be called a Nazarene." Several items invite our attention here. (1) The most straightforward observation is that Matthew identifies Jesus as the one who came from the town called Nazareth. People did not have last names in ancient times, so they were identified in other ways. Since "Jesus" was a fairly common name, one person named "Jesus" was set off from others with the same name by expressions such as "Jesus, the carpenter's son" or

---

16. Walker, *Jesus and the Holy City*, 33–34. Wallace (*Greek Grammar*, 403–5) and Turner (*Syntax*, 25–26; BDF, par. 141) resolve the difficulty grammatically by suggesting that this is an example of a "categorical plural," in which the plural is used to draw attention away from the particular actor (here, Herod) and onto the action (here, that the child's life is no longer in danger and therefore can return safely to Israel).

17. James F. Strange, "Nazareth (Place)," *ABD*, 4:1050–51.

"Jesus from Nazareth." The term "Nazarene" (*Nazoraios*) derives from "Nazareth" (*Nazaret*) to indicate a person from that town. Matthew uses these expressions "Jesus of Nazareth" and "Jesus the Nazarene" interchangeably to specify Jesus' hometown (see 21:11; 26:71).[18]

(2) Matthew's wordplay intends to suggest deeper significance, because by calling Jesus a Nazarene, it "fulfilled what was said through the prophets." Since we cannot find any direct Old Testament prophecy with this wording, Matthew intends the expression to be a form of indirect discourse. His reference here alludes to several Old Testament prophecies that relate to the wordplay conjured up by "Nazareth/Nazarene."

(a) One suggestion builds on the relationship between "Nazareth" and the Aramaic word for "vow" (*nezer*), suggesting that the founders of the village were members of a religious sect whose vows formed the focus of their practices, such as the Nazirite vows of ascetic separation found in Numbers 6:1–21: abstaining from strong drink, not cutting hair, and avoiding contact with the dead. This view suggests further that since the expression "Nazirite of God" was used interchangeably with "holy one of God" in the LXX (cf. Judg. 13:7; 16:17), "Nazarene" is linked with "Nazirite" (*nazir*) to indicate that Jesus was a Nazirite, a sort of second Samson (cf. Num. 6:1–21 with Judg. 13:5, 7; 16:17). In this case, Matthew may be emphasizing that Jesus took on certain vows as "the holy one of God" (cf. Mk 1:24). He was a man of purity and holiness.[19]

But the portrait of Jesus from the Gospels does not square with him as a Nazirite. Indeed, John the Baptist was more like this than Jesus. Jesus chided the people of Israel for rejecting John because he was an ascetic, and they rejected Jesus because he was "a glutton and a drunkard, a friend of tax collectors and 'sinners'" (11:16–19). Jesus would have violated the vow when he drank wine and when he touched the dead as he raised them (9:23–26).[20]

(b) A more likely suggestion is that Nazareth was originally settled by people from the line of David, who gave the settlement a consciously messianic name, connecting the establishment of the town with the hope of the coming *neser* ("Branch") of Isaiah 11:1:

A shoot will come up from the stump of Jesse;
from his roots a Branch [*neser*] will bear fruit.

---

18. See also Mark 1:24; 10:47; Luke 4:34; 18:37; John 18:5, 7; 19:19; Acts 2:22; 3:6; 4:10; 6:14; 22:8; 26:9). Jesus' followers were later identified as the "sect of the Nazarenes" (Acts 24:5) to specify them as followers of the Jesus who came from the town Nazareth. See H. H. Schaeder, "Ναζαρηνός, Ναζωραῖος," *TDNT*, 4:874–79.

19. See Brown, *Birth of the Messiah*, 210–13; Davies and Allison, *Matthew*, 1:276–77.

20. See Hagner, *Matthew 1–13*, 41.

---

The prophecy of Isaiah 11:1–5 was one of the most popular texts of Davidic messianism in early Judaism,[21] so it is not unlikely that a group returning from the Exile and establishing a new village would give their town a name that reflects that hope.[22] The believing remnant of Israel also are called "the branch" (*neṣer;* NIV "shoot") in Isaiah 60:21, demonstrating the solidarity of the remnant with the promised Branch of Isaiah 11:1. The theme of a messianic "branch" or "shoot" surfaces strikingly in other Old Testament contexts as well, using synonyms for *neṣer*, such as *ṣemaḥ* ("sprout, branch, horn"; e.g., Ps. 132:17; Isa. 4:2; 53:2; Jer. 23:5; 33:15; Ezek. 29:21; Zech. 3:8; 6:12), *ḥoṭer* ("shoot"; e.g., Isa. 11:1), and *yoneq* ("young plant") and *šoreš* ("root"; Isa. 53:2).

Although *neṣer* only occurs in Isaiah 11:1 and 60:21 in a messianic sense, the concept of the Branch became an important designation of the Messiah in the rabbinic literature[23] and targums, and it was also interpreted messianically by the Qumran community, where "Branch of David" became a favorite appellation for the expected Messiah.[24] This is important to note, because the term used to refer to the *neṣer* of Isaiah 11:1 in the Qumran literature is *ṣemaḥ*, demonstrating a direct equivalent usage of the terms. The expression is also used with reference to the messianic promise of 2 Samuel 7:12–14,[25] the promise of a permanent sovereign from the tribe of Judah in Genesis 49:10,[26] and other messianic contexts.[27]

---

21. Richard Bauckham, "The Messianic Interpretation of Isa. 10:34 in the Dead Sea Scrolls, 2 Baruch and the Preaching of John the Baptist," *DSD* 2 (1995): 202–16. Bauckham claims this is "the most popular" text (p. 202).

22. For a plausible reconstruction, see Adrian M. Leske, "Isaiah and Matthew: The Prophetic Influence in the First Gospel," in *Jesus and the Suffering Servant: Isaiah 53 and Christian Origins*, ed. W. H. Bellinger Jr. and W. R. Farmer (Harrisburg, Pa.: Trinity Press International, 1998), 162–63, and Rainer Riesner, "Archeology and Geography," *DJG*, 36.

23. Note, for example, the Eighteen Benedictions recited in the synagogue: "Cause the Branch of David thy servant speedily to sprout, and let his horn be exalted by thy salvation" (Ben. 15 [14]).

24. E.g., 4QWar Scroll[g] 5:3–4: "the Branch of David. Then [all forces of Belial] shall be judged," and "the prince of the congregation, the Bran[ch of David,] will put him to death." See also 4QIsaiah Pesher[a] 3:18 (4Q161 [4QpIsa[a]]): "The interpretation of the word concerns the shoot of David which will sprout in the final days."

25. "This refers to the 'branch of David', who will arise with the Interpreter of the law who will rise up in Zion in the last days" (4QFlorilegium [4Q174] 10–12).

26. 4QGenesis Pesher 5:1–5 (4Q252[4QpGen[a]]).

27. Allusions to a shoot or branch describing a messianic age are found in 1QH[a] 14:15; 15:19; 16:5–10 [= 1QH[a] 6:15; 7:19; 8:5–10] and 4QIsaiah Pesher[a] 3:15–26 (4Q161[4QpIsa[a]]. For overviews of messianism in the Qumran literature, see Marinus de Jonge, "Messiah," *ABD*, 4:777–88; Craig A. Evans, "Messianism," *DNTB*, 700–703; and Lawrence H. Schiffman, "Messianic Figures and Ideas in the Qumran Scrolls," *The Messiah:*

Together, these strands point to a significant, recognizable Old Testament theme of a messianic Branch of the line of David who would bring deliverance to Israel. The indirect discourse of Matthew's allusion to "the prophets" allows him to draw on both the Isaiah 11:1 *neṣer* prophecy as well as the substance of several Old Testament prophecies that relate to the wordplay conjured up by the "Branch" motif. The founders of Nazareth apparently were members of a movement who identified with this prophetic tradition. They were both waiting for the messianic "Branch" (Isa. 11:1) as well as living out the role of the faithful of Israel as the "branch of God's planting" (60:21). This messianic content should, in turn, be related to the announcement of Jesus' conception as the Immanuel of Isaiah 7:14.[28]

(c) Matthew also uses "Nazarene" as a slang or idiomatic expression for an individual from a remote, despised area. He draws a connection between the divinely arranged association of Jesus with Nazareth and various Old Testament prophets who foretold that the Messiah would be despised (see, e.g., Ps. 22:6–8, 13; 69:8, 20–21; Isa. 11:1; 49:7; Dan. 9:26). The theme culminates in Isaiah 53:2, especially in the contrast of the powerful Branch that is ignominious:

> He grew up before him like a tender shoot [*yoneq*],
>    and like a root [*šoreš*] out of dry ground.
> He had no beauty or majesty to attract us to him,
>    nothing in his appearance that we should desire him.

The relative ignominy of Nazareth, in comparison with Jerusalem or even Bethlehem, becomes the hometown of the Messiah.

The infancy narrative has led up to this theme. This Messiah did not come with fanfare or glory but was born in relative obscurity in Bethlehem. He and his family fled with powerless humility in the night to Egypt, and his arrival in history was surrounded with grief and sorrow when the Bethlehem infant boys were slaughtered. The child would not be raised even in Bethlehem with its Davidic overtones, but rather in the even more obscure town of Nazareth. Nathaniel displayed popular opinion when he asked, "Nazareth! Can anything good come from there?" (John 1:45–46). Matthew consistently returns to the theme of Jesus as an unpretentious figure (Matt. 8:20; 11:16–19; 15:7–8) and therefore is the One who fulfills the Old Testament

---

*Developments in Earliest Judaism and Christianity*, ed. James H. Charlesworth (Minneapolis: Fortress, 1992), 116–29. Qumran texts cited are from Florentino García Martínez, *The Dead Sea Scrolls Translated: The Qumran Texts in English*, 2d ed., trans. Wilfred G. E. Watson (Grand Rapids: Eerdmans, 1992).

28. See discussion in Brown, *Birth of the Messiah*, 211–13, 217–19; Hagner, *Matthew 1–13*, 41; Davies and Allison, *Matthew*, 1:277–79.

prophecies that the Messiah would be despised. The consistent reference to Jesus the Nazarene presumed some kind of negative overtone as an expression of sneering scorn. This scorn was also attached to Jesus' followers when they were ridiculed as "the sect of the Nazarenes" (Acts 24:5).

(3) Matthew's reflection on Jesus' early life thus intends for his readers to see a double meaning in the expression "Jesus the Nazarene." On the one hand, Jesus is the fulfillment of the hope for a messianic *neṣer*—the "Branch" out of the line of David. On the other hand, Jesus' association with lowly Nazareth gives notice that his coming is not in glory but in humble surroundings. As the Branch from the royal line, Jesus would be "hacked down to a stump and reared in surroundings guaranteed to win him scorn."[29] Used by his followers, the expression "Jesus the Nazarene" denoted faith in him as the messianic deliverer (Acts 2:22; 3:6; 10:38), but used by his enemies, it was a title of scorn to deny his messianic identity (Matt. 26:71; Mark 14:67).

Matthew says nothing about Jesus' early years in Nazareth. Recent archaeological discoveries can fill in some of the blanks about what life may have been like during those years. Education was valued highly in the people of Israel even among the poor, so most young children received the rudiments of schooling, including reading and writing. Jewish education was directed to learning the Old Testament Scriptures and perhaps learning local expressions of Judaism. Especially in the country, participation in the synagogue influenced the values, practices, and worldview of a young child.

Jesus' education would have also included learning the skills of his father— carpentry (see comments on 13:55) and other skills necessary to train a young boy for adult responsibilities, such as tending the family fields. Jesus may have had to take on adult responsibilities early, because it is likely that Joseph died sometime after the trip to Jerusalem when Jesus was twelve (Luke 2:41–51) and before the beginning of his public ministry when he was thirty (Luke 3:23).[30] The loss of a father was hard on a family, placing extra burden and expectations on the rest of the family (see comments on 12:46–50; 13:55–58).

Jesus grew up in a multicultural environment in which a number of languages were spoken by the common people. The Gospels all record Jesus' life and teachings in Greek (common language for trade and commerce of the Roman Empire), but the common language of the Jews in Galilee was Aramaic. A few of Jesus' statements in Aramaic have been brought over into the

---

29. Carson, "Matthew," 97.

30. Mary and Jesus' siblings are mentioned during his ministry (e.g., 12:46–50; 13:55–58; cf. Acts 1:14), but there is no mention of Joseph, suggesting that he is no longer alive. With Matthew's focus on Joseph's role throughout chs. 1–2, we would esp. expect to hear of him in Matthew's Gospel if he were still alive.

Gospels.[31] Devout Jews also knew at least some form of vernacular and literary Hebrew, as is evidenced by Jesus' reading the Hebrew Scriptures in the synagogue at Nazareth (Luke 4:16–20). The common people also knew some Latin, which was spoken especially by Roman military personnel. For example, the sign Pilate had nailed on Jesus' cross included a Latin title (John 19:20). Like other public people in the region of Galilee, Jesus was most likely multilingual.[32]

In sum, the picture of Jesus in Matthew 1–2 is an unfathomable equilibrium of human and divine elements. Jesus has a human lineage and a supernatural conception and birth. He is born into very human circumstances, but those circumstances are guided supernaturally. While Jesus' human development was similar to other young boys of his day, Matthew has already underscored the uniqueness of his divine nature as Immanuel, "God with us."[33] Yet none of the Gospel writers separates Jesus' human and divine natures. Both belong to the one man, Jesus of Nazareth, the Messiah, whose public ministry becomes the central focus in Matthew's ensuing chapters.

*Bridging Contexts*

MATTHEW'S PORTRAIT OF JESUS. Matthew introduced a theme in chapter 1 that becomes one of the leading characteristics of chapter 2, namely, the "fulfillment formula" (e.g., 2:14). As he records the historical details of the earthly life of Jesus, he looks beyond to the Old Testament Scriptures and declares to his readers that Jesus' life fulfills ancient prophetic pronouncements. This theme is a significant clue to understanding Matthew's purpose for writing his Gospel. He varies the theme from direct predictive prophecy to analogical (or typological) correspondence to demonstrate the way that Jesus fulfills Old Testament prophecies. Both ways give a more complete picture of Jesus as the anticipated Messiah of Israel.

(1) The first occurrence of the fulfillment formula points to Jesus' conception and birth, which fulfills the predictive prophecy that the messianic

---

31. E.g., *rhaka* ("fool"; Matt. 5:22), *Kephas* ("rock," John 1:42; cf. Matt. 16:18), *Talitha koum* ("little girl, get up!"; Mark 5:41), *Abba* ("father"; Mark 14:36), *Eloi, Eloi, lama sabachthani* ("My God, my God, why have you forsaken me?" Matt 27:46; cf. Mark 15:34).

32. For a good overview supporting Jesus' potential multilingual capacity, see Michael O. Wise, "Languages of Palestine," *DJG*, 434–44; F. F. Bruce, "Latin," *ABD*, 4:220–22; Stanley E. Porter, "Jesus and the Use of Greek in Galilee," in *Studying the Historical Jesus: Evaluations of the State of Current Research*, ed. Bruce Chilton and Craig A. Evans (NTTS 19; Leiden: Brill, 1994), 123–54.

33. Luke too accentuates this element by an event during Jesus' boyhood that displayed an early awareness of his unique relationship with God as "my Father" (Luke 2:39–50).

deliverer will be born of a virgin. The child will be known as Immanuel, which prepares Matthew's readers for the incarnational truth guaranteed in the birth of the child Jesus, that "God is with us" (1:22–23; cf. Isa. 7:14).

(2) Jesus' birth in Bethlehem of Judea fulfills the predictive prophecy of the coming Messiah who will be born in David's own ancient birthplace and who will rule and shepherd the people of Israel (2:6; cf. 2 Sam. 5:2; Mic. 5:2).

(3) Jesus fulfills analogically/typologically the correspondence between Israel as God's son being rescued and delivered from Egypt by God and Jesus as God's Son being protected from harm as he goes down and comes back from Egypt under divine protection (2:15; Hos. 11:1). The covenant with Israel that was initiated with the Passover and Exodus is now fulfilled in the arrival of Jesus to initiate the new covenant.

(4) Jesus' life events fulfill analogically/typologically the correspondence between Israel's mothers sorrowing over their exiled children at the time of the Babylonian captivity and Bethlehem's grieving mothers at the slaughter of the innocent boys. Herod's attempts to eliminate the newborn king of the Jews correspond analogically to an earlier attempt by a foreign power to wipe out God's chosen people, but Jesus' advent also marks the arrival of the comfort to Israel promised to the Jews who had been sent into exile in Babylon (2:17–18; Jer. 31:15).

(5) Finally, Jesus' hometown roots in Nazareth point toward his identity as the One who fulfills both the direct prophecy of the messianic Branch, a king from David's line who will judge with righteousness and strike the earth with the rod (2:23; cf. Isa. 11:1–5; also Jer. 23:5), and the direct prophecy of the despised, messianic suffering Servant (Matt. 2:23; cf. Isa. 52–53).

Matthew paints a bold picture of Jesus by drawing together strands of prophecy from the Old Testament that challenge sectarian expectations within Israel. Jesus is as much as any of them could have hoped for, but he is far more. He is the incarnate God who has come to be their King.

**History prophesied or prophesy historicized?** Some critics today charge Matthew with composing an account of Jesus' life that is a fanciful manipulation of facts to try and fit what the prophets have said. They claim that Matthew either fabricated details or else manipulated the facts of Jesus' life to try to make it appear that he fulfilled Old Testament prophecies about the coming of the Messiah. For example, some suggest that Matthew, writing to a Jewish audience, intentionally made up a life story about Jesus that fulfilled such prophecies as being born of a virgin in Bethlehem, or going to Egypt, or being raised in Nazareth.[34] What about this? Did Matthew write

---

34. E.g., John Dominic Crossan, *Jesus: A Revolutionary Biography* (San Francisco: HarperSanFrancisco, 1994), 15–21.

an accurate account of what happened in history that fulfilled ancient prophecies, or did Matthew create stories about Jesus to make it appear that he fulfilled those prophecies?

Our claim is the former: Matthew recorded accurately what happened in the historical life and ministry of Jesus, and those events were the miraculous fulfillment of ancient prophecies regarding the coming Messiah. Evangelical scholars have satisfactorily answered charges of critics along four basic lines.[35] (1) The creation of falsified historical accounts to substantiate a claim to prophetic fulfillment is not a staple of Jewish interpretive history. As a Jewish author, Matthew had no precedent for such a blatant disregard for Jewish interpretation of Old Testament prophecies. Moreover, he would have been subject to intense criticism from the Jewish interpretive community for falsifying predictive prophecy.

(2) The apostles, including Matthew, were so gripped by the reality of Jesus as the Messiah that they willingly suffered persecution at the hands of the Jews, and most of them later experienced martyrdom. They would not likely have been willing to suffer because of a lie about a person who really was not the Messiah.

(3) When the Gospels were written and circulated, there were still many people living who had see the events of Jesus' life. They would have confronted Matthew with his fabrication. But no such record of this kind of accusation against Matthew surfaces from any ancient record.

(4) The Jewish people themselves would have used any so-called fabrications as a way of discrediting the claims that Jesus was the Messiah. If Jesus had not been born in Bethlehem, or if his claim to being Messiah were not in line with Old Testament prophecies, Jews familiar with the details would have readily denied their reality. However, we don't hear of any such accusations, not even from the Talmud, which at points speaks derogatorily about Jesus and his followers but never accuses them of falsification of Jesus' life to fit messianic prophecies.

---

35. For a rebuttal of the scholarly charge that Matthew was a creative midrashic interpreter, see R. T. France, "Scripture, Tradition and History in the Infancy Narratives of Matthew," *Gospel Perspectives*, Volume II: *Studies of History and Tradition in the Four Gospels*, ed. R. T. France and David Wenham (Sheffield: JSOT Press, 1981), 239–66; Charles L. Quarles, "Midrash as Creative Historiography: Portrait of a Misnomer," *JETS* 39 (1996): 457–64; idem, "The *Protoevangelium of James* as an Alleged Parallel to Creative Historiography in the Synoptic Birth Narratives," *BBR* 8 (1998): 139–49; Craig Blomberg, *The Historical Reliability of the Gospels* (Downers Grove, Ill.: InterVarsity Press, 1987), 43–53. For an overview of Old Testament prophecies and their fulfillment in Jesus, see Kaiser, *The Messiah in the Old Testament*, 13–35, 231–35, passim. For a popular overview, see the interview with Louis S. Lapides, "The Fingerprint Evidence: Did Jesus—and Jesus Alone—Match the Identity of the Messiah?" in Lee Strobel, *The Case for Christ* (Grand Rapids: Zondervan, 1998), 171–87.

**The death of Herod the Great.** Matthew's manner of recording the death of Herod is another poignant clue to the way he has designed to record the life and ministry of Jesus Messiah. Whereas Josephus gives a rather graphic picture of Herod's death,[36] mainly to emphasize how God was inflicting punishment on Herod for his lawless deeds and impiety, Matthew merely states that Herod died, prompting the angel of the Lord to recall Joseph, Mary, and the infant Jesus from Egypt. His record of Herod's death, therefore, is another explanatory incident in the divine guidance of the infant Messiah's life.

Matthew may have had thoughts similar to those of Josephus about divine retribution on Herod because of the repugnancy of his murderous deeds, but he doesn't vent them. Instead, he concentrates exclusively on the events of the infant Jesus' life and how those events fulfilled Old Testament messianic prophecies. His passing reference to Herod's death serves only to mark the sovereign work of God in protecting the infant Jesus Messiah so that he can return to his homeland to be raised in preparation for his future work of proclaiming the gospel of the kingdom of God (cf. 4:23).

**Modern calendars and the date of Jesus' birth.** When Christians first learn that Jesus was most likely born anywhere from 6–4 B.C., they are confused. Doesn't the dating of Western calendars assume the birth of Jesus in A.D. 1? Could this mean that our New Testament records are in error? A little investigation helps us to see that the discrepancy does not arise from the biblical record but from the attempts in later centuries to establish a birth date for Jesus.

Modern calendars begin the present era, often called the "Christian era," with Jesus' birth. Dates after his birth are designated A.D. (Lat., *anno domini,* "in the year of our Lord") and dates before his birth are designated B.C. ("Before Christ").[37]

The first person to develop this system was the Christian monk Dionysius Exiguus in A.D. 525. Prior to him the Romans had developed the dating system used throughout the Western world, using the designation "AUC" (*ab urbe condita*—"from the foundation of the city [of Rome]"—or *anno urbis conditae*— "in the year of the foundation of the city"). Dionysius believed that it would be more reverent for calendrical dating to begin with Jesus' birth rather than the foundation of Rome. So with the historical records available to him, Dionysius reckoned the birth of Jesus to have occurred on December 25, 753 AUC (i.e., approximately 754 years after the founding of Rome). That placed

---

36. Josephus, *Ant.* 17:168–71 (cf. Nikos Kokkinos, "Herod's Horrid Death," *BAR* 28/2 [March–April 2002]: 28–35, 62).

37. Some, out of sensitivity to other religious traditions, are now using the designations C.E. ("Common Era") and B.C.E. ("Before Common Era").

the commencement of the Christian era at January 1, 754 AUC (allowing for lunar adjustment), or under the new reckoning, January 1, A.D. 1.

However, Dionysius did not have all of the historical data now available to scholars to make a more precise dating. We now know that King Herod died in March/April 750 AUC. Since Matthew states that Jesus was born while Herod was still alive, Jesus was actually born according to the Roman calendar between 748–750 AUC, four to six years earlier than Dionysius's calculations. Thus, a more accurate dating of the birth of Jesus places it in 4–6 B.C. This has nothing to do with the accuracy of the biblical records, only the historical accuracy of the well-intentioned but misguided Dionysius Exiguus.

JESUS MESSIAH CAME into the world to save it, but from the beginning he received threats. Yet in the middle of the threatening forces of the world, God's protective, guiding forces came to play in the life of the infant Jesus and family. Two points call for our attention here.

**He will be called a Nazarene.** The one named Jesus, who will save his people from their sins, Immanuel, "God with us," who is hailed as "king of the Jews," is also the one called a "Nazarene." Such is the way that Matthew concludes his astonishing narrative of Jesus' infancy. Matthew's identification of Jesus with this epithet is a double entendre that focuses on him as the fulfillment of the contrasting Branch and Servant prophecies. Jesus is both the powerful Branch of righteous redemption for Israel, but he is also the despised suffering Servant, who will take away our infirmities and will be pierced for our transgressions. The name "Nazarene" was for Jesus a title of honor as he became for Israel the long-awaited redemptive messianic Branch. But it also was a title of scorn as he became for Israel the despised suffering Servant.

**We are called "Christians."** The earliest Christians were called "the sect of the Nazarenes" by the Jews (Acts 24:5), bringing over the contempt with which they held Jesus' disciples. Soon, pagans began to call Jesus' disciples "Christians," which also had a double significance. The book of Acts indicates that in the large metropolis of Antioch, with its many competing cults and mystery religions, those who spoke so much about being disciples of the *Christos* were soon called *Christianoi*, "Christ's people." But wearing the name "Christian" was considered a badge of contempt (Acts 26:28).[38] Peter tries to shore up the resolve of the persecuted church by saying that when pagans regard them with hostility, the name "Christian" is a badge of honor (1 Peter

---

38. Agrippa spoke derisively to Paul when he said, "Do you think that in such a short time you can persuade me to be a Christian?"

4:16). Early in the second century, those accused of believing in Jesus Christ were asked by Roman officials whether or not they were "Christians." If they admitted to the name, they were killed (or, if Roman citizens, were sent to Rome for trial).[39] In the days of persecution of the early church, the use of the term was dangerous, because it clearly marked out to the Romans those who believed in a God who was not the emperor.[40]

As the name "Nazarene" was for Jesus, so the name "Christian" is a badge of honor, but it is also a badge of scorn and a designation for persecution. For many in the world today, wearing the name "Christian" is similar to what it was like for the early church. In places like Indonesia, buildings are burned just because they are known to be "Christian" houses of worship. In communist China, people are placed in jail simply because they possess and distribute "Christian" literature. And in the face of worldwide radical Islamic terrorism, persecution for being a Christian has come even closer to home.

When Mark and Lara, two of our former students, graduated from college, they married and joined an international mission organization. They trained for several years to become Bible translators and finally fulfilled their dreams by participating in translation work in a primarily Muslim country. My wife and I recently woke up on a Sunday morning to hear the television news that an international church in the city where they live had been terrorized by two men who walked in during the services and tossed several hand grenades at the parishioners. The news was sketchy at first, but it was known that five people had been killed, two of them Americans. At least forty others had been wounded, perhaps as many as ten of them Americans. Later we cringed as we heard Mark's name read over the news as having been wounded.

The country Mark and Lara live in is only about 2 percent Christian. They say that the people by and large are extremely kind and helpful to them. But there were these extremists who attacked the church only because it was a "Christian" house of worship.

The newspapers interviewed Mark a day or so after the incident. Lara and their two children were safe. When asked if they were going to leave, he said that they have contingency plans to leave if necessary, but they'd like to stay. In a gripping part of the interview, he acknowledged that he had been attacked *because he was a Christian*, but then he said that he would like to stay, *because he is a Christian*: "I'm a Christian. I believe my safety lies in God's hands, not in man's."[41]

---

39. See Pliny the Younger, *Letters* 10.96.

40. Michael J. Wilkins, "Christian," *ABD*, 1:925–26.

41. For Mark and Lara's safety, I have kept their identity, location, and newspaper interview anonymous.

---

That is the example of Jesus the Nazarene at work in his life. Today many of us wear the name "Christian" with relative ease. But in our own way, the name indicates for us both honor and scorn or suffering. Discipleship to Jesus will come to mean in Matthew's Gospel that we become like him (10:24–25). This is also the consistent theme of the other New Testament authors (e.g., 2 Cor. 3:18; 1 Peter 2:21). And if we become like him, we also will bear his name, with both positive and negative associations.

Torture and persecution for being a Christian seem far from a possibility in most of our everyday worlds. Yet persecution may become much more familiar to each of us than we expect. The increasing secularization of Western culture does not bode well for us. Christians are discouraged from denouncing practices condemned in Scripture, whether it is obscenity, pornography, or homosexuality. In the name of "freedom of religion" many of the normal practices of faith once enjoyed—such as public prayers or even displays of a manger scene at Christmas—have been stripped away. The agenda of much public policy seems more like freedom *from* religion.

It is not by accident that Jesus grew up in Nazareth and was identified with it. It was a town whose name was given in recognition of the hope of the coming messianic "Branch" in Isaiah 11:1. But his relationship to Nazareth means additionally that Jesus came to be identified not with the center of the religious and political establishment in Jerusalem. Jesus was not part of the political, religious, or militaristic establishment. Rather, he fulfilled the prophecy of a messianic figure who came from the common people, who was a man of sorrows, who was often despised, but who was ultimately the messianic Servant to justify the many and carry their iniquities (e.g., Isa. 52:13–53:12). Although his messianic sacrifice is unique, we are nonetheless provided in Jesus' incarnation an example of humility and servanthood that will challenge our own self-serving desires for comfort, fame, fortune, and glory.

Therefore, our walk with Jesus in this world will involve some kind of suffering for his name. Jesus suffered when doing the right and good thing. Persecution marked the fate of the church from its earliest days, yet it did not dim their passion for following Jesus, no matter what the cost. Paul tells young pastor Timothy, "all who desire to live godly in Christ Jesus will be persecuted" (2 Tim. 3:12).

**Joseph, the adoptive father.** A unique thrust of Matthew's Gospel is the way that Jesus' earthly father, Joseph, stands out significantly. In only his Gospel does Joseph have any prominence. So along with our Christological focus on the portrait of Jesus that emerges from the infancy narrative, we also rightly look to see in Joseph's role in the account the contemporary significance of the lessons that Matthew intended to pass on to his readers.

Having started out in Nazareth when the angel appeared to him with the announcement of the miraculous conception of the baby who would become king, Joseph appears for the last time in Matthew's Gospel as he leads the family back to Nazareth. The amazing events that transpired in less than three years must have made this young father's head spin. He was a silent but strong figure as he steadfastly guided and protected his little family. What tremendous love for his wife and son must have sustained him!

In chapter 1 we see his love for his wife displayed as he first desires to protect her from disgrace and then as he obeys the direction of the angel and takes his betrothed to be his own wife, in spite of the overwhelming *human* evidence of unfaithfulness. And in chapter 2 we see his love for his wife and son displayed as he goes against all the forces of the political and religious establishment to obey God and protect his family. As a father, I am humbled to the point of obedience to God myself as I see his example.

Yet, we must remember that this is not Joseph's biological son. We might comprehend more readily the sacrifice that Joseph made if this child were of his own blood, but it causes us to honor his obedience even more when we recognize that this is his adopted son. The bond between them did not derive from the deep emotional and spiritual tie of father and genetic son. It derived from the deep bond of obedience to the true Father of this Son.

In this way, Joseph continues to be a powerful example to all of us as parents, because our children also are truly not our own. They are a gift to us from God, their true Father. That, I believe, is one of the most powerful lessons to be learned from infant dedication services, or whatever your church tradition may call them. Young parents must start out their parental privilege by giving their own little baby back to the Father.

We learned that dramatically with our first child, Michelle. The pastor of the church we were attending while I was going through seminary stressed in the dedication service that we were not only dedicating our little baby girl to God, but we were dedicating ourselves to raise her for God, because she is his child on loan to us. Just a month later she developed a severe influenza that steadily weakened and dehydrated her. One rainy, dark evening her vomiting and diarrhea had become so severe that on doctor's orders, we rushed her to the hospital. The examining doctor said that if we had waited until the morning, she would have died of dehydration. So we left our little four-month-old baby girl—"Squeaky," the nurses nicknamed her because she hadn't the strength to give a real moan—in their care and drove home. Lynne and I cried on the way home through the wetness of that eerie night, recognizing how close we had come to losing her. But in our tears we reaffirmed to God that Michelle was his. We had given her back to him and had dedicated ourselves to raise her for him. So, in our tears we loosened our grip on Michelle and said that we would follow his will for her life, for he is her true Father.

This is what Joseph teaches us as an obedient father of an adoptive son. For all of us, whether biological or adoptive, parenting means to obey our child's true Father. Walter and Thanne Wangerin have raised children born to them as well as children adopted. They understand deeply the differences, especially the heart-wrenching that occurs when an adoptive child seeks to find her biological parents. But they learned deeply from Joseph the holy mystery of parenting another's child. And in that lesson, they also share with all parents the fact that loving our children aright means to raise them for their heavenly Father, in whose image they were created. Wangerin writes expressively:

> In all our children's faces is the image of their Creator. When any parents, by loving God, love their children right; and when, by following God, they lead their children out of the house, into adulthood and the purpose for which they were born, then in that fullness they, too, will find the face of God the Father, who had lent them the children in the first place.[42]

This was the lesson that he learned from Joseph, who had raised his adoptive Son for his heavenly Father—a fitting lesson for us all.

---

42. Walter Wangerin Jr., "A Stranger in Joseph's House," *Christianity Today* 39 (Dec. 11, 1995): 16–20 (quote on p. 20). Wangerin recounts in the article the heart-wrenching but heart-warming process of allowing their adoptive daughter to find her birth parents.

# Matthew 3:1–17

I
N THOSE DAYS John the Baptist came, preaching in the
Desert of Judea ²and saying, "Repent, for the kingdom of
heaven is near." ³This is he who was spoken of through the
prophet Isaiah:

> "A voice of one calling in the desert,
> 'Prepare the way for the Lord,
>     make straight paths for him.'"

⁴John's clothes were made of camel's hair, and he had a
leather belt around his waist. His food was locusts and wild
honey. ⁵People went out to him from Jerusalem and all Judea
and the whole region of the Jordan. ⁶Confessing their sins,
they were baptized by him in the Jordan River.

⁷But when he saw many of the Pharisees and Sadducees
coming to where he was baptizing, he said to them: "You
brood of vipers! Who warned you to flee from the coming
wrath? ⁸Produce fruit in keeping with repentance. ⁹And do
not think you can say to yourselves, 'We have Abraham as our
father.' I tell you that out of these stones God can raise up
children for Abraham. ¹⁰The ax is already at the root of the
trees, and every tree that does not produce good fruit will be
cut down and thrown into the fire.

¹¹"I baptize you with water for repentance. But after me
will come one who is more powerful than I, whose sandals I
am not fit to carry. He will baptize you with the Holy Spirit
and with fire. ¹²His winnowing fork is in his hand, and he will
clear his threshing floor, gathering his wheat into the barn and
burning up the chaff with unquenchable fire."

¹³Then Jesus came from Galilee to the Jordan to be baptized by John. ¹⁴But John tried to deter him, saying, "I need to
be baptized by you, and do you come to me?"

¹⁵Jesus replied, "Let it be so now; it is proper for us to do
this to fulfill all righteousness." Then John consented.

¹⁶As soon as Jesus was baptized, he went up out of the
water. At that moment heaven was opened, and he saw the
Spirit of God descending like a dove and lighting on him.
¹⁷And a voice from heaven said, "This is my Son, whom I love;
with him I am well pleased."

**Original Meaning**

WITH THE PHRASE "in those days John the Baptist came," Matthew jumps from Jesus' infancy to his adulthood. More than twenty-five years elapse from the time Joseph took his family to Nazareth to the time John the Baptist appears in the Judean desert.[1] The infancy narrative provided crucial background to clarify the identity of Jesus as the long-awaited Messiah of Israel. But now Matthew moves the calendar forward to focus the lens of his story on the public ministry of Jesus.

## John the Baptist Prepares the Way (3:1–6)

JOHN'S MESSAGE (3:1–3). John the Baptist appears prominently at the beginning of all four Gospels. In Matthew, he is the first person to appear when the public ministry of Jesus is recounted.[2] John is an immensely important historical figure, especially because he is the link between God's saving activity in the Old Testament and his saving activity in the ministry of Jesus. Jesus will say of him, "among those born of women there has not risen anyone greater than John the Baptist" (11:11).

Luke informs us of John's background (Luke 1:5–25, 39–80)—born to pious parents, both of the priestly line, who were well advanced in age. John's mother Elizabeth was a female relative[3] of Jesus' mother (1:36). Growing up in Judea, John probably had limited contact with Jesus, who grew up in Nazareth. The Fourth Gospel tells us that John "did not know him" (John 1:31, 33), indicating that it was not until the baptism that John knew definitely that Jesus was the Messiah.

Prior to embarking on his public ministry, John lived for some period of time in the desert (Luke 1:80). Sometime after A.D. 26 he made his public appearance to Israel, preaching in "the Desert of Judea" (Matt. 3:1). This was probably the barren desert area in the lower Jordan River valley and hills to the west of the Dead Sea. The desert was an important place in Israel's history. The law was given in the Desert of Sinai (Ex. 19), the prophets often went to the desert near Jordan to commune with God (e.g., 1 Kings 17:2–3; 19:3–18), the Maccabees carried out guerrilla warfare from the desert (e.g., 1 Macc. 5), and the desert had messianic overtones for diverse groups

---

1. Jesus was "about thirty years old when he began his ministry" (Luke 3:23).

2. For a discussion of the structure of Matthew's Gospel that stresses the appearance of John the Baptist, see Gerd Häfner, "'Jene Tage' (Mt 3,1) und der Umfang des matthäischen 'Prologs': Ein Beitrag zur Frage nach der Struktur des Mt-Ev," *BZ* 37 (1993): 43–59.

3. The Greek word for "relative" is *syngenis*, which could refer to an aunt or a cousin but is often rendered simply "kinswoman."

within Israel who associated it with God's forthcoming deliverance (e.g., Essenes of the Qumran community).[4]

While John's place of ministry at the Jordan River was close to the Qumran community's location and some scholars have wondered if John was a part of that community, we should note that John did not require those who adopted his message and baptism to withdraw from the rest of the nation and remain in the desert, as Qumran did. Moreover, John's message was more like that of the prophets of the Old Testament than of Qumran. The Qumran community was preparing itself for a final cosmic conflict in which they would join God's deliverer to do battle; John's message emphasized the coming end of the age with the judgment of God. Moreover, John's one-time baptism of repentance and the repeated ritual cleansings at Qumran are quite different. Thus, most scholars today conclude it is doubtful that John was ever associated with this community.[5]

John the Baptist has one central message, in which he urgently calls the people to "repent, for the kingdom of heaven is near" (3:2–3). This is the same message Jesus announces (4:17) and the Twelve preach on their missionary tour through Israel (10:5). John's call to repentance sounds similar to the prophets of the Old Testament, calling the people into a right relationship with God that must affect every aspect of their lives.[6] Indicating "to change one's mind," repentance in the Old Testament always called for a change in a person's attitude toward God, which would then impact one's actions and overall direction in life. External signs of repentance regularly included confession of sin, prayers of remorse, and abandonment of sin.

But as similar as John's message is to the Old Testament prophets, there is a distinctly new sound to it. He calls the people to repent because "the kingdom of heaven is near." The kingdom has come near in the soon-arriving Messiah (see comments on 4:17).[7] John is the one foretold by Isaiah who would

---

4. See Joseph Patrich, "Hideouts in the Judean Wilderness," *BAR* 15/5 (September–October 1989): 32–42. For an overview of these groups, see Richard A. Horsley and John S. Hanson, *Bandits, Prophets, and Messiahs: Popular Movements at the Time of Jesus* (Minneapolis: Winston, 1985).

5. See Ben Witherington Jr., "John the Baptist," *DJG*, 384; John P. Meier, *A Marginal Jew: Rethinking the Historical Jesus* (ABRL 2; New York: Doubleday, 1994), 49–52; Bock, *Luke 1:1–9:50*, 198; Rousseau and Arav, *Jesus and His World*, 80–82, 262; Todd S. Beall, *Josephus' Description of the Essenes Illustrated by the Dead Sea Scrolls* (SNTSMS 58; Cambridge: Cambridge Univ. Press, 1988); John C. Hutchison, "Was John the Baptist an Essene From Qumran?" *BibSac* 159 (April–June 2002): 187–200.

6. The present imperative "Repent!" gives a moral regulation; cf. Buist M. Fanning, *Verbal Aspect in New Testament Greek* (Oxford: Clarendon, 1990), 355–64.

7. The nuance of the Greek perfect in *engiken* is that the kingdom of heaven has come near to people in the soon-arriving person of the Messiah, and in his person it actually confronts them permanently (see comments on 4:17). The way in which the kingdom "is

be privileged to prepare the way for the Lord's arrival and his kingdom: "A voice of one calling in the desert, 'Prepare the way for the Lord, make straight paths for him'" (3:3; cf. Isa. 40:3).

John wasn't just another religious zealot drumming up support for a new following. As a road must be cleared of obstacles before an approaching king, John is calling for the people to clear the obstacles out of their lives that might hinder their reception of the Lord. He calls for the people to get themselves ready—to prepare their heart and life—for the arrival of the Coming One with the kingdom of heaven. In this sense, then, we can say that the kingdom of God has come near in the person of Jesus, but the full manifestation of that kingdom had not yet arrived.

The expression "the kingdom of heaven" is typical religious language of the Jewish people. Found only in Matthew's Gospel (thirty-three times), "kingdom of heaven"[8] is interchangeable with the expression "kingdom of God,"[9] which is found in the other Gospels (cf. 19:23–24; Mark 10:24–25; Luke 18:24–25). Matthew's "kingdom of heaven" reflects the Hebrew expression *malkut šamayim*, found abundantly in Jewish literature. A feeling of reverence and a desire not to blaspheme inadvertently the name of God (Ex. 20:7) led the Jews at an early date to avoid as far as possible all mention of the name of God. "Heaven" is one of the usual substitutions for the name of God (e.g., 1 Macc. 3:18–19; 4:10; 12:15; *m. ʾAbot* 1:3, 11).

By this time the people of Israel had had their fill of other kingdoms and rulers dominating them. They wanted a return to the glories of the ancient monarchy under David and Solomon and their descendants. They had a

---

near" is somewhat different for the message of Jesus (cf. 4:17) and for the Twelve (cf. 10:7). John is looking ahead to the arrival of the kingdom with the Coming One, while Jesus and the Twelve announce entrance to the kingdom because of its presence in the ministry of Jesus Messiah (cf. also 12:28).

8. The term "heaven" in the expression "kingdom of heaven" is actually plural, a typical Jewish conception of the world above that includes the air one breathes, the starry world, and the realm of spirits, but also the throne of God. The plural occurs esp. in Matthew; cf. Helmut Traub, Gerhard von Rad, "οὐρανός, κ.τ.λ.," *TDNT*, 5:497–53; Hans Bietenhard, "Heaven, Ascend, Above," *NIDNTT*, 2:184–96.

9. Most commentators concur that the expressions are interchangeable, although some have suggested that Matthew intends two different aspects of the kingdom in the use of the two phrases; e.g., the kingdom of God is a present reality that prepares individuals for the eschatological kingdom of heaven, a wholly future phenomenon in Matthew: Willoughby C. Allen, *A Critical and Exegetical Commentary on the Gospel According to S. Matthew*, 3d ed. (ICC; Edinburgh: T. & T. Clark, 1912), lxvii–lxviii, 232; Margaret Pamment, "The Kingdom of Heaven According to the First Gospel," *NTS* 27 (1981): 211–32. A distinction was also drawn between the two expressions by earlier dispensational writers, but this has been largely abandoned; see Robert L. Saucy, *The Case for Progressive Dispensationalism: The Interface Between Dispensational and Non-Dispensational Theology* (Grand Rapids: Zondervan, 1993), 19.

brief tantalizing experience of semi-independence during the Maccabean revolt and the rule of the Hasmoneans, but that had long ended. Once again another power, Rome, ruled over them. The thirst for independence was strong in Israel. The prophecies of David's house and kingdom enduring forever (2 Sam. 7:11–16; 1 Chron. 17:23–27) seemed as if they would never be actualized.

John the Baptist ignites those hopes anew by preaching that "the kingdom of heaven is near." John's mission is like that of a courier who preceded the king to proclaim his coming and the need for the citizens to ready themselves for that arrival. Their readiness was indicated by their repentance from sin and sinful ways to await the kingdom. But what kind of kingdom did they expect? What did John expect would occur now that the kingdom of God was near? As the story unfolds we will look closely to separate the various expectations from what God actually intended to accomplish.

**John's appearance (3:4).** Like his message, John's appearance—especially his clothing and food—stirred up recollections of the prophecies of Elijah's return to prepare the way for God's vengeful appearance (cf. Mal. 3:1; 4:5–6). John appears in the desert wearing garments made of camel's hair, with a leather belt around his waist (cf. 2 Kings 1:8). Goat's hair or camel's hair was often woven into a thick, rough, dark cloth, which was used as an outer garment or cloak, particularly by nomadic desert dwellers. The garment was so dense that it was virtually waterproof and could protect from most weather elements. It was proverbially the garb of poorer people, in distinction from the finery worn by those in the royal court (11:8). Moreover, garments of woven hair were sometimes worn as a protest against luxury and as a symbol of distress or self-affliction,[10] so John the Baptist's garment of camel's hair probably visualized the repentance to which he called the people (cf. Neh. 9:1; Jer. 6:26).

John's food was locusts and wild honey, not an unusual diet for people living in the desert.[11] The locust is a migratory grasshopper and was permissible food for the people of Israel to eat (Lev. 11:20–23). They are an important food source in many areas of the world, especially because they are a ready source of protein and are abundant even in the most desolate areas. They are often collected and then dried or ground into flour. John's diet of locusts and honey from wild bees supplied him with a crude but fairly balanced diet.[12]

---

10. Heb. 11:37; cf. Gen. 37:34; 2 Sam. 3:31; 2 Kings 6:30.

11. As evident in the *Damascus Document* of Qumran (CD-A 12:13–15).

12. See the interesting presentations by G. S. Cansdale, "Locust," *ZPEB*, 3:948–50, and Edwin Firmage, "Zoology (Animal Profiles): Locusts; Bees," *ABD*, 6:1150.

But more important, John's diet causes him to stand out as one who has rejected the luxuries of life. His diet and clothing combine with his message to cast a powerful demand for repentance in the light of the nearness of the kingdom. He embodies in his lifestyle the message of repentance he preaches.[13] The last Old Testament prophet, Malachi, brought his thundering message to a climax with a prophecy of the Lord sending Elijah the prophet before the great and dreadful day of the Lord, who would "turn the hearts of the fathers to their children, and the hearts of the children to their fathers" (Mal. 4:6). Many Jews were awaiting God's intervention.

No wonder, then, the remarkable response of the people to John. Although Matthew does not mention the connection yet (cf. 11:2–19; 17:9–13), here is another like Elijah. God is again speaking to his people through a prophet!

**John's baptism (3:5–6).** The response to John's call to repentance is extraordinary, as throngs of people go out to him from the city of Jerusalem, from all over Judea, and from the region of the Jordan River valley. John's message seems to have taken hold of every stratum of Israel. But they do not go out just to watch a show. It was no easy matter to go into the desert, especially for city dwellers. But, gripped by his startling declaration of the nearness of God's kingdom, they demonstrate their repentance by "confessing their sins." The ordinary people of Israel indicate by their radical repentance that they have heard in John's message a warning from a prophet of God. In the light of the imminent judgment, they must be forthright with God. The nearness of God's kingdom leaves no room for doubt. They must get everything out in the open. They must show God by their actions and by words that they are indeed putting their old ways behind and are ready for the arrival of his kingdom.

Thus, they are baptized by John in the Jordan River. Of all John's activities and characteristics, his baptism was the most strikingly unique and reminiscent of his ministry. This one-time baptism as preparation for the arrival of the coming kingdom was so distinctive that it gave him the byname "the Baptist" (see 3:1; Josephus, *Ant.* 18:116).

John's baptism was both similar to, yet distinct from, other forms of baptism in Israel at the time.[14] Accompanying as it did repentance and confession of sin, it was symbolic of purification. But in contrast to forms of baptism such as those at Qumran and by the Pharisees—both of which were highly structured and had regular, repeated washings—John's was a one-time baptism. It did have some similarity to proselyte one-time baptism,[15] but it was

---

13. See Meier, *A Marginal Jew*, 2:49.

14. For further background, see Wilkins, "Matthew," 24.

15. The dating of "proselyte" baptism is debated, some suggesting that it did not occur until around the Christian era, when Judaism admitted Gentile proselytes with baptism,

far different since it was Jews, not Gentiles, who were being baptized by John. Those responding heeded the call to the presence of the kingdom and the Coming One announced by John. His baptism called for a personal commitment to God's new activity within Israel. It became the backdrop of Jesus' and his disciples' practice (John 3:22–24; 4:1–3) and of the early church's baptism.

## The Impact of the Kingdom of Heaven (3:7–12)

AMONG THE CROWDS who went out to hear John were some of the religious leadership, including Pharisees and Sadducees. They appear here by name for the first time in Matthew's narrative,[16] although their presence is implied in the reference to the Jerusalem leadership in the infancy narrative (e.g., 2:3–4).

**Warning to the religious leaders of Israel (3:7–10).** "The Pharisees" probably derived their name from the Hebrew/Aramaic *perušim* ("the separated ones"), alluding to both their origin and their characteristic practices. They held a minority membership on the Sanhedrin, the ruling religious body in Jerusalem. The Pharisees were a lay fellowship or brotherhood connected with local synagogues and thus were popular with the common people. Their most-pronounced characteristic was their adherence to oral tradition, which they obeyed rigorously in order to make the written law relevant to daily life. "The Sadducees," by contrast, were a small group with aristocratic and priestly influence who derived their authority from the activities of the temple. They held the majority membership on the Sanhedrin but were removed from the common people by economic and political status and their support of Rome's rule over them.

Despite the fact that the Pharisees and Sadducees normally opposed one another (cf. Acts 23:7–8), they are united in coming to where John is baptizing.[17] They appear to join the crowds responding to John's call to repent. Perhaps they are coming to John as the official leadership of Israel to validate (or perhaps investigate) his ministry. John sees through their hypocrisy and has harsh words for them, calling them a "brood of vipers" (cf. 12:34; 23:33)—a clear reference to the dozen or more small, dangerous snakes that can emerge from a mother snake. Vipers are proverbial for their subtle

---

circumcision, and sacrifice; e.g., Meier, *A Marginal Jew*, 2:52; Scot McKnight, *A Light Among the Gentiles* (Minneapolis: Fortress, 1991). Others contend, however, that proselyte baptism for ritually impure Gentiles seems likely at the time of John; e.g., Craig S. Keener, *The Spirit in the Gospels and Acts* (Peabody, Mass.: Hendrickson, 1997), 63–64, 146–49.

16. For further background, see Wilkins, "Matthew," 25.

17. Matthew will note two other occasions when the Pharisees and Sadducees are listed together—in their opposition to Jesus (16:1–4, 5–12).

approach and attack, as was the original serpent (Gen. 3). These religious leaders have ulterior motives, either attempting to ingratiate themselves with the crowds who are drawn by John or coming to see if they can find fault in this prophetic figure who is outside their circles and is attracting such a following.[18]

John clarifies what will occur with the coming of the kingdom: (1) It will bring wrath on those who do not repent (3:8–10), and (2) it will be inaugurated with the arrival of the Coming One, with his baptism of the Holy Spirit and fire (3:11–12). The coming of the kingdom of heaven will be accompanied by the wrath of God and the fire of eternal punishment (3:8, 10). Those who respond to John's message and repent will escape God's wrath. But it must be an individual's personal response to God; one's religious or ethnic heritage will not help. People must come to God as repentant individuals without prior religious claims to advantage with God. This is, therefore, not a call solely for those living in blatant sin, as if repentance is only for "backsliders" or the "marginal." It is a call of repentance for all in Israel, including the religious leaders. Unfortunately, religious activity and pedigree can often blind a person to the deficiency of his or her own life before God.

John is not attempting to subvert the Pharisees and Sadducees, the official leadership of Judaism, by publicly ridiculing them. Rather, he is calling them to their proper responsibility as examples for the nation. Of all people, they should be the ones who honestly and openly prepare their hearts for the coming of the Messiah. They have had the privilege of studying Scripture more carefully. They should have been the first to prepare themselves to receive kingdom life. Instead, they will receive judgment.

Furthermore, repentance must be validated as being real through fruit in one's life. Talk is cheap. Hypocrisy is real. John will not tolerate any religious game-playing simply to gain a following. He articulates a theme that will characterize Jesus' ministry as well. The evidence of real inner spiritual life is always the fruit of a changed external life. The arrival of the kingdom will bring with it real spiritual life that produces change from the inside out. Jesus says later that false disciples are those who do not have the life of the true vine. They are dead branches, good only to be thrown into the fire (John 15:6). The decisive identifying mark of a living tree is the fruit that it bears.

---

18. This interpretation makes the best sense of the preposition *epi* in the clause *erchomenous epi to baptisma autou* (NIV "coming to where he was baptizing," instead of implying that they were "coming for baptism," NASB); cf. Gary Yamasaki, *John the Baptist in Life and Death: Audience-Oriented Criticism of Matthew's Narrative* (JSNTSup 167; Sheffield: Sheffield Academic Press, 1998), 86.

The decisive identifying mark of the kingdom of God is a life that has repented from sin and bears the fruit of repentance (cf. Paul's message in Acts 26:20).

Those who do not receive spiritual life will receive God's wrath. They have rejected his call to repentance, they have not received the life of the kingdom of heaven, and they therefore will receive the full penalty of God's judgment on their sin. John fully expects that the axe of God's judgment is quickly to be laid at the deadwood that does not bear the life and the fruit of the kingdom of heaven. And the expected messianic deliverer,[19] to whom John now gives public testimony, will wield that axe.

**The coming of Messiah (3:11–12).** Here we get to the core of John's ministry. He points ahead and beyond himself to another person. John has a powerful place in God's history of salvation, but he knows it is only preparatory to the main event. Calling the nation to repentance is not the main issue. The main event is the appearance of the One who will actually inaugurate God's kingdom on earth. Although there is continuity between their messages and ministry, John especially emphasizes the contrast between himself and the Coming One. That contrast is seen in the Coming One's identity and baptism.

(1) John points to "the one who is coming after me," an expression with strong messianic expectation.[20] John is rugged, marked by the rigors of the desert and the harshness and loneliness of his calling as a prophet. It takes personal strength of body and soul to endure such hardships. But John looks to One who is "more powerful," who will arrive with the power of God to inaugurate messianic rule. As a servant to a king, John realizes that he is not worthy even to carry the sandals of this messianic deliverer. His language is not self-degrecating. He is not lacking an adequate self-image. He knows himself and knows clearly the identity of the One to come. John is the herald; the Coming One is the messianic deliverer.

(2) John accentuates further the contrast between himself and the Coming One by differentiating their baptisms: John baptized "with" (or "in"; cf. NIV text note) water for repentance, but the Coming One will baptize "with" (or "in") the Holy Spirit and fire. Once again, John displays a straightforward understanding of his own role and place in God's plan of redemption. John's baptism will be superceded by the coming baptism.

John's baptism was uniquely associated with repentance (see comments above; see also Mark 1:4; Luke 3:3; Acts 13:24; 19:4). But as unique as it

---

19. For a thorough analysis of the messianic implications, see Bauckham, "The Messianic Interpretation of Isa. 10:34 in the Dead Sea Scrolls," 202–16.

20. Cf. Ps. 118:26 with Matt. 11:3; 21:9; 23:39; Heb. 10:37.

was, it was only preparatory to the baptism associated with the Coming One. He will inaugurate a baptism that brings both eschatological blessing and judgment (both "wheat" and "chaff"; cf. also Joel 2:28–29).[21] The Coming One will baptize the repentant—those who are prepared to receive him—with the blessing of the Holy Spirit. But the unrepentant—those who are not receptive to the Coming One—he will baptize with the judgment of eternal fire. Jesus regularly links his messianic ministry to John's by use of this dual theme: He has come to bring healing and good news to the poor and oppressed (Matt. 11:4–5) and rest for the weary (11:25–30), yet those who reject his ministry and message face certain judgment (11:20–24; cf. John 3:31–36; 5:25–35).

By the use of a second metaphor, John declares that the time of this baptism is near. Drawing on a scene common to the experience of his listeners, he declares that the coming Messiah already has the winnowing fork in his hand. The harvest is ready to begin. At the end of a harvest season, the farmer brought the harvested wheat into the threshing floor, a stone or hard-packed dirt surface, often with a short wall around the perimeter. He then took a large pitchfork and tossed the wheat into the air, where the wind blew the lighter chaff away, leaving only the good wheat heads in the threshing floor. The wheat was then stored in the granary for later grinding into flour to make bread, but the chaff was raked into piles and burned.

The impact of this message on his audience must have been profound, because they are gathered with mixed motives. John is drawing a line in Israel that is intended to test the hearts of all who hear. Those who have come out to hear him with impure motives are even now being warned that the Messiah will bring judgment on them, a judgment that ultimately will be eternal. But those who have come out to hear him with sincere motives of repentance and confession of sin will be prepared for the coming of the Messiah and the outpouring of the Spirit. The repentant will form the nucleus of those who receive the Expected One's gracious ministry.[22]

This message turns upside down the religious and social norms in Israel. The ones often considered most worthy because of their training, commitment, and dedication, such as the Pharisees and Sadducees, are the ones singled out for the most stinging criticism. But turning upside-down the norms

---

21. For further discussion, see J. D. G. Dunn, *Baptism in the Holy Spirit* (Philadelphia: Westminster, 1970), 10–11, 13–14; R. Alastair Campbell, "Jesus and His Baptism," *TynBul* 47 (1996): 191–214; Hagner, *Matthew 1–13*, 51–52; Robert A. Guelich, *Mark 1–8:26* (WBC 34A; Dallas: Word, 1989), 27–28.

22. For a discussion of the religious and social dynamic addressed to the general audience, see Robert L. Webb, *John the Baptizer and Prophet: A Socio-Historical Study* (JSNTSup 62; Sheffield: JSOT Press, 1991), 289–300.

in Israel is not new. The prophets were well known for criticizing the religious and political establishment. John's message simply harks back to the standards of judgment and blessing that God had already established as the messianic ideal (see, e.g., Jer. 23). And that day of messianic revelation is at hand.

## John Baptizes Jesus Messiah (3:13–17)

FOLLOWING THE THUNDERING, prophetic message of judgment that John the Baptist has given, anticipation is high for the arrival of the messianic deliverer. Up to this point the "Coming One" has not been identified. Now Jesus appears on the scene to lay claim to that identification.

What an unlikely figure! John has prepared us for a powerful figure coming with the might of the Holy Spirit and the judgment of fire. We might have expected the Coming One to arrive in Jerusalem, reclaiming the throne of David and the temple of Solomon. Or perhaps he would come out of the desert as a military conqueror, like the ancient warrior David, or a prophetic clarion, like John himself. Instead, Matthew says simply, "Then Jesus arrived from Galilee." He comes as a solitary figure from the insignificant agricultural region of Galilee.

Perhaps the most unlikely feature is that Jesus asks to be baptized by John, like any of the rest of the crowd. Even John seems surprised, as he tries to stop Jesus from being baptized. John's baptism is only with water and is preparatory to the greater baptism of the Holy Spirit and fire that the Messiah will inaugurate. Why does the expected Messiah want to be baptized by his forerunner?

Without a careful reading of the text, one might conclude that Jesus thought that he also needed conversion and purification, as did the crowd (3:2, 6).[23] But John quickly dispels that possibility, because he knows Jesus' identity as the One bringing the messianic baptism: "I need to be baptized by you, and do you come to me?" This is the more powerful One who inaugurates the kingdom that John has been proclaiming. Only at Jesus' insistence ("Let it be so now") does John consent to baptize Jesus, because "it is proper for us to do this to fulfill all righteousness" (3:15). Jesus' baptism has far more significance than we might think. No wonder all four Gospels narrate this incident in one form or another (cf. Mark 1:9–11; Luke 3:21–22; John 1:29–34). This is the beginning of the ministry that will forever forge the direction of God's relationship with his people.

What does Jesus mean that in his baptism he and John will "fulfill all righteousness"? The word "fulfill" (*pleroo*) continues the theme of "fulfillment"

---

23. Such is the speculative conclusion of the skeptical account of Jesus' life by Donald Spoto, *The Hidden Jesus: A New Life* (New York: St. Martin's, 1998), 45–46.

that has been so prominent in the beginning narrative of Matthew's Gospel. Jesus' conception, birth, and infancy fulfilled both specific and general prophecies (chs. 1–2), the appearance of John fulfills Old Testament expectations of the forerunner (3:3), and now Jesus' baptism will "fulfill all righteousness." Righteousness (*dikaiosyne*) is another important concept in Matthew's Gospel (cf. 5:6, 10, 20; 6:1, 33; 21:32). Some suggest that Jesus means this in an ethical sense, that the baptism will fulfill all of the righteous expectations of the law, similar to what Jesus will declare in the Sermon on the Mount (cf. 5:17).[24] However, the present context does not imply an ethical submission to God's commands. Nowhere in the Old Testament is there a divine command to submit to John's baptism. Therefore, submission to his baptism can hardly be thought of as an act of righteousness, and certainly no thought of fulfilling *all* righteousness.

Most likely Jesus means this in a salvation-historical sense. God's saving activity prophesied throughout the Old Testament is now being fulfilled with the inauguration of Jesus' ministry, culminating in his death on the cross. Perhaps Jesus has in mind the righteousness of Isaiah 53:11: "After the suffering of his soul, he will see the light of life and be satisfied; by his knowledge my righteous servant will justify many, and he will bear their iniquities." Jesus will accomplish God's will in the sense of God's saving activity. This is supported by the similar salvation-historical reference to John the Baptist in 21:31–32.[25] Jesus is expressing his obedience to God's plan of salvation that has been revealed in the Scriptures.[26]

The public baptism, therefore, provides concrete salvation-historical continuity between John's and Jesus' ministries. As Jesus identifies himself with John in the baptism, this represents an endorsement of John's ministry and message and links Jesus' cause to John's. Moreover, as Jesus goes into the waters of baptism, he identifies with his people in their need; that is, he identifies with the sinful humanity he has come to save, and especially at this point in time, with the believing remnant of Israel who come to be baptized.[27] Leon Morris paints a graphic picture:

> Jesus might well have been up there in front standing with John and calling on sinners to repent. Instead he was down there with the

---

24. Especially see Benno Przybylski, *Righteousness in Matthew and His World of Thought* (SNTSMS 41; Cambridge: Cambridge Univ. Press, 1980).

25. Donald A. Hagner, "Righteousness in Matthew's Theology," in *Worship, Theology and Ministry in the Early Church: Essays in Honor of Ralph P. Martin*, ed. Michael J. Wilkins and Terence Paige (JSNTSup 87; Sheffield: JSOT Press, 1992), 116–17.

26. Keener, *Matthew* (1999), 132.

27. George R. Beasley-Murray, *Baptism in the New Testament* (Grand Rapids: Eerdmans, 1962), 45–67.

sinners, affirming his solidarity with them, making himself one with them in the process of the salvation that he would in due course accomplish.[28]

Jesus now will bring to fulfillment the ministry John began. He is the "more powerful" One to whom John pointed, who fulfills the hope of righteousness as the Davidic King and righteous Servant. But more important, he is also Immanuel, "God with us," and Jesus, the one who will "save his people from their sins" (1:21–23). He identifies with John's salvation-historical ministry, but he does so from the water, identifying with the very people he has come to save. Hence, Jesus will now receive the anointing of the Spirit and the confirmation of the Father to accomplish his mission, further indications of the reason for his baptism.

Imagine the scene. John has declared openly and firmly his expectations about the judgment to accompany the powerful Coming One. The people have banked their future on the hope of the coming of the kingdom of God. And now the One recognized by John to embody those dreams simply goes into the waters of the Jordan River to be baptized like any of the people. It seems so anticlimactic, and even paradoxical. But out of that unassuming scene comes a dramatic enactment of God to present Jesus for his messianic mission, as he experiences a threefold revelation: He sees the heavens open; he sees the Spirit of God descend as a dove on him; and he hears God's voice acknowledge him as his beloved Son.

(1) As Jesus comes up from the water,[29] "heaven was opened." This "divine passive"[30] hints that God himself is opening the communication gates of heaven to reveal something momentous. This is a common expression in Scripture to refer to significant times of God revealing something important to his people (cf. Isa. 64:1; Ezek. 1:1; John 1:51; Acts 7:56; 10:11).

(2) Jesus then "saw the Spirit of God descending like a dove and lighting on him." The Spirit does not take the form of a dove but rather some visible manifestation, indicating the real descent of the Spirit on Jesus. The dove symbol expresses characteristics often associated with a dove, such as gentleness

---

28. Morris, *Matthew*, 65.

29. Meier concludes that the form of the baptism is most likely immersion, implied by the statement that after Jesus' baptism he "came up out of the water" (3:16; Mark 1:10). He supports this conclusion by two factors outside of Matthew: (1) John baptized at the Jordan River and at Aenon near Salim, "because there was plenty of water" (John 3:23); (2) Josephus states that John baptized not to cleanse souls but to purify bodies (*Ant.* 118; see Meier, *Marginal Jew*, 2:93 n. 152).

30. That "heaven was opened" is an example of the fairly common passive voice used without the agent expressed, but the context is clear that God is the obvious agent of the action; see Wallace, *Greek Grammar*, 435–38.

and peace in contrast to judgment (recall the dove sent out by Noah to determine whether God's time of judgment had ended, Gen. 8:10), or the superintending and creative action of the Spirit hovering over the waters of the new creation (Gen. 1:2).

The descent of the Spirit alludes to the anointing of the Servant of the Lord by the Spirit in Isaiah 42:1—which will be the words quoted by the heavenly voice in Matthew 3:17 (cf. 12:18)—and the anointing of the Davidic Branch by the Spirit in Isaiah 11:2. Jesus' anointing by the Spirit is both the coronation of Israel's Messiah and the commissioning of God's righteous Servant for the work he will now carry out in the power and presence of the Spirit.[31] The One who is to baptize with the Spirit (Matt. 3:11), who will be guided and empowered by the Spirit (4:1), who will inaugurate the messianic age of salvation through the Spirit (12:18–21; cf. Isa. 42:1–4; 61:1), is now anointed by the Spirit for his public messianic ministry.

This is not to suggest that in his baptism Jesus receives the Spirit for the first time. His conception itself was "through the Holy Spirit" (1:20), which indicates that even as John the Baptist was filled with the Spirit from the womb, so was Jesus. Rather, the descent of the Spirit in the baptism is a formal anointing that inaugurates Jesus' public ministry. John the Baptist declares elsewhere that the Spirit's descent on Jesus is what confirmed for him that Jesus was indeed the Son of God (John 1:32–34). This is the visible, confirming sign that Jesus is the long-expected Messiah, the One for whom John has been preparing the way.

(3) The symbolism of the dove is made explicit as a voice sounds out from heaven. For the Jewish people of the time, although they considered that prophecy had ceased with Malachi, a voice from God could still be heard. But that voice was indirect and did not have binding authority.[32] Now sounds a voice that is far different. The presence of the Messiah brings with him the direct voice from God with all of its authority. With the arrival of the prophetic figure John the Baptist, with the descent of the Spirit on the anointed Messiah, and with a voice from the Father, God is resuming direct communication. The voice gives a dual pronouncement of the identity and nature of Jesus through citing excerpts of two messianically significant passages: Psalm 2:7 and Isaiah 42:1.

---

31. For an intertextual analysis that draws upon the themes of judgment, deliverance, and suffering in the Jewish tradition images of the dove (e.g., Gen. 8; Ps. 74:19; 2 Esd. 5:21–6:34), see David B. Capes, "Intertextual Echoes in the Matthean Baptismal Narrative," *BBR* 9 (1999): 37–49; cf. N. T. Wright, *Jesus and the Victory of God: Christian Origins and the Question of God* (Minneapolis: Fortress, 1996), 2:536–37.

32. For background and discussion, see Davies and Allison, *Matthew*, 1:335–36.

(a) The statement "This is my Son, whom I love" calls to mind the well-known image of father and son in Psalm 2:7: "I will proclaim the decree of the LORD: He said to me, "You are my Son." The title "Son of God" had clear messianic significance prior to Jesus' ministry.[33] The expression "whom I love" may have evoked images of Isaac, who is called Abraham's "son, your only son . . . whom you love" (Gen. 22:2), but more important is the relationship that is declared between Jesus and the voice. Jesus is the Son, the voice is from the Father, and at the heart of their relationship is love. Nothing is said here of when that relationship began, but Matthew has already informed us that Jesus' conception has marked him out as of divine origin (1:20, 23; cf. 2:15). This is not the language of adoption but of confirmation of an existing relationship of divine love between the heavenly Father and his Son.[34]

(b) The statement "with him I am well pleased" takes our understanding of Jesus' mission one step further by drawing on Isaiah 42:1 for another messianically significant figure—the "Servant."

> Here is my servant, whom I uphold,
> my chosen one in whom I delight;
> I will put my Spirit on him
> and he will bring justice to the nations.

In the declaration of the Father, Jesus is heralded as the Servant who is enabled by the Spirit's anointing to bring justice to the nations. This link will be made explicit as the narrative unfolds, when Matthew cites Isaiah 42:1–4 in the context of clarifying the purpose of Jesus' ministry (cf. Matt. 12:17–21).

As the background to the Father's declaration, these passages point out two distinct emphases of Jesus' identity, self-understanding, and mission. (1) He is the divine Son and the suffering Servant, a pronouncement that recalls the double entendre of the Nazarene allusion (2:23) and will be repeated by the voice in the Transfiguration (17:5). The Father has placed into the hands of his beloved Son the mission of the Servant to bring salvation to the nations (Isa. 42:1, 4). Love and obedience will sustain the relationship and actualize the mission, because the Father's will for the beloved Son must include obedience to the cross as the Son takes on himself the iniquity of his people (Matt. 26:39, 42; cf. Isa. 53).

(2) Through the anointing by the Spirit, the Father formally inaugurates Jesus into his public ministry as the unique Son, who is the triumphant

---

33. See Ben Witherington III, *The Christology of Jesus* (Minneapolis: Fortress, 1990), 148–55.

34. In the rich associations connected with "Son of God," it is important to understand the intended contextual force. Carson notes, "As it is wrong to see ontological sonship in every use, so is it wrong to exclude it prematurely" ("Matthew," 109).

messianic King (Ps. 2), yet the humble Servant (Isa. 42). He will accomplish his Father's will in coming to his people Israel (Matt. 10:6; 15:24), yet he brings hope to the nations (Matt. 28:18). These are the themes that will characterize the unfolding story of Jesus Messiah.

THE CELEBRATED JEWISH novelist Chaim Potok has written a history of his people, which he entitled *Wanderings.* He narrates a grand and gripping story, tracing the Jewish people back through the ancient wanderings of Abraham among ancient paganism, through the centuries of the Diaspora as his kinspeople wandered through Islam and Christianity, up to the contemporary Jewish people wandering inside modern secular paganism.

In the introduction, Potok tells of his father's Judaism. It was a Judaism based on hope, but a hope that had to be worked out in the difficulties of this life. His father had served in a Polish unit of the Austrian army during World War I and often spoke of his Jewish heritage in military terms. For him the Jews were the reconnaissance troops of God's vanguard, and they

> would succeed one day in establishing the Kingdom of God on earth. Of that he had no doubt.... My father saw history as the path that led from the creation of the world by God almost six thousand years ago to the future coming of the Messiah and the redemption, first of Jewry and then of all mankind.[35]

That was the Judaism in which Potok was raised and instructed. But Potok's own Judaism has been reshaped. As he left the confines of his father's world and encountered both the loveliness and the suffering of other cultures that existed outside Judaism, the "neat antique coherence of my past came undone," Potok writes.[36] He has spent much of his adult life trying to make sense of the uniqueness of his people, who have endured so much suffering, who have clung so tenaciously to their hopes, yet whose hopes no longer seem relevant in the modern world. Reshaped and transformed especially were his father's hope of the coming kingdom of God, the hope of a future Messiah, and the hope of redemption. Now the hopes seem so hopeless.

**Expectations of the Messiah.** The Jews of the first century experienced various kinds of reshaping and transformation as well, and Matthew wrote

---

35. Chaim Potok, *Wanderings: Chaim Potok's History of the Jews* (New York: Fawcett Crest, 1978), 11.
36. Ibid., 13.

his Gospel to address their hopes. He looked out on the same Jewish heritage and narrates another kind of story—a story of *arrivals*. Hundreds of years of wandering through exile and oppression were real for his audience. But the prophetic message that sustained their hope was now fulfilled. John the Baptist, that fiery messenger of God, announced that the hoped-for kingdom of God, the hoped-for Messiah, and the hoped-for redemption of Israel and the entire human race had indeed arrived.

But it was a different kind of hope than many in Israel expected. Various groups within Israel had reshaped their hopes for a coming kingdom of God or for a coming Messiah. Some were engrossed in ritual practices to purify themselves. Others immersed themselves in meticulous study and interpretation of their Scriptures in an attempt to make relevant an old message. Some thought of a conquering king approaching, while others thought of a kingdom in which the temple and its priestly sacrifices and purity would be paramount. Still others thought of God's judgment and wrath poured out. Finally, some had nearly given up hope of God's intervention and took their hopes into their own hands, whether through political action or violent revolution. Different groups within Israel took their same Hebrew Scriptures and focused on specific strands of prophecy to end up with diverse expectations of what God would do when he sent his messianic deliverance at the end of the age.[37]

Chaim Potok's reshaping of his own understanding of his Jewish faith is not so new. It was occurring in the first century. That reshaping often caused people to have their expectations so entrenched that they had difficulty actually accepting God's work among them.

Matthew declares that Jesus is the Expected One foretold by John the Baptist in fulfillment of the Old Testament prophets, but it is a far more astounding truth than most in Israel had anticipated. It will blow away their expectations. Their thinking will need to be reshaped, and that is what Matthew does. On the one level he tells the story, but on another level he reshapes his readers' understanding to reconform their hopes to those revealed through the prophets.

---

37. Among others, Jacob Neusner refers to the phenomenon of diverse expectations as "Judaisms and their Messiahs." He explains: "A Messiah in a Judaism is a man who at the end of history, at the eschaton, will bring salvation to the Israel conceived by the social group addressed by the way of life and world view of that Judaism. Judaisms and their Messiahs at the beginning of Christianity therefore encompass a group of religious systems that form a distinct family, all characterized by two traits: (1) address to 'Israel' and (2) reference to diverse passages of the single common holy writing ('Old Testament,' 'written Torah')." See his "Introduction" to *Judaisms and Their Messiahs at the Turn of the Christian Era*, ed. Jacob Neusner, William S. Green, and Ernest Frerichs (Cambridge: Cambridge Univ. Press, 1987), ix.

**The gospel of the kingdom.** Matthew writes for us, therefore, not a biography in the modern sense of an exhaustive account of a person's life; rather, he writes for us a "gospel,"[38] an account of the good news that Jesus Messiah has brought salvation to his people. He focuses on significant events and teachings in the life of this one born "king of the Jews" (2:2), which establish Jesus' rightful claim as the One who will "save his people from their sins" (1:21). Matthew uses the noun "gospel" (*euangelion*) only four times, and three of those four occur in his unique phrase "gospel of the kingdom" (4:23; 9:35; 24:14).[39] The "good news" that Matthew stresses for his readers is that the age of the kingdom of God has finally dawned. Matthew's quotation of the kernel of John's message in 3:2 captures a theme that will be central to his message. It is the same message Jesus will announce at the beginning of his public ministry (4:17) and the Twelve will preach on their missionary tour through Israel (10:5).

We have seen how Matthew emphasized the genealogy of Jesus as One who has a right to the throne of David, the miraculous conception of the One who will save his people from their sins, and the birth and divine protection of this One born "king of the Jews." Now he focuses on the prophesied herald and the actual arrival of the Coming One on the scene of Israel's religious landscape. No doubt many who heard John were highly devout individuals who recognized in his message the prophetic voice of God. Many were at least nominally religious. But John's baptism called for a personal commitment of all the people to God's new activity within Israel. Those responding were heeding the call to the presence of the kingdom and arrival of the Coming One whom John announced.

**The mind-boggling truth of Jesus as Son of God.** We are all probably too familiar with Jesus to recognize how difficult it was for people in the first century, including later even his own disciples, to comprehend fully who he was. We have learned from our earliest years in Sunday school, youth groups, and Bible studies that Jesus is both God and human. We have recited doctrinal creeds and heard countless sermons discuss Jesus' divine and human natures. But our familiarity with the truth numbs us to the reality. As Malcolm Muggeridge says, "The coming of Jesus into the world is the most stupendous event in human history."[40]

It is not just the religious significance of Jesus' ministry to which Muggeridge refers. He refers especially to the mind-boggling truth that God

---

38. For a detailed analysis of the genre "gospel" in the light of ancient "biographies," see Richard A. Burridge, *What Are the Gospels? A Comparison with Greco-Roman Biography* (SNTSMS 70; Cambridge: Cambridge Univ. Press, 1992).

39. See comments on 4:23.

40. Malcolm Muggeridge, *Jesus: The Man Who Lives* (New York: Harper & Row, 1975), 1.

actually became a human and lived among us. It will remain for Paul and the apostle John to explain the significance of the Incarnation for human redemption. Matthew writes to recount the good news of the Incarnation's reality. He has already given his readers a behind-the-scenes understanding of Jesus' identity as he unfolded the messianic pedigree (1:1–17), and narrated accounts of the divine conception (1:18–25) and prophetically anticipated messianic infancy (ch. 2). Now he gives further insight to Jesus' true identity in his baptism (3:13–17). He is the anointed Messiah, the beloved Son, and the suffering Servant. We should note two points here.

(1) In 3:16–17 we have the appearance of the Spirit, the presence of the Son, and the voice of the Father. As Leon Morris states, "Matthew has certain trinitarian interest."[41] He will conclude his Gospel with another Trinitarian allusion in Jesus' instruction that new disciples are to be baptized in the singular name of the Father, Son, and Holy Spirit (28:19). Matthew lays out a clear picture of Jesus' deity by drawing on Old Testament prophecies. Prior to the Incarnation the strong divine language of some of these prophecies could not be adequately understood and led to the diversity of views concerning the nature of the Messiah. But for Matthew, the reality of the Incarnation now makes clear God's revelation: Jesus is the divine Son of God.[42]

(2) John said that Jesus would baptize with the Holy Spirit and fire (cf. Acts 2), and now in his baptism Jesus is anointed by the Spirit. This inaugurates the age of the Spirit foretold by the prophet Joel (Joel 2:28–29). The consistent Christological picture in the New Testament reveals Jesus as a person who is fully divine in his essence and attributes during his time on earth, yet he does not operate in glorious display of his deity. Rather, he lives a fully human life in the power of the Spirit, giving his followers the ultimate example of a Spirit-led and empowered life, the example of how true human life is to be lived.

The reality of Jesus as the incarnate Son of God is a mind-boggling truth, if we allow ourselves to reflect deeply on the story that Matthew unfolds. It truly is the only sufficient answer to the hopes of the Jewish people in the first century—and the hopes for all people today.[43] As we reflect on this truth, we will find that the story will reshape our own expectations of what kingdom life is all about.

---

41. Morris, *Matthew*, 68.

42. See Kaiser, *The Messiah in the Old Testament*, for a discussion of the chronological unveiling of the messianic prophecies of the Old Testament.

43. For an overview of the historical New Testament Christological development, see Martin Hengel, "Christological Titles in Early Christianity," in *The Messiah*, 425–48. For a theological overview, see Grudem, *Systematic Theology*, esp. 547–53.

**Contemporary Significance**

AT THIS POINT in Matthew's account, he has not revealed the full story of what the announced kingdom of heaven will be like. John has announced its arrival, and Jesus has been anointed by the Spirit and confirmed by the Father to undertake its establishment. We will have to look closely at Jesus' ministry and teaching as it unfolds through-out this Gospel to understand the kingdom's characteristics and activities. But Matthew has already given us some important clues, especially as the arrival has confronted the expectations of many within Israel. The expectations of the people, of the religious leaders, and even of John himself must be either overturned or reshaped.

While many of us do not have backgrounds that contribute to a fully developed concept of a kingdom, our own expectations similarly will need to be either overturned or reshaped as we consider the implications of our life in the kingdom of heaven. I emphasize this to my students through an acted analogy.

Walking into a classroom full of students, I shout out, "I'm the king!" After letting them recover from their shock, I ask them what came to their mind first when they heard me.

"King Arthur and his round table," said one student.

"I'm the king of the world!" shouted out a student, as he thought of the scene from the blockbuster movie *Titanic*.

Another student yelled, "There's been another sighting of Elvis Presley!"

And another sang out, "If I ... were the king ... of the foreeeeeest!" bringing to mind the whimsical lion from *The Wizard of Oz*.

We all carry around different mental memories and pictures of what a "king" and "kingdom" are like, depending on our past experiences and mindset. If you were to walk up to a person on the street and invite her or him to come enter the kingdom, you would have to do a lot of explaining about what you meant, because she or he has already formed a mental picture of what she *remembers* and what he *wants*.

In other words, our own expectations will likely need to be either overturned or reshaped. What is your expectation of the kingdom? At the least, we can see from the incidents surrounding John the Baptist's announcement of the kingdom, along with Jesus' baptism and anointing as the Messiah of the kingdom, several important implications.

**A warning of judgment, but also an invitation to life and change.** First, the arrival of God's kingdom in the preaching of John the Baptist is a warning of judgment, but it is also an invitation to life and an expectation of real change in the lives of those who respond. This will be explained more fully as Jesus' ministry unfolds, but the arrival of the kingdom of God promises to bring with it kingdom life. John fully expected the Coming One to bring wrath and final judgment on the unrepentant. But he also fully expected the coming of the kingdom to include the gathering of the repentant into safekeeping and their baptism with the Holy Spirit. Within the kingdom is life; outside the kingdom is death.

The preaching of John the Baptist was a definite intrusion into the lives of those around him. Not many of us would relish giving this kind of "hell and brimstone" sermon. We don't like to offend. Many a pastor, sitting by the bedside of a dying patient who has consistently rejected the tender message of salvation, struggles with the appropriateness of giving such a terrifying message of judgment to the very end. But John does warn us, as will Jesus later (11:20–24), of the coming judgment for those who reject the message of the arriving kingdom of God. We must be clear about this warning for ourselves and for those around us.

Although John's chronology of the arrival of messianic judgment has yet to be accomplished, it surely will come. We can create a warped view of God and the gospel by overemphasizing the judgment to come, but we just as surely distort people's view if we minimize the reality of judgment. There is no more painful, helpless, utterly desperate feeling than thinking of a loved one who has just gone into eternity with fist clenched against God. But great is the peace when thinking of a loved one safely in the receiving arms of God because he or she has heeded the warning and turned to the Savior.

But John isn't just holding out death. He is inviting those who respond to his message to experience life, to escape from the wrath to come, and to await the baptism of the Holy Spirit that the Coming One will bring. No message of judgment should ever be given without the accompanying message of promised life for those who respond.

This isn't just an escape into the future by and by. Real life promises real change in the present realm of our daily lives. The change of mind and direction of life that is one's responsibility in repentance is obvious. But John does not hold out the latest self-help promotion. Instead, he points to the source of real change: the Holy Spirit. The promised age of the pouring out of the Holy Spirit in Joel (Joel 2:28–29) is described by Ezekiel as the age of God's new covenant, when he will put his Spirit in his people (Ezek. 36:26–27). What kind of change will this be? Ezekiel promised purification and the ability to be obedient to God's law. But he connects all of this to the new heart that will be put into new covenant people. These are the beginning hints of the theme of regeneration through the Spirit, a theme that will later characterize not only Jesus' teaching (cf. John 3:3–7) but will be a foundational truth of Paul and the early church (Titus 3:4–7).

Change is not only possible, but it is the reality of those who experience the "new birth" and transforming power of the Spirit. All of this is hinted at in John's message in his reference to bearing fruit. He points to inner life and inner change that will ultimately produce external change. Profession is not enough; bearing fruit is required. "Profession" is the external assertion that a person has repented and has received new life, but "bearing fruit" is the external evidence that the new life is real. The inner life-giving force of a tree will always produce fruit in keeping with the nature of the tree. The arrival of the kingdom will be accompanied by the Spirit, who will give life to all who respond.

**The snare of spiritual pedigree.** Religious pedigree does not guarantee participation in the kingdom of heaven. John pays no homage to the ancestral pedigree of the Pharisees and the Sadducees, who have Abraham as their father (3:2, 9). We might find this surprising, since the covenantal promises to Abraham marked the beginning of the people of Israel (Gen. 12:1–3; 15:1–19). But in his warning to the religious leaders, John does not strike out anew. A consistent theme of the prophets all along has been that Israel ought not rely on pedigree or marks of the covenant, such as circumcision, but rather to "circumcise [their] hearts" (e.g., Jer. 4:4). God was the one who had established his people by choosing them as a covenantal people, and if he chose to do so, he could create a new people for himself even from stones (Matt. 3:9). Participation in the kingdom of God is a *heart* matter. Repentance means first and foremost to have one's heart rightly directed toward God, which will then be evidenced by the fruit of one's life.

I shudder at times when I remember that I am a "professional Christian." I am paid to study the Bible, to teach the Scripture, to stand and pray before my classes and the church. When it comes right down to the specifics of who we are as people, the Pharisees and Sadducees are not much different from you or me. There will be some of these religious leaders, such as Nicodemus and Joseph of Arimathea, who will acknowledge the movement of God in John's message and Jesus' ministry and will repent and turn to the arrival of the kingdom of heaven. But others will be so filled with the duties of their religious life and a commitment to their own understanding of God's message in the Old Testament that they ignore, and later reject, Jesus' offer to enter the kingdom of heaven. The privilege of their inclusion in the people of Israel and the added privilege of their leadership position are no guarantee of inclusion in the arrival of the kingdom.

This is no minor issue for us. To be born into a Christian home is a tremendous privilege. It is a privilege to have Christian parents who attempt to live out a godly lifestyle and who try to guide their children into the kind of life God has intended for us. Christian parents are privileged to have the guidance of Scripture and the Spirit to help them raise their children in the right way.

But Christian parents and children alike need to remember that there are no guarantees. The privilege of a Christian home must be accompanied by accountability. Christian parents must be diligent to lead their children not simply to church activities, but most important to understand what it means to present their hearts to God. And children of Christian families must not bank on the faith of their parents. Each of us will stand alone before God to render accountability with what we have done with our lives.

Also, we who are privileged to be involved in full-time Christian ministry must remember the trap of professionalism that John, and Jesus throughout his ministry, consistently warn against. So I shudder when I recognize the possibility of becoming like those Pharisees and Sadducees who hardened their heart to God through empty religious activities (see comments on 6:1–18). I must open my own heart to God to live in sincerity before him and experience the ministry of God in my own life, leading me to experience the fruit of a life lived in humble dependence on the Spirit of God.

**Humility.** We must take God's calling on our lives with deadly seriousness, but we must not get caught up with appearances. This third implication surfaces from observing the character qualities of John and Jesus as they fulfill their callings. John not only had a large following; he also demonstrated authority as he rebuked the religious leaders for their hypocrisy. But he did not get carried away with his own importance. He understood clearly his role and knew that there was One coming after him who would be greater, who would have a greater role. John did not balk at being surpassed. Jesus was the greater One, the Messiah, the divine Son of God, who was ready to assume his momentous redemptive role. Yet Jesus assumed a position of subservience as he submitted himself to the waters of baptism by John. He did not balk at appearing lesser.

This is a tremendous lesson on self-understanding in carrying out God's calling on our lives. Neither John nor Jesus got carried away with appearances. They demonstrated strength in carrying out their roles in the plan of salvation, yet that strength also included diminishing the appearance of their own importance. The key word here is *humility*, a term that does not get much good press in our day. We hear much more of *rights*. Perhaps it is not new, because the picture that John and Jesus give every age is the incongruity of their humility relative to the significance of their roles. We do not like to give up our appearance of importance. Thus, John and Jesus give us a powerful example of humility. Knowing God's purposes and not allowing our self-promotion to get in the way enable us to accomplish God's calling for our lives as well.

The one who can make us most uncomfortable here is, of course, Jesus. How hard, really, was it for him to appear humbly at the waters of John's baptism? Did he really wrestle with such mundane things as self-image, and appearances, and his role? I think so. He was that human. All the things that we struggle with, he experienced (cf. Heb 4:14—16). That is why he is our example. That is a key element for his entrance to history. He not only accomplished salvation for us, but he also gave us the model of what a real human life lived in the power of the Spirit is like. This does not in any way diminish his deity. Instead, it gives us a beginning glimpse of what his Incarnation entailed. He laid aside both the glory and the independent exercise of his deity to live a life like you and me. That is why he is the very real, very tangible example of what our lives are being transformed into (see 2 Cor. 3:18).

We can be uncomfortable with such a Savior. We would much rather focus on his strength—as so we shall. But his strength comes from his humble dependence on the same Spirit that you and I depend on. That is the nature of his Incarnation, to which Matthew now turns as he narrates Jesus' entrance into the cosmic battle through his temptations from Satan.

# Matthew 4:1–11

**T**HEN JESUS WAS led by the Spirit into the desert to be tempted by the devil. ²After fasting forty days and forty nights, he was hungry. ³The tempter came to him and said, "If you are the Son of God, tell these stones to become bread."

⁴Jesus answered, "It is written: 'Man does not live on bread alone, but on every word that comes from the mouth of God.'"

⁵Then the devil took him to the holy city and had him stand on the highest point of the temple. ⁶"If you are the Son of God," he said, "throw yourself down. For it is written:

"'He will command his angels concerning you,
and they will lift you up in their hands,
so that you will not strike your foot against a stone.'"

⁷Jesus answered him, "It is also written: 'Do not put the Lord your God to the test.'"

⁸Again, the devil took him to a very high mountain and showed him all the kingdoms of the world and their splendor. ⁹"All this I will give you," he said, "if you will bow down and worship me."

¹⁰Jesus said to him, "Away from me, Satan! For it is written: 'Worship the Lord your God, and serve him only.'"

¹¹Then the devil left him, and angels came and attended him.

**Original Meaning**

AFTER HIS BAPTISM Jesus enters his ministry as the Spirit-anointed and Father-confirmed messianic deliverer. But his beginning as deliverer is as incongruous as was his appearance for baptism. Instead of initiating a public reformation, he goes to the desert to fast! But this will be more than a place of spiritual retreat. The desert is the place of the first showdown between competing kingdoms and their rulers, between two figures who lay claim to the hearts and souls of men and women. Rather than retreat, Jesus now advances the kingdom of God.

## The Setting of the Temptations (4:1–2)

JESUS' MINISTRY BEGINS in the desert, probably once again referring to the highlands of the Judean desert west of the Jordan River and the Dead Sea. This is likely the same desert in which John the Baptist appeared (3:1). But unlike John, Jesus will not first preach. He will fast. Throughout his public ministry Jesus will often get away to lonely places by himself to prepare for a particularly significant event (e.g., 14:13, 23). Here his entire ministry stretches out in front of him, so he spends solitary time in the desert to prepare himself spiritually for the events to come, just as Israel had at one time lived in the desert before beginning her task in the Promised Land.

This seems to be the point of this concentrated time of fasting. Fasting was often used as a means for focusing one's attention in prayer (see comments on 9:14–15) through disciplining oneself. Jesus was readying himself for his public ministry through this extensive time of communion with his Father, who had just confirmed their relationship in the baptism.

But there is more to the story than spiritual preparation. Matthew tells us that Jesus goes into the desert for the expressed purpose of being tempted by the devil. A battle is brewing while Jesus is fasting. Matthew gives key insights in these first two verses.

(1) Jesus is Spirit-led. The Spirit came on him at his baptism (3:13–17), and now the Spirit leads him to the desert. Increasingly Matthew shows us that the Spirit is no impersonal force. He is the personal agent who will be intimately involved in guiding Jesus every step of the way in his earthly life. Jesus has come to accomplish the will of the Father who sent him (26:39, 42), and it is the Spirit who guides him as he accomplishes the Father's will. That is, Jesus is in the desert not only to commune with the Father but also to engage the enemy. That same Spirit will give power to Jesus in order to withstand Satan's temptations.

(2) The devil is the real adversary. Entering for the first time on the scene of Matthew's story is the one who already has been behind efforts to circumvent the arrival of Jesus Messiah. Although Herod was the first human adversary of Jesus, the real enemy is now revealed as "the devil," or, as he is called later, Satan (4:10; 12:26; 16:23). The Greek term *diabolos* ("accuser") occurs here preceded by the definite article to indicate Jesus is uniquely tempted by "*the* devil" (cf. also 4:5, 8, 11; 13:39; 25:41). This is not a symbol for depravity or an emblem of the propensity toward corruption. Rather, as Clinton Arnold states, "the devil is an intelligent, powerful spirit-being that is thoroughly evil and is directly involved in perpetrating evil in the lives of individuals as well as on a much larger scale. He is not an abstraction, either

as a personification of the inner corrupt self or in the sense of a symbolic representation of organized evil."[1]

As the real enemy of God (13:39), the devil leads a host of other powerful spiritual beings that assist him in trying to thwart God's purposes. Paul calls him "the ruler of the kingdom of the air" (Eph. 2:2). So the battle line traced in the sands of the Judean desert is really a battle line in the sands of all time, because the outcome will have implications for all of humanity. This is the first skirmish, as the ruler of the kingdom of the air undertakes to halt the advance of the kingdom of God.

The picture we see here is consistent with the picture we see of Satan's strategy elsewhere.[2] The enemy will not make a frontal attack. Instead, he will try to sidetrack Jesus through a variety of temptations.

The word "tempted" is the verb *peirazo*, which can mean either "I tempt" or "I test."[3] A "temptation" is an enticement to get a person to go contrary to God's will, as Satan will try to do to Jesus. A "test" tries to get a person to prove himself or herself faithful to God's will, with the good intention that the person passes the test. Scripture is clear that God never *tempts* anyone to do evil (James 1:13), but God does use circumstances to *test* a person's character or resolve with the intended purpose of promoting good ends (e.g., Heb. 11:17).

In a sense, temptation and testing are flip sides of the same coin. Satan intends to get Jesus to go contrary to the Father's will, but in the middle of those circumstances, the Father uses Satan's evil intention to a good purpose of strengthening Jesus for his messianic role. In other words, Satan does not act independently of God. Note how Satan tried to get Job to curse God and go contrary to God's will, but God was in control of the situation, so that when Job turned to God, he was strengthened. In the case of Joseph, his brothers intended harm by selling him into slavery to Egypt, but God used those same circumstances for good (Gen. 50:20). Temptation must be seen in the context of testing, because God is in control of both the tempter and the circumstances, and he will never allow a person to be tempted beyond what he or she is able to endure (1 Cor. 10:13).

This is why some refer to Jesus' temptations as the *testing* of God's Son.[4] The Father does not send the Son for evil but for good. A temptation in the

---

1. Clinton E. Arnold, *Three Crucial Questions about Spiritual Warfare* (Grand Rapids: Baker, 1997), 35.

2. See Job 1–2 [esp. 1:6–12]; Zech. 3:1–12; 1 Chron. 21:1; Luke 10:18; Rev. 20.

3. BDAG, 646. This is true as well for the noun *peirasmos*, which can mean either "temptation" or "test."

4. E.g., Birger Gerhardsson, *The Testing of God's Son (Matt 4:1–11 and Par.)* (ConBNT 2.1; Lund: Gleerup, 1966); Don B. Garlington, "Jesus, The Unique Son of God: Tested and Faithful," *BibSac* 151 (July–September 1994): 284–308.

hands of Satan becomes a test in the hands of God.[5] The temptation is real, but the good outcome is assured as the Son yields to the leading and the power of the Spirit in accomplishing the Father's will. As Jesus is led away by the Spirit into the desert, Satan will try to get the Son to go contrary to the Father's will, but that very temptation is used by the Father to establish the Son in the Father's will.[6]

Jesus' confrontation with the devil at the outset of his public ministry is not coincidental. As Matthew paints his historical narrative of these events, he indicates three significant purposes that are accomplished through Jesus' victorious clash with the evil one.[7]

(1) The victorious encounter surpasses the experience of Adam. Jesus as the Son of God will fulfill what Adam, the first "son" of God in the creation, failed to accomplish.[8] The first Adam failed in the best conditions, Jesus as the last Adam succeeds in the worst. Death was the result of Adam's sin, but Jesus' suffering and temptation will enable him to make atonement for his people and bring life. Jesus will be tempted on other occasions, and he demonstrates his qualifications to bear the sin of others by resisting sin himself (Heb. 2:17—18).

(2) The victorious encounter surpasses the experience of Moses and Israel. Matthew's prior allusions to Israel's history should lead us to correspond Jesus' experience of forty days of fasting in the desert to Israel's forty years of testing in the desert (Deut. 8:2–3).[9] Both in type and in direct fulfillment, Jesus'

---

5. The same term, *peirazo*, is used of the religious leaders coming to query Jesus later in his ministry (16:1; 19:3; 22:34–35). The context determines their motives, whether for good or bad.

6. Cf. Morris, *Matthew*, 71ff.

7. Jesus' forty-day vigil of fasting was preparing him for the redemptive ministry he would undertake, which does not imply that he was fasting to make himself intentionally vulnerable to Satan. We must be careful in drawing implications for spiritual life today. The temptation accounts have been used as models for ascetic practices that may be unwarranted, such as entering into extreme periods of fasting, almost to the point of death, in order to experience intimacy with Jesus' experiences.

8. Many have noted the parallels to Adam, beginning already with the early fathers such as Irenaeus (see D. Jeffrey Bingham, *Irenaeus' Use of Matthew's Gospel: In Adversus Haereses* [Traditio exegetica graeca 7; Louvain, Belgium: Peeters Leuven, 1998], 274–81). The parallels to Adam are more pronounced in Luke and Mark (see Davies and Allison, *Matthew*, 1:356–57).

9. The number "forty" (and multiples, such as 80 and 120) is often used for a typical round number, whether to designate the years of a generation, maturity (e.g., of a person's life), or a symbolic period of time (e.g., cf. Ex. 24:18). The period of "forty days" takes on special significance in Scripture, and it was often associated with hardship, affliction, or punishment, but was also a time of preparation for a particularly significant involvement in God's activities (see Ex. 24:18; Deut. 9:25; 1 Kings 19:8; Ezek. 4:6).

early life has paralleled the history of Israel. This point will be made all the stronger when we see that each of Jesus' replies to the tempter comes from Deuteronomy, Moses' final narration to the Israelites. But most important, harking back to Israel's experience emphasizes Jesus' victory. Jesus Messiah fulfills the nation of Israel's experience. Although Israel had the endowment of the Spirit given to them (cf. Num. 11:17, 25, 26, 29; 14:24; 24:2, 18), Jesus will be fully obedient to the Spirit's leading where the nation was not. The temptations reenact Israel's history, but victoriously.

(3) The victorious encounter confirms Jesus' identity and mission as the unique Son of God. There are larger issues at stake than simply recording Jesus' spiritual temptations. The allusions to the fall of Adam and the wanderings of Israel in the desert cry out for God's new beginning. The darkness of the chaos of sin looms over humanity, and Jesus is called upon as the unique Son of God to rectify the previous failures. But the beginning of the end of darkness must come out of the weakness of the Incarnation, because the obedient Son becomes the prototype of victory over temptation for all who follow him (Heb. 4:14−16). So, after forty days and nights of fasting, when he is most vulnerable, the tempter comes to him. Satan tries to foil God's plan for humanity's redemption by disqualifying Jesus as a sinless Savior and obedient Son.[10]

### First Temptation: Turn Stones into Bread (4:3−4)

THREE TIMES SATAN approaches Jesus, and three times Jesus thwarts those temptations. We can observe a pattern that is displayed regularly in Jesus' ministry. This pattern is also important for our own resistance to temptation.[11]

The nature of the temptations is expressed in the tempter's first words: "If you are the Son of God. . . ." This key phrase, repeated in the second temptation (4:6) and assumed in the third (4:9), reflects the tempter's overall intent to manipulate Jesus: "If you are the Son of God, tell these stones to become bread."[12] The voice from heaven recently confirmed the identity and the

---

10. Donald Guthrie, *A Shorter Life of Christ* (Grand Rapids: Zondervan, 1970), 81−82.

11. This pattern is important to observe and establish in our own spiritual development, in spite of modern attempts to deny the existence of a real satanic being, and hence, real personal temptation. For a historical survey of popular literature and the persistence of seeing a pattern for spirituality, albeit somewhat removed from Jesus' example, see Christian Davis, "Where Are We Going, Where Have We Been? The Temporality of Spirituality in Satanic Temptation Narratives," *Christian Scholars Review* 29 (Spring 2000): 455−69.

12. This is a first-class condition, "If you are the Son of God," which reflects Satan's attempt to manipulate Jesus. For point of argument he assumes the identification to be true and then uses it as a w pay of attempting to manipulate Jesus. See Richard A. Young, *Intermediate New Testament Greek: A Linguistic and Exegetical Approach* (Nashville: Broadman & Holman, 1994), 229−30.

relationship to Jesus as "my Son, whom I love" (3:17). Satan does not doubt Jesus' identity as the Son of God, nor is he trying to get Jesus to doubt it; rather, he is trying to get Jesus to misuse his prerogatives as the Son of God. He is subtly playing off Jesus' identity, almost even flattering him, to trick him into going contrary to the Father's will for the Son. "If you are the Son of God, why should you stay hungry? Just turn those stones into bread, which you are capable of doing, and feed yourself," the tempter seems to be implying.

Jesus has it within his powers to perform such a miracle, because later he miraculously multiplies loaves and fishes to feed five thousand and four thousand people. But it is not God's will for him to acquire food miraculously here. Jesus has come to live a truly human life, one that goes through the normal means of acquiring food. For Jesus to have turned the stones into bread would lead Jesus outside of the Father's will for the Son's incarnational experience.

Temptations are one of the enemy's ways of trying to get a person to go contrary to God's specific will. Therefore, a temptation is not always trying to get a person to do something that is inherently sinful. It is not inherently wrong to turn stones into bread. But the Father's will for the Son at this time is to fast, not to eat. Therefore, turning stones into bread will lead Jesus astray. The question really is, What is the Father's will for the Son?

Jesus responds to Satan by quoting a passage from Deuteronomy. This demonstrates the link between Jesus' temptations and Israel's experience in the desert. In Deuteronomy 8:2 Moses reminded the people of Israel that God had led them those forty years in the desert to humble and to test them. One of the tests was through hunger and God's miraculous provision of manna. The purpose of that test was to teach them that "man does not live on bread alone, but on every word that comes from the mouth of God" (Deut. 8:3).

That very lesson Jesus now quotes in his response to Satan's temptation. Israel should have taken God at his Word that he would care for them, even when they were in an area that had no apparent means of feeding so many. If it was God's will for them to be there, they needed to trust him when he said that he would take care of them. In like manner, since it is the Father's will for Jesus to be in the desert as a human who relies not on his own abilities to create food but on his Father to supply it, he cannot go contrary to the Father's will for this specific situation and for his entire incarnational experience. Jesus will trust what the Father has revealed to be his will.

The first temptation undertakes to get at the core of Jesus' *personal* trust in the Father's leading. Even though the present circumstances—he is hungry and hurting after forty days of fasting—seem to contradict the voice declaring his status as the Son of God whom the Father truly loves, Jesus maintains that the essence of life is trusting God's Word. He does not need to turn stones into bread in order to confirm his identity or to supply his needs. The Father has declared him the Son, the Spirit has led him into the desert, and he will not go contrary to the Father's will. Although there is no apparent circumstantial support in his present circumstances that he is the Son, the Spirit led him there and he must take the Father at his word that he will take care of Jesus even if his body is crying out for food.

### Second Temptation: Jump off the Temple (4:5–7)

IF THE FIRST temptation attacks the personal life of the Son in relationship to the Father's will, the second temptation[13] is an attack on the Son's *national* responsibility. The devil takes Jesus to Jerusalem, the holy city, and sets him on the highest point of the temple. This "highest point" probably refers to the southeast corner of the temple area, which loomed some 450 feet high over the Kidron Valley, or to a high gate of the temple. Satan approaches Jesus again with the words, "If you are the Son of God," but this time he quotes from Psalm 91:11–12, where the psalmist asserts God's protecting care for the faithful in Israel. The devil urges Jesus to throw himself down from that high place so that his loving Father will send angels to rescue him (Matt. 4:6).

Jesus has the ability to do what the devil tempts him to do. Later in Matthew, just prior to his arrest and crucifixion, Jesus states that if he wanted, he could call on his Father to rescue him by sending more than twelve legions of angels (26:53). So the devil's quotation is a blatant misuse of Scripture to try to manipulate Jesus. The original Old Testament context does not imply that God will send protecting care for every harmful situation. Jesus sees through the devil's Scripture-twisting to the sinister motivation behind it, by replying from Deuteronomy: "It is also written: 'Do not put the Lord your God to the test'" (4:7; cf. Deut. 6:13).[14]

---

13. Matthew and Luke reverse the order of the second and third temptations. This is a good example illustrating how each evangelist narrates incidents for his particular purpose. Matthew is intent on narrating chronological sequence, while Luke has a more theological purpose in placing the temple temptation last (Luke 4:3–12; cf. I. Howard Marshall, *Commentary on Luke* [NIGTC; Grand Rapids: Eerdmans, 1978], 166–67; Nolland, *Luke 1–9:20*, 180–81). Matthew's chronological intention is revealed by his use of the sequential adverb "then" (*tote*, 4:5), which he elsewhere uses regularly to note chronological progression (e.g., 3:13; 4:1, 17), and "again" (*palin*, 4:8), which continues the thought of chronological progression.

14. Christoph Kähler, "Satanischer Schriftgebrauch: Zur Hermeneutik von Mt 4,1–11/Lk 4, 1–13," *TLZ* 119 (1994): 857–68. This incident of the temptation of Jesus is unique in that it uses citations of Scripture and understands misuse of Scripture.

Satan is trying to get Jesus to test his Father in two ways (see comments on *peirazo* at 4:1–2, the root verb used here). (1) By intentionally putting himself in harm's way, Jesus would be inappropriately testing his Father's love, trying to manipulate him to send a rescuing force of angels (cf. Gideon's fleece in Judg. 6:36–40). True faith asks no such demands. (2) If Jesus were to cast himself off the high place of the temple and the angels rescued him, think of the reaction of the people! Such a spectacular display would gain Jesus a messianic following, but not by the Father's pathway—obediently proclaiming the gospel of the kingdom and suffering whatever consequences may come.

Jesus is being challenged to confirm the relationship he has to the Father. Does the Father really love him? Prove it by sending help. Does the Father really know the best way to gain a national following? Watch the reaction a jump will produce. But Jesus does not need to get the Father to prove to him that they have this Father-Son relationship. The Father declared the relationship at the baptism; the Son needs no further confirmation. This is the essence of biblical faith: taking God at his Word and being obedient to it without needing other confirmation.

### Third Temptation: Worship Satan (4:8–10)

NOT ONLY DO the temptations have personal and national elements, but now the devil reveals a *universal* dimension as well. He takes Jesus to a high mountain,[15] shows him all the kingdoms of the world and their splendor (4:8), and then makes an astounding offer: "All this I will give you," he said, "if you will bow down and worship me."

What a cruel enticement! Those kingdoms are the very reason Jesus has laid aside his own glory. His ultimate purpose is to gather the nations into the kingdom of God (cf. 25:31–34). But before he sits on his royal throne, he must hang on the cross. So the devil offers a shortcut. Jesus can bypass the ignominy of this human travail and the suffering of the cross. But taking the shortcut requires an immense condition: He must give up the will of his Father in heaven to worship the devil on earth. The Father's will for Jesus' life is the cross (see 16:21–27; 26:36–46), but Satan tries to sidetrack him from that mission by getting him to take a shortcut to gain the kingdom that will someday be his the hard way.

So Jesus emphatically declares, "Away from me, Satan! For it is written: 'Worship the Lord your God, and serve him only.'" In this response Jesus

---

15. This may indicate that at least this temptation came through some type of visionary experience, since no known mountain could make visible all of the kingdoms on the earth's sphere. Satan used whatever forces are at his disposal for very real temptations. Some supernatural powers were surely at work here to tempt the Son of God.

exerts his rightful authority over Satan by issuing his first command (cf. 16:23)[16] and quotes for the third time the book of Deuteronomy (Deut. 6:13). As powerful as Satan may be, and as frail as Jesus must be because of the extended fasting and the intensity of the temptations, Jesus vanquishes him with a word.

There are three important points here. (1) In Luke's parallel account, Satan emphasizes that he has been given authority over the kingdoms of the world, and he can give it to whomever he wishes (Luke 4:5–6). Satan does have significant influence over the people and powers of this world (2 Cor. 4:4; Eph. 2:1–2; Rev. 13:1–2), but his influence is limited. His offer to Jesus indicates his own "diabolical self-delusion."[17] The time of his demise is at hand, but he fights on, thinking that he can sidetrack the very one who comes to curtail his power (John 12:31; 14:30; 16:11).

(2) Temptations involve the twisting of reality, so the antidote comes from the *truth* of Scripture. Jesus does not get involved in a spiritual arm-wrestling match, pitting his power as Son of God against Satan's power. Instead, he uses the truth of Scripture to guide his understanding of reality.

(3) The Father alone is worthy of worship. Satan's demand for Jesus to worship him indicates his overall objective and is indeed the essence of sin. Sin desires to cast off God's will and have one's own way, to make oneself out to be the god of one's own life. Satan desires to supplant God. The pictures of the king of Tyre (Ezek. 28:2, 11–19) and the king of Babylon (Isa. 14:12– 14) epitomize this obsession and have often been understood as pointing beyond those earthly diabolical rulers to Satan himself. Worship of God is the tangible demonstration that a person has given over the rule of one's life to God's will, not one's own. This also has implications for understanding Jesus' own identity as the divine Son of God, because he has received, and will continue to receive, worship.[18]

## Outcome of the Temptations (4:11)

MATTHEW'S FINAL COMMENT on the temptation narrative gives a comforting conclusion, but it also gives insight to the bigger picture behind Jesus' conflict with Satan. (1) The immediate outcome of Jesus' rebuke of Satan was, "Then the devil left him." Although this is only the first of the many attacks

---

16. The one called "the devil" throughout (e.g., 4:1, 5, 8) is now called "Satan" (4:10), "the Adversary."

17. Bock, *Luke 1:1−9:50*, 376.

18. "Jesus' insistence on worshiping God alone makes the characteristic Matthean theme of worshiping Jesus (e.g., 2:2; 8:2; 9:18; 14:33; 15:25; 20:20; 28:17) all the more significant as evidence for his divinity" (Blomberg, *Matthew*, 85–86).

Jesus will experience throughout his ministry, it establishes the precedent for his, and all, spiritual warfare. Jesus must stay fixed on the Father's will, no matter what the circumstances or whatever temptations may come. Resisting the devil's onslaught through standing firm on the truth of God will cause Satan to flee (cf. James 4:7; 1 Peter 5:9).

(2) Matthew adds a comforting, if not touching, comment: "and angels came and attended him." That is, angels attend to Jesus' physical needs after his long period of fasting. But more important, this comment indicates the cosmic significance of the scene that has just been played. The Son has begun the invasion of Satan's domain. We read in Hebrews 1:6: "When God brings his firstborn into the world, he says, 'Let all God's angels worship him.'" It's as though angels have been watching this initial skirmish from heaven and now give due homage to the Son. This has been a momentous initial victory in the cosmic battle, and it will result ultimately in the conquest of all evil and the establishment of God's reign throughout the universe. All of heaven knows the significance, and the angels serve the Son, who now advances the kingdom.

*Bridging Contexts*

"*WHAT DID JESUS do, and could he do, only because he was God?*" Take a couple of minutes to think deeply about that question. You may think about his walking on the water. That certainly seems like something only God could do. But then we remember that Peter got out of the boat and also walked on the water for a while. He wasn't God, yet he walked on water.

Jesus' raised people from the dead, such as Lazarus. But other people in Scripture also raised persons from the dead, such as when Elijah raised the widow's son (1 Kings 17:17–24) or Peter raised Tabitha (Acts 9:36–42). Neither Elijah nor Peter was divine.

You may think of Jesus' performing various other miracles, like multiplying the fishes and loaves to feed the five thousand, or healing the crippled, or predicting future events. But other people in the Bible also performed similar deeds, such as Elisha's causing the widow's oil to multiply (2 Kings 4:1–7), Peter's commanding the crippled beggar to walk (Acts 3:1–10), or Nathan's predicting the Messiah to come through the line of David (2 Sam. 7:8–17).

You may rightly then think of Jesus' forgiving sin as an indication of his deity (Mark 2:6–12) or his atoning work on the cross. These certainly could be done only because he was God. Yet in general, when we think of all that Jesus did in his earthly ministry, only a few things were accomplished that are not paralleled by other human biblical figures.

I am not trying in any way to minimize the deity of Jesus. I became a Christian because I was absolutely convinced that Jesus was God incarnate, come to earth to die for the sins of the world and to rise in attestation of that fact. I am willing to die for that truth. Scripture is absolute in declaring that Jesus is the divine Son of God, the second person of the Trinitarian Godhead.

But many of us are what I call "functional Gnostics." We so emphasize Jesus' deity that we almost negate his humanity. The world today tends to deny the deity of Jesus and acknowledge only his humanity. As a result, we defend Jesus' deity vigorously and become suspicious of anyone who talks too much about his humanity.

The New Testament is not uneasy about either Jesus' deity or his humanity. It declares emphatically both natures (e.g., Rom. 1:3–4). Matthew readily emphasizes both Jesus' divine conception *and* his human lineage. In the baptismal scene, Matthew has clearly emphasized Jesus' divine nature as the beloved Son of God. But he just as clearly emphasizes that Jesus was Spirit-led into the temptation and was a human combatant in his victory over Satan.

**The Spirit-anointed messianic mission.** Jesus did what he did in his earthly ministry not primarily because he was operating in his powers as God, but because he was operating as the Spirit-anointed Messiah. Jesus came to live a fully human life, just like you and me, which meant voluntarily limiting himself to his human attributes. He performed miracles, healed people, even raised people from the dead, because he drew on the power of the Spirit. Notice Peter's recounting of Jesus' activities in his sermon at Pentecost: "Men of Israel, listen to this: Jesus of Nazareth was a man accredited by God to you by miracles, wonders and signs, which God did among you through him, as you yourselves know" (Acts 2:22). God performed the miracles, wonders, and signs through Jesus.

Moreover, Jesus lived a godly, pure life because he relied on the power of the Spirit. In a later message Peter said:

> You know what has happened throughout Judea, beginning in Galilee after the baptism that John preached—how God anointed Jesus of Nazareth with the Holy Spirit and power, and how he went around doing good and healing all who were under the power of the devil, because God was with him. (Acts 10:38–39)

In other words, Jesus fulfilled the messianic promises as the Spirit-anointed human descendant of David. His redemptive mission included living a fully human life that overcame all temptation in the power of the Spirit so that he could offer an unblemished human life on the cross as a sacrifice for the sins of humanity. True, that sacrifice could only be sufficient because the humanness of Jesus' sacrifice was sustained by his divine nature, as the God-man endured the cross. But while retaining full deity, he limited himself to full human experience.

Try to imagine Jesus as a baby, lying in a manger in Bethlehem. He looks up into the sky and thinks, "What a wonderful world I have created. I remember when my heavenly Father and I discussed creating this world. How beautiful it is!" As he lies there he thinks further, "I'm hungry and I'm wet. I'd sure like for Mother Mary to change me. But poor Mom. She's had a rough time of it. That donkey ride from Nazareth was tough. So I think that I'll just let her sleep through the night. I'll wait until the morning to eat and be changed. Or, better yet, I'll just get up and get a bottle and change myself."

Does that sound reasonable? Of course not! Jesus experienced full humanity. He thought the thoughts of a normal baby and had the same reactions as a normal baby. He cried when he was hungry and wet. He slept when he was full and dry. He was dependent on his human mother and father. Although Jesus was fully God, he became fully human with all of the typical human experiences.

Therefore, while Jesus was fully God with all of the attributes of deity, he limited their use so that he could fulfill the promises of God's sending a very human messianic deliverer from the line of David. He lived the same kind of life that you and I live, but he did so perfectly because he was perfectly obedient to the will of the Father in the power of the Spirit. The beginning of Jesus' public ministry was marked by the Spirit's coming on him at his baptism (3:13–17), and it was the Spirit who led Jesus immediately to be tempted (4:1). It is that same Spirit to whom Jesus turned in his humanity to receive power to withstand Satan's temptations.

**The supreme example of the Spirit-led life.** We are in deep theological waters here, but it is important for us to grasp this.[19] It is important not only so that we understand the truth of Jesus' experience in his life and ministry, but important practically for us as well, because Jesus is the example of perfect humanity lived perfectly in the power of the Spirit.

That same Spirit is available to us. While we will not attain his perfection in this life (e.g., Phil. 3:12), we look to him for an example of the kind of life lived in the Spirit that is available to us. That same Spirit is now transforming us into his image. As the apostle Paul says, "And we, who with unveiled faces

---

19. An overview of the theological issues can be found in any standard systematic theology, such as Grudem, *Systematic Theology*, esp. 547–53. Some theologians emphasize that Jesus operated exclusively in his humanity during his stay on the earth and that displays of supernatural activity are accounted for through the Spirit's power (cf. Acts 2:22–23; 10:38). Others emphasize that on occasion Jesus operated in his divine nature while on earth. All agree, however, that Jesus lived a fully human life in the power of the Spirit.

all reflect the Lord's glory, are being transformed into his likeness with ever-increasing glory, which comes from the Lord, who is the Spirit" (2 Cor. 3:18).

Jesus came to show us how to live human life the way God intended it to be lived. In his human nature he lived a victorious life because he lived perfectly in the power of the Spirit. Some of us may not perform extraordinary miracles, unless that is God's will for our lives, but we can all live victoriously through the Spirit by following Jesus' example in all areas of life.[20]

**The supreme example of how to overcome temptations.** Thus, although Jesus' temptations are unique to his mission as the messianic inaugurator of the kingdom, his temptations are also common to human experience and give us an example of what we can do in our own spiritual warfare. In his deity Jesus could not be tempted (James 1:13), but in his humanity he was tempted at all points like we are, yet without sin (Heb. 2:18; 4:15–16).[21] The temptations were directed to his human nature, and he experienced the maximum level of temptation that the demonic world could throw at him. The Garden of Gethsemane scene clearly indicates that temptation was a real, agonizing experience (see Luke 22:44). His will, fully focused on accomplishing that of his heavenly Father, directed him to resist the temptation.

The apostle Paul also narrates a powerful promise that allows us to take seriously Jesus' example: "No temptation has seized you except what is common to man. And God is faithful; he will not let you be tempted beyond what you can bear. But when you are tempted, he will also provide a way out so that you can stand up under it" (1 Cor. 10:13). God promises that no temptation can defeat us, for if we consistently and consciously turn to him in every temptation and rely on the Spirit's enabling resources, we can be victorious. The temptation is real, but we don't have to give in to it. Will we fail at times? Yes, unfortunately, until we leave this life. But the more we learn to stay focused on God's promised resources, the more we will grow in our ability to resist the temptations that come and then stand with the help of the Spirit.

One young college student of mine had never really grasped the truth of this verse until one day in class. Her eyes popped wide open and she said out loud to the class, "If I really believed that verse, my life will never be the same. I don't *have* to give in!" She went on from there to really believe it and practice it, and she has become a dynamically victorious Christian woman in the power of the Spirit.

---

20. I have developed this more fully in my *In His Image*.

21. The centuries-long debate of whether or not Jesus *could* have sinned is beyond our discussion here, but I agree with those theologians who believe that Jesus could *not* have sinned. How then was it a real temptation? The possibility of not sinning does not make the temptation any less severe. For more on this, see Grudem, *Systematic Theology*, 537–39, but also M. Erickson, *Christian Theology* (Grand Rapids: Baker, 1983), 2:718–20.

That is where Jesus' example comes in. His will was so mighty in its determination to do good that no matter how powerful the temptation addressed to his human experience, it could not defeat him. As our will is fixed with determination to do the Father's will for our lives, we can learn from Jesus' example as he carried out the Father's will for his life. We will not attain the same perfection that Jesus lived since we still live in the fallenness of this world, but the restoration process has begun through the redemptive work of Jesus, in whose steps we now follow (1 Peter 2:21).

ALL OF US have a variety of temptations that can sidetrack us. What is the source of your most distressing temptation? A difficult temptation for one person may not even faze another person. For example, I've never liked eating sweets, so waving a box of chocolates in front of me won't get my attention. For some people, chocolate is a severe temptation. But put me in a well-stocked bookstore and I'll have to restrain myself from buying all those wonderful reference books! For some people, they would never even consider buying some of the "nerd" books that I am always tempted to think that I "need"!

If you were to quiz your friends and colleagues about the source of their most severe temptations, you might be surprised to find an intriguing phenomenon. Their temptations are not usually bad things. A temptation is not usually something inherently "evil" but rather a good thing used for wrong purposes. Chocolate is not inherently evil. Books are not inherently evil. Chocolate eaten to an extreme can produce all kinds of problems, including tooth decay, weight problems, and poor nutrition. Books can be put to bad purposes, such as pornography or heretical teaching. Books can captivate a person in such a way that he or she escapes from responsible living in the real world. In the context of Jesus, we noted that eating bread is a necessity for life, but creating bread by yielding to Satan's suggestion would indeed have been a sin for him.

The very nature of a temptation is that it can be subtly construed to be a good thing, not a bad thing, by perverting a good thing to a bad use. The sexual relationship between men and women is God-ordained, but for a restricted range of relationships. The temptation to have a sexual relationship outside of marriage turns a good thing to a bad use.

Therefore, one of the most important considerations when addressing temptation is to understand the proper purpose for anything we face. Said in another way, what does God want for us in a situation? A right understanding of the way in which our bodies are created will give us a clear understanding of how much chocolate we eat, or what kind of sexual relationship to have, or whether or not we talk about a person behind her back, or anything else we encounter. When we face any kind of temptation, if we use 1 Corinthians 10:13 as a guideline in the way suggested above, we can learn how to draw on all of God's resources to be victorious. Being tempted is not a sin. Succumbing to the temptation is when it becomes sin (cf. James 1:13–15). Temptations in the hands of Satan become a test in the hands of God. God will use them as a test and strengthening of our character.

**Jesus' example for Christian leadership.** Henri Nouwen's compelling little book *In the Name of Jesus* uses Jesus' temptations as a case in point for Christian leaders.[22] A variety of temptations confront Christian leaders when they engage in ministry. We think immediately of moral or ethical temptations, because most of us have cringed as we heard the media expose sinful behavior by Christian leaders. But Nouwen focuses our attention elsewhere, on temptations that many of us may think are good things: (1) the temptation to be relevant—to do things, show things, prove things, build things that demonstrate the ability to make a difference in people's lives; (2) the temptation to be spectacular—to do something that will win great applause and popularity; (3) the temptation to be powerful—to use political, economic, spiritual, and even military might as instruments for establishing the kingdom of heaven on earth.[23]

These reflections on Christian leadership came after Nouwen left behind twenty years of teaching pastoral psychology and theology at Notre Dame, Yale, and Harvard in order to be a live-in minister at a community for the mentally handicapped. He had found that for much of his life he looked at being relevant, popular, and powerful as ingredients of an effective ministry, but it was in looking at Jesus' example that he found the key elements for resisting temptation and becoming a truly Christlike leader: prayer as a way of life, vulnerability to others in shared ministry, and trust in God's leadership for us and our people. He concludes by saying, "I leave you with the image of the leader with outstretched hands, who chooses a life of downward mobility. It is the image of the praying leader, the vulnerable leader, and the trusting leader."[24]

Some of Nouwen's points may stretch the Matthean context, but they hit home nonetheless, for these temptations readily surface as we attempt to influence people for Christ. To be relevant, popular, and powerful are not bad

---

22. Henri Nouwen, *In the Name of Jesus: Reflections on Christian Leadership* (New York: Crossroad, 1989).

23. Ibid., 16–17, 38–39, 58–59.

24. Ibid., 73.

per se, but a desire for them can corrupt ministry. Looking at Jesus' pattern, we will find a better example for our own leadership.

**Jesus' example for daily temptations and spiritual warfare.** Not only do Jesus' temptations bear relevance for developing Christlike leadership, they also are important examples for our personal daily victory over temptations and the spiritual warfare we will encounter in our own experience. These temptations of Jesus are unique to his entrance into his messianic ministry, but they have long been noted to have a rough parallel to the temptations of Eve in the Garden of Eden and the temptations from the world that John warns the church to resist.

| Temptation | Matthew 4:1–11 | Genesis 3:1–7 | 1 John 2:15–16 |
| --- | --- | --- | --- |
| Physical relevance | Turning stones to bread | The fruit of the tree was good for food | Cravings of sinful man |
| Confirm God's love and will | Rescued from a temple fall by angels | You will not die, but it is pleasing to the eye | Lust of the eyes |
| Pride and power | Have all the kingdoms of the world | You will be like God | Boasting of what we have and do |

Jesus succeeded under similar temptations where Adam and Eve failed, and the way he succeeded becomes the example for the way we can succeed under similar types of temptations. This is the powerful truth that has sustained Christians all through the ages under every type of temptation imaginable. We can summarize Jesus' example like this: *Resist the devil in the power of the Spirit through the guidance of the Word to accomplish the will of God.*

(1) *Resist the devil.* The first principle we see at work in Jesus is that he resisted the devil. Two people who knew Jesus better than anyone else and who saw up-front many of his spiritual confrontations give the same advice. James, the brother of Jesus, writes, "Submit yourselves, then, to God. Resist the devil, and he will flee from you" (James 4:7). The apostle Peter, who will succumb to the temptation to save his skin by denying Jesus, writes, "Your enemy the devil prowls around like a roaring lion looking for someone to devour. Resist him, standing firm in the faith, because you know that your brothers throughout the world are undergoing the same kind of sufferings" (1 Peter 5:8–9). This is powerful advice for every Christian. When temptation arrives, the beginning of the victory comes in saying "No!" We have been called to put on the full armor of God and to take our stand against the devil's schemes (Eph. 6:10–18).[25]

(2) *In the power of the Spirit of God.* But we cannot resist the devil in our own strength; our power must come from the Holy Spirit. Jesus was guided and

---

25. Clinton Arnold discusses nine convictions and actions that contribute to successful resistance of the devil; see Arnold, *Three Crucial Questions about Spiritual Warfare*, 30–41, 116–29.

empowered by the Spirit in his temptations. He was never alone in his struggle, even at the most difficult moments. The Spirit was there as his guide and his resource for power. Two tricks of the devil are important to note. (a) He wants us to think that in our temptation God has abandoned us. But Paul emphasizes in his treatise on life in the Spirit in Romans 8 that all those who belong to Christ have the Spirit (Rom. 8:9–11), and the Spirit is there with us even in our darkest moments. (b) Satan wants us to think that we can handle temptation on our own, in our own resources. In true spiritual warfare, we must rely on the Spirit to guide us through the thickest parts of the skirmish (cf. Eph. 6:10–18). As we claim the same power that Jesus drew upon through the Spirit, we are able to resist the devil, who *will* flee from us (James 4:7).

(3) *Through the guidance of the Word of God.* If temptation is essentially getting us to go contrary to God's will for us, then knowing that will is what keeps us on track. The Bible has been given to show us the truth of life in contrast to the lie of the world, the flesh, and the devil. Compare the Word of Jesus to the words of the world, and we will understand both how to confront the lie and how to follow the Father's will (cf. John 8:31–32). Satan twists the context of Scripture for the purposes of temptation, but in his temptations, Jesus exemplifies for us the right use of Scripture.

(4) *To accomplish the will of God the Father.* By knowing God's Word we will be able to discern his will for us. The ultimate goal in life is to hear at the end, "Well done, good and faithful servant" (25:21, 23). How do we know what we should do? We must understand God's purposes for our life—purposes in the little details as well as in the larger decisions of life. This is stated elsewhere in Matthew: "Seek first his kingdom and his righteousness"; "he must deny himself and take up his cross and follow me"; and "love the Lord your God with all of your heart and with all your soul and with all your mind" (6:33; 16:24; 22:37).

The psalmist's instruction is helpful here: "Delight yourself in the LORD and he will give you the desires of your heart" (Ps. 37:4). Delighting in God, or loving God, may be the most important guideline for all of the decisions of our lives, big and small, because if we truly love God, we will not do anything contrary to his Word and will for us. At the same time, when we delight in our walk with God, we are freed up to pursue our own desires and dreams.

Thus, when the temptation comes, we should ask regarding any contemplated action, "Is this what God wants for me? Can I do this and truly love God and delight in him?" Jesus is our ultimate example of the One whose most basic sustenance was carrying out the Father's will. "My food," said Jesus, "is to do the will of him who sent me and to finish his work" (John 4:34). When we have that aspiration before us, we will indeed be able to resist the devil in the power of the Spirit through the guidance of the Word to accomplish the will of God.

# Matthew 4:12-25

WHEN JESUS HEARD that John had been put in prison, he returned to Galilee. [13]Leaving Nazareth, he went and lived in Capernaum, which was by the lake in the area of Zebulun and Naphtali—[14]to fulfill what was said through the prophet Isaiah:

[15]"Land of Zebulun and land of Naphtali,
the way to the sea, along the Jordan,
Galilee of the Gentiles—
[16]the people living in darkness
have seen a great light;
on those living in the land of the shadow of death
a light has dawned."

[17]From that time on Jesus began to preach, "Repent, for the kingdom of heaven is near."

[18]As Jesus was walking beside the Sea of Galilee, he saw two brothers, Simon called Peter and his brother Andrew. They were casting a net into the lake, for they were fishermen. [19]"Come, follow me," Jesus said, "and I will make you fishers of men." [20]At once they left their nets and followed him.

[21]Going on from there, he saw two other brothers, James son of Zebedee and his brother John. They were in a boat with their father Zebedee, preparing their nets. Jesus called them, [22]and immediately they left the boat and their father and followed him.

[23]Jesus went throughout Galilee, teaching in their synagogues, preaching the good news of the kingdom, and healing every disease and sickness among the people. [24]News about him spread all over Syria, and people brought to him all who were ill with various diseases, those suffering severe pain, the demon-possessed, those having seizures, and the paralyzed, and he healed them. [25]Large crowds from Galilee, the Decapolis, Jerusalem, Judea and the region across the Jordan followed him.

**Original Meaning**

JESUS' RETREAT TO the desert to fast may have seemed inconsistent with what some anticipated from a messianic deliverer. But although he was weak at the end of a fast, Jesus vanquished Satan with a word of command. This "deliverer" did not fit stereotypical messianic molds, because the power and authority Jesus displayed was neither militaristic nor political. But his authority and power were staggering nonetheless. Jesus was powerful enough to conquer the devilish ruler of this world, universal enough to include both Jews and Gentiles in his messianic gospel, authoritative enough to transform simple men into leaders of a movement that changed the course of history, and effective enough to attend to the basic needs of the people—body, soul, and spirit. This is the kind of messianic deliverer that advances the kingdom of God.

### Jesus Messiah Begins His Galilean Ministry (4:12–17)

JESUS' MINISTRY HAS traditionally been reckoned as lasting three years: a year of obscurity, a year of popularity, and a year of increasing rejection.[1] The Synoptic Gospels largely omit the first obscure year, but it is implied in the introduction to Jesus' Galilean ministry: "When Jesus heard that John had been put in prison, he returned to Galilee" (4:12). We hear nothing in Matthew about that first year between Jesus' baptism by John the Baptist and John's arrest. For some details here, we must read John 1:26–4:3.

The motivation for Jesus' return to Galilee is that John the Baptist is put in prison. Behind the expression "had been put in prison" is the same verb (*paradidomi*) that will come to be associated with Jesus' own arrest, imprisonment, and eventual execution (cf. 17:22; Mark 15:1; Rom. 4:25; 8:32; 1 Cor. 11:23). Matthew does not explain why John was arrested, apparently because this was a well-known story to his audience. Josephus underscores that Herod Antipas imprisoned John for political reasons; that is, he feared that John's popularity with the people, along with his preaching and baptism, might lead the people to some form of sedition.[2] Matthew fills in later an additional moral reason behind John's arrest: John the Baptist had publicly condemned Herod Antipas for having an affair with, and eventually marrying, Herodias, his half-brother Philip's wife (see comments on 14:1–12).

---

1. For a brief overview of the chronological issues, see Robert Stein, *Jesus the Messiah* (Downers Grove, Ill.: InterVarsity Press, 1996), 51–60. For a more technical discussion, see Hoehner, *Chronological Aspects of the Life of Christ*, 45–63.

2. Josephus, *Ant.* 18.116–19.

Jesus *returns* (lit., "withdraws") to the Galilee region to begin his ministry. "Withdraw" (*anachoreo*) has been used several times already in Matthew,[3] and in each case the "withdrawing" is associated with some negative issue. Here the negative issue is the imprisonment of John the Baptist. We might assume that Jesus withdraws from the area of John's arrest to distance himself from danger.[4] But when we realize that Herod Antipas ruled the region of Galilee, Jesus is not going to Galilee to escape danger from him. Herod's capital city, Tiberius, is only eight and a half miles down the coast of the Sea of Galilee from Capernaum, the base of Jesus' ministry. One commentator even suggests that Jesus goes to the center of Herod's realm of authority as a challenge to him.[5] Whether or not this is the case, Jesus certainly is not fleeing danger.

An ominous plot is unfolding. Jesus' temptations have alerted us to the spiritual conflict that rages between the Father's plan and Satan's opposition. John the Baptist's scathing attack on the hypocrisy of the Pharisees and Sadducees warns us about the religious collision between the message of the gospel and the activities of the religious establishment. Matthew's allusion to the arrest of John cautions us that there is political conflict between the hopes of the people of Israel and the rule of the Roman occupiers. Jesus undertakes his Galilean ministry in the teeth of a gathering storm.

Returning to Galilee, Jesus goes first to his hometown of Nazareth, where apparently his mother and brothers and sisters are still living. Matthew says only that "leaving Nazareth,"[6] Jesus goes to Capernaum, but Luke fills in some of the details of his time in his former hometown. Jesus attends the synagogue, and as a returning successful preacher, reads from Scripture. However, he offends the townspeople's ethnic sensitivities when he reveals that his ministry will include Gentiles, so they attempt to kill him (see Luke 4:16–31).

Animosities between Jews and Gentiles ran high. Non-Jewish populations surrounded the tribes of Israel in the north on three sides, so the region was described as "Galilee of the Gentiles" (4:15). Although Jesus went first to the Jews to fulfill God's promises to the nation (10:5–7), he goes on to display an increasing openness to Gentiles. That openness reflects the intention of the original Abrahamic covenant to include Gentiles and is the foundation of the later apostolic mission to the Gentiles (28:18). But many Jews, including those in his former hometown, could not overcome their antipathy toward Gentiles.

---

3. See 2:12, 13, 14, 22; 4:12; cf. 14:13; 15:21; 27:5.

4. Good, "The Verb ANAXΩPEΩ in Matthew's Gospel," 1–12.

5. See Floyd V. Filson, *A Commentary on the Gospel According to St. Matthew*, 2d ed. (Black's New Testament Commentaries; London: Adam & Charles Black, 1971), 72.

6. The NIV's "But instead of going to Nazareth" obscures the normal rendering of *kataleipo*, which carries the sense of "leaving behind" (cf. BDAG, 520–21).

After leaving hostile Nazareth, Jesus makes Capernaum his base of operations and his new hometown for the length of his ministry in Galilee (4:13; cf. 9:1). Capernaum is the Greek form of the Hebrew *Kefar Nahum*, which means the "village of Nahum." Matthew narrates later that Capernaum, Chorazin, and Bethsaida were the cities "in which most of his miracles had been performed" (11:20). This area of operation is referred to by some as the "Evangelical Triangle," the central location of Jesus' proclamation of the gospel.[7] Capernaum, a Galilean frontier town, lies in the middle of the base of the triangle.[8]

Jesus' arrival in Zebulun and Naphtali in Galilee provides a fertile place of ministry and fulfills another Old Testament prophecy. Matthew 4:15–16 quotes from Isaiah 9:1–2. This is the sixth Old Testament prophecy so far, and the fifth using the distinctive Matthean fulfillment formula (see 1:22–23; 2:5–6, 15, 17–18, 23). Zebulun and Naphtali were two of the twelve tribes that settled in the northernmost region near the Sea of Galilee. Nazareth was in the territory of Zebulun, while Capernaum was in Naphtali. The "way to the sea" (4:15) was the trade route that ran through this region to the Mediterranean Sea. Matthew recognizes that Jesus' ministry will extend far beyond the physical confines of Jewish Galilee. It will influence those traveling through the region, people from beyond the Jordan, and ultimately the Gentiles.

Ever since the Assyrian campaign reduced it to a province under an Assyrian governor in 732 B.C. (2 Kings 15:29), this region had experienced turmoil and forced infiltration of Gentile influence. The inhabitants are called "the people sitting in darkness" (Matt. 4:16), a description of Jews who awaited deliverance while living among the hopelessness of the Gentiles.[9] Here, where the darkness was most dense and so far removed from the center of Jewish religious life in Jerusalem, these Jews are the first to see the great light of God's deliverance in Jesus. It will bring hope to those who understand most clearly the hopelessness of death. This light presages the universal message of hope, because from this same region Jesus will send the disciples to carry out the commission to make disciples of all the Gentiles (28:18). The message that begins to unfold is of messianic grace, for it comes first to those least expecting it.

---

7. Bargil Pixner, *With Jesus Through Galilee According to the Fifth Gospel* (Israel: Corazin, 1992), 33–35.

8. For an archeological overview of the history of Capernaum, see John C. H. Laughlin, "Capernaum: From Jesus' Time and After," *BAR* 19/5 (1993): 55–61, 70; Pixner, *With Jesus Through Galilee*, 35.

9. The term "people" (*laos*) in Matthew regularly refers to Israel (cf. comments on 1:21; 27:24–25).

The phrase "From that time on Jesus began. . ." (4:17) marks a significant turning point in Matthew's narrative.[10] This phrase indicates that the preparations for Jesus' messianic ministry are complete. The prophesied miraculous birth and infancy of Messiah have been established. The prophetic forerunner has announced his arrival. He has been anointed for ministry by the Spirit and confirmed by the Father. He has established his authoritative power as the Son over Satan. Now with John's public ministry terminated by his arrest, Jesus Messiah proceeds to the land of prophesied deliverance, where he preaches his message of God's breaking into history.

Matthew's summary of Jesus' message is the same as that of John the Baptist: "Repent, for the kingdom of heaven is near" (4:17; cf. 3:2).[11] In neither case is the arrival of the kingdom defined, probably indicating that certain expectations about the arrival of the kingdom came to mind among those who heard them preach.[12] But the way in which Jesus develops his ministry and the response of many to him reveal different understandings and expectations of the way that God's kingdom "is near."

Donald Gowan underscores a generally consistent prophetic hope that lent itself to a variety of expectations within Israel. "God must transform the human person; give a new heart and a new spirit. . . . God must transform human society; restore Israel to the promised land, rebuild cities, and make Israel's new status a witness to the nations. . . . And God must transform nature itself."[13] Some within Israel focused on a transformed nature, while others focused on Israel's restoration. Some focused on a new heart, while others focused on new cities. Many expected imminent judgment and restoration to be dispensed with the arrival of the Coming One, looking for God's wrath to be poured out on the unrighteous and for his blessing to be poured out on the righteous. When people hear Jesus announce that the kingdom of

---

10. The phrase will recur at 16:21 at another decisive turning point, where Jesus begins to tell in the first of his passion predictions of his forthcoming crucifixion. This phrase has been seen as a key to the structure of Matthew's Gospel, suggesting that Matthew uses it to divide the Gospel into three primary sections: 1:1–4:16; 4:17–16:20; and 16:21–28:20. See, e.g., Jack Dean Kingsbury, *Matthew: Structure, Christology, Kingdom* (Philadelphia: Fortress, 1975). While its appearance obviously marks a crucial transition in the narrative, it is doubtful that it would have held much significance for an aural audience, separated as far apart as are the two occurrences.

11. See comments on 3:2 for the expression "kingdom of heaven/God" in John's preaching.

12. The definitional silence assumes that Jesus and his forerunner, John the Baptist, would be understood by those who heard them preach, and that certain associations with the announcement of the kingdom would be called to mind. See Dale Patrick, "The Kingdom of God in the Old Testament," *The Kingdom of God in Twentieth Century Interpretation,* ed. Wendell Willis (Peabody, Mass.: Hendrickson, 1987), 71.

13. Donald E. Gowan, *Eschatology in the Old Testament* (Philadelphia: Fortress, 1986), 2.

heaven is near, they expect Jesus to inaugurate the kind of kingdom consistent with their hopes.

But Jesus has his own agenda. He will indeed bring a form of judgment insofar as the wrath of God remains on those who do not obey him and as he judges the ruler of this world (cf. John 3:36; 16:11). He also will bring a form of restoration as he presents the kingdom to Israel (cf. Matt. 10:5–7; 15:24). He initiates a form of restoration righteousness as a qualification for entrance to the kingdom of heaven (5:20). But the way in which this fulfills the Old Testament prophetic hope is different from what many in Israel are expecting.

The crux of Jesus' inauguration of the kingdom of heaven has to do with how people respond to him as their Messiah.[14] He is the Coming One prophesied by John (cf. 3:13–17; 11:2–6), but he preaches the "good news" of the kingdom for all who come to him. As Jesus remains faithful to his mission, people are forced to make a decision. They will either be with him, requiring that they adjust their expectations to accept what he reveals to be God's present program, or they will be against him. The tragedy of the latter choice is fully exposed at the Roman trial, when the crowd chooses the revolutionary brigand Barabbas over Jesus. Jesus has bitterly disappointed the crowd's expectations of what the kingdom should bring, so they turn against him (see 27:15–26).

God's ways are not always what humans expect. Jesus will indeed fulfill the prophetic hope. But he will bring this hope to complete fulfillment only when he returns as the Son of Man in glory (cf. 24:29–31). This dual phenomenon is what scholars today generally refer to as the "already–not yet" nature of the kingdom. Jesus has *already* inaugurated the kingdom, but it has *not yet* reached its final form.[15] As we proceed through Matthew, we will try to understand what exactly Jesus inaugurated and what awaits fulfillment. The kingdom is now present with the arrival of the messianic king of the line of David, and its arrival will confront a variety of expectations among those who

---

14. As Cranfield states, "The kingdom of God has come close to men in the person of Jesus, and in his person it actually confronts them" (C. E. B. Cranfield, *The Gospel According to St Mark* [CGTC; Cambridge: Cambridge Univ. Press, 1972], 68).

15. While there is diversity of opinion as to what was fulfilled in Jesus' first advent and what awaits his second, the "already–not yet" general position is a large consensus. For the most complete survey of recent positions, see Mark Saucy, *The Kingdom of God in the Teaching of Jesus: In Twentieth Century Theology* (Dallas: Word, 1997). For a brief overview of widely held evangelical perspectives, see the March 1992 issue of *JETS*, in which is an article by George R. Beasley-Murray, "The Kingdom of God in the Teaching of Jesus," *JETS* 35 (1992): 19–30, a response by Craig Blomberg (31–36), a rejoinder by Beasley-Murray (37–38), and a separate article by Carl F. H. Henry, "Reflections on the Kingdom of God," 39–49.

experience its impact. But some of what others expected to occur immediately—especially full judgment and restoration—awaits final fulfillment.

## Jesus Messiah Calls Fishers of Men (4:18–22)

THE KINGDOM OF God advances in a unique way as Jesus walks along the shore of the sea of Galilee, probably near Capernaum, and calls fishermen to join him.[16] The "Sea of Galilee," located about sixty miles north of Jerusalem, is called "Sea of Kinnereth" in the Old Testament.[17] Elsewhere in the New Testament it called (1) the "Sea of Tiberias" (John 6:1; 21:1), because Herod Antipas's capital city, Tiberias, lay on the west shore; (2) "Lake of Gennesaret" (Luke 5:1), derived from a town and plain by that name situated above the west/northwest shore;[18] and (3) sometimes simply "the lake" (Luke 5:2; 8:22; 23:33).

This lake is located in the great Jordan rift valley, at least 636 feet below sea level. The Jordan River enters the lake in the north and exits to the south, where it finally terminates in the Dead Sea about 65 miles to the south. Ancient writers all acclaim the Sea of Galilee for its fresh waters and pleasant temperatures, unlike the Dead Sea. It had clear sandy beaches rather than swampy marshes along the seashore, and it was well stocked with fish.[19] The lake's low elevation provides it with relatively mild, year-round temperatures, so that people could sleep outdoors in the surrounding areas (e.g., 15:32; Mark 8:2). However, encompassed as it is with mountain ranges to the east and west that rise over 2,650 feet from the level of the lake, its low-lying setting results in sudden violent downdrafts and storms (cf. Matt. 8:24; Mark 4:37; Luke 8:23; John 6:18).[20]

As Jesus walks along, he sees two men, Simon Peter and Andrew his brother, "casting a net" (lit., "throwing a cast net") into the sea (4:18). The "cast net" (*amphiblestron*) was used by a single fisherman. It was circular, about 20–25 feet in diameter, with lead sinkers attached to the outer edge. Gathering the net on his arm, the fisherman would throw it out onto the water, either while standing in a boat or in shallow water. The net was pulled down by the

---

16. The connection of Jesus' message with the immediate ministry context in Matthew's narrative is highlighted by Warren Carter, "Narrative/Literary Approaches to Matthean Theology: The 'Reign of the Heavens' As an Example (Mt. 4.17–5.12)," *JSNT* 67 (September 1997): 3–27.

17. Num. 34:11; Deut. 3:17; Josh. 12:3; 13:27.

18. "Lake Gennesaret" is a Hellenized version of the Hebrew "Lake of Kinnereth."

19. Strabo, *Geography* 16.2; Pliny, *Natural History* 5.15, 71; Josephus, *J.W.* 3.506.

20. See Seán Freyne, *Galilee from Alexander the Great to Hadrian: A Study of Second Temple Judaism* (Wilmington: Michael Glazier, 1980); idem, "Galilee, Sea of," *ABD*, 2:900; Rainer Riesner, "Archeology and Geography," *DJG*, 37.

sinkers on the outer ring (like a parachute), sinking to the bottom with fish trapped inside. This is tedious work.[21]

Jesus approaches these men and calls out, "Come, follow me ... and I will make you fishers of men" (4:19). Surprisingly, in the middle of their workday, they immediately leave their nets and follow him (4:20). The expression "left their nets" implies that they are leaving behind everything, including livelihood and home. Peter states it emphatically later: "We have left everything to follow you!" (19:27). Peter turns his home, in which his wife and mother-in-law live (cf. 8:14–15), into the base of operations for Jesus' Galilean ministry. They heed Jesus' call to change their primary occupation from fishing for fish to fishing for human souls.

Next, Jesus sees a bit farther down the beach two other brothers, James and John, the sons of Zebedee, who are mending their fishing nets (*diktya*) in their boat with their father. These nets are most likely the trammel net, which is a compound net of three layers, made up of five units each over a hundred feet long, which were used by at least two crews of boats at night when the fish couldn't see the entangling nets.[22] The recent extraordinary discovery in 1986 of an ancient fishing boat at Galilee from the time of Jesus gives us an idea of the kind of boat the sons of Zebedee may have owned. It was equipped for cooking during nightlong commercial fishing expeditions on the lake.[23]

Probably after a night of fishing with their father and others of their hired crew (cf. Mark 1:20), James and John are preparing their nets for the next commercial excursion on the lake. Caring for this equipment took up much of a morning after a night of fishing. But as with Peter and Andrew, Jesus interrupts their busy activities and calls them. They also leave everything behind to follow Jesus, including their boat and their father (4:21–22). By obeying Jesus' call, they are relinquishing commitment to the family business, their assets, and their livelihood, surely having an impact on varied family relationships, responsibilities and obligations.

Several important points underscore the significance of Matthew's account of this scene of Jesus' first public activity. (1) *Focus on Jesus.* The primary focus of this incident is on Jesus and the kingdom of heaven he has announced. The calling scene especially highlights Jesus' authority. When he calls, people

---

21. For full description and illustrations, see Mendel Nun, *The Sea of Galilee and Its Fishermen in the New Testament* (Kibbutz Ein Gev: Kinneret Sailing Co., 1989), 23–37; idem, "Cast Your Net Upon the Waters: Fish and Fishermen in Jesus' Time," *BAR* 19/6 (1993): 52–53.

22. Nun, *The Sea of Galilee and its Fishermen*, 16–44.

23. For the fascinating story of the discovery and excavation of the boat by the lead excavator, see Shelley Wachsmann, *The Sea of Galilee Boat: An Extraordinary 2000 Year Old Discovery* (New York: Plenum, 1995).

obey. It is by virtue of Jesus' authority alone that one can embark on the life of discipleship and sustain it.[24] Jesus is the Spirit-anointed messianic Son, in whom the kingdom has arrived. The only appropriate response is to obey immediately.

(2) *Kingdom workers.* Jesus is enlisting workers to join him in his kingdom mission and offers a promising outcome: "I will make you fishers of men" (4:19). In the future, "they will be as effective in seeking men as they have been in catching fish."[25] They not only will be sent out on a short-term mission with Jesus' message of the arrival of the kingdom (cf. 10:5–7), but they also will go out on a worldwide mission making disciples of all the nations (28:18–20). These four will become the inner circle among the Twelve around Jesus (see comments on 10:1–4), and Peter himself will provide much of the leadership in the early days of the apostolic church (see comments on 16:17–20).[26]

(3) *A prior relationship.* It is important to note that the call and response of the four brothers is based on an extended prior relationship that they had enjoyed with Jesus.[27] This is not the first encounter between them and Jesus. The Fourth Gospel helps to fill in some of the background to the relationship. Andrew was one of the two disciples of John the Baptist who left him to become a disciple of Jesus, and he immediately brought his brother Peter to Jesus (John 1:35–42). The other unnamed disciple has been traditionally identified as the apostle John.[28] In all likelihood at least, Andrew, Peter, and John (and perhaps James?) were the ones who accompanied him to the wedding at Cana, where they observed the miracle and believed in Jesus (2:1–2, 11). They also most likely are the disciples of Jesus who ministered with him in Judea during the first year of his ministry (cf. 3:22–23; 4:1–3).

Thus, by the time of the incidents here in Galilee, about a year later, they have had plenty of time to consider Jesus' mission. We are nowhere told why they had gone back to fishing, but Matthew highlights the urgency of

---

24. Jack Dean Kingsbury, "On Following Jesus: The 'Eager' Scribe and the 'Reluctant' Disciple (Matthew 8.18–22)," *NTS* 34 (1988): 49, states of the calling scene: "It serves to accentuate the great authority with which Jesus calls persons to become His disciples and the absolute obedience and commitment with which those summoned answer His call."

25. David Hill, *The Gospel of Matthew* (NCB; London: Oliphants, 1972), 106.

26. See Warren Carter, "Matthew 4:18–22 and Matthean Discipleship: An Audience-Oriented Perspective," *CBQ* 59 (1997): 58–75.

27. Scot McKnight, *Turning to Jesus: The Sociology of Conversion in the Gospels* (Louisville: Westminster John Knox, 2002), 40–42. I discuss the developing relationship of the disciples to Jesus more fully in Wilkins, *Following the Master*, ch. 6.

28. By remaining unnamed, the author of the Gospel of John gives a subtle signature that he is that unnamed disciple (cf. also "the disciple whom Jesus loved"). See D. A. Carson, *The Gospel According to John* (Grand Rapids: Eerdmans, 1991), 154.

their response to Jesus' call by emphasizing with identical wording in 4:20, 22: (lit.) "immediately leaving . . . they followed him." This was no emotional, spur-of-the-moment decision. They must have been waiting for this momentous occasion to join Jesus as he embarks on his kingdom mission, so they respond at once when he calls.

(4) *Personal commitment to Jesus.* While the emphasis of the story is primarily on calling the four to join in Jesus' kingdom mission, that task is accomplished above all as an outgrowth of their relationship to Jesus: "'Come, follow me,' Jesus said" (4:19). Allegiance to his person is *the* decisive act.[29] But what might this tell us about the spiritual condition of the brothers at the time of their call, and how much do they know about Jesus? As noted, these four had extensive prior acquaintance with Jesus and even believed in him as Messiah (cf. John 1:41; 2:11). We should emphasize that they are responding as much as they can to as much as they understand.[30]

Throughout Jesus' ministry there is an increasing understanding of who he is, and that increased understanding requires a corresponding adjustment of their commitment to him. Comparing incidents in the later ministry, we see Peter making a confession about Jesus' identity that is only at a later point revealed to him (16:16), and the Fourth Gospel tells of an incident some time later in which Peter makes a statement of commitment to Jesus for eternal life (John 6:66–68). As we watch various persons encounter Jesus, we must always recognize that this is a unique time, where the full significance of the entrance of the God-man to history is only slowly comprehended. In fact, it takes the resurrection and Pentecost to finally bring full comprehension. Although the explicit intention of the call is to join Jesus in fishing for men, these brothers are first and foremost being called to commit themselves to Jesus.

(5) *A distinctive call to a unique form of discipleship.* Finally, this "call" sets a distinctive mark on Jesus' form of discipleship. Although Matthew does not here refer to the four as "disciples," they are the ones assumed to be in view when Jesus sits down and teaches his "disciples" in the following scene at the Sermon on the Mount (5:1–2). On the surface, Jesus has many of the characteristics of a Jewish rabbi. He teaches in their synagogues and on the Sabbath, he teaches in accordance with Jewish customs, he is given respect due

---

29. See Leon Morris, "Disciples of Jesus," in *Jesus of Nazareth: Lord and Christ—Essays on the Historical Jesus and New Testament Christology*, ed. Joel B. Green and Max Turner (Grand Rapids: Eerdmans, 1994), 116; Eduard Schweizer, *Lordship and Discipleship*, rev. ed. (SBT 28; Naperville, Illinois: Allenson, 1960), 20.

30. For a critical analysis of Gospel perspectives on Peter's call, see S. O. Abogunrin, "The Three Variant Accounts of Peter's Call: A Critical and Theological Examination of the Texts," *NTS* 31 (1985): 587–602.

a teacher of the law, his disciples follow him around, and he is even called "rabbi" (26:49; Mark 9:5; John 1:49).

But as Jesus' ministry unfolds, he establishes a form of discipleship that is unlike that of the rabbis. The normal pattern in Israel was for a prospective disciple to approach a rabbi and ask to study with him (e.g., 8:19).[31] Later rabbinic disciples followed their master around, often imitating the master's teaching of Torah, because "imitating the master is imitating Moses' imitation of God."[32] In the early stage of the Jesus movement various people came to Jesus in similar fashion (e.g., John 1:38, 49; 3:2). But at the inauguration of his kingdom mission, Jesus establishes a new pattern, because he is the one who takes the initiative to seek out and call these brothers to enter into a permanent relationship with him.[33]

Even though it is probable that Jesus' disciples memorized much of his teaching and passed it on as the tradition of the church, they were ultimately committed to his person, not just his teaching. The goal of a Jewish disciple was someday to become a master, or rabbi, himself, and to have his own disciples. But Jesus' disciples were always to remain disciples of their Master and Teacher, Jesus, and to follow him only (cf. 23:1–12). This had long-reaching implications. Discipleship to Jesus was going to be different from what many might have anticipated. It was not going to be simply an apprenticeship program. Discipleship was a life that began in relationship with the Master and moved into all areas of their experience. This is the beginning of kingdom life.[34]

## Jesus Messiah Displays the Gospel of the Kingdom (4:23–25)

ONCE JESUS CALLS the four brothers to join him in fishing for human souls, he embarks on the first of at least three extensive ministry tours in Galilee, an area with a population of around three hundred thousand people in two hundred or more villages and towns. Matthew gives an insightful summary of the activities on that tour: "Jesus went throughout Galilee, teaching in their synagogues, preaching the good news of the kingdom, and healing every disease and sickness among the people." That summary is largely duplicated in 9:35, forming a literary device often called an "inclusio," a sort of

---

31. Joshua b. Perahyah said, "Provide thyself with a teacher and get thee a fellow disciple" (*ʾAbot* 1.6), which Rabban Gamaliel echoed, "Provide thyself with a teacher and remove thyself from doubt" (*ʾAbot* 1.16).

32. Jacob Neusner, *Invitation to the Talmud: A Teaching Book* (New York: Harper & Row, 1973), 70.

33. Martin Hengel, *The Charismatic Leader and His Followers* (New York: Crossroad, 1981), 42–57.

34. Wilkins, *Following the Master*, 100–109, 124–25.

bookends that emphasize the material in the chapters between them. In chapters 5–7 Jesus is presented as the *Messiah in word* in the incomparable Sermon on the Mount, and in chapters 8–9 Jesus is presented as the *Messiah at work* in the collection of miracle stories. Presenting Jesus in this way, Matthew's readers will know clearly the nature of the kingdom of heaven that Jesus has inaugurated.

The threefold profile of Jesus' ministry is highlighted by three participles and their objects. (1) "Teaching" is often related to explanation of truth to those already familiar with the content: Jesus will "teach" the disciples in the Sermon on the Mount (see comments on 5:1–2).

(2) "Preaching" is generally related to the proclamation of truth to those unfamiliar with the content. The gospel of the kingdom will be "preached" to the world as a witness to the Gentiles (24:14). While too much can be made of either the distinction or the overlap between teaching and preaching, [35] their juxtaposition here may indicate the variation of methods Jesus employed on different occasions for different types of audience. When in the Jewish synagogues, Jesus clarified the nature of his message from the Old Testament Scriptures, demonstrating that he was the expected messianic deliverer (cf. Luke 4:16–30). When he was in the countryside, where there were likely many not proficient in the Old Testament Scriptures, Jesus gave a straightforward proclamation of the message.

At the core of all Jesus' teaching and preaching is the message of the "gospel of the kingdom" (4:23). Matthew uses the noun "gospel" (*euangelion*) only four times, and three of them occur in the phrase "the gospel of the kingdom," found only in Matthew.[36] The real "good news" is that the age of the kingdom of God has finally dawned in the ministry of Jesus.

Matthew speaks of "their" synagogues (4:23), which may reflect the time of his writing, when Christians have already begun to meet separately from their Jewish compatriots to worship in a distinctly Christian setting. Or it may reflect the distinction that occurred early between the Jewish leadership and Jesus. The religious leaders, especially the Pharisees and teachers of the law who had their greatest following from the synagogues, early on set themselves in opposition to Jesus and his message, and the phrase "their synagogues" may show the separation between them and Jesus (see 9:35; 10:17; 12:9; 13:54; cf. 23:34).[37]

---

35. For an overview of recent discussion of these two words, see J. I. H. McDonald, *Kerygma and Didache: The Articulation and Structure of the Earliest Christian Message* (SNTSMS 37; Cambridge: Cambridge Univ. Press, 1980).

36. See 4:23; 9:35; 24:14. Many translations render the phrase in Luke 16:16 as "good news of the kingdom" (NIV) or "gospel of the kingdom" (NASB), but this is actually different from Matthew's expression. Luke uses the verb *euangelizo*, not the noun *euangelion*.

37. Morris, *Matthew*, 86.

(3) This good news is not only taught and preached, but it is also demonstrated through Jesus' "healing" every disease and sickness among the people. Healing signals once again that Jesus has authority over the powers of this world and confirms the arrival of the kingdom of God (11:4–6). "Every disease and sickness" indicates that nothing is beyond Jesus' ability to heal, an authority he will likewise give to the Twelve on their mission tour in Israel (10:1). These healings take place "among the people [*laos*]," the term that specifies the people of Israel. Both proclamation and miracle announce that Israel's hoped-for kingdom promise is at hand.

The response to Jesus' teaching, preaching, and healing is stunning. As news of his ministry spreads outside the borders of Galilee, even to the Gentile region of Syria in the north (4:24), people begin bringing to Jesus those beset with all kinds of afflictions. Matthew emphasizes the impact of Jesus' comprehensive healing ministry by stacking up a list of illnesses: "those suffering severe pain," the "demon-possessed" (indicating Jesus' continuing power over the devil's realm), "epileptics" (an illness associated with demon-possession in 17:14–21), and "paralytics" (a distressing affliction at a time when foot-travel was most common). Matthew's recurring focus on healing[38] emphasizes throughout the narrative that the arrival of the kingdom is confirmed by Jesus' power over all realms of human existence, spiritual, physical, or emotional.

Great crowds respond to Jesus' healing ministry by following him. The term "follow" has just described the response of the four brothers to Jesus' call, so we might assume that Matthew considers the crowds also to have entered into a discipleship relationship with Jesus. But in the immediately following introduction to the Sermon on the Mount, Matthew makes a distinction between the crowds and the disciples. Therefore, to "follow" Jesus can be understood in a metaphorical sense to describe discipleship, but it is also used in a spatial sense to describe literal movement. The context will determine how Matthew is using it on any particular occasion.[39]

The crowds who now follow Jesus have responded to his message and healing ministry with enough interest and enthusiasm to come from all over the surrounding regions. They come not only from Galilee but also from the Roman region of the Decapolis, which is the generally Gentile district to the south and east of the Sea of Galilee. Crowds also arrive from the center of Jewish life in Jerusalem and Judea. Moreover, part of the crowd also

---

38. Matthew uses the term for "heal" (*therapeuo*) sixteen times, more than in any other New Testament book (Hagner, *Matthew 1–13*, 81).

39. See Wilkins, *The Concept of Disciple in Matthew's Gospel*, 148–50, 170–71; Jack Dean Kingsbury, "The Verb AKOLOUTHEIN ('To Follow') as an Index of Matthew's View of His Community," *JBL* 97 (1978): 56–73.

comes from the region known as "beyond the Jordan," a common expression to designate the region of Perea, or more generally the territory north and east of the Jordan River.[40]

The areas that Matthew names in 4:24–25 take the reader to the regions that encompass the whole of the area that is populated with Jewish people. While some of these regions were populated extensively with Gentiles (e.g., the Decapolis), it is doubtful that Matthew means to imply that there is a widespread Gentile following. Those coming to Jesus are still primarily Jews, but they come from everywhere. Jesus is generating a tremendous stir in Israel with his message of the arrival of the kingdom, which has been validated by such widespread healings.

JESUS AT CENTER STAGE. The story that Matthew recounts has a variety of settings and characters that move on and off the narrative stage. If we think back through chapters 1–4, several situations and persons immediately spring to mind. In the remote village of Nazareth, Joseph, with his remarkable integrity, takes center stage in chapter 1 as he receives the announcement of the miraculous conception of his betrothed, Mary. In chapter 2, several diverse scenes and characters receive the limelight: the Magi arriving from the east, evil King Herod carrying out his dastardly deeds from the holy city of Jerusalem, Joseph heroically saving the threatened child and mother by fleeing Bethlehem to go to Egypt and then returning to Nazareth.

From the Judean desert John the Baptist makes a grand entrance in chapter 3 as the long-awaited prophet who commands repentance from the people of Israel, including the religious leaders. At the Jordan River the descent of the Spirit and the voice of the Father add dramatic effect to the baptismal scene of Jesus. We hiss in chapter 4 as the epitome of evil arrives on the stage in the person of the devil, but we applaud as he is beaten in the first skirmish of the war between Jesus and Satan. By the Sea of Galilee, we try to put ourselves in the sandals of the four fishermen as they amazingly sacrifice their livelihood to go fish for souls. Excitement rises as people from all over Galilee and the surrounding regions experience healing from many maladies.

Each of these scenes and characters captures our attention as the story unfolds—and rightly they should, since each plays an important role in the

---

40. See Bastiaan Van Elderen, "Early Christianity in Transjordan," *TynBul* 45 (1994): 97–117. Van Elderen suggests that this indicates the area of northern Transjordan, which would comport with the summary reference to "all of Syria" in 4:24.

historical narration. However, as we think back through these characters, one figure often is left out of the picture—Jesus. We are often so focused on other characters and details of the narrative scene because of what we can learn from them that we overlook the one about whom the entire story is told. Jesus almost seems to recede into the backdrop.

But as we discussed in 1:18–25, although we will learn from the roles of other characters and the scenes in which they appear, center stage always belongs to Jesus. From 1:1, where he is declared to be the culmination of the line of David and of Abraham, to 28:20, where he declares that he will be with his disciples until the end of the age, Jesus is the One about whom this entire Gospel is written.

Although this may seem obvious, unfortunately it is a fundamental hermeneutical principle that is violated on a regular basis by those reading the Gospels and by those teaching or preaching from them. In our search to make the bridge from the text to our world, we can be so focused on the supporting cast and details that most intrigue us that we look right past the primary figure about whom the story was written. Although other characters and the scenes in which they appear serve an invaluable role by highlighting various facets of Jesus and his ministry, first and foremost Matthew tells a story about Jesus.[41] This is evident from the present passage, as Matthew features significant truths about Jesus from the setting of his ministry, the four supporting figures, and the multitudes who respond to him.

**Galilee.** Surprisingly, the scene where Jesus conducts his public ministry is Galilee. One familiar with Israel's history may have expected Messiah to focus his ministry on Jerusalem, the center of religious power and prestige and prophetic hope. Galilee is the antithesis of Jerusalem. But Jesus does not associate with the high and the mighty, and he does not attend to the religious hierarchy. He goes to the land of darkness, where the light of the gospel will shine the brightest. The prophetic hope of Isaiah 9:1–6 will be fulfilled, but it begins in Galilee, far from Jerusalem, where many hoped the restoration of power and glory would come to the house of David. It is in Galilee that the hint of the Old Testament hope for all the nations begins. The incidents unfolding in Galilee require that the people's expectations of the messianic ministry must be adjusted.

**The brothers.** The response of the two sets of brothers is hugely significant, but only because of what it tells us about Jesus' call. Their response is

---

41. This is a basic principle for reading any of the Gospels, which Robert Stein illustrates from Mark: "The Gospel of Mark is a Gospel about Jesus. From Mark 1:1 to 16:8 Jesus is the focus of attention. There is no narrative in the book that does not in some way center on him. He is the main content, the focus, and the object of the entire Gospel" (*Playing by The Rules: A Basic Guide to Interpreting the Bible* [Grand Rapids: Baker, 1994], 159).

remarkable evidence that Jesus wields a different kind of messianic authority. Without army, without sword, and without the backing of the religious establishment, Jesus' authority as the inaugurator of the kingdom demands unqualified obedience. When he calls, people must obey. Matthew's abrupt narration of the calling of the four brothers assumes a prior relationship with Jesus, and they join Jesus as fellow workers in his kingdom mission.

But Matthew's account of the call is general enough that it could summon readers at various stages of faith—for example, the person being called to repentance and faith in Jesus as the messianic Savior, or the person hearing a call to leadership in the church, or the person being called to repent of half-hearted devotion and give himself or herself fully to Jesus. Discipleship to Jesus is different from what is found among relationships to other religious leaders. Jesus is the authoritative inaugurator of the kingdom, which indicates for Matthew's readers that their lives will find true fulfillment only as they follow Jesus' call to join him in the advancement of the kingdom of God.

**The crowds.** The crowds are also evidence of the nature of Jesus' identity and ministry, but their testimony is mixed. On the one hand, the crowds are an enthusiastic witness that the inauguration of the kingdom includes compassionate care for all of the vagaries of the fallen human condition: physical, emotional, and spiritual. Jesus heals all types of conditions. But on the other hand, the enthusiasm of the crowds is fickle. The response of the crowds at first seems to set an assured, optimistic future for Jesus' ministry.

But we know a different ending. What happened to change the response of the crowds? Apparently the initial enthusiasm was more of a testimony to their own needs being met than a testimony of their commitment to Jesus as Messiah. Perhaps Matthew wants to encourage his own audience that appearances can be deceiving. If the crowd that followed Jesus enthusiastically at the beginning could turn and reject him at the end, then the response to Matthew's readers' mission may need a "reality check." The initial response of the crowds is not the final validation of Jesus' messianic ministry.[42]

THE APPROPRIATE BRIDGE from the narrative of Matthew's text to contemporary significance lies in determining what the various characters and settings tell us about Jesus and his historical ministry. When we have traversed that bridge, we are much more likely to draw appropriate significance for our own situations. Three points surface from the inauguration of Jesus' ministry to Israel.

---

42. Warren Carter, "The Crowds in Matthew's Gospel," *CBQ* 55 (1993): 54–67.

**The light that dispels darkness brings life.** The geographical region into which Jesus goes to initiate his ministry was Galilee of the Gentiles, which Matthew says is metaphorically a land of darkness, a land under the shadow of death. But the sun doesn't shine any less brightly in Galilee than in Jerusalem or Bethlehem. The disease rate in Galilee is no higher than Judea or even Samaria. Rather, "darkness" in both the Old and New Testaments is an evocative word. If light symbolizes God, darkness connotes everything that is anti-God: the wicked (Prov. 2:13–14; 1 Thess. 5:4–7), judgment (Ex. 10:21; Matt. 25:30), and death (Ps. 88:13).

But few in Galilee can see the darkness or the shadow of death. The Galilee region to this day is one of the most beautiful areas in all of Palestine. The magnificent lake, flowing rivers, rolling hillsides, and luscious agriculture all are found in Galilee. The mansions and theater at Sepphoris and the palaces and stadium at Tiberias indicate that Galilee was not a cultural backwater. Nonetheless, the darkness of this world is real, even though most do not notice it. It is a region under the influence of Gentiles, with their gods, their lifestyles, their worldview.

Although darkness is opaque to humankind, it is transparent to God (Ps. 139:12), and long ago he promised to send light. With the arrival of Jesus a great light now shines in the darkness (Matt. 4:16). Those responding to the light were ushered into the sphere of life in which darkness and even the shadow of death are dispelled (cf. Job 22:28; Ps. 27:1). Other New Testament authors emphasize this theme, declaring that Jesus is life-giving light in whom is life (John 1:4), and those who follow him "will never walk in darkness but will have the light of life" (John 8:12). Believers are "sons of light" (John 12:36; Eph. 5:8) and "children of light" (1 Thess. 5:5). Light possesses powers essential to true life, so "to be in the light" comes to mean simply "to live." This indicates life eternal, but also life temporal on earth. The one who comes into the light of Jesus Messiah is brought into the life that is characterized by light.[43]

This is an essential theme for us to lay hold of. The darkness of our own world is real even when we, or those around us, don't notice it. Darkness is most directly the absence of light, so to be away from Jesus is to be in darkness. This is a necessary perspective to maintain as we go about our day-to-day activities. We don't have to be among the dregs of society to find ourselves in darkness. I live in a beautiful little beach community in Southern California, where the sun shines brightly for most days of the year. Yet

---

43. Cf. Luke 16:8; John 3:19ff.; 12:36; 2 Cor. 6:14; Col. 1:12–13; 1 Thess. 5:5; 1 Peter 2:9. Michael J. Wilkins, "Darkness," "Light," *Baker Theological Dictionary of the Bible*, ed. Walter A. Elwell (Grand Rapids: Baker, 1996), 142–43, 486–87.

even in the brightness of this little world, people are without Jesus and are living under the cloud of the darkness of this world. We can't let the superficial appearances of people mask the real needs that even they might not recognize. To reach them most effectively we must take as our calling the joy of living in the light of Jesus and continually allowing our lives to shine into theirs with the true kingdom life.

**Jesus' call today.** On the historical level, the call of the brothers serves foremost to highlight Jesus' authority to enlist mission workers as the inaugurator of the kingdom. The brothers' response illustrates how obedience is the only appropriate answer to Jesus' authoritative call. When Jesus calls, we also must obey. Jesus has authority over every area of a disciple's life, and to whatever he calls us, we must immediately obey.

While this does have significance for those who are heeding a call to salvation, because of the significant prior relationship between the brothers and Jesus, we cannot assume that Matthew intends this scene to be understood predominantly as a paradigm for evangelism. As John Calvin states, this is "not merely a general description of the call to faith, but a particular one for a certain task."[44] Modern readers must hear in Jesus' call a challenge for all of us to put aright our lifelong ambitions. These four brothers were already Jesus' disciples, ones who had committed themselves to Jesus as Messiah (cf. John 1:41; 2:2, 11). But in this scene they are being called to put their profession in proper perspective in the light of the needs of reaching their world with the message of salvation. As the four are ultimately called to a role as apostles in the foundation of the church, they personally will be required to leave their prior profession.

But not every disciple of Jesus is called to leave behind his or her profession. One of the more striking examples we will see later is Joseph of Arimathea, who was a disciple of Jesus but retained his position in society, along with his great wealth, and offered an indispensable service to Jesus at the moment of greatest need that only he could offer (cf. 27:57–60). Whatever our profession, whether preacher or plumber, teacher or technician, hotel maid or hospital orderly, discipleship means that we place as the priority of our lives joining with Jesus in reaching our daily world with the good news of life in the kingdom of heaven. I cannot reach non-Christian police officers as efficiently as committed Christian police officers. No pastor can enter into the complex world of corporate finance as effectively as a committed and knowledgeable Christian businessperson. We each have a privileged place of ministry that is unique to following Jesus in our own daily lives.

---

44. John Calvin, *A Harmony of the Gospels Matthew, Mark and Luke* (Grand Rapids: Eerdmans, 1972), 1:572.

Nor does the brothers' immediate obedience deny common sense or appropriate accountability to their personal, familial, and professional responsibilities. Although they "left everything," Peter continues to live in his own home with his wife and mother-in-law, and likely so does his brother Andrew and his family (8:14–15). There is a sense in which Peter and the rest of the Twelve give up everything to play their foundational role in the church, yet we never hear of them abandoning their responsibilities to provide for their families. The apostle Paul will later rebuke believers who were ministerial busybodies and did not care for the needs of their family (2 Thess. 3:6–13; 1 Tim. 5:8).

On one level the passage gives insight to the historical circumstances of Jesus' announcement of the kingdom of heaven and his recruitment of four crucial partners in that historically unique pronouncement. Yet the incident is a paradigm for disciples of all ages to recognize that we must see ourselves as fishers of men in whatever our calling. Our lives find fullest meaning as we follow Jesus' call to join him in advancing the kingdom of heaven.

**A life-transforming message of the kingdom of God.** Al Green is a modern-day "fisherman." He was the superstar singer of soul hits in the 1970s, such as "Love and Happiness" and "Let's Stay Together." As uplifting as those early melodies were, he experienced a change in his career path that brought an even more powerful message in song. He was "born again" at the height of his popularity, and today he is "the Reverend Al Green," pastor of a church in Memphis, Tennessee, where he sings hits like "Saved," and "Straighten Out Your Life." An interviewer for a secular magazine seemed stumped by the transformation he saw in Green's life, which he describes as "his chameleon-like nature."[45]

But the tale of Green's life is not simply a decision to change styles of music. In his words, it was a calling. While performing a soul concert in Cincinnati in 1979, he slipped from the stage, miraculously avoiding serious injury. Al Green interpreted the event as a calling from God to retire from secular music and lift his voice in praise unto God.[46] His calling brought peaceful wholeness to his life, where he could use his natural talent in the service of the kingdom of God. The rewards of fame don't hold the same attraction, he says. "Now they have become unimportant to me. The riches are in the souls of men."[47]

Whether or not our calling is as dramatic as Al Green's, the story of the ancient call of the four fishermen provides enough incentive for each of us

---

45. Richard Todd, "Let's Pray Together," *Civilization: The Magazine of the Library of Congress* (February–March 1999), 48.

46. Testimony given about Al Green from his personal website at www.algreen.com.

47. Quote from Todd, "Let's Pray Together," 48.

to recognize our responsibility to serve Jesus in the mission of the kingdom of God. Jesus describes his disciples as light and light-bearers (Matt. 5:14–16), and Paul indicates to the churches in Asia Minor and Macedonia that believer's lives are a shining light of witness to the world around them (Eph. 5:8; Phil. 2:15). So it is our task now to pass on the divine light we have received, because the world out there will die eternally without it. What we have received in the secret intimacy of the community of believers we are to proclaim fearlessly "in the light" (Matt. 10:27; Luke 12:3). All those who have entered into the light now bear the responsibility as missionaries of Christ, shining out as "lights in a dark world" with the light of Jesus himself (Phil. 2:15).

In a chapel message at our seminary, guest speaker and pastor E. V. Hill made the statement that the church throughout the centuries has struggled with the temptation to be "keepers of the aquarium instead of fishers of men." Those words hit home to each of us in attendance. There is a world of hurt outside the walls of our churches and organizations, but we can be so intent on building our ministries that we don't go to where people are hurting. Instead, we just take care of our own. As Jesus' disciples, we all have the incredible privilege, and obligation, to carry the message of the gospel of the kingdom to those who live in the darkness all around us.

# Matthew 5:1–2

NOW WHEN HE saw the crowds, he went up on a mountainside and sat down. His disciples came to him, ²and he began to teach them, saying:

THE INITIAL PHASE of Jesus' ministry has been narrated briefly yet powerfully: Jesus announced his kingdom mission (4:17), called his first coworkers (4:18–22), and conducted an extraordinary teaching, preaching, and healing tour of Galilee (4:22–25). Matthew now records an extensive message that develops in detail the kind of life available to those who respond to the arrival of God's kingdom.

Matthew has a special interest in Jesus' messages. While Mark and Luke give summaries of several different messages and John's Gospel records the extended Upper Room Discourse Jesus gave on the night before his crucifixion, Matthew has preserved for us five major messages or discourses, which alternate with narratives about Jesus' activities. As discussed in the introduction, these discourses are a key to understanding at least one of Matthew's purposes for writing his Gospel. He has gathered together a collection of Jesus' messages that enable the church for all ages to carry out a crucial component of Jesus' final commission: "teaching them to obey everything I have commanded you" (28:20).

This first of Jesus' discourses, traditionally called the Sermon on the Mount (SM), is undoubtedly the most widely known. From the time Jesus first uttered these words up to the present day, people from all backgrounds and traditions have been galvanized by its potent expression of the moral and ethical life. In the twentieth century, Mohandas K. Gandhi, the Hindu *Mahatma* (Sanskrit for "Great Soul"), was profoundly influenced by this Sermon as he established India's freedom through a nonviolent revolution. Likewise, Martin Luther King Jr., the American Protestant preacher who became a legendary international civil rights leader, strove to make the teachings of the Sermon the basis of his political program and his ideological commitment to nonviolence and civil disobedience.

This Sermon as recorded in Matthew 5–7 is almost certainly a summary of a much longer one. One can read through it in thirty minutes or less. Jesus' regular practice was to spend extended time teaching and preaching, to the point that on at least two occasions he spent an entire day speaking to the multitudes and ended up miraculously feeding five thousand and four thousand (14:13–21; 15:32–38). But this summary is not just a collection of randomly selected thoughts. The structure of this message is a unified whole.

The context of the SM is Jesus' inauguration of the kingdom of heaven. As the one born "king of the Jews" (2:2) and as one who has demonstrated power over sickness and the devil (4:23–25; cf. 9:35; 10:1), Jesus gives a powerful statement of the reality and availability of kingdom life for his followers, which includes practical instruction on how to carry out kingdom life. Thus, at the center of the SM is Jesus' message about the kingdom of heaven. Its opening words speak of the kingdom of heaven as a present possession (5:3, 10), declare different levels of status for those in the kingdom (5:19), and announce the terms of entering it (5:20). The model prayer Jesus teaches his disciples has the coming of the kingdom as its central theme (6:10), and his admonition related to daily priorities of life emphasizes seeking first the kingdom (6:33). The ultimate reward for those who truly know Jesus and do the will of his Father is to enter the kingdom of heaven (7:21–23).

The discourse gets its name from the geographical setting, "on a mountain" somewhere in Galilee (5:1). The traditional site, as well as the most recent consensus, identifies it above Tabghah, near Capernaum, on a ridge of hills just to the west of the town. This ridge is likely the place referred to in the Gospels where Jesus went "into a solitary [*eremos*] place" (14:13; cf. Mk 1:35). Ancient tradition named the top of the hill "Eremos." At the foot of Eremos lies the area of seven springs, which carried the Greek name *Heptapegon* ("Seven Springs"), later roughly transliterated into Arabic as *et-Tabgha*.[1] Eremos offers a magnificent overview of the Sea of Galilee and the surrounding villages. The cragginess of the hill meant it was left uncultivated, which could have enabled Jesus to gather large crowds around him without causing damage to the surrounding farmlands.[2]

Jesus goes to a mountain as a special place of divine revelation several times for significant events in Matthew's narrative.[3] Expositors have wondered whether Matthew draws parallels with Old Testament incidents or themes, such as Moses' going up to Mount Sinai to receive the Law (Ex. 19–20).[4] It is

---

1. Pixner, *With Jesus Through Galilee*, 34. Pixner also equates the place with Magadan (see comments on 15:39).

2. Ibid., 36.

3. E.g., the mountain of temptation (4:8); this mountain (5:1–2); the mountain of transfiguration (17:1); the mountain of olives (24:3); the mountain of resurrection appearance and commission (28:16).

4. The most complete recent study is Terence L. Donaldson, *Jesus on the Mountain: A Study in Matthean Theology* (JSNTSup 8; Sheffield: JSOT, 1985).

doubtful, however, that Jesus is to be seen as a new Moses giving a new Torah in the five discourses, as some have suggested. Jesus does not give a new law; rather, he is the One whose life and teaching fulfills the law (cf. 5:17–20). If anything, he is contrasted with the oral traditions of the scribes and Pharisees. Jesus, the authoritative Messiah, fulfills the intention of the Law, because his teaching penetrates to the full meaning of God's commandments.[5]

Matthew's wording to specify the audience of the SM is important. Jesus sees the crowds, then goes up on the mountain and sits down. Sitting down is the typical position from which a teacher in Judaism taught (cf. 23:2), a position Jesus takes regularly (cf. 13:1–2; 15:29; 24:3–4; 26:55). His disciples then come to him, and "opening his mouth" (KJV, another Jewish idiom), he begins to teach them. Since the nearest antecedent to "them" is "his disciples," Matthew specifies that Jesus leaves the crowds so that he can teach his disciples. Who are the "crowds" and who are the "disciples"? What is the significance of his teaching the disciples, not the crowds?

"Crowd" (*ochlos*) is the same term used to designate the large group of people who followed Jesus around in 4:25. The term "disciple" (*mathetes*) occurs here for the first time in Matthew; almost certainly they are the four brothers who have just been called to follow Jesus (4:18–22), along with any others who have made a commitment to him by this time. The designation "disciple" was a general term used to represent a follower of a variety of different kinds of masters within Judaism, but Jesus fashioned its use throughout his ministry in a unique way to describe his own followers.

Matthew specifies three primary groups of people around Jesus in his earthly ministry: his disciples, the religious leaders, and the crowds.[6] The *disciples* are those who have made a commitment to Jesus as the Messiah. The *religious leaders* are Jesus' opponents for much of his ministry, represented especially by the Pharisees (12:22–32). The *crowd* is basically neutral, a curious group of people who are astounded by his teaching and ministry (7:28–29) but who have not yet made a commitment to him.

Jesus' objective was to make disciples from among the crowd. As he teaches and preaches, the sign of faith is when one comes out of the crowd to call Jesus "Lord," at which time that person becomes a disciple/believer (cf. 8:18, 21; 17:14–15). At first the crowds are amazed at Jesus' teaching (7:28–29) and miracles (9:8) and receive his compassionate attention (9:35–38; 14:13–14). But they increasingly demonstrate hardness of heart (cf. 13:2–3,

---

5. So also Hagner, *Matthew 1–13*, 86. For a cautious exploration of the Mosaic theme, see Davies and Allison, *Matthew*, 1:422–24.

6. Wilkins, *The Concept of Disciple in Matthew's Gospel*, esp. 163–72; idem, *Following the Master*, 179–83. For a similar perspective, see Cousland, *The Crowds in the Gospel of Matthew*.

10–17, 34–36), until at the end the religious leaders persuade the crowd to ask for the death of Jesus (27:15–25). At this early point in his ministry, Jesus will teach the disciples in the Sermon, but he will also have an eye on the crowd, extending to them an invitation to become disciples.

We should emphasize as well that the "disciples" are not identical to the "Twelve," because some of them have yet to be called (e.g., Matthew the tax collector in 9:9; cf. 10:2–4). The Twelve are a more restricted group within the larger group of Jesus' disciples. Note Luke 6:13: "When morning came, he called his disciples to him and chose twelve of them, whom he also designated apostles." The term *disciple* here designates those who have come to believe in Jesus, while the term *apostle* designates specific disciples as leaders of the church to come.[7] As disciples the Twelve are like any others who have responded to Jesus' call to eternal life in the kingdom, but as apostles they have responded to an additional call to leadership (cf. 10:1–2).

Since Jesus' teaching in the SM is designed primarily for disciples, it can be designated as training in discipleship. It is the first basic instruction for those who have made a commitment to Jesus and his proclamation of the gospel of the kingdom. In addition, the SM also contains at certain points an invitation to the crowd to enter the kingdom of heaven (e.g., 5:20; 7:28–29).

**Relationship to Luke's "Sermon on the Plain" (Luke 6:17–49).** A message with striking similarity occurs in Luke 6:17–49. Both sermons come in the context of Jesus' widespread speaking and healing ministry (Matt. 4:23–25; Luke 6:17–19), both begin with beatitudes, both give significant ethical teaching on love and judging, both emphasize the necessity of bearing fruit, and both conclude with the parable of the builders. But there are significant differences as well. For example, Matthew does not include the "woes" after Luke's beatitudes (Luke 6:24–26), Luke does not include the majority of the antitheses found in Matthew 5:21–48, and Luke's version of the Lord's Prayer does not occur in his sermon but in Luke 11:1–4.

Reconciling the similarities and differences have led to different conclusions by interpreters. (1) The similarities lead some to assert that Matthew and

---

7. Matthew also speaks of disciples other than the Twelve (8:21) and indicates a wider circle of disciples who receive his teaching and obey his radical summons to follow him (10:24–42). He also acknowledges through a related verb the existence of a named disciple other than the Twelve, Joseph of Arimathea (27:57). Moreover, the women who attend Jesus' crucifixion are described with discipleship terms (see comments on 12:46–50; 27:55–56, 61; 28:1–8). For discussion see Michael J. Wilkins, "Named and Unnamed Disciples in Matthew: A Literary/Theological Study," *SBLSP* 30 (Atlanta: Scholars Press, 1991); idem, "Women in the Teaching and Example of Jesus," in *Women and Men in Ministry: A Complementary Perspective*, ed. Robert L. Saucy and Judith K. TenElshof (Chicago: Moody Press, 2001), 91–112; Przybylski, *Righteousness in Matthew*, 108–10.

Luke present two distinct summaries of the same message given by Jesus.[8] (2) The differences lead others to suggest that Matthew and Luke record two different sermons, given by Jesus on separate occasions when he repeated some of the same or similar content.[9] (3) Still others propose that either Matthew or Luke (or both) gathered together teachings that Jesus gave on separate occasions to make one sermon.[10] The latter is usually suggested because there are parallels to Matthew's sermon scattered throughout Luke's Gospel.[11]

Since Matthew and Luke both imply that their sermons were given on one occasion, the third view is less likely. The first view is strengthened by observing the same general context, the general order, and the similar geographical setting (mountainous area) of both sermons.[12] The second view is strengthened by recalling that Jesus went about teaching and preaching all through the countryside of Galilee for nearly two years, and he almost certainly repeated much of the same content on numerous occasions. Since nothing of great importance relies on the solution to this question, it may be best to say that until further insight is gained, either the first or second view is preferable.

**Bridging Contexts**

INTERPRETATIONS OF THE **Sermon on the Mount.** Throughout church history, expositors have subjected the SM to a variety of interpretations.[13] Those interpretations have led to diverse applications, ranging from those who place the SM at the center of their present civil and social agenda to those who limit the applicability of the details of the SM

---

8. E.g., Carson, "Matthew," 125–26; Bock, *Luke 1:1–9:50*, 553; Thomas and Gundry, *The NIV Harmony of the Gospels*, 70–71 note c.

9. E.g., Morris, *Matthew*, 93; Blomberg, *Matthew*, 96.

10. E.g., Hagner, *Matthew 1–13*, 69; Robert A. Guelich, *The Sermon on the Mount: A Foundation for Understanding* (Waco, Tex.: Word, 1982), 35; Hans Dieter Betz, *The Sermon on the Mount: A Commentary on the Sermon on the Mount, Including the Sermon on the Plain (Matthew 5:3–7:27 and Luke 6:20–49)*, ed. Adela Yarbro Collins (Hermeneia; Minneapolis: Fortress, 1995), 44–45.

11. E.g., cf. Matt. 5:13 in Luke 14:34–35; Matt. 5:14 in Luke 11:33, etc. See Hagner, *Matthew 1–13*, 83 for a complete listing.

12. Some contend for one sermon shared by Matthew and Luke by appealing to the existence of the Sermon in the Q source. But since the hypothetical Q may only be the places where Matthew and Luke share material not found in Mark, this begs the question.

13. For brief, helpful overviews of the history of interpretation, see Guelich, *The Sermon on the Mount*, 14–22, and David Crump, "Applying the Sermon on the Mount: Once You Have Read It What Do You Do with It?" *Criswell Theological Review* 6/1 (1992): 3–14. A more extensive survey is found in Warren S. Kissinger, *The Sermon on the Mount: A History of Interpretation and Bibliography* (Metuchen, N.J.: Scarecrow, 1975).

to a future time when Christ reigns on the earth. Each of these interpretations results primarily from understanding the way Jesus intended his kingdom mission to be applied to present-day life. Literally dozens of interpretations have resulted, which may be summarized under the following headings.[14]

(1) *Entrance requirements to the kingdom.* Many have understood Jesus' statements about entering the kingdom (e.g., 5:20) to mean that the SM is primarily an invitation to enter the kingdom of God and that one finds within Jesus' ethical and moral teaching explicit requirements for entering that kingdom. This approach is quite varied, shared at least in part by some within Protestant liberalism, existentialism, and the social reformers. While these approaches do not necessarily advocate a works-legalism adherence to the details of the SM, they do believe that the essence of the SM is to define the means by which one actualizes the kingdom of God. That attainable, essential element may be found in maintaining the sermon's ethical ideal (Adolph Harnack), or in carrying out authentic human existence before God (Søren Kierkegaard), or in achieving the ideal of personal and social nonviolence (Leo Tolstoy).

This approach to the SM acknowledges the radical nature of the kingdom of God that Jesus announces, but it confuses the *results* of participating in kingdom life with the *means* of obtaining kingdom life. The kind of life to which Jesus points in the SM will be the Spirit-empowered result of those who have already responded to the gospel of the kingdom, not the means by which one enters it. The sermon must be read within the context of Jesus' overall earthly ministry, which includes the redemptive work of the cross. Jesus' followers will actualize these ethical and moral ideals, not as a means of entering the kingdom but as an outgrowth of the kingdom life that will be theirs through the empowering of the Spirit.

(2) *An impossible ideal.* Martin Luther recognized that the SM cannot be an articulation of the means of entering the kingdom of God because it is impossible for humans apart from God's grace to carry out its stringent demands. Therefore, he understood the SM to be similar to Paul's statement of the role of the law (Rom. 3–4; Gal. 3). It gives God's perfect expression of his moral will, which is impossible for humans to maintain, and therefore forces us to recognize our sinfulness and cry out for God's grace in repentance.

Luther did not clearly differentiate the audience of the sermon. Jesus addresses disciples who have already responded to his kingdom mission, which includes their prior repentance (3:2; 4:17). While the SM does indeed

---

14. Some of the more helpful summaries are found in Carson, "Matthew," 126–28; W. D. Davies and Dale C. Allison Jr., "Reflections on the Sermon on the Mount," *SJT* 44 (1991): 283–309; and Blomberg, *Matthew*, 94–95. An extensive listing of interpretations is found in Clarence Bauman, *The Sermon on the Mount: The Modern Quest for Its Meaning* (Macon, Ga.: Mercer Univ. Press, 1985).

articulate an ideal that is impossible for fallen humans to attain, it is an ideal that disciples will strive to live out under the grace of God and the power of the Spirit in their everyday world (see 5:48). Jesus not only gives the ideal of the kingdom in the SM, but his description of life in the kingdom includes the enablement to attain the ideal.

(3) *An example for another age.* Other approaches to the SM do not see it as having direct relevance to the present age. Some suggest that Jesus gave these instructions to his disciples as a rigorous emergency ethic to prepare them for the imminent arrival of the kingdom of God with Jesus' return. But since Jesus didn't return, the rigorous ethic of the SM is inappropriate for the present age (Albert Schweitzer). In a completely different direction, others suggest that since Jesus did not establish the literal kingdom of God to Israel at his first advent, the literal application of the SM awaits a future time when the kingdom of heaven will be established on the earth during the millennial reign of Christ (e.g., C. I. Scofield). Both of these views find principles within the SM that present-day believers must heed, but the primary application is for another age.

While these two approaches are poles apart theologically, they both take seriously their understanding of the nature and timing of the establishment of the kingdom. Both generally conclude that Jesus either established the kingdom literally then, or it is not at all present now. However, if we understand the inauguration of the kingdom by Jesus to be a combination of the "already−not yet," then we do not have to go for an either-or extreme that both of these approaches take. As we discussed in Matthew 4, certain aspects of the kingdom were inaugurated with the arrival of Jesus while other aspects await a final fulfillment. Since Jesus teaches his disciples about how their lives are impacted by the arrival of the kingdom, then the SM is addressed in principle to disciples of every age, including now.

(4) *An optional elitism.* Several others suggest that the SM was given for a select group of highly committed believers pursuing a higher standard of ethical and moral life. This view was suggested by the medieval theologian Thomas Aquinas, who claimed that there were two levels in Jesus' teaching. One level was for the average Christian (generally the "laity"), while the higher level was for those who were seeking a higher level of righteousness (especially the clergy and various priestly/monastic orders). Similarly, some today suggest that the "crowds" represent average believers while the "disciples" represent those who are either more highly committed to serious spiritual formation or who are in training to be leaders of the church.[15]

---

15. For an overview of these traditions, see Michael J. Wilkins, "Eliminating Elitism from Our Traditions Through the Biblical Reunification of Spiritual Formation and Discipleship," in *Spiritual Formation: An Evangelical Perspective*, ed. Richard E. Averbeck and Michael P. Green (Grand Rapids: Eerdmans, forthcoming).

We must certainly agree that the SM is a high standard of ethical and moral life, but rather than being directed toward a select few, it is the high calling of all believers. A two-level ethic that artificially separates Christians into lower and higher categories has consistently been attempted but rightly rejected, as the Reformation doctrine of the "priesthood of all believers" emphasized. Further, while we agree that there is a distinction between the "crowds" and the "disciples," the distinction is not between two categories of believers (e.g., disciples are more committed than are the average "crowds" of believers). Instead, the distinction is between believers and unbelievers—that is, disciples are those who have made a commitment to Jesus as Savior, while the crowds are interested but have not yet made a decision to believe on Jesus for eternal life. Becoming a disciple occurs at conversion. Therefore, the SM is a high calling, but it is a light yoke of obligation for all Christians.[16]

**The essence of kingdom life for disciples of all ages.** Each of the above views have some truth to their claim. A majority of interpreters, however, with some variation, understand the SM to be Jesus' declaration of the essence of life in the kingdom that he has announced. Several key elements are involved in this general approach to the SM.

(1) We must hear clearly the messages intended specifically for disciples and crowds. One of the primary interpretive keys to understanding the SM is to clarify the message that is intended for either the disciples or the crowds. The disciples are those who have made a commitment to Jesus as the inaugurator of the kingdom of God and so receive direct teaching about kingdom life. The crowds are those who are interested but who have not yet made a commitment to Jesus' gospel of the kingdom. Since the SM is designed primarily for disciples, it can be designated as training in Christian discipleship for believers of all eras.

To make a distinction, the SM is primarily *instruction* for disciples about how life is to be lived on this earth in the light of the radical truth that the kingdom of heaven has arrived. But secondarily it holds out an *invitation* (not entrance requirements) to the crowds to enter the kingdom (e.g., 5:20). Some overlap will occur, because the crowds that Jesus left at the beginning of the sermon (5:1) appear at the end of the sermon, exclaiming that Jesus was "teaching them" with an authority not found in the teachers of the law (7:28–29). Even when directly teaching his disciples, Jesus has an eye on the crowd, hoping to persuade them to become his

---

16. David Crump, "Applying the Sermon on the Mount," 4, states: "Prior to the medieval period it is clear that the Sermon on the Mount was viewed as a straightforward presentation of Christian ethics."

disciples. His teaching is a tantalizing attraction to the crowds within hearing range.[17]

(2) We must recognize the targets of criticism within the historical religious setting. The teachers of the law and the Pharisees at that time were the most influential interpreters of the Old Testament Scriptures. They were the predominant caretakers and examples of righteous religious life among the common people. However, some of their interpretations and applications were leading the people astray from the intended will of God as revealed in the Law and the Prophets. Therefore, on the one hand, the teachers of the law and the Pharisees are the targets for Jesus' implicit and explicit criticism because of their faulty teaching and hypocritical example (e.g., 6:1–18). On the other hand, Jesus demonstrates throughout the SM how the kingdom life that he has inaugurated correctly fulfills the Old Testament Scriptures (5:17–20).

A subtle shift occurs in the SM, so that the relatively positive note at its beginning gets increasingly harsher. In chapter 5 Jesus calls for a higher form of righteousness than that exhibited by the teachers of the law and the Pharisees (e.g., 5:20), in chapter 6 the hypocrites are "outside" (addressed as "them"), but in chapter 7 the hypocrites are addressed directly (addressed as "you"), taking on the adversaries directly who are leading the people astray.[18] So at virtually every point in the SM we must determine how Jesus confronts an erroneous interpretation or a hypocritical application of the Old Testament that is being advanced by the Jewish leaders. Jesus shows the intended meaning of God's will by bringing the Old Testament to its fulfillment, and he does so by addressing the religious life of the common people as they have seen it speciously interpreted and modeled by the teachers of the law and the Pharisees (5:17–20).

(3) We must view the Sermon as the realistic, though ideal, model of the Christian life. The SM gives the ideal of discipleship (e.g., 5:48), yet that goal is set within a realistic understanding of everyday human life as it will be transformed through participation in new covenant life (26:26–29). The new covenant that Jesus inaugurates includes both forgiveness of sins and transformation of lives, because it is the basis of Spirit-produced regeneration and spiritual growth (cf. Ezek. 36:26–32; Titus 3:4–7). Although he does not mention the Holy Spirit explicitly in the SM, as the Spirit-anointed messianic inaugurator of the kingdom of God (3:16–4:1), Jesus exemplifies the kind of life that is empowered by the Spirit to live out the radical teaching included in the SM.

---

17. See Randall Buth, "Singular and Plural Forms of Address in the Sermon on the Mount," *BT* 44 (1993): 446–47.

18. Ibid.

Jesus' disciples will participate in real forgiveness of sins through the redemptive work of Christ on the cross, they will experience the real beginnings of kingdom life that comes through the new covenant regenerative work of the Spirit, and they will experience real transformation by the Spirit into the image of Christ (cf. 10:24–25; Rom. 8:29; 2 Cor. 3:18). Jesus displays in his own life and teaching the perfection of the Father that is laid before the disciples as the ideal goal toward which they are to strive. The wonderful truth behind the goal is that there is a realistic promise of initiation and ultimate realization, even though they will not attain the goal perfectly in this life (see comments on 5:48). The ideal life that Jesus lives and teaches becomes the goal that all of his disciples are to strive toward in this life.

Jesus interprets the unchanging principles of God's divine will already embodied in the Law and the Prophets for those who live in the already–not yet kingdom of God. The emphasis in the SM will be on inside-out transformation. Jesus will continually go to inner motivation, not external performance. The inner life will naturally transform the outer life. The heart that treasures the kingdom of heaven above all else will be the starting point for transformation of the entire life.

MATTHEW'S INTRODUCTION TO the SM brings important implications to our attention that will be helpful when understanding more clearly how to develop our own discipleship to Jesus.

**The SM delineates the foundation of our discipleship to Jesus.** The kind of kingdom life elucidated in the SM is the foundation for each Christian's personal discipleship to Jesus. The mandate of the Great Commission that concludes Matthew's Gospel is to "make disciples" of all the nations (28:19). As a person is converted, he or she becomes a disciple of Jesus, which is synonymous with being a Christian. The final participle of the Great Commission directs new disciples to be taught to obey everything that Jesus commanded (28:20). And the SM is the first major teaching of Jesus found in the Gospel, delineating the core of what it means to live as Jesus' disciple. I emphasize this especially to counteract some who understand discipleship to be reserved for an advanced stage of commitment. From the biblical point of view, all Christians are disciples, so the teaching in the SM is not for a few more-committed believers. This is the heart of Jesus' teaching for all Christians.

**Matthew's discourses develop a full-orbed description of our discipleship to Jesus.** It is no coincidence that all five major discourses in Matthew's Gospel are directed to Jesus' disciples and that these discourses are the most extensive and intentionally organized collection of Jesus' teaching ever recorded. Thus, when we understand that disciples are to be taught to obey all that Jesus has commanded, these five discourses give us the most complete articulation of the kind of discipleship life that Jesus intends for each of us. That is why I refer to Matthew as a "manual on discipleship," because throughout most of church history, this Gospel was used to provide the content of instruction on full-orbed Christian living.

We will develop this more fully as we study each of the discourses, and we will consider the ramifications for using this Gospel as a teaching tool when we examine Jesus' final Great Commission. But as an overview, we can see the kind of disciples that will develop when taught to obey the content of Jesus' discourses.

- Kingdom-life disciples. The SM, or the Kingdom-Life Discourse, unpacks what it means for Jesus' disciples to live out a radical kingdom life in their everyday world (Matt. 5–7).
- Mission-driven disciples. The second discourse is the Mission Mandate, which describes how Jesus' disciples are to go out and live out the message of the gospel of the kingdom of God to an alien and often hostile world (Matt. 10).
- Clandestine-kingdom disciples. The third discourse is the Parabolic Disclosure, which reveals what it means for Jesus' disciples to live as kingdom subjects in a world not yet fully manifested with God's power (Matt. 13).
- Community-based disciples. The fourth discourse is the Community Prescription, which focuses on discipleship to Jesus that is expressed through a church characterized by humility, purity, accountability, forgiveness, and reconciliation (Matt. 18).
- Expectant-sojourner disciples. The fifth discourse is the Eschatological Forecast, traditionally called the Olivet Discourse, which culminates Jesus' teaching on discipleship by describing how his disciples are to live each day in expectant preparation for his return with power (Matt. 24–25).

There is a progression of teaching in these discourses that addresses the fullness of the disciple's life. Matthew was the favorite Gospel of the early church throughout much of church history because it was a natural catechetical tool designed to develop wholistic disciples. The basic thrust of each discourse points to that kind of intentional well-roundedness. We would do well to return to Matthew on a regular basis throughout our lives, both for guidance in our own development as Jesus' disciples, but also for our use in guiding others within our ministries.

A balanced understanding of the SM will mature our discipleship to Jesus. Jesus' teaching in the SM gives some of the most radical challenges to our discipleship found in Scripture. It takes a careful understanding of what Jesus actually intends in his teachings for us to be truly radical in our discipleship to him and yet not take his teachings to unwarranted extremes. Some of his teachings have been misunderstood and either wrongly applied or rejected because Jesus uses intentional exaggeration to make his point (see comments on 5:29; 6:31–33). The use of normal Bible study practices and hermeneutical principles will help us to glean accurately what Jesus intends and allow us to avoid misinterpretation and faulty application.

Some specific tips for a balanced interpretation of some of the more problematic teachings of Jesus in the SM may help. Here are a few suggestive illustrations.

(1) Take the passage at face value and attempt to understand the meaning of Jesus' statement. Most problems can be resolved by looking at the literary and cultural context and seeing the intent of Jesus' saying within the larger setting. For example, when Jesus says that we are not to swear at all (5:34), the saying must be understood within the context of religious leaders trying to manipulate themselves out of their stated obligations to fellow Jews. Jesus is not condemning giving an oath of allegiance or vowing to fulfill a contract.

(2) Glean the principle being taught in the passage. An important part of understanding the SM is recognizing that when Jesus says that he has come to fulfill the Old Testament, he is taking us to the level of the intent and motive of Old Testament passages that were misinterpreted by religious leaders of his day. Behind specific instructions, such as turning one's cheek or giving up one's cloak (5:39–40), lay principles that are easily transferable to our own lives.

(3) Check to see if the passage needs to be balanced with another biblical principle in order to understand the full counsel of God. As in standard polemical argumentation, Jesus often gives one extreme with regard to an issue to drive home his point. He is not implying that other, equally important principles are invalid. For example, Jesus' statements about not being anxious about what we eat or drink or wear need to be balanced with the consistent theme of Scripture that godliness includes honest work to supply our own needs (e.g., 2 Thess. 3:9–12; 1 Tim. 5:8).

(4) Once your understanding is balanced, go back to the passage in the SM and attempt to live that principle out radically. Balancing Jesus' teachings does not water them down or mute their radical significance. Rather, truly radical discipleship means taking *all* of Jesus' teachings and living them all in the manner in which they were intended to be lived. For example, Jesus

warns against laying up treasures for ourselves on earth (6:19–21). We should live that principle fully. But he later uses a parable of sound investment of funds to warn equally against irresponsibility in investing what God has given to us to use for his service (25:14–30). Living with both of those principles at the same time will allow us to be radical disciples who live with God's perspective on our values and service.

With these guidelines for reading the SM, we must look for our discipleship to Jesus to be challenged and strengthened and to become more practical in its outworking. We look for Jesus to become more real, both as our Lord, who provides the power to live out the wonderful life he offers, and as our example, who provides the model for us to follow.

# Matthew 5:3–16

³"Blessed are the poor in spirit,
  for theirs is the kingdom of heaven.
⁴Blessed are those who mourn,
  for they will be comforted.
⁵Blessed are the meek,
  for they will inherit the earth.
⁶Blessed are those who hunger and thirst for
    righteousness,
  for they will be filled.
⁷Blessed are the merciful,
  for they will be shown mercy.
⁸Blessed are the pure in heart,
  for they will see God.
⁹Blessed are the peacemakers,
  for they will be called sons of God.
¹⁰Blessed are those who are persecuted because of
    righteousness,
  for theirs is the kingdom of heaven.

¹¹"Blessed are you when people insult you, persecute you and falsely say all kinds of evil against you because of me. ¹²Rejoice and be glad, because great is your reward in heaven, for in the same way they persecuted the prophets who were before you.

¹³"You are the salt of the earth. But if the salt loses its saltiness, how can it be made salty again? It is no longer good for anything, except to be thrown out and trampled by men.

¹⁴"You are the light of the world. A city on a hill cannot be hidden. ¹⁵Neither do people light a lamp and put it under a bowl. Instead they put it on its stand, and it gives light to everyone in the house. ¹⁶In the same way, let your light shine before men, that they may see your good deeds and praise your Father in heaven."

THE BEATITUDES OPEN the Sermon on the Mount with a sober yet dazzling vision of the operation of the kingdom of heaven among God's people. More than simply a formal literary introduction,[1] the Beatitudes summarize the essence of the sermon's message, giving in a nutshell the way in which the kingdom makes its impact on the lives of those who respond to it. The character of this kingdom life contravenes the values that most people hold dear, because God's blessing rests on the unlikely ones—the poor in spirit, mourners, the meek, the persecuted. "Thus the Beatitudes line an upside-down reality, or—more precisely—they define reality in such a way that the usual order of things is seen to be upside down in the eyes of God."[2]

## The Beatitudes of the Kingdom of Heaven (5:3–12)

APART FROM THE Lord's Prayer, these are the most familiar verses of the SM. The name "beatitude" is derived from the Latin *beatitudo/beatus*, because the first word of each statement in the Latin Vulgate is *beati*, which translates Matthew's Greek word *makarios* (traditionally translated "blessed"). Some recent versions translate *makarios* as "happy" or "fortunate," which can be good renderings, but the modern usage of those terms tends to trivialize the meaning by simply suggesting a temporary emotional or circumstantial state. The somewhat ambiguous English "blessed" perhaps is still the best term to describe Jesus' statements.

*Makarios* is a state of existence in relationship to God in which a person is "blessed" from God's perspective even when he or she doesn't feel happy or isn't presently experiencing good fortune. This does not mean a conferral of blessing or an exhortation to live a life worthy of blessing; rather, it is an acknowledgment that the ones indicated are blessed.[3] Negative feelings, absence of feelings, or adverse conditions cannot take away the blessedness of those who exist in relationship with God.

---

1. Betz, *The Sermon on the Mount*, 92: "As a musical masterpiece begins with an introitus, the SM opens with an extraordinary sequence of statements, the so-called Beatitudes."

2. Richard B. Hays, *The Moral Vision of the New Testament—Community, Cross, New Community: A Contemporary Introduction to New Testament Ethics* (San Francisco: HarperSanFrancisco, 1996), 321.

3. The sacramental aspect of conferring a blessing is not emphasized in Jesus' ministry, and we will see below that the Beatitudes are not imperatives. See Guelich, *The Sermon on the Mount*, 63–66. For a similar discussion of whether a *conferral* or *acknowledgment* of blessing is made on Peter in 16:17, see Wilkins, *Discipleship in the Ancient World and Matthew's Gospel*, 187. The latter is more likely in 16:17.

**Structure.** Each beatitude is composed of two poetic clauses. The first clause begins with the statement of blessing ("blessed") followed by a statement of the identity of the ones who are blessed (e.g., "the poor in spirit"), a structure similar to the opening verse of Psalm 1.[4] The second clause begins with "because" (*hoti*), giving the reason for what precedes it (e.g., "theirs is the kingdom of heaven").

Eight primary statements of blessing make up the Beatitudes, with the ninth statement of blessing (5:11–12) being an extension and personalization of the eighth beatitude for Jesus' disciples who experience persecution.[5] The overall structure of the Beatitudes gives an important clue to their theme. The first and the eighth beatitudes (5:3, 10) form a sort of bookends, another example of the common Hebrew literary device called an inclusio,[6] because the causal clause of the first beatitude is repeated in the last beatitude—"for theirs is the kingdom of heaven" (cf. 5:3, 10). The repetition of the present tense clause signals the main theme of the Beatitudes, that the blessedness of the kingdom of heaven is a present possession and operation among those who respond to Jesus' ministry. However, the second through seventh beatitudes (5:4–9) have a future tense in the causal clause, indicating that the kingdom is also a future expectation and hope.

**1. Blessed are the poor in spirit … (5:3).** The "poor" are those who have encountered unfortunate circumstances from an economic point of view (19:21; 26:11), but also persons who are spiritually and emotionally oppressed, disillusioned, and in need of God's help.[7] Those who have experienced the harsh side of life in which deprivation and hunger are their regular lot have no resources of their own to make anything of their lives. This also includes those who recognize that they can produce no spiritual or religious self-help before God. They are spiritually bankrupt.[8] We hear this in the psalmist as he cries out in Psalm 40:17:

---

4. The initial *makarios* without the verb "to be," which is the fixed pattern of each beatitude, occurs also in LXX Ps. 1:1 and frequently elsewhere in the LXX (cf. Gen. 30:13; Ps. 2:12; Isa. 30:18; Dan. 12:12). For an exhaustive though critical recent analysis of the poetic nature of the Beatitudes, see H. Benedict Green, *Matthew, Poet of the Beatitudes* (JSNTSup 203; Sheffield: Sheffield Academic Press, 2001).

5. The structure of the eight first statements of blessing are virtually identical. Since the theme of persecution continues on into the ninth statement of blessing but its structure differs significantly (a switch from the third person to the second person "you," the copula "are" appears for the first time, and the regular two-clause structure disappears), it is generally accepted that the ninth statement is an extension of the eighth beatitude.

6. See W. G. E. Watson, *Classical Hebrew Poetry* (JSOTSup 26; Sheffield: JSOT, 1984), 282–87. The inclusio is also found in narrative (see comments on 4:23; 9:35).

7. BDAG, 735.

8. The dative of sphere "in spirit" should be understood to be practically equivalent to an adverb, indicating "the spiritually poor" (cf. Wallace, *Greek Grammar*, 155).

> Yet I am poor and needy;
>> may the Lord think of me.
> You are my help and my deliverer;
>> O my God, do not delay.

This attitude of humility in the harsh realities of life makes a person open to receive the blessings of the kingdom of heaven.

**. . . for theirs is the kingdom of heaven.** The kingdom of God belongs to those who know they have no resources, material or spiritual, to help themselves before God. These are the "poor" to whom Jesus has come to announce "good news" (11:5) and to whom the kingdom of heaven belongs. This first beatitude undercuts the predominant worldview that assumes that material blessings are a sign of God's approval in one's life and that they automatically flow from one's spiritual blessings. Instead, Jesus teaches that the norm of the kingdom of heaven is spiritual bankruptcy, unlike the spiritual self-sufficiency that was characteristic of the religious leaders. Jesus' disciples will experience their most complete personal fulfillment as they draw on the resources of the kingdom of heaven to guide their lives.

**2. Blessed are those who mourn . . . (5:4).** Those who are bankrupt are also those who mourn. The loss of anything that a person counts valuable will produce mourning, whether it's one's financial support, or loved ones, or status in society, or even one's spiritual standing before God. The psalmist understands this latter kind of mourning, for he says, "Streams of tears flow from my eyes, for your law is not obeyed" (Ps. 119:136). Those who are self-satisfied are tempted to rejoice in themselves and their accomplishments, but those who have reached the bottom of the barrel, whether it is spiritual or emotional or financial, or those who see the bankruptcy of those around them, will mourn.

**. . . for they will be comforted.** But, "Comfort, comfort my people" (Isa. 40:1), God says to those who have realized their loss and mourn over it. The arrival of the kingdom of heaven in Jesus' ministry brings the first taste of God's comforting blessing. The poor in spirit and those who mourn now experience the fulfillment of the messianic blessing promised in Isaiah 61:1–3. Jesus has come to save his people from their sins (Matt. 1:21; 11:28–30), but they will receive final comforting in the presence of the heavenly Lamb, when "God will wipe every tear from their eyes" (Rev. 7:17).

Mourning does not exclude the joy that is to typify Jesus' followers, but instead characterizes life in the already–not yet presence of the kingdom. We weep with those who weep and rejoice with those who rejoice (Rom. 12:15). But our mourning does not turn to the grief of those who have no hope (1 Thess. 4:13). We mourn oppression and persecution, but we do not despair, because we know the end of the story. We mourn over personal sin and social evil, because we mourn the things that God mourns. But as we mourn, we become instruments of the good news of the kingdom of heaven as we bring the comfort of God with which we ourselves have been comforted (2 Cor. 1:3–7).

**3. Blessed are the meek . . . (5:5).** The domineering, the aggressive, the harsh, and the tyrannical are often those who attempt to dominate the earth and establish their own little kingdoms. But Jesus says that it is the "gentle" who will inherit the earth, harking back to the psalmist who encourages those who have been treated harshly by evildoers (Ps. 37:9, 11). This shifts the focus from individual personal qualities ("poor in spirit," "those who mourn") to interpersonal attributes ("the gentle"), to people who do not assert themselves over others in order to advance their own causes. This does not imply weakness, however, for this same term is applied to Jesus, who describes himself as "gentle and humble in heart" (11:29; cf. 21:5). Jesus was not afraid to confront the religious leaders when necessary or to rebuke his own disciples for self-centeredness. He will be strong enough to face the most torturous death possible as he endured the cross.

**. . . for they will inherit the earth (5:5).** Jesus exemplifies best what it means to be gentle. It takes tremendous strength to bring others into God's will, but when that strength is coupled with a selfless nonassertiveness, it produces a gentle person who can patiently endure much to bring about God's purposes for his people. Such gentle persons "will inherit the earth." Jesus assumes this gentle posture as he preaches good news, proclaims freedom, and announces the arrival of the Lord's favor (11:5), and blessed are those who do not take offence at his gentle messianic ministry (11:6). Ultimately this points to the reign of Christ on this earth (25:35), but even now Jesus' disciples have entered into their spiritual inheritance (e.g., Eph. 1:18; Col. 1:12; Heb. 9:15).

**4. Blessed are those who hunger and thirst for righteousness . . . (5:6).** Persons who "hunger and thirst" are in dire need. They will perish if they are not filled. Such is the passion of those who desire righteousness. In the context of the preceding beatitudes, righteousness includes several facets. It includes "justice" for those who have been downtrodden or who have experienced injustice. It includes the idea of personal ethical righteousness for those who desire a life lived above the entanglements of sin. And as in 3:15, it includes the salvation-historical sense of God's saving activity. Those who hunger and thirst for righteousness desire to see justice executed on earth, they long to experience a deeper ethical righteousness in their own lives, and most of all they crave God's promised salvation come to the earth.[9]

---

9. For discussion see Donald A. Hagner, "Righteousness in Matthew's Gospel," in *Worship, Theology and Ministry in the Early Church*, 116–17.

**... for they will be filled (5:6).** The ultimate source of this kind of righteousness is God himself (cf. Ps. 42:1–2; 63:1). His enablement is the only satisfaction for those who long for his standard of righteousness written in his law (119:10–11, 20, etc.).[10] Although the teachers of the law and the Pharisees focus on attaining righteousness through studying and interpreting the law, their efforts result in self-righteousness, which will not enable them to enter the kingdom of heaven (cf. 5:20). But for those who deeply long for God's multifaceted righteousness, they will be filled. That divine satisfaction will come in a final sense in God's future reign, but it will be experienced in the present by those who respond to Jesus' invitation to kingdom life and enter into a relationship with him as he fills their deepest personal hunger and thirst for righteousness (cf. 12:1–8; 26:26–29; John 4:13–15; 6:35ff.).

Jesus' disciples see firsthand the contrast between the self-righteousness of the religious leaders and God's righteousness in Jesus' life and ministry. As they continue to experience the transformation that accompanies life in the realm of the kingdom of heaven, their hunger and thirst for God's righteousness remains real as they live in the already–not yet of the present age, experiencing a passionate concern for the right things in kingdom living. This passionate pursuit of righteousness flows from a transformed heart. Jesus' disciples will be vessels of God's righteousness as they strive for justice, as they exemplify a life of righteousness, and as they bring God's gift of salvation to a world still held in the sway of the evil one (Eph. 2:1–10).

**5. Blessed are the merciful ... (5:7).** Mercy is a central biblical theme, because in God's great mercy he does not give humans what they deserve; rather, he gives to them what they do not deserve (see Ps. 25:6–7; cf. Prov. 14:21). Likewise, the merciful are those who demonstrate forgiveness toward the guilty and kindness for the hurting and needy. The religious leadership in Jesus' day tended toward being merciless because of their demand for rigorous observance of the law. Their motive was commendable in that it was driven by a desire for the people of Israel to be pure, but it was inexcusable because their unbending demands produced harshness and condemnation toward those who did not meet their standards.

**... for they will be shown mercy (5:7).** Without sacrificing God's standard of holiness, Jesus commends those who demonstrate mercy toward the needy, because the mercy that they show others will be shown toward them. Showing mercy toward others does not earn a person entrance to the kingdom; rather, it is a heart attitude that opens a person to receive the offer of mercy that Jesus has proclaimed in his gospel of the kingdom. The religious leaders cannot receive God's mercy because they have become so self-satisfied

---

10. See Morris, *Matthew*, 99–100.

with their own religious attainments that they don't believe that they need mercy.

Jesus' disciples learn from this beatitude that God's good requirement has always been mercy. Recall the classic statements of Micah: "He has showed you, O man, what is good. And what does the LORD require of you? To act justly and to love mercy and to walk humbly with your God" (Mic. 6:8). Those who receive mercy will demonstrate mercy, a theme reemphasized somewhat differently in the parable on forgiveness (Matt. 18:33). The true disciple has experienced God's merciful forgiveness toward an undeserving sinner, which in turn will produce such overwhelming gratitude and deep understanding of forgiveness that he or she will in turn demonstrate that same mercy toward other undeserving sinners.

**6. Blessed are the pure in heart ... (5:8).** In the sixth beatitude Jesus goes to the core of human life, the heart. Purity or cleanliness was an important religious theme in Jesus' day. Observing all the Old Testament laws of being clean could bypass the most important purity of all, purity of the heart. Jesus declares here that a pure heart is what produces external purity, not vice versa (e.g., 15:1—19). In this beatitude Jesus continues an important Old Testament theme in which a pure heart describes a person whose single-minded loyalty to God affects every area of life. "He who loves a pure heart and whose speech is gracious will have the king for his friend" (Prov. 22:11; cf. Ps. 24:3—6; 73:1).

While the people of the Old Testament knew clearly that the human heart was evil (see Prov. 20:9; Jer. 17:9), they knew equally well that God's work in an evil heart could bring purification and a new motivation for following him. "Create in me a pure heart, O God, and renew a steadfast spirit in me" (Ps. 51:10). The pure in heart are those who have not necessarily attended to all of the ritual purification ceremonies of the Pharisees but who nonetheless have given undivided loyalty to God and his ways.

**... for they will see God (5:8).** The undivided devotion of the pure in heart will be rewarded by their greatest hope: "They will see God." While no human can look fully at the glorious face of God (Ex. 33:20), the hope that culminates this age is that "they will see his face, and his name will be on their foreheads" (Rev. 22:4). But Jesus' pronouncement of this beatitude to those of his day also has an immediate fulfillment of their hopes. Jesus is Immanuel, "God with us" (1:23). For those who have set their heart on God and not simply religious ritualism and who respond to Jesus' message of the gospel of the kingdom, they are invited to enter into a fellowship with him in which they will experience the unthinkable; they will see God in Jesus.

**7. Blessed are the peacemakers ... (5:9).** The seventh beatitude focuses on "the peacemakers." The theme of "peace" (Heb. *šalom*; Gk. *eirene*) permeates the biblical record. It indicates completeness and wholeness in every area of life, including one's relationship with God, neighbors, and nations (cf. Ps. 28:3; Eccl. 3:8; Isa. 26:3). The zealots of Jesus' day attempted to bring self-rule back to Israel through the guerrilla-warfare tactic of divide and conquer, while the religious leaders brought as much division within Israel by their sectarian commitments. But the real peacemakers are those who bring the good news that "your God reigns," who brings ultimate harmony between all peoples (cf. Isa. 52:7). Making peace, therefore, has messianic overtones (cf. "Prince of Peace" in Isa 9:6–7), and the true peacemakers are those who wait and work for God, who makes whole the division created by humans.

**... for they will be called sons of God (5:9).** Jesus turns aside the various political, religious, and militaristic attempts of those within Israel to establish their supremacy. They have created even more division; thus, he turns to those who want God's peace. With the inauguration of the kingdom of heaven, Jesus himself is the supreme peacemaker, making peace between God and humans, and among humans (Eph. 2:11–17; Col. 1:20). Those who have waited for God's messianic peace can now respond to Jesus' invitation, and they will receive the ultimate reward: to be called "sons of God," fulfilling the role that Israel has assumed but taken for granted (Deut. 14:1; Hos. 1:10). Those who respond to Jesus' ministry are heirs of the kingdom and reflect the character of their heavenly Father as they carry Jesus' mission of peacemaking to the world.

**8a. Blessed are those who are persecuted because of righteousness ... (5:10).** The eighth beatitude makes it once again clear that the Beatitudes are not entrance requirements to the kingdom of God, or else Jesus would be sanctioning torture or martyrdom as a way of earning one's entrance to the kingdom. At the same time, this again makes clear that the Beatitudes are not ethical demands for personal behavior, or else Jesus would be implying that it would be good for his disciples to seek out persecution in order to gain his blessing.

Instead, in the eighth beatitude Jesus comforts those who have suffered undeserved persecution.[11] Persecution for one's own sin or foolishness may

---

11. The perfect passive participle forms a substantive, "those who have been persecuted." The use of the perfect tense here is difficult to explain. From Jesus' perspective, none of his disciples has been persecuted for righteousness up to this point. Who then would qualify to say that his is the kingdom of heaven? It cannot refer to Old Testament prophets (to whom Jesus will allude in the next verse), because they were like John the Baptist, prior to the inauguration of the kingdom, and thus the kingdom did not belong to them. Others avoid the historical situation by saying that Matthew is making a statement by selecting the perfect tense, in order to tell something to his readers. The perspective of "pronouncement" seems to offer the best explanation.

be deserved (cf. 1 Peter 2:20; 3:14; 4:14–15), but these people have been persecuted because of their stand for righteousness. With his comforting words, Jesus emphatically pronounces condemnation on those doing the persecuting. Although the persecutors are not named, Luke's parallel beatitude pronounces a "woe" on those who receive religious acclaim from the masses, as did the false prophets of the Old Testament (cf. Luke 6:26). This implicates once again the religious leadership of Jesus' day, who persecuted those who did not adopt their particular brand of righteousness.

Persecution can take the form of physical or verbal abuse, or both, but it especially points to the way that the religious leaders hounded the populace and excluded from their fellowship any who did not meet up to their standards (cf. Luke 6:22; Matt. 23:34).[12] Sadly and ironically, the religious leaders were persecuting in the name of their self-righteousness the very people who stood for true righteousness.

**. . . for theirs is the kingdom of heaven (5:10).** As difficult as is the persecution, the reward far outweighs the hazard, because "theirs is the kingdom of heaven." This is a present tense declaration that duplicates the causal clause of the first beatitude (5:3).[13] Jesus here gives hope to the people of his day who have stood up and contended for God's form of righteousness against the self-righteousness of the religious leaders. Although they have been persecuted for it, Jesus says that the kingdom of God belongs to them, not the religious leaders, and all they need to do now is to respond to his invitation to join the kingdom.

**8b. Blessed are you when people insult you . . . (5:11–12).** The emphasis shifts more and more from *pronouncement* on the crowds and the religious leadership to *instruction* for Jesus' disciples. This is made explicit by the shift from the general third person plural ("those who") to the second person plural ("you"), the disciples whom Jesus teaches in the SM (cf. 5:1–2). The religious leadership will insult, persecute, and utter evil against the disciples in God's name, but Jesus will reveal these leaders to be no different than the hypocritical leaders of the Old Testament, who persecuted God's true prophets. The harrassment his disciples receive is more specific than "because of righteousness" (5:10); it is "because of me" (5:11). Since Jesus himself will experience opposition and persecution, his disciples should expect the same.[14]

In this instruction Jesus prepares his disciples for the time when persecution will indeed come to them, offering them the hope that no matter how

---

12. Gundry, *Matthew*, 72.

13. See comments on the literary *inclusio* that this forms and the attendant implications for the meaning.

14. This is a central New Testament theme (cf. 10:24–25; John 11:16; 15:18–25; 2 Tim. 3:12; 1 Peter 4:13–14).

hard the circumstances, they are truly heirs of the kingdom. Although the kingdom belongs to them, it does not at this time usher in a time of peace and safety. In fact, Jesus indicates that their reward will not come in an earthly kingdom but "in heaven." He looks down the long corridor of time until the kingdom is established on earth in its final form and offers hope during those times when it seems doubtful that his kingdom will ever arrive. It may not look like it from a religious, economic, or social perspective, but the kingdom is theirs nonetheless—and in this they will truly rejoice.

## Salt and Light (5:13–16)

IN THE BEATITUDES Jesus gave a *pronouncement* to the crowds and religious leaders and *instruction* to his disciples concerning the nature of life in the kingdom of heaven. Now with two piercing metaphors, he focuses on his disciples and declares how they will impact this world with the kingdom life they possess. Into the world in which they can expect to find persecution (5:10–12), Jesus' disciples are to go as "salt" and as "light" (5:13–16). These metaphors reveal the nature of kingdom life that pervades those who belong to Jesus, the impact that life will have on a watching world, and the responsibility of Jesus' disciples as they live in this world and await the coming of the kingdom of God.

**You are the salt of the earth (5:13).** Salt had a variety of natural qualities and uses in the ancient world. It was so important that it was used as a medium of exchange in commercial ventures across the Mediterranean, Aegean, and Adriatic seas.[15] The variety of uses for salt leads to different interpretations of what Jesus meant to communicate with the analogy. (1) A primary use for salt until recent years was as a preservative. In a society with no refrigeration, salt could be rubbed into meat or fish to slow decay. Some suggest that with this analogy Jesus was indicating the influence his disciples would have on the moral decay of a fallen world.[16]

(2) Salt is also an essential element in the diet of human beings and other warm-blooded animals. For humans, salt is normally ingested as a seasoning added to foods, while animals commonly ingest salt from natural or artificial salt licks. This is the most familiar use of salt to modern readers, so many suggest that Jesus indicates that his disciples will provide a God-enhanced, kingdom seasoning to this world with their presence.[17]

---

15. The English word "salary" is derived from *salarium*, the Latin term referring to the salt allotment issued to soldiers serving in the Roman army. See Robert P. Multhauf, *Neptune's Gift: A History of Common Salt* (Baltimore: Johns Hopkins Univ. Press, 1978); John Challinor, *A Dictionary of Geology*, 6th ed. (Oxford: Oxford Univ. Press, 1986).

16. E.g., Carson, "Matthew," 138.

17. E.g., Luz, *Matthew 1–7*, 250.

(3) Salt was also used in small quantities as a fertilizer when applied to certain types of soil ("earth"). Thus, some suggest that Jesus' disciples will enhance the growth of God's work in this world.[18]

(4) A widely held view suggests that since salt had a varied use in the ancient world, Jesus is not pointing to one specific application but is using it in a broad, inclusive sense to refer to a vital necessity for everyday life. Sirach echoed such a perspective (Sir. 39:26), and Pliny commented that "there is nothing more useful than salt and sunshine."[19] Taken in this way, the metaphor indicates that Jesus' disciples are vitally important to the world in a general religious sense.[20]

This last suggestion is appealing because to stress too closely one particular application of salt can lead to inappropriate allegorizing. In other words, Jesus indicates with this metaphor that his disciples themselves ("*you* are the salt") are necessary for the welfare of the world. That is, the disciples have experienced a transformation in their lives as they have come into contact with the kingdom of heaven. They are now different from the people of this earth, and their presence is necessary as God's means of influencing the world for good.

Jesus' next statement has caused considerable discussion: "But if the salt loses its saltiness, how can it be made salty again? It is no longer good for anything, except to be thrown out and trampled by men" (5:13). Strictly speaking, salt cannot lose its saltiness, because sodium chloride is a stable compound. What then did Jesus mean?

(1) One possibility is that Jesus is alluding to rock formations that contained deposits of sodium chloride. Meat and fish were packed in these rocks to preserve them. After a period of time the salt leached out of the rocks, so the rocks were not good for anything and so thrown out. As believers, we are either a preservative or a worthless rock!

(2) Jesus may also have had in mind the salt that was collected from the Dead Sea by evaporation. This salt often included crystals of another mineral, gypsum, which is formed by the precipitation of calcium sulfate from seawater. Salt and gypsum were often mixed in various saline deposits. When people went to collect salt, this impure mixture of salt and gypsum could easily be mistaken for pure salt. But the mixture was not usable for either preservation or seasoning, so was regarded as having lost its usefulness.[21]

---

18. E.g., Gundry, *Matthew*, 75. See the interesting discussion of this view by a professor of agriculture, Eugene P. Deatrick, "Salt, Soil, Savior," *BA* 25 (1962): 41–48.

19. Pliny, *Nat. Hist.* 31.102.

20. E.g., Hagner, *Matthew 1–13*, 99; Davies and Allison, *Matthew*, 1:473.

21. E.g., Hagner, *Matthew 1–13*, 99, who cites F. Hauck, "ἅλας," *TDNT*, 1:229.

(3) Jesus may be alluding to the use of salt blocks by Arab bakers to line the floor of their ovens. After some time the intense heat eventually caused the blocks to crystallize and undergo a change in chemical composition, finally being thrown out as unserviceable.

(4) A quotation attributed to Rabbi Joshua ben Haninia (c. A.D. 90) may offer some help. When rebuffing a trick question, Rabbi Haninia alludes to a proverbial saying when he asks, "Can salt lose its flavor?" The context of the saying implies that it is impossible for salt to lose its flavor, because he parallels the saying by asking, "Does the mule (being sterile) bear young?" (*b. Bek.* 8b). Sterile mules can no more bear young than salt can lose its flavor.

If this last option is the background, Jesus is citing a known proverbial saying on impossibilities to describe an equally impossible characteristic of his disciples.[22] As they go out into the world as salt, they must recognize that the proof of the reality of their profession is in the nature of their lives. True disciples cannot lose what has made them disciples, because they have become changed persons, made new by the life of the kingdom of heaven. However, imposter disciples, who simply attempt to put on the flavoring of the kingdom life, will be revealed. Their salt is only an external flavoring, not a real personal change. This imposter cannot be made salty again because he or she never had that kingdom life in the first place.

Jesus' next statement drives home the seriousness of the issue: "It is no longer good for anything, except to be thrown out and trampled by men." The response to imposter disciples is rejection and judgment by the very people for whom they are to have value. Imposters will be known for what they are. They have nothing to offer the world, because they are no different from the world. So the world turns on them for their arrogant hypocrisy. The challenge is for professing disciples to examine their nature and to confess honestly whether or not they have been transformed by the life of the kingdom of God.

**The light of the world (5:14–16).** Jesus' disciples are not only "the salt of the earth" but also "the light of the world." The light metaphor continues the salt metaphor and takes it one step further to illustrate Jesus' point. "Light" is an important theme in Scripture, normally emphasizing the removal of darkness in the unfolding of biblical history and theology. The literal contrast between physical light and darkness provokes a profound metaphorical contrast between metaphysical good and evil, God and evil forces, believers and unbelievers. Jesus later declares that he is "the light of

---

22. This may be similar to Jesus' saying about the impossibility of a camel going through the eye of a needle (19:24).

the world" (John 8:12; 9:5), who has come as the light that enlightens all people (1:4–14), so that those believing in him will no longer be in darkness (12:46).

In the same way as Jesus' life and message of salvation bring light to those in darkness (Matt. 4:15–16), his disciples are a living demonstration of the arrival of the kingdom of heaven. The light of revelation from God that accompanies Jesus' announcement of the kingdom is not just carried by his disciples; they *are* that light (Matt. 5:14–16; cf. Eph. 5:8; Phil. 2:15).

Jesus continues the proverbial "impossible" language he used in the salt metaphor by stating that "a city on a hill cannot be hidden," and "neither do people light a lamp and put it under a bowl." The city to which Jesus refers may be Jerusalem, which sits on Mount Zion, since Israel with Jerusalem as the holy city was considered light to the world (Isa. 2:2–5; 42:6; 49:6). But since Jesus is now in Galilee near Capernaum, he may be using a local city as his illustration, because he often used images from his surroundings to illustrate his teaching.[23] In either case, it is impossible to hide a city located on a hill.

The lamp used in a typical Palestinian home was a partially closed reservoir made of clay. It had a hole on top to pour oil in and a spout on one end into which a wick of flax or cotton was set. It was a fairly small lamp, which gave off only a modest light; thus, to give maximum illumination it was placed on a lampstand. Since many Jewish homes were often modest one-room structures, such an elevated lamp could give light to everyone in the house. Lamps were essential for finding one's way in enclosed areas during the night and were placed under a measuring bowl only to extinguish the light (cf. *m. Šabb.* 16.1).[24]

Jesus' disciples are called to be the light of the world. They cannot be hidden, for their very nature, the kingdom life within them, is living testimony to those in the world who do not yet have that light. Their good works are produced by the light and life that come from God. It is not of their own making, because those who see them in action will glorify not them but their "Father in heaven" (cf. the motive of the religious leaders in 6:1). The title "Father" is used in Matthew here for the first time, introducing the special relationship that exists between God and Jesus' disciples. Jesus has been declared

---

23. One possible such city is Hippos, a Greek city of the Decapolis situated on a rounded hill above the southeastern shore. It was clearly visible from the Capernaum area, esp. when it was lit up at night (see Rousseau and Arav, "Hippos/Susita," *Jesus and His World*, 127–28).

24. See Wilkins, "Matthew," 36, and John Rea, "Lamp," *ZPEB*, 3:865–66, for pictures of excavated lamps from patriarchal times to the New Testament era; cf. Carol Meyers, "Lampstand," *ABD*, 4:141–43.

to be the beloved Son (3:17), and now those who have received the kingdom light are children of the heavenly Father as well (cf. John 1:7–13).[25]

Jesus' disciples possess kingdom life, which produces good deeds from a changed life. Bearing the light of the gospel in both message and life will bring people to know that the kingdom of heaven truly is in the world, and they will glorify their heavenly Father. The Beatitudes hinted at this direction, but the metaphors of salt and light are the first explicit indication that the presence of the kingdom produces changed lives.

WE THE PEOPLE of the United States, in order to form a more perfect union, establish Justice, insure domestic tranquility, provide for the common defense, promote the general welfare, and secure the blessings of liberty to ourselves and our posterity, do ordain and establish this Constitution for the United States of America.[26]

The Preamble of the Constitution of the United States is one of the most memorable statements in American history. It states succinctly the ethos of the nation to be, and provides a summarization of the articles of the constitution to follow. It gives insight to the intention of the framers of the Constitution, the details of which are enumerated in the articles. The preamble is a hint that the Constitution would be a boldly original attempt to create an energetic central government at the same time that the sovereignty of the people was preserved.[27]

In a similar manner, the Beatitudes serve as a sort of preamble to the SM, but they are an even more memorable treasure for humanity. They give a succinct statement of the ethos of the kingdom of heaven that Jesus has announced and summarize the principles of kingdom life that he will articulate in the Sermon that follows. We find in them an abstract of Jesus' history-altering intention for establishing the kingdom of heaven as well as a clue to Matthew's organization of his Gospel. The Beatitudes are a radically bold statement of Jesus' intent to establish the kingdom of heaven on earth, which

---

25. The use of the expression "Father" has metaphorical significance (e.g., Aída Besançon Spencer, "Father-Ruler: The Meaning of the Metaphor 'Father' for God in the Bible," *JETS* 39 [1996]: 433–442), but here it is laden with theological significance to underscore the relationship between the Father and Son, and even between God and believers.

26. The text of the Preamble was taken from the website of the United States House of Representatives: http://www.house.gov/house/Educat.html.

27. http://www.house.gov/house/Constitution/Foreword.html.

will bring true peace and freedom for all who dare to follow him as his disciples. It is through those disciples that his kingdom will bring blessing to all of the peoples of the earth.

**Interpreting the Beatitudes.** The Beatitudes and the Sermon on the Mount as a whole must be interpreted according to Jesus' original intention, or else we will find ourselves going contrary to his objective for establishing the kingdom of heaven on earth. When approaching the Beatitudes we must avoid sliding into various extremes. (1) We must not conclude that Jesus is calling his listeners to a meritorious attempt at earning salvation by living out these character qualities in order to enter the kingdom. Jesus' Beatitudes are statements of grace, not law. (2) We must avoid making these into burdensome ethical demands on those who are members of the kingdom. There are no imperatives here, except to "rejoice" when one experiences the blessing of God in the middle of persecution (5:12). (3) We must not conclude that these are eschatological blessings that only will be realized at the end of the age. The kingdom blessings are found in both the present tense (5:3, 10) and the future tense (5:4–9).[28]

Jesus uses the Beatitudes to speak to a variety of listeners and to communicate several messages about the kingdom of heaven. Specifically, he makes a pronouncement about the kingdom to Israel as a whole, and at the same time he gives instruction about the nature of kingdom life to his disciples.

(1) *Pronouncement.* In fulfillment of the prophecy of Isaiah 61:1, Jesus is the Coming One, who is endowed with the Spirit and anointed by the Lord to preach good news to the poor and to proclaim freedom for the captives and release for the prisoners (cf. 11:5). The kingdom of heaven belongs to those who respond. The boundaries that separate successful from unsuccessful, clean from unclean, righteous from unrighteous, have tended to be of human creation, and they are now broken down. In these eight brief declarations, Jesus makes two sweeping pronouncements.

(a) A pronouncement of invitation to those awaiting God's blessing. The kingdom of heaven is available to the oppressed in the land, to those who doubt themselves or are declared to be unworthy of the kingdom. The statement of blessing in the first half of each beatitude responds to the character qualities of those in the Old Testament who have sought God. "Blessed are the poor in spirit, for theirs is the kingdom of heaven" is Jesus' eschatological reply to the cry of the psalmist, "This poor man called, and the LORD heard him; he saved him out of all his troubles" (Ps. 34:6). Not the rich, not the powerful, not the high and the mighty, but the poor in spirit are those who seek God.

---

28. For discussion see Guelich, "The Beatitudes: 'Entrance Requirements' or 'Eschatological Blessings'?" in *Sermon on the Mount*, 109–11.

So begins Jesus' pronouncement about the arrival of the kingdom of heaven. The poor in spirit, those who mourn, the meek, those who hunger and thirst for righteousness, the merciful, the pure in heart, the peacemakers, those persecuted because of righteousness—these are the people who have pursued God by rejecting pride and self-sufficiency, which is the path of sin and idolatry. They are indeed blessed, because now Jesus invites them to respond to his message of the arrival of the kingdom of heaven.

(b) A pronouncement of condemnation on those who think that they have God's blessing. The second pronouncement is one of condemnation on those who have rejected God's ways and have found satisfaction in the pleasures of life apart from God. This is especially emphasized in Luke's version of the Sermon, where Jesus gives four woes to counterbalance the pronouncements:

> But woe to you who are rich,
>> for you have already received your comfort.
> Woe to you who are well fed now,
>> for you will go hungry.
> Woe to you who laugh now,
>> for you will mourn and weep.
> Woe to you when all men speak well of you,
>> for that is how their fathers treated the false prophets.
> (Luke 6:24–26)

These "woes" suggest that we look for a note of condemnation in Matthew's record of the Beatitudes. This pronouncement of condemnation is especially directed to the religious leaders of Israel. Jesus will stun the crowds and his disciples by declaring that the teachers of the law and the Pharisees are not in the kingdom of heaven (Matt. 5:20). They have found self-satisfaction in their self-righteousness, which has excluded them from the blessing that has arrived with Jesus' ministry.

Thus, each of Jesus' Beatitudes contains an explicit pronouncement of invitation to those seemingly unworthy of the kingdom, but each also contains an implicit pronouncement of condemnation on those who think themselves to be worthy but are not. For example, in the first beatitude Jesus graciously pronounces that the kingdom belongs to those who see themselves as having no spiritual resources worthy of the kingdom. But at the same time he pronounces condemnation on the religious elite who are full of pride in their religious accomplishments. Indeed, the religiously wealthy must humble themselves before God to recognize that they have no spiritual resources that warrant entrance to the kingdom of God.

Rooting the Beatitudes in the historical context of the original meaning of Jesus' ministry helps us avoid contemporary misinterpretation. The SM was intended, at least in part, as a historical indictment of the religious establishment's way of satisfying God. The teachers of the law and the Pharisees are held up throughout the Sermon as a foil to Jesus' declaration of kingdom life, because they are setting a wrong example of righteousness,[29] namely, the performance of a specific interpretation of the law. The tendency of these Jewish leaders was to develop external righteousness without due regard to inner righteousness. External righteousness that masks inner corruption is what Jesus refers to as "hypocrisy" (cf. 23:27). He declares, by contrast, that the righteousness of the kingdom of God is first internal, a matter of the heart, which will in turn affect outward behavior (15:16–20). Thus, each beatitude contains an implicit condemnation of religious hypocrisy that the people are to reject.

But it is not enough only to hear a pronouncement. While the Beatitudes are not entrance requirements, they do offer an invitation to the crowd to respond to Jesus' announcement of the kingdom of heaven. There are only two choices: the way of the kingdom or the way of the religious establishment. As Jesus pronounces the availability of the kingdom to all, he offers the way to life. But the door to life is narrow—as narrow as Jesus (cf. 7:13–14). All must come through him.

(2) *Instruction.* The Beatitudes also have special instructional value for his disciples. The qualities that exemplified the godly person in the Old Testament are now made an eschatological reality with the arrival of the kingdom of God. These qualities will accompany the transformation that occurs in the life of each disciple as each submits to the operation of kingdom life through the Spirit. In the Beatitudes, and indeed in the SM as a whole, the emphasis is on a righteousness that begins with the transformation of the inner life and then moves to conform external behavior to inward values (e.g., 5:20–48).

The problem with the teachers of the law and the Pharisees was their tendency to promote external righteousness first (cf. 15:6–9; 23:25–28). Jesus focuses instead on the transformation of the heart by the arrival of the kingdom of heaven, which will then direct the transformation of the entire person—word, thought, action, and deeds. This had been God's intention from the original creation, but now with arrival of the kingdom of heaven in the ministry of Jesus, discipleship to him will bring congruency between inner and external life (cf. 5:17–20). The Beatitudes are statements of reality about the kind of characteristics that will be produced in the disciple who participates in kingdom life.

---

29. In 5:20, Jesus identifies the teachers of the law and the Pharisees as those on whom he pronounces condemnation. Without actually naming them in the rest of the SM, they are the obvious objects of his criticism.

Therefore, the Beatitudes are not imperatives or required standards that disciples must perform in order to procure God's approval. If that were the case, they would not be much different than the rigorous demands for purity found among the Jewish leaders, and they would lead to the same kind of religious hypocrisy that Jesus condemns. Instead, they provide guidelines for the kind of life that God intends to produce in his disciples. With the arrival of the kingdom of God in each disciple, these character qualities become a concrete reality. This is the link between Jesus' teaching on discipleship and later New Testament discussions of regeneration and sanctification through the work of the Holy Spirit. Note, for example, Peter's description of the transformational process for those who have been born anew by the living and enduring word of God in 1 Peter 1:22–2:3. As Jesus' disciples face the daily challenges lived in the realities of a fallen world, they must reject the evil path and allow God's Spirit to produce these Christlike characteristics in them.

As such, the Beatitudes contrast Jesus' values with the values of the world. Larry Richards displays this contrast of Jesus' values and those of the world in the following way:

| Jesus' values | Countervalues |
|---|---|
| *poor in spirit* | self-confident, competent, self-reliant |
| *mourn* | pleasure-seeking, hedonistic, "the beautiful people" |
| *meek* | proud, powerful, important |
| *hunger and thirst for righteousness* | satisfied, "well adjusted," practical |
| *merciful* | self-righteous, "able to take care of themselves" |
| *pure in heart* | "adult," sophisticated, broad-minded |
| *peacemakers* | competitive, aggressive |
| *persecuted because of righteousness* | adaptable, popular, "don't rock the boat"[30] |

Each of these can be explored more fully, but they help illustrate the values that Jesus establishes with the arrival of the kingdom of heaven. The Beatitudes are bold statements of the nature of kingdom life. It begins with abandoning pride in one's spiritual accomplishment before God and proceeds as one allows God to produce kingdom life in his disciples' everyday lives.

Contemporary Significance

THE APPLICABILITY OF the Beatitudes. The Beatitudes with which the SM begins are pronouncements of blessing on those waiting for God's messianic activity, pronouncements of condemnation on the religious establishment who have attempted to secure

30. Lawrence O. Richards, *The Teacher's Commentary* (Wheaton, Ill.: Victor, 1987), 541.

God's blessing through their own efforts, and instructions for Jesus' disciples about the life that is truly "blessed" from God's perspective. But many people grate under them because they can seem so foreign to our ideas of human aspiration. Who really wants to be poor, to mourn, to be meek... ?

Dallas Willard's influential book *The Divine Conspiracy* is a forceful development of Christian discipleship, concentrating on the Gospel of Matthew and the SM in particular as his biblical foundation. In his discussion of the Beatitudes, he recounts how a woman told him that her son had dropped his Christian identification and left the church because of the Beatitudes. This son, a strong, intelligent, military person, had had an unhappy experience:

> As often happens, he had been told that the Beatitudes—with its list of the poor and the sad, the weak and the mild—were a picture of the ideal Christian. He explained to his mother very simply: "That's not me. I can never be like that."[31]

I understand this young man's experience. In my teens I also renounced my Christian identity and church for similar reasons. I clearly remember sitting in youth group meetings where the characteristics of the Beatitudes were held up as ideals for us to emulate. I remember snickering in the back row with my buddies as the youth leaders cajoled us to cease being cocky and macho and become meek and mild. The four of us were three-sport athletes in high school, and the picture of the Christian life that was held up for us from the Beatitudes seemed lamely pathetic. As I think back, our youthful cockiness and machismo were probably just as pathetic, but the Christian life painted by that church had nothing to offer us as a viable, robust alternative.

Not too many years after ruling out the Beatitudes for real life, I sat under the brilliant stars in a jungle in Vietnam and their significance overwhelmed me. I was a member of a cocky airborne infantry combat battalion. We were a well-trained, exceedingly efficient war machine. One night as I sat on guard duty after one especially ravaging battle, I experienced the reality of what Jesus addressed in the Beatitudes. I had killed gleefully that day. I had ripped the life from other young men without a twinge of conscience. I saw the

---

31. Dallas Willard, *The Divine Conspiracy: Rediscovering Our Hidden Life in God* (San Francisco: HarperSanFrancisco, 1998), 99. Awarded book of the year by *Christianity Today* in 1998, *The Divine Conspiracy* is a helpful application of the Sermon on the Mount, and Matthew's Gospel generally, to spiritual development. The exposition that Willard offers of the Beatitudes is an attempt to avoid extremes, and caricatures, of the characteristics of the Beatitudes. He rightly rejects the extremes, but his alternative explanation is problematic because he sees the individual characteristics as negative conditions. This overlooks the consistent positive use of these themes in the Old Testament as well as in the rest of the New Testament.

bodies of my nineteen- and twenty-year-old squad members ravaged by other young men who were our hated enemies, yet probably none of us on either side could really offer any adequate explanation for our animosity.

That night I experienced brokenness. I became poor in spirit as I recognized the depth of my depravity and shuddered as I considered the possibility of my fate before God, if he existed. I mourned at the evil in me and at the evil that I saw emerge so quickly in all of us. For the first time in my young life, I understood that I was not the invincible captain of my ship. I could be killed at any moment. So from that very night I began to realize that there was indeed a very different way to live. I did not articulate it that night in these words, but meekness, righteousness, mercy, purity, and peacemaking all became so much more clearly preferable than the way that I had been pursuing significance and success.

I now realize I was experiencing the beginnings of the *pronouncement* aspects of the Beatitudes. I saw for the first time the horror of my life as a human apart from God. I desperately needed something, but what it was, I had no clue. I experienced the condemnation of my old cockiness and self-sufficiency, and above all, the condemnation of my arrogant abuse of people in my quest to satisfy my own lusts. This transition in my life readied me and enabled me to accept Jesus' invitation to the life of the kingdom of heaven two years later.

I didn't try to do anything to get to this place. It came about as it should in any person who takes an honest look at the way of humans apart from God. It came about as I realized in the depth of my soul that there truly is an either-or choice in life—Jesus' way of the kingdom of God or the world's way to destruction. It is no coincidence that Jesus culminates the SM with these either-or choices (7:13–27).

No, I didn't do anything to get to this place, but I now know that someone else did. Jesus says later, in the last fateful night before his crucifixion, that he would send another in his place: a Counselor, the very Spirit of God, who will "convict" the world of sin and righteousness and judgment (John 16:8). That's what happened to me—and that's what happens to every person apart from Jesus and the kingdom of heaven, because that is the only way a person can repent and turn to God. It is the Spirit's work of conviction that brings a person to the place where she or he can respond to the invitation to the gospel of the kingdom, and in that they are blessed.

In the same way that the Beatitudes express the blessedness that comes to the crowds from the convicting work of the Holy Spirit, they also express the blessedness that comes from the renewing work of the Holy Spirit in the life of a disciple. I don't believe I have ever tried to be poor in spirit or consciously wanted to mourn or be meek. I tend to be repulsed by people who talk too much about wanting to be righteous, merciful, or pure, or who talk about making peace and will gladly suffer for Jesus' sake. But remarkably, I have seen these characteristics produced in this formerly cocky, arrogant young man as I have focused my life on walking with Jesus.

The individual characteristics of the Beatitudes are not self-produced, nor can we simply learn or emulate them in an attempt to bring them about in our lives. They are products of a life energized by the Spirit of God. They are, like the listing Paul gives in Galatians 5:22–23, the fruit of the Spirit. They are a wholistic view of what the Spirit will produce in the life of a disciple of Jesus who is walking in his ways and is being transformed into his image.

So it does help tremendously to study the Beatitudes, because they reveal the values of the kingdom of heaven. As in any study of Scripture, they show us God's ways in distinction from the world's ways and help us to know the right path. But the wonderful truth behind the study of the Beatitudes and our obedience to their truth as the Word of God is that the characteristics of the Beatitudes are ultimately produced by the Spirit of God.

The young man mentioned earlier had turned away from Christianity because of the perception he had of the Christian life displayed in the Beatitudes. Two things are probably at play here. (1) Like me, he is a product of a world that glories in self, in personal and institutional strength and bravado. The Beatitudes turn those values on end to show what humanity rightly related to God and to each other will be through the arrival of the kingdom of God.

(2) He quite likely has seen faulty applications of the Beatitudes in his church experiences. Throughout church history the Beatitudes have been subjected to faulty interpretation that has led to extremes. Many years later I came to understand that the church I left in my teens was theologically liberal. They really did believe that the Beatitudes were an expression of the ideal life that humans need to pursue to find God. They rightly recognized that the Beatitudes are an ideal statement of the Christian life, but they mistakenly thought that they could do it on their own. Some groups have contended that these characteristics are not for today's rough-and-tumble, sin-wracked world, but await some far-off future kingdom. Still others have based entire personal and ecclesiastical practices of pacifism and nonviolence on the Beatitudes' overriding centrality for a present-day theological system.

No wonder the young man did not see what Jesus meant to communicate. The Beatitudes are neither a means of entering nor of advancing in the kingdom. They are expressions of Spirit-produced kingdom life, revealing to the entire world that a transformation of creation is beginning in Jesus' disciples. That is why we are blessed.

**The applicability of the sayings on salt and light.** Throughout history humans have attempted to establish their own little kingdoms on the earth, whether through a Nazi blitzkrieg, a Communist revolution, or an Islamic jihad. It is a real temptation for humans to resort to such means, for fallen creatures want to impose their ways on others. But Jesus has brought the kingdom of God in a very different way. It is the way of regeneration and renewal by the Spirit. Spirit-produced poverty in spirit, mourning, meekness, righteousness, mercy, purity, and peace are the characteristics of Jesus' disciples that allows God to establish his kingdom in his way. The sayings on salt and light are natural outgrowths of the Beatitudes, since the kingdom life found in Jesus' disciples is demonstrated in their lives in this world.[32]

The salt metaphor informs us that our lives are important to this world. Regardless of our status or profession, the kingdom life that we possess is invaluable for the preserving/seasoning/fertilizing effect it will have in our daily realm. The metaphor also has a warning for imposter disciples, because the kingdom life that is transforming the lives of true disciples cannot be imitated or manufactured. The light metaphor continues the thought, but emphasizes more directly the positive influence disciples will make in this sin-darkened world. We not only carry the light of the gospel of the kingdom of God, but we *are* that light. Because of the work of the Spirit in our lives, our transformation has produced kingdom light in us, affecting every aspect of our being.

Two implications from these truths call for our attention. (1) Scripture speaks directly to the need of Christians to meet together regularly for support, encouragement, and training (e.g., Heb. 10:24–25). The church is our haven, our hospital, and our training center. But to be salt and light, we must go out into the world of people who are dying without the message of the gospel. This emphasis was initiated in the calling scene of chapter 4, where Jesus called two sets of brothers to be fishers of men. The people we are to reach are in the world around us. They are our next-door neighbors, our mail delivery person, our children's friends and parents and teachers, our coworkers at the office, our server in the local restaurant, and on and on. The church or Bible study or retreat center performs an invaluable service to support, guide, and prepare us for life, but life is mostly played out beyond those confines. Disciples who are salt and light are called to be intentional sojourners in the world.

---

32. Hays, *The Moral Vision of the New Testament*, 321: "The community's vocation to be 'salt' and 'light' for the world (5:13–16) is to be fulfilled precisely as Jesus' followers embody God's alternative reality through the character qualities marked by the Beatitudes."

(2) Intentional sojourning in the world as salt and light requires that we know who we are and what makes us different from the world. It isn't just a religious title. We must *speak* the truth of the gospel for people to know it, but we are called to *live* the truth of the gospel for people to see that it is real. The light of the kingdom will produce a changed life in us, "that they may see your good deeds and praise your Father in heaven" (5:16). The Beatitudes emphasize the change produced in the character of disciples who are transformed by the arrival of the kingdom. Intentional sojourning in the world requires us to be alert to the stark difference between our discipleship and the world's values and habits, and to live out the kingdom values summarized in the Beatitudes and revealed more fully in the rest of the SM.

Much of this is accomplished in the ordinariness of life. We may think that being salt and light will be carried out in dramatic ways as we preach, witness, or go on a short-term missions. But if, as we have suggested, the world to whom we are to go are people found in the everyday routines of life, they will see our transformed life in our everyday activities. It is the transformation of those everyday activities that will cause them to praise our Father in heaven. Everyday people are so affected by sin that they are less than what God has created them to be. They lie when they don't want to, they cheat just to try and get ahead, they hurt most the ones they most love. Many people we encounter don't really want to be like that, but they have no cure for the sin that has distorted who they are as created in the image of God.

Others have developed a "who cares" attitude. They speak into a cell phone as if they were the only person for blocks. They curse like Madonna on the David Letterman show; their kids think the world is their personal playground, and they drive like maniacs. A recent poll by the research group Public Agenda found that rudeness is getting worse in America. Seventy-nine percent of those surveyed said that lack of respect and courtesy is a serious problem. Eighty-eight percent said that they often or sometimes come across people who are rude or disrespectful. Poor customer service has become so rampant that nearly half of those surveyed said they have walked out of a store in the past year because of it. But interestingly, the people surveyed had few solutions. Thirty-six percent said that when confronted with rude behavior, the right thing is to respond with excessive politeness. Twenty percent said it is best to point out the bad behavior. But forty-two percent said the best thing to do is walk away.[33]

It may seem trivial, but this is what the Beatitudes address, as well as Jesus' sayings on salt and light. Yes, we have and must declare the saving message

---

33. Matt Crenson, The Associated Press, "Poll: Manners Lost in America," *Orange County Register* (April 3, 2002), Nation and World, 1.

of the gospel. People can't change until they have heard the message. But the old adage is so true that actions speak louder than words. We must show by our lives that we are different. Otherwise we are hiding our light from the world. Are we rude and disrespectful? Do we go along with the crowd that is ridiculing a player on an opposing team? Do we give the best service to our customers, whether they are customers in Wal-Mart, students at your school, or parishioners in your church? Jesus tells us that his disciples won't be rude and disrespectful if we allow the kingdom life to do its full work in us. And when we are respectful, courteous, considerate, and service-oriented, the world around us will see that Jesus really does make a difference.

Donald McCullough has written a fascinating book with practical advice in this direction.[34] While this book is not targeted primarily toward Christians, he is a professing Christian, and he bases the respect that we owe one another on the fact of humanity's creation in the image of God. Clever titles of chapters range from "Don't Show Up at the Wedding in a Baseball Cap," to "Kneel Down to Speak with Children," to "Leave a Tip Worth Working For." His intention in writing about these seemingly insignificant issues is worth our attention:

> I'm more interested in the little things, such as remembering to say "thank you" and to call your mom on Mother's Day. These things may not seem very important when compared with the major problems facing our culture. Yet they may be the best place to begin; they may be the only honest place to begin. If a person can't remember to say thank you to her housekeeper, it probably won't matter much if she writes a major philosophical treatise on kindness; if a person is rude to his family, the angels probably won't give a holy rip if he preaches soaring sermons on the nature of love.[35]

Likewise, Jesus teaches us that we witness to the reality of the presence of the kingdom of God in little kindnesses. Disciples who are poor in spirit will mourn over rudeness and abuse, and we will be gentle, pursuing righteousness, practicing mercy, and being peacemakers, even if it brings us grief. In so living, we will be revealed as sons of God, the true salt of the earth and the glowing light of the world.

---

34. Donald McCullough, *Say Please, Say Thank You: The Respect We Owe One Another* (New York: Perigee, 1998).

35. Ibid., 8.

# Matthew 5:17-20

**D**O NOT THINK that I have come to abolish the Law or the Prophets; I have not come to abolish them but to fulfill them. ¹⁸I tell you the truth, until heaven and earth disappear, not the smallest letter, not the least stroke of a pen, will by any means disappear from the Law until everything is accomplished. ¹⁹Anyone who breaks one of the least of these commandments and teaches others to do the same will be called least in the kingdom of heaven, but whoever practices and teaches these commands will be called great in the kingdom of heaven. ²⁰For I tell you that unless your righteousness surpasses that of the Pharisees and the teachers of the law, you will certainly not enter the kingdom of heaven.

**Original Meaning**

JOHN THE BAPTIST'S initial announcement of the forthcoming arrival of the kingdom of heaven brought tension between the religious establishment and the kingdom's projected activity (3:7–12). Jesus' implicit and explicit criticism of the religious establishment will bring increasing tension and outright opposition (12:22–32). At the center of that tension and opposition is the suspicion that Jesus is not fully orthodox in his commitment to the Old Testament. Thus, in his first major discourse in this Gospel, Jesus makes clear his understanding of and commitment to the Old Testament.

But he will not simply affirm one of the interpretative schools of thought. He will not offer just another application of the ancient law to his contemporary circumstances. Instead, he will give the authoritative interpretation of the Old Testament's original intended meaning, elevating himself above all the rabbinic debates. These four verses provide the key to interpreting the SM, but also in many ways the key to understanding Jesus' inauguration of the kingdom, and by extension, the understanding of Matthew's purpose for writing his Gospel.

**Fulfilling the law (5:17).** Some might see Jesus' announcement of the arrival of the kingdom of heaven (4:17) as though he is starting a new work that will bring him into conflict with the Old Testament Scriptures. But Jesus categorically declares, "Do not think that I have come to abolish the Law or the Prophets." The expression "do not think" suggests that Jesus is countering a suspicion that he is attempting to set aside God's former revelation with his announcement of the arrival of the kingdom of God.[1] Such an attempt would be the ultimate mark of a heretic.[2] So Jesus makes clear at the beginning of his teaching ministry that the arrival of the kingdom does not do away with God's prior revelation through the Law and the Prophets.

The "Law" or "Torah" refers to the first five books of the Old Testament, called the Books of Moses or the Pentateuch. The "Prophets" includes the major and minor prophets of the Old Testament. The expression "the Law and the Prophets" (cf. 7:12; 11:13; 22:40; Rom. 3:21) is a way of referring to the entire Hebrew Scriptures. This is similar to the expressions "the Law of Moses, the Prophets and the Psalms" (Luke 24:44) or simply "the Law"[3] (Matt. 5:18; 1 Cor. 14:21). Instead of doing away with what God had revealed about his will for his people in the Hebrew Scripture, Jesus' purpose for his earthly ministry is wrapped up in this formula: "I have come to fulfill them."[4]

In Matthew's narrative, the term "fulfill" (*pleroo*) has already become an important indicator of Jesus' significance in God's historical program, because Jesus' life and ministry fulfill Old Testament prophecies and expectations (e.g., 1:22–23; 2:15, 17–18, 23; 4:14–16). Throughout the New Testament, various other writers also point to the way that Jesus fulfills, for example, the Old Testament roles of prophet,[5] priest,[6] and king.[7] But here Jesus points in an additional direction when he declares that he has come to fulfill *all* of Old Testament Scripture.

The idea of "fulfillment" is more than his obedience (i.e., keeping the law), although that is included. The context, especially as worked out in the "antitheses" to follow (5:21–48), indicates that Jesus not only fulfills certain anticipated roles, but also that his interpretation of the Scriptures completes and clarifies God's intent and meaning through it.[8] Everything that the Old

---

1. The polemic of the SM (cf. 5:20; 6:1–18; 7:28–29) indicates that the antagonism between Jesus and the religious leaders is already well underway (cf. Hagner, *Matthew 1–13*, 104–5; contra Robert Banks, *Jesus and the Law in the Synoptic Tradition* [SNTSMS 28; Cambridge: Cambridge Univ. Press, 1975], 65ff.; Carson, "Matthew," 141–42).

2. Keener, *A Commentary on the Gospel of Matthew* (1999), 176 n. 46.

3. In the coming pages, we will attempt to use uppercase "Law" if it refers to the Pentateuch or the entire Old Testament, but lowercase "law" if it refers to the legal sections of the Old Testament.

4. Warren Carter, "Jesus' 'I have come' Statements in Matthew's Gospel," *CBQ* 60 (1998): 44–62.

5. Deut. 18:15–19; Matt. 21:11; Acts 3:22.

6. Lev. 16:11–19; Isa. 56:7; Matt. 21:13; Heb. 2:17–18; 4:14–16; 5:1–10; 7:24–25; 9:11–14.

7. Isa. 62:11; Zech. 9:9; Matt. 2:2; 21:5; Luke 2:11; 1 Tim. 6:15; Rev. 17:14; 19:16.

8. For helpful overviews and guides to the literature, see Guelich, *Sermon on the Mount*, 138–42, and J. Daryl Charles, "The Greatest or the Least in the Kingdom? The Disciple's Relationship to the Law (Matt 5:17–20)," *TrinJ* 13 n.s. (1992): 139–62.

Testament intended to communicate about God's will and hopes and future[9] for humanity finds its fullest meaning in Jesus. Jesus has come to actualize the Scripture and take his disciples to a deeper understanding of its intended meaning—and this in distinction from many Jewish leaders, who have misunderstood and misapplied the Scripture's intent.[10]

**The lasting validity of the Old Testament (5:18).** Jesus emphatically affirms the lasting validity of "the Law" (the entire Hebrew Scriptures) as the revealed will of God for his people until the end of this age brings a consummation of all that God has purposed. The two "until" clauses in 5:18 are parallel and essentially synonymous, used to emphasize the lasting validity of the Old Testament. "Until everything is accomplished" also seems to include some features of "fulfillment" that point to Jesus' consummation of specific Old Testament hopes; for example, in the antitheses Jesus reiterates the lasting validity of the Old Testament but does not make legally binding certain specific prescriptions (see comments on 5:33–37).

The Old Testament endures forever as a revelation of God's will for humans throughout history until all is "accomplished." While some elements of Scripture will be accomplished in Jesus' ministry, the Old Testament remains a valid principle. For example, the teaching of death and the shedding of blood to atone for sin is no longer expressed through temple sacrifices but rather has been "fulfilled/accomplished" once for all in Christ's atonement on the cross (cf. Heb. 9:11–14). Thus, this commandment from the Old Testament is no longer legally binding as a practice. Nevertheless, the Old Testament principle of penalty and payment for sin remains valid and needs to be taught and understood as God's will.[11]

Therefore, Jesus confirms the full authority of the Old Testament as Scripture for all ages (cf. 2 Tim. 3:15–16), even down to the smallest components of the written text. Those components are the "smallest letter" (*iota*; KJV "jot") of the Hebrew alphabet (*yod*) and "the least stroke of a pen" (*keraia*; KJV "tittle"), which most likely refers to a serif, a small hook or projection that differentiates various Hebrew letters.

This has implications for understanding Jesus' view of the inspiration of Scripture, which extends to the actual words, even letters and parts of letters.

---

9. See Matt. 11:13 where the Law and Prophets prophesy until the new age arrives with John.

10. For a discussion of the contrast to the contemporary religious establishment, see J. Daryl Charles, "Garnishing with the 'Greater Righteousness': The Disciple's Relationship to the Law (Matthew 5:17–20)," *BBR* 12 (2002): 1–15.

11. David A. Dorsey, "The Law of Moses and the Christian: A Compromise," *JETS* 34 (1991): 321–34. Dorsey's article attempts, commendably, to clarify the continuity and discontinuity of the law for the Christian.

This is in accord with a "verbal plenary" view of inspiration; that is, the very words, and all of the words, of Scripture are inspired. Scripture does not simply contain the Word of God; the words of Scripture are the very Word of God.[12]

**Doing and teaching the commandments (5:19).** The consequences of one's treatment of the Old Testament are immense. The rabbis recognized a distinction between "light" and "weighty" Old Testament commandments and advocated obedience to both (*m. ʾAbot* 2:1; 4:2). Light commandments are those such as the requirement to tithe on produce (cf. Lev. 27:30; Deut. 14:22), and weighty commandments are those such as profaning the name of God, misusing the Sabbath, or refusing to enact social justice (Ex. 20:2–8; Mic. 6:8). Since the Old Testament remains the valid expression of God's will, even down to the "jot" and "tittle," Jesus likewise demands a commitment to both the least of the commandments as well as the greatest, but at the same time condemns those who pervert the light into weighty (cf. Matt. 23:23).[13]

Jesus directs his comments specifically to his own followers. The "least" and "great in the kingdom of heaven" are those who have responded to his announcement of the gospel of the kingdom. Jesus drives home the binding authority of Scripture. Since he does not "abolish" the Law and the Prophets but fulfills them (5:17), his disciples likewise must not "abolish" or "break"[14] the commandments but must instead practice and teach them (5:19). The wordplay here warns his disciples how to conduct themselves with regard to the Old Testament *as he now fulfills it.* The entire Old Testament is the expression of God's will, but it is to be obeyed and taught from the perspective of how Jesus "fulfills" it through his interpretation of its intent and meaning. A disciple's status in the kingdom of heaven accords with whether one trifles with the revealed will of God or one obeys and teaches it as truly the Word of God.

The rank of "least" should not be taken to indicate exclusion from the kingdom, because in the next verse Jesus makes a distinction between those inside and outside of the kingdom. "Least" and "great" are ways to acknowledge in this present life those who have been faithful in word and deed to the revealed will of God as it is taught by Jesus.

**"Inside-out" righteousness (5:20).** From a warning and commendation to his disciples, Jesus next turns his attention to the broader audience—

---

12. For overviews, see John W. Wenham, "Christ's View of Scripture," in *Inerrancy*, ed. Norman L. Geisler (Grand Rapids: Zondervan, 1980), 1–36; Grudem, *Systematic Theology*, esp. 73–104.

13. Charles, "Greatest or Least in the Kingdom," 154–56.

14. "Abolish" is the verb *katalyo*, and "break" is the root verb *lyo* without the prepositional prefix *kata*.

those who are not in the kingdom of heaven. "For I tell you that unless your righteousness surpasses that of the Pharisees and the teachers of the law, you will certainly not enter the kingdom of heaven" (5:20). This may have been Jesus' most shocking statement, because the teachers of the law and the Pharisees were the epitome of ethical righteousness.

The "teachers of the law" or scribes (*grammateus*) were not only curators of the text of the Old Testament, but they also taught the Law (7:29), held themselves responsible to interpret and preserve the Law (Mark 7:5–8), elaborated doctrine from the Law (Matt. 17:10), and gathered around themselves disciples whom they could train to carry on the profession and their teachings. Today the equivalent might be a professor or scholar of biblical studies and theology. The "Pharisees" (see comment on 3:7) were members of the sect that was committed to fulfilling the demands of the Old Testament through their elaborate oral tradition. Their scrupulous adherence to the written and oral law was legendary in Israel, yet Jesus says that it does not gain them entrance to the kingdom of heaven.

But how could anyone possibly surpass their righteousness? If the scribes and the Pharisees had not gained entrance, what hope was there for anyone else? Does this mean an intensification of a doctrine of salvation by works? Does this mean that one must exceed the scribes and the Pharisees in performing all the 613 commandments[15] and do them one better? No, replies Jesus. His disciples are called to a different *kind* and *quality* of righteousness, not an increased quantity. As was recognized in both Jesus' interaction with John the Baptist (3:15) and the statement of the Beatitudes (5:6), righteousness in the preaching of Jesus is not primarily a personal attainment of ethical purity. Righteousness belongs in the realm of grace. Jesus' proclamation of good news is that the kingdom of heaven is now available to those who respond to him. God's saving activity has arrived on the earthly scene to deliver his people, and this will produce a radical change in their lives.[16]

The shock of that declaration strips away current precedents for gaining favor with God and serves both as an introduction to the "antitheses" to follow (5:21–48) and as a tacit disclosure of the central principle of life in the kingdom of heaven, namely, that kingdom righteousness operates from the inside-out, not from the outside-in. This is not a new principle, however.

---

15. The number 613 is the traditional number of combined commandments and prohibitions reckoned by the rabbis.

16. Hagner, "Righteousness in Matthew's Theology," 116–17. Hagner sees primarily the element of ethical righteousness in 5:20, but his argument for God's salvific deliverance in 3:15 and 5:6 could also be applied here, which he does more directly in his commentary (Hagner, *Matthew 1–13*, 109).

God's people knew that external acts of righteousness could not take away sin or gain favor with God unless they were preceded by a repentant heart. Psalm 51 is perhaps the archetype, where David seeks inner cleansing and purification of his heart after his dreadfully sinful affair with Bathsheba (Ps. 51:2, 7, 10). His understanding of the inside-out operation is explicit:

> You do not delight in sacrifice, or I would bring it;
> you do not take pleasure in burnt offerings.
> The sacrifices of God are a broken spirit;
> a broken and contrite heart, O God, you will not despise.
> (Ps. 51:16–17)

David did later offer sacrifices and offerings and he did receive God's favor, but he knew they had to be preceded by inner repentance and God's work of cleansing and purification.

Yet throughout Israel's history there was a tendency to reverse the operation, as was the case with the scribes and Pharisees of Jesus' day. The assumption seemed to be that if one worked hard enough to clean up the outside, then the inside was automatically clean. Jesus later condemns this procedure explicitly when he says:

> Woe to you, teachers of the law and Pharisees, you hypocrites! You are like whitewashed tombs, which look beautiful on the outside but on the inside are full of dead men's bones and everything unclean. In the same way, on the outside you appear to people as righteous but on the inside you are full of hypocrisy and wickedness. (Matt. 23:27–28).

Since entrance into the kingdom of heaven is not gained by external acts of righteousness, Jesus leads the audience to recognize that people must seek a different kind of righteousness—an inner righteousness that begins with a transformation of the heart, an undertaking David knew could only be accomplished by God (Ps. 51:10).

The arrival of the kingdom of heaven produces spiritual transformation in the disciple's heart, which will ultimately produce transformation in the disciple's external ethical life (see comments on 15:16–20). If entrance into the kingdom of heaven can only be accomplished by an inner work of transformation, so also personal growth within the kingdom must proceed from inside to out. That principle underlies the next series of examples Jesus uses to explain how he fulfills the Old Testament. His disciples themselves will fulfill God's intention and will (as revealed in Scripture) as they conform their inner life to his Word and then have that inner transformation guide their external behavior.

Without doubt, Jesus' declaration in 5:20 is an interpretive key to the entire Sermon on the Mount and, by extension, to life in the kingdom of heaven. It is the same reality that underlies Paul's understanding of justification and sanctification. So Jesus in no way sets aside or abolishes the Law, but he affirms and fulfills its complete authority. In the antitheses to follow, Jesus contrasts his internal, spiritual interpretation with the external, legalistic interpretation of the Pharisees, which dead-ends in an external, superficial self-righteousness.

*Bridging Contexts*

BASED ON THE stringent attitude toward God's law found in these words of Jesus, critical scholars have often tried to pit Matthew and Paul against each another, as though Paul advocated a gospel of grace that was antinomian, which Matthew intentionally countered with a gospel of law.[17] But the contrast between Paul and Matthew is overplayed. While Matthew records Jesus' sayings that uphold the binding validity of the law (5:17–20), he also has strong language of rebuke for the Pharisees who legalistically applied the Old Testament in such a way that they were cutting people off from the kingdom of heaven (e.g., 23:13–15). Matthew also focuses on Jesus' message of transformation from the heart, not salvation by works (e.g., 15:1–20).

Paul likewise upholds the law as holy, righteous, and good (Rom. 7:12) and has strong words of condemnation for the Judaizing legalists (e.g., Gal. 1:8), focusing on salvation by grace alone (e.g., Eph. 2:8–9). Both Matthew and Paul go back to Jesus for the declaration that the Old Testament Scripture is the written, revealed will of God. The Old Testament is and will remain Scripture (2 Tim. 3:16), but Jesus brings it to its intended meaning and goal.

**Fulfilling the Law.** Matthew has prepared his readers well for Jesus' staggering pronouncement, "I have not come to abolish the Law and the Prophets … but to fulfill them," by consistently pointing to the way that Jesus fulfills certain Old Testament prophecies or themes. Now comes the overwhelming pronouncement that Jesus fulfills *all* of the Old Testament. Rampant must have been the rumors that Jesus and his followers had set aside the Old Testament. So Matthew points out directly to his readers that Jesus *fulfills* the Old Testament.

But the way in which Jesus fulfills the Law here in 5:17–20 takes us in a slightly different direction than in prophecy-fulfillment in the first two chapters. There, specific Old Testament prophecies of a coming messianic

---

17. E.g., F. W. Beare, *The Gospel According to Matthew: Translation Introduction and Commentary* (San Francisco: Harper & Row, 1981), 141.

deliverer were fulfilled in Jesus' life and ministry (1:22–23, 2:5–6, 15, 17–18, 23). Here Jesus brings to fulfillment all that the Old Testament had revealed about God's will for humanity. (1) This means that Jesus' life of perfect obedience to the will of God as revealed in the law enables him to be the perfect sacrifice for sins in his death. (2) Moreover, his obedience provides the means by which his disciples are able to live lives of obedience to God's law, because Jesus will soon assist his followers in understanding and obeying God's original intention of his law.

It will not be enough to conform one's behavior to an external obedience of any particular law. Rather, Jesus' disciples will understand the realities to which the Law pointed and will have a heart transformation and obedience that is accomplished through new covenant life in the Spirit. The pathway to greatness in the kingdom of heaven is through obeying and teaching his commands (5:19), which is an overarching characteristic of Great Commission disciples (28:19–20). "The command to live under God's dominion, first given to Adam and Eve at creation, can therefore be restored with the inauguration of the kingdom, since the power of God's presence in our midst is the dawning of the new creation. Jesus' demands flow from his gifts."[18]

This is an increasingly clear indication of the arrival of those new covenant promises. The prophet Ezekiel had prophesied:

> I will sprinkle clean water on you, and you will be clean; I will cleanse you from all your impurities and from all your idols. I will give you a new heart and put a new spirit in you; I will remove from you your heart of stone and give you a heart of flesh. And I will put my Spirit in you and move you to follow my decrees and be careful to keep my laws. (Ezek. 36:25–27; cf. Jer. 31:31–34)

Jesus guides his disciples into the true intention of God's law, which focuses on inner righteousness as opposed to mere external righteousness. They gain entrance to the kingdom by repenting and confessing their sins (cf. 3:1–6; 4:17), which allows the Spirit to enter into their life to bring purification through applying Jesus' atoning righteousness to their heart. In this way, Jesus' disciples are more righteous than the scribes and the Pharisees, because they have received regeneration as they enter the kingdom.

Moreover, Jesus' disciples progress in righteousness through their transformation into the image of Christ. This statement lays the foundation for the later New Testament doctrines of justification (imputed righteousness)

---

18. Scott J. Hafemann, *The God of Promise and the Life of Faith: Understanding the Heart of the Bible* (Wheaton: Crossway, 2001), 202. All of Matt. 9 is a helpful overview of Jesus' relation to the Law and the implications for his disciple's obedience.

and sanctification (imparted righteousness), which will be special emphases of the former "righteous" Pharisee, the apostle Paul.

> Small wonder Paul, that most faultless of Pharisees (Phil. 3:4–6), when he came to understand the Gospel of Christ, considered his spiritual assets rubbish. His new desire was to gain Christ, not having a righteousness of his own that comes from the law, but one which is from God and by faith in Christ (Phil. 3:8f.).[19]

**THE CHRISTIAN'S RELATION to the law.** The issues surrounding the Christian's relationship to the Old Testament Scripture (Law) are complex. Some contend that none of it applies to Jesus unless it is explicitly reaffirmed in the New Testament, while others say that all of the Old Testament applies unless it is explicitly revoked in the New Testament.[20] Both of these extremes should be avoided in the light of Jesus' statements in 5:17–20. While these issues are beyond what we can address here, some basic principles can be suggested.

(1) The law is a revelation of God's will for humanity. It reveals a standard of God's perfect righteousness. We trifle with God's will if we set aside some aspects of his Word. For example, it may be commendable to oppose abortions, but when antiabortion activists resort to violence and murder, they have set aside God's commands.

(2) We need to understand God's purpose for giving his law if we are to rightly understand the law itself. The law had several purposes. It was designed to instruct God's people in his will so that they might fulfill his purpose for them as "a kingdom of priests and a holy nation" (Ex. 19:6). But they were not to rely on its requirements as the means of finding forgiveness (Ps. 51:14–17). The law was given to point out humanity's sinfulness and need for God (Rom. 7:7) and to lead humanity to Christ, by whom they will be justified by faith (Gal. 3:24).

(3) When reading the Gospels in general and the antitheses in particular (Matt. 5:21–48), we must keep in mind that Jesus is here objecting to misinterpretations of the law, not the law itself. A tendency existed in Pharisaic Judaism to make their interpretations and traditions just as binding as the law itself. Jesus rejected their practices, not the law. He continued to uphold the law as the will of God.

---

19. D. A. Carson, *The Sermon on the Mount: An Evangelical Exposition of Matthew 5–7* (Grand Rapids: Baker, 1978), 39.

20. Blomberg, *Matthew*, 103–4.

(4) Jesus fulfilled the law and proved to be the perfect God-man, who is therefore able to become the means of our justification or right standing with God (Matt. 5:17–20; Rom. 5:18–21; Heb. 5:7–10). Therefore, we are not under the law as a means of gaining salvation.

(5) At the same time, Jesus is the interpreter of the law, showing what is binding principle and what is the temporary symbolic ritual (Matt. 12:1–8; Heb. 9:11–10:13). We should seek Christ's mind for a proper interpretation and application of the law and understand the Old Testament in the light of the new covenant he inaugurates. He emphasized that ultimately the law was given to aid humans to live life the way God intended it to be lived, not to keep us under a binding set of religious rules (Matt. 12:3–5, 9–14). As Jesus gives his interpretation of the law, he reveals its intent and motive that were lost behind the external legalism of the scribes and Pharisees. He then demonstrates how principles of the law are valid guidelines to show God's will for his people (5:21–48).[21]

(6) Jesus demonstrates that the entire Old Testament hangs on love for God and neighbor (22:38–39), which truly brings to fulfillment all of the Law. The "law of love" becomes an important key to determine how the Christian is to live out the will of God (5:21, 27, 38, etc.).

**Inside-out transformation.** The "inside-out" nature of Jesus' teaching on kingdom life can be illustrated by thinking of his disciple as concentric layers that eventually penetrate to the core of the person. We are "soulish persons," which indicates that we are a complex of immaterial and material realities. Our outermost layer consists of social relations. What I know first about a person are the relationships I share with or see the person engaged in, whether in a class, or in a family, or on the street. The next inward layer is the body, including what the person wears, how she carries herself, the way she talks, what she looks like, and so on. The next inward layer is the mind of the person. The mind is where the person reasons, considers emotions, and experiences spiritual realities. Then the innermost core of the person is the heart, which includes the person's will and spirit.

The gospel Jesus preached was energized by the Spirit of God, penetrating through social relations and the body to the mind of the listener. Jesus' teaching, logic, and appeal to the person were all at odds with those

---

21. Dorsey, "The Law of Moses and the Christian, 331: "If on the one hand the evidence strongly suggests that the corpus is no longer legally binding upon Christians, there is equally strong evidence in the NT that all 613 laws are profoundly binding upon Christians in a revelatory and pedagogical sense." For a helpful discussion of "principlism" in applying the Old Testament, see William W. Klein, Craig L. Blomberg, and Robert L. Hubbard Jr., *Introduction to Biblical Interpretation* (Dallas: Word, 1993), 278–83; and J. Daniel Hays, "Applying the Old Testament Law Today," *BibSac* 158 (January–March 2001): 21–35.

of the religious leaders who opposed him. At the same time, the Spirit of God convicts and draws the person, yet the forces of evil try to persuade the person that Jesus' gospel message is a fraud. The battle is waged in the mind, but the war is for the heart. If the person says "yes" to Jesus in the will of his or her heart, the Word of God energized by the Spirit penetrates to the heart, bringing new covenant transformation—justification, regeneration, and renewal of life. The person has become a disciple of Jesus and entered the kingdom of heaven.

This attempts to illustrate what Jesus meant when he said that "unless your righteousness surpasses that of the Pharisees and the teachers of the law, you will certainly not enter the kingdom of heaven" (5:20). The innermost core of the disciple has experienced new covenant transformation, which includes justification (declared forensically righteous before God) and the beginnings of sanctification (the experience of personal growth in righteousness). This far surpasses the righteousness of the scribes and Pharisees, which was external and self-produced.

As the disciple continues to respond obediently to the Word of God taught and preached by Jesus and energized by the Spirit, the newly transformed heart directs the transformation of the person from the inside to the outside. The heart-will of the person in the power of the indwelling Spirit directs the renewing of the mind (cf. Rom. 12:1–2), the disciplining of the body (1 Cor. 6:12–20), and the purifying of social relations (1 Cor. 5:9–13; Heb. 10:24–25) so that the disciple says "yes" to God with his or her entire "soulish person." The disciple bears the fruit of the Spirit in a life given to God that is being transformed to be like Jesus.

The schematic on the following page attempts to illustrate these truths. This is the process of discipleship, in which the truth of the gospel sets a person free to become Jesus' disciple. As he or she continues to compare the words of the world to the words of Jesus, the person is truly free to grow in discipleship to Jesus (John 8:31–32). The Spirit of God takes up residence in the life of the disciple, producing Christlike characteristics, including especially love (John 13:34–35) and the fruit of the Spirit (John 15:7–8). As we look at the SM unfold, this schematic will help us to appropriate Jesus' teaching and promote growth to be transformed more and more like him.

# Inside-Out Transformation of Jesus' Disciples to Become Like Him*

**The disciple says "yes" to God with his/her entire person**

## Soulish Person
**(social relations, body, mind, heart)**

**Social Relations**

**Body**

**Mind**

**Heart**

**(1) The Gospel and the Spirit.**
The Words of Jesus' Gospel, energized by the Spirit, penetrate social relations and the body to the mind. The battle rages in the mind of the would-be disciple, but the war is for his or her heart.

**(2) The Obedience of the Would-Be Disciple.**
The heart-will makes a decision for or against Jesus. As the heart says "yes" to Jesus, the truth of the Word of God energized by the Holy Spirit penetrates to the heart, bringing regeneration and setting the person free to become Jesus' disciple (John 8:31–32).

**(3) Transformed to Love As Jesus Loves.**
The regenerated heart is the beginning of the transformation of the disciple into the image of Christ, particularly to love like Jesus loves (John 13:34–45). The Spirit–indwelt heart directs the inside-out transformation process of mind, body, and social relations.

**(4) Becoming Like Jesus in Our Entire Person.**
The disciple who continues to say "yes" to the Word of God is transformed to bear the fruit of the Spirit (John 15:7–8). The disciple is enabled to say "yes" to God with his or her entire person. The process of inside-out transformation goes on throughout the entire life, as the disciple continually appropriates the truth of the Word in the Spirit to become more like Jesus.

*Adapted from Dallas Willard, *Renovation of the Heart: Putting on the Character of Christ* (Colorado Springs: NavPress, 2002), 38. I have adapted the schematic to illustrate the person that Jesus describes as entering and living in the kingdom of heaven.

# Matthew 5:21–48

"Y<sup>OU HAVE HEARD</sup> that it was said to the people long ago, 'Do not murder, and anyone who murders will be subject to judgment.' <sup>22</sup>But I tell you that anyone who is angry with his brother will be subject to judgment. Again, anyone who says to his brother, 'Raca,' is answerable to the Sanhedrin. But anyone who says, 'You fool!' will be in danger of the fire of hell.

<sup>23</sup>"Therefore, if you are offering your gift at the altar and there remember that your brother has something against you, <sup>24</sup>leave your gift there in front of the altar. First go and be reconciled to your brother; then come and offer your gift.

<sup>25</sup>"Settle matters quickly with your adversary who is taking you to court. Do it while you are still with him on the way, or he may hand you over to the judge, and the judge may hand you over to the officer, and you may be thrown into prison. <sup>26</sup>I tell you the truth, you will not get out until you have paid the last penny.

<sup>27</sup>"You have heard that it was said, 'Do not commit adultery.' <sup>28</sup>But I tell you that anyone who looks at a woman lustfully has already committed adultery with her in his heart. <sup>29</sup>If your right eye causes you to sin, gouge it out and throw it away. It is better for you to lose one part of your body than for your whole body to be thrown into hell. <sup>30</sup>And if your right hand causes you to sin, cut it off and throw it away. It is better for you to lose one part of your body than for your whole body to go into hell.

<sup>31</sup>"It has been said, 'Anyone who divorces his wife must give her a certificate of divorce.' <sup>32</sup>But I tell you that anyone who divorces his wife, except for marital unfaithfulness, causes her to become an adulteress, and anyone who marries the divorced woman commits adultery.

<sup>33</sup>"Again, you have heard that it was said to the people long ago, 'Do not break your oath, but keep the oaths you have made to the Lord.' <sup>34</sup>But I tell you, Do not swear at all: either by heaven, for it is God's throne; <sup>35</sup>or by the earth, for it is his footstool; or by Jerusalem, for it is the city of the Great King. <sup>36</sup>And do not swear by your head, for you cannot make even

one hair white or black. [37]Simply let your 'Yes' be 'Yes,' and your 'No,' 'No'; anything beyond this comes from the evil one.

[38]"You have heard that it was said, 'Eye for eye, and tooth for tooth.' [39]But I tell you, Do not resist an evil person. If someone strikes you on the right cheek, turn to him the other also. [40]And if someone wants to sue you and take your tunic, let him have your cloak as well. [41]If someone forces you to go one mile, go with him two miles. [42]Give to the one who asks you, and do not turn away from the one who wants to borrow from you.

[43]"You have heard that it was said, 'Love your neighbor and hate your enemy.' [44]But I tell you: Love your enemies and pray for those who persecute you, [45]that you may be sons of your Father in heaven. He causes his sun to rise on the evil and the good, and sends rain on the righteous and the unrighteous. [46]If you love those who love you, what reward will you get? Are not even the tax collectors doing that? [47]And if you greet only your brothers, what are you doing more than others? Do not even pagans do that? [48]Be perfect, therefore, as your heavenly Father is perfect.

Original Meaning

THE NEXT SECTION of the SM is commonly called "the antitheses," because six times we hear similar statements: "You have heard it said ... but I say to you." Jesus' declaration is the antithesis of what has gone before. This has been mistakenly interpreted to mean that Jesus makes his teaching the antithesis of the Old Testament.[1] But if we look closely, we will see that Jesus is contrasting his interpretation of the Old Testament with faulty *interpretations* and/or *applications*. In each antithesis, Jesus demonstrates how the Old Testament is to be properly interpreted and applied and, thus, how the Law and the Prophets are fulfilled (cf. 5:17). This · elevates Jesus above all interpreters, making his pronouncements equivalent with Scripture itself. Such a self-claim is incredibly difficult for his followers to comprehend fully and becomes a grievous point of contention with his enemies in the religious establishment.

---

1. E.g., Luz, *Matthew*, 1:277–79. Several have attempted to show both continuity and discontinuity but tend to emphasize discontinuity between the Mosaic law and Jesus' teaching; e.g., Banks, *Jesus and the Law*, 203–26; Frank Thielman, *The Law and the New Testament: The Question of Continuity* (New York: Crossroad, 1999), 49–58.

The historical level is important to keep before us. Jesus is speaking in a religious context in which the teachers of the law and the Pharisees held sway over the lives of the common people. The Pharisees had mapped out what they considered to be the proper course for attaining righteousness through their interpretation and application of the Old Testament. One facet of this regimen was a tendency to require legalistic, external obedience to the law without calling attention to an inner obedience from the heart. They were therefore "hypocrites" in their practice of the law (see comments on 6:1–18) and were leading the people into hypocritical practices.

Jesus here looks at several examples of how they do this and demonstrates how correct interpretation and application of the law must be based on proper *intent* and *motive*. He does not say, "Hear what the Old Testament says"; rather, he says, "You have heard it said." Jesus is not negating the Old Testament but the people's understanding and application of it. He confronts faulty interpretation by giving his authoritative pronouncement, showing the original intention of the law.[2] By living with proper intent and motive, those in the kingdom of heaven will live a righteousness that surpasses that of the scribes and Pharisees (cf. 5:20).

A pattern emerges in the antitheses. (1) Jesus introduces an Old Testament passage with the distinctive expression, "You have heard that it was said [to the people long ago]." The passive verb "was said" is an example of a "divine passive," implying that God is the One who spoke the command to the Old Testament author, who in turn gave it to the people.

(2) Then Jesus either cites (e.g., 5:43) or alludes to a current popular interpretation or traditional practice of the Old Testament passage he has quoted. That current understanding is causing the people to apply the law in a faulty manner.

(3) Next Jesus gives an authoritative pronouncement that takes his audience to the intended meaning and application of the Old Testament passage. He does not abrogate the law but brings it to fulfillment. This does not always mean something completely unexpected or unknown. We can indeed find persons within the Old Testament and Judaism who understood the intention of the law the same way Jesus does and were moving in that direction.

## Murder . . . Nurturing Relationships (5:21–26)

JESUS BEGINS WITH the sixth commandment of the Decalogue, "You shall not murder" (Ex. 20:13; Deut. 5:17). Although Hebrew possesses seven words for

---

2. Carson, *Sermon on the Mount*, 40: "Jesus appears to be concerned with two things: 1) overthrowing erroneous traditions, and 2) indicating authoritatively the real direction toward which the OT Scriptures point."

killing, the verb used in Exodus 20:13 makes "murder" (*raṣaḥ*) a more accurate rendering than "kill." It denotes premeditation and deliberateness. This does not apply to killing animals (Gen. 9:3), defending one's home (Ex. 22:2), accidental killings (Deut. 19:5), the execution of murderers by the state (Gen. 9:6), or involvement with one's nation in certain types of war. It does apply, however, to self-murder (i.e., suicide), accessory to murder (2 Sam. 12:9), or those who have responsibility to punish known murderers but fail to do so (1 Kings 21:19).[3] Penalty for murder was death; it was not reducible to any lesser sentence (Num. 35:31).

The expression "and anyone who murders will be subject to judgment" is not a direct statement of the Old Testament but is a common understanding based on a number of Old Testament passages that require judgment for murder. The fact that men and women have been created in the image of God (Gen. 1:26–27; 9:6) lies behind this prohibition. This penalty was already in force before the Sinaitic law in the decrees to Noah (Gen. 9:6).

Jesus' declarative statement "But I tell you," introduces three ways that a person's life is removed besides the physical act of murder. In each case, punishment is due. (1) The first case is anger: "Anyone who is angry with his brother will be subject to judgment" (5:22). Jesus here gets at the source of murder, which is anger (cf. 1 John 3:15). Anger alone is a violation of the law and was the original intent of the murder prohibition in the Old Testament. When we are inappropriately angry with people, we attempt to take their identity and value as God's creature away from them, the ultimate form of which is the physical act of murder. The righteousness expected of God's subjects is not only in avoiding murder but in eliminating anger from our relationships.

The disciple who is angry with his "brother" (another name for Jesus' disciples; cf. 12:46–50) is "subject to judgment" (5:22), which may refer to the ruling of local religious authorities, the local Sanhedrin found in larger cities, or God's final judgment.

(2) The second case is calling another disciple "Raca," a transliteration of an Aramaic term implying "empty-headed." This term of contempt was a personal, public affront. Name-calling was highly insulting in Jewish culture because a person's identity was stripped away and an offensive identity substituted. The significance attached to one's real name is removed from the person. The national "Sanhedrin" was the official adjudicating body of the Jews (similar to a supreme court), which the Roman authorities allowed to handle Jewish cases unless they impinged on Roman rule.

(3) The third case is saying "you fool [*more*]" to a disciple (5:22). This likewise was highly insulting in Jewish culture, because moral connotations

---

3. Walter C. Kaiser Jr., "Exodus," *EBC*, 2:424–25.

were attached to the term (cf., e.g., Prov. 10:23). *More* is most likely a case form of the Greek word *moros* (the origin of the English word "moron"), indicating a person who consistently acts like an idiot. To treat one's brother with such contempt was to strip away his personal identity and wrongly make the person into something he or she was not.

The expression "fire of hell" is *geenna*, from which we get the English transliteration "Gehenna." It is a transliteration of the Aramaic form of the Hebrew *ge ben-hinnom* ("valley of the son of Hinnom"), a valley west and southwest of Jerusalem. Here Ahaz and Manasseh sacrificed their sons to Molech,[4] which caused Josiah to defile the place (2 Kings 23:10). Later the valley was used to burn refuse from Jerusalem, so the constant burning made the valley an appropriate reference to fires of punishment. Jewish apocalyptic writers began to call the Valley of Hinnom the entrance to hell, later hell itself (4 Ezra 7:36). By the time of Jesus the term was used to indicate the state of final punishment (cf. Matt.18:9).

Jesus illustrates his declarative statement of the seriousness of anger and identity theft by focusing on the antidote, which is reconciliation with "your brother" (5:23–24) and "your adversary" (5:25–26). (1) In the first situation, the expected subject is reversed—the brother has something *against you*. Jesus is dealing with occasions when his disciples have offended another person, not when they have been offended. Reconciliation is the responsibility of the one who has wronged someone else, though a reciprocal attitude is understood (cf. 18:21–22; Mark 11:25). The expression "offering your gift at the altar" assumes a sacrifice being given in the temple at Jerusalem. To leave immediately indicates the importance of reconciliation, because Jesus' audience was from Galilee and the effort to attend the temple sacrifice was significant.

(2) The second scene is on the way to court, where a litigant is taking a disciple, apparently over some dispute about money (5:26). This probably assumes a Gentile legal setting, since we have no record in Jewish law of imprisonment for debt. Before the legal process is put into action, Jesus' disciples are to "settle matters quickly" (lit., "to make friends quickly") with one's adversary.[5] More than simply discharging legal affairs, Jesus' disciples are to seek a kind of reconciliation that creates friendships out of adversarial relationships.

Remaining imprisoned until a debt is repaid down to the last penny elicits a sense of impossibility (5:26; cf. 18:34), since the debtor had no chance to work to create funds. The "penny" (*kodrantes*) is the Roman bronze/copper

---

4. See 2 Kings 16:3; 21:6; Jer. 32:35; cf. 7:31–32; 19:1–13.
5. BDAG, 409.

coin *quadrans*, the smallest Roman coin.[6] Jesus uses this scenario to return to the seriousness of the problem of anger. Unreconciled anger is the inner equivalency of murder, which is impossible to repay. To leave problems unreconciled is to allow the sin that has been created to continue to destroy relationships between people.

Fulfilling the law's command "Do not murder" is not accomplished simply by avoiding legal homicide. Jesus reveals that the intent of the law is to nurture relationships. Jesus' disciples must have a daily urgency about maintaining the healthy life of their relationships, both with other disciples and with nondisciples. Anything we do that strips away the personal distinctiveness of a brother or sister is sin, and it is our responsibility to become reconciled.

### Adultery . . . Marital Oneness (5:27–30)

IN THE SECOND antithesis, Jesus quotes directly the seventh commandment of the Decalogue, concerning adultery (Ex. 20:14; Deut. 5:17), and alludes to the tenth, concerning covetousness (Ex. 20:17; Deut. 5:21). Adultery in the Old Testament involved sexual intercourse with mutual consent between a man, married or unmarried, and the wife of another man. The term and the penalty (death) applied equally to both the man and the woman (Lev. 20:10; cf. Deut. 22:22). A betrothed woman was counted in this context as a wife (Deut. 22:23–24).

Adultery was considered one of the most serious offenses because it broke the relationship that was a reflection of God and his people. Adultery was often used to describe the way in which the people of Israel went after gods other than Yahweh (cf. Ezek. 16:32; Hos. 4:13b). Joseph recognized that adultery not only would have been an offense to Potiphar but was especially a "sin against God" (Gen. 39:9). King David, after his adulterous affair with Bathsheba, confessed his sin to God by saying, "Against you, you only, have I sinned" (Ps. 51:4). The Old Testament strongly denounces all extramarital sexual relationships, condemning the male offender even more strongly than the female (cf. Hos. 4:14).

Jesus' pronouncement reaffirms the Old Testament commitment to the unity of the marriage bond and takes it to its deepest intended meaning[7]: "But I tell you that anyone who looks at a woman lustfully has already commit-

---

6. For a helpful discussion and numerous illustrations of various coinage see D. H. Wheaton, "Money," *IBD*, 2:1018–23; also John W. Betlyon, "Coinage," *ABD*, 1:1076–89; Rousseau and Arav, "Coins and Money," *Jesus and His World*, 55–61.

7. Note that here no explicit interpretation is countered, although this antithesis goes with the next, which enunciates interpretations common in Jesus' day.

ted adultery with her in his heart" (Matt. 5:28). It is not enough only to maintain physical purity. The purity of marriage includes exclusive devotion to one another with every aspect of their lives, and this commitment excludes wanting another person or giving oneself in any way to another person.[8] Looking lustfully at another woman breaks the bond of oneness that a man has with his wife.

The basis of this principle lies in the relationship between God and his people. Ezekiel graphically condemns the people of Israel for spiritual adultery not just when they actually worship pagan idols, but when Israel's heart and eyes desired other gods. God laments, "How I have been grieved by their adulterous hearts, which have turned away from me, and by their eyes, which have lusted after their idols" (Ezek. 6:9). Oneness with a wife means that her husband gives himself to her, and her alone. When a man even looks with desire at another woman, he has rejected his wife and given himself to another. Lust originates in the heart (15:19), which is the core of a person's identity and will. Adultery, therefore, is not only physical sexual intercourse but also mentally engaging in such an act of unfaithfulness.

Jesus illustrates the seriousness of lust destroying the marriage bond through two graphic examples: "If your right eye causes you to sin, gouge it out and throw it away" (5:29), and "if your right hand causes you to sin, cut it off and throw it away" (5:30). Most people being right-handed, the right side often stood for the more powerful or important side. The eye is the medium through which the temptation first comes to stimulate the lust, and the hand represents the instrument by which the lust is physically committed. So Jesus uses hyperbole (deliberate exaggeration) for the sake of emphasizing the seriousness of single-hearted devotion—single-eyed and single-handed commitment to one's spouse.[9]

Early in church history, people such as Origen of Alexandria wrongly took the sayings here and in 19:12 literally. Jesus is not advocating physical self-mutilation, but through dramatic figures of speech indicates the kind of rigorous self-discipline that committed disciples will display. A person who intends to carry out God's ordinance should be willing to go to any lengths to maintain the unity of the bond of marriage. Sin is essentially an inner issue and condemns the person who rests complacently on his or her external acts of righteousness.[10] Our actions indicate the state of our hearts, and

---

8. See the powerful allegory on marital faithfulness in Prov. 5:15–23.

9. Davies and Allison, *Matthew*, 1:524–26. Jesus gives similar warnings in 18:8–9 in the context of maintaining the oneness of the community.

10. For a thought-provoking call to sexual purity, see John R. W. Stott, *The Message of the Sermon on the Mount (Matthew 5–7): Christian Counter-Culture* (BST; Downers Grove, Ill.: Inter-Varsity Press, 1978), 86–91.

one who destroys the marriage bond is worthy of eternal condemnation, because the sin reveals that he or she is not a disciple of Jesus. Life in the kingdom of heaven does not produce otherworldly persons, but disciples who live out human relations, including marriage, the way God originally designed.

## Divorce . . . Marriage Sanctity Inviolate (5:31–32)

IN THE THIRD antithesis, Jesus carries forward the thinking about the sanctity of marriage by alluding to the Mosaic pronouncement on certificates of divorce (Deut. 24:1; see also comments on 19:3–12). Since divorce was a widespread phenomenon in the ancient world, God instituted a regulation through Moses that was designed to do three things: (1) protect the sanctity of marriage from "indecency" defiling the marital relationship; (2) protect the woman from a husband who might simply send her away without any cause; (3) document her status as a legitimately divorced woman so that she was not thought to be a harlot or a runaway adulteress.

By Jesus' time, the essence of the sanctity of marriage was being lost among those interpreting and debating the Mosaic regulation, especially the meaning of "indecency" in Deuteronomy 24:1. The discussion assumed that divorce was necessary and legal. The more conservative school of Shammai allowed divorce only for reasons of unchastity. The more liberal school of Hillel stated that the Mosaic stipulation of "indecency" allowed a man to divorce his wife "even if she spoiled a dish for him" (*m. Giṭ.* 9:10). Later rabbis declared that divorce was required when adultery was committed (*m. Soṭah* 5:1; *m. Yebam.* 2:8), because adultery produced a state of impurity that, as a matter of legal fact, dissolved the marriage.[11]

Jesus goes back to the original intention both for God's institution of marriage and for the Mosaic regulation. God intended marriage to be a permanent union of a man and woman into one (Gen. 2:24). God "hates" divorce, because it tears apart what should be considered a permanent union (cf. Mal. 2:16). Therefore, Jesus states categorically that divorce creates adultery, the despicable nature of which he has just declared (5:27–30), because an illicit divorce turns the woman into an adulteress when she remarries.

However, as did Moses, Jesus allows for an exception. Even though God sees marriage as permanent, sometimes the marriage bond has been violated to such a degree that a spouse has already torn apart the marriage union, namely, when a person has committed *porneia*, which the NIV appropriately renders "marital unfaithfulness." Since "adultery" has already been specified

---

11. Markus Bockmuehl, "Matthew 5.32; 19.9 in the Light of Pre-Rabbinic Halakah," *NTS* 35 (1989): 291–95; D. C. Allison Jr., "Divorce, Celibacy, and Joseph," *JSNT* 49 (1993): 3–10.

by another word (*moicheuo*; 5:27–28), *porneia* must be something less specific than sexual infidelity but, following the Mosaic intention, more than something frivolous. *Porneia* includes any sinful activity that intentionally divides the marital relationship. Jesus states unequivocally the sacredness of the marital relationship but allows divorce to protect the nonoffending partner and to protect the institution of marriage from being a vulgar sham.

## Oaths . . . Transparent Honesty (5:33–37)

THE FOURTH ANTITHESIS begins not with a quotation of one command but a summary of various "oath" passages.[12] In the Old Testament, God often guaranteed the fulfillment of his promises with an oath (Gen. 9:9–17). In the same way, the Old Testament permitted a person to swear by the name of God to substantiate an important affirmation or promise. An oath or vow helped a person remain faithful to commitments. The law demanded that a person be true to any oath sworn (cf. Lev. 19:12; Num. 30:2), such as the vow to the Lord that was part of the Old Testament system of sacrificial offerings (Deut. 23:21). Although not required, oaths properly handled received approval from God. The rabbis developed a highly structured hierarchy of oaths, later comprising an entire tractate in the Mishnah, *Šebuᶜot* ("Oaths").

Some interpreters of Jesus' day tended to make the Old Testament's permission mean that only oaths that invoked the name of the Lord were binding. If a person wasn't really serious about an oath, he would swear by "less sacred" things (e.g., "I swear by heaven," "by earth," "by Jerusalem," etc.; cf. Matt. 23:16–22). Since the person didn't invoke the literal name of God, the oath wasn't considered binding. This increasing tendency to find loopholes in an oath led to their devaluation, causing some to warn against using any kind of oath. Josephus says of the Essenes, "Any word of theirs has more force than an oath; swearing they avoid, regarding it as worse than perjury, for they say that one who is not believed without an appeal to God stands condemned already."[13]

Jesus goes to the heart of the law's intent regarding oaths when he says that his disciples are not to swear "at all." This does not mean "profanity" or "cursing" but invoking God's name, or substitutes for it, to guarantee the truth of what one says. Jesus understands the duplicity of the human heart, for people sometimes invoked an oath in order to conceal an attempt to deceive. By contrast, Jesus' disciples should be people of such integrity of character and truthfulness of heart that whatever they say is absolutely believable and dependable. A person of integrity is one who in daily conversation

---

12. See Ex. 20:7; Lev. 19:12; Num. 30:2; Deut. 23:21–23.
13. Josephus, *J.W.* 2:135; see also Sir. 23:9, 11; Philo, *On the Decalogue* 84–95.

is so truthful, dependable, genuine, guileless, and reliable that his or her words are believed without an oath.

In other words, a simple "yes" or "no" should be enough for a trustworthy person (cf. 2 Cor. 1:15–24), a saying of Jesus that James passes on (James 5:12). It is true that Paul invoked an oath because the people did not know him well enough to be certain of his character yet, so we can see that oaths are not wholly disallowed in the New Testament (2 Cor. 1:18; Gal. 1:20). But Jesus' point is that a disciple's simple word should be considered as trustworthy as a signed document or contract. When he goes further to suggest that "anything beyond this is evil," Jesus indicates that swearing by something in order to deceive can only have one source—the evil one, Satan (cf. Matt. 6:13; 13:19, 38).

## Eye for an Eye . . . Servanthood (5:38–42)

IN THE FIFTH antithesis Jesus condemns the way that the law of retaliation (*lex talionis*) had been abused to promote personal revenge. Found in similar form in the Code of Hammurabi (# 196–200), the *lex talionis* is prominent in the Torah as God's means of providing justice and of purging evil from among his people: "The rest of the people will hear of this and be afraid, and never again will such an evil thing be done among you. Show no pity: life for life, eye for eye, tooth for tooth, hand for hand, foot for foot" (Deut. 19:20–21; cf. Ex. 21:23–25; Lev. 24:18–20). In some ancient societies punishment was handed out without regard for individual cases, and often the penalty far exceeded the crime. The law of retaliation was established as a check to inappropriate punishment. If a person harmed the eye of another person, the eye of the offender was to be given as equal punishment. Most commentators doubt that it was intended to be applied literally in every case, but it was a graphic metaphor to establish equivalence of loss in a given circumstance.[14] The law was intended as an equalizer of justice.

The *lex talionis* was to be imposed by the civil authorities and civil courts to protect the public, punish offenders, and deter crime. It was not to be administered by individuals (cf. Deut. 19:15–21). In fact, the civil statute was intended to *discourage* private revenge (cf. Prov. 20:22; 24:29),[15] because the person offended was too liable to be biased in retaliation. Where governing authorities were responsible to administer justice, God's people were then liberated from the need to exact personal retribution and were able to

---

14. See John E. Hartley, *Leviticus* (WBC 4; Dallas: Word, 1992), 412–14. The Mishnah speaks of financial recompense for a variety of offenses but speaks of literal life for life for murder (cf. *m. B. Qam.* 8:1–6).

15. Ibid., 412; Earl S. Kalland, "Deuteronomy," *EBC*, 3:126.

pursue a higher ethical standard; they were able to love and serve one another. The Lord spoke to his people directly about this alternative: "Do not seek revenge or bear a grudge against one of your people, but love your neighbor as yourself. I am the LORD" (Lev. 19:18).

However, in the turbulent world of Jesus' day, when Jews were under the rule of the Roman occupying forces, it was easy to lose sight of this higher purpose and begin to use the law of retaliation to justify personal revenge. The common person was at the mercy of the Romans everywhere—on the street, in the court, in the presence of the military occupying forces, and in the everyday world of financial need. Jewish leaders had little or no power to execute justice to protect their people. Those who were hurt wanted to strike back, especially when there was no apparent justice to protect them, so personal retaliation through violent resistance was a burning issue among the Jews. Even some of the Jewish leaders sought retaliation by gathering a following among the people to resist the Romans,[16] which led to popular resistance movements throughout the land at the time of Jesus.[17]

Within this oppressive atmosphere, Jesus points to the motivation of the individual disciple who has been taken advantage of and wronged. "But I tell you, Do not resist an evil person" (5:39). It is not the disciple's personal responsibility to "resist" (*anthisemi*)[18] or set oneself against the offending person. On a personal level, the disciple's first responsibility is to reverse the dynamic of the situation from taking to giving. The evil person has attempted to take, but Jesus' disciples are to give to the offender by serving him or her. Jesus' disciples are not to think first about retribution. Even when they are being abused, they must think of ways to advance the kingdom of heaven and its influence on this earth.

Jesus then uses four illustrations from the everyday life of his disciples under oppression to emphasize how they can serve those who offend them. Their ultimate goal is to seek "an opportunity for the enemy to be converted to the truth of God's kingdom."[19] (1) The first scene appears to be in an arena where the disciple is insulted publicly: "If someone strikes you on the right cheek . . ." (5:39). It is not so much the hurt as the insult that is here in mind, because it was a symbolic way of affronting a person's dignity and honor (cf. *m. B. Qam.* 8:6). Crude military personnel were known to demean subjugated people in this way. To turn the other cheek indicates that Jesus' disciples are

---

16. Saul Lieberman, *Greek in Jewish Palestine: Studies in the Life and Manners of Jewish Palestine in the II-IV Centuries C.E.* (New York: Jewish Theological Seminary of America, 1942), 179–83.

17. For background, see Horsley and Hanson, *Bandits, Prophets, and Messiahs,* 30–43.

18. *BDAG,* 80. Only occurring here in Matthew, the term connotes taking justice into one's own hands.

19. Hays, *The Moral Vision of the New Testament,* 326.

so secure in themselves that they do not need to retaliate with more evil the evil done to them (cf. Rom. 12:19–21; 1 Thess. 5:15). By turning the other cheek. they place themselves in a position of greater indignity and vulnerability, but this provides opportunity to serve the offender, as the next two scenes illustrate.

(2) The second scene shifts to a legal setting: "And if someone wants to sue you ..." (5:40). A disciple is being taken to court in an attempt to sue for his tunic. The simple clothing of a person in the first century was a loincloth, covered by one or more body-length tunic(s), the outer cloak, a girdle acting as a belt, a head covering, and sandals.[20] The "tunic" (*chiton*) was the basic garment, a long-sleeved inner robe similar to a nightshirt that a person wore next to the skin. Jesus instructs his disciples that if someone tries to sue for their tunic, they should let him have their "cloak" (*himation*) as well. The cloak was the outer robe (cf. 27:35),[21] which was an indispensable piece of clothing. When it was given as a pledge, it had to be returned before sunset since it was used by the poor for a sleeping cover (Ex. 22:26–7; Deut. 24:12; Ezek. 18:7; Amos 2:8.). Jesus makes a startling demand of his disciples. They must reverse the dynamic. Instead of defending themselves or seeking retaliation, they must give to this person who is so unfairly attempting to take their most basic necessities.

(3) The third illustration draws a military scene: "if someone forces you to go one mile ..." (5:41). In ancient practice, governmental or military personnel could requisition the help of local civilians for official business. Officers of the Persian royal postal system could force a civilian to carry official correspondence, and Roman military personnel could organize bands of unpaid laborers from the common people to construct roads, fortifications, and public buildings. They could requisition individuals on the spot to help an operation. The most familiar New Testament scene is that of Simon of Cyrene, forced by the Roman guards to carry Jesus' cross (27:32; Mark 15:21). Jesus tells his disciples that when they are commandeered to go "one mile" (*milion*[22]), they should go two.

(4) The last illustration relates to uncomfortable people: "Give to the one who asks you ... the one who wants to borrow from you" (5:42). This carries Jesus' point one step further by referring to two kinds of uncomfortable peo-

---

20. Douglas R. Edwards, "Dress and Ornamentation," *ABD*, 2:232–38.

21. John distinguishes between Jesus' outer garment (*himation*), which the soldiers divided, and the "undergarment" (*chiton*), which was seamless (John 19:23–24). He uses the same two words as Matthew.

22. This word means "a thousand paces" (BDAG, 651) or approximately one mile. For a helpful chart showing equivalent distances, see H. Wayne House, *Chronological and Background Charts of the New Testament* (Grand Rapids: Zondervan, 1981), 26.

ple who might intrude into the everyday lives of his disciples. Not only are Jesus' disciples to respond with positive treatment to those who ill-treat them, but they are also to give to those who beg and borrow. The word "ask" (*aiteo*) in this context indicates a poor person who begs for alms. The person who wants to "borrow" (*danizo*) may likewise have been poor, since the use of this same verb in Luke 6:34 indicates loaning to a person unable to repay. Giving alms to the poor was a central exercise of Jewish piety (see comments on 6:2—4). The Old Testament was likewise clear about the obligation that the people of Israel had to lend to the poor among them (Deut. 15:7–11).

Jesus, however, widens the obligation with powerful images of generosity. The one begging may not be poor legitimately or may not require charity, but give to him anyway. The one seeking a loan could be unscrupulous or even one's enemy and may not intend to repay the loan, but don't turn her away.[23] The parallel in Luke's Gospel explicitly indicates the disciples are to extend loans to one's enemies (see Luke 6:35). With these sayings Jesus removes the obligation of judging the merit of the request for charity or the loan. His disciples are free to live generously without question. The Old Testament gives a low status to sluggards who fall into poverty from their own laziness (Prov. 6:1–11) and regards as wicked those who consistently seek loans and do not repay them (cf. Ps. 37:21). But to give freely to whomever seeks assistance, especially to those who may not really need charity and to those from whom there is little chance of repayment, is the height of generosity.

Jesus himself lived out this radical principle and became a vivid example for his followers (cf. 1 Peter 2:20–25). He loved so much that he gave himself for sinners (Rom. 5:8). The obligation of his disciples is not first to retaliate for the evil done to them or to protect themselves and their personal interests. Their primary obligation is to serve those around them, both those who seem to deserve it and even those who don't. As with the other antitheses, this principle surely created uneasiness for those who initially heard it as well as those who later read it. Other passages of the New Testament seem to be at odds with the principle stated so starkly here.[24] But however much one might, or perhaps even should, desire to harmonize the teaching of this antithesis, the intensity of a disciple's obligation to serve others must not be minimized. This teaching prepares for the next antithesis, in which disciples are not to hate their enemies but are to love both neighbor and adversary.

---

23. The verb *apostrepho* has the basic meaning "to turn away, turn back," though it can also be used to mean "to defraud" (BDAG, 122–23). The former is more likely here.

24. E.g., Acts 22:29; 1 Thess. 3:10. See below for discussion.

## Love and Hatred . . .
## Unconditional Commitment (5:43–47)

JESUS BEGINS THE last antithesis by quoting one of the central truths of the Old Testament: "You have heard that it was said, 'Love your neighbor'" (5:43). Love for one's neighbor was one of God's commands through Moses (Lev. 19:18). When answering the test of a legal expert about the greatest commandment in the law, Jesus replied with the command to love God and to love one's neighbor as oneself (Matt. 22:36–40).

The next statement of the antithesis, "hate your enemies," is not found explicitly in the Old Testament. In fact, Moses directed the people to assist an enemy in need (Ex. 23:4–5). But as much as love of neighbors was at the heart of Old Testament teaching, God's hatred of evil was also a central theme in the Old Testament. The psalmist states, "You are not a God who takes pleasure in evil; with you the wicked cannot dwell" (Ps. 5:4; cf. 45:7; Deut. 7:2; 30:7). God hates evil. In fact, the psalmist takes it one step further in the next verse: "The arrogant cannot stand in your presence; you hate all who do wrong" (Ps. 4:5). In turn, those who desire to be righteous learn to adopt God's hatred of evil, so that the psalmist could say in another place, "Do I not hate those who hate you, O LORD, and abhor those who rise up against you? I have nothing but hatred for them; I count them my enemies" (Ps. 139:21–22; cf. 26:4–5).

Later groups within Israel took this further by identifying "neighbor" exclusively with those within their Jewish community and the "evildoer" as Gentiles or those outside of their community and therefore God's and their enemies. The starkest extreme is found at Qumran. *The Rule of the Community* gives instructions for seeking God and doing what is good and just, with the purpose "that they may love all that he has chosen and hate all that He has rejected; that they may abstain from all evil and hold fast to all good" (1QS 1.3–4). The instructions then go one step further, "that they may love all the sons of light, each according to his lot in God's design, and hate all the sons of darkness, each according to his guilt in God's vengeance" (1QS 1.9–11).[25] Because God hates evil, those who embody evil are understood to be God's enemies. It was natural to hate God's enemies.

But Jesus takes the competing attitudes of love for neighbor and hate for enemy and brings them together in a way that undoubtedly stuns his audience but is actually what God intended from the beginning: "But I tell you: Love your enemies and pray for those who persecute you" (5:44). God does

---

25. Using the translation of Geza Vermes, *The Dead Sea Scrolls in English*, 2d ed. (New York: Penguin, 1975), 72. See also Hill, *Matthew*, 129; Ito, "Matthew and the Community of the Dead Sea Scrolls," 27–28.

hate evil, but his intent is to bring reconciliation. As such, the old saying is true, "God loves the sinner but hates the sin." That is what drives Jesus' saying about the requirement to love one's enemies. It is a radical saying in that it goes contrary to what was occurring in many quarters in Israel, but it actually preserves the love God has for all humans. All of God's creatures are his own, and he loves them and desires that all will come to repentance (cf. 2 Peter 3:9). Jesus' disciples are to look at people in this world as God does and to love them enough to reach out to them with the message of reconciliation, even to "pray for those who persecute" them as Jesus' disciples.

When Jesus states "that you may be sons of your Father in heaven" (5:45), he is not giving the means by which one becomes a child of God but indicates that love makes explicit the relationship between God the Father and Jesus' disciples. The children of Israel were God's sons by his calling, and that calling included the obligation to carry out his will. But anyone who responds to God's will in the ministry of Jesus is a "son" or "daughter" of the heavenly Father (cf. 12:48–50). That family relationship includes the obligation to act like a son or daughter, which means loving as the Father loves.[26]

Jesus follows up with two examples of God's common grace given to all people, both evil and good, to demonstrate why his disciples are to love both neighbor and enemy. (1) God's sun rises on both evil people and good people, and rain falls on both. All of God's creatures are worthy of his care in this life. Ultimately each will be accountable for his or her choice of evil or good, and God will someday judge those who choose to do evil. But in this life, his common grace extends to all. It prepares for the extension of the offer of the grace of salvation, because of his desire that the evil and the unrighteous, the tax collector and the pagan, will all respond to his summons to the kingdom and so become children of the heavenly Father.

(2) Jesus next draws on natural relationships and how God's love goes beyond normal human ties. All groups take care of their own members. Tax collectors love their friends and colleagues, their wives and children, who love them in return, so there is no special recognition for Jesus' disciples in loving one another (5:46). Gentiles (NIV "pagans") "greet" or extend peace and blessing on their own associates and family members (5:47; cf. 10:12), so bringing other disciples into the intimacy of Jesus' community is nothing out of the ordinary. All groups take care of their own and to some degree look on those outside their group as "enemies."

But God does not see the same groupings that humans have created. He transcends human boundary markers and loves all persons, even those who have rejected him. That is the kind of love Jesus advocates, which is the

---

26. Spencer, "Father-Ruler," 440–41.

basis for the worldwide neighborhood of God, in which Jesus' disciples have no enemies but consider all of God's creatures worthy of our love. There will be a special love of Jesus' disciples for one another as members of the family who do the Father's will (John 13:34–35; cf. Matt. 12:46–50), but love is to be extended to all whom God has created. This sixth antithesis takes his disciples to the pinnacle of understanding the way that Jesus fulfills the Old Testament and the way that their righteousness as subjects of the kingdom of heaven will surpass that of the teachers of the law and the Pharisees (cf. Matt. 5:20).

## Conclusion: The Pursuit of Perfection (5:48)

"THEREFORE" INTRODUCES A powerful concluding charge: "Be perfect ... as your heavenly Father is perfect" (5:48). It is a fitting conclusion to the sixth antithesis, because the perfect love of God toward his creatures is the example of the love Jesus' disciples are to display toward their enemies and those who persecute them. God always acts perfectly toward his creatures in love, because he is love (1 John 4:16). In the same way, if Jesus' disciples strive to have the Father's love for all humans, they will always give to others what they need from God's perspective.

At the same time, this statement serves as a fitting conclusion to all of the antitheses in 5:21–47. To love one's enemies is to pursue a primary characteristic of God (5:45), but Jesus' disciples are to emulate God in every area of life. In the antitheses, Jesus has used representative selections from the Old Testament to clarify its intent as God's will for his people. The Old Testament is a reflection of God himself. Therefore, as the disciples pursue its intent and motive as Jesus has clarified it, they are in fact pursuing the perfection of God himself. Matthew's use of the future tense here (lit., "you shall be perfect") has an imperatival thrust, as the NIV indicates.

But we may also see something of a goal and a promise in the future indicative. A present imperative, "keep being perfect" or "be continually perfect," would place an impossible demand on Jesus' disciples. Instead, the future tense holds out an emphatic *goal* that is to shape the disciples' entire life—they are to set nothing less than the perfection of God as the ultimate objective of their behavior, thoughts, and will. Furthermore, the future tense also implies a *promise*, because the Father is not only the divine goal but also the divine enabler. "Jesus puts his command in such a way that disciples may look for divine help as they press toward God's goal for them."[27]

Jesus' disciples are to pursue the perfection that is God himself. The word "perfect" (*teleios*) is also used in the LXX in Deuteronomy 18:13: "You

27. Morris, *Matthew*, 133.

shall be perfect before your God." The word used in the Hebrew text (*tamim*) denotes the idea of wholeness or completeness (Lev. 23:15, 30; Josh. 10:13), specifying the soundness of sacrificial animals (Ex. 12:5) or the complete commitment of a person to God, including ethical blamelessness (Gen. 6:9; 17:1; Deut. 18:13; 2 Sam. 22:24–27). The Greek term *teleios* carries the same connotations: the end, completion, or complete thing, that which is made whole or perfect. But it can also indicate a person who has attained spiritual maturity.[28] But with the Father as the goal, Jesus is not saying, "Be mature as your heavenly Father is mature." He is saying, "Be perfect, like your heavenly Father." The disciples are to pursue the Father's perfection as the goal of their lives.

So Jesus' saying is a command, a promise, and a statement of hope. His disciples are engaged in the process of regeneration, now made objectively real in a revolutionary way with the arrival of the kingdom of heaven. The necessity of the new birth to enter the kingdom of heaven (cf. John 3:1–7) makes possible, and real, his disciples' transformation into his image (Matt. 10:24–25; Rom. 8:29; 1 Cor. 3:18). Since Jesus is both the perfection of the image of God in humans as a full human being and the perfect image of the invisible God as the divine Son of God (Col. 1:15–20), he is the ultimate example for his disciples to follow as they hear the command, "Be perfect, as your heavenly Father is perfect." That statement implies a realistically ideal goal that Jesus' disciples are to pursue with restful dissatisfaction in this life until their final perfection in eternity.

THE ARRIVAL OF the kingdom of heaven in Jesus' life and ministry is accompanied by extraordinary power and a revolutionary change of life—not the power of a mighty army or of the revolution of an armed insurrection, but the power to fulfill the Law and Prophets with a revolutionary transformation that exceeds the righteousness of the scribes and Pharisees. With six brief antitheses, Jesus elevates himself above any of the religious leaders of Israel's past or present and declares the essence of God's will for all humanity.[29] The inauguration of kingdom life does not enable Jesus' followers to obey merely the externals of God's commands, but

---

28. E.g., 1 Cor. 14:20; Eph. 4:13; Heb. 5:14; 6:1. This is the meaning adopted by William Hendriksen, *Exposition of the Gospel According to Matthew* (NTC; Grand Rapids: Baker, 1973), 317–19.

29. See Keener (*A Commentary on the Gospel of Matthew*, 181–82) for discussion of Jesus' teaching method in relationship to parallels within Judaism.

it takes them to the very core of the Old Testament's intent and motive so that they can obey God's will from the heart.[30]

**A radicalization of the Old Testament in Jesus' disciples.** With Matthew's purpose to lay out the words of Jesus so that his disciples will have a guideline for their continual growing obedience to God's will,[31] he has distilled in the five discourses the essence of discipleship. The Sermon on the Mount is the key directive to understanding the way that kingdom life will transform Jesus' disciples. If there is any truth in our earlier suggestion that the Beatitudes function as a sort of "preamble" to the SM, which itself functions as the "constitution" of the kingdom of heaven, Jesus' declarations about the Old Testament and the righteousness of the kingdom of heaven in 5:17−48 may be seen as the "bill of rights" for Jesus' disciples.

The Bill of Rights to the U.S. Constitution was adopted as a way of assuring that the new government would not thwart the intent of the framers to bring liberty and justice to individual citizens.[32] Similarly, in Jesus' declarations he reassures his listeners and chastens his opponents, who perhaps believe that Jesus' announcement of the arrival of the kingdom of heaven will abolish the Law and the Prophets. Rather than abolishing the Old Testament, Jesus radicalizes it in the lives of his disciples as their progressive transformation fulfills its intent, motive, and purpose. The antitheses provide crucial examples of how the Law and Prophets are fulfilled in Jesus' disciples and provide key directives for disciples of all ages.

Jesus likely gave many authoritative interpretations that confronted faulty interpretations and applications of the Old Testament, but Matthew records only these six antitheses. A brief summary of each illustrates the direction Jesus takes discipleship in the kingdom of heaven.

- True disciples not only avoid murder but are transformed so that they do not strip away the personhood and identity of others through anger or defamation (5:21−23), and they continually produce reconciliation in offended relationships (5:23−26).
- True disciples not only shun physical acts of adultery but are so completely committed to God's purpose for marriage that they have eyes and hands only for a spouse (5:27−28) and discipline every thought and action to be singly focused on the spouse (5:29−30).
- True disciples not only respect the purity of the marital relationship but have God's values for the original design for marriage and are unreservedly committed to its permanence and sanctity (5:31−32).

---

30. Kingsbury, *Matthew As Story*, 66.
31. See the introduction as well as comments on 28:20.
32. See the United States National Archives and Records Administration website: http://www.nara.gov/exhall/charters/billrights/billmain.html.

- True disciples do not need to give oaths in order to confirm their trustworthiness, because their faithful lives repeatedly confirm the reliability of their words (5:33–37).
- True disciples are so secure in their transformed kingdom identity that when they are wronged, they do not merely adhere to legal retribution but use every opportunity to serve others, both good and evil people, so that the reality of God's grace in their lives woos them to the kingdom of heaven (5:38–42).
- True disciples not only love what God loves and hate what God hates, but they have the renewed heart of God that enables them to love the world of sinners for whom Jesus will eventually give his life (5:43–48).
- Climactically, true disciples have experienced the powerfully life-changing presence of the kingdom of heaven in such a way that their progressive transformation into the image of Jesus, the Son of God, secures their progressive growth into the very perfection of God the Father (5:48).

**Internal heart attitudes and external actions.** The reality of kingdom life affects both internal heart attitudes and external actions, because they are in a systemic relationship with each other. Jesus does not endorse one over the other, for both internal and external attentiveness are necessary for wholistic discipleship. However, the internal attitudes of the heart are the proper foundation and source of external actions. The heart that is properly rooted in and built on Jesus will produce good fruit and withstand the storms of life (7:20, 25). Thus, our discipleship to Jesus often requires us to focus on the heart attitude (cf. 5:3–10), which will naturally overflow into a witness to the world (5:13–16) and produce a life of righteousness that fulfills God's will for our lives (5:20–48). This does not eliminate the need to be deliberate in our actions, because doing things out of a sense of duty (5:24a) and even with an eye on reward (6:18) can play a role in redefining our inner motives and make our external obedience more consistent.

The virtues of the Beatitudes are a foundational internal component for true discipleship, enabling us to repent and hear Jesus' invitation to enter the kingdom of heaven. But they are also foundational for the heart and life transformation that is exhibited in the antitheses. I don't believe that Matthew makes an intentional parallel between the eight Beatitudes and the six antitheses, but there is remarkable connection of emphases in them. The virtues of the Beatitudes provide impetus for the obedience of the antitheses.

- The poor in spirit (5:3) do not think more highly of themselves than they should (cf. Rom. 12:3), so they will not be inappropriately angry with or defame another person (5:21–26).

- Those who mourn (5:4) over the sinfulness of this world will have an eternal perspective on relationships that will prevent them from lusting for a person other than their spouse (5:27–30).
- Those who are meek (5:5) do not impose their will on others, so they will understand God's purposes for marriage and will not seek to divorce a spouse (5:31–32).
- Those who hunger and thirst for righteousness (5:6) do not need an oath to vouch for their honesty but will always speak the truth (5:33–37).
- The merciful (5:7) do not retaliate, because they have been shown mercy and will in turn give mercy to others (5:38–42).
- The pure in heart (5:8) will love both friend and foe, the entire world for whom Jesus gave his life (5:43–47).
- The peacemakers (5:9) are sons of God and sons of their Father in heaven as they love those who persecute them (5:44–45).
- Those who are persecuted because of righteousness (5:10) have entered the kingdom of heaven through the righteous gift of God and have received the promise and goal and enablement of continual growth in the righteous perfection of the Father (5:48).

Our obedience to Jesus' teaching should overflow from a heart attitude that is rightly oriented toward God. We must not be satisfied simply with following the letter of the law, which takes us back to the error of the scribes and Pharisees, but we must seek the intent and motive of the law. The antitheses are tangible, real-world examples of the obedience expected of all disciples—an obedience that becomes qualitatively more righteous as we operate from the proper motive behind them. Jesus did not come to abolish the intention of God as expressed in the law but brings us back to it, expressed most fully in his reaffirmation of the Old Testament imperative to "love the Lord your God with all your heart and with all your soul and with all your mind . . . and . . . [to] love your neighbor as yourself" (22:37).

OF THE DOZENS of books on my shelf that are devoted to the study of the Sermon on the Mount, one has the most intriguing title of all: *Did Jesus Use a Modem at the Sermon on the Mount?* I must confess that I bought the book sight unseen over the Internet because of the title. When I received it, I discovered that the book really isn't a study of the SM but is rather a collection of devotionals. The author is a full-time computer trainer, who wrote the book originally as a series of "Internet Devotionals" for his Sunday school class, using a clever computer analogy to illustrate Christian principles for job and home. He includes a catchy little poem to begin the book:

> Did Jesus use a modem
>   At the Sermon on the Mount?
> Did He ever try a broadcast fax,
>   To send His message out?
> Did the disciples carry beepers,
>   As they went about their route?
> Did Jesus use a modem
>   At the Sermon on the Mount?[33]

Did Jesus use a modem?! My word! How far removed are the activities and technology of our everyday world from those of the days of Jesus! We live very different lives than in the first century, with instantaneous digital communication, nonstop international travel, and an expanding global community. We might think that our hi-tech sophistication would make Jesus' teaching completely irrelevant. But how prevalent in your world are murder, adultery, divorce, fraudulent, vengeance, and hatred? Every time I turn on the television or read the local newspaper, these issues are everyday occurrences. So although we are worlds apart technologically from those first-century audiences, we are just as needy.

I am stunned by the brilliance of Jesus' teaching that transcends these centuries, because for all people that have ever lived, in every culture on the face of the earth, his solution to the problems of humanity are immediately germane. He didn't produce provincial religious practices that became antiquated after his place and time, but went to the heart of universal human dilemmas and provided timeless, supracultural guidance. The discipleship he advocates in these antitheses, and throughout the SM—indeed, in all of his teaching—is the same as discipleship today. Full books have been written on each of these antitheses, another indication of the continuing importance, but a few general comments will indicate their relevance for our developing discipleship.

**Treating people with dignity (5:21–26).** The striking feature of the first antithesis is its emphasis on the dignity of the human being created in the image of God. Not only are we not to take the physical life of a human, but we are not to do anything that demeans a person's dignity. C. S. Lewis referred to this as the "weight of glory" in one of his most profound sermons, calling

---

33. Ellis Bush Jr., *Did Jesus Use a Modem at the Sermon on the Mount? Inspirational Thoughts for the Information Age* (Mukilteo, Wa.: Winepress, 1997), 7.

for us to pattern our lives so that we promote our neighbor's glory. "The load, or weight, or burden of my neighbor's glory should be laid daily on my back, a load so heavy that only humility can carry it, and the backs of the proud will be broken."[34]

Another important feature of the first antithesis is our responsibility to be ministers of reconciliation so that human relationships reflect the glory of God. Jesus' illustration of hurrying to make reconciliation even if the disciple is offering a sacrifice accentuates the urgency of maintaining healthy relationships. Religious activity that attempts to appease our relationship with God is meaningless if it is not based on purity in our human relationships. We are not to come to worship with the knowledge that we have treated someone wrongly.

As ministers of reconciliation, however, there are limits to what we can accomplish. We cannot force another person to forgive us. Sometimes it takes time for another person to trust us after we have hurt them. The obligation still remains for us to pursue reconciliation, but it may not be according to our timetable. That is why we should be so careful with our words and actions. We can never take back a word uttered, and a hurt inflicted often leaves lasting scars.

Jesus' sayings require us to think carefully about what he is *not* saying. It is possible to be angry and not to sin (Eph. 4:26). Throughout Scripture we see evidence of righteous indignation against sin, which is called anger. Jesus demonstrated this in the cleansing of the temple (21:12–17), and in his parables God displays anger and wrath (18:34; 22:7). In the invectives against the religious leadership during his final fateful week in Jerusalem, Jesus referred to the teachers of the law and Pharisees as "blind fools" (23:17), using a related term to what he prohibits in 5:22. But this was not flippant name-calling. They really were fools, because they were blindly allowing their religious practices to distort their lives with God.

Jesus' teaching is sometimes used to advocate opposition to capital punishment. But the prohibition of the Old Testament that Jesus continues to uphold is against murder, not killing per se. Moreover, Jesus is addressing personal activity, not governmental responsibility. The judicial taking of life in punishment for crime is authorized in Exodus 21 and is the most likely intention of Paul's statements in Romans 13:1–5. There are four areas where taking of life is sometimes justified according to these passages: capital punishment, maintaining law and order, self-defense, and a just war. We will discuss this more fully when we address the fifth antithesis.

---

34. C. S. Lewis, *The Weight of Glory and Other Addresses*, repr. (Grand Rapids: Eerdmans, 1965), 14–15.

**Purity in marriage (5:27–30).** The second antithesis balances the stringency of the seventh commandment of the Decalogue, "You shall not commit adultery" (Ex. 20:14), with the radicalism of the tenth commandment, "You shall not covet your neighbor's wife" (20:17). It is one thing for a husband to say that he has never committed adultery, but it is another to say that he has never violated the marriage through flirting with another woman or through looking at pornography. The apostle Paul understood the difference, because he viewed himself as righteous until he grasped fully the significance of the command not to covet. Then he saw the depth of his own sinfulness (Rom. 7:7–13). The arrival of the kingdom of heaven in Jesus' ministry enables his disciples to have the kind of marriage that God originally designed. Following on the point of the first antithesis, to give myself solely and only to my wife treats her with the dignity she deserves as a woman created in the image of God. Anything less demeans her.

It is no coincidence that in the listings of qualifications for leadership in the church, Paul emphasizes the health of leaders' marriages, so that they can be examples for the church of the depth of commitment displayed in their lives (1 Tim. 3:2, 12; Titus 1:6). There is perhaps no more powerful testimony to the reality of the presence of the kingdom of heaven than leaders who have an unreserved commitment to their spouses, which means to pursue an unqualified purity in all relationships.

I remember starkly the first time I saw a pastor violate this high calling. I had been a Christian only a couple of years and was recently married. The music pastor and a woman in the ensemble carried on a flirtatious relationship. Other people seemed to think little of it, but it turned my stomach. It was offensive to both of their spouses and cheapened the standards of the ministry of that church. Eventually they ended up leaving their marriages and essentially abandoning the faith. It started out as "just a little flirting," but it ended up defiling numbers of lives. Jesus calls us to be severely honest with ourselves and to commit ourselves to our spouses with the same single-mindedness of commitment we have to him.

**Faithfulness in marriage (5:31–32).** Respecting the purity of marriage also allows Jesus' disciples to understand God's original design for marriage and to be unreservedly committed to its permanence and sanctity. The point of the third antithesis is to take the marriage covenant so sacredly that it should never be broken except when the most extreme conditions make it impossible to remain married. God has designed a pattern for the ongoing health of the human race. As a man and woman enter into a marital relationship, they commit themselves to each other as one indivisible unit. To be unfaithful to the relationship is to be unfaithful to God, who brought the two together. To stay firmly committed to the relationship—in action, words, thoughts, emotions, and priorities—is to experience the fullness of relationship that God has designed humans to experience and to use for the maintenance of life in this world.

I recommend that pastors spend time with every couple before they get married, discussing what it means to commit themselves to each other "for better or for worse, for richer or for poorer, in sickness and in health, to love and to cherish, till death do you part." Those words can run off the lips pretty easily, but in our culture where approximately half of all marriages end in divorce, couples must understand what they are getting into and what resources are available to enable them to maintain their commitment. Moreover, couples must go into marriage without divorce being an option. Yes, Jesus gave it as an exception when blatant sinfulness has already destroyed the marriage bond, but an exception is not the same as an easy option when the going gets tough.

We should also be careful not to read into Jesus' statement what he did not imply. He did not declare the exception of *porneia* to require divorce. Reconciliation and forgiveness are always the goal of any disruptions in the community of faith (cf. 18:15–35), including the biological community of faith. If all attempts at reconciliation fail, then divorce is possible; but it is not the first step, and it is not mandatory. Jesus also did not state that remarriage in the case of a legitimate divorce is invalid. Further, he did not state that illegitimate divorce and even illegitimate remarriage are unpardonable sins. While there are always consequences for going contrary to Jesus' intentions for us, we must be careful not to create oppressive burdens that cancel out God's grace and restoration.[35] We will touch on this more fully in chapter 19.

**Keeping our word (5:33–37).** In the fourth antithesis, Jesus stresses that his disciples do not need to utter oaths as additional confirmation of their trustworthiness since their faithful lives continually confirm the reliability of their word. Once again, this is a test of the heart. What we speak with our lips comes from our inner being. A dependable heart will utter dependable words. A person with an honest heart will speak honestly. If we add to our "yes" or "no" anything, such as "Yes, I swear!" does it mean that when we don't add "I swear" we don't mean it as much? A simple "yes" should always be as binding as with any oath.

Truthfulness is one of the basic necessities in the daily activities of life (Ex. 23:1–3; Lev. 19:16). When each person's word is honest, we are liberated to trust each other freely. When a person's word or handshake on a matter cannot be trusted, we must bring in all kinds of legal safeguards, which compli-

---

35. For a helpful overview, see David Instone-Brewer, *Divorce and Remarriage in the 1st and 21st Century* (Grove Biblical Series 19; Cambridge: Grove, 2001), and his longer treatment, *Divorce and Remarriage in the Bible: The Social and Literary Context* (Grand Rapids: Eerdmans, 2002).

cate daily life. Taken further, we have to bring additional safeguards into our daily lives to protect ourselves from malicious people who through false testimony would harm our reputation, destroy our character, or cheat us out of what is rightfully ours.

But Jesus is not suggesting that all oaths are wrong. He himself testified under oath in his trial before the Sanhedrin (26:63–64). In a court of law a person is operating under the jurisdiction of governing authorities who are trying to establish human norms. To submit to taking an oath is complying with those norms and, by extension, is submitting to God (Rom. 13:1–7; cf. Heb. 6:16–18). For example, in the earlier days of the U.S. judicial system when a person gave an oath in court, such as, "So help me God," it provided a standard of judgment. If a person lied under that oath before God, that person was liable to God's judgment.

Paul also made oaths when he invoked God as a witness to try to convince his readers that his word was true (2 Cor. 1:18; Gal. 1:20). His readers were not familiar enough with his character to have justifiable trust in his plain statements. We live in a world where lying is so commonplace that we don't know whom to trust. When a person doesn't know us well, they have no reason to trust us. If we invoke God as our witness, we are saying that we really are Christians. If we lie, it is a demonstration that we don't know God.

**Securely serving one another (5:38–42).** The fifth antithesis is one of the best known, though often the most misunderstood. "Turning the other cheek" has become a proverbial saying that some have used to promote absolute pacifism, others to stereotype Christians as wimps, and still others to excuse their own cowardice. Once again we must emphasize that Jesus is not countering the Old Testament law of retribution. Justice is as much a theme of Jesus as it was in the Old Testament. Sin needs a check against the destructiveness it can do in the lives of people. Sin must be punished. Jesus does not deny justice in any way; as he goes to the cross, he will be the ultimate payment for the penalty of sin.

What Jesus counteracts in the fifth antithesis is the way that the law of retaliation was used to excuse *personal* retribution. That's when it strikes home to me. I've been a fighter most of my life. I have mellowed quite a bit, but I still want to get back at people who hurt me. I want to go after a person who blatantly runs a red light. I want to stop the snowboarder who blasts down a hill without any regard for the safety of the older person on skis. And I don't think that I'm completely wrong for this. It is right to want to see justice prevail. But it is wrong when my ego gets in the way—when I retaliate to prove that I am strong, that I am superior to the other person, that I am the almighty righteous cop for God. In large part this is because of my own insecurity. I'm still trying to prove something.

There may be times that God will use me to bring justice, but for the most part that is left to governing authorities, whether the police on the street or the ski patrol on the hill. Instead, what is left to me is to give service to others so that they see a better way in me. That's fundamentally what Jesus is getting at. As disciples of Jesus, we should be so secure in our transformed kingdom identity that when we are wronged, we do not merely adhere to legal retribution, but we use every opportunity to serve others, both good and evil people, so that the reality of God's grace in our life woos them into the kingdom of heaven.

This is right in line with Paul's teaching. On the one hand, he tells the believers in the church at Rome not to repay evil for evil, to be at peace with all people, and not to take revenge (Rom 12:17–19). He is telling them not to advance *personal retaliation*. Why? Because, on the other hand, he emphasizes that God's wrath is the avenger (12:19–20), and he has established governing authorities for the task of executing judgment on evildoers (13:1–7). The individual Christian's responsibility is to do good to our enemies (12:20–21).

This does not rule out, however, Christians serving on the police force or in the military. But they must keep their personal identity clearly rooted in Christ while they serve as tools of God's righteousness. This can be a difficult balance to maintain, for it requires Christian officers to make value judgments about what is right or wrong from God's perspective, not necessarily the civil law, as one might have to do if living in a communist country. It requires Christian soldiers to make judgments about what is a just war.[36] The apostles were ready to disobey the Jewish governing authorities when ordered to quit preaching the gospel, because, as Peter said, "We must obey God rather than men" (Acts 5:29).

I almost hesitate to mention this next point, because it is easy to rationalize personal vengeance, but we might want to balance the fifth antithesis with other biblical principles. For example, Paul avoided scourging by demanding his rights as a Roman citizen (Acts 22:22–29; 25:11–12). This indicates that there are times when one should avoid personal harm, and there are times that we ought not let people walk over us, unless that is God's will for us at that time. In another example Paul declared the rule to the church, "If a man will not work, he shall not eat" (2 Thess. 3:10). There were people in the church who were religious busybodies and were expecting the church to provide for them. Paul, however, expects them to get a job and provide for themselves. Giving or loaning to such persons would be foolhardy.

---

36. A just war is noted to have seven distinctives: (1) just cause; (2) just intention; (3) last resort; (4) formal declaration; (5) limited objectives; (6) proportionate means; (7) non-combatant immunity; see Arthur F. Holmes, "The Just War," in *War: Four Christian Views*, ed. Robert G. Clouse (Downers Grove, Ill.: InterVarsity Press, 1981), 120–21.

The fifth antithesis emphasizes the goal of servanthood in Jesus' disciples. This means not to think first about our own harm but about the other's good. We are to give to the person what is needed for his or her good. Our ultimate example is Jesus himself:

> When they hurled their insults at him, he did not retaliate; when he suffered, he made no threats. Instead, he entrusted himself to him who judges justly. He himself bore our sins in his body on the tree, so that we might die to sins and live for righteousness; by his wounds you have been healed. (1 Peter 2:23–34)

**Loving as God loves (5:43–47).** The sixth antithesis continues the thought of the fifth, but it focuses on the driving energy that enables Jesus' disciples to give. We are to love as God loves. In the same way that today we might hear the word "love" used to express a variety of kinds of definitions, ranging from infatuation to brotherhood and goodwill to sexual activity, the words for love in the ancient world expressed a variety of attitudes, emotions, and behaviors. The New Testament writers took those same terms, especially the verb *agapao* and the noun *agape*, and reinvested them with new meanings befitting Jesus' teaching and example.

This radical reorientation is found in two verses that are probably known so well by Christians that they lose their impact and meaning. The first is John 3:16: "For God so loved the world, that he gave his only begotten Son, so that everyone who believes in him should not perish, but have eternal life." The key to understanding this kind of love is the word "gave." God the Father gave his Son, and the Son freely gave his life so that we might live. As Jesus was prepared to go to the cross, the apostle John tells us, "Having loved his own who were in the world, he now showed them the full extent of his love" (13:1). The full extent of his love meant giving his life for us on the cross. That is the profound nature of Jesus' love toward us, and it becomes the example of the sacrificial love that we can have for others, including our enemies.

The other verse comes from Romans 5:8: "But God demonstrates his own love toward us, in that while we were yet sinners, Christ died for us." The impact is felt even more deeply as Paul goes on to say, "For if, when we were God's enemies, we were reconciled to him through the death of his Son, how much more, having been reconciled, shall we be saved through his life!" (5:10). This kind of love is a motivating force that includes emotional attachment and personal feelings, but it goes beyond those to the action of giving oneself for the benefit of others. To love one's enemies doesn't mean that Jesus' disciples must condone their behavior, but it does mean that we are so engaged in their lives that we are used by God to reconcile them to him and to bring them into alignment with God's will for their lives. We are to love as God loves.

There are two important clues to the reason why we must love as God loves. (1) We have a new heart of love. Through the new birth, a change has been made in the spiritual heart of the believer by God's love for us (cf. Acts 15:9; also Ezek. 36:26). This new heart impels us to love with God's love. We love, not because we are so loving but because God first loved us and made a change in our hearts, which *impels* us to love (cf. 1 John 4:12–21).

(2) We have an endless supply of God's love by which the new heart can continually pour forth love. It is God's love that has brought us life, and it is his love in us that guarantees we will love others, even our enemies. God is love, and he is infinite, so he has an infinite supply of love. As we open our hearts to him, his love pours into our hearts and then overflows to those around us.

But what does it really mean to love someone? I define love as *an unconditional commitment to an imperfect person in which I give myself to bring the relationship to God's intended purpose.* Whatever it is that God has designed for my various relationships, I give myself to them unconditionally. That varies from the love commitments that I have for my wife or children or students or next-door neighbors. It will look differently as I give myself to people I don't like or who don't like me. But what I am asking in each is, "What does God want for this relationship, and how can I best give myself to bring it about?" It's with this kind of guidance that we can give ourselves wisely and maturely, even to our enemies.

There are dangerous, devious forces at work in our own day, ranging from ultra-rightwing patriot militias and ethnic supremacists to ultra-left-wing gay activists and political anarchists. After the terrorist attacks in New York and Washington, D.C., on September 11, 2001, we all understand much more clearly the reality of evil persons who declare us to be their enemies, although we have never even met them. There are forces in this world that are blatantly opposed to biblical truth and seek to undermine Christ's church and his values. Yet, do we love them? Not just at arm's length. Not just theoretically. But do we attempt to get to their hearts and win them for Jesus, even when they reject our love? I can't always say that I do. But I must, because their eternal destiny is at stake. That is the astonishing love that Jesus demonstrated, even at the cross, when he said, "Father, forgive them, for they do not know what they are doing" (Luke 23:34).

Do we love the way Jesus loved? Probably not as much as we think we do, because to love with his kind of love will mean our full obedience to God's will for our lives, the continuing transformation of our personal, corporate, and family life, and our dedicated outreach to the world around us.

Ultimately, that is what it means to truly love God with all our heart, soul, mind, and strength, and our neighbors as ourselves.[37]

**Be perfect (5:48).** Jesus concludes the antitheses with his climactic summons, "Be perfect, therefore, as your heavenly Father is perfect" (5:48). In its simplicity this may be one of the purest statements of spiritual formation in all of Scripture. But we may become uneasy before its magnitude. Some are uneasy because it may imply that we can attain a state of perfection in this life.[38] Others, rejecting that possibility, might become equally uneasy about postulating a goal that is unattainable in this life, because it could sound like wishful thinking. Or we might be uneasy about implying there are measurable points of progress toward a goal because of the cancer of comparison that can be produced in those involved in the process. Or we might be uneasy about the whole concept of "Christlikeness." Is this really an attainable goal?

But the uneasiness may dissipate by considering an important theological distinction—positional and experiential perfection. Although it awaits Paul's full theological development, positional perfection is the "imputed righteousness" of Christ that is the basis of the Christian's justification in a forensic or legal manner. Experiential righteousness is the "imparted righteousness" of Christ experienced by the Christian in the process of sanctification through the work of the Spirit. The latter is in view in 5:48, but it assumes and builds on the former. This implies an imperfect process that goes on throughout this life and accepts it as a goal that will be fully realized only in the future.[39]

Instead of being uneasy before Jesus' magnificent summons, we can practice a balance of what I call "restful dissatisfaction." I rest content with what Christ has done in my life and with the growth that has occurred, yet at the same time I balance that contentment with the desire to move on. At any one point in my life I want to be satisfied with what God has been doing in my life, yet I want to be dissatisfied to the degree that I press on to complete maturity. I accept my imperfection, yet I have the courage to press on to perfection. I rest in the indicative of what God has accomplished in Christ's work of redemption and regeneration (Titus 3:4–7), I rest in the assurance

---

37. For a popular treatment, see Michael J. Wilkins, "What Jesus Loved," *Moody Magazine* 100.3 (January–February 2000): 25–27.

38. Tasker (*Matthew*, 70) is uneasy about using "perfect" to render Matt. 5:48, calling it a "misleading translation of *teleios*, and is largely responsible for the erroneous doctrine of 'perfectionism.'"

39. Guthrie, *New Testament Theology*, 663: "The pursuit of the ideal will never be understood unless some element of the impossible is recognized in Jesus' demands. No man who considers himself to have attained perfection already has a right understanding of perfection."

that transformation is, at this very moment, being accomplished (2 Cor. 3:18), and I rest in the promise that ultimately we will be like him (1 John 3:2). But I am dissatisfied when I see immaturity or impurity in my heart, mind, and life; I am dissatisfied with the state of this world apart from Christ; I am dissatisfied with loving less than the way Jesus loves.

If we focus solely on our positional perfection, we can become complacent about our present growth. If we focus solely on our experiential imperfection, we can become distraught over our present state. We must rest in the positional perfection that Christ has brought through the cross, while being relatively dissatisfied with our experience in this life, pressing on toward greater growth in Christ. It is possible for each of us to live with unrealistic expectations of ourselves and what God wants from us. We can put ourselves on a performance standard where we expect certain behavior before we believe we are loved or accepted. Or we can fall into the trap of unrealistically comparing ourselves with the accomplishments of others in such a way that our uniqueness is lost. "Restful dissatisfaction" means that when we have given our best in our discipleship to Jesus, we are able to find contentment in our growth and accomplishment.

At the same time we must refuse to capitulate to our imperfections and press on toward further growth. Jesus' disciples experience the powerfully life-changing presence of the kingdom of heaven in such a way that becoming more like the Son produces the very perfection of God the Father. That is what I hear in Jesus' summons to be perfect as our heavenly Father is perfect.

# Matthew 6:1–18

<sup>1</sup>B E CAREFUL NOT to do your 'acts of righteousness' before men, to be seen by them. If you do, you will have no reward from your Father in heaven.

<sup>2</sup>"So when you give to the needy, do not announce it with trumpets, as the hypocrites do in the synagogues and on the streets, to be honored by men. I tell you the truth, they have received their reward in full. <sup>3</sup>But when you give to the needy, do not let your left hand know what your right hand is doing, <sup>4</sup>so that your giving may be in secret. Then your Father, who sees what is done in secret, will reward you.

<sup>5</sup>"And when you pray, do not be like the hypocrites, for they love to pray standing in the synagogues and on the street corners to be seen by men. I tell you the truth, they have received their reward in full. <sup>6</sup>But when you pray, go into your room, close the door and pray to your Father, who is unseen. Then your Father, who sees what is done in secret, will reward you. <sup>7</sup>And when you pray, do not keep on babbling like pagans, for they think they will be heard because of their many words. <sup>8</sup>Do not be like them, for your Father knows what you need before you ask him.

<sup>9</sup>"This, then, is how you should pray:

"'Our Father in heaven,
hallowed be your name,
<sup>10</sup>your kingdom come,
your will be done
on earth as it is in heaven.
<sup>11</sup>Give us today our daily bread.
<sup>12</sup>Forgive us our debts,
as we also have forgiven our debtors.
<sup>13</sup>And lead us not into temptation,
but deliver us from the evil one.'

<sup>14</sup>For if you forgive men when they sin against you, your heavenly Father will also forgive you. <sup>15</sup>But if you do not forgive men their sins, your Father will not forgive your sins.

<sup>16</sup>"When you fast, do not look somber as the hypocrites do, for they disfigure their faces to show men they are fasting.

I tell you the truth, they have received their reward in full.
¹⁷But when you fast, put oil on your head and wash your face,
¹⁸so that it will not be obvious to men that you are fasting,
but only to your Father, who is unseen; and your Father, who
sees what is done in secret, will reward you.

THE KINGDOM TRANSFORMATION that produces inner "heart righteousness" (5:20) will also produce external "acts of righteousness" (6:1) as a disciple becomes more like the heavenly Father (5:48). So Jesus turns to teach his disciples how the righteousness of the kingdom of heaven works out in the details of three primary arenas of everyday life: *public* religious life (6:1–18), *personal* interior life (6:19–34), and *interpersonal* relational life (7:1–12).

## Acts of Righteousness (6:1)

JESUS FIRST ADDRESSES the arena of public religion, because this is the place where a person's spirituality is developed and tested: "Be careful not to do your 'acts of righteousness' before men, to be seen by them." The expression "acts of righteousness" (*dikaiosyne*) is a good rendering of the same word that is rendered simply "righteousness" in 5:20. There it indicated God's inner transformation of the heart, which brings a person into the kingdom of heaven; here it indicates the external activities of the ongoing process of transformation to be more like the heavenly Father (5:48). The public religious life is crucial for the development of one's spirituality, because it is here that the people of God gather for worship, gain instruction in the Scriptures, and encourage one another in personal piety.

But this arena is also hazardous, because public religious practices can be carried out primarily to be seen by people. Because of this possibility, Jesus lodges criticism against the Jewish religious leaders of his day. Although they are not mentioned by name, the "teachers of the law and the Pharisees" are the most likely objects of this censure (cf. 5:20). They are the most public and influential religious figures among the common people, so Jesus denounces them for their faulty example. They perform religious acts in the public arena in order to receive the respect of their peers and the admiration of the common people (see 6:2, 5, 16, 18).

If Jesus' disciples fall into the same attention-seeking display of public piety, "you will have no reward from your Father in heaven" (6:1). The term for "reward" is *misthos*, which can indicate payment of "wages" (20:8) or, as here, the recompense of a person's good deeds with a good prize. It is an affirmative recognition and recompense by God for the praiseworthy moral quality of a disciple's acts of righteousness (6:1–2; cf. 5:12).[1] The notion that God rewards good behavior and punishes bad behavior is common in the Old Testament and in Jewish literature. Deuteronomy 28 lists a series of rewards and punishments that are distributed according to Israel's faithfulness to the covenant, a theme developed by later prophets (e.g., Isa. 65:6–7; 66:6). *The Rule of the Community* at Qumran presents lists of virtues and vices with their corresponding present world and future life rewards and punishments (1QS 4:2–14).[2]

But Jesus warns his disciples that obedience in the public arena does not guarantee a reward from God, because motive is more important than simple activity. Jesus goes on to demonstrate this by three examples of Jewish piety—giving to the needy (6:2–4), praying (6:5–15), and fasting (6:16–18). These acts of piety are valuable in the process of developing personal righteousness, and God will reward the disciple who practices them sincerely before him. But they can also be practiced "hypocritically"—that is, for the acclaim of people and the approval of the religious establishment. In such cases, there will be no reward from God (cf. 6:2, 5, 16).

The reward that Jesus promises follows the central message of the SM—the righteousness of the kingdom of heaven. Those who perform them out of the fullness of a heart transformed by God's righteousness will be rewarded with inner growth in kingdom righteousness in this life, and final perfection in the afterlife.

## Giving to the Needy (6:2–4)

A STATEMENT IN the apocryphal book of Tobit highlights the interdependence of the practices of giving to the needy, praying, and fasting but underscores the special importance within Judaism of giving alms:

> Prayer with fasting is good, but better than both is almsgiving with righteousness. A little with righteousness is better than wealth with wrongdoing. It is better to give alms than to lay up gold. For almsgiving saves from death and purges away every sin. Those who give alms will enjoy a full life, but those who commit sin and do wrong are their own worst enemies. (Tobit 12:8–10 NRSV)

---

1. BDAG, 653; Louw-Nida, "μισθός—38.14, 57.173," 491, 577; it can be used also to indicate recompense for evil deeds.

2. The reward for walking in obedience to the covenant would be rewarded with a profound visitation of God's blessing: "And the visitation of those who walk in it will be for healing, plentiful peace in a long life, fruitful offspring with all everlasting blessings, eternal enjoyment with endless life, and a crown of glory with majestic raiment in eternal light" (1QS 4:6–8).

The esteemed high priest at the time of Alexander the Great, Simeon the Just, is credited with the statement, "By three things is the world sustained: by the Law, by the [Temple-]service, and by deeds of loving-kindness" (*m. ʾAbot* 1.2).[3] Giving to the needy was one of the pillars of religious life. Poverty was widespread in ancient agrarian societies, and the people of Israel took seriously the obligation to provide for the poor (cf. Deut. 15:11). By the time of Jesus the phrase "to do mercy" had become a technical expression of caring for the poor by giving alms.[4]

The truly spiritual person recognized the plight of the needy and attended responsibly to their care. But Jesus says, "Do not announce it with trumpets" (6:2). Some suggest a literal trumpet is in mind, either to call the people to fasts with accompanying almsgiving or to signal an especially large gift being given. Or perhaps this denotes the sound of coins being tossed into the trumpet-shaped money chests in the temple used for collecting alms (*m. Še-qal.* 2:1). But more likely Jesus is drawing on a vivid piece of typical irony—those who seem to be the most humanitarian often want the most human glory and will make it known that they have been magnanimous in their concern for the poor. In our day the same metaphor is well known as a person who wants to "toot his own horn."

Jesus calls the persons engaged in this perilous self-promotion "hypocrites." The term "hypocrite" (*hypokrites*)[5] was originally used for actors on a Greek stage who put on various masks to play different roles. Jesus here censures the religious leaders, especially the Pharisees, for a particular form of hypocrisy: performing external acts of righteousness that mask, even from themselves, their own inner corruption (cf. 23:25–26). Their hypocrisy is *doing right things for the wrong reasons.* They perform external religious acts of piety in order be "honored" (*doxazo;* "glorified") by people and the religious establishment.[6] The tragic irony is that they will "receive in full" the reward of public and professional acclaim for their pious activities, but they will receive no reward from God. Unless prompted by the right motives, religious activities, including doing good deeds to others, are of no real spiritual value and receive no commendation from God. It does matter greatly *why* we do *what* we do.

Jesus then contrasts the way his disciples are to perform acts of righteousness with the way of the religious leaders: They are to go to the opposite extreme and keep secret their acts of piety (6:3a). They are to have such

---

3. "Simeon the Just," *DJBP,* 586.

4. See Acts 9:36; 10:2; 24:17; cf. Tob. 1:3, 16; 4:7–8; Sir. 7:10.

5. The term occurs thirteen times in Matthew, but elsewhere in the New Testament only four times.

6. See I. Howard Marshall, "Who Is a Hypocrite?" Part 2, "Four 'Bad' Words in the New Testament," *BibSac* 159 (April–June 2002): 131–50 (see esp. 137, 149–50).

pure motives of concern for the poor that when giving, they should have no self-awareness and no self-servingness at all. Don't even praise yourself for your giving, Jesus advises. It doesn't matter whether anyone ever knows what good deed has been done, because the Father sees the most secret action: "Then your Father, who sees what is done in secret, will reward you." God will reward Jesus' disciples with inner righteousness in this life and complete perfection in the afterlife. Human acclaim for giving to the needy cannot be compared to the value of being recognized by God for secret giving.

## Praying (6:5–15)

A SECOND PRACTICE of Jewish piety was prayer. Although individual prayer was appropriate at any time, pious Jews prayed publicly at set times. Commonly, there were morning, afternoon, and evening prayers (Ps. 55:17; Dan. 6:10; Acts 3:1).[7] Josephus points out that sacrifices, including prayers, were offered "twice a day, in the early morning and at the ninth hour."[8] Jesus indicates that an appropriate attitude is to be applied on any occasion one prays.

**The pretentious prayer of hypocrites (6:5–6).** As with giving to the needy (6:2), prayer can be perverted from a true act of piety into an act of hypocrisy when the external act masks an inner corrupt motive. As a set time of prayer arrived, pious Jews would stop what they were doing and pray. This could be done discreetly, or it could be done with pretentious display. Some people were sure to find themselves in a place where they would be noticed, such as the synagogue or on a street corner. In those cases, the inner motivation for offering public prayer was public recognition and acclaim of their piety, which has no value with God. This kind of hypocritical prayer receives the same reward as hypocritical almsgiving: acclaim from people.

In contrast, Jesus directs his disciples, when they pray, to go to their "inner room." Since most people did not have separate, private quarters in their homes, the meaning is most likely a metaphorical one to emphasize privacy. The saying continues the emphasis on the privacy of one's heart.[9] The focus is on the intimacy of communion with God in one's heart, which is at the center of all prayer, whether it happens to be given publicly or privately. That Jesus does not prohibit or condemn any and all public prayer is indicated by his own public prayers (see 14:19; 15:36). Note too that in the model

---

7. For a historical overview of the practice within Judaism, see Lee I. Levine, *The Ancient Synagogue: The First Thousand Years* (New Haven, Conn.: Yale Univ. Press, 2000), 510–23.

8. Josephus, *Ant.* 14.65.

9. I. Howard Marshall, "Jesus—Example and Teacher of Prayer in the Synoptic Gospels," *Into God's Presence: Prayer in the New Testament*, ed. Richard N. Longenecker (McMaster New Testament Studies; Grand Rapids: Eerdmans, 2001), 126.

prayer to follow, the disciples are to address God as "our Father" (6:9), which indicates a corporate type of prayer. But when praying publicly, disciples must watch carefully their motivation.

**The repetitious prayer of pagans (6:7–8).** Jesus goes on to warn his disciples against repetitious prayer: "Do not keep on babbling like pagans." The term "pagans" is *ethnikoi*, the regular expression for the Gentiles in Matthew, and "babbling" (*battalogeo*) indicates a person who repeats the same words over and over without thinking.[10] The priests of Baal continued from morning until noon, crying out, "O Baal, answer us" (1 Kings 18:26), and the multitude in the theater at Ephesus shouted for two hours, "Great is Artemis of the Ephesians" (Acts 19:34). God is always ready to listen, but he cannot be manipulated through ritual prayer. "Babbling" to get God's attention and to manipulate him to get what we want is foolish, because the Father is aware at all times of his children's needs even before they ask (Matt. 6:8).

Jesus illustrates in his own life and teaching two additional points about this statement. (1) Though God already knows, we should not hesitate to ask. Jesus' disciples don't pray to give him information but to express their desires, their needs, and their dependence on their heavenly Father. This is a central theme of the Lord's Prayer. (2) Long continued prayer is not improper, because Jesus himself prayed through whole nights (cf. Luke 6:12). He also commended in a parable the perseverance of the widow in prayer (Luke 18:1–8) and repeated the same request in his prayer to the Father in the garden (Matt. 26:44). Prayer is much about changing *us*, our character, our will, and our values, even while we seek for God's response. There is a better way of petitioning the Father than either the hypocrites or pagans, as Jesus now instructs his disciples.

**The model prayer for disciples: "The Lord's Prayer" (6:9–13).** Jesus now gives an example of how his disciples should pray. While it is commonly referred to as "The Lord's Prayer," it is actually "the disciple's prayer," because it is an example for them to follow.[11] Several points help to give a context for the prayer.

1. The prayer is offered not so much as a command to pray but as an *invitation* to share in the prayer life of Jesus himself.[12]
2. Jesus gives guidelines for the way in what his people should conduct their regular prayer life. It is a *model* for them. But he doesn't necessi-

---

10. BDAG, 172.

11. M. M. B. Turner, "Prayer in the Gospels and Acts," *Teach Us to Pray: Prayer in the Bible and the World*, ed. D. A. Carson (Grand Rapids: Baker, 1990), 64. The actual text of one of Jesus' prayers is found in John 17, which is the Lord's own intercessory prayer.

12. N. T. Wright, "The Lord's Prayer as a Paradigm of Christian Prayer," *Into God's Presence*, 132.

tate verbatim repetition of these words, because frequent repetitive use may lead to the sin of formalism that he here condemns.[13]

3. The *priorities* of the prayer are in line with the consistent Old and New Testament practice of establishing the primacy of God in national and personal life. In the first three petitions Jesus calls the disciples to focus on the preeminence of God, while in the final three petitions he guides them to petition for their personal needs in a community context.[14]

4. The *range* of the prayer extends from the grand themes of God's name, his kingdom, and his will to the everyday themes of bread, debts, and temptations.

5. The *theological themes* of this prayer are explicated more fully in the rest of the SM and in Matthew, indicative of the unity of Jesus' teaching as recorded in this Gospel. These themes form a trajectory of Jesus' theological program.

*Invocation* (*6:9*). The prayer begins by invoking God: "Our Father in heaven." The term for "Father" is "Abba," a name used by children for their earthly fathers that denotes warmth and intimacy in the security of a loving father's care. While children may have used it as a form of endearment, similar to the English expression "Daddy," it had a much more profound use in adult religious life.[15] The motif of a "heavenly Father" occurs throughout the Old Testament (e.g., Deut. 14:1; 32:6; Ps. 103:13; Hos. 11:1; Jer. 3:4; 31:9), growing increasingly popular during the Second Temple period in prayers for protection and forgiveness.[16] Adult Jews often referred to God in prayer as "our Father" (Heb. *'abinu*).[17] The way Jesus uses "*my* Father" (11:27) to address his heavenly Father is exceptional because Jesus is the unique Son (cf. 3:17). But by calling his disciples to share in the kingdom of heaven, they now have entered into a relationship with his Father as well.[18] Moreover, God is "*our* Father," expressing the relationship we have with one another as disciples and with Jesus as our brother, and the corporate intimacy we have with the same Father.

---

13. See Michael J. Wilkins, "Prayer," *DLNTD*, 947.

14. Hendriksen, *Matthew*, 325.

15. See Geza Vermes, *The Religion of Jesus the Jew* (Minneapolis: Fortress, 1993), 152–83.

16. E.g., *Jub.* 1:24, 28; 19:29; *Jos. Asen.* 12:14; Sir. 23:1, 4; Wisd. Sol. 2:16–20; 14:3; Tob. 13:4; 4Q372; 1QH 9:35. See "Father, God As," *DJBP*, 224.

17. For examples, see James H. Charlesworth, "A Caveat on Textual Transmission and the Meaning of *Abba*: A Study of the Lord's Prayer," in *The Lord's Prayer and Other Prayer Texts from the Greco-Roman Era*, ed. James H. Charlesworth with Mark Harding and Mark Kiley (Valley Forge, Pa.: Trinity Press International, 1994), 7.

18. This image is prevalent throughout the SM (cf. 5:16, 45, 48; 6:26, 33; 7:11).

(1) *God's name* (6:9). The first petition is directed toward God's name: "Hallowed be your name," or "Let your name be made holy." The purpose of hallowing the name (the name signifies the person) is that God might be "sanctified" or set apart as holy among all people and in all actions, that he will be treated with the highest honor. The Jewish Qaddish ("holy") prayer of the synagogue, which likely goes back to Jesus' time, begins similarly: "Exalted and hallowed be his great name in the world which he created according to his will. . . ."[19] This affirms the typical Jewish expectation that God must be treated with highest honor. To hallow God's name means to hold it in reverence—hence, to hold *him* in reverence, to honor, glorify, and exalt *him*. This is the essence of the first three of the Ten Commandments: "You shall have no other gods before me. You shall not make for yourself an idol in the form of anything. . . . You shall not misuse the name of the LORD your God . . ." (Ex. 20:3–7; Deut. 5:7–11).

Over the centuries there developed within Israel a reluctance to utter God's name, especially the unique name Yahweh (YHWH). Various substitutions were used, such as "Lord" (*Adonai*). The people of Israel were not only called to wipe out the names of the pagan gods, but they were to worship God in the sanctuary, the place where he chose to place his Name (Deut. 12:3–5, 11). Jesus' disciples will honor God's name in their prayers, but especially as they submit to his power and authority when they present themselves to baptism in the *name* of the Father, Son, and Holy Spirit (28:19).[20]

(2) *God's kingdom* (6:10). The second petition expresses the hope of God's people throughout all of history: "Your kingdom come." The Qaddish continues similarly, "May he rule his kingdom in your lifetime and in your days and in the lifetime of the whole house of Israel, speedily and soon."[21] Israel looked for God to send his Anointed One to rule the earth, and now that Jesus has inaugurated the kingdom of heaven, his disciples live with the anticipation of the completion of that program. God's anointed Messiah is here and at work, bringing the sovereign and saving rule of God. As the disciples pray "your kingdom come," they align themselves with Jesus' own practice of prayer and join his kingdom movement and seek God's power in furthering its ultimate fulfillment.[22]

---

19. B. T. Viviano, "Hillel and Jesus on Prayer," *Hillel and Jesus: Comparisons of Two Major Religious Leaders*, ed. James H. Charlesworth and Loren L. Johns (Minneapolis: Fortress, 1997), 449–50. See also James D. G. Dunn, "Prayer," *DJG*, 617.

20. See "Name," *DJBP*, 448.

21. Viviano, "Hillel and Jesus on Prayer," 449.

22. Wright, "The Lord's Prayer," 135.

This petition is reflected in a prayer expressed in the early church's appeal, "Come, O Lord!" (*marana tha*),[23] the oldest Christian prayer of which we have record. Jesus' disciples had invoked the name of their covenant God as "Lord" in the synagogue worship, but they now apply the same divine title to Jesus the Messiah, who has inaugurated the kingdom of heaven and who will bring its final manifestation.[24]

(3) *God's will* (6:10). The third petition speaks of God's will coming to pass: "Your will be done on earth as it is in heaven." This appeal is to be linked with the preceding petition. Wherever the kingdom of heaven exerts its presence, God's will is experienced. God reigns in heaven absolutely, which means that all of heaven experiences his perfect will. Jesus prays that earth will experience that same rule of God. The term for "will" is *thelema*, which can indicate God's purpose (e.g., Eph. 1:11) and desire (e.g., Luke 13:34). But as here, the term can express God's will of command, as in the psalmist's exclamation, "I desire to do your will; your law is within my heart" (Ps. 40:8).

Jesus' own utmost act of obedience in his earthly ministry was to submit to will of God the Father. He declared this allegiance at the outset: "My food ... is to do the will of him who sent me and to finish his work" (John 4:34), and he faithfully carried it out to the end, as he affirmed in the Garden of Gethsemane: "My Father, if it is possible, may this cup be taken from me. Yet not as I will, but as you will" (Matt. 26:39, 42). With the inauguration of the kingdom, those who carry out the Father's will in Jesus' ministry become his disciples (12:50) and display the reality of the kingdom of heaven as they remain faithful to that will for their lives (cf. 5:13–16). The complete experience of God's will on earth will occur only when his kingdom comes to earth in its final form, causing an overthrow of all evil rule (Rev. 20:1–10) and completing the regeneration of this earth (cf. Rom. 8:18–25). But Jesus' disciples are the present living testimony to the world that God's will can be experienced today.

The invocation and first three petitions give Jesus' disciples the right priorities, for we are less likely to pray frivolously or selfishly for God's will if we have first, and meaningfully, glorified God as "Father" and entreated him to bring his kingdom to earth.[25] Then the next three petitions can be properly focused on the needs of the individual disciples—their sustenance, their sin, and their spiritual battle.

(4) *Sustenance* (6:11). The fourth petition focuses on the disciples' sustenance: "Give us today our daily bread." The reference to "bread" is an example

---

23. See 1 Cor. 16:22; *Did.* 10.6; cf. Rev. 22:20.

24. Wilkins, "Prayer," 947; Ralph P. Martin, *Worship in the Early Church*, rev. ed. (Grand Rapids: Eerdmans, 1974), 32–33.

25. Turner, "Prayer in the Gospels and Acts," 65.

of synecdoche, a part-whole figure of speech for "food" (4:4), but especially referring to all of the believer's needs, both physical and spiritual. Disciples are to rely on God for all of their needs.[26] The adjective translated "daily" (*epiousios*) occurs in the New Testament only here and in the parallel in Luke 11:3.[27] Its connection with "bread" has been broadly debated, with the suggestions "for the present day," "for necessary existence today,"[28] "for the coming day,"[29] and "for the Day" (i.e., the blessing today of the coming eschatological Day of the Lord).[30]

Since the wording recalls Israel's daily reliance on God for manna in the desert (Ex. 16), the first view seems most likely.[31] In the same way that manna was only given one day at a time, disciples are to rely on daily provision for life from God, helping them to develop a continuing, conscious dependence on him. The emphatic position of "today" at the end of the Greek sentence emphasizes that the present day is to be the center of attention, which squares with Jesus' later admonition not to be anxious about the future (6:34). If God cares for us today, then surely he will provide for us every day of our lives. The best way to prevent anxiety is to consciously trust God for today's bread, and trust him for tomorrow's bread (cf. 6:34; Phil. 4:6). Jesus does not renounce responsible activity for his disciples to take care of their needs and those of their loved ones, as he indicates in his sound rebuke of the Pharisees when they avoided providing for parental needs (15:3–6). He only denounces anxiety about the future.[32] We are to rely on God for all physical sustenance but be concerned only one day at a time.

(5) *Sins (6:12).* The fifth petition addresses the disciples' debt of sin: "Forgive us our debts, as we also have forgiven our debtors." The word for "debt" is *opheilema*, whereas Luke uses *hamartia*, "sin" (Luke 11:4). These are basically equal expressions, but with the additional nuance in Matthew that humans

---

26. See Osborne, *The Hermeneutical Spiral*, 100–101, 108.

27. For overviews of this word, see Betz, *Sermon on the Mount*, 396–99; Davies and Allison, *Matthew*, 1:607–10; Hagner, *Matthew* 1:149–50; Morris, *Matthew*, 146 n. 43.

28. This is the view of Betz, *The Sermon on the Mount.*

29. A reference to a prayer one gives at the very beginning of a day or before one retires for the night, asking for provision for the next day. "Give us bread for the day that is beginning." Davies and Allison, *Matthew*, 1:609 adopt this view.

30. "Bread for the coming day," with reference to the eschatological day of the Lord and the eschatological banquet. The disciples are to pray for the experience of that blessing today. This eschatological reading is taken by Hagner, *Matthew* 1:149–50.

31. BDF, 123[1]: this is "conceptually and grammatically the most plausible explanation." The difficulty is that this seems redundant with *semeron*, "today," = "give to us today our bread for the present day." But see discussion.

32. Paul will later help the church achieve a rightful balance (e.g., 2 Thess. 3:6–15; 1 Tim. 5–6).

owe obedience to God. Sin creates an obligation or "debt" to God that we cannot possibly repay. This sentiment is commonly found in Judaism: "Forgive your neighbor the wrong he has done, and then your sins will be pardoned when you pray" (Sir. 28:2). But it is radicalized in Jesus' ministry. A hallmark of his new covenant ministry is his expiating role in the forgiveness of sins (26:28), which scandalized his opponents (9:1–8).

Jesus' disciples have responded to his charge to repent, and their sins are now forgiven. But they are not simply to relish their own state of forgiveness; they are also to forgive others. Those who have received forgiveness are so possessed with gratitude to God that they in turn will eagerly forgive those who are "debtors" to them. This does not teach that humans must forgive others before they can receive forgiveness themselves; rather, forgiveness of others is *proof* that that disciple's sins are forgiven and he or she possesses salvation (cf. 18:21–35). Disciples are to forgive those who have wronged them to maintain a joyful experience of our salvation (cf. 6:14–15). Doing so serves as evidence that a person has truly been forgiven his or her debt of sin.[33] If we don't forgive, it is evidence that we haven't experienced forgiveness ourselves.

(6) *Spiritual battle (6:13).* The final petition addresses the disciples' battle with evil forces: "And lead us not into temptation, but deliver us from the evil one." Since God is not one who tempts his people to do evil (James 1:13), and the word rendered "temptation" (*peirasmos*) can be used for either temptation or testing (cf. Matt. 4:1–11; James 1:12–13), this petition indicates that the disciples should pray either for relief from testing (Ex. 16:4; Deut. 8:16; 1 Peter 1:7) or for their testing not to become an occasion for temptation. This is similar to a standardized Jewish morning and evening prayer:

> Bring me not into the power of sin,
> And not into the power of guilt,
> And not into the power of temptation,
> And not into the power of anything shameful.[34]

Jesus directed the disciples to pray this way in the Garden of Gethsemane, "Watch and pray so that you will not fall into temptation. The spirit is willing, but the body is weak" (26:41).

The second clause of this petition, "but deliver us from the evil one," indicates that disciples must be conscious that life is a spiritual battle. The occurrence of the definite article with the word "evil" probably indicates Satan, "the

---

33. See P. S. Cameron, "Lead Us Not into Temptation," *ExpTim* 101 (1990): 299–301.

34. *b. Ber.* 60b, cited in Joachim Jeremias, *New Testament Theology: The Proclamation of Jesus* (New York: Scribner's, 1971), 202.

evil one" (cf. 5:37), although it can also be understood to indicate evil gen-erally (cf. 5:39).[35] Satan's influence is behind every attempt to turn a testing into a temptation to evil, so Jesus teaches his disciples that they must rely on God not only for physical sustenance and forgiveness of sins, but also for moral triumph and spiritual victory in all of the spiritual battles of life.[36]

*Liturgical ending.* The doxological ending that many Christians are accus-tomed to pray—"For yours is the kingdom and the power and the glory for-ever. Amen" (cf. NIV text note)—did not originally conclude the Lord's Prayer in Matthew's Gospel. The best and oldest manuscripts do not have it, and the earliest commentaries on the Lord's Prayer do not mention it. Neither does it appear in Luke's parallel prayer (Luke 11:2–4). This doxology does occur in a variety of forms in many later manuscripts. Although it was not originally in Matthew's Gospel, it is in line with many other scriptural concepts and probably reflects early Christian practice of adapting the prayer for liturgi-cal use in the church, perhaps on the basis of 1 Chronicles 29:11.[37]

**Forgiveness and prayer (6:14–15).** Jesus concludes his instruction on prayer by reiterating the emphasis of the fifth petition on forgiving others (6:12). Salvation does not rest on human merits but only on the grace and mercy of God. Once disciples have received forgiveness and salvation, they are to forgive with the same forgiveness with which they have been for-given. This is the evidence that they are indeed forgiven (see also comments on 18:21–35).

## Fasting (6:16–18)

JESUS RETURNS TO his condemnation of the hypocritical practices of the reli-gious leaders, especially the teachers of the law and the Pharisees, now con-centrating on fasting, the third pillar of Jewish piety (see comments on 6:1–2). Since the religious leaders fasted in order to get recognition from the people, that is all the reward that they will receive. "Acts of righteousness," such as fasting, are of no value if not done with the right motives.

Various kinds of fasts were commonly practiced throughout much of Israel's history, always as a symbol of some deeper meaning than simply abstaining from food.

---

35. Morris, *Matthew,* 148–49, takes it in the latter sense. Others have suggested that this is a "litotes," a figure of speech that expresses one thing by negating the opposite; e.g., the expression "not a few" means "many." Disciples are to pray that God will lead them, not into temptation, but away from it, into righteousness, into situations where, far from being tempted, they will be protected and kept righteous; Carson, *Sermon on the Mount,* 70.

36. Bruce Chilton, *Jesus' Prayer and Jesus' Eucharist: His Personal Practice of Spirituality* (Val-ley Forge, Pa.: Trinity Press International, 1997), 46–47.

37. For discussion, see *TCGNT,* 13–14; Betz, *Sermon on the Mount,* 414–15.

---

- *Normal fast.* A person abstained from all food, solid or liquid, but not from water—usually to prepare for some significant event. Jesus fasted for forty days in preparation for his temptations from Satan and the inauguration of his public ministry (Matt. 4:1–2; Luke 4:1–2).
- *Partial fast.* Sometimes people entered into a partial restriction of diet, but not total abstention. For a three-week period of mourning, Daniel ate no meat or drank no wine, and he applied no lotion to his body (Dan. 10:3).
- *Absolute fast.* During a relatively short, urgent period of time, people could abstain from all food and water to discern God's leading. Esther neither ate nor drank for three days during a period of national crisis (Est. 4:16), and at Paul's dramatic conversion he abstained from eating and drinking for three days (Acts 9:9).
- *Private and corporate fasts.* Fasting is usually a private affair, but at times the people of God came together for corporate or public fasts, such as on the Day of Atonement (Lev. 23:37), in times of national emergency (2 Chron. 20:1–4), or for seeking God's guidance in prayer (Ezra 8:21–23).

The Old Testament law required only one fast a year—on the Day of Atonement (Lev. 16:29–34; 23:26–32). The expression used in Leviticus for fasting is literally "deny yourselves" (NIV) or "humble your souls" (NASB). This indicates that in addition to abstaining from food, the people were to demonstrate a humbling of their souls by wearing sackcloth, mourning, and praying (cf. Ps. 35:13; Isa. 58:3).[38] As time passed, fasts multiplied for legitimate purposes, such as national repentance and seeking God's mercy (e.g., Ezra 8:21–23). Certain days of the year became regularly anticipated days of fasting (Neh. 9:1; Zech. 8:19).

Jesus' teaching draws on that national history. He assumes his disciples will fast, because he says simply, "When you fast" (6:16). Giving to the needy, praying, and fasting were an assumed part of regular devotion. Jesus does not prohibit his disciples from fasting, but neither does he make it a required practice. Later in a confrontation over the fasting practices of the disciples of the Pharisees and the disciples of John the Baptist, Jesus declares that his disciples were to celebrate while he was with them; fasting was inappropriate. When he was taken away, fasting would once again be an important spiritual exercise, but was not mandatory (see 9:14–15).

Fasting was practiced regularly twice a week among some sectarians (cf. Luke 18:12), usually on Monday and Thursday, because Moses is said to

---

38. BDB, 776, 847; see Hartley, *Leviticus*, 242; R. Laird Harris, "Leviticus," *EBC*, 2:591.

have gone up on Sinai on those days. In fasting on those days, they felt they were emulating Moses' rigorous approach to God and his holiness. But this can also lead to a deceptive trap of self-aggrandizement when people attempt to elevate their religious status in the eyes of the people and their peers by broadcasting their religious accomplishments. Thus, Jesus says, "do not look somber as the hypocrites do, for they disfigure their faces to show men they are fasting."

"Disfigure" (*aphanizo*) here indicates making one's face unrecognizable from a normal perspective, with the intent to publicize the physical hardships endured while fasting. The hypocrites certainly did not want to be completely unrecognizable, which would defeat the purpose of trying to gain attention for their pious deed. During the fasting period they might disfigure their face by remaining ungroomed or perhaps by sprinkling ashes on their head and face as a sign of contrition. This was a deceptive way of letting others know of their extensive efforts to increase their personal piety.

Jesus' disciples are to have a different approach, because fasting is to be a heart issue between God and the individual. "But when you fast, put oil on your head and wash your face." This kind of anointing and washing is social, not religious. It signifies that a person has prepared herself or himself to enjoy life, similar to the expression in Ecclesiastes, "Go, eat your food with gladness, and drink your wine with a joyful heart, for it is now that God favors what you do. Always be clothed in white, and always anoint your head with oil" (Eccl. 9:7–8). Rather than making a public display of fasting, which would destroy any spiritual value, Jesus' disciples are to celebrate life while fasting. Other people do not need to know of their religious discipline.

Like the practices of giving to those in need and praying, fasting is to be done in the secrecy of the heart, with only God the Father as audience. The reward for fasting is the same as the reward for other "acts of righteousness"—continued development of inner righteousness in this life and the final perfection of righteousness in the afterlife (6:1–4). But the spiritual value of fasting will only be rewarded to those who seek God's favor and attention, and his alone.

**Bridging Contexts**

JESUS CAME TO fulfill the Old Testament revelation of God's will for his people, but he did not come into a vacuum. Many other people and groups were also trying to live out the Old Testament's directives. How different from these other groups will be the form of discipleship that Jesus introduces? What will make Jesus' teaching stand out from the leading religious figures of his day? These are important issues for Matthew as he writes his Gospel, because his record of the SM is an important foundational statement of what discipleship to Jesus entails. Since disciples in all ages are to be taught to obey all that Jesus has commanded (28:20), Matthew wants to state clearly and precisely the kind of discipleship Jesus desires.

Thus, after recording six representative examples of the way that Jesus' interpretation and application of the Old Testament is the antithesis of current practices (5:21—48), he records three representative ways that the discipleship of Jesus surpasses the external, legalistic, pious life of the leading religious figures of his day. Jesus may have given other examples, because the original SM was likely much longer, but these three powerfully refute the hypocritical example of the religious leaders. Obedience is central to Jesus' form of discipleship, as it was to other forms of discipleship within Judaism, but Jesus calls his followers to adhere to the *motive* behind obedience to the Old Testament, not simply to carry out external compliance.

**Motives.** Why do we do the good things that we do? Because of our gratitude to Jesus for inviting us to the kingdom of heaven, or because of the rewards that he offers? Because it is the right thing to do, or because we want to be recognized by people? Giving to the needy, praying, and fasting can be valuable in developing personal righteousness, and God will reward those who practice them sincerely before him. But they can also be practiced "hypocritically" (6:2, 5, 16) for the acclaim of people, the approval of the religious establishment, and the accumulation of material blessing in this life. In such cases there will be no reward from God. Those who engage in such activities for the acclaim of people will grow in increasing self-righteousness, and the only reward they receive will be the approval of people (6:2, 15).

Why do we do what we do? Philosophers, psychologists, and educators have long debated whether motivation is innate (genetically programmed) or acquired (learned), whether it is primarily the result of internal needs or external goals, or whether it is principally either mechanistic (automatic) or cognitive (active processing). Not surprisingly, most researchers concur that many of the real-life situations that we encounter undoubtedly require a combination of each of these.[39] That is borne out by looking at Jesus' teaching in this section. The criticism he lodges against the religious leaders is directed at their inner corruption, their hypocrisy, which is the sinful disease of self-glorification. But that corruption was also stimulated by the external reward they received when desire for attention was satisfied by being "honored" by the people and by the religious establishment. They are a classic example of "mixed motives," where good and bad motivating forces are

---

39. For a clearly developed overview, see Herbert L. Petri, "Motivation," *Encyclopedia Britannica* <http://www.britannica.com/eb/article?eu=115599> [Accessed April 27, 2002].

unwisely or wickedly united. Intentionally acting out of mixed motives is what Jesus directly condemns.

While avoiding "mixed" motives, we can see in Jesus' teaching that a variety of motivational elements will influence our own discipleship. The *transformed disposition* of the disciple's inner heart motivates us to discipline our lives to be like the Father (5:48). We are different because the arrival of the kingdom of heaven in Jesus' ministry brings new covenant salvation and transformation through the cross. A true disciple operates out of *gratitude* to the Savior who has rescued us (see comments on 20:1–16). But Jesus also holds out *rewards* as an external motivating factor. We discipline ourselves to be obedient to Jesus' teachings so that we can receive from the Father the reward of continual development of righteousness in this life and the promise of the completion of that process in the afterlife.

So why do we do what we do? Keeping these forces in balance is critical for our discipleship, because going too far in any direction will distort our motivation. Since motivation is personal and internal, motives are a quick gauge of a person's heart. I once had a friend tell me that his primary motivation as a pastor is the rewards that he will receive from God at the end of this life. I've always considered that a bit unbalanced, especially when I consider the other motivating forces that are at our disposal. The following may be a way of developing an appropriate balance.

In the hierarchy of Christian motives, a strong case should be made that the highest-placed motive is showing gratitude for the grace of God in sending his Son to be a ransom for humanity (20:1–28). Unlike other high-level motives that are often advanced by secular ethicists, this motive is directed away from self.[40] Gratitude is developed as a motivating force by continually looking away from self to the finished work of Jesus' ministry and considering deeply the alternative consequences of our fate without it.

A second, and consequent, motive is love in response to God's love for us (5:43–47; cf. 1 John 4:7–21). To have experienced real love from God will move us mightily to love him and to love others. We might then be motivated by the desire to emulate Jesus, as a disciple will become like his or her Master (10:24–25; 2 Cor. 3:18).

There is also the motivation to avoid loss of joy (Ps. 51:12). And, of course, there is the motive of our own future reward. Those who give to the needy, pray, and fast in the secrecy of the heart will be rewarded (6:4, 6, 18). But Jesus did not present rewards as the primary motivating force. Rewards are mentioned as the by-product of a life free from self-advancement.

---

40. Ronald C. Doll, "Motives and Motivation," *Baker's Dictionary of Christian Ethics*, ed. Carl F. H. Henry (Grand Rapids: Baker, 1973), 437–38.

New Testament scholar Harold Hoehner contends, "Believers' motivation in this life should not be the obtaining of rewards as an end in itself. Our motivation should be to please God wholeheartedly in gratitude for what he has done for us through Christ."[41] To regard our own rewards as our primary motivation is to center on ourselves, the very hypocrisy Jesus condemns.[42] A horizontal and vertical balance will keep us rightly motivated: "The worthiest of motives are directed vertically in an effort to give gratitude, obedience, and honor to God, and then horizontally in quest of the spiritual welfare and also the physical and material welfare of one's fellows."[43]

CONGRUENCY OF INNER **life and external practice.** Jesus expects us to practice "acts of righteousness." He does not advocate this in order to earn entrance to the kingdom of heaven or to achieve advanced standing with the Father, but these acts are intentional ways of conforming the external expression of our lives to the inner work of God in our hearts. Acts of righteousness (popularly called "spiritual disciplines") bring congruency between the inner righteousness that God initiates when a disciple enters the kingdom of heaven, and the development of experiential righteousness in this life as the disciple pursues the directive, "Be perfect, therefore, as your heavenly Father is perfect" (5:48). The apostle Paul advises young pastor Timothy likewise: "Train yourself to be godly. For physical training is of some value, but godliness has value for all things, holding promise for both the present life and the life to come" (1 Tim. 4:7–8).

The transformation that God has begun in the inner life is reflected in our acts of righteousness. Jesus emphasizes three practices that illustrate this principle. The transformation that occurs in the heart of a disciple causes him to love with God's love, which will be expressed in giving to the needy (6:2–4). The intimacy of the relationship with God that has occurred in the inner person of the disciple will be expressed in an intimate form of personalized prayer between her and the Father (6:5–15). The inner life of the disciple who has experienced true humility and mourning over one's own sin and the sorry sinful state of the world apart from God will urge her or him to undertake the discipline of fasting in order to examine one's personal life and to focus on prayer for the world's repentance (6:16–18).

---

41. Harold H. Hoehner, "Rewards," *NDBT*, 740.

42. Cf. ibid.: "A soldier's primary motivation should be to serve his country, though he may receive medals as a reward for his service. In the same way, true servants of God should not be centred on themselves but on the Lord whom they love and serve."

43. Doll, "Motives and Motivation," 438.

Throughout church history the practice of the full panoply of spiritual disciplines has been a key to spiritual growth. These "disciplines" are viewed from different perspectives. One way is to view them as a threefold unity: *inward disciplines* (meditation, prayer, fasting, study), *outward disciplines* (simplicity, solitude, submission, service), and *corporate disciplines* (confession, worship, guidance, celebration).[44] Another way is to view them is from a twofold opposite perspective: *disciplines of abstinence* (solitude, silence, fasting, frugality, chastity, secrecy, sacrifice) and *disciplines of engagement* (study, worship, celebration, service, prayer, fellowship, confession, submission).[45] However we might view them, the important point is to remember that the righteousness of the kingdom of heaven is an inside-out process, which Jesus intentionally orients to counteract the hypocritical practice of operating only on the surface.

One of the gravest dangers is to practice these disciplines in a rote way for the approval of the people around us or to satisfy the expectations of the church tradition of which we are a part. Another grave danger is to fall into the opposite trap, neglecting the practice of the disciplines because we are afraid of becoming legalistic. Perhaps the most important example is in Jesus' own life, who not only calls us to practice these disciplines but sets the example himself of how to practice them as a natural outgrowth of his inner godliness. Donald Whitney states, "The Lord Jesus not only expects these Disciplines of us, He modeled them for us. He applied His heart to discipline. He disciplined Himself for the purpose of Godliness. If we are going to be Christlike, we must live as Christ lived."[46]

Personal transformation begins in the inner person through the work of the Spirit of God, which produces change on the outside as we discipline ourselves to be more Christlike. We must develop an inside-out mentality so that Spirit-produced growth of the inner person is in harmony with outward obedience.

**Being seen by men (6:1).** Jesus reveals here an important distinction to be maintained by his disciples. Earlier he urged them to "let your light shine before men, that they may see your good deeds" (5:16). Here he admonishes them to "be careful not to do your 'acts of righteousness' before men, to be seen by them" (6:1). On the surface this may seem like a contradiction, but when we look more closely, we see that the difference in each case is the disciples' *motive* in performing public acts of piety.

---

44. Richard J. Foster, *Celebration of Discipline: The Path to Spiritual Growth*, rev. ed. (San Francisco: Harper & Row, 1988).

45. Dallas Willard, *The Spirit of the Disciplines: Understanding How God Changes Lives* (San Francisco: Harper & Row, 1988), 156–75.

46. Donald S. Whitney, *Spiritual Disciplines for the Christian Life* (Colorado Springs: NavPress, 1991), 21.

In the former case, the public display of good works is not for the purpose of drawing attention to the disciple but for people to "praise your Father in heaven" (5:16). Disciples could easily be afraid to let their light of good works shine because it might bring persecution (5:10), so Jesus calls them to think courageously of their heavenly Father's glory as the motive for public displays of righteousness. In the latter case, Jesus addresses religious vanity, in which case disciples face the temptation to perform public acts of piety and good works to gain the admiration of other people (6:1). A way of balancing the temptation from both personal cowardice and religious vanity was proposed over a hundred years ago by A. B. Bruce, who suggested that we try this formula: "Show when tempted to *hide*, hide when tempted to *show*. The Pharisees were exposed, and yielded, to the latter temptation."[47]

**Eliminating elitism.** Another element that surfaces from Jesus' confrontation of the hypocritical practices of the religious leaders is what we might refer to as "elitism." Each of the spiritual disciplines noted above, including the three Jesus addressed directly, are practices rooted in biblical prescriptions, and each should rightfully be incorporated into faithful Christian living. But, as with the Pharisees, the flawed practice of these disciplines can create an elitist distinction.

Within church history the expectations of performance often became so demanding within certain traditions that only a few people could really devote themselves to the full practice of the disciplines. This was one of the problems with certain ascetic monastic movements. Some traditions became exclusivistic in the sense that their tradition alone was the primary means of attaining spirituality, so that an elitist distinction developed between nominal Christians and those committed to the practices of a particular tradition. This was surely not the original intent, but it became the unfortunate result, with the average Christian often despairing of being "spiritual." From there it led to the clergy-laity distinction that the Reformers tried to rectify.

The prevalence of elitism in many traditions partially explains why scores of people are frustrated in their Christian lives. A two-level conception of the Christian life promotes apathy among those who haven't yet chosen to be committed, and it suggests that the higher level of commitment is optional, which in the daily world of most Christians means that commitment to Christlikeness is optional. One of Jesus' purposes in the SM, and particularly in addressing the practice of "acts of righteousness" in this section, is to eliminate an elitist conception of discipleship. The practice of the disciplines is a normal outgrowth of discipleship to Jesus. Since all true believers are

---

47. Alexander Balmain Bruce, "The Synoptic Gospels," *The Expositor's Greek Testament* (1897; repr.; Grand Rapids: Eerdmans, 1976), 1:116.

disciples of Jesus Christ and, correspondingly, all true believers have been born anew to spiritual life by the Spirit of God (cf. Rom. 8:9; Titus 3:3–7),[48] Jesus calls all believers to his form of discipleship, which means faithfully practicing the "acts of righteousness" in devotion to the Father.[49]

**Practicing disciplines in secrecy.** Jesus further emphasizes that one key solution to religious hypocrisy is to be sure that an act of righteousness is carried out "in secret" (6:4, 6, 18), which means essentially that the deed be performed in the privacy of one's heart.

*Giving to the needy in secret (6:2–4).* Inner motivation drives outward actions, so Jesus' disciples are to give to the needy from the secrecy of their heart. Jesus is not saying that his disciples should never give to the needy publicly. Practically all such giving required a public service to the needy, far different than today when we can send money anonymously through the mail or via a bank transfer. Although the various acts were carried out in the public arena—such as giving to the street corner beggar, or the poverty-stricken family in the community, or the widowed mother in the worshiping community—the motive of the heart was to be one of secrecy; Jesus' disciple desires no public adulation.

A thoughtful, appropriate balance is required. I was somewhat surprised to receive in the mail a magazine from a Christian college that listed every alumnus of that institution that had donated to the school and then went on to make a pretty strenuous appeal for those who hadn't given to become more supportive. It seemed a bit manipulative to me, although it seems not to have offended others. Nevertheless, it might be extreme to require that only anonymous donations are appropriate. One church I attended did not pass offering baskets because they wanted to avoid manipulating their people and to maintain as much anonymity as possible. So they put offering boxes on the wall into which members dropped their offering when leaving. That can be even more public than offering baskets!

Again, Jesus is addressing the *motive* of the person giving, not any particular format. We are not to give with mixed or ulterior motives of gaining public acclaim for our giving. But we are not to wait until our motives change by themselves. Dealing with our motives can be a paralyzing issue, because in the process of our growth in Christ we will continue to be influenced daily by the temptations of this world. God doesn't require us to be perfect; he just tells us to pursue it—and that includes our motives.

Years ago, before giving a prayer for the offering in the little church where

---

48. See D. A. Carson, "When Is Spirituality Spiritual?" *JETS* 37 (September 1994): 381–94.

49. See a more complete development of this theme in Wilkins, "Eliminating Elitism" (forthcoming).

I was pastor, I used to tell the people that if they were grudging that morning in their giving (2 Cor. 9:5), or if they were tempted to give to be noticed by the pastoral staff or the leadership, or even their own family, they should put their wallet or purse away. God doesn't need their money given with bad motives. The elders of the church gasped almost visibly. But then I went on to say that even if they had mixed motives in giving, God could change their hearts in a beat. So if they were ready, we could pray and ask God to purify their motives. The elders were much happier! It is within our responsibility to check our motives, to ask the Spirit of God to purify our motives, and then to move on, knowing that he will continue to cause us to grow in this area, if we really desire it.

*Praying in secret (6:5—15).* Prayer is also to be conducted in the secret privacy of the disciple's heart (6:6).[50] There are no set requirements for attaining this privacy; it means primarily to find ourselves in such a situation where we are addressing the Father alone. Some people find that privacy in special times of the day, others through journaling, others through a particular pattern of prayer. Jesus' own public prayers (14:19; 15:36) and the communal nature of prayer to "our Father" (6:9) allow us to see that he is not prohibiting or condemning all public prayers. Public prayer is to be a part of the community of disciples who join their hearts in one accord to seek God's leading and petition for his activity on their behalf (cf. Acts 2:42; 4:23–30). But when prayers are given in public, the one offering the prayer is to operate out of the privacy of his or her heart, with God alone as audience.

We've all been conscious at times of being in a prayer group when it seemed as though the one praying is addressing us more than God. Or our grand prayers were really aimed at impressing the audience more than reaching God. I've learned over the years when praying in public to address God intently from the privacy of my heart, but also to recognize that I am charged with leading the people, and even instructing them, in my prayers. This seems to be the purpose of Jesus' high-priestly prayer (John 17) and Paul's prayers for the churches (e.g., Eph. 3:14–21). The motivation of private prayer is the intimacy of communion with God in our heart, which is at the center of all prayer, whether it happens to be given publicly or privately.

*Fasting in secret (6:16—18).* Like giving to the needy and praying, fasting is also to be conducted in the privacy of the disciple's heart. It takes rigorous self-control to undertake a fast, so it is a significant temptation to let others know of our efforts or even of our victories. This may be done innocently, but Jesus allows us to see that broadcasting our fast in any way can become a dangerous form of religious pride and self-delusion.

---

50. Marshall, "Jesus—Example and Teacher of Prayer in the Synoptic Gospels," 126.

But as in the other disciplines, Jesus does not prohibit corporate fasting. Of the sixteen or so references to fasting in the New Testament, roughly half speak of corporate fasts, including those that seem to indicate that it was the regular practice of the early church (Acts 14:23; 23:12; 27:9, 33).[51] As with individual fasts, corporate fasting encouraged the church to express sorrow for sin, seek community forgiveness, concentrate on the work of God, and seek his guidance. But even corporate fasting needs to be conducted in the privacy of the heart, with no self-adulation of the church taking pride in its serious rigor. Fasting has lost much appeal in the modern church. This is a sad misreading of Jesus' teaching. He does not condemn fasting, not even corporate fasting, but only fasting with the motive of receiving acclaim from the people.

---

51. For a listing of references to fasting in the Bible and their classification as individual or corporate, see Kent D. Berghuis, "A Biblical Perspective on Fasting," *BibSac* 158 (January–March 2001): 86–103, esp. 97–101.

# Matthew 6:19–34

"DO NOT STORE up for yourselves treasures on earth, where moth and rust destroy, and where thieves break in and steal. [20]But store up for yourselves treasures in heaven, where moth and rust do not destroy, and where thieves do not break in and steal. [21]For where your treasure is, there your heart will be also.

[22]"The eye is the lamp of the body. If your eyes are good, your whole body will be full of light. [23]But if your eyes are bad, your whole body will be full of darkness. If then the light within you is darkness, how great is that darkness!

[24]"No one can serve two masters. Either he will hate the one and love the other, or he will be devoted to the one and despise the other. You cannot serve both God and Money.

[25]"Therefore I tell you, do not worry about your life, what you will eat or drink; or about your body, what you will wear. Is not life more important than food, and the body more important than clothes? [26]Look at the birds of the air; they do not sow or reap or store away in barns, and yet your heavenly Father feeds them. Are you not much more valuable than they? [27]Who of you by worrying can add a single hour to his life?

[28]"And why do you worry about clothes? See how the lilies of the field grow. They do not labor or spin. [29]Yet I tell you that not even Solomon in all his splendor was dressed like one of these. [30]If that is how God clothes the grass of the field, which is here today and tomorrow is thrown into the fire, will he not much more clothe you, O you of little faith? [31]So do not worry, saying, 'What shall we eat?' or 'What shall we drink?' or 'What shall we wear?' [32]For the pagans run after all these things, and your heavenly Father knows that you need them. [33]But seek first his kingdom and his righteousness, and all these things will be given to you as well. [34]Therefore do not worry about tomorrow, for tomorrow will worry about itself. Each day has enough trouble of its own.

THE KEY SAYING of this section is Jesus' famous imperative, "But seek first his kingdom and his righteousness" (6:33). It continues the overall priority and teaching of the SM. The preceding section (6:1–18) indicates the kind of religious life that Jesus' disciples will experience in the public realm under the influence of the kingdom of heaven. Their "acts of righteousness" (6:1) brings congruency between the initial gift of positional righteousness by which they gained entrance to the kingdom of heaven (5:20) and their experiential growth in righteousness as they pursue the ultimate goal of the perfection of their heavenly Father (5:48). This section continues the teaching on the pursuit of kingdom righteousness (6:33), but here the spotlight is on the kind of personal interior life that Jesus' disciples will experience in their everyday world.

On the one hand, Jesus warns against the everyday concerns about wealth (6:19–24) and worry (6:25–34), which can rob disciples of the kingdom's priority in their personal lives. On the other hand, he teaches how his disciples can properly live with the priority of the kingdom of heaven and its righteousness, including their ideals, vision, priorities, and security.

## Choose Your Master: God or Wealth (6:19–24)

IN THE PURSUIT of the perfection of the Father (5:48), Jesus' disciples will encounter a number of everyday concerns that have the potential to deter them from undivided loyalty to the kingdom and its righteousness. The first one he discusses is wealth.

**Two treasures of the heart (6:19–21).** Material wealth was important to the people of Israel since it was often seen as a sign of God's blessing and the reward for obedience to him. One ancient rabbi said:

> A man should always teach his son a cleanly [or easy] craft, and let him pray to him to whom riches and possessions belong, for there is no craft wherein there is not both poverty and wealth; for poverty comes not from a man's craft, nor riches from a man's craft, but all is according to his merit. (*m. Qidd.* 4.14)

But Jewish writers also regularly warned the people that wealth is not the final determination of one's spiritual standing before God.[1] Wealth could be acquired illegitimately, and all too often the wicked are the ones who prosper. Jeremiah laments: "You are always righteous, O LORD, when I bring a case before you. Yet I would speak with you about your justice: Why does the way

---

1. Cf. 1QS 10.18–19; Sir. 31:8–11.

of the wicked prosper? Why do all the faithless live at ease?" (Jer. 12:1). *First Enoch* speaks of the ultimate destruction of those who accumulate wealth illegitimately: "For your wealth shall not endure but it shall take off from you quickly for you have acquired it all unjustly, and you shall be given over to a great curse" (*1 En.* 97:8–10).

The accumulation of wealth for its own sake is deceptive, because one can find in material treasure a false sense of security or an inaccurate assessment of one's spirituality. So Jesus says, "Do not store up for yourselves treasures on earth." The term behind the negative imperative "do not store up" is *thesaurizo*, which is related to the noun "treasure" (*thesauros*). The wordplay can be rendered woodenly, "Do not treasure up for yourselves treasure on earth." "Treasure" represents the accumulation of what is valuable.

But those things that some people value are subject to the destructive effects of life in a fallen world, "where moth and rust destroy, and where thieves break in and steal." The moth was commonly recognized as a destroyer of the most basic materials of life.[2] The finest garments could be destroyed by a little devouring insect. The term "rust" is a general term for "consuming," which points not only to a destructive action on metals but also a deterioration of a more wide-ranging nature. It destroys a variety of materials—crops, vines, and even teeth.[3] The most valuable possessions are subject to being consumed. The kind of "thief" Jesus has in mind here robs from the rich to serve himself. Moth, rust, and thieves represent those forces that cause earthly treasures to diminish in value and finally be destroyed.

Rather than collecting material valuables in this life, Jesus says, "store up for yourselves treasures in heaven." He does not identify these treasures, but the idea of storing up good works before God was prominent in Israel's history. Sirach exhorts, "Lose your silver for the sake of a brother or a friend, and do not let it rust under a stone and be lost. Lay up your treasure according to the commandments of the Most High, and it will profit you more than gold" (Sir. 29:10–11 NRSV). Jesus may have in mind the "acts of righteousness" of the preceding section—giving to the poor, praying, and fasting—or any other valuable deeds that his disciples perform. Paul refers to the gold and silver of the Christian's work for the kingdom that will be rewarded at the Day of Judgment (1 Cor. 3:12–15).

But the contrast of "treasures on earth" with "treasures in heaven" more importantly implies a contrast of values. Jesus goes beyond good works to focus on the heart, "For where your treasure is, there your heart will be also."

---

2. Job 4:19; Isa. 50:9; 51:8.

3. E.g., Mal. 3:11. See BDAG, 184–85. Greek has another word for rust that destroys metal—*ios* (see James 5:3).

The "heart" represents the core of a person's being, the real inner person, the causative source of a person's spiritual, emotional, and psychological life. What a person values is driven by the nature of a person's heart (see 5:8, 28).

Jesus has already indicated that the heart is the source of our good or evil deeds (5:28; cf. 15:18–19). That thought carries here as well, but with the additional element that whatever the disciple has placed as his or her highest value is a gauge of the condition of the heart.[4] The righteous value must be God himself. Rewards are important, but the greatest treasure in heaven is the Father. If Jesus' disciples keep their hearts fully focused on the Father in heaven, then all other treasures of this world will pale in comparison. This will set a trajectory for healthy discipleship, including one's priorities, motives, righteous deeds, ambitions, security, personal self-worth, and relationships.

**Two eyes of the heart (6:22–23).** These difficult verses must be connected to the preceding (6:19–21) and following (6:24) passages to make sense of them—the disciple must make a choice between competing treasures. Jesus continues the theme of "treasure" by addressing the "eye" as the conduit to the inner person, "The eye is the lamp of the body. If your eyes are good, your whole body will be full of light." While the "good" eye and the "bad" eye can be understood physically to speak of a healthy and diseased eye, we should follow the metaphorical meaning here. Some Greek and Jewish writers spoke of the eye as a lamp that contained its own source of light that shone outward to illuminate objects; this indicated the vitality of life in a person (e.g., eyes become dimmed; Gen. 27:1; 48:18).[5] But here Jesus uses the eye in a different metaphorical sense, as a lamp that illumines a person's inner life.

There was a close connection between the heart and the eye in Jewish literature.[6] By using the symmetry in this passage, the "good" eye can either mean a "generous" eye, a person who is ready to give away one's wealth,[7] or it can mean "single" in the sense of singleness of purpose or undivided loyalty.[8] The latter is more in line with the preceding and following sayings. Since the heart is the true repository of treasure, Jesus now indicates that

---

4. The saying is personalized to the individual disciple by the switch from the second person plural "you" in 6:19–20 to the second person singular in 6:21.

5. See D. C. Allison Jr., "The Eye Is the Lamp of the Body (Matthew 6.22–23 = Luke 11.34–36)," *NTS* 33 (1987): 61–83.

6. See *T. Iss.* 3:4; 4:1–2, 5–6; 5:1.

7. Susan Eastman, "The Evil Eye and the Curse of the Law: Galatians 3.1 Revisited," *JSNT* 83 (September 2001): 69–87, esp. 77.

8. See BDAG, 104 for this sense of *haplous*: "motivated by singleness of purpose so as to be open and above board."

when the eye focuses on something of value, it becomes the conduit that fills the heart with what has been focused upon. If the eye is good, it is the conduit that allows the heart to be filled with the light of God's treasure.

But there is also an evil eye: "But if your eyes are bad, your whole body will be full of darkness." The word "bad" here connotes moral evil.[9] The "evil eye" in the ancient world is one that enviously covets what belongs to another; it is a greedy or avaricious eye.[10] This expression occurs similarly in 20:15, where the literal expression "evil eye" indicates envy (cf. NIV "envious"). The parallelism here indicates once again singleness of vision, but it is an evil vision. If a disciple's eyes are fixed on earthly treasure as her or his value, personal significance, and earthly security, then the heart will likewise be full of darkness.[11] When we focus on something evil, the eye becomes the conduit by which evil fills the inner person.

**Two masters of the heart: God and money (6:24).** Two treasures (6:19–21) and two eyes (6:22–23) prepare for the climax about choosing between two masters: "No one can serve two masters." The word for "master" is *kyrios*, which has sufficient flexibility that it can indicate a landowner (18:25; 20:8), a master in a typical teacher-disciple relationship (10:25), Jesus as Son of Man, who is Lord of the Sabbath (12:8), Jesus as the arriving messianic king (21:3), the Messiah as David's Lord (22:44), and the returning Son of Man as Lord (24:42–44). The usage here indicates a general principle on both the level of commitment to an earthly master as well as to God as one's ultimate Master. The term for "serve" is *douleuo*, indicating the work of a slave, not an employee. One might be able to work for two employers, but a slave is sole property of one master, which implies an exclusive owner who demands exclusive service.

Loyalty to one's master is extreme: "Either he will hate the one and love the other, or he will be devoted to the one and despise the other." The biblical notion of "hate" and "love" understands them to be patterns of life, not simple emotional reactions. "Do I not hate those who hate you, O LORD, and abhor those who rise up against you? I have nothing but hatred for them; I count them my enemies" (Ps. 139:21–22; cf. Matt. 5:43; 1QS 1.9–11). This prepares for Jesus' radical summons of unconditional commitment to him, to the point that one must hate, or completely reject, anything that hinders attachment to him, and love him, or give oneself completely to him (cf. Matt. 10:34–39; 12:30; Luke 14:26).

---

9. See Davies and Allison (*Matthew*, 1:639–41) for discussion of the background.

10. G. Harder, "πονηρός," *TDNT*, 6:555–56. See also *T. Benj.* 4:2–3; cf. 6:5–7.

11. Hagner, *Matthew*, 1:159: "Metaphorically speaking, a generous eye or the single eye of discipleship is the source of light; an evil, covetous eye is the source of darkness."

The metaphors on choosing between masters culminate in the saying, "You cannot serve both God and Money." There can be no divided loyalties with God. Jesus personifies wealth or possessions of all kinds as a rival god, "Mammon." This word is the Greek *mamona*, from a Hebrew/Aramaic word *mamon*, meaning "wealth, riches, property." The temptation to worship the god of materialism was well known in Judaism. A heart-rending confession from the second century B.C. *Testament of Judah* (19:1–2) states: "My children, love of money leads to idolatry, because once they are led astray by money, they designate as gods those who are not gods. It makes anyone who has it go out of his mind. On account of money I utterly lost my children." The writer goes on to say, "The prince of error blinded me" (19:4), pointing to Satan's activity in using material idolatry to lead astray the children of God.

Greed and covetousness are favorite snares of the evil one, so commands and warnings against greed and covetousness are common in the Old Testament (e.g., Ex. 20:17; Deut. 5:21; Job 31:24–25; Ps. 49; Eccl. 2:1–11), in Judaism (Sir. 11:18–19; *T. Jud.* 18–19; *1 En.* 97:8–10), and in the early church (Col. 3:5; 1 Tim. 6:10; 2 Peter 2:3). Ultimately, there is only one choice—service, love, and devotion to God or to Satan. Loving God is not merely a matter of the emotions but of serving and giving oneself to him completely—heart, soul, mind, and strength (see Matt. 19:16–22; 22:37).

## Choose Your Provider: God or Worry (6:25–34)

BUT THE QUESTION might be, "If I choose God as my Master and place my value and worth and source of security in heaven, who will take care of my daily needs on earth?" So Jesus directs the attention to the issue of "worry." In particular, this Master will take care of the basic needs of Jesus' disciples so that they can give attention to more important issues of life, especially summed up in the expression, "seek first his kingdom and his righteousness" (6:33).

**The principle about worry (6:25).** The principle about worry is expressed in the imperative, "Do not worry [*merimnao*] about your life." Sometimes *merimnao* expresses an appropriate feeling of intense concern and care for something, such as the Lord's work (1 Cor. 7:32) or someone's welfare (Phil. 2:20).[12] In this case we can render this word in English as "concern." Concern is appropriate when it is directed toward right things, kept within bounds, and causes us to do our proper duty. However, *merimnao* also expresses intense feelings of anxiety about issues of life, such as what to say when arrested for preaching the gospel (Matt. 10:19), about many less important things (Luke 10:41), or about the pressing daily matters of life. Paul uses this meaning

---

12. BDAG, 632.

when he says, "Do not be anxious about anything, but in everything, by prayer and petition, with thanksgiving, present your requests to God" (Phil. 4:6). Worry is inappropriate or wrong when it is misdirected, is in wrong proportion, or indicates a lack of trust in God. It is this latter sense that Jesus addresses here.

Jesus then directs a question to his disciples that assumes an immediate answer and response: "Is not life more important than food, and the body more important than clothes?" The implied natural answer should be, "Yes, of course my life and my body are more important than food and clothing!" And the natural response to the argument should be, "If God has given me life and a body, he certainly will give me food and clothing."

But the poor had difficulty getting their eyes off such basic necessities, since it wasn't always easy to supply them. Jesus is speaking to people familiar with life's daily struggles. Much of their daily routine was spent trying to get enough supplies for day-to-day existence. The poor especially did not have extensive supplies, so that the question of what one would eat tomorrow was a real one, especially with the vagaries of seasonal famine, fire, or flood. Thus, Jesus is forcing even the poorest among them to agree that they must focus on the more important issues of life. For the poor, this is a radical challenge, because if they become unconcerned about supplying each day's food and clothing, their families could be in immediate trouble. Jesus calls for them to live in the immediate challenge of daily trusting God's care in everyday situations.

**The example of life and food (6:26–27).** The first reason Jesus gives as to why his disciples should not worry is the Father's care for his creatures: "Look at the birds of the air; they do not sow or reap or store away in barns, and yet your heavenly Father feeds them." Birds expend energy in doing what is natural, such as building nests and collecting food for their young, yet it is actually God who feeds and clothes them (cf. Ps. 104:10–16; *Pss. Sol.* 5:8–10). The point is that when Jesus' disciples are responsible to carry out the proper ways of life as ordained by God, God is faithful to carry out his end of the order.

In a common style of arguing "from the lesser to the greater," also regularly used by the rabbis, Jesus queries with another rhetorical question, "Are you not much more valuable than they?" Humans are the crown and ruler of God's creation (Ps. 8:3–8), and their needs will receive appropriate attention from God. Jesus advances the argument with further rhetorical questions, "Who of you by worrying can add a single hour to his life?" The NIV has a good rendering of a curious expression in Greek, which reads, "add one forearm length [*pechys*] to his age/stature [*helikia*]." *Pechys* is a standardized unit of measure the typical length of a forearm, or about eighteen inches, called a "cubit."[13] The term *helikia* usually designates a measure of age or maturity (e.g., Heb. 11:11), but occasionally it is used for physical stature (e.g., Luke 2:52; 19:3). The present context makes no sense to refer to adding physical height, but instead indicates a measure of time of life. Worrying cannot extend the duration of one's life.

**The example of clothing (6:28–30).** Jesus then gives the second reason why his disciples are not to worry: "See how the lilies of the field grow." This expression draws to mind God's provision in nature for flowers growing wild, which probably surrounded Jesus, the disciples, and the crowd as he spoke. Even today, red and purple anemones with crowning ten-inch stalks, along with blue irises, grow wild on the hillside above the Sea of Galilee.[14] The beautiful flowers surrounding Jesus elicit a striking contrast to Solomon's royal robes: "Not even Solomon in all his splendor was dressed like one of these." Solomon's wealth prompted the visit from the Queen of Sheba and his life became a proverbial success story (see 1 Kings 10:1–29; 2 Chron. 9:1–28). Yet God's provision for wild flowers causes them to be more beautiful, if one would only look.

The emphasis shifts slightly to regard lilies as the clothing of "the grass of the field" (6:30). The green grass of spring when cut, dried, and bundled was a natural source of fuel for fire ovens and was a common biblical metaphor for dramatic changes of fortune and for human frailty and transience.[15] If God's sustaining care extends to such a transitory part of his creation, "will he not much more clothe you, O you of little faith?" Those with eyes of effective faith will see the beauty of God's creation in contrast to human efforts at splendor and will learn daily how to follow God's guidance and how to trust in his gracious provision. "Little faith" (*oligopistos*) is a favorite expression of Jesus, found mainly in this Gospel.[16] It is only directed to Jesus' disciples, indicating that "little faith" is not *absence* of faith but *deficiency* of faith.

**The Father's interest in all things (6:31–32).** The third reason why the disciples are not to worry is because that is the pattern of unbelievers who do not understand the Father's care: "For the pagans run after all these things, and your heavenly Father knows that you need them." The term "pagans [*ethne*]," rendered elsewhere in Matthew as "the nations" (12:21; 25:32; 28:19), commonly designates non-Jews or Gentiles. Here, the emphasis is on those who operate outside of God's values. Those with faith in God's provision

---

13. Marvin A. Powell, "Weights and Measures," *ABD*, 4:899.

14. Irene and Walter Jacob, "Flora," *ABD*, 2:813; Pixner, *With Jesus Through Galilee According to the Fifth Gospel*, 37.

15. Ps. 37:2; 102:4, 11; 129:6; Isa. 40:6–8; quoted in 1 Peter 1:24–25; James 1:10; see "Grass," *DBI*, 348–49.

16. See 6:30; 8:26; 16:8; 14:31, 17:20; Luke 12:28; cf. also *oligopistia* in Matt. 17:20.

---

will not worry and will reject the pursuits and values of unbelievers. An absence of inappropriate anxiety derives from an appropriate understanding of God's provision and his creatures' responsibilities and priorities of life.[17] Morris comments, "This attitude removes people from preoccupation with their own worldly success; it discourages the wealthy and the comfortable from concentrating on their own success and the poor and uncomfortable from concentrating on their own misery."[18]

**The proper priority (6:33).** Jesus' reasoning culminates in the famous directive, "But seek first his kingdom and his righteousness." This climactic admonition draws the listeners back to the key verse of the sermon, where Jesus declared, "Unless your righteousness surpasses that of the Pharisees and the teachers of the law, you will certainly not enter the kingdom of heaven" (5:20). The use of the imperative "seek" does not mean to look for something not present, for Jesus has already announced the arrival of the kingdom. In this context it means that his disciples are to make the kingdom of heaven the center of their continual, daily priorities. They have already entered the kingdom of heaven and are to live with that reality, drawing on God's ordering of their daily lives.[19] In doing so they will "seek ... his righteousness."

The conjunction of righteousness and the kingdom maintains a special theme in the SM (5:6, 10, 20; 6:1). It does not mean to pursue salvation, because the disciples' entrance to the kingdom secured them that kind of "imputed" righteousness (5:20). It means that they are to pursue their experiential growth of "imparted" righteousness, which is to pursue the increasing perfection of the Father (5:48) through their practice of "acts of righteousness" (6:1). The theological articulation of these themes becomes a major focus of the early church, especially Paul. But their foundation is laid in Jesus' teaching here. When his disciples pursue God's kingdom and his righteousness in their daily priorities and activities, they will have all of their needs met by their ever-caring, ever-watching heavenly Father—"and all these things will be given to you as well."

**Eliminating worry (6:34).** Having given the climactic imperative to guide every area of the disciples' lives, Jesus returns to the specific issue—worry about God's daily care for their needs. If God's ordering of the disciples' lives includes his provision for all of their daily needs, "therefore" one certainly should not worry about tomorrow. Learned reliance on God's care for present needs will cause his disciples to develop trust in him for their future needs.

---

17. Craig Blomberg, "On Wealth and Worry," *Criswell Theological Review* 6 (1992): 72–89, esp. 82.

18. Morris, *Matthew,* 157.

19. Thomas E. Schmidt, "Burden, Barrier, Blasphemy: Wealth in Matt. 6:33, Luke 14:33, and Luke 16:15," *TrinJ* n.s. 9 (1988): 171–89, esp. 174–75.

The two expressions in this verse, "for tomorrow will worry about itself" and "each day has enough trouble of its own," reiterate the same basic truth. All the worry in the world today can do nothing about the cares and problems of tomorrow. As disciples learn to let God care for them today, including their "daily bread" (6:11), they will become increasingly secure in his care for them tomorrow, regardless of whatever evil may come.

Since no exact parallel to this maxim exists,[20] Jesus' saying apparently became proverbial, because James gives an admonition that appears to draw on this truth (James 4:13–15). Jesus' disciples don't know what tomorrow will bring, but the Father does. It takes a great deal of worry from us when we live that way daily.

 **LIFE IN THE ancient world.** Everyday life in the cities of the ancient world was far different than even the most difficult circumstances of urban life in the modern world. With limited water and means of sanitation, the incredible density of humans and animals is beyond our imagining.

> Tenement cubicles were smoky, dark, often damp, and always dirty. The smell of sweat, urine, feces, and decay permeated everything. Outside, on the street, it was little better—mud, open sewers, manure and crowds. In fact, human corpses—adult as well as infant—were sometimes just pushed into the street and abandoned.[21]

Matthew writes to a community of believers who live in this everyday world, probably in a urban setting. For the most part, they are probably among the poor. They look out from their dismal, everyday existence and try to figure out how they can get by for the next day, how they can get ahead in any way, and how they can supply for a future of their children. They may think that the world of Jesus' original ministry in rural Galilee offered a more idyllic setting, with its rolling green hills, open blue skies, and expansive boundaries.

But life in both settings is hard. The people to whom Jesus is speaking in the SM may have included some of the wealthy, but the vast majority of them are peasants, who live most of their lives hand to mouth, eking out a living from the Galilean countryside. What they can produce from the land

---

20. But for similar sayings, see Prov. 27:1; *b. Sanh.* 100b; *b. Ber.* 9a; Hagner, *Matthew,* 1:166.

21. Rodney Stark, "Antioch as the Social Situation for Matthew's Gospel," *Social History of the Matthean Community: Cross Disciplinary Approaches,* ed. David L. Balch (Minneapolis: Fortress, 1991), 194.

goes for food supplies until the next harvest, feed for their work animals, extra seed for next year's crops, and enough to sell or barter for other necessities. But whether they work their own land or are tenant farmers, they are required to pay any surplus as taxation to the dominant group of rulers, who use it to underwrite their own high standard of living.[22] Not surprisingly, one of the significant phenomena of this time period was the rise of revolutionary movements that sought to elevate the plight of the poor by overturning the backbreaking grip that the wealthy landowners had on the economic and political life of the region.[23]

Negatively, Jesus warns against the everyday trouble about wealth (6:19–24) and worry (6:25–34) that can rob disciples of the kingdom's priority in their personal lives. Placing trust in earthly treasures is foolish and will not bring true security, because the things of the world are perishable. If their minds are directed at the same time toward earthly and heavenly things, their view will actually end up distracting, confusing, and darkening their inner life. It is impossible to be God's servants and the servants of Mammon at the same time, because desire for wealth and worry about daily needs actually supplants God.

Positively, Jesus teaches how his disciples can live securely in the middle of their daily difficulties. The way for them to attend to their personal life is to prioritize their values so that nothing in this world supplants God as their Master (6:19–24) and Provider (6:25–34). This is accomplished overall as they "seek first his kingdom and his righteousness" (6:33). If their base of security is in earthly treasures, then no matter how much "concern" they have, they will never be able to satisfy their needs. If they place their security in their heavenly Father, he will naturally take care of all of their needs.

**Avoiding extremes.** A proper perspective on wealth and worry will help us to avoid some distressing extremes. (1) One extreme is to deny all material concern to the point of asceticism, such as that found in some quarters of Judaism.[24]

(2) Another extreme is to think that making provision for future physical needs demonstrates a lack of faith. Common sense tells us that God's regular pattern for his people has always been responsible stewardship of resources to care for daily needs. For example, a significant part of God's law regulated life so that there would be abundant provisions to supply offerings

---

22. Horsley and Hanson, *Bandits, Prophets, and Messiahs*, 53–54.

23. See Seán Freyne, "Economic Realities and Social Stratification" and "How Revolutionary Was Galilee," *Galilee from Alexander the Great to Hadrian*, 155–255.

24. See, e.g., *1 En.* 108:8–9: "Those who love God have loved neither gold nor silver, nor all the good things which are in the world, but have given over their bodies to suffering—who from the time of their very being have not longed after earthly food, and who regarded themselves as a (mere) passing breath."

and sacrifices (e.g., Ex. 22–23). The sluggard is the one who expects to be supported by his neighbor, so he must learn from the ant the common sense of gathering during the summer for the needs of the winter (Prov. 6:6; 30:25). God's orchestration of Joseph's life included advising Pharaoh to store up grain for future use during the seven years of drought, which God used to save Joseph's family (Gen. 42:33–36; 45:7). And responsible parents save up for their children (2 Cor. 12:14). God want us to use our common sense to provide for future needs as one means by which he maintains his place as Master and Provider of his people.

(3) A third extreme is to think that Jesus is teaching that it is a lack of faith to engage in business and commerce for the purpose, at least in part, of making a profit. Again, God's ordering of life for his people includes wise business sense, as the commendation of the virtuous wife teaches (Prov. 31:10–31). Jesus commends wise business and banking practices in the parable of the talents (Matt. 25:14–30). James appears to draw on Jesus' statement in Matthew 6:34 by setting a right balance for wise business planning: "If it is the Lord's will, we will live and do this or that" (James 4:15). We cannot foresee the future, but God does, so the wise businessperson seeks God's will.

(4) A final extreme is to think that all wealthy people have bowed the knee to Money as their God and cannot be Jesus' disciples. As we noted, one sign of God's blessing can be material wealth. Abraham was very wealthy (Gen. 13:2), yet he is called the friend of God (2 Chron. 20:7; Isa. 41:8; James 2:23). After Job's testing, the blessing of God on his life was his doubled prosperity (Job 42:10–15). At Zacchaeus's conversion he was a wealthy tax collector, yet he gave away only half of what he had, promising to repay four times the amount he had cheated anyone, implying that he had plenty left over (Luke 19:2–10). And Joseph of Arimathea was a disciple of Jesus who was wealthy (Matt. 27:57); he is an example of a disciple whom God allowed to keep his wealth so that he could provide privileged service to his Lord.

The key thing for all disciples is to have no other god—whether it is money or success or self—before Jesus as our Master and Provider as we seek first his kingdom and his righteousness.

A COUPLE OF well-known bumper stickers I've seen many times express the idolatry of the modern world: "He who dies with the most toys wins." "You can't take it with you." According to the philosophy behind those maxims, this life and the afterlife have no real meaning, so make it your ambition to play hard and find your worth in the materialism and pleasure of this world.

Israel went into captivity in Babylon as a punishment for worshiping pagan idols (Jer. 25:1–11). While they never again succumbed as a nation to this form of idolatry once they returned from captivity, other forms of idolatry plagued them, such as serving the god of materialism, Mammon. We in the modern world may never consider bowing down to a pagan idol, but we must learn from Israel's temptation to make materialism and its pleasure a very real god. Materialism is a rampant cancer that is now a worldwide temptation, which consequently produces untold worry in people as to how they will be able to maintain the kind of lifestyle they require.

**The idol of materialism.** There are several reasons why people accumulate "treasure" on earth.

- *Security.* We want to know that we are taken care of, so what brings us the greatest security of life and soul is to have material security.
- *Personal worth, esteem, and value.* Material possessions and wealth often indicate that people are successful in what they have done with their lives. We feel good about ourselves if we dress, drive, dine, and decorate well.
- *Power.* With wealth and material success, we believe that we can have and get and be what we want. Wealth gives us control over our own fate and over other people.
- *Independence.* With wealth I can be my own "god" and not rely on anyone else.
- *Pleasure.* With wealth we can indulge our every fantasy, whether it is the exotic vacation, the luxurious wedding, the finest dining, or the most decadent home.

The psalmist gives us a wise perspective on those who have dedicated their lives to the pursuit of wealth and reverses the philosophy of the cliché bumper stickers.

> Do not be overawed when a man grows rich,
>   when the splendor of his house increases;
> for he will take nothing with him when he dies,
>   his splendor will not descend with him.
> Though while he lived he counted himself blessed—
>   and men praise you when you prosper—
> he will join the generation of his fathers,
>   who will never see the light of life.
> A man who has riches without understanding
>   is like the beasts that perish. (Ps. 49:16–20)

The pursuit of material wealth is a feeble attempt to fill the dark void that can only be filled by a good eye fixed on Jesus as our sole Master and Provider. We will all do well to ask ourselves frequently, "What is the most valuable thing in my life?" And then we should evaluate where we have spent our time, what we have invested our life pursuing, and where we have spent our money. Good accounting—whether of time, relationships, or money—is a good gauge of our values.

Money, wealth, and possessions have at least three primary purposes in Scripture: (1) to give appropriate care for one's own family and prevent them from becoming a burden to others (1 Thess. 4:11–12; 2 Thess. 3:6–15; 1 Tim. 5:8); (2) to help those who are in need, especially the family of faith (Prov. 19:17; Acts 11:27–30; Rom. 15:25–27; 2 Cor 8:1–15; Gal. 6:7–10; Eph. 4:28; 1 Tim. 5:3–7); and (3) to encourage and support God's work in spreading the gospel of the kingdom both at home and around the world (1 Cor. 9:3–14; Phil. 4:14–19; 1 Tim. 5:17–18). If we put Jesus at the center of our lives to serve and love him with all that we are and have, we will use appropriately all the blessings of life and avoid the modern idolatry of materialism.

**The idolatry of worry.** We probably do not think of worry as a form of idolatry, but it is when we allow it to take our eyes off of Jesus. We substitute despair, hopelessness, or fear in place of God and turn to our own efforts at trying to control our environment. This can be a harsh world, and worry about the outcome can consume us. A recent cover story in *Time* magazine provides evidence that anxiety as a biological, emotional, and psychological response to current national and world affairs is high. More than ever people are worrying themselves sick.[25]

I've often been struck by the way that mothers deal with these issues. The article posits this all-too-frequent scene:

> It's 4 a.m., and you're wide awake—palms sweaty, heart racing. You're worried about your kids. Your aging parents. Your 401K. Your health. Your sex life. Breathing evenly beside you, your spouse is oblivious. Doesn't he—or she—see the dangers that lurk in every shadow? He must not. Otherwise, how could he, with all that's going on in the world, have talked so calmly at dinner last night about flying to Florida for a vacation?[26]

Mothers have special concerns. As they carry their child during pregnancy, they have the concern of the birth itself and then the ongoing care of this fragile little blessing. They're concerned about the healthy growth and

---

25. Christine Gorman, "The Science of Anxiety," *Time* 159 (June 10, 2002): 46–54.
26. Ibid., 46.

the proper friends and influences; they think about whom their children will marry and whether they, as mothers, can handle all these responsibilities. Then they become concerned about their own failures as a mother, whether they give enough discipline and love, enough guidance and freedom, or appropriate reward and restriction. Of course, fathers are all involved in these same activities, but the special role of a mother often leads to more direct concern about the past and the future in raising their children.

While teaching for a short stint at another seminary, I heard Warren Wiersbe make this comment during a chapel message: "It is often said that we are continually being crucified between two thieves—the regrets of yesterday and the worries about tomorrow."[27] When a mother turns her eyes off Jesus, responsible concern often turns to the worry of despair, or fear, or hopelessness.

A woman in our neighborhood is having a significant bout with worry. Her children have all caused her a measure of grief, but they are basically good kids. Her husband is a hard-working man, but he is not a very good businessman. They have had significant financial problems in the past and are now considering bankruptcy. They are not believers, and worry has consumed her. She rarely sleeps through the night, she talks incessantly about the bleak outlook for their future, and she is now developing high blood pressure and heart problems. Her greatest need is to be able to let loose of the regrets about yesterday and relinquish her worries about tomorrow.

Max Lucado has written a little devotional book for mothers, and in it he has a selection cleverly entitled "Whaddifs and Howells: The Burden of Worry." He asks what a mother may very well ask, "'Whaddif I marry a guy who snores?' 'Howell we pay for our baby's tuition?'"[28] Commenting on Jesus' statement in Matthew 6:34, Lucado uses a rendering, "God will help you deal with whatever hard things come up when the time comes." He goes on to give sound advice to mothers, especially focusing on the phrase "when the time comes":

> "I don't know what I'll do if my husband dies." You will, *when the time comes*.
>
> "When my children leave the house, I don't think that I can take it." It won't be easy, but strength will arrive *when the time comes*.
>
> The key is this: Meet today's problems with today's strength. Don't start tackling tomorrow's problems until tomorrow. You do not have tomorrow's strength yet. You simply have enough for today.[29]

---

27. Chapel message for the Doctor of Ministry students and faculty at Trinity Evangelical Divinity School, November 9, 1998.

28. Max Lucado, *Traveling Light for Mothers* (Nashville: W Publishing Group, 2002), 65.

29. Ibid., 74–75.

My wife and I are working with our young friend the anxious mother to help her find today's strength in a relationship with Jesus. But Lucado's advice is good for all of us. We have all probably at one time or another awakened at night fretting about a looming bill, or a teenager not yet home from a night out, or a pressing deadline at work. We have probably all wondered at times whether we will be able to handle the next phase of parenting or marriage. The popular secular song advises: "Don't worry. Be happy." We'd like to be happy, but the wishing won't make it happen. The key to overcoming worry is to learn how to utilize God's strength to accomplish what is set before us today, because today's accomplishment is tomorrow's lesson.

I believe that one of the most important ways of actually carrying this out is to learn to express regularly our gratitude to God for what he is doing, and has done, in preparation for relying on him tomorrow. A way of reversing the trend toward anxiety is to look around at what we have and what God has done and then say, "Thank you." That is the theme of the heartfelt chorus "Give Thanks with a Grateful Heart," which most of us have sung at one time or another.[30] Whether we are weak or strong, poor or rich, Jesus' teaching on wealth and worry is rooted firmly in what has done for us. He is our Master and Provider, the one who has given us kingdom life, kingdom priorities, and kingdom values, by which we can truly say, "Thank you."

---

30. Henry Smith, "Give Thanks with A Grateful Heart," words and music: © 1978 Integrity's Hosanna! Music, Glyndley Manor, Stone Cross, Pevensey, East Sussez BN24 5BS.

# Matthew 7:1-12

"**D**O NOT JUDGE, or you too will be judged. ²For in the same way you judge others, you will be judged, and with the measure you use, it will be measured to you. ³"Why do you look at the speck of sawdust in your brother's eye and pay no attention to the plank in your own eye? ⁴How can you say to your brother, 'Let me take the speck out of your eye,' when all the time there is a plank in your own eye? ⁵You hypocrite, first take the plank out of your own eye, and then you will see clearly to remove the speck from your brother's eye.

⁶"Do not give dogs what is sacred; do not throw your pearls to pigs. If you do, they may trample them under their feet, and then turn and tear you to pieces.

⁷"Ask and it will be given to you; seek and you will find; knock and the door will be opened to you. ⁸For everyone who asks receives; he who seeks finds; and to him who knocks, the door will be opened.

⁹"Which of you, if his son asks for bread, will give him a stone? ¹⁰Or if he asks for a fish, will give him a snake? ¹¹If you, then, though you are evil, know how to give good gifts to your children, how much more will your Father in heaven give good gifts to those who ask him! ¹²So in everything, do to others what you would have them do to you, for this sums up the Law and the Prophets.

**Original Meaning** — JESUS NOW SHIFTS from warning his disciples about their own personal temptations concerning wealth and worry to temptations that can surface in their relationships with each other. This carries forward his theme about the nature of kingdom life for his disciples. After giving the interpretive principles of kingdom life that fulfills God's original intention in the Old Testament (5:17–48), Jesus turned to teach his disciples how they are to develop true kingdom life in the real world (6:1–7:12). The present section is the third of three sections that deal with this theme (see comments at the beginning of 6:1–18). Here he address the disciples' *interpersonal* kingdom spirituality in their community relationships (7:1–12).

Jesus spent considerable time condemning the religious leaders for their hypocrisy, the outward appearance of righteousness for the acclaim of people (6:1−18). Now he acknowledges that his own disciples can fall into hypocrisy (7:1−5). Then he adds a word of caution against the opposite extreme—being undiscerning (7:6). To avoid both extremes is an impossible task in one's own power, so Jesus includes a section on prayer to show his disciples how to live in balance, both in this problem and in all others (7:7−12). Kingdom life allows his disciples to live properly in relationship to others. It will free them from both improper judgmental attitudes as well as guard them from gullibility toward the truly hurtful people in this world.

## Judging Others Inappropriately (7:1−5)

JESUS WARNS, "DO not judge, or you too will be judged." This warning sets the principle for the section to follow (7:1−5). The specific issue being judged is nowhere identified but allows for a broad application. The verb "judge" (*krino*) has a number of different nuances, depending on the context—ranging from ordinary discernment or evaluation (cf. Luke 7:43), to judicial litigation (Matt. 5:40), to bestowal of reward (19:28), to pronouncement of guilt (John 7:51), and to absolute determination of a person's fate (5:22; 8:16). The latter two senses are in view here: Jesus warns his disciples against setting themselves over others and making a pronouncement of their guilt before God. We should be careful in making these kinds of judgments, because we too will be judged for committing a sin worse than that which we are accusing. A similar sentiment is found in Sirach 18:20: "Before judgment comes, examine yourself; and at the time of scrutiny you will find forgiveness"; and James warns, "There is only one Lawgiver and Judge, the one who is able to save and destroy. But you—who are you to judge your neighbor?" (James 4:12).

The principle of the warning is reemphasized, "For in the same way you judge others, you will be judged." The Greek text is emphatic: "With the judgment you judge you will be judged." We can understand the rationale behind the warning if we recognize that it reiterates earlier principles of the SM.[1] The warning about judging is the reverse of the positive blessing Jesus advocated in the fifth beatitude: "Blessed are the merciful, for they will be shown mercy" (5:7). The warning also recapitulates the point of the fifth petition of the Lord's Prayer: "Forgive us our debts, as we also have forgiven our debtors" (6:12). True disciples, who have been impacted by the mercy of God in the arrival of

---

1. Bruner interestingly calls the first four pericopes in ch. 7 "the Sums," because they sum up much of the earlier teaching of the SM; Frederick Dale Bruner, *Matthew 1−12, The Christbook: A Historical/Theological Commentary* (Waco, Tex.: Word, 1987), 272.

the kingdom of heaven, will exhibit mercy toward one another, not judgment. Because true disciples have received forgiveness, they will forgive one another.

In other words, to fall into a pattern of life in which we judge others is to show that we are not true members of the kingdom of heaven. Absolute judgment is a categorical pronouncement of the guilt of another person as though this is the final word on a matter. At fault is a person who makes himself and his way of doing things and his opinion the absolute standard. He or she has usurped the place of God because only God can judge in this way.

When disciples have developed this critical, condemning attitude as a pattern of life, they have forced love out of their relationships with others. The kind of love that Jesus offers enables his disciples to give what is good to others, not to condemn them. If we don't have that love, but instead have vindictive condemnation in our hearts, we demonstrate that we really do not know God's mercy and forgiveness. The divine passive, "you will be judged," points to God as the judge, who alone can judge absolutely.

The warning continues with a parallel admonition, "And with the measure you use, it will be measured to you," which is similar to a cautionary note found in a rabbinic ruling on adultery: "With what measure a man metes it shall be measured to him again" (*m. Soṭah* 1.7). The "measure" can be a scale, a vessel, or a rod used for calculating weight or distance, but which was often used figuratively, as here, to designate God's uniform justice (cf. 23:32).

The illustration Jesus uses indicates that the specific issue that the accuser condemns is of no major consequence. Once again he uses hyperbole (intentional exaggeration; cf. 5:29–30) as a figure of speech to illustrate his point: "Why do you look at the speck of sawdust in your brother's eye and pay no attention to the plank in your own eye?" The metaphor may surface from Jesus' own background as the carpenter's son (13:55). The "speck" (*karphos*) refers to a small twig or stalk, something quite insignificant in contrast to a "plank" (*dokos*) or large beam. The contrast illustrates the difference between the insignificance of the problem of the accused in comparison to the magnitude of the accuser's problem. The accuser cannot help anyone else because his spiritual vision is impaired by the plank in his own eye.

The real problem is that the accuser is a "hypocrite" (7:5). Jesus uses the singular vocative, "You hypocrite," here, which personalizes the accusation, implying that the hypocrisy is detected among Jesus' own followers. As earlier (cf. 6:2, 5, 16), hypocrisy means to perform external acts of righteousness that mask, perhaps even from oneself, one's own inner corruption. In this case, the hypocrite thinks he can see clearly the sin of a fellow disciple and is condemning her before God. However, he has not seen his own self-righteous, judgmental attitude. On the one hand, the hypocrisy may be a remediable sin that the disciple can eliminate through self-examination and confession (7:5). On the other hand, the hypocrisy may reveal a more ter-minal sin. Throughout Jesus' ministry certain people attached themselves to him, but they never truly believed. The primary example is Judas Iscariot, but there were many others who once called themselves disciples, yet never truly believed (e.g., John 6:60–66).

Jesus calls the nominal disciple to examine himself or herself, because a hypocrite in the latter sense does not know God (see comments on 6:1–2). Religiosity in either case blinds the disciple to the hypocrisy.[2] He must seek God to bring forgiveness and spiritual healing to himself before he can in any way even know what is wrong with others. When the disciple removes the plank of self-righteousness, she is then able to see with eyes of humility the speck that other brothers or sisters may have. A mark of the discipleship community is the responsibility that disciples have to help each other remove the "speck" of sin from each others lives (cf. 18:15–20), but it must come from a humble and self-examined life that has removed the plank of self-righteous judgment (cf. Gal. 6:1–5). Then restoration can occur with the right attitude: "After self-criticism takes place, relationships are based on redemp-tive empathy rather than condemning detachment."[3]

## Evaluating Others Appropriately (7:6)

JESUS NEXT ADDRESSES a problem at the opposite extreme of judging hypo-critically: naive acceptance. He calls for the appropriate discernment of right and wrong or good and bad (7:6, 15–23), because in their everyday world disciples will have to make regular evaluations. They are to be wise and dis-cerning.[4] In the first place, "Do not give dogs what is sacred." To modern read-ers the mention of "dogs" conjures up images of well-groomed household pets, but in the ancient world dogs lived in squalor, running the streets and scavenging for food (Ps. 59:14–15). To refer to a person as a dog was a grave insult, reducing the person's status to among the lowest in the social scale (2 Sam. 16:9). As a metaphor, "dog" was a humiliating label for those apart from, or enemies of, Israel's covenant community.[5] But the reference here

---

2. Morris, *Matthew*, 167: "Jesus is drawing attention to a curious feature of the human race in which a profound ignorance of oneself is so often combined with an arrogant presump-tion of knowledge about others, especially about their faults."

3. William F. Warren, "Focuses on Spirituality in the Sermon on the Mount," *Theologi-cal Educator* 46 (1992): 121.

4. See also comments on 7:16–20; 10:11–15; 16:6, 12; 18:17–18; cf. 1 Cor. 5:5; 1 John 4:1.

5. See 1 Sam. 17:43; Ps. 22:16; Prov. 26:11. For further background, see comments on Matt. 15:26–28; see also the sidebar on "Dogs and Pigs in the Ancient World," in Wilkins, "Matthew," 51.

seems wider, in that it includes all those who are hostile to Jesus' disciples. "What is sacred" in this context most likely refers to the message of the gospel of the kingdom, indicating that this holy message must not be defiled by those who are unreceptive to, or have rejected, Jesus' invitation.[6]

The image of the dog is reinforced by the parallel image of a pig: "Do not throw your pearls to pigs." The pig in the ancient world is far different than modern cartoon characters like "Porky Pig." Although pork was a highly prized food among many people in the ancient Mediterranean world, it was rejected by Jews (and perhaps some ancient priestly Egyptians), probably because pigs, like dogs, were scavenging animals. Their omnivorous habits occasionally led pigs to feed on decaying flesh, a practice deplorable to Jews. Pigs were often dangerous because they ravaged fields (Ps. 80:13), and while running wild in city streets were often responsible for the death of little children.[7] "Pearls" symbolize the value of the message of the kingdom of heaven (see comments on 13:45–46). Something so valuable should not be given to those who have no appreciation for such precious truths; their nature is demonstrated by their rejection of that message.

Jesus' disciples are not "judging" people to be beasts but are simply taking them at face value. By their actions these are people who have demonstrated themselves to be enemies of the kingdom of heaven. Dogs and pigs are linked elsewhere in Scripture (Isa. 66:3; 2 Pet. 2:22) as dangerous and ritually unclean animals. The bizarre behavior of these wild animals produced fear, because their often-intense hunger could cause them to attack and eat humans (cf. Ps. 22:16–17). The image here warns disciples of the danger of those who have rejected the message of the kingdom of heaven. It is a warning against mistaken zeal in proclaiming the gospel of the kingdom to those whose only intent is mockery or ridicule, or worse.

## God's Guidance in Relationship to Others (7:7–12)

THE CONNECTION OF these verses to the preceding seems somewhat disjointed until we see that Jesus is now drawing the SM to a close. In these verses, he focuses on the source of the disciples' stability as they learn to live a true kingdom life in this fallen world.

**Ask, seek, and knock (7:7–8).** For the application of the principles not to judge, yet to evaluate others wisely and appropriately, the disciples should approach the Father with expectation she or he will receive: "Ask . . . seek . . . knock and the door will be opened to you." Jesus' disciples may find it difficult

---

6. Hagner, *Matthew*, 171–72.

7. See "Dog," "Pork," *DJBP*, 172; "Animals," "Dogs," "Swine," *DBI*, 29, 213–14, 834–35; Edwin Firmage, "Zoology," *ABD*, 6:1130–35, 1143–44.

to be at the same time both merciful and forgiving, yet wisely discerning; to give other disciples the benefit of the doubt, yet to be on guard for those who would harm the community; to judge no one, yet to be wisely observant to see the true character of people and deal with them accordingly. But through the divine enablement that is supplied by God as Jesus' disciples pray, they can avoid the extremes of 7:1–5 and 7:6.

To "ask" naturally indicates prayer, but "seek" and "knock" are also metaphors for prayer. In the apostle John's vision, the risen Jesus "knocks" so that the church will hear and open themselves to the intimacy of his fellowship (Rev. 3:20).[8] Although some see the present imperatives "ask, seek, knock" as practically equivalent,[9] it seems better to suggest that Jesus is indicating a rising scale of intensity in one's prayers and points to the persistent manner of life lived before the Father.[10] "Ask" indicates coming to God with humility and consciousness of need, as a child fittingly comes to her father. "Seek" links one's prayer with responsible activity in pursuing God's will, as when a person prays for a job and at the same time checks out leads. "Knock" includes perseverance in one's asking and seeking, as when the disciple perseveres in praying for his unbelieving family's salvation and speaks and lives the gospel throughout his lifetime.[11] Jesus' disciples are to ask the Father continually as a manner of life, to be constantly responsible in pursuing God's will, and to maintain an unremitting determination in expecting the Father to answer.

But if these present imperatives teach that the disciples are to exhibit *persistence* in prayers, then the parallel responses teach that they are to know the *certainty* of the answer of their prayers to the Father. The predictive responses—"it will be given," "you will find," and "the door will be opened" (7:7)—are reiterated to give a remarkably universal certainty of the answer to the disciples' prayers. It isn't just a few who will have their prayers answered, but "everyone," meaning all those who have followed Jesus as his disciples.

**Bread ... stone ... fish ... snake (7:9–11).** Jesus clarifies the open-ended teaching on the certainty of the answer to the disciples' prayers by demonstrating that the Father will answer with what he knows is good for his children. "Which of you, if his son asks for bread, will give him a stone? Or if he asks for a fish, will give him a snake?" (7:9–10). Staple food in a Jewish daily diet included bread and fish. A responsible father would not be

---

8. Wilkins, "Prayer," *DLNTD*, 941–48.

9. John Broadus, *Matthew: An American Commentary* (Valley Forge, Pa.: Judson, 1886), 158.

10. France, *Matthew* (1985), 144.

11. Hendricksen, *Matthew*, 361–62.

mean and trick his children with stones that resembled bread (cf. Jesus' first temptation, 4:1–4), nor would he be hurtful by tricking them with snakes that resembled fish. So if a responsible father will supply his children precisely what they need on a daily basis, the heavenly Father, who is absolutely trustworthy, will always give to the disciples what they really need.

Jesus closes with an a fortiori argument (arguing from an accepted conclusion to an even more evident one), called in Jewish rabbinic interpretation *qal waḥomer*.[12] "If you, then, though you are evil, know how to give good gifts to your children, how much more will your Father in heaven give good gifts to those who ask him!" (7:11). If the lesser is true (the activity of earthly fathers who are tainted by the evil of this fallen world), "how much more" the greater will be true (the response of the heavenly Father). Earthly fathers have an innate sense of doing right by their children and are not primarily mean or hurtful to them, even though they are still evil by way of the entrance of sin to all humanity through the sin of Adam and Eve (cf. Rom. 5:12–14). How much more will the heavenly Father, who is inherently perfectly holy and good, always give to his children what they need when they ask him.

**The Golden Rule (7:12).** The primary teaching of the SM is drawing to a close, so Jesus takes the way of the kingdom to its zenith in one precept: "So in everything, do to others what you would have them do to you, for this sums up the Law and the Prophets" (cf. Luke 6:31). The maxim is commonly called the "Golden Rule," with the Emperor Alexander Severus reputedly having it written on his wall in gold.[13] The word "so" (*oun;* "therefore") introduces the saying as a summarizing conclusion to the core of the SM. The statement "for this sums up the Law and the Prophets" forms an inclusio to the similar saying that signaled Jesus' initial intent for the SM (5:17).[14] Jesus' teaching in the SM "fulfills" (*pleroo*) the Law and the Prophets (5:17), while his Golden Rule "sums up" the Law and the Prophets (7:12). So the Golden Rule summarizes the essence of God's will for his people in the Old Testament, and now for Jesus' disciples. After this concluding saying, Jesus will call for his audience to make a decision between two ways: either with him or against him (7:13–27).

This moral maxim of the Golden Rule occurs in various forms in other traditions, stated both positively and negatively (see below). The precept appears to have been a common theme in Judaism of the time, with Hillel

---

12. For extensive examples see Keener, *A Commentary on the Gospel of Matthew* (1999), 247 n. 231.

13. France, *Matthew* (1985), 145.

14. Guelich, *Sermon on the Mount*, 361–62; France, *Matthew* (1985), 145; Carson, "Matthew," 188; Morris, *Matthew*, 172; Davies and Allison, *Matthew*, 1:688–89.

the Elder supposedly having as his motto, "What is hateful to you, do not do to your neighbor." Rabbinic literature attributes the saying to Hillel the Elder, who goes on, "That is the whole Torah. The rest is commentary. Go and learn!" (*b. Šabb.* 31a).[15]

In Jesus' Golden Rule we find a liberating basis for personal and community life. What is the right thing to do? Think of the way that you would like to be treated and then use that as a guideline for how you will treat others. In this way we have a summary rule that expresses all that God intended in the Old Testament for the righteousness of the community and that Jesus expects from the kingdom community of his disciples.

Jesus' teaching on prayer and the Golden Rule brings to the light two significant points about stability in one's discipleship. (1) Stability will come as his disciples learn how to depend on their heavenly Father—their one constant in this world. Whatever needs the disciples have, whether material or spiritual, they must develop a healthy dependence on their heavenly Father (7:7–11). To love God is to trust him to take care of us.

(2) Stability will also come through a healthy commitment to live for the benefit of others (7:12). To truly love others is to give to them for their benefit. When there is truly mutual love, both persons completely trust one another to take care of the other's needs. When appropriate trust in another's care is linked with trust in the Father's care, Jesus' disciples never have to think about their own needs being met; those needs are met in the loving community of disciples who emulate the Father's commitment to care for us.

*Bridging Contexts*

AS HE HAS done throughout the SM, Jesus moves the motivating force for discipleship to the heart, so that what impels obedience begins with God's work in the inner person. True disciples will not judge one another inappropriately, because they have experienced God's mercy and forgiveness and so will extend to others that same mercy and forgiveness out of gratitude to God (7:1–5). True disciples will learn whether it is advisable to share their gospel with those who are apt to scorn it (7:6). The continual development of the disciples' inner growth is found in a persistent prayer relationship with the Father, who promises to answer their requests with what is good for them (7:7–11). And the determination of what is the "good" comes from the values of the kingdom, which to this point are explicated most clearly in the full teaching of the SM.

---

15. See P. S. Alexander, "Jesus and the Golden Rule," in *Hillel and Jesus*, 363–88.

**The Golden Rule.** So with the culminating Golden Rule, Jesus articulates in one statement the essence of God's will as revealed in the Old Testament and the essence of kingdom life for his disciples. As a benchmark for human relations, this moral maxim has been expressed in other contexts throughout history in both positive and negative forms. The ancient Roman philosopher and statesman Seneca (4 B.C.–A.D. 65) expressed the principle positively: "Let us show our generosity in the same manner that we would wish to have it bestowed on us" (*De beneficiis* 2.1.1), while the Chinese philosopher Confucius (551–479 B.C.) stated it negatively, "Do not do unto others what you would not want others to do unto you!" (*Analects* 15:23).[16]

The precept appears to have been a common theme in Judaism of the time of Jesus. Tobit gives a negative form of the principle, "Watch yourself, my son, in everything you do, and discipline yourself in all your conduct. And what you hate, do not do to anyone" (Tobit 4:14b–15 NRSV). We noted above that Hillel the Elder (c. 70 B.C.–A.D. 10) had a similar motto. But whereas other expressions of this saying in the ancient world indicate *ethical aspiration*, Jesus declares that the Golden Rule is the *normative manifestation* of his followers' discipleship.

As such, the Golden Rule truly "sums up the Law and the Prophets" (7:12; cf. 5:17–20), because it localizes the motivating force for discipleship in the heart. As he has done throughout the SM, Jesus indicates that this was God's original intent for the Old Testament. Moses pointed in this direction when he declared that the commandments were to be impressed upon Israel's heart (Deut. 6:6), not simply performed externally. Ethical obedience must operate out of the fullness of a person's heart. A person may say that he or she lives by the Golden Rule as the expression of a utilitarian ethical ideal, but it will become a futile effort, or possibly even self-serving, unless it is generated from the heart.

In other words, the Golden Rule must be lived in conjunction with the greatest commandment. Later when asked what is the greatest commandment in the law, Jesus replied, "'Love the Lord your God with all your heart and with all your soul and with all your mind.' ... And the second is like it: 'Love your neighbor as yourself'" (Matt. 22:37–40; cf. Deut. 6:4–5 and Lev. 19:18). The practice of the Golden Rule as an outgrowth of discipleship to Jesus is at the core an expression of the life of a person who loves God and neighbor.

In this we find a liberating basis for personal and community life. Love for God enables us to love others, which means in its most practical sense to do to others as we would want to have done to us. But we do not always know what is best for us. Each of the ancient expressions of the Golden Rule had

---

16. For other examples, see Betz, *The Sermon on the Mount*, 509–16.

expectations of what people wanted to have done or not done to them. So the practice of the Golden Rule assumes that Jesus' disciples know what is best for them, which they can use as a standard for doing unto others. That standard is the impact of the kingdom of heaven in their lives.

In responding to the gospel of the kingdom, Jesus' disciples have experienced what is truly best for them. They have, for example, experienced the Father's love for them as his children, so they will love not only their neighbor but their enemy (5:43–47), which establishes love as the central standard of the discipleship community. They have experienced God's mercy, so they will extend mercy, which establishes mercy as a realistically reciprocal standard of their mutual discipleship (5:7). They likewise have received forgiveness, so they will forgive others, establishing forgiveness as a mark of reciprocal discipleship (6:12). They understand what solitary dedication means in their relationship with the Father, so they will extend to their spouse solitary dedication, eliminating lust, adultery, and divorce from the community (5:25–32).

In this way, all of Jesus' teachings in the SM become the standard by which a realistic practice of the Golden Rule can be conducted. It is an ethical ideal that fulfills the deepest inclination of the person created in the image of God, liberating Jesus' disciples from external legalistic obedience to extend in concrete activities the very love of God to others that they have experienced in their reception of kingdom life.

SEVERAL YEARS AGO two speakers came to our university to give a series of messages in the undergraduate chapel during a missions conference. The speakers were trying to help the students understand how to find God's will for their lives. The first message had as its theme passage Psalm 46:10: "Cease striving and know that I am God; I will be exalted among the nations. I will be exalted in the earth" (NASB). The speaker entitled the message, "Let Go, and Let God." The second message had as its theme passage Matthew 7:7: "Ask and it will be given to you; seek and you will find; knock and the door will be opened to you." This speaker entitled the message, "Knocking Down Doors."

The first message advocated letting go of the problem and turning it over to God. The focus was on letting God take control of their lives and then finding peace about what they wanted to do in their lives. They were encouraged to find a quiet corner and seek the mind of God. They were admonished to let go of their own ambitions, their own planning, their own struggle to find God's will, and instead to allow God to be the God of their lives. "Let go and let God!"

The second message advocated personal responsibility. The focus was on exercising faith as a means to discovering God's will for their lives. The students were encouraged to go enlist godly advice, to explore possibilities, and to attempt various alternatives. They were advised that it is only in taking a step of faith that they will find God's will. An illustration used was that a car that is moving steers easier than a car that is parked. "Knock Down Doors for God!"

Many students were visibly confused by those seemingly contradictory messages. The speakers seemed to be telling them opposite things. Were they contradictory? I would say yes, and no. Yes, in that each gave a correct biblical principle, and in our limited perspective they are seemingly contradictory. But no, in that they don't have to be opposed to each other. Instead of living with one or the other, both principles can have crucial significance in the attempt to discover God's will for us as individuals.

**Balance.** One of the most significant keys to my life as a disciple of Jesus Christ is *balance*. I do not go so far to say that balance is *the* key, but rather is *a* key that has helped me to deal with many difficult issues. The kind of balance I affirm arises from a phenomenon that pervades much of life. In our day-to-day existence and in some of our most profound intellectual pursuits, we often encounter dilemmas produced by paradox. By *dilemma* I mean "a situation requiring a choice between equally undesirable alternatives" or "a choice between alternatives which both appear to be true." By *paradox* I mean "any person, thing, or situation exhibiting an apparently contradictory nature."[17]

The important point is that the opposing alternatives are not necessarily contradictory, but from the perspective of the observer they appear to be contradictory. What makes for a dilemma is that the alternatives are both apparently true and therefore both apparently must be retained, yet the observer is not able to understand how the alternatives can be retained at the same time. In addition, one alternative often appears to be more desirable than the other. Some dilemmas are found when we pursue the great truths of history, some are produced through our attempt to understand God and his revelation to us, and others are experienced in the daily routines of life.

The dilemmas that are so much a part of our intellectual, ethical, and daily lives bring out a grave tendency in many of us. That tendency is toward "polarization" or "extremism." When we are confronted with two seemingly opposite truths, our tendency is to cling to one and then ignore, exclude, or attack the other. Three issues contribute to this tendency: our finite capabilities simply will not allow us to grasp fully how both can be true, life situations demand that we make a decision immediately before we can really grasp the

---

17. These definitions are from *Webster's Encyclopedic Unabridged Dictionary of the English Language* (Avenel, N. J.: Gramercy, 1989).

complexity, and the pendulum of history swings from one alternative to the other as being more desirable.

The kind of balance I advocate means to take two seemingly opposite truths and live with them both at the same time, even though we may not be able to understand completely how they fit together. Some avoid the concept of balance because it may seem as if it leads to compromise or fence-straddling, which we certainly want to avoid. But what I mean by balance is much different. It is a process that includes the following points.

1. Think sensibly! Don't be carried away by emotional reactions. Such reaction to apparent contradictions may cause us to become immobilized or carried away to an extreme.

2. Be honestly open to both truths, regardless of past experience or background.

3. Hold those seemingly opposing truths at the same time. If they are both biblical, they will both have value in the decision-making process and ultimately will reveal themselves as complementary, not contradictory.

4. Apply both sides of the issue to life at the same time. Since Scripture is a guide to life, both principles may be more easily lived out than fully comprehended.

For example, although we may not be able to understand completely how God's sovereignty and our responsibility coexist (for that is a major underlying issue in Scripture), we all have the experience of seeing both principles worked out in the day-to-day experiences of life. We need both to hear God's direction and seek out his direction. Both principles are essential for helping us function effectively as we walk with God in real life. At first it may be simpler just to take one side of the issue or the other, but we will be wiser, better informed, and more well rounded with a balance of both.

Throughout the SM we have had to resort to balance to understand Jesus' full teaching on the nature of kingdom life. We saw, for example, that Jesus exhorted his disciples to "let your light shine before men, that they may see your good deeds and praise your Father in heaven" (5:16); yet later he admonished, "Be careful not to do your 'acts of righteousness' before men, to be seen by them" (6:1). A balance of both advises us to avoid the temptation from both personal cowardice and religious vanity by the adage, "Show when tempted to *hide*, hide when tempted to *show*."[18]

Or again, we are not to be anxious about what we eat or drink (6:25–34), yet if a person refuses to work, he is not to be supplied with food from the oth-

---

18. Bruce, "The Synoptic Gospels," 116.

ers in the church (2 Thess. 3:10). This calls for a balance of God's ever-present care and our own personal responsibility. We are told by Paul that we can rest in who we are because of our positional righteousness in Christ (Rom. 8:1), yet Jesus tells us that we should press on toward perfection (Matt. 5:48). I find a balance of those principles in the expression "restful dissatisfaction."

In this section we come across a number of issues that require us to balance two truths. (1) We are not to judge (7:1), yet we are to be wisely discerning (7:5). To be an accurate judge, a person must know the accusation, have all of the evidence, hear both sides, render a verdict impartially, and then carry out the punishment according to the law. Absolute judgment (which only God can do) is prohibited, yet a relative judging or evaluation of a person's behavior is required.

(2) We are not to give what is holy to dogs or give pearls to swine (7:6), yet we must continually proclaim the gospel with love to those who are even our enemies (5:43–47). Think of what it is like trying to share the gospel with a belligerent drunk or trying to share the beauty and power of the name of Jesus with someone who has just used it in vain. An old saying goes, "Never try to teach a pig to sing. It wastes your time and annoys the pig." Yet some who we think are dogs or pigs will respond to the pearls that we have. We shouldn't make a hasty "judgment." Remember that Jesus saw much more in the tax collectors and sinners and the thief on cross than did the religious establishment—perhaps even more than they saw in themselves.

(3) In following the exhortation to ask, seek, and knock (7:7), we should balance it with the advice from the psalmist, "Cease striving and know that I am God" (Ps. 46:10). That is what I helped our students to discover.

Living with a sense of balance has been a very helpful tool in my interpretation of Scripture and in applying it in my own personal life. But sometimes the attempt to be balanced can cause us to read into truths a balance that is faulty or unnecessary. We can be so focused on finding balances that we become blind to real contradictions. In that case striving for balance can actually lead us to error or compromise. The analysis of paradoxes can also be such a consuming process that we can end up in intellectual burnout, leading to immobilization. Rightly approached, proportional living is a fulfilling way of thinking and exploring all of life, because it leads us into the fullest realization of truth. But it is also the most demanding, because we are always thinking and weighing our actions and thoughts. We must recognize that we are always in process. But the pursuit of the goal to understand and apply all of God's truth is what will enable us to keep balanced.[19]

---

19. I developed this fully in Michael J. Wilkins, "Balance as a Key to Discipleship," *Ratio: Essays in Christian Thought* 1/1 (Spring 1993): 45–64.

# Matthew 7:13-29

"ENTER THROUGH THE narrow gate. For wide is the gate and broad is the road that leads to destruction, and many enter through it. ¹⁴But small is the gate and narrow the road that leads to life, and only a few find it.

¹⁵"Watch out for false prophets. They come to you in sheep's clothing, but inwardly they are ferocious wolves. ¹⁶By their fruit you will recognize them. Do people pick grapes from thornbushes, or figs from thistles? ¹⁷Likewise every good tree bears good fruit, but a bad tree bears bad fruit. ¹⁸A good tree cannot bear bad fruit, and a bad tree cannot bear good fruit. ¹⁹Every tree that does not bear good fruit is cut down and thrown into the fire. ²⁰Thus, by their fruit you will recognize them.

²¹"Not everyone who says to me, 'Lord, Lord,' will enter the kingdom of heaven, but only he who does the will of my Father who is in heaven. ²²Many will say to me on that day, 'Lord, Lord, did we not prophesy in your name, and in your name drive out demons and perform many miracles?' ²³Then I will tell them plainly, 'I never knew you. Away from me, you evildoers!'

²⁴"Therefore everyone who hears these words of mine and puts them into practice is like a wise man who built his house on the rock. ²⁵The rain came down, the streams rose, and the winds blew and beat against that house; yet it did not fall, because it had its foundation on the rock. ²⁶But everyone who hears these words of mine and does not put them into practice is like a foolish man who built his house on sand. ²⁷The rain came down, the streams rose, and the winds blew and beat against that house, and it fell with a great crash."

²⁸When Jesus had finished saying these things, the crowds were amazed at his teaching, ²⁹because he taught as one who had authority, and not as their teachers of the law.

THE DISCIPLES HAVE been the primary object of Jesus' teaching in the SM (cf. 5:1–2), but throughout he has had an eye on the crowds and religious leaders. He has extended an invitation to the crowds to enter the kingdom of heaven and cautioned both his disciples and the crowds about the erroneous leadership of the religious establishment, especially the teachers of the law and the Pharisees (cf. 5:20).

Jesus now concludes the SM with warnings directed to all three groups because eternal destiny is at stake. He warns his *disciples* to examine themselves to be sure that they are truly members of the kingdom of heaven, not simply those who profess allegiance. He warns the *crowds* to consider carefully the alternative of following him or following the popular religious leadership. And he warns the *religious establishment* about their culpability for leading the people in the wrong direction. In each of the four basic warnings—two gates and roads (7:13–14), two kinds of prophets (7:15–20), two kinds of disciples (7:21–23), and two foundations (7:24–27)—a choice must be made: Are you with Jesus or against him? There is no middle ground, no other choice, and a decision must be made—a decision with eternal consequences.

## Narrow and Broad Gates and Roads (7:13–14)

"ENTER THROUGH THE narrow gate" initiates the final section of the SM. The image of two paths in life was common in Judaism, whether speaking of separate paths that lead to paradise or to Gehenna (*b. Ber.* 28b), or of a narrow path of life's hardships that ultimately lead to a broad path of eternal blessing (e.g., 2 Esd. 7:3–9). Jesus' use of the imagery is specific and straightforward. Those who enter the wide gate will find themselves on a broad road that leads to destruction, but those who enter the narrow "gate" will find themselves on a narrow road that leads to life.

The broad gate and road is inviting, offering plenty of room for those who would follow the cultural and pious norm of the religious leaders. The terms "wide" and "broad" are spatial, but they also evoke a sense of ease and comfort. One can enter and travel comfortably and unmolested on this roomy road.[1] However, the comfort is deceiving, because it ends in "destruction" (*apoleia*), a common word for eternal punishment (cf. 2 Peter 3:7; Rev. 17:8).

The narrow gate and road is much more restrictive, because it is limited to Jesus and his manner of discipleship. His is the minority way insofar as few will dare abandon the popular opinion of people and the religious establishment. The terms "small" and "narrow" are also spatial, but they balance the

---

1. Cf. Hagner, *Matthew*, 1:179.

metaphor by evoking images of difficulty. This is especially the case in the latter word, which can indicate trouble and affliction (e.g., 2 Cor. 1:6; 4:8).[2] Those traveling this narrow road will experience difficulty, especially because the challenge of Jesus' way of discipleship will prompt oppression, even persecution, from those of the majority way.

There are two important and related interpretative distinctions to be made of the metaphorical intention. (1) Which comes first, the road or the gate? (2) Is entrance through the gate, whether wide or narrow, something that occurs in this life or at the end of this life? The answers to both of those questions have important related implications. Some contend that the road is first, leading to the gate, and that with this metaphor Jesus challenges his audience to embark on the way of righteousness set forth in his teaching in the SM so that they may enter the gate to the kingdom at the end of their life's journey.[3] But the majority of interpreters contend, I think rightly, that Jesus intended the order as it is actually found in the text, the gate first and then the road, and that it speaks of a decision that is made in this life.[4]

Jesus himself is the narrow gate through which people pass as they respond to his invitation to the kingdom of heaven. The way of discipleship then stretches throughout one's years on earth, ultimately leading to life eternal. The false prophets and religious opposition offer the people what is on the surface a more appealing invitation, for theirs is the easier way to fit into conventional wisdom. But those who choose to enter the gate to popular opinion by rejecting Jesus' invitation will find that it opens onto a road that leads to eternal destruction.

## True and False Prophets (7:15–20)

ON THAT NARROW road disciples are to "watch out for false prophets." Jesus has already warned against religious leaders who lead the people astray with their false form of righteousness (5:20; 6:1–18), but now he warns further against revolutionary leaders who lead the people astray with their false form of prophecy. Warnings of false prophets form an important theme in Matthew's Gospel (e.g., 7:21–23; 24:11–12, 24), similar to how the Old Testament gave analogous warnings (e.g., Jer. 6:13–15; 8:10–12; Ezek. 13:1–23; 22:27–29; Zeph. 3:1–4). These were warnings against those who

---

2. The verb used here is a form of *thlibo*, which is a cognate with the common word for "tribulation" (*thlipsis*), normally indicating persecution.

3. E.g., Tasker, *Matthew*, 82; Richard B. Gardner, *Matthew* (Scottdale, Pa.: Herald, 1991), 136.

4. E.g., Betz, *Sermon on the Mount*, 524–26, Carson, "Matthew," 189–90; Davies and Allison, *Matthew* 1:697–99; France, *Matthew*, 146–47.

attempted to lead God's people by falsely speaking for God. Josephus tells of a variety of popular prophets who led the people to insurrection: "Deceivers and imposters, under the pretense of divine inspiration fostering revolutionary changes, they persuaded the multitude to act like madmen, and led them out into the desert under the belief that God would there give them tokens of deliverance."[5]

False prophets first seem to be genuine members of God's flock by their talk and association with the group, but their intentions are evil, like a wolf who ravages a flock for its own gratification: "They come to you in sheep's clothing, but inwardly they are ferocious wolves." This expression draws on the natural enmity of sheep and wolves (e.g., Isa. 11:6; 65:25) and is the basis of the apostle Paul's later warning to the Ephesian elders (Acts 20:29) and the early church father Ignatius's warning to the church at Philadelphia (Ign. *Phil.* 2:1–2).[6]

Maintaining the earlier balance of not judging another brother or sister (7:1–5), yet not being naively accepting either (7:6), Jesus tells his disciples to be wisely discerning when prophets come into their midst. "By their fruit you will recognize them." "Fruit" is the product of a person's essential life. All that a person says and does reveals who he or she is (James 3:9–12). John the Baptist earlier rebuked the Sadducees and Pharisees for coming for baptism, telling them to "produce fruit in keeping with repentance" (Matt. 3:8). Repentance in their heart will produce a repentant life that rejects sin.

In a similar vein, Paul later tells the church at Galatia to examine their own lives and the lives of the false teachers, because those who truly belong to Christ will bear the fruit of the Spirit, not the works of the flesh (Gal. 5:16–24). The mark of a church that is growing in Christ is the fruit of righteousness and good works (Phil. 1:11; Col. 1:10). And the apostle John calls the church to test the spirit of prophets to see whether they are led by the Spirit to confess that Jesus indeed has come in the flesh (1 John 4:1–3).

So Jesus calls his disciples to evaluate carefully any prophets who come into their community, not only to look at their message to see if it is consistent with the narrow way advocated by Jesus in the SM, but also to look at their works and lives to see if they are consistent with the kingdom life of righteousness he has advocated in the SM. "Do people pick grapes from thornbushes, or figs from thistles?" Grapes and figs were the staple diet in Palestine, and thornbushes and thistles were hurtful weeds. The latter

---

5. Josephus, *J.W.* 2.259. Among the more popular of these leaders of movements were Theudas (c. A.D. 45; see *Ant.* 20.97–98), the prophet from Egypt (c. A.D. 56; see *Ant.* 20.169–71; *J.W.* 2.261–63), and Jesus son of Hananiah (c. A.D. 62–69; see *J.W.* 6.300–309). For an overview of these groups, see Horsley and Hanson, *Bandits, Prophets, and Messiahs*, 160–89.

6. See also 2 Cor. 11:11–15; 2 Peter 2:1–3, 17–22.

choke off nutrients from the soil from other plants and are harmful also to humans because of their sharp thorns. A harmful weed cannot produce healthful fruit. Without the moving of God in their lives, false prophets cannot speak God's message and cannot display the kingdom righteousness he produces.

A vine or tree will only produce fruit that is consistent with its nature— good to good, and bad to bad—so as before (cf. 7:6), Jesus admonishes his disciples to be "fruit inspectors" of those passing themselves off as prophets. False prophets will produce bad fruit, which from an Old Testament perspective includes leading the people away from God to follow false gods (Deut. 13:1–18) or speaking prophecies that are not fulfilled (18:21–22). Bad trees are good for nothing except to be used for firewood (Matt. 7:19), a striking metaphor of the judgment to come for false prophets. Jesus then repeats 7:16, "Thus, by their fruit you will recognize them" (7:20), another example of an inclusio to bracket off this important warning (cf. 5:3, 10).

## True and False Disciples (7:21–23)

NOT ONLY WILL false prophets enter the community, but some within the community itself will be false disciples: "Not everyone who says to me, 'Lord, Lord,' will enter the kingdom of heaven." This is an individual who has confessed Jesus as Lord but whom Jesus knows has not truly repented as a condition for entering the kingdom of heaven. At this stage of the Jesus movement, it is doubtful that calling Jesus "Lord" (*kyrios*) implied the full divine significance that the title carried in the postresurrection period (e.g., John 20:28). During Jesus' ministry the term is used by people mostly as a title of respect (e.g., Matt. 18:21; 26:22).

But we must notice that the use of *kyrios* in Matthew's Gospel also has much more significance. "Lord" is the title that is regularly used by people who approach Jesus in search of divine aid (e.g., 8:2, 5; 9:28; 15:22, 25; 17:15; 20:30, 31, 33), including his own disciples when they need divine assistance (e.g., 8:25; 14:30).[7] As Jesus' ministry unfolds, his disciples use the title with increasing deference, for he is turning out to be more than they had originally understood him to be. He is connected with God's power and has a relationship with God as the Son that can only be addressed with a title normally reserved for God, "Lord" (e.g., 14:28; 16:25; 17:4). This is particularly momentous when they see his miraculous deeds, call on him as "Lord," and then worship him (14:33), an activity reserved solely for deity.

---

7. Günther Bornkamm, "End-Expectation and Church in Matthew's Gospel," *Tradition and Interpretation in Matthew*, ed. Günther Bornkamm, Gerhard Barth, and Heinz Joachim Held, trans. Percy Scott (Philadelphia: Westminster, 1963), 41–43.

"Lord" is also one of the titles, like "Son of Man" (see comments on 8:20), that Jesus uses to refer to himself in a way that increasingly reveals his divine identity.[8] As the only one who refers to God in heaven as "my Father" (used here for the first time in Matthew[9]) and the one who has authority to banish false prophets to eternal judgment (7:22–23), Jesus is indeed more than any mere respected master.

So this false disciple who calls on Jesus as "Lord, Lord" has said more than he knows, but those reading the account in Matthew's community will catch the full significance. An oral confession of Jesus as Lord can mask an unrepentant heart, so Jesus says that entrance to the kingdom of heaven is reserved for those who do "the will of my Father who is in heaven" (7:21). The same basic phrase occurs later to indicate the qualification for entrance to Jesus' family community (12:50; cf. 6:10; 21:31; 26:42). This does not mean simply to obey the Old Testament law as God's will. The will of the Father means obedience to the call to the kingdom of heaven that will result in true righteousness. Since Jesus is the fulfillment of the Old Testament (5:17), he is the ultimate example of the Father's will obeyed (26:42). To follow his example in discipleship and become like him will enable his disciples to do God's will on a daily basis.

These false disciples claim prophetic status and point to their charismatic activity as a sign of their discipleship: "Did we not prophesy in your name, and in your name drive out demons and perform many miracles?" Exorcism and performance of miracles regularly accompany the gospel proclamation of Jesus (e.g., 4:24; 8:3, 16) and the Twelve (cf. 10:1, 7–8); such activities confirm the authenticity of the message. False disciples are able to gain power "in Jesus' name," but their activities are meaningless for their own eternal destiny. They do not come to Jesus as the true gate to the kingdom and so do not engage in these activities according to Father's will (7:21).

Jesus never emphasizes the external as being the highest sign of authenticity. He demands our inward allegiance to God's will, which will produce the fruit of a changed life. In accomplishing his goals, God may use a person (even "many" persons) who professes the name of Jesus, even if the person has deceived himself or herself and others. However, the ultimate revelation of the authenticity of one's life will come at the time of judgment.

So Jesus evokes an eschatological scene of eternal judgment and banishes them from him. "Then I will tell them plainly, 'I never knew you. Away

---

8. See 9:38; 21:3; 22:43–45; 23:38; 24:42; 25:37, 44. France, *Matthew: Evangelist and Teacher*, 287–88.

9. See also 10:32, 33; 11:27; 12:50; 16:17; 18:10, 19; 20:23; 25:34; 26:39, 42, 53.

from me, you evildoers!'"[10] This is a stark, straightforward rejection of a person who does not have a true relationship with Jesus as his disciple (cf. 25:13). For Jesus to place himself as the One who has the authority to determine who enters the kingdom and who is banished to eternal punishment is to accrue to himself the highest Christological claim. Throughout the Old Testament God is said to "know" those whom he has chosen to be his people (Jer. 1:5; Hos. 13:5; Amos 3:2), a theme reiterated throughout the New Testament to speak of a saving relationship found with God through Jesus Christ (cf. Gal. 4:8–9; 2 Tim. 2:19). Here Jesus claims that divine prerogative to know the inner recesses of a person's heart.

## Wise and Foolish Builders (7:24–27)

JESUS GIVES THE parable of the wise and foolish builders as an illustrative challenge and conclusion to the SM (cf. also Luke 6:47–49): "Therefore everyone who hears these words of mine and puts them into practice. . . ." "Everyone" includes the disciples, who are the primary recipients of the teaching of the SM, but also the crowds, to whom Jesus has consistently extended an invitation to the kingdom of heaven (see comments on 5:1–2, 20). Most likely in attendance also, probably surreptitiously, are representatives of the religious establishment whom Jesus has consistently held up as negative examples of those who are leading the people away from God's righteousness to their own self-righteous hypocrisy (cf. comments on 5:20; 6:1–2).[11]

The delightful little Sunday school song ("the wise man built his house upon the rock. . .") might soften the stark historical contrast in the parable. Jesus calls for a decision between himself and the religious establishment. This is the same theme to which he returns over and over: "You are either with me or against me." He calls on those who have heard the words of the SM to put them into practice, drawing a dividing line between him and any other foundation of life. The allusion to rising water is typical Jewish figurative language, as is reflected in Qumran literature (1QH 6.26; 7.8–9) and in an early second century Tannaitic saying: "A man of good deeds who has studied much Torah, to what may he be likened? To someone who first lays stones and then bricks. Even when much water rises and lies against them, it does not dislodge them. . . ."[12] But Jesus' saying reflects a more specific reference to his surroundings and the object of his criticism.

---

10. For a scholarly discussion of fiery judgment in Matthew's Gospel, see David C. Sim, *Apocalyptic Eschatology in the Gospel of Matthew* (SNTSMS 88; Cambridge: Cambridge Univ. Press, 1996), esp. 130–39.

11. Guelich, *Sermon on the Mount*, 419–21.

12. Attributed to Elisha ben Abuyah in *Abot de-Rabbi Nathan*, A 24 (p. 77); cited in Vermes, *The Religion of Jesus the Jew*, 102.

Jesus demonstrates familiarity with current building techniques in this parable, perhaps a reflection of his own training in his father's trade as a carpenter (13:55): "like a wise man who built his house on the rock ... like a foolish man who built his house on sand" (7:24–25). The locale of the sermon near the Sea of Galilee finds a natural setting for this parable. The alluvial sand ringing the seashore was hard on the surface during the hot summer months. But a wise builder would not be fooled by surface conditions. He would dig down sometimes ten feet below the surface sand to the bedrock and there establish the foundation for his house. When the winter rains came, causing the Jordan River pouring into the sea to overflow its banks, houses built on the alluvial sand surface would have an unstable foundation. But houses built on bedrock would be able to withstand the floods. Excavations in the late 1970s in the region uncovered basalt stone bedrock that was apparently used for the foundation of a building in antiquity.[13]

The audience of the SM would readily understand the surface meaning intended in the parable, because they would know how foolish a person was who would choose the easy way and did not build on bedrock. "The rain came down, the streams rose, and the winds blew and beat against that house, and it fell with a great crash." But would they see beyond the parable to Jesus' point? Would they reject the present secure but shallow sifting sands of the religious leadership of the scribes and Pharisees and choose instead Jesus' words as the foundation for their lives? The religious establishment was advocating a form of surface righteousness that masked an unstable foundation of religious hypocrisy. Eventually its instability would be revealed as not having the answers to the deepest needs of the people. In this parable Jesus continues to give an invitation to the bedrock of true life in the kingdom of heaven, but it is the unpopular way, even the troubled way, because those who follow him leave behind the way of comfort found in identifying with the popular religious establishment.

The wise person shows that he or she has carefully viewed the shifting sands of life's teachings and understands that Jesus is the only secure truth of life (cf. 1 Cor. 3:10–11). The wise person thinks ahead to when there will be storms and sacrifices and builds his or her life on the rock of Jesus' words. The choice is no less stark in our own day. Wise men and women build their lives on Jesus, regardless of the cultural or religious weather.

## The Reaction of the Crowds (7:28–29)

THE WORDS MATTHEW uses to signal the conclusion of the SM recur as an identical formula after each of the five major discourses in his Gospel: "when Jesus

---

13. Gordon Franz, "The Parable of the Two Builders," *Archaeology in Biblical World* 3 (1995): 6–11.

had finished..." (7:28; cf. 11:1; 13:53; 19:1; 26:1). This formula is part of a pattern that marks off these discourses, since they will be used as the primary content that his disciples will use throughout history to teach new disciples to obey everything Jesus has commanded in his earthly ministry (28:20).

Although Jesus intended the SM primarily as teaching for his disciples, "the crowds" have been in the background listening (cf. 5:1–2). In fact, Jesus directed some of his challenges to the crowds as an invitation to enter the kingdom of heaven (5:20), especially toward the end (e.g., 7:24).[14] So Matthew records their reaction here: "The crowds were amazed at his teaching, because he taught as one who had authority, and not as their teachers of the law" (7:28–29). This is eloquent testimony to the authority of Jesus' teaching, which accentuates Matthew's primary intention. The teachers of the law were the legal experts of the Old Testament in Jesus' day (see comments on 5:20; 8:19). Their authority among the people came from their expertise in citing earlier authorities and in formulating new interpretations. But ironically, their practices had muted the authority of the Old Testament because they added so many traditions and legal requirements that the power of Scripture was defeated (e.g., 15:1–9). Thus, they could not speak with authority, for they had muted the only source of authority.

But Jesus has inherent authority. This is seen not only in his repeated declaration in the antitheses, "but I say to you," showing how he fulfills the Old Testament (see 5:21–48), but also in his dramatic declaration as the judge of a human's eternal destiny, "I will tell them plainly, 'I never knew you. Away from me, you evildoers!'" (7:23). From Moses (Ex. 11:4) to Elijah (1 Kings 21:23) to Isaiah (Isa. 3:16) to Zechariah (Zech. 8:3), prophets and writers of the Old Testament did not speak of their own authority; instead, they declared, "This is what the LORD says." Jesus' teaching is so forceful that it clearly indicates he bears God's own authority.

But Matthew's conclusion is ironic. Amazement at Jesus' teachings does not indicate acceptance. The term "amazed" is the passive form of *ekplesso*, which in Matthew is not a description of faith. It indicates a variety of emotional responses but not a commitment to Jesus' messianic ministry. The word is used to describe Jesus' hometown's unbelieving reaction to his ministry (13:58), his own disciples' astonished response at the difficulty of a rich man being saved (19:25), and the crowds' astonishment at Jesus' teaching on marriage at the resurrection (22:33). Amazement is not the same as a commitment of faith. Only when a person accepts Jesus' invitation and enters the kingdom of heaven does he or she become a disciple.[15]

---

14. Wilkins, *Discipleship in the Ancient World and Matthew's Gospel*, 150–52.
15. Kingsbury, "The Verb *AKOLOUTHEIN*," 61.

On the one hand, Matthew applauds the crowds who have exalted Jesus, for they have recognized Jesus' authority in contrast to the religious establishment of that day. On the other hand, he expresses a warning to the crowds. Jesus does not want people simply to listen and go away amazed. He wants them to listen and to make a decision for him. To make a decision is to come out of the crowd and become Jesus' disciple.[16]

This is the remarkable impact of the SM. It is intensely life-challenging. It is a profoundly disturbing indictment of the religious establishment, those who have attempted to establish their own pious enterprise that has supplanted God's original intention. It is also an amazing challenge to the crowds, those attracted to Jesus' uniquely authoritative pronouncement about life's realities but not yet placing their faith in him. And it is the highest aspiration, the most realistic guideline of life, for Jesus' disciples, who will find that Jesus' words in the SM are a continual fount of God's guidance as they live out the wondrous reality of life in the kingdom of heaven.

*Bridging Contexts*

"IT FELL WITH a great crash" (7:27). Jesus' final words of his magnificent SM end on a tragic note. This may not be the way that many modern preachers choose to conclude a sermon. It sounds a bit like too much "fire and brimstone." We would rather to end with more of a note of encouragement. Obviously, Jesus didn't always conclude his messages in this way. In the final recorded message of his earthly ministry, the Upper Room discourse given to his disciples the night before his crucifixion, he ended on a very different note: "I have told you these things, so that in me you may have peace. In this world you will have trouble. But take heart! I have overcome the world" (John 16:33).

But the mixed audience of the SM calls for a different challenge. At this early stage of the Jesus movement, Jesus challenges his disciples to examine themselves carefully so that they do not deceive themselves about the authenticity of their commitment to him, for someday they will be called to an eternal accounting for their profession. He challenges the crowds to take up his invitation to the kingdom of heaven, because their choice either for or against him has eternal consequences. And he challenges the religious leaders to consider carefully their pious hypocrisy, which may lead them and the crowds to eternal destruction. So the note of doom with which Jesus

---

16. Wilkins, *Discipleship in the Ancient World and Matthew's Gospel*, 229–30; Guelich, *Sermon on the Mount*, 419–21; T.W. Manson, *The Teaching of Jesus*, 2d ed. (Cambridge: Cambridge Univ. Press, 1935), 19.

concludes the SM is urgently appropriate to the time and audience and draws attention not so much to the judgment but to Jesus as the One who will dispense that judgment.

The amazement of the crowds at his teaching underscores the authority with which he has spoken throughout the SM; thus, the final spotlight is on Jesus himself. Matthew wants his readers to see that Jesus' words have authority because of who he is. In chapters 1–4, Jesus was introduced as the Messiah of Israel through the genealogy and infancy narrative, in the thunderous preaching and ministry of John the Baptist, in the skirmish with the devil in the desert, in the arrival of Jesus in Galilee to announce the arrival of the kingdom of heaven, and in the calling of his first coworkers to become fishers of men. In chapters 5–7, Jesus is presented as the Messiah in word, in the matchless SM, and in chapters 8–9 to follow, Jesus will be presented as the Messiah at work in a collection of miracle stories. The spotlight shines fully on Jesus as the authoritative Messiah of Israel's hopes.

But as Messiah, Jesus is also highlighted as the authoritative adjudicator of humanity's destiny. In these four brief scenes that conclude the SM, all of humanity stands before Jesus, and he asks each, "What will you do with me?"

- 7:13–14: Will you enter the gate to life in the kingdom of heaven and embark on a life of following me? Or will you reject me for the popular road that leads to destruction?
- 7:15–20: Will you find in me the inner source of transformation that will produce the good fruit of life? Or will you follow the prophetic voices of this world that hype a promise of life but will only take you into the fires of hell?
- 7:21–23: Will you obey my Father's will and come to me as your only Lord? Or will you chase after false manifestations of spirituality that result in eternal banishment?
- 7:24–27: Will you build your life on me as your solid rock? Or will the pleasant ease of your life cause you to be unprepared for the storms that will come in this life and that will ultimately wash you away into the desolation of the afterlife?

These pictures of eternal punishment are not pretty, but they are urgently necessary for Jesus' audience and for Matthew's readers, including us. The years that we have been allotted on this earth have eternal significance. They may end sooner than we think, so we must be prepared at all times for what lies beyond. What's more, the way we live these years is important, because what we sow here is what we reap there. This should cause us to live with an eternal perspective, which will influence our priorities in our work and play, in our relationships and commitments, and in our stewardship and service.

Thus, Jesus' concluding tragic note is instructive for our own preaching and teaching and for our own personal lives and ministries. I doubt that I will go to the other extreme and become a complete "hellfire and damnation" preacher, but I have a responsibility in my ministry and leadership to call people to consider their eternal responsibility to what they have done with Jesus. As Jesus did, I must ask: "Are you with Jesus or against him? Are you clear about the consequences either way, both for this life and the afterlife?"

"A BAD PERSON cannot perform good works, nor can a good person perform bad works."[17] These are striking words from the ancient church father and theologian Augustine in his commentary on Jesus' metaphor of the good and bad trees (7:15–20). For over two thousand years the SM has been studied, preached, memorized, and used as a pattern for life by devout disciples of Jesus Christ. We in the twenty-first century are often all the poorer because we have not had our studies informed by their experience. With the advent of the printing press, more recent studies of the SM, such as those by the Reformers, have been available for modern students, but those of earlier centuries were often inaccessible. However, in recent years the church has been enriched by affordable translations and collections of earlier church father's commentaries and homilies on Scripture.[18]

As we might expect, we find a mixed bag of good and poor among these ancient expositions, not too dissimilar to what we find when surveying commentaries written today. And we can find some theological quirks in these writings that centuries of theological reflection and modern archaeological discoveries have helped to settle. Nonetheless, I find it rewarding to survey the views of the church fathers when looking at the four warnings that conclude the SM. The problems Jesus first addressed here are similar to those of the early church and of today. The perspectives of the ancient fathers are helpful when compared with modern writers to show us how Jesus' words have been guidelines throughout church history. We are wiser when we learn from both ancient and modern reflections on Jesus' stark warnings here.

**Narrow and wide gates and roads (7:13–14).** A perpetual problem of those who consider Jesus' invitation to the kingdom is that it is not the popular way. "Few find it" (7:14). We cannot always discover God's will by

---

17. Augustine, *Sermon on the Mount* 2.24.79. All citations of the early church fathers in this section are from the collection by Simonetti, *Matthew 1–13*, 152–58. Later authors are all cited directly.

18. A recent example is the ongoing Ancient Christian Commentary on Scripture series, Thomas C. Oden, gen. ed.

appealing to the majority, because our ways are not always God's ways. "'Everybody does it' will not be a very helpful criterion in Christian ethics,"[19] quirks modern scholar and pastor Dale Bruner. When we are motivated by a desire to please people, we will find that it might not at all please God. Reformer John Calvin writes:

> How is it that men knowingly and willingly rush on, carefree, except that they cannot believe that they are perishing, when the whole crowd goes down at the same time. Contrarily, the small numbers of the faithful make many cowards, for it is hard to induce us to renounce the world, and to pattern our life upon the ways of a few.[20]

So Jesus calls us to a courageous commitment to him as the entrance to the road of life in the kingdom of heaven. There we will find the community of disciples with whom we will share a common appreciation for kingdom values and fellowship.

But another problem of those who consider Jesus' invitation to the kingdom is that it is not the easy way. The words "wide" and "broad" not only clue us to the numbers of those who will take the highway to hell, but they also imply an easy way, without the troubles and oppression and rigor of the "small" gate and "narrow" way of discipleship to Jesus. Jesus will say later that "my yoke is easy and my burden is light" (11:30)—a reassurance that he will be yoked together with us as we walk the road of discipleship and that we will receive strength to endure. But he calls us to count the cost of what this narrow road will mean in our daily lives. Bruner goes on:

> There is no need to fool ourselves by saying that Jesus' ethic is not difficult. Jesus' Sermon on the Mount requires red blood and moral investment. It is a tough way. . . . The successism of both secularity and superspirituality lacks the moral fiber and intellectual meaning found in life lived in obedience to Jesus' demands.[21]

But the early church father Chrysostom finds encouragement in the difficulty of the road as he looks ahead to the crowns of eternal reward.

> For this road ends in life! The result is that both the temporary nature of the toils and the eternal nature of the victor's crowns, combined with the fact that these toils come first and victor's crowns come afterward, become a hearty encouragement.[22]

---

19. Bruner, *Matthew*, 1:283.
20. Calvin, *Matthew, Mark, and Luke*, 1:233.
21. Bruner, *Matthew*, 1:283.
22. Chrysostom, *The Gospel of Matthew*, Homily 23.5.

So Jesus calls would-be disciples to consider carefully the alternative of life in the kingdom of heaven, as narrow and as difficult as it may be, with the popular road that leads to destruction.

An additional problem that can surface from Jesus' challenge of the gates and roads is that if we don't get the order right, we may think Jesus is implying a system of works. In the theologically liberal churches where I went to Sunday school as a little boy, I remember clearly the teacher saying that the road came first, then the gate. That is, we had to choose one road, either the narrow road, which was synonymous with living a good life, or the wide road, which was synonymous with an immoral life. At the end of our years on earth, if we didn't stray from the narrow road, we were promised that we would go through the narrow gate and enter heaven. This teacher was advocating that we work our way to heaven.

But by looking closely at Jesus' saying, we have seen that the gate comes first. Jesus offers by grace this invitation to life. He is the narrow gate through whom we must enter the kingdom of heaven and eternal life. Like the gate, the road is as narrow as Jesus himself, indicating the life of discipleship on which one embarks after entering the gate. The wide gate and road indicate the decision to choose the world's path over Jesus. The decision either for or against him comes in this life, and it is the most important decision any of us will ever make. Jesus offers by grace the invitation to salvation and a life of walking with him.

**Good and bad fruit (7:15–20).** When warning against deceptive prophets, Jesus implies by the metaphor of the wolf in sheep's clothing that they are within the community. The only way of telling them from true disciples is by the fruit of their lives. Early in church history Augustine wrote against a group of wolves in sheep's clothing, the Manichaeans, a dualistic group that advocated two opposing natures inherent in every person—one good and one evil, the supreme God and the Power of Darkness. They used the saying of Jesus about the two trees to support their claim, so Augustine comments to combat their error: "The tree, of course, is the soul itself—that is, the person—and the fruits are the person's works. So a bad person cannot perform good works, nor can a good person perform bad works."[23] Augustine is not implying that an evil soul cannot be changed into a good soul. He contends that the soul itself in its goodness or badness produces either good or bad fruit. The soul will bear fruit in keeping with its nature, good or bad.[24]

Two important implications draw our attention. (1) Real transformation is the test of the reality of the impact of the kingdom of heaven in a person's

---

23. Augustine, *Sermon on the Mount* 2.24.79.
24. Simonetti, *Matthew 1–13*, 155 n. 19.

life. The virtuous life of the kingdom of heaven that Jesus taught in the SM cannot be produced by a person who has not experienced the kingdom's transforming power. Ancient father Chrysostom says, "As long as a person is living in a degenerate way, he will not be able to generate good fruit. For he may indeed change to virtue, being evil, but while continuing in wickedness, he will not bear good fruit."[25]

(2) We are called to examine the fruit of those who profess a message from God, for they may be impostors. If there is any lesson of history from which we should learn, it is that churches, denominations, schools, and mission groups have been, and are, susceptible to false teaching.[26] It is our responsibility to guard the flock from vicious wolves who attempt to draw disciples away from the faith through their perversion of the gospel (cf. Acts 20:28–30).

The popular twentieth-century expositor William Barclay tells of a thorn-bush called the buckthorn, which has little blackberries that resemble little grapes, and a thistle bush that has a flower that from a distance can be mistaken for a fig. He uses these examples to illustrate the way that we might see a superficial resemblance between a true and false teacher, but the nature of his or her life will eventually reveal the veracity of the message. Barclay suggests that the basic fault of the false teacher is *self-interest*:

> The true shepherd cares for the flock more than he cares for his life; the wolf cares for nothing but to satisfy his own gluttony and his own greed. The false prophet is in the business of teaching, not for what he can give to others, but for what he can get to himself.[27]

Barclay then cautions those of us who are in the ministry of the gospel about three ways in which a teacher can be dominated by self-interest: He may teach solely for *gain;* she may teach solely for *prestige;* or he may teach solely to *transmit his own ideas,* not God's truth.[28] Jesus' warning of false prophetic voices is as relevant today as it has been throughout church history. A multitude of false messengers hype a promise of life, but it will only take them and their followers into the fires of hell.

**Hearers and doers of the Father's will (7:21–23).** In the third warning, Jesus addresses those who make profession of faith in him, who even perform

---

25. Chrysostom, *The Gospel of Matthew*, Homily 23.7.

26. Keener, *Matthew* (IVPNTC; Downers Grove, Ill: InterVarsity, 1997), 164: "We who should be challenging unjust reasoning in the world instead often find ourselves fighting a defensive battle within our own ranks."

27. William Barclay, *The Gospel of Matthew*, rev. ed. (DSB; Philadelphia: Westminster, 1975), 1:284.

28. Ibid., 1:284–85.

miraculous deeds in his name, but who are really not his own. Ancient father Cyril of Alexandria instructs his church:

> There may be some who, in the beginning, believed rightly and assiduously labored at virtue. They may have even worked miracles and prophesied and cast out demons. And yet later they are found turning aside to evil, to self-assertive deception and desire. Of these Jesus remarks that he "never knew them."[29]

Cyril rightly emphasizes that self-assertive deception and desire characterize false disciples, because they deceive themselves and other believers and desire the attention they will receive for the spectacular displays. It is no different today. It is discouraging to see how many are attracted to preachers who assert the authenticity of their message by dramatic exhibitions of "spiritual" power. Jesus warns us that signs and wonders are not proof of his Father's will since they can come from sources other than God, including the demonic world and human creation (cf. Acts 19:13–16; 2 Thess. 2:9–12; Rev. 13:13–14). As Craig Blomberg notes, charismatic activity has a tendency "to substitute enthusiasm and the spectacular for more unglamorous obedience in the midst of suffering. But these external demonstrations prove nothing."[30]

The final proof of any ministry is whether it promotes obedience to the Father's will. Modern pastor John Stott remarks, "We recite the creed in church, and sing hymns expressive of devotion to Christ. We even exercise a variety of ministries in his name. But he is not impressed by our pious and orthodox words. He still asks for evidence of our sincerity in good works of obedience."[31] Anything else is the product of "evildoers" (7:23), which will result in eternal banishment. Cyril continues, "Even if they at the outset had lived virtuously, they ended up condemned. God knows those whom he loves, and he loves those who single-mindedly believe in him and do the things that please him."[32]

**Wise and foolish builders (7:24–27).** Jesus' fourth warning compares the wisdom of finding one's righteousness in Jesus' proclamation of the kingdom of heaven with the foolishness of pursuing the self-righteousness of the religious establishment. Chrysostom refers to the foolish person who labors to build a house on sand as "brainless," because that effort will gain immediate benefit but eternal destruction.[33] "Brainless" is an apt expression today as

---

29. Cyril of Alexandria, *Fragment* 88.
30. Blomberg, *Matthew*, 133.
31. Stott, *Sermon on the Mount*, 208.
32. Cyril of Alexandria, *Fragment* 88.
33. Chrysostom, *The Gospel of Matthew* 157.

well when we consider the choice between building our lives on Jesus as our life's foundation or any other way.

The popular pastor and expositor James Montgomery Boice suggests that there are two mistakes that a person can make with respect to this choice. One error is to say, as many young people might, that they need no foundation. The other error is to say, as many of an older generation may, that any foundation will do.[34] The former we see in the postmodern skepticism about finding absolute truth. The latter we see in the politically correct pluralism of modern culture. But the solid rock that has provided true stability, security, and hope throughout church history is none other than Jesus, and him alone, and the life of kingdom righteousness that he has announced in the SM. This is expressed so beautifully in the old, yet not so old, hymn, "My Hope Is Built on Nothing Less."

> My hope is built on nothing less
> Than Jesus' blood and righteousness;
> I dare not trust the sweetest frame,
> But wholly lean on Jesus' name.
> On Christ the solid Rock I stand;
> All other ground is sinking sand,
> All other ground is sinking sand.[35]

My prayer is that our study of this Sermon will have caused us to be more than "amazed" at Jesus' teaching—that we are not simply giving an emotional response but that we respond as disciples who have left all to follow Jesus' way. It will cause us truly to exalt Jesus as the One who has all authority, the One whose teaching is the true foundation and fountain of life.

---

34. James Montgomery Boice, *The Sermon on the Mount: An Exposition* (Grand Rapids: Zondervan, 1972), 310–11.

35. William B. Bradbury, "My Hope Is Built on Nothing Less" (1863).

# Matthew 8:1–9:8

W HEN HE CAME down from the mountainside, large
crowds followed him. ²A man with leprosy came
and knelt before him and said, "Lord, if you are
willing, you can make me clean."

³Jesus reached out his hand and touched the man. "I am
willing," he said. "Be clean!" Immediately he was cured of his
leprosy. ⁴Then Jesus said to him, "See that you don't tell anyone. But go, show yourself to the priest and offer the gift
Moses commanded, as a testimony to them."

⁵When Jesus had entered Capernaum, a centurion came to
him, asking for help. ⁶"Lord," he said, "my servant lies at home
paralyzed and in terrible suffering."

⁷Jesus said to him, "I will go and heal him."

⁸The centurion replied, "Lord, I do not deserve to have you
come under my roof. But just say the word, and my servant will
be healed. ⁹For I myself am a man under authority, with soldiers
under me. I tell this one, 'Go,' and he goes; and that one,'Come,'
and he comes. I say to my servant, 'Do this,' and he does it."

¹⁰When Jesus heard this, he was astonished and said to
those following him, "I tell you the truth, I have not found
anyone in Israel with such great faith. ¹¹I say to you that many
will come from the east and the west, and will take their places
at the feast with Abraham, Isaac and Jacob in the kingdom of
heaven. ¹²But the subjects of the kingdom will be thrown outside, into the darkness, where there will be weeping and
gnashing of teeth."

¹³Then Jesus said to the centurion, "Go! It will be done just as
you believed it would." And his servant was healed at that very hour.

¹⁴When Jesus came into Peter's house, he saw Peter's mother-
in-law lying in bed with a fever. ¹⁵He touched her hand and the
fever left her, and she got up and began to wait on him.

¹⁶When evening came, many who were demon-possessed
were brought to him, and he drove out the spirits with a word
and healed all the sick. ¹⁷This was to fulfill what was spoken
through the prophet Isaiah:

"He took up our infirmities
and carried our diseases."

¹⁸When Jesus saw the crowd around him, he gave orders to cross to the other side of the lake. ¹⁹Then a teacher of the law came to him and said, "Teacher, I will follow you wherever you go."

²⁰Jesus replied, "Foxes have holes and birds of the air have nests, but the Son of Man has no place to lay his head."

²¹Another disciple said to him, "Lord, first let me go and bury my father."

²²But Jesus told him, "Follow me, and let the dead bury their own dead."

²³Then he got into the boat and his disciples followed him. ²⁴Without warning, a furious storm came up on the lake, so that the waves swept over the boat. But Jesus was sleeping. ²⁵The disciples went and woke him, saying, "Lord, save us! We're going to drown!"

²⁶He replied, "You of little faith, why are you so afraid?" Then he got up and rebuked the winds and the waves, and it was completely calm.

²⁷The men were amazed and asked, "What kind of man is this? Even the winds and the waves obey him!"

²⁸When he arrived at the other side in the region of the Gadarenes, two demon-possessed men coming from the tombs met him. They were so violent that no one could pass that way. ²⁹"What do you want with us, Son of God?" they shouted. "Have you come here to torture us before the appointed time?"

³⁰Some distance from them a large herd of pigs was feeding. ³¹The demons begged Jesus, "If you drive us out, send us into the herd of pigs."

³²He said to them, "Go!" So they came out and went into the pigs, and the whole herd rushed down the steep bank into the lake and died in the water. ³³Those tending the pigs ran off, went into the town and reported all this, including what had happened to the demon-possessed men. ³⁴Then the whole town went out to meet Jesus. And when they saw him, they pleaded with him to leave their region.

⁹:¹Jesus stepped into a boat, crossed over and came to his own town. ²Some men brought to him a paralytic, lying on a mat. When Jesus saw their faith, he said to the paralytic, "Take heart, son; your sins are forgiven."

³At this, some of the teachers of the law said to themselves, "This fellow is blaspheming!"

⁴Knowing their thoughts, Jesus said, "Why do you entertain evil thoughts in your hearts? ⁵Which is easier: to say, 'Your sins are forgiven,' or to say, 'Get up and walk'? ⁶But so that you may know that the Son of Man has authority on earth to forgive sins...." Then he said to the paralytic, "Get up, take your mat and go home." ⁷And the man got up and went home. ⁸When the crowd saw this, they were filled with awe; and they praised God, who had given such authority to men.

As JESUS CONCLUDES the Sermon on the Mount and comes down from the mountain, large crowds of people follow him (8:1). His initial public ministry attracted large crowds (4:23–25), and his teaching in the SM has amazed the crowds (7:28), so they begin to follow him around the countryside of Galilee. Matthew now brings together several miracle stories to show that Jesus not only has a great messianic message but also a great messianic mission.[1] Jesus is not only Messiah in word (chs. 5–7) but is also Messiah at work (chs. 8–9).

Jesus' miracles may be divided into at least three general classes: healings, exorcisms, and nature miracles, with raisings of the dead a subcategory of the last (or a separate category). Matthew will focus on each of these types of miracles here as a demonstration that the kingdom of God truly has arrived (cf. 12:28).

But Jesus' messianic mission will not unfold as many may have expected. First, he will heal the marginalized (8:1–17), disappoint current discipleship expectations (8:18–22), and overpower Satan's strongholds, including nature, demons, and disease (8:23–9:8). Then he will reveal an unexpected form of discipleship (9:9–17), heal the unexpected (9:18–35), and enlist workers to go out with his messianic authority to extend his mission (9:36–10:4).

## Healing the Marginalized (8:1–17)

IN THREE BRIEF scenes, Matthew demonstrates how Jesus' messianic ministry brings restoration to people who were often marginalized within Jewish culture: lepers (8:1–4), Gentiles (8:5–13), and women (8:14–15). In this way Jesus breaks down purity, ethnic, and gender barriers so that all may respond to his invitation to the kingdom of heaven.

---

1. The miracles in chs. 8–9 are not in the chronological order followed by standard harmonies of Jesus' life. See, e.g., the placement of the miracles in Thomas and Gundry, *The NIV Harmony of the Gospels*, 22–26. Matthew has theological purposes in mind as he gathers these miracle stories together in one place.

**Cleansing the leper: purity boundaries (8:1–4).** The narrative opens abruptly: "A man with leprosy [*lepra*] came and knelt before him." The modern conception of leprosy brings to mind the dreaded and debilitating illness known as Hansen's disease, prevalent in low, humid, tropical, or subtropical areas of the world (mostly in Asia, Africa, South America, and the Pacific Islands). While it is not highly contagious, the horror of the illness, which can waste away human limbs and extremities such as ears and noses, has led to the isolation of people with the disease.

But in the ancient world leprosy was more generally associated with a variety of skin diseases, such as dermatosis, psoriasis, lupus, ringworm, and other suspicious skin disorders. The Old Testament provided specific guidelines for the examination and treatment of those with these diseases (see Lev. 13–14), since many of the disorders were considered highly contagious.

This leper must have heard of Jesus' widespread healing ministry (Matt. 4:23–25), because he kneels before Jesus and says, "Lord, if you are willing, you can make me clean." The vocative title "Lord" (*kyrie*) is the title that people commonly use when they approach Jesus for divine aid.[2] This leper does not presume to dictate Jesus' agenda but appeals to him as one bearing God's healing purity. The line between medical and spiritual impurity was often blurred because of the uncertainty of diagnosis. All those with leprosy were required to be examined by the priest, who after examination might pronounce the person clean or unclean (Lev. 13:2ff.). If found to be leprous, the diseased individual was to be isolated from the rest of the community and was required to wear torn clothes, cover the lower part of his or her face, and cry out, "Unclean! Unclean!" (Lev. 13:45–46; Num. 5:2–4).

The source of the healing of this leper is in Jesus, who only has to *will* to effect an immediate cure. As he reaches out to touch the leper, Jesus does not violate the Old Testament purity laws, for instead of becoming unclean himself, he cleanses the leper with his healing hand and spiritual purity. By commanding the leper to perform the prescribed ritual of presenting himself to the priest (8:4), Jesus fulfills the law required of lepers for reentry into society (Lev. 14:1–32). As Jesus fulfills the Mosaic law, it becomes a "testimony" (*martyrion*) to the priesthood and to the people of his true messianic identity (Matt. 8:4).

But the leper is instructed, "See that you don't tell anyone." A regular aspect of Jesus' ministry was to demand secrecy about his identity and activity, which is especially emphasized in Mark's Gospel, but also in Matthew (cf. 9:30; 12:16; 16:20; 17:9). Jesus' desire for silence is not some theme con-

---

2. E.g., 8:2, 5; 9:28; 15:22, 25; 17:15; 20:30, 31, 33; see Bornkamm, "End-Expectation and Church in Matthew's Gospel," 41–43.

trived by the Gospel writers to explain the nonmessianic tradition they received,[3] but is a theme that characterizes Jesus' historical mission. He carefully avoids stirring up in the crowds a misunderstanding of his messianic identity. Although miracles will attest the authenticity of his gospel message about the arrival of the kingdom of heaven, Jesus does not want crowds clamoring for the miracles alone. They may easily misunderstand his message to mean that he has come to effect only physical healing or to bring national and military liberation. He will guide his disciples and the crowds to understand that his primary mission is to bring forgiveness of sins (see 9:1–8; 20:28; 26:28), which brings true cleansing.

**Healing the centurion's servant: ethnic boundaries (8:5–13).** Not only do we find in this narrative an astounding account of Jesus healing a person from a distance, but we also find a staggering reversal of ethnic and religious expectations. At this early stage of Jesus' ministry and Matthew's narrative, a Gentile is healed, a promise of Gentile inclusion in the kingdom of heaven is revealed, and the nation of Israel is warned of exclusion from God's program of redemption if they do not repent. This certainly must have shocked Jesus' audience and is a stark reminder to Matthew's readers of the true nature of discipleship.

Returning again to Capernaum, the base of his Galilean ministry (see comments on 4:13), Jesus encounters a centurion, a Roman military officer. The *centuria* (century), a group of a hundred soldiers, was the smallest unit of the Roman legion. Each one was commanded by a centurion, the principal professional officer in the armies of ancient Rome. Although there was little tangible evidence of a *centuria* being stationed in Galilee until A.D. 44,[4] recent excavations reveal that a military garrison at Capernaum had its quarters to the east of the Jewish village. These excavations shed fuller light on the centurion of Capernaum. He must have been an able and responsible official, who maintained good relations with the Jewish populace.

In each of the miracle scenes in chapters 8–9, Matthew abbreviates the narrative to get at the primary figure or action of the incident. He has the centurion approach Jesus directly[5] with a request, not for himself but for his

---

3. This is a popular interpretation among some critical commentators, beginning in 1901 with William Wrede, *The Messianic Secret,* trans. J. C. G. Greig (Cambridge: James Clarke, 1971) and revisited in a variety of forms to the present; e.g., C. M. Tuckett, ed., *The Messianic Secret* (Philadelphia: Fortress, 1983).

4. A. N. Sherwin-White, *Roman Society and Roman Law in the New Testament* (Oxford: Clarendon, 1963), 123–24.

5. In Luke's version (Luke 7:1–10), which gives greater detail, the actual request for healing of the servant is brought by some Jewish elders and then other Jewish friends. They

servant: "My servant lies at home paralyzed and in terrible suffering." Jesus has already cured the same malady (paralysis) of those brought to him by the crowds in 4:24, so the centurion has probably heard about Jesus' power over this disease. This servant is suffering terribly. The source of the paralysis is unknown, but the descriptions have led some to suggest that the cause was poliomyelitis, a scourge of many ancient societies.

Using the same title uttered by the leper, "Lord" (8:2), this Roman centurion displays a remarkable sensitivity for Jewish traditions by considering himself unworthy to receive the Jewish teacher into his Gentile home: "Lord, I do not deserve to have you come under my roof." Entering the home of a Gentile rendered a Jew ceremonially unclean (cf. Acts 10:28). But the centurion goes beyond the Jewish aversion to Gentile homes in his recognition of Jesus' personal superiority as the One who can heal his servant. "But just say the word, and my servant will be healed. For I myself am a man under authority, with soldiers under me." The Roman military exercised profound control over the lives of their own troops, as was necessary in readiness for combat situations. But this centurion pays homage to an even greater authority in Jesus, whose word alone, like God's word (cf. Ps. 107:20), can heal.

The likelihood that this centurion is a Gentile God-fearer will not alone account for the statement of praise from Jesus to his followers: "I tell you the truth, I have not found anyone in Israel with such great faith." The centurion understands that in Jesus is the hoped-for Deliverer, whom Israel as a nation should have recognized. Hence, Jesus' statement both singles out the centurion for exemplary faith and censures Israel for its lack of faith. Jesus' praise and indictment turn to language of promise to Gentiles and judgment against Israel: "I say to you that many will come from the east and the west, and will take their places at the feast with Abraham, Isaac and Jacob in the kingdom of heaven."

The phrase "east and west" points to the breadth of peoples who will come from the ends of the earth. The Old Testament had anticipated the inclusion of all the peoples of the earth in the eschatological banquet (Isa. 25:6–9; 56:3–8).[6] The covenant made with Abraham to be a blessing to all the nations of the earth, which has been fulfilled with the arrival of Jesus (cf. 1:1; Gen. 12:1–3; 22:18), is now made public in the pronouncement to the centurion. The peoples of the earth will join the patriarchs at the eschatological banquet in the kingdom of heaven.[7]

---

approach Jesus out of gratitude to the centurion because he had built a synagogue for them. The centurion sensitively recognizes his own unworthiness as a Gentile to approach Jesus (7:7).

6. Gene R. Smillie, "'Even the Dogs': Gentiles in the Gospel of Matthew," *JETS* 45 (March 2002): 73–97, esp. 91–97.

7. See Scot McKnight, *A New Vision for Israel: The Teachings of Jesus in National Context* (Grand Rapids: Eerdmans, 1999), 150–55.

At the same time that Jesus assures the inclusion of Gentiles, he dramatically foresees the exclusion of those who seem to have an assured place: "But the subjects of the kingdom will be thrown outside." The expression "subjects of the kingdom" (lit., "sons of the kingdom") is a Semitism pointing to national Israel,[8] whose leaders took exclusive claim to God's kingdom through their Abrahamic heritage (3:8–9). With remarkable passion, Jesus continues the theme of judgment that John the Baptist announced (cf. 3:7–12). Israel's claim to the kingdom will leave outside any who have not repented, unless they follow the path of faith in Jesus that the centurion has exemplified (see comments on 21:43–46). Jesus goes on to paint a woeful picture of the future of unrepentant Israel with terms common to descriptions of hell or Gehenna (22:13; cf. *4 Ezra* 7:93; *1 En.* 63:10): "into the darkness, where there will be weeping and gnashing of teeth."

This declaration must have shocked Jesus' listeners, but it is consistent with the Old Testament prophets, who consistently called Israel back to God. Jesus will continue to appeal to Israel to repent and enter the kingdom he has inaugurated. This fulfills the covenantal promises to Israel made through Abraham, Isaac, and Jacob, which includes attendance at the eschatological banquet. Attendance at that banquet has one primary requirement for all of God's children, regardless of ethnic identity: faith in Jesus as Messiah. Gentiles who believe will join Jews who believe.[9] Those who do not turn to him in faith as the messianic deliverer will receive just punishment, whether Jew or Gentile. The Gentile mission has not yet been declared, but Jesus' reply to the centurion indicates that the door to the kingdom is open to whoever believes.[10]

The actual healing is not in *proportion* to the amount of the centurion's faith (see comments on 17:20), nor is the healing *caused* by the centurion's faith (see comments on 15:28), but it is in *response* to his faith in Jesus as the One who can heal. Accounts of miraculous healing within Judaism are rare and were considered extraordinary, so Jesus' healing in this story would have been regarded as astonishing. For example, the much-discussed story of Rabbi Hanina ben Dosa that is told in the Babylonian Talmud (*b. Ber.* 34b) indicates that the rabbi knew he was only a prayer intermediary and did not have even the stature of a prophet.[11] But Jesus knows that he is himself the source of the healing (8:7), which the centurion knows as well (8:8). Jesus'

---

8. E.g., Luke 16:8 refers to "sons of light," and 1QM 17.8 refers to "sons of his truth" and "sons of his covenant."

9. McKnight, *A New Vision for Israel*, 150–51.

10. Charles H. H. Scobie, "Israel and the Nations: An Essay in Biblical Theology," *Tyn-Bul* 43 (1992): 283–305, esp. 293–94; Carson, "Matthew," 203.

11. See Wilkins, "Matthew," 55, for a recounting of the rabbi's prayer for healing.

authority as the One who heals sets him apart from all others, a prerogative that only a divine Messiah could claim and validate.

**Healing Peter's mother-in-law: gender boundaries (8:14–15).** Jesus has crossed purity (8:1–4) and ethnic (8:5–13) boundaries, and in this third healing miracle, he breaches a gender boundary to heal a woman, another person often marginalized in some circles of Judaism. Similar to the previous healing story, the incident of the healing of Peter's mother-in-law is abbreviated in Matthew (cf. Mark 1:21–31; Luke 4:31–39). Matthew focuses only on the healing incident rather than other elements surrounding it.

The scene takes place in Peter's house in Capernaum. Peter and Andrew have apparently moved the family fishing business from their hometown in Bethsaida (John 1:44) to Capernaum and established a home there. Jesus enters Peter's house. This may surprise the reader because of the earlier response of Peter and Andrew to Jesus' call, "At once they left their nets and followed him" (4:20). Obviously following Jesus did not necessitate Peter to abandon his home or his family members (though see 19:27). Peter's call to become a fisher of men meant to follow Jesus' will for his life, but it did not mean to compromise his familial responsibilities or to assume an ascetic lifestyle in which he gave up all material possessions.

Interestingly, in 1968 excavations were undertaken on a site that traditionally was said to be the actual home of Peter. Sifting down through the remains of centuries-old churches, excavators came to what was originally a house, built in approximately 63 B.C. All of the historical and archaeological evidence has led the majority of scholars to the conclusion that the site actually was the original home of Peter in Capernaum during Jesus' ministry.[12] The excavation of a nearby synagogue is consistent with Mark and Luke's narratives, which imply that the synagogue was near Peter's home. The lowest level of this latter excavation is a black basalt first-century synagogue, probably the synagogue in which Jesus preached, just a few steps from Peter's home.[13]

Mark informs us that the home belonged to both Peter and Andrew (Mark 1:29). Perhaps it was a home of their parents but was now occupied by the sons and their extended families, including at least Peter, his wife, and her parent(s). Matthew's expression "lying in bed with a fever" indicates that Peter's

---

12. See Wilkins, "Matthew," 56.

13. For popular discussions of the excavation of both Peter's house and the synagogue, see Charlesworth, *Jesus Within Judaism*, 109–15; James F. Strange and Hershel Shanks, "Synagogue Where Jesus Preached Found at Capernaum," *Archaeology and the Bible: The Best of BAR, Volume II: Archaeology in the World of Herod, Jesus and Paul* (Washington, D.C.: Biblical Archaeological Society, 1990), 200–207; Rousseau and Arav, "Capernaum (Capharnaum)," *Jesus and His World*, 39–47.

mother-in-law is in the throes of a severe illness, perhaps malaria, because fever was considered a disease, not a symptom (cf. John 4:52; Acts 28:8).

Jesus' personal presence commands authority over this diseased-ravaged world as he heals the woman with a touch. The miracle is effective and instantaneous: "And she got up and began to wait on [*diakoneo*] him." The straightforward implication is that the woman serves Jesus a meal. But Matthew's use of *diakoneo* has significance beyond simple meal preparation. The woman's actions indicate instantaneous gratitude for being healed, a strikingly significant motivation for all discipleship to Jesus (see comments on 20:1–15).

**Exorcising and healing many (8:16–17).** Since Matthew does not record the Sabbath synagogue exorcism found in Mark 1:21–28 and Luke 4:40, he gives only a general comment on the time of day: "when evening came." Because the Sabbath ended with sunset, people can bring their demon-possessed and sick relatives and friends to Jesus without breaking Sabbath laws. As with the centurion's servant, Jesus' powerful "word" is all that is needed to heal.

Matthew once again emphasizes that Jesus' life and ministry is the fulfillment of the Old Testament (cf. 1:23, 25; 2:15, 23; 4:14), specifying that his healing ministry fulfills the prophecy of Isaiah 53:4: "Surely he took up our infirmities and carried our sorrow." This is another allusion to the Servant of Isaiah's prophecy,[14] now focusing on the Servant's role as the one who brings healing. The Greek text of Matthew's quotation gets at the heart of the meaning of the prophecy, in which both sin and sickness are in view. The quotation is from the larger "Servant Song" of Isaiah 52:13–53:12, which has substitutionary atonement as one of its central themes. The Servant bears the sicknesses of others through his own suffering and death. Matthew draws on this prophecy to link Jesus' healing ministry with the substitutionary theme. Jesus does not himself become ill but takes and removes illness by his healing power.

While this does not yet explicitly introduce Jesus' vicarious suffering and death for sin, it certainly prepares the way for it.[15] Jesus came to save his people from their sins (1:21), and his healings point beyond themselves to the cross and his initiation of the new covenant in his blood, which is poured out for the forgiveness of sin (26:27–28). All sickness and death is ultimately rooted in the entrance of sin to human existence, so Jesus' entire ministry in his inauguration of the kingdom of heaven begins to reverse the cycle of death and suffering.[16]

---

14. See 2:23, the "Branch" of Isa. 53:2; cf. also Matt. 12:17–21; 26:28; 27:12; 27:38.
15. Millard Erickson, *Christian Theology* (Grand Rapids: Baker, 1984), 836–41.
16. Carson, "Matthew," 206.

Some modern critical scholars doubt that first-century Jews interpreted Isaiah 53:4 messianically,[17] but later rabbinic texts did know a messianic interpretation of the passage.[18] So it is more than likely that at least some Jews of Jesus' day saw the messianic significance of the Suffering Servant of Isaiah 53, as Matthew indicates.[19] Matthew makes explicit that in Jesus the Servant has come to take away the sickness of his people. The full disclosure of Jesus' vicarious suffering for sin will be made clearer as Jesus' ministry unfolds (e.g., 20:18–19, 28; 26:27–28).

### Expected Discipleship Disappointed (8:18–22)

WE MAY BE surprised by Jesus' actions after these healings, for when he sees the crowds, he goes away from them (see 5:1 for a similar note; see comments). Here Jesus sees the crowd and departs to be with his disciples (8:18). This is a consistent contrast in Matthew. The crowd is the object of Jesus' ministry of proclaiming the gospel and healing, inviting them into the kingdom of heaven to become his disciples. The disciples are those who have responded, and Jesus gives them specialized teaching that enables them to live kingdom life and serve others. The following incident records two individuals who come forward, already apparently Jesus' disciples but deficient in their understanding of what discipleship to Jesus entails. To these two, Jesus declares the crux of discipleship in individual fashion for both of their shortcomings.

**A would-be disciple's professional expectations (8:18–20).** Jesus directs his disciples "to cross to the other side of the lake" (8:18). The expression "other side" usually marks Jesus' movement across the Sea of Galilee, on this occasion from the primarily Jewish region on the west side to the primarily Gentile region on the east side (cf. 8:28; 9:1). But before they depart, "a teacher of the law" comes to him (8:18; see also comments on 5:20). This person was a *grammateus* ("scribe"), an expert in handling written documents. In the ancient world only a few people could read and write. Although the Jews had a higher percentage of the population trained in reading and writing, only a special group regularly worked with written materials, and even fewer had access to books or Scriptures. The capabilities of scribes went far beyond simple secretarial skills to include teaching, interpretation, and regulation of laws.

---

17. E.g., Hooker, "Did the Use of Isaiah 53 to Interpret His Mission Begin with Jesus?" 88–103.

18. Hill, *The Gospel of Matthew*, 161; e.g., *b. Sanh.* 98a-b: "Surely he hath borne our griefs and carried our sins, yet we did esteem him stricken with leprosy, and smitten of God and afflicted."

19. For an extended discussion of the identification of the prophesied Davidic messianic King with the Suffering Servant of Isaiah 52:13–53:12, see Van Groningen, *Messianic Revelation in the Old Testament*, 619–50.

In Galilee the scribes appear as lower-level officials who acted in the synagogue as teachers or interpreters (7:28–29), while in Jerusalem they were high-level officials linked with the chief priests and the Sanhedrin (2:4). Scribes joined with the Pharisees to question Jesus in Galilee (15:1) and Jerusalem (23:13) and linked forces with the chief priests in Jerusalem in their condemnation of Jesus (21:15). They were experts in Scripture according to their sectarian beliefs (hence the NIV "teacher of the law").

The teacher of the law in 8:19 had been a disciple of a rabbi until he finished his course of study and then became a legal expert himself. He comes to Jesus with that background, referring to Jesus as "teacher," the equivalent of the Hebrew title "rabbi" (see comments on 23:7–10). "I will follow you" normally indicates a desire for a discipleship relationship, but this man has in mind the kind of master-disciple relationship in which a potential disciple examines various masters and then enlists himself with the most popular or the best-equipped one.[20]

Jesus' response to the teacher of the law's volunteerism is surprising: "Foxes have holes and birds of the air have nests, but the Son of Man has no place to lay his head" (8:20). Jesus is most likely drawing on a familiar metaphor to explain the uniqueness of his form of master-disciple relationship. This noticeably stern reply checks this enthusiastic recruit, because Jesus' form of discipleship is a different sort from what the scribe has experienced in his prior training. Rabbis enjoyed a relatively high status within Judaism, but Jesus has no school or synagogue or prestigious place of honor among the religious establishment. He stays at the home of friends, relatives, and disciples through most of his ministry (e.g., 8:14). So the expression "no place to lay his head" does not indicate a homeless, Cynic-type philosopher but rather that his ministry will not result in an institutional establishment with comfortable benefits, and this will also be the lot of those who follow him.[21]

The expression "Son of Man" (8:20) would have struck a relatively ambiguous chord with this teacher of the law. He would have remembered its use in Ezekiel, where God refers to the prophet with the expression "son of man" over ninety times (e.g., Ezek. 2:1, 3, 6, 8, etc.; cf. Dan. 8:17), stressing Ezekiel's frailty as a human before the mighty God revealed in the vision.[22] But the teacher of the law would also have recalled how Daniel used "Son of Man" to refer to a glorified Sovereign, the apocalyptic messianic figure who rules forever with the Ancient of Days (Dan. 7:13–14). This latter sense of

---

20. See Martin Hengel, *The Charismatic Leader and His Followers*, trans. James Greig (New York: Crossroad, 1981), 3–15; passim.

21. Jack Dean Kingsbury, "On Following Jesus: The 'Eager' Scribe and the 'Reluctant' Disciple (Matthew 8.18–22)," *NTS* 34 (1988): 47–52, esp. 49.

22. Allen, *Ezekiel 1–19*, 38.

the expression found its way into Judaism, because it occurs in the pseude-pigraphal writings *1 Enoch* and *4 Ezra* 13. The reference in *1 Enoch* is particu-larly interesting because it probably precedes the time of Jesus:

> Pain shall seize them when they see that Son of Man sitting on the throne of his glory. (These) kings, governors, and all the landlords shall (try to) bless, glorify, extol him who rules over everything, him who has been concealed. For the Son of Man was concealed from the beginning, and the Most High One preserved him in the presence of his power; then he revealed him to the holy and the elect ones (62:5–7).[23]

But this title was not widely used. With such an ambiguity, it was for Jesus a convenient vehicle to convey his messianic identity. It did not have pop-ular associations attached to it, such as were attached to titles like "Messiah," "Son of David," or even "Son of God." Instead, he could teach the true mean-ing of his identity by referring to himself as "the Son of Man," which is indeed Jesus' favorite self-designation.[24] With a general threefold progres-sion, Jesus uses the expression to clarify who he is and what his ministry is.[25]

1. The Son of Man is the humble Servant who has come to forgive the sins of common sinners in his earthly ministry (8:20; 9:6; 11:19; 12:8, 32, 40).
2. The Son of Man is the suffering Servant, whose atoning death and resurrection will redeem his people (16:13, 27–28; 17:9, 12, 22; 20:18, 28; 26:2, 24, 45).
3. The Son of Man is the glorious King and Judge who will return to bring the kingdom of heaven to earth (10:23; 13:37, 41; 19:28; 24:27, 30, 37, 39, 44; 25:31; 26:64).

---

23. Although the dating of this portion of Enoch is debated, current scholarly opinion dates it at around the time of Herod the Great; cf. E. Isaac, "1 (Ethiopic Apocalypse of) Enoch," *The Old Testament Pseudepigrapha*, ed. James H. Charlesworth (Garden City, N.Y.: Doubleday, 1983), 1.7.

24. In every instance in the Gospels except two, the title is found only on the lips of Jesus, but even in these (1) the audience uses this title because Jesus previously used it as a self-designation (John 12:23), and (2) the angel is simply repeating Jesus' own words (Luke 24:7). In the rest of the New Testament the title is used of Jesus only once (Acts 7:56), except for three Old Testament allusions or quotations (Heb. 2:6 = Ps. 8:5; Rev. 1:13 and 14:14 = Dan. 7:13).

25. For a helpful overview by an evangelical scholar, see Robert H. Stein, *The Method and Message of Jesus' Teaching*, rev. ed. (Louisville: Westminster John Knox, 1994), 135–51. For an interesting discussion by a Jewish scholar, see David Flusser, *Jesus*, in collaboration with R. Steven Notley, rev. ed. (Jerusalem: Magnes, 1998), 124–33.

Jesus' mission is not always understood because of the misperceptions and faulty expectations of the people, the religious leaders, and even his own disciples. But at the end, after he has used this ambiguous title to clarify his identity and ministry, he uses it for the last time at his trial before Caiaphas and the Sanhedrin, where it is perfectly clear that he is claiming to be the divine Messiah of Israel (cf. 26:63–68).[26]

 **A would-be disciple's cultural expectations (8:21–22).** Now "another disciple" comes forward. Some suggest that the term "another" (*heteros*) makes a distinction between the teacher of the law (8:19) and this person, so that the former is a would-be disciple and the latter a true disciple.[27] It is more helpful to view both of these individuals from the historical perspective of the Jesus movement. At the early stage of Jesus' ministry people come to him and ask to join his movement. They come with their expectations of what discipleship to Jesus is like, based primarily on their past experiences. But in the later stages of his ministry, Jesus teaches explicitly what his form of discipleship is like, in distinction from other forms in Judaism. So these two individuals are disciples in the loose sense of the term. Neither is one of the Twelve, but is one of the broader circle of disciples who early on gather around Jesus (cf. Luke 6:13, 17), many of whom do not fully understand what Jesus' form of discipleship entails.

But Jesus will have no disciples except under his own conditions, so he tests this disciple's commitment. He later will do so to a large group of his disciples, at which time it is revealed that they have never truly believed (John 6:60–66).[28]

The disciple asks, "Lord, first let me go and bury my father." Burial of the dead superseded other religious obligations in Israel, even for the priests, who were allowed to be defiled by touching the dead if it was a family member (Lev. 21:2). The obligation to care for the dead came implicitly from the command to "honor your father and your mother" (Ex. 20:12; Deut. 5:16; cf. also Gen. 50:5; Tobit 4:3; 6:15). Note this statement in the Mishnah about caring for one's dead: "He whose dead lies unburied before him is exempt from reciting the *Shema*, from saying the *Tefillah* and from wearing phylacteries" (*m. Ber.* 3.1). The Talmud carried it one step further: "He who is confronted by a dead relative is freed from reciting the *Shema*, from the Eighteen Benedictions, and from all the commandments stated in the Torah" (*b. Ber.* 31a).

---

26. E.g., Gerhardsson, "The Christology of Matthew," in *Who Do You Say That I Am?* 20–21: "In the Gospel of Matthew, the status of Jesus—both in his humiliation and in his exaltation—and his entire work are covered by Son of Man sayings."

27. E.g., Kingsbury, "On Following Jesus," 47–52.

28. See Wilkins, *Following the Master*, ch. 6.

Jesus' response is surprising, if not shocking: "Follow me, and let the dead bury their own dead." He later rebukes the Pharisees and teachers of the law for not rightly honoring father and mother (15:1–9), so he is not advocating that this disciple contravene the Old Testament prescription. Trying to understand Jesus' response has led to a number of explanations. Some think that the person's father has not yet died, and he wants to stay with him until then. Or perhaps he is returning to fulfill the second stage of burial by transferring the bones of his father a year after death to an ossuary. Still others look for explanation in a metaphorical allusion in Jesus' language, such as: "Let those who are *spiritually* dead bury the *physically* dead."[29] In any case, Jesus is elevating his call to "follow me" above all other allegiances. Anything that gets in the way of unqualified commitment to him must be set aside.[30]

This calls for wise thinking. Jesus' disciples must be guided by God's mandate to honor their parents, but the supremacy of Jesus as their Master must always be heeded. This was a typical struggle in that culture, trying to balance responsibility to family with commitment to God, because on several occasions Jesus challenges the crowd and even his own disciples not to have any family commitment take priority over commitment to him (10:37–39; Luke 14:25–26.).

## Overpowering Satan's Strongholds (8:23–9:8)

THE FIRST SKIRMISH between Jesus and Satan resulted in Jesus' victory over the temptations (4:1–11). He continues to invade and overpower three of Satan's primary strongholds: the realm of nature as he calms the storm (8:23–27), the sphere of the spirit world as he exorcises the demoniacs (8:28–34), and the domain of disease and sin as he heals a paralytic (9:1–8).

**Calming a storm: authority over nature (8:23–27).** The desire of the teacher of the law ("I will follow you," 8:19) and the command of Jesus ("follow me," 8:22) are now exhibited by his disciples: "Then he got into the boat and his disciples followed him." The term "follow" (*akoloutheo*) is a synonym for discipleship (cf. 4:20, 22), marking a transition from the scene of the two would-be disciples to the story of Jesus with his disciples on the lake. In contrast to the preceding two, the disciples do follow Jesus, and their participation in the nature miracle demonstrates both the deficiency as well as the expected growth of their discipleship to Jesus.

These disciples, only four of whom have been named (Peter, Andrew, James, and John; see 4:18–22), have probably crossed the sea many times,

---

29. See Hagner, *Matthew*, 1:218.

30. For discussion of the social setting, see Joseph H. Hellerman, *The Ancient Church As Family* (Minneapolis: Fortress, 2001), 72–73.

being professional fishermen. But they are in for a trip that will mark them forever. "Without warning, a furious storm came up on the lake." Ancient writers all acclaim the Sea of Galilee for its fresh waters and pleasant temperatures, unlike the Dead Sea. It had clear sandy beaches along the seashore and was well stocked with fish.[31] The lake's low elevation (636 feet below sea level) provided it with mild year-round temperatures, permitting sleeping outdoors as a common practice (e.g., 8:25).

However, surrounded by mountain ranges to the east and west that rise over 2,650 feet from the level of the lake, especially infamous was an east wind that blew in over the mountains, particularly during the spring and fall (cf. 14:19, 24; John 6:1–4). The lake's low-lying setting resulted in sudden violent downdrafts and storms (cf. Mark 4:37; Luke 8:23; John 6:18) that produced waves seven feet and more, easily able to swamp a boat.[32]

Traversing the Sea of Galilee by night was a common experience for fishermen, who used trammel nets throughout the night.[33] Many boats needed a crew of at least five to handle the boat (four rowers and one rudderman), though it could carry as many as sixteen. There was enough room for a person to lie down in the stern and sleep when not on duty, with perhaps a ballast sandbag for a pillow (cf. Mark 4:38).[34]

This must have been a most powerful storm for these disciples to be afraid. They cry out, "Lord, save us!" Under these circumstances their plea indicates that they understand Jesus to be powerful enough to turn to when they cannot control their fate. If he were a mere mortal, he would not have been able to do anything more than they could do for themselves.

But their appeal to him isn't quite enough, because Jesus chides them, "You of little faith [*oligopistos*], why are you so afraid?" The disciples have faith, but it is not functioning properly (see comments on 6:30; 17:17, 20). Jesus calls them to understand more clearly who he is and then act on it. True faith will enable them to trust in God's care even when the circumstances do not look promising.

To give them a clearer view of who he really is, Jesus "got up and rebuked the winds and the waves, and it was completely calm." As a human Jesus was extremely tired after an exhausting day, but with divine power he quiets the storm by a mere word of command. He is able to command even the forces of nature, in the same way that in the Old Testament God "rebuked" the sea, a demonstration of his sovereign control over all of nature (cf. 2 Sam. 22:16;

---

31. Strabo, *Geography* 16.2; Pliny, *Natural History* 5.15, 71; Josephus, *J.W.* 3.506.

32. Freyne, "Galilee, Sea of," *ABD*, 2:900; Rainer Riesner, "Archeology and Geography," *DJG*, 37.

33. Nun, *The Sea of Galilee*, 16–44.

34. Wachsmann, *The Sea of Galilee Boat*, 326–28.

Ps. 18:15; 104:7; 106:9; Isa. 50:2; Nah. 1:4). This is an obvious miracle, because if a storm suddenly stopped naturally, the wind might cease but the waves would be disturbed for quite some time.

The reaction of the disciples says much about whom they are beginning to understand Jesus to be: "The men were amazed and asked, 'What kind of man is this? Even the winds and the waves obey him!'" The term for "amazed" is *thaumazō*, a different word from the one used to describe the reaction of the crowds to the SM (7:28). But it is similar in that it does not indicate a clear understanding of Jesus' identity.[35] Perhaps Matthew signals this deficiency by calling them here simply "the men" (8:27) instead of the usual "his disciples" (8:23).

It is still too much for the disciples to grasp fully, for what Jesus has just accomplished is something only God can do. When Jonah tried to run from his calling to preach to Nineveh, God caused the calming of the storm, which produced a similar reaction from the sailors (Jonah 1:16). In the Psalms Yahweh is celebrated as the master of the storm and sea (Ps. 65:7; 89:9; 104:6–7; 107:23–32).

In other words, Jesus is far more than the disciples have up to this time supposed. And he is far more than what we have often understood as well. It is a challenge for all of us to look clearly at Jesus as the divine-human Messiah, to allow him to amaze us, and even beyond amazement, to move us to follow him as his true disciples. We would do well to humble ourselves and call on him at our time of need, as self-sufficient as we might think we are.

**Exorcising the demoniacs: authority over the spirit world (8:28–34).** After the miraculous calming of the storm, Jesus and the disciples continue their trip across the Sea of Galilee. The next incident focuses entirely on Jesus; there is no mention of the disciples. Matthew draws our attention further to Jesus to help answer the exclamatory question, "What kind of man is this?"

The group arrives "at the other side in the region of the Gadarenes." Jesus is now in the predominantly Gentile region of the Decapolis, which explains why pigs are being raised, an animal unclean to Jews (Lev. 11:7; Deut. 14:8). "Gadarenes" refers to both the village of Gadara, located about five miles southeast of the Sea of Galilee, as well as to the surrounding region, which probably included the little village of Gerasa (modern Khersa or Kursi), which lay on the eastern shore of the Sea of Galilee and is the traditional site of the exorcism.[36]

---

35. The verb indicates being extraordinarily impressed or disturbed by something and so to "wonder, marvel, be astonished." Context determines whether this is a good or bad sense; see 8:10; 15:31; 22:22; 27:14 (cf. BDAG, 445–46).

36. Van Elderen, "Early Christianity in Transjordan," 100–102. This is the best accounting for the variant readings in the Synoptics.

As Jesus arrives in the region of the Gadarenes, "two demon-possessed men coming from the tombs met him." Mark 5:1–20 and Luke 8:26–39 record only one demoniac here. But rather than assuming that Matthew has added a second demoniac for a theological purpose, such as wanting two witnesses to the exorcism for legal reasons,[37] we can infer that Matthew has independent knowledge of the second man.[38] Matthew often gives only general details of a narrative, so he simply mentions two demoniacs, whereas Mark and Luke single out the spokesman and describe him in more detail, citing his name as "Legion"—a figurative expression for the amount of demons possessing the men. A Roman army legion had six thousand men.

Contact with the dead rendered a Jew ceremonially unclean,[39] which may have been why the demon-possessed men come out to accost this Jewish contingent. But the mention of tombs also casts an ominous pall of death and evil on the scene. The danger is heightened by noting that these two men are "so violent that no one could pass that way." Apparently they are well known among the populace and feared.

The demons immediately recognize Jesus' true identity as the "Son of God" (cf. Satan in 4:3, 6). This is a title that eventually the disciples will use (14:33; 16:16; cf. 27:54) as they gain increased clarity of his uniqueness as the One whom the Father has revealed to be his beloved Son (3:17; 17:5). But from the demons, the use of the title trumpets their recognition that another stronghold of Satan, the sphere of the spirit world, is being invaded and overpowered. These demons apparently know quite well an appointed time when the forces of Satan will be judged. "What do you want with us, Son of God?" they shout. "Have you come here to torture us before the appointed time?" The author of *1 Enoch* 16:1 says graphically:

> From the days of the slaughter and destruction, and the death of the giants and the spiritual beings of the spirit, and the flesh, from which they have proceeded forth, which will corrupt without incurring judgment, they will corrupt until the day of the great conclusion, until the great age is consummated, until everything is concluded (upon) the Watchers and the wicked ones.[40]

In Jesus' ministry the "time" has already begun with his ministry of exorcism. It indicates the arrival of the kingdom (4:17; 12:28) and the invasion and

---

37. Hagner, *Matthew*, 1:225; cf. Deut. 17:6; 19:15.
38. Carson, "Matthew," 217.
39. Num. 19:11, 14, 16; Ezek. 39:11–15.
40. Cf. Jude 6; Rev. 20:10; *Jub.* 10:8–9; *T. Levi* 18:12; 1QS 3:24–24; 4:18–20; the "Watchers" is a reference to the fallen angels (see Metzger, *1 Enoch*, 13 n. 1).

conquest of Satan's strongholds, even though the time of final judgment awaits Jesus' coming in glory.

The demons' plea to be sent into a nearby herd of swine would not be an unhappy thought to Jews, who considered swine and demons of the same order. Jesus warns his disciples not to throw pearls before swine (7:6). Peter regards false teachers as those who will return to their (swinish) pagan nature (2 Peter 2:22). But since the east shore of the Sea of Galilee is a Gentile region, this was not a wild herd but pigs being raised for market. Their owners would be upset at the loss of this large herd, which Mark numbers at about two thousand (Mark 5:13).

The request of the demons to enter the pigs has an added sinister purpose. Demons are elsewhere known to cause injury and pain to God's creatures (e.g., 17:14–20), and they do whatever they can to stimulate opposition to Jesus and his invasion of Satan's stronghold. The destruction of the pigs leads the Gentiles of the region to ask Jesus to leave (8:34). This response is a sad commentary on the perversion of their values, for one would think they would rejoice at a victory over Satan's demons. But as one commentator states, "all down the ages the world has been refusing Jesus because it prefers the pigs."[41] The darkness of the scene implies that the legion of demons go from the drowned swine looking for others to inhabit, an ominous thought for these people who have rejected Jesus. Jesus does not destroy the demons; rather, he allows evil to run its course in this world until "that day" when all will be rectified.

Matthew does not tell us the outcome of the exorcism, but Mark and Luke mention that the Gerasene demoniac begs to accompany Jesus. But Jesus tells him to go home and tell his family and friends how much God has done for him (Mark 5:18–19; Luke 8:38–39). The former demoniac sees the disciples with Jesus and desires to become one like them. But Jesus returns the man to his native place to witness. The Twelve will be fishers of men in one way, but this Gentile who has now become Jesus' disciple will fish for men in another way, among his own people.

**Healing the paralytic: authority over sin (9:1–8).** Jesus has stilled the storm, demonstrating his authority over the realm of nature (8:23–27). He has exorcised the demon-possessed men, demonstrating his authority over the spirit world (9:28–34). Now he heals a paralytic, demonstrating his authority over Satan's domain of disease, illness, and, surprisingly, sin. He does so back on the Jewish side of the Sea of Galilee, in "his own town"— undoubtedly Capernaum, the home base of his ministry in Galilee (cf. 4:17; 8:5; 11:23).

---

41. Paul P. Levertoff, cited in Tasker, *Matthew*, 94.

Probably back at Peter's home (see 8:14–15), "some men brought to him a paralytic, lying on a mat" (9:2). This is the parallel account of the famous scene in which the paralytic is brought by four men and lowered through a thatched roof (see Mark 2:1–12; Luke 5:17–26). Jesus has already cured paralysis (Matt. 4:24), so the men have probably heard of Jesus' supernatural healing ability and now bring their companion to him for healing. Jesus sees that they have faith in his ability to heal their companion, and they expect he will do so.

But Jesus' supernatural ability goes beyond healing: "Take heart, son; your sins are forgiven." The connection between sin and sickness was suggested earlier (8:17), but now Jesus states explicitly that they are related. The entrance of sin to the world brought corruption and death, and the only way of reversing this worldwide phenomenon is to have the sin problem corrected. God had promised to bring healing to Israel if they repented of their sin and sought forgiveness (2 Chron. 7:14; cf. Ps. 103:3). While individual sin is usually not the direct cause of a person's sickness (see John 9:2–3), at the heart of humanity's problem is sin. In 4:23–25, healing confirmed Jesus authority to announce the arrival of the kingdom of heaven, and healing now confirms that forgiveness of sin accompanies that arrival. Once sin is forgiven and redemption has occurred, all sickness and death will ultimately be abolished (cf. Isa. 25:8–9).

But not all rejoice at Jesus' arrival to inaugurate the prophesied day of salvation, for "some of the teachers of the law said to themselves, 'This fellow is blaspheming!'" This is the first time that the teachers of the law appear in explicit opposition to Jesus in Galilee. Blasphemy is an act in which a human insults the honor of God. This extends to misusing the name of God, which is cursed or reviled instead of being honored, the penalty for which is death by stoning (Lev. 24:10–23; 1 Kings 21:9–14). The teachers of the law charge Jesus with blasphemy because they believe that he is dishonoring God by taking to himself the prerogative to forgive sins, something only God can do (cf. Mark 2:7; Luke 5:21).

We may wonder why the teachers of the law so often oppose Jesus. They were the officials charged with preserving the law and its traditions. But now Jesus claims to speak and act for God. From the beginning of Jesus' public ministry the people see that Jesus gives new teaching with authority, in direct contrast with the teachers of the law (cf. 7:28–29). They see Jesus as a threat to their power and position in several ways.

- Jesus is a challenge to scribal interpretation and application of the Old Testament (5:17–48).
- Jesus threatens their understanding of the way God works, including healing on the Sabbath (12:1–14) and now forgiving sins (9:1–8).

- Jesus threatens their professional security as guardians of the law, because he contrasts his way of righteousness with theirs (5:20).
- Jesus is a threat to their popularity because his ministry is attracting the following of the people (21:15).
- The teachers of the law see Jesus as a threat to national security because of the popular excitement caused by his radical ministry (21:12–13).

The teachers of the law rightly understand that Jesus is making a profound equation of himself with God as he offers forgiveness of sin, but they have evil thoughts against him. They assume Jesus is wrong and label him with the charge of blasphemy. Later the Sanhedrin (which includes teachers of the law) likewise charge Jesus with blasphemy and condemn him to death because he tells the truth of who he actually is (26:63–68), thus presenting a threat to the establishment (cf. Luke 19:47–48).

Jesus turns on the offensive and questions them, "Which is easier: to say, 'Your sins are forgiven,' or to say, 'Get up and walk'?" This rhetorical question assumes, of course, that it is easier to say your sins are forgiven, because there is no way of confirming whether or not it has happened. It is obviously much more difficult to declare a person healed, because it can be immediately confirmed by the person's ability to walk. Then Jesus, using his title "Son of Man" again (see comments on 8:20), reveals another aspect of his identity by declaring that he has authority to forgive sins. As the teachers of the law have already ascertained, this is tantamount to an explicit claim to be divine.

The evidence of Jesus' authority is demonstrated as the man gets up and goes home. Not only have the teachers of the law witnessed the miraculous healing and authoritative claim to forgive sins, but the crowds also are witness; "they were filled with awe; and they praised God, who had given such authority to men." This is similar to the crowd's reaction at the conclusion of the SM (7:28–29), except now instead of amazement, they are "filled with awe [*phobeo*]," a word that normally connotes an element of fear. The crowds still do not get the full implication of Jesus' identity, because they think that the authority to forgive sins has been given "to men," not to the Son of Man. But Matthew's readers, including us, recognize that in Jesus an entirely new era has dawned—the age of forgiveness of sins, the reason for which Jesus was born (1:21).

*Bridging Contexts*

THE SERMON ON the Mount and the two subsequent chapters are sandwiched between two almost identical summaries of Jesus' ministry of preaching, teaching, and healing (cf. 4:23–25 and 9:35–36). Those summaries form a literary inclusio, because, like two bookends, they set off the material between them. This leads many to the conclusion that the SM and the chapters of Jesus' miracles form a literary diptych, or double panel, of the ministry of Jesus.[42] Jesus is not only Messiah in word (chs. 5–7) but is also Messiah at work in his miraculous deeds (chs. 8–9).

**Authority.** A central theme that characterizes Jesus as Messiah in word and work is "authority" (*exousia*). Of the nine times Matthew uses the word, five occur in this section. The crowds are amazed at Jesus' teaching with authority (7:29), the centurion recognizes Jesus' inherent authority to heal (8:9), Jesus declares that the Son of Man has authority to forgive sins (9:6), to which the crowds react with astonishment (9:8), and Jesus will soon delegate this authority to the Twelve to work miraculous deeds to confirm the same message of the kingdom of heaven (10:1, 7).[43] As Jesus establishes his messianic authority in word and work in the early stage of his Galilean ministry, he lays an authoritative foundation for the rest of his earthly ministry and subsequent ministry through his disciples (28:18–20).

Chapters 8–9 are generally recognized to have been organized by Matthew as collections of three groups of miracle stories, each of which is followed by sayings of Jesus. As is typical of Matthew's emphasis, this arrangement highlights both authoritative Christology and discipleship. Each miracle highlights particular aspects of Jesus' person and mission as the central figure of the narrative, and then the sayings clarify how discipleship to Jesus demands an allegiance to him and his calling that is strikingly different from other forms of discipleship in the ancient world.[44] These are important preparations for the pinnacle of Matthew's Gospel in Jesus' crucifixion and resurrection and the Great Commission.

People have authority in an area when they are able to back up their claims about some specific area of knowledge. When we look at court cases, people are said to be experts if they have the credibility and the ability to back up their claims. Jesus' healings in the Galilean narrative certainly point to his compassion, but they especially highlight his authority regarding the message of the kingdom that he brings—his disciples can trust him and should adopt his vision for life. Jesus did not present the SM as being optional or culturally conditioned; rather, it was a necessary foundation for life. Now in these chapters he backs up his authority to make this kind of claim with his powerful actions.

---

42. For an overview of Matthew's perspective of Jesus' miracles, with special reference to Matthew 8–9, see Graham H. Twelftree, *Jesus the Miracle Worker: A Historical and Theological Study* (Downers Grove, Ill.: InterVarsity Press, 1999), 102–24.

43. The other uses of *exousia* are 21:23, 24, 27; 28:18; a related verb, *katexousiazo*, "exercise authority over," occurs in 20:25.

44. For a similar understanding see Blomberg, *Matthew*, 136–37.

Those who encounter Jesus are attracted to, or threatened by, his authority. In this section we see what an appropriate response to him should be in the face of his authoritative person and mission. One response is to come with trust, having a humble recognition that he alone is adequate to handle the needs of all who come, regardless of whether society considers them worthy or not. Jesus has the power to break down purity boundaries, so the leper comes to Jesus, saying, "Lord, if you are willing, you can make me clean" (8:2). Jesus can also break down ethnic barriers, so the centurion comes to Jesus and says, "Lord, I am not worthy. . . . Just say the word, and my servant will be healed" (8:8). This results in glowing commendation from Jesus about his faith (8:10) and rebuke for the unfaithfulness of his own people who have not trusted him. Jesus has the authority to break down gender barriers, so he takes the initiative to reach out to Peter's mother-in-law to heal her (8:15).

Another appropriate response to Jesus' authority is unqualified allegiance to his person and mission. We are to place him at the center of our world. His authoritative work in our lives should cause us to serve him (8:15), to follow him and him alone (8:18–23), and always to turn to him in the moment of our deepest fears (8:26), because he has authority over the ravages of nature (8:26), the oppression of the spirit world (8:29–32), and the most devastating malady of humanity, sin (9:2–6).

But the tragedy is that not all who encounter his authority respond with trust in and allegiance to his person and mission. Many see Jesus' authority as a threat. Some come to Jesus with mixed motives and find that following him is a threat to their comfortable lifestyle (8:18–20). Others come with dual allegiances and find that commitment to Jesus threatens their social and cultural acceptability (8:21–22). Still others become so fixated on the consequences of Jesus' assault on the powers of this world that they are threatened by the consequences in their own lives if they allow him to take up residence in their personal, everyday world (8:34). And still others find that Jesus' claims threaten the very core of their religious worldview, and they flatly refuse the paradigm shift in their thinking and belief structure that will allow him the authoritative role in their lives that he deserves and demands (9:3–4).[45]

When exposed to the reality of Jesus' identity and ability, the proper response is unqualified trust in and allegiance to his authoritative person and mission. He deserves our awe and reverence, but he demands that we follow him wherever he calls, regardless of the cost and of the threat to our status quo.

---

45. For a scholarly perspective on Matthew's view of the conflict, see Evert-Jan Vledder, *Conflict in the Miracle Stories: A Socio-Exegetical Study of Matthew 8 and 9* (JSNTSup 152; Sheffield: Sheffield Academic Press, 1997), 243–53.

**Contemporary Significance**

**FACING FEARS.** I have lived most of my life near the ocean, and I never tire of its beauty and vastness. Every day brings a different wave size, swell direction, and atmospheric marine layer. One day the water sparkles with blue-green iridescence, but the next day dark rolling waves surge with foaming white tips as a storm passes through. The ocean can provide the most relaxing ambiance as the surf rocks gently against the coast. But it can also be a most frightening place when rogue, monster waves threaten the heartiest of souls. One thing every wise person learns early on when adapting to the ocean is that it deserves a healthy respect and an appropriate fear of its awesomeness.

Several years ago my daughters gave me the best-selling book by Sebastian Junger, *The Perfect Storm.* I was gripped by the magnitude of the storm and the immensity of the waves. Most of all, I was gripped by the terror that those caught in the storm experienced. Not only skilled recreation boaters but also well-trained and well-equipped Coast Guard veterans and experienced merchant sailors were traumatized by the storm's immensity—and especially those seasoned, professional fishermen who lost their lives on the commercial fishing boat, the *Andrea Gail.* They had gone out fishing for swordfish in beautiful, calm weather in the fall of 1991, but they fatally experienced the full brunt of nature's most powerful force—the hurricane. Junger describes the intensity of this phenomenon of nature.

> A mature hurricane is by far the most powerful event on earth; the combined nuclear arsenals of the United States and the former Soviet Union don't contain enough energy to keep a hurricane going for one day. A typical hurricane encompasses a million cubic miles of atmosphere and could provide all the electric power needed by the United States for three or four years.[46]

The Sea of Galilee is a microcosm of the ocean, where the disciples of Jesus also face the full force of nature's wrath. For these veteran fishermen to express their fear and plea for help to a *carpenter* indicates that they know he can do what they cannot do for themselves. But what do they think he will do? After all, when he calms the storm they ask, "What kind of man is this?" (8:27). They have faith, because they place as much confidence in Jesus as they think he can accomplish. But it is "little faith," because it is deficient to the task at hand. A more complete knowledge of who he really is and what he is able to accomplish would allow them to trust him fully and without fear.

---

46. Sebastian Junger, *The Perfect Storm: A True Story of Men Against the Sea* (New York: Norton, 1997), 127–29.

**Facing sin's fears.** They are not the only ones who face their fears in these scenes. Disease, spiritual oppression, social ostracism, and, of course, the ravages of nature's storms all produce fear. But the final scene depicts the most fearful of all life's challenges—*sin*. The other fearful challenges can ultimately result in physical death, but sin results in death for eternity. Facing death with the prospect of eternal consequences can evoke the greatest of all fears.

But just as faith in Jesus' ability to care for his disciples in the most fearful situations of life will get them securely through a storm of nature, so faith in Jesus' ability to forgive us our sins will guide us securely through life's storms to our eternal destiny. We know that sin, the greatest threat to our well-being and security, has been vanquished. It's important to keep this perspective, because it allows us to take in stride other fear-inducing challenges we face.

Think of the stark fear that a woman experiences when she finds the lump in her breast, or the terrifying paranoia that a person feels when he discovers his house has been broken into. Consider the horror that a parent experiences when discovering that her child was killed in a car accident, or the gut-wrenching dread that can overcome someone who has just been informed he has been laid off. Or even the anxiety many brides and grooms feel just before the wedding as they consider the prospect of their own inadequacy or the faithlessness of their future spouse.

All of these are very real storms of life. But first things first. Having the right perspective on our eternal destiny enables us to have a different perspective on daily challenges. With our sins forgiven, we know that our own mortality will eventually lead to a secure eternity. The knowledge that our loved one's sins are forgiven will give us a peace beyond comprehension as we turn his or her care over to the Savior. And when we experience suffering in this life, we can rest secure in the knowledge that the Savior who suffered death on the cross for the forgiveness of our sins not only awaits us in our eternal resting place but also travels with us as we endure the travail of this life.

Likewise, if we ignore eternity, we close our eyes to the consequences of the choices we make in this life. Our priorities change when we recognize that there will be an accounting for all that we do now. Rebellion against God and his ways is less prevalent in the person who realizes that there will be no future possibility for rectifying mistakes made today.

Thus, author Gary Thomas drolly advises us that "wise Christians clip obituaries"[47]—not out of a morbid preoccupation with death but out of a

---

47. Gary Thomas, "Wise Christians Clip Obituaries," *Knowing and Doing* (Spring 2002): 12–15, 23.

practical way of keeping a right perspective on life and eternity. We should remember the accomplishments of Christians who have lived life God's way, and we should follow their example. Let us rejoice at the prospect of eternal life so that we do not fear the challenges of earthly storms. The authority of Jesus over all of life's challenges enables us, with an eternal perspective, to trust him fully wherever he may call us to follow him.

# Matthew 9:9–38

❦

AS JESUS WENT on from there, he saw a man named Matthew sitting at the tax collector's booth. "Follow me," he told him, and Matthew got up and followed him.

¹⁰While Jesus was having dinner at Matthew's house, many tax collectors and "sinners" came and ate with him and his disciples. ¹¹When the Pharisees saw this, they asked his disciples, "Why does your teacher eat with tax collectors and 'sinners'?"

¹²On hearing this, Jesus said, "It is not the healthy who need a doctor, but the sick. ¹³But go and learn what this means: 'I desire mercy, not sacrifice.' For I have not come to call the righteous, but sinners."

¹⁴Then John's disciples came and asked him, "How is it that we and the Pharisees fast, but your disciples do not fast?"

¹⁵Jesus answered, "How can the guests of the bridegroom mourn while he is with them? The time will come when the bridegroom will be taken from them; then they will fast.

¹⁶"No one sews a patch of unshrunk cloth on an old garment, for the patch will pull away from the garment, making the tear worse. ¹⁷Neither do men pour new wine into old wineskins. If they do, the skins will burst, the wine will run out and the wineskins will be ruined. No, they pour new wine into new wineskins, and both are preserved."

¹⁸While he was saying this, a ruler came and knelt before him and said, "My daughter has just died. But come and put your hand on her, and she will live." ¹⁹Jesus got up and went with him, and so did his disciples.

²⁰Just then a woman who had been subject to bleeding for twelve years came up behind him and touched the edge of his cloak. ²¹She said to herself, "If I only touch his cloak, I will be healed."

²²Jesus turned and saw her. "Take heart, daughter," he said, "your faith has healed you." And the woman was healed from that moment.

²³When Jesus entered the ruler's house and saw the flute players and the noisy crowd, ²⁴he said, "Go away. The girl is not dead but asleep." But they laughed at him. ²⁵After the

crowd had been put outside, he went in and took the girl by the hand, and she got up. [26]News of this spread through all that region.

[27]As Jesus went on from there, two blind men followed him, calling out, "Have mercy on us, Son of David!"

[28]When he had gone indoors, the blind men came to him, and he asked them, "Do you believe that I am able to do this?"

"Yes, Lord," they replied.

[29]Then he touched their eyes and said, "According to your faith will it be done to you"; [30]and their sight was restored. Jesus warned them sternly, "See that no one knows about this." [31]But they went out and spread the news about him all over that region.

[32]While they were going out, a man who was demon-possessed and could not talk was brought to Jesus. [33]And when the demon was driven out, the man who had been mute spoke. The crowd was amazed and said, "Nothing like this has ever been seen in Israel."

[34]But the Pharisees said, "It is by the prince of demons that he drives out demons."

[35]Jesus went through all the towns and villages, teaching in their synagogues, preaching the good news of the kingdom and healing every disease and sickness. [36]When he saw the crowds, he had compassion on them, because they were harassed and helpless, like sheep without a shepherd. [37]Then he said to his disciples, "The harvest is plentiful but the workers are few. [38]Ask the Lord of the harvest, therefore, to send out workers into his harvest field."

**Original Meaning**

THE MIRACLE STORIES and sayings on discipleship in 8:1–9:8 have emphasized the messianic authority of Jesus' person and mission as he demonstrated the power of the kingdom of heaven. But Jesus' messianic mission has not unfolded as many expected. He did not cater to the religious or social elite; instead, he healed the marginalized, breaking down purity, ethnic, and gender barriers to the kingdom (8:1–17). He disappointed the discipleship expectations of some who wanted to follow him, indicating that his discipleship was not based on economic well-being or cultural expectations (8:18–22). He demonstrated that the authority of his messianic kingdom has not come with military or political might but with a goal to overpower Satan's strongholds within nature, the demonic world, disease, and most importantly, sin.

The unexpectedness of Jesus' mission now begins to elicit opposition. People do not like to have their worldview rattled or challenged. As Jesus calls unexpected and unappreciated types of people to follow him, he encounters resistance from the religious establishment (9:9–17). As he heals surprising types of people, the crowds react with amazement, but the religious leaders hint that his mission is really not from God but from Satan (9:18–35). Yet this does not deter Jesus. In fact, his compassion for the crowds is in stark contrast to the religious leaders, who have made life even more cruel for the people. So Jesus expands his mission to Israel by sending out others with his authoritative message and power (9:36–38).

## Unexpected Discipleship Revealed (9:9–17)

MATTHEW CALLED (9:9). The form of discipleship that Jesus institutes is unexpected and shocking, because he breaks down barriers between social classes, overturns religious conceptions of well-being, and abolishes slavish adherence to religious cultural traditions. It begins with the calling of a local tax collector, Matthew.

Taxes in ancient Rome were collected by the highest bidders for a collection contract, but in Palestine tax collectors were employed as representatives of the Roman governing authorities, collecting the prescribed duties and generally seeing to public order. They usually came from the native population, so that they knew the local people and local customs. They were required to collect a certain amount of tax money for the Roman authorities, and whatever extra they collected constituted their own commission. A tendency to excessive extortion made them despised and hated by their own people (cf. Luke 19:8), and they became proverbial of a person with a self-seeking outlook (Matt. 5:46).

Matthew's tax booth probably stood at some place where the Via Maris passed close by the lakeshore on the outskirts of Capernaum.[1] He may have collected tolls from the commercial traffic traveling through this area or taxes for the fish caught on the Sea of Galilee, for both of which Herod Antipas was responsible. The expected tax revenue was a heavy toll to extract from the people of Galilee, who already had a hard life. So Matthew is likely not well respected in the region. In fact, the population probably considers him a traitor, selling out his own people to Roman occupation and rule.[2]

Then Jesus shows up. "'Follow me,' he told him, and Matthew got up and

---

1. Pixner, *With Jesus Through Galilee*, 35.
2. Keener, *A Commentary on the Gospel of Matthew* (1999), 291–93.

followed him." It is possible that this a dramatic first encounter between Jesus and Matthew and that the forcefulness of Jesus' authoritative person and call demands immediate obedience.[3] But more likely this is the culmination of a prior relationship, similar to the call of the two sets of brothers—Peter and Andrew, James and John (see comments on 4:18–22).[4] The wording of Matthew's call is somewhat different from that used of the four,[5] but it carries the same connotation, and the wording used to describe his response is identical—he "followed him."

This leads us to assume that Matthew has probably been under the influence of Jesus for some time. The public healings, exorcisms, preaching, and teaching have been going on in Galilee and are primarily taking place in the Capernaum region. Matthew has likely witnessed them and is now ready to join Jesus. If the prior call of the brothers extends the pattern further, it may mean also that this is not as much of a conversion story as it is a call to join the four in their training to become fishers of men as members of the twelve apostles. The lists of the Twelve each place Matthew in the second group of four. In its list, this Gospel calls him "Matthew the tax collector" (10:3).

For Jesus, Matthew is a notorious convert. For Matthew, discipleship has an immediate cost, for collecting taxes not only filled the coffers of the governor but also meant a lucrative income for the tax collector (cf. Zacchaeus, Luke 19:1–10). A fisherman could always go back to fishing, but it is less likely that a tax collector could return to the booth. But our author doesn't expand on what that sacrifice entails, perhaps a subtle indication of the identity of the humble Matthew as author of this first Gospel.

In recounting the call of the tax collector, this Gospel refers to him as "Matthew" (9:9), while Mark refers to him as "Levi son of Alphaeus" (Mark 2:14) and Luke simply as "Levi" (Luke 5:27). Some scholars have attempted to show that Levi was not one of the Twelve and therefore different from Matthew, but this is unwarranted speculation, since the circumstances of the calling is the same in Matthew and Mark/Luke.[6]

Much speculation surrounds the reason for the name variation, but most scholars suggest that this tax collector has two names, Matthew and Levi. Some speculate that "Levi" is his Jewish birth name and "Matthew" a name given to him after conversion, similar to Saul/Paul.[7] Others suggest that

---

3. Thomas Long, *Matthew* (Westminster Bible Companion; Louisville: Westminster John Knox, 1997), 103–4.

4. McKnight, *Turning to Jesus*, 40–43.

5. "Follow me" versus "Come after me."

6. For the evidence equating Matthew and Levi as one person, see France, *Matthew: Evangelist and Teacher*, 66–70.

7. Hagner, *Matthew*, 1:237–38.

"Matthew Levi" is a double name given to him from birth, since there is little evidence for "Matthew" being a Christian name.[8] The name "Levi" may indicate he is from the tribe of Levi and therefore familiar with Levitical practices.[9] Mark refers to him as "son of Alphaeus," which some have understood to mean that he is the brother of "James son of Alphaeus" (cf. Mark 3:18). But since the other pairs of brothers are specified to be brothers and are linked as such, it is unlikely that Matthew-Levi and James are brothers.

Little else is known of Matthew-Levi except for the widely attested tradition from the second century on that he wrote the Gospel that now bears his name. As a tax collector he would have been trained in secular scribal techniques, and as a Galilean Jewish Christian he would have been able to interpret the life of Jesus from the perspective of the Old Testament expectations.[10] Eusebius said that Matthew first preached to "Hebrews" and then to "others," including places such as Persia, Parthia, and Syria.[11] The traditions are mixed regarding Matthew's death, with some saying that he died a martyr's death and others that he died a natural death.[12]

**Tax collectors and sinners (9:10–13).** Matthew immediately follows Jesus and arranges a banquet for him and his other disciples at his own home (cf. Luke 5:29–30). Since tax collectors were generally better off financially and yet despised by the local populace because of their extortion practices, Matthew's calling and response are completely out of the ordinary and require nothing short of a miraculous turnaround in his life. To the banquet are invited "many tax collectors and 'sinners,'" most likely Matthew's closest companions up to this point.

Table fellowship was an important social and religious convention among many groups in the ancient world. Boundaries were established that designated who were included and excluded from a meal, and that also served to delineate religious and ethical obligations toward the participants. Within Judaism the Therapeutae, Essenes, and Pharisees were especially known for the role that table fellowship played in defining their group identities.[13] The shared meal was a formal occasion when group members consumed food made sacred through various ritual practices such as ceremonial washings or tithing. Participants were often marked out by a prior required initiation, such as circumcision or immersion.[14]

---

8. Carson, "Matthew," 224.

9. Albright and Mann, *Matthew*, clxxvii–clxxviii, clxxxiii–clxxxiv.

10. Cf. France, *Matthew: Evangelist and Teacher*, 70–74; Gundry, *Matthew*, 609–22.

11. Eusebius, *History* 3.24.6.

12. Wilkins, *Following the Master*, 161–62.

13. See, e.g., Philo, *Vita. Cont.* 40–89; 1Qsa 2.

14. Dennis E. Smith, "Table Fellowship," *ABD*, 6:302–4; Neusner and Green, "Table Fellowship," *DJBP*, 613.

The derision that many felt generally for tax collectors was aggravated because they were regarded as ceremonially unclean through their continual contact with Gentiles and because they worked on the Sabbath.[15] Therefore, the Pharisees are aghast that Jesus is eating with them and with "sinners," so they ask, "Why does your teacher eat with tax collectors and 'sinners'?"

The term "sinner" (*hamartōlos*) is often used by the Pharisees to point to an identifiable segment of the people opposed to God's will as reflected in their understanding of obedience to the law and their interpretations (e.g., Luke 7:36–50; cf. Matt. 26:45).[16] These are people who willfully ignore rightful boundaries of appropriate Jewish behavior. Matthew's cohorts are not only traitorous tax collectors but also other Jews who live outside of the law. In the minds of the Pharisees, for Jesus to share a meal with these types of persons indicates that he includes them within his own fellowship; it also suggests to them that he condones their behavior.[17]

Jesus must now clarify who he is and what his mission entails by using the metaphor of a doctor: "On hearing this, Jesus said, 'It is not the healthy who need a doctor, but the sick.'" One of the most distinctive features of Jesus' message and ministry is the promise of salvation to "sinners."[18] But in an incisive play on words, Jesus shows the Pharisees that he has a different view of what it means to be a sinner than they do. To the Pharisees, a sinner is a person who has violated the law according to their interpretations. But to Jesus, a sinner is any person who remains opposed to God's will. The Pharisees consider themselves to be righteously healthy before God because they define righteousness by their observance of the law—their "sacrifice." But they are blind to their real sinfulness before God.

Therefore Jesus continues: "But go and learn what this means: 'I desire mercy, not sacrifice.' For I have not come to call the righteous, but sinners." The motley crew assembled with Jesus cannot avoid their own sinfulness. Matthew has been one of them, but he has experienced Jesus' merciful call to salvation, so now he brings his sinful companions to Jesus. He wants his friends to find the same healing for their souls. It is to these that Jesus has come[19] to bring his message of mercy. His offer of salvation to sinners apart from factional observances threatens the way of life of the Pharisees, yet is at the heart of the gospel Jesus announces.[20]

---

15. J. H. Harrop, "Tax Collector," *IBD*, 3:1520–21.

16. For background to the various uses of "sinner" in the Gospels, see Michael J. Wilkins, "Sinner," *DJG*, 757–60; Keener, *A Commentary on the Gospel of Matthew* (1999), 294–96.

17. I. Howard Marshall, "'Sins' and 'Sin'," *BibSac* 159 (January–March 2002): 3–20.

18. E. P. Sanders, *Jesus and Judaism* (Philadelphia: Fortress, 1985), 174.

19. See Warren Carter, "Jesus' 'I have come' Statements in Matthew's Gospel," *CBQ* 60 (1998): 44–62.

20. Wilkins, "Sinner," *DJG*, 760.

The calling of Matthew and the following feast shows us Jesus' great mercy. He reaches out to blatant sinners and social outcasts, and he even takes one of them and calls him to be an apostle, one of the foundational leaders of the church to come (10:1–4; Acts 1:13). The Pharisees are so engrossed with their religious self-righteousness that they cannot see their own hard-hearted sinfulness. Jesus' merciful outreach demonstrates for us our own calling, to seek out those who are sinfully sick and to invite them to experience healing of their souls and come into the fellowship of our discipleship to Jesus.

**Discipleship and religious traditions (9:14–17).** Jesus' banquet with tax collectors and sinners is offensive to the Pharisees, but it also is offensive to the disciples of Jesus' forerunner, John the Baptist. They come to Jesus and ask: "How is it that we and the Pharisees fast, but your disciples do not fast?" These people gathered around John as the prophet who would usher in the messianic age. They assisted him in baptizing those who came to him and engaged in strict religious practices such as fasting and prayer (Luke 5:33; 11:1). The "disciples of the Pharisees" (see Mark 2:18; cf. Matt. 22:16) are most likely those in training to become full initiates to their brotherhood. They have been immersed in the oral law and rigorous practice of their traditions.

Fasting was only prescribed in the Old Testament for the Day of Atonement (cf. Lev. 16:29, 31; 23:27, 32), though other occasions for voluntary fasting arose (for more on fasting see comments on Matt. 6:16–18). John's disciples do not understand why Jesus' disciples do not regularly fast as a sign of repentance or as an indication of their spiritual discipline. In his response, Jesus alludes to himself as the "bridegroom," who in the Old Testament is Yahweh (cf. Isa. 62:5; Hos. 2:19–20): "How can the guests of the bridegroom mourn while he is with them?" The arrival of the kingdom of heaven has brought to fulfillment the promises of Israel, which is cause for a time of rejoicing, such as what would be experienced during marriage ceremonies (cf. Matt. 25:12–13). It is not an appropriate time to fast. However, fasting will be appropriate when Jesus is "taken away," perhaps suggesting violence to the suffering Servant (Isa. 53:8b; Matt. 8:17) that Jesus will experience at the crucifixion.[21]

Jesus' response is an important guideline for a proper perspective on spiritual growth and traditional practices. Spiritual growth is not automatically assured through ritual observance of certain spiritual disciplines. In the SM, Jesus said that disciplines such as fasting, prayer, or giving to the needy are worthless unless they express a heart that humbly desires to grow into the Father's likeness (5:48–6:18). Moreover, such practices must be carried out

---

21. France, *Matthew: Evangelist and Teacher,* 169.

appropriately, not legalistically. Traditions are what humans have designed to apply biblical principles to everyday life, but they are not commands from God. They can be helpful if practiced appropriately, but they can be stifling if they become more important than scriptural revelation itself.

Jesus illustrates these perspectives on spiritual growth and traditional practices by using two examples from everyday life, which today have become proverbial. He has not come simply to shore up the traditional practices of the Jews. Rather, he has come to offer an entirely new approach to God. Jesus' kingdom life is an entirely new garment and entirely new wine, which must have appropriate traditional practices.

(1) Jesus uses an example from clothing. "No one sews a patch of unshrunk cloth on an old garment." If a person puts an unshrunk new patch on an old, washed, shrunk garment, the new patch will shrink when washed and will tear away from the old cloth, leaving a larger hole. Jesus has not come just to patch up the old religious traditions; rather, he offers a new garment. He does not specify the garment, but if his key statement about entrance to the kingdom in 5:20 is linked with the required wedding garment in the parable of the wedding feast (22:11–13), we can conclude that Jesus is pointing to the righteousness of the kingdom of heaven. Jesus has not come to patch up the traditional acts of righteousness within religious Judaism; he offers real growth in true righteousness through discipleship in the kingdom of heaven.

(2) Next Jesus uses an example from common wineskins: "Neither do men pour new wine into old wineskins." Wineskins were made from tanned and sometimes skinned animal hides. Over time they stretched to their limit and eventually became brittle. New wine that is still fermenting expands and will cause old skins to burst if new wine is poured into them. The new wine and old skins will both be lost. New wine requires new wineskins. In other words, Jesus has not come to fill the old Jewish system of traditions with new life. They are inadequate to the new life of the kingdom. Rather, new forms are needed for his kingdom, and new practices must accommodate the new life of discipleship to Jesus. This does not supercede or abolish the Old Testament, which Jesus has come to fulfill (5:17); instead, it indicates that discipleship to Jesus supercedes rigid legalistic adherence to traditional practices of Judaism.

## Unexpected Miracles Demonstrate Extraordinary Compassion (9:18–34)

MATTHEW'S COLLECTION OF miracle stories and discipleship sayings in chapters 8–9 authenticates Jesus' authority as the Messiah at work. But the unexpected nature of his messianic mission continues to astound the crowds (e.g., 7:28; 8:8; 9:33) and provoke opposition from the religious establishment

(9:3–4, 11, 14). In the first cycle of three miracles Jesus demonstrated that he has not come to cater to the religious or social elite but instead to heal the marginalized (see comments on 8:1–17). In the second cycle of three miracles he showed that the authority of the messianic kingdom is not military or political might but instead spiritual might to overpower Satan's strongholds in nature, the demonic world, and disease/sin (see comments on 8:23–9:8). In this third and final cycle of three miracle stories, Jesus demonstrates extraordinary compassion as he performs unexpected miracles, so that the dead have life (9:18–26), the blind have sight (9:27–31), and the mute have voice (9:32–34).

The response of the crowds becomes increasingly vocal as Jesus' fame spreads throughout the region (9:31), which contributes to further hostility in the religious leaders as they connect Jesus' miraculous power with the prince of demons (9:34). Nevertheless, Jesus will model for his disciples how compassion for the harassed and helpless should compel them to minister to the crowds with the gospel and power of the kingdom of heaven (9:35–38).

**The dead have life (9:18–26).** The first miracle story of this cycle includes a healing of a hemorrhaging woman but climaxes with the raising of a ruler's daughter (9:18–25). It results in a positive response throughout the region (9:26).

After the encounters with the religious leaders over Jesus' practices, one of the leaders of the Jewish community comes forward with a pressing need. Matthew's reference to him as a "ruler" (*archon*), which denotes either a community leader or the head of a synagogue board (Mark 5:22 and Luke 8:41 specify the latter). Perhaps in a smaller community this man (named Jairus in Mark and Luke) functions as both a community and a synagogue leader.[22] By kneeling before Jesus he indicates the extreme honor he gives to him, because kneeling is the appropriate position one takes before God (e.g., Gen. 22:5; Ex. 4:31; Deut. 26:10; Ps. 5:7) or a king or superior (e.g., 1 Sam. 24:9; 1 Kings 1:16, 23).

The ruler's request is urgent: "My daughter has just died. But come and put your hand on her, and she will live." The ruler has the same confident trust in Jesus' ability to heal as did the leper (8:2–4), the centurion (8:5–13), and the paralytic and his friends (9:2–7), but his trust is profound enough to believe that Jesus can raise his daughter from the dead. Jesus has not yet raised anyone from the dead, but Old Testament emissaries of God like Elijah (1 Kings 17:17–24) and Elisha (2 Kings 4:32–37) were known to have done so. Matthew again condenses the narrative. In his account the daughter is already dead (9:18), while in Mark 5:23 and Luke 8:42 she is at the point

---

22. Levine, *The Ancient Synagogue*, 402–3.

of death. Jesus' compassion is immediate, because he "got up and went with him, and so did his disciples."

Jesus' emergency trip to Jairus's home is interrupted briefly by another dire need—"a woman who had been subject to bleeding for twelve years." Most likely this woman's condition is menorrhagia, a disease in which the menstrual flow is abnormally prolonged, which usually produces anemia as well.[23] This condition is all the more difficult because she would be considered ritually unclean and excluded from normal social and religious relations, since others making contact with her would also become unclean (Lev. 15:25–30).

She has suffered with her condition for twelve years and has sought help from all known medical care (cf. Mark 5:26; Luke 8:43). Nothing has brought healing, so she approaches Jesus and touches "the edge [*kraspedon*] of his cloak." The term *kraspedon* is rendered "tassel" in 23:5, which may be the meaning here as well. On the four corners of a garment worn by men were "tassels" attached with a blue cord, conforming to Numbers 15:37–42 and Deuteronomy 22:12. These tassels reminded the wearer to obey God's commands and to be holy to God.

Like Jairus and others who have heard of Jesus' healing powers, this woman has unwavering trust in his ability to heal her: "She said to herself, 'If I only touch his cloak, I will be healed.'" Matthew once more has an abbreviated account. In Mark's and Luke's account her healing causes Jesus to recognize that power has gone out from him and he stops to investigate who has touched him (Mark 5:29–30; Luke 8:44–45). Matthew simply records Jesus' final statement: "Take heart, daughter . . . your faith has healed you."

Jesus' expression "Take heart, daughter" again underscores his compassion, while his declaration "your faith has healed you" points to the source of healing. Faith itself does not heal; God does. The woman has faith in Jesus' ability to heal her, which has brought her into this precarious public arena to seek out his healing. The centurion believed that Jesus could heal his servant without being present, and this woman believes that any kind of contact with Jesus, even without him knowing it, will bring healing. So her faith brings her to the place where God can heal her. By making her healing pubic with his announcement, Jesus removes the public stigma of her physical condition and thus facilitates her reentry into normal social and religious life

But Jesus also wants her and any others observing, such as his disciples, to be clear that it is not a magical coat that has healed her; it is God. The flow of healing power comes through the sovereignty of God and the exercise of her faith. Healing power does not just flow continually from Jesus; this is

---

23. D. H. Trapnell, "Health, Disease and Healing," *IBD*, 2:619.

God's activity. Matthew may indicate that an even more profound event has transpired in this woman's life because both Jesus' statement ("has healed)" and Matthew's narrative ("was healed") use the verb *sozo*, which normally is used in the sense of "saved." It may well be that her act of faith in coming to Jesus for h7ealing is also the moment in which she exercises faith in Jesus as the One who can save her from her sins (cf. 1:21).

Jesus now continues on to Jairus's home, where he encounters a typical Jewish mourning scene—"flute players and the noisy crowd." In the family of a prominent person like the ruler, many professional mourners would have joined the family and friends in expressing their grief. Jesus, however, indicates that the death of the little girl is merely "sleep," at which the mourners laugh. So he clears the house of the skeptics. With the same compassionate touch that healed Peter's mother-in-law (8:15), Jesus takes the girl by the hand and brings her out of her sleep of death. This scene confirms for all believers that death is merely a state of sleep of one's body while awaiting the final resurrection (1 Cor. 11:30; 15:20–23, 51–55; 1 Thess. 4:13–18).

This first account of raising someone from the dead fuels the furor about Jesus as "news of this spread through all that region." Jesus will later emphasize to John that Baptist that the dead being raised is another sign that he is the Messiah (11:2–5).

**The blind have sight (9:27–31).** The second miracle story records the healing of two blind men. Blindness was one of the grimmest maladies in the ancient world and was considered to be only a little less serious than being dead.[24] Nonetheless, it was quite common. Here the two blind men "follow" (*akoloutheo*) Jesus. This verb sometimes simply indicates spatial movement (e.g., 4:25), but it can also indicate the following of discipleship to Jesus (4:20, 22; 9:9). The context in each case determines the usage.[25] The blind men's understanding of Jesus' true identity may indicate the latter. They call out, "Have mercy on us, Son of David!" They understand Jesus to be the "Son of David," the first time Jesus is called by this title (cf. 1:1).

This expression refers to the promise of the messianic deliverer from the line of David whose kingdom will have no end (2 Sam. 7:12–16; cf. *Pss. Sol.* 17:23). The messianic age promised to bring healing to the blind (Isa. 29:18; 35:5; 42:7), which Jesus told John the Baptist was one of the signs that he indeed was the expected Coming One (Matt. 11:2–6). The Old Testament records no healing of blindness,[26] and none of Jesus' followers is ever recorded

---

24. Twelftree, *Jesus the Miracle Worker*, 83–84 (see also *b. Ned.* 64b).

25. Wilkins, *Discipleship in the Ancient World and Matthew's Gospel*, 137–41.

26. In the Apocrypha, Tobit is cured of blindness with the gall of a fish by his son Tobias (Tobit 11:7–15).

to have given sight to the blind.[27] But Jesus' healing of the blind is one of his most frequent miracles (9:27–31; 12:22–23; 15:30–31; 20:30–34; 21:14–15). These men have profoundly connected Jesus with the prophecies of the Son of David who will heal blindness (cf. 12:22–23; 21:14–15), and they ask for that gift of messianic mercy.

They follow Jesus indoors, where Jesus elicits from them a statement of their faith: "Do you believe that I am able to do this?" They reply, "Yes, Lord." Like each of those in the preceding healing scenes, they trust in Jesus' ability to heal them. Linked with their affirmation that Jesus is the "Son of David," calling him "Lord" (*kyrios*) may indicate that they see in Jesus more than any mere prophet. Once again (cf. 8:15; 9:25) Jesus' compassionate touch accompanies his word of command to bring healing: "Then he touched their eyes and said, 'According to your faith will it be done to you.'" As he indicated to the hemorrhaging woman (9:22), Jesus emphasizes to the blind men that their faith in his ability and desire to heal them has prompted them to come to where they can receive his miraculous gift.

As their sight is restored, Jesus warns them, "See that no one knows about this." The demand for secrecy is a regular aspect of Jesus' ministry (see comments on 8:4; cf. 12:16; 16:20; 17:9) and may be a reason why he waits to heal them until they are indoors. He carefully avoids stirring up in the crowds a misunderstanding of his messianic identity. Although miracles will attest the authenticity of his gospel message about the arrival of the kingdom of heaven, Jesus does not want crowds to clamor for the miracles alone or to think of him simply as a messianic wonder-worker; he is the Savior, who has come to bring salvation from sin.

At the same time, the public celebration of Jesus' miracle-working ministry soon leads to further opposition from the religious leaders (cf. 9:34). But the blind men's enthusiasm over their healing cannot restrain them, because contrary to Jesus' warning, "they went out and spread the news about him all over that region." Obedience to Jesus is not yet an established characteristic of their faith in him. Little do they know that their celebration of healing will contribute to even more opposition to Jesus being aroused in the religious leaders.

**The mute have voice (9:32–34).** The final miracle in this collection of miracle stories involves both healing and exorcism. "While they were going out, a man who was demon-possessed and could not talk was brought to Jesus." Demon-possession takes a variety of external forms. In the case of

---

27. The "scales" that fell from Saul's eyes when Ananias laid hands on him could be an exception, although this seems different, because Ananias did not pray for healing but rather arrived as the conduit for the giving of the Holy Spirit (Acts 9:17–19).

the two demoniacs in the area of the Gadarenes, the manifestation produced violent behavior that threatened people (8:28). Here the phenomenon in some way prohibits the man from speaking (see also 12:22). The exorcism of the demon and the concurrent healing of muteness is a most powerful demonstration that the kingdom of heaven has finally arrived.

At the conclusion of the miracle stories the crowd is amazed and exclaim, "Nothing like this has ever been seen in Israel." Jesus is Israel's Messiah, but a Messiah quite unlike what many were expecting. He did not come with militaristic power or regal fanfare. Rather, he came with a powerful message and a unique ministry that amazed the crowds (cf. 7:28–29).

But if the uniqueness of the miracles is a sign to the crowds of God's activity in Jesus' ministry, it also confirms to the religious establishment that God does not work in this way. And if God is not the source of Jesus' miraculous exorcism powers, it must be "by the prince of demons that he drives out demons" (9:34; cf. 9:3).[28] Without eyes of faith the Pharisees cannot see beyond their parochial experience that God is doing something unique in Israel in the word and work of Jesus. So they gather their opposition to Jesus, both protecting their religious domain and thinking they are protecting the people from Jesus. This is an ominous tone, which tragically sets a trajectory for the cross that will inevitably come.

## The Messiah at Work Enlists Workers (9:35–38)

MATTHEW CONCLUDES HIS collection of miracle stories and discipleship sayings with the same narrative expression that he used to mark the beginning of Jesus' ministry in Galilee: "Jesus went through all the towns and villages, teaching in their synagogues, preaching the good news of the kingdom and healing every disease and sickness" (9:35; cf. 4:23). These verses form an inclusio, creating a "bookends" effect that sets off the material in the chapters between them. In chapters 5–7 Jesus is the authoritative Messiah in word in the Sermon on the Mount, and in chapters 8–9 he is the Messiah at work in the miracle stories.

The crowds continue to be the object of Jesus' ministry, and the motivating force is his compassion. "When he saw the crowds, he had compassion on them." The verb "have compassion" is *splanchnizomai* ("to be moved in the inward parts"), which usually indicates deep feelings in the heart and affections. Elsewhere this word describes Jesus' motivation to heal and feed the crowd (14:14; 15:32) and heal the blind (20:34; cf. 18:27).[29]

---

28. They reiterate that charge in 12:24, where they identify the prince of demons as Beelzebul and where Jesus responds to that charge.

29. BDAG, 938.

In this instance, the need Jesus sees is that the crowds are "harassed and help-less, like sheep without a shepherd." The metaphor of sheep and shepherd was well known in Israel's history, ranging from the sacrificial lamb of the Day of Atonement and the Passover (Ex. 12:1–4; 29:35–42) to the relationship that God as shepherd has with Israel his sheep (Isa. 40:10–11) and the psalmist's utter dependence on God as his shepherd (Ps. 23). The Davidic Messiah will establish the everlasting covenant with Israel as a shepherd (Ezek. 37:24).

The leaders in Israel's history had also been likened to shepherds. Joshua was appointed leader after Moses, so that "the LORD's people will not be like sheep without a shepherd" (Num. 27:17).[30] But that is what Israel is like in Jesus' day. The leaders have not fulfilled their responsibility to guide and protect the people, and therefore the people are "harassed" and "helpless." These crowds are experiencing distressing difficulties and are unable to care for themselves. The job of the shepherd is to make sure that the sheep are led peacefully beside still waters and that they lack for nothing, but these lead-ers are harassing the helpless crowds. They are suffering under the oppres-sion of the occupying Roman forces, plus they have all of the daily concerns, heartbreaks, and difficulties of life beating down on them.

In the preceding miracle stories (chs. 8–9), Jesus has healed the diseased and sick, raised the dead, calmed the stormy sea, and exorcised demons. Those needs are hugely important, but woven throughout the scenes is Jesus' recognition of an underlying destitution that is far worse. In a word, the problem is "sin." Jesus is the promised Suffering Servant, who will take on him-self not only the infirmities of his people but also their sins (8:17; cf. Isa. 53:4–5). The deeper illness of the paralytic and the spiritual sickness of tax collectors and Pharisees alike is their sin (9:2, 13). So the real downfall of the leaders of Israel is that they are not giving proper care to the spiritual needs of the people. Jesus sees deeply into the need of the crowds and has been bringing healing to both body and soul.

The metaphor changes from sheep that are harassed and helpless to a bountiful harvest in need of harvesters (9:37–38). Although the metaphor changes, the meaning remains the same. The "harvest" is the crowds within Israel who have such tremendous needs, as the following mission discourse makes clear (see esp. 10:5–23). The theme of harvest was common in Judaism. A rabbi from around A.D. 130 said, "The day is short and the task is great and the labourers are idle and the wage is abundant and the master of the house is urgent" (*m. ʾAbot* 2.15). Even as Jesus' mission is to bring the gospel of the kingdom to the needy, he wants his disciples to join him, because "the harvest is plentiful but the workers are few."

---

30. "Sheep, Shepherd," *DBI*, 782–85.

While Matthew normally emphasizes a small group of disciples around Jesus, it need not be restricted to the Twelve here. The disciples are all those who have responded to his summons to the kingdom of heaven. Jesus will send out the Twelve on a special mission within Israel (10:1–15), but as long as there are needy crowds, he calls disciples throughout the ages to become harvest workers (10:16–23). Jesus will later expand on this harvest metaphor and use it to denote a time of judgment (13:30, 39; cf. Isa. 17:11; Joel 3:13; Rev. 14:14–20).

The disciples are to "ask the Lord of the harvest ... to send out workers into his harvest field." The "Lord of the harvest" is God, who will respond to their prayer for harvest workers. But dramatically it is Jesus who steps forward in answer to their prayers to commission the Twelve to go out and minister. The harvest mission includes the immediate assignment of the Twelve to take the gospel message only to Israel (10:1–15), but also the long-range mission of the disciples throughout the world until the Son of Man returns (10:16–23).

CHRISTOLOGY AND DISCIPLESHIP are two of the most important themes of Matthew's Gospel. The alternating miracle and teaching scenes throughout chapters 8 and 9 have accentuated those themes. They draw us into the heart of Jesus' ministry by revealing his identity and mission, which in turn lead us to understand much more clearly the implications for our discipleship to him. Underlying the phenomenal external displays of power are issues that reveal his kingdom mission. Jesus' miracle-working ministry astounds the crowds and threatens the religious establishment, but those with eyes of faith see that the miraculous power has implications for daily discipleship.

**Healing for sinners.** From the beginning of Jesus' ministry, the arrival of the kingdom indicates that the greatest miracle is often the one least noticed. It is the miracle of forgiveness. When Jesus called Matthew, one of the notorious tax collectors, he made a momentous announcement of his kingdom mission—to bring healing to a sin-sick world. His compassion extends to unexpected individuals that were often despised or neglected by the religious elite.

Sin is not cured by religion. In the encounter of Jesus with the Pharisees, who question his practice of dining with the dregs of society, we see that sin is an inner spiritual sickness that must be honestly acknowledged to be incurable by one's own attempts at religious righteousness. Sin is cured only by the Great Physician. Moreover, sin is the real culprit of humanity's distress. The physical suffering of the hemorrhaging woman and the blind men was real, and Jesus attended to their needs, but in pointing to their faith in him, he indicates that there are deeper spiritual issues at stake. The crowds seem to want healing without attending to their deeper needs of salvation from sin. And to compound the problem, the crowds are harassed and helpless by religious leaders, who were oppressing them with religious activity that masked the sin problem.

The concerns that we often think are our greatest needs may not be. As we put ourselves into God's hands, he understands our lives better than we do, and at times he is more concerned with the development of our hearts than he is with the comfort of our lives. There is no question that God enjoys giving good gifts to his children (7:11) and has compassion on our suffering (9:18–34). But sometimes what we think is the greatest gift does not always address the deepest needs in our lives. Our hearts have been tainted severely by the effects of sin, and sin hits the center of our affections and our ability to have a relationship with God. God is always concerned with what is best for us, but what is best may not always be what we think or pursue for our own well-being. The healing of physical suffering is only cosmetic if a sinful heart is not given into the care of the Great Physician.

**Spiritual warfare.** The second issue that underlies Jesus' supernatural displays of power is that they are indicators of the cosmic spiritual warfare in which he is engaged. The people of Israel heard for centuries that God was in control and that he would someday send a Messiah to deliver them from evil, hatred, and hurts. But they are now more oppressed than ever. Where is God's promise of relief? Where is God?

Into that hurt and despair Jesus comes with his authority over evil spirits, with his message, and with his ministry of healing. His casting out of evil spirits and healing of disease and sickness are external validation of the reality of the presence of the kingdom of heaven, and people should now turn to Jesus as the messianic deliverer. His authoritative mission is an invasion of Satan's realm. No longer is Satan the uncontested ruler of this world. He has met his match, and more, in the arrival of Jesus. And Satan's evil forces will continue to be confronted, as Jesus' emissaries go out with his authority to bring release to the harassed and helpless.

But spiritual warfare is deceptive. It does not necessarily make people more "religious." Because Jesus does not conform to the religious expectations of the Pharisees and does not lead those being exorcised into the religious life advocated by the Pharisees, he is considered to be a demonic fraud (9:34). Jesus' spiritual liberation intends to lead people into the righteousness of kingdom life that he has promoted in the SM, not the expectations of the religious establishment. The Pharisees are so consumed with scrupulous adherence to external acts of righteousness such as table fellowship and fasting that they are unaware of the spiritual warfare battling for their own hearts.

**Contemporary Significance**

WHEN I WAS a boy growing up in the 1950s, there were certain words or expressions that evoked powerful images. One was "Pearl Harbor," which immediately brought to mind not only the surprise attack on the U.S. naval force in Hawaii but also symbolized the U.S. entrance into four years of worldwide bloody warfare. Another expression was "cold war," which elicited the near hysterical fear of nuclear annihilation as well as the insidious threat of worldwide communism. As the years went by, these expressions lost their emotional impact, either because the memories had faded or the threat had gone away.

But in the last few years other terms have taken on powerful significance. "Columbine" is a name that evokes powerful images, not of the flower by that name but of the horror of mass, cold-blooded murder carried out by two young high school students that many of us watched unfold on live television. "9/11" is a number that used to bring to mind the emergency telephone number but now evokes the horror of mass, cold-blooded murder carried out by terrorists who flew passenger airplanes into occupied buildings, also scenes that many of us watched unfold on live television. Both of these new expressions have brought a tragic awareness that something is terribly wrong, that there is real evil in this world. For all of our modern advancement technologically, it seems only to have given opportunity for more widespread evil and terror.

Ancient Israel also had terms with evocative images. "Egypt" called to mind images of slavery and national suffering. "Nebuchadnezzar" evoked painful memories of later national suffering in the Babylonian deportation and the destruction of the holy temple in Jerusalem. On an individual level, expressions like "Unclean!" evoked the horror of disease for which there was no physical cure and which meant the emotional dreadfulness of ceremonial and social isolation.

But Israel also had other expressions that brought hope. "Passover" brought to mind the annual ceremony that celebrated Israel's deliverance by God from Egyptian slavery. "Day of the Lord" was an expression that offered hope that Israel's enemies would one day be vanquished and Israel would be reestablished in Jerusalem (Joel 1:15; 2:1, 11, 31; 3:14—21). "Son of David" expressed hope of the Anointed One of the line of David who would usher in the messianic age that promised healing and cleansing (2 Sam. 7:11—16; Isa. 35:1—10; 42:1—7). These powerfully evocative expressions of hope also have significance for us as we look at this passage.

**Evil is real.** Columbine and 9/11 are painful reminders that evil is real. This world lies in the grip of sin, and the evil one has not yet been fully vanquished. Death too is a real phenomenon that stares each of us in the face. Whether one ever sees or experiences personally an encounter with a demon (and I don't suggest that you go looking for them!), this world is a spiritual battleground.

But there is evil of less dramatic sorts as well. In our passage, there was the evil of religious elitism that the Pharisees demonstrated toward the tax collectors and sinners (9:10–13). There was the evil of disease that kept a woman locked up in physical suffering and social and religious impurity (9:20). There was the evil of physical handicaps like blindness and of demon possession that locked a man up in his muteness (9:27, 32). There was the evil of oppression of common people from military and religous powers (9:36). And with ironic tragedy, there was the evil of religious opposition to God's liberating plan of deliverance (9:34).

These are scenes of evil that you and I see on a daily basis. Whether it is going through suffering with loved ones who are experiencing disease and death, watching the tragedy of an unwitting young idealist entrapped by a religious cult, or observing the incredible cruelty of city gangs, evil is real in this world. We must live with that as a reality. In spite of the blind confidence of some political and religious optimists, the world is not getting better spiritually, ethically, or morally through modern progress.

But into these overwhelming scenes of evil, Jesus' messianic mission comes to offer hope. The liberation from slavery to sin that the Passover symbolized for Israel is now fully realized in Jesus as "the Lamb of God, who takes away the sin of the world" (John 1:29), and as the Great Physician who has "not come to call the righteous, but sinners" (Matt. 9:13). He healed the sick, exorcised the demons, and confronted religious hypocrisy in the first century, and he brings the same salvation to our sin-sick world. Today that includes sinners like you, me, and the raucous neighbor down the block. He has come with mercy and grace to save us from our own helpless state.

Only a couple of days after the Columbine tragedy, I was in the grocery store where my eye was caught by the bold letters on the cover of a national magazine. "MY GOD, MY GOD!" with pictures below of the parents of the high school kids. Those words were both an exclamation of horror and a cry for help from the people of Littleton, Colorado. They are no different than the people of our communities who need to know and hear from us that only in Jesus will we find deliverance from the evil.

**Opposition will come.** It's a well-known phenomenon of Christian experience that when we are doing a good work for the Lord, we can expect opposition. But it's most heartbreaking when we find that the opposition comes from within. Israel was often Israel's worst enemy. The nation's history was checkered by a number of occasions when the people suffered oppression, usually because of their own penchant for engaging in adulterous relationships with the idols of surrounding nations (e.g., Jer. 3:6–10). Nebuchadnezzar's invasion and destruction of Jerusalem were a painful judgment by God for Israel's own faithlessness (cf. Jer. 21–22).

As Jesus came with his plan of deliverance, he almost immediately encountered opposition, but the heartbreak is that it came primarily from his own people, especially the religious leaders of Israel. They objected to his associations with sinful people as he reached out with his call to kingdom repentance (9:11). They objected to his disciples' supposed lack of commitment to spiritual disciplines (9:14). They objected to Jesus' form of spiritual liberation, because it did not fit their religious parochialism (9:34). These religious leaders, especially the Pharisees, had elevated their traditions to the point where they could not hear or see the truth of Jesus' gospel message. Their human traditions and interpretations supplanted God's Word and distorted Jesus' message. He will warn the Pharisees of this dangerous tendency in their "traditions of the elders" (15:1–9). A day of judgment awaits those who continue down this path (e.g., ch. 23).

We too will face opposition if we are doing God's work in God's way. We will not be popular with the current secular culture and will often find opposition if we speak the truth about sin or give a biblical evaluation of current trends in film or entertainment or even in educational philosophies. We should expect opposition, but the heartbreak will be when it is from within. It may be when one of your extended family members opposes your decision to go on the mission field. Opposition might come when the pastor tries to take the church in a direction that will mean asking a popular music leader to resign because of a difference of vision for worship.

The listing could be endless, but it also should be added that it may not be easily determined in each situation who is in the right. A bit of tension in relationships should encourage us to open up lines of communication so that we listen to one another and try to ascertain clearly the Lord's principles and leading in each different scenario. I am certain that the Pharisees thought that they were right in opposing Jesus. They felt that Jesus was unjustly opposing their leadership among the people. Their hard-heartedness prevented them from hearing Jesus' message and from allowing the Spirit to guide them to the truth. We should expect opposition if we are doing something right, but our own humility must cause us to admit also that we may be wrong.

**Jesus is compassionate.** We may think that the evil and opposition Jesus encountered would harden him, but one of the most striking pictures in these scenes is his compassion. Compassion is an emotion that Jesus feels for the crowds throughout his ministry. But in Jesus it is not simply "emotional." He gathers with sinners so that they can hear his message (9:10). He reaches out and touches those who are dead and diseased (9:25, 29). He continually goes to the crowds with his salvation mission of preaching and healing (9:36). As the "Son of David" he compassionately touches the eyes of the blind as a sign that the messianic mission brings healing and cleansing. Jesus' empathy is guided by a deep understanding of the real needs of people.

That compassion provides us with an important object lesson. As we see the needs of people all around us, we must allow our hearts to feel deeply with them. But we cannot stop there. We must get close enough to them to see how we can bring the healing touch of the gospel of the kingdom to their deepest needs. For Jesus, the message of the kingdom's saving power was primarily a ministry of spiritual healing.

But this is not license for the church to neglect the role of ministering to the whole person. We should do all we can to alleviate suffering. Caring for the physical, emotional, or psychological needs of an individual can be vital to displaying Jesus' compassion for individuals and is often instrumental in creating a responsive attitude to the message of the gospel. This is the approach of a mission that reaches out to the inner city homeless. The message of the gospel will likely fall on deaf ears if the immediate physical needs are not addressed. It is hard to convince an individual that God cares if he is dying of AIDS or if she is suffering emotional and physical abuse from an alcoholic husband.

A proper sense of balance comes from keeping an eternal perspective on our compassion. Our responsibility for being salt and light among the evil of this world will not result in the eradication of evil. Regardless of how much healing of physical, emotional, or psychological problems we provide, each individual will someday have an eternal reckoning. Our compassion for the world is insincere unless we keep this eternal perspective. Humanity is dying without the Great Physician, and we are the ones who must go next door or around the world carrying his healing touch, because they will either be gathered in this harvest of grace or face the next harvest of judgment. It is a weighty and marvelous charge that Jesus gives to disciples of all ages.

# Matthew 10:1–42

H E CALLED HIS twelve disciples to him and gave them
authority to drive out evil spirits and to heal every
disease and sickness.

²These are the names of the twelve apostles: first, Simon
(who is called Peter) and his brother Andrew; James son of
Zebedee, and his brother John; ³Philip and Bartholomew;
Thomas and Matthew the tax collector; James son of
Alphaeus, and Thaddaeus; ⁴Simon the Zealot and Judas Iscar-
iot, who betrayed him.

⁵These twelve Jesus sent out with the following instructions: "Do not go among the Gentiles or enter any town of
the Samaritans. ⁶Go rather to the lost sheep of Israel. ⁷As you
go, preach this message: 'The kingdom of heaven is near.'
⁸Heal the sick, raise the dead, cleanse those who have leprosy,
drive out demons. Freely you have received, freely give. ⁹Do
not take along any gold or silver or copper in your belts;
¹⁰take no bag for the journey, or extra tunic, or sandals or a
staff; for the worker is worth his keep.

¹¹"Whatever town or village you enter, search for some
worthy person there and stay at his house until you leave.
¹²As you enter the home, give it your greeting. ¹³If the home is
deserving, let your peace rest on it; if it is not, let your peace
return to you. ¹⁴If anyone will not welcome you or listen to
your words, shake the dust off your feet when you leave that
home or town. ¹⁵I tell you the truth, it will be more bearable
for Sodom and Gomorrah on the day of judgment than for
that town. ¹⁶I am sending you out like sheep among wolves.
Therefore be as shrewd as snakes and as innocent as doves.

¹⁷"Be on your guard against men; they will hand you over
to the local councils and flog you in their synagogues. ¹⁸On
my account you will be brought before governors and kings as
witnesses to them and to the Gentiles. ¹⁹But when they arrest
you, do not worry about what to say or how to say it. At that
time you will be given what to say, ²⁰for it will not be you
speaking, but the Spirit of your Father speaking through you.

²¹"Brother will betray brother to death, and a father his child;
children will rebel against their parents and have them put to

death. ²²All men will hate you because of me, but he who stands firm to the end will be saved. ²³When you are persecuted in one place, flee to another. I tell you the truth, you will not finish going through the cities of Israel before the Son of Man comes.

²⁴"A student is not above his teacher, nor a servant above his master. ²⁵It is enough for the student to be like his teacher, and the servant like his master. If the head of the house has been called Beelzebub, how much more the members of his household!

²⁶"So do not be afraid of them. There is nothing concealed that will not be disclosed, or hidden that will not be made known. ²⁷What I tell you in the dark, speak in the daylight; what is whispered in your ear, proclaim from the roofs. ²⁸Do not be afraid of those who kill the body but cannot kill the soul. Rather, be afraid of the One who can destroy both soul and body in hell. ²⁹Are not two sparrows sold for a penny? Yet not one of them will fall to the ground apart from the will of your Father. ³⁰And even the very hairs of your head are all numbered. ³¹So don't be afraid; you are worth more than many sparrows.

³²"Whoever acknowledges me before men, I will also acknowledge him before my Father in heaven. ³³But whoever disowns me before men, I will disown him before my Father in heaven.

³⁴"Do not suppose that I have come to bring peace to the earth. I did not come to bring peace, but a sword. ³⁵For I have come to turn

> "'a man against his father,
>> a daughter against her mother,
>> a daughter-in-law against her mother-in-law—
> ³⁶ a man's enemies will be the members of his own
>> household.'

³⁷"Anyone who loves his father or mother more than me is not worthy of me; anyone who loves his son or daughter more than me is not worthy of me; ³⁸and anyone who does not take his cross and follow me is not worthy of me. ³⁹Whoever finds his life will lose it, and whoever loses his life for my sake will find it.

⁴⁰"He who receives you receives me, and he who receives me receives the one who sent me. ⁴¹Anyone who receives a prophet because he is a prophet will receive a prophet's

reward, and anyone who receives a righteous man because he is a righteous man will receive a righteous man's reward. [42]And if anyone gives even a cup of cold water to one of these little ones because he is my disciple, I tell you the truth, he will certainly not lose his reward."

JESUS' MISSION IS now well established. He has announced his central message (4:17), called his first coworkers (4:18–22), articulated his pro-grammatic standard of discipleship (chs. 5–7), and demonstrated his authoritative power (chs. 8–9). Now is the time to expand his influence by sending out his disciples with the same message and power, because opposition is building. Jesus will send them first to his people Israel because of their salvation-historical primacy (10:5–15). But he will also prepare them for a worldwide mission among the Gentiles (10:16–23). Jesus' training will address directly the characteristics that his disciples will need to embody as they carry out the mission (10:24–42).

## Commissioning the Twelve for Mission (10:1–4)

TWELVE DISCIPLES (10:1). In answer to the prayer for the Lord of the harvest to send out workers into his harvest field (9:38), Jesus calls his twelve disciples to him, the highest of Christological clues to Jesus' divine identity.[1] Although this is the first time Matthew mentions the Twelve explicitly, the informal way in which they are introduced suggests that they became a recognized group earlier.[2] Matthew is the only New Testament writer to refer to the "twelve disciples" (11:1; 20:17), although the title "the Twelve" occurs regularly elsewhere.[3] Up to this point in the narrative, Matthew has introduced only five of his named disciples—Peter, Andrew, James, John, and Matthew (4:18–22; 9:9); here he names the entire group. Mark and Luke name the Twelve in the context of their *calling* (Mark 3:13–19; Luke 6:12–16), while Matthew names them in the context of their *commissioning*.

---

1. Eduard Schweizer, *The Good News According to Matthew*, trans. David E. Green (Atlanta: John Knox, 1975), 235–36; Filson, *The Gospel According to St. Matthew*, 125.

2. For discussions of the historicity of the Twelve within Jesus' ministry, see Scot McKnight, "Jesus and the Twelve," *BBR* 11 (2001): 203–31; John P. Meier, "The Circle of the Twelve: Did It Exist During Jesus' Public Ministry?" *JBL* 116 (1997): 635–72; idem, *A Marginal Jew:* Volume III: *Companions and Competitors* (New York: Doubleday, 2001), 3:125–63; contra the minority opinion in Robert W. Funk and the Jesus Seminar, *The Acts of Jesus: The Search for the Authentic Deeds of Jesus* (San Francisco: HarperSanFrancisco: 1998), 71.

3. E.g., 26:14, 20; Mark 4:10; 6:7; Luke 8:1; 9:1; John 6:67, 70; Acts 6:2; etc.

"Twelve" has obvious salvation-historical significance. The number corresponds to the twelve patriarchs of Israel, the sons of Jacob, from whom the tribes of Israel descended. The twelve disciples symbolize the continuity of salvation history in God's program as Jesus sends them out to proclaim to the lost sheep of the house of Israel that the kingdom of heaven has arrived (cf. 10:5–6).[4] But there is discontinuity as well, because the Twelve will sit on twelve thrones judging the house of Israel (cf. 19:28). The arrival of the kingdom of heaven in Jesus' ministry demands an appropriate response from his chosen people Israel. In the gathering of the twelve disciples, we find the hint that Jesus is indeed the messianic king of Israel who has come to unite the people of God in all ages.[5] The same authority that characterized Jesus' ministry in chapters 8–9 is now given to the Twelve. Like Jesus, this authority enables them to drive out evil spirits and to heal every kind of disease and sickness (10:1; cf. 4:23; 9:35). All that the Twelve will accomplish is based on their having received Jesus' authority. Disciples of every era will find their own authority only by submitting to Jesus. In their call, disciples were conscripted to kingdom service (4:18–22); in their instruction of the Sermon on the Mount, disciples learned how to live the kingdom life (chs. 5–7); now in their commission, disciples go out with the power and message of the kingdom (10:1–5; cf. 9:6, 8; 28:18–20).[6]

"Evil" or "unclean" spirits are mentioned only one other time in Matthew's Gospel (12:43), but they are the same malevolent spirit beings called "demons" elsewhere (e.g., 8:28–32). The advance of the kingdom of heaven in Jesus' ministry continually encounters spiritual warfare. Unclean spirits are in rebellion against God and are capable of inflicting mental, moral, and physical harm on humans. Demon-possessed people are healed alongside other illnesses (e.g., 4:25), and demons being cast out indicate that the time of God's judgment has begun upon the stranglehold of evil over this world (8:16, 17, 29).

As the Twelve cast out demons and heal diseases, it validates the reality of the presence of the kingdom of heaven, so that people should turn to Jesus as the messianic deliverer. But their authoritative mission is also an exercise of control over Satan's realm of rule on this earth. No longer is Satan the uncontested ruler of this world. He has met his match, and more, in the arrival of Jesus. And Satan's evil forces are similarly subdued, as Jesus' emissaries go out with his authority to bring release to those held captive.

**Twelve apostles (10:2–4).** The disciples are also "apostles" (10:2). The

---

4. Cf. McKnight, "Jesus and the Twelve," 220–31; Karl H. Rengstorf, "δώδεκα," *TDNT*, 2:326.

5. Cf. Seán Freyne, *The Twelve: Disciples and Apostles. A Study in the Theology of the First Three Gospels* (London: Sheed & Ward, 1968), 23–48; A. B. Bruce, *The Training of the Twelve* (repr.; Grand Rapids: Kregel, 1971), 32–33.

6. Hagner, *Matthew*, 1:265.

term *apostle* has a significantly different meaning than *disciple*. The latter designates anyone who has believed in Jesus, while *apostle* designates one who has been commissioned to be his representative. This is a clue to the role of the Twelve. As disciples the Twelve are examples of what Jesus accomplishes in all believers; as apostles the Twelve are set aside as the leaders within the new movement. Further, this is a clue that the Twelve will transition from the time of Jesus' historical earthly ministry, when they are sent out as disciples to Israel (10:5–15), to the time of his ascended ministry, when they are sent out as apostles to the nations (10:16–23).

Matthew uses the word "apostle" only here, and he is the only Gospel writer to use the expression "the Twelve apostles" (cf. Rev. 21:14). "Apostle" has narrow and wide meanings in the New Testament. The narrow sense, as here, is the usual meaning, signifying the special authoritative representatives chosen by Jesus to play a foundational role in the establishment of the church.[7] Paul normally used the term to refer to the Twelve, but he includes himself among them as a special apostle to the Gentiles (1 Cor. 15:8–10). The wide sense of "apostle" derives from the verb *apostello*, "I send" (e.g., 10:5), and therefore can mean merely "messenger" (John 13:16), refer to Jesus as "the apostle and high priest whom we confess" (Heb 3:1), or designate an individual such as Barnabas, Titus, or Epaphrodites within the group of missionaries larger than the Twelve and Paul.[8]

"The Twelve" are significant in the foundational days of the early church. They appear in the days before Pentecost, and they function as a group in the earliest days after Pentecost. They provide leadership for the distribution of food in the dispute between factions of the disciples (Acts 6:2). From that point on, however, we do not find the title "the Twelve" used in the narrative of Acts, nor does the title appear in the New Testament letters. Four times a listing of the Twelve occurs in the New Testament.

## Lists of the Twelve

| *Matthew* 10:2–4 | *Mark* 3:16–19 | *Luke* 6:13–16 | *Acts* 1:13 |
|---|---|---|---|
| **First group of four** | | | |
| 1. first, Simon (who is called Peter) | Simon (to whom he gave the name Peter) | Simon (whom he named Peter) | Peter |

---

7. Cf. Gal. 1:17, 19; 1 Cor. 9:1–5; 15:7; Eph. 2:19–22.

8. Barnabas in Acts 14:4, 14; Titus in 2 Cor. 8:23; Epaphroditus in Phil. 2:25; probably Timothy and Silas also in 1 Thess. 1:1; 2:6; cf. Andronicus and Junias in Rom. 16:7. James the brother of Jesus seems to be included among the apostles in Jerusalem as a "pillar of the church" (Gal. 1:17; 2:9).

| Cont. | Matthew 10:2–4 | Mark 3:16–19 | Luke 6:13–16 | Acts 1:13 |
|---|---|---|---|---|
| 2. | his brother Andrew | James son of Zebedee | Andrew | John |
| 3. | James son of Zebedee | John | James | James |
| 4. | his brother John | Andrew | John | Andrew |

**Second group of four**

| | | | | |
|---|---|---|---|---|
| 5. | Philip | Philip | Philip | Philip |
| 6. | Bartholomew | Bartholomew | Bartholomew | Thomas |
| 7. | Thomas | Matthew | Matthew | Bartholomew |
| 8. | Matthew the tax collector | Thomas | Thomas | Matthew |

**Third group of four**

| | | | | |
|---|---|---|---|---|
| 9. | James son of Alphaeus | James son of Alphaeus | James son of Alphaeus | James son of Alphaeus |
| 10. | Thaddaeus | Thaddaeus | Simon the Zealot | Simon the Zealot |
| 11. | Simon the Zealot | Simon the Zealot | Judas son of James | Judas son of James |
| 12. | Judas Iscariot, who betrayed him. | Judas Iscariot, who betrayed him | Judas Iscariot, a traitor. | |

The structure of the list of the Twelve is significant.[9]

1. Matthew organizes the names in pairs, which is especially recognizable in the Greek text, corresponding to Mark's statement that Jesus sent the Twelve out two by two (Mark 6:7).[10]
2. Within the Twelve is a recognizable division into three groups of four. The first name in each group remains the same in all the lists (the first, fifth, and ninth place is occupied, respectively, by Peter, Philip, and James of Alphaeus). The order of the rest of the names varies. The

---

9. See the discussion in Wilkins, *Following the Master*, ch. 8; idem, "Disciples," *DJG*, 179–81. See also Meier, *A Marginal Jew*, vol. 3, ch. 27. For discussions of the apocryphal traditions about the Twelve, see Hennecke, *New Testament Apocrypha*, 2 vols.

10. Pairs of two names are set off from each other and connected with the simple conjunction "and" (*kai*): e.g., "Philip and Bartholomew; Thomas and Matthew"; see Carson, "Matthew," 237.

sequence of the groups is the same in each list. This grouping suggests that the Twelve were organized into smaller units, each with a leader.[11]

3. The first group is composed of those two pairs of brothers who were the first called—Peter and Andrew, James and John (Matt. 4:18–22), commonly called the "inner circle." However, on some significant occasions only Peter, James, and John accompanied Jesus, such as the healing of Jairus's daughter (Mark 5:37–40) and the Transfiguration (Matt. 17:2); they were the audience of the Olivet Discourse (Mark 13:3; Andrew is included), and they were with Jesus during his agony in the Garden of Gethsemane (Matt. 26:37).

4. Peter heads all the lists. He is regularly the spokesman for the Twelve,[12] and during the days of the early church he fulfills Jesus' prediction that he will play a foundational role as the rock of the church and holder of the keys of the kingdom of heaven.[13] Peter is called "first" (e.g., 10:2) in the sense that he is first among equals as the leader of the Twelve.[14]

5. The Twelve are normally mentioned as a group, with only occasional focus on individuals. Not much is known about the individual lives of the Twelve, except what is known from brief biblical data and from some statements by the early church fathers.

6. The Twelve display a remarkable personal diversity, which may have been part of the reason for their effectiveness in reaching Israel (see Contemporary Significance).[15] Peter, Andrew, James, and John were partners in a successful business in the fishing industry on the Sea of Galilee (see 4:18–22). Matthew was a hated tax collector (see comments on 9:9). Simon the Zealot had been a zealous revolutionary, willing to die for his cause of liberating Israel from Rome by guerilla warfare tactics. At any other occasion these men might have been ready to stick a knife into each other, but here they are all part of one group around Jesus.

7. Judas Iscariot, always listed last, is also noted as the one "who betrayed him." "Iscariot" most likely denotes Judas's place of origin, since his

---

11. Meier, *A Marginal Jew*, 3:130–31; Bruce, *The Training of the Twelve*, 36–40.

12. Matt. 14:28; 15:15; 18:21; 26:35, 40; Mark 8:29; 9:5; 10:28; John 6:68.

13. Matt. 16:17–19; cf. Acts 1:8; 2:14; 8:14; 10:34.

14. See Wilkins, *Disciples in the Ancient World and Matthew's Gospel*, 174–75; also, Oscar Cullmann, *Peter: Disciple—Apostle—Martyr. A Historical and Theological Essay*, trans. Floyd V. Filson, 2d ed. (Philadelphia: Westminster, 1962), 19; Joseph Fitzmyer, *To Advance the Gospel* (New York: Crossroad, 1981), 112–13.

15. Keener, *A Commentary on the Gospel of Matthew* (1999), 311.

father is described as "Simon Iscariot" (John 6:71). Judas was the treasurer for the apostolic band (John 12:4–6); hence, we may assume that he displayed positive characteristics recognizable by the others.

## Instructions for the Short-Term Mission to Israel (10:5–15)

THE INSTRUCTIONS FOR the disciples/apostles' mission is the second of the five major discourses in Matthew's Gospel (see the introduction). This discourse is divided into three basic sections: missionary instructions for that particular historical context (10:5–15), a preview of the disciples' role as missionaries in the future (10:16–42), and principles of discipleship for disciple-missionaries of every era (10:24–42)

**The prohibition** (10:5–6). Jesus begins with a surprising prohibition: "Do not go among the Gentiles or enter any town of the Samaritans. Go rather to the lost sheep of Israel." The mission is apparently restricted to Jewish Galilee, which was surrounded on all sides by Gentile country except to the south, where lay Samaria.[16] The full expression is "lost sheep of the house of Israel," which does not denote a certain portion of Israel that is lost but rather the whole lost Israel, which is being called to make a decision about the gospel of the kingdom.

The key to the prohibition is found here. This is a special mission of Jesus' disciples during his ministry to the crowds of Israel, who are like harassed and helpless sheep without a shepherd (9:36). Jesus goes first to Israel (cf. 15:21–28) to fulfill the salvation-historical order that God established, with Israel being the tool he will use to bring blessing to the world.[17] Then he will charge the Eleven to continue the historical outworking by going to the nations (28:19–20). Paul later saw this as the priority of the Jews in salvation, for God's plan is "first for the Jew, then for the Gentile" (Rom. 1:16; 2:9–10).[18] Jesus' attention to Israel underscores God's faithfulness to his covenant promises, the continuity of his purposes, and his plan for Israel.

Why does Jesus even bother to give such a prohibition, given the fact that the Twelve would not likely go the Gentiles and Samaritans anyway (cf. the antipathy of the early church in Acts 10; 11:1–4; 15)? Most likely, Jesus is

---

16. Hill, *Matthew*, 184–45; Morna D. Hooker, "Uncomfortable Words X: The Prohibition of Foreign Missions (Mt. 10:5–6),'" *ExpTim* 82 (1971): 364.

17. E.g., Gen. 12:2–3; 22:18.

18. Douglas J. Moo, *The Epistle to the Romans* (NICNT; Grand Rapids: Eerdmans, 1996), 69, 139; Wayne A. Brindle, "'To the Jew First': Rhetoric, Strategy, History, or Theology," *BibSac* 159 (April–June 2002): 221–33. See also J. Julius Scott, "Gentiles and the Ministry of Jesus: Further Observations on Matt. 10:5–6; 15:21–28," *JETS* 33 (1990): 161–69.

dispelling any doubt as to whether he truly is the Messiah who fulfills the promises given to Israel and God's program of salvation history. But there is also a warning here. The eschatological ingathering is beginning. This is Israel's opportunity, and from here on it will be fully responsible for its own decision.[19]

**Message and miracles** (10:7–8a). The message of the disciples is the same as that of both John the Baptist and Jesus: "The kingdom of heaven is near" (see comments on 3:2; 4:17). They also go with the same authority as Jesus (10:1)— to "heal the sick, raise the dead, cleanse those who have leprosy, drive out demons." The power of the Twelve is clearly an extension of Jesus' own power and is to be exercised in the same manner. The commission to raise the dead harks back to Jesus' stupendous miracle of raising Jairus's daughter (9:25–26).

**Equipment for the mission** (10:8b–10). The disciples have benefited from the gift of the kingdom of heaven—in the message they have believed, in their authority over unclean spirits, disease, and sickness (10:1), and in the commission they now receive. They likewise are to give this ministry of the gospel freely to the lost sheep of the house of Israel: "Freely you have received, freely give." They are not to accept payment from those to whom they minister, which would otherwise make it a mercenary venture. Jesus gives them their authoritative power as a gift, so they must not take payment for performing miracles.

Furthermore, they are not to "take along any gold or silver or copper in your belts; take no bag for the journey, or extra tunic, or sandals or a staff; for the worker is worth his keep." Jesus is not prohibiting them from owning these items but rather is stressing the urgency and requirements of the mission. The Twelve are not to spend time procuring extra supplies as though they are going to be out in foreign lands for an extended period of time.

There are two reasons for this prohibition. (1) This is a relatively quick preaching tour through the Galilean countryside. To procure extensive supplies is unnecessary. (2) Jesus insists that "the worker is worth his keep." On this brief mission tour the Twelve are to accept the hospitality extended to them as traveling missionaries, so they will not need money or extra clothing or equipment. It is the responsibility of those to whom they minister to support their mission (10:10).[20] Although they may not charge for their ministry, the Twelve are to accept the hospitality extended to them for those to whom they minister (cf. 3 John 5–8).

---

19. Kingsbury, *Matthew: Structure, Christology, Kingdom*, 22–23; Broadus, *Matthew*, 219.

20. Alfred Plummer, *Matthew: An Exegetical Commentary on the Gospel According to Matthew* (London: Stock, 1909), 149. The apostle Paul later calls upon this principle as a rationale for the support of full-time Christian workers (1 Cor. 9:14; 1 Tim. 5:18; cf. *Did.* 13:1–2).

**Worthy of the mission (10:11–14).** While the Twelve are on the mission journey, they must "search for some worthy person." The word "worthy" (*axios;* trans. "deserving" in 10:13) does not point to a person who has a high moral or religious stature but indicates someone who responds positively to the message proclaimed by the disciples.[21] An individual, a house, or a city (10:11, 12, 14) that receives the greeting—which Luke tells us is "Peace be to this house" (Luke 10:5)—recognizes that the Twelve are emissaries of God and thus receives their message. If the household does not receive God's message and messengers, then the missionaries are to shake the dust off of their feet when they leave. It was a sign used by Jews when leaving Gentile regions that they have removed completely unclean elements (*b. Sanh.* 12a). For the missionaries it is an acted parable of judgment on those rejecting the mission message.[22] Paul practiced this symbol when he left regions where his message was rejected (Acts 13:51).

**Judgment for rejecting the mission (10:15).** The element of judgment implied thus far is now explicit: "I tell you the truth, it will be more bearable for Sodom and Gomorrah on the day of judgment than for that town." The preaching of the gospel becomes for Israel a threat as well as a promise. Increased light of God's revelation makes for increased responsibility, and those who have been exposed to Jesus' ministry and the witness of the disciples have greater responsibility for that privilege (see also 11:20–24). The whole scene exudes urgency because the time of Jesus' earthly ministry is short and both the blessings of the kingdom and the punishment of judgment are awaiting a decision from Israel.

## Instructions for the Long-Term Mission to the World (10:16–23)

SHEEP AMONG WOLVES (10:16a). The theme of judgment on Israel for rejecting the mission of the Twelve leads to a surprising reversal of the sheep metaphor: "I am sending you out like sheep among wolves." Up to now the disciples are to go to the sheep—that is, the crowds who are harassed and helpless, the lost people of Israel (9:36; 10:6). But now they themselves are the sheep, being sent out among wolves (cf. also Luke 10:3). Why this reversal? Because Jesus is dealing with a different subject. In the first part of the commissioning, he gave instructions to the disciples about their short-term mission to Israel during his earthly ministry. Now he is giving them instructions about their long-term mission throughout the world after that ministry.[23]

---

21. Albright and Mann, *Matthew*, 212.

22. G. E. Ladd, *A Theology of the New Testament*, 2d ed. (Grand Rapids: Eerdmans, 1993), 88.

23. Köstenberger and O'Brien, *Salvation to the Ends of the Earth*, 92–93.

How do we know? (1) Jesus changes from the present tense to future tense. The future tense marks off a distinctively different future ministry. (2) This ministry involves a witness to "Gentiles" (10:18), whom the Twelve were warned to bypass (10:5). This suggests the worldwide mission of the Great Commission (28:18–20). (3) Throughout this second section Jesus prepares the disciples for intense persecution, which they did not experience during Jesus' earthly ministry. (4) The appearance of similar warnings in 24:9–13 and Mark 13:9–13, which record Jesus' message of the end times, indicates that he is here including warnings about the treatment that missionary disciples will endure until the coming of Jesus at the end of the age.

Matthew makes no reference to the Twelve either actually going out or returning from their mission. In this way, the commission is sufficiently open-ended to include both instructions for an immediate mission to Israel and the ongoing mission to the nations until the end of the age. The historical setting of Jesus' sending of the Twelve to the people of Israel has provided an occasion for him to lay down instruction for Christian missions to all nations.

**Wise serpents, harmless doves (10:16b).** Along with the reversal of the sheep metaphor, Jesus warns his disciples that wariness, yet innocence, will be necessary in the future mission. They must venture out as defenseless sheep in the midst of ravenous wolves, but what will keep them alert to dangers is to be "wise as serpents and innocent as doves" (10:16). The serpent was the emblem of wisdom, shrewdness, and intellectual keenness (Gen. 3:1; Ps. 58:5), while the dove represented simple innocence (Hos. 7:11). This is a difficult but necessary balance to maintain. Without innocence the keenness of the snake is crafty, a devious menace; without keenness the innocence of the dove is naive, helpless gullibility. Schweizer notes, "The caution of the disciples is to consist not in clever diplomatic moves but in the purity of a life that is genuine and wears no masks"[24] (cf. also Rom. 16:19).

**Flogging in the Jewish synagogue (10:17).** Jesus' warning is now explicit: "Be on your guard against men; they will hand you over to the local councils and flog you in their synagogues." This language echoes Jesus' prophetic statement of the way that Jewish religious leaders will mistreat missionaries (cf. 23:33–34). The synagogue was not only the place of assembly for worship but also an assembly of justice, where discipline was exercised (cf. John 9:35). Note that it is not "our" or "your" synagogues; it is "their" synagogues. The synagogue belongs to those opposed to Jesus' disciples.[25]

**A witness to Gentiles (10:18–20).** The disciples' future mission will bring them "before governors and kings as witnesses to them and to the

---

24. Schweizer, *Matthew*, 240.
25. For more on flogging, see Wilkins, "Matthew," 69.

Gentiles." Acts records times in which early church leaders were first called before Jewish officials of the national council (Acts 4:1–22; 5:17; 7:12.), later before the ruling authorities in Israel (12:1–4; 21:27–23:11), and finally before the rulers of the Roman world (14:5; 16:19–34; 17:1–9; 18:12–17; 23:24–26:32; 28:17–31). At the time of their trials, the mission-disciples will witness to these ruling figures of the truthfulness of the gospel message brought by Jesus.

In their future mission, the disciples are to depend on the Holy Spirit to speak through them in the moment of their most difficult opposition. The Spirit is the creative, empowering, guiding force in Jesus' own life (1:18, 20; 3:11, 16; 4:1; 12:18, 28). Through this same Spirit his disciples will find their own empowering and guidance to give their witness.

**The disciples' opposition and endurance (10:21–23).** Not only will opposition come from Jewish and Gentile officials but also from the disciples' close family relations: "Brother will betray brother to death, and a father his child; children will rebel against their parents and have them put to death." Moses had warned the people that even if one's own brother or sister or wife or closest friend tries to beguile a person into idolatry, this person was to be stoned (Deut. 13:6–11). In the future, some may think that the disciples are leading the people into idolatry with their call to worship Jesus; as a result, the mission-disciples will be delivered over to persecution and death.[26] This will be a tragic misperception of Jesus' identity and message.

Along with family betrayal because of their commitment to Jesus' exclusivity, his disciples will feel the wrath and hatred of "all men . . . because of me" (cf. also 24:9). An element of hyperbole may be included, but this statement indicates an unavoidable consequence that comes from attachment to Jesus and his message. The phrase "because of me" is literally "because of my name" and is an important Christological expression (cf. 5:11; 24:9) that harks back to the Old Testament significance of God's name as representing his person as the sole focus of Israel's worship and allegiance (e.g., Ex. 3:15; 6:3; 9:16; 20:7). Jesus' disciples will have the privilege of carrying his name, but it also brings suffering, because the hatred directed against him will naturally fall on his followers (cf. John 15:21; 2 Tim. 3:12; 1 Peter 4:13–14).

But Jesus promises that "he who stands firm to the end will be saved" (see also 24:13). By this statement Jesus gives great assurance that in spite of an increase in persecution, the hatred of humanity will not overcome his disciples. Active resistance may be included in standing firm, but much more in view is their enduring fortitude under any circumstance, including the most

---

26. See D. Neale, "Was Jesus a *Mesith?* Public Response to Jesus and His Ministry," *TynBul* 44 (1993): 89–101, esp. 94–98.

---

hateful persecution. Those who endure until the end of the age, when the Son of Man comes, or to the end of their lives will be saved.

"Saved" here does not mean rescue from death, for many Christians have been martyred. Instead, Jesus gives both a concrete promise and a cautionary reminder. His *promise* is that the one who remains committed to his name to the end will not be consumed by the persecution but will experience the full blessing and peace of kingdom's salvation. The *reminder* is that the test of a disciple's real commitment to Jesus is whether he or she remains steadfast to the end. Jesus through his Spirit will provide the resources to withstand whatever difficulties may come (10:19–20); in fact, Jesus himself will be with them to the end of the age to see them through (28:20).

With the mention of "the end" (10:22), Jesus culminates the prophetic aspect of the commissioning with a remarkable statement: "I tell you the truth, you will not finish going through the cities of Israel before the Son of Man comes." This is one of the most problematic verses in the Bible. What does "before the Son of Man comes" mean in this context?[27] Some suggest that Jesus is promising the disciples that they will witness the final coming of the Son of Man while they are on their first Palestinian mission, or at his resurrection, or at Pentecost, or at the destruction of Jerusalem in A.D. 70.[28] Others contend that this promise is to be associated with the coming of the Son of Man at the end of the age.

The latter seems to fit the larger context here. While the Jews have priority of salvation (10:6) and of judgment (10:15), their judgment will not permanently exclude them from God's eschatological promises. The ongoing mission to the nations includes both Jew and Gentile (see comments on 28:18–20). As Jesus offers comfort to the mission-disciples about their ultimate salvation (10:22), he warns them not to abandon Israel. When persecuted in one city, they should flee to the next, because the mission to Israel will not conclude before the Son of Man returns.

In other words, there will be a continuing mission to Israel alongside the mission to the Gentiles until the Parousia.[29] In spite of Israel's hard-heartedness, God will remain faithful to his covenant promises to her. The mission-disciples must remain faithful to their calling to preach to everyone regardless of persecution, family alienation, and ostracism. This is a powerful apologetic to the Jews both in Jesus' ministry and to those within hearing of Matthew's

---

27. Ben Witherington III, *Jesus, Paul, and the End of the World: A Comparative Study in New Testament Eschatology* (Downers Grove, Ill.: InterVarsity Press, 1992), 39–42.

28. For discussion of these and other views, see Carson, "Matthew," 250–53, who holds to the latter.

29. Blomberg, *Matthew*, 176; Davies and Allison, *Matthew*, 2:189–90. So also Gundry, *Matthew*, 194, though he doubts the authenticity of the saying.

Gospel: God has not abandoned his covenantal promises. It is also a challenging, yet sober call to the mission-disciples to endure to the end with the message of the gospel to all peoples—both Jew and Gentile.

## Characteristics of Missionary Disciples (10:24–42)

JESUS' MISSION CHARGE has included instructions to his disciples during his earthly ministry (10:5–15) and instructions to apostles/disciples in a worldwide mission until his return at the end of the age (10:16–23). This last section gives characteristics of discipleship that are to guide all disciples as they carry out Jesus' mission to the world.

**Disciples and the Master in mission (10:24–25).** This section opens with sayings that are central in importance: "It is enough for the student to be like his teacher, and the servant like his master." The word "student" is *mathetes*, the common word for "disciple." The ultimate goal of a disciple is to be like the master—a general principle of master-disciple relations in Judaism and the Greco-Roman world. This general principle of discipleship also applies to relations with Jesus as Teacher and Master. His disciples have received his authority, so they go out with his message and power (10:1, 7–8). The harsh treatment that he is now beginning to receive from the religious leaders will be their lot as well in the ongoing mission.

The Pharisees had accused Jesus of casting out demons by the "prince of demons" (9:34), another name for Satan. That identity is further revealed to be "Beelzebub"[30]—or better, "Beelzeboul" (meaning "master of the house"), as Jesus' play on words with "head of the house" (*oikodespotes*) indicates: "If the head of the house has been called [Beelzeboul], how much more the members of his household!" The term Beelzebub most likely comes from an identification of the chief of the evil spirits with Baal Shamayim, whose worship was installed in the temple by Antiochus Epiphanes IV.[31] The accusation that Jesus has formed an alliance with Satan to carry out his work will naturally be lodged against his disciples as well.

**Fearless followers (10:26–31).** Since the charges against Jesus are false and unfounded, "do not be afraid of them." Jesus then gives three reasons why his followers should not be afraid. (1) The truth about his ministry will become known: "There is nothing concealed that will not be disclosed, or hidden that will not be made known." Eventually the subversive opposition to his ministry conducted in the hidden counsel of the religious leaders will be revealed as false.

---

30. Baal Zebub, meaning "lord of the flies" in Heb.; cf. also 12:24, 27.
31. Neusner and Green, "Beelzebul," *DJBP*, 84.

Jesus also knows that shallow exuberance and vicious opposition will come from revealing his true identity and mission, because the crowds will misunderstand it and it will be a threat to the religious establishment. Thus, he has consistently called for secrecy (see comments on 8:4; 9:30). But the time is approaching when the secret message will be broadcast universally, as if a person climbed to the top of the flat roof of one's home and shouted across the city.

(2) The next reason why mission-disciples should not be afraid is because their eternal destiny is secure. The sober call to mission commitment until the end of the age included the stark reality that persecution may result even in loss of life (10:21), so Jesus gives his disciples reassurance why they should not be afraid: "Do not be afraid of those who kill the body but cannot kill the soul." This is a call to courage in the face of persecution. Jesus' disciples might abandon their mission out of fear, so their work should take precedence over what anyone might do to them. Hell is near (10:28), and one who is afraid of confessing Jesus as Messiah is in danger of a far greater judgment than physical death. Therefore, to carry on the mission is to receive the blessings of the Father (10:32). Jesus' sayings bring comfort and encouragement, for there is a limit to what humans can do to them. If the disciples persevere, they will be rewarded, but if they are disloyal to the truth of the gospel message, they will face ultimate condemnation.

(3) His disciples should not be afraid as they embark on their mission in this world, because of the Father's unrelenting sovereign supervision over their lives, as testified in 10:29–31. The "sparrow" is proverbially the smallest of creatures and the penny (*assarion*) is one of the smallest and least in value of the Roman coins (cf. *quadrans* in 5:26). If the heavenly Father gives constant sovereign supervision to such insignificant creatures, surely he will for mission-disciples whose every detail, even to the number of hairs on their head, he knows. It is to these disciples that their Father has sent his beloved Son (3:17), so he will surely give them absolute sovereign care. Do not fear when persecution comes, for God is aware and in control.

**Acknowledging Jesus' supremacy in public (10:32–33).** The test of a disciple's commitment to Jesus and his mission will come when opposition arises. The easiest way to avoid persecution is to deny that one is Jesus' disciple. But the true disciple does not fear death (10:28), so she will publicly acknowledge or confess Jesus as her Master (10:24–25) and God, the Son of the heavenly Father (10:32). This public discipleship to Jesus is eternal, for Jesus will likewise acknowledge her to his Father, another statement of the exclusive relationship that Jesus and the Father enjoy (cf. 7:21). But the disciple who attempts to avoid persecution by public denial of Jesus reveals that he is not a true disciple and has not publicly confessed Jesus as his Master and God. Such denial results in eternal rejection by the Father.

**Allegiance to Jesus' supremacy at home (10:34—39).** We have here another statement of Jesus' explanation of the reason for which "I have come."[32] The public nature of discipleship will test the disciples' confession, and the private nature of discipleship will test their absolute allegiance to Jesus. The latter testing comes at home. In the first place, confession of Jesus will divide family members: "a man against his father, a daughter against her mother, a daughter-in-law against her mother-in-law." This is one of the truly radical sayings of Jesus in the social milieu of first-century Judaism, showing that he has not come simply to mollify the status quo.

The "sword" in 10:34 is a metaphorical sword, as proven by Jesus' rebuke of those who took up an actual sword to defend him in the Garden of Gethsemane (26:52). The sword can be a metaphor of God's judgment (Ps. 7:12) or, as here, a metaphor of separation between those who believe and those who don't, even if it is in one's family. Earlier Jesus revealed that opposition to his mission would come from the disciples' closest family relations (see comments on 10:21—23). Thus, Jesus' claim to messianic identity and authority is a divider between people, including one's own family. One either believes in Jesus or rejects him; there is no middle ground. Before Jesus' own family finally came to recognize his true identity and mission, they also opposed him (13:53—58; Mark 3:21; John 7:3—5). So, like their Master, Jesus' disciples can expect division to occur in their family as members try to prevent them from furthering Jesus' mission.

Furthermore, discipleship to Jesus means that he has unqualified supremacy over the disciples' lives: "Anyone who loves his father or mother more than me is not worthy of me; anyone who loves his son or daughter more than me is not worthy of me." In a return to the expression "worthy" (*axios;* see comments on 10:11), Jesus indicates his form of discipleship calls for giving him ultimate supremacy beyond parents or children, something not even the most esteemed rabbi would demand. This is an implicit declaration of his deity, because only God deserves higher place of honor than one's father and mother. A precedent for this is found in Moses' commendation to the tribe of Levi:

> He said of his father and mother,
> "I have no regard for them."
> He did not recognize his brothers
> or acknowledge his own children,
> but he watched over your word
> and guarded your covenant. (Deut. 33:9—10)

---

32. Carter, "Jesus' 'I have come' Statements in Matthew's Gospel," 44—62.

Giving rightful place to family presumes giving obedience first to God, which will then enable a person to honor appropriately one's father and mother, sons and daughters. The strength of attachment to family in Israel had a tendency at times to supplant commitment to God (see comments on 8:21–22). Jesus' statement here is in line with the call there to give priority to Jesus as God above all else, even one's dearest loved ones.[33] To take up one's cross is a metaphor that means to take up God's will for one's life, in the same way that the cross was the Father's will for the Son's life. Taking up God's will for one's life will result in gaining true life as Jesus' disciple (see comments on 16:24–26).

**Reward for receiving Jesus' mission-disciples (10:40–42).** Jesus concludes this Mission Discourse by reiterating that the mission is his, because the missionaries go out with his message and his authority (10:1, 7). He speaks directly to the disciples/apostles, who have been the subject of the discourse throughout (cf. 10:1–2, 5): "He who receives you receives me, and he who receives me receives the one who sent me." The mission-disciples include the original Twelve (10:5–15) and all future disciples until the Son of Man returns (10:16–23, 24–25). Mission-disciples go in the authority and with the message of Jesus himself, so to receive them is to receive Jesus. This includes a "prophet," a "righteous man," and a "little one."

The "prophets" and the "righteous" are linked elsewhere (13:17; 23:29); here they refer to Christian prophets (cf. 23:34) and righteous persons (cf. 13:43, 49; 25:37, 46). These distinctions are not mutually exclusive. "Prophet" refers to one who speaks for God (cf. 5:10–12; 7:15–23); "righteous man" is a generic category for one who has the righteousness of the kingdom that comes from obeying Jesus (cf. 5:20), including the righteous people of earlier generations who by faith looked forward to the arrival of God's gracious redemption (cf. Rom. 4:1–25). To receive either means to receive Jesus' gospel of the kingdom and live under its authority and so receive life's greatest reward—kingdom salvation and kingdom life. Prophets and righteous men have already been blessed with that reward upon their own entrance to the kingdom of heaven, and their great privilege is to share it with others (cf. 5:12).

The context of the reward for receiving missionary disciples who have sacrificed and experienced persecution blends with reward for treating well the "little ones," a theme that will resurface significantly in the eschatological discourse (cf. 25:31–46). "Little ones" points explicitly to needy disciples and emphasizes that they are often the ones excluded from care, since attention is given usually to prominent members of the discipleship community. This

---

33. Hellerman, *The Ancient Church As Family*, 20–21.

is in line with the admonition Jesus gave to the disciples as they were arguing about who was the greatest in the kingdom of heaven (18:1). There, he
advised them to become like children, because receiving children in his name
is like receiving Jesus (18:2–5).

This is also in line with James's rebuke of his church for showing partiality to the rich in the church while dishonoring the poor (cf. James 2:1). So
Jesus affirms that believers are to care for one another, but especially the
least and insignificant among them, particularly those who are most needy
but have given unqualified commitment to Jesus' mission.

IN THIS SECOND discourse of Jesus in this Gospel,
Matthew provides us another crucial collection of
Jesus' commands that disciples are to be taught to
obey (28:20). In the Sermon on the Mount (chs.
5–7), Jesus delineated the principles for his followers that are to characterize their lives as "kingdom-life" disciples in our everyday world. This second
discourse, the Mission Discourse, develops what it means to be "mission-
driven disciples." Jesus' disciples are to go out to share and live the message
of the gospel of the kingdom of God to an alien and often hostile world. Four
primary topics surface here.

**Mission.** The first is "mission."[34] This includes several important features.

1. Jesus lays out God's salvation-historical mission of redemption. The
   disciples first go to Israel to fulfill God's covenantal promises (10:6),
   but then they are to go to the Gentiles (10:18). They will continue
   with the two-pronged mission to Jews and Gentiles throughout the
   age until Jesus returns (10:23). The mission-disciples must be appropriately equipped in each phase. The urgent mission to Israel during
   Jesus' historical ministry required preparation unique to that setting
   (cf. 10:5–15), which should be wisely evaluated so that no unwarranted application is made to the later worldwide mission (10:16–42).
2. The disciples are to go with the same authoritative message and
   power that characterized Jesus' mission (10:1–8).
3. Since the mission charge is addressed to disciples, mission is a responsibility of all believers (10:24–24, 40–42), not just a special category
   of persons. It occurs in both public confession to the world (10:32–
   33) and in private commitments to one's family (10:34–39).

---

34. Cf. Köstenberger and O'Brien, *Salvation to the Ends of the Earth*, 87–109; Donald Senior
and Carroll Stuhlmueller, *The Biblical Foundations for Mission* (Maryknoll, N.Y.: Orbis, 1983),
250–51.

4. Like Jesus, disciples can expect opposition and persecution (10:24–25) from Jews and Gentiles alike, as well as one's own closest family and companions (10:17–21). Jesus is the dividing line between the entire world and his disciples (10:22).
5. The source of the disciples' power and guidance is the Spirit (10:19–20) and the source of their care and control is the sovereign will of the Father (10:28–33). Disciples, therefore, should have no fear (10:26–27).
6. Mission is a community issue, as the one who receives shares the reward of the one who carries the message (10:40–42).
7. Mission includes not only proclamation and displays of God's power but also care for the needy among them (10:42).
8. Mission includes spiritual transformation. The centrality of Jesus in the life of the disciples is the most vital characteristic of the mission, so that the disciples increasingly grow to be like the Master (10:24).
9. All of these issues prepare and equip Jesus' disciples to undertake with boldness and effectiveness the mission with which Matthew concludes his Gospel, the Great Commission (28:18–20), which is the key to understanding Matthew's overall purpose for writing.

**Particularism and universalism.** One of the well-known difficulties of studying Matthew's Gospel is to try to understand the tension between the particularistic thrust, where Jesus emphasizes a mission only to the lost sheep of Israel (10:6; 15:24), and the universalistic thrust, where Jesus emphasizes a mission to all the nations (28:19). Jesus reserved an undisguised declaration of the universal mission until after the resurrection, but all throughout Matthew there are hints of its coming. This is part of Jesus' own earthly economy of salvation history, and Matthew emphasizes it for his own apologetic message to his Jewish kinsmen and Jewish-Christian community (see comments on 10:6).[35] The double horizon of the mission to Israel and then to the nations instructs all disciples of its present universal responsibilities.

To emphasize too heavily Matthew's particularistic themes could lead one to accuse him of ethnic prejudice, but to emphasize too heavily the universal theme could lead one to accuse him of ethnic anti-Semitism. A proper balance is found in recognizing God's plan of salvation history—to the Jew first, then to the nations. Jesus' admonition to the disciples to give singular attention to Israel (10:6) underscores God's faithfulness to his covenant promises, but by bearing witness to the Gentiles (10:18), the mission accomplishes his salvific purposes for all of humanity while declaring that his plan for Israel will not be finished until the Son of Man returns (10:23).

---

35. John P. Meier, "Salvation-History in Matthew: In Search of a Starting Point," *CBQ* 37 (1975): 203–15.

**Discipleship.** Another emphasis of the Mission Discourse is discipleship. Matthew has emphasized that there is an incontrovertible solidarity between Jesus and his disciples, including authority (10:1), message (10:1), activity (10:7, 8), mission (10:18), suffering (10:18, 24–25, 38), confession (10:32), and reception (10:40). Since the Twelve represent the relationship that disciples throughout the ages will enjoy with Jesus (see 28:16–20), the open-ended historical nature of this discourse posits specific examples for our own mission.

However, as we noted above, the Twelve's urgent mission to Israel during Jesus' earthly ministry (e.g., 10:5–15) must be understood historically so that we do not draw unwarranted application. This discourse encourages us to understand that disciples of Jesus will engage in mission and be transformed to meet life's demands by being continually transformed to be like the Master. Discipleship begins by taking up one's cross, which symbolizes God's will for a person's life, and by following Jesus into every situation while on earth. The extended section on the characteristics of mission-disciples draws together those two themes. The form of discipleship Jesus has explicitly instituted connects discipleship and mission—all believers are disciples/missionaries, and each role affects the other as they carry out that mission to the world.

**Persecution and suffering.** Persecution and suffering will be a regular part of discipleship and mission, just as it was of Jesus' life (10:24–25). Several points may help us to see Jesus' perspective on persecution and suffering.

1. How one bears up under persecution is basically determined by whether one is a disciple or not, which has eternal implications (10:32–34).
2. Persecution may include rejection, alienation, being hated, and ultimately martyrdom (10:21–22, 28, 38–39).
3. The severity of persecution and suffering requires us to give unqualified allegiance to Jesus. Jesus warns us not to give priority to any other relationship and not to deny allegiance to him because of fear of persecution. The disciple is not to fear those who can only kill the body; rather, we must fear the One who can destroy both body and soul in hell (10:28). To deny Jesus here on earth is to be denied by the Father in heaven (10:33).
4. Jesus' disciples can expect to be maligned and to have falsehood spread about their message and character, for the same was done to Jesus (10:25). However, they are not to fear this subversive persecution, because eventually they will be vindicated (10:26).

5. Most important, while experiencing persecution the Spirit will provide power and guidance to speak the right words of witness for the situation (10:19–20), and the Father will exercise sovereign control over all circumstances, so the mission-disciples are not to fear that the persecution is out of God's control (10:29–31).

TELEVISION NEWS ANCHOR Tom Brokaw wrote a best-selling, gripping tribute to what he calls *The Greatest Generation*.[36] It is a collection of stories about the generation that grew up in the Great Depression, which was shaken out of everyday life to help save the world by fighting the Second World War on two fronts, and which then immediately undertook the daunting task of rebuilding the economies and political institutions of their own homeland and those of their former enemies.

One of the most important themes that Brokaw wanted to get across is that these were common people who all joined together to face these challenges. It wasn't just an elite group who made up this greatest generation. They were ordinary men and women who answered the call to serve their country in whatever capacity they were gifted and equipped. Some were on the front lines fighting hand to hand with the enemy, while others were on the home front nursing the wounded back to health. Some heroes humbly received Medals of Honor, while other heroes served nobly in the obscurity of a factory. The Allied victory in World War II and the rebuilding of the war-ravaged world could not have been accomplished except for the full mobilization of an entire generation.

When we read the story of Jesus' mission of the Twelve, we can also think of them as the greatest generation of the church. They were called out of the hardship of occupation by the Roman Empire, but they went on to fight a battle, not with swords and chariots but with the good news of the arrival of the kingdom of heaven and a message of transformation. They went on to lay the foundation of the church, and most suffered martyrdom for the name of their Lord Jesus.

Scripture likewise speaks of our own discipleship using the language of warfare, although it is not a war against flesh and blood (e.g., Eph. 6:10–20; cf. 1 Tim. 2:18). Christians are everyday people who have been called to advance the kingdom of God in an alien and hostile world. We are the church, the body of Jesus Christ, some of whose service results in external and public honor while others carry out their service in the humility of obscu-

---

36. Tom Brokaw, *The Greatest Generation* (New York: Random House, 1998).

rity. But each individual is vitally necessary to the proper functioning of the church in this world.

Martin and Gracia Burnham are everyday people. They began serving as missionaries with New Tribes Mission in the Philippines in 1986, where they raised their three children. Martin grew up in the Philippines with his missionary parents, and he wanted to be a mission aviation pilot his entire life. He and Gracia were examples of grace and servanthood both to other missionaries and the Filipino people. While celebrating their eighteenth wedding anniversary at Dos Palmas Resort off Palawan Island, they were kidnapped May 27, 2001, by the Abu Sayyaf Group, terrorist Filipino rebels. They were held hostage for 376 days in the jungles of Basilan and Mindanao. When a Filipino military group attempted to rescue them, Gracia was wounded and Martin was killed. During their captivity they shared with their captors the food that was sent to them, and they also shared the gospel with them, challenging the rebels' Muslim beliefs.

After Gracia was reunited with her family and children in Rose Hill, Kansas, she said, "We want everyone to know that God was good to us every single day of our captivity. Martin was also a source of strength to the other hostages. He was a good man, and he died well." Dan Germann, an executive with New Tribes Mission, said of Martin and Gracia, "These are people who loved God and didn't reluctantly move toward a mission field. They did it gladly, because their eyes were fixed on Him. In that sense, they are our modern day heroes."[37]

Martin and Gracia are examples to all of us in our own everyday worlds, for Jesus' missionary discourse is directed to all who are courageous enough to call themselves his disciples. As Martin once said, "I'm not called to the Philippines or to be a missionary. I'm called to serve Christ." And he did—and so shall we, with God's grace. In that sense, every generation of the church is called to be the greatest, because if it is not for the mobilizing of all disciples, the war for the hearts and souls of lost men and women will be lost.

**Mission-driven discipleship.** *Every disciple is a missionary.* Some of us tend to avoid passages like the Mission Discourse by saying, "Well, how does this relate to me? Those were the twelve apostles. I'm not like them!" But while it does have special significance for the Twelve in their historical ministry, it has immediate relevance for disciples in every era. As Jesus calls the twelve disciples to him and gives them authority (10:1), all of us should identify with

37. Ted Olsen, "Special Report," *Christianity Today* 46/8 (July 8, 2002): 18–22. The New Tribes Mission website (www.ntm.org/connect/burnham/update.shtml) gives further information and background.

them *as disciples*. If we call ourselves Christians, we are disciples of Jesus (cf. 5:1–2; 28:18–20), and this passage should impel us to see that mission activity is a vital part of our discipleship to him. The authority and purposes of God have not changed, and thus the principles outlined in this discourse are as relevant today as they were to the original disciples.

*Every disciple is a missionary, but not every missionary goes overseas.* Equally as important, not all of Jesus' disciples are missionaries who go away from home to a mission tour. Even in Jesus' day many of his disciples did not follow him around or go out on a tour. The Gadarene who had had a demon begged to go with Jesus but was sent back home to tell his townspeople what Jesus had done for him (Luke 8:38–39). We have no evidence that Joseph of Arimathea or Nicodemus ever left Jerusalem or their occupations, yet they were disciples of Jesus and were used at a critical time to provide him a burial place (Matt. 27:57–61; John 19:38–42). The woman named Tabitha did not leave her hometown, yet she was a servant of God who affected the entire region, both by her actions and the miracle of being raised from the dead (Acts 9:36–43).

While all of us may not become full-time missionaries, it is clear that all disciples are called to join in mission in some fashion. And whether we are more directly involved in mission or conduct more of a support role, the rewards are the same (10:41–42). The specifics of how one engages in mission should be tailored to one's giftedness and abilities, but a disciple of Jesus will see that carrying the message of salvation to the world is a vital part of our discipleship.

*Support of worldwide mission is the responsibility of all disciples.* Much of the evangelistic and teaching ministry of the early church was performed by traveling missionaries who served the various churches and were dependent on the hospitality and gifts of the members of the churches they visited. One striking example is Gaius, who was especially faithful in exercising hospitality (3 John 6); many traveling missionaries shared with John's church how generous Gaius had been. John commends Gaius for his hospitality and encourages him to continue, because these missionaries would not accept help from the unconverted. To receive aid from such people might give the appearance of selling the gospel, reducing the missionaries to the level of various popular philosophers and religious preachers seeking payment for services.

This speaks to our own responsibility to support the mission work of the church beyond our own personal mission work. When we stay home and support those who go, we are fellow workers with them (3 John 8). And we are to support missionaries "in a manner worthy of God" (3 John 6). God gives generously to us, his disciples, so we should likewise give generously to mission-disciples involved in full-time mission. As Howard Marshall states,

"Christian ministers and missionaries live in the faith that God will encourage his people to provide for their needs; it is better that such provision err on the side of generosity than stinginess."[38]

**Transformational discipleship.** Discipleship refers to the process of how Christians are equipped and transformed for this life and battle, to be light in a dark world to those still held in the clutch of the prince of the power of the air. Those first Twelve disciples/apostles are a great deal more like us than we usually imagine. We each can look at these men, and the many other men and women who were Jesus' disciples, and find that we are not much different from them. Look at the brief description of each and see if you can identify with one or more of them:

- Peter—a businessman who was regularly in a leadership position
- Andrew, his brother—a person highly sensitive to God's leading, though overshadowed by his brother Peter
- James son of Zebedee—who left a successful family business to follow Jesus but was the first apostle martyred
- John, his brother—who had a fiery temper but also a profound love for God
- Philip—never quite one of the inner circle, yet took a leadership role among the lesser-known apostles
- Bartholomew—known for his outspoken honesty (he is probably the one called Nathaniel in John 1:43–51)
- Thomas—a skeptical rationalist who eventually had one of the most profound theological understandings of Jesus' identity as the God-man
- Matthew the tax collector—formerly a traitor to his own people to support himself and his family but became a missionary to them by writing his Gospel
- James son of Alphaeus—either younger, shorter, or less well known than the other James, faithful throughout his life but never given much recognition for it
- Thaddaeus (or Lebbaeus)—also called Judas son of James, often confused with Judas Iscariot and didn't develop much of his own reputation
- Simon the Zealot—before accepting Jesus as Messiah, a guerrilla fighter who wanted to bring in God's kingdom by force
- Judas Iscariot, who betrayed him—love of money and power may have drawn him to abandon and betray even his closest friends

---

38. I. Howard Marshall, *The Epistles of John* (NICNT; Grand Rapids: Eerdmans, 1978), 86.

The Twelve are not to be idealized. We can look at each of them and find that they are not much different from you or me. I don't say that to try to bring them down to our level but rather to emphasize that we are more like them than we may realize. Try identifying realistically with even one of the Twelve, with their individual strengths, yet also with their foibles and failings. Which one are you most like? Can you see the same faults in you that are in one of them? Can you see the same potential for your own unique ministry? If God could transform their lives, he can transform ours as well. That is the overwhelming passionate story of Jesus' ministry. Our call is to be what Jesus wants to make of us, wherever we happen to be.

You and I may not be involved in a large-scale assault on the evil of this world, but the transformation of those who will respond to the gospel message begins with us, in our own world. The Twelve had to start with a clear understanding that each of us needs transformation. The apostle John, for example, was called one of the Sons of Thunder, most likely because of his fiery temper. On one occasion he and his brother James wanted Jesus to call down fire from heaven to consume a village of Samaritans that had disrespected Jesus (Luke 9:51–55). But as his own heart was transformed to learn how to love with God's love, he later actually went to those same Samaritans with the gospel (Acts 8:14–17). This is a real transformation that we can all understand. It is a transformation of the heart that ultimately affects every aspect of our being.

**The persecution and suffering of discipleship.** Persecution is another issue in this Mission Discourse that we may think is not relevant to our daily lives. Many of us live in a culture and society that does not experience the same degree of persecution that the early Christians faced. But there are broader principles here that apply to us. Regardless of how comfortable a life we may live, there are always daily choices that demonstrate our allegiance and submission to the Lord. And invariably, opposition and persecution will follow.

Persecution is closer than we think. Believers who stand for the name of Jesus as we enter the third millennium are increasingly facing persecution similar to that experienced in the first centuries of the church's existence. Wherever communism, Islam, or nationalism is struggling for dominance, there is a new outbreak of anti-Christian violence and oppression. This has resulted not only in the arrest and imprisonment of Christians but also their torture and execution.[39] In Saudi Arabia, for example, in spite of its strong ties with

---

39. Kim A. Lawton, "The Suffering Church," *Christianity Today* 40 (July 15, 1996): 54–61, 64. See also Susan Bergman, ed., *Martyrs: Contemporary Writers on Modern Lives of Faith* (San Francisco: HarperSanFrancisco, 1996).

the United States and other Western countries, persecution and execution of Christians are common. As an Islamic theocracy, the government believes it must preserve a narrow Qur'anic purity and the shrines in Mecca and Medina, which means that denial of religious freedom is integral to its identity.

Oswaldo (Wally) Magdangal, a Filipino pastor whose house church in Riyadh, Saudi Arabia, grew too noticeable for the authorities, was arrested for blaspheming Islam. Shari'ah law requires beheading for "apostates"— those who renounce Islam. Religious police tortured every part of Magdangal's body, trying to force him to renounce his faith, and he was beaten throughout 210 minutes of mocking interrogation. During that time no Friday passed without at least one execution in the public square, and Pastor Wally was sentenced to be executed on Friday, December 25, 1992. But through the combined efforts of Western human rights organizations and his close friends in the Saudi government, God miraculously intervened and Pastor Wally was deported; he is now president of Christians in Crisis, an advocacy group based in Sacramento, California.[40] His goal is to wake up the church to the real persecution that Christians around the world experience every day.

Moreover, the increasing secularization of Western culture does not bode well for us. Christians are discouraged from denouncing practices condemned in Scripture, such as obscenity, pornography, and homosexuality. In the name of "freedom of religion" many of the normal practices of faith once enjoyed— such as public prayers or even displays of a manger scene at Christmas—have been stripped away. The agenda of much public policy seems more like freedom *from* religion, and the consequences for those who decry this secularist public policy will grow increasingly harsh.

Jesus suffered when doing the right and good thing, and persecution marked the fate of the church from its earliest days. Yet it did not dim passion for following Jesus, no matter what the cost. Paul tells young pastor Timothy that "all who desire to live godly in Christ Jesus will be persecuted" (2 Tim. 3:12). But our consolation is that our suffering unites us to Christ, and we will find a rare fellowship with him when we identify with the suffering he endured, whether in life or in death (Phil. 3:10). The apostle Peter reiterates the same theme that he had heard Jesus give in this Mission Discourse, which will be increasingly relevant for us in the third millennium:

---

40. Pastor Magdangal's story is given by Jeff M. Sellers, "How to Confront a Theocracy," *Christianity Today* 46 (July 8, 2002): 34–40. The website for Christians in Crisis (www. christiansincrisis.org) gives further details and describes the organization's mission: "CIC exists to help spread the Gospel and serves as an advocate and a voice for God's people who are faced with crisis and persecuted due to their faith in the Lord Jesus Christ."

Dear friends, do not be surprised at the painful trial you are suffering, as though something strange were happening to you. But rejoice that you participate in the sufferings of Christ, so that you may be overjoyed when his glory is revealed. If you are insulted because of the name of Christ, you are blessed, for the Spirit of glory and of God rests on you.... If you suffer as a Christian, do not be ashamed, but praise God that you bear that name. For it is time for judgment to begin with the family of God; and if it begins with us, what will the outcome be for those who do not obey the gospel of God? (1 Peter 4:12–17)

For the Christian, suffering is *not* something to be avoided at all costs. Suffering, when it comes, can be a means of furthering our union with Christ, who promises to be united with us in our deepest hour of need.[41]

**Guarding our hearts in the real world.** One of the central cautions of Jesus in this Mission Discourse is that as we live out our lives with him in the world, our hearts become vulnerable to hurt, temptation, and spiritual attacks. Proverbs tells us, "Above all else, guard your heart, for it is the wellspring of life" (Prov. 4:23). As we take up the armor of God in spiritual warfare, the breastplate of righteousness will guard our hearts (Eph. 6:14). But Jesus warns us that a delicate balance must be maintained while we walk in this world as mission-disciples: We must guard our hearts from hurt, yet at the same time we must not develop a heart that is so protected that it becomes hardened. As Jesus gives his prophetic vision to his disciples being sent out into the world, he says, "See, I am sending you out like sheep into the midst of wolves; so be wise as serpents and harmless as doves" (Matt. 10:16).

Jesus did not call us out of the world into a safe haven of rest. We must venture out as defenseless sheep in the midst of ravenous wolves, so we must guard our hearts. Guarding them means being wise as serpents. We are to know the ways of the world, especially the traps that await us. We must understand clearly how people can hurt and abuse us. There are people in this world who want to dominate us to perpetuate their own self-serving agenda. We must guard ourselves and those for whom we are responsible. We are to be wise about the temptations that will come our way and know how to escape.

At the same time, we are to be innocent as doves. We must not allow our hearts to become so protective and distrustful of the wolves in the world that we harden them. We should not learn the craftiness of the snake so well that we acquire the heart of a snake. I have said many times in the past, "I don't

---

41. For further discussion, see Wilkins, *In His Image*, 192–93.

trust anyone." That statement came from a heart that had been hurt by people. While it is true that many people can't be trusted, I took it too far. I became so distrustful of people that I hurt them by my accusations of false motives or unfaithfulness. A dove doesn't hurt others. A dove brings grace and beauty. The dove is the symbol of peace.[42]

Guarding our hearts in this world is a difficult yet necessary balance as we, mission-disciples, carry the message of the gospel of the kingdom to a world that is dying, eternally, without its message of grace and salvation. I don't fancy myself as a part of a "greatest generation," but I do know that I am called to unwavering commitment to bring the gospel of the kingdom to my generation and to those who follow. That is the clarion call of Jesus' Mission Discourse to every generation of the church.

---

42. See Wilkins, *In His Image*, 179–80.

# Matthew 11:1-30

❦

**A**FTER JESUS HAD finished instructing his twelve disciples, he went on from there to teach and preach in the towns of Galilee.

²When John heard in prison what Christ was doing, he sent his disciples ³to ask him, "Are you the one who was to come, or should we expect someone else?"

⁴Jesus replied, "Go back and report to John what you hear and see: ⁵The blind receive sight, the lame walk, those who have leprosy are cured, the deaf hear, the dead are raised, and the good news is preached to the poor. ⁶Blessed is the man who does not fall away on account of me."

⁷As John's disciples were leaving, Jesus began to speak to the crowd about John: "What did you go out into the desert to see? A reed swayed by the wind? ⁸If not, what did you go out to see? A man dressed in fine clothes? No, those who wear fine clothes are in kings' palaces. ⁹Then what did you go out to see? A prophet? Yes, I tell you, and more than a prophet. ¹⁰This is the one about whom it is written:

> "'I will send my messenger ahead of you,
>     who will prepare your way before you.'

¹¹I tell you the truth: Among those born of women there has not risen anyone greater than John the Baptist; yet he who is least in the kingdom of heaven is greater than he. ¹²From the days of John the Baptist until now, the kingdom of heaven has been forcefully advancing, and forceful men lay hold of it. ¹³For all the Prophets and the Law prophesied until John. ¹⁴And if you are willing to accept it, he is the Elijah who was to come. ¹⁵He who has ears, let him hear.

¹⁶"To what can I compare this generation? They are like children sitting in the marketplaces and calling out to others:

> ¹⁷"'We played the flute for you,
>     and you did not dance;
> we sang a dirge,
>     and you did not mourn.'

¹⁸For John came neither eating nor drinking, and they say, 'He has a demon.' ¹⁹The Son of Man came eating and drink-

ing, and they say, 'Here is a glutton and a drunkard, a friend of tax collectors and "sinners." ' But wisdom is proved right by her actions."

²⁰Then Jesus began to denounce the cities in which most of his miracles had been performed, because they did not repent. ²¹"Woe to you, Korazin! Woe to you, Bethsaida! If the miracles that were performed in you had been performed in Tyre and Sidon, they would have repented long ago in sackcloth and ashes. ²²But I tell you, it will be more bearable for Tyre and Sidon on the day of judgment than for you. ²³And you, Capernaum, will you be lifted up to the skies? No, you will go down to the depths. If the miracles that were performed in you had been performed in Sodom, it would have remained to this day. ²⁴But I tell you that it will be more bearable for Sodom on the day of judgment than for you."

²⁵At that time Jesus said, "I praise you, Father, Lord of heaven and earth, because you have hidden these things from the wise and learned, and revealed them to little children. ²⁶Yes, Father, for this was your good pleasure.

²⁷"All things have been committed to me by my Father. No one knows the Son except the Father, and no one knows the Father except the Son and those to whom the Son chooses to reveal him.

²⁸"Come to me, all you who are weary and burdened, and I will give you rest. ²⁹Take my yoke upon you and learn from me, for I am gentle and humble in heart, and you will find rest for your souls. ³⁰For my yoke is easy and my burden is light."

Original Meaning

ALTHOUGH JESUS GAVE authority to his disciples to go to Israel (10:1–7) and later to all nations (10:16–23; 28:18–20), he has not yet transferred his work to them completely. He now himself goes to Israel to teach and preach. He still confines his ministry to "the towns of Galilee" (11:1), but soon the populace will have had their opportunity to hear the gospel message (cf. 4:13–17; 11:20–24). Then Jesus will expand his ministry throughout the surrounding cities of Israel and the Gentile regions (15:21–34). Restrained resistance to Jesus' ministry has appeared occasionally (9:3–4), but now overt opposition begins. The altercation begins innocently enough through questions from John the Baptist (11:2–19), but it quickly escalates into opposition and hostility from the Jewish religious leaders (12:1–45).

## John the Baptist Questions Jesus (11:1–6)

TRANSITION (11:1). THE conclusion to the Mission Discourse is signaled by the stylized formula, "After Jesus had finished" (11:1; cf. 7:28; 13:53; 19:1; 26:1). This formula also serves as a transition to the next section of narrative (chs. 11–12). Matthew says nothing about the Twelve's actual mission (cf., by contrast, Mark 6:30; Luke 9:10). The next time the disciples appear in this Gospel, they are accompanying Jesus on his short trip.

John questions Jesus through his disciples (11:2–3). Early in the narrative Matthew noted the arrest of John the Baptist as the impulse for Jesus to begin his Galilean ministry (4:12). John had been imprisoned by Herod Antipas at the fortress Machaerus,[1] where ultimately he was put to death (see 14:1–14). As he awaited his fate, John heard about "the deeds of the Messiah" (11:2; NIV "what Christ was doing"), presumably the teaching (chs. 5–7), miracles (chs. 8–9) and mission (ch. 10) in Galilee. Matthew uses the title "the Christ" or "the Messiah" (*ho Christos*) for the first time since his opening chapters (see 1:1, 16, 17, 18, 2:4), making explicit that John wanted clarification about Jesus' identity and ministry as the Messiah.

John sends some of his disciples to Jesus. These disciples were committed followers who had gathered around him to assist him in his ministry as the prophet preparing the way for the Messiah, who would usher in the messianic age (John 1:35–42; 3:22–4:3; see comments on Matt. 9:14). They apparently stayed as close to John as they could while he was in prison, and evidently John was able to communicate with them.

Along with John they were becoming increasingly alarmed as to the future of the messianic program. Earlier they had questioned Jesus about the incongruity of their own practice of fasting with Jesus' disciples lack of participation in that activity (see comments on 9:14–17). Armed with John's question, they travel from the fortress Machaerus north through Perea alongside the Jordan River, crossing into Galilee near Capernaum (where Jesus was ministering)—nearly a hundred miles on foot.

John instructed his disciples to ask of Jesus, "Are you the one who was to come, or should we expect someone else?" The expression "the one who was to come" is an allusion to the Messiah, the Coming One, the expression John used to refer to Jesus at the beginning of the public ministry (3:11). This phrase draws on expressions such as "Blessed is he who comes in the name of the LORD" in Psalm 118:26 and recalls Zechariah's prophecy, "See, your king comes to you, righteous and having salvation, gentle and riding on a donkey, on a colt, the foal of a donkey" (Zech. 9:9)—the prophecy Jesus fulfilled at his entry to Jerusalem (Matt. 21:4).

---

1. See Josephus, *Ant.* 18.112, 119.

John's question seems out of character with his earlier bold and courageous declaration of Jesus as the Coming One (cf. 3:1–14). Some commentators have explained John's question as intended not for himself but for his disciples' clarification. But Jesus directs his answer back to John himself. Others suggest that John's question reflects a state of depression that has come on him from being imprisoned. But the question implies more concern for the arrival of Messiah than for his own condition. Most likely, John is concerned because his present experience does not match the message he gave about the Coming One's arrival, which promised blessing on those who repent and judgment on those who do not.

It is natural for John to experience perplexity as he languishes in prison, much as had earlier prophets such as Elijah (e.g., 1 Kings 19:1–18) when their human experience did not fully correspond with God's message through them. John rightly expected the Messiah to be a judging figure, so events are not unfolding as he anticipated. The divine judgment and time of messianic blessing do not seem to have arrived as he projected. Jesus is not carrying out judgment; rather, he seems to be concentrating on healing and helping. John needs to have his understanding of the messianic program reconfirmed.[2]

**Jesus responds to John's questions (11:4–6).** Jesus reiterates to John's disciples that the way his ministry has unfolded (chs. 8–9) is in line with the prophetic promises. In Jesus' ministry are fulfilled Isaiah's prophecies that described the coming messianic ministry in these very terms: The blind receive sight (9:27–32; Isa. 29:18; 35:5), the lame walk (Matt. 15:30–31; cf. Isa. 35:6), those who have leprosy are cured (Matt. 8:1–4; cf. Isa. 53:4), the deaf hear (Mark 7:32–37; cf. Isa. 29:18–19; 35:5), the dead are raised (Matt. 10:8; cf. Isa. 26:18–19), and the good news is preached to the poor (Matt. 5:3; cf. Isa. 61:1).[3]

> Therefore Jesus explicitly confirms that in his ministry the messianic age of blessing has arrived. But the implications are even more profound because the miracles accomplished by Jesus fulfill expectations previously associated with God and the eschatological Day of the Lord. Jesus indicates that he has come in the place of God performing the work of God.[4]

So Jesus confirms for John that the blessings of the messianic age have arrived with his ministry. But Jesus likewise mildly rebukes John and his disciples by calling them to see the bigger picture in his ministry: "Blessed is the man who

---

2. Witherington, *The Christology of Jesus*, 43.

3. There is a close parallel from Qumran in 4QMessianic Apocalypse (4Q521) 1, 6–8, 11–13, which lists these activities as characteristic of the coming Messiah's ministry; see John J. Collins, "The Works of the Messiah," *DSD* 1 (1994): 71–97; Flusser, *Jesus*, 260.

4. Edward Meadors, "The 'Messianic' Implications of the Q Material," *JBL* 118 (1999): 259.

does not fall away on account of me." This beatitude (see comments on 5:3) functions as both a warning and a challenge. It is a warning to those who fail to understand correctly Jesus' identity and ministry and so fall away from faith in his saving activity. It is a challenge to those with eyes of faith to stand firm in what God has revealed about Jesus in John's own message and in Jesus' ministry.

John and his disciples need to see the bigger picture of God's timing and manifestation of blessing and judgment in Jesus' messianic ministry. On the one hand, the Old Testament prophets often telescoped near and far events in God's program, so that future events appear alongside of present events. John and his disciples should look for God's timing of the complete fulfillment of blessing and judgment in Jesus' present and future ministry (cf. 24:36–42). On the other hand, each of the prophecies to which Jesus alludes as being fulfilled in his ministry includes in the immediate context references to both blessing and judgment (Isa. 35:4–6; 61:1–2). John and his disciples must use eyes of faith to recognize both blessing and judgment. Jesus has brought the blessing of healing and good news to the poor and oppressed (11:4–5), yet those who reject his ministry and message face certain judgment, which even now is pronounced by Jesus (11:20–24; cf. John 3:31–36; 5:25–35).[5]

## Jesus' Tribute to John the Baptist (11:7–19)

AFTER MILDLY REBUKING John for not seeing with eyes of faith the full picture of his messianic program, Jesus speaks to the crowds about John, giving a glowing tribute to this greatest of those born of women (11:11–15). He then rebukes the crowds and the religious leaders for not responding to John's ministry as well as his own (11:16–19).

**John is more than a prophet (11:7–10).** John was immensely influential among the people of Israel (3:1–6). The crowds may have heard of his questions about Jesus' messianic identity, and if John was experiencing doubt, they may be following his lead and be experiencing doubt as well. So Jesus compels them to recall the tremendous impact that John's ministry had originally had among them.

He begins his tribute by inducing the crowds to specify correctly John's identity and mission, which in turn will lead them to an accurate understanding of Jesus' own identity and mission. Jesus asks, "What did you go out into the desert to see?" John's call to repentance was extraordinary, as throngs of people continually went out to him (3:5). Through three rhetorical questions Jesus gives the crowds contrasting options about John, which will force them to acknowledge his true identity and mission.

---

5. Yamasaki, *John the Baptist in Life and Death,* 106–10; Robert L. Webb, "Jesus' Baptism: Its Historicity and Implications," *BBR* 10 (2000): 305–7.

(1) Was John a "reed swayed by the wind?" The metaphor of tall reed grasses growing along the shores of the Jordan suggests weakness and vacillation with every changing wind of opportunity or challenge. John, by contrast, languishes in prison because of the strength of his resolve to confront every challenge and speak the truth.

(2) Was John "a man dressed in fine clothes?" The expected answer is "Of course not!" John consistently lived an ascetic lifestyle in keeping with his call for repentance. John's question about Jesus did not come from materialistic opportunism.

(3) The crowds should recall that they went to the desert to see the first prophet sent from God in four centuries. John was like the Old Testament prophets because he was God's spokesperson who called the nation to repentance and declared God's program of salvation.

But John was more than any prophet of the Old Testament because he was the one about whom a prophecy had been given—the prophet who would announce the arrival of the Messiah and the inbreaking of the kingdom of heaven. Because Malachi 3:1 refers to preparing *God's* way, Jesus dramatically implies his own divine status, although it is doubtful that the crowds or even Jesus' disciples understand that distinction at this point in his ministry.[6]

**John's greatness and the greatness of the messianic kingdom (11:11).** Jesus continues to defend John by pointing to the greatness of his ministry, yet he gives a surprising twist by pointing to the greatness of those in the kingdom of heaven: "I tell you the truth: Among those born of women there has not risen anyone greater than John the Baptist; yet he who is least in the kingdom of heaven is greater than he." The phrase "among those born of women" contrasts ordinary human birth (Job 14:1; 15:14; 25:4) with the birth of those born anew into the kingdom of heaven. The contrast is not between human accomplishments but between eras. The arrival of the kingdom of heaven ushers in an incomparably greater era than any preceding it.

John is a transitional figure who has prepared the way for the Coming One, but Jesus implies here that John will not live to see the full arrival of the kingdom.[7] Jesus' institution of the new covenant in his blood is a dividing line.

---

6. Gundry, *Matthew*, 214; Keener, *A Commentary on the Gospel of Matthew* (1999), 338. By substituting "you/your" for the first person ("me/[the]) in his quotation of Malachi, Jesus makes it clear that he personifies the coming of Yahweh and the eschatological Day of Yahweh.

7. The majority of interpreters follow this reasoning, including Blomberg, *Matthew*, 187; Carson, "Matthew," 264–65; France, *Matthew*, 194–95; Hagner, *Matthew*, 1:305–6; Morris, *Matthew*, 280–81. A minority view is represented by Witherington, *The Christology of Jesus*, 46–47, who attempts to include John in the kingdom of heaven by suggesting that the comparison is between two ways of evaluating the human condition. But this misses the intended comparison of the stages of redemptive history; cf. Flusser, *Jesus*, 261–64.

---

The complex of events including the cross, resurrection, ascension, and sending of the Spirit at Pentecost brings the arrival of the kingdom's redemptive life, by which time John was executed. John is the greatest of those born during the Old Testament era because of his crucial role in preparing the way for the Messiah and his kingdom. His mission was great because of the greatness of the One he introduced. But those in the kingdom are greater because of their privilege actually to have entered it.

**Violence and the kingdom of heaven (11:12).** Jesus continues his tribute to John by harking back to the beginning stages of his announcement that the kingdom of heaven will soon arrive in the ministry of the Coming One: "From the days of John the Baptist until now, the kingdom of heaven has been forcefully advancing, and forceful men lay hold of it." This saying of Jesus has been widely debated, with the difficulty arising primarily because the verb *biazo* (NIV "forcefully advancing") and the noun *biastes* (NIV "forceful men") can be taken in either a positive or a negative way.[8]

The interpretations come down to whether the two clauses are to be interpreted positively, or negatively, or a combination of both. (1) On the positive side, some suggest that Jesus is pointing to the powerful advance of the kingdom and the zeal and courage of those who dare to accept the invitation to enter.[9] (2) On the negative side, others contend that Jesus is pointing to the violence that the kingdom of heaven has suffered at the hands of evil, violent men.[10] (3) Still others suggest that Jesus is pointing to a combination of positive and negative features—the kingdom is advancing powerfully, but evil men are attacking it violently.[11]

View (2) is supported by the fact that the noun *biastes* is normally, if not always, rendered in a negative way to designate "violent men." Since the verb *biazo* and the noun *biastes* are related, Matthew intends them to reflect a parallel expression by Jesus, meaning that both clauses should be interpreted more naturally with the same force. Thus, in the light of the negative circumstances of John the Baptist and the rising opposition to his own ministry, Jesus points to the ongoing opposition that the kingdom of heaven has encountered since the days of John the Baptist. The first clause proba-

---

8. Davies and Allison, *Matthew*, 2:254–55, list no fewer than seven different interpretations. For the history of interpretation, see P. S. Cameron, *Violence and the Kingdom: The Interpretation of Matthew 11:12* (Frankfurt: Peter Lang, 1984).

9. The rendering of the NIV suggests this view; also Hendriksen, *Matthew*, 489–90; Brad H. Young, *Jesus the Jewish Theologian* (Peabody, Mass.: Hendrickson, 1995), ch. 6.

10. Blomberg, *Matthew*, 187–88; Davies and Allison, *Matthew*, 2:256; France, *Matthew*, 195–96; Hagner, *Matthew*, 1:306–7; Morris, *Matthew*, 281–32; Witherington, *The Christology of Jesus*, 46–49.

11. Carson, "Matthew," 266–68.

bly indicates opposition from the religious establishment generally, while the second clause probably points to the forces of specific evil people, such as Herod Antipas, who has even now imprisoned John. The saying foreshadows the gathering opposition to Jesus, which will come to a climax in his arrest, trial, and execution by the Jewish high priest, Caiaphas, and the Roman governor, Pontius Pilate.

**John and Elijah (11:13–15).** Jesus' tribute to John peaks with a powerful testimony to the role John has played. Jesus used the expression "Law and the Prophets" to refer to the entire Old Testament revelation (5:17); now he reverses their order, perhaps emphasizing the prophetic role of both the Old Testament and John himself: "For all the Prophets and the Law prophesied until John." John is the culmination of a long history of prophecy that looked forward to the arrival of the messianic kingdom. That prophetic hope has been realized in John's preparation for Jesus' inauguration of the kingdom of heaven.

Thus, Jesus turns to the crowds and announces, "And if you are willing to accept it, he is the Elijah who was to come." Malachi prophesied that Elijah would prepare the way for Messiah (Mal. 3:1; 4:5). Malachi did not imply a reincarnation of Elijah or that Elijah would return to life in a whirlwind the way that he left. Perhaps that is why John earlier had denied that he was Elijah (John 1:21). John fulfilled Malachi's prophecy in that at his conception he was designated as the one who would minister in the "spirit and power of Elijah" (Luke 1:17). For those who receive John's ministry, he is the fulfillment of Malachi's prophecy (see Matt. 17:10–13).

Therefore, Jesus summons the crowds to exercise faith in both John's preparatory message and Jesus' identity as the messianic deliverer: "He who has ears, let him hear." This phrase calls for a response from the crowd and, at the same time, introduces Jesus' rebuke of Israel generally for rejecting John's role of preparing for Jesus Messiah and the establishment of the kingdom of heaven. This call to recognize John as the fulfillment of Malachi's prophecy is even more dramatic when we recall that Elijah would prepare for the coming of the Lord himself in the great and terrible day of the Lord (cf. Mal. 3:1; 4:5–6). Jesus equates his ministry as Messiah with God's own arrival, another awe-inspiring revelation of his divine identity.[12]

**The discontented generation (11:16–19).** Jesus now rebukes the present generation. The expression "this generation" recurs often in Matthew's Gospel pejoratively to designate the current generation of Israel's people—including the crowds and the religious leaders—who have rejected John's and Jesus'

---

12. Cf. 11:10; France, *Matthew*, 194, 196; idem, *Jesus and the Old Testament* (Downers Grove, Ill: InterVarsity Press, 1971), 91–92, 155.

ministries (cf. related expressions, such as "a wicked and adulterous generation").[13] This is not a blanket condemnation of Israel, because Jesus' own disciples are Jews and large crowds of Jews still follow him around (cf. 14:13–
21), but it points sadly to the fact that only a small minority of the current
generation will enter the narrow gate to the kingdom by accepting John's and
Jesus' invitation (7:13–14).

Jesus taps into the current cultural setting by drawing on games that children played in the marketplace. In many villages the marketplace was the regular playground for children while their parents shopped, bartered, and
exchanged local news. But Jesus intriguingly compares the innocence of
child's play with the deviousness of this generation of adults who are playing an evil game. The difference is between *childlike*, which is positive (cf.
18:1–5), and *childish*, which is essentially selfish, petty, and insistent on having one's own way.

When children invite other children to join them in playing games, childish children insist on having their own way. The current generation is like
such children, who continually want to set the agenda of games. They are
like pouting, petulant children who criticize other children because they
wouldn't go along with their agenda. When they announce to everyone by
playing a flute that the game they want to play is "wedding," they become
upset when other children don't go along by dancing. Then when they
change the game and announce a funeral game by singing a "dirge," they are
upset when the other children don't immediately fall in line by putting on a
face of mourning. Selfish childishness insists on having its own way.

Likewise, this generation rejects the invitation to the kingdom of heaven
because John and Jesus don't play the game that they want. They rejected
John because he did not dance when they wanted to be merry, and they are
rejecting Jesus because he does not mourn when they want to fast (e.g.,
9:14–17). Like hardhearted sinners, the generation of Jesus' day expected
John and Jesus to conform to their expectations and refused to allow God's
agenda to alter their own.

"For John came neither eating nor drinking, and they say, 'He has a
demon.'" The expression "neither eating nor drinking" contrasts everyday,
carefree indulgence with John's rigorous personalization of his message of
repentance in the light of the soon-arriving kingdom of heaven (see comments on 3:1–11). Those who rejected John's message interpreted his rugged
appearance and ascetic desert habits as proof that he was demon-possessed,
like the demoniacs who chose to live in tombs or in the desert (8:28; 12:43).
The same people will also accuse Jesus of being demon-possessed when he

---

13. Cf. 12:39, 41–42, 45; 16:4; 17:17; 23:36; 24:34.

exorcises a demon on the Sabbath, bringing him into conflict with their Sabbath rulings (12:24). It is the way of those with hardened hearts to try to rationalize their decision to reject the message by falsely accusing the messenger.

Reversing the accusation, when Jesus came eating and drinking, they accused him of being "a glutton and a drunkard, a friend of tax collectors and 'sinners'" (11:19). By referring to himself once again as the "Son of Man" Jesus gives another reference to his unique messianic identity as the great physician who sought out those who needed his healing touch of salvation from sin (see comments on 8:20). It is a hardhearted generation that distorts Jesus' salvific association with those who need spiritual healing (see comments on 5:46; 9:9–13) into an accusation of him being a rapacious and inebriated party animal.

But, as Jesus, says, "wisdom is proved right by her actions." Wisdom (*sophia*) was often personified in Judaism as a woman giving her children practical guidance in everyday affairs (Prov. 8; cf. Wisd. Sol. 7–8; Sir. 51:13–30). The personification exemplified the way in which those who are guided by God's practical approach to life make right decisions. The saying here appears to be proverbial. Some interpret it to be Christological, with Jesus identified as Wisdom incarnate.[14] Elsewhere in the New Testament Jesus is referred to as "the wisdom of God" (1 Cor. 1:24, 30), and the message of the gospel is "God's wisdom" (1 Cor. 2:7), which has become reality through Jesus' death on the cross (1 Cor. 2:8).[15] In this view, as Wisdom incarnate, Jesus' deeds, including those criticized by his opponents, will ultimately vindicate him.

However, since the emphasis in the passage is not primarily Christological but salvation-historically attuned to the developing ministries of John and Jesus, it is better to understand "wisdom" here in its more usual sense in association with God's wisdom. God's wisdom will be "proved right" (or "vindicated") by her actions in the ministries and lifestyles of John and Jesus. Wisdom is the application of knowledge to life in such a way that a person's activities are a concrete example of a life lived well in God's presence. If this generation had taken John the Baptist and Jesus for who they said they were, the knowledge of them as forerunner and Messiah would have been proved right by their actions, as seemingly opposite as were their lifestyles. This interpretation appears to explain best its occurrence in this context.[16]

---

14. See M. Jack Suggs, *Wisdom, Christology, and Law in Matthew's Gospel* (Cambridge, Mass.: Harvard Univ. Press, 1970), 36–58; followed by Boring, "Matthew," *NIB*, 8:269; Davies and Allison, *Matthew*, 2:264–65; Hagner, *Matthew*, 1:311; Keener, *A Commentary on the Gospel of Matthew* (1999), 343.

15. For a brief discussion of the wisdom motif, see Eckhard J. Schnabel, "Wisdom," *NDBT*, 843–48.

16. Cf. Carson, "Matthew," 270–71; France, *Matthew*, 197.

## Judgment and Invitation (11:20–30)

HAVING REBUKED THE crowds and the religious leaders for not responding to his ministry and that of John, Jesus speaks words of judgment on those who do not repent (11:20–24). He goes on, however, to give one of the warmest invitations to the crowds to become his disciples and find rest in relationship with him (11:25–30).

**The privileged unrepentant cities (11:20–24).** Jesus turns up the heat by "denouncing" the cities who have rejected his gospel message. Capernaum, Korazin (or Chorazin), and Bethsaida—what some call the "Evangelical Triangle"—were the cities in which most of Jesus' miracles had been performed (11:20).[17] They have rejected Jesus' mission, so on them each are pronounced a series of "woes" (see comments on 23:13). Tyre and Sidon were Gentile cities in northwest Philistia/Phoenicia. In the Old Testament they became proverbial for pagan peoples, often linked as the object of condemnation from Old Testament prophets for their Baal worship and arrogant pride in their power and wealth.[18]

The privilege of witnessing Jesus' miraculous ministry should have moved the people within the Evangelical Triangle to repent and accept the invitation to the kingdom of heaven. Repentance was the appropriate response to Jesus' miracles, which validated his message of the kingdom (cf. 4:23; 9:35). "Sackcloth and ashes" were familiar symbols of repentance (cf. Est. 4:1–3; Jonah 3:5–8).

The contrast is heightened when Jesus refers to Capernaum, his own city (9:1, 9; cf. 4:13), which was privileged to be the headquarters of his Galilean ministry. Its prideful self-exaltation will result in its being condemned to "Hades" (NIV "depths"; cf. Isa. 14:12–15).

Sodom was the consummately proverbial city of sin.[19] Yet Sodom too, had it been privileged with the revelation of Jesus' miracles, would have been gripped by the reality of the gospel of the kingdom and would have repented. The gradation of punishment for Sodom in comparison to Capernaum indicates that the punishment given will accord with the light of revelation received (cf. 11:22, 24).

**A prayer of praise to the Father (11:25–26).** The intimacy of Jesus' relationship with God is again revealed as he addresses him as "Father" (6:9; cf. Sir. 51:10). In the context of question, rejection, and judgment (cf. "at that time"), Jesus praises the Father for his wise plan of redemption. The expression "Lord of heaven and earth" is a title of sovereignty that brings comfort

17. For more on these cities, see Wilkins, "Matthew," 74.
18. E.g., Isa. 23:1–17; Jer. 25:22; 27:3–7; Ezek. 26:2–9; Joel 3:4–8; Zech. 9:2–4.
19. Gen. 18:16–19:29; Ezek. 16:48; cf. *m. Sanh.* 10.3.

and security, as is expressed in Jewish literature, "Take courage, my daughter; the Lord of heaven grant you joy in place of your sorrow" (Tobit 7:16).

Jesus praises his Father "because you have hidden these things from the wise and learned, and revealed them to little children." The things that are both hidden and revealed are presumably the activities of the good news of the presence of the kingdom of heaven that required humble eyes of faith to see God's hand in them. These things are "what Christ was doing" (11:2) that John and his disciples should have recognized as pointing to Jesus' identity as the "one who was to come" (11:3–5)—things for which the present generation is being judged (11:16–24). The "wise and learned" are not academic specialists but those who stubbornly refuse to repent and learn from Jesus the true way to God (i.e., the current generation in Capernaum, Korazin, and Bethsaida; cf. also 23:25–28). "Little children" are those who innocently (not naively) receive Jesus' revelation from the Father (cf. 18:1–5). The Father's divine sovereignty and the respondents' responsibility are thus held in perfect balance.

The contrast is between those whose pride and self-sufficiency have caused them to reject Jesus' message and those whose humility and recognition of their own neediness allow them to be open to God's unqualified care through Jesus' announcement of the arrival of the kingdom. Jesus will use his teaching in parables as a way to test the hearts of the people, so that those who are spiritually responsive will learn more while those who refuse to repent will have their hearts and ears closed (cf. 13:10–16). Jesus praises the Father's sovereignty and wise plan of redemption, but also the Father's motivation behind it, which was his "good pleasure" (11:26). It is the Father's will that all receive his care in the same way, as humble and repentant children.

**The unique relationship between Father and Son (11:27).** Jesus follows his brief prayer with an astonishing statement of his relationship to the Father—a statement that has been called "the most important passage for the study of Synoptic Christology"[20]: "All things have been committed to me by my Father. No one knows the Son except the Father, and no one knows the Father except the Son and those to whom the Son chooses to reveal him." Jesus has a profound divine self-consciousness. He was validated at the baptism as the Son (3:17), tested as the Son of God (4:2–10), worshiped as the Son of God (14:33), confessed as the Son of the living God (16:16), validated at the Transfiguration as the Son (17:5), alludes to himself as the Son in the parables of the landowner and wedding banquet (21:23–46; 22:1–14), refers to himself as the Son of the Father (24:36), emphasized as Son of God strongly in the trial and crucifixion (cf. 26:39, 63; 27:43, 54), and associated

---

20. Ladd, *A Theology of the New Testament*, 164.

with the Father and Holy Spirit in the baptism of new disciples (28:18–20). The Son theme is one of the high points of Matthew's Christology as well as Synoptic Christology generally.[21]

In both his incarnate and eternal state as Son, Jesus and the Father know each other in an exclusive way, which in biblical language means that they enjoy an exclusive relationship. For Jesus as Son, the Father is "my Father."[22] They enjoy a direct, intuitive, and immediate knowledge that is grounded in their divine relationship as Father and Son. As such, what the Father and Son share stands apart from all human relationships and all human knowledge.[23] Thus, Jesus' sonship involves more than a unique filial consciousness; it involves an exclusive essential relationship between Father and Son.[24]

In his incarnate state, Jesus received from the Father the exclusive authority to reveal the Father, which does not imply the Son's inferiority to the Father but the process of revelation.[25] Humans can know the Father only through the sovereign will of the Son's revelation. Therefore, a crucial element of Jesus' messianic mission is to impart to people a mediated knowledge of God, which indicates that sonship and messiahship are not the same. Sonship precedes messiahship and is the basis for the entire messianic mission. God's program of salvation history derives from the unique, divine relationship of Father and Son.

**An invitation to the weary and burdened (11:28–30).** With an invitation found only in Matthew's Gospel, Jesus, who alone reveals the Father and the divine plan of redemption, calls out, "Come to me, all you who are weary and burdened, and I will give you rest." Jesus had called Peter and Andrew with a similar expression (4:19), but there it was (lit.) "Come after me," while here it is "Come to me," a tender call to intimacy with him for all those who are weary and burdened. "Weary" evokes the image of persons exhausted from their work or journey, while "burdened" indicates persons weighted down with heavy loads. They are like the crowds whom Jesus said earlier are harassed and helpless, like sheep without a shepherd (9:36).

In the light of the following statements, the scribes and Pharisees seem once again to be the target of Jesus' criticism (cf. 5:20; 6:1–18). Jesus will later condemn outright the Jewish leaders for the burden that their legalistic traditions has put on the people (23:4), so this is an invitation to the crowds to become his disciples and find a rest in him that cannot be found in the legal casuistry of the Pharisees.

---

21. Stein, *The Method and Message of Jesus' Teachings*, 131–35.

22. Not "the Father"; cf. also, 7:21; 10:32, 33; 12:50; 16:17; 18:10, 19; 20:23; 25:34; 26:39, 42, 53.

23. Ladd, *A Theology of the New Testament*, 165–66.

24. Ibid., 166.

25. Guthrie, *New Testament Theology*, 307.

---

He extends the invitation by saying, "Take my yoke upon you and learn from me, for I am gentle and humble in heart, and you will find rest for your souls." The "yoke" (*zygos*) was the wooden frame joining two animals (usually oxen) for pulling heavy loads; this image was used metaphorically to describe one individual's subjection to another. In that latter sense, the yoke is a common metaphor in Judaism for the law: "He that takes upon himself the yoke of the Law, from him shall be taken away the yoke of the kingdom [troubles from those in power] and the yoke of worldly care; but he that throws off the yoke of the Law, upon him shall be laid the yoke of the kingdom and the yoke of worldly care."[26]

Sirach invited people to the yoke of studying Torah through personified wisdom: "Acquire wisdom for yourselves without money. Put your neck under her yoke, and let your souls receive instruction; it is to be found close by" (Sir. 51:25–26; cf. 6:23–31). The Sirach passage is often cited as the background for Jesus' statement and recently has generated much discussion about Jesus claiming to be Wisdom incarnate.[27] But the contrast between Sirach and Jesus' saying is distinct. Sirach invites his readers to the "house of instruction" for the study of Torah (Sir. 51:23). The developing rabbinic tradition understood discipleship to entail learning from Pharisaic authorities and carrying out scrupulous observance of the oral law.[28] Because the oral law was considered to be of divine origin, its massive obligations became far more burdensome than Scripture itself, and with the passing of years and the addition of more and more prescriptions, the rabbis could not lessen the burden without overthrowing the whole system.

In addition, the yoke is also a familiar metaphor in the Old Testament to describe Israel's subjection to foreign oppression: "With a yoke on our necks we are hard driven; we are weary, we are given no rest" (Lam. 5:5 RSV). Israel's return from the Egyptian captivity is described as release from the heavy yoke of servitude: "I am the LORD your God, who brought you out of Egypt so that you would no longer be slaves to the Egyptians; I broke the bars of your yoke and enabled you to walk with heads held high" (Lev. 26:13; cf. Ex. 6:6–8). And the prophets promised a time when God would break off the yoke of foreign oppression and give rest to the people of Israel when they repented and were restored to the land (e.g., Isa. 14:25; Jer. 2:20; 5:5; 30:8; Ezek. 34:27).[29]

---

26. *m. ʾAbot* 3:5; cf. *m. Ber.* 2:2.

27. Suggs, *Wisdom, Christology and Law in Matthew's Gospel*, 107; Celia Deutsch, *Hidden Wisdom and the Easy Yoke* (JSNT 18; Sheffield: JSOT Press, 1987), 130.

28. The New Testament elsewhere refers to the yoke of legalism (Acts 15:10; Gal. 5:1).

29. B. Charette, "'To Proclaim Liberty to the Captives': Matthew 11.28–30 in the Light of OT Prophetic Expectation," *NTS* 38 (1992): 290–97.

Jesus' invitation is in stark contrast to the religious burden of Pharaisism or the militaristic burden of foreign oppressors. His yoke—a metaphor for discipleship to him—promises rest from the weariness and burden of religious regulation and human oppression, because it is none other than commitment to him. His disciples learn directly from him. As the messianic inaugurator of the kingdom of heaven, Jesus offers rest in himself for their souls through his authoritative understanding of God's truth. His yoke will bring true learning, which takes us back to the Sermon on the Mount, where he declares that has come to fulfill the Law. To learn from Jesus is to learn from his revelation of what the Law truly intends (cf. 5:17–48).

The yoke of discipleship brings rest because (*hoti;* NIV "for") Jesus is "gentle and humble in heart" (11:29). Jesus exemplifies the very characteristics his disciples will display as members of the kingdom of heaven—gentleness (5:5) and humility (James 4:6; 1 Peter 5:5). He has castigated the scribes and the Pharisees for their hypocritical self-righteousness (5:20; 6:1–18) and will condemn them for their prideful religious regalia, places of privilege, and elitist titles (23:5–7). But Jesus does not need to strut his authority. He has come gently, preaching and teaching the good news of the arrival of the kingdom of heaven, and in humble human form he has brought healing to sin-sick humanity. This is the true eschatological rest for which Israel has long hoped, "a realization of a deep existential peace, a *shalom*, or sense of ultimate well-being with regard to one's relationship to God and his commandments."[30] Jesus' teaching is the true fulfillment of the Law, and those who come to him will enter into a discipleship that produces rest for the soul (cf. Jer. 6:16).

While discipleship to Jesus brings relief from the burden of Pharisaic regulations, it is not lawlessness. He goes on to say, "For my yoke is easy and my burden is light." These two clauses are in synonymous parallelism to emphasize Jesus' way of discipleship. His discipleship is an easy or serviceable yoke because his teaching equips us most effectively to live out God's will in the way life was designed to be lived. Furthermore, his discipleship is not the oppressive burden of Pharisaic legalism (23:4) but instead turns the load of life into one that is manageable (cf. Gal. 6:5). Jesus does not release his disciples from burdens, just as he did not escape the burdens of human life in his Incarnation. Illness and calamity and tragedy remain a part of this fallen world until the final renewal, but for those in the kingdom of heaven there is a promise of Jesus' sustaining help as we carry his yoke of discipleship.

In fact, in Jesus' interpretation of the Law the challenge of following him may be seen as even more demanding than the Pharisees, because he calls us to fulfill the Law from the obedience of the heart, not simply through exter-

---

30. Hagner, *Matthew*, 1:324.

nal obedience (5:21–47), and he calls his disciples to be perfect, as their heavenly Father is perfect (5:48). But Jesus' demands are still a yoke that is easy to bear and a burden that is light to carry, because in the coming of the kingdom and the inauguration of the new covenant, his Spirit provides the same strength to carry the load that Jesus himself relied upon to carry his own load of redemptive service to humanity.[31]

However, in the quest to learn from Jesus how to live God's truth, it is critical to remember that Jesus' disciples can also turn his yoke into an unbearable burden unless we consciously recognize that discipleship to Jesus is not essentially a religious obligation. Rather, ours is an intimate relationship with the One who calls, "Come to me" and "learn from me." As complicated as life may become, discipleship is at heart simply walking with Jesus in the real world and having him teach us moment by moment how to live life his way.

WITH JESUS' MESSIANIC message (chs. 5–7) and miraculous ministry (chs. 8–9) established and the disciples' mission to Israel commissioned (ch. 10), Matthew tracks a change. Crowds still follow, but the mood is different. There is a beginning dissatisfaction with Jesus, which is an ominous harbinger of a swing to reject Jesus as Israel's Messiah. In chapter 11 we find a number of questions raised about Jesus' identity and mission, while in chapter 12 we find outright opposition. Israel has been privileged to be given the first opportunity in salvation history to receive Messiah, and Jesus will continue to give them further opportunity to acknowledge him as their Messiah, but the time is drawing near for accountability to their decision, either for or against him. Privilege and responsibility are two paramount themes throughout chapter 11.

**The incomparable privilege of bearing witness to Jesus Messiah.** The culmination of God's salvation history has occurred in the deeds of the Messiah, with the generation of that time being one of the most, if not *the* most, privileged in all of history. (1) They were privileged to witness these events unfold. Jesus points to his activities of healing and preaching as explicit confirmation that he is indeed the Messiah (11:4–5). Both the crowds and the religious leaders of the cities that witnessed these miraculous messianic deeds were also among the most privileged (11:20–23).

(2) That generation was the most privileged because they had been honored to witness John the Baptist's ministry. John should be recognized as a

---

31. Hafemann, *The God of Promise and the Life of Faith*, 203.

great man in his own right (11:11). He was the first prophet to speak in Israel in hundreds of years. He was an immensely important historical figure, because he was the link between God's saving activity in the Old Testament and his saving activity in the ministry of Jesus Messiah. The people were privileged to witness this one who was more than a prophet, the one who himself was privileged to fulfill Malachi's prophecy of Elijah preparing the way for God's arrival.

(3) The honor that John had was almost nil in comparison to those with the faith and courage to respond to Jesus' messianic ministry and enter the kingdom of heaven (11:11). It was a great privilege to belong to this era of God's salvation history. But beyond that privilege was the even greater one of being in relationship to Jesus, to have experienced forgiveness of sins and transformation of regeneration by the Spirit (26:26–29), to belong to the church, the body of Christ (16:18–19), and to be involved in the Great Commission to bring the nations to Jesus as new disciples (28:18–20). Greatness according to Jesus is not primarily related to accomplishment, which is the prevailing yardstick of the world. Jesus measures greatness simply in one's acquisition of the redemptive work of Jesus and one's service to others in advancing the cause of the kingdom (cf. 18:1–4; 20:20–28). Privilege in the kingdom of heaven does not come from jockeying for positions of greatness but by being a member of the new order that Jesus brings and bearing witness to him. Jesus offers privilege to *all* who receive it.

(4) This generation was honored to be the first witnesses of the astonishing revelation of the relationship between Father and Son and now to be included in that relationship. Father and Son from eternity had a uniquely transparent knowledge of one another (11:27). They intensely and intuitively knew each other's essential being and shared each other's thoughts, emotions, and will. And with the Incarnation, Jesus' mission was to reveal that relationship to humanity and include in it those who dared to respond to such an astounding revelation. And miracle of miracles, those who enter this relationship will find rest from the human toil of trying to figure this whole thing out on their own. We enter into a discipleship to Jesus in which we learn from him directly. Jeremiah had prophesied of this sort of new covenant life:

> I will be their God,
>> and they will be my people.
> No longer will a man teach his neighbor,
>> or a man his brother, saying, 'Know the LORD,'
> because they will all know me,
>> from the least of them to the greatest. (Jer. 31:33–34)

Isaiah too prophesied of a coming day for Israel when they would experience a relationship with God in which he would give direct guidance to their daily lives:

> Although the Lord has given you bread of privation and water of oppression, He, your Teacher will no longer hide Himself, but your eyes will behold your Teacher. And your ears will hear a word behind you, "This is the way, walk in it," whenever you turn to the right or to the left. (Isa. 30:20–21 NASB)

The Old Testament theme of God with his people finds explicit fulfillment in the relationship of Jesus with those privileged to undertake the easy yoke and light burden of discipleship to him.[32]

Do we think of discipleship to Jesus in this way? Do we understand how much of a privilege it is to be a part of the kingdom of heaven? I suspect that too often we take for granted our relationship with Jesus, our peace with the Father, and the reality of the church as the body of Christ. We may even forget that it was out of God's voluntary great love and sacrifice that our current spiritual existence is even possible, and that the nature of this existence is greater than any that came before Jesus.

This information should encourage us to take the most advantage of the benefits of kingdom discipleship to Jesus by fully realizing who we were meant to be as human beings—those who fully love and serve God and others out of a renewed and loving spirit, not from compulsion (cf. chs. 5–7). This should also energize us to pursue intentionally our spiritual development.

**The unavoidable responsibility that accompanies privilege.** The second major theme of this chapter is that with privilege and opportunity come unavoidable responsibility. When we witness the acts of the Messiah, our responsibility is to respond humbly in belief. John and his disciples were privileged to prepare the way for Jesus, but that privilege brought personal responsibility to continue humbly to believe in Jesus Messiah's mission, even when things weren't going as they anticipated. But it also brought them a wider responsibility, because if they did not in faith continue to hail Jesus as Messiah, they would lead others astray.

With the advantage of witnessing John's and Jesus' ministries came the unavoidable responsibility to exercise one's will (11:14), to open's one's ears to hear (11:15), and to respond to the message that John fulfilled the prophecy about Elijah coming to prepare for God's arrival and the Day of the Lord (cf. 11:10; Mal. 3:1; 4:5–6). But instead, that generation childishly demanded their own agenda, refusing both John's and Jesus' message and

---

32. See further on the fulfillment of this theme in Wilkins, *Following the Master*, 51–69.

libelously condemning both messengers (11:16–19). But God's wisdom in salvation history will prove this wicked generation wrong, and they will bear the full responsibility for rejecting God's messengers.

The privilege of the people in the cities of Korazin, Bethsaida, and Capernaum to have witnessed Jesus' messianic deeds had an accompanying responsibility to repent and acknowledge Jesus as Messiah. Instead, their privilege led them to self-exaltation so that they rejected Jesus. Their privilege and abandonment of the accompanying responsibility now leads to greater culpability, and their judgment will be greater than the most infamously sinful cities in the ancient world (11:20–24).

And with the benefit of receiving the revelation of the knowledge of the relationship between the Father and Son (11:25–27) comes the responsibility not to dishonor the sacredness of that relationship. To reject that knowledge is to commit blasphemy against God, but to receive that knowledge from Jesus is to humbly receive the yoke of discipleship to him and to bear with dignity the honor of serving him. With the words of Jesus so accessible to us, as we now daily learn from him (11:29), we have a greater responsibility to know exactly what it is to be his disciple—what he calls us to do and who he calls us to be. To neglect this responsibility is to fail to be a faithful follower.

Thus, for us as Jesus' disciples, privilege is balanced with responsibility. The more we know, the more we are responsible, both to be obedient to that knowledge and to share that knowledge with others. However, in all of our privilege and responsibility, we should never forget that Jesus says that our yoke is easy and our burden is light. Why? Primarily because Jesus shares the yoke and burden with us. Doug Webster comments on both the challenge and the promise of the easy yoke and light burden that Jesus extends to us:

> His easy yoke is neither cheap nor convenient. The surprising promise of the easy yoke was meant to free us from a self-serving, meritorious, performance-based religion. It is easy in that it frees us from the burden of self-centeredness; liberates us from the load of self-righteousness; and frees us to live in the way that God intended us to live. . . . The easy yoke sounds like an oxymoron. Plowing a field or pulling a load is hard work! And nowhere does Jesus promise soft ground for tilling or level paths for bearing the load. What he does promise is a relationship with Himself. The demands are great but the relationship with Jesus makes the burden light.[33]

---

33. Doug Webster, *The Easy Yoke* (Colorado Springs: NavPress, 1995), 8, 14.

REST. Of the many different types of people who gather together in Christian worship each week, one group deserves special attention: those who come to the Lord with a questioning heart in need of rest. It may be a person who suffers at work under an uncaring boss; it may be a person in a marriage with an uncaring or cheating spouse; it may be a faithful parent with a spiritually wayward child; or it may be a young person who has lost a friend in a tragic death. Oftentimes these kinds of people will come into a worship setting to question—sometimes respectfully, other times not—the Lord's control of life. They are seeking some kind of resolution in their heart to a big question in their lives for which they have no answer and for which they may even doubt that God has an answer. What they need is rest.

It is the wise pastor or youth worker or Sunday school teacher who recognizes how many people come to church with this need of rest. Jesus extends the same invitation to rest to each, though not all will respond to him in the same way.

(1) *Experience and expectations.* Some come with questions because their experience does not match up with how they expect God's will to be carried out. As God's prophet preparing the way for the Messiah, John the Baptist had special revelation about Jesus' messianic identity. However, his present experience of being in prison awaiting execution did not jive with his expectations of the judgment that the Messiah's arrival would bring. Jesus' reply forced John to look at the facts of his ministry and adjust his expectations to fit God's activity (11:1–6).

Many people can relate to John's situation. The young mother of three children whose husband is diagnosed with terminal cancer may plead with God to understand how he could leave her with this unexpected, lonely burden. The youth pastor who is unexpectedly forced out of the church by the new senior pastor may question what it really means to follow God's leading. The veteran missionary couple who have sacrificed throughout their lives to spread God's message only to discover that their denominational retirement fund has unexpectedly been dissolved may question their own wisdom and God's provision. These are just three real-life situations that come to mind; each of us can think of dozens of others where our own experience does not match what we expected from following God's leading. From Jesus' reply to John's question we may infer three guidelines to such questions.

(a) Jesus' reply displays compassion for John's circumstances and suffering, which is always a necessary element to be included in any of our responses to those whose questions stem from suffering. The young wife and mother whose husband died of cancer needed years of compassionate care by our community of faith, which gave her the strength to trust God's wisdom even in the most difficult circumstances.

(b) Jesus did not allow John's current climate of questioning to cancel out John's prior, lifetime courageous ministry. Jesus' tribute to John may have been the reminder he needed to call himself back to the message that he had preached for so long. The youth pastor ousted from his former position needed to be reminded that even if he is not appreciated by one person, that does not cancel out the thousands of lives that he touched throughout his years of ministry. He needs to learn from this difficult experience, but not allow it to cancel out the memory of the effectiveness of his past ministry or deter him from future ministry.

(c) Perhaps most important, Jesus pointed to the fulfillment of Scripture in his healing and preaching ministry. John's expectations must continually be guided by the reality of God's Word. The retired missionary couple had leaned on God's Word throughout their career, and it is what brought them back to a realistic understanding of God's purposes in their lives. Even though humans failed them, God's Word promised that he would be faithful to them, and they found remarkable peace in the middle of their dilemma. As a result, the Christian community responded with an outpouring of love and support for them, by which God was proven once again to be faithful in their lives.

I should add one additional element that jolts me as I read this passage. On the one hand, John's question reassures us that if this great prophet has questions, it's all right for us to have questions as well. I need to be honest when I encounter situations that tax my faith or my understanding and be able to express when my experience baffles my expectations. This is where it is especially important to have colleagues and confidants who understand and can help us through situations that we may not have encountered before and which catch us unexpectedly off-guard. Jesus acted as a stalwart friend to John in this situation.

But, on the other hand, we may have the potential to lead others astray with our questions. John mildly rebukes John for not seeing clearly the fulfillment of Scripture in his ministry (11:6). If John continues to allow his circumstances to take his eyes off of the reality of God's activity in Jesus' ministry, he will not only stumble himself but will almost certainly continue to lead his own disciples astray and the crowds who venerated him as God's prophet. There are times when we may need to endure silently our circumstances and trust God's leading. I've seen Christian leaders virtually destroy their ministries because they bring home every detail of their ministry to their spouse, needing a sympathetic ear to whom they can ventilate their struggles. One friend did this so regularly that he and his wife came to despise the people of their ministry because they only spoke of the bad, virtually never sharing together the good. They repeated this in their last two callings and are now out of that ministry.

Our present experiences exert a powerful influence on the way we view God's activities in our lives and in the lives of others. We will find the fortitude to endure when we experience compassion, respect, and a clear understanding of God's will according to his Word.

(2) *Agendas and motives.* There are also those whose personal agenda for God's work causes them to question and to distort the motives of God's messengers. Jesus compares the current generation to children who stubbornly demand that other children play the game they want, and when they won't go along, they slander their character. There was no way of pleasing that generation, because ultimately they did not want to submit their own religious agendas to God's plan of salvation. John was too ascetically religious, and Jesus was not pious enough.

The response of this generation suggests a couple of points. (a) As convinced as we may be about our own agendas for what we believe to be the right way of doing God's work, having a healthy personal humility allows room for God to adjust our agendas. The religious leaders and even the crowds missed, and even distorted, the message of both John and Jesus because of their stubborn refusal to hear God's voice in their messages.

One of my colleagues has been a leader in evangelical academia and scholarship for over forty years, and he is firm in his doctrine and his understanding of the way in which ministry and academia should be conducted. It would be quite an undertaking for someone to try to change his views of the kingdom or how leadership within the church and school should be accomplished. Yet what keeps him continually alert to grow in his understanding of God's Word and work is his deep-seated humility. He would rather ask my opinion on an issue than demand that I hear his. This does not suggest that we cannot have a healthy skepticism about suggestions or have a healthy confidence in what God has taught us. But it does suggest that we need to have hearts that are soft enough to be receptive to Jesus and the ministry he brings to us through others.

(b) In Jesus words, "But wisdom is proved right by her actions" (11:19), he gives the comforting assurance of being vindicated in the midst of rejection. Jesus and John were both rejected, and those who follow Jesus now may experience rejection. Jesus continually lays out the hardship of those who follow him. However, there is a level of vindication that will become self-evident in the deeds of the individual, and ultimately in the hands of a just God, that should give us strength and confidence. When we are confident of the truth of God's Word and follow that truth, the truth itself will vindicate our actions. Obviously this needs to be tempered with the points above, that we must be careful of prideful attachment to our own agendas. But when lived out with healthy humility, we can find confidence in contending for the truth of God's Word.

(3) *Smugness and a hardened heart.* The self-serving agenda of those who question the motives of the messengers eventually leads them to reject Jesus, and the smugness of their hardened heart leads them to impending eternal judgment. This was the fate of people in Korazin, Bethsaida, and Capernaum (11:20–24), and it is the fate of those today whose privileged position leads them to question Jesus' identity and message. This is the sad story often found within liberal Christian academia, where scholars may have been raised in churches where they confessed Jesus as Savior but whose increasing secularism leads them into a profound skepticism about Jesus.

New Testament scholar Robert Funk, founder of the infamous Jesus Seminar, tells of his own journey, which led him from a youth where he confessed Jesus as his personal Savior, to the point where in his early adulthood he rejected a life of ministry and later ultimately rejected Jesus as any kind of divine Savior. He prefers instead to create a picture of Jesus that conforms more comfortably with his modernist agenda, smugly contending that those who continue to believe in the Jesus of the New Testament and the creeds of the church are "compliant, mindless adherents of the received tradition."[34] His is a sad commentary.

A very different New Testament scholar, Dale Bruner, warns all who have had the privilege of experiencing the risen Christ's miraculous presence to see whether we have given him his rightful place in our lives. Capernaum seems to have had a sort of town motto based on Isaiah 14:13, "lifted up to the skies" (11:23), indicating perhaps a sense of civic pride in having Jesus' ministry based in their city, but they smugly rejected him as their Messiah. In the same way, modern countries that have been privileged to experience Jesus' miraculous presence through the work of the church and Word and who may even boast, "In God We Trust," as we do in America, are called to account for what we have done with Jesus. Bruner writes:

> *Christian* countries are in special trouble on judgment day, not because Jesus has not really been in their communities but because he has. Jesus' presence, without change, can lead to a damnation deeper than Sodom's.... Capernaum stands for all self-conscious Christianity, for

---

34. Robert W. Funk, *Honest to Jesus: Jesus for a New Millennium* (San Francisco: HarperSanFrancisco, 1999), 12. Much of his journey is recounted in ch. 1 (pp. 1–14) and is articulated in the chapter "Jesus for a New Age," 297–314.

all Christianity smug in its possession of Jesus, in its being the center of Jesus' work. . . . Jesus is not always impressed. It is going to go better in the judgment day for notorious pagans than for self-satisfied saints. The sum of the matter is this: *Christians* should take Jesus seriously. When they do, they escape judgment; when they do not, they invite it.[35]

These are serious words, but no less serious than Jesus' warning to the cities that had been privileged to witness his ministry but then rejected him out of their own smugness and hardened heart.

(4) *Weariness and rest.* Finally, there are those who have eagerly desired an intimate relationship with God, but by following the practices of the self-righteous religious leaders, they have only become weary and increasingly burdened. Jesus invites them to know true rest, for their weariness and burdens can only be released by rest in Jesus' yoke of discipleship (11:28–30). Ironically, we find ultimate rest in the easy yoke and light burden of discipleship. There seems to be something counterintuitive to finding rest in a way of discipleship that demands the highest commitment imaginable, where seeking the kingdom of heaven is to be placed before personal comfort and where we are guaranteed rejection by those whose hearts are hardened to the message of the kingdom. However, this yoke is what Jesus offers to us as being the greatest privilege imaginable.

Why is that? It is easy to find comfort in places other than Jesus himself, whether it be television, alcohol, escapist vacations, pornography, or a myriad of other things that dull us to the pain of life. We can find peace in that reality, not in other things that masquerade as true life. Much of what we use to dull the pain of life really does exactly the opposite, giving us fleeting pleasure and leaving us empty in the end. But this is exactly what Jesus offers us—true life (John 10:10), one that forms us from the inside out (see comments on Matt. 5:20) and makes us into the kinds of people who love and serve God from a renewed nature under his easy yoke of discipleship. Webster concludes his study of the easy yoke with these penetrating words:

> Apart from the grace of Christ and the saving work of the Cross, it would be impossible to convince people that the easy yoke is doable, let alone easy. But for those who live under the yoke there is absolutely no other way to live. Who in their right mind would go back to the gods of Self, Money, Lust and Power? Who would return on bended knee to the shrines of pious performance and judgmentalism? Is not

---

35. Bruner, *Christbook: Matthew 1–12*, 425, 28.

love better than hate, purity better than lust, reconciliation better than retaliation? And is not "better" really "easier" when measured in character rather than convenience, rest for the soul rather than selfish pride?[36]

Such is the rest that comes with Jesus' easy yoke of discipleship.

---

36. Webster, *The Easy Yoke*, 201.

# Matthew 12:1–50

AT THAT TIME Jesus went through the grainfields on the Sabbath. His disciples were hungry and began to pick some heads of grain and eat them. ²When the Pharisees saw this, they said to him, "Look! Your disciples are doing what is unlawful on the Sabbath."

³He answered, "Haven't you read what David did when he and his companions were hungry? ⁴He entered the house of God, and he and his companions ate the consecrated bread—which was not lawful for them to do, but only for the priests. ⁵Or haven't you read in the Law that on the Sabbath the priests in the temple desecrate the day and yet are innocent? ⁶I tell you that one greater than the temple is here. ⁷If you had known what these words mean, 'I desire mercy, not sacrifice,' you would not have condemned the innocent. ⁸For the Son of Man is Lord of the Sabbath."

⁹Going on from that place, he went into their synagogue, ¹⁰and a man with a shriveled hand was there. Looking for a reason to accuse Jesus, they asked him, "Is it lawful to heal on the Sabbath?"

¹¹He said to them, "If any of you has a sheep and it falls into a pit on the Sabbath, will you not take hold of it and lift it out? ¹²How much more valuable is a man than a sheep! Therefore it is lawful to do good on the Sabbath."

¹³Then he said to the man, "Stretch out your hand." So he stretched it out and it was completely restored, just as sound as the other. ¹⁴But the Pharisees went out and plotted how they might kill Jesus.

¹⁵Aware of this, Jesus withdrew from that place. Many followed him, and he healed all their sick, ¹⁶warning them not to tell who he was. ¹⁷This was to fulfill what was spoken through the prophet Isaiah:

¹⁸"Here is my servant whom I have chosen,
  the one I love, in whom I delight;
 I will put my Spirit on him,
  and he will proclaim justice to the nations.
¹⁹He will not quarrel or cry out;
  no one will hear his voice in the streets.

> [20] A bruised reed he will not break,
>     and a smoldering wick he will not snuff out,
>     till he leads justice to victory.
> [21]   In his name the nations will put their hope."

[22] Then they brought him a demon-possessed man who was blind and mute, and Jesus healed him, so that he could both talk and see. [23] All the people were astonished and said, "Could this be the Son of David?"

[24] But when the Pharisees heard this, they said, "It is only by Beelzebub, the prince of demons, that this fellow drives out demons."

[25] Jesus knew their thoughts and said to them, "Every kingdom divided against itself will be ruined, and every city or household divided against itself will not stand. [26] If Satan drives out Satan, he is divided against himself. How then can his kingdom stand? [27] And if I drive out demons by Beelzebub, by whom do your people drive them out? So then, they will be your judges. [28] But if I drive out demons by the Spirit of God, then the kingdom of God has come upon you.

[29] "Or again, how can anyone enter a strong man's house and carry off his possessions unless he first ties up the strong man? Then he can rob his house.

[30] "He who is not with me is against me, and he who does not gather with me scatters. [31] And so I tell you, every sin and blasphemy will be forgiven men, but the blasphemy against the Spirit will not be forgiven. [32] Anyone who speaks a word against the Son of Man will be forgiven, but anyone who speaks against the Holy Spirit will not be forgiven, either in this age or in the age to come.

[33] "Make a tree good and its fruit will be good, or make a tree bad and its fruit will be bad, for a tree is recognized by its fruit. [34] You brood of vipers, how can you who are evil say anything good? For out of the overflow of the heart the mouth speaks. [35] The good man brings good things out of the good stored up in him, and the evil man brings evil things out of the evil stored up in him. [36] But I tell you that men will have to give account on the day of judgment for every careless word they have spoken. [37] For by your words you will be acquitted, and by your words you will be condemned."

[38] Then some of the Pharisees and teachers of the law said to him, "Teacher, we want to see a miraculous sign from you."

³⁹He answered, "A wicked and adulterous generation asks for a miraculous sign! But none will be given it except the sign of the prophet Jonah. ⁴⁰For as Jonah was three days and three nights in the belly of a huge fish, so the Son of Man will be three days and three nights in the heart of the earth. ⁴¹The men of Nineveh will stand up at the judgment with this generation and condemn it; for they repented at the preaching of Jonah, and now one greater than Jonah is here. ⁴²The Queen of the South will rise at the judgment with this generation and condemn it; for she came from the ends of the earth to listen to Solomon's wisdom, and now one greater than Solomon is here.

⁴³"When an evil spirit comes out of a man, it goes through arid places seeking rest and does not find it. ⁴⁴Then it says, 'I will return to the house I left.' When it arrives, it finds the house unoccupied, swept clean and put in order. ⁴⁵Then it goes and takes with it seven other spirits more wicked than itself, and they go in and live there. And the final condition of that man is worse than the first. That is how it will be with this wicked generation."

⁴⁶While Jesus was still talking to the crowd, his mother and brothers stood outside, wanting to speak to him. ⁴⁷Someone told him, "Your mother and brothers are standing outside, wanting to speak to you."

⁴⁸He replied to him, "Who is my mother, and who are my brothers?" ⁴⁹Pointing to his disciples, he said, "Here are my mother and my brothers. ⁵⁰For whoever does the will of my Father in heaven is my brother and sister and mother."

THE ADVANCE OF Jesus' ministry has experienced an underlying opposition from the religious establishment of Israel, especially from the teachers of the law and the Pharisees. Now that opposition comes out into the open. These religious leaders are convinced that Jesus' ministry is not from God. So out of their self-deceived sense of duty to protect the people and to further God's cause, they set out to trap Jesus into being condemned by outright, flagrant violations of God's law. They focus on violations of the Sabbath (12:1–14) and then turn to accuse him of being in league with Satan (12:22–37).

But Jesus vindicates himself as God's true Lord of the Sabbath (12:8), God's true Servant of justice (12:18), the Spirit-endowed inaugurator of the kingdom of God (12:28). As such he pronounces a judgment of condemnation on these religious leaders for their hard-hearted blasphemy (12:30–45). Yet he is the hope of justice for the oppressed nations (12:18–21), who are now invited to obey the Father's will and so become Jesus' disciples, his closest family (12:46–50).

## Confrontations with the Pharisees
## over the Sabbath (12:1–14)

THE ROUND OF confrontations between Jesus and the Pharisees begins with two accusations against his disciples and himself about violating the Sabbath. God gave the Sabbath as a day of rest and holiness. The fourth commandment specified that no work was to be performed on the Sabbath, so that the day would be kept holy to God (Ex. 20:8–10). Over time the Sabbath became one of the most distinctive characteristics of the Jewish people, along with circumcision and dietary laws. But the mandate not to work was understood differently by sectarian groups within Israel, so it had to be interpreted for the people. With their emergent oral tradition, the Pharisees developed an extensive set of laws to guide the people so that they would not violate the Sabbath.

The two following incidents are recorded by each of the Synoptic Gospels (cf. Mark 2:23–3:6; Luke 6:1–11) and give a profound principle for the place of the Sabbath for Jesus' disciples. Like Jesus' interpretation of the Law and the Prophets in the Sermon on the Mount (cf. 5:17–47), he gives a stunning authoritative pronouncement about the Sabbath that takes us to the heart of God's intent and motive in giving that commandment.[1] This passage, therefore, should be read in the light of the preceding chapter, where Jesus condemned the current generation whose religious leaders, especially the Pharisees, had wearied and burdened the people with legal obligations of their traditions. Jesus has come to bring rest to those who take on his yoke of discipleship (cf. 11:28–30), the kind of true rest to which the Sabbath rest was designed to point.

**The Pharisees' accusations against Jesus' disciples (12:1–2).** The first controversy arises as the Pharisees confront Jesus about his disciples "working" on the Sabbath. Jesus regularly attended the synagogue services on the Sabbath (cf. Mark 1:21), after which he and the disciples gathered together, apparently often in Simon Peter's and Andrew's home in Capernaum (Mark

---

1. For theological significance see Yong-Eui Yang, *Jesus and the Sabbath in Matthew's Gospel* (JSNTSup 139; Sheffield: Sheffield Academic Press, 1997), 305–6.

1:29; cf. Matt. 8:14). Sometime during the day, Jesus, accompanied by his disciples, took a walk presumably within the allowable Sabbath restrictions[2] (Matt. 12:1).[2] Pathways formed borders of family fields (e.g., 13:4), which allowed travel from village to village.

While walking along, "his disciples were hungry and began to pick some heads of grain and eat them." It would have been easy for them to reach down and pick a few grains of wheat to quell the afternoon hunger as they walked along the paths that bordered agricultural fields. The law made provision for people who were hungry to eat from a neighbor's field (Deut. 23:24–25). Similarly, the edges of a field were not normally harvested, so that the poor and hungry, foreign travelers, and orphans and widows might have grain available to them. This also included olives and grapes left after the first harvest (24:19–22; cf. Ruth 2:2–3).

While it is doubtful that Pharisees regularly patrolled the fields watching for people violating the Sabbath, with the mounting opposition to Jesus' ministry they are now likely looking for opportunities to accuse him and his disciples of crimes against the law.[3] "When the Pharisees saw this, they said to him, 'Look! Your disciples are doing what is unlawful on the Sabbath.'" The expression "what is unlawful" can refer to an explicit Old Testament directive (e.g., 12:4; 14:4) or to an interpretation of an Old Testament command (e.g., 12:10; 19:3; 27:6). The disciples could have been guilty of several rabbinic rules as they plucked grain heads, separated the chaff from the grain, and ground the grain in their hands to prepare it to eat. But not everyone shared the Pharisees' view of the Sabbath, which heightens our awareness of the tension that is growing between Jesus and the Pharisees.[4]

**Jesus defends his disciples (12:3–7).** Jesus' reply puts the Pharisees on the defensive because he uses the Old Testament itself, on which they prided themselves as experts, to combat their accusations against his disciples. Instead of rebuking his disciples, Jesus cites two Old Testament examples that render ineffective the Pharisees' charge and then goes on to give a third response that clarifies his use of these examples. He is not entering into their rabbinic debate but, as in the SM, will show how his authoritative arrival and teaching has fulfilled the law.

(1) The first example is the incident when David was fleeing from King Saul, who was trying to kill him (1 Sam. 21:1–7; 22:9–23). The "consecrated

---

2. The Qumran community restricted travel to less than a quarter of a mile (CD 10.21), the rabbis to a little over half a mile (*m. Soṭah* 5:3). The only New Testament reference to this travel restriction is in Acts 1:12.

3. M. Casey, "Culture and Historicity: The Plucking of the Grain (Mark 2.23–28)," *NTS* 34 (1988): 1–23, esp. 4–5.

4. Keener, *A Commentary on the Gospel of Matthew* (1999), 351–54.

bread" refers to the twelve loaves of bread stipulated to be baked and placed in the tabernacle on each Sabbath as an offering representing the covenant made by God with the twelve tribes of Israel. This bread was only to be eaten by the priests (Lev. 24:5–9). Jesus indicates that technically David and his men did what was unlawful, but what is important to note is that Scripture does not condemn them for eating the bread, nor does it condemn the priest, Ahimelech, for allowing them to do so.

Jesus' intention in his appeal to this Old Testament incident and its relationship to the charge against Jesus' disciples has been understood variously.[5] Apparently Ahimelech understood that as God's anointed, David was serving God and was thus entitled to the bread at his time of need. The significance of Ahimelech's action in giving the bread to David becomes clear later, when Saul ordered Ahimelech and the others of the family of priests to be put to death because he aided David, the future king, and his men (cf. 1 Sam. 22:9–23). Ahimelech served God's purposes by feeding the fleeing David. The intent of the law is to serve God's people, not for God's people to serve the law. The next two responses clarify this point.

(2) The next Old Testament incident referred to by Jesus alludes to the directive in the Pentateuch that required priests to make sacrificial offerings on the Sabbath (e.g., Num. 28:9–10): "Or haven't you read in the Law that on the Sabbath the priests in the temple desecrate the day and yet are innocent?" Priests regularly violated the Sabbath when they performed their duties on the Sabbath, yet they were considered guiltless. Since God's law required them in their duties to work on the Sabbath, God made allowance within the law. Like the incident of David and his men, the law made allowance for violations when God called people to a task that would put them into conflict with a strict interpretation of the law.

Jesus presses the point by giving his rationale. "I tell you that one greater than the temple is here." Using typical rabbinic logic, Jesus emphasizes that if the guardians of the temple were allowed to violate the Sabbath for the greater good of conducting the priestly rituals, how much more should Jesus and his disciples be considered guiltless when doing the work of God given to them. After all, he is someone greater than the temple. This must have been a stunning remark to the Pharisees. What could be greater than the temple? And what is the "greater" that is now here? This word points to either the min-

---

5. Davies and Allison (*Matthew*, 2:310–11) list eight different interpretations. The most influential interpretations propose that Jesus indicates (1) that human necessities take precedence over legal technicalities, (2) that Jesus attacks the oral tradition, not the written Torah, (3) that doing good may condone breaking a commandment, or (4) that David as the anointed representative illustrates Jesus' messianic authority. The interpretation offered here combines some of the truth of each of these perspectives.

istry of Jesus and his disciples in proclaiming the arrival of the kingdom of heaven, to Jesus himself, or to a combination of both. The following comments that focus on Jesus' Christological status seem to indicate that "greater" refers to Jesus himself, but focuses on the quality of superior greatness in his ministry more than his personal identity.[6]

(3) Jesus' third response takes the argument one step further by quoting a second time from Hosea 6:6 (cf. 9:13): "If you had known what these words mean, 'I desire mercy, not sacrifice,' you would not have condemned the innocent." Jesus' disciples are the innocent ones who deserved mercy from the Pharisees, not condemnation. God in his great mercy has given the Sabbath to give his creatures relief from daily burden, not so that people would perform weekly sacrifice. The disciples were not guilty according to the Old Testament law but only according to the Pharisaic interpretation of the law. If they had not just read the prophet but had understood him, they would have known that in their adjudication of the Sabbath, they should have extended mercy, not demanded more sacrifice. Jesus attacks the very core of the Pharisaic tendency to add burdens to the daily lives of people by their accumulation of oral traditions.[7]

**Lord of the Sabbath (12:8).** Jesus concludes the argument with another remarkable clarification of his identity and authority: "For the Son of Man is Lord of the Sabbath." The arrival of the greater work of the gospel of the kingdom is centralized in Jesus as the Lord of the Sabbath, which gives a further clarification of his identity through this Son of Man saying (see 8:19). Jesus has revealed himself to Israel as their long-anticipated Messiah—the One who has come to fulfill the Old Testament law (5:17–20). In similar fashion to the way that Jesus points in the SM, the Sabbath law has been fulfilled in the rest brought by Jesus' yoke of discipleship (11:25–30). The messianic Son of Man has the authority to give the true interpretation of the law (5:17–48), including the role of the Sabbath.

In other words, Jesus does not challenge the Sabbath law itself but the prevailing interpretation of it. Even though David had lied to the priest Ahimelech about his mission and he and his men ate the bread in the tabernacle that was not designated for them, it was the mercy of God that did not condemn David. It is the mercy of God that does not strike dead the priests who minister on the Sabbath in the temple, because his mercy is the basis that underlies the entire sacrificial system.[8]

---

6. Gundry, *Matthew*, 223; Davies and Allison, *Matthew*, 2:314.

7. Cf. Yang, *Jesus and the Sabbath in Matthew's Gospel*, 187–88.

8. A classic statement of this appeal to mercy is found in David's psalm of contrition (Ps. 51:16–17).

So Jesus answers the charge against his disciples by showing from the Old Testament itself that the Sabbath is not fulfilled by the scrupulous observance of the Pharisees but in living out the intent and motive of the Sabbath, which was designed to bring rest.[9] Increased sacrifice brought greater burden. As the Lord of the Sabbath, Jesus gives the true interpretation of its intent, bringing rest under his easy yoke and light burden of discipleship (cf. 11:28–30).

**Healing on the Sabbath (12:9–13).** Matthew moves quickly to another Sabbath controversy that apparently takes place on a different Sabbath (cf. Luke 6:6): "Going on from that place, he went into their synagogue, and a man with a shriveled hand was there. Looking for a reason to accuse Jesus, they asked him, 'Is it lawful to heal on the Sabbath?'" The cause of the deformity to the man's hand is not specified, but it may have been some form of paralysis.

The identity of Jesus' accusers is not stated, but presumably they are the Pharisees of the preceding controversy (12:2), who plot Jesus' demise at the end of this confrontation (12:14). They have seen Jesus heal and pronounce forgiveness of sins (9:1–7), which they consider blasphemy (9:3). They have just witnessed his pronouncement about his authority over the Sabbath and the preference of mercy over sacrifice (12:7–8). So they provoke the controversy in an attempt to entrap him. Rabbinic teaching allowed that only in extreme cases of life and death could the Sabbath be violated.[10] The man with the withered hand has likely had the condition for some time, and his life certainly is not in danger, so he could wait until the next day. According to the Pharisees, he is not a proper candidate for healing.

Jesus counters with a question of his own. "If any of you has a sheep and it falls into a pit on the Sabbath, will you not take hold of it and lift it out?" The question is not simply rhetorical. There was active debate in Judaism at the time on just such a point. In many ways the debate centered on how much a person was willing to sacrifice to give honor to God and his holy day. The Qumran community was more rigorous on this matter than most: "No-one should help an animal give birth on the Sabbath day. And if he makes it fall into a well or a pit, he should not take it out on the Sabbath" (CD 11:13–14). In the same document they contend that even if a living man fell into water, they were not to take him out by using a ladder or a rope or a utensil (CD 11:16–17).

---

9. Keener, *A Commentary on the Gospel of Matthew* (1999), 357.

10. E.g., "If a man has a pain in his throat they may drop medicine into his mouth on the Sabbath, since there is doubt whether life is in danger, and whenever there is doubt whether life is in danger this overrides the Sabbath" (*m. Yoma* 8:6).

Jesus presses the argument further because most Pharisees and other Jewish interpreters would have agreed with his example of rescuing an animal on the Sabbath. Using another typical rabbinic method of argumentation, Jesus contends that the higher principle is not simply abstaining from activity on the Sabbath but doing good on the Sabbath (12:12). This line of reasoning also follows from the preceding example of the priests performing their good work of temple service on the Sabbath and being considered guiltless (12:5).

To make an immediate confirmation of his claim, Jesus says to the man, "'Stretch out your hand.' So he stretched it out and it was completely restored, just as sound as the other." The miracle confirms Jesus' authority to make these pronouncements about the Sabbath, once more validating his claim to be the messianic Son of Man (cf. 9:1–8; 12:8).[11] Without uttering a command of healing or even touching the withered limb, Jesus heals the man's hand completely. This is similar to the way Yahweh had control over Moses' diseased hand (Ex. 4:6–7).

**Plot of the Pharisees (12:14).** The seriousness of these issues is now revealed, for in reaction to Jesus' actions and pronouncement about the Sabbath, the Pharisees plot to put Jesus to death (12:14). As vigorously as they debated legal rulings, they would never consider putting another person to death over a difference of interpretation. Thus, this verse shows that they understand clearly that Jesus' claim to messianic authority to interpret the law is, in their eyes, a heretical claim worthy of death. They are now convinced that Jesus is not God's agent.

The law prescribed the death penalty for cases of extreme Sabbath desecration (Ex. 31:14; 35:2), but under the Roman occupation the Jews did not have arbitrary power to impose or to carry out a death penalty (cf. John 18:31). But as the narrative will reveal, the collaboration and plotting of the Pharisees with Caiaphas, the chief priests, and the rest of the Sanhedrin are eventually sufficient to persuade the Romans to put Jesus to death for them (cf. 27:1–2).

## God's Spirit-Anointed Servant (12:15–21)

ONCE AGAIN IN response to a threat, Jesus withdraws (cf. 2:14, 22; 4:12; 14:13). He is not trying to escape opposition but to keep it at bay until the time for his predicted betrayal, arrest, and death (cf. 16:21; 17:22–23; 20:17–19; 26:45). He is still in full public view, because "many followed him, and he healed all their sick" (12:15). From the beginning of his public ministry people came to Jesus for healing from the surrounding countryside (cf. 4:24–25;

---

11. Yang, *Jesus and the Sabbath in Matthew's Gospel*, 209.

9:35), now including people from as far away as Idumea, over a hundred miles away (see Mark 3:7–8).

Not only does Jesus heal all who come, but he warns "them not to tell who he was." We have already seen that a regular aspect of Jesus' ministry is to demand secrecy about his identity and activity (8:4; cf. 12:16; 16:20; 17:9). Jesus carefully avoids stirring up in the crowds a misunderstanding of his messianic identity. The typical person in Israel hoped for liberation from oppression by the Roman occupation and the fulfillment of the promise of a Messiah who would restore the dignity of the Davidic kingdom to Israel. Jesus wants the people to see that his purpose in coming will not always meet their expectations. As Matthew now clarifies, Jesus is indeed the Messiah, but he has come meekly to bring justice to the Gentiles. Although miracles will attest the authenticity of his message about the arrival of the kingdom, Jesus does not want crowds clamoring for miracles alone. They may misunderstand his message to mean that he has come to effect only national and military liberation.

Matthew uses his typical fulfillment formula (cf. 1:22; 2:15) to introduce the longest Old Testament quotation in his Gospel, which identifies Jesus with the messianic Servant in Isaiah 42:1–4: "This was to fulfill what was spoken through the prophet Isaiah: 'Here is my servant whom I have chosen the one I love, in whom I delight; I will put my Spirit on him, and he will proclaim justice to the nations.'" The context in Isaiah's prophecy is the section often called the Servant Songs (Isa. 40–52). The identity of the Servant is perplexing, because it vacillates between the nation of Israel as the Servant (41:8–10; 44:1–3, 21; 45:4 [49:3?]) and an individual who leads the nation (42:1–4; 49:5–7). That individual emerges as the Servant Messiah who has a ministry and mission both to Israel and the nations.[12] The phrase "the one I love, in whom I delight" takes the reader back to Jesus' baptism and forward to Jesus' transfiguration, where the Father expresses the same delight in his beloved Son (3:17; 17:5).

In this fulfillment quotation, Matthew gives one of the clearest declarations of Jesus' intent as Messiah: He is the gentle, Spirit-endowed, Suffering Servant, who advances a mission of justice to the nations.[13] Later Peter will proclaim that God had anointed Jesus with the Holy Spirit in order to do good and to heal (Acts 10:37–38). Ultimately, the same Spirit impelled Peter to go to the Gentile centurion Cornelius with the message of the gospel (10:44–48). The age Jesus inaugurated with the arrival of the kingdom is

---

12. For brief overviews of this complex subject, see Kaiser, *The Messiah in the Old Testament*, 173–81; Van Groningen, *Messianic Revelation in the Old Testament*, 575–618.
13. Richard Beaton, "Messiah and Justice: A Key to Matthew's Use of Isaiah 42.1–4?" *JSNT* 75 (September 1999): 5–23.

the age of the Spirit. Thus, to speak against the working of the Spirit is blasphemy, which is the sin that cannot be forgiven (see comments on Matt. 12:28, 31–32). The "justice" Jesus brings to the "nations" combines the sense of grace and judgment that has characterized the theme of inward righteousness that accompanies the arrival of the kingdom of heaven (e.g., 5:20). The Servant will pronounce the arrival of the kingdom that is an invitation to kingdom life, but it is also a sentence of judgment on the rulers of this world.

This Servant has an unexpected demeanor. Far from painting a picture of an imposing figure of conquest, Matthew continues his citation of the Suffering Servant theme from Isaiah:

> He will not quarrel or cry out;
> > no one will hear his voice in the streets.
> A bruised reed he will not break,
> > and a smoldering wick he will not snuff out,
> till he leads justice to victory.
> > In his name the nations will put their hope.

This is a picture of a gentle Servant Messiah, who will not brazenly demand allegiance with his proclamation of justice but will gently and humbly invite those who are the most in need (11:28–30). The double metaphor of a bruised reed and smoldering wick emphasizes that the Servant will compassionately care for those who have been abused and who are about to expire because of misuse—pictures that find relevance in the harassed and helpless (9:36) and the weary and burdened (12:28) who are being oppressed not only by the foreign invading forces of Rome but also by the legalistic burdens from Israel's religious establishment.

The Suffering Servant's advance of justice will not break those who are abused, nor will it smother those who are nearly out of resources; rather, he will provide the ultimate victory for those who respond to the invitation to enter the kingdom. The strong and the mighty are often victorious in this life because they advance their own causes by abusing others and withholding care from the needy. But even as Isaiah knew that evil would not have the ultimate victory, so Matthew points to Jesus and declares that victory is at hand for those who seek God's justice.

But it is not only for Israel. All "the nations" will put their hope in the name of this Servant, the One who Matthew declares is none other than Jesus of Nazareth (cf. 2:23; 12:21). The "name" in 12:21 stands for the whole of the person, including his identity and mission. Jesus Messiah is a Suffering Servant who is Spirit-endowed and who offers hope, because the advance of the kingdom of heaven promises victory for all the nations of the world.

## Confrontations with the Pharisees over the Source of Jesus' Miraculous Power (12:22–37)

THE PHARISEES ACCUSE Jesus of demonism (12:22–24). The connector "then" in 12:22 ties together thematically the accusations from the Pharisees about Jesus' and his disciples' activities on the Sabbath with accusations about Jesus' healing and exorcisms. The controversies come to a head as a demon-possessed man who is blind and mute is brought to Jesus. Jesus heals the man by exorcizing the demon "so that he could both talk and see" (cf. 17:18, where Jesus heals a boy of epilepsy by casting out a demon). As we noted earlier (cf. 9:27–31), healing the blind is one of the most common of Jesus' miracles and a signature of his messianic identity.[14]

The people are astonished at Jesus' healing of this blind and mute demoniac, so they exclaim, "Could this be the Son of David?" (12:23). Different Jewish groups had difficulty putting together all of the varied messianic promises of the Old Testament (e.g., prophet, priest, king). The common people especially seemed to focus on David as warrior and king, so that the messianic son of David would be a liberator. Thus, they are perplexed here and ask, "Can the coming Messiah be both a liberator and an exorcist?" Although David was not considered a miracle worker, he is the only person recorded to have exorcised a demon in the Old Testament (1 Sam. 16:14–23). It is perhaps stretching the crowds' understanding to comprehend that this gentle healing person (8:17; 12:18–21) is indeed the Son of David who will shepherd his people and bring the time of covenantal peace (Ezek. 34:23–31; 37:24–28).

The focus of the narrative, however, is on the continuing confrontation between the Pharisees and Jesus. In contrast to the reaction of the crowds, the Pharisees see the exorcism as more fuel for their charges against Jesus (see 9:3, 11, 34; 12:14). It causes them to condemn him as being in league with Satan (12:24). In the ancient world, exorcists used a variety of incantations and spells, potions and herbs, rings and earrings as magical things in an attempt to manipulate the spirit world.[15] But Jesus' form of exorcism has been far different. He commands the demons from his own authority, and they immediately submit. The exorcisms are meant to confirm the in-breaking of the kingdom of God in his words and deeds.

---

14. See also 9:27–31; 15:30–31; 20:30–34; 21:14–15; Twelftree, *Jesus the Miracle Worker*, 127.

15. For a brief background see Mark Strauss, "Demonization and Exorcism in the First Century," in "Luke," *ZIBBC* (Grand Rapids: Zondervan, 2002), 397. See Hans Dieter Betz, ed., *The Greek Magical Papyri in Translation* (Chicago: University of Chicago, 1986). The closest Hellenistic parallel to Jesus' form of exorcism appears in Philostratus, *Life of Apollonius of Tyana*, 4:20 (LCL), a third century A.D. document.

Nonetheless, the Pharisees accuse Jesus of drawing upon the power of "Beelzebub" (or better, "Beelzeboul," the ruler of the demons; see comments on 10:24–25) to cast out the demon from the blind and mute man. The Pharisees do not deny the miracle but instead attribute Jesus' power to Satan.[16] This is a most serious charge, because practicing magic under the influence of Satan was a capital offense, punishable by stoning.

**Jesus' defense (12:25–29).** Jesus first defends his ministry of exorcism with two short parables, then he follows it with two scathing denunciations of the Pharisees (12:30–37). (1) The power behind an exorcism could come from either God or Satan. Since the Pharisees have already concluded that Jesus is not God's agent (cf. 12:14), they cite the source of his power as Satan. They assume that since a demon has come out of the man, it must be evidence that the demon is obeying Satan as the ruler of the demons. But Jesus shows the illogical nature of their thinking (12:25–26). If Satan wants to maintain rulership of this world, he would not work against himself by exorcising a demon that had control of a person. That would be counteracting his own attempt to maintain control of this world. The only logical conclusion is that if the man has been liberated from a demon, healed of blindness, and enabled to speak, it indicates that the source of Jesus' power is God in his battle against Satan's kingdom.

Since Satan's kingdom is being overcome by Jesus' exorcisms, they are concrete evidence that the "kingdom of God" has arrived (12:28). The power that underlies Jesus' exorcisms is the Spirit of God, not Beelzebul. As with his healings, Jesus' exorcisms validate the message that he is inaugurating the blessings of the eschatological age. This is one of the clearest statements in Matthew's Gospel about the present reality of the kingdom of God. Only seldom does the expression "kingdom of God" occur in Matthew (19:24; 21:31, 43), who usually prefers the expression "kingdom of heaven." These are equivalent expressions (see comments on 3:2), but here it may emphasize the opposition between God and Satan. The power of the Spirit of God operating through Jesus in exorcising Satan's demons is tangible confirmation that the kingdom of God has arrived.[17]

At the same time, miracles are not compelling proofs. The cities of Korazin, Bethsaida and Capernaum did not repent, even though they witnessed the majority of Jesus' miraculous deeds (11:20–24), and these Pharisees, who are eyewitnesses, do not believe either. The true significance of

---

16. Later Judaism continued this charge into the early centuries of the church era, branding him a sorcerer (e.g., *b. Sanh.* 43b: "He [Yeshu] is going forth to be stoned because he has practiced sorcery and enticed Israel to apostasy").

17. John P. Meier, *Matthew* (New Testament Message 3; Wilmington, Del.: Michael Glazier, 1980), 135.

miracles is recognizable only by faith in the person of Jesus Messiah. The exorcisms are, as it were, "chinks in the curtain of the Son of God's hiddenness."[18] The exorcisms do reveal the reality of the arrival of the kingdom of God, but hearts that are hardened against Jesus' messianic identity are even more blinded than the man from whom Jesus has just exorcised the demon.

(2) Jesus continues his response to the Pharisees' charge that he casts out demons by Beelzebul with a second short parable: "Or again, how can anyone enter a strong man's house and carry off his possessions unless he first ties up the strong man? Then he can rob his house." Jesus alludes to his role of inaugurating the kingdom as entering a well-guarded house (the household of Satan and his demonic cronies) and plundering the possessions of the owner. Before Jesus can release through exorcism those held captive, he must "bind" Satan. Jesus declares here that Satan's powers are now limited because of the arrival of the kingdom of God.

**Jesus' offense (12:30–37).** Jesus now goes on the offensive and declares with two scathing denunciations of the Pharisees the consequences of those who oppose his messianic ministry. (1) He begins by throwing down the gauntlet: "He who is not with me is against me, and he who does not gather with me scatters." There is no middle ground with Jesus. He is either Messiah, or he isn't. The Pharisees have already determined that he is not, so they will oppose him, as they have already demonstrated. But this saying has great relevance for all those within hearing. The crowds have been offered many opportunities to repent and enter the kingdom, but their day of opportunity will not last long. "To refuse to decide positively for Jesus is already to have decided against him."[19] The tragedy is that many in the crowds will ultimately follow the persuasiveness of the religious leaders and join them in asking for Jesus' execution (27:20–25).

The Pharisees have been mounting charges of blasphemy against Jesus, but now Jesus shows that all of their charges are actually blasphemy themselves: "And so I tell you, every sin and blasphemy will be forgiven men, but the blasphemy against the Spirit will not be forgiven." The Old Testament regarded deliberate, defiant sin against God and his ordinances to be blasphemy, the guilt of which remained (Num. 15:30–31). The Jews considered such defiant sin as unforgivable (see, e.g., *Jub.* 15:34). Rejection of Jesus' ministry as validated by the Spirit is the same sort of defiant, deliberate sin. By attributing the work and power of the Spirit to Satan, the Pharisees are displaying the highest dishonor to God. To reject the evidence of exorcisms and healings and miracles is to reject the kingdom's offer of forgiveness of sins.

---

18. C. E. B. Cranfield, *The Gospel According to Saint Mark*, 2d ed. (CGTC; Cambridge: Cambridge Univ. Press, 1972), 83.

19. Meier, *Matthew*, 135.

As long as the Pharisees continue to reject that evidence, they cannot enter the kingdom and receive forgiveness.

This also goes along with the role of the Spirit in convicting individuals of sin, righteousness, and judgment (John 16:8). As long as one rejects the Spirit, one can never find forgiveness for sins. Apparently Jesus knows the state of these Pharisees' hearts and knows that they have now reached a point where they have hardened their hearts beyond the point of return.

This passage has caused many unknowing believers anguish, thinking that somehow they have committed this sin through a verbal assault on the Holy Spirit, resulting in eternal condemnation. Rather, this is a heart sin of unchangeable rejection whereby the Jewish leaders rejected the ministry of the Holy Spirit in their lives. Ralph Martin comments:

> The verse is a solemn warning against persistent, deliberate rejection of the Spirit's call to salvation in Christ. Human unresponsiveness inevitably leads to a state of moral insensibility and to a confusion of moral issues wherein evil is embraced as though it were good.... In such a frame of mind repentance is not possible to the hardened heart because the recognition of sin is no longer possible, and God's offer of mercy is in effect peremptorily refused.[20]

This sin can be committed today only by unbelievers who reject the ministry of the Holy Spirit leading them to salvation. To the believer who fears that he or she has committed this sin, Cranfield says wisely, "It is a matter of great importance pastorally that we can say with absolute confidence to anyone who is overwhelmed by the fear that he has committed this sin, that the fact that he is so troubled is itself a sure proof that he has not committed it."[21]

Jesus continues the offensive by distinguishing between rejection of him and the rejection of the work of the Holy Spirit: "Anyone who speaks a word against the Son of Man will be forgiven, but anyone who speaks against the Holy Spirit will not be forgiven, either in this age or in the age to come." To speak against the Son of Man implies that a person does not know the full identity of Jesus. Through greater revelation and understanding, that deficiency can be overcome, the person can repent, and the person can then find forgiveness of sin. By yielding to the Spirit's evidential and convicting work a person can be led to that very point. But to reject continually the Spirit's work will result in a person never being able to reach that point.

Ultimately, once a person has either hardened his or her heart to an irretrievable point in this life (see comments on 13:14–15) or has died without

---

20. Ralph P. Martin, "Blasphemy of the Spirit," *IBD*, 1:201.
21. Cranfield, *Mark*, 142.

repenting, the chance for forgiveness has passed. It is only what one does in this life that matters for eternity. Thus the only true "unpardonable sin" is when a person consciously, willfully, rejects the operation of the Spirit bearing witness to the reality of Jesus as the Savior. The person who does not receive this work of the Spirit cannot come to Jesus and therefore cannot receive forgiveness.

(2) Jesus' second offensive strike forces the Pharisees to recognize that their charges against him come from their own evil nature. Like the challenge that Jesus addressed to the disciples and crowds in the Sermon on the Mount (7:15–20), Jesus tells the Pharisees to examine the fruit of their own lives—good trees bear good fruit and bad trees bear bad fruit, because of the nature of the tree (12:33; cf. 3:8). With the same scathing invective that John the Baptist used to address the Pharisees and Sadducees, Jesus declares, "You brood of vipers, how can you who are evil say anything good? For out of the overflow of the heart the mouth speaks. The good man brings good things out of the good stored up in him, and the evil man brings evil things out of the evil stored up in him."

The expression "brood of vipers" (cf. 3:7; 23:33) refers to the dozen or more small, dangerous snakes that can emerge at birth from a mother snake. Vipers are proverbial for their subtle approach and attack, as was the original serpent (Gen. 3). The Pharisees attempt to hide their own wicked blasphemy by calling Jesus a blasphemer. But Jesus reveals the crux of the problem of the Pharisees—their hearts are evil. As with false prophets who lead the people astray with the false words of prophecy, eternal judgment awaits the Pharisees and teachers of the law who have attempted to dissuade the crowds from following Jesus by slandering him with accusations of blasphemy. But their slander is actually blasphemy of the Spirit of God. Since they refuse to repent, they will be held accountable for every word at the judgment.

## Confrontations with the Pharisees over Their Demand for a Sign (12:38–42)

THE CONFRONTATIONS BETWEEN Jesus and the Pharisees over the Sabbath (12:1–14) and the source of his miraculous powers (12:22–37) lead to another attempt to entrap Jesus. They ask Jesus to show them "a miraculous sign" (12:38). A "sign" is some kind of visible mark or action that conveys an unmistakable message, such as the mark of Cain that warned people not to kill him (Gen. 4:15) or the way that the act of speaking in tongues is a sign to unbelievers of the reality of the gospel message (1 Cor. 14:22). Jesus' return as the glorious Son of Man is the sign that announces the eschatological consummation of the age (see Matt. 24:29; cf. 16:27; 26:64).

The problem with a sign is that it can be interpreted in different ways.[22] The Pharisees here ask Jesus to perform some kind of on-demand spectacular display of power that will irrefutably convince them that his power is from God, not from Satan. However, although their request appears innocent enough, they are not asking in good faith. They are asking for a sign that they can use against him. Jesus has already performed many miracles publicly, some of which the Pharisees have witnessed first-hand (cf. 12:9–14). If the Pharisees were open to God's message, they would have accepted that Jesus truly is the Messiah. Instead, their hard hearts have rejected the miracles' authenticating power, and they have used those same miracles as the basis of the charge that he is a satanic tool (12:24). Jesus recognizes their evil motive, so he refuses to fall into their trap of giving them further ammunition for their charges against him.

Then Jesus turns around the deceptive attempt of the Pharisees to entrap him and confronts them about their own duplicitous motivation and their impending condemnation. "A wicked and adulterous generation asks for a miraculous sign! But none will be given it except the sign of the prophet Jonah."[23] When Jonah appeared among the people of Nineveh, he was the sign to them that his message was from the God who had rescued him from death (Jonah 3:1–5). The generation that has heard Jesus' message and seen his ministry have enough validating proof in his miracles that he is the Messiah. Instead of repenting when seeing his miracles, they have attempted to use them as the basis of the charge that he is in league with Satan (12:24). Because of their evil intention, the only other sign that Jesus will give to them is a sign of God's coming judgment on them, as Jonah was to the people of Nineveh.[24]

"For as Jonah was three days and three nights in the belly of a huge fish, so the Son of Man will be three days and three nights in the heart of the earth." The expression "three days and three nights" is not incompatible with the synoptic picture of Jesus being buried late Friday afternoon and rising on Sunday morning. Jesus repeatedly said that he would be raised "on the third day" (16:21; 17:23; 20:19). If he was a literal three days and three nights in the tomb, he would have been raised on the fourth day. But the Old Testament regularly reckoned a part of a day as a whole day,[25] and in rabbinic

---

22. James D. G. Dunn, "Sign," *IBD* 3:1450.

23. Note that "the sign of . . . Jonah" is not some kind of sign that Jonah brings. Rather, Jonah is the sign.

24. Hans F. Bayer, *Jesus' Predictions of Vindication and Resurrection: The Provenance, Meaning and Correlation of the Synoptic Predictions* (WUNT 2/20; Tübingen: J.C.B. Mohr [Paul Siebeck], 1986), 141–45, 182.

25. Cf. Gen. 42:17–18; 1 Sam. 30:12–13; 1 Kings 20:29; 2 Chron. 10:5, 12; Est. 4:16; 5:1.

thought, a part of a day was considered to be a whole day.[26] Three days and three nights is almost a proverbial expression and means no more than the combination of any part of three separate days.

The culpability of the Pharisees and teachers of the law for not repenting at the arrival of Jesus extends to the entire generation who followed their misguided lead. They have had the greatest privilege (11:20–24), but the ones who will point a figure of condemnation are those who had far less privilege—the pagans of Nineveh—who repented when God's messenger, Jonah, arrived (12:41). "One greater than Jonah is here."

A second figure of condemnation against the Pharisees is another pagan—"the Queen of the South" (12:42), that is, the queen of Sheba (1 Kings 10:1–29). She too allowed God's revelation to penetrate to her pagan heart. In his comparison to Solomon, Jesus once again makes a messianic claim to be "greater" than Solomon. "To claim that Jesus is greater than [Solomon] is to claim that he is the true Messiah; that he will build the eschatological Temple; that through him the Davidic kingdom will be restored."[27]

In sum, the three ways in which Jesus is greater than the temple, the prophet Jonah, and wise king Solomon (12:6, 41, 42) elevate Jesus' person, proclamation, and inauguration of the kingdom to be greater than, and therefore the fulfillment of, the three greatest institutions in Israel—priest, prophet, king. Jesus' arrival with the kingdom of God has exceeded all that Israel has witnessed in her history. But tragically, and ironically, the Gentiles see what the Pharisees and that fateful generation do not.[28]

## This Wicked Generation and the Return of the Evil Spirit (12:43–45)

AFTER THE SCENE of judgment for rejecting Jesus Messiah's inauguration of the kingdom of heaven, Jesus gives a parabolic revelation of the warfare within that adulterous generation. The incident of the demon-possessed man who was blind and mute had instigated the entire interchange with the Pharisees (12:22–37), so Jesus returns to the topic of exorcism to make a final point. The Pharisees have accused him of exorcising demons by Satan's power, but in an ironic twist, Jesus shows that these religious leaders and those of that generation who are following their lead are themselves under the influence of Satan's evil spirits.

---

26. See *y. Šabb.*, 12a, 15, 17 (cf. *b. Naz.* 5b; *b. Pesaḥ* 4.2); cited in Gerhard Delling, "ἡμέρα," *TDNT*, 2:949–50.

27. Wright, *Jesus and the Victory of God*, 535.

28. Hagner, *Matthew*, 1:355.

Jesus begins with a general statement of how demons operate: "When an evil spirit comes out of a man, it goes through arid places seeking rest and does not find it." The verb "comes out" implies that the demon has come out through an exorcism. Demons are often associated with desert (waterless) places as their home (Isa. 13:21; 34:14; Tobit 8:3; *1 En.* 10:4). The "rest" implies that although a demon can exist in a disembodied state, its evil purpose is best performed in an embodied state.

The demon seeks reownership of a person's entire immaterial/material self: "I will return to the house I left" (lit., *"my* house"—that is why it is called demon *possession*). Demons tend to be persistent in wanting to maintain ownership of a person. So "it goes and takes with it seven other spirits more wicked than itself, and they go in and live there." The number seven is linked in Scripture with completion, fulfillment, and perfection.[29] Here it may point to the completeness of demon-possession once the demon returns.

The evil generation that Jesus addresses has experienced his powerful ministry, especially through his exorcisms. That has been a good thing for Israel. But Israel has not repented and turned to the kingdom of heaven. Therefore, that generation is more susceptible to the power of the evil one than ever before. The tragic point of the parable is in the statement, "And the final condition of that man is worse than the first." If the present generation continually rejects Jesus, they too will be like a repossessed demoniac— their final condition of judgment will be worse than before Jesus came to them (cf. 12:32, 36).

The passage is parabolic in nature, drawing on real-life situations to tell a story to make a point. It has relevance for the generation as a whole, but it is instructive for individuals as well. That is, the parable points to an unbeliever who has been exorcised but who does not come to Jesus and enter the kingdom (cf. 12:28). The exorcised person must respond to Jesus' invitation to believe in him as Messiah, enter the kingdom of God, and experience new life through his Spirit. The implication here is that this person has not entered the kingdom. Without kingdom transformation, a "cleaned-up" person is more vulnerable to the renewed and persistent attack of the demon world to take back ownership. He can easily be repossessed by the demon and seven more wicked cronies and will be in far worse shape, completely dominated by the entourage of wickedness. But if this person does receive Jesus and the kingdom, Satan will flee from the presence of God in this disciple's life (James 4:7; 1 John 4:4).

---

29. From earliest times seven also had sacred associations; Gen 2:2; 4:24; 21:28; Ex. 20:10; Lev. 25:2–8.

## Jesus' Disciples Are His True Family (12:46–50)

THE CONFRONTATIONS WITH the religious establishment have brought to light the incontrovertible differences between Jesus' proclamation of the gospel of the kingdom and the expectations of the crowds and the religious establishment of Israel. As he brings the law to its fulfillment as the Lord of the Sabbath (12:8), he releases those who respond to him from an oppressive slavery to the burdens of Pharisaic legalism and the oppression of Satan's demonic kingdom. But there are other forces at work that may attempt to deter Jesus and his followers. This passage prepares for one of the most significant transitions in Jesus' ministry (see comments on 13:1–17) by declaring clearly the distinguishing signature of Jesus' own life and ministry as well as that of his followers: obeying the will of the Father (12:50).

The expression "while Jesus was still talking to the crowd" transitions the narrative from the preceding section that focused on those outside (i.e., the crowds and the Pharisees) to those within (i.e., the disciples). Matthew's narrative has maintained a striking contrast between three groups: the disciples, the crowds, and the religious establishment of Israel (see comments on 5:1–2). Disciples are those who have responded positively to Jesus' invitation to the gospel of the kingdom. The crowds are those who are interested in Jesus' message and ministry but who have not yet made a decision to enter the kingdom and become Jesus' disciples. The religious leaders are those who consistently oppose Jesus' message and ministry.

Matthew 12:9–45 did not include any reference to the disciples. This is a clue that the topics discussed there were about entrance into the kingdom, not instruction about life within it. Now, however, as Jesus continues to address the crowd (12:46), "his mother and brothers stood outside, wanting to speak to him." Jesus has focused upon proclaiming the gospel of the kingdom to all with an open-ended invitation. That invitation continues, but he now begins to require accountability of those to whom the invitation has been extended.

The omission of "father" may indicate that Joseph has died by this time. Matthew gives no reason for why his family wishes to speak to him, but Mark indicates that earlier his family apparently went out from Nazareth to Capernaum because they heard reports of the commotion that Jesus' ministry was causing. They wanted to take control of Jesus and alter his ministry, because they thought that he was out of his mind, considering the claims he was making and his disruption of the religious status quo (Mark 3:21; cf. John 7:5).[30] Along with this, it may be that they intend to bring Jesus to his

---

30. See R. T. France, *The Gospel of Mark* (NIGTC; Grand Rapids: Eerdmans, 2002), 164–65; Guelich, *Mark 1–8*, 172–73; George Aichele, "Jesus's Uncanny 'Family Scene,'" *JSNT* 74 (June 1999): 29–49.

senses as the eldest son, the one responsible to care for his mother and younger brothers and sisters after the death of Joseph.

Those who have contended for the perpetual virginity of Mary have tried here to interpret "brothers" to indicate either Joseph's sons by an earlier marriage or cousins of Jesus, Mary's sister's sons. There is no historical evidence for a prior marriage of Joseph with children. If there were, that firstborn son, not Jesus, would have been the legal heir to the throne of David through Joseph.[31] And although "brother" can have a broader meaning to include cousin, there is no contextual warrant for reading that meaning here.[32] The most natural reading of this passage, especially in the light of the infancy narrative (see comments on 1:24–25) and the later mention of Jesus' brothers and sisters (13:55–56) is that once Jesus was born, Joseph and Mary had normal sexual relations and had other children, who are Jesus' half brothers and sisters.

With that context in mind, Mary and Jesus' brothers arrive at the place where Jesus is speaking in order to escort him back to Nazareth. Someone tells Jesus, "Your mother and brothers are standing outside, wanting to speak to you." But Jesus will not be deterred from his messianic mission, even if it means disruption of biological loyalties. "'Who is my mother, and who are my brothers?' Pointing to his disciples, he said, 'Here are my mother and my brothers.'" Jesus has already accentuated to his disciples the inevitable separation that will occur between family members because of a commitment to him (10:34–39; cf. 8:21–22). He has not come to abolish the family, for later he upholds the law that demands children honor their parents and rebukes those who develop traditions that allow them to circumvent such care (15:3–9). And we will see that after the Parable Discourse, Jesus does return to Nazareth, where his family is still living, to preach in the synagogue (13:54–58). But Jesus is here demonstrating the preeminence of commitment to him and the kingdom of heaven, which places people in a new spiritual family.

Jesus specifies the central feature that creates and characterizes this spiritual family: "For whoever does the will of my Father in heaven is my brother and sister and mother." The theme of doing the will of the heavenly Father is a motif that runs throughout Matthew's Gospel and reflects deep Jewish roots (cf. 6:10; 7:21; 18:14; 21:31; 26:42).[33] The will of the Father means

---

31. Carson, "Matthew," 299.

32. Leading Roman Catholic Matthean scholars today acknowledge the difficulty of reading "brothers" as anything other than Mary's children; e.g., Harrington comments, "It is doubtful that Matthew knew the tradition about the perpetual virginity of Mary"; Daniel J. Harrington, S.J., *The Gospel of Matthew* (Sacra pagina 1; Collegeville, Minn.: Liturgical, 1991), 191. For an overview of this entire issue, see Richard J. Bauckham, "Relatives of Jesus," *DLNTD*, 1004–6.

33. Senior, *Matthew*, 145.

obedience to the call to the kingdom of heaven that will result in true right-eousness. A person's genealogical relationship to Israel does not guarantee a place in the kingdom of heaven, nor does a person's family relationship. Each individual must respond to the will of the Father and obey Jesus' call to the kingdom and become his disciple. Jesus is the ultimate example of the will of the Father revealed and obeyed (11:27; 26:42), so to follow his example in discipleship and become like him will enable his disciples to do the Father's will on a daily basis.

Jesus intentionally broadens the gender references to include women as his disciples by not only referring to mother and brother but also by bring-ing in "sister."[34] His message and ministry initiate a unique form of disciple-ship. Within Judaism at that time, especially among the rabbis, only men could become a disciple of a rabbi and study the Torah. But with Jesus, any person—woman or man, young or old, Gentile or Jew—who responds to the gospel of the kingdom and believes on him for eternal life is his disciple. In other words, discipleship to Jesus is not defined by rabbinic models but by relationship to Jesus, which means obedience to the will of the Father.[35] The Old Testament prepared for this concept by stressing the importance of both the nation and the individual walking in the ways of God, which is now ful-filled in a discipleship to Jesus that creates a new family of God.[36]

This form of discipleship culminates in Jesus' final Great Commission, where the central imperative is to "make disciples of all nations" (28:19). This includes both men and women, which the book of Acts confirms. In the earliest days of the church, "disciple" refers to men and women (Acts 6:1–7; 9:10, 36; 16:1), called "believers" (5:14), or the "church" (8:3).[37] All disciples are to be taught to obey all that Jesus commands (cf. Matt. 28:19–20), which ultimately leads to obeying the Father's will on a moment-by-moment, day-by-day basis.

MATTHEW HAS ORGANIZED his Gospel around large chunks of material that reveal clearly Jesus' true identity and ministry. He has carefully revealed Jesus' divine origin (chs. 1–2), his prophetic and Spirit-led preparation (chs. 3–4), his authoritative messianic message (chs. 5–7) and miraculous ministry (chs. 8–9), and his messengers' mission of pro-

---

34. Hagner, *Matthew*, 1:360.
35. See Wilkins, "Women in the Teaching and Example of Jesus," 91–112.
36. Wilkins, *Following the Master*, 66–68; Hellerman, *The Ancient Church As Family*, 64–70.
37. See Wilkins, *Following the Master*, ch. 13.

claiming his own messianic message (ch. 10). With Jesus' mission fully established, Matthew dedicates two full chapters to reveal opposition that is mounting in Israel against Jesus. Not only did John the Baptist, his own prophetic forerunner, question the reality of his mission (11:1–6), but those who have had the greatest opportunity to witness his teaching and miracles have rejected him, to their own condemnation (11:7–24). And now we see that the religious leaders, those with the most responsibility to acknowledge Jesus and point Israel to him, becoming Jesus' primary opponents.

These scenes of controversy illustrate the conflict Jesus endured in his earthly ministry, so they have face value for our understanding of what he and the arrival of the kingdom of heaven encountered. But there are several valuable themes that Matthew has emphasized in this chapter. Why do the Pharisees and the teachers of the law challenge and oppose Jesus? Why could they not recognize the hand of God in Jesus' ministry? He has come as the messianic initiator of the kingdom of heaven, yet those most responsible for recognizing him are the most blinded. This should cause us to pause. When we challenge Jesus' role in our lives, we may be more like the Pharisees than we care to admit. Thus, a careful look at the motivating forces behind the confrontations will provide some valuable lessons.

**Jesus' opponents appear to have sincere motives.** The advance of Jesus' ministry has experienced an underlying opposition from the religious establishment of Israel, especially from the Pharisees and teachers of the law. But now that opposition comes out into the open. These leaders are now convinced that Jesus' ministry is not from God. Their suspicions arise because they believe that he blasphemes by attributing to himself prerogatives to act in ways that only God can act (e.g., forgiving sins, 9:3), because he associates with sinful people (9:11), and because he has control over evil spirits (9:34).

Surely no person—whether prophet, priest, or king—has ever performed in such a way in Israel's history. In their way of thinking Jesus must not be God's emissary, let alone his Messiah. They believe he is leading the people in the wrong direction—away from God, not toward him. Therefore, he must be stopped. He is not simply a variant teacher of God's law. Rather, Jesus is a law-breaker, whose crimes are worthy of death (12:14).

Nor is he simply a radical prophet of God, like John the Baptist. Rather, he is a demonic emissary of Satan, and his activities warrant a death penalty. So they try to entrap Jesus and confront him on two basic counts: violation of the Sabbath (12:1–14) and working miracles by Satan's power (12:22–37). The religious leaders believe they are acting in good conscience by protecting the people, the law, and God from the evil that they perceive in Jesus' ministry.

**Jesus' opponents are sincerely wrong.** But the true story must be told. In spite of their seemingly sincere motives and efforts, the Pharisees are wrong.

And it is not just that they have been mistaken; they have a more serious, deadly condition. They are so blinded and hardened in heart that they cannot see that the very activities for which they have accused Jesus are actually validations of the divine source of his ministry of teaching and healing. So as they oppose him, Jesus turns each confrontation into an opportunity to reveal further the true divine source of his teaching (12:8), healing (12:12), and identity (12:15–21).

Jesus also turns each confrontation around to refute the Pharisees about the disastrous effects of their own ministry. Not only have their traditions twisted the blessing of God's law into a weary and burdensome load of guilt upon the people (11:28–29; 12:7), but the evil they are attempting to perpetrate by condemning Jesus comes from their own evil hearts (12:34–37). As the Spirit-endowed Son of Man, Jesus pronounces the judgment on these religious leaders for their blasphemy and sinful hardness of heart that cannot be forgiven (12:31, 37, 41, 45).

**Jesus is the fulfillment of Israel's greatest institutions.** As Jesus counters the hardhearted opposition, he vindicates himself as God's true Lord of the Sabbath (12:8), revealing that God's intent in giving his law was not mere compliance but bringing good to those in need (12:3–7, 11–13). He is also God's true Servant (12:18), the Spirit-endowed inaugurator of the kingdom of God (12:28), who has come to bring justice to those caught in the legalistic trap of the religious leaders (12:18–21). And Jesus is also greater than the temple (12:6), greater than the prophet Jonah (12:41), and greater than wise King Solomon (12:42). His person, proclamation, and inauguration of the kingdom are greater than, and therefore the fulfillment of, the three greatest institutions in Israel — priest, prophet, king. Jesus' arrival with the kingdom of God has exceeded all that Israel witnessed in her history and should have been a day of great rejoicing. But tragically, the Pharisees and that fateful generation hardened their hearts against him.

**The surprising victims of demonic activity.** An ironic predicament that surfaces from these confrontations is the very real presence of demonic activity and their surprising victims. Jesus' power over demon-generated maladies produced charges that he was in league with the prince of demons, which Jesus quickly refutes (12:25–37). But Jesus uses the analogy of an exorcised man to illustrate that the Pharisees, and all those of that generation who follow their lead in opposing Jesus, are the self-inflicted victims of demonic domination (12:43–45). They are likened to the exorcised man who attempts to "clean up" his house, but because they have not experienced the transformation that accompanies those who respond to the gospel of the kingdom, they will be inflicted with more than seven times the original demonic possession. Those who thought themselves to be the experts at diagnosing demonic activity are the victims of their own accusations.

**The unexpected recipients of justice.** But in the midst of the confrontation between Jesus and the Pharisees and the teachers of the law, another theme is sounded. Jesus is not only the authoritative Lord of the Sabbath (12:8); he is the Spirit-endowed Servant who brings justice to the nations (12:18). He has not come brazenly to demand a hearing for himself, but he has come gently and meekly with the hope of justice for the oppressed nations (12:15–21). Those with the closest relationship to Jesus Messiah are not those of his own biological household (12:46–49), nor those who have exercised authority in the religious household. Rather, as Jesus reveals the will of his Father, all who dare to obey will become his disciples, his closest household family members (12:50).

Contrary to the religious leaders, whose evil hearts are the source of their accusations against Jesus (12:33–37), Jesus' disciples will experience a transformation of heart that will enable them to understand and carry out the intention of the law (12:1–6), follow Jesus, and become his emissaries of hope to the nations as he leads justice to victory (12:20–21), speak good words that typify people of the kingdom (12:35), and obey the will of their heavenly Father (12:49–50).

The battle between Jesus and the religious leaders is not a simple debate among Jewish leaders but a symptom of the cosmic spiritual warfare being waged ever since Jesus' first arrival. He had been a threat to King Herod, the false claimant to the throne of Israel, and the religious establishment in Jerusalem, who tried to have him killed. Behind that opposition lurks Satan, who knows that his stranglehold on this world is being challenged. Through the temptations, Satan attempted to deter Jesus from reclaiming this sin-sick world (4:1–11). In chapter 12, sadly we see that Satan has deceived the religious leaders into opposing Jesus, to their own condemnation. Those the most responsible for recognizing him are the most blinded and severely influenced by all of Satan's demonic forces. But to those who humbly receive him as God's messenger of justice, victory over those evil forces is a very real hope.

THE CONTROVERSIES BETWEEN Jesus and the Pharisees and teachers of the law end on a somewhat unexpected note. Jesus turns away from his own biological family, points to his disciples, and says, "Whoever does the will of my Father in heaven is my brother and sister and mother" (12:50). With that statement, Jesus puts into perspective the entire series of confrontations. He has come to do his Father's will (11:27; 26:42), and those who receive his message and ministry obey the Father. Those who deny him—or worse, oppose him—deny and oppose the Father. The religious leaders of Israel had the greatest opportunity to know the Scriptures that prophesied of the arrival of Messiah, and with eyes of faith they should have recognized Jesus and pointed the people to Jesus as the fulfillment of those prophetic hopes. But instead of obeying the leading of the Spirit, they hardened their hearts against the Spirit and instead followed the lead of demonic forces.

**Obedience to the Father's will.** There are several points of application for us as modern readers of this account, but obedience to the Father's will stands at the center. Rightly applying the Old Testament by imitating Jesus' example,[38] encountering persecution while engaging in spiritual warfare, and developing community discipleship are all themes of this chapter. And all hinge on rightly obeying the Father's will as it is now revealed by Jesus Messiah.

This has been the consistent battle cry of persecuted disciples of Jesus throughout church history. The contemporary Christian music group dc Talk teamed up with the Christian ministry The Voice of the Martyrs to write the gripping book called *Jesus Freaks: Stories of Those Who Took a Stand for Jesus*. It is a collection of worldwide testimonies targeting teens across America with the message of the uncompromising persecuted church. In an introduction to the book, Michael Tait explains its purpose: "In a world built on free will instead of God's will, we must be the Freaks. While we may not be called to martyr our lives, we must martyr our way of life. We must put our selfish ways to death and march to a different beat. Then the world will see Jesus."[39] The book is filled with almost 150 personal testimonies and quotes from around the world and throughout church history of people who obeyed God's will, most to the point of death. It has a powerful message for every Christian as we follow a conquering Savior who is able to carry us through any situation in life.

The book recounts the story of Geleazium, who was martyred in St. Angelo, Italy, in the Middle Ages. He is quoted as saying: "Death is much sweeter to me with the testimony of truth than life with the least denial."[40] That is an awe-inspiring commitment of obedience to the will of the Father.

---

38. For principles of applying the Old Testament today, see Contemporary Significance section of 5:17–20.

39. dc Talk and The Voice of the Martyrs, *Jesus Freaks: Stories of Those Who Stood For Jesus, the Ultimate Jesus Freaks* (Tulsa: Albury, 1999), 8.

40. Ibid., 135.

In our day it is no less imperative to cling to the truth of God's Word and treasure it, even at the risk of our well-being.

Tom White, the director of The Voice of the Martyrs, who was himself imprisoned in Cuba for seventeen months for distributing evangelistic literature, understands clearly the necessity of obedience, which he saw exemplified in the suffering endured by Christians in Vietnam. He writes, "I was in the central highlands in Vietnam when someone remarked about how the Christians suffer there. One Vietnamese Christian remarked, 'Suffering is not the worst thing that can happen to us. Disobedience to God is the worst thing.'"[41]

**Evaluating the opposition that will come.** Opposition to the work of the kingdom of God is real. Jesus was opposed by the religious leaders of his time. In our obedience to the Father's will for our lives, we too can expect opposition. As he sent the Twelve out on their first mission, Jesus gave a grim prediction: "It is enough for the student to be like his teacher, and the servant like his master. If the head of the house has been called Beelzebub, how much more the members of his household!" (10:25). The harsh treatment that Jesus received from the religious leaders will be the lot of his disciples until the end of this age.

The opposition that we encounter will be of a variety of different types. In the increasingly secular society of the twenty-first century, we will encounter opposition to our faith from popular culture. The Christian community in the United States was rocked during the summer of 2002 when a panel of the U.S. 9th Circuit Court of Appeals struck down a 1954 law passed by Congress that added the reference "under God" to the Pledge of Allegiance. The court said these words violate the establishment clause of the First Amendment, which requires the separation of church and state. The case was brought by an atheist doctor with a law degree, who argued that the First Amendment rights of his school-age daughter were violated when she was forced to listen as her teacher led her classmates in the pledge proclaiming that ours is "one nation under God."[42] At this writing the legal appeals have not been concluded, but this incident clearly indicates that our culture is increasingly opposed to the public display of any acknowledgment of the reality of God and his will for us.

As with Jesus, we may encounter opposition from our own family if they do not understand the way in which we want to serve God. I remember a young man who announced to his family that he was going to leave the state

---

41. Ibid., 40.
42. Evelyn Nievese, "Judges Ban Pledge of Allegiance from Schools, Citing 'Under God,'" *New York Times* (June 27, 2002), National Desk, 1.

university that he was attending on full scholarship in order to go to a Christian college and prepare for Christian ministry. His stepfather took him aside and said, "It will be a terrible waste of a brilliant mind to throw it away on Christian studies." And throughout his studies he received resistance instead of his family's support.

On a more drastic level, Christians can expect opposition when we proclaim the message of the gospel. A recent, unforgettable color photograph from Africa illustrated a special report entitled "The Global Persecution of the Faithful." It was a picture of a Sudanese man sitting on a donkey, with a caption that read, "Still preaching." The man's feet had been chopped off to keep him from evangelizing village to village. But that horrific act would not stop him. He now rides the donkey to spread the gospel of Jesus Christ. The article, included in a publication of the *Washington Times*, went on to document the rise of persecution around the world with this startling statement: "More Christians were killed in the twentieth century than in the previous nineteen centuries combined."[43]

**Emulating Jesus' response to opposition: tips for wounded disciples.** Within Jesus' prediction of the inevitability of opposition, we also should look for his example in dealing with it. Matthew develops his narrative in such a way that as one looks at the life of Jesus, one not only learns what it is for Jesus to be Messiah, but also what it is to be his disciple by emulating the life he lived. Jesus was hurt deeply in all ways possible, as those he came to rescue rejected him (11:20–24), as his own forerunner questioned him (11:1–6), as his family members attempted to deter him (12:46), and ultimately how his own people, including the crowds and the religious leaders, sought ways to have him arrested and executed (27:17–25). But Jesus did not allow his own massive hurt to dislodge him from his mission. He remained ever obedient to the Father's will for his life, ever faithful as the Spirit-endowed Servant who brings justice to the nations (12:18). In the Sermon on the Mount Jesus had declared that his disciples were to love their enemies and pray for those who persecute them (5:44). In each of his responses to opposition we can safely assume that he was loving his enemies.

Every person who reads these words, every person to whom we minister, has been hurt. Not as deeply as we see in Jesus, but we have all been hurt by seemingly well-intentioned people who, in their own misguided sincerity, have attacked us, called into question our motives, or perhaps even slandered us. How should we respond? How do we maintain our commitment to the Father's will while loving those who oppose us and who have hurt us?

---

43. "The Global Persecution of the Faithful," *World & I* (December 2000), 18.

Earlier I suggested a definition of love that goes to the heart of how Jesus loved: *Love is an unconditional commitment to an imperfect person in which we give our-selves to bring the relationship to God's intended purpose.*[44] As we encounter opposition, or at the least difficulties, in our relationships, we must love as Jesus loved. Here are some "tips for wounded disciples," with suggestions for learning how to love and serve those who have hurt us. Except for the first three, they are not in any particular order.

(1) *Give yourself to others, not just your duties and responsibilities.* In the ultimate sense, it was the person of Jesus that accomplished God's work. It was his love, his character, his embodiment of grace that permeated this world. God gave his Son to save this world, and the Son freely gave himself to those who did not deserve it (John 10:14–18). The world needs to see in us the embodiment of Jesus' love, compassion, and character, not just a perfunctory performance of our job. Relationships become cold and lifeless if based only on duty. When we give ourselves, not just our duties and responsibilities, to others, we establish real relationships.

One Christian employer whom my wife worked for several years ago had continual personnel problems. He was a rather gruff older man and kept his distance from the employees. My wife one day tried to talk to him about the problems it was creating with excessive turnover and poor morale among the working staff, and his rebuff was to say, "I'm paying their salary; I don't have to be their friend too." That may be a bit of an extreme, but it illustrates the point. Each of us can create our own relational problems when we think it is enough simply to carry out our responsibilities without giving ourselves.

Jesus exemplifies the kind of servant leadership in which he entered into personal relationships with his disciples, not simply carrying out a formal aca-demic relationship so typical among the rabbis. Developing an appropriate role as leader or employer may be difficult, but even the smallest ways of giv-ing ourselves to create an appropriate relationship with those who work for us is critical. Likewise, husbands and fathers, we may have fulfilled our duties to our wives or children by bringing home the paycheck, but have we given ourselves? I have had many conversations with adult children who lament the fact that mothers or fathers or both were so consumed with providing for the family economically that they never really gave themselves relationally to their children.

(2) *Reverse the dynamic of the relationship from taking to giving.* When we follow Jesus' example of ministry, we find that he came to give, not take, as was the Father's entire purpose in sending his Son (John 3:16; Rom. 5:8). He came not to be served but to serve and to give his life as a ransom for his people

---

44. See on the Contemporary Significance section of 5:43–47.

(Matt. 20:28; cf. Mark 10:45). Such an attitude of giving should also characterize our closest relationships.

Ask most people why they want to get married, and they will usually describe their reasons in terms of *getting*: "I will become more fulfilled in marriage"; "I have always wanted to have a husband and children and a home of my own." These motivations are not necessarily bad, but marriage as God intended it is a relationship of giving ourselves to another for their enrichment. Spouses who are so consumed with having their own needs met by their partner often cannot get their eyes off their own needs long enough to care for another's needs, and the relationship becomes parasitic. The tug-of-war of needs between people demands that we continually take in order to have our needs met.

Even in relationships that cause us the most pain, what often changes the tenor is when we give. As Jesus entered Jerusalem for his final week to present himself as Israel's Savior, he wept over the city because he knew that the nation would deny him and be judged (Luke 19:41). In the life he offered as a living sacrifice for the sins of his people, he asked for forgiveness for those who crucified him (Luke 23:34). Jesus' giving of himself is the model for our own discipleship: "Whoever wants to become great among you must be your servant, and whoever wants to be first must be your slave" (Matt. 20:26–27). This certainly opens us up to being taken advantage of by those who would hurt us, so we are to be wisely discerning as a serpent, but harmless as a dove (10:16). But the wonderful promise is that God, who is love, will continually pour his love out upon our lives. And as we receive God's love, we can in turn give it to others, even to a brother or sister who has hurt us (1 John 3:11–16; 4:7–21).

(3) *Give yourself to God's expectations for the relationship.* Jesus maintained a clear perspective of his Father's will for his life and ministry and was not deterred by what others expected him to be. He was the Messiah of Israel offering forgiveness for the sins of the people and remained fully focused on that calling. Our lives and ministries will stay focused when we try to bring any of our relationships to what God desires, not necessarily what we, or what others, may want. Others may try to manipulate us, or they may sincerely think that they know what is best for us. We should maintain a listening attitude and a genuine humility that is open to the voice of God through others, but we must be wise enough to know what God wants and not be swayed by the pressure of politics or heavy-handed personalities.

(4) *Enter into the other's experiences of life.* Two important words here are immensely important: "I understand." Jesus clearly understood the religious and emotional atmosphere of his time. He felt with the crowds and their suffering under Rome and under the religious leaders. He empathized with

the Pharisees' desire for scrupulous purity before God. This allowed him to bring his messianic ministry to their deepest needs. In understanding them he was able to treat people as individuals and accept even those who opposed him the most.

Try to put yourself in the place of people who oppose you to understand what makes them think the way they do. Put yourself in the place of your teenage son or daughter who is rebellious and try to understand them. Try to understand how difficult it is for your elderly parents to lose control over their health and independence and realize why they may be so difficult to live with at times. It may change the way that you deal with them.

(5) *Give others a vision of Jesus in each area of your life and actions.* In the middle of the narrative about the controversies, Matthew inserts a powerful vision of Jesus as the Spirit-endowed Servant, who does not quarrel or cry out, who deals gently with the hurting and oppressed, but who does not waver in leading justice to victory (12:18–21). This is a striking example of a balance of strength and gentleness, conviction and compassion, unwavering commitment to do what is right, yet humble servanthood that does not have to beat others down. Those who have hurt us need to see Jesus in our lives. Whenever we encounter opposition or difficulties in our relationships, our transformation into the image of Christ is the most tangible (cf. 2 Cor. 3:18). This is when we want to act like Jesus, think like Jesus, speak like Jesus, and bear the fruit of the Spirit as Jesus did in each encounter.

My uncle Leon is a retired pastor. He and my aunt Mary come to our town in Southern California each winter for two months or so to escape the snows of their home in the mountains of rural Colorado. One morning during our weekly walk and breakfast we were reflecting on our years of pastoral service. He summarized much of his philosophy of ministry by recalling a bit of ministerial lore: "The old preacher once said to the young pastor, 'You don't have to tell people they should be good. They already know that. You've got to show them *how* to be good.'" Give others a vision of Jesus in each area of your life and actions.

(6) *Choose carefully the "hills" on which you will "plant your flag and die."* Jesus knew clearly that his mission of establishing the kingdom of heaven would lead him to the cross for the redemption of humanity. He did not get caught up in petty rabbinic squabbles about the law. To use modern parlance, he majored on the majors, not on the minors. He chose carefully how to accomplish his life's mission by setting his face toward the hill called Golgotha. There are many issues that confront us each day, and to expend energy battling each one is exhausting and can cause us to lose sight of the bigger picture. Wisdom distinguishes what is most crucial. Not every hill of opposition or controversy is worth fighting for. The older I get, the more I realize how

few issues are really worth dying for; yet earlier in my life it seemed like I was ready to fight at the drop of every theological hat. Choose carefully the hills on which you will plant your flag and die.

(7) *Distinguish between "liking" and "loving" people.* I can imagine that Jesus encountered many disagreeable people. Some of the Pharisees strike me as unbearably narrow, bigoted know-it-alls. But Jesus came to love them all and to offer all the invitation to the kingdom of heaven. There are likely some disagreeable people in your church, perhaps even some in your own family. We don't necessarily have to like their personality or their tastes. Some people will rub us the wrong way. There are people with whom we will not click personally. It is important to distinguish between liking disagreeable people and loving them with God's love.

There have been times when I have been unbearable with my wife, when I have been insensitive or rude or selfish. She has said with teeth clenched tight, "I don't like you right now. But I love you, so I will bear with you." We won't always like the way some people act, but we are called to love them, that is, to give ourselves to them for what God desires to accomplish.

(8) *Broaden your vision to have God's perspective on your relationships with others.* In addition to giving ourselves to God's expectations for our relationships (# 3), we need to maintain God's perspective on our relationships. At all times Jesus knew who he was and what he came to accomplish in his life's mission. Others questioned his identity and his purpose, but he did not allow their opposition to deter him from the Father's will for his life. God has a vision for our relationships that is probably bigger than what we understand.

As a pastor I grew to understand that I was not just an employee of the church or just a preacher. True, some people saw me almost exclusively in those terms. But in my growing understanding of God's vision for my relationships with others, even those who were the most disagreeable, I realized there was a bigger picture. I was called to be God's agent of love and encouragement in the process of transforming the lives of people. It is comforting to broaden our vision to have God's perspective on our relationships with others, especially when others have a narrower vision of what they want from us.

(9) *Avoid gossip sessions about your relationships.* Gossip is a sin (e.g., 2 Cor. 12:20), so we can safely conclude that Jesus the sinless Savior never gossiped about those who opposed him. But gossip is a favorite pastime of many people. Both men's locker rooms and women's tea rooms often house regular conversations that degenerate into complaining about nagging wives or lazy husbands, and often much worse. The latest hurtful argument is aired so that a spouse can find solace in others who can commiserate with their hurt. But the reputation of the spouse has just been sabotaged.

Unfortunately, I've also been in many pastors' conferences where the favorite topic is bashing hurtful parishioners or deacons. There are many pastors who have been unjustly hurt, but creating an atmosphere of woundedness seldom brings healing. Instead, it reinforces an "us-versus-them" mentality, where the people of the church become the bad guys. I counsel young couples and young pastors to develop a pattern of life in which they never say anything negative about their spouse or parishioners to other people. If counsel must be sought, do so from qualified people, not those that will only reinforce your negative attitudes.

(10) *Protect your closest relationships from negative outside influences.* As Jesus left the Pharisees, he went into the house where his disciples were gathered. Perhaps he took them away from his conflicts with the Pharisees. We do know that later Jesus did have them clearly in mind in his great high priestly prayer. Although they would be sent out into the world, he asked the Father to protect them, keep them safe from the evil one, and sanctify them by the truth (John 17:11–17). In our closest relationships we must cling to the truth as a way of protecting them from evil.

I have a friend who was an administrator at a well-known seminary. He experienced struggles with other administrators, which is not uncommon and was not really bad. However, each night when he went home he shared those struggles with his wife. It was his way, he thought, to vent his problems. Unfortunately, he wouldn't emphasize the many positive things that occurred on campus. He assumed she knew about those. What soon happened was that she became so hardened and embittered that she had no good thoughts at all about the school. Most of what she felt was not justified. He eventually resigned to go elsewhere. To this day his wife carries bitterness toward the former school, and actually toward seminaries in general.

I've seen the same mistake made by many spouses as they go home and vent about their work situation or their church. There are many negative experiences that I have had in ministry that I have never told my wife. I may feel temporarily better by venting, but she can't know the full context of the good and the bad I have experienced that day. I want to protect her from unjustly becoming hardened or embittered from my negative experiences. This once again takes discernment to know when to share and when not to, but a good guideline for me is to ask whether my temporary ventilation of my problems will help her to help me, or whether it will simply put a burden on her that is unwarranted.

(11) *Differentiate between criticism of issue and criticism of you personally.* Jesus displays a healthy objectivity even when attacked and slandered. When accused of performing exorcisms by the power of Satan, he dismantles the attack with calm logic and doesn't get caught up in an angry personal defense. He

recognizes the deeper spiritual issues. The slander lodged against him as Son of Man is actually resistance against the Holy Spirit (12:32). Jesus kept his eyes on the real issues and didn't get caught up in simply defending himself.

There are times when we may become too sensitive and lose that distinction. There are times when people are intentionally hurtful, but many times we take criticism of our ministry or our work or our efforts in parenting too personally. It is always helpful to back off a moment and try to separate the issue from our feelings. We may win over opposition if we objectively deal with the issues and don't allow our feelings to get hurt. But even if we don't win them over, if we maintain our objectivity, we should not get caught up in childish, ad hominem name-calling, which may cause us to lose sight of God's objectives. We need to learn how to differentiate between criticism of issues and criticism of us personally.

We have all encountered opposition. We've all been hurt. The opposition Jesus encountered and the hurt he experienced in his earthly life is beyond comprehension. But for those of us who may be his wounded disciples, his example is necessary to guide us in our response to opposition and to those who have hurt us. His example is the most profound display of love imaginable, of giving himself to bring others to God's intended purpose for their lives.

# Matthew 13:1–52

T HAT SAME DAY Jesus went out of the house and sat by the lake. ²Such large crowds gathered around him that he got into a boat and sat in it, while all the people stood on the shore. ³Then he told them many things in parables, saying: "A farmer went out to sow his seed. ⁴As he was scattering the seed, some fell along the path, and the birds came and ate it up. ⁵Some fell on rocky places, where it did not have much soil. It sprang up quickly, because the soil was shallow. ⁶But when the sun came up, the plants were scorched, and they withered because they had no root. ⁷Other seed fell among thorns, which grew up and choked the plants. ⁸Still other seed fell on good soil, where it produced a crop—a hundred, sixty or thirty times what was sown. ⁹He who has ears, let him hear."

¹⁰The disciples came to him and asked, "Why do you speak to the people in parables?"

¹¹He replied, "The knowledge of the secrets of the kingdom of heaven has been given to you, but not to them. ¹²Whoever has will be given more, and he will have an abundance. Whoever does not have, even what he has will be taken from him. ¹³This is why I speak to them in parables:

"Though seeing, they do not see;
though hearing, they do not hear or understand.

¹⁴In them is fulfilled the prophecy of Isaiah:

"'You will be ever hearing but never understanding;
you will be ever seeing but never perceiving.
¹⁵For this people's heart has become calloused;
they hardly hear with their ears,
and they have closed their eyes.
Otherwise they might see with their eyes,
hear with their ears,
understand with their hearts
and turn, and I would heal them.'

¹⁶But blessed are your eyes because they see, and your ears because they hear. ¹⁷For I tell you the truth, many prophets

and righteous men longed to see what you see but did not see it, and to hear what you hear but did not hear it.

[18]"Listen then to what the parable of the sower means: [19]When anyone hears the message about the kingdom and does not understand it, the evil one comes and snatches away what was sown in his heart. This is the seed sown along the path. [20]The one who received the seed that fell on rocky places is the man who hears the word and at once receives it with joy. [21]But since he has no root, he lasts only a short time. When trouble or persecution comes because of the word, he quickly falls away. [22]The one who received the seed that fell among the thorns is the man who hears the word, but the worries of this life and the deceitfulness of wealth choke it, making it unfruitful. [23]But the one who received the seed that fell on good soil is the man who hears the word and understands it. He produces a crop, yielding a hundred, sixty or thirty times what was sown."

Jesus told them another parable: "The kingdom of heaven is like a man who sowed good seed in his field. [25]But while everyone was sleeping, his enemy came and sowed weeds among the wheat, and went away. [26]When the wheat sprouted and formed heads, then the weeds also appeared.

[27]"The owner's servants came to him and said, 'Sir, didn't you sow good seed in your field? Where then did the weeds come from?'

[28]"'An enemy did this,' he replied.

"The servants asked him, 'Do you want us to go and pull them up?'

[29]"'No,' he answered, 'because while you are pulling the weeds, you may root up the wheat with them. [30]Let both grow together until the harvest. At that time I will tell the harvesters: First collect the weeds and tie them in bundles to be burned; then gather the wheat and bring it into my barn.'"

[31]He told them another parable: "The kingdom of heaven is like a mustard seed, which a man took and planted in his field. [32]Though it is the smallest of all your seeds, yet when it grows, it is the largest of garden plants and becomes a tree, so that the birds of the air come and perch in its branches."

[33]He told them still another parable: "The kingdom of heaven is like yeast that a woman took and mixed into a large amount of flour until it worked all through the dough."

³⁴Jesus spoke all these things to the crowd in parables; he did not say anything to them without using a parable. ³⁵So was fulfilled what was spoken through the prophet:

"I will open my mouth in parables,
   I will utter things hidden since the creation of
      the world."

³⁶Then he left the crowd and went into the house. His disciples came to him and said, "Explain to us the parable of the weeds in the field."

³⁷He answered, "The one who sowed the good seed is the Son of Man. ³⁸The field is the world, and the good seed stands for the sons of the kingdom. The weeds are the sons of the evil one, ³⁹and the enemy who sows them is the devil. The harvest is the end of the age, and the harvesters are angels.

⁴⁰"As the weeds are pulled up and burned in the fire, so it will be at the end of the age. ⁴¹The Son of Man will send out his angels, and they will weed out of his kingdom everything that causes sin and all who do evil. ⁴²They will throw them into the fiery furnace, where there will be weeping and gnashing of teeth. ⁴³Then the righteous will shine like the sun in the kingdom of their Father. He who has ears, let him hear.

⁴⁴"The kingdom of heaven is like treasure hidden in a field. When a man found it, he hid it again, and then in his joy went and sold all he had and bought that field.

⁴⁵"Again, the kingdom of heaven is like a merchant looking for fine pearls. ⁴⁶When he found one of great value, he went away and sold everything he had and bought it.

⁴⁷"Once again, the kingdom of heaven is like a net that was let down into the lake and caught all kinds of fish. ⁴⁸When it was full, the fishermen pulled it up on the shore. Then they sat down and collected the good fish in baskets, but threw the bad away. ⁴⁹This is how it will be at the end of the age. The angels will come and separate the wicked from the righteous ⁵⁰and throw them into the fiery furnace, where there will be weeping and gnashing of teeth.

⁵¹"Have you understood all these things?" Jesus asked.

"Yes," they replied.

⁵²He said to them, "Therefore every teacher of the law who has been instructed about the kingdom of heaven is like the owner of a house who brings out of his storeroom new treasures as well as old."

THE CONFRONTATIONS BETWEEN Jesus and the religious leaders in chapters 11–12 culminated with the scene where Jesus pointed to his disciples as his closest family and declared that "whoever does the will of my Father in heaven is my brother and sister and mother" (12:50). Jesus came to do the will of his Father (11:27; 26:42), and those who receive his message and ministry obey the Father. Those who deny him, or worse oppose him, deny and oppose the Father. The contrast between Jesus' disciples and the religious leaders is now established explicitly. Jesus' disciples obey the Father's will; the religious leaders do not. They have rejected his invitation to the kingdom of heaven.

But what of the crowds? They have followed Jesus around, received his invitation to the kingdom, heard his messages, and witnessed his miracles. But will they follow the lead of Jesus' disciples and obey the Father's will to enter the kingdom and become disciples? Or will they follow the lead of the religious leaders and reject Jesus? They have had ample opportunity, so now Jesus tests their responsiveness.

At the same time, Jesus also instructs his disciples about the manifestation of the kingdom of heaven. All along many were expecting Jesus to establish the throne of David in Israel, but Jesus continually directs them first to attend to their hearts. Entrance to the kingdom occurs with the establishment of God's righteousness in the heart of a believer, which results in becoming a disciple of Jesus (see comments on 5:20). This is a strikingly different manifestation of the kingdom than many had anticipated, even his disciples, so Jesus clarifies what the kingdom is really like at this point in God's program of salvation history.

The specific means of both testing the crowds and instructing the disciples is the use of parables. Thus, in this discourse, popularly called the Parabolic Discourse, Jesus turns to this form of teaching.

## The Setting for the Parabolic Discourse (13:1–3a)

DURING MUCH OF chapter 12, Jesus has been in "the house" (13:1), most likely Peter's and Andrew's home in Capernaum (see 8:14). Jesus now leaves the house to go sit "by the lake," that is, the Sea of Galilee. Sitting was the typical posture for teachers (cf. 5:1–2). The crowds apparently understand that he is ready to continue his teaching ministry, so they come in great numbers to hear him. Such large crowds only heighten the animosity of the Pharisees, who up to now have been popular with the people and see their influence continuing to shift to Jesus.

On another occasion large crowds also pressed on Jesus so that he taught from a boat (Luke 5:1–3). The boat on that occasion belonged to Peter, so

Jesus may have used it again here. Local tradition locates this discourse at a distinctive cove or inlet called the "Cove of the Parables." The land surrounding the cove slopes down like a natural horseshoe-shaped amphitheater, providing environmental acoustics for Jesus' voice to carry over one hundred meters from the boat to a crowd of hundreds gathered on the shore. Israeli scientists have tested the acoustics in modern times and found them realistic for Jesus' parables to have been heard.[1]

At the beginning of the Sermon on the Mount, Jesus left the crowds to sit down and teach the disciples, but on this occasion he speaks to the crowd[2] in parables. Later, Jesus will explain the parables to his disciples (13:10–23, 36–52). Parables have distinctively different purposes for the crowd and for the disciples. Prior to this Jesus had given several individual parables,[3] but this is the first time Matthew uses the term "parable." Underlying this term is the Hebrew *mašal*, which refers to a wide spectrum of ideas based on comparison or analogy.[4] As used by Jesus, the parable is a way of communicating truth through a narrative analogy in the service of moral or spiritual argument.

Among the types of parables Jesus used are proverb (6:22–23), simile (10:16), similitude (13:33), story (20:1–16), and allegory (21:28–32).[5] By using vigorous figures of speech he arouses interest and curiosity and holds the attention of the audience by drawing on common experience, which disarms the listener and addresses particular needs.[6] While the analogies or comparisons Jesus uses to make his point come from everyday experiences, they press the listener to search for the intended spiritual meaning. That is why in popular preaching Jesus' parables are often referred to as "an earthly story with a heavenly meaning." But parables are often deeply, even frustratingly, perplexing, because the story may take an unexpected turn and cause offense to the audience when personal application is made.[7] As Jesus

---

1. Charles R. Page II, *Jesus and the Land* (Nashville: Abingdon, 1995), 85; Pixner, *With Jesus Through Galilee According to the Fifth Gospel*, 40.

2. The term *ochlos* in 13:2b is best rendered "crowd," not "people" as in NIV (cf. 4:16; 26:24–25).

3. E.g., 5:14–15; 7:24–27; 9:16, 17; 11:16–19; 12:27–29, 43–45.

4. Including byword, proverb, wisdom sayings, story, and allegory. For an overview of the relationship to Jewish usage, see Vermes, *The Religion of Jesus the Jew*, 90–97. For an extensive discussion of parables within Jewish rabbinic literature, see David Stern, *Parables in Midrash: Narrative and Exegesis in Rabbinic Literature* (Cambridge, Mass.: Harvard Univ. Press, 1991).

5. Robert H. Stein, "The Genre of the Parables," *The Challenge of Jesus' Parables*, ed. Richard N. Longenecker (Grand Rapids: Eerdmans, 2000), 30–50.

6. Mark L. Bailey, "Guidelines for Interpreting Jesus' Parables," *BibSac* 155 (January–March 1998): 29–38.

7. John W. Sider, *Interpreting the Parables: A Hermeneutical Guide to Their Meaning* (Grand Rapids: Zondervan, 1995), 88–89.

will make clear, his parables can function in different ways for different people, with dramatically different results. For the crowd they hide truth, while for the disciples they communicate truth.

The history of interpretation of Jesus' parables has swung from extremes. Early interpretation was allegorical, where every minor element of the parable was understood to teach something. More recently the parables were said only to have one point, with the surrounding details being simply stage props.[8] Most interpreters have now swung partway back to suggest that the parable may accomplish Jesus' intended analogy through points associated with each major character or groups of characters.[9] We will see from the first parable that there is a sower with a seed and four particular types of soils, each of which has radically different results from sowing. This leads us to ask the meaning of each.[10]

## The Parable of the Sower and Soils (13:3b–9)

THE BRILLIANCE OF Jesus' parables is that they come directly from the everyday experiences of his listeners. This first parable uses the story of a farmer who went out to sow his seed (13:3). Jesus' listeners are well aware of farming techniques, since most of these listeners take care of their own fields and gardens or work the fields of their landlords.

Many commentators place primary emphasis on the sower in this parable. As such they interpret this primarily as a Christological parable, focusing on Jesus' work of proclaiming the gospel of the kingdom of God.[11] However, the sower appears only at the beginning of the parable. This figure sets in motion the parable, but then the focus shifts to the soils. The parable does accentuate Jesus' arrival with the gospel message, but it also emphasizes significantly the contrast between good and bad soils and their response to the seed.[12]

---

8. E.g., Joachim Jeremias, *The Parables of Jesus*, rev. ed. (New York: Scribner's, 1972). A recent literary approach that tends to this view is Warren Carter and John Paul Heil, *Matthew's Parables: Audience-Oriented Perspectives* (CBQMS 30; Washington, D.C.: Catholic Biblical Association of America, 1998), 1–22.

9. Cf. Klyne R. Snodgrass, "From Allegorizing to Allegorizing: A History of the Interpretation of the Parables of Jesus," *The Challenge of Jesus' Parables*, ed. Richard N. Longenecker (Grand Rapids: Eerdmans, 2000), 3–29. One who has swung back the farthest to suggest that the parables are allegories is Craig L. Blomberg, *Interpreting the Parables* (Downers Grove, Ill.: InterVarsity Press, 1990), 29–69.

10. E.g., David Wenham, *The Parables of Jesus* (Downers Grove, Ill.: InterVarsity Press, 1989), 41–48.

11. Ibid.

12. Blomberg, *Interpreting the Parables*, 226–29; cf. Guelich, *Mark 1–8:26*, 192.

---

(1) *Seed on paths* (13:4). Seed was sown "broadcast" style by scattering it in all directions while walking up and down the field. Fields were apparently plowed both before the seed was sown and then again after, plowing across the original furrows to cover the seeds with soil. The desired depth of plowing under wheat seed was usually one to three inches, though it could be less where the topsoil was shallow. It was common for seeds to be scattered accidentally on the hard paths that surrounded the fields. Birds would swoop down and eat those seeds.

(2) *Seed on rocky places* (13:5–6). Conditions for farming in many areas of Israel were not favorable. In many places the terrain was uneven and rocky, with only thin layers of soil covering the rock. Seed that landed on this shallow soil would begin to germinate more quickly than seed sown in deep soil, but it couldn't put down deep roots and had to collect what little moisture lay in that parched thin layer of earth.[13] The sprouting seed would soon wither and die in the hot sun (13:6; cf. James 1:11).

(3) *Seed among thorns* (13:7). In the third scene, seed fell among thornbushes. The plants battled for nutrients from the soil, and the wild thorny plants were well adapted to rob whatever they needed from the soil. As the thorny plants grew up with other plants, they choked out the less hardy agricultural plants.

(4) *Seed on good soil* (13:8). In the fourth example, seed fell on "good soil." As the seeds germinated and matured, they kept on yielding a range of a hundred, sixty, or thirty times what was sown. The straight meaning of the parable is that only seed sown on good earth yielded a crop. But the implication of the yield amount has been variously understood. Some see this as implying an extraordinary, superabundant, perhaps even miraculous, crop, suggesting that typical Palestinian harvests yielded only about five to ten times the quantity sown.[14] Others understand the yield of thirty, sixty, and a hundredfold to signify a very good harvest, typical of a harvest blessed by God but not supernatural.[15] The latter view is supported by reports such as Isaac's harvest: "Isaac planted crops in that land and the same year reaped a hundredfold, because the LORD blessed him" (Gen. 26:12). Thus, seed sown on good soil yielded to the maximum what it was created to produce, with varying amounts that reflected individual potential.

---

13. Oded Borowski, "Agriculture," *ABD*, 1:97–98; idem, *Agriculture in Ancient Israel* (Winona Lake, Ind.: Eisenbrauns, 1987).

14. Joachim Jeremias, *The Parables of Jesus*, 149–51; Rousseau and Arav, "Agriculture, Cereals," *Jesus and His World*, 8–12; Keener, *A Commentary on the Gospel of Matthew* (1999), 377–78.

15. Philip Barton Payne, "The Authenticity of the Parable of the Sower and Its Interpretation," *Gospel Perspectives*, ed. R. T. France and D. Wenham (Sheffield: JSOT Press, 1980), 1:181–86; Carson, "Matthew," 305; Bailey, "The Parable of the Sower and the Soils," 183–84.

*Spiritual ears (13:9).* It may seem that Jesus is simply giving an agricultural seminar, until he utters the catchphrase, "He who has ears, let him hear" (13:9; cf. 11:15; 13:43). This alerts the audience that a deeper meaning is intended; the parables have a theological purpose in the plan of God. The following explanatory narrative will clarify who has ears (13:10–11), who will hear and understand (13:12–17), and what truth is communicated (13:18–23). This summons to hear means either (1) that not everyone has ears to hear or the ability to hear, or (2) that those who do, do not always use their ears or hear. When we see the statements in 13:10–17, the emphasis falls on the former: The parable is not for just anyone to hear, but rather is for those with spiritual ears who have the ability to hear the spiritual message embedded in the parable.

### Jesus' Purpose for Speaking in Parables (13:10–17)

JESUS HAS ALREADY given two major discourses in Matthew's Gospel—the Sermon on the Mount (chs. 5–7) and the Mission Discourse (ch. 10). He will later give the Community Discourse (ch. 18) and the eschatological Olivet Discourse (chs. 24–25). Each of those other discourses is addressed primarily to Jesus' disciples. But here Jesus is sitting in a boat, speaking parables to "the crowds" that stand on the shore (13:2). Since it is somewhat out of the ordinary to address the crowd apart from the disciples, Jesus' disciples approach him and then ask why he has been speaking to the crowd in parables (13:10). The distinction between the disciples and crowd is crucial in order to understand Jesus' purpose for speaking in parables. He uses the parables to cause the listener to make a decision about the kingdom of God.

**The secrets of the kingdom of heaven (13:11).** The reason why Jesus speaks to the crowd in parables is because[16] God has given (cf. the use of the divine passive "has been given") "the secrets of the kingdom of heaven" to the disciples, not to the crowd, to know. "Secrets" is the Greek *mysteria* ("mysteries"), which draws on a Semitic background that speaks of an eschatological secret (Aram. *raz*) passed on in veiled speech to God's chosen. The term is found explicitly in Daniel 2:18–19: "During the night the mystery was revealed to Daniel in a vision" (cf. also Job 15:8; Ps. 25:14; Prov. 3:32; Amos 3:7). Jesus' message from the beginning has declared that the kingdom of heaven has arrived, but it hasn't always been apparent to those observing. Jesus gives to his disciples an understanding of that kingdom as it is now, and will be, operating in the world. The kingdom is present, but not in its fully manifested power. George Ladd notes:

---

16. Jesus begins his answer to the disciples' question with a causal conjunction "because" (*hoti*; not reflected in NIV), indicating the reason why he speaks to the crowd in parables.

The mystery is a new disclosure of God's purpose for the establishment of his Kingdom. The new truth, now given to men and women by revelation in the person and mission of Jesus, is that the Kingdom that is to come finally in apocalyptic power, as foreseen in Daniel, has in fact entered into the world in advance in a hidden form to work secretly within and among humans.[17]

The mysteries are not that God will establish his kingdom, which was a well-known prophetic hope within Israel, but that it has arrived in a form different from what was anticipated. This is a secret now being revealed in veiled speech to God's chosen, Jesus' disciples. So, on the one hand, the parables reveal to the disciples how the kingdom of God will operate in this world before its final, powerful manifestation (which Jesus will reveal in chs. 24–25). On the other hand, the truth that is revealed to the disciples is concealed from the crowd because of their spiritual unresponsiveness (see 13:12–13). The initial understanding of the secrets of the kingdom of heaven that the disciples now have, as given by God through Jesus, will be enlarged upon, so that they will have full understanding. But whatever understanding the crowd has, even that will be taken away. In other words, not only do the parables *not* reveal truth to the crowd; they even take away what the crowd already has.

**Sovereignty and responsibility (13:12–13).** The clause rendered "though seeing they do not see" is introduced by the subordinating conjunction *hoti* (not trans. in NIV), which normally is causal; this indicates that the parables' blinding force is a result of the crowd's own spiritual hard-heartedness. Mark, however, has the subordinating conjunction *hina* here, which often introduces a purpose clause, such as "in order that" (Mark 4:12); this indicates that Jesus gives parables with the purpose of blinding the crowd. While some commentators prefer to emphasize either result or purpose, it is best to take both accounts together to give a broader perspective of the spiritual activity of the parables in the lives of the crowd.

The crowd has a mixture of attitudes toward Jesus. Some are leaning toward becoming his disciples, while others are leaning toward following the Pharisees and opposing Jesus. Still others are riding the commitment-fence. But Jesus has insisted there is no middle ground (e.g., 12:30). The crowd must make a decision, and the parables force the issue. God knows those who will harden their heart against Jesus' message, so the parables are used to harden sovereignly the person's heart to the point where eventually he or she will be unable to respond (13:15). God also knows those who will respond to the message of the gospel, so the parables elicit a positive response to

---

17. Ladd, *Theology of the New Testament*, 92.

come to Jesus, become his disciple, and ask for explanation (cf. 13:10). Thus, both sayings balance God's divine sovereignty with each individual human's responsibility.[18]

**Hard-hearted crowds (13:14–15).** Jesus quotes Isaiah 6:9–10 to indicate that even as Israel had a long background of unbelief and rejection of God's prior prophets, so the crowd is now hardened against him. The crowd mirrors the people of Israel to whom the prophet Isaiah ministered. They rejected the message because they were spiritually deadened. The subordinating conjunction *mepote,* "lest" or "otherwise" (NIV in 13:15), denotes the purpose of the divine hardening and parallels the thought in Mark 4:12.[19] The parables stimulate a hardening in those who have rejected Jesus, which prohibits them from turning for God to heal them. The unbelievers among the crowd are like the Pharisees who have committed the unpardonable sin (12:31–32) and have sinned away their day of opportunity.

Note how the parables are given after the section on the increasing rejection and opposition by Israel. God does not force anyone to accept the message of the kingdom, so the crowd's response to the parables is dictated by the nature of their heart. If a person in the crowd has no spiritual ears, his or her heart will be increasingly hardened and will turn away from Jesus and the healing that comes with the kingdom of heaven (13:15).

**Blessed disciples (13:16–17).** Jesus' disciples, on the contrary, are spiritually alive, with spiritual eyes and ears that see and hear the reality of the kingdom of heaven (13:16). The significance of the catchphrase that concluded the parable of the soils (13:9) is now revealed. Jesus' parables are designed to test the spiritual "ears" or life of his audience. The spiritually alive disciples will seek further understanding from Jesus, causing their life and understanding to be enhanced. All that the prophets and righteous people of the Old Testament had longed to see, Jesus' disciples are privileged to take part in.

"The prophets" are those who spoke for God, and "the righteous" are those in the Old Testament who eagerly awaited the arrival of God's gracious redemption and kingdom but who died before its arrival (cf. Rom. 4:1–25). In this way the unhearing crowd parallels the spiritually blind and ignorant of Isaiah's day (Matt. 13:14–15), while the disciples parallel the prophets and righteous people of the Old Testament who faithfully responded to God's revelation.

Therefore, we can say generally that with the parables Jesus accomplishes two important feats. (1) The parables test the heart of the listener. They act

---

18. For further discussion, see Carson, "Matthew," 308–10.
19. BDAG, 648.

as a spiritual examination, prompting a response from the listener that will indicate whether the person's heart is open to Jesus' message or is hardened. If the latter, the parable will stimulate confusion or outright rejection and prompt the listener to turn away from Jesus and the truth (13:11–15). But if a person's heart is open to Jesus' message, he or she will come to Jesus for further clarification about its meaning, as the disciples do (13:10). Jesus' revelation of truth and the disciples' obedient receptivity is the required distinction in understanding and not understanding.

(2) The parables give instruction to those who are responsive. They teach Jesus' disciples about the nature of the kingdom of heaven, clarifying its mysteries, which thus shows how the kingdom operates in this world in a very different way from that expected by the religious leaders and the crowds. By this Parabolic Discourse Jesus gives indications of the development of the kingdom (sower: 13:18–23, 36–43; weeds: 13:24–30; mustard seed: 13:31–32; leaven: 13:33), the incomparable value of the kingdom (treasure: 13:44; pearl: 13:45–46), membership in the kingdom (net: 13:47–50), and service in the kingdom (teacher of the law: 13:51–52).

Although this does not idealize the disciples, it implies their spiritual sensitivity. Their positive response prompts them to ask for further explanation (13:10, 36), and their request is rewarded (13:18–23, 37–43) with additional truths about the mysteries of the kingdom (13:44–52). While the disciples are not perfect in understanding, they possess the potential and desire to progress. Ultimately, they *will* understand because they have been obedient to listen and hear (13:51).

## Interpretation of the Parable of the Sower and Soils (13:18–23)

JESUS CONTINUES TO address the disciples and explains the parable to them. They are privileged to receive this clarification of God's program of salvation history and so are blessed beyond what Old Testament saints have witnessed (13:16–17). They have spiritual ears that enable them to hear the truths about the secrets of the kingdom. Whatever understanding the disciples had prior to this is now increased, because they are spiritually responsive.

**Hard hearts (13:19).** Jesus' proclamation of the kingdom of God is the setting for each of the four types of soil. In his explanation of the parable of the soils Jesus indicates that it is the Son of Man who sows the good seed (13:37). He is like the farmer sowing seed in the hearts of the people of Israel.[20] The seed represents "the message about the kingdom" (13:19), a phrase equivalent to one of Matthew's favorite expressions, "the gospel of the

---

20. Bailey, "The Parable of the Sower and the Soils," 179.

kingdom" (cf. 4:23; 9:35; 24:14).[21] Thus, all of Jesus' seeds are good, so the emphasis falls on the type of soil, whether it is good or bad.[22]

In contrast to the disciples, some in the crowd have hardened their hearts against Jesus' message. That hardness of heart prevents the seed of the gospel from taking root, and they cannot understand its truth. It makes them vulnerable to Satan, the "evil one," who snatches them away. In other words, the preaching of the gospel of the kingdom did not impact this type of person. They are like the teachers of the law and the Pharisees, who were against Jesus from the start.

**Shallow hearts (13:20–21).** The seed sown on rocky places with shallow soil signifies the type of heart that has sufficient receptivity to allow the seed to sprout up, but it is not deep enough to develop any root. It is important to recognize that the life is in the seed, not in the soil. When the environment is suitable, the life in the seed will begin to germinate. There is potential in the soil for the seed to send out life, but it is only superficial. This type of heart exhibits a superficial reception of the gospel ("at once receives it with joy"), but it does not take root. This is like those of the crowd who have not made a personal commitment to be Jesus' disciple. The seed of the gospel message was not able to penetrate to produce the change of regeneration in the person's heart.

Jesus predicted difficult times ahead for those who followed him in the kingdom of heaven (5:11–12; 10:16–25), so these professing disciples should have expected it. But under the burning heat of troubles and persecution (cf. 13:6, 21), the professing disciple's true nature is revealed, while others stumble or fall away. This one is like the false prophet who does not bear kingdom fruit and who will be cast into judgment (7:15–20; cf. 12:33–37).

**Thorny hearts (13:22).** The third type of soil is crowded with thorns. This type of heart receives the gospel but has competition from the world. As with the second soil, this type of heart has enough potential for productivity that the life in the seed begins to develop. But the competition from the thorns is too much, and the young seedling is choked out. The message of the gospel is not able to transform the person into a true disciple because of his or her competing priorities. The "worries of this life" indicate that the person has not yet placed the kingdom above all else and so tries to manage his or her own life. Jesus has already warned about such worrying in the SM (cf. 6:25–34), but the worry here tragically chokes out the life of the seed.

---

21. Donald A. Hagner, "Matthew's Parables of the Kingdom (Matthew 13:1–52)," *The Challenge of Jesus' Parables*, 106.

22. Brad H. Young, *The Parables: Jewish Tradition and Christian Interpretation* (Peabody, Mass.: Hendrikson, 1998), 251–76.

The "deceitfulness of wealth" combines with worry to choke out the life of the seed for the one who is trying to manage his or her own life apart from God and is tempted to find the solution in worldly resources.[23] The noun behind "deceitfulness" (*apate*) can be used to express both "pleasure" (2 Peter 2:13) and "deception" (Col. 2:8; 2 Thess. 2:10), which may be combined here to warn how wealth can be a deceptive pleasure (cf. Paul's warning in 1 Tim. 6:9). Note too how in addition to warnings about worry, Jesus warned in the SM about the power of the deceptive pleasure of wealth (cf. 6:19–24). The combined priorities of worry and wealth choke out the life of the message of the kingdom of heaven, so that it is unable to bear fruit.

**Receptive hearts (13:23).** Only the fourth soil is called "good." This represents the person who not only hears the gospel message but understands it and allows it to take full root in his or her heart so that it can produce fruit. This soil represents a true believing disciple. Only those whose hearts have been receptive to the work of Jesus' message will produce the fruit of kingdom life, the evidence that they are truly children of the kingdom. Jesus has already said that the fruit reveals the character of the tree (7:15–20; cf. 12:33–37), so he now declares that if the seed-message of the gospel does not bear a kingdom crop, there is no life in the person. There may be varying amounts of yield in each person, but there must be a yield.

Note that neither here nor in the giving of the parable is the fruit identified. Many think that it refers to converts won to Christ through the believer. This is no doubt partially correct, but in this context it refers to something more fundamental—the transformation of a person who has encountered the kingdom of heaven. In the fourth soil, the fruit represents the outworking of the life of the seed (cf. 1 John 3:9), with special reference to the production of the fruit of the Spirit (cf. Gal. 5:22–23) and the outworking of the Spirit in his gifts in the believer's life (1 Cor. 12). This results in the creation of the fruit of Spirit-produced righteousness and good works (e.g., Col. 1:10) and, indeed, new converts won through the believer's testimony (e.g., Rom. 1:13). The fruit produced is the outward evidence of the reality of the inward life of the kingdom.

As noted above (see comments on 13:8), the implication of the yield amount does not indicate supernatural amounts but rather signifies a harvest blessed by God. Seed sown on good soil will yield to the maximum what it has been created to produce, with varying amounts that reflect individual potential.[24]

---

23. The two phrases "worry of this life" and "deceitfulness of wealth" are the double subject of the verb "choke," indicating a combined thorny threat to kingdom life.

24. Payne, "The Authenticity of the Parable of the Sower and Its Interpretation," 181–86; Bailey, "The Parable of the Sower and the Soils," 183–84.

## Further Parables Told to the Crowds (13:24–35)

JESUS NOW SWITCHES to speak in parables to the crowd again (cf. 13:34–36). He gives three parables that all focus on the nature of the kingdom of heaven, describing what must have been a perplexing concept for the crowds. It is indistinguishable from weeds (13:24–30), it begins insignificantly but then becomes a huge roosting place for birds (13:31–32), and it permeates like yeast (13:33). This certainly isn't what many were expecting with the arrival of the kingdom, so these parables qualify well for explanation of its secret character (13:11). After these parables, Jesus leaves the crowd and spends the rest of the discourse with his disciples (13:36–52).

**The parable of the wheat and the weeds (13:24–30).** Jesus introduces each of the three parables with a distinctive expression: "The kingdom of heaven is like...." The theme of the kingdom of heaven pervades Jesus' ministry,[25] but this introduction implies that he will compare the activity of the kingdom with everyday experiences. His first example is that of "a man who sowed good seed in his field." Like the parable of the sower and soils, Jesus begins with a man sowing seed. Now, however, the seed is described as good seed and is contrasted with an enemy of the farmer, who attempts to disrupt the growth of good wheat by sowing among it *zizanion*, a kind of weed referred to as "darnel" or "tares." This is a weedy rye grass with poisonous seeds, which in early stages of growth looks like wheat but can be distinguished easily at harvest time.

When the servants report the growth of weeds, the "owner" (lit., "master of the house") immediately recognizes that this was the work of his enemy. But the destruction of the weeds must wait until the time of the harvest. Were they to attempt to uproot the weeds, they would endanger the wheat, because the weeds grow so closely intertwined with the wheat that both would come up.[26] The servants are not blamed for their failure to prevent the crime. It is the deviousness of the enemy that is to be blamed. The servants' task at the end of the age will be to distinguish between the good and the worthless and then to burn the weeds.

Jesus sounds an eschatological note with this parable that resounds throughout the rest of the discourse. The kingdom of heaven has indeed come into this world, but its advance does not mean that the enemy will be completely vanquished during this age. That awaits the final judgment, which is surprisingly delayed.[27] Jesus will later explain the meaning of the parable to his disciples at their request (see 13:36–43).

---

25. E.g., see comments on 3:2; 4:17; 5:3–20; 10:7; 11:11–15; 13:11.

26. Keener, *A Commentary on the Gospel of Matthew* (1999), 387.

27. Hagner, "Matthew's Parables of the Kingdom," 110; Vermes, *The Religion of Jesus the Jew*, 100.

**The parable of the mustard seed (13:31–32).** The next parable also begins with "the kingdom of heaven is like . . ." (cf. 13:24). Once again Jesus uses a common phenomenon to illustrate the activity of the kingdom of heaven; it is like "a mustard seed, which a man took and planted in his field." The mustard seed was the smallest seed known in Palestine at that time. Apparently, the remarkable contrast of the tiny seed of the mustard plant with its final large results took on proverbial status in Judaism (cf. 17:20).

Although the parable of the sower and soils and the parable of the wheat and weeds both receive Jesus' interpretation, neither the parable of the mustard seed nor the parable of the yeast does. But the disciples are expected to understand the meaning, because the parables reveal truth to their spiritually sensitive ears and hearts (cf. 13:10–11, 16–17).

The proverbial smallness of the mustard seed as a metaphor that describes the kingdom of God would have shocked the crowd. Israel always believed that when God's kingdom was established on the earth, it would be great; they were not prepared for an insignificant beginning. But through this parable Jesus declares that the kingdom is already present, although only as a tiny manifestation. Such a beginning may cause some among Jesus' opponents and the crowd to despise this manifestation of the kingdom. But the crowd should not let that belie the kingdom's ultimate greatness.[28] "What may not look like much to the world will in fact fulfill all God's promises."[29] The image of a large tree with birds alighting on its branches recalls several Old Testament references to a great kingdom (cf. Ezek. 17:22–24; 31:2–18; Dan 4:9–27).

**The parable of the yeast (13:33).** In this fourth and final parable given to the crowd, Jesus continues the thought of the parable of the mustard seed. With another surprising twist to what Israel had expected with the arrival of the kingdom, Jesus declares that "the kingdom of heaven is like yeast that a woman took and mixed into a large amount of flour until it worked all through the dough." Jesus reverses the common evil connotation associated with yeast for the purpose of once again prompting the crowd to try to understand the presence of the kingdom.

Yeast is any number of different forms of fungi that multiply rapidly because of fermentation. Bread required a bakers' yeast to cause it to rise (or "leaven"). Thus, a small piece of fermenting, acidic dough, set aside from an earlier baking, was "mixed" or "hidden" in the flour and kneaded. Scripture uses leaven almost exclusively as a negative metaphor, probably because fermentation implied disintegration and corruption (Ex. 12:8, 15–20). But Jesus

---

28. Ladd, *Theology of the New Testament*, 96.
29. Blomberg, *Matthew*, 220.

uses yeast to symbolize the positive, hidden permeation of the kingdom of heaven in this world.

The Jews rightly understood that the arrival of the kingdom would mean the transformation of the order of things in this world. But Jesus' arrival did not bring the expected immediate, external, dramatic change. So his parable teaches the crowd that they must not let the present, inconspicuous form of the kingdom fool them from understanding what will be its final result. The kingdom of heaven is indeed active, although it is not at that time fully observable, because it begins with an inner transformation of the heart.

The parables of the mustard seed and yeast work together to reveal the nature of the kingdom of heaven in Jesus' ministry. The mustard seed emphasizes an inconspicuous beginning of the kingdom of heaven with its growth into external greatness, while the yeast suggests its inconspicuous permeation and transformation. In spite of its small inauspicious beginnings, the kingdom of heaven will pervade the world and eventually produce the prophesied greatness.

**Parables that reveal hidden things (13:34−35).** Matthew concludes Jesus' parabolic messages to the crowd by stating: "He did not say anything to them without using a parable." This emphasizes Jesus' relationship to the crowd, which he had previously clarified to the disciples (see 13:10−17). The crowd has had the opportunity to hear Jesus' proclamation of the gospel of the kingdom. Now they must respond. The parables are one of the means by which he tests the hearts of those in the crowd, prompting them either to be with him or against him (12:30). Their day of opportunity is nearly over. They cannot stay in the middle ground forever.

Matthew draws upon an Old Testament precedent for Jesus' relationship to the crowd: "So was fulfilled what was spoken through the prophet: 'I will open my mouth in parables, I will utter things hidden since the creation of the world.'" The psalmist Asaph reflected on Israel's history and clarified through parables the meaning of God's salvation-historical events so that the people would learn from their history and not be a stubborn and rebellious people with hearts hard to God's saving work (Ps. 78:2, 8). Matthew's standard fulfillment formula (see comments on 1:22; 2:15) says that Jesus is doing a similar service to Israel in his day, revealing in his parables the secrets of the kingdom of heaven that have been hidden since the beginning.[30]

The entire Old Testament has looked forward to the inauguration of the kingdom of heaven, and in Jesus' ministry he has drawn together the many strands of prophetic hope that seemed disparate to some.[31] His revelation of

---

30. Morris, *Matthew*, 354−55.
31. Ito, "Matthew and the Community of the Dead Sea Scrolls," 29−30.

the secrets of the kingdom of heaven in parables has brought to the light God's program of salvation and redemption. The significance for the crowd is their response. Those spiritually alive will come to Jesus for clarification and understanding and become his disciples; those spiritually dead will turn away.

## Explanations and Parables Told to the Disciples (13:36–50)

THE "HOUSE" THAT is a safe haven from the pressing crowd is once again probably Peter's and Andrew's home in Capernaum (see comments on 8:14; 13:1), where his disciples again ask for a clarification of a parable, this time the one regarding the weeds (cf. 13:10). After Jesus gives the explanation, he gives three final parables, this time not to the crowds but to the disciples themselves (13:44–50). They demonstrate their sensitivity to spiritual truth by acknowledging that they understand the meaning of the parables (cf. 13:10–15, 51). While the number of disciples has grown by now, Matthew consistently emphasizes the smaller group of Twelve, not only as an example of growth in discipleship for his readers, but also as an example of the way that Jesus trains them for leadership in the church to come.[32]

**Interpretation of the parable of the wheat and weeds (13:36–43).** The explanation of the parable of the wheat and weeds is unique for the way in which Jesus identifies the main elements of the story, leading to an eschatological conclusion. Each of these elements is helpful for interpreting other parables. Several elements are not identified (e.g., the servants and their sleep; 13:25), which reminds us that not every element has significance in the metaphor.

- The *sower* of good seed is Jesus, the Son of Man (see 8:20). By extension we can imply that the sower can be any of Jesus' disciples who proclaim the Word of God.
- The *field* is the world. The kingdom of heaven will expand beyond Israel throughout the world. The secret of the kingdom is its present but hidden working in the world.[33] It is important to note that Jesus is not giving lessons on the activities of the church in this parable. The church will be a visible institution throughout this age in service of the kingdom, but Jesus does not equate the two (see comments on 16:18–19; 18:15–20). His parables describe the activity of the kingdom during this age. To interpret these as characteristic of the church's activity produces many misconceptions and misapplications.

---

32. Wilkins, *Following the Master*, 176–93.
33. Ladd, *Theology of the New Testament*, 94–95.

For example, many have mistakenly equated this parable with the church's characteristic of true and false believers. While it may be true that we can find in many churches true and false believers, it is defeatist to suggest that Jesus declares that this is the norm. Instead, Jesus shows how the kingdom of heaven will exist alongside the sons of the devil throughout this age. "The parable deals with eschatological expectation, not ecclesiological deterioration."[34]

- The *good seed* is the people of the kingdom. These are the ones who have been receptive to the preaching of the message of the kingdom and have become Jesus' disciples. They are the "good soil" of the parable of the sower and soils and the wheat of this parable.

- The *weeds* are the people who belong to the evil one. They are the unbelievers of Jesus' day and all those throughout this age who reject the gospel message.

- The *enemy* that sneaked in and planted weeds among the wheat is called "the devil," the same term used of Satan in Jesus' temptations (see comments on 4:5, 8). The devil operates in this world as a swooping bird (13:19) and (here) as an enemy farmer attempting to disrupt the growth of good wheat (disciples).

- The *harvest* is the end of the age, a reference to the judgment that will accompany the coming of the Son of Man to consummate the establishment of the kingdom (24:3).

- The *harvesters* are Jesus' angels (13:39), who will accompany him to establish his kingdom and bring judgment (24:31).

With the primary players of the parable identified, Jesus gives additional explanation of the events that will transpire at the end of the age. As he consummates his kingdom on the earth, Jesus will send his angels to remove all sin and sinners from this world, now called for the first time "his kingdom" (13:41). His divine sovereignty will be visibly established over all creatures of this world at this time. Judgment of the sons of the evil one will commence in the fiery furnace (cf. 3:11; 5:22), where there will be "weeping and gnashing of teeth" (13:42; cf. 8:12). These are Jesus' typical expressions of eternal judgment.

At that time "the righteous" (13:43)—Jesus' disciples, who have experienced inner transformation and who are the wheat that has grown up throughout this age—will experience the full manifestation of the kingdom's glory and "will shine like the sun." Jesus' disciples are the light of the world during this age while they await its consummation (6:14–16), but at that time they will shine with unhindered brilliance. The expression "the kingdom of their Father" is not to suggest that there is a distinction between the king-

---

34. Carson, "Matthew," 317; Morris, *Matthew*, 350. See below at 13:36.

dom of the Son and another kingdom of the Father, but that the Father's will has been fully accomplished on earth through the activity of the Son. There is full congruence between the will and activity of Father and Son.

Jesus' instruction on prayer to the Father for the coming of the kingdom and the establishment of his will on earth (6:10) is now answered in full. So Jesus concludes his explanation of this parable with the familiar refrain to yield to the will of the Father as it is being proclaimed by Jesus—anyone who is willing to hear should listen and understand!

**The parable of the hidden treasure (13:44).** Jesus for the first time speaks in parables to his disciples. They are still away from the crowds in the house (13:36), so the intent of the parables is not to conceal but to reveal further secrets about the kingdom (see comments on 13:10–17). The parables of the treasure and pearl make a similar point. In contrast to the parable of the wheat and weeds, which looks forward to the Parousia and the consummation of the kingdom, these two parables emphasize the present value of the partially inaugurated kingdom.

The kingdom of heaven is likened to "a treasure hidden in a field. When a man found it, he hid it again, and then in his joy went and sold all he had and bought that field." Treasures were often hidden in fields, because there were no formal banks as we know them today (cf. 25:25).[35] It was not uncommon for people to hide valuables when a marauding army approached. If the homeowner did not survive the invasion, the treasure would be forgotten and unclaimed. The land could change hands several times without anyone being aware of hidden treasure.

So the kingdom of heaven is like a treasure that lies unnoticed because of its hidden nature. However, Jesus stresses that the man is not searching for the treasure. He happens upon it and instantly recognizes its value. By selling all that he has to purchase the field, he is gaining something far more valuable than any of his possessions and far more valuable than the field itself.[36] As with ethical issues in other parables, surreptitiously buying land known to contain treasure is not condoned nor even the point. The surprising find simply heightens the drama.[37] The emphasis is on the supreme worth of the treasure that is unseen by others; it is worth far more than any sacrifice one might make to acquire it.

Although the religious leaders and the crowd are blind and ignorant of the presence of the kingdom (11:25; 13:13–15), Jesus' parables reveal its

---

35. The intriguing Copper Scroll found at Qumran lists sixty-four places in Palestine where treasures were apparently hidden.

36. The Mishnah required a contractual statement specifying that the sale of land included its contents (*m. B. Bat.* 4.9); cf. Vermes, *The Religion of Jesus the Jew*, 107.

37. Hagner, "Matthew's Parables of the Kingdom," 117.

surpassing value to the disciples (13:11–12, 16–17). No sacrifice is too great to live in God's will and experience a discipleship relationship with Jesus as Master.[38] The contrast will be sadly displayed in the rich young ruler, who would not abandon all that he had to follow Jesus (19:16–22). The apostle Paul understood clearly the surpassing value of a discipleship relationship to Jesus: "I consider everything a loss compared to the surpassing greatness of knowing Christ Jesus my Lord, for whose sake I have lost all things" (Phil. 3:8). In this parable Jesus is not speaking to self-sacrifice so much as joyful abandonment to obtain the kingdom of God.[39]

**The parable of the costly pearl (13:45–46).** Jesus expresses continuity with the thought of the preceding parable regarding the value of the kingdom of God. In this one, however, instead of unexpectedly stumbling across a hidden treasure, we find a merchant who is out deliberately searching. He is apparently a wholesale pearl dealer on a professional trip looking for fine pearls for his business. "When he found one of great value, he went away and sold everything he had and bought it."

As with the parable of the treasure, this one stresses the incomparable quality of the kingdom of God. But a contrast between the two primary figures illustrates that instead of simply stumbling across a hidden treasure, a diligent search by one well qualified to know its value will ultimately lead to the kingdom. Moreover, as an expert, the merchant knows that even if he sells all that he has, the pearl he possesses surpasses all his former accumulated wealth.

The point is not on buying one's way into the kingdom but on recognizing its supreme value.[40] Earlier Jesus used a pearl to illustrate the precious nature of the gospel that could not be appreciated by pigs (7:6). The religious leaders of Jesus' day were certainly those whose expertise qualified them to understand the magnitude of the kingdom of God that Jesus announced, but they were blinded by their hypocrisy and their desire for a pious reputation and honor from people (6:1–3). Jesus' disciples are to understand that there is nothing more valuable in all of the world than possession of the kingdom of God.[41]

**The parable of the dragnet (13:47–48).** Jesus concludes with a brief parable about the net and immediately follows it with a brief explanation of its meaning. The parable climactically focuses on the eschatological consequences of the choice one makes with regard to the kingdom of God. The

---

38. See Young, *The Parables*, 199–221.
39. See Wenham, *The Parables of Jesus*, 206–7.
40. Young, *The Parables*, 199–221.
41. Hagner, "Matthew's Parables of the Kingdom," 118.

net is the large seine or dragnet (*sagene*), the oldest type of net used on the lake and until recently the most important fishing method. It was shaped like a long 750 to 1,000 foot wall, upwards of 25 feet high at the center, and 5 feet high at the ends. The foot-rope was weighted with sinkers, while the head-rope floated with attached corks, enabling the net wall to be dragged toward shore by both ends, trapping fish inside (see also comments on ancient fishing at 4:18–22).[42] Separating good fish from bad fish was an ancient tradition in Israel. Among those considered "bad fish" included those without fins and scales, which were unclean (Lev. 11:9–12).

Jesus uses this metaphor to describe the end-of-the-age judgment when the good will be separated from the bad, similar to the way that the parable of the wheat and weeds depicted an end-of-age separation (13:24–30, 36–43). When Jesus comes in power, he will consummate the establishment of his kingdom on the earth. He will send his angels to initiate judgment by separating the wicked (those who have denied the message of the gospel) from the righteous (those who have responded to the gospel and have entered the kingdom of heaven; cf. 5:20). The statement of judgment of the wicked reiterates verbatim the words of 13:42. The final arrival of the kingdom of heaven will then extend its net throughout the world, and "no race or category of person will escape the final judgment. All will be sorted into one of two groups, those God accepts and those he rejects."[43]

## The Parable of the Householder's Treasure (13:51–52)

AFTER GIVING THE final parable of the secrets of the kingdom of heaven to the disciples in the house, Jesus asks them, "Have you understood all these things?" As a climax to the entire discourse, Jesus has in mind their understanding of both explained and unexplained parables, which implies their understanding of the secrets of the kingdom. They did not have full understanding earlier when they requested explanation from Jesus (13:10, 36), but now their narrative reply is swift and confident: "Yes." In contrast to the crowd, the disciples understand Jesus' parables, as he said they would (13:10–17). As true disciples they are growing in their understanding. But unless they give unwavering attention and obedience to Jesus' teaching, they will display an obtuseness similar to the crowd (e.g., 15:16). Their confidence may be more than appropriate, given their later vacillation, but they are indeed growing in understanding.

---

42. Nun, *Sea of Galilee and its Fishermen*, 16–44.
43. Blomberg, *Interpreting the Parables*, 202.

Jesus responds to their affirmative reply with a parable about their present privileged status and their future role. "Therefore every teacher of the law who has been instructed [*matheteuo*] about the kingdom of heaven is like the owner of a house who brings out of his storeroom new treasures as well as old." In light of usage of *matheteuo* elsewhere, a preferable rendering here is "has become a disciple [*mathetes*]" or "has been made a disciple."[44]

Since Jesus is speaking to disciples here about the consequence of their understanding (cf. "therefore," 13:52), he now likens them to teachers of the law, who are in turn likened to "owners of a house" (*oikodespotes*). An *oikodespotes* is used in Jesus' parables to refer to God (21:33), Jesus (10:25; 13:27), or Jesus' disciples (24:43) and is sometimes pictured as distributing his wealth, whether as wages for his workers (20:1–16) or as a rental property for farmers (21:33–43).[45] Jesus extends the metaphor here to indicate that the householder brings from his treasure box both new and old things. He does not do so simply to ogle his wealth but to dispense it for the benefit of others.[46]

The contrast is thus drawn between the teachers of the law within Judaism and the disciples of Jesus. The Torah-trained teachers of the law studied under great rabbis and passed on their traditions and interpretations. But all those who have become disciples of the kingdom of heaven have Jesus alone as their teacher, and they will in turn faithfully pass on to others what Jesus has taught them. They not only understand how to draw spiritual truths from the parables properly (13:51), but they understand how Jesus' arrival has fulfilled the promises of the coming of the Messiah and the messianic kingdom (e.g., 1:22; 2:5, 15, 17, 23; 3:15; 4:14–17) and how Jesus truly fulfills the Law and the Prophets (5:17–20).[47]

This marks an important development in the training of the disciples for their future role throughout the ages. In the same way that Jesus has developed them, they are to make disciples of all the nations and teach these new disciples all that they have been taught by Jesus (28:19–20). Jesus is not merely describing the disciples, "but as usual in parables is challenging them to fulfill a role: they have received 'treasure' through his instruction; now they are to 'bring it out' in teaching others."[48] Jesus' disciples are to give close attention to the priority of the kingdom in their lives so that they may continue to be the treasure of Jesus' revelation to a watching world.

---

44. Hagner, *Matthew*, 1:401–2; see Wilkins, *Discipleship in the Ancient World and Matthew's Gospel*, 160–63.

45. BDAG, 695.

46. Carson, "Matthew," 332.

47. David E. Orton, *The Understanding Scribe: Matthew and the Apocalyptic Ideal* (JSNTSup 25; Sheffield: JSOT Press, 1989), esp. 140–53.

48. France, *Matthew*, 231.

*Bridging Contexts*

THE PARABOLIC DISCOURSE occupies a pivotal position in Matthew's presentation of Jesus Messiah and his gospel of the kingdom of heaven. This is the third of Jesus' major discourses that Matthew has preserved for his readers, and it records parables that both tested the hearts of the crowd and provided instruction for Jesus' disciples. But these parables will likewise test and instruct readers throughout this age, because in the five discourses that Matthew has collected, he has provided us the largest collection of Jesus' instructions, which is the basis of what disciples are to be taught to obey in the development of their lifelong discipleship to Jesus (28:20).

**Discourses and discipleship.** A brief overview of the type of disciple described in each of the discourses will give us a context for understanding the place of the Parabolic Discourse in Jesus' intentional development of our own discipleship to him.

(1) In the first discourse, the Sermon on the Mount (chs. 5–7), Jesus develops what it means to be *kingdom-life disciples*. He expounds the reality of a radical everyday discipleship lived in the presence and power of the kingdom of God. This kind of discipleship involves an inside-out transformation into the righteousness of the kingdom (5:20). The ultimate example of this righteousness is Jesus himself, who has come to fulfill the Old Testament revelation of God's will for his people (5:17, 21–47), so that Jesus' disciples can pursue clearly the goal to be perfect as their heavenly Father is perfect (5:48). Kingdom life, therefore, addresses all aspects of what discipleship to Jesus means during this age, including ethical, religious, marital, emotional, and economic dimensions.

(2) The Mission Mandate develops what it means to be *mission-driven disciples* (ch. 10). Jesus commissions all his disciples to go out to live and share the gospel of the kingdom with an alien and often hostile world until his return. Mission in this age is a responsibility of all believers (10:24–25, 40–42), not just a special category of persons. It occurs in both public confession to the world (10:32–33) as well as in private commitments to one's family (10:34–39). Like Jesus himself, the disciples can expect opposition and persecution (10:24–25) from Jews and Gentiles, from the religious and political world, and from one's own closest family and companions (10:17–21). Yet they need not fear because the Spirit will provide power and guidance (10:19–20) and the Father will exercise sovereign care and control (10:28–33). The centrality of the presence of Jesus in the disciples' life is the most vital characteristic of the mission, so that the disciples increasingly grow to be like the Master (10:24).

(3) The center discourse, the Parabolic Disclosure (ch. 13), develops what it means to be *clandestine-kingdom disciples*. This discourse acts as a transition from simple presentation of the gospel of the kingdom to a time of examination for the crowds following Jesus, and also to a time of instruction for Jesus' disciples about the surprising nature of the kingdom of heaven. We will look at this a bit more carefully below.

(4) In the fourth discourse, the Community Prescription (ch. 18), Jesus will develop what it means to be *community-based disciples*. He will declare how the life of the kingdom is to be expressed through the church, which he will establish on earth through his disciples. The church is to be characterized by humility, purity, accountability, forgiveness, reconciliation, and restoration.

(5) The final major discourse is the Olivet Discourse (chs. 24–25), which unfolds what it means to be *expectant-sojourner disciples*. Jesus looks down the long corridor of time and prophesies to his disciples about his return, the end of the age, and the establishment of his messianic throne. This discourse culminates his teaching on discipleship by describing how his disciples are to live each day in this age of the "already–not yet" consummation of the kingdom of God, in expectant preparation for his return with power.

**Clandestine-kingdom disciples.** Thus, in chapter 13 Jesus indicates that his disciples will live out their discipleship in a manifestation of the kingdom that is clandestine. Many in the crowd that followed him around were hoping for the arrival of the kingdom with an overt display of political and militaristic might. Their attraction to Jesus was not based so much on what Jesus intended in announcing the arrival of the kingdom, but on what they expected to get out of it—the blessings of the messianic age.

Hoping for the blessings is not bad, but it leads them to overlook the real message Jesus is announcing. In fact, the hope for physical and material blessings hardens them from recognizing their own spiritual condition. They are increasingly influenced by the religious leaders, especially the Pharisees, who prided themselves on their own accomplishments and ignored their own spiritual destitution. Because of the influence of the religious leaders, the crowd eventually becomes so hardened against Jesus' form of the kingdom that they call for his execution in preference for the rebel leader Barabbas, a man involved with plotting to overthrow Rome and establishing a physical kingdom of Israel (see comments on 27:20).

Jesus' own followers still do not fully understand the uniqueness of the manifestation of kingdom of God that Jesus is instituting. While imprisoned, John the Baptist, his privileged prophetic forerunner, had questioned Jesus' messianic identity because his kingdom program didn't coincide with what John anticipated (cf. 11:2–6). And when it is evident that Jesus will be crucified instead of claiming his throne, even his closest disciples abandon him.

So in this third major discourse, Jesus develops what it means to be "clandestine-kingdom disciples." Through his parables Jesus tests the hearts of the crowd to reveal whether the message of the kingdom has taken root and is producing fruit or whether it has been unproductive (13:18–23). They must decide whether they are with him or against him. In addition, through these parables Jesus reveals to his disciples the secrets of the kingdom of God, making known that during this age the kingdom will exist in a hidden form. It will be an undercover kingdom, not the overpowering political and militaristic cultural manifestation of God's rule that many expect (13:31–33). So the parables reveal what it means for Jesus' disciples to live as kingdom subjects in a world that has not yet experienced the fully consummated kingdom of God.

The parables further reveal that Jesus' disciples are to be demonstrably different from others in this world. The inside-out transformation that he articulated in the Sermon on the Mount will produce fruit in them that will mark them out clearly as his disciples. But it is only at the end of this age that a final separation will make fully known who belongs to kingdom of heaven and who does not (13:41–43, 49–50). The incongruity of its hiddenness and inconspicuousness causes many to overlook and even reject the kingdom of God, yet to those who discover its presence, it is the most precious reality of this age (13:44–46). Therefore Jesus' disciples must give closest attention to the priority of the kingdom in their lives so that they will continue to be the treasure of revelation to a watching world (13:51–52).

**Who is responsible for a hardened heart?** With this revelation in parables of the secrets of the kingdom of heaven, the reader might think that the crowds should be excused if they don't understand these cloaked messages. But we noticed above that when Jesus explained his purpose for speaking in parables, he put the blame squarely on those who have hardened themselves against his message and ministry: "though [or 'because'] seeing they do not see; though hearing, they do not hear or understand" (see comments on 13:13). When taken together with Mark's emphasis on this quotation as the purpose of speaking in parables (Mark 4:11–12), we saw that these two accounts together give a broader perspective of the spiritual activity of the parables in the lives of the crowd.

With a mixture of attitudes toward Jesus within the crowd—some leaning toward becoming Jesus' disciples, while others leaning toward following the Pharisees and opposing Jesus, and still others riding the commitment-fence—Jesus uses the parables to force a decision. God knows those who will harden their heart against Jesus' message, so the parables are used to harden sovereignly the person's heart to the point where eventually he or she will be unable to respond (13:15). God also knows those who will respond to the message of the gospel, so the parables elicit a positive response to come to Jesus, become his disciple, and ask for explanation (cf. 13:10). Thus the use of the saying in Matthew and Mark balances God's divine sovereignty with each individual human's responsibility.

**Balanced Christian thinking and living.** This causes us to return to the concept of "balance" that Matthew tends to maintain with seemingly contradictory truths.[49] We saw, for example, that Jesus exhorted his disciples to "let your light shine before men, that they may see your good deeds and praise your Father in heaven" (5:16), yet later he admonished, "Be careful not to do your 'acts of righteousness' before men, to be seen by them" (6:1). One might hastily emphasize only one truth, to the sad neglect of the other. A balance of both advises us to avoid the temptation from both personal cowardice and religious vanity (cf. 6:1–2).

There are many issues in Matthew's Gospel, and Scripture generally, that demand a balancing of extremes that at face value seem contradictory. Unfortunately, the human tendency is to alleviate the dissonance by taking one side of the issue, often neglecting or reinterpreting the other body of scriptural evidence to support the position. The right kind of balance means taking two seemingly opposite truths and living with them both at the same time, even though we may not be able to understand completely how they fit together.

The truths in this section—God's sovereignty and humanity's responsibility—require a careful balance. I encourage the following process when encountering two seemingly opposite truths: (1) Think sensibly! Don't be carried away by emotional reactions. Emotional reaction to apparent contradictions may cause us to become immobilized or be carried away to an extreme.

(2) Be honestly open to both truths, regardless of past experience or background. Our denominational background or church experience may cause us to reject out of hand the truth that is less emphasized in our theological tradition. We must be open to the truth of God's Word.

(3) Hold those seemingly opposing truths at the same time. If they are biblical truths and not simply someone's opinion, they will both have value in the decision-making process and ultimately will reveal themselves as complementary, not contradictory.

(4) Apply both sides of the issue to life at the same time. Since Scripture is a guide to life, both principles may be more easily lived out than fully comprehended. Although we may not be able to understand completely how God's sovereignty and our responsibility coexist, we all have the experience of seeing both principles worked out in the day-to-day experiences of

---

49. See the Contemporary Significance section of 7:1–12.

life. We must recognize that God is absolutely in control of all that happens in this life, yet we each are individually responsible for our own actions and will be accountable eternally.[50]

The parables of Jesus are a remarkable demonstration of the way in which those truths are balanced. God's sovereignty does not eliminate personal responsibility as a factor in entering the kingdom. His control over each human's fate is rightly balanced with the moral responsibility of each human to respond appropriately to God.[51] A balanced position affirms both realities.

**The law of progressive spiritual atrophy or consecutive spiritual assimilation.** As the crowd hears Jesus' parables, their hearts are tested and they are given an opportunity to receive God's divine revelation. But it will impact each person differently. One person may hear the parable and immediately harden his or her heart against the truth it teaches and turn away from Jesus. Each time he hears and rejects the truth of a parable, his heart is further hardened. Another person will hear the parable and immediately respond to its truth, turn to Jesus, become his disciple, and learn from him. Each time that she hears and responds positively to the truth of a parable, her heart increases in Christlikeness. One commentator calls this the law of "progressive spiritual atrophy" or "consecutive spiritual assimilation." He describes it in this way:

> The judgment is written plain for those who hear and fail to appropriate: their capacity for apprehension and appropriation of spiritual truth dwindles until it disappears. Contrariwise, the more of God's revealed truth that we assimilate, the more our capacity for assimilating truth will grow, in a sort of spiritual geometric progression.[52]

He concludes by stating that "spiritual perception of God's truth is perilous: it condemns us unless we act upon it. Increased knowledge merely brings increased responsibility (Lk. xxii. 48)."[53]

This is the frightening situation of the unbelievers within the crowd. Jesus' parables present them with truths about the kingdom of heaven. To reject those truths is to start on the long path to denial of reality and a heart that will eventually be hardened beyond the possibility of return. This becomes the situation of the Pharisees, who already have denied the working of the Spirit leading them to the truth of the gospel and who eventually

---

50. For a more complete discussion, see Wilkins, "Balance as a Key to Discipleship," 45–64.

51. Hagner, *Matthew*, 1:373.

52. Alan Cole, *The Gospel According to St. Mark: An Introduction and Commentary* (TNTC; Grand Rapids: Eerdmans, 1961), 91.

53. Ibid.

are hardened beyond the possibility of restoration (cf. 12:30–32). Their rejection of Jesus' message is the epitome of self-deception, because they rationalize their judgment of Jesus as though they were God's authorized dispensers of religious verdicts.

But such is the situation of every person who rejects Jesus' message. They ultimately elevate their own opinion over God's. Each time a person hardens his heart against the gospel, he deceives himself into thinking that he knows the truth about reality and rationalizes his conclusion about Jesus. This is done by those who believe the gospel to be too exclusivistic for modern pluralistic tolerance. It sounds so narrow-minded to speak of only "one way" to God. Or it can be done by those who think that Jesus' message about the righteousness of the gospel is too archaically prudish for enlightened and liberated modern people. It sounds so legalistic to suggest that a person deny herself to take up her cross and follow Jesus. This is what it means, however, to really want God to be the God of our lives. Dallas Willard writes somberly:

> *The ultimately lost person is the person who cannot want God.* Who cannot want God to be God. Multitudes of such people pass by every day, and pass into eternity. The reason they do not find God is that they do not want him or, at least, do not want *him* to be God. Wanting God to be God is very different from wanting God to help me.[54]

Such is the case of the unbeliever. But what about the believer? Believers also must be wary, because rejecting the truth of the gospel can lead to a heart hardened against God. The primary interpretation of the parables deals with the initial response of the hearer to the kingdom message, but Jesus' interaction with his disciples allows us to see that they must also maintain an openness to the truth embedded in the parables for them to continue to understand and obey.

We are all too aware of public Christian leaders who have been revealed to have had a long-term illicit sexual relationship while continuing to serve in a leadership position. They have continually rejected the conviction of the Spirit and the truth of God's Word about their sin and so have hardened their hearts against God. Such is also the case of any believer who lives with a sin, such as gossip or bigotry or gluttony or pride, and rationalizes its appropriateness. These are sins that are less visible but nonetheless can point to a heart hardened against God's leading.

I do not believe this implies that a believer has lost his or her salvation. A heart that is regenerated cannot be unregenerated. However, we must

---

54. Willard, *Renovation of the Heart*, 58; his emphases.

consider the possibility that a person who continues to harden his or her heart against the truth of God's Word was never regenerated in the first place. Or it may be like the case of the Corinthian believers, who sinned blatantly within the community of believers and so were disciplined by God with illness and even death so that purity would be maintained within the community. The sick and dead are not threatened with eternal loss, but God's discipline is understood as that in which a loving God is correcting his children.[55] A heart that is sensitive to God will display a genuine remorse for sin committed. Without it there is no possibility of growth in Christlikeness. Willard continues:

> . . . *without this realization of our utter ruin* and without the genuine revisioning and redirecting of our lives, which that bitter realization naturally gives rise to, *no clear path to inner transformation can be found*. It is psychologically and spiritually impossible. We will steadfastly remain on the throne of our universe, so far as we are concerned, perhaps trying to "use a little God" here and there.[56]

Jesus admonishes, "He who has ears, let him hear" (13:9), because it is only in hearing and obeying the truth that a person's heart is given over to the rule of God's kingdom and the possibility of personal growth in Christlikeness.

HIDDEN BUT POWERFUL. During the occupation of Europe by Nazi Germany during World War II, millions of people experienced unspeakable horror. Concentration camps mushroomed throughout Europe where minority groups, chiefly Jews but also gypsies, homosexuals, and anti-Nazi civilians, were at first confined and later executed. The fear of arrest that everyday people felt turned to a paralyzing terror. Daily life was dominated by the presence of the German military and the dreaded SS (*Schutzstaffel*, German for "Protective Echelon") forces.

But there arose within the terror another response—the underground "resistance"—made up of various secret and clandestine groups that opposed Nazi rule. From southern France to the northern reaches of Scandinavia to the distant Soviet Union, widely diverse groups of civilians as well as armed bands of partisans or guerrilla fighters worked secretly against the occupation. Their activities ranged from publishing clandestine newspapers to

---

55. Gordon D. Fee, *The First Epistle to the Corinthians* (NICNT; Grand Rapids: Eerdmans, 1987), 566.

56. Willard, *Renovation of the Heart*, 60; his emphases.

assisting the escape of Jews and Allied airmen shot down over enemy territory to committing acts of sabotage and ambushing German patrols. These were brave men and women, who could not overtly resist the powerful German forces but who covertly operated to bring freedom to their people.

But the will and the ability to fight on covertly was in large measure kept alive by one abiding hope—the rumored coming Allied invasion. From the first German Blitzkrieg of Poland in 1939 to those in the successful German invasions of Belgium, the Netherlands, and France in 1940, millions of people were oppressed for years. The effort, ability, and resources of the resistance would most likely have waned except for that hope of the coming of liberation. As the months and years dragged on, one of the most important efforts of the resistance was preparing for and coordinating with the invasion by conveying intelligence information to the Allies. Finally, on June 6, 1944, D-Day, also called Operation Overlord, the Allied invasion of western Europe began.

On the surface of German-occupied Europe all appeared horrifically helpless and hopeless. But hidden among the terrorized were those people who dared to resist, in large part because they were joined with the powerful Allied forces that promised liberation. We shouldn't idealize them since some of them, like many of those in the Soviet Union who supported Joseph Stalin, had ideological agendas that were later used to subjugate their own people. But the resistance does provide a modern illustration of the *effectiveness of hidden power*. It proved dramatically effective in keeping the Nazi war machine off balance, it gave inspiration to the common people throughout Europe, and in spite of its apparent helplessness the resistance drew on the promised hope of the Allied invasion to coordinate its efforts at liberation.[57]

The power that Jesus brought with his announcement of the arrival of the kingdom of heaven did not have the perception of power that many people expected. Jesus could indeed perform powerful miracles, but they were short-lived and selective. The complete regeneration of the world that many associated with the messianic age of blessing had not arrived. Rome still dominated the land, and ruthless leaders still induced fear of imprisonment and execution. People still died. Hunger and disease were still daily experiences.

So Jesus clarifies with his parables that the kingdom of heaven has secrets associated with it. It is hidden but powerful in its spiritual transformational working. It is small in its beginning, but it will bring the reality of salvation from sin to all those who dare to come to it with eyes of faith and an open heart. God's judgment of the evil one and his followers is certain and will

---

57. "Resistance," *Encyclopædia Britannica*, http://www.britannica.com/eb/article?eu=64876 [Accessed August 12, 2002].

come with power, but it may not always appear that way during the age that follows. Jesus' return in glorious power to liberate this sin-sick world is a concrete promise that energizes us and gives us purpose for our own lives. These are the truths of the parables that reveal the secrets of the kingdom of heaven and that have provided guidance and hope and revelation of God's powerful, yet hidden operation during this age.

Before we look briefly at the contemporary significance of the parables in this grand discourse, we should take an overview of the principles of their interpretation so that we hear clearly the message that Jesus intended to communicate in each.

**Interpreting the parables of the secrets of the kingdom of heaven.** Every good teacher or preacher understands the significance of illustrating a lesson with examples from everyday life. This serves to make an abstract concept relevant and concrete to the audience. But illustrations are not intended simply to entertain, otherwise the teacher or preacher is only a storyteller. As Sidney Greidanus cautions, "one ought to select illustrations not simply to create interest, but to elucidate the truth or to concretize the application of a particular passage."[58]

Jesus was a master storyteller, but he was far more than that. His parables not only captivated interest, but they produced conviction and demanded a response. The same is true for their impact on modern readers. Jesus' repeated refrain, "He who has ears, let him hear" (13:9), and related expressions about the blessedness of those who hear and the dire consequences of those who don't (e.g., 13:13–17) calls us to a careful acquisition of the truth he is communicating in his parables.

Jesus used parables earlier and elsewhere in his ministry, but the collection of parables in Matthew 13 had a unique purpose in his historical ministry. With these parables he intended to test the hearts of the crowds and to force them to commit either to be with him or against him. At the same time, he used them to unveil the secrets of the kingdom to his disciples and to communicate truth to them about its operation in this world until his return in glory. Although there is variation among scholars about the details of interpreting Jesus' parables, the following basic principles are widely acknowledged to be crucial in understanding their purpose.[59]

---

58. Sidney Greidanus, *The Modern Preacher and the Ancient Text: Interpreting and Preaching Biblical Literature* (Grand Rapids: Eerdmans, 1988), 340–41.

59. Cf., e.g., Bailey, "Guidelines for Interpreting Jesus' Parables," 29–38; Blomberg, *Interpreting the Parables*, 29–69; Sider, *Interpreting the Parables*, 13–26, 171–246; Klyne R. Snodgrass, "Parable," *DJG*, 591–601; idem, "From Allegorizing to Allegorizing," 3–29; Robert H. Stein, *An Introduction to the Parables of Jesus* (Philadelphia: Westminster, 1981), 15–41; Wenham, *The Parables of Jesus*, 11–25, 225–38.

---

(1) We should attempt to understand the first-century historical, cultural, and religious setting of Jesus' ministry. This includes understanding the circumstances that prompted the parable and the significance of the issues addressed. This step is necessary since so many of Jesus' parables were drawn from experiences common to first-century listeners but are foreign to modern readers. For example, the social status of landowners and tenants, the Old Testament background related to the approaching kingdom of God, or the religious orientation of the Pharisees within Judaism is vital to understand clearly Jesus' message in its original setting.

(2) We should attempt to understand the literary and theological setting of these parables within Jesus' ministry, within each particular Gospel, and within the New Testament as a whole. We should search the context of Jesus' overall ministry and his teaching elsewhere for clues to the parables' interpretation, because Jesus interpreted several of the parables for his disciples (e.g., 13:18–23, 37–43, 49–50).

Moreover, each Gospel writer has a unique perspective on the parables. Matthew, for example, has a purpose for the Parabolic Discourse that is important to understand within the structure of his overall record. We should be guided by the contextual and other interpretative hints given by the evangelists, which are some of the earliest clues to the interpretation of the parables. Nor should we neglect the broader context of other New Testament teachings, because the teaching of Jesus was foundational to the thinking and teaching of the early church.

(3) We should attempt to determine the central truth that the parable intends to teach. When giving an illustration that appropriately highlights a sermon or teaching lesson, the speaker usually tries to make a primary, overarching point. However, the supporting details add subpoints that are crucial to the intended lesson. This appears to have been Jesus' method. Most interpreters now recognize that the parables accomplish Jesus' intended analogy through a central point, yet each major character or groups of characters provide additional points or subpoints.[60] We should not overinterpret by assigning unwarranted significance to minor details, but neither should we underinterpret by missing the significance of intended supporting elements. We should try to evaluate details in relation to the whole.

(4) We should attempt to isolate the point Jesus is making about the kingdom of heaven. The repeated introduction, "The kingdom of heaven is like" (e.g., 13:24, 31, 33, 44, 45), alerts us to the central place that instruction about the kingdom holds in this discourse. We will see below that this means

---

60. Cf. Snodgrass, "From Allegorizing to Allegorizing," 3–29; Blomberg, *Interpreting the Parables*, 29–69.

to understand the kingdom's transforming power, its looming judgment, its surprising appearance, its incalculable value, and the disciples' responsibility to its spread.

(5) We should attempt to determine how the central truths of the parables apply to the life of the individual unbeliever or believer. The spiritual application was always relevant to the hearer's needs; therefore, it is important to uncover the need that prompted the parables. The parables can be deeply, even frustratingly, perplexing, because the story may take an unexpected turn and cause offense to the audience when personal application is made. The parables were intended to reveal the secrets of the kingdom of heaven to Jesus' disciples (cf. 13:10–17). They provide concrete illustrations of the way we can apply the truths of the kingdom of heaven to our own discipleship to Jesus while we live in this world that is under the sway of the evil one.

(6) We should attempt to establish how the truth of the parable can be applied to the life of the church, both throughout the ages and today. Reflection about the contemporary message of the parable should be based on the historical meaning of the parables,[61] which includes recognizing that one of the secrets of the kingdom is its present but hidden working in the world (cf. 13:37–43). In these parables we are attuned to Jesus' original intent to show how the kingdom of heaven will exist throughout this age. He is not giving lessons directly on the activities of the church. The church will be a visible institution throughout this age in service of the kingdom of God, but Jesus does not equate the kingdom with the church (see comments on 3:2; 4:17; 16:18–19; 18:15–20). Nonetheless, appropriate application to the church can be derived from the parables.

With these guidelines for interpreting Matthew's parabolic discourse, we can now focus on the specific truth Jesus intended to communicate in each parable and briefly how that might be applied to our contemporary Christian discipleship. Since some of the seven primary parables about the secrets of the kingdom in this discourse overlap in the truths they communicate, we can summarize them under four primary headings: (1) the kingdom's transforming power, (2) its looming judgment, (3) its surprising appearance, and (4) its incalculable value.

**The transforming power of the kingdom of heaven—the parable of the sower and soils (13:1–9, 18–23).** The parable of the sower and soils in many ways is a parable about the parables. It illustrates how the truth that is embedded in the parables will impact the life of those who hear its message. Although the gospel of the kingdom of heaven will be preached and taught indiscriminately in this world (4:23–25; 9:35–38), there are varied

---

61. Wenham, *The Parables of Jesus*, 237–38.

responses to it. One's external response indicates the inward spiritual condition of his or her life. The life-giving force is in the seed, not in the soil, so how the soil responds to the seed indicates the impact of the life of the kingdom in a person's heart. This includes whether it is rejected outright by a hard heart, or is received in a shallow fashion but does not take full rootedness, or is choked out by competing priorities. Only the person who receives the message deep into his or her heart has allowed the life-giving gospel of the kingdom to take root and produce fruit.

Since the primary focus is not on the sower but on the soils, we can safely assume that the one sowing the message of the gospel in this world applies not only to Jesus in his historical ministry but also to the Twelve as they went out on the short mission tour (10:5–15)—and to disciples throughout this age who carry this message (10:16–42; 28:16–20). This teaches us that just as Jesus had varied responses to his message, so will we. Faithfulness in sowing the gospel message is paramount, not the numbers that respond.

Likewise, we should recognize that the disproportionate response of those who do not respond fully to the gospel in comparison with those who bear fruit is consonant with Jesus' statement that many enter the broad gate and way to destruction while only a few enter the narrow gate and way to life (7:13–14). The results are ultimately in the hands of God as well as in the choice of the individual. Our responsibility is to sow the seed, as did Jesus, to trust God, and to understand that inevitably there will be mixed responses. Nothing is comparable to the gospel message itself. It alone has potential power to produce life in dead soil. There are many stories of missionaries who labor for years in a foreign country before seeing even one conversion. Contentment comes through obedience and trusting God with the results.

There is a clear, unmistakable distinction made between those who are outright hardened against the gospel message in the first soil and those who produce fruit in the fourth soil. But there is a perplexing middle ground in those who initially receive the word but who then fall away. Some hear the word and fall away because of the trials and hardships of life (13:20–21), and others get sucked into the priorities of the world over kingdom values (13:22). This is a warning to those who respond to the kingdom to guard against and be prepared for those things that prevent them from producing fruit. Ultimately, it is the ongoing production of fruit that differentiates those who have truly responded to the kingdom from those who have not.

And it is that very fruit that gives us the hope of personal transformation. The person who receives the gospel of the kingdom into his or her heart will experience the transformation of kingdom life, the very life that Jesus described in the Sermon on the Mount (e.g., 5:3–16, 21–48). So we should not just hope for transformation but should expect it as a result of the life-giving power of the gospel of the kingdom as energized by the Spirit of God. Those who inherit the kingdom will experience transformation from former fleshly practices into personal characteristics produced by the Spirit (Gal. 5:16–23) and will experience the gifts of the Spirit in their lives (1 Cor. 12:1–31). The transformation will extend to the creation of the fruit of Spirit-produced righteousness and good works (e.g., Col. 1:10) and participation in gospel outreach produces the fruit of new converts won through the believer's testimony (e.g., Rom 1:13). Seed sown on good soil will result in maximum yield according to individual potential.

We should perhaps extend the analogy one step further to note that the responsibility for the production of fruit lies in the life-giving operation of the Spirit-empowered gospel, but that does not eliminate the disciple's own responsibility. We must be careful to supply proper nutrients and care for our well-being by continually being watered with the Word of God and enfolded in a protecting community of other believers. We likewise must be careful not to allow the weeds of this world to choke us, as the next parable points out.

**The looming judgment of the kingdom of heaven—the parables of the wheat and weeds (13:24–30, 36–43) and the dragnet (13:47–50).** Although the kingdom of heaven has been inaugurated in this world through the sowing of the gospel and many have become Jesus' disciples, the arrival of the kingdom has not vanquished the enemy or prevented the survival of evil people in this world. On a surface level, Jesus' disciples may not look different from others in this world, but there is an inherent difference as a result of the transformation that is produced by the impact of the kingdom in a person's life. The wheat and fish of the kingdom of heaven are "good" (13:38, 48) and "righteous" (13:43, 49). This is the righteousness of the kingdom that produces personal transformation (cf. 5:20).

But these parables make another important point. We will not see the uprooting or elimination of evil until the end of this age. There will be a mixed nature in the world, which will continue in a form that seems counterintuitive to contemporary notions of God's reigning kingdom. Jesus does not give a full theodicy with the parable, only a rock-solid basis for hope. Evil derives from the evil one, not from God. We should expect spiritual warfare throughout this age as we live in an environment contaminated by evil. But there looms on the horizon of history certain rescue for Jesus' disciples and certain judgment for those who are aligned with the evil one. Jesus' disciples are not called out of the world during this age, but we are promised to have Jesus' continual prayer for the Father's protecting hand upon us (cf. John 17:15–19).

While the parables speak of the coexistence of the sons of the evil one and the sons of the kingdom in this world, there is secondary application to the church. The parable of the wheat and weeds allows us to be aware of the plans of the enemy—that Satan will attempt to infiltrate the church. We must be aware of how to be on guard, which should encourage us to pray against the plans of Satan. Although Satan will operate in this world until the judgment, we can reduce his influence by not allowing sinful activities that give him a foothold in our communities (Eph. 4:27) and by dealing effectively and quickly with sin within the community (18:15–20).

Moreover, like a large dragnet, the kingdom of heaven will have all sorts respond to it in the preaching of "fishers of men" (4:19). The true nature of those who are gathered in will not always be readily apparent, as Judas Iscariot sadly exemplifies. Only at the judgment will the full implication be known.[62]

**The surprising appearance of the kingdom of heaven—the parables of the mustard seed and yeast (13:31–32, 33).** These two parables combine to emphasize one of the primary secrets of the kingdom of heaven—it has come in a surprisingly hidden manner. Jesus does not deny the greatness and glory that the kingdom will ultimately manifest, but he does emphasize that during this age it will exist in a hidden and inconspicuous form. This contrasts the partial inauguration of the kingdom with its final consummation. During this age the beginning presence of the kingdom will be inauspicious, yet it will permeate this world and operate with hidden transformation in the hearts of the sons and daughters of the kingdom.

These parables should caution us about the popularity of our faith. In centuries past these parables were understood as referring to the church as the manifestation of the kingdom. The church has experienced remarkable growth at various periods of time in the world's history, but often at the expense of contamination from the world. This should again caution us against equating the kingdom of God and the church. Only with the arrival of the Son of Man will the kingdom be established in visible power and glory.

We live at a time when the popularity of the church has waned in much of the Western world but is dynamically alive in much of the Third World. The parables of the mustard seed and yeast caution us against expecting the popularity of the kingdom of heaven during this age. It will remain inconspicuous and hidden except to eyes of faith, awaiting its final manifestation. As citizens of the kingdom we are the salt of the earth and the light of the world (5:13–16), and we seek to bring people into a loving community within the church, but our popularity is never to be the final gauge of the real influence of the kingdom.

---

62. Cf. Keener, *A Commentary on the Gospel of Matthew* (1999), 393.

The incalculable value of the kingdom of heaven—the parables of the hidden treasure (13:44) and costly pearl (13:45–46). These parables focus on the incalculable value of the kingdom of heaven. Continuing the thought of the inconspicuousness of the mustard seed and yeast (13:31–32, 33), the parable of the hidden treasure emphasizes that the kingdom has a value that far outweighs what anyone looking on an open field might have expected. The parable of the costly pearl emphasizes that the well-trained expert will discover, upon finding the reality of the kingdom, that nothing is comparable in worth. Whatever cost a person expends is nothing in comparison to the benefit of belonging to it. Salvation and the righteousness of the kingdom is a greater treasure than all that the world has to offer, and it is the source of greatest joy (13:44). When we recognize fully the value of life in the presence of the Savior now and life eternal, all of the sacrifice we make cannot compare to the joy of experiencing its present reality.

Unfortunately, it is all too easy to lose sight of this value and so lose the joy. This is the danger of those who grow up in fine Christian homes and good churches but who take this for granted. If a person has always known the message, he or she may not really grasp the value of the gospel and the reality of the presence of the kingdom of God. However, if early on in life a clear distinction is made about spiritual realities, a profound, humble gratitude for the precious gift of the gospel can be learned and an equally profound, humble compassion for those without the gift of the kingdom of God can be lived out.

This is also a danger for those of us in ministry, who are paid to study the Bible, to teach about Jesus, and to pray for our students and the people in our churches. We can become so familiar with the things of God that we lose sight of the incredible worth of what we teach. One of the greatest privileges of life is to be in our ministry situations. Talking about Jesus, praying with other believers, attempting to be a servant of Christ in our daily affairs, exegeting difficult passages of Scripture, defending the faith against enemies of the cross—all these are our regular activities.

Nevertheless, each of these activities can become drudgery when we are overworked or unappreciated, or when we receive opposition. Every day that we carry out our responsibilities, it is important to recall what a privilege it is to help others hear Jesus more clearly, walk with him more closely, and serve him more happily. We are ambassadors of the kingdom of heaven, the greatest treasure of this world, and each day we should repeatedly give thanks for the incredible value of this gift that we handle. Therein lies our true joy.

# Matthew 13:53–14:36

❧

HEN JESUS HAD finished these parables, he moved on from there. 54Coming to his hometown, he began teaching the people in their synagogue, and they were amazed. "Where did this man get this wisdom and these miraculous powers?" they asked. 55"Isn't this the carpenter's son? Isn't his mother's name Mary, and aren't his brothers James, Joseph, Simon and Judas? 56Aren't all his sisters with us? Where then did this man get all these things?" 57And they took offense at him.

But Jesus said to them, "Only in his hometown and in his own house is a prophet without honor."

58And he did not do many miracles there because of their lack of faith.

14:1At that time Herod the tetrarch heard the reports about Jesus, 2and he said to his attendants, "This is John the Baptist; he has risen from the dead! That is why miraculous powers are at work in him."

3Now Herod had arrested John and bound him and put him in prison because of Herodias, his brother Philip's wife, 4for John had been saying to him: "It is not lawful for you to have her." 5Herod wanted to kill John, but he was afraid of the people, because they considered him a prophet.

6On Herod's birthday the daughter of Herodias danced for them and pleased Herod so much 7that he promised with an oath to give her whatever she asked. 8Prompted by her mother, she said, "Give me here on a platter the head of John the Baptist." 9The king was distressed, but because of his oaths and his dinner guests, he ordered that her request be granted 10and had John beheaded in the prison. 11His head was brought in on a platter and given to the girl, who carried it to her mother. 12John's disciples came and took his body and buried it. Then they went and told Jesus.

13When Jesus heard what had happened, he withdrew by boat privately to a solitary place. Hearing of this, the crowds followed him on foot from the towns. 14When Jesus landed and saw a large crowd, he had compassion on them and healed their sick.

¹⁵As evening approached, the disciples came to him and said, "This is a remote place, and it's already getting late. Send the crowds away, so they can go to the villages and buy themselves some food."

¹⁶Jesus replied, "They do not need to go away. You give them something to eat."

¹⁷"We have here only five loaves of bread and two fish," they answered.

¹⁸"Bring them here to me," he said. ¹⁹And he directed the people to sit down on the grass. Taking the five loaves and the two fish and looking up to heaven, he gave thanks and broke the loaves. Then he gave them to the disciples, and the disciples gave them to the people. ²⁰They all ate and were satisfied, and the disciples picked up twelve basketfuls of broken pieces that were left over. ²¹The number of those who ate was about five thousand men, besides women and children.

²²Immediately Jesus made the disciples get into the boat and go on ahead of him to the other side, while he dismissed the crowd. ²³After he had dismissed them, he went up on a mountainside by himself to pray. When evening came, he was there alone, ²⁴but the boat was already a considerable distance from land, buffeted by the waves because the wind was against it.

²⁵During the fourth watch of the night Jesus went out to them, walking on the lake. ²⁶When the disciples saw him walking on the lake, they were terrified. "It's a ghost," they said, and cried out in fear.

²⁷But Jesus immediately said to them: "Take courage! It is I. Don't be afraid."

²⁸"Lord, if it's you," Peter replied, "tell me to come to you on the water."

²⁹"Come," he said.

Then Peter got down out of the boat, walked on the water and came toward Jesus. ³⁰But when he saw the wind, he was afraid and, beginning to sink, cried out, "Lord, save me!"

³¹Immediately Jesus reached out his hand and caught him. "You of little faith," he said, "why did you doubt?"

³²And when they climbed into the boat, the wind died down. ³³Then those who were in the boat worshiped him, saying, "Truly you are the Son of God."

³⁴When they had crossed over, they landed at Gennesaret. ³⁵And when the men of that place recognized Jesus, they sent word to all the surrounding country. People brought all their sick to him ³⁶and begged him to let the sick just touch the edge of his cloak, and all who touched him were healed.

TO SIGNAL THE conclusion of the Parabolic Discourse and the transition to the continuing narrative description of Jesus' ministry, Matthew uses the formulaic expression that concludes each of the discourses in his Gospel ("when Jesus had finished," 13:53; cf. 7:28; 11:1; 19:1; 26:1). From the conclusion of the Parabolic Discourse in chapter 13 until the Community Discourse in chapter 18, Matthew narrates a major new emphasis in Jesus' earthly ministry. Jesus gives increasing clarification to his disciples of his identity as Messiah, culminating in Peter's confession (16:15–19) and the Transfiguration (17:1–8). But he also begins to prophesy of his impending suffering sacrifice (16:21–28; 17:22–23; 20:17–19).

The amazing popularity of Jesus' Galilean ministry continues with the feeding of the five thousand (14:13–21), but the mood turns somber as Jesus increasingly sets his face toward Jerusalem and the final fateful encounter on the cross. This somberness begins with two incidents of prophets of God who are given no honor by their people—Jesus at his own hometown of Nazareth (13:54–58) and John the Baptist at the fortress of Machaerus (14:1–12). Yet in a dramatically different manner, Jesus is given the honor that is his due as his disciples fall down to worship him as the Son of God after he stills the storm (14:33).

### Jesus Rejected at Nazareth (13:54–58)

JESUS RETURNS TO his hometown, Nazareth, the village of his family and the place where he spent his childhood (see comments on 2:23). Matthew does not give the reason for this return except to say that "he began teaching the people in their synagogue." Luke records a preaching scene in the synagogue at Nazareth at the beginning of Jesus' public ministry, at which time the townspeople were incensed at his inclusion of the Gentiles in God's salvation-historical outreach program and attempted to kill him (Luke 4:16–30).

Many scholars see Matthew's account as a thematic abridgment of the one recorded in Luke.¹ It is possible, however, that this is a later return to Galilee

---

1. E.g., Blomberg, *Matthew*, 227; Davies and Allison, *Matthew*, 2:452–54; France, *Matthew*, 232.

for a second visit (see also Mark 6:1–6). Note the reference to "wisdom and
... miraculous powers," which were not a significant part of Jesus' ministry
until after the visit to Nazareth as recorded in Luke. If so, the antagonism of
the earlier visit is now somewhat mitigated because of Jesus' increasing popularity throughout Galilee as a result of his teaching, preaching, and his miracle-working ministry. The allusion to "leaving Nazareth" in Matthew 4:13
is more likely parallel to events in Luke.[2]

The return to Nazareth is somewhat surprising because, prior to the
beginning of the Parabolic Discourse, Jesus' mother and brothers attempted
to make contact with him, and Jesus seemingly rebuffs their visit (see comments on 12:46–50). Perhaps as he returns to Nazareth, he is acceding to the
request from his mother and brothers to return home. A similar pattern may
be discerned in Jesus' reaction to Mary's comment, made at a wedding in
Cana, about no wine, where he appears to rebuff Mary but eventually assents
to her request (cf. John 2:1–10). Jesus will not allow himself to be deterred
from his ministry, but he refrains from rejecting his family outright.

The four brothers (James, Joseph, Simon, and Judas) apparently did not
accept Jesus' authority before the resurrection (cf. Mark 3:21; John 7:5). The
risen Jesus appeared to James (1 Cor. 15:7), and three years after Paul's conversion James was known as one of the pillars of the Jerusalem church (Gal.
1:19; 2:9). After King Herod Agrippa I of Judea beheaded the apostle James
son of Zebedee, and Peter escaped from Jerusalem (Acts 12:1–17; c. A.D.
44), James assumed an even more significant leadership role. He was the
chief spokesperson for the Jerusalem church at the pivotal Jerusalem Council regarding Paul's mission to the Gentiles (Acts 15:13) and during Paul's
final visit to Jerusalem (Acts 21:18). Later tradition notes his moral and godly
behavior. James is most likely the author of the book that bears his name.

Another brother of Jesus, Judas (= Jude), is the traditional author of the
letter of Jude. Nothing of any substantial historical value is known of Jesus'
other brothers or his sisters. On the theories as to how these "brothers" and
"sisters" are related to Jesus, see comments on 12:46–50.

As Jesus begins to teach in the synagogue, the people of his hometown
are amazed and ask, "Where did this man get this wisdom and these miraculous powers?" At the beginning of his ministry (Luke 4:16–30), the townspeople were incensed by his inclusion of Gentiles in God's plan of salvation,
but now they are incredulous at the reports of the wisdom and miracles that
he has demonstrated throughout Galilee. Like the Pharisees in Capernaum
(12:24), they question the source of his mighty powers. Is he operating from
God's authority or from some other source?

---

2. E.g., Carson, "Matthew," 335; Morris, *Matthew*, 364.

They already have their answers in mind as they pose a number of questions. Since they know his human roots, with the town carpenter as father, the well-known Mary as mother, and his equally well-known brothers and sisters, he cannot obviously be anything special. He is a hometown son who is trying to be more than he possibly can claim. Thus, the townspeople conclude that since Jesus had no other training than that of a carpenter,[3] he cannot be a proper source of wisdom, nor can he lay claim to supernatural powers.

So instead of allowing Jesus' wisdom and miracles to testify to his divine origin, the townspeople "took offense at him" (*skandalizo;* 13:57), an expression in Matthew that indicates an obstacle to faith (5:29; 11:6). Like the crowd in Capernaum who has rejected his true identity and messianic mission (13:10–17), the people of his own hometown cannot rise above their provincialism. Jesus responds: "Only in his hometown and in his own house is a prophet without honor." In what was likely a proverbial saying, Jesus uses the title of prophet to refer to himself.

Jesus, in other words, aligns himself with the Old Testament prophets who revealed God's will for the nation, which was not always palatable.[4] Those messengers had consistently been rejected by the people of Israel. Jesus is likewise rejected. No prophet had spoken in Israel for hundreds of years, but even now in Jesus' hometown, the people harden themselves against his ministry of declaring God's truth. Moreover, the puppet-leadership of Israel, represented by Herod Antipas, will put John the Baptist, the other prophet, to death. It is a sad day in Israel.

Because of the hardness of their hearts, they are not open to Jesus' ministry. "And he did not do many miracles there because of their lack of faith." While Jesus could apparently heal people elsewhere whose faith was not a significant factor in the miracle,[5] hard-heartedness and rejection prevent the ministry of the Spirit's healing, even as it prevents the forgiveness of sin (12:31–32).

## John the Baptist Beheaded by Herod Antipas (14:1–12)

MATTHEW NOW GIVES an account of Herod Antipas's execution of John the Baptist that fits the developing story line. Not only is Jesus Messiah a prophet without honor in his hometown (13:57), but the prophet John the Baptist is dishonored with execution. John had been imprisoned about a year and a half prior to this, and he had heard reports about Jesus' activities. Jesus replied to

---

3. Mark 6:3 calls Jesus a carpenter.
4. Morris, *Matthew*, 366.
5. E.g., the Gadarene demoniacs (8:28–34) and the lame man in John 5.

John through his disciples with a full accounting of what he had accomplished (cf. comments on 11:2–6). John may have been executed some months prior to the events of chapter 14. Matthew's narrative about the execution is likely a historical flashback.

Nearing the end of his nearly two-year ministry in Galilee, Jesus' teaching and miracle-working powers have drawn the notice of the highest-level ruler in the region, Herod Antipas (14:1). After his father, Herod the Great (see comments on ch. 2), died, the kingdom was divided among three of his sons. Herod Antipas became tetrarch of Galilee and Perea for many years (4 B.C.–A.D. 39). His chief infamy in the New Testament comes from his execution of John the Baptist and from his interview of Jesus prior to his crucifixion (cf. Luke 23:6–12).

Herod Antipas's capital city, Tiberias, was only eight and a half miles down the coast of the Sea of Galilee from Capernaum, the base of Jesus' ministry. Somehow Jesus' widespread popularity among the masses of people throughout Israel, Perea, and the Decapolis reaches the ears of Herod. Herod's reaction reveals a curious blend of emotion, theology, and superstition: "This is John the Baptist; he has risen from the dead! That is why miraculous powers are at work in him." Herod's guilty fear for having executed John combines with a confused notion of resurrection, probably based in part on Pharisaic beliefs along with semi-pagan superstitious ideas of returning spirits.

Herod Antipas had married the daughter of King Aretas IV of Nabatea, probably a political marriage arranged by Emperor Augustus to keep peace in the region. The marriage lasted over fifteen years, until Antipas fell in love with Herodias,[6] the wife of his half-brother Herod Philip I. This man was a private citizen who lived in Rome with his wife. On a trip to Rome, Antipas stayed at their house and fell in love with Herodias. They determined to marry, but Herodias demanded that Antipas first divorce his wife.[7] Some years later (A.D. 36), King Aretas IV attacked and conquered Antipas's military forces, at least in part to seek revenge for repudiating his daughter.[8]

When Antipas married Herodias, the highly popular John the Baptist publicly condemned him for marrying his half-brother's wife, who was also his half-niece. John stated categorically, "It is not lawful for you to have her" (14:4). Such a marriage would have been considered an incestuous affront to

---

6. Herodias was the daughter of Aristobulus (son of Herod the Great) and Bernice (daughter of Herod the Great's sister, Salome), which made her the half-niece of her husband Herod Philip I and Herod Antipas.

7. Josephus, *Ant.* 18.5.1 §§109–15.

8. For a brief overview, see Harold W. Hoehner, "Herodian Dynasty, *DJG*, 322–25. For the most extensive treatment of the era, see idem, *Herod Antipas: A Contemporary of Jesus* (Grand Rapids: Zondervan, 1980).

God's law (Lev. 18:16; 20:21). Both Josephus and the Gospel writers agree that Herod Antipas had John arrested and executed because of his influence with the people. Beyond that, they give helpful different perspectives on the underlying motivation for arresting John. According to Matthew, "Herod wanted to kill John, but he was afraid of the people, because they considered him a prophet." Josephus surmises that God judged Herod for his treatment of John.[9]

On Herod's birthday a great celebration was held in his honor at the palace at Machaerus, where John was imprisoned.[10] On this fateful occasion, Herodias's daughter (named Salome, according to Josephus) performs a dance for Antipas. The girl is probably only twelve to fourteen years old, but in this degraded, deceptive setting she dances what is likely a highly sensual dance, for she "pleased Herod so much that he promised with an oath to give her whatever she asked."

Herodias steps in immediately to orchestrate the elimination of another threat to her husband's reign. She prompts Salome to ask for the head of John the Baptist on a platter, because she wants to eliminate his accusing voice. This was a relatively common practice among ruthless leaders. Herod the Great, for example, had his own wives and children put to death out of his paranoid fear of anyone usurping his throne. Herod Antipas knows that John is a prophet, popular with the people, and does not want to execute him. But he does not want to lose face in front of his guests, so "he ordered that her request be granted and had John beheaded in the prison. His head was brought in on a platter and given to the girl, who carried it to her mother."

John's disciples have remained loyal to the prophet throughout his imprisonment, and now they perform the duties of loyal followers, since John's family is likely deceased by this time. They take his body and give it a proper burial. Then they come to Jesus in Galilee again, bearing the tragic news of John's death (14:12). We hear of other disciples of John throughout the next few decades, although they were increasingly separated from his true message (Acts 19:1–7). The natural transition should have been for them to follow Jesus.[11]

## Compassionate Healer and Supplier (14:13–21)

JESUS HAS BY this time returned to Capernaum from Nazareth. The rejection of Jesus by his hometown people (13:53–58) and the execution of John the

---

9. See "John the Baptist's Execution by Herod Antipas as Recorded by Josephus," in Wilkins, "Matthew," 90.

10. On John's imprisonment at Machaerus, see Josephus, *Ant.* 18.112, 119.

11. Wilkins, *Following the Master,* 86–88, 253–56.

Baptist by Herod Antipas (14:1–12) signal an escalation of the opposition to the establishment of God's kingdom. But in the teeth of this gathering storm, Jesus resolutely presses on with his own agenda.

**Beginning withdrawal from Galilee (14:13–14).** Matthew's narrative comment strikes a melancholy note: "When Jesus heard what had happened, he withdrew by boat privately to a solitary place." The implication may be that Jesus hears about the death of John and withdraws for a period of personal contemplation and mourning.[12] But since John was most likely executed some months prior to this, others suggest that Jesus' withdrawal is connected to Herod Antipas's reaction to Jesus' ministry (14:1–2).[13]

But perhaps Matthew intends to link these two factors. The beginning of Jesus' ministry was prompted by a withdrawal to Galilee when he heard that John had been imprisoned by Herod Antipas (4:12). That was not a fearful flight from Herod but an intentional initiation of his ministry after seeing the momentous turn of events. Likewise, here Jesus is not fleeing from Herod, but after seeing the rising opposition initiated by John's death and Antipas's paranoiac response, Jesus purposefully commences a new phase of his ministry. Herod's cowardly execution of John symbolically demonstrates that Galilee will not repent, so Jesus begins his withdrawal. Galilee has been the primary place of his ministry (see comments on 4:12–17). However, the opposition from Herod Antipas, the misguided enthusiasm of the crowd, the gathering hostility of the religious leaders, the increasing focus on training the Twelve for their apostolic role in the age to come, and Jesus' resolute will to face the cross in Jerusalem require that he withdraw from Galilee.

Twice in this narrative Jesus goes off alone (14:13, 23), which he often did at a momentous time in his ministry. He used these occasions to prepare himself for upcoming, significant events, where he needed to have all of the spiritual strength possible that accrued from time spent alone with his heavenly Father (cf. Matt. 4:1–2; 26:36–46; Mark 1:35; Luke 5:16; 6:12). A key to his ministry was the way he listened to and then obeyed his Father's will, which often took place through the discipline of solitude. With his impending withdrawal from Galilee in order to make the final destined trip to Jerusalem and the cross, Jesus seeks the fellowship, solace, and guidance of his Father.

Thus, Jesus crosses the sea of Galilee to go "to a solitary place." However, his popularity with the people has not diminished. Word spreads that he is on the move, and many from the surrounding towns follow him on foot along the shore. When he lands, a large crowd is there to meet him. Even though the crowd is a fickle lot (cf. 13:10–17), Jesus has compassion for

---

12. France, *Matthew*, 236; Hagner, *Matthew*, 2:417.
13. Carson, "Matthew," 340–41; Morris, *Matthew*, 417.

them. They have carried the sick to him from out of the towns, so Jesus heals them (14:13–14).

**Feeding the five thousand (14:15–21).** This isolated place with the crowd gathered becomes the scene of the climactic feeding of the five thousand, the only miracle from Jesus' earthly ministry recorded in all four Gospels.[14] Matthew's record is the barest account. The traditional site of the miracle is west of Capernaum, just a mile or so beyond the "Cove of Parables" (cf. 13:1–3).[15]

After the day of travel and healing, Jesus' disciples approach him with a logistical problem. The remote region offers no food for the people to eat, so they suggest that Jesus dismiss the crowd "so they can go to the villages and buy themselves some food." Such a large crowd might have presented problems to any surrounding villages, since abundant staples were not usually on hand.[16] Thus, Jesus turns the problem back to the disciples and tells them to give the crowd something to eat, showing them the importance of compassion for the needs of people.

The crowd has either already eaten their food for the day, or else in their haste to follow Jesus and bring their sick to him they have not brought along anything to eat. Apparently the disciples have no more food of their own either, but they scrounge around and come up with five loaves of bread and two fish (14:17). Bread and dried or pickled fish were staple food and suitable for taking on a short journey into the hills. The season is spring, when the grass is lush and the streams are running full, so Jesus directs the crowd to sit down on the grass. He takes the loaves (about bun-size) and the fish and looks up to heaven, a typical posture for prayer (cf. John 17:1). He gives thanks or offers a blessing and breaks the loaves (14:19). Jesus does not bless the bread but blesses God for what will be the miraculous supply of bread.

Now the disciples are able to do what Jesus asked them to do—give the crowds something to eat. He gives the disciples the miraculously multiplied bread, and they in turn pass among the crowd and give the pieces to the people. Matthew narrates almost casually that the crowd eats until they are satisfied, and "the disciples picked up twelve basketfuls of broken pieces that were left over." The number twelve is obviously significant for both the twelve tribes of Israel and the twelve disciples/apostles, but the significance here is uncertain. It is perhaps another indication of the fulfillment of Jesus'

---

14. See Mark 6:32–44; Luke 9:10–17; John 6:1–15.

15. There are harmonization difficulties in connection with Mark's reference to Bethsaida as the location the disciples head toward after this miracle (Mark 6:45) and Luke's reference to the feeding miracles as occurring at Bethsaida (Luke 9:10); it is beyond the scope of this commentary to solve them.

16. Keener, *A Commentary on the Gospel of Matthew* (1999), 403–4.

messianic ministry (cf. 10:1–6; 19:28). The crowds in this region will not experience this miraculous provision again, so gathering up the leftovers demonstrates that they should not neglect what God has already provided.

Matthew is the only evangelist to note that the number five thousand associated with the feeding counts only men, not women and children. The total number may have stretched to ten thousand or more, far larger than the populations of most villages surrounding the Sea of Galilee. Many Jews expected the Messiah to appear in the spring at the Passover season, when he would repeat the miracle of feeding Israel by manna as had occurred through Moses.[17] In connection with this, perhaps, John points out that the crowd now surges forward to make Jesus their king, but he withdraws again from them (John 6:14–15). The crowd apparently thinks that Jesus will now restore the throne to Israel. They cannot get their eyes off their physical needs long enough to hear Jesus' message. So Jesus leaves to focus on those who will accept his offer of salvation.

But the miracle also has a lesson for the disciples. They see the size of the need and the smallness of the human resources available. They must learn to see as Jesus sees, who "recognizes the size of the need and the greatness of God's resources available."[18]

### The Son of God Is Worshiped (14:22–36)

AFTER THE DRAMATIC feeding of the five thousand, which authenticates Jesus' authoritative power to heal and supply the needs of the crowds, Jesus reveals himself as the true Son of God, who has authoritative power over the elements of nature and so deserves the worship that is due to God alone.

**Jesus walks on the water (14:22–27).** This has been a strenuous day for Jesus and his disciples. He intended to go away to a solitary place to reflect on the potential threat from Herod Antipas and the death of John the Baptist, but he ends up preaching to and healing a huge crowd of people. Jesus and the disciples did not prepare to spend the night away from home, and there certainly is no place for such a large crowd to sleep, so he charges the disciples to go in the boat to the other side to find shelter while he directs the crowd to return to their homes.

After the crowd and disciples leave, Jesus is finally alone. On a mountainside he spends concentrated time in prayer with his heavenly Father throughout the evening and into the night (see comments on 14:13–14). At this significant turning point in his ministry, Jesus is readying himself for the journey into Gentile regions, with the cross in Jerusalem looming on ahead.

---

17. Hagner, *Matthew*, 2:418.
18. Keener, *A Commentary on the Gospel of Matthew* (1999), 405.

While Jesus is alone on the mountain in prayer, the disciples are having a difficult time trying to cross the Sea of Galilee. They were likely in one of the fishing boats outfitted to handle the sudden storms that blow up on the lake (see comments on 8:23–27). The disciples must have been both sailing and rowing the boat, because they are well out onto the water.

Matthew narrates portentously that they are "buffeted by the waves because the wind was against it." The winds against the boat may indicate that they were moving from west to east, because the most severe storms came down the mountains to the east. "A considerable distance" out on the lake in Greek is literally "many stadia" (a *stadion* is about six hundred feet), which probably means they are two to three miles out on the lake. They battle the storm for over nine hours—from before sundown until the "fourth watch" (3:00 to 6:00 A.M.). In the previous incident of stilling the storm, Jesus was with the disciples, although he was sleeping in the stern of the boat (8:24). Now he comes walking to them on the sea.

The disciples were afraid of dying in the earlier storm (8:25), but this time they are afraid when they see Jesus walking on the water, thinking that he is a "ghost" (*phantasma;* 14:26). In Greek literature this word is used for dream appearances or spirit appearances, but in the Old Testament it means a "deception" (Isa. 28:7; Job 20:8 LXX; cf. Wisd. Sol. 17:14).[19] The disciples may be thinking that some evil spirit is attempting to deceive them. Jesus gives them immediate assurance that he is no deceptive evil spirit but truly their Master: "Take courage! It is I. Don't be afraid." The expression "It is I" (lit., "I am") may allude to the voice of Yahweh from the burning bush (Ex. 3:14) and the voice of assurance to Israel of the Lord's identity and presence as their Savior (Isa. 43:10–13). Throughout this section Jesus continues to reveal his true nature to the disciples, and this powerful statement accords with his miraculous calming of the storm.

Jesus' walk on the water to the disciples in the storm is intended to elicit faith in his true identity and mission as the Son of God. The time has come for the disciples to step forward to claim their responsibility as leaders in the Jesus movement, which Peter will falteringly attempt to exemplify.

**Peter walks on the water (14:28–32).** Amazingly, as Peter hears the voice of Jesus, he shouts back above the storm, "Lord, if it's you, tell me to come to you on the water." The expression "Lord" (*kyrios*) was used elsewhere to address Jesus with a title of respect (e.g., 8:21) or as a false declaration of faith (e.g., 7:21), but here it means far more. Jesus is walking on the water in the middle of a furious storm, something that elevates him above any

---

19. R. Bultmann/D. Lührmann, "φάντασμα," *TDNT*, 9:6. The term occurs only here and in Mark 6:49.

other figure that Peter has ever known. But likewise, if Jesus truly is the Lord and not an apparition, there is no need for fear. Peter's focused faith in Jesus' true identity enables him to overcome his fear, to call out to him, and to recognize that Jesus can enable Peter also to come to him on the water. Peter doesn't say "walk" on the water but "come," a fitting qualification to the request, since as far as he knew, this was not going to be a simple stroll on the lake.

In reply to Peter's request, Jesus authoritatively says, "Come." Peter obeys by getting down out of the boat and miraculously walks on the water toward Jesus. We are not told how far or for how long he walks on the sea, but suddenly reality hits. He sees the wind, meaning the effects of the wind, produce billowing whitecaps, surging seas, and wind-blown spray, and he realizes where he is and becomes afraid. Experienced fisherman that he is, he knows the danger. Peter demonstrates tremendous courage in this incident, but at the same time his courage to go to Jesus on the water becomes the occasion for failure. He loses his focused faith in Jesus' divine identity and begins to sink beneath the seas. But then most importantly, Peter cries out, "Lord, save me!" The same Lord who could walk on the water himself and then enable Peter to walk on the water is more than able to save him from sinking.

Jesus immediately catches Peter by the hand to rescue him and says, "You of little faith, why did you doubt?" "Little faith" (*oligopistos*) is not the same as the "no faith" of the hardhearted townspeople of Nazareth (13:58). A person with no faith would not recognize Jesus and call out to him. Peter has faith; it is just not functioning properly. It is "ineffective faith" (cf. 17:20). Peter's faith enables him to recognize Jesus' true identity and to request to come out to him on the water, but it is like a burst of emotional energy. It is effective enough to motivate him but not effective enough to sustain him. The key element is keeping his eyes firmly focused on Jesus instead of the danger of the wind-swept sea. Jesus thus directs Peter to understand more clearly who he is and then act upon it. Faith is not like a commodity of which Peter needs more. Rather, faith is consistent trust in Jesus to accomplish what Peter is called to do.

The emphasis in this story is on the grace and power of Jesus. Once Jesus and Peter climb into the boat with the other disciples, the wind dies down. This is the second time the disciples have witnessed the miraculous calming of the sea during a storm (see 8:26). Matthew does not record Jesus' words or actions here but only notes that the winds abate. The wind that has so frightened Peter (14:30) is now under Jesus' control.

**Jesus is worshiped as the Son of God (14:33).** All of these compelling events—Jesus' walking on the water in the storm, enabling Peter to walk to him, saving Peter, and now calming the winds—overwhelm the disciples, and

Matthew narrates unequivocally: "Then those who were in the boat worshiped him, saying, 'Truly you are the Son of God.'" Worship is an action in Scripture reserved for God. One may prostrate oneself before other esteemed personages as a symbol of respect, such as David before King Saul (1 Sam. 24:8) or Abigail before David (25:23). But in the context of such works of divine significance, the disciples are gripped with the reality that Jesus is much, much more; he is the Son of God, and so they worship him.

This is the first time that the disciples use the title "Son of God" to address Jesus. How much they understand is uncertain (cf. Mark 6:51–52), because only at the resurrection do they fully grasp the radical truth of Jesus' divine identity. But their understanding is increasing, because they worship him— an act of reverence reserved for God alone. Recognizing Jesus as God's Son will be part of the continuing revelation that is expressed later in Peter's climactic confession: "You are the Christ, the Son of the living God" (16:16). They are understanding more clearly that Jesus is uniquely related to God the Father. Connected with the confession, their worship of Jesus is similar to the spontaneous reaction of people in the Old Testament to divine disclosures (e.g., Gen. 24:26–27a; Ex. 34:8). Baffled as they must be as to who Jesus really is, they give homage to him in a way that is only rightly accorded to God.[20]

**The Son of God heals at Gennesaret (14:34–36).** After the storm, Jesus and the disciples land at Gennesaret. This place is probably a plain extending about three and a half miles by one and a half miles along the northwest shore of the Sea of Galilee. This plain is the only easily tillable land bordering the Sea of Galilee and was known for its fertile soil that allowed the growth of walnuts, palm trees, figs, and olives. It was heavily populated during Jesus' day and lay close to the urban centers of Tiberias, Herod Antipas's elaborate and bustling capital city, and Magdala, the hometown of Mary Magdalene.[21]

The region of Gennesaret did not figure prominently in Jesus' ministry as recorded in the Gospels. We have no record of any prior ministry here, but Jesus' reputation must have been well known. When the people recognize who he is, they spread the word throughout the surrounding country, and the response to him is remarkable. They bring their sick to him, believing that if they only touch the edge of his cloak, they will be healed. Behind the expression "edge of his cloak" is the term *kraspedon* (see comments on 9:20). Touching the fringe or tassels does not imply that the people of Gennesaret have a superstitious belief in the healing power of Jesus' garment; rather,

---

20. Peterson, *Engaging with God*, 85–86.
21. Douglas R. Edwards, "Gennesaret," *ABD*, 2:963.

they understand that his power is so great that only this derivative contact with him is necessary to bring healing. As on the occasion of the woman with the hemorrhage (9:20–22), "all who touched him were healed." This is a remarkable display of faith, in stark contrast to the Pharisees and teachers of the law in the next few incidents, whose legalistic religiosity soon blinds them to their need of Jesus' cleansing (15:1–20).

MATTHEW'S TRANSITIONAL SCENE from the Parabolic Discourse finds Jesus back in his hometown of Nazareth. He explained in the discourse that his parables will test the hearts of those who hear his message, hardening those who reject him but giving understanding of the operation of the kingdom of heaven to those who are receptive to him. These dual themes of rejection and reception continue to mark Matthew's narrative throughout the rest of his Gospel.

**Rejection.** The majority of Israel, including the crowds and the religious leaders, will ultimately reject Jesus as their Messiah. Even now they are turning away from him. That tragic scene will be played out, but it is critical to note that Jesus continues to attempt to minister to those rejecting him. As Matthew emphasized in his record of Jesus' explanation for speaking to the crowd in parables, the responsibility for a hard heart lies with each individual (13:10–17). But in spite of their hardhearted rejection of him, Jesus persistently presents an invitation to the kingdom of heaven and brings his compassionate care to bear on their needs.

Matthew emphasizes this theme of rejection by two scenes where God's prophets are rejected by those who have had the greatest privilege. (1) Jesus is the ultimate prophet, who is God's message incarnate. When he returns to Nazareth to preach in the synagogue, he and his message are rejected by his hometown people, who cannot rise above their hardhearted provincialism. They cannot believe that God has brought the Messiah through a humble local family. Since Mary and Joseph and his brothers and sisters aren't anything special, then neither can Jesus be anything but an ordinary man. They have no explanation for why he speaks with such wisdom and performs such profound miracles, but their hard hearts reject him and his miraculous work in their own lives. They have the greatest privilege of human history to be in the hometown of the Messiah, but that privilege is their fateful undoing. The old expression is true—*familiarity breeds contempt.*

(2) Matthew also records the rejection of the prophet John the Baptist. But the one who rejects him is Herod Antipas. Herod had the privilege of being in a political leadership position in Galilee, with his capital city just over

eight miles down the coast of the Sea of Galilee. Recognizing that privilege should have impelled him to listen carefully to the prophetic voice of John and to try to rule with sensitivity to the ethical and moral standards of Israel. But he is driven by his own passions and manipulated by his opportunistically ruthless wife. So he capitulates even though he knows he is wrong, rejects the message of John, and orders him to be executed.

Rejection of God's gospel message through his prophets has not ceased. Much of the secularist Western world is also familiar with Jesus. They pride themselves on being ultramodern or postmodern and cannot conceive how such an ancient message is relevant to our world. Jesus is like a comfortable old shoe that they can sing about at Christmas, but he isn't serviceable for everyday life. Thus, they reject him as being of any value for understanding the reality of life in the twenty-first century. Something new is needed to explain our world, such as more pluralistic doctrines that include many ways to God or an explanation for life origins and meaning that rejects the existence of God.

Then there are those whose familiarity with Jesus comes from their own personal church and family background. Somewhere in the daily and weekly exposure to Jesus they have lost the perspective of Jesus as the God of their lives. They continue to call themselves Christians since they aren't Buddhists or atheists, but they do not have a worldview that places Jesus as the central priority and joy of their lives. He is not an urgent and absolute guideline to their everyday activities, nor is he a present companion in their thoughts and values. Thus, they increasingly reject Jesus and his message.

Jesus is also rejected by those who find that the message of the kingdom places too overtly stringent ethical and moral demands on their lives. Jesus and John preached a message of righteousness about an inner transformation that impacts external behavior. That message is just as offensive today to those who are driven by their passions, who manipulate the passions of others, or who are intent on demanding their "rights." Many prefer a tolerant message that is acceptant of deviant lifestyles, and so they reject Jesus' kingdom standards.

But Jesus' compassionate mercy continues to be extended to those who are not yet committed to him. He tries to heal the people in Nazareth even after they have rejected him, although their hard-heartedness prevents its effectiveness (13:58). Later the crowd of five thousand exhibits characteristics of increasingly rejecting his message, yet Jesus continues to heal them and care for their physical needs (14:13–21).

This mercy of his extends to our own day and is most evident in our own actions toward those who have rejected him and his message through us. We are to be wise and not cast the pearl of the gospel message to those who would harm us or defame the kingdom (7:6). But we cannot always be certain of who have rejected the gospel and who are still open. So our challenge is to seek to follow Jesus' example of wisdom in recognizing hard hearts (12:30–32), yet compassion in offering a continuing open call to the kingdom of God.

**Reception.** To those who are courageously receptive to his gospel of the kingdom and have become his disciples, Jesus will continue to carry out his program of transformation. The power of the kingdom changes everyday men and women into the likeness of their Master, Jesus. Matthew was the recipient of that transforming power, and he gives profound insights into that process. Up to this point none of the disciples has figured prominently as an individual actor on Matthew's narrative stage. We do know a little about two pairs of brothers—Peter and Andrew, James and John (4:18–22)—and Matthew himself (9:9), all of whom have responded to Jesus. Beyond that the disciples have functioned as a relatively nameless, faceless group.[22] But at this juncture, Peter begins to play an increasingly important role. In the next five chapters, Matthew narrates five incidents in which Peter figures prominently.[23]

His focus here is twofold. (1) He focuses on Peter's personal life and characteristics as an example of the way in which Jesus transforms his disciples. Peter becomes an example for all disciples of the developmental process of discipleship to Jesus.

(2) Matthew focuses on Peter's leadership role and the way Jesus develops him into the kind of leader who will be instrumental in the coming church. Peter becomes an example to others of the developmental process of leadership under Jesus. Significantly, in the listing of the Twelve in the mission discourse Peter is designated "first," an indication of his role as a leader and spokesman for the disciples (see comments on 10:2). Later Jesus will prophecy of Peter's pivotal role in the church to come (16:17–19), which will offer an example for leaders throughout the ages (cf. 18:18; John 20:23; 21:15–19).

Through these two foci, Matthew emphasizes Peter's increasing importance, but he also shows how Peter is both an imperfect disciple and leader in process of development. The difference between growth and failure rests on whether Peter continues to be receptive to God's revelation and will. When he remains open to the things of God, he grows both in his personal discipleship and in his leadership responsibility. When he does not remain receptive to the things of God, he fails in both. These stories function as warnings for disciples and leaders within the church throughout the ages. Like Peter, the difference is the kind of faith we display in Jesus.

---

22. Cf. Wilkins, *Discipleship in the Ancient World*, 163–72.
23. See 14:28–31; 15:15; 16:17–19; 17:24–27; 18:21.

Myron Augsburger sets the stage for understanding the events of this section with the following insights:

> The work of Christ is limited by our unbelief. There is doubtless much that God would prefer to do for us and for society, but He limits His action to function where and when its results are recognized to be of God and not by our own achievements. To say that God moves where it brings glory to Him is to recognize the integrity of His grace.[24]

The hardhearted rejection of Jesus by the people of Nazareth and the villainous murder of John the Baptist by Herod Antipas demonstrate the epitome of unbelief that prevents God's working in their lives. The continuing curiosity and desperate need of the crowd impels them to follow Jesus, seeking his healing touch and experiencing his gift of miraculous provision, but they have not yet responded to his grace and mercy with the kind of effective faith in Jesus that will lead them to become disciples. Jesus' disciples' faith, however, is on the move. They increasingly recognize his divine identity and power, when the feeding of the five thousand teaches them that Jesus is adequate to meet any need, no matter how impossible the circumstances. A recognition of his divine identity impels one of them to walk in faith toward Jesus on a stormy sea and to call out for help when his faith fails. Their experience of his miraculous power to calm those seas drives them to their knees to worship him as the Son of God. Such rejection and reception provide warnings and encouragement for us today.

THE WIDE RANGE of reactions to Jesus' gospel of the kingdom that are found in this narrative hinge on one common element: an exercise of faith in Jesus' identity and message. The people of Nazareth reject a hometown boy who simply cannot be who he says he is, while John the Baptist has courageously held to the message that he announced of Jesus' arrival, even though he experienced personal doubt and persecution to the point of death. In the feeding of the five thousand and the mind-boggling experience of Jesus' walking on the water, the disciples' faith is stretched to see in Jesus something no one has before understood to be possible—divine nature in human form. The faith of people today ranges from the same extremes, with similar results. These narratives offer helpful growth in our own faith in Jesus' identity and message.

---

24. Myron S. Augsburger, *Matthew* (The Communicator's Commentary; Waco, Tex.: Word, 1982), 182.

**Offensiveness of the message and messenger.** Earlier we noted Jesus' and our response to opposition (chs. 10–12). Opposition may come from family (10:21, 34–39) or foe (10:24–25), religious leaders (10:17) or secular leaders (10:18). But all opposition is not simply a rejection of the message that we bear; it may be a rejection of us personally. Both Jesus and John the Baptist draw to our attention the fact that in addition to the offensiveness of their message, they are personally offensive to those who reject them.

*Too familiar with Jesus' background.* Jesus is offensive because his background is not much different from that of his own hometown, Nazareth. The people there have known Jesus and his family well, and since he did not display distinguishing characteristcs or miraculous powers as a boy or teenager, they continue to confine him to that box. They cannot see beyond their provincialism to the person that he has become.[25]

People don't like to forget others' pasts. If a person is not particularly striking or gifted at one point in life, then family, friends, and neighbors often won't let them grow into something more significant. It's usually an ego issue. If Jeff can remember when Mitchell was just the boy down the block, then all the hype about Mitchell's accomplishments must be an obvious fraud or delusion. Otherwise Jeff begins to doubt his own accomplishments. Or else he tries to ride the coattails of Mitchell and to pride himself for being the real contributing factor for any good that Mitchell has accomplished. Pride and ego, the twin towers that define sin, are the source of the cancer of comparison. And in the battle, sinful comparison always causes someone to lose inappropriately, because pride and ego must be fed.

This is an issue that almost every church has wrestled with at some point or another. Those of the older generation ought to keep wisely in mind that the upcoming generation is often a threat to their own identity. It is sometimes difficult for older people, even older pastors, to resist the influence that younger people who have grown up in the church begin to exert. They resist the new styles, not only of clothes and cars but also of styles of teaching or innovations in worship. True, sometimes these new ways are simply fads that end up doing more harm than good. But does the older generation allow the younger the opportunity to earn their respect by giving them a chance to prove their giftedness and calling from God? Or are they rejected out of hand simply because they are too familiar with them?

*Too threatened by John's message.* The devious rejection and execution of John the Baptist foreshadows Jesus' own betrayal and execution, but we should also

---

25. Hagner, *Matthew*, 1:406: "The primary mistake of the people of Nazareth was their automatic limitation of Jesus to the familiar framework in which they had previously known him. This made them unable to evaluate Jesus in terms of his message and deeds."

consider the ramifications for anyone bearing God's message. Not only did John arouse the ire of Herod Antipas for calling into question his illicit marriage to his brother's wife, but he was personally a threat to Herodias's political aspirations, and the only way to get rid of that threat was to get rid of John. In the non-Christian circles in which we move, we will also be an embodiment of moral evaluation. On the mild side, people will stop swearing when we enter a room, or they may refrain from that off-color joke. More offensive will be the effect of our presence when we come to a family gathering where a family member is having an affair or is living together with a boyfriend before marriage.

But the viciousness of an attack on the messenger is especially unleashed when our message gets in the way of another's ambition. To call into question a colleague's motivation, to point out a lie, or to reveal a cover-up of an unethical business practice threatens one's power track to success, and you may find yourself facing not only anger but also bodily or emotional danger. But such is sometimes the responsibility of disciples, who are to be salt and light in a dark world (see comments on 5:14—16).

*Two caveats.* I must interject two caveats about these lessons from Jesus' and John's experiences of rejection. (1) We must learn to live with the consequences if we attempt to minister to people who are too familiar with us. We cannot demand respect; we have to earn it. If we do not earn others' respect, we must accept the consequences of rejection, but we should keep on loving those who reject us. It is difficult to love those who reject us, but Jesus is our example. Love them and then go on graciously to where the message will be received with gratitude.

Or if we go into a setting where we believe that we are called to establish an ethical or moral judgment, we must recognize that there may be personal consequences. It may not mean something as drastic as our own death, like Jesus and John, but it may mean alienation from family members, or perhaps the loss of a promotion for confronting a superior, or perhaps even harassment from neighbors for not allowing our children to attend neighborhood parties that are a bad influence. We may be personally offensive because of the message we embody. Jesus and John contended for the message but accepted the consequences bravely.

(2) We must recognize that sometimes the *inappropriate* offensiveness of the messenger causes a rejection of the message. There are Christians out there who are jerks. They have poor social skills and poor manners. They treat people, both Christian and non-Christian, with disrespect. They run roughshod over others in the name of their own crusade. Some Christians are so legalistically narrow-minded that no one is right about anything except them.

I have met many Christian leaders who are as arrogant and pompous as any pagan leader. These people often are completely blind to their own *inappropriate* offensiveness. They are actually a hindrance to the gospel message, and others cannot see beyond their offensiveness to the message of grace that they say they carry. This is why it is important to have people around us who are not afraid to tell us the truth about us and who will call us into accountability if we are developing an edge to our personality, if we need to grow in kindness and goodness, or if we are beginning to think more highly of ourselves than is fitting. Jesus and John embodied a powerfully truthful message that called the nation into accountability, but they did so with appropriate, not inappropriate, personal offensiveness.

**Eliciting discipleship and leadership through faith and worship.** After the long day of ministry, Peter might have been delighted to send the crowd away to find their own food (14:15). But he learns from the feeding of the five thousand that Jesus is the source of help for problems. He learns from the incident of his own walk on water that Jesus is also the solution for disasters. Peter is learning to grow in leadership, because he and the other disciples are discovering what they will need to display as future church leaders. These events teach us that both discipleship and leadership, under Jesus, demand effective faith in his divine power and humble worship of his divine identity.

*Effective faith in Jesus' divine power.* Peter emerged as the leader of the twelve disciple/apostles. In the listing of the Twelve, Matthew describes him as "first," and he consistently becomes the spokesman for others (e.g., 15:15; 16:16; 17:4, 24).[26] He also seems the most human, because his story is one of repeated successes and failures. He is impulsive, brazen, and proud, yet also passionate, devoted, and repentant. This contributes to one of Peter's widely recognized character qualities—swings from extreme highs of faith in Jesus to extreme lows of lack of faith and even denial of Jesus.

- Peter swings from great faith by obeying Jesus' summons to walk on the water, but then demonstrates ineffective faith by taking his eyes off Jesus.
- He swings from making a great confession of Jesus' identity; then immediately switches to being a tool of the devil (16:16–19, 22–23).
- He is privileged to be with the inner three with Jesus on the Mount of Transfiguration, but then he makes a bumbling statement about pitching tents (17:1, 4).

---

26. Pheme Perkins, *Peter: Apostle for the Whole Church* (Studies on Personalities of the New Testament, gen. ed. D. Moody Smith; Columbia, S.C.: Univ. of South Carolina Press, 1994), 18–21.

- He exercises faith to catch a shekel-loaded fish, but then he haggles over how many times he should forgive a brother (17:24–27; 18:21).
- He is among the inner three with Jesus in his final hours at Gethsemane, yet he is singled out for not staying awake to watch and pray with Jesus (26:37, 40–41).
- He boasts that his faith in Jesus will remain even if all the others fail, and he follows Jesus to the courtyard where he is tried by the Sanhedrin, but he disappears in Matthew's Gospel after his predicted threefold tragic denial of Jesus (26:33–41, 58, 69–75).[27]

Matthew gives more prominence to Peter's leadership than any other Gospel writer, yet he does not paint an idealistic picture of him as an infallible leader. Instead, he focuses on how Jesus is preparing Peter for a leadership role in the early days of the church, including how Peter must learn to overcome seriously deficient character qualities.[28]

Specifically, we see that leadership under Jesus demands effective faith in his divine power. Peter is often criticized by modern preachers for being presumptuous to ask to go out on the lake. But Jesus does not reprimand Peter for getting out of the boat; he only mildly chides him for failing once he got out there. It took much courage to follow Jesus on the water, probably more than most of us would have had. Peter does fine on the water until he looks at his circumstances ("seeing the wind," 14:30). As soon as he takes his eyes off Jesus, he finds himself afraid and in trouble.

But through this momentary failure Peter learns something that only his courage in getting out of the boat to obey Jesus' summons can teach. We may focus on the failure, but his obedience became the training ground for future growth in faith in Jesus' sustaining power. As John Ortberg writes:

> ... only Peter knew that when he sank, Jesus would be there, and he was wholly adequate to save. The other disciples could not know because they never got out of the boat. This is the fundamental truth: If you want to walk on water, you've got to get out of the boat. If you want to experience the power of God in your life, you've got to take a step of faith. It involves risky obedience.[29]

---

27. See the graph in the introduction that plots Peter's actions in Matthew's Gospel, dramatically illustrating his vacillation of faith.

28. For Matthew's portrait of Peter and his developing leadership role, see Wilkins, *Discipleship in the Ancient World and Matthew's Gospel*, 173–216, 264.

29. John Ortberg, "If You Want to Walk on Water, You've Got to Get Out of the Boat," *Pathways* 1/1 (Fall–Winter 2001), 11. This is an excerpt from the book of the same name (Grand Rapids: Zondervan, 2001).

We all face many circumstances for which we are unprepared. The difficulties we face change from day to day. But the one constancy we have in this life is Jesus. As we go through life focused on an intimate walk with Jesus through each and every circumstance, we learn how to apply his consistency to our situations. We may never be in such a position as Peter was, but we can learn from him. When the Lord called him, whether to get out of the boat or later to become a leader in the early church, Jesus was always there to see him through.

Some thirty years later we find Peter, now an older man, perhaps in his mid-sixties, exemplifying this change. When he speaks of the great day of coming salvation with the return of Christ, he gives a stirring expression of perseverance of faith:

> In this you greatly rejoice, though now for a little while you may have had to suffer grief in all kinds of trials. These have come so that your faith—of greater worth than gold, which perishes even though refined by fire—may be proved genuine and may result in praise, glory and honor when Jesus Christ is revealed. Though you have not seen him, you love him; and even though you do not see him now, you believe in him and are filled with an inexpressible and glorious joy, for you are receiving the goal of your faith, the salvation of your souls. (1 Peter 1:6–9)

Gone is the braggadocio. But gone also is the ineffective faith. Even though Peter and his readers cannot see Jesus now, they have learned the lesson of never taking their eyes of faith off him. No matter what Peter is called by his Lord to do, faith simply means saying yes to that summons. As a leader of the early church, Peter exemplifies that kind of faith, and the people of the church carefully followed his example.

Peter's lifelong story emphasizes for us the astonishing grace and gentle restoring power available in Jesus. None of us has failed so many times that God cannot use us for his purposes. But we must continue to focus on Jesus instead of becoming unsettled by circumstances we have never encountered. This is the key for a consistent Christian lifestyle and for consistency in whatever leadership role we may be given. We can rely on his presence in our lives. He will be there with us to help us make the right decisions, to give us courage in the face of fearful opposition, or to comfort us in sorrowful situations. This is a vital ingredient for a Christlike life in this world. Let me suggest three ways we can live this out.

(1) Learn to practice the presence of Jesus. Learn to open your conscious attention to Jesus everywhere you go and to develop a line of communication with him in all of your circumstances. I talk with Jesus as though he is

in the car seat next to me when I drive to an important meeting or expected confrontation. I ask him for advice (silently!) when I am counseling a person, because only Jesus knows precisely the advice that is needed. I gauge my spiritual health at least in part by the degree to which I allow Jesus' presence to invade every moment of my day.

(2) Understand that your circumstances are not the measure of Jesus' love for you. He will never leave you, and he never loves you less, even though your conditions cause you to doubt him. Life in this world is hard at times. Some of the health-and-wealth messages of recent years suggest that only those who succeed physically or materially have true faith and that those blessings are an indication of God's love. But even as Jesus' purpose in life was to suffer on the cross for us, we have been called to suffer for his sake (Phil. 1:29), whether the suffering comes directly from persecution for our faith, from engaging in the spiritual warfare of this life, or from living in a world that is still under the curse of sin and death. Jesus loves us no less, even though we may feel he is far away.

(3) Consciously open yourself up to Jesus' power, presence, and love in the most difficult of times. This point follows from the fact that our circumstances are not the measure of Jesus' love for us. When we know that he is near, we can, and must, call on him. This was Peter's exercise of faith in calling out for Jesus' saving help even at the time that he was failing.

My wife and I learned this lesson early in the raising our children. Our older daughter fell into a feverish coma with spinal meningitis when she was just four years old. At the emergency room the doctors said that she would not live through the night. A wave of panic washed over us when we heard those words, and we began to sink into a pit of despair. But in the middle of our desperation, my wife and I held each other and cried out to God. We consciously gave our little Michelle back to her heavenly Father, knowing that he loved her even more than we did. But we also asked for the healing touch of Jesus in her life. We experienced the warmth of God's peace flood our souls that night. But we also experienced the miraculous healing of our daughter.[30]

We have had many other difficult situations since that time, not all of which turned out so well. But that night we learned the reality that the outcome isn't what really matters. It was our blessing to have her healed, but if the Lord would have taken her home to be with him, we know that he would have somehow sustained us in that crisis. What matters is that we continually call on the power, presence, and love of Jesus in all of our circumstances.

The apostle Peter, and we, have learned that Jesus is with us all the time, that he has power over all circumstances, and that he never stops loving us,

---

30. I recount this story more fully in Wilkins, *In His Image*, 157—59.

even though it doesn't seem like it in the middle of those trying times. To focus on intimacy with Jesus instead of circumstances enables us to trust him no matter what comes our way and no matter what the outcome. Discipleship and leadership under Jesus demand effective faith in his divine power.

**Humble worship of Jesus' divine identity.** The events of this narrative also teach us that discipleship and leadership under Jesus demand humble worship of his divine identity. The townspeople of Jesus' hometown Nazareth had a faulty understanding of Jesus that caused them to reject him. But as the disciples saw Jesus heal and feed the crowd, then saw him walk to them on the water, enable Peter to walk on the water, save him, and then calm the storm, they had a very different understanding of Jesus.

This passage is tied into a more developed understanding of Jesus' identity, which is progressively revealed throughout Matthew 14–17. These events help answer the question, *Who is Jesus?* We see that he is *compassionate*, expressed in both his healing and his provision of food for the hungry. He also *provides* as a result of this compassion, not only to bring healing wholeness (14:14, 35) and physical sustenance (14:19–21) but also to bring the security of his presence to his needy disciples (14:22–33). Ultimately, he *has authority over all creation*, which he demonstrates in the calming of the sea (14:32–33). All of these factors point strongly to his identity, and the narrative is capped off with the disciples worshiping him as they proclaim his identity: "Truly you are the Son of God" (14:33). Thus the events play on two levels: They point to his identity as the Son of God in order to show what kind of Messiah he is for his people.

It is vitally important for us to develop a clear vision of Jesus. For many people, an understanding of Jesus is cluttered with fragmented or distorted images. We are often more familiar with the pieces of Jesus' image that our culture, denomination, church, or fellowship group has excised for its own use than we are with the full biblical picture.

Individual churches and denominations and parachurch organizations tend to focus on certain characteristics of Jesus, especially those that support an understanding of their theology or mission. These stereotypes give a slice of truth about Jesus but often fail to tell the whole story. They may focus on Jesus as Savior, shepherd, teacher, Lord, friend, revolutionary leader, or provider. A partial image of Jesus can never provide a complete understanding of who he is, what he means to our Christian lives, and what it is that he wants to accomplish in us. If Jesus is only a friend to us, perhaps we do not understand that he is also the powerful Lord of the universe, who can supply us with the power necessary to accomplish whatever God calls us to in life. If Jesus is only our gentle shepherd, perhaps we do not recognize him as the religious revolutionary who despised religious hypocrisy.

Jesus is all of these images, and more. A balanced, rounded understanding of Jesus needs to incorporate all aspects of his character and nature. A faulty vision of Jesus will cause us to reject him or to base our lives on only a partial understanding of what he has come to accomplish in our lives. But a clear and accurate vision of Jesus will cause us to worship him, which means ultimately to give our lives completely to him as our God. In the earlier incident of the calming of the storm the disciples were amazed (8:27), but now after coming to a more complete understanding of who he is, they worship him (14:33). A proper appreciation for Jesus' power should produce worship, not simply astonishment.

Worship involves honoring, serving, and respecting God, and abandoning any loyalty or devotion that hinders an exclusive relationship with him. It is an expression of a personal and moral fellowship with God relevant to every sphere of life. The starting point of New Testament worship is the conviction that God fully and finally has manifested himself in the person of his Son. Jesus Christ is the ultimate meeting point between heaven and earth and the decisive means of reconciliation between God and humanity.[31]

As we come to see who Jesus really is, we are affected by his compassion, provision, and protection, which is grounded in his authority over nature. We know that Jesus cares for us and our present circumstances. He will provide for us, out of this compassion. As we venture out in faith, we can trust that Jesus will be with us. As we walk through this world we need not fear, because he walks with us. We all start out with a level of ineffective faith like Peter, but it grows as Jesus shows himself faithful to us over time. The reason we can trust Jesus is because he has authority over all creation. What can hurt us without his permission?

Max Lucado imagined what a journal would have been like if one of the disciples had made his entry on the morning after Jesus calmed the storm. The imaginary reflections strike a realistic chord of what that disciple experienced. He writes:

> I had never seen Jesus as I saw him then. I had seen him as powerful. I had seen him as wise. I had witnessed his authority and marveled at his abilities. But what I witnessed last night I know I'll never forget.
>
> I saw God. The God who can't sit still when the storm is too strong. The God who lets me get frightened enough to need him and then comes close enough for me to see him. The God who uses my storms as his path to come to me.
>
> I saw God. It took a storm for me to see him. But I saw him. And I'll never be the same.[32]

---

31. Peterson, *Engaging with God*, 283–85.
32. Lucado, *In the Eye of the Storm*, 182.

The story of Peter and the other disciple on the stormy waters is surpassed only by the perfect walk of our Lord Jesus upon the lake. In that walk we see God. And when we see him clearly and obey his summons upon our lives, we too will never be the same.

T HEN SOME PHARISEES and teachers of the law came to Jesus from Jerusalem and asked, ²"Why do your disciples break the tradition of the elders? They don't wash their hands before they eat!"

³Jesus replied, "And why do you break the command of God for the sake of your tradition? ⁴For God said, 'Honor your father and mother' and 'Anyone who curses his father or mother must be put to death.' ⁵But you say that if a man says to his father or mother, 'Whatever help you might otherwise have received from me is a gift devoted to God,' ⁶he is not to 'honor his father' with it. Thus you nullify the word of God for the sake of your tradition. ⁷You hypocrites! Isaiah was right when he prophesied about you:

⁸"'These people honor me with their lips,
   but their hearts are far from me.
⁹They worship me in vain;
   their teachings are but rules taught by men.'"

¹⁰Jesus called the crowd to him and said, "Listen and understand. ¹¹What goes into a man's mouth does not make him 'unclean,' but what comes out of his mouth, that is what makes him 'unclean.'"

¹²Then the disciples came to him and asked, "Do you know that the Pharisees were offended when they heard this?"

¹³He replied, "Every plant that my heavenly Father has not planted will be pulled up by the roots. ¹⁴Leave them; they are blind guides. If a blind man leads a blind man, both will fall into a pit."

¹⁵Peter said, "Explain the parable to us."

¹⁶"Are you still so dull?" Jesus asked them. ¹⁷"Don't you see that whatever enters the mouth goes into the stomach and then out of the body? ¹⁸But the things that come out of the mouth come from the heart, and these make a man 'unclean.' ¹⁹For out of the heart come evil thoughts, murder, adultery, sexual immorality, theft, false testimony, slander. ²⁰These are what make a man 'unclean'; but eating with unwashed hands does not make him 'unclean.'"

²¹Leaving that place, Jesus withdrew to the region of Tyre and Sidon. ²²A Canaanite woman from that vicinity came to him, crying out, "Lord, Son of David, have mercy on me! My daughter is suffering terribly from demon-possession."

²³Jesus did not answer a word. So his disciples came to him and urged him, "Send her away, for she keeps crying out after us."

²⁴He answered, "I was sent only to the lost sheep of Israel."

²⁵The woman came and knelt before him. "Lord, help me!" she said.

²⁶He replied, "It is not right to take the children's bread and toss it to their dogs."

²⁷"Yes, Lord," she said, "but even the dogs eat the crumbs that fall from their masters' table."

²⁸Then Jesus answered, "Woman, you have great faith! Your request is granted." And her daughter was healed from that very hour.

²⁹Jesus left there and went along the Sea of Galilee. Then he went up on a mountainside and sat down. ³⁰Great crowds came to him, bringing the lame, the blind, the crippled, the mute and many others, and laid them at his feet; and he healed them. ³¹The people were amazed when they saw the mute speaking, the crippled made well, the lame walking and the blind seeing. And they praised the God of Israel.

³²Jesus called his disciples to him and said, "I have compassion for these people; they have already been with me three days and have nothing to eat. I do not want to send them away hungry, or they may collapse on the way."

³³His disciples answered, "Where could we get enough bread in this remote place to feed such a crowd?"

³⁴"How many loaves do you have?" Jesus asked.

"Seven," they replied, "and a few small fish."

³⁵He told the crowd to sit down on the ground. ³⁶Then he took the seven loaves and the fish, and when he had given thanks, he broke them and gave them to the disciples, and they in turn to the people. ³⁷They all ate and were satisfied. Afterward the disciples picked up seven basketfuls of broken pieces that were left over. ³⁸The number of those who ate was four thousand, besides women and children. ³⁹After Jesus had sent the crowd away, he got into the boat and went to the vicinity of Magadan.

*Original Meaning*

MANY PHARISEES AND teachers of the law were so focused on external acts of purity that they regulated even the most mundane activities of their life in order to develop purity before God. But Jesus makes explicit what he has implied throughout his teaching, that true purity comes from a heart that has been made righteous by God (cf. 5:20).

## The Traditions of the Jewish Elders (15:1–9)

THE CHARGE AGAINST Jesus' disciples (15:1–2). The ministry of Jesus has disturbed the local Pharisees (12:1–14), so they apparently send word to the highest level of their leadership in Jerusalem, who arrive in Galilee to confront Jesus about the practices of his disciples.[1] The primary point of contention is that Jesus does not recognize the binding authority of the oral law, here called the "tradition [*paradosis*] of the elders." This phrase became a technical expression to refer to interpretations of Scripture made by past esteemed rabbis and passed on orally to later generations. This is connected later with the Mishnah's *halakah*, which sets forth laws to guide the faithful in their walking, and living, in consistency with Scripture.[2] According to Jewish tradition, "Moses received the [Oral ]Law from Sinai and committed it to Joshua, and Joshua to the elders, and the elders to the Prophets; and the Prophets committed it to the men of the Great Synagogue [supposedly a leadership group begun by Ezra]" (*m. ʾAbot* 1.1).

The earlier charge of the Pharisees against Jesus' disciples was that they defiled the Sabbath (12:1–7). Now the Pharisees and teachers of the law from Jerusalem lodge a charge against the disciples that "they don't wash their hands before they eat." Bodily cleanliness was valued highly in the ancient world. The heat and dust made frequent washing necessary for both health and refreshment. Within ancient Israel, a host provided travelers with water for their feet so that they could be refreshed and cleansed from their journey and be ready for a meal (Gen. 18:4; 19:2; 1 Sam. 25:41; cf. John 13:1–10). The hands were a particular concern for cleanliness, as something unclean could be transmitted to oneself and others, so the priests were required to wash their hands and feet prior to offering their service (Ex. 30:18–21). The Pharisees adapted the concern for hygienic cleanliness to ceremonial purity and applied it to common Israelites.

---

1. On Pharisees and teachers of the law, see 3:7; 5:20; 8:19. See also D. R. de Lacey, "In Search of a Pharisee," *TynBul* 43.2 (1992): 353–72.
2. Samuel Sandmel, *Judaism and Christian Beginnings* (New York: Oxford, 1978), 103.

**Jesus' countercharge (15:3–9).** Jesus counters the Pharisees' charge against his disciples by asking why they and teachers of the law transgress God's command because of a commitment to their "tradition" (15:3). In this question he goes to the heart of the problem, which is the relationship of the developing oral law to the written law. The tradition of the elders was not simply a preferred way of living, but it became equal in authority to the written law. Jesus makes it clear to them that the Old Testament came from God, while their traditions are simply the pronouncements of human elders.

The specific example concerns the way that the Pharisees' tradition regarding vows made to God have actually caused them to violate the Old Testament's directives about honoring parents. God made it clear that the Israelites were to give unreserved honor to their parents: "For God said, 'Honor your father and mother' and 'Anyone who curses his father or mother must be put to death.'" But the Pharisees' commitment to human traditions regarding gifts given to God caused them to violate God's law: "But you say that if a man says to his father or mother, 'Whatever help you might otherwise have received from me is a gift devoted to God' he is not to 'honor his father' with it."

The expression "gift devoted to God" reflects the Hebrew term *qorban* (cf. "Corban" in Mark 7:11), a technical term designating a formal vow made to God, which is here a gift for the support of the temple. The Pharisees developed a complicated series of rulings regarding vows and oaths. For example, a person could make a vow of dedication, which rendered a thing forbidden in the future for common use (as in 15:5). Such a formal vow allowed a person to be exempt from one's other responsibilities, such as the support of one's aging parents here.

Jesus drives home the point that their tradition has caused them to violate the law, so that they "nullify the word of God" in their zeal to practice a human tradition (15:7). The Pharisees, like most Jews, demanded honor of father and mother. They would have rightly considered honoring parents to include supporting them in their old age. But as Jesus sees it, their human traditions of allowing vows was actually supplanting Scripture. They have considered anyone who broke a vow (i.e., a human law) in order to help one's needy parents (i.e., God's law) to have committed a serious sin. Jesus, therefore, lays down the gauntlet: The written word of God is of higher authority than the tradition of humans, and when humans make their traditions legally binding, they make the Word of God empty of true authority.

Earlier Jesus condemned as "hypocrites" the religious leaders who performed acts of righteousness for the purpose of being honored by people (6:1–18). There he explicitly addresses them as "You hypocrites!" (15:7). He goes on to use the similar situation from Isaiah's experience to condemn the

Pharisees' motivation in developing their traditions. Isaiah had condemned religious leaders from Jerusalem who formalistically developed rituals and teachings as though that deserved merit from God. That prophetic word of God stands as a judgment against all generations of God's people. The Pharisees and teachers of the law perform religious rituals externally, but their primary motivation has not been to commit their entire inner person to God. Therefore, not only does their human tradition and teaching nullify God's Word (15:6, 9), but their worship is empty of any real meaning (15:9). This is a disturbingly sweeping indictment by Jesus of Israel's leading religious establishment.

## Purity and Impurity from the Heart (15:10–20)

A WARNING TO the crowd (15:10–11). Since the Pharisees and teachers of the law are so influential among the common people, Jesus turns to the crowd to warn them of falling into the same trap. The warning also answers the charge of these Jewish leaders by declaring the source of purity and impurity. In 15:15, the disciples call this warning a parable, which is in line with the stated purpose of Jesus' parables earlier (13:10–17). They will test the spiritual receptivity of the audience, calling them to respond further to his teaching so that they can understand God's will. Those in the crowd who are unreceptive will turn away from this saying to follow the Pharisees and teachers of the law, while those who are receptive will respond by becoming his disciples and seeking further understanding through his teaching (15:15–20).

Jesus states categorically that spiritual impurity is not contracted through eating foods that are not ceremonially cleansed: "What goes into a man's mouth does not make him 'unclean.'" He thereby renounces publicly the Pharisees' tradition that required ritual cleansing before eating. He is not speaking of hygienic cleanliness but of spiritual purity. Ceremonial cleansing is not the key element in producing godliness. A hypocritical show of devotion to God can mask a heart that is more intent on gaining a religious reputation than it is on seeking to do God's will as revealed in the Old Testament (cf. 6:1–18).

In challenging Jesus about conformity to the tradition of the elders, the Pharisees reveal that their inner life is unclean. They have not repented in the light of the arrival of the kingdom of heaven and received the righteousness that is Spirit-produced. They continue to rely on their own practice of external righteousness, which does not allow them entrance to the kingdom (see comments on 5:20). They have not only deceived themselves but have misled the people with their traditions, so Jesus gives due warning to the crowd.

A warning from the disciples (15:12–14). It was one thing for Jesus to rebuke the Pharisees privately, but when he publicly warns the crowd about their wrong-headed approach to spiritual purity, the Pharisees are personally "offended" (*skandalizo*) at having their reputation besmirched in front of the people. The disciples hear about it, and when they gather away with Jesus again in the house (probably Peter's; cf. 8:14), they tell Jesus. They are probably worried not only about Jesus finding himself at odds with these religious leaders, but also with those who are influenced by them. And they are also probably worried about their own reputation. The Pharisees, in contrast to the Sadducees (see comments on 3:7), were increasingly influential in Israel as the authoritative interpreters of Scripture and the most righteous in their daily behavior.[3] They rightly understand that Jesus has elevated himself as a critic of their entire religious tradition, which will undercut their influence with the people.

Jesus replies to the disciples' warning with two parables. (1) He likens the fate of the Pharisees to that of a plant: "Every plant that my heavenly Father has not planted will be pulled up by the roots." Reminiscent of the parable of the weeds and the wheat, this saying declares that the Pharisees have not been planted by the Father. Jesus elevates his pronouncements about the true intent of the Old Testament over the Pharisees' traditions and points to their future judgment, when they will be uprooted (cf. 13:29). As in the parable of the weeds, the implied consequence of uprooting is to be cast into the furnace of divine judgment (13:42).

(2) Jesus also likens the Pharisees to blind guides: "Leave them; they are blind guides. If a blind man leads a blind man, both will fall into a pit." Not only does the hypocrisy of the Pharisees blind them to their own inner impurity, but in their blindness they lead the people astray because they cannot see the truth of God's will in the Old Testament (cf. 23:16–22).

**A question from Peter (15:15–16).** As a spokesman for the disciples (see comments on 10:2; 14:28–31), Peter asks for the interpretation of the parables. That Peter is not asking alone is revealed in Mark, where the disciples as a whole ask this question (Mark 7:18; note that in Jesus' reply in Matt. 15:16, he uses the plural "you"). Understanding Jesus' parables and teaching is a key element of discipleship, because true disciples have spiritual ears to hear and spiritual eyes to see the truth of Jesus' teaching, something the crowd does not have (cf. 13:10–17, 51). But Jesus rebukes the disciples here for not being as spiritually perceptive as they should. As elsewhere, the real key to understanding is Jesus' teaching, so he goes on to give an explanation of the parable.

---

3. Comparing the Sadducees and the Pharisees, Josephus said that they had significant differences, among them, "the Sadducees having the confidence of the wealthy alone but no following among the populace, while the Pharisees have the support of the masses" (Josephus, *Ant.* 13.10.6§298).

---

**Jesus' explanation of the role of the heart in spiritual purity (15:17–20).** In his explanation, Jesus outlines to the disciples the central role that the heart plays in spiritual purity. Food that goes into the mouth does not affect the spiritual heart; it simply goes through the digestive system and is excreted (15:17). Food or ceremonial purification rites attendant to eating food do not affect a person's inner purity. Jesus thus renders superfluous the Pharisaic fastidious and obsessive preoccupation with dietary purity laws—especially here the washing of hands. These traditions of the elders have nothing to do with true spiritual cleanness, because they only focus on the external physical activities. They do not make a person unclean before God. God's judgment concerns behavior that originates in the heart of a person.

The implication is that the spiritual heart is naturally evil (cf. 7:11) and needs the righteousness that Jesus has initiated with the arrival of the kingdom of God. The Pharisees' charge about violating traditions regarding ritual purification before eating (15:2) lead to the general statements Jesus makes about all human activities, namely, that inward, spiritual defilement is more deadly than outward, ceremonial defilement. The spiritual heart is evil, and it must first be cleansed, which will then produce lives that exemplify righteous purity in word, thought, motivation, deed, and relationships.

This is an explicit statement about the heart that was implied in Jesus' teaching in the Sermon on the Mount. Jesus came to fulfill the Old Testament revelation about God's will for his people and to bring about the righteousness of the kingdom of heaven in those who respond to his message. That righteousness is an inside-out transformation that begins with the heart and works throughout the process of the disciple's life to produce external righteousness while pursuing the perfection of the Father (cf. 5:17–48).

## Healer and Provider for Gentiles (15:21–39)

JESUS WITHDRAWS TO **Gentile regions (15:21).** Jesus may have stayed for some time in the Jewish region of Gennesaret on the northwest coast of the Sea of Galilee (14:34), but he now explicitly withdraws to Gentile territory, to the infamous cities of Tyre and Sidon (on these cities, see comments on 11:20–24). The Jews of Galilee have been privileged to hear and see Jesus' message and miracles that authenticated his announcement of the arrival of the kingdom of heaven (4:12–17), but their lack of repentance condemns them (11:20–24). Rejection of Jesus by his hometown people of Nazareth (13:53–58), the arrest and execution of John the Baptist, and his own threatened public peril from Herod Antipas (14:1–2) combine to signal the end of the Galilean ministry, so Jesus "withdraws" (see comments on 4:17; 14:13). He and his disciples proceed to Gentile regions before heading to Judea and the final destination, Jerusalem.

**A Gentile woman acknowledges Jesus as the Son of David (15:22–28).** His first encounter in this Gentile region is with a Canaanite woman. She comes to him, crying out, "Lord, Son of David, have mercy on me!" This woman, a "Canaanite" (i.e., a pagan non-Jew) demonstrates familiarity with Jewish messianic tradition by calling Jesus "Son of David" (see comments on 1:1; 9:27), and she pleads for his merciful, miraculous ministry of exorcism for her daughter. A temple dedicated to Eshmun, a god of healing, was located three miles northwest of Sidon.[4] This woman was likely familiar with the pagan deity, but Jesus' reputation has preceded him, and she comes instead to Jesus for healing for her daughter. Her use of "Lord" three times (15:22, 25, 27) is probably a title of great respect, but she is saying more than she realizes.

Jesus does not reply to the woman's cry for help, which the disciples apparently take as his way of rebuffing the woman's request. So they urge him to "send her away, for she keeps crying out after us." The disciples perhaps remember Jesus' charge that included the directive about not going to Gentiles but only to the lost sheep of Israel (cf. 10:5–6). Indeed, in this Gentile region Jesus maintains his commitment to fulfill that mission for which he was sent as he says, "I was sent only to the lost sheep of Israel" (15:24). "Lost sheep of Israel" does not mean the lost sheep *among* Israel, as though some were lost and others not. The expression indicates the lost sheep *who are* the house of Israel. Jesus comes as the Suffering Servant to save all Israel. Jesus must first go to Israel in fulfillment of the promises made to the nation (cf. Isa. 53:6–8), so that the Gentiles themselves will glorify God for his promises made to his people (cf. Rom. 15:8–9).

But this woman's great need to have her daughter exorcised drives her to be persistent, which is a sign that she knows that Jesus certainly can come to her aid. She kneels in humble obeisance before Jesus and calls him "Lord" a second time as she seeks his help (15:25). But Jesus still maintains his commitment to his mission to Israel as he replies, "It is not right to take the children's bread and toss it to their dogs." The "children's bread" emphasizes the care that God promises to provide for his covenant children, Israel (see Deut. 14:1–2; Hos. 11:1). As a metaphor, "dogs" is a humiliating label for those apart from, or enemies of, Israel's covenant community (1 Sam. 17:43; Ps. 22:16; Prov. 26:11).[5] Jesus used the metaphor similarly in the Sermon on the Mount to indicate that the holy message of the gospel of the kingdom must not be defiled by those who are unreceptive to, or have rejected, Jesus' invitation (7:6).

---

4. Cf. Rousseau and Arav, "Tyre and Sidon," *Jesus and His World*, 327–28.
5. See "Dog," *DJBP*, 172; "Animals," "Dogs," *DBI*, 29, 213–14.

The woman continues the metaphor but uses it to emphasize that dogs too had a caring relationship with "their master." Most dogs at this time were nondomesticated, living in squalor, running the streets, and scavenging for food (Ps. 59:14–15). Some dogs were trained for guarding flocks (Job 30:1) and humans (Isa. 56:10; Tobit 6:2; 11:4), but they were not normally brought into the home. However, some were more domesticated as household watchdogs, and they were fed in the house (cf. *Jos. Asen.* 10:13). This perceptive woman, who has already confessed Jesus as the messianic Son of David, now presses Jesus by calling on the extended blessings promised to the Gentiles. Although Israel receives the primary blessings of the covenant, Gentiles also were to be recipients of blessing through them (see Gen. 12:3; see comments on Matt. 1:1; 8:5–13).[6] The woman draws on that promise to seek the aid of Jesus Messiah.

She understands the program of God to go to Israel first, but she persists. In a sense, Jesus is testing her. Will she see through the salvation-historical distinction between Israel and the Gentiles and recognize that God ultimately desires to bring healing to all people? She passes with flying colors because she acknowledges that as the Messiah of Israel, Jesus is the master of all, and he will care for the needs of all, whether Jews ("children") or Gentiles ("dogs"). Her response is called by Jesus an exercise of "great faith," which is rewarded by having her daughter healed that very hour (15:28).

Even though God has a program, he responds to true faith.[7] The privileged people of Nazareth did not respond in faith and so could not receive Jesus' healing ministry (13:58). But this Gentile woman has an openness to Jesus that allows his healing ministry to operate. Here we understand that faith is essentially accepting the revelation and will of God as one's own reality and purpose for life. The "greatness" of faith points to the fact that such an unlikely person—a Gentile woman living outside of Israel—demonstrates one of the clearest understandings of God's salvation-historical program and Jesus' participation in it. This is another incident where exorcism is called "healing" (cf. 12:22–23) and is a continuation of the confirmation of Jesus' messianic ministry. By healing this Gentile woman's daughter, Jesus demonstrates that he also has an eye on the ultimate ingathering of all peoples (8:5–13).[8]

---

6. See F. Gerald Downing, "The Woman from Syrophoenicia, and Her Doggedness: Mark 7:24–31 (Matthew 15:21–28)," *Women in the Biblical Tradition*, ed. George J. Brooke (Studies in Women and Religion 31; Lewiston N. Y.: Edwin Mellen, 1992), 129–49.

7. Smillie, "'Even the Dogs': Gentiles in the Gospel of Matthew," 73–97; esp. 93–95; T. W. Manson, "Only to the House of Israel?" in *Facet Books Biblical Series* 9 (Philadelphia: Fortress, 1964), 22–23.

8. Scott, "Gentiles and the Ministry of Jesus," 161–69.

**Many Gentiles glorify the God of Israel (15:29—31).** Jesus returns to the Galilee region, but Mark specifies that he goes to the Decapolis (Mark 7:31), the primarily Gentile region on the southeastern coast of the Sea of Galilee. Here Jesus performs many miracles among the crowds, thus authenticating his message that the kingdom of God has arrived. When juxtaposed with the preceding story that emphasized the salvation-historical priority of Israel first and then the Gentiles, the dropping of "crumbs" to the Gentile mother and daughter prepares for a turning to the Gentiles in general with the miraculous feeding of the four thousand.

Gentiles increasingly become the focus of Jesus' ministry now that the religious leadership is working to turn the people away from him.[9] As Israel rejects the kingdom, Gentiles frequently come into view as recipients of his message and healing. Like the crowd in Israel, they are amazed when they see his miraculous ministry, and they "glorify the God of Israel" (15:31; cf. 9:33). But like Israel's crowd, it is not enough to be amazed. They must believe on him as the Messiah of Israel and become his disciples.

**Feeding the four thousand (15:32—38).** This is the second time that Jesus feeds a crowd of thousands miraculously after spending time healing those brought to him, although this time he is in the Gentile region of Decapolis.[10] As in the earlier feeding, Jesus has compassion on the crowd that has gathered to receive his healing ministry. They have been with him for three days (15:32), and their reserves of resources and their strength are exhausted, and they will not be able to get to adequate supplies before they collapse (15:32). Jesus addresses the disciples with the needs of the crowd, challenging them to recall the earlier miraculous supply of the five thousand. But the disciples still have not fully grasped the magnitude of Jesus' identity, because they question where they will find supplies to feed such a massive group. Once again Jesus will teach them with a miraculous illustration.

In this feeding the number of small bread cakes is seven, and there are seven baskets left over. If the number of twelve baskets left over in the feeding of the five thousand is symbolic of Israel, as most suppose, then the number seven here, which is normally symbolic of perfection or completion, may symbolize the completion or fullness of God's meeting the needs of all peoples, now including Gentiles.[11] As in the feeding of the five thousand, Matthew alone specifies that the four thousand that are fed are men, besides women and children. Again, this indicates a number most likely close to ten thousand.

---

9. Carson, "Matthew," 356—57.
10. For further discussion, see the feeding of the five thousand in 14:13—21.
11. Cf. Hagner, *Matthew*, 451—52; less convinced is Carson, "Matthew," 359.

**A brief return to Jewish territory (15:39).** The miraculous feeding concluded, Jesus sends the crowd away. He once again traverses the Sea of Galilee by boat, which means he now returns to Jewish territory. The name "Magadan" occurs only here in the New Testament (Mark 8:10 has Dalmanutha). The identity of the town or region is puzzling, because there are no historical or archaeological records to confirm the identity. The most promising proposal is that Magadan is a variant spelling for Magdala, the home of Mary Magdalene (27:55; cf. Luke 8:2).[12]

Magdala is generally identified with Migdal Nunya ("Tower of Fish") of Talmudic times, about three miles north of Tiberias on the Gennesaret plain.[13] The name suggests that this town was the center of Galilee's fish-processing industry, making it one of the most important fishing centers on the Sea of Galilee and the administrative seat of the surrounding region.[14] Archaeologists uncovered in Magdala, in the ruins of a first century A.D. home, a decorative mosaic depicting a boat with a mast for sailing and oars for rowing.[15]

**Bridging Contexts**

IN THIS GEM of a chapter that marks a transition away from the Galilean ministry of Jesus, Matthew highlights explicitly three themes that characterize Jesus' inauguration of the kingdom of God and his form of discipleship—the supremacy of the Word of God, the centrality of the heart, and the necessity of faith for all people. These themes have been surfacing implicitly, but now they arise explicitly as the confrontation between Jesus and the religious leaders heats up. Jesus' way of kingdom life for his disciples demands a departure from the ways of human religious efforts. Matthew shows how the hardening of the hearts of the people of Israel against Jesus and their preference for traditional religious practices result in his increasingly turning away from them and preparing for a door to be opened to all peoples who have true faith in him.

**The supremacy of the Word of God.** The confrontation between Jesus and the religious leaders from Jerusalem highlights one of the most signifi-

---

12. Gundry, *Matthew*, 322; Keener, *A Commentary on the Gospel of Matthew* (1999), 420; Rousseau and Arav, "Magdala," *Jesus and His World*, 189–90.

13. Some conjecture that removing the first syllable of *Migdal Nunya* could give rise to a form Dalnunya, similar to Dalmanutha (Mark 8:10); cf. Gundry, *Matthew*, 322; Blomberg, *Matthew*, 247 n. 87.

14. James F. Strange, "Magdala," *ABD*, 4:463–64.

15. Dodo Joseph Shenhav, "Loaves and Fishes Mosaic Near Sea of Galilee Restored," *BAR* 10 (1984): 22–31. Only a mile from here the famous first-century fishing boat was found (see comments on 4:21).

---

cant dividing lines between them—the supremacy of the Word of God over any other authority. Matthew assumes his audience is familiar with the traditions of the Pharisees.[16] The Pharisees and teachers of the law came from a long history of teachers and interpreters who attempted to make the Old Testament practical and relevant for contemporary life. While the Jews were in captivity after the temple had been destroyed, the Old Testament prescriptions for sacrifice and offerings for sin seemed irrelevant. So teachings and interpretations were developed that applied those prescriptions to daily life in such a way that the Jewish interpreters believed that they had fulfilled God's desire for purity. Rabbis debated which interpretation was authoritative until consensus was reached.[17]

Jesus saw this authoritative position of the traditions of the elders developing and confronted the Pharisees and teachers of the law about its conflict with the written Word of God. Some of their traditions were in conflict with the Old Testament commands, but they must now intentionally abandon such traditions. Tragically, however, their traditions had become so entrenched in their authoritative pronouncements about how to achieve right standing with God that they were blind to the conflict, and they hardened themselves against the truth of God's Word. But Jesus' pronouncement is clear: The Word of God alone is the supreme statement of truth about every realm of reality, whether it is religious, social, relational, ethical, political, or whatever. Every human tradition or teaching or interpretation or reasoning must bow before the written Word of God.

But Jesus is not saying that all the Pharisees were necessarily practicing their traditions or worshiping with evil ulterior motives.[18] Many Pharisees made their vows in good faith, not intentionally avoiding the obligation to parents but also not realizing that their vow would eventually put them at odds with honoring their parents. But their zeal for observance of their traditions supplanted true commitment from the heart to God's intention in the Old Testament. As they take issue with Jesus and his disciples over one

---

16. This is different from Mark, who gives an extended description of the Pharisaic practices, explaining for his audience what lies behind this controversy (Mark 7:3–4).

17. Note that after the permanent destruction of Jerusalem and the temple in A.D. 70 and the scattering of the Jews, the need for relevant and authoritative application of the Old Testament to daily life became even more pronounced, and ultimately the binding traditions of the elders were codified and written to produce the Mishnah.

18. An evil motive would be like a son who intentionally wanted to avoid the obligation of giving something useful to his needy parents. He then would dedicate it to God for a future offering, so that giving it to anyone else was prohibited. In the meantime the son retained possession and use of the item for himself, and he intentionally dishonored the obligation to his parents.

of their purity laws, their actions reveal hearts that are becoming hardened against God's purposes.

Some who heard Jesus' declaration recognized the conflict. Pharisees like Nicodemus saw that Jesus held the true understanding of the Old Testament and became his disciples (John 3:1–9; 7:50–51; 19:38–39). Later Saul, a prominent member of the Pharisees, when confronted with the risen Christ, was dramatically converted and recognized that the traditions of humans must all yield before the gospel of Jesus Christ (cf. Gal. 1:13–16). As the apostle Paul, he warns, "See to it that no one takes you captive through hollow and deceptive philosophy, which depends on human tradition and the basic principles of this world rather than on Christ" (Col. 2:8).

This is not to assume that all tradition is wrong per se. Paul uses the same term "tradition" (*paradosis*) to refer to the gospel truths he passed on to the churches (1 Cor. 11:2; 2 Thess. 2:15; 3:6), and the related verb (*paradidomi*) to refer to the fundamental truths of the cross and resurrection that he had received and passed on to the church (1 Cor. 15:1). Tradition is also a helpful way of passing on the teaching of earlier generations so that each new generation is not required to reinvent the proverbial wheel of doctrinal truth. The essential difference between these forms of tradition and those developed within Judaism rests on the fact of Jesus' incarnation. Jesus is the revelation of God embodied, and Paul declares, therefore, that the traditions he received and passed on to the church have derived from God himself through the revelation of Jesus Messiah. That is a crucial dissimilarity.

The determining feature is the supremacy of the Word of God as declared in the Old Testament, fulfilled in Jesus' ministry, and revealed through his apostolic messengers. For example, Jesus' reiteration of God's truth concerning the family in this confrontation with the Pharisees should be compared with the opposite reversal of priorities that he addresses elsewhere. The traditional obligation to family was so highly valued among the Jews that Jesus challenged his disciples and would-be disciples to be careful that duty to parents does not supplant following him and honoring him as their Master (cf. 8:21–22; 10:34–39; cf. Luke 14:26). The role of the biological family as a primary training ground of faith is reemphasized, but Jesus' clarification of the Father's will creates a complementary spiritual family, which must not be supplanted by one's biological family (see comments on 12:46–50).

Jesus' main emphasis is that all traditions must yield to the supremacy of God's Word. When tradition takes priority over or supplants God's written Word, tradition is faulty.

**The centrality of the heart.** Jesus has repeatedly contrasted the external and internal in his teachings about the role of the heart in a person's life. The pure in heart will see God (5:8), but the hypocritical self-righteousness of the Pharisees and teachers of the law will not be rewarded by God (cf. 5:20; 6:1–18). Purity of heart and righteousness that surpass the Jewish leaders comes through yielding to Jesus' call to repent and enter the kingdom of heaven (see comments on 5:20). The righteousness of kingdom life is found in obedience from the heart to Jesus' fulfillment of the Law and the Prophets (cf. 5:17, 28; cf. 5:21–48). One's external treasure reveals the priorities and values of one's inner heart (6:21).

External weariness and the burdens of religious legalistic activity can never produce the rest for one's soul that is found in being yoked to the gentleness and meekness of Jesus' heart (11:28–30). The words one utters are the external evidence of either a good or evil inner heart (12:34–35). Ultimately, the seed of the Word of God planted in one's heart will reveal externally whether one has received Jesus' message of the kingdom or has hardened his or her heart against it (13:10–23).

In Jesus' compelling rebuke of the Pharisees for elevating their traditions over the Word of God in their pursuit of religious cleanliness, he articulates the central problem—their heart. The wickedness of the natural heart was well known. The prophet Jeremiah stated forthrightly, "The heart is deceitful above all things and beyond cure. Who can understand it?" (Jer. 17:9). A desire for a new heart should be the aspiration of the wicked (Ezek. 18:31). The Pharisees know that this is God's desire, but they focused on the wrong order. God's law will someday be written on the heart (Jer. 31:33), but the Pharisees focus on external laws of ceremonial purification rites in order to purify their hearts. Thus, Jesus declares that attending to the wicked heart must be understood as the priority, not external observations, because it is out of the heart that all evil thoughts, actions, and words proceed (Matt. 15:18–19).

This becomes the distinguishing mark of discipleship to Jesus. With the institution of the new covenant in his blood (26:26–29), Jesus brings the new heart for which Israel and all humanity long. This inward transformation will be empowered by God's Spirit, not human law, and will produce genuine obedience from the heart, not hypocritical legalism, as Ezekiel prophesied: "I will give you a new heart and put a new spirit in you; I will remove from you your heart of stone and give you a heart of flesh. And I will put my Spirit in you and move you to follow my decrees and be careful to keep my laws" (Ezek. 36:26–27).

It now remains for Jesus and the new community of faith to articulate how this inside-out transformation from the heart to the entire person is carried out. A couple of hints are given in the succeeding narratives, where Jesus declares that forgiveness of other believers stems from the heart (18:35), and love for God and neighbor begins with love from the heart (22:37–40).

This is a rich portend of what discipleship to Jesus is to be like in the community of believers.

**The necessity of faith for all people.** In this chapter, Matthew emphasizes that true faith in Jesus as the messianic inaugurator of the kingdom of God is a requisite for all people, whatever their race, nationality, or gender. The people of Jewish Galilee, privileged to be the first to hear and receive Jesus' invitation to the kingdom, have had their opportunity, but the verdict is clear. Like Jesus' own hometown of Nazareth, they have hardened their heart against his message.

By contrast, the disciples will continue to be characterized as having faith, though it is in process of development. At times their faith is effective, at other times not. Peter was rewarded for his faith in Jesus' true identity by being called to walk on the stormy seas, but his "little" or ineffective faith caused him to sink (14:27–31). The disciples' faith caused them to worship Jesus when he calmed the seas (14:32–33), but their faith in him did not fully extend to understanding his ability to provide for the needs of the people. They have not learned their lesson about his ability to feed the five thousand, because they soon question Jesus about where they will get the resources to feed the four thousand (cf. 14:15–21; 15:33).

The Canaanite woman, however, is a person of "great faith," which allows Jesus to reward her with her request of healing for her daughter (15:28). Great faith does not imply a large quantity but rather an immovable steadfastness in trusting God's Word and will against all odds and circumstances. This persistent Gentile mother's faith indicates that in spite of the odds against finding a person who clearly understands God's Word and his will for humanity in a pagan territory, she is such a person in her steadfast resolution to find healing for her daughter in Jesus. Her openness to his true identity and mission allows his healing ministry to operate. She accepts God's revelation and will as her reality and purpose for life, which is the central defining element of faith. Matthew highlights the necessity of true faith in such an unlikely person and place, which offers hope to men and women of every generation. Jesus' compassionate care is available to all who take his Word and will as their reality and purpose for life.

THE THREE AREAS described in the Bridging Contexts section have challenged us to have no other tradition or authority supplant the Word of God, to understand that the workings of God in the transformation of lives begin with the heart and proceed outward, and to realize that faith is the conduit through which God brings his saving and healing touch into our lives. In the Reformation these three clarion calls were articulated in the central tenets of the *solas: sola scriptura, sola gratia,* and *sola fidei. Scripture* alone is the authority for people, not the church and its councils. Salvation is a work of God in a person's heart that is by *grace* alone. We receive this salvation by *faith* alone, not by works, the church, or sacraments.

**The ultimate authority of the Word of God.** Throughout the centuries men and women have attempted to discover God's will for their lives. That search is conducted on the personal and the community level. The search must finally be answered in the daily role of the Scriptures as the ultimate authority in our lives.

Some today, however, attempt to discover God's will through human spiritual experiences. Scripture is important to them, but often human knowledge or reason or experience is their final judge. Those who reject the full inspiration of Scripture often adjudicate seemingly contradictory passages in Scripture by what they can reconcile with their own understanding.

Others who contend for a high view of divine inspiration of Scripture reject teachings that seemingly reflect old cultural values that are not relevant in our contemporary world. An inflammatory example among some groups is the practice of homosexuality. In many places within Western culture, homosexual activity is accepted, condoned, and protected. Some mainline denominations have groups within them that declare homosexuality to be an acceptable lifestyle for ordained ministers.[19] Proponents of such causes often contend that their reasoning and experience have forced them to deny the Bible's teaching. In this case human reasoning and experience becomes more authoritative than the Bible itself.

Still others attempt to articulate God's will through various ecclesiastical traditions. The struggles of the Reformation centered on this issue, where the teaching authority of the Roman Catholic Church was elevated to an equal level of revelation. Recently the *Catechism of the Catholic Church,* initiated by Pope John Paul II, reaffirmed that the divine revelation of the gospel is transmitted in two forms: sacred Scripture and the teaching tradition of the church.[20] An elevation of the authority of tradition is also found in the Orthodox Church, where

---

19. For example, a group within the Presbyterian Church (USA) has tried for several years to have an amendment adopted that would remove from the PC(USA)'s constitution a provision requiring that candidates for ordination "live either in fidelity within the covenant of marriage between a man and a woman, or chastity in singleness." Proponents of the amendment hoped to clear the way for the ordination of gay and lesbian Presbyterians. This has been voted down consistently by the presbyteries, but appears to continue to be an inflammatory issue within the denomination. For a recent report on this controversy, see *http://www.pcusa.org/pcnews/02389.htm.*

20. *Catechism of the Catholic Church* (Mahwah, N.J.: Paulist, 1994), par. 81.

the doctrinal definitions of the historic ecumenical councils of the church are considered infallible and are placed alongside Scripture as having equal authority.[21]

Jesus' confrontations with the religious leaders of his day, especially the political rationalism of the Sadducees and the religious authoritarianism of the Pharisees, give us the right guidance to understanding God's will in our own day. The Word of God as revealed in Scripture must be understood as the sole authority that contains all that is necessary for salvation and the spiritual life. That Word must be elevated above any human tradition (15:2–9). It is in God's Word that we have the clearest understanding of God's will for our daily lives and the life of our communities of faith. Teachers, preachers, and doctrinal formulations are helpful guides to individuals and churches, but Scripture must continually be upheld as the final authority.[22]

In a practical way, we can accomplish this as we compare the words of the world with the Word of God and continually give ourselves to what God has to say about our daily choices and priorities and standards for life. This is precisely the directive of Jesus in the Great Commission, where new disciples must be taught to obey everything Jesus commanded as their means of growth (28:20). We must develop a habit of life in which we acquire and obey the teachings of the Word of God.

This is not simply an academic exercise, because when we interact with God's Word, it is a spiritual activity. Note Hebrew 4:12: "For the word of God is living and active. Sharper than any double-edged sword, it penetrates even to dividing soul and spirit, joints and marrow; it judges the thoughts and attitudes of the heart." As we acquire the teachings of God about any subject, they alter our values, motives, and goals in life. We are set free from sinful habits to live out God's will. Our entire person—physical, mental, emotional/social, spiritual—is then brought into conformity with the will and personality of God.

Martin Luther's commitment to God's Word not only was the driving force behind his commitment to the Reformation but was also the driving force in his own life transformation:

> Since these promises of God are holy, true, righteous, free, and peaceful words, full of goodness, the soul which clings to them with a firm faith will be so closely united with them and altogether absorbed by them that it not only will share in all their power but will be saturated and intoxicated by them. If a touch of Christ healed, how much more

---

21. E.g., Timothy Ware, *The Orthodox Church* (London: Penguin, 1993), 202.

22. For a helpful overview of these issues, see Robert L. Saucy, *Scripture: Its Power, Authority, and Relevance* (Nashville: Word, 2001), 230–40.

will this most tender touch, this absorbing Word of God, communicate to the soul all things that belong to the Word.[23]

His description of the power and role of the Word of God in daily life are instructive for us who also await its tender touch.

**Transformation from the heart.** Jesus' condemnation of the Pharisees for elevating human traditions over the Word of God brought to the light a precipitating problem—the evil of one's heart cannot be cleansed by religious activity. Along with the Old Testament prophets, the Pharisees knew that the evil inclinations of the human heart were inherent in men and women living under the Fall, but their attempts to rectify the problem through religious ritual were futile.

While Jesus does not give the full prescription here, he prepares the way for his own later teaching and that of the apostles concerning the role of the Spirit in bringing about the regenerated heart of the new covenant (e.g., 26:27–29; John 13–16; Titus 3:4–7; 1 John 4:21). It is only through this activity that the heart that has been hardened against God can be transformed to function as our spiritual heart is intended to function. This is true in the first place in unbelievers, who need the regenerating work of God, but it is also true in believers as they experience the ongoing sanctifying work of God.

Spiritual hearts become hardened in two primary ways. (1) Hearts harden from the inside when we say no to what God wants from us. Put simply, our hearts harden when we sin. We are resistant to the Spirit, who is trying to convict us. While we live in a condition of saying no to God with our sin, we harden our hearts more and more.

(2) But hearts also harden against the outside when we try to protect ourselves from being hurt. Every person reading these words has been hurt by other people, and we often try to protect ourselves from being hurt again by hardening our heart against those who might bring pain into our lives. This kind of hardening of the heart can result in fearfulness, arrogance, or bitterness as means of protecting ourselves.

We must be starkly honest with ourselves because we can mask a hard heart. One primary way a hard heart can be masked is behind external acts of religion. There are many people in churches today with hard hearts. They regularly attend church and appear to be religious, but their hearts are hardened to God and to his people. A hard heart can also be masked behind glitzy performances, whether the performance is preaching or singing or praying. Religious heart diseases are often not seen by the one who has the disease, yet they eat away at the spiritual health of the person and are usually

---

23. Martin Luther, "The Freedom of a Christian," *Luther's Works*, 31:349; cited in Saucy, *Scripture*, 248.

masked by religious activities that feed the disease instead of healing the person. As we noted above, Jesus reserved his harshest criticism for the religious figures of his day who hid a hard heart behind hypocrisy.

The only cure for spiritual heart disease is through the penetrating, transforming work of the kingdom of God in a person's life. As we allow Jesus to unleash the power of the Spirit in our hearts, we will experience an inward transformation that will begin to influence our thoughts, our actions, our emotions, and our relationships.

Jesus does not dismiss the importance of obedience. However, right action as an end in itself without grounding it in a heart regenerated by the kingdom's power of love loses the moral worth of the action. As John Piper adroitly asks, what would be the morally better action, and which would be appreciated more by a man's wife—bringing her roses on their anniversary because it was his duty or because he delights in bringing her this little show of devotion?[24] So it is with our life with God and our worship of him. As Piper contends,

> If God's reality is displayed to us in his Word or his world, and we do not then feel in our heart any grief or longing or hope or fear or awe or joy or gratitude or confidence, then we may dutifully sing and pray and recite and gesture as much as we like, but it will not be real worship. We cannot honor God if our "heart is far from him."[25]

Religious obedience, whether demanded by first-century Pharisees or twenty-first century legalists, is only as worthy as is the impulse of the heart.

**Great faith and ungrateful privilege.** In this passage, it is initially shocking that Jesus seems ready to ignore the request of the woman simply because she is a non-Israelite, and some commentators have been scathing in their criticism of Jesus for his lack of ethnic sensitivity.[26] But as noted above, Jesus does not demonstrate ethnic bigotry against Gentiles but salvation-historical privilege for Israel. His mission is initially to Israel, but eventually the whole world will be blessed through Israel. Jesus will develop this plan further, but we get a peek of the broader picture here that has as its scope the entire world (28:19) and all people groups (21:43).

While there is no real evidence that Jesus lifts his particularistic priority of Israel during his earthly ministry,[27] we can see an initial hint of Jesus' desire

---

24. John Piper, *Desiring God: Meditations of a Christian Hedonist*, expanded ed. (Sisters, Ore.: Multnomah, 1996), 83–84.

25. Ibid., 83.

26. E.g., Beare, *Matthew*, 341–42.

27. Frederick W. Schmidt, "Jesus and the Salvation of the Gentiles," in *Through No Fault of Their Own? The Fate of Those Who Have Never Heard*, ed. William V. Crockett and James G. Sigountos (Grand Rapids: Baker, 1991), 97–105.

to reach beyond the ethnic borders of Israel to help the non-Israelite woman (cf. also the centurion's son, 8:5). This shows his heart. In the same way that he had compassion on the harassed and helpless people of Israel, who were like sheep without a shepherd (9:36), he has compassion on a little girl and her mother, who are like dogs without a scrap of hope, and he responds. In either case, his response is to those who have opened eyes of faith to see and respond to him. The vast majority of those within Israel who are privileged to see and hear him first ultimately reject him. So this woman of great faith gives us due warning and instruction.

Privilege demands accountability, and faith in Jesus' identity and mission brings the touch of the kingdom's blessing. This blessing is not that of wealth—quite possibly the woman already had that—or even that of health, for the mother herself receives nothing, and her little daughter will eventually die physically. Rather, like the centurion, this Gentile woman of great faith is a foretaste of the promise of the eschatological feast of salvation that all those from every point of the compass will enjoy who respond to Jesus' summons to the kingdom (8:10—12).

I live in great privilege, both materially and physically. I also have been blessed to grow up in a culture where the gospel has been freely proclaimed. But privilege can also be a hindrance to spiritual realities. The kingdom's blessing turns upside-down many of our typical concepts of privilege. I have been remarkably touched by a different kind of advantage I have seen in men and women of great faith around the world. The sheer delight of poor church people in the slums outside Manila in the Philippines results from an understanding of their privilege to experience their newfound eternal life in Christ. The steadfast courage of a group of pastors from Muslim countries in central Asia results as they rejoice in their "gift" of being able to suffer for the name of Jesus. The unfathomable peace of patients in intensive care wards in hospitals around the world results from their recognition that they are loved by the One who holds the health of their souls in his tender hands.

This wonderful story of the persistent mother warns and instructs us that Jesus always responds to those who have the courage to come to him with their desperate need, because true privilege comes through openness to him in faith.

# Matthew 16:1–28

T HE PHARISEES AND Sadducees came to Jesus and tested him by asking him to show them a sign from heaven.
²He replied, "When evening comes, you say, 'It will be fair weather, for the sky is red,' ³and in the morning, 'Today it will be stormy, for the sky is red and overcast.' You know how to interpret the appearance of the sky, but you cannot interpret the signs of the times. ⁴A wicked and adulterous generation looks for a miraculous sign, but none will be given it except the sign of Jonah." Jesus then left them and went away.

⁵When they went across the lake, the disciples forgot to take bread. ⁶"Be careful," Jesus said to them. "Be on your guard against the yeast of the Pharisees and Sadducees."

⁷They discussed this among themselves and said, "It is because we didn't bring any bread."

⁸Aware of their discussion, Jesus asked, "You of little faith, why are you talking among yourselves about having no bread? ⁹Do you still not understand? Don't you remember the five loaves for the five thousand, and how many basketfuls you gathered? ¹⁰Or the seven loaves for the four thousand, and how many basketfuls you gathered? ¹¹How is it you don't understand that I was not talking to you about bread? But be on your guard against the yeast of the Pharisees and Sadducees." ¹²Then they understood that he was not telling them to guard against the yeast used in bread, but against the teaching of the Pharisees and Sadducees.

¹³When Jesus came to the region of Caesarea Philippi, he asked his disciples, "Who do people say the Son of Man is?"

¹⁴They replied, "Some say John the Baptist; others say Elijah; and still others, Jeremiah or one of the prophets."

¹⁵"But what about you?" he asked. "Who do you say I am?"

¹⁶Simon Peter answered, "You are the Christ, the Son of the living God."

¹⁷Jesus replied, "Blessed are you, Simon son of Jonah, for this was not revealed to you by man, but by my Father in heaven. ¹⁸And I tell you that you are Peter, and on this rock I will build my church, and the gates of Hades will not overcome it. ¹⁹I will give you the keys of the kingdom of heaven;

whatever you bind on earth will be bound in heaven, and whatever you loose on earth will be loosed in heaven." ²⁰Then he warned his disciples not to tell anyone that he was the Christ.

²¹From that time on Jesus began to explain to his disciples that he must go to Jerusalem and suffer many things at the hands of the elders, chief priests and teachers of the law, and that he must be killed and on the third day be raised to life.

²²Peter took him aside and began to rebuke him. "Never, Lord!" he said. "This shall never happen to you!"

²³Jesus turned and said to Peter, "Get behind me, Satan! You are a stumbling block to me; you do not have in mind the things of God, but the things of men."

²⁴Then Jesus said to his disciples, "If anyone would come after me, he must deny himself and take up his cross and follow me. ²⁵For whoever wants to save his life will lose it, but whoever loses his life for me will find it. ²⁶What good will it be for a man if he gains the whole world, yet forfeits his soul? Or what can a man give in exchange for his soul? ²⁷For the Son of Man is going to come in his Father's glory with his angels, and then he will reward each person according to what he has done. ²⁸I tell you the truth, some who are standing here will not taste death before they see the Son of Man coming in his kingdom."

CHAPTER 16 IS a pivotal chapter in Matthew. After the increasing opposition of the Jewish religious leaders to his messianic ministry (12:9–14, 22–37) and the increasing threat of the local political machine (14:1–13), Jesus has been turning to his disciples to help them to understand more clearly his unique identity and mission. He is a prophet, even though he is without honor among his own people (13:53–58). He is the compassionate healer and supplier of Israel's needs, even though they misperceive his earthly mission (14:13–21). He is the Son of God who can walk on water and calm stormy seas and who is worthy of worship, even though his own disciple(s) falter in fixating on him (14:22–36). He is the true teacher of God's Word, even though this may threaten the social security of his disciples (15:1–20). He is also the compassionate healer and provider for the needs of the Gentiles, even though his disciples sometimes forget that fact (15:21–31).

Jesus has led his disciples along slowly so that they can try to grasp the magnitude of his true identity. The religious leaders and the crowds have had their opportunity to acknowledge him as their Messiah, but their hardness of heart prevents them from perceiving him clearly (cf. 13:10–17). They will receive no more signs. But the disciples, who have been open to his identity and mission, now receive from the Father the most penetrating revelation of Jesus' identity (16:13–20). This revelation in turn leads to further revelation from Jesus about his life's mission—he will be killed and be raised up again (16:21). These are not easy revelations for the disciples to handle, as we will see. The disciples, especially Peter, continue to both understand yet not understand. They stride forward in faith when they focus on God's revelation, yet falter when they rely on their own understanding (16:22–23).

## Jesus Gives No More Signs of His Identity and Mission (16:1–4)

BACK IN JEWISH territory after landing at Magadan (15:39), Jesus and his disciples are confronted again by the religious leaders, possibly the same earlier contingent of leading officials from Jerusalem (15:1). But this time the Pharisees are joined by the Sadducees. Although they were often bitter opponents, the Pharisees and Sadducees joined forces when they saw a threat to their leadership, as they had when John the Baptist arrived on the scene (cf. 3:7).

The Pharisees and Sadducees come to Jesus to test him by asking him to show them a sign from heaven (16:1). A "sign" (*semeion*) is some kind of visible mark or action that conveys an unmistakable message, such as when Hezekiah asked Isaiah for a sign from God to certify his healing (2 Kings 20:8–11; Isa. 38:7–8). The Pharisees asked for a sign earlier as irrefutable proof that Jesus' power was from God, not Satan (see comments on 12:38–42).

But a sign can be interpreted different ways.[1] The Pharisees and Sadducees want a sign from God, most likely one that will be displayed in the skies. Although their request appears innocent enough, Matthew emphasizes that they are not asking in good faith. They are looking to "test" or "tempt" (*peirazo*) Jesus, the same word used for Jesus' temptations by Satan (4:1). They want a sign that they can use against him.

Jesus sees through their ruse and calls them to be accountable for the signs of his messianic identity and mission that he has already displayed (cf. 11:2–6): "You know how to interpret the appearance of the sky, but you cannot interpret the signs of the times." People who live close to nature are aware of daily patterns and irregularities in those patterns that might portend

---

1. James D. G. Dunn, "Sign," *IBD*, 3:1450.

future natural phenomena. There are numerous maxims or proverbial expressions that capture such signals from nature. Mariners, for example, are notorious for developing maxims that predict the patterns of weather, which they must heed daily, if not hourly, in order to conduct safe passage on the seas, such as the well-known saying, "Red skies at night, sailor's delight; red skies in the morning, sailor's warning."

Jesus uses a similar maxim drawn from his cultural milieu to contrast the religious leaders' familiarity with natural phenomena in the "sky" (*ouranos*, 16:3) with the supernatural phenomena from "heaven" (*ouranos*, 16:1) that they request, but about which they are so spiritually blind that they cannot recognize it. Because the Jewish religious leaders are not seeking in good faith, the only validating sign Jesus will give them of his messianic authority will be his resurrection, which will be like the appearance of Jonah to the Ninevites (see 12:40–41).

"The sign of Jonah" is not some kind of sign that Jonah brings. Rather, Jonah is the sign. His appearance was the sign to the people of Nineveh that his message was from the God, who had rescued him from death (Jonah 3:1–5). Jesus' resurrection from the dead will be the sign of judgment to the generation that hears his message.[2] The actions of the pagan people of Nineveh who repented at Jonah's preaching forms the judgment on all who do not repent at Jesus' announcement of the arrival of the kingdom of God, including the Jewish religious leaders who stubbornly refuse (Jonah 3:1–5; cf. Luke 11:29). The apostle Peter in his dramatic sermon at Pentecost will point to Jesus' resurrection as the conquest of Hades that seals the guilt of the house of Israel for crucifying Jesus (cf. Acts 2:22–36).

Jesus has already performed many miracles publicly, some of which the religious leaders witnessed firsthand (cf. 12:9–14, 22). To those with eyes of faith, his miracles validate his identity as the Messiah. If the religious leaders were open to God's message, they had enough of a sign that Jesus truly is the Messiah. Instead, their hard hearts have rejected the miracles' authenticating power and use those same miracles as the basis of the charge that he is a satanic tool (12:24). Jesus recognizes their evil motive, so he refuses to fall into their trap of giving them further ammunition, and Matthew narrates ominously, "Jesus then left them and went away."

## Spiritual Leaven of the Pharisees and Sadducees (16:5–12)

ONCE MORE CROSSING the Sea of Galilee, Jesus and the disciples apparently traverse from the Jewish sector on the northwest shore to the Gentile northeast shore, heading to the district of Caesarea Philippi (cf. 16:13). Jesus has

---

2. Bayer, *Jesus' Predictions of Vindication and Resurrection*, 141–45, 182.

wrapped up the bulk of his Galilean ministry and will return to Jewish Galilee (17:22, 24) only to prepare for his journey south to Judea (cf. 19:1).

Since the disciples have forgotten to bring along provisions for what now appears to be an extended trip (16:5–17:20), Jesus takes the occasion to instruct them about the Pharisees and Sadducees who have just tried to entrap him: "Be on your guard against the yeast of the Pharisees and Sadducees." Jesus earlier used yeast as a positive metaphor to represent the permeating nature of the kingdom of heaven (see comments on 13:33). Now he uses it as a negative metaphor to indicate how the evil of disintegration and corruption can permeate what is good (e.g., Ex. 12:8, 15–20).

The prior use of yeast in the parable of the mystery of the kingdom of heaven should have prepared the disciples to understand that he was using it metaphorically again, but they are so preoccupied with their physical needs that they overlook the direction of Jesus' spiritual teaching. Discipleship to Jesus implies that they should be spiritually sensitive to his teaching, for they have received spiritual eyes and ears for understanding (13:10–17). Their lack of understanding implies that they are not acting like true disciples; instead, they are acting like the crowds, or worse yet, like the Pharisees and Sadducees, who demand spectacular signs. The disciples have not remembered the miracles, which all along have acted as a confirmation of his identity and were designed to induce faith in those with receptive ears and hearts.

But Jesus patiently leads these fumbling disciples into the meaning that he intends them to understand. "Then they understood that he was not telling them to guard against the yeast used in bread, but against the teaching of the Pharisees and Sadducees." Their openness to his teaching about the yeast of the Pharisees and Sadducees leads to their understanding the threat that these religious leaders are to Jesus and his mission.[3]

The way Matthew refers to "the teaching [yeast] of the Pharisees and Sadducees" implies a teaching that these two groups hold in common. Jesus knows full well that there are significant differences between the teachings of the Pharisees and the Sadducees (see comments on 22:23–33; see also Acts 23:6–10). Jesus is not suggesting here that the Pharisees and Sadducees share the same overall theological outlook, but he is aware that these two groups have a united conviction about him that is evil. They are cooperating in their opposition to him. Jesus cannot be the fulfillment of messianic expectations because he does not fulfill their nationalistic expectations. In their own unique ways, the Pharisees and Sadducees were each expecting a political/militaristic fulfillment of Israel's gaining universal preeminence among the nations. Since

---

3. I have explored this perspective more fully in Wilkins, *The Concept of Disciple in Matthew's Gospel*, 134, 165–66, 230–31.

Jesus is not fulfilling their expectations, these groups attempt to dissuade the crowds, and even Jesus' disciples, from following him.

## Who Is the Son of Man? (16:13–14)

JESUS CONTINUES TO move away from Galilee, going into the predominantly Gentile area to the north-northeast of the Sea of Galilee called Caesarea Philippi. This region was governed by Philip the Tetrarch, one of Herod the Great's three sons.[4] Philip was sixteen years old when he was given the region, and he ruled for thirty-seven years. He married Salome, the daughter of Herodias, the girl who had danced at the infamous scene at which Herod Antipas beheaded John the Baptist (cf. 14:6–11; Josephus, *Ant.* 18.5.4 §§136–37).

At the time that Jesus and his disciples traveled there, Caesarea Philippi was an important Greco-Roman city, whose population was primarily pagan Syrian and Greek. This region, long a bastion of pagan worship to Baal, then to the Greek god Pan, and then to Caesar, becomes the site where Jesus calls for a decision about his own identity. It is here that the Father reveals to Peter that Jesus is truly the prophesied Messiah (16:13–20).

To this point in his ministry Jesus has used the relatively enigmatic expression "Son of Man" as a title to reveal his true identity and mission (see comments on 8:20; occurrences of this title up to here include 9:6; 10:23; 11:19; 12:8; 13:37–43). Other titles that he may have rightfully claimed, such as Messiah or Son of David, evoked popular militaristic and political images among the people that would have caused them to overlook his uniqueness and the message of spiritual salvation and liberation. Jesus will continue to use the expression Son of Man to clarify his identity and mission (see 16:27–28; 17:9–12; 19:28; 20:18, 28; 24:27, 30, 37, 39, 44; 25:31; 26:2, 24, 45, 64), but at this pivotal time, having basically concluded his Galilean mission, he attempts to elicit from his disciples not only what the people have gleaned, but also what his disciples have come to understand about him.

Thus, Jesus asks, "Who do people say the Son of Man is?" (16:13). The disciples' response is striking. They have heard several reports from the people about their understanding of the identity of the Son of Man, including some who say that he is John the Baptist, Elijah, Jeremiah, or one of the prophets (16:14). Each response indicates a prophet, in line with one of the popular messianic expectations held in Israel. This goes back to the strand of prediction about a great prophet who would arise. Included in this strand are the eschatological prophet of Moses' prophecy (Deut. 18:15–18),[5] the return of Elijah (Mal. 4:5; see comments on Matt. 17:12–13), and the

---

4. See Wilkins, "Matthew," 102.
5. Cf. John 6:14; 7:40, 52; Acts 3:17–22; 7:37.

anticipated return of Old Testament prophetic figures such as Isaiah and Jeremiah (*4 Ezra* 2:18).[6]

Like the earlier reaction by Herod Antipas (14:2), some think Jesus is John the Baptist raised from the dead, perhaps revealing a curious strand of superstitious belief in reincarnation. A few Jews like Philo were influenced by Plato and other sources and so accepted reincarnation within their worldview. However, most Palestinian Jews believed in the bodily resurrection antici-pated at the end of the age (Dan. 12:2).

Those who thought that the Son of Man was Jesus as John the Baptist raised from the dead possibly thought of the temporary resuscitations that Elijah and Elisha performed in the Old Testament (1 Kings 17:22; 2 Kings 4:34–35). Matthew alone among the Synoptics mentions Jeremiah as one of the prophets associated by the people with Jesus as the Son of Man. Jeremiah is a recurring prophetic voice within this Gospel,[7] perhaps recalling the Old Testament prophet as one whose message and ministry were rejected by Israel, just as Jesus' will be.[8] But even the people who have identified him with Jeremiah do not have a clear view of Jesus' true identity.

## Peter's Confession of Jesus' Identity (16:15–16)

IT IS NOT enough simply to connect the Son of Man with the prophetic expectation generally. Through the instruction that Jesus has given his dis-ciples about his identity and mission by using the title, they must now give account for whom they understand him to be. So Jesus asks them, "But what about you? . . . Who do you say I am?"

Peter steps forward once again as a leader and spokesperson for the oth-ers (cf. comments on 10:2[9]). He declares, "You are the Christ, the Son of the living God" (16:16). Prior to this, the expression "Christ" has occurred only in Matthew's narrative; now it is used for the first time by a person to address Jesus directly. "Christ" is a title, the transliteration of the Greek term *Chris-tos*, which is a translation of the Hebrew term for "anointed" (*mašiaḥ*). It occurs thirty-nine times in the Old Testament to describe kings (e.g., 2 Sam. 1:14, 16; cf. 1QSa 2:14, 20), priests (e.g., Ex. 28:41; cf. 1QS 9:11), and prophets (e.g., Ps. 105:15; cf. CD 2:12; 5:21–6:1).

---

6. Flusser, "Son of Man," *Jesus*, 124–25.

7. The prophet Jeremiah is named three times in Matthew and nowhere else in the New Testament; see comments on 2:17 and 27:9.

8. Knowles, *Jeremiah in Matthew's Gospel*, 81–94.

9. Since Jesus posed the question to the group of disciples (the "you" is pl. in 16:15), Peter functions at least in part as spokesman for the Twelve. This is the third of five incidents unique to Matthew in which Peter figures prominently (14:28–31; 15:15; 16:17–19; 17:24–27; 18:21).

"Anointed one" came to be linked in the Jewish mind to David as the anointed king of Israel, with the promise of an "anointed one" who would be the light of hope for the people of Israel. In spite of David's shortcomings, God had promised him through Nathan the prophet that the house and throne of David would be established forever (2 Sam. 7:11b–16).[10] That promise became a fixture of the hope for a coming age of blessing for the nation (e.g., Isa. 26–29, 40), inaugurated by a figure who would bring about the eschatological reign of David's line (cf. Ps. 2:2; Dan. 9:25–26). By the time of the first century, the term *Messiah* or *Christ* denoted a kingly figure who, like David, would triumph in the last days over Israel's enemies.[11]

Peter further expresses Jesus' identity as "the Son of the living God," an expression that has special significance in the area of Caesarea Philippi with its plethora of ancient Baal, Pan, and Caesar worship. Jesus is the Son of the God who is living, not like those mythical, superstitious figures etched in stone. Even more significantly, this expression bears witness to a relationship that has characterized Jesus and God throughout Matthew. Jesus is uniquely God's Son—testified as such in his conception (1:21–23), in his return from Egypt (2:15), at his baptism (3:17), at his temptations (4:2, 5), and during exorcisms (8:29). Throughout this Gospel, Jesus continually lays claim to a unique relationship with his heavenly Father.[12]

This also points back to the profound prophecy of David's line, "I will be his father, and he will be my son" (2 Sam. 7:14), which spoke immediately of Solomon, but also of the future messianic line. The successor to the line was to be God's Son, as the Old Testament and later Jewish writings reveal. Psalm 2, one of the magnificent royal psalms that speaks of the consecration and coronation of the Lord's Anointed, the Davidic King, declares, "I will proclaim the decree of the LORD: He said to me, 'You are my Son; today I have become your Father'" (Ps. 2:7; cf. 89:27). The first century B.C. *Psalms of Solomon* express a combined hope of son and king: "Behold, O Lord, and raise up unto them their king, the son of David, at the time you have foreseen, O God, to rule over Israel your servant" (*Pss. Sol.* 17:21).[13]

---

10. For overviews of the prophecies in Samuel, see Ronald F. Youngblood, "1, 2 Samuel," *EBC*, 3:879–96. Somewhat differently, see Philip E. Satterthwaite, "David in the Books of Samuel: A Messianic Hope?" in *The Lord's Anointed*, 41–65.

11. See, e.g., Lawrence H. Schiffman, *The Eschatological Community of the Dead Sea Scrolls: A Study of the Rule of the Congregation* (SBLMS 38; Atlanta: Scholars Press, 1989).

12. See 7:21; 10:32–33; 11:25–27; 12:50; 15:13; 18:35; 20:23; 24:36; 25:34; 26:39, 42; 26:53; 28:19.

13. For an overview, see Marinus de Jonge, "Messiah," *ABD*, 4:777–88; for an evaluation of the concept, as well as explicit terminology, see Edward Meadors, "The 'Messianic' Implications of the Q Material," *JBL* 118 (1999): 253–77.

Peter's confession is not the first recognition of Jesus as Messiah, but it is the fullest to this point.[14] The proper sense of Jesus as the "Christ" can only be understood in conjunction with Peter's additional statement that he is the "Son of the living God." He has a special relationship to God that sets him apart from any other kind of messianic figure. Jesus is Messiah with a unique status as the Son of God (see the confirmation of this in 16:17).[15]

But Peter confesses more than he really understands about Jesus' identity, and he does not yet fully understand Jesus' mission, because he will soon attempt to deter Jesus from his redemptive objective (cf. 16:22). But his understanding is certainly increasing, as is that of the rest of the Twelve, as they pay attention to God's revelation of who Jesus is and what he has come to accomplish.

## Jesus' Pronouncements About Peter (16:17–20)

ONCE PETER MAKES his grand confession about Jesus, Jesus in turn makes a grand pronouncement about Peter. These verses have an obvious parallelism that helps to understand Jesus' words. There are three parallel groups of three clauses (tristichs), with the first line of each unit setting the theme or making a pronouncement about Peter, and the second and third lines (composed in antithetic parallelism) forming an explanation or consequence of each first line.[16]

> (1) Blessed are you, Simon son of Jonah,
>     for this was not revealed to you by man,
>     but by my Father in heaven. (16:17)
> (2) And I tell you that you are Peter,
>     and on this rock I will build my church,
>     and the gates of Hades will not overcome it. (16:18)
> (3) I will give you the keys of the kingdom of heaven;
>     whatever you bind on earth will be bound in heaven,
>     and whatever you loose on earth will be loosed in heaven. (16:19)

**(1) Peter is the recipient of blessed revelation (16:17).** Jesus' first statement concerns the blessing that Peter has received. The Greek word for "blessed" (*makarios*) is the same as that found in the Beatitudes of the SM (see comments on 5:3). As there, this is not a *conferral* of blessing but an *acknowledgment* that Peter has been blessed personally by a revelation from God, Jesus' Father (cf. 5:3–11; 11:6; 13:16; 24:46). Peter's blessed condition results

---

14. See the additional perspective that John's Gospel gives in John 1:41; 3:28; 4:25–26, 29.

15. Keener, *A Commentary on the Gospel of Matthew* (1999), 424–25, n. 72.

16. See Wilkins, *The Concept of Disciple in Matthew's Gospel*, 186–87.

from the privilege of receiving revelation from Jesus' Father.[17] Jesus contrasts what humans have discerned about him on their own ("Who do people say the Son of Man is?") to what his disciples have gleaned through his instruction and the Father's revelation.

Although Peter apparently acts as spokesman for the group, Jesus' reply is directed to Peter himself. Each of his pronouncements about Peter is the second person singular: Peter is the *personal* recipient of revelation from the Father, which is a *personal* blessing to him. Nevertheless, what Peter confesses has already been confessed by all the disciples (cf. 14:33),[18] and the expression of blessedness is similar to that already attributed to all the disciples, who have received a revelation of the mysteries of the kingdom of heaven (cf. 13:11, 16).[19]

Peter is obviously singled out, yet he is still within the circle of disciples, so he is not being set apart from or above the rest.[20] Indeed, as spokesman he represents the common view of the group, and the blessing and revelation may be obliquely directed to the group as well. His confession is an answer *for* the disciples (16:15–16) and provokes a charge *to* all the disciples (16:20). Perhaps it is best to say that Peter is individually singled out for his act of leadership in making the confession, yet his leadership role is from *within* the circle of disciples. Even with the pronouncement about Peter's special role, the rest of the disciples will also be included in similar roles (e.g., 18:18–20).

Peter is "Simon son of Jonah," which harks back to his original Jewish name (4:18; 10:2; cf. John 1:42, which gives an Aramaic alternative, "son of John"). By calling attention to the full name, Jesus may be emphasizing the "humanness" of Simon and his natural father as opposed to the "supernaturalness" of the revelation-inspired confession from the divine Father of Jesus.

**(2) Peter, the rock, and the everlasting church (16:18).** The second tristich begins with "and I tell you," a phrase that carries a tone of consequence stemming from Peter's statement in 16:16. Jesus calls Peter here by the name he had given him when Simon was first called, transliterated from Aramaic in John 1:42 as *Kephas*. As John specifies, the name Peter (*Petros*) is the Greek

---

17. Cf. P. Bonnard, *L'Evangile selon Saint Matthieu*, 2d ed. (CNT; Neuchâtel: Delachaux et Niestlé, 1970), 244.

18. Most commentators agree that the significant feature of the Christological statement concerned the confession of Jesus as "Son of God," which is the similar confession of 14:33; cf. Jack Dean Kingsbury, "The Figure of Peter in Matthew's Gospel as a Theological Problem," *JBL* 98 (1979): 74 n. 25; idem, *Matthew*, 78–83; Carson, "Matthew," 367; Gundry, *Matthew*, 330; Schweizer, *Matthew*, 340; Hill, *Matthew*, 260; Tasker, *Matthew*, 159.

19. M. D. Goulder, *Midrash and Lection in Matthew* (London: SPCK, 1974), 387.

20. Contra Beare, *Matthew*, 354; T. W. Manson, *The Sayings of Jesus*, 2d ed. (London: SCM, 1999), 204.

equivalent for *Kephas*. Jesus' earlier statement was prophecy, now it is fact. Some understand this to be the occasion of the giving of the name,[21] but more likely this is a pronouncement prompted by the confession of Peter who already bears the name.[22]

This is one of the most discussed, debated, and researched verses in Scripture,[23] and it contains three significant features that must be interpreted to understand clearly Jesus' intention for Peter and the church to come: the relationship of Peter to "this rock," the nature of the "church," and the meaning of the "gates of Hades" in relationship to the church.

*(a) Peter and the rock.* The first feature is a well-known wordplay in Greek: "You are Peter [*Petros*], and on this rock [*petra*] I will build my church." In Aramaic, almost certainly the language Jesus spoke on this occasion, the same word (*kepha*ʾ) would have been used for both "Peter" and "rock." Translating it into Greek, Matthew would naturally use the feminine noun *petra* for "rock," since it is the most common and closest equivalent to *kepha*ʾ.[24] But when it came to recording the wordplay in Greek, Matthew had to use the less common masculine noun (*petros*) in the first half of the wordplay, for he would not refer to Peter with a feminine noun.[25] Nevertheless, the use of the two different Greek words does not change the basic meaning of the wordplay, for *petros* and *petra* were at times used interchangeably.[26] In essence Jesus is saying: "You are Rock, and on this rock I will build my church."

This helps interpret the meaning of the wordplay, which has been interpreted in three primary ways. (i) Drawing on the close relationship of the terms in both Aramaic and Greek and the syntactical prominence of the person confessing, one view stresses that the most obvious intent of the wordplay is to refer to Peter. Peter will play a foundational role in the establishment of Jesus' church.[27]

---

21. E.g., Schweizer (*Matthew*, 341) calls this the Matthean bestowal of the name.

22. Cf. W. Mundle, "πέτρα," *NIDNTT*, 3:383; Josef Blank, "The Person and Office of Peter in the New Testament," trans. Erika Young, in *Truth and Certainty*, ed. Edward Schillebeeckx and Bas van Iersel (Concilium 83; New York: Herder & Herder, 1973), 50.

23. For an overview of the history of this discussion see Oscar Cullmann, *Peter: Disciple–Apostle–Martyr. A Historical and Theological Essay*, 2d ed. (Philadelphia: Westminster, 1962), 155–70; J. A. Burgess, *A History of the Exegesis of Matthew 16:17–19 from 1781 to 1965* (Ann Arbor: Edwards Brothers, 1976); and Raymond E. Brown, Karl P. Donfried, and John Reumann, eds., *Peter in the New Testament* (Minneapolis/New York: Augsburg/Paulist, 1973).

24. Fitzmyer, "Aramaic *Kepha*ʾ and Peter's Name in the New Testament," in *To Advance the Gospel*, 115.

25. Cullmann, *Peter*, 18–19; Mundle, "πέτρα," 3:383.

26. Colin Brown, "πέτρα," *NIDNTT*, 3:386.

27. This was the interpretation of most of the early church fathers, although very early many fought against its use for establishing any kind of papacy (e.g., Ignatius, Justin,

(ii) The second view rejects any notion of the church being built on a human person and bases its argument on the distinction between *Petros* and *petra*. The demonstrative pronoun "this" points away from Peter as a person and specifies an *aspect* of him.[28] In this view it is the truth of Peter's confession[29] or his faith[30] expressed in his confession that is the rock on which the church will be built.

(iii) The last view likewise claims that Jesus intends a contrast between *Petros* and *petra*, but it differs by observing that other New Testament passages refer to Christ as the "rock"[31] and the "foundation"[32] and that Jesus refers to *himself* as the rock on which the church will be built. This view likewise contends that the demonstrative pronoun "this" points away from Peter, but it points to Jesus himself.[33]

Each view has its strengths, but several considerations combine to point to the first view—Jesus intends Peter as the antecedent to "this rock" on which he will build his church. (i) Jesus' pronouncement is directed toward Peter personally, both before and after the wordplay, and it is unlikely that a change of reference would have been made without some explicit indication. (ii) The copulative "and" (*kai*) more naturally signals *identification* of the halves of the wordplay than *contrast*: "You are Peter *and* upon this rock...." Contrast is necessary if the saying points to the confession or Christ. (iii) "Peter" is the nearest explicit antecedent to "rock," and in general the nearest antecedent is preferred over an implied or more distant antecedent unless something in the

---

Origen, Tertullian, Cyprian, Firmilian; see Cullmann, *Peter*, 159–62). This became the view of the Roman Catholic Church and is held today by scholars such as those represented in Brown, Donfried, and Reumann, *Peter*, 92–93. However, it is the dominant view held of those of a broader confessional background, such as Albright and Mann, *Matthew*, 647; Carson, "Matthew," 367–69; France, *Matthew*, 254–55; Morris, *Matthew*, 422–24; Stendahl, "Matthew," 787.

28. This view was held early in church history by John Chrysostom and attested to by Origen, Eusebius, Ambrose, and Theodore of Mopsuestia (cf. Cullmann, *Peter*, 162; Brown, Donfried, and Reumann, *Peter*, 93). More recently this has been proposed by Allen, *Matthew*, 176; Alan McNeile, *The Gospel According to St. Matthew* (London: Macmillan, 1915), 241; Mundle, "πέτρα," 384–85, and Chrys C. Caragounis, *Peter and the Rock* 58 (BZNW 58; Berlin: de Gruyter, 1990).

29. Caragounis, *Peter and the Rock*, esp. 88–119.

30. This is a view held by Luther (cited in Cullmann, *Peter*, 162) and early this century by A. B. Bruce, "The Gospel According to Matthew," *The Expositor's Greek Testament*, vol. 1 (Grand Rapids: Eerdmans, repr. 1976), 224; cf. also Tasker, *Matthew*, 162.

31. E.g., 21:42, though the term used is *lithos*; 1 Cor. 10:4, where *petra* occurs.

32. E.g., 1 Cor. 3:11; 1 Peter 2:4–8.

33. This view was held as early as Origen and Augustine (cf. Cullmann, *Peter*, 162; Brown, Donfried, and Reumann, *Peter*, 93 n. 216). This was also the major view of Luther, Calvin, and many of the Reformers (cf. Cullmann, *Peter*, 162–63).

---

context specifies another referent. (iv) The Aramaic substratum almost certainly identifies Peter as the intended antecedent (as does the interchangeability of the terms *petros* and *petra*). The likelihood of Jesus speaking Aramaic on this occasion is more probable than positing that Jesus was speaking Greek.[34]

Thus, the most natural reading of the wordplay is to see that Jesus points to Peter as one who will play a foundational role in the establishment of his church. This notion is consistent with the way in which from the beginning Peter has been spokesman and leader of the Twelve. Jesus recognizes the leadership role Peter is beginning to assume by this time and promises to extend it in laying the foundation of the church.

This facet is borne out in the historical record. Jesus appears to Peter after the resurrection (Luke 24:34) and gives him special encouragement to feed Jesus' sheep (John 21). Peter holds a leadership position among the disciples prior to Pentecost (Acts 1:15–26), at Pentecost (2:14, 37–38), and after Pentecost (e.g., 3:4, 6, 12; 4:8; 8:14–25; 10:9–11:18). Peter has a unique function and position in laying the foundation of the church. This does not mean that he builds the church (Jesus says, "*I* will build my church"), but he is important in the first days of its formation. Note that he disappears from the narrative of Acts after the foundation is laid (Acts 16 and on).[35]

Although Peter's foundational role was later taken to an extreme by the Roman Catholic Church to invest Peter with an authority and a succession of leadership,[36] we should not go to the opposite extreme and deny the natural reading of the wordplay. As D. A. Carson notes, "if it were not for Protestant reactions against extremes of Roman Catholic interpretation, it is doubtful whether many would have taken 'rock' to be anything or anyone other than Peter."[37]

*(b) Peter, Jesus, and the church.* The second phrase of this first saying to Peter gives a prediction of Jesus' new community, the church. Matthew is the only evangelist to use the term "church" (*ekklesia;* cf. 18:18), which brings to mind the "community/assembly [*qahal*] of the LORD" (Deut. 23:3; cf. 5:22). In his selection of the twelve disciples/apostles to go with his message of fulfillment to Israel (Matt. 10:1–6), Jesus here points ahead to the time when his disciples, his family of faith (12:48–50), will be called "my church." This will be the fellowship of disciples who, unlike national Israel, will believe in Jesus' identity as the Messiah, the Son of the living God (16:16), and will leave all

---

34. See Carson, "Matthew," 367–69, for other valuable support.

35. Cf. Oscar Cullmann, "πέτρος," *TDNT*, 6:108.

36. Some refer to this as a prime example of biblical exegesis losing to theological eisegesis; cf. Cullmann, *Peter*, 214ff.; Colin Brown, "The Teaching Office of the Church," *Churchman* 83 (1969), 187ff.

37. Carson, "Matthew," 368.

other allegiances behind as they receive mercy and forgiveness of sin and likewise demonstrate toward each other mercy and forgiveness (see comments on 18:15–35).

Jesus will build his church, but it will come about through the foundational activity of the apostles and prophets (Eph. 2:20). Peter will be the leader among the apostles, but once he has fulfilled that role, he will pass off the scene. His position is not passed on to others. And it will soon be apparent that unless Peter continues to be open to the leading of Jesus' Father, he will compromise his leadership role (Matt. 16:22–23).

But even though Peter appears to be the antecedent to "this rock," the reference should not be understood too narrowly. "Peter" denotes more than just the person. It is the characteristics that make Simon a "rocky ledge" that comprise the wordplay. Note the demonstrative "this." *This rock* is everything that Peter is at this very moment. It refers to him as the courageous confessor who steps forward, as the representative spokesman for the disciples, as the blessed recipient of revelation, as the first individual to make a public confession of Christ, and as the one who leads the disciples forward into realms of expression of faith. Upon *this Peter* Jesus will build his church. If Simon functions in this way, he is the rock; if he does not, he can become a stumbling block (16:23).

At the same time, Jesus' pronouncement is not a conferral of unique, individual supremacy. Peter is given a special recognition for all he is and is to be, but he is never placed above or apart from the disciples. This is also borne out in New Testament church history. Peter is almost always together with other disciples. Early in Acts he appears as the recognized leader, but at the Jerusalem council James shares the leadership (cf. Acts 15:13–21). Thereafter Peter disappears from the narrative and Paul is the one who receives special notice for continuing the work of the church. Peter is crucial for his role in the foundation of the church, but he is not the only part of the foundation (cf. Eph. 2:19; Rev. 21:14).

*(c) Jesus and his everlasting church (16:18).* As Jesus looks down the long corridor of history and even at the corridor that leads him to the cross, he gives an absolute promise that his church will endure to the end of the age: "I will build my church, and the gates of Hades will not overcome it" (18:18). Hades, or Sheol, is the realm of the dead, and the word "gates," which are essential to the security and might of a city, indicates power. So the expression "gates of Hades" in the Old Testament and later Jewish literature,[38] which is basically the same as the "gates of death,"[39] referred to the realm and

---

38. Isa. 38:10; Wisd. Sol. 16:13; 3 Macc. 5:51; *Pss. Sol.* 16.2.
39. Job 38:17; Ps. 9:13; 107:18; cf. 1QH 6:24–26.

power of death. Jesus thus promises that death will not overpower the church, his own family of faith (cf. Matt. 12:48−50).

In just a short while Jesus will give the first of four predictions of his coming death. This will be hard for his disciples to handle, so here Jesus gives not only an enigmatic allusion to his coming death but also to his power over death. Even though his enemies will kill him, death will not prevail over him.[40] Note Peter's own first powerful sermon at Pentecost, when he declared that in Jesus' resurrection the reality of the prophetic hope of the conquest of Hades ("death" in NIV) had occurred (Acts 2:31). And even though the new community will face martyrdom and persecution, the church will never die. Jesus' victory over death is living proof that he will continue to build his church against all the forces of death.[41]

(3) **Peter, the keys, and binding and loosing (16:19).** The building metaphor of the preceding pronouncement leads naturally to a discussion of "keys" in this final pronouncement about Peter. In all cases here, the pronouns used or implied are second person singular.

*(a) The keys of the kingdom of heaven.* The "keys" metaphor could point to a "generic power" given to Peter alone[42] or to his "authority" over the house of God.[43] But the building metaphor of the preceding saying more closely prepares for Jesus to pronounce Peter's role in opening or shutting the doors to the kingdom of heaven.[44] This saying gives a declaration about entrance to the kingdom, but authority is not too far removed: Peter is given the authority to admit entrance to the kingdom of heaven.

In this way Peter stands in contrasts to the scribes and Pharisees, who shut off entrance to the kingdom (23:13).[45] Peter's mission is to give people access to the kingdom, and this mission involves especially his preaching of the gospel.[46] Peter, the representative disciple who gives the first personal declaration of the Messiah's identity, is the one in the book of Acts who opens the door of the kingdom to the Jews on Pentecost (Acts 2), to the Samaritans (Acts 8), and finally to the Gentiles (Acts 10). The entrance image is fore-

---

40. McNeile, *Matthew*, 242.

41. For an historical overview of this saying, see Jack P. Lewis, "'The Gates of Hell Shall Not Prevail Against It' (Matt 16:18): A Study of the History of Interpretation," *JETS* 38.3 (1995): 349−67.

42. Brown, Donfried, and Reumann, *Peter*, 96, 100−101.

43. Blank, "Peter," 51; Manson, *Sayings*, 205; Stendahl, "Matthew," 787.

44. Bonnard, *Matthieu*, p. 246; Kingsbury, "Peter," 76 n. 27.

45. Cf. a similar saying in Luke 11:52, where Jesus charges the scribes and Pharisees with taking away the "keys of knowledge." See Dietrich Müller, Colin Brown, "κλείς," *NIDNTT*, 2:732; Donald Guthrie, *New Testament Theology* (Downers Grove, Ill.: InterVarsity Press, 1981), 714.

46. Müller, Brown, "κλείς," 732.

most in view, and therefore "the keys refer to the fact that chronologically Peter, acting as the representative of Jesus, was the first to announce the message."[47] Note that even though the Samaritans had "believed" through the preaching of Philip (8:4–13), Peter had to go there in order for them to receive the Holy Spirit as confirmation to the early church that God had now included the Samaritans (8:14–17).[48] Once Peter used the keys to open the door to the kingdom of God, he passes from the scene. The door to the kingdom now stands open throughout the ages, so the keys are no longer needed.

(b) *Binding and loosing.* In rabbinic literature, "binding and loosing" describes the authority of the rabbis in teaching and discipline to declare what is forbidden or permitted and thus to impose or remove an obligation by a doctrinal decision.[49] Some therefore suggest that Peter is given authority as a "supreme rabbi" who applies binding interpretations in the life of the church.[50] However, since the keys metaphor suggests that Peter is given authority to open the door to the kingdom of heaven, the binding and loosing metaphor continues that theme by indicating that Peter is the one who is given authority to declare the terms under which God grants entrance to, and exclusion from, the kingdom.

Peter's authority is tied directly to his confession. Through the revelation of the Father and the personal confession of Jesus as the Messiah, the Son of the living God, Peter receives a blessing and becomes the foundation of the church. His confession is a condensation of the gospel, and through Peter's preaching of the gospel and the preaching of others who follow him, sins are forgiven and entrance gained to the kingdom.

Two passages that help clarify the meaning are Matthew 18:18 and John 20:22b–23. (i) The former passage describes forgiveness or retention of sins within the church and illustrates that the disciples as a whole have a responsibility for declaring the terms under which sins are forgiven or a brother is excommunicated from the fellowship of the local church. As parallel statements, these sayings of Jesus are the basis for entrance or banishment from the kingdom (16:19) and the local church (18:18).[51] Both sayings relate to forgiveness of sin.

---

47. Guthrie, *Theology*, 714.

48. Müller, Brown, "κλείς," 732; Guthrie, *Theology*, 714.

49. See Friedrich Buchsel, "δέω (λύω)," *TDNT*, 2:60; who cites Str.-B., 1:739, *b. Mo'ed Qat.* 16a; *b. Menah* 34b.

50. E.g., Stendahl, "Matthew," 787; Beare, *Matthew*, 355.

51. The saying in 16:18–19 draws a distinction between the "church" (16:18) and the "kingdom of heaven" (16:19), but with the inclusion of the parallel saying on binding and loosing occurring in a church discipline passage (18:16–18), the requirement for entrance is the same for both: forgiveness of sins.

(ii) John 20:22b–23 also concerns the forgiveness of sins. The reception of the Holy Spirit by all the disciples will enable them to declare the terms under which God has forgiven or retained sins. The periphrastic future tense in Matthew 16:19 (lit., "shall have been bound ... shall have been loosed") has the same flavor. The passive voice of these verbs and the phrase "in heaven" are Semitic circumlocutions for describing the action of God.[52] In other words, what Peter and the disciples do in this present age has already been determined by God.[53] Peter is only an instrument God uses, because God alone can grant forgiveness of sin and entrance to the kingdom. He is given authority to declare the terms under which God forgives or retains sins.[54]

This third pronouncement isolates both the unique and representative roles of Peter. Peter alone receives the keys because once the door to the kingdom of heaven is unlocked, there is no more need for keys. Once Peter opens the doors to Jews, Samaritans, and Gentiles, all the disciples will continue to proclaim the gospel because all of them share the authority of "binding" and "loosing" (cf. 18:18; John 20:22b–23). People who receive the gospel are loosed from their sins so that they can enter the open door to the kingdom. People who reject the gospel message are bound in their sins, which will prevent them from entering the kingdom.

**Jesus warns against his public identification as the Christ (16:20).** A regular feature of Jesus' ministry was to demand secrecy about his identity and mission (see comments on 8:4; cf. 9:30; 12:16; 16:20; 17:9). He carefully avoided stirring up in the crowds a misunderstanding of his messianic identity. The title "Christ/Messiah" carried for the populace connotations of political-military liberation, and they could easily misunderstand his message to mean that he had come to begin the revolution. Peter's confession has released Jesus' identity as the Messiah/Christ, but it is still subject to misunderstanding by the crowds and even by his own disciples, as even Peter will soon display. So Jesus warns his disciples not to disclose further to the crowds that he is the Messiah. His message must be understood to focus on entrance to the kingdom of heaven, which will come about as people are loosed from their sins.

---

52. Brown, Donfried, and Reumann (*Peter*, p. 96 n. 220) cite C. H. Dodd, *Historical Tradition in the Fourth Gospel* (Cambridge: Cambridge Univ. Press, 1963), 347–49. Note that John too has divine passives in John 20:23.

53. Gundry, *Matthew*, 335; see the excellent discussion in Carson, "Matthew," 370–74.

54. Cf. Bonnard, *Matthieu*, 246; Carson, "Matthew," 370–74; Cullmann, *Peter*, 205; Müller, Brown, "κλείς," 733; Nickelsburg, "Enoch, Levi and Peter," *JBL* 100 (1981): 594–95. Guthrie (*Theology*, 714) points out that Peter is the first historically to proclaim a loosing from sins (Acts 2:38) and a binding (5:3).

---

## Jesus Messiah Predicts His Suffering and Resurrection (16:21–23)

MATTHEW NOTES THE transitional nature of this scene in Caesarea Philippi with the phrase "from that time on" (16:21). This phrase has occurred earlier only in 4:17, where it marked the initiation of Jesus' mission to Israel in Galilee. Here it marks the conclusion of his Galilean mission and the initiation of his journey to Jerusalem and the mission of the cross. The revelation of Jesus' true identity by his heavenly Father to Peter is now matched by Jesus' revelation of his true mission to the disciples. It is not an optional mission. Even as the religious leaders came from Jerusalem to try to catch him and his disciples in a transgression of the law, they are even now assembling against him. So he "must go to Jerusalem" to face his suffering at their hands.

The consciousness of the coming cross clearly is not a new idea to Jesus. We do not know when he first understood this to be the fate of his earthly mission, even as we do not know when he first understood his messianic identity. As a boy of twelve he had at least the rudiments of understanding his uniqueness, when "my Father's house" had a special significance in his self-identity (Luke 2:49). Now he reveals that his earthly mission must involve suffering, and more.

**The suffering and risen Messiah (16:21).** This is the first of four times in which Jesus predicts his arrest and crucifixion (16:21; 17:22–23; 20:17–19; 26:2), but as much as he tries to get his disciples to understand the necessity of that mission, they continually misapprehend its significance. Instead of being a revolutionary liberator, Jesus will be a suffering Messiah, something that even his own disciples, let alone the crowds, have great difficulty fathoming. By claiming the necessity of suffering death at the hands of the religious leadership of Jerusalem, Jesus begins to reveal the ultimate destiny and purpose for his life's ministry. Nothing must deter him from his mission. While this in a sense is martyrdom (the act of choosing death rather than renouncing one's religious principles), it is not martyrdom in the traditional sense.[55] While others in Jewish history had experienced martyrdom, it was for them a *consequence* of their convictions; for Jesus it is the *purpose* of his entrance to history (cf. 20:28).

The single article that refers to three groups responsible for Jesus' suffering ("the elders, chief priests and teachers of the law") indicates the combined leadership of Jerusalem. "Elders" is a generic title for anyone whose age, experience, and character has resulted in a position of leadership within

---

55. See James D. Tabor, "Martyr, Martyrdom," *ABD*, 4:574–79; Arthur J. Droge and James D. Tabor, *A Noble Death: Suicide and Martyrdom Among Greeks and Romans, Jews and Christians in the Ancient World* (San Francisco: HarperSanFrancisco, 1992).

groups such as the Pharisees and Sadducees. The "chief priests" are part of the ruling aristocracy over primarily Judea during the reigns of the Hasmoneans, Herod, and the Roman governors. They came from four prominent families of chief priests who dominated Jewish affairs in Jerusalem at the time of Jesus up to A.D. 70. They alternately supplied the offices of the high priest, captain, and treasurers of the temple.[56] The "teachers of the law" or "scribes" were professional interpreters of the law, especially associated with the Pharisees in the Gospels (see comments on 8:19; cf. 12:38; 21:15).[57]

But not only does Jesus give the first prediction of his impending suffering and death at the hands of the official leadership in Jerusalem, he also gives the first prediction of his resurrection: "and that . . . on the third day [he] be raised to life" (16:21). The passive voice used here testifies to the Father's activity in protecting his Son from the "gates of Hades" (16:18). Jesus' earlier allusion to being in the earth three days and three nights is now directly related to his death, burial, and resurrection.[58] "After three days" is the typical way of referring to any portions of days and nights (see comments on 12:40). Jesus' resurrection will be the event that transforms his disciples into the foundation of the church (see comments on 28:1–20), though for now they cannot understand the significance of what Jesus predicts.

**Peter's presumption (16:22–23).** With audacious presumption Peter steps forward, likely once again as spokesman for the rest of the shocked disciples, to try to save his Master from the announced fate of suffering. Within Jewish master-disciple relationships it was unthinkable that a disciple would correct his master, let alone "rebuke" him,[59] as Peter does here. By addressing him as "Lord," Peter is not thinking of Jesus as his divine Master but rather is once again trying to fit him into his human understanding, so the title reflects only a respectful form of address. By attempting to admonish Jesus, Peter sinks to new depths of human misunderstanding. The Greek construction used here (*ou me* plus a future tense verb) is one of the strongest negations in Greek, as though Peter himself will intervene and not let his Master suffer and die at the hands of the religious leadership in Jerusalem.

Although this may appear to reflect appropriate concern, Jesus understands the source of Peter's admonition: "Get behind me, Satan! You are a stumbling block to me; you do not have in mind the things of God, but the things of men." Satan tried to tempt Jesus away from carrying out the Father's

---

56. Annas the high priest, whose daughter married Caiaphas, the head priest at the time of Jesus' arrest and crucifixion (26:3), was the head of one of those powerful priestly families.

57. For an overview of these groups, see Brown, *The Death of the Messiah*, 1425–29.

58. Bayer, *Jesus' Predictions of Vindication and Resurrection*, 182–88.

59. Wilkins, *Discipleship in the Ancient World*, 116–24.

will at the start of his earthly ministry (see comments on 4:1–11). Now he uses a different strategy by trying to hinder Jesus' mission through Peter, one of Jesus' own disciples, the same one who has just been privy to a revelation from God the Father (16:17). A "stumbling block" is an obstacle in a path, but it becomes a metaphor for something that causes a person to sin or falter in one's faith (cf. 13:41; 18:7; the cognate verb occurs in 11:6).[60] Peter has his own ideas about the path of the Messiah, but he must know God's plans. There are only two choices: God's way or Satan's way. God's ways are often quite different from human ways.

Peter here sets his mind on human ways, not on God's. He may have gotten carried away with his own significance in understanding Jesus' identity and mission, which made him vulnerable to Satan's temptation. He undoubtedly thinks he is protecting Jesus. But as one commentator notes, "Jesus recognizes here His old enemy in a new and even more dangerous form. For none are more formidable instruments of temptation than well-meaning friends, who care more for our comfort than for our character."[61] Jesus will now show Peter that God's way is the way of the cross, for him and for all disciples.

## The Cost of Discipleship (16:24–28)

JESUS NOW TURNS from Peter to all of the disciples to reveal one of the central principles of discipleship: A disciple must take up his (or her) own cross and follow Jesus.

**Taking up one's cross (16:24).** In the first century, crucifixion was one of the most feared forms of execution, used effectively by the Romans as a strong deterrent against insurrection or rebellion in the provinces of the empire. It was a dreadful way to die. Condemned victims were often forced to carry a crossbeam to the scene of crucifixion (see comments on 27:26, 35). There they were nailed to the crossbeam, which in turn was nailed to the upright beam, and the entire cross was hoisted into place.

The horror of the cross will be Jesus' tragic fate. Among the Jews crucifixion was viewed as a terrible and shameful death,[62] but it could also be associated with an innocent sufferer or martyr.[63] Jesus follows on the latter understanding. But in what must have been to the disciples a shocking shift of emphasis, he uses the cross and crucifixion as an image of discipleship.

---

60. In other words, Peter "the rock" becomes Peter "the stumbling stone."

61. A. B. Bruce, "The Gospel According to Matthew," 226.

62. E.g., 4QNahum Pesher, frag. 3–4, col. 1.6–8 and 11QTemple Scroll 64:7–13.

63. David W. Chapman, "Perceptions of Crucifixion Among Jews and Christians in the Ancient World," *TynBul* 51 (2000): 313–16.

Although the image is often understood by modern society as bearing up under some personal hardship or life's cruel fate, as used here by Jesus the cross has a much more profound significance: One must die to his or her own will and take up God's will (cf. 16:25–26).

Jesus' path of suffering and death on the cross is the ultimate example of obedience to the Father's will.[64] Indeed, the cross symbolizes the central purpose for Jesus' life, as he will cry out to the Father in the garden just prior to his betrayal and crucifixion, "Yet not as I will, but as you will" (26:39). The cross is for Jesus and those who follow him in discipleship a metaphor of the Father's will for a disciple's life. It involves the negative, "denying self" (a person's own will for his or her life), and the positive, "taking up the cross" (accepting God's will) and "following Jesus" (putting it into practice).

The apostle Paul points to the cross as the historical event in which Jesus' death is bound up with all components of salvation and the development of the Christian life, among which are justification (Rom. 3:21–26), reconciliation (Col. 2:11–14), and regeneration (Gal. 2:19–20). This makes the cross not only a horrid reminder of the death of the Son of God but also an irreplaceable symbol of grace and a stark, matchless image of the Christian life of discipleship.

**The reasons for taking up one's cross (16:25–28).** Verses 25–27, each beginning with "for" (*gar*; the NIV does not translate *gar* in v. 26), give three related reasons for the necessity of taking up the cross of discipleship.[65] The first two reasons, set forth in paradoxical rhetorical parallelism, emphasize the urgency of the preeminence of God's will for a person's life by a person's responding to and remaining in Jesus' summons to experience life in the kingdom of God. The Greek word *psyche* is behind "life" in 16:25 and "soul" in 16:26; the emphasis is the same in both verses, for this word indicates existence beyond physical survival and success.

(1) *Saving and losing one's soul (16:25).* The person who tries to hang on to his own will and reject what God desires for him ultimately loses eternally all that he is attempting to protect in this life. Paradoxically he might go to the most extreme lengths to preserve physical existence or to try to discover the essence of his existence, but in the end, apart from being in the center of God's will, there is nothing for him but death for his soul. On the other hand, the person who lets loose of her own self-centered desires and accepts God's will for her discovers true life—salvation and righteousness and the fulfillment that she gains as she receives the reality of life in the kingdom of heaven.

---

64. "Cross," *DBI*, 184.
65. Hagner, *Matthew*, 1:27.

Losing one's life to Jesus means giving over one's own will to follow him alone in discovering God's will as the central, driving force for one's life. This concept echoes later in Paul's declaration, "Therefore, if anyone is in Christ, he is a new creation; the old has gone, the new has come!" (2 Cor. 5:17). The new life of the kingdom of God is discovered only by giving over to Jesus one's old life and finding new life in following him.

(2) *The value of a kingdom soul (16:26).* All of the physical riches, pleasures, and powers of this world will do no one any ultimate good if one "forfeits" his or her spiritual existence. The word "exchange" (*antallagma*), found in the New Testament only here and in the parallel in Mark 8:37, occurs twice in Sirach, both expressing something beyond comparative value: faithful friends and a devoted wife (Sir. 6:15; 26:13—14). Here the term emphasizes the incomparable value of discovering true restoration of life and salvation for one's soul within Jesus' summons to the kingdom of heaven. We come into this life with empty hands, and we will go out just as empty. The acquisition of all the world has to offer cannot match the blessed riches of finding true life through obeying God's will in following Jesus' summons to the kingdom of God. At the end of this life we are each measured by the health of our souls, not the wealth of our estates. The apostle Paul understood clearly the comparative value of his old life in the religious establishment of Israel versus the life he found in his discipleship to Jesus:

> But whatever was to my profit I now consider loss for the sake of Christ. What is more, I consider everything a loss compared to the surpassing greatness of knowing Christ Jesus my Lord, for whose sake I have lost all things. I consider them rubbish, that I may gain Christ and be found in him, not having a righteousness of my own that comes from the law, but that which is through faith in Christ—the righteousness that comes from God and is by faith. (Phil. 3:7—9)

(3) *The reward of gaining kingdom life for one's soul (16:27—28).* It is urgently necessary to take up one's cross in discipleship, because the coming of the Son of Man will bring an abrupt accounting as to whether each person has taken up God's will by responding to Jesus' call to kingdom life (16:27). Whether at the end of one's life or at the unexpected time of the return of the Son of Man in glory, we must all account for the choices we have made.

Although the Son of Man will die (16:21), he will also come in glory, an allusion to the prophecy of Daniel 7:13—14 (see further comments by Jesus in Matt. 19:28; 24:30—31; 25:31). The juxtaposition of Jesus' dying and coming in glory provoked misunderstanding in at least some of his first disciples (cf. 20:17–22), and it also provokes discussion of Jesus' intended meaning among modern interpreters. Behind the expression "the Son of Man is going to come" is the verb *mello* (lit., "I am about to"), which is ambiguous. The verb can be used to indicate something that is going to be undertaken in the near future. For example, it is used in the predictions of Jesus' forthcoming crucifixion (17:12, 22; 20:22; cf. also its use in 2:13 for Herod's impending search for Jesus). But the verb also refers to the indeterminate time of judgment that John the Baptist said was "about to come" (3:7); it also refers to the age "to come" (12:32) and to the wars and rumors of wars that the disciples "will" hear throughout this age until the end (24:6).

So what does Jesus mean by saying that the Son of Man "is going to come" in his glory? As a general principle, the arrival of the Son of Man in glory with his angels will mean judgment for those who have not taken up the cross and reward for those who have. That is a principle that extends throughout the ages for all those presented with the gospel invitation.

But then Jesus gives a specific application to the Twelve standing there with him: "I tell you the truth, some who are standing here will not taste death before they see the Son of Man coming in his kingdom." The phrase "I tell you the truth" typically introduces an important declaration. Here it signals a concluding clarification of the reward that will be given to those who have followed Jesus' form of discipleship by taking up God's will as symbol-ized in the cross. The expression "taste death" is an idiom for "die." Some of the Twelve standing with Jesus in Caesarea Philippi will remain alive until they see the Son of Man coming in his kingdom.

Thus, the time frame of judgment and reward is narrowed to a near-future event for the Twelve, but this interpretation is also debated. Does Jesus refer to his transfiguration that immediately follows (17:1–8),[66] his resurrection,[67] the coming of the Spirit at Pentecost, the spread of the kingdom in the preaching of the early church,[68] the destruction of the Temple and Jerusalem in A.D. 70,[69] or the Parousia, with the second coming and judgment and final establishment of the kingdom?[70]

With no other hint in the passage, the immediate context suggests that

---

66. Blomberg, *Matthew*, 261.

67. Davies and Allison, *Matthew* 2:679.

68. France, *Matthew*, 261; Carson, "Matthew," 382; they somewhat combine this with an allusion to the resurrection.

69. Hagner, *Matthew*, 2:487.

70. Those who hold to this view either suggest that the prophecy was mistaken about coming in the lifetime of those with Jesus, or else this is a Matthean redaction; cf. Davies and Allison, *Matthew* 2:679–81.

the event Jesus intends as signaling his coming as Son of Man in his kingdom is the Transfiguration, which immediately follows (see also Mark 9:2–10; Luke 9:28–36). It may seem strange to speak of "some who are standing here will not taste death" to refer to three disciples who will witness the transfiguration in a mere six days.[71] But we must remember that Jesus is continuing to call for an urgent response to his kingdom mission that is now headed to the cross. Even among his closest followers Peter has tried to hinder him under the influence of Satan (16:23), and Judas under the possession of Satan will soon betray him (26:21–25, 47–50; cf. John 13:27). The time is drawing short for those in his public ministry to respond to his invitation to enter the kingdom of God. Taking up the cross in discipleship is not something that a person can put off, because death or the coming of the Son of Man will bring with it certain accountability and judgment.

In other words, Jesus is saying to the Twelve that they must weigh carefully whether or not they have truly taken up their cross, because judgment is sooner than they think. Although they may believe that they have an extended time to weigh the options, judgment will come soon, as Judas finds out. Peter, who has just experienced the highs and lows of his own commitment in bearing the cross of kingdom obedience, will later connect the Transfiguration with Jesus' coming in power, which may have struck him as his own flirtation with judgment.[72] He writes in 2 Peter 1:16–18:

> We did not follow cleverly invented stories when we told you about the power and coming of our Lord Jesus Christ, but we were eyewitnesses of his majesty. For he received honor and glory from God the Father when the voice came to him from the Majestic Glory, saying, "This is my Son, whom I love; with him I am well pleased." We ourselves heard this voice that came from heaven when we were with him on the sacred mountain.

Jesus' saying, therefore, in this context points to the urgency of his disciples' taking up their cross. As they will see, Jesus will be transfigured in kingdom glory in just a few days. They must not themselves delay to take up their cross and adopt God's will for their lives, because in some sense, every day brings with it the possibility of impending reward or judgment.

---

71. E.g., Carson, "Matthew," 380; Hagner, *Matthew*, 2:486.

72. Peter's later comment brings congruency between Jesus' prediction in Matthew and that in Mark, who records Jesus as saying that "some who are standing here will not taste death before they see the kingdom of God *come with power*" (Mark 9:1). Jesus' transfiguration is a display of the authoritative establishment of the kingdom with God's full power, which demands immediate obedience to his calling upon their lives (cf. France, *Mark*, 344–46).

THE GOSPEL OF Matthew, like the other Gospels, is a story about the arrival of Jesus Messiah and his announcement of the kingdom of God. Other characters and issues come on and off the stage and occupy our attention. When we come to chapter 16, we see the spotlight fixed on Jesus. Matthew calls his readers to see Jesus and his mission on his terms, not their own.

**Jesus' identity.** Throughout chapter 16, Matthew's readers are consistently called to view Jesus from God's perspective, not from a human perspective. The religious leaders want signs of Jesus' messianic identity on their own terms, not Jesus', which results in a pronouncement of judgment that will be sealed with Jesus' resurrection. As a group, Jesus' own disciples will be able to discern the evil intentions of the religious leaders only as they pay attention to the revelation of Jesus' identity that comes from the Father. Human opinion of Jesus' identity is not adequate, because it only partially understands the Old Testament prophetic hopes. Even Peter's confession of Jesus' identity, inspired as it is by a revelation from God, is subject to limitation when satanic influence tempts him to fit it all into his human understanding. Those who would understand Jesus most clearly must be guided by the revelation of God the Father as it is clarified by Jesus' own teaching about his identity and mission.

Matthew knows firsthand the danger of relying on only human understanding. During their time together he watched Judas, who was privy to all that was being revealed about Jesus' identity and mission. But at the end Judas refused to accept that revelation and took matters into his own hand by betraying Jesus for a human ambition (26:14–16). Matthew also watched Peter, who first confessed Jesus' identity but then almost immediately attempted to hinder him from God's intended will of going to the cross (16:22–23). Matthew also will later watch Peter deny he even knows Jesus (26:69–75), a sure sign that Peter is still operating with human insight, not God's.

Matthew allows us to see that even partial human understanding is ultimately catastrophic. He calls his readers to accept Jesus' identity and mission on God's terms, not their own. Peter's confession of Jesus as the Christ/Messiah, the Son of the living God, is certainly the core creed of Matthew and his church,[73] but it is much more than humans can comprehend on their own. As Messiah, Jesus is more than even Peter fully knows on this occasion and more than the kind of deliverer that many of the oppressed crowds of Israel expect. Jesus is the Messiah, who will deliver his people from their

---

73. See Gerhardsson, "The Christology of Matthew," in *Who Do You Say That I Am?* 20.

sins. The route he will take to Jerusalem will not be one of political and military conquest but of suffering, dying, and rising again (16:21). Jesus has been revealing in his miraculous ministry his role as the anticipated Suffering Servant (cf. 8:17), but now he explicitly reveals that this is the Father's purpose for his life.

So to discover Jesus' identity and mission, Matthew's readers, including modern readers, must not decipher it according to their own understanding but give over their minds and their hearts to God's revelation. It is only in doing so that we will find the true life that comes, paradoxically, from Jesus' cross, and the cross that all those must take up who want to follow him (16:24–27).

**Jesus' church and the kingdom of heaven.** Arising from a God-revealed awareness of Jesus' identity and mission comes a clarification of God's purposes throughout history. Jesus' announcement of the kingdom reveals God's purposes in a way not fully understood by most people. Jesus' pronouncements to Peter about his role in the foundation of the church and entrance to the kingdom reveal some important markers of God's purposes in this age.

(1) One mark of God's purposes in this age is the relationship of Jesus to Israel. Jesus came as a Jew to the Jewish people with the offer of the kingdom of God. But, by and large, Israel rejected Jesus and his message about the kingdom. Nonetheless, a substantial group within Israel did respond in faith. Discipleship to Jesus was commitment to him, which meant that a new disciple could enter into the presence of the kingdom of God in the person of Jesus.

The kingdom, therefore, has entered history in the person of Jesus, and its blessings are demonstrated in the lives of his disciples.[74] While some suggest that as the recipients of messianic salvation they replace Israel,[75] several passages lead us to conclude that Israel will still have a role in the future. We will later see that the role of carrying out God's purposes through his kingdom has been taken away from the nation of Israel in the present age, and that Jesus' disciples currently enjoy both the blessings of the kingdom and the role of carrying the message of the gospel (21:43). But Israel is still kept in view as someday receiving the eschatological fulfillment of Jesus' kingdom promises (Matt. 10:23; 23:37–39; cf. Rom. 11:25–32; 15:7–13; Rev. 7:1–8).[76] The Twelve represent the fulfillment in part of the promises to Israel, but they do not replace Israel or become Israel.

---

74. Cf. Ladd, *Theology of the New Testament*, 104–6.

75. Ladd is representative of this view: "Jesus' disciples are the recipients of the messianic salvation, the people of the Kingdom, the true Israel" (*Theology of the New Testament*, 106).

76. E.g., Scott Hafemann, "Eschatology and Ethics: The Future of Israel and the Nations in Romans 15:1–13," *TynBul* 51 (2000): 161–92.

(2) Furthermore, the juxtaposition of sayings concerning the church (16:18) and the kingdom of heaven (16:19) gives us further clarification about God's purposes during this present age. As we noted earlier in Jesus' ministry, although the kingdom has been inaugurated, its full establishment awaits a future arrival of the King in glory. Therefore, this passage helps us to understand four points about the relationship of the kingdom and the church. (a) The kingdom of God is not the same as the church. The kingdom is the presence of the king who has come to inaugurate the fulfillment of God's salvation-historical redemptive plan by establishing the new covenant blessings of the Spirit. Confession and forgiveness of sin by God allows one to enter it.

(b) The arrival of the kingdom with its salvation-historical fulfillment of God's plan of redemption creates the church. Jesus challenged men and women to respond to him and enter the kingdom (5:20), which brought them into a new discipleship fellowship in Jesus (12:46–50). The community he created and will build in this age is the church, which is made up of people who have responded to his invitation and entered into the kingdom in the name of the king and now enjoy the blessings of the new covenant. Those who respond to this invitation and receive the work of the Spirit in their lives in regeneration and sanctification in this age are those who make up the body of Christ, the church.

(c) The church has as its central mission to proclaim the reality of the presence of kingdom of God. It must display in this present evil age the life and fellowship of the reality of the kingdom of God, which is an anticipatory witness to the full establishment of the kingdom in power in the age to come. This witness is especially evident in the humility that disciples display as they serve others, not themselves (20:20–28), and in the forgiveness that those who have been forgiven display as they forgive others (18:23–35).

(d) The church is the guardian and instrument of the kingdom. The declaration to Peter that he will be given the keys to the kingdom of heaven indicates that Peter is the one who offers the message that allows entrance to the kingdom. Peter used the keys to open the doors of the kingdom to all people (16:18); that was a one-time act in history. However, all disciples use the same principle as they carry out the Great Commission (28:18–20), declaring the terms under which God forgives sin and allows entrance to the kingdom (cf. 18:15–20; John 20:22–23). The church during this age is the instrument by which the presence of the kingdom is made known through the work of the Spirit.[77] And with the resurrection of Jesus the power of

---

77. Cf. Ladd, *Theology of the New Testament*, 106–14.

death is broken, a sure promise that the gates of Hades will not prevail against the church (Matt. 16:18).

(3) The selection of twelve disciples/apostles shows both continuity with Israel and discontinuity. The church, no longer Israel, is the primary witness to and guardian of the gospel message in this present age. However, this does not deny Israel its future role as witness (e.g., Rev. 7:1–8), nor does it replace Israel's promise of being recipients of the gospel message as a nation (Matt. 10:23; 23:37–39; Rom. 11:25–33; 15:7–13). At some time in the future, repentant Israel[78] will again play a central role, but in this age the church as the body of Christ is the visible manifestation of the reality of kingdom life.

**Peter's role.** This is by far the most important passage in Matthew concerning the role of Peter. Jesus' pronouncement reveals at least six significant features.[79]

(1) Peter personally is the recipient of revelation from the Father, which makes him blessed. Peter functions as a leader of the Twelve by acting as their spokesman in his confession, and Jesus designates him to have a personal leadership role in the foundation of the church and in the use of the keys of the kingdom.

(2) Peter acts as the spokesman for the disciples. As he declares Jesus' identity, Peter's confession represents the confession of all of the disciples. Therefore, as he receives blessing and honor, Peter represents the blessing and honor that all disciples receive.

(3) Peter functions in at least two important ways in the early days of the church. On the one hand, he leads the church as the confessor. His revelation from the Father and his personal courage to give his confession leads all of the disciples into a clearer understanding of Jesus' identity and mission. This plays a foundational role and sets a trajectory for the ongoing confession of the church and its future growth. On the other hand, Peter leads the fledgling church to accept all peoples as recipients of God's kingdom blessings. His presence on three critical occasions (Acts 2, 8, 10) signified that God had bestowed his Spirit on all peoples—Jews, Samaritans, and Gentiles. As the utilizer of the keys of the kingdom of heaven, Peter signifies that God has opened the door of salvation-historical blessing for all peoples.

(4) Peter is especially recognized for all he says and does among the disciples, but is never said to rise above them. His leadership is from within; it is a *primus inter pares* ("first among equals"). Peter will function foundationally in the church, but the other apostles will share a foundational role in the church as well (Eph. 2:20). Although Peter alone receives the keys of the

---

78. E.g., Zech. 12:10–14.
79. For extended discussion, see Wilkins, *The Concept of Disciple in Matthew's Gospel*, 208–16.

---

kingdom, he shares with the disciples the binding and loosing of sins for exclusion or entrance to the kingdom once the doors are opened (Matt. 18:18; John 20:23).

(5) Because of the personal nature of the passage, all that is directed to Peter is temporally limited to his lifetime. It is therefore right for us to give due regard to this blessed apostle as one used in a special way in opening the doors of the kingdom of God and in the establishment of the church. But nowhere does Jesus indicate that Peter will play a perpetual role through successors.

(6) Peter represents all the disciples, and since the disciples in Matthew serve as an example for all believers,[80] Peter acts as a personal example for all believers. His confession is a model confession for all believers. His courage in stepping forward exemplifies boldness in the face of diverse opinions about Jesus. The way he acts as a spokesman typifies boldness. He is also an example of how entrance is made to the kingdom: through confession and forgiveness of sin. At the same time, with his unique role as a leader among the Twelve, Peter functions as an example for all church leaders. But as we have seen, Peter is also a negative example, as when he follows his own thinking in trying to deter Jesus from the pathway to the cross.

CONSISTENCY. My wife and I raised our daughters and still live in a nice beach community in Southern California, located about halfway between the metropolises of Los Angeles and San Diego. Two blocks from our house is one of my favorite surf spots. The incoming ocean swells encounter a submerged reef about a hundred yards offshore, causing waves to form and break in deep water. The waves take shape like a big A-frame in a center peak that peel off for both right and left hand rides. Taking off on one of those waves, a person can carve the face of the wave all the way in, where on the inside beach-break the wave reforms for a nice barrel ride.

But although this is a really good wave, I've only surfed there maybe two or three times in the last year. That may seem surprising. If this place is so good, why don't I surf there more often? Am I too busy? No, I try to surf other places at least once a week. Is it too dangerous? No, it's deep enough so there is no real danger of hitting the reef. Is it too crowded? No, you hardly ever see anyone surfing there. Are there sharks there? No again.

Then why don't I surf there more often? One word—*consistency*. On a good day, when the circumstances are just right, when the swell is big enough

---

80. This aspect of discipleship is central to Matthew's theological purposes and a foundation mark of Jesus' entire earthly ministry; cf. Wilkins, *Following the Master*, 174–93.

and the tide is low enough, and all the conditions are just right, this place breaks beautifully. But on a bad day, you won't see any wave out there. That's why our local break isn't known as a great surf spot, for the circumstances determine the wave. And the right configuration of circumstances happens sometimes only once or twice a year, if that.

Now you may wonder where I'm going with this, but we don't have to look too far when we consider the characters in this chapter. A key element for Peter and the rest of the disciples is learning *consistency* in their discipleship to Jesus. That means especially not allowing their circumstances to determine their faithfulness.

The disciples' lifelong story emphasizes for us the astonishing grace and gentle, restoring power available in Jesus. None of us has failed so many times that God cannot use us for his successful purposes. But we must learn to continue to focus consistently on Jesus instead of becoming unsettled by circumstances we have never encountered before. This is a major key for consistent discipleship. We can rely on his presence in our lives whatever the circumstances. He will be there to help us make the right decisions, to give us courage in the face of temptation or opposition, or to comfort us in sorrowful situations. This is a vital ingredient for a Christlike life in this world.

The apostle Peter stands throughout history as a significant example of this principle. His personal potential was noteworthy. He was a successful fisherman in the most important Galilean industry. He was a partner in a flourishing business and a homeowner in an area of dire poverty. He was a Jew committed to accepting the unfolding revelation and establishment of God's salvation-historical program in history. He displayed remarkable courage, spiritual sensitivity, openness to God's revelation, and willingness to be used in the establishment of God's purposes on this earth. But he also was swayed by the circumstances of personal fear, public opinion, political trends, and religious legalism.

It is easy for us to judge Peter. But if I am honest with myself, I see my own propensities to be swayed by the variation of my circumstances. I need to appreciate deeply the powerful, courageous stand and role that Peter played in the outworking of salvation history. Yet I must also learn from Peter's failures. Again, the key is consistency. If we want to be significant in the outworking of God's plan, we must yield ourselves consistently to his leading in our lives.

Peter's greatness in his role in the early church did not come from his personal abilities or giftedness. What led to Peter's great role in church history ultimately comes down to the development of consistency in his commitment to Jesus in all areas of his life. He was able to give himself consistently to God's ways, God's work, God's will—not his own—whatever the circumstances. For that Peter becomes an important example of the way in which our lives can count for God in his calling in our lives—at our work, in our families, in our church, and in our neighborhood—when we develop consistency in our commitment to Jesus as our Master.

Therefore, in Matthew 16 we can see at least three areas where we must develop consistency in our daily walk with Jesus, regardless of our circumstances: consistency in our spiritual perception and reception, consistency in our motivation to know Jesus on his terms rather than ours, and consistency in our willingness to live with the cross.

(1) *Consistency in spiritual perception and reception.* The perceptiveness of our hearts is different from the perceptiveness of our intellect or mind. We may be the smartest people intellectually with reference to the material world, but we can also be blind to realities that should guide our spiritual development. Often the fundamental problem is an issue of spiritual receptivity. A heart open to spiritual cues will hear God's voice, whereas a heart hardened against God cannot hear him or see him.[81] Matthew draws a continual contrast between bad and good receptivity to Jesus. The religious leaders reject him, guarding their spiritual blindness with a desire for a "sign," while Jesus' disciples are learning to be open to him. Jesus refuses to give a sign to the religious leaders because he knows no sign will convince them. But an indication of faithful discipleship is receptivity to the Father's revelation of Jesus' identity, even if the disciples do falter.

For us, too, openness to God as his disciples is related to spiritual perception. Jesus is still looking for obedient disciples who have hearts that are sensitive enough to hear God and to respond to his guidance. As Dallas Willard writes, "Hearing God—as a reliable, day-to-day reality for people with good sense—is for those who are devoted to the glory of God and the advancement of his kingdom. It is for the disciple of Jesus Christ who has no higher preference than to be like him."[82]

The voice of God is heard first in the Word of God, but also is heard in the wisdom of godly counsel, in the daily ordering of our path, and in his providential care for our daily lives. Willard comments further on those who consistently say that they do not hear the voice of God and therefore are not obedient to him: "Perhaps we do not hear the voice because we do not expect to hear it. Then again, perhaps we do not expect it because we know that we fully intend to run our lives on our own and have never seriously considered anything else."[83] Obedient discipleship means being receptive to God's voice.

---

81. Hagner, *Matthew*, 2:456.

82. Dallas Willard, *Hearing God: Developing a Conversational Relationship with God* (Downers Grove, Ill.: InterVarsity Press, 1999), 70.

83. Ibid., 71.

---

A specific issue in this passage illustrates the point that sensitivity to Jesus' teaching and trust in him opens the door to spiritual growth. Lack of trust that focuses too much on trivial concerns prevents us from understanding or even hearing the message of Jesus. The issue surfaces with what may seem like an insignificant narrative aside: "When they went across the lake, the disciples forgot to take bread" (16:5). This little notation is a hint of something deeper, because an intriguing interchange immediately occurs between Jesus and the disciples. They are confused about their own forgetfulness about bringing provisions for the trip and what they hear in Jesus' teaching on the yeast of the Pharisees and Sadducees. This distraction over their own inadequacy prevents them from hearing Jesus' real teaching. Only because Jesus persistently probes their obtuseness and explains what he really means are they able finally to get his point. They have not learned appropriate dependence on Jesus to care for their needs.

The disciples should have been prepared. They have just witnessed the feeding of both the five thousand and the four thousand (14:15–21; 15:32–38), so they should be ready to allow Jesus to take care of their material needs, even if their own forgetfulness gets them into difficulty. And they should have remembered clearly Jesus' earlier teaching in the Sermon on the Mount, where they were taught to pray, "Give us today our daily bread" (6:11), and where they were admonished not to worry about what to eat or drink or wear (6:31). When Jesus' disciples seek first the kingdom, their Father will supply what they need (6:32–33).

This is a tangible example of what it means to seek first the kingdom of God—placing ourselves in a position where we can learn from Jesus about spiritual realities and then receiving what he desires to give us. We are each called to do so. The disciples get into the boat, so they are in physical proximity to learn. But the condition of their spiritual hearts does not allow them to receive his teachings. Their forgetfulness about their personal responsibility to bring bread causes them to be distracted, so they cannot attune their "spiritual ears" to really hear Jesus' message. Moreover, their forgetfulness about Jesus' providential care for their needs in the past causes them to overlook his provision in the present.

That is an important balance. One side of the balance focuses on our responsibility. Appropriate attention to our daily responsibilities—paying our bills, spending time with our children, doing our homework, caring for the elderly neighbor—lessens the emotional distractions that keep us from hearing God's voice. We can sometimes become so distraught because of our failures that we tune God out. Remember that the devil wants us so discouraged when we've failed that we think that God doesn't care about us any more.

The other side of the balance focuses on God's providential care. God is the One who supplies all that we have, even if we think that it is through our own successful education that we receive a job, that it is through our own careful manipulation of our budget that we are able to care for our children's educational needs, or that it is through our own brilliant industriousness that we have received a promotion that enabled us to give to the church fund. The difference between us and pagans is that we know and experience God's hand in every area of our lives. But it takes careful spiritual sensitivity to see his hand. Each time we see his hand operate in our lives, it strengthens our confident reliance on his sustaining hand in the future.

A right kind of balance lives daily, moment by moment, with both truths. One of the most wonderful experiences of our family life has been learning, often with great difficulty, how to live out this balance. For most of our married life my wife and I, and later our children, lived from month to month. We watched carefully our budget and didn't get into debt. But at several critical junctures God called us to make sacrifices. For a control person like me, it was difficult not to know for sure how the bills would be paid that month. But in each time of sacrifice he miraculously provided for our needs: going to seminary, doing a church planting, starting doctoral work, and leaving a significant income to teach in a Christian college and seminary.

In each of those situations we continued to watch our budget closely and never went into debt, but when we heard God's voice calling us to a time of sacrificial service, we knew that he would not call us to anything for which he did not supply our needs. I would literally moan and groan and pull at my hair at the beginning of the month as I looked at the budget books. We had been so scrupulous about groceries and buying our daughters adequate clothing, but the month ahead looked bleak. But during the month I'd get an unexpected odd job. Or the family across the street brought over a supply of groceries from the family reunion that didn't come off. Or my wife's parents would say that they got an unexpected bonus check and wanted us to have it. I'm an overly proud person and often resisted these acts as though they were an affront to my adequacy. But my wife, who is often much more spiritually attuned to God's graciousness, would point to God's hand behind the act. Each time that we saw his providential care, we were more firmly prepared to trust him at the next time of need.

This reinforces the importance of placing ourselves in proximity to where we can learn, such as in a church setting or an individual or group Bible study. But mere proximity doesn't guarantee adequate reception. Our receptivity to God's leading and teaching must balance appropriate personal responsibility with adequate reliance on God's provision.

(2) *Consistency in knowing Jesus on his terms, not ours.* As we have seen at regular stages through Matthew's Gospel, consistency was an urgent need for Peter's development. Peter had his own ideas about the path of the Messiah, but he needed to know God's plans. God's ways are often different from our human ways. Peter partially understood Jesus' messiahship, but when it came to an aspect of God's program that he did not understand (i.e., Jesus' going to the cross), he tried to force it into his own understanding. Jesus then referred to him as a "stumbling block." This was an ominous pronouncement, for it shows that without consistency in his sensitivity to God's will, Peter "the rock" becomes Peter "the stumbling stone." Peter has set his mind on human interests, not God's (cf. 16:21–23).

Peter is often described as a person who is "up and down" in his spiritual development, which we have graphically displayed on page 31 in the introduction. In this passage Peter goes from the highest high to the lowest low. I doubt that there is a Christian who has not shuddered at the potential consequences for Peter, but also for all of us as followers of Jesus, and especially for Christian leaders. We must cling to the restoring grace of God, because in the next chapter Peter will be called with the others in the inner circle to witness Jesus' transfiguration (17:1). Peter will continue his up-and-down pattern until that fateful time when he denies Jesus. With the coming of the Spirit at Pentecost we can see a dramatic empowering, although he will continue to experience highs and lows in his spiritual development.

The one primary lesson that I take away from Peter's experiences is that I must not force Jesus into my own understanding but must allow his presence in my life to transform me into his image. That means that in my own personal life as well as in my life as a Christian leader, I must know my God-given potential and then focus on maximizing all to which God has called us. Peter likely got carried away with his importance as the "rock man" and overstepped his responsibilities. At times his passion for living bordered on arrogance. No self-respecting disciple of a rabbi in the first century would have dared rebuke his teacher. Yet Peter tried to hinder Jesus, whom he had just declared to be more than any other rabbi. This was a satanically induced temptation to determine Jesus' fate.

Arrogance, cockiness, and self-sufficiency are all counterfeits of confidence. Confidence is simply the recognition of what God has given us to do and that we can do it in his strength. To conduct ourselves appropriately as Jesus' disciples is to understand that we can do nothing of eternal value apart from clearly knowing his will and to experience deeply his enablement. We can each display a rocklike consistency in our lives if we know who we are as created and gifted and called by God (and no more!), and if we then commit ourselves to maximizing all God wants to do through us as his uniquely gifted vessels. To do so is to be motivated only to know Jesus on his own terms, not ours, and to take his calling on our life with deadly seriousness—but not take ourselves too seriously in the process.

(3) *Consistency in living with the cross as both invitation and instruction.* Another way of learning consistency in our discipleship to Jesus is illustrated by the metaphor of the cross. It not only is the cruel instrument of Jesus' death and the symbol of the purpose for his incarnation, but it is also emblematic for following him in our own lives. Consistency in our discipleship involves a continual willingness to live with the cross, because taking up our cross to follow Jesus involves both the initiation of the Christian life as well as the ongoing standard of discipleship.

A comparison of the parallel in Mark's Gospel makes this plain. Mark 8:34 tells us that along with directing this saying to the disciples, Jesus calls the crowds and addresses the saying to them as well. This follows a regular pattern in the Gospels. When Jesus addresses the crowds, he is *inviting* them to enter the kingdom of God to find salvation in discipleship to him—evangelism. When he addresses the disciples, he is *instructing* them about their developing life of discipleship—edification (see comments on 5:1–2). Therefore, this saying not only characterizes the way that we enter into the Christian life of discipleship, but also the way in which our devotion to Jesus develops.

This ongoing kind of denial, cross-bearing, and following Jesus is not meant for solitary periods of isolation from regular life, regardless of how helpful some may find those times. Rather, Jesus shows how we are to conduct ourselves in the everyday routines of life. We must learn consistency in living with the cross. To deny ourselves and take up our cross points to the overriding principle of adopting God's will for our lives over our own will. This initiates our discipleship as we find God's gracious salvation through Jesus' own sacrifice of his will to accomplish our redemption on the cross.

But denying our own will for our lives in exchange for God's will should also characterize our discipleship to Jesus. Do we regularly, day by day, moment by moment, examine what we want in the light of what God wants for us? The further we get along in the kind of exchange, the further our hearts are transformed to love like Jesus (John 13:34–35; 15:12) and the more our minds are trained to think like Jesus (Rom. 12:1–2; Phil. 2:5). We will then experience the kind of life where our daily actions reflect him (2 Cor. 3:16), and the kinds of prayers where we can ask anything in Jesus' name and have it answered (John 15:7).[84]

---

84. Matthew hints at this in the construction of the saying. He switches from the aorist imperatives "deny himself" and "take up his cross" to the present imperative "follow me," which suggests the ongoing life of following him (cf. Turner, *Syntax,* 76).

We should note also that Jesus, in directing this teaching to the disciples, is calling them to evaluate themselves even after having made a commitment. He must be poignantly directing this at least in part to Judas, who has not truly denied himself and taken up his cross to follow Jesus. He is a false disciple. He remains his own man, not truly Jesus' man, with his own eternal dark destiny of judgment. We should not emphasize examining ourselves so heavily that we dissolve the confidence that we should have when we believe on Jesus as the true Son of God for eternal life (cf. 1 John 5:13—15). But persons who have truly denied themselves and have taken up the cross will stand out in this world as they follow Jesus and live his kingdom values in transformed lives.

# Matthew 17:1–27

A FTER SIX DAYS Jesus took with him Peter, James and John the brother of James, and led them up a high mountain by themselves. ²There he was transfigured before them. His face shone like the sun, and his clothes became as white as the light. ³Just then there appeared before them Moses and Elijah, talking with Jesus.

⁴Peter said to Jesus, "Lord, it is good for us to be here. If you wish, I will put up three shelters—one for you, one for Moses and one for Elijah."

⁵While he was still speaking, a bright cloud enveloped them, and a voice from the cloud said, "This is my Son, whom I love; with him I am well pleased. Listen to him!"

⁶When the disciples heard this, they fell facedown to the ground, terrified. ⁷But Jesus came and touched them. "Get up," he said. "Don't be afraid." ⁸When they looked up, they saw no one except Jesus.

⁹As they were coming down the mountain, Jesus instructed them, "Don't tell anyone what you have seen, until the Son of Man has been raised from the dead."

¹⁰The disciples asked him, "Why then do the teachers of the law say that Elijah must come first?"

¹¹Jesus replied, "To be sure, Elijah comes and will restore all things. ¹²But I tell you, Elijah has already come, and they did not recognize him, but have done to him everything they wished. In the same way the Son of Man is going to suffer at their hands." ¹³Then the disciples understood that he was talking to them about John the Baptist.

¹⁴When they came to the crowd, a man approached Jesus and knelt before him. ¹⁵"Lord, have mercy on my son," he said. "He has seizures and is suffering greatly. He often falls into the fire or into the water. ¹⁶I brought him to your disciples, but they could not heal him."

¹⁷"O unbelieving and perverse generation," Jesus replied, "how long shall I stay with you? How long shall I put up with you? Bring the boy here to me." ¹⁸Jesus rebuked the demon, and it came out of the boy, and he was healed from that moment.

¹⁹Then the disciples came to Jesus in private and asked, "Why couldn't we drive it out?"

²⁰He replied, "Because you have so little faith. I tell you the truth, if you have faith as small as a mustard seed, you can say to this mountain, 'Move from here to there' and it will move. Nothing will be impossible for you. "

²²When they came together in Galilee, he said to them, "The Son of Man is going to be betrayed into the hands of men. ²³They will kill him, and on the third day he will be raised to life." And the disciples were filled with grief.

²⁴After Jesus and his disciples arrived in Capernaum, the collectors of the two-drachma tax came to Peter and asked, "Doesn't your teacher pay the temple tax?"

²⁵"Yes, he does," he replied.

When Peter came into the house, Jesus was the first to speak. "What do you think, Simon?" he asked. "From whom do the kings of the earth collect duty and taxes—from their own sons or from others?"

²⁶"From others," Peter answered.

"Then the sons are exempt," Jesus said to him. ²⁷"But so that we may not offend them, go to the lake and throw out your line. Take the first fish you catch; open its mouth and you will find a four-drachma coin. Take it and give it to them for my tax and yours."

AFTER RECEIVING PETER'S confession of his identity as the Messiah, the Son of the living God, and after giving the first prediction of his suffering and resurrection, Jesus directs his earthly ministry toward the final preparation of his disciples for the impending events of Passion Week. In chapter 17 Jesus reveals his divine glory in the Transfiguration (17:1–8), and Matthew shows us (1) how the ministry of John the Baptist's ministry does, yet does not, fulfill the prophesied arrival of Elijah the prophet (17:9–13), (2) how unbelief and ineffective belief can thwart God's will (17:14–22), (3) how Jesus' impending death will come about through betrayal (17:22–23), and (4) how institutional religious rules have no claim on him or his disciples (17:24–27).

## The Transfiguration of Jesus (17:1–8)

A HIGH MOUNTAIN (17:1). On the seventh day after the climactic events of Peter's confession and Jesus' first prediction of his suffering and death, the even more dramatic event of Jesus' transfiguration occurs. Apparently Jesus stays for a week with the disciples, probably the Twelve and some others (cf. 16:13), in the area around Caesarea Philippi.[1] Jesus takes with him the inner circle of disciples—Peter, James, and John—and goes up "a high mountain." Luke tells us that the purpose for this was to pray (Luke 9:28). However, Jesus is also probably taking the inner circle to give them extra experience for their future leadership roles within the church.

This mountain is not identified. Mount Tabor has been favored by much of church tradition. It is only six miles from Nazareth and twelve miles from the Sea of Galilee, but few today contend for this as the site, primarily because we now know that it was occupied by a Roman garrison during Jesus' time. Moreover, since Matthew seems to imply the mountain is outside of Galilee (cf. 17:22), most scholars favor Mount Hermon. Jesus and the disciples have been in the region of Caesarea Philippi, and this mountain is immediately accessible. It is the most majestic peak in the region, rising 9,166 feet about sea level. Its primary peak is snow-capped for much of the year, with a series of two other peaks rising at less altitude. If this is the location, Jesus and the disciples probably do not ascend to the top but go to a secluded spot.

The primary difficulty with identifying Mount Hermon with the transfiguration scene is that when Jesus and the others descend from the mountain, they are met by a crowd of people and a man seeking healing from Jesus, among whom are "teachers of the law" (Mark 9:14). This is an unlikely scene for a pagan region. Nevertheless, Mount Hermon remains the most likely spot, although it is still debated.[2]

**Jesus is transfigured (17:2).** The urgency of the preceding call for the disciples to take up their cross in the light of Jesus' soon-coming glory (cf. 16:24–28) is now readily understood, because three of them receive an unmistakable revelation of Jesus' identity. There must be no hesitancy or delay in following Jesus with all one's heart and soul, for unreserved commitment to Jesus Messiah is required from those who have witnessed his glory.

The Synoptic Gospels indicate that while Jesus is on the mountain with Peter, James, and John, he is "transfigured" (Mark 9:2–10; Luke 9:28–36). Matthew uses the passive of the verb *metamorphoo*, indicating that God is behind the transformation. Paul uses the same verb to describe the spiritual transformation that believers experience as a result of regeneration (Rom. 12:2; 2 Cor. 3:18). But here Jesus experiences a physical transformation visible to the disciples. It is a reminder of Jesus' preincarnate, divine glory (John

---

1. Alternatively, the reference to "after six days" (17:1) may signify the time it took to travel to the site where Jesus is transfigured.

2. For more discussion see Wilkins, "Matthew," 106 ("The 'High Mountain' of Jesus' Transfiguration").

1:14, 18; 17:5; Phil. 2:6—7) and a preview of his coming exaltation (2 Peter 1:16—18; Rev. 1:16). That glory designates the royal presence, for in his person the kingdom of God is with his people. The inner circle of disciples witness this profound revelation of Jesus' identity as well as his mission.

**Moses and Elijah appear (17:3).** During this transfiguration, two of the greatest Old Testament figures appear, Moses and Elijah. Their arrival represents the Law and the Prophets as witnesses to Jesus the Messiah, who fulfills the Old Testament (cf. 5:17). Moses is the one whom God used to give the Law, and Elijah is the one who connects the earlier charismatic prophecy of the days of Samuel with the later writing prophets. Moses is also considered the model prophet (Deut. 18:18) and Elijah the forerunner of Messiah (Mal. 4:5—6; cf. Matt. 3:1—3; 11:7—10).

Both Moses and Elijah had visions of the glory of God on a mountain—Moses on Mount Sinai (Ex. 24:15) and Elijah on Mount Horeb (1 Kings 19:8—16). Both of them had unique endings—Elijah was taken directly to heaven (2 Kings 2:11—12), while Moses, whose grave was never found (Deut. 34:6), is said by rabbinic tradition also to have been taken directly to heaven (cf. *As. Mos.; b. Soṭab* 13b). Both are mentioned together in Malachi 4:4—6: the giving of the Law through God's servant Moses and the sending of the prophet Elijah before the coming Day of the Lord. Their appearance on the mountain with Jesus indicates the greatness of Jesus, who transcends them both as the One who will be declared the Son of God.

**Peter's response (17:4).** Peter "answers,"[3] which indicates that he is stepping forward once again as a leader and spokesman for the others as he tries to respond to these spectacular appearances. This is the fourth of five incidents in which Matthew emphasizes a prominent role for Peter (14:28—31; 15:15; 16:17—19; 17:24—27; 18:21). Each incident reveals a forcefulness of character that will be used for his leadership role, but which also reveals that he is an imperfect leader in the process of growth.

It is difficult to understand Peter's comment and suggestion: "Lord, it is good for us to be here. If you wish, I will put up three shelters—one for you, one for Moses and one for Elijah." He may be indicating what a privilege it is for the three disciples to witness the event, although "good" seems rather weak. Or he may actually be posing a question, "Is it good for us to be here?"—voicing the fear that they may be experiencing at this frightening event.[4] The offer to build three "shelters" may recall the Old Testament

---

3. Lit., "And answering, Peter said"; this is a typical Matthean stylistic phraseology in his narrative (e.g., 3:15; 4:4; 8:8; 11:4; 16:16, 17); the NIV drops a reference to "answering."

4. Randall E. Otto, "The Fear Motivation in Peter's Offer to Build τρεῖς σκηνάς," *WTJ* 59 (1997): 101—12 (esp. 105).

tabernacle, since the word "tent" is the same one used in the LXX for the tabernacle (Ex. 25:9). But it also is the word used for the shelters erected for the Old Testament Feast of Tabernacles (Lev. 23:42).

Perhaps the best that can be made of Peter's suggestion is that he, in trying to make sense of this overwhelming transfiguration of Jesus and the appearance of these great figures, wishes to make some sort of memorial fitting to their stature. As the next verses indicate, however, Peter does not grasp fully the stature of Jesus, for he is not just another Old Testament figure like Moses and Elijah. Jesus is superior in every way, and his transfiguration confirms the eschatological inauguration of the kingdom of God.

**The Father's declaration (17:5).** The glorious scene continues, interrupting Peter's feeble attempt to make sense of the situation. A "bright cloud" appears, reminiscent of the way that God appeared at different times in the Old Testament. The cloud of God's presence appeared to Moses on Sinai (Ex. 34:5–7, 29–35), his Shekinah glory filled the tabernacle (40:34–35), the cloud of God's presence guided the Israelites during their wandering in the desert (13:21–22; 40:36–38), and the cloud of the glory of the Lord filled Solomon's temple (1 Kings 8:10–13). Isaiah looks ahead to the day when the Branch of the Lord will bring restoration to Jerusalem, as the cloud of the glory of the Lord shelters Zion (Isa. 4:1–6). The cloud of the glory of the Lord was recognized in Jewish literature as the time when the Messiah would gather his people and reveal the location of the ark of the covenant (2 Macc. 2:7–8).

The voice of God the Father from the cloud gives the same public endorsement of Jesus that was given at his baptism (see comments on 3:17), combining elements prophesied in Psalm 2:7 ("this is my Son") and Isaiah 42:1 ("with him I am well pleased"), indicating that Jesus is both Son and Suffering Servant. Jesus has fulfilled both the Law and the Prophets (cf. 5:17), now made clear in that he is superior to Moses and Elijah, whose revelations point ultimately to Jesus. Jesus is the embodied Son of God, the ultimate Prophet who fulfills Moses' prophetic expectation (Deut. 18:15–22), so the disciples must listen to him to understand his messianic mission. The gloriously transfigured Jesus Messiah will be the divine sacrifice on the cross (17:12), but he will be raised from the dead (17:9) to live forever as their messianic deliverer.

At the sound of the voice of the Father coming from the cloud of his presence, the disciples "fell facedown to the ground, terrified" (17:6). An experience of the awesome reality of God's presence commonly produced fear in the people of the Old Testament whether they observed the presence of God in a cloud or heard his voice.[5] But Jesus tenderly touches his frightened

---

5. See, e.g., Ex. 19:16; 20:18; 34:30; Deut. 4:33; 5:5, 23–27; Hab. 3:2–6, 16.

disciples and tells them not to fear (17:7). This gives them reassuring confirmation that he is the same Master that they have known, even though they have just experienced a stunning revelation of his divine nature.

When the disciples look up, they see no one except Jesus (17:8). Their focus is now exclusively on Jesus, the way Moses and Elijah would have desired, for their ultimate significance was in preparing the way for Messiah, the Son of God, and his redemptive mission.[6] The disciples have received the most explicit revelation of Jesus' identity, but they still do not comprehend fully what they have experienced.[7]

### John the Baptist and the Coming of Elijah (17:9–13)

THE NEED FOR SILENCE (17:9). As they are coming down the mountain, Jesus instructs the disciples for the final time not to tell anyone what they have seen (cf. 8:4; 9:30; 12:16; 16:20). They may tell others of the stupendous events of the Transfiguration only after he has been raised from the dead. Otherwise, the disciples and the crowd may think that Jesus' transfiguration and meeting with Moses and Elijah indicates that the time has come to effect national and military liberation, thus misunderstanding his mission. Jesus' message must be understood to focus on forgiveness of sins through his suffering on the cross. Through the Spirit of holiness, Jesus will be declared with power to be the Son of God by his resurrection from the dead (cf. Rom. 1:3); then all will finally understand who he is and what he has come to accomplish. (For comments on "Son of Man," see 8:20.)

**Elijah and John the Baptist (19:10–12).** The need for silence is immediately illustrated in the question the disciples ask: "Why then do the teachers of the law say that Elijah must come first?" After having seen Jesus transfigured and Elijah appear, Jesus' disciples do not understand how Malachi's prophecy of Elijah as the forerunner can be fulfilled in Jesus if he truly is the Messiah. Jesus is there with them, and Elijah has only now appeared on the mountain. He has not preceded Jesus, so how can Jesus be the fulfillment of Malachi's prophecy? The further talk of Jesus being raised from the dead confuses them even more.

Congruent with the prophecy that Elijah would come before the day of the Lord, Malachi prophesied that at that time all things will be restored, particularly the hearts of the fathers to their children and the hearts of the children to their fathers (Mal. 4:5–6). Jesus confirms that all things will be

---

6. Cf. Markus Öhler, "The Expectation of Elijah and the Presence of the Kingdom of God," *JBL* 118 (1999): 461–76.

7. See James A. Penner, "Revelation and Discipleship in Matthew's Transfiguration Account," *BibSac* 152 (April–June 1995): 201–10.

restored with Elijah's arrival (17:11), but to be clear, it is not Elijah who will restore all things, otherwise he would be the Messiah. Instead, John's appearance signaled the beginning of these events, indicating that the Messiah would soon arrive to carry them out.

So Jesus clarifies Malachi's prophecy in the light of John the Baptist's ministry, his own arrival, and the response of the people of Israel to both John's and Jesus' announcement of the kingdom of God—John's ministry was a partial fulfillment of Malachi's prophecy. "But I tell you, Elijah has already come, and they did not recognize him, but have done to him everything they wished. In the same way the Son of Man is going to suffer at their hands." Malachi's prophecy drew on the memory of Elijah as a fiery prophetic voice to point ahead to the time when another prophetic voice like Elijah's would announce God's restoration and judgment through the Messiah. Apparently some of the religious leaders misunderstood Malachi's prophecy to mean that Elijah would return personally. Their hope was focused primarily on a militaristic/political Elijah for a militaristic/political Messiah. But John the Baptist clarified that he was not a reincarnated Elijah (John 1:19– 27).[8] Reincarnation was a superstitious pagan belief.

The correct understanding of the prophecy is that John had come "in the spirit and power of Elijah" (Luke 1:17). John was the fulfillment of the arrival of the anticipated Elijah, in that he was the prophet sent by God to prepare the way for Jesus as Messiah (Matt. 3:1–3; 17:12–13). Had the people and religious leadership repented fully and accepted John's and Jesus' message of the gospel of the kingdom, John would have been the complete fulfillment of Malachi's prophecy (11:14). But neither John's nor Jesus' ministry was accepted fully. Instead, John was executed, as will be Jesus. Thus, the complete fulfillment of Malachi's promise of restoration and judgment cannot now be accomplished. Another Elijah-type figure will have to come in the future (17:11), again preparing the way, but then for the final consummation of the Day of the Lord prophesied in Malachi, preparing the way for the returning Son of Man who will at that time restore all things and bring God's wrath on the unrepentant.[9]

**The disciples understand (17:13).** Jesus' clarification of the role that the prophesied Elijah figure will play jogs the disciples' memory. Jesus had earlier connected John the Baptist with Malachi's prophecy (11:14), so now they understand the connection. In Matthew, understanding is a key ingre-

---

8. Commenting on John's vehement denial that he is Elijah, B. F. Westcott (*The Gospel According to St. John,* 2 vols. [London: John Murray, 1908], 18) comments: "The denial of the Baptist is directed to the Jewish expectation of the bodily return of Elijah."

9. The "two witnesses" (Rev. 11:3) are sometimes identified with Moses and Elijah.

dient of Jesus' disciples. But as we saw in the Parabolic Discourse, their understanding is not some special quality with which they have been endowed. Rather, it results from Jesus' teaching (see 13:10–17, 51).

We can observe this crucial distinction by comparing Mark and Matthew's narrative. On several important occasions Mark notes that the disciples do not understand who Jesus is or what he is talking about (Mark 6:52; 8:21; 9:10, 32), whereas in related passages Matthew says that the disciples come to understand the implications of what Jesus has said (Matt. 14:33; 16:12; 17:13, 23; cf. 13:51). Just as it served Mark's purpose to emphasize the profound historical and theological difficulty of understanding Jesus' identity and teaching, so Matthew goes one step further and clarifies how, in the midst of confusion and misunderstanding of each of those incidents, Jesus goes on to give teaching or revelation that finally brings the disciples to the point of understanding. Matthew emphasizes how Jesus and his teaching bring enlightenment in the path of discipleship.[10]

## The Healing and Exorcism of an Epileptic Boy (17:14–20)

JESUS AND THE inner circle of three disciples come down the mountain of transfiguration to rejoin the remaining disciples. The next scene appears to be in a Jewish setting, because Mark tells us that teachers of the law are arguing with the disciples (cf. Mark 9:14). This may indicate either that they have traveled out of the Mount Hermon and Caesarea Philippi region into Galilee proper, or that the mountain is actually in a Jewish region. But it may also indicate that the teachers of the law have been tailing Jesus and his disciples wherever they go, looking for more evidence against them of violating the law (cf. 12:2; 15:1).

**The epileptic boy not healed by Jesus' disciples (17:14–16).** As they come down the mountain, a crowd has gathered because of an argument about the attempted healing of an epileptic boy. The boy's father approaches Jesus with great reverence and says, "Lord, have mercy on my son. . . . He has seizures and is suffering greatly. He often falls into the fire or into the water." The man respects Jesus as an esteemed pious master by calling him "Lord," but he goes beyond that to anticipate that Jesus can extend mercy to heal his son. He has apparently heard of Jesus' reputation as a miracle worker and seeks help for his beleaguered son. The boy's lack of control over motor skills causes him to suffer greatly.

While Jesus was on the mountain with the inner three, the father sought help from the remaining disciples. The father had such confidence in Jesus'

---

10. Cf. Wilkins, *Discipleship in the Ancient World*, 164–66.

ability to heal that he assumes that his disciples have this ability as well. But his confidence has been dashed: "I brought him to your disciples, but they could not heal him."

**The generation's "no faith" (17:17–18).** Jesus' response is noticeable insofar as he points beyond his disciples' inability to heal the boy and condemns the entire generation. "'O unbelieving and perverse generation,' Jesus replied, 'how long shall I stay with you? How long shall I put up with you?'" Jesus here points to all who have witnessed his miracles that have attested his identity as the long anticipated Messiah and calls them "unbelieving and perverse." "Unbelieving" (*apistos*) indicates that the current generation has not as a whole placed their faith in Jesus as the anticipated Messiah; "perverse" (*diestrammenos*) indicates that they have become distorted in their evaluation of Jesus, likely a result of their own willfulness in rejecting Jesus' demand for repentance as well as the influence of the religious leaders on them.

Jesus clearly understands that this world is not his real home ("how long shall I stay with you?") and that his departure is based at least in part on the recognition that this world will not fully turn to him ("how long shall I put up with you?"). He reveals a conscious understanding not only of the contrast between the glory of his transfiguration and the realities of this world, but of his heavenly origin with his Father. Jesus will only return to his heavenly glory after going through this world of demonic activity, faithlessness, and eventually the cross. Demonstrating that he has ultimate authority over the satanic source of this illness, he directs the father to bring the boy to him. Then Jesus rebukes the demon, it comes out of the boy, and he is immediately healed.

This is another incident in which the casting out of an evil spirit produces healing of a physical infirmity (cf. 9:32–33). It reveals a wholistic understanding of the interplay of spiritual and natural forces in this world. While not all illness or disease is a direct result of demonic activity, the fallenness of this world does impact our entire being. True healing involves the whole person—physical, emotional, and spiritual. The tendency for many of us in the modern world is to fragment people by not recognizing the way our human condition is intertwined.[11]

**The disciples' "little faith" (17:19–20).** Once they hear Jesus condemn that generation for having "no faith," his disciples come to him in private to

---

11. A recent example of this fragmentation is an editorial article I read on the causes of schizophrenia in the prestigious *New England Journal of Medicine*. The author acknowledged the complexities surrounding the causation of schizophrenia, but she focused almost exclusively on finding neurological causes, without mention of other possible causes, including spiritual or emotional. See Nancy C. Andreasen, "Understanding the Causes of Schizophrenia," *New England Journal of Medicine* 340 (1999): 645–47.

ask about their inability to exorcise the demon to heal the boy. Jesus says that it was because of their "little faith." The generation of Israel at that time is "unbelieving" (lit., "having no faith," 17:17), because as a whole it has not repented and believed in Jesus as their Messiah. The disciples do have faith in Jesus and his mission, but here it is not functioning properly; it is "little faith," or defective faith (17:20; see also comments on 13:58; 14:31). Apparently in the present incident the disciples were either relying on their own abilities to do the exorcism, or else they were doing something that God had not called them to do; perhaps they were trying to put on a show for their own acclaim.

**The accomplishments of "effective faith" (17:20).** Instead of the ineffective faith that the disciples have displayed, Jesus presents a memorable contrast to show what effective faith can accomplish: "I tell you the truth, if you have faith as small as a mustard seed, you can say to this mountain, 'Move from here to there' and it will move. Nothing will be impossible for you." Jesus does not point to the amount of faith but rather to its effectiveness. By using the contrast to the mustard seed, the smallest seed known in Palestine, he declares that even the smallest amount of faith can accomplish tremendous feats. The disciples' themselves would declare that they have a larger amount of faith than that the size of a mustard seed. So Jesus is getting them to look at the real nature of faith. It is not the *amount* of faith that is in question, but rather its *focus*.

Faith is not a particular substance, the more of which the disciples have, the more they can accomplish. It is not a gift of magic that can be manipulated at will. Rather, faith is confidence that we can do what God calls us to do—it is "taking God at his word." Therefore, the disciples should not place confidence in what they have but have confidence that if God calls them to do something, they can do it in his strength.

Moving a mountain is proverbial in Jewish literature for doing what is virtually impossible (Isa. 40:4; 49:11; 54:10; *b. Sanh.* 24a; cf. Matt. 21:21–22).[12] Faith simply means that if God calls a person to do something, it will be accomplished through his power and the person's obedience. Even the most absurd things from the world's point of view can be accomplished if God calls us to do it.

This whole section centers on "faith." Faith is either existent (as in the disciples) or non-existent (as in that generation), but it can also either be functioning effectively or defectively. Jesus does not so much condemn the little faith as he points out that if faith is placed in God's will and power, even though it is "little," all things can be accomplished. Even the smallest amount

---

12. Keener, *A Commentary on the Gospel of Matthew* (1999), 442.

of effective faith can move mountains; misdirected faith, even if it is of the largest amount, can do nothing.

## The Second Passion Prediction (17:22–23)

JESUS AND THE disciples now return to Galilee. This is the final visit to that region prior to the final journey to Jerusalem. Jesus gives his second prediction of the fate that awaits him there: "The Son of Man is going to be betrayed into the hands of men. They will kill him, and on the third day he will be raised to life." Jesus gave his first prediction of these impending events after the profound confession that Peter made of Jesus' identity (cf. 16:16–17). Now after the profound revelation of Jesus' divine nature as revealed in his transfiguration and the voice from the Father (17:1–9), he reveals again that he will be killed but raised to life (17:22–23). This is the Father's will for his life's mission, which will unfold step by step throughout the rest of Matthew's narrative. Thus, as the obedient Suffering Servant, Jesus resolutely gives himself to the redemptive sacrifice that lies behind the prediction and ahead of him as his ultimate task.

This second prediction adds an ominous element: Jesus will not just be arrested by the religious leaders—he will be betrayed. Along with an increased understanding of the tragedy ahead, the knowledge that a duplicitous, evil betrayal lies behind it causes the disciples to be "filled with grief." Little do they know they will experience even greater grief upon discovering that the traitorous betrayer is one of their own (cf. 26:21–25, 47–50; 27:3–5) and that they themselves will abandon Jesus at his moment of greatest human need (cf. 26:56).

## Paying the Temple Tax (17:24–27)

JESUS AND THE disciples arrive in Capernaum and are accosted by religious tax collectors with a question: "Doesn't your teacher pay the temple tax?" The Old Testament directed that at the annual census, each person over twenty had to give a half-shekel offering to the Lord for the support of the tabernacle (Ex. 30:11–16), which was later applied for the support of the temple. The half-shekel temple tax was the equivalent of the Greek silver *didrachma*, a "two-drachma piece" coin. But the most common coin used among the people was the denarius, equivalent to a day's wage. So those coming to collect the tax from one person would have received two denarii, since the *didrachmon* was seldom minted. Or two persons could have paid for their combined temple tax with the Tyrian *stater* or Greek *tetradrachma* (cf. 17:28).[13]

---

13. For a table of equivalent weights and coinage at the time of Jesus, see Wilkins, "Matthew," 116.

These collectors of the temple tax are not tax collectors of the sort Matthew had been prior to his call, who had worked for the Roman occupying forces (cf. 9:9). Rather, they represent the Jewish religious establishment in Jerusalem overseeing the temple. The high priest was in charge of collecting the temple offering. In the Diaspora on the fifteenth of Adar,[14] local community leaders collected the half-shekel tax by installing in conspicuous community centers containers similar to those found in the temple that were shaped like trumpets, into which the local people placed the temple tax.[15] In Palestine, representatives of the Jerusalem priesthood went throughout the land collecting the temple tax.[16]

Instead of approaching Jesus himself, the tax collectors approach Peter, the leader among his disciples, which may have been a practice in deference to the esteem of a popular teacher (cf. 9:11).[17] The grammatical structure of the question indicates that these temple tax agents are attempting to elicit an affirmative response: "He does pay the tax, doesn't he?" This may mask an attempt to embroil Jesus in a contemporary debate among the religious leaders about who should pay the tax.[18] These representatives from the temple establishment may have been attempting, with duplicity, to confirm charges of Jesus' disloyalty to the temple.

Peter knows of Jesus' loyalty to the law (5:17–19), so he answers in the affirmative. He is correct on one level, but once Jesus gets him alone in the house, he gives Peter a more profound insight to the issue. Jesus has apparently overheard the interaction. He calls Peter by his given name, "Simon," which is Jesus' usual way of referring to him in this book (except for 16:18–19). This leads to his question about the "duty and taxes," which are civil tolls and poll taxes that a ruler exacts from his subjects (see comments on 22:17). He asks: "From whom do the kings of the earth collect duty and taxes— from their own sons or from others?"

---

14. With annual variation, it occurs approximately in the middle of March.

15. See *m. Šeqal.* 1.3; 2.1; *y. Šeqal.* 6:1, 5; Josephus, *War* 5.5.2 §200; *Ant.* 18.9.1 §§312–13.

16. Cf. Josephus, *Life* 12 §§62–63. Powell, "Weights and Measures," pp. 905–8; Rousseau and Arav, "Temple, Treasury," *Jesus and His World*, 309–11; "Tax Collectors" and "Taxes," *DJBP*, 618–19.

17. They call him *didaskalos*, a title used commonly in Matthew to address Jesus by nondisciples; cf. 9:11; 12:38; 19:16; 22:16, 24, 36.

18. Evidence for this debate is found at Qumran, where some contended that the census tax had to be paid only once in a person's lifetime (4QOrdinances 1.6–7) and in *m. Šeqal.* 1.3–7. For overviews of the debate within Judaism, see W. Horbury, "The Temple Tax," *Jesus and the Politics of His Day*, ed. E. Bammel and C. F. D. Moule (Cambridge: Cambridge Univ. Press, 1984), 265–86; David E. Garland, "Matthew's Understanding of the Temple Tax (Matt. 17.24–7)," *SBLSP* 1987, ed. Kent H. Richards (Atlanta: Scholars Press, 1987), 190–209.

---

Peter's reply is expected: Rulers do not collect taxes from their own children but from their subjects. This completes the analogy, as Jesus concludes, "Then the sons are exempt." The temple is his Father's own house, so since Jesus is the Son of God his Father, he is exempt from the temple tax. And Jesus' disciples, now part of the Father's family (12:48–50), are likewise exempt. This is a profound Christological statement, indicating not only Jesus' relationship by analogy to his Father, the ultimate King, but also the way in which he is the fulfillment of the law. There will no longer be a need for sacrifice in the temple because his cross will be the final sacrifice (cf. Heb. 7:26–28). Hence, there will be no temple tax for Jesus' disciples.

Jesus, and by extension his disciples, are not under obligation to pay the tax. But so as not to offend the conscience of those Jews who have not yet experienced liberation through Jesus and his end to the temple, they will both pay the tax. For the Jews to go against their conscience by Jesus' example would lead them to sin. Here Jesus enunciates the principle of not giving offense to the Jerusalem authorities or "causing them to stumble" unnecessarily (*skandalizo*; cf. 1 Cor 8:13). This same principle later guides the apostle Paul in resolving problems for life among pagans (cf. Rom. 14:13–23; 1 Cor. 8:13–9:1, 12, 22).

To make a striking impression on his disciples that they will long remember, Jesus instructs Peter to throw out a fishing line, where he will find the coin for paying the tax. Although line and hook were used regularly for fishing on the Sea of Galilee, nets were the most effective means of commercial fishing (see 4:18–22). All other references to fishing in the New Testament indicate the use of a net. The fish known popularly, but probably inaccurately (since it feeds only on plankton), as "Saint Peter's Fish" in commemoration of this event, is the *musht*. Most likely Peter caught the *barbell*, a voracious predator of the carp family. The coin found in the fish's mouth was the *stater*, the equivalent of two *didrachmas*—hence, one shekel.[19]

The miracle is both of foreknowledge (cf. 21:2) and of divine provision. God may have arranged providentially for a fish to swallow a shiny coin at the lake's bottom, which is not an unknown phenomenon, or this may have been a uniquely arranged miracle. Either way it is a sign for the disciples, like the cursing of the fig tree (21:19), but here it indicates Jesus' superiority to the temple (cf. 12:6). The age of God's kingdom has dawned. The temple, which has stood as the ultimate hope of God's coming redemption and forgiveness of sins, now has its hopes fulfilled in Jesus' steadfast stride toward the cross.

---

19. For further discussion and a table of equivalent weights and coinage at the time of Jesus, see Wilkins, "Matthew," 116.

**Bridging Contexts**

THE EVENTS RECORDED in chapter 17 further clarify the revelations in chapter 16. The Transfiguration, the healing of the epileptic boy, and the miraculous provision of the temple tax confirm the reality of Jesus' true identity as the messianic Son of God (cf. 16:16–17), whose mission, quite askew of the common expectation, is to die and rise again. Matthew especially emphasizes how one must listen to Jesus' words about himself and follow his model of obedience to the Father, in which true life is found. The connection is Jesus' words about those who truly want to follow him is that they should take up their cross and lose their lives in finding real life (16:24–28). If they submit to God's will for their lives, only then will they find true life. One should do this since submitting to God's plan or failing to do so has eternal consequences.

However, Jesus' teachings often fell on reluctant or deaf ears. So in Jesus' transfiguration his disciples see the proof of his mission in a grand and powerful way, grounded in the Father's direct confirmation of Jesus' mission: "This is my Son. . . . Listen to him!" If they have not taken Jesus' words seriously before, they surely must now! Those events on the mountain had such a dramatic effect on Peter that he mentions them later as one of the profound confirmatory evidences of Jesus' true identity (2 Peter 1:16). They served not only to confirm Jesus' words about his present mission (reflected in the presence of Moses and Elijah being precursors to the Messiah) but they also foreshadowed his glorious state after his resurrection. The transfiguration cements and confirms in a powerful way Jesus' identity and mission.

**Proximity to Jesus can screen a clear vision of him.** Those with the privilege of close proximity to Jesus were often screened from fully comprehending his identity and mission by their own preconceptions. Peter and the other disciples were honored to have physical proximity to Jesus, yet that very closeness impeded them from comprehending the magnitude of his person and mission. They had preconceptions of what the Messiah was to be, which hindered them from seeing who Jesus actually was. They were so close to Jesus physically that they could not understand the immensity of his incarnation. Jesus was the man with whom they had walked and talked and shared meals. They believed him to be God's Messiah, the divinely endowed deliverer of Israel. But it took the transfiguration to drive home that he was not just divinely endowed but was actually himself divine.

Our own closeness to Jesus can also hinder us from seeing him for who he really is. We are privileged to have proximity to Jesus through the original disciples' preaching and writings, along with two thousand years of theological reflection. Through the careful formulations of church history, we have a precise understanding of the Trinitarian relationship of Father, Son, and Holy Spirit. We have an orthodox understanding of the hypostatic union of the two natures, human and divine, that constitute the one person, Jesus Christ. We have a more carefully formulated comprehension of Jesus than did even those first followers. Yet our familiarity with Jesus can screen us from realizing the sheer immensity of the truth of his incarnation. We can be so comfortable with our theological formulations that we lose the impact of the uniqueness of his person and work.

But God does not want us to be too comfortable, nor will he consign us to our propensities to blindness. As he continues to nudge Peter and the other disciples along toward fuller understanding, so he patiently continues to reveal himself to us through his Word so that we can align our awareness and expectations of Jesus' identity and mission to his own purposes. The social, religious, and philosophical barriers to a clear understanding of Jesus' identity and mission in the first century were overcome by the Father's intentional revelation, and those same barriers in our contemporary world can be overcome by heeding clearly the message that Matthew has recorded for our guidance.

**The mountain of transfiguration alters our worldview.** Peter's prior confession in 16:16–17 said even more than he understood. So in this scene on the mountain, God continues to nudge him and the other disciples to comprehend more fully Jesus' uniqueness. The disciples must recognize that Jesus is not another lawgiver, as great a privilege as that was for Moses. He is not just another prophet, as powerful a role as that was for Elijah. He is not even just a divinely endowed messianic deliverer, as significant as that was in the hopes and dreams of Israel. Instead, Jesus is the One to whom the greatest Old Testament figures, Moses and Elijah, defer. Jesus is himself in his very being divine, not just divinely endowed.

This is the stunning truth that thunders from the mountain of Jesus' transfiguration. The Father not only reveals the divine glory of Jesus' preexistent form (Phil. 2:5–7) and his end-time apocalyptic form (Dan. 7:13–14; Matt. 24:30), but he also reveals the glory that exists in Jesus as the Son of God at that very moment. The divine glory that he retained as the Son of God, but was hidden in his incarnation, is now transfigured to the outside world. Dale Bruner remarks that "what Jesus *was within* was once made visible without."[20] The theological function of the Transfiguration was to demonstrate to the disciples that the seemingly inauspicious history of Jesus always contained the divine dimension as the ontological Son of God.[21]

---

20. Bruner, *Matthew*, 2:602.
21. Ibid.

So the mountain of transfiguration demands a radical shift in the disciples' worldview. They cannot remain the same, for such an unthinkable reality had never before been considered, much less occurred. Jesus as the ontological Son of God in human form does not fit into any of their philosophical or religious or theological categories. So they must change. And the change will affect everything—every thought about reality, every activity in their religious behavior, every dream and ambition in their personal lives.

The shift in their worldview will come slowly, since it is too immense to handle at once. Peter shows that he doesn't quite yet get it when he attempts to put his arms around this truth by memorializing it. It remains for the events of the cross and resurrection and the coming of the regenerating and illuminating Spirit at Pentecost for the disciples to finally get it. And get it they do, because their view of the world was never the same after that. Their understandable fright on the mountain gave way to unthinkable courage as they went everywhere to proclaim the message of Jesus as Savior and God, which eventually challenged every religious, philosophical, and political establishment around the world.

Jesus' transfiguration also demands the transformation of our own worldview. When we see him for who he is truly as the ontological Son of God incarnate, it promises for us a completely new way of looking at reality. Jesus is, as John records, *the* way, *the* truth, and *the* life (John 14:6). Jesus is not just the only way to the Father, as vitally important as that is for life eternal, but he is the sole truth that brings all reality into focus, and he is the sole access in this world to the kind of life that allows us to live the way God intends us to live. If Jesus truly is the Son of God, which the events of his transfiguration declare him to be, then it demands that we view everything through his ordering of this world.

Our view of reality will never be the same once we allow Jesus to transform our worldview, whether in the realm of the religious or scientific or economic or political or social. All of the world's ideologies must be examined in the light of the revelation of Jesus that we see on this mountain. There cannot be a religious pluralism that makes all ways to God equally valid. There cannot be a scientific materialism that accounts for the origin of life or the explanation of reality apart from God. There cannot be a Marxist dialectical or historical materialism that accounts for a progress of history through class struggles. There cannot be a social objectivism that elevates the individual whose egoism and genius prevail over altruism, social conformism, and sacrifice for others.[22] With Jesus at the center of our worldview, all of these ideologies need to be adjusted.

---

22. As expressed in Ayn Rand's *The Fountainhead* (1943), *Atlas Shrugged* (1957), and *The Virtue of Selfishness* (1965).

---

Our view of this world will be transformed when we place Jesus, the Son of God, at the center of our reality. Not only ideologies, but also our daily priorities and values must be evaluated in the light of Jesus' revelation. After all, the Father declares, "Listen to him!" We must listen to his guidance on the way that we live our lives—how much television and what kind of movies we watch, the way we budget our income, the respect we display toward our spouses and children, the kind of car we drive, the style of clothes we wear, the language that proceeds from our mouths. Everything that we are is impacted by the centrality of Jesus in the way that we view the world and live in it as his disciples.

ON A LOCAL news broadcast the anchor ridiculed a recent advertisement. The ad that he mocked was entitled "What Would Jesus Drive?" He had a great deal of fun spoofing the Christians who had created the ad, convincing his viewers that Jesus probably wouldn't care at all, and if he did, he'd probably drive a donkey. I was a bit embarrassed at first, thinking that this was just another gimmick by Christian car salesmen trying to pitch their model of automobile. But as I looked into it more closely, I saw the point. In a recent issue of *Christianity Today*, there was a full-page ad with the same title, "What Would Jesus Drive?" placed beside The Evangelical Environmental Network (EEN). In the ad they make the following claims:

> Of all the choices we make as consumers, the cars we drive have the single biggest impact on all of God's creation. Car pollution causes illness and death, and most afflicts the elderly, poor, sick and young. It also contributes to global warming, putting millions at risk from drought, flood, hunger and homelessness.... Transportation is now a moral choice and an issue for Christian reflection. It's about more than engineering—it's about ethics. About obedience. About loving our neighbor. So what *would* Jesus drive?[23]

You may not agree with that argument, but the ad rightly challenges Christians to put Jesus' values at the center of our worldview. Not every Christian thinks through from the perspective of Jesus' values the car that he or she drives. But we should. We could say the same for our every action, every word, every thought, every choice. That is the impact that Jesus should have on us. His living presence in our lives radically challenges all that we are.

---

23. *Christianity Today* 47/1 (January 2003): 17. See also the website www.WhatWould-JesusDrive.org.

The picture of Jesus that we see displayed in this chapter is awesome. He is transfigured to show his divine relationship to his heavenly Father, which now places a radical challenge on our worldview and in turn affects all we do, say, and think. That is the impact he makes on those who surround him in these incidents. Matthew presents three primary scenes—from the mountain of transfiguration to the village of faulty faith to the sea of the miraculously supplied coin—to demonstrate the centrality of Jesus Messiah in God's program of salvation history and to persuade his followers to give him ultimate centrality in their worldview. This in turn affects all of our relationships, all of our ministries, and all of our priorities.

**Obedience means to listen to Jesus.** The stunning revelation of Jesus as the ontological Son of God on the mountain of transfiguration prompted an almost comical response from Peter about building three tents. We suggested above that Peter is probably doing his best to get his mental and spiritual arms around this stupendous revelation, so he stumbles around and suggests that he build a memorial. Then from out of the glorious cloud that envelopes them on the mountain, the voice of God the Father declares again his relationship to Jesus his Son and demands authoritatively, "Listen to him!" This is an overarching command that demonstrates that Jesus' ministry fulfills the law as represented in Moses and the Prophets as represented in Elijah.

Jesus is the unrivaled, authoritative revelation of God, and "mortal people should take heed to all that he says."[24] This especially goes for Peter, whose enthusiasm consistently causes him to stumble. It's as though the Father is saying, "Peter, if you really want to understand who Jesus is and what he has come to do, be quiet, stop trying to figure it out on your own, and listen to what he reveals to you." Throughout the rest of the chapter, and indeed throughout the rest of his ministry, Jesus will lead Peter and the others to a clearer comprehension, and all that is required is that they stop talking long enough to listen to him.

As rational, reasoning humans, we can go a long way toward understanding this world in which we live, but the revelation of God through Jesus is the final and ultimate word. Thus, we must learn to submit ourselves to the authority of Jesus, which means to evaluate our lives in the light of his revelation, being obedient to what he calls us to be and to do. Once we hear his words, we cannot pick and choose which ones we like. Hardship may accompany being one of his disciples, but if we want to find true life, we must embrace that to which he calls us.

**Faith means to stay focused on Jesus.** The second incident occurred in the village where the remaining disciples were not able to heal the epileptic

---

24. Morris, *Matthew*, 441.

boy. This is one of the most striking demonstrations of the function of faith in our personal lives and in our ministries. The generation of that day was described as being "without faith" (17:17) while Jesus' disciples were described as having "little faith" (17:20). That Jesus was not talking about the *amount* of faith in the disciples is indicated by the analogy to the smallest of all seeds, the mustard seed. Instead of amount, Jesus pointed to the *effectiveness* of faith. The smallest faith can accomplish the greatest deeds, such as moving a mountain, if it is properly focused. We do not accomplish anything on our own. It is God who is at work through us, and our role is to yield ourselves to him so that he can accomplish what he wants. Thus, the important thing once again is to listen to Jesus, hear what he calls us to do, and then simply say yes to his will for us.

I saw this up close in the first pastorate that my wife and I served. The wife of one of our elders was gravely ill and hospitalized. The doctors gave her only days to live. Her husband called me one evening and asked if I would gather the other elders and come to pray for her. I was a young and completely inexperienced pastor, but they looked to me to offer some hope. As we gathered in her hospital room, we prayed and anointed her. I went home that night exhausted with the ordeal of her condition but peaceful with the way in which we had placed her in God's hands. The next day her husband called early in the morning with intense excitement in his voice. His wife was showing improvement! The doctors were amazed at her recovery, and within two to three weeks she was released from the hospital. Although she was in her seventies and suffered repercussions from her illness, she went on to live four more years.

It was a miraculous healing that profoundly affected the entire church. One of the other elders in the church also had a bedridden wife, suffering from a severe spinal injury. She likewise asked us to come to pray over her. I was feeling as if a whole new ministry was opening up! As we gathered around her bed, we prayed the same prayers, used the same anointing, and had the same hope. But this woman was not healed. In fact, she got worse.

Did we have more faith when we prayed in the first incident than in the second? No, I don't believe so. I believe that we acted out of the same primary motivation: We were seeking God's will for each woman. In the first case it was God's will that she be healed; it wasn't God's will in the second case. We were God's instruments by which he demonstrated his will. The second woman later declared to us that not being healed was the best thing that ever happened to her, because she learned to rely on God in the middle of her suffering. This eventually led to her developing a ministry to others in like circumstances.

It is not the amount of our faith that works miracles. It is the focus of our faith on Jesus who will work miracles through us according to his will. Jesus' point is that anyone with any amount of faith can do the most unthinkable things, if that is what God has called us to do. Therefore, we should not place confidence in what we have; rather, we should be confident that if God calls us to do something, we can do it in his strength, even the most absurdly impossible-sounding things from the world's point of view. That is the primary point of the apostle John's statement, "This is the confidence we have in approaching God: that if we ask anything according to his will, he hears us. And if we know that he hears us—whatever we ask—we know that we have what we asked of him" (1 John 5:14–15).

**Freedom means the ability not to demand our rights, but to do the right thing.** The incident back at the Sea of Galilee where Jesus told Peter to find the coin in the fish's mouth for paying the temple tax has two important implications for us. (1) We have a preview here of the effect of Jesus' forthcoming atoning work on the cross. The temple ritual and sacrificial system are to be fulfilled by Jesus' own sacrifice, setting his disciples free from sin's bondage. The recognition of what Jesus will accomplish on the cross brings us to understand deeply the applicability of his sacrificial death, for which he has paid the price for our sins. Jesus will pay the ransom for our sin with his own life (20:28).

(2) We see in this incident that the freedom brought by Jesus' sacrifice now gives us the ability to do the right thing for others. As Jesus directs Peter to pay the temple tax so that it will not cause others to stumble into sin, he indicates that true freedom is not serving ourselves but in serving others. By paying the temple tax, even though he was free from the obligation to do so, Peter discovers he has another form of freedom—the ability to go beyond himself to serve others.

We often think of freedom as simply the ability to do what we want to do. There is truth in that concept. But there is another sense of freedom that comes from the biblical understanding of the effect of sin on humanity. Humanity after the fall does not have the ability to do consistently the right thing (cf. Rom. 3:9–18). Humanity is under the curse of sin, which chains us to self-centeredness and rebellion against what God wants us to do. But when we come to know the truth from Jesus about our sinfulness and receive his atoning sacrifice, we are set free from our bondage to sin (Rom. 6:1–14; cf. John 8:31–32). That freedom enables us to do the right thing, which we were not able to do before.

Therefore, true freedom does not mean the unrestricted ability to do whatever we want, but the ability to sacrifice ourselves for the good of others. This is the principle that the apostle Paul enunciated for the church as they attempted to live within their pagan culture with the varied practices that individual believers brought into the church from their diverse backgrounds (cf. Rom. 14:13–23; 1 Cor. 8:13–9:1, 12, 22). The kingdom life characterizes the church, and our walk of discipleship in this world is not so much about asserting our rights as it is the freedom to benefit and serve others. As Martin Luther stated, "A Christian is the most free lord of all, and subject to none; a Christian man is the most dutiful servant of all, and subject to every one."[25]

25. Martin Luther, "Concerning Christian Liberty," *The Harvard Classics*, trans. R. S. Grignon (New York: Collier & Son, 1910), 36:353.

# Matthew 18:1–35

A T THAT TIME the disciples came to Jesus and asked, "Who is the greatest in the kingdom of heaven?" ²He called a little child and had him stand among them. ³And he said: "I tell you the truth, unless you change and become like little children, you will never enter the kingdom of heaven. ⁴Therefore, whoever humbles himself like this child is the greatest in the kingdom of heaven.

⁵"And whoever welcomes a little child like this in my name welcomes me. ⁶But if anyone causes one of these little ones who believe in me to sin, it would be better for him to have a large millstone hung around his neck and to be drowned in the depths of the sea.

⁷"Woe to the world because of the things that cause people to sin! Such things must come, but woe to the man through whom they come! ⁸If your hand or your foot causes you to sin cut it off and throw it away. It is better for you to enter life maimed or crippled than to have two hands or two feet and be thrown into eternal fire. ⁹And if your eye causes you to sin, gouge it out and throw it away. It is better for you to enter life with one eye than to have two eyes and be thrown into the fire of hell.

¹⁰"See that you do not look down on one of these little ones. For I tell you that their angels in heaven always see the face of my Father in heaven.

¹²"What do you think? If a man owns a hundred sheep, and one of them wanders away, will he not leave the ninety-nine on the hills and go to look for the one that wandered off? ¹³And if he finds it, I tell you the truth, he is happier about that one sheep than about the ninety-nine that did not wander off. ¹⁴In the same way your Father in heaven is not willing that any of these little ones should be lost.

¹⁵"If your brother sins against you, go and show him his fault, just between the two of you. If he listens to you, you have won your brother over. ¹⁶But if he will not listen, take one or two others along, so that 'every matter may be established by the testimony of two or three witnesses.' ¹⁷If he refuses to listen to them, tell it to the church; and if he refuses

to listen even to the church, treat him as you would a pagan or a tax collector.

¹⁸"I tell you the truth, whatever you bind on earth will be bound in heaven, and whatever you loose on earth will be loosed in heaven.

¹⁹"Again, I tell you that if two of you on earth agree about anything you ask for, it will be done for you by my Father in heaven. ²⁰For where two or three come together in my name, there am I with them."

²¹Then Peter came to Jesus and asked, "Lord, how many times shall I forgive my brother when he sins against me? Up to seven times?"

²²Jesus answered, "I tell you, not seven times, but seventy-seven times.

²³"Therefore, the kingdom of heaven is like a king who wanted to settle accounts with his servants. ²⁴As he began the settlement, a man who owed him ten thousand talents was brought to him. ²⁵Since he was not able to pay, the master ordered that he and his wife and his children and all that he had be sold to repay the debt.

²⁶"The servant fell on his knees before him. 'Be patient with me,' he begged, 'and I will pay back everything.' ²⁷The servant's master took pity on him, canceled the debt and let him go.

²⁸"But when that servant went out, he found one of his fellow servants who owed him a hundred denarii. He grabbed him and began to choke him. 'Pay back what you owe me!' he demanded.

²⁹"His fellow servant fell to his knees and begged him, 'Be patient with me, and I will pay you back.'

³⁰"But he refused. Instead, he went off and had the man thrown into prison until he could pay the debt. ³¹When the other servants saw what had happened, they were greatly distressed and went and told their master everything that had happened.

³²"Then the master called the servant in. 'You wicked servant,' he said, 'I canceled all that debt of yours because you begged me to. ³³Shouldn't you have had mercy on your fellow servant just as I had on you?' ³⁴In anger his master turned him over to the jailers to be tortured, until he should pay back all he owed.

³⁵"This is how my heavenly Father will treat each of you unless you forgive your brother from your heart."

AS THE OPPOSITION from the religious establishment to his ministry increased (cf. 12:22–32;
15:1–20; 16:1–12), Jesus has twice predicted that
he will soon suffer at their hands, be crucified,
but then be raised again (16:21; 17:22–23). He knows that the conclusion
of his earthly ministry is approaching, so he has spent considerable time
with his disciples clarifying his identity and mission (chs. 14–17). With his
impending absence from them, he now also spends time instructing them
about the kind of community life that should characterize their relationships
with one another and with the world at large.

This extended instruction comprises the fourth of five discourses by Jesus
that Matthew has recorded in his Gospel (see the introduction). This fourth
discourse, the Community Prescription, delineates the church as the community of disciples that witnesses to the reality of the presence of the kingdom
throughout this age. Their witness comes both through their declaration of the
gospel message and living it out as a family of faith characterized by humility,
purity, accountability, discipline, reconciliation, restoration, and forgiveness.

Much of this material is unique to Matthew, especially noted by the occurrence of the term *ekklesia* in 18:17, a term that only appears in the Gospels in
Matthew (cf. 16:18). The broad prescription of the church's community life
continues through chapter 20. Thereupon, Jesus and the disciples leave Galilee
for the final time, heading for Jerusalem by passing through the Transjordan
region of Judea called Perea (19:1) and entering Judea at Jericho (20:29).

## The Greatness of Humility (18:1–4)

IN 17:24–27, JESUS and his disciples were in Capernaum. Although Matthew
does not narrate their location during the Community Prescription, he does
tell us in 19:1 that they leave Galilee. Thus, Jesus most likely gathers with
his disciples for a final time in Capernaum, perhaps again at the home of
Simon Peter and Andrew, the headquarters for the Galilean ministry (see
comments on 8:14).

The event that precipitates this discourse is a surprising question from
Jesus' disciples[1] about who is the greatest in the kingdom of heaven. They
are still developing an understanding of what it means to be Jesus' particular
type of disciple, which is different from other forms of disciples within

---

1. As is typical in Matthew's Gospel, the mention of "disciples" calls to mind the Twelve,
but the wider circle of Jesus' disciples is in view as well. This wider circle includes all who
have responded to his invitation to kingdom life (cf. Wilkins, *Concept of Disciple in Matthew's
Gospel,* 163–72).

Judaism and the wider Greco-Roman world. Discipleship in the ancient world often involved a significant commitment to a rigorous course of study and disciplined lifestyle in order to attain to the master's level of expertise.

The ambition to achieve greatness is a pursuit central to human accomplishment, and on the strictly natural level it is not inappropriate. Jesus pointed to the greatness of John the Baptist as the culminating prophet of the old order, though he did state, shockingly, that the person who is least in the kingdom of heaven is greater than John (11:11). Jesus' disciples most likely have remembered that comparison, and they seek to advance to the kind of greatness in the kingdom that they think Jesus indicated. They have all sacrificed significantly by following him around the countryside these last two to three years, and they want to attain to the highest level of commitment to Jesus' kingdom agenda (cf. also, later, 20:20–28).

But as the following interaction indicates, the disciples have a different type of greatness in mind from what Jesus meant. When he spoke of John's greatness and the greatness of those who are least in the kingdom of heaven, Jesus meant the honor of serving God by preparing for the Messiah and of experiencing the arrival of the blessings of the new covenant through his blood (see comments on 11:11). The disciples understood him to mean primarily the greatness that comes from human endeavor and heroic accomplishments. One of Jesus' primary goals in chapter 18 is to revise their understanding of "greatness" to the way God thinks about it.[2]

Jesus begins this process with a visual aid by calling a little child and having him stand among them. He then makes a startling statement: "I tell you the truth, unless you change and become like little children, you will never enter the kingdom of heaven." Jesus is not commending an inherent innocence of children. The Old Testament has a balanced view of both the sinfulness and the value of children. They can be rebellious and be subject to severe punishment (e.g., Deut. 21:18–21), and the psalmist knows of his sinfulness from conception (Ps. 51:5). But children are also a wonderful creation of God (139:13–14), and Jewish tradition regarded them as a blessing and gift from God (127:3–5; 128:3–4; *Pss. Sol.* 1:3).

Instead of pointing to the innocence of a child, Jesus uses the little child as an object lesson on humility that comes from their vulnerability: "Therefore, whoever humbles himself like this child is the greatest in the kingdom of heaven." In the ancient world, children were valued primarily for the ben-

---

2. For a study that emphasizes the disciples' consistent lack of understanding Jesus' message and mission in Matthew, see Jeannine K. Brown, *The Disciples in Narrative Perspective: The Portrayal and Function of the Matthean Disciples* (SBL Academia Biblica 9; Atlanta: SBL, 2002), esp. 147–52.

efit that they brought to the family by enhancing the workforce, adding to the defensive power, and guaranteeing the future glory of the house. But they had no rights or significance apart from their future value to the family and were powerless in society. The humility of a child consists of the inability to advance his or her own cause apart from the help and resources of a parent.

Yet Jesus celebrates the humility that comes from the child's weakness, defenselessness, and vulnerability. The child can really do nothing for himself or herself and will die if left alone. It is this kind of humility that Jesus uses as a visual aid to contrast the world's form of greatness to the greatness of the kingdom of heaven. Like the values established in the Beatitudes (5:3–10), this is an explicit pronouncement of grace to those who seemingly are unworthy of the kingdom, but it is also a pronouncement of condemnation on those who think themselves to be worthy but are not. Those who wish to enter the kingdom must turn away from their own power and self-seeking, and in childlike humility call on God's mercy to allow them to enter the kingdom of heaven. The child becomes a metaphor to Jesus of the values of discipleship.[3]

Therefore, childlikeness is a characteristic of all true disciples, because it is only through God's mercy that a person can enter his kingdom and find the greatness that comes from having one's sins forgiven and being invested with kingdom life. Note especially that Jesus is speaking to those who are disciples already (cf. 18:1). He is still clarifying his form of discipleship against other forms found in Judaism at the time and against the expectations of those who have responded to his message and confessed themselves to be his disciples. Some of these have attached themselves to him according to their own agendas—most noticeably Judas, but also others who did not truly believe in Jesus' identity and mission (cf. John 6:60–66). Those who would follow Jesus must understand his form of discipleship.

This encounter is an important time for the disciples to check themselves. If they do not yet truly believe, even though they may be "disciples" in name, they must repent, be converted, and enter the kingdom of heaven. Not all who call themselves disciples of Jesus are so truly. The proof will be, at least in part, in their character of childlike discipleship, which is solely a product of humbling oneself to receive the new life produced by entering the kingdom.

## Shelter for the Humble (18:5–9)

JESUS GOES ON to indicate that in the same way one must humbly receive God's mercy in order to enter the kingdom of heaven and become his

---

3. Warren Carter, *Households and Discipleship: A Study of Matthew 19–20* (JSNTSup 103; Sheffield: JSOT Press, 1994), 96–97.

disciple (18:1–4), humility must continue to characterize a life of discipleship.[4] The disciples must learn to let God direct their path even while they serve within his kingdom. Childlike humility that comes from vulnerability is a primary characteristic of discipleship to Jesus because it enables his disciples to receive God's mercy consistently instead of priding themselves on human accomplishments. This reverses typical human notions of how to achieve greatness and how to grow in greatness.

**Care for humble disciples (18:5).** But in advocating a childlike humility for his disciples that comes from weakness, defenselessness, and vulnerability, Jesus encourages others to care for them: "And whoever welcomes a little child like this in my name welcomes me." The "little child" is the true disciple who has humbly received God's enabling mercy to enter the kingdom and who is now serving God. Jesus harks back to the parallel saying in the mission mandate (10:40–42), where he stated that whoever "receives" (*dechomai;* "welcome" in 18:5) childlike disciple-missionaries who carry the message of Jesus, receive Jesus himself. Receiving a little child in the name of Christ means accepting and believing the witness of a Christian disciple.

**Warning about taking advantage of humble disciples (18:6–7).** Jesus not only encourages care for humble disciples but also warns any who would take advantage of them that disciples will have the strength, protection, and invincibility of the kingdom to shelter them as they serve their Master. Jesus switches from the term "child" as a metaphor of discipleship to the "little ones who believe," but the meaning is essentially the same.

Using hyperbole reminiscent of sayings in the SM (e.g., 5:27–30), Jesus emphasizes the seriousness of causing a person to stumble on the path of discipleship (18:6). The phrase "cause to sin" does not indicate a single isolated indiscretion. Rather, drawing on the metaphorical nature of the verb *skandalizo* ("cause to stumble"), it points to a person who has been led astray into sin and fallen badly in his or her walk with God.[5] To practice a lifestyle that regularly leads Jesus' humble disciples to sin indicates that one is headed for eternal damnation, so it would be better to cut one's life off quickly than to risk staying on that trajectory.

The crescendo of warning increases as Jesus pronounces, "Woe to the world because of the things that cause people to sin! Such things must come, but woe to the man through whom they come!" As in the earlier "woes" pro-

---

4. Bruner comments: "Matthew 18:1–4 calls us *to* humility, then v.5 gives us a major way to *practice* humility" (*Matthew*, 2:637), which indicates that 18:1–4 are a call to *enter* the kingdom and 18:5 is the *life of service in* the kingdom.

5. "Cause to stumble" = "cause to sin" (NIV). The use of *skandalizo* links back to 17:27, but here the use of the term indicates *cause to apostatize* by losing faith and falling away from God rather than *cause offense* (Davies and Allison, *Matthew*, 2:761–62; Blomberg, *Matthew*, 274).

nounced on certain unrepentant cities (11:21), Jesus does not dispassionately pronounce doom on the world. "Woe to the world" is a pronouncement of judgment on those who persist as instruments of causing others to sin. Even though such inducements to sin happen, no one is personally free from responsibility if he or she leads others to sin. This pronouncement later falls on Judas for his culpability in betraying Jesus (26:24).

**Warning about allowing one's own passions to lead oneself into sin (18:8–9).** Jesus now addresses the disciples directly about their personal responsibility for their own actions. Lest they deceive themselves into thinking that all sinful behavior is the result of others causing them to sin, Jesus declares that they must take responsibility for their own tendencies to cause themselves to sin (again *skandalizo*, as in 18:6). Similar to the hyperbole in the SM (5:29–30), Jesus indicates that cutting off one's hand or foot or plucking out one's eye in this life (18:8–9) is no comparison to the eternal judgment destined for allowing the passions of one's own life to lead one into sin. Jesus is not advocating physical self-mutilation, but through dramatic figures of speech he indicates the rigorous self-discipline needed for committed disciples.

A disciple's actions indicate the state of his or her heart (15:19), and the person who consistently yields to sin is worthy of eternal condemnation since such sin reveals that he or she is not a disciple of Jesus. The fires of the eternal hell of Gehenna await those who receive God's judgment.[6]

## Angelic Protection of the Little Ones (18:10)

JESUS CONTINUES HIS warning to those who may try to take advantage of his disciples. The expression "little ones" here are disciples who have humbled themselves to be like powerless children (cf. 18:2–6), although there may be dual attention paid to literal children among the disciples. Since the disciples have humbled themselves not to be self-seeking and now display childlike humility of weakness, defenselessness, and vulnerability (cf. 18:1–4), they, and those who might take advantage of them, can be sure that the heavenly Father will watch out for their welfare through angels, who are in constant communication with him.

Angels are well known to be active in the affairs of humans, but in a strikingly personal way, Jesus refers to "their angels."[7] Scripture speaks of angelic

---

6. For discussion of the way that the valley of Hinnom became a metaphorical reference for the eternal fires of hell, see comments on 3:12; 5:22; 25:42.

7. Carson cites approvingly B. B. Warfield's view that the "angels" of the "little ones" are the spirits of deceased believers after death who are always in the presence of the heavenly Father ("Matthew," 401). But the majority of commentators rightly emphasize that the context speaks of disciples and their protection by angels in this *present life* (cf. Morris, *Matthew*, 464–65; Davies and Allison, *Matthew*, 2:768–72).

care for individual persons such as Jacob (Gen. 48:16; cf. Ps. 34:7; 91:11), individual churches (Rev. 1:20), and nations (Dan. 10:13). Jewish literature has a consistent emphasis on angels as guardians of individual persons.[8] Whether or not Jesus' statement implies guardian angels who watch over individual believers on an ongoing basis,[9] it does confirm that the heavenly Father uses angels to care for childlike disciples (cf. Heb. 1:14). Although some Jewish literature pictures only the higher echelons of the angelic orders who can approach God,[10] Jesus' statement that they "always see the face of my Father" indicates that the disciples' angels have constant access to and communication with God. "My Father" reemphasizes the unique relation between Jesus and his heavenly Father.[11]

## The Divine Search for Lost Sheep (18:12–14)

JESUS CALLS FOR the disciples to make the connection between the angelic care for the "little ones" and the following parable of the sheep ("What do you think?").[12] The key is a concern for his humble followers who have gone astray through others' causing them to sin (18:6–7) or through their own sinful choices (18:8–9). The Father will not only send angels to try to bring them back to discipleship but will himself expend every effort to bring about their safe return.

Jesus uses a parable concerning safe and wayward sheep to make his point. The secure image of God's people as his sheep is replete throughout the Old Testament (e.g., Ps. 23; Isa. 53:6; Jer. 13:17; Zech. 10:3; 13:7), as is the distressful image of some who stray (e.g., Ps. 119:176; Isa. 53:6; Jer. 23:1–4; 50:6; Ezek. 34:1–30). The metaphor naturally becomes associated with Jesus, as he here seems to imply,[13] as a central part of his mission both to Israel and to all of humanity (cf. John 10:7–18; 1 Peter 5:2–4; Rev. 7:17). Since shep-

---

8. E.g., Tobit 12:13–22; *1 En.* 100:5; *Jub.* 35:1; *T. Levi* 5.3; *T. Jac.* 2.5–6. For further literature, see Keener, *A Commentary on the Gospel of Matthew* (1999), 450–51; Davies and Allison, *Matthew,* 2:770.

9. Most commentators see a possible reference to guardian angels here, but the passage falls short of final proof for lack of evidence elsewhere in the New Testament; e.g., Blomberg, *Matthew,* 276; Davies and Allison, *Matthew,* 2:771–72; Hagner, *Matthew,* 2:527; Keener, *A Commentary on the Gospel of Matthew* (1999), 450–51; Morris, *Matthew,* 464–65.

10. Cf. *1 En.* 14:21; 40:1–10.

11. Cf. 7:21; 10:32–33; 11:27; 12:50; 16:17; 18:19; 20:23; 25:34; 26:39, 42, 53.

12. Since the transition between Jesus' statement about angelic care for the disciples and the parable of the sheep seems somewhat rough, several manuscripts have inserted an additional v. 11 (see NIV text note): "For the Son of Man came to save what was lost." The phrase is lacking in the best manuscripts.

13. See Davies and Allison, *Matthew,* 2:773–74.

herds often worked with one another as their sheep grazed the hillsides, to leave the ninety-nine is of no real concern, since other shepherds would keep an eye on them. A hundred sheep is an average size for a flock, easily cared for by a shepherd.[14]

Then Jesus makes a remarkable statement: "And if he finds it, I tell you the truth, he is happier about that one sheep than about the ninety-nine that did not wander off." The joy of finding the lost sheep does not mean that it has more value than the others. Rather, the shepherd's joy demonstrates the depth of his concern, care, and love for all his sheep. The depth of that love is often only experienced when faced with the possibility of loss.

Jesus then gives the point of the parable: "In the same way your Father in heaven is not willing that any of these little ones should be lost." The mention of the "little ones" again indicates disciples who have stumbled off the path of discipleship because of mistreatment and temptations to sin that came through other people, including professing, but false, disciples (cf. 18:6–7), or else their stumbling into sin came through their own passions (18:8–9).

Note that the similar parable in Luke 15:3–7 has the lost sheep representing unsaved sinners, while here it implies a believer who has gone astray. Perhaps Jesus spoke this similar parable on two occasions with different purposes in view, or else his intent is to illustrate in his care and restoration of the wayward disciple his concern for all those who are lost.[15] Either way, Jesus' emphasis in Matthew's account is on the recovery of backslidden disciples who are in danger of eternal judgment. The danger comes from the real possibility that they may not be disciples at all. Judas is lurking on that wayward trail, which would be a stark reminder for Matthew's readers. The Father will not force anyone to repent, as Judas so grievously illustrates, but God has commissioned the community of disciples to do everything possible to retrieve their straying brothers and sisters, for they must have the same heart as does their heavenly Father.

## Disciplining Wayward Disciples (18:15–17)

THIS PERICOPE (UNIQUE to Matthew's Gospel) follows logically from the preceding warnings about sin committed by disciples. Jesus gives the steps of discipline (18:15–17) and the method of confirmation (18:18–20) that the community must apply to sinful situations.

---

14. Edwin Firmage, "Zoology (Animal Profiles): Sheep," *ABD*, 6:1126–27; Keener, *A Commentary on the Gospel of Matthew* (1999), 452.

15. Blomberg, *Matthew*, 275–76, seems to lean toward the former, while the latter is understood by Young, *The Parables*, 191–200.

Jesus begins by specifying the problem: "If your brother sins against you. . . ." The "little one" who went astray is now called a "brother" who has committed sin. "Brother" harks back to the scene where Jesus emphasizes that his disciples, who have obeyed the will of the Father by following Jesus, are his mother, and brother, and sister (cf. 12:46–50). The gender of the disciple is not in view here, we can apply this to any member of the family of faith. Jesus addresses what the community of believers must do if one in the family commits a sin. The basis of the process is rooted in Deuteronomy 19:15–18, as his quotation of this passage in Matthew 18:16 indicates.[16]

Jesus enunciates four steps for dealing with a sinning member of the discipleship community, which has as its intended goal the restoration of the sinning brother or sister to a state of purity and the reestablishment of the fellowship of the body.

(1) *Personal confrontation.* "Go and show him his fault, just between the two of you. If he listens to you, you have won your brother over." Either the person who has been offended or a member of the community who has knowledge of the brother's sin must go to the person who has sinned and lay out his fault. Such an encounter must be undertaken with privacy so that if it is resolved, no undue attention will be given to the tragedy of sin committed by a member of the community. The ultimate objective of the encounter is not punishment but restoration—winning over a brother so that he can be restored to the faithful path of discipleship.

(2) *Witnesses to the confrontation.* If the first step does not result in repentance, one or two other members of the community should go back to witness the confrontation (not that they were eyewitnesses to the original sin) and the sinning brother's refusal to repent. They will be able to help arbitrate, or in the case of stubborn rebellion, become witnesses of nonrepentance. This follows the guideline provided in Deuteronomy 19:15: "One witness is not enough to convict a man accused of any crime or offense he may have committed. A matter must be established by the testimony of two or three witnesses."

(3) *Involvement of the church.* The third step, in the case of nonrepentance, is to bring the complaint before the church: "If he refuses to listen to them, tell it to the church." This is the second time that the word "church" (*ekklesia*) occurs in Matthew's Gospel, both times used by Jesus. This is a look ahead by Jesus to the future functioning of his family of disciples as the community of believers in this present age (see comments on 16:18).

---

16. The Lev. passage also stands behind a three-stage process of discipline found in the Qumran community: individual confrontation, witnesses, and, if necessary, final judgment by the community leaders (see 1QRule of the Community 5:24–6:1; cf. also CD 9:2–4).

Again with the goal of restoring wayward disciples ("sheep"; 18:12–14), the intent of including the church in the disciplining process is to involve the broader body of believers in trying to get the sinning brother to acknowledge his sin. Those who have shared the fellowship of the community may persuade the sinning brother to accept responsibility for his action(s).

The way in which this was carried out in the small home churches of the early church may be quite different than today. Such a sin would become immediately evident to the community. Today some churches actually publish a list or make an announcement from the pulpit. I personally have seen this work most effectively when the church leaders are made aware of the situation and are brought into the process of attempted restoration rather than making a public announcement.

(4) *Treat as an unbeliever.* The fourth step of discipline is to treat the sinning brother who refuses to repent like a pagan (*ethnikos;* lit., "Gentile") or tax collector, the common titles for those who are consciously rebellious against God and his people. The Old Testament prescriptions for exercising punishment (Deut. 25:1–3) were later applied by Judaism as a responsibility of the synagogue. The synagogue was not only the place of worship, instruction, and fellowship, but also the place of discipline. Extreme discipline included flogging and expulsion from the community (*m. Mak.* 3.1–2; see comments on 10:17). Jesus focuses instead on spiritual exclusion from the fellowship of the church, which is symbolic of spiritual death.

Again, the way that this is carried out today must be determined by individual circumstances. Some suggest that the person not be allowed to participate in any activities of the church. However, since unbelievers are encouraged to come to the assembly to hear the gospel, it must mean something other than strict removal. Rather, this is best carried out when the church considers the sinning individual not to be a believer. Confessing disciples who live with unconfessed sin indicate by their lives that they are not truly members of Jesus' spiritual family and are not to be allowed to enjoy its fellowship. They should be treated as unbelievers, with the same compassion and urgency needed to encourage them to repent; they are not to receive the same openness to the inner fellowship of the community that is reserved for fellow disciples.

## Consensus on Community Discipline and Life (18:18–20)

JESUS GOES ON to emphasize that the responsibility of the community of disciples is to come to a corporate consensus in which there is correspondence between heaven and earth in carrying out the will of the Father.

**Consensus in discipline (18:18).** That means in the first place to seek the Father's will about the activities of brothers and sisters who are accused of sinful behavior and then seek to bring God's will to bear on the situation. Jesus states, "I tell you the truth, whatever you bind on earth will be bound in heaven, and whatever you loose on earth will be loosed in heaven." This saying is virtually identical to the pronouncement made of Peter's role in the foundation of the church (see comments on 16:19), except with the striking difference that here the verbs are plural, indicating that Peter's foundational authority is extended to the entire community of disciples. In this context, the community of disciples, the church, is given authority to declare the terms under which God forgives or refuses to forgive the sin of wayward disciples.

In other words, the disciples as a whole have a responsibility for declaring the terms under which sins are forgiven or how a person is to be excluded from the fellowship of the local church. As parallel statements, these sayings of Jesus are the basis for entrance into or banishment from the kingdom (16:19) and the local church (18:18).[17] Both sayings relate to forgiveness of sin. A third passage, John 20:22b–23, also concerns the forgiveness of sins, and is a threefold saying of almost identical construction. The periphrastic future tense indicates that what Peter and the disciples do in this present age has already been determined by God.[18]

The church is the instrument of God, who alone can grant forgiveness of sin or consign a person to judgment. The passive voice of "will have been bound" and "will have been loosed" and the phrase "in heaven" are Semitic circumlocutions for describing God's actions.[19] But the church does have the authority to "bind and loose," that is, to declare the terms under which God either forgives or retains sins (cf. John 20:22b–23). Jesus' statement assures the church that God in heaven confirms its judgment on a sinning brother.

**Consensus in praying for God's will in the community (18:19).** The correspondence sought in the community of disciples between earth and heaven also promises to guide the church's attempt generally to carry out the will of the heavenly Father on earth (cf. 6:10; 26:39–42): "Again, I tell you that if two of you on earth agree about anything you ask for, it will be done for you by my Father in heaven." The confirmation of the action of the community in binding and loosing the sins of church members is expressly related to the action and will of the Father in carrying out the requests of the community.[20]

---

17. The saying in 16:18–19 draws a distinction between the "church" (16:18) and the "kingdom of heaven" (16:19), but with the inclusion of the parallel saying on binding and loosing occurring in this church discipline passage (18:16–18), the requirement for entrance is the same for both: forgiveness of sins.

18. Gundry, *Matthew*, 335; Carson, "Matthew," 370–74; see comments on 16:19.

19. For discussion see comments on 16:19.

20. See David McClister, "'Where Two or Three Are Gathered Together': Literary Structure As a Key to Meaning in Matt 17:22–20:19," *JETS* 39 (1996): 556–57.

**Consensus in experiencing Jesus' presence within the community (18:20).** Jesus' third statement expands on the first two, indicating that the fellowship that the community enjoys in reaching consensus about disciplining a fellow believer is actually brought about by the presence of Jesus: "For where two or three come together in my name, there am I with them." Jewish councils required a minimum of three judges to decide regarding minor cases in the local community, assuming that the Shekinah remains with a just court.[21] Likewise, when two men gathered to discuss the law, the Shekinah was present: "But if two sit together and words of the Law are spoken between them, the Divine Presence rests between them" (*m.* *ʾAbot* 3:2).

But in a striking declaration, Jesus himself assumes the place of the divine presence among his disciples, guaranteeing that when his followers reach a consensus as they ask in prayer for guidance in matters of discipline, his Father in heaven will guide them as they carry it out. The basis of the assurance is Jesus' continual presence among his disciples who gather in his name. This looks ahead to the promise that he will be with his disciples forever in his resurrected presence (see comments on 28:20).

Although these verses are commonly understood to be a promise regarding consensus in prayer (and there may be an appropriate application in this regard), the promises here specifically concern the unity of the church in rendering a decision about a sinning member. But the principle underlying this saying goes beyond the matter of church discipline. Within the broader context of the Community Prescription, the promised presence of Jesus in their midst is a real empowerment when God's "little ones" gather in Jesus' name.

A special emphasis of Matthew is that the presence of Jesus endows his people with Immanuel, God with us (1:24), an abiding presence that goes on until the end of the ages (28:20). David Kupp states that the presence of Jesus within the gathering of his disciples "is the social and religious experience of his gathered people being filled with divine authority, focus and coherence for the ordinary and extraordinary events in the life of their community."[22] Jesus' risen presence within his community brings radical transformation so they steadfastly carry out the Father's will in imitation of Jesus' own unswerving commitment to his Father's will.

### Forgiveness in the Community Toward Sinning Disciples (18:21–35)

REPEATED FORGIVENESS (18:21–22). Restoration of a sinning brother to the path of discipleship is the purpose of discipline within the church, which must

---

21. Cf. *m.* *Sanh.* 1:1; *b.* *Ber.* 6a; "Shekinah" means the divine presence.
22. Kupp, *Matthew's Emmanuel*, 199.

be ready to forgive and restore anyone who repents. But the wise disciple recognizes that those who are repenting and seeking forgiveness may only be putting on a show and will soon scurry back to their sinful ways. Such people can cause considerable damage in the lives of others and disrupt the proper functioning of the community. In this brief interaction that is unique to Matthew's Gospel, Peter seems to be thinking this way as he approaches Jesus and asks, "Lord, how many times shall I forgive my brother when he sins against me? Up to seven times?"

We must probe the Jewish background to understand the larger issues that prompt Peter's question. Forgiveness in the Old Testament came from the God of grace, who instituted sacrifices that benefited only because he gave the means of making atonement through the shedding of blood (Lev. 17:11). But as God himself declared, the same God who forgives wickedness, rebellion, and sin "does not leave the guilty unpunished; he punishes the children and their children for the sin of the fathers to the third and fourth generation" (Ex. 34:6–7). In the everyday world, persons can get caught up in a regular pattern of sinning and seeking restoration.

The teaching within Judaism (based on Amos 1:3; 2:6; Job 33:29, 30) is that three times was enough to show a forgiving spirit. Rabbinic Judaism recognized that repeat offenders may not really be repenting at all: "If a man commits a transgression, the first, second and third time he is forgiven, the fourth time he is not" (*b. Yoma* 86b, 87a). The Mishnah is even less forgiving: "If a man said, 'I will sin and repent, and sin again and repent,' he will be given no chance to repent ... for transgressions that are between a man and his fellow the Day of Atonement effects atonement only if he has appeased his fellow" (*m. Yoma* 8.9).

Peter's question appears to be following in that line, wondering how many times he should forgive a person who repeatedly sins against him. His offer to forgive the person seven times, more than double the above-mentioned statements, is magnanimous, reflecting a desire for completeness that the number seven usually evokes. But he wonders whether this is where the limit should be drawn on his generosity of spirit.

Jesus' astonishing response is that Peter must forgive not the magnanimous number of seven but countless times: "I tell you, not seven times, but seventy-seven times." The meaning of the number that Jesus uses is unclear. One can read "seventy-seven times," which is the same wording found in the LXX of Genesis 4:24, or the less likely "seventy times seven."[23] In essence, Jesus seems to be saying that the number doesn't matter. Peter and the rest of the disciples are to continue to forgive without keeping

---

23. See BDF §248(2), 130; the KJV and NASB have this.

count. The reason for such an unheard of thought is given in the parable that immediately follows—Peter should go on forgiving because the reality of his own forgiveness is demonstrated in the way in which God forgives others.

**The parable of the unforgiving and unmerciful servant (18:23–35).** Introducing the parable in the same way as he did the parables of the mysteries of the kingdom of heaven (cf. 13:24, 31, 44, 45, 47), Jesus tells Peter and the other disciples what forgiveness is like for those who have encountered the kingdom. That kingdom is like a king who wanted to settle accounts with his servants (18:23).

*The first servant (18:23–27).* The expression "settle accounts" rings an ominous note of judgment by setting the stage for an accounting of what is owed the king. The amount owed by one person (10,000 talents) was incomprehensible. This amount indicates hyperbolically the incalculable debt owed by the servant. Perhaps he was a governor of a region and collected taxes for the king but has squandered the amount.

The exact monetary value is difficult to determine, because the "talent" was not a coin but a unit of monetary reckoning. A silver talent was about seventy-five pounds, valued at six thousand denarii. Since a denarius was the equivalent of a day's wage for a common laborer (see comments on 17:24–27) and if we use the year 2001's minimum wage of $5.15 an hour in the United States, a common laborer could expect $41.20 a day. A talent, therefore, would be worth approximately $247,200 (cf. 25:15).[24] Altogether, therefore, the man owes at least two and a half billion dollars. As extreme as those figures are, comparisons are difficult to appreciate since such a sum in first-century Palestine would be far more disproportionate to the same sum in modern times. Some estimate that the amount is the equivalent of hundreds of billions of dollars (see also comments on 25:15). In any case, the hyperbole of the parable is dramatic.[25]

Since the man is unable to pay such an astronomical figure, he and his family are to be sold to repay the debt, implying that the king will sell them into slavery, a practice common in the ancient world. Debtors were often forced to sell their children as slaves or gave their children as slaves to a creditor (cf. 1 Kings 4:1; Neh. 5:4–8). Debtor's slavery was often designed more as punishment than repayment, for as in this case, it was impossible to repay the amount owed.

---

24. See Wilkins, "Matthew," 115, for a table of weights and measures and coinage at the time of Jesus.

25. For an overview of the parable within its Jewish context, see Young, *The Parables: Jewish Tradition and Christian Interpretation*, 127–44.

The servant of the king makes a ridiculous petition, suggesting that with just a bit of patience he can repay the debt (18:26). But his overwhelming plight evokes pity from the king, and prompts him to give to the servant what he does not deserve: He cancels the debt and releases him (18:27). Those hearing the parable would have recalled here the theme of forgiveness that introduced the parable (18:21–22). This first scene is a powerful display of the forgiveness that God, who alone is king, displays toward those who have offended him.

*The second servant* (18:28–30). In this next scene, the servant who has been forgiven the unthinkable amount of ten thousand talents finds a fellow servant who owes him one hundred denarii. Using the same figures to compare the amount owed, the second slave owed just a little over four thousand dollars, a pittance in comparison to the billions owed by the first slave. But the one who has been forgiven so much does not respond with the same pity but rather the opposite. "He grabbed him and began to choke him. 'Pay back what you owe me!' he demanded." The second servant pleads with almost the identical actions and words as the first servant used when begging for leniency from the king. But instead of reacting with the same compassion and grace, the first servant delivers physical punishment by choking him and, instead of selling him into slavery, throws him into the debtor's prison, an even more severe punishment than that threatened him by the king, which made repaying the debt impossible (18:29–30).

*The first servant's punishment* (18:31–34). But the ungrateful servant cannot get away with his treachery, because other servants of the king are grieved when they see the unfair treatment and tell the king (18:31). The true nature of the servant is revealed, as he is called "wicked."

The king asks the wicked servant: "Shouldn't you have had mercy on your fellow servant just as I had on you?" The mercy and benevolence of the master toward the first servant should have so impacted his life and values that he would shower mercy and benevolence on others. Instead, his wicked nature has only taken selfish advantage of the master. Now he will receive the punishment that he deserved in the first place. He is handed over to the "torturers," that is, those jailers in a debtor's prison who not only guarded against escape but inflicted torture on inmates. Since it would be impossible for the servant to repay the vast amounts owed, the scene concludes with the grim certainty that he will experience that punishment forever, a harsh metaphorical allusion to an eternal destiny of judgment (cf. 8:12; 10:28; 13:42, 49–50; 24:51).[26]

---

26. For a scholarly discussion of fiery judgment in Matthew's Gospel, see Sim, *Apocalyptic Eschatology in the Gospel of Matthew*, esp. 130–39.

*The parable's principle (18:35).* The core of the meaning of the parable is found in the final verse: "This is how my heavenly Father will treat each of you unless you forgive your brother from your heart." "Mercy" is *not giving* to a person what he deserves, while "grace" is *giving* to a person what he *does not* deserve. This takes us to a central principle of the kind of kingdom life that Jesus has inaugurated. A person who has truly experienced the mercy and grace of God by responding to the presence of his kingdom will be transformed into Jesus' disciple, which, in a most fundamental way, means experiencing a transformed heart that produces a changed life that gives the same mercy and grace one has received from God (cf. Isa. 40:2).

Such a transformation will be evident in the words and actions of a disciple's life (12:33–37; 13:8, 23; 15:17–20). A person who has not truly experienced God's grace and mercy will not experience his forgiveness. He will, like the first servant, accept the personal benefits, but it will be only superficial. It will not penetrate a hard and wicked heart to produce transformation. Such a person will thus experience eternal condemnation. Jesus' disciples must be forgiving to others, for through God's grace and mercy they have experienced his forgiveness.

Peter and the other disciples are thus brought up to an incomprehensible truth that will mark their lives forever. As they continue to see Jesus' life and ministry come to a close and then come to understand the significance of the cross and empty tomb, they will be gripped by the compassionate mercy and grace of God demonstrated in their loving Savior Messiah, their Master, Jesus. Such a transformation will occur in their own lives that the mercy of God becomes a preeminent characteristic of the community of disciples. Peter later writes in 1 Peter 2:9–10:

> But you are a chosen people, a royal priesthood, a holy nation, a people belonging to God, that you may declare the praises of him who called you out of darkness into his wonderful light. Once you were not a people, but now you are the people of God; once you had not received mercy, but now you have received mercy.

**Bridging Contexts**

THE FIVE LENGTHY discourses that Matthew has recorded are the most extensive collection of Jesus' teachings found in Scripture. They are a treasure of kingdom principles that have guided the church throughout its history. They are directly linked to Jesus' purposes for all his followers, since they comprise the primary material from which all disciples are to be taught to obey everything that Jesus commanded (cf. 28:18–20; for more on this, see the introduction). This fourth discourse, the Community Prescription, delineates the church as the community of disciples that witness to the reality of the presence of the kingdom throughout this age. Their witness comes both through their declaration of the gospel message and through their example of living out the gospel message as a family of faith that is characterized by humility, purity, accountability, discipline, reconciliation, restoration, and forgiveness.

The first and third discourses primarily were addressed to Jesus' disciples, though the crowds were included for other particular purposes (see comments on 5:1–2; 7:28–29; 13:1–2, 10–17) and the religious leaders were an implied object of rebuke (5:20; 6:1–18; 12:24–32, 46–50). But like the second and fifth discourses, this one is directed exclusively to Jesus' disciples. The uniqueness of this material accentuates Jesus' urgency to prepare them for the time when a new community of faith will replace Israel during this age as Jesus' body that functions as his witness to the reality of the presence of the kingdom.

The uniqueness of this prescription for community life also accentuates the way that the presence of the kingdom of heaven turns upside down the values of this world and how the new community, the church, will be a living witness to this reversal. The discourse displays the values of the community in several ways.

**The greatness of kingdom life.** Greatness is not achieved through one's personal accomplishments but through humility in receiving God's grace. The pattern of the world is to count up one's accomplishments, especially if they involve personal sacrifice. The disciples have committed themselves to that kind of effort for the kingdom of heaven and are now looking to see who has accomplished the most and is therefore the greatest among them in the kingdom.

But Jesus turns that value upside down as he demonstrates through the example of a little child that the truly transformed life cannot be achieved by personal efforts but only by humbly allowing God to bring his spiritual renewal within a person's life. That renewing activity brings a person into the realm of the kingdom of God. This is much the same message as the Beatitudes of the SM, where those who have cast aside all self-effort at achieving status before God will be enabled to receive the gift of kingdom life (cf. 5:3–16). As one humbly receives this gift of life, one becomes Jesus' disciple and is privy to all of the greatness that comes from an intimate relationship to Jesus and to his Father (18:4).

Perhaps we can use an example of ancient royal families. A girl born into a royal family did not become a princess through her own efforts. There was no cause for pride in what she was gifted to be. Rather, a wise princess would be humble. She, like every other little baby, was born weak, defenseless, and vulnerable. It was only the gift of her birth into the royal family that established the greatness of her position. As she grew in her royal role, she realized that her greatness as a future queen would come only as she gave herself to serve her subjects. All of her accomplishments could only come about because of the privilege of being born into her position.

Likewise, it is not what you or I have done that brings greatness, but only in what we are already on account of what God has done in our lives to bring us into his kingdom. From that beginning we are able to dedicate our lives to following Jesus' pattern of servanthood for the sake of the kingdom that allows us to progress in that kind of humble greatness (cf. 20:25–28).

**Responsibility for the others' purity.** Jesus further demonstrates that his community is responsible to pattern a life for others that will not lead them to sin. Since the context concerns individual efforts to achieve greatness (18:1–4), we can assume this is Jesus' starting point. "Little ones," perhaps new disciples, are weak, defenseless, and vulnerable as they humbly enter the kingdom of heaven. They look at the pattern of those disciples who have preceded them, and they are highly susceptible to following their example. Although all disciples must enter the kingdom by becoming like a humble child (18:3), the world's pattern of greatness is a dangerous temptation to those within the community of disciples. Members of the community may start counting their accomplishments, comparing their achievements, and condemning their brothers' and sisters' endeavors, all in the pursuit of greatness according to the world's standards.

If this is the pattern adopted by the community, new disciples will be tempted to pattern their new life of discipleship after that model. Therefore, Jesus declares that we must take seriously our responsibility for other disciples, because if they follow a faulty pattern, they will be led into the sin of worldly greatness instead of kingdom humility.

Thus, a core value for the community of faith is responsibility for other disciples' purity of life, starting first with one's attitude of personal greatness. This is apparently why Jesus' warnings are directed to our responsibility both for other's sinful behavior (18:5–7) and for our own behavior (18:8–9). The world's pattern is to look out for oneself primarily, but all that we do within the community of faith will impact everyone else. Thus, it should be a high value within the community to develop a pattern of life in which all disciples are committed to living out our responsibility to each other's purity.

**Accountability for restoration.** Following on from the responsibility the community bears for each other's purity is the accountability we share for restoring those who have gone astray. The parable of the lost sheep (18:10–14) reveals God's heart. The shepherd could have settled for bringing back ninety-nine sheep. That's a good percentage. Loss of some of the flock is expected in the wilds of nature. He wouldn't have been condemned for losing only one. But just as God sends protecting angels over each of his little disciples (18:10), he considers each wayward disciple nonexpendable. We can assume that the leadership of the community bears significant responsibility for bringing back those who have gone astray, but all members are accountable for whatever lengths we can go to restore wayward brothers and sisters.

It is sometimes easier to beat a brother or sister who has fallen, punishing such a one for a lack of faithfulness or trying to get even with that person for the hurts he or she has caused. But what is needed is for us to accept such people back into the community so they can be strengthened by our unity and faithfulness. The community is accountable to the Shepherd to give unreserved commitment to restoring those who have fallen.

**Discipline and reconciliation.** Likewise, the community has a responsibility to protect its purity from those who have brought sinful activity into the fellowship. It is sometimes easier to compromise the purity of the community than to confront the sin. Or, as is the maxim of the world, it is easier to "live and let live" because of the difficulty of sustaining absolute standards. "Who am I to judge when I'm not perfect myself" is often another guideline. But courageous concern for members of the community of faith will take seriously the plight of the individual who is practicing sin and the purity of the community that allows the sin to infect the fellowship.

Two of the most important guidelines for exercising discipline within the community are the intended goal and the ultimate source of discipline. (1) The intended goal is *reconciliation*. If a brother or sister accepts discipline, the goal is to win him or her over (18:15). A disciple who continues in sin is alienated both from God and from pure fellowship with other believers. When he or she confesses that sin, fellowship with God and other believers is restored.

(2) The ultimate source of the discipline is *God himself*. God alone can forgive or retain sin, so it is the responsibility of the community to understand God's standards, seek for the unity of the Spirit that leads to an understanding of God's will, and follow the leading of the presence of Jesus within the community (18:18–20). The community that disciplines its own members displays the love, compassion, and purity of God the Father, who draws its members together truly as brothers and sisters in Christ.

**Unconditional forgiveness.** Perhaps the kingdom value most difficult for the world to comprehend is the kind of forgiveness Jesus articulates in the discourse. It is not a conditional acceptance but an unqualified removal of all that we hold against others. At least one reason why the world cannot really understand this value is that hurt is real in offended relationships. When we have been hurt, we don't want to be hurt again. We won't allow ourselves to be used. We want to get even with those who have abused us. If we do forgive others, it is often conditionally based on the actions of the one we are forgiving. But what Jesus shows is that when we experience God's unqualified forgiveness, it will influence all that we are and will impact all of our relationships. Mercy experienced will produce mercy demonstrated.

This is what ties the Community Discourse together. The individual who has experienced God's mercy and has received his forgiveness has humbly entered into the life of the kingdom of heaven. All of the former values of the world are turned upside down. I no longer need to be on top. I don't need to be the greatest, for when I do, I am estranged from others who also want to be the greatest. Unhealthy competition and comparison are now eliminated from our fellowship; I am here now to seek your best, not my own. I can elevate your good as my aspiration to serve.

That is what is so unique about the community Jesus has established, which today is visible as the church, the body of Christ. Whatever else we may use as guidelines for the health of the church, Jesus says that his community of disciples is the primary witness to the reality of the presence of the kingdom throughout this age. Our witness comes through both our declaration of the gospel and living out that gospel as a family of faith. What will characterize our fellowship is humility, purity, accountability, discipline, reconciliation, restoration, and forgiveness

**COMMUNITY.** The renowned pollsters George Gallup Sr. and his son George Gallup Jr. have studied the habits and preferences of the people of the United States since the 1930s. In one of the younger Gallup's studies several years ago, he concluded that we are among the loneliest people on earth. He cited a variety of contributing factors, among which is Western individualism turned isolationism, acerbated by urbanization, technology, and consumerism.[27]

This truth points out something that many of us with our stubborn independence don't like to admit—we need each other. We pride ourselves on our ability to take care of ourselves, to get along without needing anyone. But that's not the way that we were created to be. Community is an important element of God's creation. In spite of the devastating effects of sin, community is a stabilizing force that God has established to perpetuate his creation. As the

---

27. George Gallup Jr., *The People's Religion* (New York: Macmillan, 1989), passim.

crown of God's creation, humans are designed as the exemplary apex of community. It was not good for Adam to be alone, so God created him a helper. It has never been good since then for humans to be alone.

Community is an element that is built into us from our birth. It is also an element found in the broader creation. In biology, a *community* is an interacting group of various species in a common location. For example, a biological community may be a forest of trees and undergrowth plants, inhabited by animals and rooted in soil containing bacteria and fungi. A variety of factors determine the overall structure of a biological community, including the number of species (*diversity*) within it, the number of each species (*abundance*), the interactions among the species, and the ability of the community to return to normal (*resilience and stability*) after a disruptive influence such as fire or drought. The growth and change of biological communities over time is known as ecological succession.[28]

God built community into the creation to enable it to sustain itself and succeed. A deer would never be able to endure without the remarkable interdependence of all the elements of the forest that make up the biological community. We of all of God's creation, created in his image, should place community as one of our highest values, because within the Godhead itself is the wonderful interplay of community in the Trinity. However, sin disrupts community, because individual humans prioritize their own good over that of the community. The very elements of community that sustain the creation, including diversity, abundance, interaction, resiliency and stability, are the factors that tend to tear us apart.

But with the arrival of the kingdom of heaven, with its radicalizing of life for those who respond to its invitation, community is now revisioned. Jesus' message in this Community Discourse provides a prescription for reversing the destructive effects of sin on human relationships to promote biblical community. In this discourse, Jesus focuses on specific issues that destroy community and must be reversed. Three destructive issues are noted: competition, independence, and retribution. Likewise, three qualities to overcome these destructive elements are also noted: humility, accountability, and mercy. This kind of church community will function faithfully as a witness to the presence of Jesus in this age.

**Humility reverses competition.** The question that prompted this discourse on community arose from the disciples' quest to know who is the greatest in the kingdom of heaven (18:1). The desire to maximize one's life is not in and of itself a bad thing. But as Jesus goes on to show his disciples, the kingdom operates under a different motivation. To operate primarily

---

28. See the entry "Community" in *Encyclopædia Britannica*.

with a goal in life to be the greatest promotes a competition that destroys relationships. Drawing on the biological parallel used above, competition results when resources such as food or space are not sufficient to fill the needs of those species that are attempting to live together in community. When that kind of competition ensues, the younger, weaker, marginalized members are cut off and often ultimately die. This is the way of creation that is dominated by sin.

I am not suggesting, however, that all competition is bad. When it is guided by appropriate humility, a healthy competition in sports can promote a common good and can help individuals maximize their potential. The New Testament itself points to the competition in athletics as a positive analogy (1 Cor. 9:24; Eph. 6:12). That analogy, however, indicates that the Christian must pursue not the crown of human accomplishment but the imperishable crown of eternal life (1 Cor. 9:25; 1 Tim. 4:8).[29] An economic system that focuses on the quality of the product and the adequate supply for consumers can profit from competition. But when promotion of self at the expense of others is the motivation, competition is destructive.

In the academic world, competition can be highly destructive to community. I warn my students every year of inappropriate kinds of competition. They can compete with each other in ways so that they become jealous, suspicious, envious, and hateful toward each other. Or they can learn to work together, appreciate each other's giftedness, and encourage each other to find their life's goals that will ultimately serve the common good of establishing the kingdom of God.

I saw this myself when I was in seminary many years ago. I was not much of a student in high school, primarily because of personal difficulties. I'd rather play sports or party. After I got out of the army, I had become a Christian and suddenly discovered a love of learning. I did well in college, and in seminary I entered into fields of study that lit up my world. So I competed with myself to maximize my time in school. I wanted Jesus to know that I was giving it my all. Besides, I was married with a newborn baby girl at home. My wife sacrificed much to get me through seminary, so when I went home, I wanted to show her good grades that meant her sacrifice was worth it. I think it was a healthy competition with myself to get the most out of my studies, which was the beginning recognition that I was headed toward a career in academics.

But a friend of mine developed a competition with me about grades that I don't think was healthy. He wanted to see how I did on my papers and what scores I got on quizzes and grades. He wanted to graduate with a higher

---

29. "Athletics," *DBI*, 54.

G.P.A. than me. I can honestly say it really didn't matter to me what his grades were, but it did to him. Somehow it affected our friendship. I was more guarded with him, and he was more aggressive with his advancement over me. To this day we remain friends, but there is still a hint of competition. I'm probably more aware today that I may have unwittingly contributed to the competition years ago, and I'm especially aware of how that kind of competition destroys community.

Jesus offers a revolutionary alternative—humility. This is not the kind of self-abnegation that beats oneself emotionally or even physically as though one has no value. That kind of self-devaluation denies the individual's worth as a person uniquely created in the image of God. Rather, the humility Jesus proposes is one in which we place ourselves in an unqualified state of vulnerability to God. That happens in this passage in two primary ways, as humility both creates and advances community.

*Humility creates community.* Instead of aggressively pursuing our own status and life goals by our efforts, we receive life as a gift of the kingdom of heaven (18:1–4). As we enter into that life, we find our own personal worth as disciples of Jesus. We are each the "greatest" because of the unqualified grace we have received as Jesus establishes us in a relationship to him. In that relationship we understand his purposes for our own life together and in relationship to others. Community is created because of our essential equality. We are part of the same family, equal brothers and sisters of Jesus with the same Father. There is no need to compete for attention or love or prominence. As we humbly experience God's grace in being established as Jesus' disciples as we enter the kingdom, community is created.

*Humility advances community.* Humility also advances community. Instead of competing with others to be personally the greatest, our unique individual relationships to Jesus allow us to serve each other for their ultimate good and for the good of his kingdom in this world. Comparison is a cancer in our relationships that robs the uniqueness of the other person as we elevate ourselves over them. Jesus emphasizes that as we enter the kingdom of heaven as little children, we are likewise to protect others who have humbly entered it (18:5–9).

Humility is a tricky characteristic to display toward others because of the extremes to which we can go. As soon as we think that we are humble, we probably are prideful. Yet the person who is too afraid of being prideful often will not have the courage to use his or her talents and gifts. We often have difficulty maintaining the right balance. I'm often reminded of this when I recall the story of the person who was called up to the front of the church to be given a pin of recognition for his lifelong humility in serving in children's Sunday school. The next week when he wore the pin to church, the pastor took it away from him because he was accused of pride. Humility is a tricky business to exercise.

I find one extreme when I congratulate a student on doing well on an exam and he says, "Oh, it wasn't me; it was the Lord." He is trying to be humble, but it certainly wasn't the Lord who studied all night, nor was it the Lord who worked through the difficult Greek syntax of a passage. I understand the student's desire to give glory to God in all things, but his response actually can be a subtle form of pride. Aren't the other students in the class also godly? Doesn't the Lord work through them too? Why didn't they receive the high grade he did? Appropriate humility acknowledges that one's talents and giftedness come from God and then offers them in the service of the Lord and others.

I find the other extreme when I encourage a student to take a position that has been offered by a church. She turns it down because she considers herself lacking to the task. She is so caught up in the awareness of her inadequacies that she is paralyzed and does not allow herself to be used by the Lord to exercise her wonderful natural abilities and her giftedness from the Spirit. She needs to humbly acknowledge that if God has called her to a task, he will supply the giftedness and the ability to carry it out.

**Accountability overcomes independence.** Independence is highly esteemed in Western culture, since it indicates freedom from the influence, control, or determination of others, especially of one country over another. It filters down to the personal level when we value not having to depend on anyone else or not having others depend on us. As valuable as that form of independence can be when pursued in a healthy way, it can be an insidious element that destroys community. We think we don't need anyone else and can get along fine by ourselves, so we develop an isolationism in which everyone is responsible only for himself or herself.

*Accountability creates community.* The fierce independence that many desire in the modern world is another evidence of a subtle sinfulness. What overcomes that independence is a proper sense of accountability—others need us. We have a young friend who had a difficult pregnancy. This young woman was strong and prided herself on her independence and ability to handle most anything that came her way. She was an outstanding athlete in high school and college. But the little baby growing inside her was a major hindrance to her independence. She was increasingly unable to compete in sports to her satisfaction as the pregnancy advanced, and she felt as if the baby was robbing her of her ability to do what she wanted, when she wanted. She even began to resent this life inside her. Such thoughts and feelings baffled her. She was sure that this wasn't right, but she couldn't help them, nonetheless.

But all of that changed as soon as the baby was born. She suddenly was gripped with the fact that this little baby needed her, and she became intensely committed to her little girl. Now her every waking thought and activity is directed toward the needs of her baby. She hardly cares about herself at all; in fact, her husband practically has to force her to get out of the house to go for a run or a swim. Now she feels she has higher priorities. It is an intriguing transformation. Her individualism has been tempered by her accountability to her child and her husband.

The Community Prescription notes how an appropriate accountability to the needs of others can overcome an unhealthy independence from others. Once we gain God's heart for his children, which prompts him to provide ministering angels for their every need (18:10), our own eyes are opened to the needs of those for whom he has given us responsibility, and an accountability relationship is established that creates God's kind of community.

*Accountability advances community.* One of the responsibilities given to Adam and Eve was to be stewards of God's creation, which illustrates the responsibilities we have within the community of disciples. We are stewards of each other. We can help take care of each other's needs when things are difficult—for example, when money is low, or when others need a place to stay or a shoulder to cry on. We can take care of people who have just moved into town and need fellowship and help moving into their house. We can involve them in significant ministry opportunities. There are multitudes of ways that this kind of care can be expressed. Essentially, we are to look after our brothers and sisters as God himself would look after them.

We see in the Community Prescription two ways in which accountability advances community: pursuing the wayward and daring to discipline. (1) The parable of the lost sheep (18:12–14) is connected to care of the wayward, but it carries over to the spiritual well-being of all disciples in the community. When we love individuals and desire to treat them with the respect their kinship in the kingdom entitles them, we care much about the direction of their lives. This parable is often interpreted to imply going after unbelievers. That is the thrust of the Lukan parallel, but in Matthew's context it implies that disciples are to go after fallen brothers or sisters, knowing that this is what God himself desires for that individual.

Over the years I have seen some of the deepest pain in the eyes of Christian parents whose children have gone astray. They doubt themselves and the reality of their own faith. Why did they not have more influence on their children? They feel guilty about their parenting, wondering whether they should have been stricter, or more lenient. Should they have forced their children into more church participation, or less? Their children may be highly successful in their careers or education, but without any Christian orientation, how different are they than any other pagan? What of their eternal destiny? What about the influence on the grandchildren? It is this kind of parent who understands the joy and sorrow that the shepherd in the parable evinces over the wayward sheep that is found. These parents do not love less or take less joy in their children who have not gone astray; they grieve the loss, spiritually, of their wayward child.

Such parents illustrate the necessity of mutual accountability within the community of disciples. A parent will almost certainly never give up on a willful child, and we within the community must not give up on recalcitrant brothers and sisters in Christ. They need to know that we love them and will continue to pursue them. We need to know the limits within which they will allow us to operate, but we must continue to pursue.

My own brother went astray into the dark path of homosexuality after he had been walking with Jesus for only a year or two. When he left, I couldn't understand him, and I almost rejected him. But I continued to pray. After nearly fifteen years I learned how best to reach him. I stopped condemning him and said I would love him regardless of his choices. Two years later he died in an AIDS hospice house. I held him and cried during his final tragic moments, but in a broken whisper he thanked me for loving him and never giving up on him. I believe that the loving Lord Jesus reached down and restored him, because my brother displayed a deep sorrow and repentance at the end. I'll never know for sure in this life, but I do know that he taught me never to give up on those who have gone astray. I may not get the results that I want, but we are nevertheless responsible for the accountability that we have for each other.

Two important points follow from this. (a) We must never get too preoccupied with our own advancement in Christian service and maturity that we forget that we are here to help other disciples on the path, including those who backslide. (b) Although God loves the ninety-nine faithful, obedient sheep and rejoices over his relationship with them, his heart is never fully settled until all are safe. Although we should participate in the joy of Christian fellowship, we must give ourselves to the prayer, pursuit, and restoration of those gone astray.

(2) The four steps of dealing with sinning brothers or sisters (18:15–19) is instructive for our day. Discipline is not usually a popular topic. Dr. James Dobson wrote a remarkably best-selling book in 1970 entitled *Dare to Discipline*,[30] which challenged the prevailing pattern of parenting. The church today likewise needs to dare to discipline those involved in sin by challenging the prevailing pattern of permissiveness. In the litigious atmosphere of

---

30. James C. Dobson, *Dare to Discipline* (Wheaton: Tyndale House, 1970).

popular culture, it is often easier to allow people to get away with sin than to try to implement the steps of discipline that Jesus develops and face the threat of a lawsuit. And in the cafeteria-style hopping from church to church that is so prominent in our day, it is sometimes easier to let people who have sinned in one church be allowed to go to another church body, since there is little mutual accountability between churches.

But it is important for us to try to work through the process practically. I am ordained in the Evangelical Free Church of America, and I was encouraged several years ago when the ministerial studied the question of discipline and restoration of those who had fallen into moral failure. Over the period of several years and several drafts, it produced a document intended to guide individual churches and the denomination in the process of disciplining and, hopefully, of restoring pastors and leaders who have been charged with moral failure. The document took its lead from Matthew 18:15–20 but also allowed the full counsel of Scripture to inform the process, including Paul's directive in 1 Timothy 5:19–22, which guards the accused and the church.

This document is one of the finest I have seen to help guide the process. While it does not resolve all the difficulties, it is a courageous attempt to follow biblical guidelines, and the document maintains a steady focus both on discipline and on restoration as the intended goal. It answered many of the tough practical questions of how to carry this out with regard to an ordained minister, but it is also helpful to any situation of a sinning brother or sister.[31]

The discipline of brothers and sisters is not a pleasant task, but as we follow Scripture's teaching, it will help contribute to a community of disciples that is a faithful witness to the presence of the risen Lord Jesus in our midst. And it is important always to keep in mind that the goal is not discipline itself, or even punishment. The intended goal of all discipline is restoration of the sinning brother or sister to a state of purity and the reestablishment of the fellowship of peace within the body.[32]

**Mercy annuls alienation.** A few years ago when bumper stickers were popular, one stood out to me: "I don't get mad, I get even." It was meant to be humorous, but it had a chilling effect on me, because it described my attitude just a few years prior. I've mentioned elsewhere that I was raised by a stepfather who caused my family and me a great deal of pain. He left our family when I was in my early teens, and I carried a deep animosity toward him for years. When I was in Vietnam, my animosity became almost obsessive,

---

31. Requests for the report may be sent through the ministerial website *http://www.efca.org/freechurch.html*.

32. For a practical application, see Ken Sande, *The Peacemaker: A Biblical Guide to Resolving Personal Conflict* (Grand Rapids: Baker, 1997).

and I vowed that the first time I saw him on my return, I would kill him. I would make him pay for what he had done to our family. I returned a few months later and within a year had become a Christian. My world began to change, and I put that stepfather out of my mind.

I had not thought about him much until about four years later, when he suddenly showed up where my wife and I and our little girl were living. He had tracked us down. My wife, being the loving person she is, invited him in. As we sat and talked politely, that vow came to my mind. I then told him, "I made a vow in Vietnam that the first time I saw you, I would kill you. Today is that day." I will never forget the look of terror that came over his face. He started to sweat and slide down on the couch. I went on, "But I now know that I'm no better a person than you. God has forgiven me. And if he can forgive a sinner like me, I can forgive you. I will not allow you to hurt my family again, so don't think that this is made out of weakness. Rather, I forgive you because I have been forgiven."

I probably was as shocked as he was. I had not thought about saying those words of forgiveness, but they came easily. I was deeply aware of the mercy and forgiveness that God had extended to me. I knew my sin better than anyone. I may not have been as abusive as my former stepfather. I may not have hurt people in the same way he had hurt our family. But I had also abused and hurt people in my own self-seeking way. When I came to that awareness, I knew that I needed mercy and forgiveness. And in receiving the gift of life that Jesus extended to me through his work on the cross, extending mercy and forgiveness to my former stepfather was a natural response. My vow had been the rash, irresponsible reaction of a deeply hurt, bitter young sinner. However, my ability later to forgive came from the eternal, loving act of grace in Jesus' sacrifice for my sin. I discovered that the key to forgiveness is to stop focusing on what others have done *to* us and focus instead on what Jesus has done *for* us.

*Mercy creates community.* I have had the privilege of getting to know a person who exemplifies this truth. His name is Tom Tarrants. He is currently the president of the C. S. Lewis Institute, an organization that sponsors conferences and a fellows program that try to break down walls between believers of varied backgrounds for a common commitment to the "mere Christianity" that C. S. Lewis articulated. Tom is well qualified to provide leadership, not least because of his background. He has been the copastor of an interracial church in Washington, D.C., and one who has learned how mercy received creates community.

A former segregationist who participated with the violent activities of the Ku Klux Klan during the 1960s and 1970s, Tom met Jesus Christ as his Savior in a Mississippi prison cell. The transformation of his life is miraculous, as his hatred was replaced by love, and his bigotry with reconciliation. Together with John Perkins, a former black activist, they have written a book entitled *He's My Brother*, which not only tells their stories but also presents a workable strategy for building bridges of understanding and reconciliation between peoples of differing backgrounds and color.[33] Their unwavering message is that racial reconciliation is impossible until individuals on both sides experience the mercy and forgiveness of God for their personal sin, which will create a community of faith based in the reconciling work of Jesus Christ. These men operate out of a deep well of gratitude to God for his mercy and forgiveness, which in turn has compelled them to demonstrate mercy and forgiveness to those they once hated.

*Mercy advances community.* The creation of a community of disciples based on reconciliation requires an ongoing process to advance community. John Perkins states it this way:

> God expects us to value our brothers and sisters the way He does. . . . I see it not as an option, but as an integral part of the Gospel. I also see reconciliation as something that takes time. The divisions in our country are deep ones. We have deep wounds that have not yet begun to heal. We have hurts and resentments that have never been dealt with. It will require time, patience and perseverance to overcome these obstacles to reconciliation.[34]

Both Tarrants and Perkins have given themselves in their personal lives and in their ministries to exemplify the reconciliation that they experienced with God and with each other. In receiving mercy, they demonstrate mercy.

You may not have the same testimony of explicit hatred of others, but our own hurt and resentment, even against those within the church, hinder true community. An unspiritual community is one that does not live in relationship to the reality of the cross and resurrection of Jesus. Rather, it lives according to the prevailing cultural paradigm of values. We may try to gather around like interests, or geographical location, or even political ideologies. But the kind of community that Jesus advances is based on having received mercy and forgiveness, which in turn will impel us to demonstrate mercy and forgiveness.

There is something powerful in the contrast between the two debts (18:23–35). The first man is forgiven such a large amount that it should truly affect the way that he responds to others' infractions against him. This debt represents the type of debt we have been forgiven by the Father. We would

---

33. John Perkins and Thomas A. Tarrants III, with David Wimbush, *He's My Brother: Former Racial Foes Offer Strategy for Reconciliation* (Grand Rapids: Baker, 1994).

34. Ibid., 228.

never be able to pay back such a huge debt, and we are granted a reprieve simply by asking. In turn, we should be as willing to pardon infractions against us, which are qualitatively much less in comparison. As we said, the key to forgiveness is to stop focusing on what others have done *to* us and focus on what Jesus has done *for* us.

The obvious application is much more than simply a toleration of the person who has offended us. It is a forgiveness "from the heart" (18:35). True reconciliation is not simply a tolerant attitude toward one another in the same living space. It is a real, personal, loving connection between individuals that Jesus desires, and without a heart attitude of forgiveness, this type of connection is not even possible.

Another important facet to consider is that often our forgiveness of others points people toward God's forgiveness of them. Forgiveness not only sustains the intimacy of the community, but it is a powerful device that allows people to make change in their own lives and move on toward deeper intimacy with God. One of my students was struck by the impact of this in the day-to-day realities of the workaday world. He worked in a print shop in which some materials were made for him, with the understanding that he would pay for it later. He eventually moved on to another job, failing to pay for the materials before he went, and the Lord prompted him later to call the owner and offer to pay for the product. He asked for forgiveness for failing to pay earlier. The owner was so quick to forgive that it moved my student to tears. It was a minor issue, but he realized that the incident gave him a living example of what God's forgiveness toward us is like. He was able to connect to the Father on a deeper level because of a godly man's immediate obedience, even in the little things, to the standard of forgiveness set out by Jesus.

# Matthew 19:1–30

W HEN JESUS HAD finished saying these things, he left Galilee and went into the region of Judea to the other side of the Jordan. ²Large crowds followed him, and he healed them there.

³Some Pharisees came to him to test him. They asked, "Is it lawful for a man to divorce his wife for any and every reason?"

⁴"Haven't you read," he replied, "that at the beginning the Creator 'made them male and female,' ⁵and said, 'For this reason a man will leave his father and mother and be united to his wife, and the two will become one flesh'? ⁶So they are no longer two, but one. Therefore what God has joined together, let man not separate."

⁷"Why then," they asked, "did Moses command that a man give his wife a certificate of divorce and send her away?"

⁸Jesus replied, "Moses permitted you to divorce your wives because your hearts were hard. But it was not this way from the beginning. ⁹I tell you that anyone who divorces his wife, except for marital unfaithfulness, and marries another woman commits adultery."

¹⁰The disciples said to him, "If this is the situation between a husband and wife, it is better not to marry."

¹¹Jesus replied, "Not everyone can accept this word, but only those to whom it has been given. ¹²For some are eunuchs because they were born that way; others were made that way by men; and others have renounced marriage because of the kingdom of heaven. The one who can accept this should accept it."

¹³Then little children were brought to Jesus for him to place his hands on them and pray for them. But the disciples rebuked those who brought them.

¹⁴Jesus said, "Let the little children come to me, and do not hinder them, for the kingdom of heaven belongs to such as these." ¹⁵When he had placed his hands on them, he went on from there.

¹⁶Now a man came up to Jesus and asked, "Teacher, what good thing must I do to get eternal life?"

¹⁷"Why do you ask me about what is good?" Jesus replied. "There is only One who is good. If you want to enter life, obey the commandments."

¹⁸"Which ones?" the man inquired.

Jesus replied, "'Do not murder, do not commit adultery, do not steal, do not give false testimony, ¹⁹honor your father and mother,' and 'love your neighbor as yourself.'"

²⁰"All these I have kept," the young man said. "What do I still lack?"

²¹Jesus answered, "If you want to be perfect, go, sell your possessions and give to the poor, and you will have treasure in heaven. Then come, follow me."

²²When the young man heard this, he went away sad, because he had great wealth.

²³Then Jesus said to his disciples, "I tell you the truth, it is hard for a rich man to enter the kingdom of heaven. ²⁴Again I tell you, it is easier for a camel to go through the eye of a needle than for a rich man to enter the kingdom of God."

²⁵When the disciples heard this, they were greatly astonished and asked, "Who then can be saved?"

²⁶Jesus looked at them and said, "With man this is impossible, but with God all things are possible."

²⁷Peter answered him, "We have left everything to follow you! What then will there be for us?"

²⁸Jesus said to them, "I tell you the truth, at the renewal of all things, when the Son of Man sits on his glorious throne, you who have followed me will also sit on twelve thrones, judging the twelve tribes of Israel. ²⁹And everyone who has left houses or brothers or sisters or father or mother or children or fields for my sake will receive a hundred times as much and will inherit eternal life. ³⁰But many who are first will be last, and many who are last will be first."

THE GREAT GALILEAN ministry has ended. Galilee was the primary focus of Jesus' earthly ministry, with the city of Capernaum the primary headquarters (see comments on 4:12; 8:14). Tremendous crowds witnessed his teaching and miracles. But Jesus' popularity began to fade when the crowds realized he was not going to establish the political, militaristic kingdom that they desired (see comments on 13:10–17). Jesus and the disciples now begin the momentous journey to Jerusalem, which will culminate with the crucifixion, burial, and resurrection in the first week of April, A.D. 30.[1]

---

1. For a discussion of the dating, see comments on 21:21; 26:17.

## Journeying Through Judea to Jerusalem (19:1-2)

THE ROUTE THAT Jesus and the disciples take from Galilee to Judea goes through the region Matthew calls "beyond the Jordan" (19:1). This is most likely Perea, the land just east of the Jordan River that lay between Samaria and the Decapolis. Along with Galilee, it was administered by Herod Antipas, with a largely Jewish population.[2] The fortress Machaerus, where John the Baptist was beheaded, was located in the southern region of Perea. Jesus' reputation from his healing ministry in Galilee has preceded him, for large crowds follow his movement through the region. Similar to his compassion demonstrated in Galilee, he heals them.

It is difficult to determine which events in Matthew's narrative of the nearly six-month journey to Jerusalem occur in Perea and which in Judea, though the final event does occur in Jericho (20:29-34), which is located in Judea. Following the Community Prescription (ch. 18), Matthew records events that reveal what life is like in his community of disciples, including the sanctity of marriage (19:3-12) and the value of the kingdom over all else, including status (19:13-15), wealth (19:16-29), rewards (20:1-15), rank (20:20-28), and capability (20:29-34).

## Sanctity of Marriage in the Community (19:3-12)

ON HIS JOURNEY to Jerusalem, Jesus is confronted several times by religious leaders who "test" him, trying to get him to incriminate himself through misinterpreting the law according to their traditions. Pharisees arrive, continuing the opposition that those in Galilee (e.g., 12:1-2) and those who traveled from Jerusalem (e.g., 15:1) carried out. They now focus on divorce by asking, "Is it lawful for a man to divorce his wife for any and every reason?"

**The question of divorce (19:3-9).** The expression "for any and every reason" is unique to Matthew, reflecting his remembrance of this controversy. A hotbed of discussion surrounded the interpretations of Moses' divorce regulation.[3] The leading Pharisees of Jesus' day debated the grounds for divorce that Moses established, who allowed a man to divorce his wife if he "finds something indecent about her" (Deut. 24:1). The debate focused on the word "indecent."

---

2. Matthew's wording in 19:1 seems to imply that Judea includes Transjordan. The parallel passage in Mark 10:1 has the word *kai*, meaning "and" ("into ... Judea *and* across the Jordan"), though this *kai* is textually uncertain. For background, see Van Elderen, "Early Christianity in Transjordan," 97-117; Diane I. Treacy-Cole, "Perea," *ABD*, 5:224-25.

3. For a very fine overview of the passage that wrestles with contemporary application, see Craig L. Blomberg, "Marriage, Divorce, Remarriage, and Celibacy: An Exegesis of Mt 19:3-12," *TrinJ* n.s. 11 (1990): 161-96. For what may be the best full-length treatment that concludes with pastoral implications, see Instone-Brewer, *Divorce and Remarriage in the Bible*.

The Mishnah tractate *Gittin* ("Bills of Divorce") records the differing interpretations (*m. Git.* 9:10). The more conservative school of Shammai held to the letter of the Mosaic law and said that the word "indecent" means "unchastity." The more liberal school of Hillel interpreted "indecency" to mean that "he may divorce her even if she spoiled a dish for him." The esteemed Rabbi Akiba, who belonged to the school of Hillel, later added, "Even if he found another fairer than she," demonstrating that divorce was being granted for the most superficial reasons.

Jesus brought up marital faithfulness and divorce in the Sermon on the Mount as an example of the way that the arrival of the kingdom of heaven brings to fulfillment the Old Testament. He used it also as an example of the way that current interpretations were causing the intention of the Old Testament to be violated (see comments on 5:31–32). Here he uses the same argumentation but addresses the Pharisees directly, who were guilty of that violation.

Jesus goes back to the beginning of creation to demonstrate God's intention for the institution of marriage. He quotes Genesis 2:24 to note that God designed his human creatures as male and female, with marriage a permanent bond of a man and woman into one new union that is consecrated by physical intercourse. God "hates" divorce, because it tears apart what should be considered a permanent union (cf. Mal. 2:16). So Jesus avoids the Pharisaic argument and demands that humans should go back to God's intention and understand that marriage is part of God's original design.[4] Divorce separates what God brought together (Matt. 19:4–6).[5]

But the Pharisees think that they have trapped Jesus, for they point to the Mosaic law that allowed a husband to give to his wife a certificate of divorce: "Why then ... did Moses command that a man give his wife a certificate of divorce and send her away?" Since sinful abuse of a marriage partner was a harsh reality in the ancient world, Moses instituted a regulation designed to do three things: (1) protect the sanctity of marriage from something "indecent" defiling the relationship; (2) protect the woman from a husband who might simply send her away without any cause; and (3) document her status as a legitimately divorced woman, so that she would not be thought a harlot or a runaway adulteress. The Pharisees insist that if Moses allowed divorce, then it must be a valid option for a marriage partner to consider.

Jesus counters by once again going to God's original intention with marriage: "Moses permitted you to divorce your wives because your hearts were hard. But it was not this way from the beginning." Somewhere in each

---

4. G. D. Collier, "Rethinking Jesus on Divorce," *Restoration Quarterly* 37 (1995): 80–96. Jesus is attacking the practice of searching for frivolous authorization for divorce and remarriage.

5. Instone-Brewer, *Divorce and Remarriage in the Bible*, 133–41.

relationship that experiences divorce, something has gone wrong that shouldn't have. So Moses gave God's prescription for dealing with sin. Jesus emphasizes that divorce should never be understood to be a morally neutral option. It always evidences the presence of sin, the hardness of heart.[6] The Pharisees are focused on the wrong issue. They are not looking at God's original intention but at Moses' prescription.[7] With the arrival of the gospel of the kingdom, the reversal of the fallen order has begun, which means the redemption of marriages as well. Hard hearts can be regenerated and the divorce certificate made obsolete.

However, as did Moses, Jesus allows for an exception to protect the nonoffending partner and to protect the institution of marriage from being an indecent sham.[8] Such an occasion occurs when a person has committed *porneia*, which the NIV appropriately renders "marital unfaithfulness." In a phrase unique to Matthew (see also 5:32), Jesus states, "I tell you that anyone who divorces his wife, *except for marital unfaithfulness [porneia]*, and marries another woman commits adultery" (19:9; my emphasis). Since "adultery" is already specified by another word (*moicheuo;* 5:27–28; 19:9), *porneia* must be something less specific than sexual infidelity, but, following the Mosaic intention, more than a frivolous excuse.

The semantic range of *porneia* includes whatever intentionally divides the marital relationship, possibly including, but not limited to, related sexual sins such as incest, homosexuality, prostitution, molestation, or indecent exposure.[9] Later rabbis declared that divorce was required in the case of adultery (putting the offending party to death as Moses prescribed in Deut. 24:1–4 was no longer practiced), because adultery produced a state of impurity that, as a matter of legal fact, dissolved the marriage (*m. Sotah* 5:1; *m. Yebam.* 2:8).[10]

---

6. Carson, "Matthew," 413.

7. See Andrew Warren, "Did Moses Permit Divorce? *Modal weqatal* As Key to New Testament Readings of Deuteronomy 24:1–4," *TynBul* 49 (1998): 39–56.

8. Allen R. Guenther, "The Exception Phrases: Except πορνεία, Including πορνεία or Excluding πορνεία? (Matthew 5:32; 19:9)," *TynBul* 53 (2002): 83–96, takes up the question of the grammatical construction, which has been often debated as to whether Jesus meant it *inclusively* ("if a man divorces his wife even though she has not been unfaithful"), *exceptively* ("if a man divorces his wife, except if she has been unfaithful"), or *exclusively* ("if a man divorces his wife—*porneia* is a separate issue"). Guenther accepts the latter exclusive interpretation, but Instone-Brewer adequately demonstrates how the traditional exceptive interpretation is demanded here and in 5:32 (Instone-Brewer, *Divorce and Remarriage*, 155–56).

9. Blomberg, "Marriage, Divorce, Remarriage, and Celibacy," 177; David Janzen, "The Meaning of *Porneia* in Matthew 5.32 and 19.9: An Approach from the Study of Ancient Near Eastern Culture," *JSNT* 80 (2000): 66–80.

10. See Markus Bockmuehl, "Matthew 5.32; 19.9 in the Light of Pre-Rabbinic Halakah," *NTS* 35 (1989): 291–95.

Jesus does not require divorce but allows it to occur to protect the person violated. Divorce without this exception creates adultery, the despicable nature of which he has declared in the SM (5:27–30), because an illicit divorce turns both parties of a new marriage into adulterers. However, if a divorce is granted under the exception of *porneia*, remarriage is permissible.[11]

The exception clause is consistent with Joseph's behavior as a "righteous" man in the infancy narrative (1:18–25). When Mary becomes pregnant through the Holy Spirit in the betrothal period, Joseph first learns of her condition without knowing of its supernatural origin. As a righteous man, it is appropriate for him to obtain a certificate of divorce because he thinks she has committed adultery. But he does not carry through with the divorce after the angel of the Lord appears and tells him his wife-to-be has not been unfaithful.

**The question of singleness in the community (19:10–12).** The disciples do not seem to catch the full meaning of Jesus' statement, so most likely after the Pharisees leave, they approach Jesus for more complete understanding (cf. 13:10; 15:12). They now understand that marriage is far more of a permanent, unbreakable commitment than even they may have treated it, but they misunderstand the commitment to mean a torturous obligation. If that is the case, they mistakenly surmise, it is better not to marry (19:10).

Although the disciples may have been making a somewhat cynical suggestion, Jesus picks up on their comment in a positive way to suggest that for some it is God's will to remain single, and it is only for them to accept it (19:11). Jesus does not contradict his earlier confirmation that the right order of God's creation is for men and women to marry and remain so permanently (19:4–6), but neither is he going to adopt the disciple's cynical attitude toward a life of singleness. Singleness is an appropriate alternative for those for whom it has been given as their lot in life, whether they are a literal (either born or man-made) or figurative eunuch (19:12).

Some eunuchs have been born without the capacity for sexual relations, such as those born without properly developed genitalia.[12] Others have been castrated for official functions, especially those in some cultures, like the Ethiopian eunuch (Acts 8:27), who were castrated in order to be officials in a court among royal women. Still others have adopted abstinence because God has made an exception for their particular work in the kingdom of heaven, such as John the Baptist and Jesus himself. Paul points out that some, on the basis of extreme situations in the church, would serve better if they were single (1 Cor. 7:7–9). But nowhere in Scripture is celibacy seen as a higher form of spirituality than being married.

---

11. Cf. Philip H. Wiebe, "Jesus' Divorce Exception," *JETS* 32 (1989): 327–33.

12. Blomberg, "Marriage, Divorce, Remarriage, and Celibacy," 185.

## The Kingdom Community Belongs to Children (19:13–15)

THE SUBJECT OF children naturally arises after marriage. "Then little children were brought to Jesus for him to place his hands on them and pray for them." Placing hands on children for blessing had a long history in Israel, primarily when passing on a blessing from one generation to another (cf. Gen. 48:14; Num. 27:18). But bringing children to Jesus for his blessing irritates the disciples, and they rebuke those bringing them. The disciples probably do not want the children brought to Jesus because they had an insignificant societal status and are interrupting what they consider to be more important matters of proclaiming the kingdom of heaven.

But the scene is reminiscent of the way in which Jesus used little children as metaphors of discipleship when counteracting the glory-seeking of the disciples. Jesus once again turns prevailing societal values on their head to show that the low position of children in society illustrates the humility necessary for entrance into the kingdom of God (19:14; see comments on 18:1–5). Childlikeness is not only a prerequisite for entrance to the kingdom but is also a necessary lifetime characteristic for Jesus' disciples. As weak, defenseless, vulnerable children, they must continue to maintain dependence on their heavenly Father for the purpose, power, and significance of their life of discipleship.[13]

Thus, Jesus confirms these values for those in his kingdom by placing his hands on the children (19:15). This is a symbolic demonstration, not an actual conferral of kingdom life, as some in church history later construe it to mean.[14] Through this act Jesus displays to his disciples and to the crowds the essential nature of the characteristics of kingdom life that are to be produced in them. The disciples will desperately need this reminder when all thought of glory, power, and greatness is removed with the arrest and crucifixion of Jesus.

The metaphorical lesson on discipleship should not displace the literal lesson concerning children. It is their very weakness and vulnerability that often enable little children to be most receptive to Jesus' message. Before hardness of heart sets in from experiencing the hurts of this life, vulnerable children can learn to trust the message of hope and salvation that is found in the gospel. Jesus' gentle openness to them, his compassionate touch, and his protective words elevate them from being marginally irrelevant to being valuable objects of his gospel outreach.

---

13. See Carter, *Households and Discipleship*, 113–14.

14. Hagner, *Matthew*, 2:553, notes that the practice of infant baptism is sometimes based on this passage, an unlikely association. There is no water in the passage, and the children are used as a metaphor, not as literal recipients of a conferral of kingdom life.

All humans are equally precious to Jesus, and this picture of Jesus' tender touch of the little children has become an emblem of missionary and humanitarian efforts for the church throughout history. The community of disciples sees in Jesus' actions a picture of how it must overcome the irritation of those first disciples and devote itself to the spiritual and physical care not only of children, but of all those who are helpless, hurting, and marginalized.

It is also important to recognize that little children bring with them as new disciples a perspective that is unique to them. We can learn much by valuing the contributions of children and seeing their spiritual growth and development not only in terms of their future development but also in what they can also contribute now. Often, children endorse attitudes and insights that we lose as we grow in discipleship. Jesus validates the unique perspectives of these little ones who correctly perceive the true nature of the kingdom, and we do well to learn from them.

### The Tragedy of the Rich Young Man (19:16–22)

THE INCIDENT OF the rich young man appears in all three Synoptic Gospels (19:16–22; Mark 10:17–22; Luke 18:23). While each writer discloses that the person is rich, they reveal his further identity somewhat differently: Matthew calls him a "young man" (19:20), Mark simply states he is a "man" (10:17), and Luke alone calls him "a certain ruler" (18:18). This young man (between twenty to forty years old) is some kind of religious lay leader, possibly a Pharisee (because of his scrupulous adherence to the law). These people often were well off financially since they were among the retainer class. In first-century Palestine the Roman occupiers allowed a form of self-rule, and within Judaism the religious leaders exercised that leadership.[15]

Addressing Jesus with a title of respect ("teacher") that acknowledges the help he can receive from his learning and mastery of Scripture, the young man evidently has experienced a need in his life to perform some kind of righteous deed that will assure him of having eternal life. "Teacher, what good thing must I do to get eternal life?"[16]

This young man seems to believe that there is something deficient in obeying the law to gain eternal life. Jesus gets the young man to focus on God alone as the Good, to whom he must come to gain eternal life (19:17). Jesus is not denying he is good or that he is equal with God, but he is trying to get the rich young man to see that only in understanding God as good can he discover that good deeds beyond the law do not obtain eternal life. Jewish writings exhorted

---

15. Saldarini, *Pharisees, Scribes and Sadducees*, 277–97.

16. On the surface it may appear as if the young man is attempting to entrap Jesus in a theological error, as other Pharisees did (e.g., 16:1; 19:3), but Matthew does not indicate that.

each person to bless God as the truly good: "For rain and good tidings he should say, 'Blessed is he, the good and the doer of good'" (*m. Ber.* 9.3).

Jesus goes on: "If you want to enter life, obey the commandments." Jesus takes the young man back to obeying the law as the expression of belief in the truly good being. The good God has written his good will for his people.[17] Connected to the preceding discussion of entering the kingdom of heaven as a child, the rich young man should display obedience to the law as the source of all good, including eternal life. This is not to *earn* life eternal; rather, it is humbly to obey the law in childlike faith in God's goodness.

Jesus approaches the concept of eternal life here from three perspectives, all of which combine to give a clearer understanding of that one phenomenon. (1) Eternal life is entering a form of existence that differs from the human existence into which one is born (19:17). One enters that form in the here and now, but it continues after one's physical death (cf. 25:46). (2) Eternal life is equal to entrance into the kingdom of heaven (19:23), which looks at one's life in the continual presence of God and his kingdom, which has both present and future, spiritual and physical, realities (see comments on 3:2; 4:17). (3) Eternal life equates to being saved (19:25), which looks at one's existence from the perspective of deliverance from the judgment that accompanies sin. It is rare to find these three perspectives in one passage.

In 19:18 the young man responds to Jesus' directive to obey the commandments by asking, "Which ones?" Jesus replies by giving a representative listing of the law, including five of the commandments in the second part of the Decalogue (cf. Ex. 20:1–17; Deut. 5:7–21) and the second of the two greatest commandments (Lev. 19:18; cf. Matt. 22:36–40). With unblinking confidence, the young man (identified for the first time as "young") declares that he has kept them all. And he does not mean only those commandments cited by Jesus, for he understands these commandments as representative of the entire law. His obedience to the law is complete.

Although it may seem presumptuous for the young man to say he has kept all the commandments, he is not alone. When Sirach called his readers to obey the law, he calls them to acknowledge the power of their own free choice and challenges them, "If you choose, you can keep the commandments, and to act faithfully is a matter of your own choice" (Sir. 15:15). When Paul recounted his former life as a Pharisee and viewed his obedience to the law, he considered himself "as to righteousness under the law, blameless" (Phil. 3:6; NRSV).

But obedience to the law still does not satisfy this young man. He senses that he still lacks something: "What do I still lack?" This is the place where he needs to be. Jesus could have challenged him further to find where some lack of obe-

---

17. Larry W. Hurtado, "First-Century Jewish Monotheism," *JSNT* 71 (1998): 3–26.

dience might be found and corrected, but the issue is not one of external performance. The Pharisees prided themselves on their righteousness accomplished
through obeying the law. Instead, Jesus takes the young man to the inner place
where his values are formed (his heart) and challenges him to see what is his most
cherished value—in essence, the ruling god of his life. Without the truly good
God ruling him, he will continue to lack. Note how Paul, when he went to the
inner place of his heart and examined himself in the light of the inner urge to
covet, realized that he was fully sinful (cf. Rom. 7:7–12).

Jesus answered, "If you want to be perfect, go, sell your possessions and
give to the poor, and you will have treasure in heaven. Then come, follow
me." The young man has almost certainly given to the poor in the past,
because the giving of alms was one of the pillars of piety within Judaism, especially among the Pharisees (see comments on 6:1–4). But giving to the poor
can be done out of the abundance that a person has. It can give a person an
even greater sense of power and personal pride. Jesus instead calls this young
man to address the central lack in his life. His wealth has become his means
to personal identity, power, purpose, and meaning in life. It has, in a real
sense, become his god. Thus, Jesus calls him to exchange the god of wealth
for following him as the one true God.[18] He will continue to lack until he
becomes like a child—powerless, defenseless, and needing his Father's influence (see 18:1–4; 19:13–15).

The response of the young man comprises one of the truly heartbreaking verses in Scripture: "When the young man heard this, he went away sad,
because he had great wealth." The young man knows that Jesus has correctly
pinpointed what is lacking in his life. He knows what issues are at stake. His
many possessions have captivated his heart, and he cannot exchange this
god for Jesus (cf. 6:21–24). So he goes away with great distress (cf. 26:22,
37), knowing deep in his heart that his decision has eternal consequences.
He knew all along what he was lacking for eternal life, and when he is offered
it by Jesus, he rejects the invitation to life.

### The Gracious Reward for Those
### Who Follow Jesus (19:23–30)

THE DIFFICULTY OF rich people entering the kingdom of heaven (19:23–
26). Jesus uses the incident of the rich young man as an object lesson for the

---

18. For a similar perspective that draws on the community pattern of the first-century
model of the Mediterranean family and Jesus' alternative spiritual pattern from Mark's perspective, see Joseph H. Hellerman, "Wealth and Sacrifice in Early Christianity: Revisit-
ing Mark's Presentation of Jesus' Encounter with the Rich Young Ruler," *TrinJ* n.s. 21
(2000): 143–64.

disciples: "I tell you the truth, it is hard for a rich man to enter the kingdom of heaven." This man illustrates a basic principle of this life—wealth is a heady intoxicant, because it provides most of the counterfeits that fool a person into thinking he or she does not need God. The wealthy person is the opposite of the child. The child has no power, no defense, and no personal resources to accomplish what he or she wants in life. To become like a child is to receive God into one's life, who will then supply what is lacking (18:1−5; 19:13−15). But the rich person is self-sufficient, having the resources to be powerful, to protect oneself from deprivation and hardship, and to make of oneself whatever one wants.

To illustrate the difficulty of a rich person entering the kingdom of God,[19] Jesus draws on an analogy using a camel, the largest land animal in Palestine, and the eye of a needle, the smallest aperture found in the home (19:24). If not for the seriousness of the issue, the analogy would bring a chuckle to Jesus' listeners as they envision the impossibility of the huge, humped, hairy, spitting beast fitting through the tiny eye of a common sewing needle. And it just may have been Jesus' intent to lighten the mood with this ridiculous mental picture, because he wants to shock the crowd into seeing that even the absurdly impossible is possible with God (19:26).[20]

The disciples are shocked at Jesus' statement about the difficulty of wealthy people entering the kingdom of God, because wealth was often equated with the blessing of divine favor (Deut. 28:1−14). Abraham's wealth was assumed to be a reward for his obedience as a God-fearing man (Gen. 13:2), and the psalmist declares of those who fear the Lord, "His children will be mighty in the land; the generation of the upright will be blessed. Wealth and riches are in his house, and his righteousness endures forever" (Ps. 112:1−3). If those who seemingly are the most blessed of God cannot be saved, then who can be (Matt. 19:25)? Notice that the disciples understand that "entering the kingdom of heaven/God" (19:23−24) is equivalent to being "saved" (19:25), which in turn is equivalent to entering and obtaining eternal life (19:16−17).

---

19. Note that Jesus uses "kingdom of God" here (19:24). It is used in parallel with "kingdom of heaven" in the preceding verse (19:23), a reminder that the expressions were interchangeable (cf. 3:2; 4:17).

20. Some unimportant manuscripts read *kamilon* ("rope, ship's cable") here rather than *kamelon* ("camel"), suggesting a rope being pulled through a needle. A popular interpretation, dating from the Middle Ages, suggests that there was a small gate in Jerusalem called "eye of the needle" and that camels had to stoop to their knees to enter it with great difficulty. There is no historical or archaeological support for this gate. Both suggestions miss the point of the analogy, which emphasizes the impossibility of rich persons entering the kingdom of heaven.

Jesus knows that riches can keep people's eyes off of God. But he also knows God's operation in the lives of people and says that even if it is impossible with humankind, if a rich person truly trusts God, God will make it possible (19:26). The rich young man has a deep-seated recognition that something is lacking in his life. Jesus points him to the inner problem, the wealth that is the ruling force in his life, and by exchanging his wealth for Jesus as his Lord, he will indeed become Jesus' disciple, enter the kingdom of heaven, and find eternal life. But the young man finds this too difficult, so he turns away. Other rich persons, such as Joseph of Arimathea (27:57) and Zacchaeus (Luke 19:9–10), did find salvation by becoming Jesus' disciples. All we need to do is to acknowledge what rules our lives and exchange that treasure for the treasure of Jesus as one's God (cf. Luke 14:25–33).

**Reward for following Jesus (19:27–30).** Once Jesus has made this dramatic statement, Peter steps forward once again as a spokesman for the disciples: "We have left everything to follow you! What then will there be for us?" Peter gets Jesus' point, but not fully. He rightly understands that the focus is not solely on the rich person but on all people, because it provides a pattern for anyone. He and the others have left all to follow Jesus (4:18–22). But Peter should have left it there. He has already entered the kingdom of heaven and found salvation. Instead, he focuses on rewards. Jesus will acknowledge the rewards they will receive, but Peter's self-seeking for rewards sets up the parable in 20:1–15, which is a subtle rebuke to that self-seeking.

In Jesus' response to Peter, the plural "them" (19:28a) implicates the rest of the disciples with Peter's question: "I tell you the truth, at the renewal [*palingenesia*[21]] of all things, when the Son of Man sits on his glorious throne, you who have followed me will also sit on twelve thrones, judging the twelve tribes of Israel." In Titus, Paul refers to individual regeneration that each person experiences who is born again by the Spirit of God as he or she enters the kingdom of heaven (cf. John 3:3; 2 Cor. 5:17; 1 Peter 1:3). But individual regeneration looks forward to the renewal Jesus refers to in Matthew 19:28. *Palingenesia* here refers to a future time of renewal, the hope that was basic to Jewish expectation of Israel's future national restoration.[22]

Although "judging" can indicate condemnation of Israel for rejecting Jesus as national Messiah,[23] the idea of Jesus as the Son of Man and the Twelve

---

21. *Palingenesia* ("renewal, regeneration") occurs only here and in Titus 3:5 in the New Testament.

22. Cf. Sanders, *Jesus and Judaism*, 103. *Contra* David C. Sim, "The Meaning of *palingenesia* in Mt 19.28," *JSNT* 50 (1993): 3–12.

23. Carson, "Matthew," 426; cf. George Beasely-Murray, *Jesus and the Kingdom of God*, 275–76.

ruling or governing is paramount (cf. Rev. 3:21; 20:6). Condemning Israel would bring no great pleasure to the disciples, but reward would, which was the point of Peter's request (Matt. 19:27). Jesus predicts a time of renewal when the Twelve will participate in the final establishment of the kingdom of God on the earth, when Israel will be restored to the land and the Twelve will rule with Jesus Messiah.[24]

Although there will be a specific salvation-historical reward for the Twelve in relation to Israel at the time of the establishment of the kingdom of heaven on earth, there will also be reward for all who become disciples of Jesus: "And everyone who has left houses or brothers or sisters or father or mother or children or fields for my sake will receive a hundred times as much and will inherit eternal life." In distinction from the rich young man who has turned away, any who examine themselves and give up their own little gods to follow Jesus in discipleship, whether that little god is family or possessions or territory (cf. 10:34–39; Luke 14:25–33),[25] will receive the reward of the full realization of their inheritance of eternal life.

Jesus ends by showing that serving him and the kingdom of heaven for the primary purpose of receiving rewards and gaining personal prominence is the least noble of motivations for a disciple (19:30). Those who serve for the purpose of gaining rewards will be last, but those who serve for the motivation of obeying Jesus' summons will be first (cf. 20:1–16).

THE TRANSITIONAL PHRASE in 19:1, "When Jesus had finished saying these things," not only marks the beginning of the narrative of Jesus' travel through Perea and Judea en route to Jerusalem, but it also marks the end of Jesus' fourth discourse. Matthew signals the conclusion of each of Jesus' five primary discourses with a similar phrase (7:28; 11:1; 13:53; 19:1; 26:1). But the themes developed in each of the discourses continue to be woven into his ministry, so that the narratives of his activities are illustrations of the revelation he has given in the discourses.

This is readily seen in the interplay of the themes found in the fourth discourse with the narrative that follows. The Community Prescription of chapter 18 delineates the church as the community of disciples who witness to the reality of the presence of the kingdom throughout this age. Their wit-

---

24. Cf. Saucy, *The Case for Progressive Dispensationalism*, 267–69.

25. Thomas E. Schmidt, "Mark 10.29–30; Matthew 19.29: 'Leave Houses . . . and Region?,'" *NTS* 38 (1992): 617–20. Schmidt suggests that the Aramaic underlying *agrous* indicates that Jesus called disciples to leave house, family, and *territory*, which is a call to a new family and nation.

ness comes both through their declaration of the gospel message and through their example of living out the gospel as a family of faith that is character- ized by humility, purity, accountability, discipline, reconciliation, restora- tion, and forgiveness. Chapters 19–20 illustrate those community themes. The community of Jesus' disciples is not a theoretical concept but the con- crete expression of the way the kingdom affects real-life relationships. They illustrate how disciples are to be taught to obey everything that Jesus com- manded (28:20). Some of those principles are portrayed through negative examples of what destroy community life.

**Hardness of heart.** With his usual incredible insight into the human con- dition, Jesus states that the reason for the Mosaic certificate of divorce is because "your hearts were hard" (19:8). We might have expected Jesus to point out specific sins; instead, he looks at the condition of the heart. Hard hearts destroy a marriage in a variety of ways. (1) A hardened heart resists the will of God for the individual and for the marriage. This kind of person wants her own way and sins against God's way. So sin enters into the rela- tionship and defiles the purity of the oneness of the marriage bond. A hard heart begins to break the oneness that God had initiated.

(2) A person with a hard heart resists opening himself to his spouse. If love is commitment to a person, then hate is rejecting a person, and there is no more appropriate illustration of those truths than in a marriage (see comments on 5:43–47). For whatever reasons, ranging from the most trivial (e.g., a spouse's loss of youthful looks by aging) to the most complex (e.g., the acci- dental loss of a child in a car accident driven by one's spouse), it is possible to start hardening one's heart to the one to whom the husband or wife used to be so committed. The spiritual, emotional, and relational openness to each other that they once enjoyed is cut off, the commitment turns gradu- ally to outright rejection, and the unity of the marriage is violated.

(3) A heart that is hardened cannot receive or extend forgiveness. This becomes the most tragic, because with this kind of hardening a person with- draws into one's own little world, recreating reality by rationalizing sinful activities and attitudes, casting blame on everyone else, and developing a veneer of bitterness that warps all relationships. This kind of person refuses to repent and accept God's forgiveness and refuses to extend forgiveness to the spouse. The wife can never measure up to her husband's expectations, or the husband to the wife's expectations, and their former oneness is destroyed.

A related kind of hardening of heart occurs when one partner in a marriage has been continually hurt by the other. Each time the hurt occurs, the one who is hurt hardens the heart toward the spouse so that he or she won't be hurt again. Lack of trust leads to hardening against restoration and to isolation, where that person may seek companionship elsewhere, destroying the relationship.

It is from these kinds of hard hearts that sinful activity emerges. God weeps over these relationships, but to keep the hardhearted person from destroying his or her spouse, divorce was permitted. Likewise, Jesus allows divorce when *porneia* issues forth from a hard heart (we will explore some of the implications below).

We have seen that Jesus' teaching in the Community Prescription reveals the antidote for hard hearts—humility, purity, accountability, discipline, reconciliation, restoration, and forgiveness—whether the hard heart is within a marriage or within the church. Jesus warns each of us to regularly check our hearts to gauge our love for our spouse and for brothers and sisters within the community of disciples. The best starting point is to join humility with forgiveness, both asking for it from God and others and extending it in the way God has extended it to us.

**Treasures on earth.** The tragedy of the rich young ruler is that he preferred the treasures of earth to the treasures of heaven (19:21), preventing him from exchanging this "god" of his life for discipleship to Jesus. The truth that astounds the disciples is that those things that they have associated with God's blessing, especially wealth, is actually what prevents the rich young man from entering into the kingdom of heaven and joining the community of disciples.

But what is true as a warning for those outside the community holds true for us within the community. The "god" of our lives that we abandoned when we followed Jesus can rise up again to lead us astray. This is the subtlety that lies behind each of the temptations to sin about which Jesus warns the community (e.g., 18:6–9). When a person humbles himself to become vulnerable like a little child, the rest of the community must look out for him and help him overcome the allure of life. As soon as Peter steps forward to trumpet what he and the others have sacrificed and to inquire about their reward, the treasures of the old life beckon. In this case Jesus gives us the clue with his subtle chiding of Peter for wanting to be first (19:30), in the same way that each of the disciples competed over who was the greatest (18:1; see also 20:20–21). Jesus' disciples are responsible not just to themselves but also to each other, to help maintain purity and accountability to the ever-present Jesus (18:20).

COMMUNITY. The kind of community that Jesus sets forth in the Community Prescription and then illustrates in chapters 19 and 20 goes far beyond what many of us think of when we consider "community." It goes to the deepest hurts and needs and scars and offers a prescription of healing that will draw disciples of all walks and backgrounds together in the name of Jesus. It becomes a workable paradigm for any location, any time, and all types of people.

Randy Frazee is the pastor of an exciting church in Arlington, Texas. As his ministry has developed over the years, he has come to recognize that community is one of the most essential needs of his people and one of the foundational features of the church. Pastor Frazee writes of the "connecting church." He illustrates how the church overcomes three problems by connecting people to three crucial ingredients of community. Biblical community overcomes individualism by connecting people to a common purpose, which overcomes the problem of isolation by connecting people to a common place, and then overcomes the problem of consumerism by connecting people to common possessions. His thoughts reflect the principles that we have seen unfolded in Matthew's fourth discourse and the following narrative.

There is much wisdom, practical advice, and experience in his book. As Frazee says himself, "the most profound thought of the book is this: *Biblical community is the life of Christ on earth today.* When the church is fully functioning, it exudes the presence, power, and purpose of Jesus Christ."[26] The life of Jesus becomes the life force of the church as we witness to the reality of the kingdom of heaven. Our witness comes through both our declaration of the gospel message and our example of living out the gospel message as a family of faith characterized by humility, purity, accountability, discipline, reconciliation, restoration, and forgiveness. Two primary areas call for our attention: the sanctity of marriage and the "god" of one's life.

**The sanctity of marriage.** Performing a wedding is one of the great joys of pastoral life. I get to spend extended hours for several months of premarital preparation with the couple. I help them explore themselves and their relationship together and understand the nature of marriage as God intended it. Then, on the day of the wedding, it is my privilege to unite them in Christ. The pure elation on those beaming young faces, often with tears of joy streaming down, brings us close to one of the pure intentions for men and women, because it was God himself who established and made holy the relationship of marriage.

In Genesis God said of his creation of Adam, "It is not good for the man to be alone. I will make a helper suitable for him" (Gen. 2:18). Solomon writes that "he who finds a wife finds what is good and receives favor from the LORD" (Prov. 18:22). The apostle Paul, writing his letter to the church at Ephesus, described marriage as like the relationship between our Lord Jesus Christ and the church. It is an intimate relationship. It is a holy and sacred

---

26. Randy Frazee, *The Connecting Church: Beyond Small Groups to Authentic Community* (Zondervan, 2001), 22.

relationship. In Paul's words, it is a relationship of mutual submission and love (Eph. 5:21–33).

Those words strike at the heart of the purest ideal for marriage. If you ask most people why they desire to be married, they will describe their reasons in terms of "getting." But a real marriage is a relationship of giving. Marriage as God intended it is unconditionally giving ourselves to each other, looking for ways of meeting the other's needs, and seeking for our partner's happiness, even above our own. The beauty of this kind of marriage is that when we unconditionally give ourselves to each other—body, mind, and spirit—what we have together is far greater than what either would have separately.

This kind of marriage sounds impossible in today's world—and it would be, except for one important point. The same God who established marriage gives the courage and the strength to complete that marriage. Those who receive the love of God in a personal relationship with Jesus Christ have an inexhaustible store of love for each other by which they can commit themselves to what God wants to do through them to serve each other. Thus, marriage is a mystical union and a source of grace to all who enter it under the blessing of God, and it remains a bond of peace with Christ at the center. This is what marriage will be, if we beautify and enrich it by our tender care, our attention to the little things, and our patience and sacrifice to each other.

*Divorce is not an option.* One of the points I emphasize from the first to a prospective bride and groom is what exemplifies unconditional commitment to each other is that they should never consider divorce to be an option. You remember the vows:

> I take you to be my wedded wife/husband, to have and to hold
> from this day forward, for better or for worse, for richer or for poorer,
> in sickness and in health, to love and to cherish, till death do us part.
> According to God's holy ordinance, I pledge you my life.

A bride and groom are committing themselves for life, for the long haul. Part of my responsibility in premarital preparation is to get them to own that commitment and to understand clearly the difficulties that will come and how to walk through them together.

Many today do not make that kind of vow. Their vow is conditional, whether they say so or not. The favorite expression of the court is that couples divorce because of "irreconcilable differences," which can describe most anything, from career goal conflicts to property rights disputes to personality differences. Divorce is considered a morally neutral option.

The Pharisees debated the meaning of Moses' exception because, in the more liberal school, the divorce certificate was becoming an option. If a husband was disinclined toward his wife, he could simply dismiss her with a divorce. Jesus condemns that attitude because it violates God's intention of the permanence of the marital union. A marriage that is centered in Christ vows from the first to remain together no matter what comes between them.

*Divorce is an exception.* So if divorce is not to be considered an option, why does Jesus allow it? As with God's allowance through Moses, Jesus allows divorce as an exception because some destructive sin has entered into the relationship and destroyed the union God established. Divorce is permitted to protect the nonoffending spouse. By allowing divorce as an exception, Jesus is condemning the hardness of heart that leads to sinful behavior and is indirectly proposing a renovation of the heart, as seen through his kingdom program, which will affect these areas of life. Allowing divorce and presenting the certificate to protect the rights of the injured party prevents further damage in a fallen world.

*Adultery and desertion.* In the case of *porneia*, which we understand to be basically equivalent to adultery but includes anything that intentionally divides the marital relationship (e.g., incest, homosexuality, prostitution, molestation, indecent exposure[27]), divorce and by extension remarriage are permitted. The apostle Paul included another exception: desertion by an unbelieving partner (cf. 1 Cor. 7:12–16).[28] Together, Jesus' and Paul's teachings address the two main components of the marriage covenant—interpersonal intimacy culminating in sexual relations and personal allegiance or loyalty. "Both infidelity and desertion break one half of the marriage covenant. Unfaithfulness destroys sexual exclusivity; desertion reneges on the commitment to 'leave and cleave.'"[29]

In our day Christians must hold up the permanence of marriage as the intended design by God and not consider divorce as a morally neutral option. As with any other sin within the community, restoration is the intended goal. Those within a marriage that is experiencing either of these exceptions should not see divorce as mandatory; they should seek all avenues to have the sinning partner repent and attempt to restore the marriage to a healthy state. This is not easy because of the hurt that has been experienced, with the resulting absence of trust. But the reality of kingdom life that Jesus advocates is just the divine source of healing and recovery that brings the Spirit's regenerative powers into all relationships within the community.

---

27. Blomberg, "Marriage, Divorce, Remarriage, and Celibacy," 177; Instone-Brewer, *Divorce and Remarriage in the Bible*, 278–79.

28. For a careful discussion, see Instone-Brewer, *Divorce and Remarriage in the Bible*, 189–212, 279–82; also Gordon Fee, *The First Epistle to the Corinthians*, 267–70.

29. Blomberg, "Marriage, Divorce, Remarriage, and Celibacy," 192.

We in the community of faith must take seriously our responsibility in supporting those going through these difficulties. Those committing the sin that breaks the marriage bond need our attention to try to bring discipline and restoration. They are the wayward sheep whom we must go after (18:10–14). Those who have experienced divorce and have been the offended party need our full acceptance. Usually they feel like second-class Christians with permanent disgrace; they need the fellowship of our community.

*The sanctity of singleness.* Those who have chosen to remain single as the expression of the way that they believe they can best serve God need us as their community of brothers and sisters. Jesus declares that celibacy *is* an acceptable lifestyle for those for whom it is given by God. Paul expands on Jesus' statement to indicate that if one remains unmarried, one is in a position to be undistracted by the amount of work that goes into taking care of one's family responsibilities, and the kingdom of God receives benefit (1 Cor. 7:27, 39–40).

Unfortunately, many of our churches endorse marriage as a sign of maturity, and those who are married tend to get the more "responsible" ministry opportunities in the church. Single people are seen as those who have not "settled down" yet. We should reevaluate the way we view and value single people within our ministries.

*Reconciliation and restoration.* We should also take seriously the reality of divorce and remarriage that falls outside these exceptions. Reconciliation and restoration are ultimate goals that come only through repentance and forgiveness. Divorce is not the unpardonable sin, but we tend to go to extremes with those who have unbiblically divorced and remarried. We either relegate them to an outcast status with permanent stigma, or else we glibly act as though it never happened. The themes of repentance, forgiveness, restoration, and reconciliation that marked Jesus' community prescription in chapter 18 must guide our thinking in all of these situations.[30]

**The "god" of a person's life.** In this chapter, the rich young man's wealth prevented him from entering the kingdom of heaven (19:23). From this we learn that one should be careful of the "deceitfulness of wealth" (cf. 13:22). This passage does not suggest that wealth is wrong, however (cf. 27:57; Joseph of Arimathea, a disciple of Jesus, was a rich man), but it does suggest that there is something about wealth that can choke off the effectiveness of the gospel and keep one from entering the kingdom. The rich young man sensed a lack in his life that could not be filled with his own religious efforts. It could only be filled with the perfection that comes through entering the

---

30. For a helpful pastoral perspective on dealing with all kinds of scenarios related to divorce and remarriage, see Instone-Brewer, *Divorce and Remarriage in the Bible*, 300–314.

kingdom of heaven and experiencing the inner transformation of heart; those two things would have set him on the path to be perfect as the heavenly Father is perfect (see comments on 5:48). The inner change will produce a transformation from the inside to the outer.

*The treasure of our lives.* It must begin by exchanging the treasure of one's life for the treasure of heaven. Jesus knew full well the controlling issue of the rich young man's life—it was his wealth, which provided him power, significance, and status. It become the god of his life; it determined his values, priorities, and ambitions. Jesus called him to exchange it for following him in discipleship in the kingdom of heaven. The young man's turning away is tragic, but it becomes a powerful illustration even in our own lives of the way we need to keep short account of what is ruling our lives. Even Christians can misplace their allegiance, so each person must be honest with himself or herself to know what is the treasure of the heart.

At stake is Jesus' place as the messianic Savior of each individual's life. Jesus wants to be God, not only of the universe but also of our individual lives if we are to find salvation and if we are to make progress in our discipleship. In any crowd of people there will be a mixture of priorities that drive individual lives. In order to claim Jesus as Savior, each person must exchange the "god" of his or her life to have Jesus as God. The cost varies from person to person according to the god of each person's life, but it must be faced.

Each of us faces the daily challenge in our growth as his disciples. Jesus still calls us to be honest about what rules our lives. It could be a drug addiction or a boyfriend. It could be the pursuit of a Ph.D., the acceptance and respect of peers, or an insatiable need for pleasure or the toys of life. The joys, securities, and comforts these pursuits temporarily offer may not appear to be bad, but they are when serving self is the real motive.

*Peter and rewards.* Peter's response shows that he too is driven by a less-than-pure treasure in heaven (19:23–30). The rich ruler refused to exchange his wealth for following Jesus, and Jesus then warned his disciples about the danger that riches pose to a person's eternal salvation. Peter flaunts the sacrifice that he and the other disciples have made to follow Jesus and boldly asks, "What then will there be for us?" (19:27). His question reveals a wrong motive. He is driven by serving Jesus and the kingdom of heaven for the primary purpose of receiving rewards and gaining personal prominence. Jesus acknowledges Peter's sacrifice and does say that he will be rewarded, but this is the least noble of motivations for a disciple. The paradoxical statement about the first and the last (19:30; cf. 20:16) declares that those who serve with the primary motivation of receiving rewards will be last, and those who serve only in order to respond in obedience to Jesus' summons will be first (cf. 20:1–16).

So what rules our lives? What must be dethroned as that which is keeping us from experiencing freedom and fullness of life? Jesus calls us to come and follow him, so that he can save us from our old way of life and offer us a new way. We must surrender that which governs us and accept a new ruler. Only under the rule of the kingdom can we be transformed into true sons and daughters of God, directed by his Word and Spirit so that we can do his will on earth.

Christians throughout the ages have had to pay the cost of surrendering their earthly pleasures and securities to follow Jesus alone, for the gods of materialism and pleasure-seeking are not new. Augustine, one of the theological giants of church history, was similarly held captive by these "gods." After his conversion he wrote:

> The very toys of toys and vanities of vanities, my ancient mistresses, still held me; they plucked my fleshy garment, and whispered softly, "Will you cast us off for ever? and from that moment shall we no longer be with you for ever?"
>
> I hesitated to burst and shake myself free from them, for a violent habit said to me, "Do you really think you can live without them?"

But as the Spirit prompted Augustine to read Paul's words to the Romans, he was set free from their power over his life:

> I seized, opened, and in long silence read that section on which my eyes first fell: "Not in rioting and drunkenness, not in chambering and wantonness, not in strife and envying; but put on the Lord Jesus Christ, and make no provision for the flesh, to fulfill its lusts" [Rom. 13:13–14].
>
> No further would I read; nor needed I: for instantly at the end of this sentence, by a light as it were of serenity infused into my heart, all the darkness of doubt vanished away.[31]

Augustine struggled with philosophical doubts about the truth of Christianity. He also struggled with his own moral depravity. Says historian Will Durant of Augustine's conversion, "Surrendering the skepticism of the intellect, he found, for the first time in his life, moral stimulus and mental peace."[32] As he gave up the pleasure gods that ruled his life and allowed Jesus to rule, Augustine discovered a reality of existence he had never before known.

---

31. *The Confessions of Saint Augustine*, trans. Edward B. Pusey (New York: Macmillan, 1961), 8.12 (pp. 129–30; I have updated Pusey's translation at points).

32. Will Durant, *The Story of Civilization*; vol. 4: *The Age of Faith* (New York: Simon Schuster, 1950), 66.

Salvation is not earned. It is received by faith through God's grace. But at the same time salvation is costly. It cost Jesus his life, and it costs us our lives as well. C. S. Lewis recognized what Jesus' challenge to count the cost of the relationship with him meant. He saw that we are called to place our lives into Jesus' hands so that he can perform the task of transforming us completely into his image. Lewis explains this powerfully from Jesus' standpoint:

> That is why He warned people to "count the cost" before becoming Christians. "Make no mistake," He says, "if you let me, I will make you perfect. The moment you put yourself in My hands, that is what you are in for. Nothing less, or other, than that. You have free will, and if you choose, you can push me away. But if you do not push Me away, understand that I am going to see this job through. Whatever suffering it may cost you in your earthly life, whatever inconceivable purification it may cost you after death, whatever it costs Me, I will never rest, nor let you rest, until you are literally perfect—until my Father can say without reservation that He is well pleased with you, as He said He was well pleased with me. This I can do and will do. But I will not do anything less."[33]

Being a disciple of Jesus is for those who have counted the cost and want real life, eternal life, received from a Savior who came to earth to seek and to save us and who lovingly, persistently, transforms us into his image. These are tough words if we fear and resist him. But they are words of hope, promise, peace, and joy if we are tired of ruling our lives ourselves.

---

33. C. S. Lewis, *Mere Christianity*, new ed. (New York: Macmillan, 1960), 158.

# Matthew 20:1–34

F OR THE KINGDOM of heaven is like a landowner who went out early in the morning to hire men to work in his vineyard. ²He agreed to pay them a denarius for the day and sent them into his vineyard.

³"About the third hour he went out and saw others standing in the marketplace doing nothing. ⁴He told them, 'You also go and work in my vineyard, and I will pay you whatever is right.' ⁵So they went.

"He went out again about the sixth hour and the ninth hour and did the same thing. ⁶About the eleventh hour he went out and found still others standing around. He asked them, 'Why have you been standing here all day long doing nothing?'

⁷"'Because no one has hired us,' they answered.

"He said to them, 'You also go and work in my vineyard.'

⁸"When evening came, the owner of the vineyard said to his foreman, 'Call the workers and pay them their wages, beginning with the last ones hired and going on to the first.'

⁹"The workers who were hired about the eleventh hour came and each received a denarius. ¹⁰So when those came who were hired first, they expected to receive more. But each one of them also received a denarius. ¹¹When they received it, they began to grumble against the landowner. ¹²'These men who were hired last worked only one hour,' they said, 'and you have made them equal to us who have borne the burden of the work and the heat of the day.'

¹³"But he answered one of them, 'Friend, I am not being unfair to you. Didn't you agree to work for a denarius? ¹⁴Take your pay and go. I want to give the man who was hired last the same as I gave you. ¹⁵Don't I have the right to do what I want with my own money? Or are you envious because I am generous?'

¹⁶"So the last will be first, and the first will be last."

¹⁷Now as Jesus was going up to Jerusalem, he took the twelve disciples aside and said to them, ¹⁸"We are going up to Jerusalem, and the Son of Man will be betrayed to the chief priests and the teachers of the law. They will condemn him to

death [19]and will turn him over to the Gentiles to be mocked and flogged and crucified. On the third day he will be raised to life!"

[20]Then the mother of Zebedee's sons came to Jesus with her sons and, kneeling down, asked a favor of him.

[21]"What is it you want?" he asked.

She said, "Grant that one of these two sons of mine may sit at your right and the other at your left in your kingdom."

[22]"You don't know what you are asking," Jesus said to them. "Can you drink the cup I am going to drink?"

"We can," they answered.

[23]Jesus said to them, "You will indeed drink from my cup, but to sit at my right or left is not for me to grant. These places belong to those for whom they have been prepared by my Father."

[24]When the ten heard about this, they were indignant with the two brothers. [25]Jesus called them together and said, "You know that the rulers of the Gentiles lord it over them, and their high officials exercise authority over them. [26]Not so with you. Instead, whoever wants to become great among you must be your servant, [27]and whoever wants to be first must be your slave—[28]just as the Son of Man did not come to be served, but to serve, and to give his life as a ransom for many."

[29]As Jesus and his disciples were leaving Jericho, a large crowd followed him. [30]Two blind men were sitting by the roadside, and when they heard that Jesus was going by, they shouted, "Lord, Son of David, have mercy on us!"

[31]The crowd rebuked them and told them to be quiet, but they shouted all the louder, "Lord, Son of David, have mercy on us!"

[32]Jesus stopped and called them. "What do you want me to do for you?" he asked.

[33]"Lord," they answered, "we want our sight."

[34]Jesus had compassion on them and touched their eyes. Immediately they received their sight and followed him.

THE PARABLE ABOUT the workers and the vineyard (20:1–16), found only in Matthew, grows out of the encounter between Jesus and the rich young man (19:16–22) and especially Peter's reaction (19:23–30). Jesus demonstrates how serving him and the kingdom of heaven for the purpose of receiving rewards and gaining personal prominence is the least noble of motivations for a disciple. The paradoxical statement about the first and the last (19:30; 20:16) declares that those who serve in order to receive a reward will be last, and those who serve only in order to respond in obedience to Jesus' summons will be first (cf. 20:1–16).

### The Parable of the Vineyard Workers: Gratitude and Service in the Kingdom Community (20:1–16)

GRAPES WERE ONE of the most important crops in the land of Israel, leading to one of the most important metaphors to describe Israel—the "vine" or "vineyard" of God (e.g., Jer. 2:21; Hos. 10:1).[1] Here Jesus uses the vineyard to represent the sphere of worldly activity (cf. Matt. 21:28–46): "For the kingdom of heaven is like a landowner who went out early in the morning to hire men to work in his vineyard." The typical introductory formula, "the kingdom of heaven is like" (cf. 13:24, 31, 33, 44, 45, 47; 18:23), is a clue that Jesus is giving a lesson on the activity of the kingdom in the world. Jesus pictures harvest time, when a landowner hired seasonal workers to help with his harvest.[2] He went early to the marketplace, where laborers gathered, waiting for landowners to hire them. The agreed-upon sum of a denarius was expected, because a denarius was a day's wage for a laborer (see comments on 17:24–27; 18:24–28).

The ancient workday was typically divided into three-hour increments, running from about 6:00 A.M. to 6:00 P.M. The landowner hired the first workers at the beginning of the day to work the entire day. At the third hour (9:00 A.M.), the landowner needed more laborers for his abundant harvest, so he went back the marketplace and found people still waiting for the chance to work. Families in the ancient world often went day to day, earning only enough for the food for that particular day (cf. 6:11). If they did not find work, they would not have enough to eat, so they continued to wait for someone to hire them. These laborers agreed to work for "whatever is right" (20:4), expecting most likely to receive a proportionate reduction from the day's regular denarius. The abundance of the harvest was such that the landowner went again at the sixth hour (12:00 noon) and the ninth hour (3:00 P.M.).

---

1. "Vine and Vineyard," *DJBP*, 657–58.
2. Young, *The Parables: Jewish Tradition and Christian Interpretation*, 74–80.

Needing still more laborers, the landowner went back to the town marketplace and found workers who were desperate enough to remain waiting for work. It was the eleventh hour (5:00 P.M.), close to the end of the workday. These workers would have expected only one-twelfth of the amount of those who worked for the denarius. They were also hired to work in the vineyard.

At the end of the day when the foreman or steward of the landowner (cf. Luke 8:3; Gal. 4:2) paid the wages, a shocking development unfolded. The laborers who were hired last were paid the full denarius, the wages expected for a full day's work. This built up the expectations that those who worked longer would receive a proportional increase in their wages. But no! Those who worked the entire long, hot day received the same wage as those who only worked an hour, which expectedly caused the first laborers to protest that the others didn't deserve equal treatment. "Little seems more unequal than the equal treatment of unequals!"[3]

With a measure of gentleness but with the intent to straighten out his attitude, the landowner addressed one of the first hired laborers as "friend." This man did not have a regular job, so getting the denarius that he had agreed upon was more than what he would have had at the end of the day except for the fortunate intervention of the landowner. He should simply be thankful that he had enough to care for the day's needs for his family. The central issue was the self-centeredness of the laborer. He was only thinking about himself, not about the generosity and intervention of the landowner or the fortune of the other laborers.

The expression "are you envious" (20:14) can be rendered literally, "Is your eye evil," indicating that the laborer could not be thankful because he was blinded by his self-centered envy. The "evil eye" in the ancient world was one that enviously coveted what belonged to another. It was a greedy or avaricious eye (see also 6:23). If a disciple's eyes are fixed on earthly, material treasure as his or her value, personal significance, and earthly security, then the darkness of that evil value is the state of that person's heart. When we focus on something evil, the eye becomes the conduit by which the evil fills the inner person.

Jesus' concluding statement in 20:16 repeats 19:30, but reverses the order to emphasize the conclusion of the parable. Those hired last were unworthy of what they received, yet they were paid first and treated with equality to those who were hired first. And those who were hired first were paid last, and from their point of view, treated unfairly as though they were equal to those who were last. The intended application to Peter (19:27) and his

---

3. Blomberg, *Matthew*, 303.

request for preferential treatment and reward is obvious. Although he and the Twelve were the first to give up all they had to follow Jesus, contrary to the rich young man, Jesus includes all true disciples as having done the same thing (19:29).

So this parable is a lesson on gratitude and motivation in service. The parable is not about salvation or gaining eternal life, because salvation is not earned by works (Eph. 2:8–9; Titus 3:5–6). Nor is the parable about rewards for service, because God will reward believers differently according to their service (1 Cor. 3:8; John 4:36). If the denarius stands for rewards, there is no distinction, because every worker got the same reward. Rather, this is a profound parable about what should be the disciple's motivation for service. We should serve out of gratitude, for it is only through the intervention of Jesus that any disciple receives anything. We should be concerned only to rejoice when others are called to the kingdom without serving as long or as hard as we have.

If we think that we deserve something because of our time, diligence, and commitment of service, we have negated the real value of what we have done. All who respond to the grace of God in Jesus' kingdom invitation are equal disciples, and we must be careful not to measure our worth by what we have done and what we have sacrificed.[4] Our calling is still one of grace, and a grateful heart will serve without thought of reward or without comparison to others. As the landowner points out, to think of rewards and to compare with others will cause us both to question the wisdom and fairness of God and to become envious of other disciples (20:15).

## The Third Passion Prediction (20:17–19)

JESUS AND THE disciples continue traveling from Galilee through Perea to Judea (19:1), with the ultimate goal of arriving in Jerusalem for the Passover. Evidently a fairly large contingent accompany Jesus, including the women disciples who ministered to Jesus' needs (Luke 8:1–3) and who will witness the crucifixion (see comments on Matt. 27:55–56). With the fateful event in Jerusalem only weeks away, Jesus takes aside the Twelve to give them another prediction of his impending betrayal. This is the third of four predictions of his arrest and crucifixion, but the drama is heightened by the first reference to Jerusalem, the first mention of the religious leaders' condemnation of Jesus to death, and the first mention of the Gentiles who will carry out the execution (see comments on 16:21; cf. 17:22–23; 26:2).

---

4. So also B. Rod Doyle, "The Place of the Parable of the Labourers in the Vineyard in Matthew 20:1–16," *ABR* 42 (1994): 39–58.

## The Example of Jesus for Community Sacrifice, Suffering, and Service (20:20–28)

As JUST NOTED, several women apparently are accompanying Jesus and the Twelve on the journey to Jerusalem. As Jesus gives the prediction of his impending crisis in Jerusalem, one of those women, the mother of Zebedee's sons (see 4:19–20), comes up to Jesus with her sons and, "kneeling down, asked a favor of him." This woman has been a faithful follower of Jesus. Later identified as Salome, she is among the women who attends Jesus at the cross and witnesses the empty tomb (cf. 27:56; Mark 15:40; 16:1). The best clarification of the listings of the women identify Salome as the sister of Mary, Jesus' mother (cf. John 19:25). So she is Jesus' aunt, and her sons, James and John, are his cousins on his mother's side. As Jesus undertakes his last fateful trip to Jerusalem, his mother and aunt may have traveled with the band of disciples. This may at least partly explain why there is no hint of scandal with the other women who travel with Jesus and the band to Jerusalem and who witness the crucifixion and resurrection (e.g., Mary Magdalene, the other Mary, and Joanna; cf. Matt. 27:55–56; Luke 24:10).[5]

As she kneels before Jesus, Salome shows her deference to Jesus as her messianic Master, but she also comes apparently to exercise her earthly kinship advantage with Jesus. Mark has these two disciples asking the favor for themselves (Mark 10:35–36), which indicates that the desire comes from them as well as their mother.

The mother's request for a favor is forthright: "Grant that one of these two sons of mine may sit at your right and the other at your left in your kingdom." She is not pushing her sons into something that they do not want, but together they are demonstrating their commitment to support Jesus in what lies ahead.[6] A mother seeking the advancement of her sons through direct petition to a person in authority was a well-known phenomenon, such as Bathsheba seeking the throne for her son Solomon from the aging King David (1 Kings 1:15–21).

This request is likely inspired by Jesus' comment in 19:28, where he announced the role that the Twelve would have in ruling with him. When Jesus sits on his glorious throne, the Twelve will sit on twelve thrones judging the twelve tribes of Israel. Since "judging" speaks more prominently of ruling than condemnation, the mother desires for her sons to have the highest positions of importance when Jesus inaugurates his future kingdom.

---

5. Emily Cheney, "The Mother of the Sons of Zebedee (Matthew 27.56)," *JSNT* 68 (December 1997): 13–21.

6. Contra Cheney, ibid., who suggests that her presence with the sons indicates their lack of commitment to the family of faith, because they have maintained their family relationship, contrary to what disciples should do (19:19).

Seated at the right-hand side is the most typical place of honor, whether it is the king's mother at the king's right side (1 Kings. 2:19), King David at God's right hand (Ps. 16:11), or the Messiah sitting at the right hand of God (Ps. 110:1, 5; cf. Matt. 22:44). The left side is reserved for the second highest position of importance to the monarch. King Saul reserved those two places for his son and general (see Josephus, *Ant.* 6.11.9 §235). Relegating a person to the left-hand side instead of gaining the right-hand side can be a place of disfavor symbolically (e.g., 25:33–46), but typically, as here, it is a place of high importance.

Jesus addresses the brothers directly, as he declares that "you [second person plural] don't know what you [second person plural] are asking" (20:22). They (and their mother) have only a faint idea of what lies yet ahead. "Can you drink the cup I am going to drink?" The "cup" throughout Scripture refers figuratively to one's divinely appointed destiny, whether it was one of blessing and salvation (Ps. 16:5; 116:13) or of wrath and disaster (Isa. 51:17; Jer. 25:15–29). Jesus is referring to his forthcoming cup of suffering on the cross (Matt. 26:39), to which he has just given his third prediction (20:17–19).

The brothers' response, "We can," indicates that they misunderstand Jesus to be challenging them to see if they are willing to endure the difficulties that lie ahead in the battle to establish the eschatological kingdom. They probably hear in the metaphor of the cup both blessing and adversity and declare that they are ready to endure any hardships for the reward of the glory that lies ahead. Perhaps they think of other heroes in Israel's history who boldly stepped forward in times of crisis and volunteered to fight for God. David, for example, volunteered to fight Goliath to defend the honor of the living God, even though he knew the one who killed Goliath was to be rewarded with wealth and the king's daughter in marriage (1 Sam. 17:25–37). The disciples will reaffirm their commitment to Jesus and his destiny in the Upper Room (26:31–35), but they have little knowledge of what lies ahead. Their bravado is commendable for its commitment to Jesus and their willingness to face difficulties for the reward of future glory, but they don't really know themselves or the future.

Jesus looks down the corridor of time to when the brothers will suffer for the kingdom of heaven: "You will indeed drink from my cup, but to sit at my right or left is not for me to grant. These places belong to those for whom they have been prepared by my Father." James became the first martyr of the church (Acts 12:2), and John experienced persecution and exile (Rev. 1:9), although apparently not martyrdom. They will share in Jesus' cup of blessing, but they must submit to the Father's will for their future, just as Jesus is doing. Jesus has come to fulfill the task assigned by the Father, which is not the path of glory but of servanthood. The disciples will see that there is no less requirement of submission for them as well.

The brothers and their mother must have taken Jesus aside for this request, so "when the ten heard about this, they were indignant with the two brothers." The other disciples are probably indignant,[7] not so much because of the immodesty of the request of James and John, but because of the attempt to use their mother's family relationship to Jesus as an unfair advantage to get what they themselves wanted. All of the disciples had earlier argued about who would be the greatest in the kingdom of heaven (cf. 18:1), and they had already been promised to sit on thrones in Jesus' eschatological rule over Israel (19:28).

Jesus then gathers all the disciples together to overturn their strictly human ambitions by making a contrast between the world's conception of greatness and that in the kingdom of heaven. Greatness among the Gentiles was measured by being in a position to "lord it over" others and "exercise authority over" others (20:25). A person who is a "ruler" or "high official," can do whatever he wants with others and can serve his own wants. What may have first come to the minds of the disciples was the Roman occupation under which Israel suffered for decades, which meant heavy taxation and foreign military rule. For oppressed people with such hardships, capturing those positions of power and authority is the best way to gain any measure of self-respect and significance. To pursue those positions of power and authority is an ambition that is valued highly among the power structures of the world.

In other words, the prevailing dictum in the world is that ruling, not serving, is the best status for a human. But Jesus gives a different, and shocking, sort of ambition that must be the chief value among his disciples: "Not so with you. Instead, whoever wants to become great among you must be your servant, and whoever wants to be first must be your slave." A "servant" (*diakonos*) worked for hire to maintain the master's home and property, while a "slave" (*doulos*) was forced into service. In human eyes, service is not dignified. These are two of the lowest positions in society's scale, yet Jesus reverses their status in the community of his disciples to being "great" and "first."

Jesus' disciples have the ambition to be greatest (18:1) and to be first (20:21), so Jesus gives them the means by which they can do so according the values of the kingdom of God. They must arrange their lives with the goal of giving themselves for the benefit of others. It is no coincidence that Paul adopts these titles to describe himself[8] and others[9] who gave their lives for

---

7. The verb *aganakteo*, "I grieve," is best rendered "indignant," indicating their anger over an anticipated loss. It is used of the disciples in 26:8 and the chief priests and scribes in 21:15.

8. E.g., *diakonos*: 2 Cor. 3:6; Eph. 3:7; Col. 1:23; *doulos*: Rom. 1:1; Gal. 1:10.

9. E.g., *diakonos*: Phoebe, Rom. 16:1; Tychicus, Eph. 6:21; Epaphras, Col. 1:23; *doulos*: Epaphras, Col. 4:12;

the welfare of humanity and the church. John later calls himself a *doulos* of Jesus (Rev. 1:1), as does Peter (2 Peter 1:1) and Jesus' own brothers (James 1:1; Jude 1).

The ultimate example for the disciples is Jesus' own life: "just as the Son of Man did not come to be served, but to serve, and to give his life as a ransom for many" (20:28). As the Son of Man (see comments on 8:20)—in which he had been revealed to be the Messiah, the Son of God (e.g., 16:16–17), to whom all glory and honor should be paid—Jesus has willingly set aside that prerogative for a higher purpose, namely, to serve by giving his life as a ransom for many. This statement gives an explicit indication of his self-understanding of the purpose for the crucifixion he will soon suffer (cf. 16:21; 17:22–23; 20:17–19).

Jesus will give his life as a "ransom" (*lytron*), which means "the price of release," a word often used of the money paid for the release of slaves. In the New Testament, "redemption" or "release" as a theological concept is based on the experience of Israel's release from the slavery of Egypt. The term may also contain an allusion to the Suffering Servant passage of Isaiah 53, especially 53:6b: "And the LORD has laid on him the iniquity of us all."

The phrase "for many" ("for" connotes "in place of"[10]) signifies the notion of exchange for all those who will accept his payment for their sins. This saying of Jesus prepares the way for the doctrine of substitutionary atonement in the work of his sacrifice on the cross, which involves the greatest cost of all, the life of the Son of Man.[11]

### Merciful Healing of Two Blind Men in Jericho En Route to Jerusalem (20:29–34)

JESUS AND THE disciples have now finished the trek from Galilee with ministry in Perea and Judea and are ready to make the ascent to Jerusalem. Their route takes them through Jericho, where a large crowd follows him and where he encounters two blind men. Jericho was an important place during the time of Jesus.[12] This city was not the ancient city of Old Testament fame

---

10. The preposition *anti* virtually never means "on behalf of" but demands the use "in place of" (cf. Wallace, *Greek Grammar*, 365–67). The "many" (*pollon*) has been understood to have either an exclusive sense, "many, but not all," restricting the application to the community of the elect (e.g., 1QS 6:1–23), or to have an inclusive sense, "many, the totality which embraces many individuals," opening the application to all without limitation. The most convincing historical and linguistic argument affirms the latter; cf. Joachim Jeremias, "πολλοί," *TDNT*, 6:536–45.

11. Cf. Sydney Page, "Ransom Saying," *DJG*, 660–62; Scot McKnight, "Jesus and His Death: Some Recent Scholarship," *CurBS* 9 (2001): 185–228.

12. For further background, see Wilkins, "Matthew," 125.

(e.g., Josh. 5), which was still inhabited.[13] The new Jericho refers to the developments surrounding a huge palace complex first built by the Hasmoneans on a three-acre site about a mile south of the ancient city mound, which was greatly expanded by Herod the Great.

Matthew records this healing as Jesus is leaving Jericho, while Luke writes that Jesus is drawing near to Jericho (Luke 18:35). This can be most easily reconciled in the light of the phenomenon of two Jerichos still being inhabited, with Jesus leaving the old site and entering the new Jericho on his way to Jerusalem.[14]

A similar scene earlier in the Galilean ministry (see 9:27–31) indicates that this type of encounter was relatively frequent as Jesus passed through new areas. His remarkable reputation preceded him. Mark and Luke speak of one blind beggar, whom Mark identifies as Bartimaeus (Mark 10:46; Luke 18:35). They apparently focus on Bartimaeus as the more prominent of the two. The blind men understand Jesus to be the "Son of David" (see comments on 9:27–31; also 11:2–6), so they ask for the gift of messianic mercy to heal their blindness. Although he has experienced increasing rejection from his own people and will face the ultimate betrayal and rejection as he enters Jerusalem, Jesus continues to have compassion on those in greatest need, so he touches their eyes and heals them. Thereupon they follow Jesus.

The contrast in this incident is on the crowds who try to silence the two blind men. Yet the two men are the ones to whom Jesus directs his ministry; the crowds remain only spectators. Those without natural ability to follow Jesus are able through his healing touch to follow him.

JESUS AND THE band of disciples are nearing Jerusalem. Soon Jesus will face his earthly life's ultimate purpose and test, as he will be arrested and crucified, but then be raised. In the same way that Jesus' physical presence has been the unifying factor among the disciples, his risen presence will continue to unite them as his community of disciples (18:20). In order to prepare them for when he will no longer be with them physically, Jesus gave the Community Prescription discourse (ch. 18). The narratives in chapters 19–20 go on to illustrate the community themes outlined in chapter 18. The community of Jesus' disciples is not a theoretical

---

13. T. A. Holland, "Jericho," *ABD*, 3:737. It survived primarily because of the fresh water from the nearby spring, making it to this day perhaps "the oldest continually inhabited oasis in the world."

14. See Morris, *Matthew*, 513–14. Others suggest that the miracle was performed as Jesus left the city (20:29; Mark 10:46), though Jesus first encountered the men as he approached the city (Luke 18:35).

concept but the concrete expression of the way that the kingdom of heaven affects real-life relationships.

**Unity in community.** Unity is an inherent component of community. Without unity, fellowship disintegrates. There will be many forces at work in this world that will tend to tear apart the community. There are external forces, such as persecution, that Jesus prepares the church to face (e.g., 10:16–25; 24:15–28). But the primary forces that tend to tear apart the unity are internal. Because of pride and self-centeredness, the discipleship community must guard against the manifestation of those characteristics in their relationships.

The arrival of the kingdom of heaven has provided the power for personal and community transformation. The witness to the world of the reality of the kingdom is the transformation of relationships within the community, especially expressed in humility, purity, accountability, discipline, reconciliation, restoration, and forgiveness (see comments on ch. 18). But there are forces at work among the disciples that can destroy their cohesion. In their inquiry about rewards and positions of prominence, Peter and the sons of Zebedee (with their mother) illustrate that the disciples are motivated by the desire for just recompense because of their sacrifice of discipleship (19:27; 20:20–21). That motivation is a stock value of the world, but Jesus turns it upside down. Yes, rewards will be given for faithful and sacrificial discipleship. But if obtaining rewards is the motivating force, it will destroy unity by producing envy, comparison, self-promotion, and competition.

How can this threat be overcome? Jesus supplants it with two kingdom-inspired motivations: gratitude and servanthood. If his disciples are impelled by these two forces, unity is maintained and strengthened, the work of the kingdom is advanced more effectively, and recompense for sacrifice of service becomes simply a by-product. These two revolutionary kingdom principles reflect the deepest aspirations of humans created in the image of God. But they are held captive by the competing forces of self-centeredness and pride.

**Gratitude.** In the parable of the vineyard and workers, Jesus illustrates that gratitude must be a compelling motivation for the discipleship community. Peter's question in 19:27 reveals that he is motivated by the thought of receiving rewards for his sacrifice of devotion to Jesus. In the light of that context, the rewards he is expecting are primarily material, since wealth was understood as a reward for godliness and service. But such self-promotion will produce envy and comparison, which will in turn tear apart the cohesiveness of the group.

We can all understand Peter's thinking, but what Jesus illustrates in the parable is that we must look deeply at what God has done for us. We who have nothing of our own have been called to the kingdom of heaven and endowed with the privilege of being Jesus' disciples, with the promise of just recompense. When we properly respect that privilege, with a clear recognition of the dire alternative of not being called to the kingdom, a deep well of gratitude is produced in our heart. All that we are, everything that we have, all that we ever hope to accomplish is a pure gift—and the only appropriate response is gratitude.

Certainly we know that we will be blessed for the work we do for our Master, but the reward pales in the light of the gift of life in the kingdom that we have already received. In the light of what our Savior has done for us, the greatest honor we can express for any crowns of reward is to cast them in grateful worship before the throne of the God who created us and all things, as did the twenty-four elders in their heavenly expression of praise (Rev. 4:10–11).

**Servanthood.** Jesus reveals in the interplay with the sons of Zebedee and their mother that servanthood and gratitude must be the twin motivation for the community of disciples. The sons are eager to endure any kind of sacrifice as long as they will be rewarded with personal prominence in the kingdom (20:20–23). But as is again true, this kind of incentive will tear apart their unity by producing manipulation and competition.

We can again understand the motivation of the brothers and their mother, because this is the way of the world that we all know so well. But when servanthood is linked with gratitude in understanding the gift of the position that we hold as members of the kingdom of God, we can take our eyes off ourselves. There will never be any higher position for us, because we are all equal brothers and sisters of one Father and all equal disciples of one Teacher and Master (23:8–12).

Since our position is established, we can turn upside down the world's pattern of greatness and find our own greatness in looking for the needs of those within the community of disciples and give ourselves to serve them. Since we can trust unconditionally that our Father supplies our every need (6:11, 25–33) and that the Master we serve has given us an easy yoke that will never take us beyond our strength (11:28–30), we can place ourselves in God's hands to guide us as we give ourselves unconditionally to the fellowship of believers.

The compelling example that goes before us is Jesus himself. He was so secure in his identity as the Son of God that he could give himself unreservedly, in spite of his earthly circumstances, to serve us. The paradigm of power is turned upside down, so that the apparent weakness of a human on a cross is the greatest display of power that the world has ever known. In that single substitutionary act of service, all of the greatest needs of humanity were met as Jesus became the ransom for sin. That act stands before us as the ultimate example of the servanthood to which we are called within the reciprocating community of disciples and to a stupefied, waiting world.

MOTIVES ARE A tricky phenomenon, primarily because there is always the temptation of having mixed motives. I may want to express unqualified love for my wife by bringing her flowers, but behind it might be the desire to manipulate her just slightly so that I won't feel guilty watching the Lakers play that basketball game on television! That might be a trivial example, but let's think about more significant mixed motives. I have a tremendous desire for our neighbors to become Christians, but is it entirely for their eternal good? Or might I just slightly think of my own reputation when word gets out of my evangelistic prowess?

We saw in the SM that Jesus derided the religious leaders for hypocrisy, which in that context meant that they were *doing right things* for the *wrong reasons*. They were motivated to perform external religious acts of piety by one overarching objective: to be honored by the people and by the religious establishment (see comments on 6:2).[15] I know I can fall into the same trap.

Now Jesus shifts the attention to his disciples. Unless we watch our motives, we also can do the right things for the wrong reasons and fall into the same kind of hypocrisy. The present situation, not unlike that of the Pharisees in chapter 6, concerns the motivation of rewards for service—both material rewards as well as rewards of personal prominence and status. So as we look at this concluding section that deals with the community of Jesus' disciples, we must evaluate our own actions in the light of two primary motivations for service—gratitude and servanthood. The more we focus on the example of Jesus in his earthly ministry, who came not to be served but to serve, the more we will be able to purify why we do what we do. As I once heard a preacher say, the Rewarder should fill our hearts, not the reward.

**The attitude of gratitude.** G. K. Chesterton is widely quoted as saying, "Gratitude is the mother of all virtues." He was continually thankful for the "birthday present of birth," and he would wish most of all to be remembered for commending to the human race a sense of gratitude. His verse expresses it well:

Give me a little time,
I shall not be able to appreciate them all;
if you open so many doors
And give me so many presents, O Lord God.[16]

---

15. Marshall, "Who Is a Hypocrite?" esp. 137, 149–50.

16. Cited in J. D. Douglas, "G. K. Chesterton, the Eccentric Prince of Paradox," *Christianity Today* (May 24, 1974), *http://www.christianitytoday.com/ct/2001/135/52.0.html*.

Gratitude is the response of the believing person to the goodness of God's grace in creation and redemption, making gratitude the authentic hallmark of the disciple of Jesus. We know there is nothing we have that we have not first received. And out of that knowledge comes the wellspring of gratitude that affects what we are, what we do and say, and how we conduct our lives. Gratitude impels our worship (Ps. 126:1–2; Eph. 5:19), motivates our service (Rom. 12:1), and inspires our continual thankfulness (Eph. 5:20; 1 Thess. 5:18). Søren Kierkegaard gives memorable expression to gratitude as the characteristic attitude of the redeemed person: "I am a poor wretch whom God took charge of, and for whom he has done so indescribably much more than I ever expected . . . that I only long for the peace of eternity in order to do nothing but thank him."[17]

Chesterton and Kierkegaard, from similar perspectives, reflect the deep truths of this community pattern. The person who has received the mercy and forgiveness of God will have the deepest sense of thankfulness for the new life he or she has received and in turn will extend mercy and forgiveness to others as a natural response. The ability to pardon comes from the eternal, loving act of grace in Jesus' sacrifice for our sin. The key to doing this is to stop focusing on what others have done *to* us and to focus instead on what Jesus has done *for* us.

*Rewards.* In the parable of the workers in the vineyard, instead of being motivated by "fairness" or reward, the most noble of motivations is gratitude. The profound significance of gratitude is that it impacts not just the one toward whom we should be grateful but all other relationships as well. Those who give to the needy, pray, and fast in the secrecy of the heart will be rewarded (6:4, 6, 18). But rewards are mentioned as the by-product of a life that is free from self-advancement. As New Testament scholar Harold Hoehner contends, "Believers' motivation in this life should not be the obtaining of rewards as an end in itself. Our motivation should be to please God wholeheartedly in thankfulness for what he has done for us through Christ."[18]

*Service.* What we do in giving ourselves in service of the kingdom of heaven flows from a grateful heart. God created the original man and woman to serve as stewards of his creation. Humans were the highest of his creatures, but he did not create them to dominate the rest of creation. Rather, they were to take care of it for God (Gen. 1:26–29; 2:15; cf. Luke 16:1–13). Tragically, with the entrance of sin came the distortion of this stewardship, so

---

17. Kierkegaard, *The Journals*, cited by Stuart B. Babbage, "Gratitude," *Baker's Dictionary of Christian Ethics*, ed. Carl F. H. Henry (Grand Rapids: Baker, 1973), 275.

18. Harold H. Hoehner, "Rewards," *NDBT*, 740.

that men and women became self-centered, with the desire to take instead of give, to dominate instead of serve, to hate instead of love.

But when God's love impelled him to give his Son, a fundamental change occurred in those who humble themselves to receive his gift. That transformation reverses the impulse from taking to giving, from self-centeredness to other-centeredness. Because of the impact of God's love in our lives, we can now love (1 John 4:19). And because of the transforming impact of God's gift of grace in our lives, we can now give ourselves to serve others.

I've mentioned before that I went oversees to spend a year of combat in Vietnam when I was only nineteen years old. It was a traumatic year, at the height of some of the most intense fighting of the war. I saw many young men lose their lives. I became a Christian just over a year after I returned from the war. Some time later a friend asked me, "Mike, where would you be right now if you had been killed in Vietnam?" And for the first time I was struck by the enormity of the eternal consequences of this life. I had been only a breath away from an eternity in hell. I was overwhelmingly struck with the realization that my life was a gift. My life was not my own but was truly a gift from God. The only appropriate response of gratitude for that gift was to give myself back to God for him to use in whatever way he wanted.

I knew clearly that it wasn't in just some abstract religious sense that I could transfer my life back to God. I could give every area of my life to God because his grace produced in me a very different sort of person than I was before. I could give to my relationships so that God's grace flowed through me to others. I could give myself to my jobs, as modest and diverse as they seemed when I was a janitor or a plumber or a Bible study leader for junior high kids, because God was producing through me the kind of product that was his workmanship in my life.

That is what lies behind the concept of the Christian life as being able to be generous and to give all day and every day as a pattern of life. The giving of ourselves—including our careers, our relationships, our talents, our resources, and our time—flows from a transformation of our lives produced by God's giving to us. The motivation for devoting ourselves to service comes simply from a grateful heart.

Why is it "more blessed to give than to receive" (Acts 20:35)? Why does God love a "cheerful giver" (2 Cor. 9:7)? Why was the poor widow's gift, while less financially, actually "more than all the others" (Luke 21:3)? In each case, it is because the gift came out of the fullness of a grateful life lived in God's presence. A faithful "giver" is one who lives in unending trust in God and so can surrender his or her entire being to others as a gift of grace. The next time you plan an afternoon off to spend with your child, or go out of your way with a word of encouragement to your secretary, or offer a day at the local homeless shelter, or make a sacrificial gift to your missionary friends so that they can perform their own gift of ministry, make sure that each gift operates out of your conscious reliance on God's grace in your life.

If you try to draw the gift out of your own resources, you will eventually become exhausted. But if you draw on God's gift of grace in your own life, you yourself will be God's gift to others in every activity of your life. The apostle Peter declares, "As each one has received a special gift, employ it in serving one another, as good stewards of the manifold grace of God" (1 Peter 4:10). That is what it means to serve the community of Jesus' disciples in the vineyard of the kingdom of heaven from the fullness of a grateful heart.

**The ambition to serve.** Each year at the seminary where I teach we have a faculty retreat. This year one of our professors led us in some wonderful times of corporate worship. In the first evening, he took us to Psalm 95, which we read together. Then he had us focus on verse 6, which says: "Come, let us bow down in worship, let us kneel before the LORD our Maker." Then he surprised us all by saying, "Why don't we all actually kneel before the Lord our Maker?"

Envision this professor. He is originally from the mountain country of Colorado, about six foot four; he looks more like a big lumberjack than a professor. But he also is very bright. He has a Ph.D. in philosophy from Oxford and has a successful career as a teacher and scholar. As he sank to his knees, it was as though all of those things that made him impressive in the eyes of the world were stripped away, and he was just plain Dave, a servant kneeling before his Master.

Then, all around the room in that dimly lit cabin in the mountains, every single faculty member slowly sank to his or her knees. Everyone there had an academic doctorate; some of them are among the most influential Christian scholars around the world; all of them are respected among church leaders throughout the nation. But everyone symbolically stripped away whatever honors they have earned, whatever positions of prestige and power they may think that they have, and they went to their knees. There, guided by the words of Psalm 95 and viewing God as our Maker and the One we serve, we worshiped God by praying and singing. To a person, everyone later declared that was one of the most powerful experiences of their lives as we united together to declare our servanthood to Jesus.

You see, the academic world and the guild of scholarship is highly competitive. You have to master your own discipline to get your degrees. You have to provide a better solution to theological and biblical problems to get published. And sometimes that means that we as Christian scholars are no more principled than any others. We can become self-serving.

*The way of the world.* Think of your own career, your involvement in community activities, or even your own church. The way of the world is getting ahead by being more aggressive, more powerful, more intimidating, more demanding than the other person. In our passage, James and John incurred the anger of the other apostles when they approached Jesus and asked for prominent positions in his kingdom. They were ready and willing to endure whatever hardship was necessary, whatever sacrifice was required, as long as they could get positions of prominence in Jesus' kingdom.

*Jesus' example.* Sacrifice is a concept that is readily understood when we think of it in terms of our own benefit. "No pain, no gain" is an old adage. It communicates a well-known and appreciated value—we must sacrifice present pleasure for personal gain. That may mean the pain of exercise for the gain of a healthy physical heart, or the pain of sacrificing to save enough to gain that long-anticipated vacation.

Jesus does not overturn that principle completely, but he does reverse the focus: "My pain, *others'* gain." Jesus' sacrificial servanthood was not directed toward his own personal benefit but for those who believe in his work on the cross and receive forgiveness of their sins. His servanthood provides us with the example we are now to display toward one another. We sacrifice for the sake of empowering others, not for what we can get out of it. Against the backdrop of human ambition, Jesus explains that in his kingdom the proper goal is not authority over others but service to them.

*Hitch ambition to selfless servanthood.* But I hasten to add that this does not mean that all ambition is bad. Ambition is bad when it is greedy, when it hurts and uses people, when it exalts us over others, when it is prideful. James and John were ambitious people. They wanted to make something of their lives, they wanted to be significant, they wanted to be of great use in the kingdom of God. Those are strengths when focused in the right way.

But the right kind of ambition involves hitching our aspirations to selfless servanthood. James's and John's strength was a weakness because it was greedy and selfish. But when ambition is selflessly directed toward service, God can use it in powerful ways. John's ambitious drive guided and nurtured the early church in Jerusalem. James's zeal resulted in his being the first apostle to suffer martyrdom, which became a turning point in the courage of the church. Disciples of Jesus are to be just as goal-oriented as anyone in the world, but our ambition must be linked to selfless servanthood—giving our lives as a source of blessing to those for whom we have responsibility. That starts with our closest relationships and then expands, including our spouse, children, neighbors, coworkers, and fellow Christians.

The reason that this kind of servanthood is possible is because Jesus' servanthood in going to the cross releases us from the power of sin, which is pride and self-centeredness. The motivation of serving ourselves is broken, and we are able to focus on serving others. Even as Jesus was the redemptive servant, our own authentic discipleship entails selfless servanthood.

The lesson that we all took away from our time of worship at the retreat is that whether we did so literally or figuratively, it was vitally important to drop to our knees before God, intentionally and regularly, and take off all those things that we do and say to impress others with who we are, and to serve Jesus by serving his people. Instead of demanding respect and honor from our students, our calling as Christian professors is to view ourselves as servants of Jesus and as servants of our students, preparing them for their own lives of service to the people of the church or on some mission field.

What we recommitted ourselves to that weekend is what we are all called to consider. The world of academia is not significantly different from the business world, the military, government work, or whatever setting you find yourself in every day. Interestingly, many cultures around the world understand this principle—politicians and government workers are often called "public *servants*." In my own home town the local police force has a motto placed on the side of every police car: "To protect and to *serve*." "Service" is also the motto of many businesses, from the restaurant to the gas company to the department store to the Internet provider. It represents a human ideal. But what gets in the way of service is *self-centeredness*. The world cannot experience true servanthood until it experiences release from the selfishness of sin.

*Tug-of-war of needs.* This principle is not much different from what can happen in our own families and churches. We have all experienced this. Servanthood ends what can be a vicious battle of emotional and relational self-centeredness by allowing us to invest ourselves in others to bring about God's blessing in their lives.

Many marriages experience what I call the "tug-of-war" syndrome, where each partner tugs to have his or her needs met by their spouse. Wives want their needs met and expect their husbands to do that. But husbands wait for their own needs to be met before they'll meet their wife's needs. They can reach a state of equilibrium when each has tugged hard enough so that they are relatively satisfied. But if you have ever been in a tug-of-war, you'll remember that the equilibrium is tenuous, because it is maintained only through tension. Many couples grow so tired of this kind of continual struggle that they give up.

However, instead of tugging, couples can be taught how to serve. I try to teach this when I take couples through premarital or marital counseling. I ask each couple to perform an experiment. They commit themselves for two months never to ask to have their own personal needs met but only to ask how each can meet the other person's needs. That is usually a huge paradigm shift, and it can be quite threatening.

Couples usually react incredulously when I propose the experiment. One young woman said, quite honestly, "I'm so used to nagging him that I'll never get him to help me around the house. He'll never take me out to dinner now! He just doesn't think about my needs."

But when we made it clear how we were going to attempt to follow God's pattern of grace toward us, she was amazed at her husband's response. He developed a whole new set of daily priorities, where he consistently asked, "What does she need today that I can supply?" In turn, she was free to make sure that he got what she knew he needed, like the regular Saturday afternoon to play basketball with his buddies. Remarkably, he would often volunteer even to give up that time if he saw that she needed him!

The experiment ends up in most cases as the basis of a new kind of marital relationship, in which servanthood is the operating guideline. The equilibrium couples attain is not one of tension but of grace and service. That kind of graceful equilibrium is possible only by a fundamental transformation when we experience God's grace and mercy in our lives.

I am awestruck when I ponder the goodness of Jesus serving us. But I am perhaps even more awestruck when I discover that his servanthood is the foundation and example for my own servanthood. Jesus deserved all the honor and glory that humanity could give him, but he thought first of humanity's needs. This world was lost in the darkness of sin, so Jesus gave up what was rightfully his to give himself as a servant to others.

In spite of whatever rights or authority we may claim, we have one primary example—Jesus, who laid aside all of the glory of heaven to take up a cross so that he could serve us. As we experience his ministry in our lives, we are enabled to experience a transformation of all of our values so that we can serve those around us.

As you consider this challenge, try getting down on your knees. It doesn't have to be literally. But remember to strip away all that you think makes you important and simply consider yourself a servant—of Jesus and of each other.

# Matthew 21:1–46

AS THEY APPROACHED Jerusalem and came to Bethphage on the Mount of Olives, Jesus sent two disciples, ²saying to them, "Go to the village ahead of you, and at once you will find a donkey tied there, with her colt by her. Untie them and bring them to me. ³If anyone says anything to you, tell him that the Lord needs them, and he will send them right away."

⁴This took place to fulfill what was spoken through the prophet:

> ⁵"Say to the Daughter of Zion,
> 'See, your king comes to you,
> gentle and riding on a donkey,
> on a colt, the foal of a donkey.'"

⁶The disciples went and did as Jesus had instructed them. ⁷They brought the donkey and the colt, placed their cloaks on them, and Jesus sat on them. ⁸A very large crowd spread their cloaks on the road, while others cut branches from the trees and spread them on the road. ⁹The crowds that went ahead of him and those that followed shouted,

"Hosanna to the Son of David!"

"Blessed is he who comes in the name of the Lord!"

"Hosanna in the highest!"

¹⁰When Jesus entered Jerusalem, the whole city was stirred and asked, "Who is this?"

¹¹The crowds answered, "This is Jesus, the prophet from Nazareth in Galilee."

¹²Jesus entered the temple area and drove out all who were buying and selling there. He overturned the tables of the money changers and the benches of those selling doves. ¹³"It is written," he said to them, "'My house will be called a house of prayer,' but you are making it a 'den of robbers.'"

¹⁴The blind and the lame came to him at the temple, and he healed them. ¹⁵But when the chief priests and the teachers of the law saw the wonderful things he did and the children shouting in the temple area, "Hosanna to the Son of David," they were indignant.

¹⁶"Do you hear what these children are saying?" they asked him. "Yes," replied Jesus, "have you never read,

"'From the lips of children and infants
   you have ordained praise' ?"

¹⁷And he left them and went out of the city to Bethany, where he spent the night.

¹⁸Early in the morning, as he was on his way back to the city, he was hungry. ¹⁹Seeing a fig tree by the road, he went up to it but found nothing on it except leaves. Then he said to it, "May you never bear fruit again!" Immediately the tree withered.

²⁰When the disciples saw this, they were amazed. "How did the fig tree wither so quickly?" they asked.

²¹Jesus replied, "I tell you the truth, if you have faith and do not doubt, not only can you do what was done to the fig tree, but also you can say to this mountain, 'Go, throw yourself into the sea,' and it will be done. ²²If you believe, you will receive whatever you ask for in prayer."

²³Jesus entered the temple courts, and, while he was teaching, the chief priests and the elders of the people came to him. "By what authority are you doing these things?" they asked. "And who gave you this authority?"

²⁴Jesus replied, "I will also ask you one question. If you answer me, I will tell you by what authority I am doing these things. ²⁵John's baptism—where did it come from? Was it from heaven, or from men?"

They discussed it among themselves and said, "If we say, 'From heaven,' he will ask, 'Then why didn't you believe him?' ²⁶But if we say, 'From men'—we are afraid of the people, for they all hold that John was a prophet."

²⁷So they answered Jesus, "We don't know."

Then he said, "Neither will I tell you by what authority I am doing these things.

²⁸"What do you think? There was a man who had two sons. He went to the first and said, 'Son, go and work today in the vineyard.'

²⁹"'I will not,' he answered, but later he changed his mind and went.

³⁰"Then the father went to the other son and said the same thing. He answered, 'I will, sir,' but he did not go.

³¹"Which of the two did what his father wanted?"

"The first," they answered.

Jesus said to them, "I tell you the truth, the tax collectors and the prostitutes are entering the kingdom of God ahead of you. ³²For John came to you to show you the way of righteousness, and you did not believe him, but the tax collectors and the prostitutes did. And even after you saw this, you did not repent and believe him.

³³"Listen to another parable: There was a landowner who planted a vineyard. He put a wall around it, dug a winepress in it and built a watchtower. Then he rented the vineyard to some farmers and went away on a journey. ³⁴When the harvest time approached, he sent his servants to the tenants to collect his fruit.

³⁵"The tenants seized his servants; they beat one, killed another, and stoned a third. ³⁶Then he sent other servants to them, more than the first time, and the tenants treated them the same way. ³⁷Last of all, he sent his son to them. 'They will respect my son,' he said.

³⁸"But when the tenants saw the son, they said to each other, 'This is the heir. Come, let's kill him and take his inheritance.' ³⁹So they took him and threw him out of the vineyard and killed him.

⁴⁰"Therefore, when the owner of the vineyard comes, what will he do to those tenants?"

⁴¹"He will bring those wretches to a wretched end," they replied, "and he will rent the vineyard to other tenants, who will give him his share of the crop at harvest time."

⁴²Jesus said to them, "Have you never read in the Scriptures:

"'The stone the builders rejected
    has become the capstone;
the Lord has done this,
    and it is marvelous in our eyes' ?

⁴³"Therefore I tell you that the kingdom of God will be taken away from you and given to a people who will produce its fruit. ⁴⁴He who falls on this stone will be broken to pieces, but he on whom it falls will be crushed."

⁴⁵When the chief priests and the Pharisees heard Jesus' parables, they knew he was talking about them. ⁴⁶They looked for a way to arrest him, but they were afraid of the crowd because the people held that he was a prophet.

THE CRESCENDO OF Jesus' messianic ministry occurs as he enters Jerusalem, the city of the great King (Ps. 48:1–2), the center of Israel's spiritual life and messianic hope.[1] The circuitous route from Galilee through Perea and Judea had given Jesus extended time with his disciples, primarily prescribing for them the characteristics they will display as his new community, his church. Galilee had been privileged to be the primary location of the display of his messianic identity and mission, but Jerusalem becomes the scene of the final revelation. In one climactic week Jesus concludes the primary purpose of his earthly mission—the redemption of humanity.

While the description of Jesus' earthly mission to this point took twenty chapters, Matthew now devotes eight chapters, nearly 30 percent of his Gospel, to this one holy week (see Bridging Contexts). These final chapters can be broken down into further subtopics. In the first days of Jesus' arrival in the city, he asserts his authority over Jerusalem, revealed in the events of his climactic (triumphal) entry (20:1–11), his temple actions (21:12–17), and his cursing the fig tree (21:18–22), in the series of debates with the religious leaders in the temple (21:23–22:46), and in the woes that he pronounces on the teachers of the law and the Pharisees (23:1–39).

Jesus then gives his final extended discourse to his disciples about the events of his return in power and glory and how his followers are to conduct themselves until his return (chs. 24–25). The events of his final Passover and institution of the Lord's Supper, his arrest, trial, crucifixion and burial are recorded in one running narrative (chs. 26–27), and then the final chapter details Jesus' resurrection and Great Commission to his disciples (ch. 28).

The extensive treatment of these final days is testimony to the immense significance of Jesus Messiah's redemptive ministry to his people Israel, and beyond to all the nations.

### The Climactic Entry into Jerusalem: Jesus' Authority As Messiah (21:1–11)

THE LAST RECORDED stop on the journey from Galilee through Perea and Judea to Jerusalem was in Jericho (20:29). The road from Jericho to Jerusalem was about fifteen miles, ascending three thousand feet through dry desert.

---

1. For an overview of the importance of Jerusalem to Israel, Christianity, and Islam, see Zitza Rosovsky, ed., *City of the Great King: Jerusalem from David to the Present* (Cambridge, Mass.: Harvard Univ. Press, 1996).

It took some six to eight hours of uphill walking, so Jesus and his disciples are eager to make it to their destination before nightfall, for the road was infamous for highway robberies (cf. Luke 10:30–35). As the road neared Jerusalem it approached the back (east) side of the Mount of Olives, passing through Bethany, the place where Jesus stayed during his final week (Matt. 21:17; cf. John 12:1–10), about two miles southeast of Jerusalem (John 11:18). The road continued over the Mount of Olives, down through the Kidron Valley, and into Jerusalem.

Rising 2,660 feet above sea level, the Mount of Olives (21:1) lies to the east of Jerusalem, directly overlooking the temple area. It is a flattened, rounded ridge with four identifiable summits. The name derived from the olive groves that covered it in ancient times. The traditional site of the Garden of Gethsemane lies near the foot of the Mount of Olives, on the western slope above the Kidron Valley.

According to the traditional accounting of the final week, Jesus and the traveling band of disciples arrive in Bethany on Friday afternoon and celebrate the Sabbath there, beginning at sundown on Friday evening through Saturday at sundown. A celebration with many of his closest followers in the Jerusalem area may have taken place on Saturday evening in Bethany, at which time Mary anointed Jesus' feet (see comments on 26:6–13; cf. John 12:1–8).[2] On Sunday morning Jesus directs the disciples to make preparations for his entry to Jerusalem.

**Preparations for the entry (21:1–7).** Near Bethany is the town of Bethphage (21:1), which Matthew tells us is the place from which Jesus directs his entrance to Jerusalem. The town is today called el-Azariyeh, named in honor of Lazarus, who was raised in this proximity (John 11:1, 17–18). The traditional site is on the southeast slope of the Mount of Olives, less than a mile east of Jerusalem. The name Bethphage (Heb. *bet pagey*) means "house of the early fig."[3]

---

2. For a brief overview of the difficulties of ascertaining the actual dates of the Holy Week using Friday Nisan 15 as a linchpin, and a helpful resolution of the various possibilities, see the brief article "Problems in Dating the Crucifixion," at the website of the Astronomical Applications Department of the U.S. Naval Observatory: *http://aa.usno.navy.mil/faq/docs/crucifixion.html*. They offer the dates of Jesus' crucifixion as either Friday, April 7, A.D. 30, or Friday, April 3, A.D. 33. For similar dating after more extensive discussion, see Kenneth F. Doig, *New Testament Chronology* (Lewiston, N.Y.: Edwin Mellen, 1990), who contends for the A.D. 30 dating. If we follow the A.D. 30 dating, Jesus arrives in Bethany late Friday afternoon on March 31, spends the Sabbath with his disciples in Bethany, then has the celebratory meal in Bethany on Saturday evening, April 1. The climactic triumphal entry occurs on Sunday, April 2, with the crucifixion Friday, April 7, and the resurrection on Sunday, April 9.

3. See Scott T. Carroll, "Bethphage," *ABD*, 1:715.

Jesus sends two disciples into Bethphage, where they are to obtain the donkey and colt for Jesus' entry into Jerusalem. They are to untie them and bring them to Jesus, and if anyone questions their actions they are to say, "The Lord needs them" (21:3). The term "Lord" (*kyrios*) can designate one's earthly master or one's deity. It is used to refer to the master of the slave in 10:24, but also to God as the Lord of the harvest (9:38), Lord of the vineyard (20:8), Lord of heaven and earth (11:20, 25), and often of Jesus as the Messiah (Acts 10:36). It is difficult to say what either the disciples or anyone else would have understood *kyrios* to mean in this context, but Jesus plainly intends it to refer to himself as the one who sovereignly superintends these events. At this climactic time of his earthly ministry, Jesus reveals himself with increasing clarity.[4]

Jesus intentionally declares his identity to the nation. The circumstances of his entry will produce a variety of reactions among the people. At the Passover season, messianic excitement tended to run high. With pilgrims crowding into Jerusalem not only from the various regions within Palestine but also from the Diaspora, hope for the appearance of Messiah was ready to be ignited. The recent raising of Lazarus stimulated renewed interest in Jesus—both the crowd's hope in him as a miraculous liberator and the religious leaders' opposition to him as a threat to the national security (John 11:45–53; 12:9–11, 17–19).

Jesus' descent from the Mount of Olives into Jerusalem evokes images of Zechariah's prophecy of the Lord's fighting against the nations with his feet on the Mount of Olives and liberating Jerusalem (Zech. 14:3–21). Further excitement is stimulated by Jesus' riding on a colt, fulfilling Zechariah's prophecy of the messianic king who comes to liberate his people (Zech. 9:9–13; cf. Matt. 21:4–5). This is no mere coincidence. The acclaim of the crowds comes from their own expectations of what they want Jesus to be. But for Jesus it is a self-disclosure to Israel, which will seal the fate of his people but will also be a testimony to his disciples once they reflect on these events with eyes of faith after his crucifixion and resurrection.[5]

The fulfillment phrase, "this took place to fulfill what was spoken through the prophet" (21:4), is most likely Matthew's comment that Jesus' entrance into Jerusalem on a colt fulfills the prophecy of Zechariah 9:9: "Your king comes to you, gentle and riding on a donkey" (21:5). The time has now come for Jesus to declare openly that he is the righteous Davidic Messiah. There may be also an allusion to Genesis 49:12, where Jacob prophesies of the kingly descendant of Judah:

---

4. Cf. also, Carson, "Matthew," 437; Gundry, *Matthew*, 593.

5. Carson, "Matthew," 437.

He will tether his donkey to a vine, his colt to the choicest branch;
  he will wash his garments in wine, his robes in the blood of grapes.

Jacob's prophecy occurs in the context of a promise to Judah of a permanent kingly line in his descendants, whose rule will include the obedience of the nations.

The Zechariah prophecy indicates the nature of Jesus' arrival: He comes as the righteous one who offers salvation, not as a conquering military leader. He comes with reconciliation, as did rulers who sometimes rode a donkey in times of peace (Judg. 5:10; 1 Kings 1:33). Through this event, Jesus delineates that he is not coming to bring military conquest.

Zechariah's prophecy specifies in synonymous parallelism that a young colt, the unbroken foal of a donkey, is the animal on which the peace-bringing king of Israel will enter Jerusalem. Of the four Gospels, Matthew alone mentions two animals, and he further says that as the disciples bring the two animals and lay their garments on them, "Jesus sat on them" (Matt. 21:7). Matthew's meticulous attention to the Old Testament prophecies does not allow him to ignore the parallelism of Zechariah's prophecy by suggesting that Jesus rides both animals. Rather, Matthew's account adds a touch of historical reminiscence: An unbroken young colt is best controlled by having its mother ride alongside to calm it in the midst of the tumult.[6]

The disciples place their outer cloaks (cf. 5:40) on both animals, but Jesus sits on the cloaks placed on the foal. There is no mistaking that he proceeds into Jerusalem as the anticipated king, the messianic Son of David. But his entry is triumphant in a paradoxical sense, because his victory will come by way of being nailed to a cross.[7]

**Jesus' climactic entry to Jerusalem (21:8–11).** The events for which Jesus has prepared the disciples now begin to unfold. As he descends from the Mount of Olives to enter the city, "a very large crowd" gathers to acknowledge his arrival in Jerusalem. Some in the crowd throw garments[8] in Jesus' path, symbolizing their submission to him as king (21:8).[9] Others cut palm fronds (cf. John 12:13) from the trees and spread them on the road before Jesus (Matt. 21:8). Palms symbolized Jewish nationalism and victory, such as when Judas Maccabeus and his followers recovered Jerusalem and the temple desecrated by Antiochus (2 Macc. 10:7; cf. 1 Macc. 13:51). Many coins

---

6. Cf. Gundry, *Matthew*, 409–10; Hagner, *Matthew*, 2:594–95.

7. Hagner, *Matthew*, 2:595.

8. Same term, *himatia*, for the cloaks that the disciples placed on the two animals (21:7).

9. When Elisha announced that Jehu would be anointed king, his fellow officers "took their cloaks and spread them under him on the bare steps. Then they blew the trumpet and shouted, 'Jehu is king!'" (2 Kings 9:13).

at the time of Jesus contain palms, expressive of nationalism generally, both Jewish and Roman.

Matthew refers to "the crowds that went ahead of him and those that followed him." John's Gospel helps us understand the picture. Crowds come out from Jerusalem to greet Jesus, apparently those pilgrims in Jerusalem for the Passover who have heard of Jesus' miraculous feat of healing Lazarus and who are caught up in the messianic expectation (John 12:12). They meet Jesus en route and turn around to form an advance processional, while those who are accompanying Jesus from Bethany, including his disciples, follow behind.

This large crowd is a mixed sort. Luke tells us that there is a multitude of Jesus' own disciples (Luke 19:37), which includes the Twelve and the larger group of his followers. Among the larger group are most likely the women disciples who followed Jesus from Galilee (Matt. 27:55–56), but also the contingent of believers in the Jerusalem region—among them Lazarus, Martha, and Mary and others who believed when Jesus raised Lazarus (cf. John 12:1–3). Within the crowd are also those who are not Jesus' disciples but who are part of the typical crowds that followed Jesus throughout his ministry. They follow with their own particular expectations, here thinking perhaps that Jesus has come to liberate Jerusalem and the people of Israel from Roman oppression. Others are there most likely out of curiosity and are caught up in the excitement. Luke further reveals that the crowd also has some religious leaders, such as the usual Pharisee contingent that opposes Jesus' claim to authority and are keeping watch on him (Luke 19:39).

The crowds shout out "Hosanna," which is the transliteration of the Hebrew expression that means "O save" (cf. 2 Sam. 14:4; 2 Kings 6:26). This draws the crowd to make a connection to the Hallel (Ps. 113–118) that was sung during the Passover season, especially expressing the messianic hopes of Israel as voiced in Psalm 118:19–29 (cf. esp. 118:25: "O Lord, save us"). They further cry out to Jesus as "Son of David" (21:9). Linked with Hosanna, the title "Son of David" is unmistakably messianic. The crowd acknowledges what Jesus has already stated in his fulfillment of Zechariah 9:9: He is the Davidic Messiah (see comments on 1:1), on whom they call to save them out of their oppression.

As the advancing crowd enters the city, "the whole city was stirred and asked, 'Who is this?'" This reminds the reader of the reaction of Jerusalem when the Magi came seeking the One born the king of the Jews—"all Jerusalem" was "disturbed" (2:3). Now as Jesus enters Jerusalem, "the whole city" is "stirred." The expression "the whole city" indicates that the religious establishment is once again paranoid of this One whom they believe may attempt to usurp their power, and they want an explanation of who Jesus intends to present himself to be.

The crowds answer generally, "This is Jesus, the prophet from Nazareth in Galilee." That answer indicates the mixed nature of those attending Jesus' entrance. Some in the crowd call him a prophet, which many in his ministry saw him to be (16:14; 21:46). This does not seem to imply that they understand him to be *the* eschatological Prophet of Moses' prophecy (Deut. 18:15–18),[10] but rather the prophet who has been creating such a stir in Galilee, whose hometown was Nazareth. Others who have called out "Hosanna" seem to expect Jesus to bring liberation, as had the kings of ancient Israel and the Maccabees of more recent times.

But Jesus has undertaken a different kind of "triumphal entry" from what many among the crowd expected. Jesus will triumph over the enemy of sin, bringing salvation to his people through his righteous sacrifice on the cross that looms ahead. Many in the crowd can only think of physical and military liberation. They cry "Hosanna" now, but soon will see that Jesus is not bringing the freedom they desire and will ultimately cry out, "Crucify him" (27:22). Although the crowd gives great acclaim, Jesus knows why they are really welcoming him. He knows their nationalistic ambitions and fickleness; thus, Luke tells us that Jesus weeps over the city (Luke 19:42–44).

## The Temple Actions: Jesus' Pronouncement on the Temple Establishment (21:12–17)

MATTHEW CONDENSES SOME of the narrative of Jesus' activities during Holy Week, which is the case with his narrative here of the chronology of the temple activities. A comparison of the other Gospels indicates a fuller sequence of events. After his climactic entry to Jerusalem, Jesus goes to the temple precinct area and surveys the activities being conducted (Mark 11:11). Later that day (i.e., Sunday afternoon), he returns to Bethany with the Twelve (11:11), where they spend the night. Early on Monday morning Jesus and the disciples return to Jerusalem, but on the way he symbolically curses the fig tree (11:12–14). After entering the city, Jesus proceeds to the temple. At this point Matthew picks up the narrative.

················································································

*John and the Synoptics on Jesus' Actions in the Temple.* John's Gospel has a narrative of a similar activity in the temple at the beginning of Jesus' ministry (John 2:13–17). Many scholars contend that John has placed this action of Jesus at the beginning for thematic purposes, while the Synoptic Gospels narrate the actual historical chronology.[11] We have seen that it is not unusual for

---

10. Cf.. John 6:14; 7:40, 52; Acts 3:22; 7:37.

11. E.g., George Beasley-Murray, *John*, 2d ed. (WBC; Nashville: Thomas Nelson, 1999), 38–42; Hagner, *Matthew*, 2:599–600.

the Gospel writers to arrange material thematically,[12] so this may account for the two different versions. Few today hold to two similar but chronologically different temple activities, one at the beginning of Jesus' ministry and the other at the end. These scholars wonder how the religious leaders would have let Jesus get away with this activity twice.

We may not have certainty on this issue, but there is much to commend the view that Jesus did go twice to the temple with a message to Israel and its leadership.[13] At the beginning of his ministry, Jesus made a declaration of the nature of his messianic ministry by the temple activity recorded in John, which was a warning to Israel. That this was not overlooked by the religious leaders is revealed in a statement by Jesus during the first temple incident that was later used against him falsely in his trial (John 2:19; see Matt. 26:61; Mark 14:58; cf. Acts 6:14).

When Jesus arrives in Jerusalem at the end of his ministry, it is obvious that the religious establishment has not led the people of Israel to repentance in the light of the arrival of the kingdom of heaven. Thus, Jesus' temple activity at the conclusion of his ministry is now a symbolic act of judgment. At the first incident they were caught by surprise, while at the second the crowds are so aligned with Jesus that the temple authorities dare not act against him in public and prevent his temple activity. But now the religious leadership cannot overlook the obvious revolutionary nature of Jesus' rejection of their authority, so they attempt to entrap him in debate with the hope that he will be denounced (21:23–27; 22:15–46). Failing that, they plot to arrest and kill him (21:46; 26:3–5) in order to avoid the threat to themselves from both the populace and from the Roman governing body.[14]

......................................................................................................................

**Jesus' action in the temple (21:12).** At the southern end of Temple Mount, Jesus enters the temple through the Huldah Gate. He then climbs another series of steps to enter the royal stoa, a long hall with four rows of forty thick columns each. Within the stoa is a market where commercial activity enables

---

12. E.g., Matthew's thematic arrangement of Jesus' miracles (chs. 8 and 9) and Luke's thematic arrangement of the order of Jesus' temptations (Luke 4:1–13; cf. Matt. 4:1–11).

13. Cf. Leon Morris, *John*, rev. ed. (NICNT; Grand Rapids: Eerdmans, 1995), 166–69; Carson, *John*, 176–78.

14. The absence of the first temple incident in the Synoptics is consistent with the overall absence of Jesus' early Judean ministry in their narratives. The absence of the second incident in John's narrative of Holy Week may belong to the difference of emphasis on Jesus' trial. The Synoptics focus on the accusations of Jesus' statements against the temple (Matt. 26:61; Mark 14:58) and on the related charge of blasphemy, while John records only a vague questioning by Annas (the former high priest) about Jesus' teaching (John 18:19–23).

pilgrims from throughout the Diaspora to participate in temple activities. Here they exchange their varied currency for temple currency, the Tyrian shekel, which is then used to pay the required temple tax (17:24–27; cf. Ex. 30:11–16) and purchase animals and other products for their sacrifices.[15]

Jesus immediately begins to drive out all who are both buying and selling and overturns the tables of the moneychangers and the benches of those selling doves (21:12). Both the moneychangers and those buying and selling are making this simply a commercial operation, and the temptation for abuse is real, since surplus tax was consigned to the temple fund (*m. Šeqal.* 2:5). Doves were the sacrifice made by the poor (who could not afford animal sacrifices) and by those making a variety of types of personal offerings (cf. Lev. 5:7; 12:6; 15:14, 29). Temple commerce was at times notorious for exploiting the disadvantaged (*m. Ker.* 1:7). Jesus' actions, of course, will not permanently halt these activities. In fact, his crucifixion will serve as a strong deterrent to any others who may want to act in a similar manner.

One might think that Jesus would be stopped immediately by the temple authorities, but he was noted to be a prophet by even the most distant of observers (21:11). As a spokesman for God, many prophets performed acts that were pronouncements of judgment, even in the temple precincts (cf. Jeremiah smashing the clay pot; Jer. 19). The whirl of popularity surrounding Jesus makes the religious leaders fearful of the crowds. But as with Jeremiah, once the crowds are swayed away from Jesus, he will be arrested.

**A den of robbers (21:13).** Jesus extends his authoritative pronouncement of judgment against the temple personnel, since they have misused the temple for commercial activity instead of its intended spiritual activity. He declares, "It is written, 'My house will be called a house of prayer,' but you are making it a 'den of robbers.'" The religious leaders are treating the temple as robbers do their dens—a place of refuge for both accumulating illicitly gained wealth and for plotting future illegal activities. The term "robber" (*lestes*) is not the word for a common thief but for one who is an insurrectionist, such as Barabbas and the two revolutionaries between whom Jesus will be crucified.[16] This may be a subtle use of the term to indicate that the temple authorities are making it a nationalistic stronghold,[17] or more subtly, a place where they are insurrectionists against God's intended plan for the temple.

Matthew leaves out the phrase about the temple being a house of prayer "for all the nations" (cf. Mark 11:17), but the rebuke is implicit, since it is the

---

15. See Kathleen Ritmeyer, "A Pilgrim's Journey," *BAR* 15/6 (November–December 1989): 43–45, for an informative insight to a journey into the temple.

16. Cf. Wilkins, "Barabbas," *ABD*, 1:607.

17. Carson, "Matthew," 442; Hagner, *Matthew*, 2:601.

outer court of the Gentiles that Jesus clears. His contemporaries are preventing Gentiles from using this one place set aside for them to pray by turning it into a den of robbers. They are robbing God of the means by which his blessing extends to all the nations.[18] The temple's primary purpose is being lost in a frenzy of religious activity. The temple leadership stands condemned.

Jesus' action here has often been called a "cleansing" of the temple, implying that Jesus is attempting to purify the temple from corrupt practices and restore it to proper usage as God intended. While corrupt practices are certainly being rebuked, Jesus goes beyond cleansing to enact intentionally a symbolic act of judgment against the religious leadership of Israel.[19] This is also a dramatic statement on Jesus' authority over the purposes of the temple sacrificial practices, which will be fulfilled with his impending crucifixion, as is so dramatically announced by God in the tearing of the veil at his death (27:51).[20]

**Healings and praise (21:14—16).** Matthew alone mentions the healings that Jesus performs in the temple after his disruption of the commercial practices and the ensuing confrontation with the chief priests and the scribes. The blind and lame were restricted from full access to temple activities to symbolize the purity that was expected to be displayed in those approaching God (cf. Lev. 21:18—19). As Jesus heals the blind and the lame, he shows his authority to create purity in all those desiring to worship God, demonstrating that as the One who is greater than the temple (12:6), he fulfills the Old Testament prescriptions for cleansing that the temple practices required to come into the presence of God.[21]

Jesus' healing activities prompt the children in the temple to mimic the chant, "Hosanna to the Son of David," which they heard earlier from the crowd during Jesus' dramatic entry to Jerusalem (21:9, 15). Jesus' actions in the temple in pronouncing judgment and healing the blind and lame should have caused the religious authorities to acknowledge his authority as the Messiah, the Son of David whom the children innocently and unknowingly identify.[22] Instead, they become "indignant" at Jesus' challenge to their authority. The word "indignant" (*aganakteo*) is the same term used of the ten disciples' reaction to the sons of Zebedee and their mother's attempt to use kinship privileges to obtain places of privilege in Jesus' kingdom (20:24).

---

18. See Peterson, *Engaging with God*, 87—90.

19. France, *Matthew*, 300—303; Morris, *Matthew*, 525—26; Davies and Allison, *Matthew*, 3:133—37; Sanders, *Jesus and Judaism*, 61—69.

20. Peterson, *Engaging with God*, 87—90.

21. Schweizer, *Matthew*, 408.

22. Rudolf Schnackenburg, *The Gospel of Matthew*, trans. R. R. Barr (Grand Rapids: Eerdmans, 2002), 203.

The religious leaders recognize Jesus as a threat to their positions of religious prominence. Jesus acknowledges the honor so unknowingly bestowed on him by the children and links it to Psalm 8:2, chiding the religious leaders for something they should have known if they truly knew the biblical witness. The psalmist applies the praise of children to God, but here the children are ascribing the praise to Jesus as the Son of David. Jesus thus admits his messiahship in receiving the blessing/praise and goes beyond what even the children know by personally receiving what was applicable in the psalm only to God (21:16).[23]

**Return to Bethany (21:17).** After the dramatic events of this Monday of Holy Week, Jesus leaves the religious leaders, most likely with their mouths hanging over and their fury beginning to boil. He will return to the city and the temple the next day to engage them in extended debate, but for now he returns to Bethany (see comments on 21:1). Jerusalem was packed with pilgrims during the Passover season, and many found shelter outside the city. Most likely Jesus stays at the home of Lazarus, whom he raised from the dead, and of his sisters, Mary and Martha (Luke 10:38–42; John 11:1–44).

## Cursing the Fig Tree: Jesus' Judgment of the Nation (21:18–22)

MATTHEW TOPICALLY DISCUSSES together both the cursing of the fig tree and the disciples' reaction to seeing it withered,[24] whereas Mark gives the more probable chronological order. The tree was cursed on Monday morning on the way into the city to enact the judgment on the temple leadership. The disciples return to Bethany on Monday night (Mark 11:19), and on Tuesday morning they react to the withering on the way back to Jerusalem (cf. 11:12–14, 20–26).

Jesus and the disciples, traveling from Bethany to Jerusalem, pass through the little village of Bethphage (see comments on 21:1). The appearance of leaves on a fig tree in this region was a promise of the sweet early fig. But the tree is unproductive, with no figs at all. This becomes an appropriate object for Jesus to use to indicate Israel's spiritual condition (cf. Hos. 9:10, where Israel is compared to a fruitful fig tree), providing a striking lesson for the disciples.[25] Just as the fig tree's fruitfulness was a sign of its health, so fruitfulness was a sign of Israel's faithfulness to the covenantal standards. Now

---

23. France, *Matthew*, 302–3; Keener, *A Commentary on the Gospel of Matthew* (1999), 502–3.

24. Cf. Matthew's topical arrangement of the miracles in chs. 8–9.

25. The fig tree also represents the new messianic age, when God's reign is established fully (cf. Zech. 3:10; Micah 4:4). For a discussion of the symbolism of the fig tree and Israel, see "Fig, Fig Tree," *DBI*, 283–84.

that Israel, especially represented by its religious leadership, has perverted the temple practices and has not repented at the appearance of Jesus Messiah proclaiming the arrival of the kingdom of heaven, Israel is being judged by God.

The disciples are amazed that the fig tree can wither so quickly, simply at the word of Jesus, but he tells them that they also can do such a thing, and even more (21:20–21). Jesus' cursing the fig tree is not a fit of temper but a symbolic act, demonstrating that God's creatures must produce that for which they were created—to carry out God's will, which means entering into a discipleship relationship with him and then demonstrating fruit from that relationship in a life of faith empowered by prayer.[26]

Using the handy object of the Mount of Olives or perhaps even the Temple Mount across the Kidron Valley, Jesus says that one with faith can throw the mountain into the sea (21:21). Then, similar to an earlier saying (17:20–21), Jesus declares, "If you believe, you will receive whatever you ask for in prayer." The point here is not the disciples' amount of faith to do great things but rather their trust in accomplishing God's will in God's power. If God directs them to move a mountain, God will supply the power for it to be accomplished. They simply must be obedient and say yes to his will.

### Controversies in the Temple Court over Jesus' Authority (21:23–27)

MOST LIKELY ON Tuesday morning of Holy Week, Jesus goes to the temple. While he is teaching the people there, the religious leaders, the subjects of Jesus' enacted symbolic judgment the previous day in the temple, confront him about his authority to do these things. Jesus gives three extended parables that reveal God's judgment on these leaders for not fulfilling their responsibility in getting the people to respond to his invitation to the kingdom of God (21:28–22:14). After that is a series of four interactions as the religious leaders attempt to entrap him, but he turns the tables to reveal his true identity as the Son of God (22:15–22:46). Jesus closes this section by pronouncing his climactic woes on these leaders (23:1–39).

The debates probably take place in one of the open-air porches surrounding the Court of the Gentiles. Jesus is confronted by "the chief priests and the elders of the people." The chief priests were high-ranking members of the priestly line who joined the high priest in giving oversight to the temple activities, treasury, and priestly orders. The "elders" (cf. also 26:3, 47;

---

26. The apostle Paul will later emphasize that the normal product of a disciple in relationship to Jesus is found especially in the fruit of the Spirit produced in our lives (cf. Gal. 4:6–7; 5:13–26).

27:1) were members of the Sanhedrin, the ruling body. They were representatives from the Sadducees and Pharisees (cf. 26:57; Mark 14:53).

Since Jesus had the previous day symbolically judged the religious leaders publicly, shaming them before the crowds over whom they exercised religious authority, they respond by asking, "By what authority are you doing these things?"[27] The reference to the authority to do "these things" most likely refers to Jesus' disrupting the commercial activities of the temple on the day before (21:12–13), but they are probably also questioning his authority to heal (21:14–16) and to teach in the temple (21:23). Jesus is, after all, neither an official priestly nor scribal authority according to their sectarian standards.

Instead of cowering before their challenge, Jesus replies, "I will also ask you one question. If you answer me, I will tell you by what authority I am doing these things." He now engages the religious leaders in a series of rabbinic-type debates that follow a typical pattern: a hostile question, followed by a counter-question, admission, and final rejoinder.[28]

Jesus' question is: "John's baptism—where did it come from? Was it from heaven, or from men?" Do they think John the Baptist had divine or human authority to carry out his ministry of calling all Israel to repentance in the light of the soon-coming arrival of the Messiah? By shifting the questioning back to the religious leaders, Jesus lays a logical trap (21:25b–26). They cannot alienate the people by saying that John's highly popular prophetic ministry was not from God. They fear that the people may turn against them and cause an uprising (21:26), which would jeopardize the Roman support of their leadership.

But neither can they endorse the very prophet who had condemned them for not repenting (cf. 3:7–10). The implication that Jesus demands them to admit is that John's authority as a true prophet was derived from God, and John had pointed to Jesus as the Messiah (cf. 3:11–17; 11:1–6; John 1:19, 26–27). If they respond that John's authority came from God, that would validate Jesus' authority to say and do what he wishes, even in the temple, which would be a clear answer their question. If these religious leaders will not endorse the prophet from God who pointed to Jesus, they surely will not endorse him as the Messiah, whose most recent actions have demonstrated that he has come to judge their leadership in Israel.

These religious leaders recognize the dilemma Jesus has put them in, so they refuse to answer. That refusal shows their dishonesty, and they must

---

27. See Joseph H. Hellerman, "Challenging the Authority of Jesus: Mark 11:27–33 and Mediterranean Notions of Honor and Shame," *JETS* 43 (June 2000): 213–28.

28. See Keener, *A Commentary on the Gospel of Matthew* (1999), 506, for background and literature.

accept their culpability. Therefore Jesus feels no obligation to answer their question about his authority, since he has forced them to accept their own responsibility for how they have responded to him. They are spiritually dishonest by not acknowledging the truth they know and have hardened their hearts against God's revelation. This is the unforgivable sin that the Pharisees committed earlier (12:30–32).

### Parables of Condemnation Directed Toward the Religious Leadership of Israel (21:28–46)

NOW THE INITIATIVE passes to Jesus as he presses the Jewish leaders with three parables (21:28–22:14). In each one it is evident that God is displeased with the officialdom of Israel. Each parable deals with their dishonesty and failure as leaders of the people.

**The parable of the two sons: The religious leadership did not heed John the Baptist (21:28–32).** The first parable is about two sons who were asked to work in their father's vineyard. This parable presses Jesus' point that the religious leaders have not rightly recognized John the Baptist's divinely endowed prophetic ministry. Grapes were one of the most important crops in ancient Israel and became one of the most important metaphors to describe Israel as the "vine" or "vineyard" of God (e.g., Jer. 2:21; Hos. 10:1). This parable and the next (21:33–46; cf. 20:1–16) bring to mind the religious leaders, who have been called to serve God by serving the nation of Israel. In the parable, one son initially refuses to go, but then does go. The other initially agrees to go, but then refuses.

Jesus presses the Pharisees and Sadducees with the question, "Which of the two did what his father wanted?" They reply with the obvious answer— the one that obeyed. By pressing them to give that answer, Jesus compels them to accept their responsibility as religious leaders of Israel. The son that originally refused but then obeyed is like those in Israel who were disobedient to the law, such as the tax collectors and prostitutes. But when John arrived with the message of true righteousness through the announcement of the arrival of the kingdom of God, they obeyed God's call through John and were repentant. By contrast, the religious leaders are like the son who agreed but did nothing. They were externally obedient to the law, but when God sent his messenger, John the Baptist, they did not obey God's message through him.

Sinners who repent will obey God and by it show their repentance. It does not matter if they once turned their backs on God. God wants obedience. The Jewish leaders are hypocritical in that they talk but do not live up to their talk. In the final analysis, it is the fruit of our lives that proves whether or not we are submissive to God's message through his messengers.

**The parable of the wicked tenants: God takes away the kingdom from Israel (21:33—46).** Jesus continues the vineyard metaphor of the previous parable. Clearly alluding to Isaiah 5:1–7, he intensifies his rebuke of the religious leadership by pronouncing God's judgment: The kingdom will be taken away from Israel and given to another people.[29]

Jesus reveals his firsthand knowledge of viticulture, because his description of the preparation of a vineyard for production conforms to the practices known from other sources from that time period. Stone walls were built around vineyards to protect them from thieves and wild animals, and some larger vineyards had watchtowers built for added security. It was common to have large farming estates in Palestine, which were owned either by foreigners or wealthy Jews and rented out to poor Jewish farmers. A wealthy landowner might employ a farmer or rent out his vineyard to tenants if he had other preoccupations.[30]

The peaceful scene of vineyards rented out to tenants turns ugly. With the arrival of harvest time, the landowner sends his servants to the tenants to collect the portion of the fruit that belongs to him. However, the unthinkable occurs: "The tenants seized his servants; they beat one, killed another, and stoned a third." Many absentee landowners were notorious for their harsh treatment of their tenants. Here, the scene is reversed, and the landowner's servants are abused when they come to collect a portion of the harvest. The landowner continues to send servants to collect what is rightfully his, but each is treated the same way (22:36). The treatment of these "servants" calls to mind the same fate that befell God's prophets throughout Old Testament history (e.g., 1 Kings 18:4; Jer. 20:1–2). Jesus will soon hold the teachers of the law and Pharisees culpable for the ill fate of the prophets and wise men sent to Israel (cf. Matt. 23:34).

Finally, the landowner sends his own son to make a collection, saying, "They will respect my son." This is an unmistakable allusion to God the Father's sending his Son, Jesus (cf. 10:40–41; cf. 3:17; 11:27; 15:24; 17:5), which is further evidence of Jesus' self-consciousness of his identity as God's unique Son (cf. 3:17; 11:27). Through this parable Jesus is making a public assertion of his divine Sonship to the religious leadership and the crowds.[31]

The story turns unthinkably ugly when the tenants say, "'This is the heir. Come, let's kill him and take his inheritance.' So they took him and threw him

---

29. For analysis, see Klyne R. Snodgrass, "Recent Research on the Parable of the Wicked Tenants: An Assessment," *IBR* 8 (1998): 187–215.

30. See Rousseau and Arav, "Viticulture," *Jesus and His World*, 328–32.

31. Kingsbury suggests that this is Jesus' first public assertion of his divine Sonship; see Jack Dean Kingsbury, "The Parable of the Wicked Husbandmen and the Secret of Jesus' Divine Sonship in Matthew: Some Literary-Critical Observations," *JBL* 195 (1986): 643–55.

---

out of the vineyard and killed him." The religious leaders have not acknowledged Jesus publicly as God's Son, nor have they publicly condemned Jesus
out of fear of the crowds (cf. 21:45–46). But Jesus foretells what they will do
to him secretly and blindly. They will condemn him for being a messianic
pretender and have him killed by the Gentiles, thinking that will enable
them to retain their claim to religious authority in Israel. Jesus has been
telling his disciples of his crucifixion at the hands of the religious leaders for
several months (16:21; 17:23; 20:18), and now he tells the rulers themselves
in parabolic form.

But the Jewish leaders cannot get away with their duplicity. Jesus concludes the parable by foretelling their demise. He places their self-
condemnation in their own mouth by asking these religious leaders what
the vineyard owner will do to those wicked tenants when he comes (21:40).
They reply with the only just thing that should be done: "He will bring those
wretches to a wretched end . . . and he will rent the vineyard to other tenants, who will give him his share of the crop at harvest time." This is fitting
self-condemnation, which Jesus makes explicit as he foretells their judgment
and rejection (21:42–44).

The crowds at Jesus' entrance to Jerusalem had sung out a portion of the
last Hallel psalm, "O Lord, save us," a quotation of Psalm 118:25–26 (cf.
Matt. 21:9). Now Jesus draws on Psalm 118:22 to point to his rejection and
future vindication: "The stone the builders rejected has become the capstone" (Matt. 21:42). God gives prominence to his suffering servant like a
"capstone" (lit., "head of the corner"), either the stone that held two rows of
stones together in a corner ("cornerstone") or the wedge-shaped stone placed
at the pinnacle of an arch that locked together the ascending stones. The suffering of the Son will be turned into the position of ultimate prominence and
importance.

Jesus climaxes his indictment of the religious leadership with a stinging
pronouncement: "Therefore I tell you that the kingdom of God will be taken
away from you and given to a people who will produce its fruit." This gives
Jesus' unambiguous conclusion to the preceding parable. The leaders are not
fulfilling the obligations to God for which they are responsible, neither in
their own lives nor in leading the nation of Israel. They have not repented
at the arrival of the kingdom of God; rather, they are rejecting the very Son
who announced its arrival. This is a statement to them personally of the
judgment they will receive, which had been enacted to the disciples symbolically in the cursing of the fig tree for not bearing fruit (21:18–21).

The privileged role of the religious leaders in caring for God's "vineyard"
is now being taken away. But this is also a hint that Israel's privileged role in
the establishment of God's kingdom will be taken away and given to another

people. "People" is the singular *ethnos*, which prepares for the time when the church, a nation of gathered people, will include both Jew and Gentile in the outworking of God's kingdom in the present age. All who become individual disciples out of the plural "nations" (28:19; *ethne*) will be brought together as one new "nation." Peter later also uses the singular *ethnos* in the context of the "stone" passage to refer to the church (1 Peter 2:9). This will not abolish the promises made to Israel nationally (cf. Rom. 11:25—33), but it does point to the transition of leadership and prominence that will be given to the church in God's program for the present age.

The kingdom of God will produce its fruit in this new nation of Jesus' disciples, which points ahead to the work of the Holy Spirit in the establishment of the new covenant. The reign of God's powerful presence is demonstrated in regenerated people through lives distinguished by the fruit of righteousness (Matt. 5:20) and good works (Col. 1:5—10), the fruit of Spirit-produced transformation of character (Gal. 5:21—24), and the fruit of new generations of disciples (Matt. 28:18—20; cf. John 15:16) that will bear witness to the reality of the kingdom on earth.

All of this could have been fruit produced in Israel, but instead it is taken away from them. Jesus continues to press the theme of judgment by saying, "He who falls on this stone will be broken to pieces, but he on whom it falls will be crushed." While different words for stone are used here than in 21:42, the meaning appears to be connected. The two parts of the stone imagery are somewhat enigmatic, but the emphasis on judgment is clear. The first half speaks of the personal culpability of individuals who stumble or fall into sin by not rightly recognizing the identity of Jesus. This probably draws on the imagery of Isaiah 8:13—15:

> The LORD Almighty is the one you are to regard as holy,
> > he is the one you are to fear,
> > he is the one you are to dread,
> and he will be a sanctuary;
> > but for both houses of Israel he will be
> a stone that causes men to stumble
> > and a rock that makes them fall.
> And for the people of Jerusalem he will be
> > a trap and a snare.
> Many of them will stumble;
> > they will fall and be broken,
> > they will be snared and captured.

The second half of 21:44 emphasizes the absolute judgment that will fall on those who stumble over Jesus, probably drawing on the well-known stone imagery in Daniel 2:34–35, 44–45. Jesus returns to the stone motif to issue a warning to Israel and her leadership. Not only will the privileged position and role in the outworking of the kingdom of God be taken away, but judgment also will come on those rejecting the Son. Those who stumble over the stone and try to destroy it, such as the religious leaders, will be destroyed. At the end Jesus will come as judge and fall on those who have rejected him (cf. chs. 24–25). "This despised stone (v. 42) is not only chosen by God and promoted to the premier place, it is also dangerous."[32]

The confrontation between Jesus and the religious leaders (now specifying "the chief priests and the Pharisees," 21:45) comes to a head. They cannot miss the point that Jesus is indicting them with his words of judgment. They understand the radical nature of what Jesus has pronounced and try to arrest him. He could stir up the crowds in such a way that all of their institutional power could be threatened. But their earlier fear of arousing the wrath of the people because of the prophet John the Baptist also prevents them from arresting Jesus, whom the crowds also perceive to be a prophet (cf. 21:45; cf. v. 11). At least for the time being, the enthusiasm of the crowd deters them from plotting his arrest. But what they fear to do in public, they plot to undertake in secrecy. In the end they themselves will persuade the crowd to ask for Jesus' death (cf. 27:20).

As JESUS ENTERS Jerusalem for his final week, everything about his person and mission comes to a climactic focus for the culmination of his earthly assignment. Everything he taught and every miracle and tender act of kindness he has performed now find their ultimate meaning in the deeds of this final week. He announces the arrival of the kingdom of heaven, and then demonstrates its good news of salvation from sin with preaching the gospel and its power with miracles of healing and exorcism of demons. This final week culminates his kingdom mission by establishing the new covenant in his blood (26:26–29). With his sacrifice on the cross, the actual atonement for humanity's sin is accomplished, which becomes the basis for the creation of a new humanity with the arrival of the Holy Spirit at Pentecost.

**Holy Week.** This week has rightly been called "Holy Week" throughout much of church history, a phrase that was used at least in the fourth century by Athanasius, bishop of Alexandria, and Epiphanius, bishop of Constantia. In some traditions this week is called "Passion Week" ("passion" comes from

---

32. Carson, "Matthew," 454.

the Latin *passio,* "suffering"). The Latin translations of the New Testament adopted the term *passio* to point to the Gospel narratives of Jesus' suffering and the attending events.

The pre-Nicene church concentrated its attention by celebrating one great feast, the Last Supper or the Christian Passover, on the night between Saturday and Easter Sunday morning. But by the late fourth century the church began separating the various events and commemorating them on the days of the week on which they occurred. Originally only Friday and Saturday were observed as holy days; later Wednesday was added as the day on which Judas plotted to betray Jesus. The commemoration of the full Holy Week then commenced with Palm Sunday to mark Jesus' dramatic entry to Jerusalem; Maundy Thursday marked Judas's betrayal and the institution of the Eucharist; the suffering, death, and burial of Jesus were commemorated on Good Friday; and his resurrection was celebrated on Easter Sunday.

Matthew, like all of the evangelists, gives special attention to Jesus' final week. The most basic message about Jesus given by the apostles concentrated on his death, burial, and resurrection, as we can see from the preaching accounts of the early church.[33] This basic message is the *kerygma* (Gk. term meaning "preaching"), which became the standardized message to unbelievers but also to believers. Therefore, as we embark on the study of the final eight chapters of Matthew's Gospel, we enter into Holy Week.

**Pictures of Jesus as prophet, priest, and king.** Matthew presents the activities of this final week to clarify the way that Jesus fulfills the various prophesied roles of the anticipated Messiah. One of the distinctive features of first-century Judaism that separated the various sects and made it difficult for them to understand Jesus' fulfillment of the Old Testament prophecies is their tendency to focus on one strand of messianic prediction, sometimes to the exclusion of others. For example, many focused on prophecies of a kingly conqueror who would arise to sit on David's throne (e.g., 2 Sam. 7:11−16). Others focused on prophecies of a great prophet like Moses, who would give the authoritative interpretation of God's law (Deut. 18:15−18). Still others looked at priestly passages and expected a mysterious figure like Melchizedek to have a messianic function (Gen. 14:18−20; Ps. 110:4).[34]

However, we do find evidence that at least some in Israel held these three prophetic strands in tension. A trilogy of messianic proof texts in a single document from the Qumran community speaks first of an eschatological prophet like Moses (Deut. 5:28−29; 18:18−19), then of a departing

---

33. E.g., Acts 2:23−36; 3:13−26; 7:51−53; 10:39−43; 13:26−31; 1 Cor 15:1−7.

34. For an overview of messianic expectation, see Craig A. Evans, "Messianism," *DJG,* 698−707.

kingly star and an arising kingly scepter from Israel who will crush their enemies (Num. 24:15–17), and finally of a priestly figure like Levi, whom Moses blessed (Deut. 33:8–11).[35] However, this probably indicates that the Qumran community expected more than one messiah. Note this famous phrase in the Rule of the Community: "until the prophet comes, and the Messiahs of Israel and of Aaron."[36] Nowhere do we find a consistent understanding that all three offices of prophet, priest and king would be fulfilled in one person.

At various times in Jesus' ministry he revealed how he fulfilled those strands, but in the passion narrative we begin to see most clearly how he fulfills all three in his messianic mission. Matthew helps us to see that as the true Messiah, the Son of David, Jesus fulfills the full Old Testament prophesied hope and expectation of the Jews by performing the eschatological functions of prophet, priest, and king. In fact, all the Gospel writers present Jesus as God's Messiah in his threefold role as teacher, sin-bearer, and ruler (i.e., prophet, priest, and king).

*Prophet.* Many within Israel looked to the prophets, who spoke for God and declared God's will for his people, both in their present time and for the future. They looked for the Messiah to be the voice of God, the greatest prophet, who would fulfill Moses' prophecy of the eschatological Prophet (Deut. 18:15–18). Jesus' arrival in Jerusalem prompts people in the crowd to herald him as the prophet from Nazareth in Galilee (Matt. 21:11), which probably indicates that they understand him to be another voice like that of John the Baptist. However, as some had earlier begun to see,[37] Jesus was indeed that great Prophet to whom Moses had pointed, who revealed and explained the Father to his people (John 1:18; 6:14; 7:40).

*Priest.* The priestly line of the Old Testament represented Israel before God to seek his forgiveness of sin. The Qumran community illustrates those within first-century Judaism who expected a priestly Messiah, as is especially seen in the phrase "the anointed one of Aaron" (e.g., 1QS 9:11). Jesus' activities in the temple and his declaration of judgment on those who perverted its function announce that he is the actualization of the priestly hopes. The unfolding activities of Passion Week, culminating in his cries from the cross and the tearing of the curtain veil, proclaim that he has fulfilled those hopes. According to the book of Hebrews, Jesus continues to intercede for his fol-

---

35. The document in question is 4QTestimonia.

36. 1QRule of the Community [1QS] 9:11. For discussion, see John J. Collins, *The Scepter and the Star: The Messiahs of the Dead Sea Scrolls and Other Ancient Literature* (ABRL; New York: Doubleday, 1995), 74–101.

37. Cf. John 6:14; 7:40, 52; Acts 3:22; 7:37.

lowers daily, demonstrating that true purity is a matter of the heart and that purity and righteousness work from the inside out (Heb. 7:24–25).

*King.* The patriarch Jacob prophesied of a kingly Messiah who would come from the tribe of Judah and reign as king: "The scepter will not depart from Judah, nor the ruler's staff from between his feet, until he comes to whom it belongs" (Gen. 49:10). This theme is expanded in classic messianic passages where David's line comprises a dynasty from which the Anointed One will arise to vanquish God's enemies and rule his people on an eternal throne in Jerusalem (2 Sam. 7:16; cf. Ps. 2:6; 110). But the distinctive strain of these prophecies is that this Anointed One extends the rule of God, not the rule of humans.

Jesus' dramatic entry to Jerusalem brings those strains together. He is the divine-human king who fulfills the Davidic prophecies of a future king but who also establishes the kingdom of heaven in a spiritual way that will allow him to reign in his followers' hearts throughout this age (Eph. 3:17). Moreover, as the human representative, Jesus fulfills the intended goal for humanity that was created to rule this world for God (cf. Gen. 1:26–28; Ps. 8:3–8). Matthew emphasizes the kingly aspects of Jesus' messianic identity as he narrates the final week of Jesus' mission, although he often presents these details tragically—as Jesus is accused of treason for claiming the title of king of the Jews (27:11–14) and as the crowds mock his kingship (e.g., 27:29).

Since the Old Testament messianic roles of prophet, priest, and king were primarily understood in Judaism to be fulfilled by separate individuals, if one person fulfilled all three offices, he would have to be an extraordinary person, more than anyone could conceive. And that is precisely how the Gospel writers present him,[38] and it is a special focus of Matthew's clarification of Jesus' messianic identity and mission. All three offices coalesce in the one person of Jesus Messiah, but the way that he fulfills these offices confounds the people of Israel.

- He enters Jerusalem as the King, not to establish the monarchy but to bring peace between God and humanity, and among humans, through his own death.
- He clears the temple, not simply to restore the institutional and ethical integrity of the priestly order but to announce that he is the Priest who will offer the final sacrifice that will make open and permanent the access of all humans to God.

---

38. These three aspects of Jesus' work are found together in the book of Hebrews, where Jesus is the messianic king who is exalted to his throne (1:3, 13; 2:9; 4:16), the great High Priest who offered himself to God as a sacrifice for our sins (2:17; 4:14–5:10; chs. 7–10), and the messenger who is the ultimate revelation of God (1:1–14; 3:1).

- He pronounces judgment on Israel like the prophets of old, not simply to restore order but to function as the Prophet who has fulfilled the Old Testament to enable his nation of disciples to live kingdom-empowered lives as his witnesses during this age.

Therefore, our discipleship to Jesus must understand him to be more than a warrior for God, more than a minister for God, and more than a spokesman for God. J. I. Packer catches the essence of this as he declares of Jesus as king, priest, and prophet:

> It is his glory, given him by the Father, to be in this way the all-sufficient Savior. We who believe are called to understand this and to show ourselves his people by obeying him as our king, trusting him as our priest, and learning from him as our prophet and teacher. To center on Jesus Christ in this way is the hallmark of authentic Christianity.[39]

Jesus is the Messiah who fulfills all of the hopes for humanity and offers an entirely new way of living.

**Jesus, Israel, and the mission of the new people of God.** Throughout the Old Testament the concept of God's kingdom includes the reign of God over the universe (1 Chron. 29:11−12; Ps. 103:19) and the coming kingdom when God's glory will be manifest on the earth (Isa. 24:23). The prophets continue that theme and emphasize that while God is King, both of Israel (Ex. 15:18; Num. 23:21; Deut. 33:5; Isa. 43:15) and of all the earth (2 Kings 19:15; Ps. 29:10; 99:1−4; Isa. 6:5; Jer. 46:18), he will become King and rule in a tangible way over his people (Isa. 24:23; 33:22; 52:7; Zeph. 3:15; Zech. 14:9ff.). This leads many to the conclusion that "while God is the King, he must also become King, i.e., he must manifest his kingship in the world of human beings and nations."[40] Therefore, God's kingdom includes both his activity of his reign and the realm of his reign.

The people of Israel were God's chosen children, through whom he covenanted to establish his kingdom on the earth. They were not to be the sole heirs of the kingdom, but rather they were to be the center of God's witness of his reality. This has been described as God's centripetal mission to the world, as the people would come to Israel to hear and witness God's revelation of his purposes for humanity.[41] The final eschatological hope revealed in the prophets is still centripetal, where God's purposes for all humanity are realized as they come to Jerusalem. This is classically pictured by Isaiah in Isaiah 2:2−3 (cf. also Mic. 4:1−2):

---

39. J. I. Packer, *Concise Theology* (Wheaton, Ill.: Tyndale House, 1993), 133.
40. Ladd, *Theology of the New Testament*, 58.
41. Cf. Köstenberger and O'Brien, *Salvation to the Ends of the Earth*, 40−42.

In the last days
the mountain of the LORD's temple will be established       •
    as chief among the mountains;
it will be raised above the hills,
    and all nations will stream to it.
Many peoples will come and say,
"Come, let us go up to the mountain of the LORD,
    to the house of the God of Jacob.
He will teach us his ways,
    so that we may walk in his paths."
The law will go out from Zion,
    the word of the LORD from Jerusalem.

Jesus came to Israel announcing that the kingdom of heaven had arrived. Israel continued as God's chosen recipients of the kingdom mission and witness. To and through Israel he ministered throughout his earthly life, expecting Israel to repent and receive his kingdom offer so that the centripetal concept would continue as Gentiles streamed to Zion to worship on the holy mountain.

But the events of the Holy Week bring to a critical juncture Jesus' relationship to Israel and the role they will play during this age. The events also clarify further the relationship and role for the disciples that Jesus was gathering around him. Throughout Matthew's narrative we have seen an uneasy tension between Jesus' compassion for the people of Israel (e.g., 9:35–38), yet the continual opposition to him by Israel's leadership (e.g., 12:24). We have also seen a puzzling tension between Jesus' commitment only to go to Israel (e.g., 10:5–6; 15:24), yet a tender responsiveness to the faith of Gentiles (8:10; 15:28). We have seen an emphasis on the present fulfillment of the covenantal promises of the kingly Davidic line (1:17; 2:2–6), yet an emphasis on the future fulfillment of the covenantal promises of the universal Abrahamic line (8:11–12). These tensions now prepare for some critical changes in both the mission, and the missionaries, of God's kingdom program. The narrative of these final chapters begins to clarify the process that led to these changes.[42]

1. Jesus came as a Jew to the Jewish people to fulfill the salvation-historical promises to Israel (10:5–6; 15:24). It was not his intention to undertake his ministry with the evident purpose of starting a new movement either within or outside of Israel.

---

42. For an overview of these issues, see Ladd, *Theology of the New Testament*, 104–6. I agree in large part with Ladd's perspective, but differ where he emphasizes that the church now replaces and becomes Israel, seemingly permanently. See also Scot McKnight, "Gentiles," *DJG*, 259–64.

2. Although Jesus' ministry was particularistic in its attention to Israel, it responded to the faith of Gentiles and held promise of a future universalistic outreach.

3. Israel as a whole, including both the leaders and the people, rejected Jesus and his message about the kingdom (12:25–32, 38–39; 13:10–17; 27:25).

4. A substantial group did respond in faith, however. Those who responded positively to his offer of the kingdom became his disciples. Discipleship entailed unreserved commitment to him, which meant that a new disciple entered the kingdom of God in the presence of the person of Jesus (5:2–16, 20).

5. Jesus declares in the events of the temple, the cursing of the fig tree, and the parables directed to the religious leaders who question his authority that the kingdom of God is being taken away from Israel (21:43).

6. The recipients of his messianic salvation become his new nation of witness to the reality of the kingdom (21:43).

7. The mission now becomes centrifugal instead of centripetal. This means that instead of the Gentiles coming to Israel to hear God's message, Jesus' disciples are to go to all the nations with the gospel of the kingdom of heaven to make more disciples (28:18–20).[43]

8. The twelve apostles will sit on twelve thrones "judging" the twelve tribes of Israel (19:28). This indicates ruling, which speaks to the future existence of Israel in God's purposes.

The role of carrying out God's purposes through the kingdom of God has been taken away from the nation of Israel in the present age, and Jesus' disciples currently enjoy both the blessings of the kingdom of God and the responsibility of the role of carrying the message of the gospel of the kingdom (21:43; 28:18–20). But Israel is still kept in view as receiving in the future the fulfillment of the promises of the kingdom (10:23; 23:37–39; cf. Rom. 11:25–32; 15:7–13; Rev. 7:1–8).[44] Jesus' disciples represent the fulfillment in part of the promises to Israel, and they now perform the role that Israel performed, but they do not replace Israel or become Israel.

---

43. Kostenberger and O'Brien, *Salvation to the Ends of the Earth*, 103–5, 135–37.
44. Cf. Hafemann, "Eschatology and Ethics," 161–92.

My earliest memory of the Easter season is as a child visiting a rather large church. All of us little children were given palm fronds, and we then lined up and walked down the aisle of the church with the choir singing at the top of their lungs. We stood on either side of the aisle, with our palm fronds extending out and above us, forming a canopy. This seemed to me like a very fun way to do church! Then I was absolutely stunned, because down the aisle came a man in a long robe riding a donkey! Riding a donkey into church! That is a good memory. It was a happy procession of children and choir and a man on a donkey, almost like a celebration. It seemed like everyone loved Jesus on that Palm Sunday.

But memories of childhood aren't all exactly correct. Several years ago someone gave me a story of a Sunday school teacher who decided to ask her little preschool class what they remembered about Easter. The first little fellow suggested that Easter was when all the family came to the house and they ate a big turkey and watched football. The teacher thought that perhaps he was thinking of Thanksgiving, not Easter, so she let a little girl answer. She seemed to think that Easter was the day when you come down the stairs in the morning and saw all the beautiful presents under the tree.

At this point the teacher was really feeling discouraged. But after explaining that the little girl was probably thinking of Christmas, she called on a little boy with his hand tentatively raised in the air. The teacher's spirits immediately perked up as the boy said that Easter was the time when Jesus was crucified on a cross and buried. Finally, she felt that she had at least gotten through to one child. Then the little boy added, "And then he came out of the grave, and if he sees his shadow we have six more weeks of winter!"

Well, when I was a little boy, I thought Palm Sunday seemed to say that everyone loved Jesus. Now that Jesus arrived on a donkey, everything is going to turn out all right. But like the little boy who confused Easter with Groundhog Day, I got only about half the story right.

Palm Sunday does speak of celebration, but we have already seen that people were celebrating for a variety of reasons, not all of which reflect Jesus' purposes for entering Jerusalem. Lots of people did shout for joy because they loved Jesus, but not all them really cared for him above their own dreams. In just a few days many of the same ones shouted with anger to have Jesus crucified. Because of Jesus' redemptive sacrifice, things will turn out right for his disciples. But for the people of Israel a different future now commences, and for many of them it spells doom.

**Walking with Jesus through the Holy Week.** The magnitude of the Holy Week events for the future of humanity must be understood correctly. We must understand what Jesus intended in the Holy Week so that our own expectations and dreams are kept in line with his. Thus, many years ago, I began a practice of what I call "walking with Jesus through the Holy Week." I try to visualize what Jesus was doing every day of that week, starting from the celebration with his disciples on the Saturday evening prior to Palm Sunday, all the way to the resurrection on Easter Sunday. I try to imagine what Jesus was doing at each hour of each day—was he enjoying the last fellowship with his disciples, or was he alone preparing for the experience of the cross? I try to put myself in his place to feel what he was feeling—was it poignant joy when Mary anointed his feet, or painful rejection as Peter and the other disciples denied him? What was he feeling as Judas betrayed him?

I also try to imagine his incredible suffering as he endured the horrors of his crucifixion and separation from God, yet I try also to imagine the incredible joy as he experienced the resurrection with his victory over sin accomplished. As I walk with Jesus through these various events, I have an incredibly wide range of experiences, from feelings of tenderness and intimacy with him, to my own anger at what others did to him, to utter amazement over the profound experience of the God-Man on the cross and out of the empty tomb.

Each year I read through a different account of the Holy Week from one of the Gospels. Mark gives the quickest chronological overview, but each Gospel records significant issues and perspectives that complement each other for a full understanding of the week's events. After a couple of years of doing this, I began memorizing each of the events so that no matter what I was doing—from preparing a sermon for Easter, or joining my daughters for an afternoon surf session, or pulling weeds in the garden—I could reflect on what Jesus was doing at that very hour. This week has become the most powerful week of my year.

I also started taking along others with me as I walked with Jesus through the Holy Week. As a youth pastor taking groups of students on Easter mission trips or ski outings, I would teach on Jesus' activities throughout the week to correspond with the individual events. I began also to ask the students to memorize the outline of the events. Later, as a professor I began challenging students to memorize these events, and then I'd give an examination to encourage them to do so! Thus, when Easter vacation came along, no matter where they were or what they were doing, they would be able to walk with Jesus through Holy Week. Literally thousands of students have done this over the years. The response I get from people who have done this is almost always that they have profited immensely from this simple discipline of focusing on Jesus and trying to plumb the depths of the historical, personal, and theological ramifications of his final week on earth. Many of these students have likewise used this in their own ministries and families to help others participate with Jesus in the most important events of human history.

To encourage you to do so, and also perhaps to use with your own people, I've reduplicated the basic events that correspond to our calendar and hours of the day. This kind of discipline has been practiced by Christians throughout history to commemorate, celebrate, commiserate, and contemplate these events with Jesus and to enter into a profound understanding of what Jesus accomplished for us. It can be done alone, with groups, or even as a family's worship time.[45]

# Walking with Jesus Through the Holy (Passion) Week
## A Harmony of the Events of Jesus' Final Week[46]
(cf. Matt. 21–28; Mark 11–16; Luke 19–24; John 12–21)

| Modern Calendar Days | Event of the Holy Week |
|---|---|
| | • Arrival in Bethany (John 12:1) |
| Saturday | • Evening celebration, Mary anoints Jesus (John 12:2–8; cf. Matt. 26:6–13) |
| Sunday | • Triumphal Entry into Jerusalem (Matt. 21:1–11; Mark 11:1–10; John 12:12–18)<br>• Jesus surveys the temple area (Mark 11:11)<br>• Return to Bethany (Matt. 21:17; Mark 11:11) |
| Monday | • Cursing the fig tree on the way to Jerusalem (Matt. 21:18–22; cf. Mark 11:12–14)<br>• Clearing the temple (Matt. 21:12–13; Mark 11:15–17)<br>• Miracles and challenges in the temple (Matt. 21:14-16; Mark 1:18)<br>• Return to Bethany (Mark 11:19) |
| Tuesday | • Reaction to cursing the fig tree on the way back to Jerusalem (Matt. 21:20–22; Mark 11:20–21)<br>• Debates with religious leaders in Jerusalem and teaching in the temple (Matt. 21:23–23:39; Mark 11:27–12:44)<br>• Eschatological Discourse on the Mount of Olives on the return to Bethany (Matt. 24:1–25:46; Mark 13:1-37) |

45. For family-focused activities, see the excellent little booklet with selections from Charles Colson, Billy Graham, Max Lucado, and Joni Eareckson Tada, *Christ in Easter: A Family Celebration of Holy Week* (Colorado Springs: NavPress, 1990).

46. Compiled with reference to A. T. Robertson, *A Harmony of the Gospels for Students of the Life of Christ: Based on the Broadus Harmony in the Revised Version* (New York: Harper & Row, 1922), and Robert L. Thomas and Stanley N. Gundry, eds., *The NIV Harmony of the Gospels* (Harper & Row, 1978).

| Wednesday | • "Silent Wednesday"—Jesus and disciples remain in Bethany for last time of fellowship |
| | • Judas returns alone to Jerusalem to make arrangements for the betrayal (Matt. 26:14–16; Mark 14:10–11) |
| **Thursday** | • Preparations for Passover (Matt. 26:17–19; Mark 14:12–16) |
| | *After sundown:* |
| | • Passover meal and Last Supper (Matt. 26:20–35; Mark 14:17–26) |
| | • Upper Room discourses (John 13–17) |
| | • Prayers in the Garden of Gethsemane (Matt. 26:36–46; Mark 14:32–42) |
| **Friday** | *Sometime perhaps after midnight:* |
| | • Betrayal and arrest (Matt. 26:47–56; Mark 14:43–52) |
| | • Jewish trial—Jesus appears in three phases in front of: |
| | —Annas (John 18:13–24) |
| | —Caiaphas and partial Sanhedrin (Matt. 26:57–75; Mark 14:53–65) |
| | —Sanhedrin fully assembled (*perhaps after sunrise*) (Matt. 27:1–2; Mark 15:1) |
| | • Roman trial—Jesus appears in three phases before: |
| | —Pilate (Matt. 27:2–14; Mark 15:2–5) |
| | —Herod Antipas (Luke 23:6–12) |
| | —Pilate (Matt. 27:15–26; Mark 15:6–15) |
| | • Crucifixion (*approx. 9:00 A.M. to 3:00 P.M.*) (Matt. 27:27–66; Mark 15:16–39) |
| **Sunday** | • Resurrection witnesses (Matt. 28:1–8; Mark 16:1–8; Luke 24:1–12) |
| | • Resurrection appearances (Matt. 28:9–20; Luke 24:13–53; John 20–21) |

**The impact of Holy Week on our lives.** The practice of walking with Jesus through the Holy Week achieves at least five important functions in my life. (1) It solidifies the historical foundation of my Christian worldview. As I mull these events, I recognize that my faith is build on the rock-solid events that Jesus performed in history—why he was arrested, why the Jewish leaders rejected him, why the Romans executed him, and why even his own followers were so frightened and perplexed. When I reach resurrection Sunday having followed Jesus through the events of this week, my faith is not wishful thinking; rather, it is founded on the facts of history revealed in God's Word. The empty tomb is the convincing fact that my faith in a risen Savior is real (1 Cor. 15:12–34).

(2) I also understand the disciples more clearly. I understand why they were frightened and cowered as a group behind closed doors to save their own necks because of their perplexity at seeing their miracle-working Master led away and crucified. But I also understand how their experience of seeing Jesus raised from the dead transformed them into courageous and bold leaders who risked everything to tell the world of this good news. They serve as an example of what my own life can be when I am gripped by the events of Holy Week.

(3) I am held under the conviction of my responsibilities as Jesus' disciple. The second point thrusts on me my responsibility as I watch the reaction of the people and leaders of Israel. They had the greatest privilege of humanity in their calling to be God's chosen people and to experience their relationship with him in person. Yet their own personal agendas and hardheartedness rejected Jesus and his message, and they have now been cut off from both their privileges and responsibilities. Those who have responded now belong to the new nation of Jesus' disciples (21:43).

There is an underlying principle for us here as well. We too can be so set on our own agenda that we harden our hearts against what Jesus wants to accomplish through us. He is patient, but if those who are in positions of responsibility drop the ball, he will give the privileges and responsibilities to those who can be trusted. We must be trusted to live lives and do ministry according to God's criteria that Jesus unfolded in his earthly ministry and that will be developed in the rest of the New Testament. If not, God will, I suspect, find people to live according to kingdom principles and carry out the work of the kingdom in the way he wants it done.

(4) My experience of these events impels me to more sincere worship. I comprehend the tragedy of the temple. One of Israel's greatest failures was to understand the fundamental significance of the temple. This failure was not just conducting sacrifices in the wrong way, or profiteering from the poor, or personal corruption among the priesthood, although all of these were included. Jesus' critique was that "the mechanics of the temple ritual were allowed to obscure the point of authentic communion with God."[47] As Jesus pronounces judgment on Israel in the temple incident and in the cursing of the fig tree, I must look to my own life. How much of what I do is simply religious ritual and self-serving hypocrisy? And how much of what I do in the everyday routines of life is lived in the conscious presence of my God and Savior, Jesus Christ?

When we do the latter, our lives are one continual act of worship. Understanding God's purposes and will means allowing him to be the God of my

---

47. Hagner, *Matthew*, 2:601.

life in all that I say and do. And when I do so—whether I am in the market or in meditation, on the freeway or facing my classroom, walking the neighbor's dog or waking up with my bride at my side—I live a worshipful life that gives adoration, praise, and glory to Jesus just simply by being alive.

(5) I am drawn into a more intimate relationship with Jesus after having walked with him through all of the events of this week. I have entered into the fellowship that he experienced with his closest followers that fateful week—the adrenaline rush of the entry into Jerusalem and clearing the temple, the tenderness of the final moments of silent Wednesday and the Upper Room supper, the heartbreak of seeing them turn away from him in his hour of greatest need and then even deny him. I have followed Jesus into the Garden, where, in utter anguish, he prays for a different path but then resolutely accepts the Father's will of going to the cross. I have drawn as close as I dare to witness his physical pain of scourging and crucifixion and have tried as feebly as I can to comprehend the abandonment he experiences from God. And I have, as Paul says, experienced being raised with him from the dead as I reconsider and reclaim my own salvation experience (cf. Rom. 6:1–14).

Our walk with Jesus through Holy Week is a time that best enables us to comprehend him as our divine-human Savior and Lord and to live in a right relationship with him today.

# Matthew 22:1–46

❧

J ESUS SPOKE TO them again in parables, saying: ²"The kingdom of heaven is like a king who prepared a wedding banquet for his son. ³He sent his servants to those who had
been invited to the banquet to tell them to come, but they
refused to come.

⁴"Then he sent some more servants and said, 'Tell those
who have been invited that I have prepared my dinner: My
oxen and fattened cattle have been butchered, and everything
is ready. Come to the wedding banquet.'

⁵"But they paid no attention and went off—one to his
field, another to his business. ⁶The rest seized his servants,
mistreated them and killed them. ⁷The king was enraged. He
sent his army and destroyed those murderers and burned
their city.

⁸"Then he said to his servants, 'The wedding banquet is
ready, but those I invited did not deserve to come. ⁹Go to the
street corners and invite to the banquet anyone you find.' ¹⁰So
the servants went out into the streets and gathered all the
people they could find, both good and bad, and the wedding
hall was filled with guests.

¹¹"But when the king came in to see the guests, he noticed
a man there who was not wearing wedding clothes. ¹²'Friend,'
he asked, 'how did you get in here without wedding clothes?'
The man was speechless.

¹³"Then the king told the attendants, 'Tie him hand and
foot, and throw him outside, into the darkness, where there
will be weeping and gnashing of teeth.'

¹⁴"For many are invited, but few are chosen."

¹⁵Then the Pharisees went out and laid plans to trap him in
his words. ¹⁶They sent their disciples to him along with the
Herodians. "Teacher," they said, "we know you are a man of
integrity and that you teach the way of God in accordance
with the truth. You aren't swayed by men, because you pay no
attention to who they are. ¹⁷Tell us then, what is your opinion? Is it right to pay taxes to Caesar or not?"

¹⁸But Jesus, knowing their evil intent, said, "You hypocrites,
why are you trying to trap me? ¹⁹Show me the coin used for

paying the tax." They brought him a denarius, 20and he asked them, "Whose portrait is this? And whose inscription?"

21"Caesar's," they replied.

Then he said to them, "Give to Caesar what is Caesar's, and to God what is God's."

22When they heard this, they were amazed. So they left him and went away.

23That same day the Sadducees, who say there is no resurrection, came to him with a question. 24"Teacher," they said, "Moses told us that if a man dies without having children, his brother must marry the widow and have children for him. 25Now there were seven brothers among us. The first one married and died, and since he had no children, he left his wife to his brother. 26The same thing happened to the second and third brother, right on down to the seventh. 27Finally, the woman died. 28Now then, at the resurrection, whose wife will she be of the seven, since all of them were married to her?"

29Jesus replied, "You are in error because you do not know the Scriptures or the power of God. 30At the resurrection people will neither marry nor be given in marriage; they will be like the angels in heaven. 31But about the resurrection of the dead—have you not read what God said to you, 32'I am the God of Abraham, the God of Isaac, and the God of Jacob' ? He is not the God of the dead but of the living."

33When the crowds heard this, they were astonished at his teaching.

34Hearing that Jesus had silenced the Sadducees, the Pharisees got together. 35One of them, an expert in the law, tested him with this question: 36"Teacher, which is the greatest commandment in the Law?"

37Jesus replied: "'Love the Lord your God with all your heart and with all your soul and with all your mind.' 38This is the first and greatest commandment. 39And the second is like it: 'Love your neighbor as yourself.' 40All the Law and the Prophets hang on these two commandments."

41While the Pharisees were gathered together, Jesus asked them, 42"What do you think about the Christ? Whose son is he?"

"The son of David," they replied.

43He said to them, "How is it then that David, speaking by the Spirit, calls him 'Lord'? For he says,

⁴⁴"'The Lord said to my Lord:
"'Sit at my right hand
until I put your enemies
under your feet.'" '

⁴⁵If then David calls him 'Lord,' how can he be his son?" ⁴⁶No
one could say a word in reply, and from that day on no one
dared to ask him any more questions.

CHAPTER 21 CONCLUDED with Jesus in direct confrontation with the religious leaders in the temple in Jerusalem (see comments on 21:23). At the
center of the confrontation was the religious lead-
ers' challenge to Jesus' authority. He had cleared the temple the prior day
(Monday of Holy Week), which was an enacted, symbolic pronouncement
of judgment on the temple establishment. It was also a precursor of the end
of the temple as an institution, because his impending crucifixion would provide direct access to God's forgiveness and salvation.

Jesus did not cower before the challenge to his authority. Instead, he turned
the tables back on them by challenging them to publicly recognize the source
of John the Baptist's authority as being from God (21:24–27). He then told
a series of three parables that challenged and pronounced judgment on their
own authority. The first two (the parable of the two sons and the parable of
the wicked tenants) are in 21:28–46 (see comments). The parable of the wedding banquet that begins chapter 22 is the third of those parables.

## The Parable of the Wedding Banquet: Responses to the Invitation to the Kingdom (22:1–14)

THE PARABLE OF the wedding banquet is unique to this context, although a
similar parable occurs in another context in Luke 14:15–24. Jesus confronts
the religious leaders with a carefully designed parable that surfaces from the
situation in the temple as he rebukes and condemns them for not responding to his invitation to the kingdom of heaven.¹ Using familiar wording to
introduce a parable about the kingdom (cf. 13:24, 13:31, 44, 45, 47, 52),
Jesus describes the consequences that will fall on the religious leaders. This
parable falls into three sections: the judgment that will befall the religious

---

1. For details see Blomberg, *Interpreting the Parables*, 237–40; for an excellent recent article on this parable, see Noel Rabbinowitz, "Matthew 22:2–4: Does Jesus Recognize the
Authority of the Pharisees and Does He Endorse Their *Halakhah?*" *JETS* 46 (2003): 423–47.

leaders for their rejection of his invitation to repent and enter the kingdom (22:1–7), a description of those who will be invited to replace them (22:8–10), and the requirements for participation in the kingdom (22:11–14).

**Rejections of the invitations to the wedding (22:1–7).** The setting of the parable is a celebration: "a king who prepared a wedding banquet for his son." This type of wedding would have been a countrywide celebration that would last for several days.

The parable takes its first surprising turn because some have apparently overlooked the initial invitation to the wedding celebration and then refuse the king's personal invitation sent through his servants (22:3). Although one might overlook a first invitation, the refusal of a direct invitation from the king would be unthinkable—a dangerous affront to the monarch. Yet the king's graciousness wins the day, and he reissues the invitation through more servants, now elaborating on the bounty of the celebration: "My oxen and fattened cattle have been butchered, and everything is ready. Come to the wedding banquet."

Some of the invitees still reject the king's invitation—with trivial excuses of preoccupation with everyday affairs (e.g., farming and business). The rest actually abuse and kill the king's messengers (22:6). This is an unbelievable insult to the king, who severely punishes his insubordinate subjects with death and fire (22:7). This kind of punishment was used only in case of the most serious treason and revolt against a king.

While not as explicit, the allusion to Israel as the vineyard of Isaiah's prophecy in the preceding parables continues, now drawing on the destruction that will come on the nation of Israel and its leaders (see comments on 21:28, 33) for despising the Holy One of Israel (cf. Isa. 5:3–12, 24–25).[2] This destruction of rebellious subjects and their city parallels other rebellions in Jewish history.[3] Even through he does not mention the temple here, Jesus may be alluding to the coming destruction of Jerusalem and the judgment of the religious establishment in A.D. 70, a theme to which he returns in the Eschatological Discourse (cf. 24:1–3).

**An open invitation to the wedding (22:8–10).** The second part of the parable draws on another inconceivable development. Instead of the privileged few being invited to the wedding, the undeserving and unworthy many ("anyone you find") receive an invitation. Those who considered themselves able to dispense with the king's invitation are now undeserving (22:8). They correspond to the religious leadership of Israel and the other self-righteous Jews who follow their leadership.

---

2. See Gundry, *Matthew*, 436–37.
3. E.g., Judg. 1:8; Isa. 5:24; 1 Macc. 5:28; *T. Jud.* 5:1–5.

This continues a theme that Jesus has emphasized throughout his ministry. It is not the externally righteous or healthy but sinners and the sick who are invited to the kingdom of heaven (5:20; 9:12–13). Only those who recognize their personal helplessness (like a sick person or child, e.g., 9:12–13; 18:3–4) cast aside their self-reliance and self-worthiness to accept the grace of God. Those on the main highways correspond to the publicans and sinners of Israel, who have been the surprising object of Jesus' ministry (9:10–11), and to the Gentiles, who will become the object of his ministry through the disciples' worldwide outreach (28:18–20). The wedding hall is filled with these undeserving guests who respond to the gracious invitation (22:10).

**Inappropriate garments for the wedding (22:11–13).** The third part of the parable focuses on one of the guests who has gained entrance to the wedding but does not have the appropriate wedding garment. Since the king sent out an open invitation to those who were not worthy of such a celebration, it is fitting that he should come to see who has responded. Although the invitation was given to all, proper attire was expected. Drawing on some evidence for a king in the ancient world supplying festal garments for guests (Gen. 45:22; Est. 6:8–9), some have understood this as an allusion to the imputed righteousness that Jesus hinted at early in his ministry (5:20) and that Paul will later enunciate (e.g., Rom. 3:21–31; 4:22–25). Others suggest that this refers to clean garments as opposed to dirty ones, not symbolizing works meriting salvation but evidential works of righteousness for those already having obtained salvation.[4]

In either case, since the individual is addressed as "friend" (see comments on 20:13) and is left speechless when confronted by the king (22:12), the implication is that the guest has proper clothing available but has declined to wear it. The man is bound and cast into the outer place of weeping and gnashing of teeth (22:13), language that commonly refers to eternal judgment (cf. 8:12; 13:42, 50; 24:51; 25:26, 30).[5]

This once again points to the accountability of everyone's response to Jesus' invitation to the kingdom of heaven. The privileged religious leaders are judged for rejecting the invitation (22:7), and the populace of Israel, who also are privileged to be the children of God, will be judged for their response to the kingdom. But even Jesus' professing disciples, such as Judas (called "friend" in 26:50), are culpable for what they ultimately do with the invitation. Not all who respond do so from the heart. This is the point of all three

4. Gundry, *Matthew*, 439; Davies and Allison, *Matthew*, 3:204 n. 53; Keener, *A Commentary on the Gospel of Matthew* (1999), 522, n. 189.

5. See Keener, *A Commentary on the Gospel of Matthew* (1999), 523.

parables of judgment (21:28–32, 33–46; 22:1–14). Any who insult God's gracious offer of the kingdom of heaven by presuming on it without honoring the Son will receive due judgment.

**Many invited, few chosen (22:14).** A pithy statement gives a concluding pronouncement to the parable of the wedding feast, but also to the other two preceding parables generally: "For many are invited, but few are chosen." "Many" (*polloi*) without the article is a common Semitic universalizing expression, which is normally translated "everyone" or "all" (cf. 20:28). In Psalm 109:30, for example, the Hebrew *rabbim* becomes *polloi* in the LXX, indicating an inclusive reference for "all" in the congregation. Similarly, in the Qumran literature, *rabbim* is a fixed inclusive title for all those in the Congregation (1QS 6:8–11) or all who exercise jurisdiction as leaders in the Congregation (e.g., 1QS 6:1).[6] By the expression "many are invited," Jesus points to a universal invitation to the kingdom of heaven.

The counterbalancing point in the second half of the saying, "but few are chosen," emphasizes that not all who are invited are chosen. This does not specify the actual amount but rather points to the divine perspective of the preceding parables. Those chosen are "the elect," which for Jesus is an alternative expression for his true disciples (cf. 11:27; 24:22, 24, 31). Israel and her leadership had been known as the "chosen," but even their privilege is lost through unresponsiveness to Jesus' invitation to the kingdom of heaven. Therefore, while there is an open invitation to the kingdom, from the divine perspective it is only God's sovereign choice that effects salvation. From a human perspective it is only those who respond to the call appropriately that are part of the banquet. Only an appropriate response reveals God's divine election.

God is the King who has invited all to the celebration of the arrival of the kingdom of heaven in the person of his Son, Jesus Messiah.[7] He has sent out an invitation to the privileged religious leaders and their followers, even to the supposedly undeserving within Israel. Israel and her leadership are held responsible for rejecting Jesus' invitation, regardless of whether they have simply refused (22:3), are preoccupied with their own affairs (22:5), are actively rebellious (22:6), or display inappropriate personal responsiveness (22:12). Instead, as Jesus predicted in the previous parable (21:41, 43), God will turn to the undeserving outside of Israel to fill his kingdom with celebrants.

---

6. Joachim Jeremias, "πολλοί," *TDNT*, 6:536–45.

7. The parable does not speak of the actual wedding feast of the Lamb in heaven (Rev. 19:5–8), but depicts responses to the invitation to the kingdom of heaven. Beyond that, it can illustrate responses of individuals in this life to the gospel message. Jesus points out the seriousness of one's response to the opportunity of being called into the family of God.

## Four Debates with the Religious Leaders Concerning Jesus' Authority and Identity (22:15–46)

THE CONFRONTATIONS CONTINUE between Jesus and the religious leaders concerning his authority to orchestrate activities in the temple and pronounce judgment on the religious establishment (cf. 21:23). Jesus now enters into four debates with various leaders: with the Pharisees' disciples and the Herodians about paying taxes to Caesar (22:15–22), with the Sadducees about remarriage in the resurrection (22:22–23), with a law expert about the greatest commandment (22:34–40), and the Pharisees about the Messiah as the son of David (22:41–46). After these confrontations, Jesus gives his fateful woes on the religious leadership (23:1–36).

**Paying taxes to Caesar: Disciples of the Pharisees and the Herodians (22:15–22).** Having been the object of Jesus' stinging pronouncement of judgment (21:45), the Pharisees went out from the temple area to develop a strategy how "to trap him in his words" (22:15). Prior to this in Galilee, the Pharisees tried to tempt (*peirazo*) Jesus to violate the law (16:1; 19:3). Similarly, but perhaps with an even more sinister motivation, they now try to trap (*pagideuo*) or ensnare Jesus in his words with the hope that he will incriminate himself in a pronouncement that they can use to take him to the Romans for execution.

*The disciples of the Pharisees and the Herodians (22:15–16).* Perhaps knowing that Jesus is savvy to their evil intentions, the Pharisees send "their disciples" to the temple area where the controversies continue to boil between Jesus and Israel's religious leadership. These disciples are most likely those in training to become full initiates to the brotherhood of Pharisees and have been immersed in the Pharisaic commitment of the oral law and rigorous practice of their traditions. But since they are not legal experts yet, on the surface they would not appear to be as much of a legal threat to Jesus. It is a seemingly innocuous group that approaches him with fawning deference, attempting to disarm him so that they might entrap him.

The disciples of the Pharisees are joined by the Herodians in this sinister maneuvering (cf. also Mark 3:6; 12:13). The Herodians were supporters of the Herodian family and dynasty (c. 55 B.C.–c. A.D. 93), most immediately Herod Antipas, the Roman client tetrarch who ruled Galilee after the death of his father, Herod the Great. They most likely are a loosely organized group with a vested economic and political interest in advancing the Herods' influence in Israel.[8] Herod Antipas never liked the fact that he did not gain control over all of his father's former territory, so his followers advance his

---

8. For an overview of the evidence and research into this shadowy group, see Meier, *A Marginal Jew*, 3:560–65. The most extensive recent study is Kokkinos, *The Herodian Dynasty*.

cause to attempt to regain Judea, which Pilate governed for Rome. Although the Herodians and the Pharisees would be at odds on many political and religious issues, here they combine to combat the common threat to their respective power bases.

Calling Jesus "teacher" is an attempt to ingratiate themselves with him by using a title of respect, the equivalent of the Hebrew title "rabbi." In Matthew it is the normal title used when nondisciples approach Jesus (9:11; 12:38; 17:24; 19:16; 22:24, 36). In this case the disciples of the Pharisees and the Herodians use the title deceptively, for Jesus has not gone through one of the rabbinical training colleges to attain the status of rabbi. They are shamelessly hypocritical in their attempt to disarm Jesus with their flattery. This address, however, is far truer than they realize and is the opposite of their own hypocrisy and that of the religious leaders whom Jesus has condemned throughout his ministry (e.g., 6:1–18). If these disciples of the Pharisees and Herodians really mean these words, they will become Jesus' disciples.

*Paying taxes to Caesar (22:17–18).* These visitors to Jesus try to ambush him with a seemingly innocent question: "Is it right to pay taxes to Caesar or not?" While the question itself may be innocent, the intent behind it is not. Either answer Jesus might give can be used against him. At question was the legal requirement of paying taxes to "Caesar," the family name of Julius Caesar, which had become a title for the following Roman emperors. Currently, Tiberius Julius Caesar Augustus was emperor of Rome.[9]

This question reveals a volatile issue in Israel. The tax mentioned is either the annual head tax or one of the more general taxes, such as the poll tax.[10] The people of Israel, indeed all of Rome's subjects, labored under heavy taxation that kept the empire operating. The Herods had long collected taxes in the name of Rome to support their own military ventures, building projects, and lavish lifestyles. They paid a tribute to Rome directly, so they were allowed to exact heavier taxes to fill their own coffers. The roman prefect of Judea and Samaria collected the land and poll taxes directly for Rome. The Jewish religious authorities also exacted their own taxes for the temple and for their other institutional expenses (cf. 17:24–27).

Thus, the people were seething at the exhausting taxation. Some estimate that a Jewish family paid approximately 49–50 percent of its annual income to these various taxes.[11] If Jesus answers that it is indeed right to pay taxes to Caesar, it will put him in disfavor with the burdened people, who will

---

9. For a chart of the Roman emperors called "Caesar" during New Testament times and later and the corresponding biblical references, see Wilkins, "Matthew," 136.

10. Colin Brown, Norman Hillyer, "Tax, Tax Collector," *NIDNTT*, 3:751–59.

11. See Rousseau and Arav, "Tax and Tax Collectors," *Jesus and His World*, 278.

think that he has capitulated and is now in league with Roman oppression. If Jesus answers that it is not right to pay taxes to Caesar, it can be used against him with the Roman authorities to support their case that he is an insurrectionist. The Pharisees know that either answer will jeopardize Jesus' mission—exactly their intent.

Jesus sees through their hypocritical ploy because he knows[12] the evil behind their motivation (22:18). The term behind Jesus' use of "trap" here is *peirazo*, the common word for "tempt" or "test." They are attempting to get Jesus to incriminate himself. They come with fawning flattery, but their intentions are evil, which is the height of religious hypocrisy.

*Giving to Caesar and to God (22:19–22).* But Jesus reverses the confrontation by taking the offensive. He asks for a coin used for paying the tax, the denarius, which they produce. He points to the coin and asks them to identify the portrait and inscription forged on it. They reply, "Caesar's." On the obverse side of a silver denarius was a profile of the head of Tiberius Caesar, with the Latin inscription on the perimeter of the coin, "Tiberius Caesar, son of the divine Augustus." On the reverse of the coin was a picture of the seated Pax, the Roman goddess of peace, with the Latin inscription "High Priest."[13]

Replying to their statement that Caesar's portrait and inscription are on the denarius, Jesus avows, "Give to Caesar what is Caesar's, and to God what is God's." Jesus is not merely attempting to wiggle out of a sticky, logical riddle by offering another. Rather, behind his answer is a profound statement of his role at this point of God's salvation-history, as well as the way those in the kingdom of God will operate in this world. (1) He has not come as a military or political threat to the established rulers of this world. His kingdom is revolutionary, but until he returns in glory, the kingdom will operate within the existing political order.

(2) Those who have responded to the invitation to the kingdom of heaven will continue to have obligations to governing authorities of this world, a fact that later New Testament writers emphasize even while living under oppressive authorities (e.g., Rom. 13:1–7; 1 Peter 2:13–17). Thus, Jesus again demonstrates that he is not establishing a political kingdom to oppose Caesar.

(3) Giving what is God's to God implies much more than paying a temple tax. God as Creator has sovereign right over all creation and everything in it. We are to pattern our lives in such a way that we show we are God's stewards of all he has created, and we are to use what is his in the way he has designed it to be used. This implies that even what belongs to Caesar is only

---

12. Cf. 12:15; 18:8; 26:10 for Jesus' form of special knowledge.
13. Rousseau and Arav, "Coins and Money," *Jesus and His World*, 55–61. For a picture of a coin that depicts Caesar Augustus, see Wilkins, "Matthew," 135.

his in a secondary way. Allegiance to God takes precedence over allegiance to Caesar, especially when Caesar attempts to usurp allegiance to God's will (cf. Acts 4:19; 5:29).

Jesus may be implying further that while the "image" of Caesar was stamped on coins, humans bear the image of God from creation (Gen. 1:26–27). Thus, God has claim on all that any person has or is.[14] Jesus is not saying that life is to be divided into two compartments, with obligations to Caesar and to God separated from one another. Both Caesar and the kingdom of God have rights in their respective areas as ordained by God, but "the obligation to God covers all of life; we must serve Caesar in a way that is honoring to God."[15]

Jesus' profound logic undoes the attempt of his enemies to entrap him with their contrived conundrum. They are amazed at how easily he has reversed the debate (22:22). Behind them stands the wisdom of Pharisaic scribal wizardry and the experience of the Herodian political dynasty, which is no match for Jesus' profound understanding of how God wants his people to operate in this world. They go away, probably back to those who sent them. They are surely chagrined at their failure to trap Jesus, because the Pharisees have sent them after carefully preparing the ambush. This could have been an opportunity for them to see the superiority of Jesus' teaching over the Pharisees' sagacity and the Herodian political schemes, but Jesus' wisdom does not break through their hard hearts to convict them of their sinful attempts at entrapment. This certainly is not the end of their attempts to snare him.

**Marriage at the resurrection: Sadducees (22:23–33).** Once the disciples of the Pharisees and the Herodians have their whack at Jesus, the Sadducees step up. This debate takes place in the temple, the stronghold of Sadducean power (see comments on 3:7). It revolves around the doctrine of resurrection. The Sadducees did not believe in the resurrection since they drew only on the Pentateuch for doctrine. Resurrection is a doctrine developed more clearly in the latter books of the Old Testament (cf. Isa. 26:19; Dan. 12:2) and in Second Temple Jewish literature and rabbinic writings.[16] Jesus will show here what he will demonstrate physically in his own experience, that resurrection has more far-reaching implications than anyone realizes.[17]

---

14. Dale Bruner states: "As Caesar's coin bears Caesar's image and belongs to Caesar, so God's humanity bears God's image and belongs to God" (*Matthew*, 2:784).

15. Morris, *Matthew*, 558. For extended discussion of the implications for church-state relationships, see Bruner, *Matthew*, 2:784–87.

16. E.g., 2 Macc. 7; *1 En.* 102; *2 Bar.* 49–51; *m. Sanh.* 10:1; *b. Roš Haš.* 16b–17a.

17. See Wilkins, "Matthew," 187, for comments on the resurrection of the dead in Judaism and in Jesus.

*The Sadducees' question of resurrection (22:23–28).* The debate begins with the Sadducees citing the Old Testament law of "levirate" marriage: "Moses told us that if a man dies without having children, his brother must marry the widow and have children for him." In this law the *levir* (the surviving brother of a childless, deceased man) was required to marry his sister-in-law. This law was designed to provide care for the widow as well as to preserve the deceased brother's genealogical line if they should bear children (Deut. 25:5–10).

Like the Pharisees, the Sadducees try to create a theological trap to demonstrate that Jesus holds to doctrines that are biblically unsubstantiated. They essentially ask what will happen if the levirate marriage is followed by each of the succeeding seven brothers and then the woman dies. They assume their question will stump Jesus theologically: "Now then, at the resurrection, whose wife will she be of the seven, since all of them were married to her?"

The case they bring could possibly have happened, but they have more malicious intentions. They hope to disclose that Jesus is not qualified as a theological leader and has no right or authority to challenge their authority. Since they do not believe in the resurrection, their question reveals a hypocritical attempt to confound Jesus and others who do believe in the resurrection. They assume that resurrection life is like the present life, which will lead to the charge that the woman was guilty of incest. This attempt at developing a logical conundrum leads to the obvious conclusion that the idea of resurrection is a make-believe absurdity.

*Know the Scriptures and know God (22:29–30).* Once again Jesus turns the logic back upon his questioners. This time he reveals that the problem is not simply their failure to develop a foolproof, logical riddle; rather, it is their faulty theological and biblical understanding of the concept of the resurrection. He starts with their underlying foundational failure and accuses the Sadducees, "You are in error because you do not know the Scriptures or the power of God." They should recognize that the rest of the Old Testament is also Scripture, where the doctrine of resurrection is clear. He also chides them for denying the reality of the resurrection, for what lies behind any thought of resurrection is the power of God to do so.

Jesus then turns to the specific issue that they have raised about the woman who married the seven brothers: "At the resurrection people will neither marry nor be given in marriage; they will be like the angels in heaven" (22:30). Jesus draws a parallel to angels in order to note that resurrected humans will not continue the practice of marriage. This line of argumentation holds a double edge, since Sadducees also denied the existence of angels (cf. Acts 23:8). Their doctrinal ignorance is based on their lack of biblical knowledge, which in turn dramatically impacts their deficient understanding of the way life is to be lived both here and in the hereafter.

Jesus does not suggest that humans become angels; rather, in the same way that angelic beings do not marry or procreate, the resurrected state ends the practice of marriage and issues in entirely new relationships between resurrected humans. With this declaration and his earlier promotion of celibacy for those who are called to such a life, Jesus rejects the "divinizing of marriage."[18] At the same time, while the state of relationships will be altered at the resurrection, this does not imply that prior earthly relationships are eliminated completely, nor does it imply that resurrected relationships are without special attachment. The wife (or husband, for that matter) of multiple spouses in this life will have an equally altered capacity and understanding of love, which will enable her (or him) to love all without measure or jealousy or possessiveness.[19]

*I am the God of Abraham (22:31–33).* Jesus develops a further clinching argument from the Sadducees' authoritative base, the Pentateuch. "But about the resurrection of the dead—have you not read what God said to you, 'I am the God of Abraham, the God of Isaac, and the God of Jacob'? He is not the God of the dead but of the living." Drawing on the present tense in Exodus 3:6 of the statement, "I *am* the God of Abraham, the God of Isaac, and the God of Jacob," Jesus states that the logical implication is that even though the patriarchs have died physically, they are still alive at the writing of the book of Exodus. They still exist as seen by the fact that God continues in a relationship with them as their God, which cannot be sustained with those who no longer exist. If they are still alive even though physically dead, and if the rest of Scripture points to the reality of resurrection, the Sadducees should believe God's power to raise the patriarchs to enjoy his continued purposes for humanity in the eternal covenant of God.

The crowds who hear Jesus' answer to the Saducean challenge are "astonished" (*ekplesso*) at his teaching (22:33). This is the same word that expresses the reaction of the crowds to his teaching in the SM (cf. 7:28) and the reaction of his townspeople at Nazareth to his preaching (13:54). While amazement can imply a continued attachment to Jesus' teaching (e.g., 19:25), in neither of the prior cases does this reaction imply they have become Jesus' disciples. In fact, in spite of his townspeople's amazement, Jesus could do no miracles in Nazareth because of their lack of faith (13:58). Here too the crowds express amazement at Jesus' profundity in responding to the Sadducees, but this is not the same as faith. The crowds will soon be swayed by the religious leaders to ask for Jesus' death (27:20–25). Astonishment is not faith; faith comes from conviction, not emotion.

---

18. Bruner, *Matthew*, 2:790.
19. Cf. Blomberg, *Matthew*, 333; Carson, "Matthew," 461–62.

**The greatest commandment: A legal expert of the Pharisees (22:34–40).**
The competition among the religious leaders to trounce Jesus in debate is
heating up. When the Pharisees hear how Jesus has silenced the Sadducees,
they get together. Now it's their turn to try to trip Jesus theologically. This
encounter is initiated by an "expert in the law" (*nomikos*) from the Pharisees
(22:35), who approaches Jesus to test him (*peirazo;* cf. 22:18).[20] The lawyer
initiates the interchange with a piercing question: "Teacher, which is the
greatest commandment in the Law?" "The Law" in this interchange is a shorthand expression for the entire Old Testament (cf. 5:17). A regular debate
went on among rabbis to determine the weighty and light commandments
(see 23:23). This legal expert is probably well aware of this discussion.[21]

Jesus' reply is not unexpected. He quotes Deuteronomy 6:5: "Love the
Lord your God with all your heart and with all your soul and with all your
mind." The twice-daily repeated Shema was well known as an overarching
obligation of each individual Jew, and it included the duty of obedience to
the other commandments given by God (see the similar logic in 5:16–20).
Love for God is not understood as simply an emotional attachment. Rather,
it means giving oneself to him with one's entire person. Heart, soul, and
mind are not rigidly separated compartments of the human existence but
reflect that the entire person is given to God.

Jesus continues by quoting from Leviticus 19:18, "And the second is like
it: 'Love your neighbor as yourself.'" The venerable Rabbi Akiba had declared
Leviticus 19:18 to be a "great principle in the Torah."[22] This opinion was
likely expressed in Jesus' day as well. Like the first commandment, Jesus is
not simply advocating an emotional attachment or an abstract love. Rather,
love here indicates a concrete responsibility, the act of being useful and
beneficial to one's neighbors, both Jew and Gentile (cf. Lev. 19:18, 34).[23] To
love is to give to someone what that person needs. In the same way that individuals are called to care for themselves responsibly and attune their lives
to carry out God's will in their lives, they are to give themselves to others
to care for them responsibly and help them attune their lives to carry out
God's will.

In this light, these two commandments are similar to the Golden Rule,
which Jesus said is a summary of the Law and the Prophets (7:12). This

---

20. Mark tells us that at the end of the interchange Jesus commends him (Mark 12:34),
which may indicate that he approaches Jesus with more sincerity than the previous questioners.

21. Hagner, *Matthew*, 2:646.

22. *Genesis Rabbah* 24.7.

23. See Abraham Malamat, "Love Your Neighbor As Yourself," *BAR* 16/4 (July–August
1990): 50–51.

helps explain what Jesus means by the expression, "All the Law and the Prophets hang on these two commandments" (22:40). The kingdom life that Jesus inaugurates fulfills the deepest inclination of humans created in God's image. Kingdom life enables his disciples to live the way God intends us to live, which means living responsibly in relationship to God and others. As such, the entire Old Testament hangs on love for God and others and truly brings to fulfillment the Law and the Prophets (cf. 5:17–20).

It may be helpful here to draw on a definition of "love" that was developed earlier in the Sermon on the Mount (see comments on 5:43–48): Love is an unconditional commitment to an imperfect person in which one gives oneself to another to bring the relationship to God's intended purposes. The person who loves God with all of her being—heart, soul, and mind—will understand that God's will for her life is revealed in the Old Testament, and she will gladly, eagerly, obey it because she knows that in doing so, she is living life the way God has designed it to be lived. In turn, her obedience to God's will transforms her entire being—heart, soul, and mind—into the image of God so that she is more like what God has intended for her to be like. Furthermore, loving her neighbor as herself means that she gives herself to other humans to help them live as God designed life to be lived, so that she helps them in their own transformation.

These are the greatest commandments because they go to the essence of the way God has created humans to live: giving oneself to God and to others to fulfill his purposes for us as the crown of his creation in displaying in our lives the glory of God's kingdom on earth. Jesus' inauguration of the kingdom enables this to be a concrete reality for his disciples.

**The son of David: Pharisees (22:41–46).** In Matthew's narrative of the Holy Week controversies, the first three encounters with the religious leaders were initiated as they formulated questions designed to trap Jesus. Still in the temple courts on Tuesday with the various groups in attendance—the religious leaders (Pharisees, Sadducees, Herodians), the multitudes, and his disciples—Jesus takes the initiative to press the debate in a critical direction. He goes on the offensive as he poses a question to the Pharisees. Jesus goes to the heart of the issue, challenging their ability to rightly interpret one of the most important messianic texts in the Old Testament. If they cannot rightly interpret this text, they cannot possibly rightly understand his identity. So he prods them: "What do you think about the Christ? Whose son is he?"

This must have seemed like a simple question to the Pharisees, who answer with, "The son of David." This is the automatic reply, based on common knowledge that the prophesied Messiah (*ho Christos*, "the anointed One") was from the line of David.[24] This is confirmed by common practice, with the recurring declarations of Jesus' messianic identity as "Son of David."[25]

But Jesus presses them further to plumb the depths of their understanding of the true identity of the Messiah from the Old Testament prophecies: "How is it then that David, speaking by the Spirit, calls him 'Lord'?" The point that Jesus is making is taken from Psalm 110:1, which he quotes—the most quoted Old Testament passage in the New Testament.

The Pharisees recognized this psalm as a messianic prophecy by David under the inspiration of the Holy Spirit.[26] In this passage David refers to the coming messianic ruler—his descendant, his "son"—as *kyrios*, "lord." Familial respect would not expect an older person, such as David, to refer to his offspring as "lord"; rather, the offspring, "son," should refer to David, his "father," as "lord." The LXX, which is almost verbatim to what Matthew records here, has *kyrios* in both instances of the word "Lord." The Hebrew, however, has Yahweh (*yhwh*) for the first and Adon (*ʾadoni;* lit., "my Lord") for the second occurrence of "Lord."

In other words, Jesus uses their own Scriptures to point out the obvious implication of these combined points, which the Pharisees cannot avoid. "If then David calls him 'Lord,' how can he be his son?" David says that the coming Messiah is One who is not just his special human descendant but is his "Lord." Psalm 110:1 further indicates that his descendant bears a unique relationship to Yahweh—he is seated at the highest position of privilege and authority at Yahweh's right hand, and Yahweh will subject all his enemies to him. This bears striking similarity to Daniel's prophecy, where the Son of Man was led into the presence of the Ancient of Days and "was given authority, honor, and royal power over all the nations of the world, so that people of every race and nation and language would obey him. His rule is eternal—it will never end. His kingdom will never be destroyed" (Dan. 7:14).

The Messiah is more than what the Pharisees have understood the "son of David" to be. He is more than a human descendant of David. Since the Pharisees do not adequately understand the Old Testament prophecies regarding the Messiah, they cannot possibly understand Jesus' identity. They do not understand the depth of the personal identity of the Messiah in relationship to Yahweh, so they cannot understand the relationship of Jesus to Yahweh. The Messiah is "Adon," the "Son of Man," who is given authority

24. See comments on 1:1; cf. 2 Sam. 7:12−14; Ps. 89:4; Isa. 11:1, 10; Jer. 23:5: cf. *Pss. Sol.* 17:21.

25. See comments on 1:20; 9:27; 12:23; 15:22; 20:30−31; 21:9, 15.

26. By extension, Jesus implies the Davidic authorship of the psalm as inspired Scripture. For a recent overview, see Barry C. Davis, "Is Psalm 110 a Messianic Psalm?" *BibSac* 157 (April–June 2000): 160−73.

by the Ancient of Days (Dan. 7:13–14). Jesus prods the Pharisees to acknowledge what they should have understood all along. The Jews did not generally believe that the Messiah would be divine, but here Jesus confounds them by showing that as David called Messiah "son" and "Lord," Messiah is indeed his human descendant, but he sustains a divine relationship to Yahweh.[27]

Throughout Jesus' ministry, his relationship to God has been increasingly revealed and clarified. He is the unique Son of God (3:17; 4:3, 6; 10:32–33, 40; 11:27), a most amazing truth that his disciples have increasingly come to recognize (14:33). Their understanding came to a climax when Peter confessed that Jesus is the Christ, who is uniquely "the Son of the living God" (16:16).

Matthew narrates the combined reaction to Jesus' final spar with the religious leaders in the temple: "No one could say a word in reply, and from that day on no one dared to ask him any more questions" (22:46). Their silence and reticence to question Jesus further is not only the conclusion to the preceding pericope but also the conclusion to the series of controversies that stretch back to 21:23. Jesus has given increasing clarification of his identity everywhere in these controversies. They have not been able to entrap him. Instead, he has revealed clearly his identity and his authority. He will now soon rebuke them severely in the series of "woes" (ch. 23) for not accepting him for who he has revealed himself to be, their long-anticipated Messiah, David's "Lord," who sustains a matchless relationship to Yahweh as his unique Son.

CHAPTER 22 BEGINS with the third of three parables that confront the religious leadership because they did not repent and seek to enter the kingdom of God (21:28–32). As a result, God will take away the kingdom from Israel and give it to another nation that will produce fruit (21:33–46). In the parable of the wedding banquet, Jesus declares that God judges all responses in Israel to the invitation to the kingdom of heaven, including the nation generally, the religious leaders especially, and individuals personally (22:1–14). Matthew's narrative takes a significant turn at the conclusion of the parables. One by one he enters into theological debate with the various leadership groups in Jerusalem, each of which has tried to undercut Jesus' messianic claims. Matthew specifies in a unique way that although they try to debate Jesus, they are all deficient in understanding the Old Testament's witness to his messianic claims.

---

27. See also Craig A. Evans, *Mark* 8:27–16:20 (WBC 34B; Nashville: Nelson, 2001), 272–75.

These controversies between Jesus and the religious leaders in the temple form the last public debates of Jesus' earthly ministry. They occur throughout much of Tuesday of Holy Week. In less than three days Jesus will again stand before the religious leaders, but then he will be on trial for his life in the secret confines of the high priest's stronghold (26:57—68). Thus, as Jesus confronts these leaders publicly this last time, everything about his earthly ministry is on trial.

But most important, Matthew reveals insights to show that it is really not Jesus who is on trial but the religious leaders themselves. In these brief scenes, Jesus takes to task each of the primary leadership groups in Jerusalem—Pharisees, Sadducees, Herodians, and even the Zealots tangentially.[28] When we compare the various Gospel narratives of these scenes, Matthew specifies each group that Jesus addresses. His precise understanding of these groups reflects his intimate familiarity with the historical details of the temple controversies, the Jerusalem sectarian leadership turf wars, and the specific areas of theological culpability for which all are guilty.

Each group has its own unique theological, political, sociological, and religious agenda. Each has its strengths and weakness from which we can learn, both how to profit from their commitments and how to avoid their errors. Jesus brings out into the open the inherent theological foibles of each group, which, unless they are rectified, result in exclusion from the kingdom of heaven and ultimately in final judgment. But he goes beyond any one group's expectations in Israel to show us how we can learn from their weaknesses and strengths to hear most clearly the message of the kingdom of heaven.

**Disciples of the Pharisees.** Only Matthew records the parable of the wedding banquet, which is a direct pronouncement of judgment on the religious leaders for rejecting Jesus' invitation to the kingdom of heaven. Likewise, only Matthew records the Pharisaic conspiracy to trap Jesus theologically as their response to Jesus' pronouncement in the parable (22:15). It is also only Matthew who specifies that it is "the disciples of the Pharisees" who are sent by their leaders to try to entrap Jesus (22:16).

This adds a unique dimension to the intrigue. These disciples of the Pharisees apparently are the Pharisees' flunkies. Since they are not legal experts or full-fledged Pharisaic leaders, they do not appear to be as much of a legal threat to Jesus; they are a seemingly innocuous group. They come with fawning flattery, expressing accurate descriptions of Jesus, but their intentions

---

28. Only the Essenes do not appear, which is consistent with their largely historical, geographical absence from Jerusalem political life and their literary absence from the New Testament.

are evil. That is the height of religious hypocrisy (22:18)—to try to disarm Jesus so that they can trap him. The painful point is that external religious performance, no matter how sincere and accurate is appears, is evil if it is driven by inner evil intentions.

**Herodians.** Matthew also records the presence of the group called the Herodians along with the disciples of the Pharisees (22:16; cf. Mark 12:13). In many ways they are on opposite side of the theological battle within Judaism. The Herodians represent the Herodian dynasty and its cutthroat representation of Rome in Israel. The Pharisees represent the vestiges of those within Israel who contend for legalistic purity and separation from ethnic defilement. That the two groups come together to confront Jesus highlights not only that politics makes strange bedfellows, but also that Jesus is a threat to every stratum of the Jewish establishment.

The question of whether to pay taxes to Caesar reveals the underlying issue of how much deference should be paid to secular political forces. The Pharisees and Herodians represent opposing methodologies. Although the Pharisees do not accept the Roman occupation, they express their opposition by separating themselves through ritual purity and praying for the arrival of a messianic deliverer.[29] The Herodians, in representing the Herodian dynasty, have capitulated to the Romans and are promoters of Greco-Roman culture. Like the Sadducees, they reject any messianic hope and see political action as the way of promoting their own interests.[30]

But Jesus will not adopt either extreme. The kingdom of heaven operates within this earthly sphere, neither relying on political or military might of any human government to advance its influence, nor withdrawing and pining for God's arrival. Jesus' kingdom disciples are not a threat to worldly governing systems, nor do they give them first allegiance. Jesus' disciples give due obligation to worldly governing systems (cf. Rom. 13:1–7; 1 Peter 2:13–17), but they seek and serve first the kingdom of heaven (Matt. 6:24, 33).

**Sadducees.** All three Synoptic Gospels narrate the instigation of the Sadducees in the third debate related to the resurrection (22:23; Mark 12:18; Luke 20:27). The Sadducees were an influential group within Jewish political circles in Jerusalem. They were the party of high priests, aristocratic families, and merchants. Within the economic system of Israel they represented the wealthier elements. Like the Herodians, they came under the influence of Greco-Roman culture and cultivated good relations with the Roman rulers. Theologically, they were basically conservative, since they accepted only

---

29. For a brief overview of the Pharisees, see Wilkins, "Matthew," 25. For an extended treatment, see Meier, *A Marginal Jew*, 3:289–340.

30. Meier, *A Marginal Jew*, 3:560–65.

the written Pentateuch (the first five books of the Old Testament) and held to a literal interpretation of the Bible. This led them to oppose the oral law of the Pharisees, but also to deny the immortality of the soul, bodily resurrection after death, the arrival of a future messianic deliverer, and the existence of angelic spirits.[31]

As the Sadducees attempt to entrap Jesus with a question about the resurrection, he reveals that their conservative posture is actually a self-serving ploy. Their view of the extent of Scripture serves their own interests. If, as their doctrine teaches, there is no real future, they need to grab all of the power and pleasure they can right now to make heaven on earth. If there is no real participation of God in history, then they may as well take life into their own hands to secure their own future. Their wealth and political power produce haughtiness, and their willingness to cooperate with the Roman rulers causes them to compromise their theological convictions. Jesus rails against them that they know neither the Scriptures nor the power of God (22:29).

Jesus contends that God is the God of both living and dead and that each person must live each moment under his lordship. All of the power and prestige and pleasures of this age cannot compensate for standing one day before him and receiving one's eternal destiny.[32]

**Crowds.** Only Matthew mentions that the crowds respond with astonishment at the way Jesus' dismantles the Sadducees' theological riddle (22:33). A superficial reading might lead one to think that this is an expression of faith and commitment to Jesus. But as Matthew has emphasized throughout his Gospel, astonishment or amazement is not the same as faith. Faith leads to discipleship, while astonishment leads to emotional attachment, which is fickle. Jesus knows that simple popularity can be accomplished by being a people-pleaser.

The crowds that shouted "Hosanna!" at Jesus' entry into Jerusalem and who are astonished at his teaching will soon be persuaded by the religious leaders to ask for the release of Barabbas and the execution of Jesus. They rely on human power to bring in the kingdom, not on the power of the kingdom of God. Matthew gives us keen insight throughout the Holy Week narrative that the crowds want things their way, not God's. Jesus is no people-pleaser, as

---

31. For a brief overview of the Sadducees, see Wilkins, "Matthew," 25. For an extended treatment, see Meier, *A Marginal Jew*, 389–444.

32. Several related points surface from this latter interaction. (1) Note that Jesus here contends for verbal inspiration of the Scriptures, since his argumentation is based on the tense of a verb from the Old Testament ("I *am*"). (2) Since the material aspect of the persons to whom Jesus points has died, the immaterial aspect sufficiently implies the real existence of these people. (3) Jesus does not explain the mode of existence of those who have experienced physical death, but only that they still have a form of personal existence.

even his enemies know (22:16), so regardless of how much acclaim he receives from the crowds, he must conduct his life on this earth to do the will of God.

**Pharisaic expert in the Law.** Matthew gives more specific insight into the intrigue behind the third confrontation. The Pharisees are keeping track of the debate, and when the Sadducees fail, they step forward by sending one of their legal experts to test Jesus. Matthew is the only evangelist to associate this expert in the law with the Pharisees (22:34–35).

A commendable quality of the Pharisees is their commitment to the Word of God and their desire to make it practical for daily life. The legal expert's response recorded in Mark allows us to see that he is a person who, in spite of the evil motivations of some of the Pharisees, is sincerely seeking the truth. Jesus tells him that his wise response reveals that he is not far from the kingdom of God (Mark 12:34).

Jesus is surrounded on every side by enemies, but even among those who are his harshest critics can be found those seeking from a sincere heart. It takes emotional restraint for Jesus to see the good intentions of the lawyer. So Matthew points his readers to the right kind of questions that should be put to Jesus. One of those is to find overarching truths that enable us to understand the essential, practical spirit of the Bible. By seeking the greatest commandments in the Law, the lawyer is finding principles that will enable him to obey the essence of the spirit of the Law. It is important to learn to principalize the Bible rather than be legalists who simply memorize rules and obey them like robots. We must understand God's purpose for giving the Scripture and what stands behind why we do what we do.

**The Pharisees.** In the fourth debate, Jesus turns to confront at the Pharisees directly with his own question (22:41–42). Their pride in their ability to rightly interpret the Bible prevents them from seeing the real meaning of the text. Jesus prods them to go beyond the pat answers of their tradition and understand that David's descendant is more than his human progeny; he is the "Adon," the "Son of Man" in Daniel's prophecy (22:43–45).

Matthew thus highlights the danger of traditionalism, which only accepts that which one's interpretive community understands and practices. The Pharisees take the stock answer from the tradition of the elders, but they do not keep pressing to see beyond the simple answer to God's intent revealed in the messianic prophecy. Tradition can be a helpful way of building on the skill, insight, and learning of prior generations, but it can also hinder hearing the voice of God, either in the biblical text or in the arrival of Jesus as God's messenger.

Had the Pharisees been open to Jesus' revelation, they would have seen even more of what this messianic psalm had to teach about Jesus' identity and mission. Later New Testament writers cite Psalm 110 more than any other

Old Testament prophecy to clarify that Jesus is Messiah (Acts 2:34–36), that he is greater than the angels (Heb. 1:13), that after his crucifixion, resurrection, and ascension he is now sitting at the right hand of God the Father in heaven (Acts 2:33–35; Heb. 6:20), and that God has placed Jesus' enemies under his feet (1 Cor. 15:25–28; Eph. 1:22; Heb. 10:13).[33]

But we should note one other important thing about the Pharisees. Contemporary expressions such as "You Pharisee!" and "She is so pharisaical" are based on the first-century setting. Emphasizing either strict legalism or hypocritical self-righteousness, such expressions today are used almost entirely to disparage a person. But in the first century, to call a person a Pharisee was to compliment him on his sincere accomplishment in applying the Bible to his life. To say that a person was pharisaical was to commend such a person for his diligence in pursuing righteousness, even though he wasn't an official member of that party.

Jesus himself, who reserved the harshest criticism for the Pharisees, also saw in the intense questioning of a legal expert the genuine pursuit of the kingdom of God (Mark 12:34). The Pharisee Nicodemus became a disciple of Jesus (cf. John 19:39), as did Joseph of Arimathea, a member of the Sanhedrin and most likely a leading Pharisee, whom Luke describes as a good and righteous man "waiting for the kingdom of God" (cf. Luke 23:50–51). They were both used by God at one of the most strategic points in history, having positions of influence that enabled them to claim Jesus' body for burial (Matt. 27:57–60; John 19:38–42).

I do not in any way want to downgrade the evil that Jesus saw in the Pharisees or lessen their responsibility for participating in the treachery that eventually led to his crucifixion, but we should bring in a bit more objectivity when we look at the Pharisees of the first century. That is likewise true of the Sadducees, whose members included the high priest and chief priests who brought those false charges against Jesus to the Romans that resulted in his crucifixion. The priest element of the Sadducees became the early church's primary antagonists (e.g., Acts 4:1–3; 6:17–18), but also many of the Sadducean priestly line became believers and influential members of the early church (Acts 6:7). Their background most likely was a factor in coming to believe in Jesus.

Such objectivity will help us to recognize that each of these first-century groups has strengths and weakness from which we can learn much, especially because they have characteristics that can be found in Christian circles today. As we look at the basic interactions of Jesus with these groups in the temple in Jerusalem, lessons abound for us.

---

33. Davis, "Is Psalm 110 a Messianic Psalm?" 172.

THE INVITATION TO **insiders to come inside.** The striking, almost frightening, point of the parable of the wedding celebration (22:1–14) is that the ones who are condemned the most severely are insiders. Jesus addresses the parables to the religious leaders, primarily Sadducees and Pharisees, and they do not miss his point (21:45; 22:15). Jesus is a threat to the Sadducean establishment in the temple and to the Pharisaic influence in the synagogues. They receive his invitation to the kingdom of God along with the rest of the people of Israel, but their commitments to their institutions blind them from seeing the truth in Jesus' summons. So they have him killed, but their punishment will be swift and severe (22:7). One who does respond to the invitation but doesn't wear the appropriate garment is condemned to eternal punishment. He likely represents insiders like Judas Iscariot, who betrays Jesus from the inside.

This parable does not speak of the wedding feast of the Lamb in heaven (Rev. 19:5–8) but depicts first-century responses in Israel to the invitation to the kingdom of heaven. Beyond that it illustrates responses of individuals in this life to the gospel. Many are called, but few are chosen. Jesus points out the seriousness of one's response to the opportunity of being called into the family of God. This has important implications for us.

The parable should cause us to take stock of our true membership within the kingdom. The apostle Peter writes, "Therefore, my brothers, be all the more eager to make your calling and election sure. For if you do these things, you will never fall, and you will receive a rich welcome into the eternal kingdom of our Lord and Savior Jesus Christ" (2 Peter 1:10). The church does contain people who are not true members of the kingdom. There are children of solid church members who are "insiders" but who have not truly responded to the invitation of the gospel. I do not believe that continual harping will necessarily make the difference, and as we suggested above, the issues of election that Jesus and Peter emphasize are a matter of God's sovereign choice. But if we follow Peter's advice, we should try to "make sure" our calling and election.

To do so both personally and with those to whom we minister, including our own churches and families, involves learning from the religious leaders of Jesus' day—those insiders who never came into the kingdom. Jesus said that the kingdom was being taken away from those not bearing fruit and would be given to those who do bear kingdom fruit. This points ahead to the work of the Holy Spirit in establishing the new covenant. The fruit produced is God's presence reigning in his regenerated people, who demonstrate his power through lives distinguished by the fruit of righteousness

(Matt. 5:20) and good works (Col. 1:5–10), the fruit of Spirit-produced transformation of character (Gal. 5:21–24), and the fruit of new generations of disciples (Matt. 28:18–20; cf. John 15:16) who bear witness to the reality of the kingdom on earth.

The encouragement from Peter is that as insiders, we can help our people, and ourselves, learn how to rightly examine ourselves. When we give unfettered allegiance to Jesus alone as our only claim to life here and eternal, then we can claim the confidence that the apostle John promised comes from obedience to his writing: "I write these things to you who believe in the name of the Son of God so that you may know that you have eternal life" (1 John 5:13). Not hope or wish or want, but that we may *know* we have eternal life. Those who are truly abiding in Jesus and his Word will see the fruit of a developing internal character that not only does the right thing but has the heart to do the right thing that leads to action.

While we go about this, let's be careful not to fall into the Pharisaic legalism that counts fruit in others. The reality of the mixed nature of those who are insiders allows us to be comforted as realists about life until Jesus' return. It *will* be a mixed bag of the good wheat and bad weeds until Jesus comes (see 13:24–30). As we learn to examine ourselves and to help others learn to examine themselves, we can back off and leave the judging to God.

**Advice for making a difference in this world.** Jesus' response to the religious leaders about paying taxes to Caesar stands as one of the most important principles for Christians living in this world until the Lord returns: "Give to Caesar what is Caesar's, and to God what is God's" (22:21). Jesus is not saying that life is to be divided into two compartments, with obligations to Caesar and to God separated from each other. Both Caesar and the kingdom of God have rights in their respective areas as ordained by God, but the way of fulfilling our obligations to earthly authorities is by first fulfilling our obligations to God.

The danger for religious leaders is a tendency to go to extremes. On the one side they either withdraw completely from Caesar, like the Essenes at the Qumran community, or withdraw socially, like the Pharisees. On the other side they may capitulate by joining league with Caesar, like the Sadducees and Herodians, or they may take matters into the own hands and fight against Caesar, like the Zealots. As we look around at the various groups within the larger world of Christendom today, we find the same kinds of extremes. Some separatist Christians withdraw to their own world, like the Amish, or stay socially separated, like some fundamentalist groups. Others go to the other extreme and capitulate, like various liberal denominations that use politics as their primary agenda, while others use violence and bomb abortion clinics to advance their cause. Jesus' words should help us stay balanced.

In the days after the terrorists brought unthinkable horror to the everyday lives of people on September 11, 2001, I clearly remember watching television as the U.S. Congress was assembled in the Senate chambers. President George W. Bush gave a passionate speech. He honored several of the firefighters and police officers who were at the devastation. He honored the wife of one of the men who had rushed the hijackers and given up their lives. I was struck by the need for healing for all those who experienced firsthand the horror of those days.

As President Bush gave his speech, I could see his resolve spread to all those assembled and to all of us watching around the nation, indeed around the world. But as I watched, I saw all of those events through very different eyes than I had over thirty years ago when I was also motivated to serve my country through enlisting to fight an enemy. At that time I was a non-Christian who was called to do my duty for my country. But this time I saw a need that only you and I can fill. We have the only real hope, the only real peace.

Some Christians do enlist in the military service and serve in combat. That is between them and the Lord to understand that calling. Some become firefighters or police officers. Some become doctors or economists or engineers or building contractors, all of whom are needed to rebuild after the ravages of terrorism and war and make it safe for our children. I hope that many will respond, for an appropriate respect and support of government is a way of honoring God.

But we as Christians must never forget this: Our first allegiance is to the kingdom of God. As a Christian I can be engaged in service by bringing justice to those who perpetrate evil. However, I have already fought a war, and I know evil of a horrendous nature. I also know the evil that lurked in my own heart as I killed, not for justice but for my own ego, my own satisfaction, without any regard for the person I gunned down.

And I know now that as I am continuing to be transformed into the image of Christ, I have a different allegiance. I must fight to overcome evil with the power of the gospel, bringing real peace through the blood of the cross of Jesus Christ. I must love my enemies and overcome their evil through the powerful working of the Holy Spirit to bring them to repentance before a loving, and yet holy and righteous God. All that we give to the government, whether it be our taxes, our participation in the military or police, or our involvement in politics, is not going to hasten the coming of the kingdom of God. And an unreserved allegiance to the state infringes on the second half of Jesus' statement; since all that is belongs to God, ultimate allegiance is to him.

In the conclusion to his insightful study of this passage, Calvin comments, "In short, the overthrow of civil order is rebellion against God, and obedience to leaders and magistrates is always linked to the worship and fear of God, but if in return the leaders usurp the rights of God they are to be denied obedience as far as possible short of offence to God."[34] Our allegiance to God should not promote aloofness from giving to Caesar or rebellion against Caesar. Nor should our allegiance to Caesar ever infringe on our allegiance to God. And when the kingdom of Caesar infringes on the kingdom of God, the penetrating proviso of Peter and the other apostles comes into play: "We must obey God rather than men!" (Acts 5:29).[35]

Jesus' statement is one that should continue to cause us daily to monitor our allegiances. Dale Bruner says wisely of Jesus' saying in Matthew 22:21:

> Jesus' great sentence does not forever settle the question of Christians' relation to the state, because every day we must ask ourselves afresh if we are giving too little or too much of our energies to the political. Jesus' Caesar sentence is a slide rule asking us perpetually to readjust our use of time and priorities.[36]

**Letting God be God.** The Sadducees' question about resurrection was an attempt to trap Jesus with what they saw to be an irresolvable dilemma within the belief system of Jesus, but it also revealed their own worldview. They rightly denied the authority of the Pharisees' oral law, but they had boxed in God's voice to the books of the Bible that they believed were inspired, which then boxed God into what they believed he could actually do in this world—and that wasn't much. No immortality, no resurrection, no intervention in history, no spirit world.

I was quite a fan of the Beatles in my youth. But as I consider the worldview of the Sadducees, they sound strangely like John Lennon's song "Imagine." In this song, Lennon calls on his listeners to imagine that there is no heaven, no hell, no countries, and nothing to kill or die for. He dreamed of a world with no religion, calling us to imagine all people living in peace. His song called for a blissfully naive fantasy world. But the tragic ending of John Lennon's life brought to an end for many what they then considered merely a pipe dream.

The Sadducees likewise came to a tragic end in A.D. 70 with the destruction of the temple and the desolation of Jerusalem. They capitulated to the Roman rule, attempting to create political alliances that would bring them power, wealth, security, and peace. They looked for truth and power in all of the wrong places. They ended up denying their own Jewish faith, because

---

34. Calvin, *Matthew, Mark, and Luke,* 3:27.
35. Passages that should be studied to help us maintain the right kind of balance are Matt. 5:38–42; Rom. 13:1–7; 1 Tim. 2:1–7; Titus 3:1–2.
36. Bruner, *Matthew,* 2:785. His treatment of the practical issues is very helpful.

they stifled God's voice in the rest of Scripture and denied his power in their own lives and in the lives of the people for whom they were responsible.

The important example for us is set by Jesus' censure of the Sadducees: "You are in error because you do not know the Scriptures or the power of God" (22:29). We must commit ourselves to knowing the full teaching of Scripture, not just those selections or books that we find comfortable or compatible with our own worldview. The Bible will make us uncomfortable with our sin. It will also point out that it is incompatible with our secularist cultural baggage and philosophies. As much of a fan of John Lennon that I was, I had to evaluate his secularist philosophies in the light of the Bible—and they were incompatible.

Furthermore, we must commit ourselves to know the power of God, which can change lives, make a difference in this world, break the chains of addictions, and enable marriages to last and flourish. The power of God is for every Christian, every day, every hour. One of my favorite prayers in the Bible is Paul's prayer for the Ephesian church in Ephesians 1:18–20:

> I pray also that the eyes of your heart may be enlightened in order that you may know the hope to which he has called you, the riches of his glorious inheritance in the saints, and his incomparably great power for us who believe. That power is like the working of his mighty strength, which he exerted in Christ when he raised him from the dead and seated him at his right hand in the heavenly realms.

That's a lot of power! No power known to humans is like that. We can run cars, propel rockets to the moon, harness energy to light up entire cities, but we cannot raise anyone from the dead. And that's the power that Paul prays will be ours to energize our lives on a daily basis. The source of that power is simply to be filled with the Holy Spirit (Eph. 5:18). That's when our individual lives and our churches reject the error of the Sadducees and demonstrate the kind of discipleship to Jesus that relies on the full teaching of Scripture and the full power of God.

**Love as God's overarching will for disciples.** Working with college and seminary students, I regularly hear them discuss God's will for their lives—what he wants them to study, what job or ministry they should pursue, where they should live, whom they should marry! All critical issues. Finding God's will for our lives is a heavily debated topic among young people. I usually toss out to the students Augustine's oft-quoted dictum, "Love [God], and do as you will." At first it sounds almost antinomian to them, but the more they think about it, usually the more helpful it is.

I think that is what the legal expert from the Pharisees was looking for— a practical handle to grasp God's will—because the Bible is God's written will for his people. As he asks what the greatest commandment is in the Law (22:35–36), he is looking for an overarching way to obey God's will, which Jesus then says is to love God and one's neighbor—and that sounds strikingly similar to Augustine's statement. If we truly do love God with all of our heart and soul and mind, our entire person is focused on giving ourselves to him. We will not want to do anything contrary to his will for us. We will love our neighbors by giving ourselves to them, and if we truly love them, we will only do to them what is for their good. There is a great deal of freedom in that orientation toward the Bible.

In our discussion of the Sermon on the Mount, I suggested a schematic in which our transformation works from the inside to the out, with the heart directing the mind, body, and social relations to say yes to God.[37] When we keep that perspective in view, it is congruent with what the lawyer seeks from Jesus and how Jesus replies. Ultimate obedience to God occurs when our entire person is directed toward loving him and others.

The nineteenth-century Christian novelist and poet George MacDonald was regarded by C. S. Lewis to be his literary master. MacDonald wrote everything from grand Victorian novels to Christian fantasies. But he also kept an extensive correspondence. In a letter to his daughter Mary when she was sixteen, MacDonald tried to extend his understanding of God's love as a determining factor to guide her life. He wrote:

> God is so beautiful, and so patient, and so loving, and so generous that he is the heart and soul and rock of every love and every kindness and every gladness in the world. All the beauty in the world and in the hearts of men, all the painting, all the poetry, all the music, all the architecture comes out of his heart first. He is so loveable that no heart can know how loveable he is—can know only in part. When the best loves God best, he does not love him nearly as he deserves, or as he will love him in time.38

That is the kind of love about which Jesus spoke to the Pharisaic lawyer. And that is the kind of love that, when practiced in giving ourselves to God so that we can love our neighbor, opens up the freedom of living in obedience to his will.

**Jesus under fire.** The Pharisees who responded to Jesus' question about the identity of the Messiah (22:42) gave an answer that satisfied the tradition of

---

37. See the Contemporary Significance section on 5:17–20.

38. Cited as the quote of the month for June 2002, at Golden Key, an "on-line resource for all things related to Victorian novelist, poet and Christian Fantasy writer George Mac-Donald (1824–1905)" (www.george-macdonald.com).

their academic brotherhood, but it did not give the full picture of the Messiah. They were left with only a human descendant of David. But that kind of messiah is not able to do much more than any other human religious figure. So Jesus brilliantly prods them to open their eyes and hearts to see what David's psalm said—that Messiah is *Adon*, the Lord, who is the divine Son of man of Daniel's prophecy. That grand, mind-opening experience should have convinced the Pharisees. They were waiting for a messianic deliverer, but this didn't fit with their preconceived ideas, so they turned away.

The upshot for us is that we must have the courage to see what Scripture truly teaches about Jesus and then act on it. Several years ago some colleagues and I put together an anthology that attempted to defend the biblical teaching concerning Jesus from modern aberrations—specifically the group known as the Jesus Seminar. We entitled the book *Jesus Under Fire*.[39] It was a wonderful opportunity to work with leading evangelical scholars from around the country, all of whom were dedicated to one thing: refuting bad modern reinventions of Jesus in the light of a more biblical understanding.

I'm not sure if many Jesus Seminar participants have reconsidered their understanding of Jesus, but it illustrates for me what Jesus encountered. He was also under fire in the first century. The traditions of the elders of the Pharisees were reinventing the messianic prophecies of the Old Testament because they couldn't figure out how the Messiah could be both human and divine. Jesus did not have to give the Pharisees a new Bible. All that they needed was already there. But since they couldn't conceive of such a tremendous truth, they revised the biblical portrait.

It is no less significant for us today. The modernist and postmodernist mindset balks at the incredible claims for Jesus that the Bible makes. But what we advanced in *Jesus under Fire* is that the New Testament claims about Jesus of Nazareth are true, and it is reasonable to believe this is so. Our hope there, as it is here, was that a study of God's Word would whet your appetite for the quest for God. If you are to live a life of integrity before God, it is imperative that your beliefs be true and that your questions have intellectually satisfying answers. Jesus provided those for the first century, and he does so for us today. Without him, we are spiritually bankrupt and hopeless. The kind of Messiah envisioned by the Pharisees or by modern reinventions cannot offer eternal salvation or the power to live life as we know we should.

These truths lie at the center of Christian claims. If Jesus is truly the One whom he declares himself to be, we have a unique message to proclaim. Jesus is unlike any figure ever to walk the earth, for he is not simply a mes-

---

39. Michael J. Wilkins and J. P. Moreland, eds., *Jesus Under Fire: Modern Scholarship Reinvents the Historical Jesus* (Grand Rapids: Zondervan, 1995).

senger but the Son of God. The religious leaders' silence is outspoken testimony that the straightforward implication of the text cannot be avoided. The Messiah has a special relationship to Yahweh, which Jesus claims for himself. Their silence is also outspoken testimony of their own hypocritical avoidance of the implications for themselves. They should acknowledge Jesus as their own Lord and Messiah. But ultimately, none of us, Christian or non-Christian, can ignore the influences for our personal lives. Jesus demands nothing less than to be accepted, served, and worshiped as our Lord.

# Matthew 23:1–39

THEN JESUS SAID to the crowds and to his disciples:
²"The teachers of the law and the Pharisees sit in
Moses' seat. ³So you must obey them and do everything they tell you. But do not do what they do, for they do
not practice what they preach. ⁴They tie up heavy loads and
put them on men's shoulders, but they themselves are not willing to lift a finger to move them.

⁵"Everything they do is done for men to see: They make
their phylacteries wide and the tassels on their garments long;
⁶they love the place of honor at banquets and the most important seats in the synagogues; ⁷they love to be greeted in the
marketplaces and to have men call them 'Rabbi.'

⁸"But you are not to be called 'Rabbi,' for you have only
one Master and you are all brothers. ⁹And do not call anyone
on earth 'father,' for you have one Father, and he is in heaven.
¹⁰Nor are you to be called 'teacher,' for you have one Teacher,
the Christ. ¹¹The greatest among you will be your servant.
¹²For whoever exalts himself will be humbled, and whoever
humbles himself will be exalted.

¹³"Woe to you, teachers of the law and Pharisees, you hypocrites! You shut the kingdom of heaven in men's faces. You
yourselves do not enter, nor will you let those enter who are
trying to.

¹⁵"Woe to you, teachers of the law and Pharisees, you hypocrites! You travel over land and sea to win a single convert,
and when he becomes one, you make him twice as much a son
of hell as you are.

¹⁶"Woe to you, blind guides! You say, 'If anyone swears by
the temple, it means nothing; but if anyone swears by the gold
of the temple, he is bound by his oath.' ¹⁷You blind fools!
Which is greater: the gold, or the temple that makes the gold
sacred? ¹⁸You also say, 'If anyone swears by the altar, it means
nothing; but if anyone swears by the gift on it, he is bound by
his oath.' ¹⁹You blind men! Which is greater: the gift, or the
altar that makes the gift sacred? ²⁰Therefore, he who swears
by the altar swears by it and by everything on it. ²¹And he
who swears by the temple swears by it and by the one who

dwells in it. [22]And he who swears by heaven swears by God's throne and by the one who sits on it.

[23]"Woe to you, teachers of the law and Pharisees, you hypocrites! You give a tenth of your spices—mint, dill and cummin. But you have neglected the more important matters of the law—justice, mercy and faithfulness. You should have practiced the latter, without neglecting the former. [24]You blind guides! You strain out a gnat but swallow a camel.

[25]"Woe to you, teachers of the law and Pharisees, you hypocrites! You clean the outside of the cup and dish, but inside they are full of greed and self-indulgence. [26]Blind Pharisee! First clean the inside of the cup and dish, and then the outside also will be clean.

[27]"Woe to you, teachers of the law and Pharisees, you hypocrites! You are like whitewashed tombs, which look beautiful on the outside but on the inside are full of dead men's bones and everything unclean. [28]In the same way, on the outside you appear to people as righteous but on the inside you are full of hypocrisy and wickedness.

[29]"Woe to you, teachers of the law and Pharisees, you hypocrites! You build tombs for the prophets and decorate the graves of the righteous. [30]And you say, 'If we had lived in the days of our forefathers, we would not have taken part with them in shedding the blood of the prophets.' [31]So you testify against yourselves that you are the descendants of those who murdered the prophets. [32]Fill up, then, the measure of the sin of your forefathers!

[33]"You snakes! You brood of vipers! How will you escape being condemned to hell? [34]Therefore I am sending you prophets and wise men and teachers. Some of them you will kill and crucify; others you will flog in your synagogues and pursue from town to town. [35]And so upon you will come all the righteous blood that has been shed on earth, from the blood of righteous Abel to the blood of Zechariah son of Berekiah, whom you murdered between the temple and the altar. [36]I tell you the truth, all this will come upon this generation.

[37]"O Jerusalem, Jerusalem, you who kill the prophets and stone those sent to you, how often I have longed to gather your children together, as a hen gathers her chicks under her wings, but you were not willing. [38]Look, your house is left to you desolate. [39]For I tell you, you will not see me again until you say, 'Blessed is he who comes in the name of the Lord.'"

**Original Meaning**

THE EXTENDED CONTROVERSIES of chapters 21 and 22 revealed beyond any doubt that the religious establishment will not lead the people of Israel in repentance and accept Jesus' invitation to the kingdom of heaven. These controversies were held in the temple courts within the public hearing of those conducting business there as well as of the crowds who gathered to hear Jesus' teaching (21:23). Traditionally these events are understood to have occurred on Tuesday of Holy Week. The time of Jesus' public interaction with the religious leaders and the crowds is winding down, as it is increasingly clear that the leaders' opposition to him is leading them to plot his demise.

Jesus gives a final scathing denunciation of the teachers of the law and the Pharisees as a warning to his disciples and to the crowds. Jesus addresses this denunciation for several reasons. These religious leaders are the most influential ones of the common people because they were located in the villages throughout Israel and participated in the life of the synagogue. The Pharisees have been Jesus' most vocal opponents throughout his ministry, primarily because he has undercut their oral law, which threatens their authoritative pronouncements and their esteem among the people. In many ways the doctrinal positions of the Pharisees on crucial items are more similar to Jesus' positions than other sects within Israel, especially the Sadducees.[1]

This series of "woes" follows closely from the parables (21:28–22:14) that revealed the culpability of these religious leaders for not leading the nation in repentance with the arrival of the kingdom of heaven, and from the debates (22:15–22:46) in which they attempted to entrap Jesus. Jesus warns the crowds and his disciples of the false leadership of these leaders and alerts them not to follow their false example (23:1–12). But he also directs the woes against them directly to confront them with their failed responsibility as leaders and with its consequences. Because of their deadly false leadership, Jesus pronounces severe judgment on them (23:13–39).

Some link these pronouncements with the following Olivet Discourse (chs. 24–25) to form the fifth and final major discourse in Matthew's Gospel. But since the subjects are quite different, it is best to see these woes as a culmination of the judgment on Israel's leadership that has been building since Jesus' climactic entrance to Jerusalem and the events in the temple. Then, as he and the disciples return to Bethany that afternoon, the discourse on the Mount of Olives takes place (see comments on chs. 24–25).

---

1. See comments on 3:7; see also Wilkins, "Matthew," 25.

## Warning the Crowds and the Disciples (23:1–12)

JESUS FIRST ADDRESSES the crowds and his disciples to warn them of the false leadership that the teachers of the law and the Pharisees have given and to warn them not to follow their example (23:1–12). "The teachers of the law" (or scribes) and "the Pharisees" are two separate groups: The scribes are interpretive experts of the Torah, while the Pharisees are theological experts (see comments on 8:19).

**Warnings about demanding legalistic performance (23:1–4).** Jesus first warns the crowds and the disciples about the burdens that the teachers of the law and the Pharisees have imposed on them because of their authoritative position in the synagogue. They sit in Moses' seat and offer pronouncements about the law that they expect the people to follow, but they offer no practical help for them to actually carry them out.

Jesus' reference to the "seat [*kathedra*] of Moses" is the earliest known literary reference to this expression.[2] Other references in rabbinic literature speak more generally of a synagogue chair on which esteemed rabbis sit when teaching.[3] This "seat" was often viewed as a figurative expression, referring to the authority of Moses. However, recent archaeological evidence points to a literal chair.[4] The purpose of the seat has been debated, though most scholars view it as the seat for a leader in the synagogue. It may be the place from which the synagogue ruler presided, or the place where the expositor sat after reading and interpreting a portion of Scripture, or the place where an honored guest or speaker sat.[5] Jesus' statement confirms the use of the "seat of Moses" as a place from which experts in the law teach.

Jesus declares, "So you must obey them and do everything they tell you." This declaration is somewhat surprising, given his antipathy toward them in the following warnings and woes. While this may be sarcasm or bitter irony,[6] Jesus' statement follows from the religious leaders' position as expounders of Moses' teaching. He gives a scathing denunciation, yet he recognizes their official capacity when exercised in the proper manner. Any and all accurate interpretation of Scripture is to be obeyed. The Pharisees had many good things to say, and their doctrine was closer to Jesus' on many crucial issues than to other groups. Jesus does not deny that their teaching is beneficial for spiritual life, and he endorses, in principle, their desire to pursue righteous ends.[7] In this

---

2. For discussion, with the latest evidence, see Levine, "Cathedra of Moses," *The Ancient Synagogue*, 323–27.

3. See *t. Suk.* 4:6, cited in ibid., 324.

4. For pictures, see Wilkins, "Matthew," 140.

5. Levine, *The Ancient Synagogue*, 326.

6. Carson, "Matthew," 473.

7. Hagner, *Matthew*, 2:654.

sense, Jesus does not condemn them for developing their teaching, but he does condemn oral tradition when it incorrectly interprets the intent of the Old Testament and inappropriately supplants it (cf. 15:1–9).

Jesus further condemns the hypocritical behavior that some (likely not all) Pharisees expressed. "But do not do what they do, for they do not practice what they preach." Jesus does not condemn the pursuit of righteousness itself; rather, he criticizes only certain attitudes and practices expressed within the effort to be righteous. Here he points to specific issues in which the Pharisees preach one value but do not practice it themselves. This is a form of hypocrisy. The hypocrisy that Jesus condemned in the SM was that the Pharisees were doing right things for the wrong reasons (cf. 6:2). Both forms of hypocrisy are included below in Jesus' criticism.

Throughout his ministry, one of Jesus' core censures of these religious leaders has been that they burden the people (e.g., 9:36; 11:28–30). As he says here, "They tie up heavy loads and put them on men's shoulders, but they themselves are not willing to lift a finger to move them." "Heavy loads" put on people's shoulders denotes the rabbinic oral tradition that was a distinctive feature of the Pharisaic branch of Judaism. It was intended to make the Old Testament relevant to life situations where it seemed irrelevant, such as the complex sacrificial system in contexts removed from the temple, both in time and in locale.

The oral tradition was also designed as a "fence around Torah" (see *m. ʾAbot* 1.1). Their interpretations, applications and solutions to problems became a means of protecting Torah itself. Since the oral law was considered to be of divine origin, its massive obligations became far more burdensome than Scripture, and with the passing of years and the addition of more and more prescriptions, the rabbis could not lessen the burden without overthrowing the whole system. This is the inherent conflict with Jesus and the Pharisaic system, because they were so committed to their system that they missed the movement of God among them in the person of Jesus.

**Warnings about pretentious public displays of piety (23:5–7).** The second warning Jesus gives to the crowds and his disciples about the teachers of the law and the Pharisees is that "everything they do is done for men to see." The expression "for men to see" is reminiscent of Jesus' criticism of the religious leaders in the SM (cf. 6:1). The specific criticism here focuses on two related practices: wearing of religious garments and positioning for religious prominence. In Jesus' view, conducting religious performance in order to enhance reputation and status among the people will actually blot out God from the people's attention.

The religious garments of the leaders come in for the first criticism: "They make their phylacteries wide and the tassels on their garments long" (23:5).

Phylacteries (*phylakteria;* Heb. *tefillim*) are small leather cubical cases containing passages of Scripture written on parchment. They were worn as an attempt to obey literally the admonition in the book of Deuteronomy, "Fix these words of mine in your hearts and minds; tie them as symbols on your hands and bind them on your foreheads" (Deut. 11:18; cf. Ex. 13:9, 13; Deut. 6:8). They were fastened to the left arm and forehead to be worn by adult males in the morning service.

The discovery of leather phylactery cases at Qumran illustrates their usage at the time of Jesus. One type, about an inch long, was worn on the forehead and contained four small inner compartments for holding four tiny scrolls on which were written, in tiny script, Exodus 13:9, 16; Deuteronomy 6:8; 11:18. The second type, approximately one-third of an inch long, was worn on the left arm and had only one compartment with a single minute scroll containing all four verses.[8] The rabbis themselves had regulations about wearing phylacteries because of the temptation to wear them too large or inappropriately to draw attention to one's piety.[9] Jesus warns the crowds and the disciples against the practice of parading such religious objects to trumpet one's piety.

On the four corners of a garment worn by men were "tassels" (*kraspeda*) that had a blue cord, conforming to the admonitions of Numbers 15:37—42 and Deuteronomy 22:12. The tassels reminded the people to obey God's commandment and to be holy to God (Num. 15:40). Jesus himself wore these tassels on his garment (see Matt. 9:20/Luke 8:44; Matt. 14:36/Mark 6:56), although the term in these contexts may refer to the outer fringe (decorated or plain) of the garment. Jesus chides these religious leaders for extending the tassels as a display of their piety, which is another way that they try to gain the admiration of the people.

Sought-after religious positions of honor come in for a second criticism: "They love the place of honor at banquets and the most important seats in the synagogues." Seating at special dinner occasions was bestowed on guests according to their rank or status. Guests reclined on couches around a U-shaped series of tables, and the place of honor was at the center table, with the host seated in the center and the most honored guests on either side. The other guests were then seated in descending order of importance (see comments on 26:26).[10]

Seating in the synagogue varied from location to location, with some synagogues having stone benches along one, two, three, or four of the walls,

---

8. "Tefillin" and "Tefillin, Archaeology of," *DJBP*, 621.

9. See Wilkins, "Matthew," 141.

10. For various customs, see Gene Schramm, "Meal Customs (Jewish)," and Dennis E. Smith, "Meal Customs (Greco-Roman)," *ABD*, 4:648—53.

with removable benches or mats brought in for the majority of the congregation. There is ample evidence that the elders and other synagogue leaders had places of prominence.[11] Benches or chairs may have been reserved on special occasions for important persons, and, if a regular part of each synagogue, the seat of Moses (23:2) was reserved for the one expounding on Scripture.[12]

Honorific public recognition to trumpet one's religious position in the community is especially odious: "They love to be greeted in the marketplaces and to have men call them 'Rabbi.'" The rabbi was generally a master of the Torah, and the title usually refers to the head of a rabbinical school. The association with these schools tended to set them aside somewhat from the populace. The school was a holy community, and the people regarded the members as a whole with great deference.[13] These academic institutions were distinguished from the synagogue, with the academy a place to promote Torah study and the synagogue a place to promote prayer.[14]

**Warnings about exploiting titles (23:8–10).** After the general warning about the hypocrisy of desiring honorific titles, Jesus warns his disciples against using three specific titles: "rabbi," "father," and "teacher." (1) The warning against being called "rabbi" continues the warning against honorific positions in the community. The ultimate goal of a disciple of a rabbi was to become a rabbi himself at the end of his course of study.[15] With Jesus, however, a new form of discipleship emerges. A disciple of Jesus will always and forever be only a disciple, because Jesus alone is Teacher. The ultimate authority within the community of disciples is Jesus, which eliminates the struggle for authoritative teaching positions among his followers. They are brothers of one family, all of whom are equal in status.

(2) Nor are Jesus' disciples to abuse the term "father": "And do not call anyone on earth 'father,' for you have one Father, and he is in heaven." This warning follows from the preceding admonition. If Jesus' disciples are all brothers, then they must have a common father. Biological fathers are not in view, since Jesus reiterates elsewhere the enduring validity of the fifth commandment to "honor your father and your mother" (15:4; 19:19; cf. Ex. 20:12; Deut. 5:16), although he does warn against elevating family loyalty over loyalty to Jesus (cf. 10:34–39).

---

11. A later rabbinic passage is representative: "How did the elders sit? Facing the congregation and with their backs to the holy [i.e., Jerusalem and the temple] ... the administrator of the synagogue faces the holy and the entire congregation faces the holy" (*t. Meg.* 3:21).

12. Levine, *The Ancient Synagogue*, 313–17.

13. "Rabbi," *DJBP*, 516; Levine, *The Ancient Synagogue*, 440–70.

14. For discussion of this distinction, see Levine, *The Ancient Synagogue*, 449–51.

15. See Wilkins, *Discipleship in the Ancient World*, 116–24.

The use of the term "father" as a title of honor, respect, and authority had deep roots in ancient Judaism, including its use by Elisha to cry to Elijah as he was ascending to heaven (2 Kings 2:12; 6:21), its reference to the Maccabean martyr Razis as "father of his people" (2 Macc. 14:37), and its later use to denote the head of a rabbinic court.[16] "Father" (*'abba*) occurs regularly in rabbinic sources as a title for esteemed scholars and rabbis.[17] The expression "father of the synagogue" was used in rabbinic times of an individual holding a place of honor and leadership within the synagogue affairs generally.

The motif of the heavenly "Father" occurs throughout the Old Testament (Deut. 14:1; 32:6; Ps. 103:13; Jer. 3:4; 31:9; Hos. 11:1), growing increasingly popular during the Second Temple period in prayers for protection and forgiveness.[18] Jesus brought his disciples into a unique relationship with God as Father, since he is the unique Son of God and they are his brothers and sisters (cf. Matt. 6:9; 12:48–50). Jesus warns against elevating religious leaders to a place where they usurp the authority due to God alone. No human leader may ever usurp God the Father's preeminence. This allows Jesus' followers to leave behind wrangling over preeminence.

(3) Matthew uses a word found only here in the New Testament to describe the third title that Jesus' disciples are to avoid—*kathegetes* ("teacher"). It is a near equivalent for the word *didaskalos* (e.g., 26:18), but it carries an additional sense of "leader" (NASB). The term *kathegetes* does not occur in the LXX, but it does occur in Greek literature to designate especially a private tutor, which may point to the individual authority an instructor has over a student.[19] Since Jesus is alluding to various titles that one might take, perhaps a better rendering is "master."[20] Jesus' disciples are not to seek out personal authority as "master" over other disciples, because as the Messiah, Jesus alone is Master (*kathegetes*). He alone has personal authority to guide his disciples (28:18, 20). The more that Jesus' disciples exalt Jesus as the Messiah, the less they will think of magnifying themselves over others.

**A new type of leadership (23:11–12).** Jesus concludes his warnings against legalistic burdens (23:1–4), public displays of piety (23:5–7), and honorific titles (23:8–10) by harking back to a saying that earlier corrected the disciples' inappropriate concern for positions of prominence (20:26–27): "The greatest among you will be your servant" (23:11). In the new order that

---

16. See Levine, *The Ancient Synagogue*, 404–6.

17. Cf. *b. Ketub.* 8a; *t. Beṣah* 1:7; see examples in *DJBP*, 2–3.

18. E.g., *Jub.* 1:24, 28; 19:29; *Jos. Asen.* 12:14; *Sir.* 23:1, 4; Wisd. Sol. 2:16–20; 14:3; Tob. 13:4; 4Q372; 1QH 9:35. See "Father, God as," *DJBP*, 224.

19. See Bruce W. Winter, "The Messiah As the Tutor: The Meaning of καθηγητής in Matthew 23:10," *TynBul* 42 (1991): 152–57.

20. E.g., Robertson, *Grammar*, 138.

supplants the prior leadership of Israel (21:43), Jesus' disciples must place servant leadership as the highest priority. Greatness in the community of the kingdom is much different from that displayed by the religious leadership of Israel. The teachers of the law and the Pharisees have patterned their leadership after the example of worldly rulers, whose primary goal is to extend their own power and authority.

Jesus offers a different model—that of the servant. The ideal servant lived to care for, protect, and make better the lives of those over him or her. Jesus' disciples had the ambition to be great (18:1) and to have the highest positions (20:21), so Jesus gives them the means by which they can do so according the values of the kingdom of God, not the kingdoms of the world. They must arrange their lives with the ambition to give themselves for the benefit of others.

Like the warnings directed to these religious leaders, Jesus warns his own disciples about trying to thwart this new servant-leader paradigm: "For whoever exalts himself will be humbled, and whoever humbles himself will be exalted." If they follow the world's thirst for power and prestige and attempt to exalt themselves, they will be humbled. Like the leaders of Israel from whom God has taken away their role in the outworking of his kingdom, Jesus' disciples who exalt themselves will also be humbled and lose their place of leadership. But those who, in the example of Jesus, came not to be served but to serve (20:28) and to live out the humble role of servant, will be exalted as true sons and daughters of the kingdom. This does not indicate exaltation over each other but the equal exaltation that all disciples of Jesus enjoy as those who are brothers and sisters of one another with Jesus as Master and his Father as their own.

### Woes on the Teachers of the Law and the Pharisees (23:13–36)

JESUS HAS WARNED the crowds and his disciples about the destructive example of the teachers of law and the Pharisees. Now he addresses these leaders of Israel directly and pronounces a series of seven "woes" on them, which flesh out the condemnation that Jesus has directed to them throughout his ministry. The interjection "woe" (*ouai*) is a mixed cry of regret, compassion, sorrow, and denunciation.

When Jesus utters this cry seven times, he is deploring the miserable condition in which the Pharisees can be found, but he is also pronouncing the fate they have brought on themselves. They seem unaware of the judgment that awaits them, living in a fool's paradise while thinking that they are the epitome of religious blessedness. Their woeful condition lies especially in their hypocrisy and blindness, in which they disfigure the truth of God's revelation through their self-deception and inconsistency. But it also results from abusing their responsibility as leaders by refusing the invitation to the kingdom of God and by leading Israel to the doom that was likewise prophesied of Korazin, Bethsaida, and Capernaum (11:20–24).[21]

**First woe: The shut door (23:13 [14]).** The first "woe" establishes the strong language, "Woe to you," which is reminiscent of Old Testament prophetic series of pronouncements of judgment.[22] Similar to Jesus' key statement in the SM (5:20), the scribes' and Pharisees' emphasis on external righteousness not only has blinded them to Jesus' gracious offer of an inward righteousness through a transformation of the heart, but their leadership role in Israel has caused the people to be blinded as well. Therefore, Jesus condemns these leaders for hypocrisy.

We saw earlier that the term "hypocrite" (*hypokrites*) was originally used for a play actor (see comments on 6:2). Jesus condemned the religious leaders in the SM for the form of hypocrisy in which they deceived themselves (cf. 6:1–18). Here he condemns them for the type of hypocrisy in which they deceive the people through their fallacious leadership. They have mounted the seat of Moses, from which they offer their teachings and traditions, but their pronouncements are false. They do not lead the people to God but away from the kingdom of heaven. Not only have they rejected the offer to enter the kingdom themselves, but their teachings and opposition to Jesus' ministry influence the people to reject that invitation as well.

This is a terrible abuse of their responsibility. Jesus condemns them for their hypocrisy, that is, attempting to bring the people into a righteous relationship with God while at the same time not being in a genuine relationship themselves.[23] The first woe sets a trajectory for those that follow.[24]

**Second woe: Entrapped converts (23:15).** Jesus continues to denounce the hypocrisy of the religious leaders, turning now to address the extent of Jewish activity of making proselytes (*proselytos;* NIV "win a convert"): "You travel over land and sea to win a single convert, and when he becomes one, you make him twice as much a son of hell as you are." Jewish history records an active propaganda directed toward gaining proselytes. Some rabbis even declared that this was the divine purpose for the exile of the Jewish people

---

21. See Norman Hillyer, "Woe (οὐαί)," *NIDNTT*, 3:1051–54.

22. E.g., six in Isa. 5:8–22; five in Hab. 2:6–20; cf. the two series of three in Rev. 8:13; 9:12; 11:14; 12:12; and 18:10, 16, 19.

23. Marshall, "Who Is a Hypocrite?," esp. 139–42.

24. Some manuscripts add an additional verse here (see NIV text note): "Woe to you, teachers of the law and Pharisees, you hypocrites! You devour widows' houses and for a show make lengthy prayers. Therefore you will be punished more severely" (23:14). The best manuscripts do not have these verses.

(cf. *b. Pesaḥ.* 87b).[25] Josephus indicates that both before and after the destruction of the Second Temple, many proselytes were made both among the masses and the upper classes in the Gentile cities surrounding Israel.[26]

Perhaps the primary point of Jesus' invective is best understood by recognizing that the Pharisees, not all of Judaism, are the primary targets here. The Pharisees were ardent advocates of their own sectarian understanding of Judaism, contending that their way was the primary avenue of living a life of true devotion. Therefore, Jesus does not condemn proselytizing per se but criticizes the way that the Pharisees, zealous to win people to their own brand of Judaism, place them under their particularly burdensome code of conduct in the oral law (cf. 23:4). They "succeed only in creating a duplicate of their own devices."[27]

These Pharisees have not entered the kingdom themselves and also block their followers from entering (23:13), so when they win adherents, they make their proselytes "twice as much of a child of hell as themselves." Literally "child of Gehenna," this is another reference to the Valley of Hinnom, the ravine just south of Jerusalem, which Jewish and New Testament writings use to portray the last judgment and place of eternal punishment (e.g., *1 En.* 26–27; see comments on Matt. 5:22). The expression "twice as much" may be literary hyperbole,[28] or it may point to the zeal of a recent convert who, knowing no other way, is more easily indoctrinated to the way of error and is far less likely to escape.[29]

**Third woe: Binding oaths (23:16–22).** This third woe addresses "blind guides." The subject is assumed to be the same, but Jesus now intentionally addresses the teachers of the law and the Pharisees by the characteristic that has so led themselves and others astray. Their clever casuistry has blinded them to the truth, which in turns causes them to lead others away from the truth (cf. 15:14). "You say, 'If anyone swears by the temple, it means nothing; but if anyone swears by the gold of the temple, he is bound by his oath.'" The Pharisees developed a complicated series of rulings regarding vows and oaths that were eventually compiled in the rabbinic Mishnaic tractates *Nedarim* ("vows") and *Šebuʿot* ("oaths").[30] Jesus addressed vows in 15:1–9, but here he addresses oaths (and in 5:34–37).

---

25. See "Proselytes," *EJR*, 312–13.

26. See, e.g., Josephus, *J. W.* 2.560–61[2.20.2]; *Ant.* 20.24–48 [2.1–4]. Tacitus in *Hist.* 5.5 criticizes the Jews for attempting to gain converts. On the issue of Jewish proselytizing (which is debated among scholars), see esp. McKnight, *A Light Among the Gentiles*, 106–8.

27. Senior, *Matthew*, 261; cf. McKnight, *A Light Among the Gentiles*, 107.

28. Hagner, *Matthew*, 2:668–69.

29. Morris, *Matthew*, 580.

30. A vow is distinct from the oath: The vow forbids a certain thing to be used, while an oath forbids the swearer to do a certain thing although that thing is not forbidden in itself.

The Pharisees distinguished between oaths made "by the temple" and those made "by the gold of the temple," and oaths made "by the altar" and those made "by the gift on it." Included in Jesus' criticism may be that they have the most important matters reversed, and they are giving more attention to minute details of the law rather than to its principles. This reflects an inconsistent hypocrisy in the religious leaders' teaching when they declare some oaths binding and others not, and also in their behavior, when they themselves are inconsistent when they take oaths.[31] Overall, as he emphasized in the SM, Jesus declares that a person should not try to play games with God or develop elaborate systems to try to remain faithful. A person who lives in moment-by-moment accountability to the presence of the living God will need only to give a simple "yes" or "no" as a binding oath (cf. 5:23, 34–37).

**Fourth woe: Neglecting the weighty matters of the Law (23:23–24).** The fourth woe combines with the third to emphasize that proper responsibility to God's law is not found only in fastidious attention to the details but especially in obeying its overarching intent. The Mosaic law specified that a tenth of all that one had was to be given to the Lord for the ongoing work of God through the Levites and the priests (e.g., Lev. 27:30–33; Num. 18:21, 24; Deut. 12:5–19). The Pharisees are so scrupulous about attending to this requirement that they measure out and pay the tithe on the smallest of garden crops—such as the herbs mint, dill, and cummin.

Jesus does not tell the Pharisees and teachers of the law to neglect the tithe, but their scrupulous attention to ceremonial detail consumes so much of their time and attention that they have no time to plan how they will daily exercise the more important matters, such as bringing justice to those who are wronged, mercy to those who do wrong, and faithfulness to those who have departed from the faith. These Jewish leaders have lost sight that the real purpose of their responsibilities to God is to bring about righteousness in this world, not simply perpetuate religious activity and burdens.

With sardonic humor Jesus shows through what may be a well-known proverbial saying that the Pharisees and teachers of the law have indeed overlooked the obviously important issues while focusing on their minute regulations: "You blind guides! You strain out a gnat but swallow a camel." The law declared that many winged creatures were unclean (Lev. 11:23, 41), which the rabbis applied by straining wine to keep out small insects that made wine unclean. While attending to the minutiae of legal matters, they overlook the largest land animal in Palestine, the camel, which was also ceremonially unclean (Lev. 11:4). This may be the clearest example of the kind of hypocrisy that demonstrates inconsistency in their personal behavior.

---

31. Marshall, "Who Is a Hypocrite?" 140.

They display partial obedience to God alongside of partial disobedience.[32] "The scribes and Pharisees play on the sea shore of religion while the great ocean of fundamental truth lies all undiscovered before them."[33]

**Fifth woe: Clean outside, filthy inside (23:25–26).** The fifth woe reveals a critical flaw of these religious leaders. They are highly committed to their purity laws that require external ceremonial purification. Time and again they criticized Jesus for eating with those who were not ceremonially pure (9:1–12) or for not requiring his own disciples to observe such purity laws (15:1–20). Jesus before warned his disciples and the crowds of this error (15:1, 10–20), but now he confronts them directly. "You clean the outside of the cup and dish, but inside they are full of greed and self-indulgence. Blind Pharisee! First clean the inside of the cup and dish, and then the outside also will be clean."

The heart is the source of all thoughts, motives, and actions. The greed and self-indulgence of the Pharisees and teachers of the law, especially their lust for public religious acclaim, are inner motivations that impact external behavior. In order to bring about true purity, their hearts need purifying. The only genuine purification is through the power of the kingdom of heaven (see comments on 5:20; 15:18–20). By rejecting the operation of that kingdom in their own lives, they are choosing to remain inwardly defiled.

A root of hypocrisy is pride, the desire to have others see one as better than one actually is. This deceptive and pretentious attitude fuels a drive for power and prestige by those in a position to take advantage of those who are vulnerable (cf. 23:4, 6–7). Moreover, hypocrisy has caused the Pharisees to miss the more important internal, moral issues that are foundational to the operation of the kingdom—justice, mercy, and faithfulness (23:23). Jesus accuses them of being clean on the outside but dirty on the inside; if the inside is clean, the outside will follow also.

**Sixth woe: Whitewashed tombs (23:27–28).** The sixth woe describes the religious leaders further as "whitewashed tombs." It was a custom to mark tombs in burial grounds with white chalk to make them conspicuous so that passersby unfamiliar with the terrain would not come in contact with a tomb and so be rendered unclean for seven days (Num. 19:16; cf. Luke 11:44). This whitewashing practice was especially prominent in Jerusalem during Passover time, when many pilgrims traveled to Judea, lest they inadvertently walk over tombs and incur pollution before the Passover (cf. John 11:55; 18:28).[34] This may be another ironic statement by Jesus, because one wonders how whitewash makes a tomb appear "beautiful."[35]

---

32. Ibid., 140–41.
33. Davies and Allison, *Matthew*, 3:295.
34. Colin J. Hemer, "Bury, Grave, Tomb," *NIDNTT*, 1:265.
35. For a discussion of the problems, see Davies and Allison, *Matthew*, 3:301–2.

At the same time, this woe probably builds on the fifth woe, alluding to the practice at the time of Jesus where ornate ossuaries (small bone-box receptacles) made of white limestone were used to retain the bones of deceased ancestors.[36] The teachers of the law and the Pharisees were like these ossuaries—on the outside they were deceptively ornate, but inside there is nothing but impure death. Jesus makes his point plain: These religious leaders give the appearance of having avoided unrighteousness by their attention to their many legal requirements, but inwardly they are unrighteous, for they have not attended to the transformation of the heart that can come by responding to Jesus (cf. 5:20; 15:17–20).

**Seventh woe: Descendants of murderers of the prophets (23:29–32).** The seventh woe continues the theme of death: "Woe to you, teachers of the law and Pharisees, you hypocrites! You build tombs for the prophets and decorate the graves of the righteous." Matthew alternates here between "tombs" for the prophets and "graves" of the righteous. On the one hand, there may be a difference between these two terms, the former indicating "burial grounds" for prophets that the Pharisees embellished, the latter indicating "monuments" (RSV) adorned for "righteous" religious leaders. The "prophets" and the "righteous" are linked elsewhere (10:41; 13:17), indicating Old Testament prophets and others who were renowned for their righteous lives lived out before God. On the other hand, this may be stylistic parallelism, because Jesus' explanation does not address two different types of people who were killed but one, the prophets (23:30–31).

We know from literary and archaeological evidence that Jews at this time began building elaborate memorials and richly ornate ossuaries, tomb facades, and sarcophagi, as well as wall paintings and graffiti (cf. 1 Macc. 13:27–30; see comments on Matt. 27:57–61).[37] The well-known tombs of esteemed figures from Israel's history (cf. Acts 2:29) apparently benefited from this development.

Like the preceding woe, this is a blatant contrast between the religious leaders' fastidious outward observance of cleanliness and the wickedness of their inward motives. They build beautiful monuments to the prophets, but Jesus declares that they are motivationally descendants of those who killed them. They deny that they would have killed the ancient prophets, but as they secretly prepare to have Jesus executed, they demonstrate their wicked, spiritually corrupt lineage to the ancient murderers.

This prepares for Jesus' final invective, in which the teachers of the law and the Pharisees are found guilty of putting to death the messengers of

---

36. For pictures and discussion of the practice, see Wilkins, "Matthew," 144, 160.
37. See Rachel Hachlili, "Burials," *ABD*, 1:789–94

God. Their hypocrisy lies in the inconsistency between honoring the dead prophets and murdering the contemporary ones, like Jesus, who will face their murderous wrath in just a few short days.[38] The religious leaders are intent on their deceptive practices, so sadly Jesus pronounces on them their own self-determined destiny: "Fill up, then, the measure of the sin of your forefathers!" (23:32).

**Final Invective: Murderers of the righteous (23:33–36).** Some place verse 33 with verses 29–32 as a concluding pronouncement of the seventh woe because the word "therefore" in verse 34 may suggest a new unit. However, 23:33 fits well with 23:34–36 as Jesus' final invective against the religious leaders. These verses do not form a separate "woe" but are a culminating pronouncement of judgment. "Snakes" as used here with "brood of vipers" are synonyms to heap up the culpability of these religious leaders. The wording is reminiscent of John the Baptist's and Jesus' earlier pronouncement against the religious leaders (see comments on 3:7; 12:34). Their activities in the last three years is sealing their eternal judgment. It is still not too late to repent and "escape," but the hardening of their hearts against Jesus' and John's message is woefully predictive of future condemnation.

Jesus gives a blood-curdling prediction: "Therefore I am sending you prophets and wise men and teachers. Some of them you will kill and crucify; others you will flog in your synagogues and pursue from town to town." This prophetic statement points ahead to the Christian era, when Israel will still be a focus of Jesus' gracious invitation through his messengers, but they will continue to reject that message. The Jewish leaders, with Roman support, were able to unfurl their wrath first on Stephen (Acts 7:54–60). The later crucifixion of Christians was at the hands of the Romans, but most likely instigated by jealous Jewish officials.

The language here echoes Jesus' prior prophetic statement of the fate of Christian missionaries (cf. 10:16–25) and adds that they will be rejected and persecuted (23:34–35). The lifting of the ban on eating certain meats (e.g., Acts 10:9–16) would make a Jewish convert to Christ unclean in the eyes of the synagogue officials and subject to flogging.[39]

Along with the prophecy that the religious leaders will murder his messengers, Jesus includes a prophecy of the judgment that will come on them for their murderous activities: "And so upon you will come all the righteous blood that has been shed on earth, from the blood of righteous Abel to the blood of Zechariah son of Berekiah, whom you murdered between the tem-

---

38. Marshall, "Who Is a Hypocrite?" 141–42.

39. See comments on 10:17; for background on flogging in the synagogue, see Wilkins, "Matthew," 69.

ple and the altar." The span from the blood of righteous Abel to the blood of Zechariah son of Berekiah includes the entire sweep of biblical history. The first righteous person in human history to be killed was Abel, slain by his brother Cain in an act of unrighteous jealousy (cf. Gen. 4:8–11). The last murder recorded in the Old Testament in the canonical order of the Hebrew Bible (Law, Prophets, Writings) is Zechariah, a son of the high priest (2 Chron. 24:20–22), murdered in the courtyard of the temple.[40]

This generation of Israel's history has been privileged to witness the culmination of salvation history. They have had the opportunity of accepting the gospel of the kingdom and seeing God establish his righteousness in Israel. But instead, like those other wicked people in Israel's history who spilled innocent blood, the religious people of this generation will continue to spill martyr's blood—Jesus' and his messengers'. And the crowds will follow their lead in asking for Jesus' death (27:20), with the result that the people of Israel of that generation declare, "Let his blood be on us and on our children!" (27:25). Israel cannot deny her responsibility for shedding innocent blood: "I tell you the truth, all this will come upon this generation" (23:36).

### Lament over Jerusalem (23:37–39)

JESUS' TONE NOW combines the denunciation of the woes with a compassionate lament. The term "Jerusalem" has stood for the leadership of the nation (cf. 2:3; 21:10), but here it seems to include a reference to the whole nation of Israel for whom Jesus is deeply burdened. Israel stands condemned for eliminating the voice of God's messengers, soon to include Jesus' voice and those whom he will send after him (23:34). But like Yahweh in the Old Testament, who provides protection for his people under his metaphorical wings (e.g, Ex. 19:4; Deut. 32:1; Ruth 2:12; Ps. 17:8; 91:4), Jesus continues to desire the gathering his people. But he will not force himself; they must determine their own fate—"but you were not willing."

---

40. The primary difficulty with this view is that Zechariah's father is there named Jehoiada, and Jesus calls him the "son of Berekiah." This latter reference fits with the prophet Zechariah, who is called the son of Berekiah, the son of Iddo (Zech. 1:1), which some then suggest is the identity of the Zechariah mentioned by Jesus, which would then make the time span from creation to the last recorded prophet (Blomberg, *Matthew*, 349). However, since the prophet Zechariah is not recorded to have had his life end in a violent death, others contend the Zechariah whose death in the temple courtyard was recorded in 2 Chronicles was either identified by a developing tradition as the prophet Zechariah (Hagner, *Matthew*, 2:677; Davies and Allison, *Matthew*, 3:319; Keener, *A Commentary on the Gospel of Matthew* [1999], 556), or he was named in Chronicles from his grandfather rather than his father, a generally common practice (Morris, *Matthew*, 589 n. 45).

Jesus is especially burdened in light of Israel's coming judgment. He predicts the destruction of Israel's "house," an expression for the temple in the Old Testament (1 Kings 9:7–8; Isa. 64:10–11; cf. John 12:7.). This is possibly its meaning here as well, although it may point more widely to judgment on Jerusalem's leadership. Jewish authority will be lost with the destruction of the temple in A.D. 70. This is the theme to which Jesus turns next (chs. 24–25).

Jesus concludes his address to the people of Israel with a dramatic prophecy: "For I tell you, you will not see me again until you say, 'Blessed is he who comes in the name of the Lord.'" This is the last time that Jesus addresses the crowds, who have had their opportunity to repent. The Christological implications of Jesus' quotation of Psalm 118:26 are profound. The same words were cited in 21:9 at Jesus' entrance to Jerusalem, shouted by those identifying him as the messianic Son of David. Now as Jesus cites the same passage, he identifies himself with God's Messiah, Israel's Savior, the "Coming One," who will once again return to his people after a time of great judgment, when they will have no other choice but to acknowledge him as Lord, either in great joy or in great sorrow.

**Bridging Contexts**

THE PHARISEES STARTED out well. Most likely their roots are found in the schism in Israel between the Hasideans, who advocated pure Jewish culture, and the Hellenists, who adopted Greek ways during the Seleucid dynasty, especially under Antiochus IV Epiphanes (175–164 B.C.). The Pharisees' name is probably derived from the Hebrew/Aramaic *perušim* ("the separated ones"), indicating that they were spiritual descendants of the Hasideans, separating themselves from all pagan practices that would defile pure Jewish religion and ways of life.

The Pharisees came to be one of the dominant forces within Jewish life because they were so influential among laypeople. But Jesus' scathing denunciation of them indicates that they had begun to accrue to themselves more authority than was warranted and were actually leading the people astray from God's intent to have the Old Testament alone as central in authority. They did not take their leadership role of directing the people to accept the invitation to the kingdom of heaven that Jesus offered as the long-anticipated and prophesied Messiah. Thus, with the arrival of the kingdom and the establishment of the church to take Israel's place as the primary instrument and witness to the gospel, the teachers of the law and the Pharisees will be removed from their positions (21:43).

Matthew has witnessed this amazing transition of leadership. He has heard Jesus' denunciations of the religious authorities, experienced his own calling as an apostle, participated as the Twelve and those around them in Jerusalem became the foundation and leaders of the church, and observed as local congregations with their own elders, pastors, and deacons sprang up throughout the Mediterranean world. A whole new set of leaders are guiding God's people. But they need guidelines to help them avoid the errors of the Pharisees and Sadducees and promote the kind of people Jesus wants. This is where Matthew steps forward.

In the development of his Gospel, one of Matthew's primary purposes is to put together a collection of Jesus' sayings to his disciples in his earthly ministry so that the church will have a resource from which they can teach new disciples to obey everything Jesus commanded them (28:19–20). The bulk of that resource is found in Jesus' five discourses that Matthew has recorded (chs. 5–7, 10, 13, 18, 24–25). But Matthew has also collected many other sayings of Jesus, including the most comprehensive collection of his warnings and woes, through which he gives cautions of what to avoid. We will briefly look here at the failure of the religious leaders that produced each warning and woe, and in the Contemporary Significance section we will look at the positive lessons we can glean from each.

**Warnings for leaders.** The section of warnings (23:1–12) cautions church leaders about the temptations that caused the teachers of the law and the Pharisees to distort and abuse their leadership privilege. (1) The first section warns about the burdens of legalism that these religious leaders impose on the people (23:1–4). They rightly teach God's Word, but their intent is not to provide an example of how it works in their own lives but simply to maintain control of other people's lives through the burden of legalistic expectations.

(2) The next section (23:5–7) warns about public displays of piety that misrepresent God's authority. The teachers of the law and the Pharisees rightly attempt to incorporate in their lives patterns of godliness, but they are wrongly drawing attention to themselves. Therefore, the patterns are external and manipulated to be seen as godly, but God is not involved in the process. Jesus' leaders must be careful of self-promotion at the expense of promoting God's authority. This kind of leader has not developed personal righteousness and has not earned respect as a leader but has manipulated the religious system to obtain respect.

(3) The final warnings are directed toward those who wear titles that usurp God's authority (23:8–10). The teachers of the law and the Pharisees have rightly studied carefully to know Scripture to become rabbis, they have rightly become trusted caregivers to whom people can turn for the strength of a father, and they have rightly given themselves to provide guidance for

the community as leaders. But when they elevate themselves by accruing these titles, they usurp God's authority.

**Woes for leaders.** The second section of this collection addressed to leaders is composed of seven woes and a final invective (23:13–39). (1) The first woe focuses on the personal and party failure of these leaders to recognize Jesus as the Messiah, which has led to a faulty leadership example that is drawing the people away from life in the kingdom of God.

(2) The second woe condemns the zeal of the teachers of the law and Pharisees to win converts to their way of thinking, not God's. By elevating their oral traditions to equal authority with Scripture, they are actually making converts of hell when people are converted to their way of thinking, because they are in error and are held captive by the legal system.

(3) The next woe addresses the oaths that the teachers of the law and Pharisees make. Jesus condemns them for playing games with God, either to get out of one's commitment or to trump a prior commitment. They supposedly use Scripture as a validation of their oath, but this is Scripture-twisting to get what one wants.

(4) The fourth woe condemns these religious leaders for majoring on minor issues, which prevents them from accomplishing God's work in this world. Moreover, their example leads the people into the same kind of burdensome preoccupation with the letter of the law.

(5) In the fifth woe Jesus censures these leaders for their failure to examine their motives of greed and self-indulgence. When motives go unexamined and are sinful, they produce self-absorbed and manipulative ministries.

(6) The sixth woe demonstrates that the religious leaders have created a superficial identity that is man-made. It masks a heart contaminated with hypocrisy and wickedness. The creation of this religious facade hopes to gain a following for its counterfeit character and calling.

(7) The final woe decries the teachers of the law and Pharisees for promoting a religious establishment that advances their own cause at the expense of God's voice. They perpetuate a religious establishment that kills anyone with God's righteousness and voice.

Jesus leads us to the conclusion that leadership has stricter condemnation ("How will you escape being condemned to hell?" 23:33; cf. James 3:1; 2 Cor. 10–13). Leaders must listen to God's message and be careful when they see themselves stifling every voice with which they disagree. God will avenge those who have lived righteously and have been abused by those who have taken God's authority into their own hands and have quashed all opposition to their own benefit. Be warned—positions of sheer power lead to abuses that manipulate vulnerable people. But God's judgment awaits those who abuse their authority.

**Contemporary Significance**

I BELIEVE THAT we as Christian leaders may be more like the Pharisees than we want to admit. I don't say this in a totally negative way, for the Pharisees had many good things about them: their personal godliness, their commitment to the Scripture, their belief in a coming Messiah and in a resurrection, afterlife, and spirit world, their leadership role in the synagogue, their desire to be separate from the sin of this world. We should all relate to those characteristics.

Nevertheless, one of the most humbling aspects of reading the Gospels (Matthew in particular) is recognizing that many of the criticisms that Jesus lodges against the Pharisees can also be lodged against us. This is especially true of Christian leaders. We have seen how Jesus pointed out many troublesome, indeed sinful, characteristics: pride, public showmanship, one-upmanship, bull-headedness, politicizing of one's position, and, of course, hypocrisy.

John Fischer, the long-time Christian musician and author, recently confessed that he is like the Pharisees. He writes:

> As I have grown to understand the gospel and learn more of God's grace, I have also become conscious of a corresponding struggle with pride and self-righteousness. Like anyone, I want to be well thought of. I am often conscious, as I am even now, of picking my words carefully, like walking through a minefield of impressions, so as to appear honest while stopping short of the naked truth that might implicate me more than I am willing. It is a problem that the Pharisees of Jesus' day sought to overcome by concealing themselves behind a whitewashed religious veneer.[41]

In his book he uses the recovery model somewhat tongue in cheek to help people unmask the intoxication of spiritual pride and prejudice that lures believers away from genuine discipleship to Jesus. The first three steps indicate the direction he takes his readers.

1. We admit that our single most unmitigated pleasure is to judge other people.
2. Have come to believe that our means of obtaining greatness is to make everyone lower than ourselves in our own mind.
3. Realize that we detest mercy being given to those who, unlike us, haven't worked for it and don't deserve it.[42]

---

41. John Fischer, *12 Steps for the Recovering Pharisee (Like Me)* (Minneapolis: Bethany, 2000), 1.
42. In addition to the book, the steps are listed at his website: www.fischtank.com/book/12step.cfm.

Matthew's Gospel is the source from which leaders can derive insight into the errors of the Pharisees as well as help in establishing more consistent leadership qualities. In the Bridging Contexts section, we listed the warnings and woes Jesus pronounced on the teachers of the law and Pharisees in order to learn from their errors. Here we will attempt to derive some positive lessons from those errors. Twelve basic lessons will help us set a positive trajectory for becoming the kinds of leaders Jesus desires.

## Lessons on Leadership from Jesus

| Context | Warnings for Leaders | Positive Lessons for Leaders |
|---|---|---|
| 1st warning | Demands of legalistic performance abuse God's authority | 1. Live by example God's message of grace |
| 2nd warning | Pretentious displays of piety misrepresent God's authority | 2. Earn respect and honor; don't demand them |
| 3rd warning | Exploiting the use of titles usurps God's authority | 3. Wear titles lightly that point to God |
| Jesus' leaders | Pursuit of greatness compromises kingdom equality | 4. Serve God's people to empower them to advance the kingdom |

| Context | Woes for Leaders | Positive Lessons for Leaders |
|---|---|---|
| 1st woe | Failing to recognize Jesus' identity prevents others also | 5. Be a signpost to the doorway to the kingdom |
| 2nd woe | Propagating extremism to entrap converts in error | 6. Make converts to the kingdom, not to yourself |
| 3rd woe | Violating commitments made to God by religious game-playing | 7. Maintain personal accounability |
| 4th woe | Majoring on the minors of religious performance | 8. Major on the majors of the kingdom |
| 5th woe | Failing to restrain impure motives of leadership | 9. Promote motives for leadership-ministry from the inside out |
| 6th woe | Creating fake exterior leadership identities | 10. Develop personal identity as a leader from the inside out |
| 7th woe | Perpetuating godless institutional establishments | 11. Choose carefully the traditions you will represent |
| Finale | Stifling righteous voices of God so that ours is louder | 12. Listen to God's other messengers, because leadership has stricter condemnation |

(1) **Live by example God's message of grace (23:1–4).** Jesus' first warning cautions against abusing the authority of God's Word by demanding legalistic performance from the people. The positive lesson that Jesus' leaders can learn from this is that we need to live out God's message of grace by example. The gospel of the kingdom is grace, not practicing works to gain God's favor. We must demonstrate grace toward those to whom we minister and love and accept them regardless of their performance. We certainly will continue to encourage them toward godliness, but the best way to do so is to provide an example of obedience in our own lives that they can follow. As leaders we must not try to maintain control of other people's lives through the burden of legalistic expectations.

(2) **Earn respect and honor, don't demand them (23:5–7).** The second warning points out that pretentious displays of piety misrepresent God's authority. A general principle of leadership is that respect is earned, not demanded. In the most basic sense, leadership simply means that we know where we are going, we know how to get there, we have the ability, training, and resources to get there, and the people trust us enough to follow us to our destination.

Young and inexperienced leaders posture themselves as if they know what they are doing and then demand the respect and honor of those below them. I saw this clearly in my own life when I was an assistant drill sergeant in the army at age nineteen. I had the technical knowledge and the position, but not the other qualities of a leader. So I postured myself as mean and experienced, trying to demand the respect of my troops. It didn't work. In fact, I lost virtually all respect from the trainees. I had to learn the hard way what it meant to earn their respect.

In Jesus' warnings, we can turn them around to understand how respect and honor are achieved. This has direct relevance to leadership in the church. We must earn respect by the daily, long-term development of our personal godliness, not in artificial and ostentatious displays of piety, but in developing our prayer life, controlling our temper, and maintaining an appropriate demeanor when in front of people. We can also earn respect by taking the less prominent positions, such as going last at church potlucks, sitting with the children at a Christmas celebration, or sharing the pulpit with associates who preach or teach better than us. We can also earn respect by developing a personal transparency that allows people to engage us intimately. It is a temptation to hide behind titles and positions and pretentiously posture as a leader, but your people need to see plain old you—a regular person like them, who is also in process of growing into the image of Christ. Don't demand respect and honor by manipulation.

(3) **Wear titles lightly that point to God (23:8–10).** Jesus also warns against exploiting the use of titles, because doing so usurps God's authority.

The warning is not so simple as to suggest that titles are always inappropriate. Rather, the warning is directed against three issues that can stifle our discipleship to Jesus. (*a*) *Rabbi*. In our desire to teach and provide others with insights into the Word of God, we should be careful to avoid *academic arrogance*. We should be careful never to supplant Jesus as the Teacher, who will guide his disciples into all truth through the Spirit-guided Word of God (cf. John 16:13, 14). (*b*) *Father*. In our desire to protect and nurture others, we should be careful to avoid *religious elitism*. All Jesus' disciples are his brothers and sisters, and we should never elevate ourselves to where we supplant our heavenly Father. (*c*) *Master*. In our desire to guide and lead others into the fullness of discipleship, we should be careful to avoid *authoritarian dominance*. Jesus is the Master, the one who has all authority, who is Lord and Head of the church.

The positive side is that we should wear lightly any titles we may have, for each points to some aspect of God's relationship with his people. The way to exercise this form of leadership is to understand the responsibilities of a title, to help the people respect the office that lies behind a title, but not to command authority by a title that usurps God's authority. It is easy to be known by who we are, by what we know, or by the degrees we have. But this produces arrogance and cockiness. We must never forget Paul's statement that "knowledge puffs up, but love builds up" (1 Cor. 8:1). Don't use your titles or degrees or education to manipulate people into following you. Use it to bless them so that they can be drawn into an even more intimate relationship with Jesus. Wear your titles lightly by allowing them to make you wiser, more understanding, and more effective as a servant of Christ.

**(4) Serve God's people to empower them to advance the kingdom of God (23:11–12).** In concluding the three warnings, Jesus gives the main principle of what it means to be the new kind of leader for his kingdom program—servanthood. This type of leadership means empowering others to do God's will. For those that have been placed in positions of prominence, such as a teacher, minister, or executive, the goal of each position is to advance the kingdom; the means is to give yourself to all so that they can best accomplish God's calling on their lives. Those who promote themselves to positions of authority in order to get acclaim and honor will find that position taken away and will be set aside from service in the kingdom. Those who care only to serve God will find themselves elevated to the level of equality as brothers and sisters of Jesus, with no prominence given to anyone but him.

**(5) Be a signpost to the doorway to the kingdom (23:13).** The first woe chides the religious leaders for failing to recognize Jesus' identity as the Messiah. What we teach and believe has tremendous influence in the lives of those who look up to our leadership position. The fifth principle for leaders is that in all that we say and do, we are to be a signpost to the doorway to the kingdom. We are to provide a personal example of the teaching concerning the reality of life lived in the power of the presence of Jesus through the indwelling Spirit of God.

(6) **Make converts to the kingdom, not to yourself (23:15).** The second woe blasts the religious leaders for propagating their extremist sectarian views to convert others to their way of thinking and living, but this entraps their converts in error, which ultimately will result in eternal punishment. This is the tragic result of those who are entrapped in a cult.

Leaders within the kingdom of heaven are to point people only to Jesus, not our own stuff—we are to make converts to the kingdom, not to ourselves. We must take God's calling on our lives seriously, for people's responses to the gospel we proclaim have eternal consequences. But we are not to take ourselves too seriously in the process. If we overstep our bounds, God will use others. Be absolutely sure to maintain a grip on the truth by sticking as close to Scripture as possible. Our idiosyncratic views or pet theological projects can lead people to error and even to judgment. We must passionately pursue converts to life in the kingdom of God, not to ourselves.

(7) **Maintain personal accountability (23:16–22).** The third woe chides the teachers of the law and the Pharisees for violating commitments made to God by religious game-playing. External forms of accountability can be helpful for staying true to our relationship with Jesus, whether they are small groups, one-on-one checkups, journals, and so on. But we can play games with each of these by lying, shading the truth, or simply hiding our thoughts and actions. It is important for leaders to maintain personal accountability by weaning ourselves from artificially imposed ways of remaining accountable to God. The most straightforward approach is the transparency of a life lived in the intimacy of a relationship with Jesus.

(8) **Major on the majors of the kingdom (23:23–24).** Jesus pronounces the fourth woe on the religious leaders because they are majoring on the minor issues of religious performance, which prevents them from accomplishing the work of God in this world. The positive principle is crucial. Jesus' leaders are to major on the major facets of the kingdom, not on the secondary points of religious performance. Like the first warning, it is easy to get caught up in minor issues that lead to legalistic demands and expectations. To understand what are the really important concerns—doctrinally, ecclesiastically, relationally—is to give our time and energies to what will really count for eternity.

(9) **Promote motives for leadership-ministry from the inside out (23:25–26).** The fifth woe reveals how the religious leaders have failed to examine

and amend their greedy and self-indulgent motives in ministry, which produces self-absorbed and manipulative ministries. Leadership can be highly self-centered and self-serving. Jesus calls all of his leaders to evaluate why we do what we do so that we promote his kingdom, not our own interests. It's easy to put on a show. Run a glitzy worship service and people are convinced that they have really worshiped. But leaders can be tempted to draw attention to themselves instead of to God. This illustrates the importance of team ministries that are honest and transparent, where others call us on our self-indulgent motives and help us promote pure motives.

(10) **Develop personal identity as a leader from the inside out (23:27− 28).** The sixth woe is similar to the fifth, except with a focus not on self-serving motives but on creating exterior leadership identities that are phony. The religious leaders have bought into the motto that "image is everything." Create a beautiful exterior, whitewash old faults, and people will never know what they are really like. How a leader postures himself or herself will often get results, which sadly underscores that the content of one's ministry or the depth of character does not matter.

Jesus calls his leaders to develop personal identity from the inside out. Instead of a superficial, external personal identity that is man-made, we must start with a deep, inner, new identity in Christ that is God-made. When considering his eternal future, the apostle Paul muses, "Now I know in part; then I shall know fully, even as I am fully known" (1 Cor. 13:12). As we open ourselves up to be known by God, we embark on one of the most important aspects of our growth as leaders: to know ourselves as God knows us. Opening up to God enables him to help us understand ourselves more accurately. Find out who you are. What makes you tick the way you do? What are your problems? Our continuing transformation will occur as we know ourselves as God knows us. Let your self-worth grow out of who you are in Christ, not what you do for him.

(11) **Choose carefully the traditions you will represent (23:29−32).** Jesus' seventh woe reproaches the religious leaders for perpetuating godless establishments. They are like murderers throughout Israel's history that put to death the prophets, even though they built monuments to them. Jesus' leaders must choose carefully the traditions we represent. There are many voices out there, but our calling is to listen to the voice of God and those who represent him.

(12) **Listen to God's other messengers, because leadership has stricter condemnation (23:33−36).** Jesus' final invective against the religious leadership calls them into accountability, which may result in their being condemned to hell. That is a chilling concept. Those who are the most privileged to lead God's people have the stricter condemnation. This recalls for us as

leaders James's equally chilling warning: "Not many of you should presume to be teachers, my brothers, because you know that we who teach will be judged more strictly" (James 3:1).

We as leaders must listen to God's message through his other messengers and be careful when we see ourselves stifling every voice with which we disagree. Jesus rebukes the religious leaders because they are muffling God's righteous voice so that their own can be heard. God will avenge those who have lived righteously and have been abused by powerful leaders. There are other people out there who speak for God; we are not the only ones. We must examine those voices, but we will be wiser, more balanced, and better equipped when we learn from others and join with them in advancing the kingdom of God.

# Matthew 24:1–35

〰

JESUS LEFT THE temple and was walking away when his disciples came up to him to call his attention to its buildings. 2"Do you see all these things?" he asked. "I tell you the truth, not one stone here will be left on another; every one will be thrown down."

3As Jesus was sitting on the Mount of Olives, the disciples came to him privately. "Tell us," they said, "when will this happen, and what will be the sign of your coming and of the end of the age?"

4Jesus answered: "Watch out that no one deceives you. 5For many will come in my name, claiming, 'I am the Christ, ' and will deceive many. 6You will hear of wars and rumors of wars, but see to it that you are not alarmed. Such things must happen, but the end is still to come. 7Nation will rise against nation, and kingdom against kingdom. There will be famines and earthquakes in various places. 8All these are the beginning of birth pains.

9"Then you will be handed over to be persecuted and put to death, and you will be hated by all nations because of me. 10At that time many will turn away from the faith and will betray and hate each other, 11and many false prophets will appear and deceive many people. 12Because of the increase of wickedness, the love of most will grow cold, 13but he who stands firm to the end will be saved. 14And this gospel of the kingdom will be preached in the whole world as a testimony to all nations, and then the end will come.

15"So when you see standing in the holy place 'the abomination that causes desolation,' spoken of through the prophet Daniel—let the reader understand—16then let those who are in Judea flee to the mountains. 17Let no one on the roof of his house go down to take anything out of the house. 18Let no one in the field go back to get his cloak. 19How dreadful it will be in those days for pregnant women and nursing mothers! 20Pray that your flight will not take place in winter or on the Sabbath. 21For then there will be great distress, unequaled from the beginning of the world until now—and never to be equaled again. 22If those days had not been cut short, no one would survive, but for the sake of the elect those days will be shortened. 23At that time if anyone says to you, 'Look, here is the Christ!' or, 'There he is!' do not believe it. ²⁴For false Christs and false prophets will appear and perform great signs and miracles to deceive even the elect—if that were possible. ²⁵See, I have told you ahead of time.

²⁶"So if anyone tells you, 'There he is, out in the desert,' do not go out; or, 'Here he is, in the inner rooms,' do not believe it. ²⁷For as lightning that comes from the east is visible even in the west, so will be the coming of the Son of Man. ²⁸Wherever there is a carcass, there the vultures will gather.

²⁹"Immediately after the distress of those days

> "'the sun will be darkened,
>     and the moon will not give its light;
> the stars will fall from the sky,
>     and the heavenly bodies will be shaken.'

³⁰"At that time the sign of the Son of Man will appear in the sky, and all the nations of the earth will mourn. They will see the Son of Man coming on the clouds of the sky, with power and great glory. ³¹And he will send his angels with a loud trumpet call, and they will gather his elect from the four winds, from one end of the heavens to the other.

³²"Now learn this lesson from the fig tree: As soon as its twigs get tender and its leaves come out, you know that summer is near. ³³Even so, when you see all these things, you know that it is near, right at the door. ³⁴I tell you the truth, this generation will certainly not pass away until all these things have happened. ³⁵Heaven and earth will pass away, but my words will never pass away.

**Original Meaning**

THE EVENTS OF this Holy Week continue to unfold in ways that must have astounded Jesus' disciples. Jesus entered Jerusalem on Sunday with what seemed to be triumphant acclaim from the crowds as the arriving Messiah (21:1–11). But after disrupting the commercial activities in the temple on Monday, things took an ominous turn (21:12–17). The entire Tuesday morning Jesus engaged in endless controversies and debates (21:23–22:46), which were followed by a shocking diatribe in which Jesus gave public warning to the crowds and his disciples about the teachers of the law and the Pharisees. He then turned to them directly with agonizing pronouncements of woe (23:1–39). Now his disciples can see that the week in

Jerusalem will be dangerous, because the religious leaders in Jerusalem are out to get Jesus to try and silence him.

So Jesus urgently turns his attention to his disciples. He can perceive the coming crisis of his arrest, so he must prepare his followers for the events that await them. For the fifth and final time in Matthew's Gospel, he directs a major discourse to the disciples that will comprise part of what all new disciples will be taught to obey (28:20). This discourse is prophecy, to prepare his disciples both for the catastrophic events of judgment that will befall the nation with the destruction of the temple and for the interval before his return in glory and triumph.

## The Setting of the Olivet Discourse (24:1–3)

APPARENTLY LATE TUESDAY afternoon after the theological debates with the religious leaders, Jesus and the disciples leave the temple and the city to make their way back to Bethany, where they stay each evening (cf. 21:17). The road from Jerusalem to Bethany traverses the Mount of Olives, giving a spectacular view of the temple behind and below them. The disciples look back over the city and point out the beautiful buildings of the temple to Jesus (24:1). According to Mark 13:1, they exclaim, "Look, Teacher? What massive stones? What magnificent buildings!"

In response to these exclamations over the beauty and magnificence of the temple, Jesus paints a dark picture of its future: "I tell you the truth, not one stone here will be left on another; every one will be thrown down." The last invective Jesus addressed to the Pharisees included a warning to the entire generation and a lament over Jerusalem and its temple (cf. 23:36–38). This must have startled the disciples, because Jerusalem was the holy city and the rebuilt temple was the pride of the nation. Jesus' statement here also must have baffled the disciples, since the temple was almost completely rebuilt by this time (cf. John 2:20).[1] Now Jesus is prophesying its destruction (which did occur in A.D. 70).

Jesus sits on the Mount of Olives, perhaps pondering his prophetic forecast, when his disciples approach him to ask his private understanding of the incredible events to which he has just alluded (24:3). Jesus' reply initiates an extended discourse forecasting the events that will stretch on down the course of history. This is the fifth and final major discourse recorded in this Gospel. As with the other discourses, Jesus directs it to his disciples and it is part of the material that new disciples must be taught to obey until his return (28:20). Here the material is apocalyptic revelation, whereas the earlier discourses included teaching (chs. 5–7), a missionary mandate (chs. 10), para-

---

1. For an overview, see Michael O. Wise, "Temple," *DJG*, 811–17.

bles (ch. 13), and sayings on the community life of the church (ch. 18). Since he gave this discourse while sitting on the Mount of Olives, the traditional name is the Olivet Discourse. All three Synoptic Gospels contain this prophecy, though Matthew gives the fullest description.

The content of the discourse is in response to the disciples' questions: "'Tell us,' they said, 'when will this happen, and what will be the sign of your coming and of the end of the age?'" The disciples ask two questions here: (1) "When will all these things be?" (2) "What will be the sign of your coming and the end of the age?" That is, this second question probes both Jesus' coming and the end of the age as descriptions of one event.[2] This is indicated in Greek by one article that governs both the phrase "sign of your coming" and the phrase "end of the age."[3]

Jesus' answer to the first question comes most directly in Luke's account (Luke 21:20; cf. Matt. 24:15), although he alludes to the abandonment of Jerusalem's temple in that generation in the conclusion to the woes on the religious leadership of Israel (Matt. 23:34). But the way in which the disciples ask both questions may indicate that to them, the destruction of the temple and the Parousia are not separated, which clues us to Jesus' reply.

In this discourse we have historical and eschatological references, with Jesus prophesying both the fall of Jerusalem and his own Parousia. Luke focuses on historical details of the destruction of the temple and the fall of Jerusalem, events that happened in A.D. 70 (Luke 21:20–24), while Matthew and Mark give details that are difficult to see completely fulfilled with the first-century events and thus point to a future fulfillment (cf. Matt. 24:15–22; Mark 13:14–20). Jesus does allude to the destruction of the temple in A.D. 70, but he uses these events to foreshadow end-time events.

George Ladd suggests that the historical and eschatological elements are purposely intertwined under a kind of "prophetic foreshortening." The near event, the destruction of Jerusalem, serves as a symbol for the far event.[4]

---

2. Cf. France, *Matthew*, 337; Gundry, *Matthew*, 476; Hagner, *Matthew*, 2:688; Ladd, *New Testament Theology*, 196–98; Stanley D. Toussaint, *Behold the King: A Study of Matthew* (Portland: Multnomah, 1981), 268–69.

3. For discussion of the "Granville Sharp Rule" as it concerns the "article-substantive-καί-substantive" (TSKS) construction, see Wallace, *Greek Grammar*, 270–90. He lists Matthew 24:3 as an ambiguous impersonal TSKS construction that is exegetically and theologically significant (Wallace, *Greek Grammar*, 288 n. 87).

4. Ladd, *Theology of the New Testament*, 198. Cf. also Hagner, *Matthew*, 2:688; Mounce, *Matthew*, 228–30. Cranfield suggests that in Jesus' own view the historical and the eschatological are mingled, and that the final eschatological event is seen through the "transparency" of the immediate historical incident (Cranfield, *Mark*, 390–94). For an attempt to balance the two, see David L. Turner, "The Structure and Sequence of Matthew 24:1–41: Interaction with Evangelical Treatments," *GTJ* 10/1 (Spring 1989): 3–27.

Jesus intertwines his answer to both of the disciples' questions concerning the destruction of Jerusalem and the Parousia. The destruction of the temple answers the questions of Jesus' disciples, but he sees beyond that day to the entire age and his coming in power and glory at the end of the age.[5]

We may see, then, three basic parts to Jesus' discourse. (1) Part one describes events, generally chronological, prior to the coming of Jesus (24:4–31). (a) He first offers a general description of events that will transpire throughout the entire age (24:4–14), with worldwide evangelistic activity consummating the age; (b) then he describes the "great tribulation" (24:15–28), which intertwines prophecy of the destruction of the temple in A.D. 70 and the final desolation at the end of the age; (c) then he describes the coming of the Son of Man during the time of Tribulation (24:29–31); (d) he concludes the first part of the discourse with a general principle of nearness concerning the destruction and Parousia (24:32–35).

(2) Part two gives lessons on watching, waiting, and being prepared for the coming of Jesus (24:32–25:30). (a) Jesus begins the lessons by declaring why his disciples are to watch, namely, that the time of his coming is unknown (24:36-41); (b) he then gives a general warning to "watch" (24:42–44), because the coming is at an unknown hour, and he follows that with three parables to instruct his disciples how they are to await his unknown time of coming (24:45–51; 25:1–13; 25:14–30).

(3) Part three concludes the discourse with a warning of judgment and a promise of reward at the time of his coming (25:31–46).

## The Beginning of Birth Pains (24:4–14)

IN THE FIRST section of the Olivet Discourse, Jesus gives a preview of general conditions on the earth that in some sense characterize the entire age before the coming of the Lord. The Twelve have been warned of some of this impending persecution and suffering they will endure on their future worldwide missionary endeavor (cf. 10:16–23), but here it is given in a discourse that anticipates suffering that will be common to all disciples as they await the return of Jesus and the end of this age.

**Sufferings throughout the world (24:4–8).** The discourse begins with a stern admonition: "Watch out that no one deceives you." Many events may deceive the disciples into thinking that the end of the age has arrived. Instead, all of these events are general characteristics of this present age of "birth pains." Jesus explicitly outlines a number of conditions that must not be seen as indicators of the end of the age.

---

5. For further discussion see below in Bridging Contexts.

*False messiahs (24:4–5).* He first warns, "Many will come in my name, claiming, 'I am the Christ,' and will deceive many." Prophetic figures and messianic deliverers had long attempted to incite revolution against occupying forces in the Second Temple period, and they continued into the years after the foundation of the church. The second-century Jewish rebel Simon Bar Kokhba (meaning "son of a star") was so named by Rabbi Akiba, proclaiming him the Messiah on the basis of the star from Jacob in Numbers 24:17. Later rabbis rejected this identification and referred to him as Bar Kosiba (lit., "son of a lie").[6] Throughout the ages, many have attempted to claim messianic identity. Jesus' disciples must not be deceived.

*Wars and calamities (24:6–7).* Jesus next warns that wars and rumors of wars will occur repeatedly throughout this age, with nations and kingdoms rising against each other. But he warns: "See to it that you are not alarmed. Such things must happen, but the end is still to come." The end is not near even though calamities may seem to indicate that it is. The Old Testament linked wars, cosmic battles, famines, earthquakes, and other catastrophic events with the end of the age, as did the apocalyptic vision of 2 Esdras 9:1–6 (note too the catastrophic events recorded in Revelation). But Jesus emphasizes that these cataclysmic activities will be a regular part of the suffering of this life until the return of Jesus begins the redemption of all creation.

*Birth pains (24:8).* These are just "the beginning of birth pains." "Birth pains" is a common metaphor from the Old Testament prophets to depict terrible human suffering generally (Isa. 13:8; 21:3; 42:14; Jer. 30:7–10; Hos. 13:13), but also the suffering that Israel specifically will endure prior to her deliverance (Isa. 26:17–19; 66:7–11; Jer. 22:23; Mic. 4:9–10). The imagery points to an expected time of suffering that will characterize the period prior to the messianic age. Although the inauguration of the kingdom of heaven brings redemption to its citizens, the whole world continues to experience birth pains as it awaits final redemption, as do even believers who have the first-fruits of the Spirit (cf. Rom. 8:22–23).

We may think that the imagery of "birth pains" contradicts Jesus' statement that the time of his coming is unknown (24:36), since such pains presage the imminent birth of a baby. But the metaphor in "birth pains" is used to highlight a different facet of the prenatal process, that the onset of childbirth is not steady but is a repeated phenomenon, coming in waves over and over again.[7] The baby does not come on the first pang, but once the pains begin, all know that the inexorable process has commenced. We do not know if the

---

6. "Bar Kosiba, Simon," *DJBP*, 77–78.

7. Conrad Gempf, "The Imagery of Birth Pangs in the New Testament," *TynBul* 45 (1994): 119–35; esp. 132–34.

baby will come on the fifth, the fifteenth, the fiftieth, or the five hundredth. Periods of wars and rumors of wars, tragic earthquakes, and famines wash over the landscape of history in repeated pains. Each reminds us that the end is coming, but no one knows when until the Son of Man appears. Throughout the labor we must remain on guard.

Some will try to mislead believers that these pains *are* the end. But Jesus warns his disciples not to be deceived. The first appearance, especially the tragedies they will witness in Jerusalem in A.D. 70, are the *beginning* of birth pains, but they will continue to recur and will characterize the entire age. The metaphor indicates the inescapability of the sequence of events once the process begins and also the repetitive nature of the waves of pain until the end.

**Sufferings of Jesus' disciples (24:9—13).** The adverb "then" (*tote*) occurs regularly in Matthew, at times to indicate chronological sequence (e.g., 2:7; 4:5, 17), and at other times only as a loose connector (e.g., 3:15; 4:11). Likewise in this chapter *tote* occurs in some cases as a loose connector (e.g., 24:10, 23), in other cases with a strong sense of temporal sequence (24:14, 16, 30). Some see chronological sequence in 24:9, indicating that the events of 24:9—14 will presage the Parousia.[8] Rather, a special emphasis of *tote* signals a change of focus.[9] Jesus switches from prophesying the suffering that the world will experience throughout this age (24:4—8) to predicting suffering that his disciples will encounter because they are his followers (24:9—13).[10]

*Persecution (24:9—11).* Reminiscent of his Mission Discourse that prepared his disciples for their responsibilities to carry the gospel of the kingdom throughout this age (ch. 10), Jesus warns them that they will encounter persecution: "Then you will be handed over to be persecuted and put to death and you will be hated by all nations because of me" (cf. 10:16—24). The disciples will be handed over to *thlipsis* ("persecution, distress, tribulation"), a word that occurs four·times in Matthew, three of which are found in this chapter (13:21; 24:9, 21, 29). In 24:21, 29, *thlipsis* points to a specific future period of unparalleled "distress" (NIV) or "tribulation" (NASB); here, as in 13:21, the term indicates a general kind of trouble or persecution. Jesus' disciples will feel the wrath and alienation from humanity for following him and proclaiming his message.

---

8. Some see a shift of increased persecution of the church signaled in 24:9 just prior to the Parousia; e.g., Robert H. Gundry, *The Church and the Tribulation* (Grand Rapids: Zondervan, 1973), 49; Brent Kinman, *History, Design and the End of Time: God's Plan for the World* (Nashville: Broadman & Holman, 2000), 80.

9. E.g., Blomberg, *Matthew*, 354—55; Carson, "Matthew," 498; Davies and Allison, *Matthew*, 3:341; Hagner, *Matthew*, 2:694.

10. France, *Matthew*, 338.

The phrase "because of me" is literally "because of my name" and is an important Christological expression[11] (cf. 5:11; 24:9) that harks back to the Old Testament significance of God's name as the representation of his person as being the sole focus of Israel's worship and allegiance (e.g., Ex. 3:15; 6:3; 9:16; 20:7). Jesus' disciples will have the privilege of carrying his name, but it also brings with it suffering, because the antagonism and hatred that is directed to him will naturally fall on his followers.[12]

*Betrayal (24:10).* Because of persecution, the faith of Jesus' followers will be tested. "Many will turn away from the faith and will betray and hate each other." It is not easy to endure persecution, and those who only hold on to Jesus because of their own comfort will find it easier to turn away from him and avoid the suffering. They not only will seek their own escape from suffering, but they will become enemies of Jesus and turn against his followers, their former fellow disciples. They will betray them to the persecutors, and the love that had characterized the relationship between them (5:43–47; 22:34–40) will be turned to hate as they utterly reject Jesus. This apostasy is the evidence that they never were true disciples.

*Deception (24:11).* Not only will false messiahs try to deceive the world (24:5), false prophets will surface within the community to try to deceive Jesus' disciples. The apostle John warns likewise of deceptive voices both within the church and in the world (1 John 2:18–27; 4:1–6), who are to be tested according to the criterion of their acknowledgment of Jesus as the incarnate Messiah (1 John 2:22; 4:2–3). This criterion will be employed throughout this age to test cults and false theology, but sadly, these false prophets will deceive many.

*Wickedness and lovelessness (24:12).* All of the preceding phenomena are described as the increase of wickedness, which points to the spiritual death of those who fall away and those who have attempted to deceive the community. The chief characteristic of spiritual death is that it causes love to grow cold. Jesus emphasized throughout his ministry that love is not primarily an emotion but is an active commitment to God and to others to promote God's will (cf. 5:43–47). Those who are spiritually dead cannot produce this kind of love, which reemphasizes that these apostates never knew God at all. The NIV expression "most" (gen. pl. of *polloi*), along with the other uses of *polloi* in this chapter that are rendered "many" (24:5, 10–11),[13] indicates that a large percentage of the community will apostatize.[14] This is a somber picture

---

11. Hagner, *Matthew*, 1:278.
12. Cf. John 15:21; 2 Tim. 3:12; 1 Peter 4:13–14.
13. Blomberg, *Matthew*, 355; Hagner, *Matthew*, 2:695.
14. The articular *ton pollon* can indicate majority, as in the NIV rendering; cf. *BDAG*, 849; Davies and Allison, *Matthew*, 3:343 n. 98; France, *Matthew*, 338.

of the community of disciples being impacted by apostasy. But it is not unlike Jesus' statements elsewhere when he emphasizes that the gate and way to life are narrow, with only a few finding it (7:13–14).

*Standing firm (24:13).* Along with the somber picture of apostasy Jesus gives a critical promise: "But he who stands firm to the end will be saved." Active resistance may be included in standing firm, but much more in view is the enduring fortitude of the disciples under any circumstance, including the most hateful persecution. The identical expression occurred in the Mission Discourse, where Jesus gave great assurance that in spite of the increase in persecution, the hatred of humanity would not overcome his missionary disciples (10:22). Here Jesus also looks to the promise that the disciple who endures to the end—that is, the end of the persecution with the coming of the Son of Man (10:23) or the end of a person's life—will be saved.

"Saved" does not speak of rescue from physical death, because many true disciples have experienced martyrdom (cf. also 24:21–22). Instead, Jesus gives both a concrete promise and a cautionary reminder. His promise is that the one who remains committed to his name until the end will not be consumed by the persecution, but will experience the full blessing and peace of kingdom's salvation with his arrival. But Jesus likewise reminds them that a disciple's real commitment to him is demonstrated in whether he or she remains steadfast. Jesus is faithful to provide the resources to withstand whatever difficulties may come, because the same Spirit who was on Jesus in his earthly ministry (12:18) will speak through the disciples when they are under pressure and persecution (10:19–20) and will provide the strength necessary to endure the persecution to the end. Jesus himself will be with them to the end of the age (28:20).

**Preaching the gospel to all nations (24:14).** Jesus cautioned the disciples against false assumptions about what will signal the end (24:6, 8); now he gives an explicit indicator of the activity that must be accomplished before the end of this age: "And this gospel of the kingdom will be preached in the whole world as a testimony to all nations, and then the end will come." The expression "gospel of the kingdom" is unique to Matthew (cf. 4:23; 9:35), combining the good news of salvation with the arrival of the kingdom of God. This is testimony or a witness to the reality of God's presence in the ministry of Jesus and his followers (cf. 8:4; 10:18). Although the increase of events in 24:9–13 indicates that the Parousia is near, the only explicit condition to be met is the proclamation of the gospel to all the nations. After that proclamation has occurred, the end will come.

During Jesus' earthly ministry, the disciples' mission was restricted to Israel (cf. 10:5–7) in fulfillment of the Davidic covenant. The future mission shifts to all the nations, which will fulfill the Abrahamic covenant, though it will include a continued outreach to Israel (see comments on 10:23; 28:19).[15] This future mission will be inaugurated with the risen Jesus' "Great Commission" (28:16–20), but it is prophesied both here in the Olivet Discourse and earlier in the Missionary Discourse (10:16–23).

This worldwide proclamation was realized in part during the first century with the preaching of Paul throughout the then-known world (e.g., Rom. 15:19), which contributed to the possibility of the imminence of Jesus' return.[16] But the priority of worldwide missionary activity is demanded by recognizing that the final fulfillment of Jesus' statement in 24:14 awaits the eschatological arrival of the events of great tribulation, to which he now turns. Jesus' disciples are to give themselves urgently to the task of preaching the gospel of the kingdom throughout this present age, because we cannot fully discern when it has finally reached into all nations.[17] Each new generation of nations does bring with it a new mission field. But once this proclamation has been fulfilled, the beginning of the time of tribulation on the earth will begin.

### Description of "Great Tribulation" (24:15–28)

THE COMBINATION OF the temporal ("when") and inferential ("so, therefore") conjunctions beginning 24:15 signals a major temporal shift: "So when you see standing in the holy place 'the abomination that causes desolation'...." Moving from general characteristics of this age until his return, Jesus now points to an event prophesied in Daniel 9:27, "the abomination that causes desolation." Some contend that at this point Jesus focuses exclusively on the destruction of the temple in A.D. 70,[18] while a wide spectrum of scholars hold that these events also presage a future time of eschatological defilement and destruction.[19] The latter view is preferred here, especially when it is compared with Paul's prediction of the eschatological man of lawlessness (2 Thess. 2:1–12) and with John's vision of the beast in Revelation 13:11–18, which are remarkably similar to Jesus' prophecy. Together they indicate some "evil, deified figure such as the AntiChrist."[20]

If one looks only at the account in Luke 21:20–24, the focus is apparently on the fall of Jerusalem. But when we look at Matthew 24:15–22 and Mark 13:14–20, with the mention of the "the abomination that causes desolation"

15. Cf. Wayne A. Brindle, "'To the Jew First'," 221–33.
16. E.g., Blomberg, *Matthew*, 356–57.
17. E.g., Davies and Allison, *Matthew*, 3:344; Morris, *Matthew*, 602.
18. E.g., France, *Matthew*, 340–41; Blomberg, *Matthew*, 357–59.
19. E.g., Davies and Allison, *Matthew*, 3:344; Gundry, *Matthew*, 485; Ladd, *Theology of the New Testament*, 675–76.
20. Gundry, *Matthew*, 482.

(notice that Luke only speaks of the desolation of Jerusalem), we can see that the focus shifts to something that did not occur at the destruction of Jerusalem in A.D. 70. This reference shifts the focus to activities at the end of the age. Jesus is thus giving a mixture of prophetic elements that speak both to his generation and to the future.

**The abomination that causes desolation (24:15).** The prophecy in Daniel refers to a period of "seven," during which in the middle of the "seven" a ruler will set up "an abomination that causes desolation" (Dan. 9:27 NIV; cf. also 8:13; 11:31; 12:11). During the days of the Maccabees, the same expression was used to describe the sacrilege of Antiochus IV Epiphanes, the Seleucid king who decreed that an altar to Olympian Zeus and perhaps also a statue of himself be erected in the temple on 15 Chislev, 167 B.C. (1 Macc. 1:54; cf. 2 Macc. 6:2). Antiochus further decreed that the Sabbath and other festal observances were to be profaned, that circumcision was to be abolished, and that swine and other unclean animals were to be sacrificed in the temple (cf. 1 Macc. 1:41–50). This was one of the lowest points of Jewish history.

But the Daniel references were also brought to the mind of the ancients in A.D. 26, when Pontius Pilate arrived as prefect to govern Judea and introduced to Jerusalem military standards bearing idolatrous symbols of the emperor.[21] Others believed Daniel's prophecy was being fulfilled when Emperor Gaius (Caligula) ordered that a gigantic statue of himself be set up in the temple in Jerusalem, although he was dissuaded by King Herod Agrippa I and died in A.D. 41 before the order could be carried out.[22]

But rather than having been completely realized in the activities of Antiochus IV Epiphanes or at any other time, Jesus quotes Daniel directly to clarify that the fulfillment of the "abomination that causes desolation" is yet future.[23] Paul harks back to Jesus' and Daniel's prophecy as he gives his own prophetic statement of the Antichrist who is yet to come (2 Thess. 2:3–4), which prefigures the Antichrist (the first beast), who will be set up by the false prophet (the second beast) as a god in the temple (Rev. 13:11–18).

Both Matthew and Mark include the phrase "let the reader understand" (cf. Mark 13:14). This is an aside intended to get the reader of Daniel to see that in Jesus' words, one will find the real fulfillment of the prophecy. With the onset of the abomination that causes desolation as spoken of by Daniel, the period of "great distress" begins (Matt. 24:21). This desolating sacrilege

---

21. See Josephus, *Ant.* 55–59; for discussion see Paul Barnett, *Jesus and the Rise of Early Christianity: A History of New Testament Times* (Downers Grove, Ill.: InterVarsity Press, 1999), 144–48.

22. Cf. Philo, *Legatio ad Gaium* 200–203; Josephus, *Ant.* 257–309; see F. F. Bruce, *New Testament History* (New York: Doubleday, 1969), 253–57.

23. For discussion of related issues, see Gleason L. Archer Jr., "Daniel," *EBC* (Grand Rapids: Zondervan, 1985), 7:111–21.

is the predominant event of this period of tribulation, which corresponds to Daniel's period of "seven," during which in the middle of the "seven" a ruler will set up "an abomination that causes desolation" (Dan. 9:27 NIV). When we look at Daniel (esp. 9:25–27) and the events of Revelation (see the number of days of 1,260 in Rev. 12:6, which equals three and a half years), this marks the second half of the seven years of tribulation, the time of "great distress [tribulation]." Apparently the first three and a half years was a time of relative peace and quiet.

As discussed in the introduction to this discourse, Jesus' prophecy is an answer to both of the disciples' questions. He predicts the destruction of Jerusalem and the temple in A.D. 70, but he looks beyond to a future time when another abomination that causes desolation will arise in Jerusalem to lead astray God's people and bring destruction on all who resist him.[24]

**Flight of believers (24:16–20).** In a series of five warnings taken from everyday life in Israel, Jesus accentuates the immediacy of danger that will accompany the fulfillment of the arrival of the abomination that causes desolation. (1) "Let those who are in Judea flee to the mountains." When the abomination occurs, those who have heeded the prophecies of Jesus will know that immediate and utter destruction is coming on Jerusalem and many will die, so they are to flee with great haste. The Christian historian Eusebius reported that Jesus' warning to flee to the mountains was fulfilled during the Jewish revolt when Christians fled to Pella.[25] But Jesus' warning is more general, since the mountains have always been a place of refuge for those beleaguered by invading armies, so Christians must find refuge there at this future time of great danger.

(2) "Let no one on the roof of his house go down to take anything out of the house." The impending destruction means that there will be no time to gather provisions in the home. The flat rooftops on many homes in Israel were a place to find a cool breeze in the evening and were considered part of the living quarters.

(3) "Let no one in the field go back to get his cloak." The outer coat was an essential garment for traveling, often used as a blanket when sleeping outdoors, and only those in the greatest hurry would think of leaving it behind.

(4) "How dreadful it will be in those days for pregnant women and nursing mothers!" The danger of travel in this perilous time is greatest for those most at risk, especially pregnant mothers and their infants. Jesus describes

---

24. It is interesting to note that there is an active movement within Judaism in Israel to rebuild the temple, which would be the Third Temple (see, e.g., the following website: *www.templeinstitute.org*).

25. Eusebius, *Eccl. Hist.* 3.5.3.

their fate with a cry of "woe," emphasizing that those who are most vulnerable and who normally rely on the help of others will suffer the most.

(5) The final warning states bluntly, "Pray that your flight may not be in winter or on a Sabbath." Flight in winter, when roads are washed out and rivers are swollen, presents even more difficulty for those fleeing the horrors of approaching ruin. In prayer the disciples must cling to God's presence and ever-ready help, even though they may have to disrupt even the most devoutly held religious traditions, such as the Jewish Sabbath.

**"Great distress" (24:21).** The adverb "then" (*tote*) occurs again, here with a strong sense of temporal sequence (see comments on 24:9; cf. 24:14, 16, 30). The appearance of the abomination that causes desolation launches the period of "great distress, unequaled from the beginning of the world until now—and never to be equaled again." While the time of the siege and destruction of Jerusalem were horrible,[26] Matthew's description here indicates a time of tribulation that did not occur during the fall of Jerusalem. The horrors that fell on the Jewish people and on the entire world with the two world wars of the twentieth century are a somber warning that the devastation that comes from humanity's unleashed depravity will yet be unequaled. The vision Jesus paints must yet be ahead. The apostle John's vision reveals such a future time of incredible horror (Rev. 7–19). The unusual piling up of negatives in Matthew 24:21 ("never to be equaled again"—*oud' ou me genetai*) makes for an emphatic negation, which points both to the unequaled climax of horror and God's promise that it will not be repeated.[27]

**The days cut short (24:22).** Jesus again reiterates the terrible suffering of those future days: "If those days had not been cut short, no one would survive, but for the sake of the elect those days will be shortened." This is a proverbial way of indicating that God is in control even of these days of horror. If the wickedness of humanity and the wrath of God were allowed to run unchecked, there would be no end to the terror and no one would survive. This is a promise that the time of tribulation will not last indefinitely, because God is in control.

The people of Israel are often referred to as "the elect" (e.g., Isa. 45:4; *1 En.* 1:1), but this is a reference to believing Christians (e.g., Rom. 11:7). In the time of future great tribulation, when Israel will once again be used of God for witness (e.g., Rev. 7:3–8) to bring in a multitude of believers from all the

---

26. See Josephus, *J.W.* 5–6,

27. Others try to account for this incredible statement of the build-up of horrors of 24:21–28 by positing that the percentage of Jews killed in Jerusalem at A.D. 70 was greater than any since then (e.g., Carson, "Matthew," 501), or by suggesting that this describes the suffering of believers throughout the entire church age from A.D. 70 until Jesus returns (e.g., Blomberg, *Matthew*, 359–60). Neither really does justice to the language here.

nations who worship God and the Lamb (Rev. 7:9–12), the expression "the elect" includes all who believe on Christ during this period (cf. Matt. 24:24, 31).

**Warnings about false messiahs (24:23–28).** Jesus once again points to the rise of false messiahs and prophets, but whereas before he noted that the presence of these charlatans would be a characteristic of the entire age until the Parousia and would not signal the end of the age (see comments on 24:5, 11), during the time of great distress there will be an unprecedented rise of miracle-working false messiahs and prophets. The signs and miracles they perform are indications of supernatural activity, but believers must be careful not to be deceived into thinking that God stands behind them. Satan himself and his evil forces are able to manipulate the supernatural, so the spiritually discerning must look for the hand that lies behind the signs and miracles to see whether it truly comes from God. False messiahs and prophets who work supernatural deeds are therefore ultimately pawns in the hands of the enemy of God, the evil one.

Believers, beware. "So if anyone tells you, 'There he is, out in the desert,' do not go out; or, 'Here he is, in the inner rooms,' do not believe it." The desert had messianic overtones for diverse groups within Israel, who associated it with God's forthcoming deliverance (e.g., Essenes of the Qumran community); messianic pretenders often gathered their followers in the desert prior to their public appearance.[28] Jesus warns that they are not to believe those "in the desert" or "in the inner rooms" who say that they are the Messiah. The Messiah will not come in a secretive manner only to his exclusive gang of followers. Rather, the Son of Man will come in a spectacular manner, like lightning that is visible to all: "For as lightning that comes from the east is visible even in the west, so will be the coming of the Son of Man."

The warnings about secret workings of false messiahs and the declaration of his own spectacular appearance prompts Jesus to give a puzzling saying: "Wherever there is a carcass, there the vultures will gather." The term *aetos* can be used to refer to an "eagle" (Rev. 4:7; 8:13), but where a carcass is mentioned, it is best to render it as "vultures" (NIV), since eagles do not gather as a group and do not normally feed on dead meat. This saying is proverbial, either quoted by Jesus or created by him to make a macabre point (cf. also Luke 17:37). Here it connects either with the appearance of false messiahs and prophets or with the coming of the Son of Man.

This proverb therefore means one of the following. (1) It may point out that the corruption of this world will draw false messiahs and prophets to converge and feed on those being deceived, who really therefore are spiritually

---

28. See Patrich, "Hideouts in the Judean Wilderness," 32–42. For an overview of these groups, see Horsley and Hanson, *Bandits, Prophets, and Messiahs*.

dead. This fits best with the warnings about false prophets.[29] (2) It may mean that just as certainly as vultures gather to devour a corpse or animal carcass, so all people will be drawn to see Christ upon his return.[30] (3) It may indicate the sphere of operation from which people can see high circling vultures converging on the carcass of a dead animal; so will be the visibility of the return of the Son of Man when he comes to bring judgment on the deadness of this corrupt world.[31] This latter view seems to make most sense in the context of Jesus' allusion to his lightning-like appearance, but it is awkward in that it seems to make Jesus parallel to a vulture. But such incongruities often characterize Jesus' proverbial sayings and parables for effect.

## Description of the Coming of the Son of Man (24:29–31)

THE PHRASE "IMMEDIATELY after the distress of those days" (24:29) introduces a temporal sequence: The Son of Man will come after that time of tribulation. Here "distress" (*thlipsis*) connects with 24:21 to point to a specific period of great tribulation. The adverbial expression "immediately after" emphasizes that the celestial signs and the coming of Jesus will occur after the time of "great distress" just described in 24:15–28.

Those who hold to these events occurring during the fall of Jerusalem emphasize that one must resort to a "pitiful prosiness"[32] in order to have these events occur literally at the end of the age. But those who see these events occurring at the end suggest that one must "wildly spiritualize"[33] these events in order to see them as occurring at the fall of Jerusalem. Once again, the mixture of prophecy referring to both the fall of Jerusalem and the end of the age should be acknowledged. Although the judgment that will be brought on Israel in A.D. 70 with the fall of Jerusalem does seem to be in Jesus' mind (cf. 23:37–39; Luke 21:20–24), the primary emphasis rests on the end of the age when he will come as the Son of Man in great universal power.

**Heavenly disturbances (24:29).** The end of the age will come with great disturbances in the heavens, with darkened skies, falling stars, the disruption of the forces of this age, and finally the coming of Jesus. At his coming he will gather the elect from the ends of heaven. These events most likely refer

---

29. Morris, *Matthew*, 608. This seems to make sense of the metaphor by connecting it with negative connotations, but doesn't really fit the context of Jesus' statement about his return.

30. Blomberg, *Matthew*, 361. This seems to make more sense of Jesus' statement in the context, but the metaphor doesn't really make a parallel with Jesus' coming; does the Parousia correspond to a carcass?

31. Hagner, *Matthew*, 2:707; though Hagner downplays the judgment aspect.

32. France, *Matthew*, 344.

33. Toussaint, *Behold the King*, 266.

to his coming at the end of the time of tribulation, which would correspond with the time of judgment of the nations (25:31–46).

Jesus uses typical apocalyptic imagery as he alludes here to passages such as Isaiah 13:10 and 34:4[34] to describe his coming with a mixture of literal and figurative language. God will cause the skies to be darkened and the heavenly bodies to be disturbed. Such language may point to both physical phenomena and political and spiritual disruptions. The darkness at Jesus' crucifixion was an indication that he had conquered the forces of evil on the cross, and the darkness during his second coming is an indication that he will now exert his rule over all forces, especially those of the demonic prince of the powers of the air.

**Heavenly appearances (24:30–31).** Along with these heavenly disturbances will come heavenly appearances: "At that time the sign of the Son of Man will appear in the sky." There is debate as to whether the "sign" is some sort of heavenly ensign or banner or whether the sign is the Son of Man himself.[35] Many have connected the "sign" with the "banner" that Messiah will raise as he gathers the nations and Israel (Isa. 11:10–12; 18:3), or the type of "banners" noted in the War Scroll that the battle formations of the congregation at Qumran raise at the final battle (cf. 1QM 3:13–4:17). Among the many theories of some sort of particular heavenly ensign, some (e.g., Chrysostom) suggested that the sign will be a cross in the sky. However, since the rest of the verse points to the coming of the Son of Man himself as that which promotes mourning, the apparent reference to Daniel 7:13 ("one like a son of man") indicates that Jesus himself is the sign of the eschatological consummation of the age (see Matt. 16:27; 26:64).[36]

As in his first coming, when Jesus' ministry and resurrection were sufficient signs that he was indeed the Messiah, the Son of God,[37] so his second coming will be the sign to "all the nations [*phylai*] of the earth," who will then mourn (24:30). The term *phylai* can be rendered either "nations" (NIV) or "tribes" (NASB). Matthew regularly uses *ethne* to refer to the nations (e.g., 24:9; 28:19), and the only other time he uses *phylai* it refers specifically to the twelve tribes of Israel (19:28); thus, here it should be rendered as "tribes,"

---

34. Cf. Ezek 32:7; Joel 2:31; 3:15; Amos 8:9; 2 Esdras 5:4–5; 7:39; *T. Mos.* 10:5.

35. In terms of Greek grammar, the question involves whether the genitive in the expression "the sign of the Son of Man" is an objective genitive ("the sign which indicates the Son of Man") or a genitive of apposition ("the sign which is the Son of Man").

36. Cf. also the messianic expectation of a person as banner in Isa. 5:26–30; see Gordon D. Kirchhevel, "He That Cometh in Mark 1:7 and Matt 24:30," *BBR* 4 (1994): 105–11.

37. The Jewish leaders had repeatedly asked for such a sign (12:38; 16:1; cf. John 2:18; 20:30–31).

calling to mind the twelve tribes of Israel. If so, "earth" refers to the land of Israel.[38] This integrates Daniel's emphasis of the time of great stress that will come on the earth with the arrival of the Son of Man with the prophet's emphasis on the coming Day of the Lord with its judgment of evil.

This language would hold special meaning to a Jewish audience, since the prophecy of Zechariah 12:10 speaks of the people of Israel mourning when they look on the One whom they have pierced. The apostle John applies this prophecy to those Jews who mourned the crucifixion (John 19:37), and he quotes the prophecy in Revelation 1:7. Those events had great import for the people of Israel, and John uses the singular noun form *phyle* to refer to each individual tribe of Israel (Rev. 7:4–8). This is a kind of mourning that produces repentance, or else it stems from recognition of their coming judgment. In the light of the place that Paul gives to Israel's future repentance and conversion (Rom. 9–11; cf. Matt. 23:39), repentance is more likely in view.

Jesus continues the description of his coming: "They will see the Son of Man coming on the clouds of the sky, with power and great glory." Coming on the clouds with power and glory cannot easily be made to refer to Christ's coming spiritually in judgment against Israel at the time of the destruction of the temple. Rather, this is eschatological language that echoes Daniel's prophecy and points to Christ's return at the end of the age. Jesus completes his self-identity through the use of the relatively ambiguous title "Son of Man" (see comments on 8:20). He is the Son of Man who displays humiliation with nowhere to lay his head (8:20), who experiences suffering as the servant who gives his life for many (20:17–19, 28), and who is now revealed as the One who will come in glorious power as the majestic sovereign designated by the Ancient of Days to receive worship as the divine King of the kingdom of God (Dan. 7:13–14).

At his appearance "he will send his angels with a loud trumpet call." Both banners and trumpets were associated in Jewish eschatological thought with the majestic arrival of the Messiah.[39] Jesus' return—accompanied by angels and a sounding trumpet—recurs in Paul's eschatological teaching (1 Cor. 15:51–2; 1 Thess. 4:16). Jesus refers elsewhere to the angelic host that accompanies his eschatological appearance for gathering and for bringing judgment (Matt. 13:39, 41, 49; 16:27; 25:31) and is at his disposal (4:11; 26:53). An angel of the Lord announced the arrival of Jesus as the incarnate Immanuel (1:20–24) and guided the family during his infancy (2:13:23), and an angel will announce the resurrected Jesus (28:2–5).

---

38. So Blomberg, *Matthew*, 362.
39. Isa. 18:3; 27:13; Jer. 4:21; 6:1; 51:27; 1QM 3–4, 8, 16, 17–18.

This picture coincides with the sovereign Son of Man accompanying the angels of heaven, who "will gather his elect from the four winds, from one end of the heavens to the other." The "elect" is another reference to all believers, both Jew and Gentile, who have come to believe on him during this time of great tribulation. The gathering "from the four winds, from one end of heaven to another" may refer to the four points of the compass (cf. Ezek. 37:9; Dan. 8:8; 11:4) and from every place under heaven, indicating the gathering of all believers who are on the earth at the time.[40] Others take the expression to refer to Jesus' angels gathering and bringing with him all of the redeemed already in heaven to join with believers on the earth (cf. Rev. 19:11–16).[41] It probably should include both, so that at the end of the period of tribulation Jesus returns both to bring with him all those believers who are with him in heaven as well as to gather believers alive on the earth.[42]

## The Lesson of the Fig Tree (24:32–35)

A SWITCH OF emphasis now occurs. Up to this point there has been a combination of historical and eschatological features in answer to the questions about the destruction of the temple and Jesus' return and the end of the age. Jesus has given a descriptive overview of the entire age. But now he deals with attitudes that should characterize those who live during this age and await his coming. He gives several lessons to equip people in preparation for the end.

The first is the parabolic lesson from the fig tree. Prior to this, the fig tree provided Jesus with an object lesson for his disciples on the irresponsibility of the Jewish leaders, who should have recognized his messianic authority in announcing the arrival of the kingdom of heaven (see 21:18–22). Perhaps Jesus is here continuing the allusion to Israel, pointing to the Messiah's future liberation of Israel and the temple from Gentile dominance, with the fig tree illustration indicating the time of future blessing for Israel.[43] But more likely Jesus uses the fig tree as a parabolic lesson taught from nature to the disciples. It teaches a principle of nearness concerning the abomination that causes desolation of the temple and the return of the Son of Man. "As soon as its twigs get tender and its leaves come out, you know that summer is near. Even so, when you see all these things, you know that it is near, right at the door."

---

40. Carson, "Matthew," 506; Keener, *Matthew* (1997), 352; Morris, *Matthew*, 611.

41. Blomberg, *Matthew*, 363.

42. Pretribulationists contend that Jesus brings with him both the deceased and the "raptured" believers who are with him in heaven, while postribulationists contend that he brings with him only the former.

43. Flusser, "Jesus Weeps over Jerusalem," *Jesus*, 240–43.

In the winter months figs lose their leaves, so just buds and new leaves in spring indicate that summer is near; so also when the events in the preceding context occur, the disciples are to be prepared for the coming of the Son of Man. Jesus stated earlier that the general distressful events of this age must not be interpreted to mean that the Lord is near (24:1–8). However, as the end grows closer, subtle increases of difficulty begin to mark the end. The budding tree can be overlooked; it is not spectacular and can even be unnoticed until too late.

Therefore, when his disciples see "all these things" (i.e., the beginning of the increase of distress and the accomplishment of the worldwide proclamation of the gospel of the kingdom), they should be alert that the end may be imminent. The ambiguous *estin* (24:33) can be rendered "it is near" (NIV), pointing back to the antecedent "summer" in the preceding verse, or "he is near" (NASB, NRSV), pointing back to the arrival of the Son of Man in the preceding section (24:30). It is better with the NIV to render it impersonally, which includes all aspects of the Parousia. All people during this age should stay alert, because the arrival of summer can come unnoticed. But for those who are alert, there are indications that the end is near, specifically the preaching of the gospel of the kingdom to all nations (24:14). Therefore, "summer" here refers to the age of blessedness and fruitfulness that will occur when Jesus has returned. This helps disciples to stay alert. But because the budding is not spectacular but subtle, it can be overlooked. The point is that people must stay alert and must be forewarned by certain signs at the very end.

Jesus next speaks of "this generation": "I tell you the truth, this generation will certainly not pass away until all these things have happened." The identity of "this generation" has vexed interpreters. Some contend it refers to the generation of Jesus' disciples alive when he spoke, who will witness the terrible events at A.D. 70.[44] Others suggest it refers to the Jewish people alive at the time of the return of the Son of Man.[45] Still others indicate that it refers to the kind of wicked people in Jesus' day who opposed him in his earthly ministry and who will again arise to oppose Jesus' disciples prior to his return.[46]

Perhaps it is best to see a twofold reference, as Jesus has done throughout the discourse. The disciples to whom Jesus is speaking on the Mount of

---

44. E.g., Davies and Allison, *Matthew*, 3:365–66; France, *Matthew*, 346.

45. E.g., Schweizer, *Matthew*, 458.

46. E.g., Gundry, *Matthew*, 491; Morris, *Matthew*, 612–13; Neil D. Nelson Jr., "'This Generation' in Matt 24:34: A Literary Critical Perspective," *JETS* 38 (September 1995): 369–85.

Olives most naturally will be "this generation" that sees the events of the destruction of the temple, which shows the applicability of the discourse to A.D. 70. Further, within the context of Jesus' statements about the coming of the Son of Man, there must be primary applicability to those at the end of the age who see the events surrounding the abomination of desolation occurring.[47] When these signs of the end of the age appear, those waiting for his arrival will recognize that their redemption is drawing near (Luke 21:28). This refers both to repentant Israel and to unrepentant wicked people. But it also refers to believers alive at that time who see these things occurring; they will be the generation of Jesus' disciples who will see their Lord appear.

In other words, the saying is a word of warning to those of the generation with Jesus and those in the future who have not yet repented that the arrival of the Son of Man will bring judgment. But the saying is also a word of encouragement to his followers that tribulation will not go on forever, as it may appear to those who are suffering in it. Summer is near.

In the final words of this section, Jesus gives a profound word of assurance to all those looking down the corridors of history and seeing the incredible events he has just described: "Heaven and earth will pass away, but my words will never pass away." This is similar to the enduring quality of the Old Testament that Jesus had declared in the SM (see comments on 5:18). As there, Jesus ascribes divine, eternal qualities to his own teaching. His words are not given by inspiration but are his own, and they have authority for that reason (24:34), with his teaching having the same divine character as God and his words.[48] Throughout history will come birth pains and tribulation that may seem as though history itself is out of control. But Jesus' rock-solid prophesying of his return to establish his kingdom on the earth provides the assurance needed by his disciples to maintain hope and determination. Even though heaven and earth will not exist in the future in the form that we know them now (cf. 2 Peter 3:10; Rev. 21:1), the firm foundation of discipleship to Jesus for eternity are his words of truth.

This ends the first major part of the Olivet Discourse, which provides an eschatological forecast of the general character of this age, the time of great tribulation with the abomination that causes desolation, and the beginning lesson on how all should await Jesus' arrival. This third lesson will be expanded in the rest of the discourse to encourage Jesus' disciples to wait alertly and in expectation of reward, but also to warn the unprepared and unrepentant about judgment.

---

47. Cf. Ladd, *Theology of the New Testament*, 196–205.

48. Daniel Doriani, "The Deity of Christ in the Synoptic Gospels," *JETS* 37 (September 1994): 333–50, esp. 343.

**Bridging Contexts**

THE WORDS OF Jesus in this Gospel, especially in the five primary discourses, contain a wealth of kingdom principles to guide the church throughout its history. They are directly linked to Jesus' purposes for all his followers, since they comprise the primary material from which all disciples are to be taught to obey everything Jesus commanded (cf. 28:18–20; see comments at the beginning of the SM [chs. 5–7], the Mission Mandate [ch. 10], the Parabolic Disclosure [ch. 13], the Community Prescription [ch. 18], and the Oliver Discourse (chs. 24–25]).

Like the other discourses, the fifth is addressed to insiders—Jesus' disciples. It intends to give to them a basic prophetic overview of the events to transpire in the near and distant future. But Jesus' intent isn't primarily to give a timetable; he focuses especially on the attitudes and character qualities that guide their discipleship to him for the days and years ahead.

**Jesus' eschatological preparation of the disciples.** While Jesus' eschatological forecast in this final discourse in Matthew's Gospel is his most complete discussion of end-time events that surround his return in glory, it doesn't cover everything. Note that Jesus issues this forecast during his final week with his disciples. They still have not comprehended his crucifixion, resurrection, and ascension, nor have they grasped that they will soon become the kingdom community called the church with the descent of the Spirit at Pentecost. Thus, Jesus here gives only a rough outline of what will transpire throughout this age. The events he discusses will be fleshed out later with additional revelation, when they are better prepared to handle a more complete picture of end-time events. But during this tumultuous week, they are not yet ready for a complete picture.

Jesus likely gave fuller details of end-time events to the apostles during the forty days before his ascension, where he spoke about the kingdom of God (Acts 1:4). Through insights and revelation from the Father through the Spirit, the apostles fill in many more details as they write later books of the New Testament (e.g., 1–2 Thessalonians; Revelation). These later descriptions of end-time and eternal activities will fill in the details of Jesus' basic outline given here in the fifth discourse. This is similar to what Jesus provided in the Missionary Discourse (ch. 10) and the Community Discourse (ch. 18), where he gave only a rough outline that later would be filled in by New Testament writers inspired by God, who will give details about missionary outreach (e.g., Acts) and the structure and function of the church (e.g., Ephesians; 1 and 2 Timothy).

Thus, we must not make Jesus' eschatological forecast in the Olivet Discourse say more than what he intended to say. Further details must be supplied by other biblical writings, the exhaustive study of which is not the purpose of this commentary. As we have done with his other discourses, we seek to understand Jesus' purpose for his disciples in giving this discourse in its historical setting and Matthew's intention as he records it for his community.

**Interpreting the Olivet Discourse.** Jesus' predictions in this discourse have produced an almost dizzying array of interpretations.[49] The primary issue is to understand the relationship of historically fulfilled prophecy to unfulfilled prophecy. We can get a grip on one of the most important issues here by subsuming the various interpretations under three broad headings.

(1) On the one extreme are those who suggest that virtually all of the events that Jesus prophesies in the discourse were fulfilled in the first century, primarily with the fall of Jerusalem and the destruction of the temple in A.D. 70.[50] One proponent suggests that the fall of Jerusalem alone is in view in 24:4–35, and that only at 24:36 does Jesus begin to discuss the Parousia.[51] This view does take seriously the context of Israel's judgment, which Jesus has just emphasized in the temple incidents, the controversies with the religious leaders, and the woes pronounced on the teachers of the law and the Pharisees (chs. 21–23). It also finds parallels in historical incidents that transpired leading up to the temple destruction in A.D. 70 that correspond to Jesus' prophecy.[52] The weakness of this view is that it minimizes some of the details of the discourse that were not fulfilled in A.D. 70,[53] as well as the remarkable parallels in other prophetic literature to the events recorded here that point to a future fulfillment (e.g., Dan. 9:27; 12:11).

(2) On the other extreme is the futurist view, the strength of which is the acknowledgment of the direct fulfillment of parallel prophetic passages like Daniel 9 and 12 in future events prophesied here by Jesus. This view suggests that virtually all the events of the discourse are fulfilled in the future when Israel is once again reestablished in God's purposes.[54] Many who hold this view suggest that the church is "raptured" prior to the events of the great tribulation, so Israel is once again the evangelistic instrument to bear witness

---

49. For helpful overviews, see Turner, "The Structure and Sequence of Matthew 24:1–41," 3–27; Ladd, *Theology of the New Testament*, 197–99; Carson, "Matthew," 488–92.

50. This is often called the "preterist" (past perspective) position.

51. E.g., France, *Matthew*, 333–36.

52. Ibid., 336–46.

53. E.g., Christians fled to Pella nearly two years prior to the fall of Jerusalem, not after, and the description of Israel's tragedy in these events as the greatest tribulation in history or in the future (24:19) does not square with later tragedies in Israel's history; cf. Ladd, *Theology of the New Testament*, 197–99; Gundry, *The Church and the Tribulation*, 132–34.

54. See Louis Barbieri Jr., "Matthew," in *The Bible Knowledge Commentary, New Testament*, ed. John F. Walvoord and Roy B. Zuck (Wheaton: Victor, 1983), 76–78.

to the gospel of the kingdom.[55] It takes seriously God's promises to Israel to be reestablished in the land in fulfillment of Daniel's seventieth week. Its weakness is that it overlooks that Jesus gives the discourse to his disciples, not to Israel, as a guide to their understanding of their own role in this age and how they are to respond to future events. The events are a guide to the church's expectations throughout this age. Moreover, this view minimizes how Daniel's prophecy of the abomination of desolation has already been partially fulfilled with the defiling activities of Antiochus IV Epiphanes (Dan. 11:31).

(3) As noted above, this commentary takes a mediating position, which finds an intentional intertwining of historical and eschatological fulfillment. There is a comprehensive theological cohesion in the discourse between Jesus' treatment of the fall of Jerusalem and the Parousia, but there is no clear dividing point between historical and eschatological fulfillment.[56] The resolution is that the two are purposely intertwined under what some call a "double reference" prophecy or "prophetic foreshortening," where a near event serves as a partial fulfillment and symbol for the fulfillment of far events.[57] In this view, the events of 24:4–14 generally describe life in the church during this age, perhaps with some increase of activity in 24:9–14. But 24:15 begins a double reference to events that will be partially fulfilled at A.D. 70 with the destruction of the temple and Jerusalem but culminate in the future fulfillment of the complex of events surrounding the return of Jesus—the abomination that causes desolation, the end of the age, and the Parousia.

This mediating position has been adopted by a wide range of interpreters, perhaps "a majority of conservative sources,"[58] including those from an amillennial perspective,[59] those from a premillennial-pretribulational perspective,[60] and those from a premillennial-posttribulational perspective.[61] A

---

55. Whatever one concludes with reference to a "rapture" in the unfolding of these events (see Bridging Contexts of 24:36–25:46), the scantiness of exegetical material, esp. in this discourse (if not absence of material here), suggests that it should not be the primary determining factor as to how in interpreting this discourse.

56. Morris, *Matthew*, 593–94 n. 4.

57. Ladd, *Theology of the New Testament*, 198.

58. Turner, "The Structure and Sequence of Matthew 24:1–41," 9.

59. Anthony A. Hoekema, *The Bible and the Future* (Grand Rapids: Eerdmans, 1979), 130, suggests that the signs given by Jesus "had their initial fulfillment at the time of the destruction of Jerusalem; since this discourse exemplifies the principle of prophetic foreshortening, however, the signs mentioned in them will have a further fulfillment at the time of the Parousia." See also Hendricksen, *Matthew*, 852–56.

60. Turner, "The Structure and Sequence of Matthew 24:1–41," passim; Alva J. McClain, *The Greatness of the Kingdom* (Chicago: Moody, 1959), 136–39; see also Ed Glasscock, *Matthew* (Moody Gospel Commentary; Chicago: Moody Press, 1997), 468: "The nature of eschatological revelation allows for a typological fulfillment at one level with a more complete fulfillment at another."

majority certainly doesn't always signify accuracy, but here it suggests caution against going too far in either direction.[62] Jesus warns of first-century historical judgment on Israel for rejecting the invitation to the kingdom, but he also provides future guidance for his disciples. Moreover, Christ anticipates the fulfillment of the covenantal promises to Israel to be restored to the land, which ushers in the messianic kingdom.[63]

PROPHECY TODAY. Prophecy is big business. A recent issue of *Time* magazine had a cover story entitled, "The Bible and the Apocalypse: Why More Americans Are Reading and Talking About the End of the World."[64] The author documented the recent rise in attention given by the general population in North America to end-time discussions. She highlighted especially the phenomenally successful series by Tim LaHaye and Jerry Jenkins. Starting with the first book, *Left Behind*,[65] which sold more than seven million copies, the series to date has ten volumes, selling more than fifty million total copies.[66] That's big business!

But prophecy is much more than simply big business. Evangelical Christians historically have been interested in prophecy, primarily because so

---

61. Robert Gundry indicates that (1) the events centering around the destruction of Jerusalem in A.D. 70 did not exhaust Jesus' prophecy, with the result that a time of future tribulation immediately before the return of Christ is yet to be fulfilled; (2) the events centering around the destruction of Jerusalem did, however, constitute a fulfillment precursive to a larger and final fulfillment at the end of the age (*The Church and the Tribulation*, 129). See also Ladd, *Theology of the New Testament*, 198.

62. Carson ("Matthew," 495) and David Wenham (*The Rediscovery of Jesus' Eschatological Discourse* [Gospel Perspectives 4; Sheffield: JSOT Press, 1984]) espouse a somewhat unique approach, which Turner calls a "revised preterist-futurist view" ("The Structure and Sequence of Matthew 24:1–41," 9–10). They suggest that Jesus first gives a general discussion of this time period (24:4–28), with a brief discussion of the fall of Jerusalem in A.D. 70 inserted as an example of God's judgment (24:15–21), and then comes the Second Advent (24:29–31), with the warning in 24:32–35 describing the whole tribulation period that stretches from the Ascension to the Second Advent (cf. Carson, "Matthew," 495). While somewhat unique, it falls generally within the broad sweep of mediating positions between the extremes of historical and futuristic interpretations, but avoids the significance of the temple and Israel in these tribulational scenes.

63. Hafemann, "Eschatology and Ethics," 161–92.

64. Nancy Gibbs, cover story: "The Bible and the Apocalypse," *Time* (July 1, 2002): 40–48.

65. Tim LaHaye and Jerry B. Jenkins, *Left Behind: A Novel of the Earth's Last Days* (Wheaton: Tyndale, 1996).

66. Gibbs, "The Bible and the Apocalypse," 44–45.

much of the Bible speaks about end times. But intriguingly, the article declares that of those reading the series, only about half are evangelicals, which suggests a much broader audience of people, including many non-Christians, who are interested. The scary situation of the world since the tragic events of September 11, 2001, have almost certainly contributed to the interest, similar to the way that the events of World War II and the creation of the nation of Israel in the land in 1948 stimulated a resurgence of interest in prophecy in the middle of the twentieth century. I have spoken to dozens of unbelievers who have read at least one of the books in the series, and they all indicate that they are looking for some kind of an answer to the world situation.

In the middle of the secularist, pluralistic, relativistic culture in which we live, it is fascinating that so many people are turning to these religious novels for help. The surveys conducted in researching the *Time* article suggested that thirty-six percent of Americans believe that the Bible is the Word of God and is to be taken literally, and that fifty-nine percent believe that the prophecies in Revelation will come true. I was taken aback by those statistics. All of this points out that prophecy is a powerful message of both hope and warning and that it should be a point of study and debate, but especially an ingredient of evangelism and spiritual formation.

That is a crucial factor in the study of eschatology. One does not have to hold the same theological position as the *Left Behind* series to observe how the authors have taken seriously the implications of their eschatological views for the daily lives of their readers.[67] All of us need to move from speculation to implication in our study of prophecy, because the Bible does not record prophecy of end-time activity simply for curiosity's sake. Many will surely undertake a study of prophecy in a vain attempt to figure out what Jesus declared to be unknown—the time of the end and his return. But prophecy about the future is always given for the purpose of affecting behavior in the present. Every Bible passage I have ever studied with a message about end times always comes in the context of exhortation and warning. That must never be forgotten.

The study in this commentary of Jesus' life and teaching understands that the offer and establishment of the kingdom of God is an already–not yet proposition—it is present and fully operative in the lives of those who respond, but it yet awaits a final manifestation, when Jesus Messiah will reign

---

67. The authors of the series espouse a pretribulational, premillennial eschatology, in which they draw first on Paul's teaching about a "rapture" (1 Thess. 4:16–17) to set the stage for the first novel, and from there draw primarily on scenes from Revelation for their novelistic recounting of end-time events.

on the earth and Israel will experience the realization of her covenantal promises. That premillennial outlook on Jesus' eschatological discourse leads to important implications.

**Godly living in the present.** The study of the future should spur us to godly living in the present. Jesus' signal statement, "See, I have told you ahead of time" (24:25), stands in the middle of his prophecy of future events. He tells his disciples these events so we are not deceived and go after false messiahs and prophets (24:23–24, 26), but also so that we may develop godly perseverance through wars, famines, earthquakes, and persecution (24:6–7, 9–10), that our love for him and each other will not falter when wickedness surrounds us (24:12), and that the testimony of our lips and lives will remain steadfast and pure to the end (24:13–14).

Jesus' message in the SM was that personal righteousness may result from entering the kingdom of heaven (5:20). Now he prophesies future events so that we will discipline ourselves to maintain and expand that personal kingdom-righteousness in our daily lives regardless of the circumstances. He does not tell us these things so that we will be obsessed with dates, events, and speculation about the minute details of his prophecy, but to encourage us to godly living.

**Conviction about the future.** A second implication is that our study of prophecy should produce conviction about what is going to happen in the future. We should admit we may be wrong on certain points, which will help us avoid a narrow dogmatism; but when we have done our homework and settle on what we believe to be the Bible's teaching, we should develop conviction, for appropriate conviction affects our character and our attitudes. People without conviction run the gamut of emotions from depression to giddiness in each change of circumstance. Superpower nations who like to flex their nuclear or biological muscles produce in people all around us the fear of unstoppable disaster. But Jesus warns us against being alarmed when international events seem to indicate that the world is going to fall apart (24:6). When we are convinced that the end of the world will only come when Jesus returns visibly and powerfully, we can maintain hope and vigilance no matter how bad things get.

Similarly, the apostle Paul gives prophetic revelation about Jesus' return so that his readers will have hope about their loved ones who have died (1 Thess. 4:13–18). One of my closest friends lost his daughter suddenly to a tragic death. It was a blow that would devastate most anyone, yet he told me that his unwavering convictions that she was present with the Lord and that he would be with her one day gave him a blanket of peace in the cold, harsh realities of this world. That conviction came only from a study of God's Word about the future.

In our personal study and in our preaching and teaching, we must not overlook the prominent position that prophetic teaching occupies in Scripture. Even though we must guard against excess and obsession with this kind of study, we will have no peace or security without a proper understanding of revelation concerning the future.

**Warning of difficult times ahead.** There is also an important warning in Jesus' prophecy of difficult times ahead. Jesus spent much of his time in the discourses preparing the disciples in advance for the harsh realities of life during this age. The power of this preparation cannot be underestimated, because much of our development as disciples comes in preparing ourselves before the fact. Jesus make us aware of rejection as we go out to do missions (10:22–23). He informs us about the mixed nature of the kingdom until his return (13:24–50). He warns us about imperfection in the Christian community until his return (18:7) and how we should respond in the light of this imperfection (18:12–20). And he repeatedly tells us of the hardships and trials that come as a result of following him.

The Olivet Discourse expands on this preparation, cueing us to the fact that there will be those who will try to deceive us as well as persecute us. Knowledge of this fact helps us to prepare ourselves mentally and spiritually for this reality and helps guard against disillusionment. When we fail to tell disciples about these things, there are chances that they will be misled by messianic pretenders or be disheartened by the difficulty of the process.

Jesus' prophetic words, as well as much of prophecy generally, are an encouragement for believers in the midst of persecution, not a handbook for future prediction or simply a hope of escape from an imperfect world. Every generation has had those who attempt to predict the time of the return of Jesus, at times even selling all worldly possessions in anticipation. These groups have been immensely disappointed, or worse, when their predictions fell flat. Prophecy is not escapism from the trials of life. The reality is that Jesus gives us this information so that we can endure and live appropriately until his return.

**Warning of impending judgment.** But there is another kind of warning in Jesus' eschatological forecast—impending judgment. Not only is prophecy an encouragement to godly living; it is a stimulus to repentance. I often hear media commentators speak disparagingly of preachers or evangelists as end-time doomsayers, but prophetic revelation does in fact teach that judgment is coming on those who reject God's day of opportunity. Whether at the end of one's life or the end of the age, judgment is coming. Here again we must guard against excess, but most churches with which I'm familiar never come close to an excess in such preaching. An appropriate preaching, teaching, and evangelism from prophetic passages must include warning of judgment, or else the full message has been ignored. This calls for wisdom in our presentations, compassion in our approach, and urgency in our message.

**Missions and evangelism.** The conviction of Jesus' return, therefore, should fuel a vigorous involvement in missions, evangelism, and church planting. When we are gripped with the fact that the souls of men and women are at stake, we will move our study of prophecy beyond academic debate or idle curiosity. Active participation in reaching out to a lost world enables people across the nation and around the world to be prepared to meet the Lord when he comes in glory. Churches and individual Christians who ignore the centrality of mission and evangelistic outreach miss an essential component of the overall plan of God. Jesus tells us that "the end" will come after the gospel has been preached as a testimony to all nations (24:14). This does not mean that we preach the gospel simply to force his return. However, the Parousia and consummation of the kingdom are closely connected with all the nations hearing the gospel.

On a different note, there is strong encouragement in Jesus' statement. Even though at times opposition appears to be insurmountable, true Christianity will assert itself in the preaching of the gospel message. The prophetic statement of Jesus assures us that nothing can stop this. To the churches around the world that persevere under governments that have legislated against evangelism or proselytizing—for example, in some Islamic or communist nations—this is a powerful, immediately relevant promise. This is also a powerful promise to those in Western countries that have become increasingly secularized. No matter how bad things may get within public opinion or the political arena, no matter how much government may legislate against Christianity, or no matter how much persecution is mounted against it, the gospel cannot be stopped until the end, when Jesus returns in glory and power.

# Matthew 24:36—25:46

N O ONE KNOWS about that day or hour, not even the angels in heaven, nor the Son, but only the Father. ³⁷As it was in the days of Noah, so it will be at the coming of the Son of Man. ³⁸For in the days before the flood, people were eating and drinking, marrying and giving in marriage, up to the day Noah entered the ark; ³⁹and they knew nothing about what would happen until the flood came and took them all away. That is how it will be at the coming of the Son of Man. ⁴⁰Two men will be in the field; one will be taken and the other left. ⁴¹Two women will be grinding with a hand mill; one will be taken and the other left.

⁴²"Therefore keep watch, because you do not know on what day your Lord will come. ⁴³But understand this: If the owner of the house had known at what time of night the thief was coming, he would have kept watch and would not have let his house be broken into. ⁴⁴So you also must be ready, because the Son of Man will come at an hour when you do not expect him.

⁴⁵"Who then is the faithful and wise servant, whom the master has put in charge of the servants in his household to give them their food at the proper time? ⁴⁶It will be good for that servant whose master finds him doing so when he returns. ⁴⁷I tell you the truth, he will put him in charge of all his possessions. ⁴⁸But suppose that servant is wicked and says to himself, 'My master is staying away a long time,' ⁴⁹and he then begins to beat his fellow servants and to eat and drink with drunkards. ⁵⁰The master of that servant will come on a day when he does not expect him and at an hour he is not aware of. ⁵¹He will cut him to pieces and assign him a place with the hypocrites, where there will be weeping and gnashing of teeth.

²⁵:¹"At that time the kingdom of heaven will be like ten virgins who took their lamps and went out to meet the bridegroom. ²Five of them were foolish and five were wise. ³The foolish ones took their lamps but did not take any oil with them. ⁴The wise, however, took oil in jars along with their lamps. ⁵The bridegroom was a long time in coming, and they all became drowsy and fell asleep.

⁶"At midnight the cry rang out: 'Here's the bridegroom! Come out to meet him!'

⁷"Then all the virgins woke up and trimmed their lamps. ⁸The foolish ones said to the wise, 'Give us some of your oil; our lamps are going out.'

⁹"'No,' they replied, 'there may not be enough for both us and you. Instead, go to those who sell oil and buy some for yourselves.'

¹⁰"But while they were on their way to buy the oil, the bridegroom arrived. The virgins who were ready went in with him to the wedding banquet. And the door was shut.

¹¹"Later the others also came. 'Sir! Sir!' they said. 'Open the door for us!'

¹²"But he replied, 'I tell you the truth, I don't know you.'

¹³"Therefore keep watch, because you do not know the day or the hour.

¹⁴"Again, it will be like a man going on a journey, who called his servants and entrusted his property to them. ¹⁵To one he gave five talents of money, to another two talents, and to another one talent, each according to his ability. Then he went on his journey. ¹⁶The man who had received the five talents went at once and put his money to work and gained five more. ¹⁷So also, the one with the two talents gained two more. ¹⁸But the man who had received the one talent went off, dug a hole in the ground and hid his master's money.

¹⁹"After a long time the master of those servants returned and settled accounts with them. ²⁰The man who had received the five talents brought the other five. 'Master,' he said, 'you entrusted me with five talents. See, I have gained five more.'

²¹"His master replied, 'Well done, good and faithful servant! You have been faithful with a few things; I will put you in charge of many things. Come and share your master's happiness!'

²²"The man with the two talents also came. 'Master,' he said, 'you entrusted me with two talents; see, I have gained two more.'

²³"His master replied, 'Well done, good and faithful servant! You have been faithful with a few things; I will put you in charge of many things. Come and share your master's happiness!'

²⁴"Then the man who had received the one talent came. 'Master,' he said, 'I knew that you are a hard man, harvesting where you have not sown and gathering where you have not

scattered seed. ²⁵So I was afraid and went out and hid your talent in the ground. See, here is what belongs to you.'

²⁶"His master replied, 'You wicked, lazy servant! So you knew that I harvest where I have not sown and gather where I have not scattered seed? ²⁷Well then, you should have put my money on deposit with the bankers, so that when I returned I would have received it back with interest.

²⁸"'Take the talent from him and give it to the one who has the ten talents. ²⁹For everyone who has will be given more, and he will have an abundance. Whoever does not have, even what he has will be taken from him. ³⁰And throw that worthless servant outside, into the darkness, where there will be weeping and gnashing of teeth.'

³¹"When the Son of Man comes in his glory, and all the angels with him, he will sit on his throne in heavenly glory. ³²All the nations will be gathered before him, and he will separate the people one from another as a shepherd separates the sheep from the goats. ³³He will put the sheep on his right and the goats on his left.

³⁴"Then the King will say to those on his right, 'Come, you who are blessed by my Father; take your inheritance, the kingdom prepared for you since the creation of the world. ³⁵For I was hungry and you gave me something to eat, I was thirsty and you gave me something to drink, I was a stranger and you invited me in, ³⁶I needed clothes and you clothed me, I was sick and you looked after me, I was in prison and you came to visit me.'

³⁷"Then the righteous will answer him, 'Lord, when did we see you hungry and feed you, or thirsty and give you something to drink? ³⁸When did we see you a stranger and invite you in, or needing clothes and clothe you? ³⁹When did we see you sick or in prison and go to visit you?'

⁴⁰"The King will reply, 'I tell you the truth, whatever you did for one of the least of these brothers of mine, you did for me.'

⁴¹"Then he will say to those on his left, 'Depart from me, you who are cursed, into the eternal fire prepared for the devil and his angels. ⁴²For I was hungry and you gave me nothing to eat, I was thirsty and you gave me nothing to drink, ⁴³I was a stranger and you did not invite me in, I needed clothes and you did not clothe me, I was sick and in prison and you did not look after me.'

<sup>44</sup>"They also will answer, 'Lord, when did we see you hungry or thirsty or a stranger or needing clothes or sick or in prison, and did not help you?'

<sup>45</sup>"He will reply, 'I tell you the truth, whatever you did not do for one of the least of these, you did not do for me.'

<sup>46</sup>"Then they will go away to eternal punishment, but the righteous to eternal life."

 ACCORDING TO THE traditional reckoning of the activities during Holy Week, Jesus spent much of Tuesday morning debating the religious leaders in the temple (see comments on chronology at 21:1). Late in the day, as he is heading with his disciples to Bethany, Jesus ponders the temple and the city of Jerusalem stretched out to the west of them as well as the long future facing his disciples (chs. 24–25). In the last chapter we looked at Jesus' discussion of the events surrounding his return (24:4–31), with the first lesson on how they are to conduct themselves until that time (24:32–35). The rest of the discourse continues here.

Jesus gives the necessary exhortation that accompanies the preparedness of his disciples. They are to watch, for they do not know when he is coming. He then tells four parables that give variations on the theme, each teaching a particular point about how and why they should be prepared: the homeowner and the thief in the night (24:43–33), the good and wicked servant (24:45–51), the ten virgins (25:1–13), and the talents (25:14–30). His disciples are to wait alertly and in expectation of reward at his return, because the unprepared and unrepentant will receive only judgment (25:31–46).

## The "Time" of Jesus' Coming (24:36–41)

IN BOTH HIS direct statement and in the parables that follow, Jesus' primary point is the imminence of his return. Although people enduring the horror of the great tribulation will surely know that they are in some of the worst incidents to have transpired on the earth, disciples until that time must live with the conviction that he can return unexpectedly at any moment.

**The day and hour of coming is unknown (24:36).** Jesus begins with a startling but central truth of his coming and the end of the age: "No one knows about that day or hour, not even the angels in heaven, nor the Son, but only the Father." This is Jesus' direct answer to the question about the time of his coming. No one knows! The expression "day or hour" is used throughout Scripture to indicate a general reference to time (e.g., 7:22; 10:19; 24:42).

This includes not only a literal day and/or time of day, but also the year and/or month. This must be seen as an answer even to the putting forth of buds and new leaves in the preceding parable (24:32–35). There may be a general indication of coming, but it is so general that no one will be able to pinpoint the time. Until the budding actually occurs, no one will be able to guess the precise moment.

The knowledge of his return was not given to angelic heavenly beings, who apparently have superhuman but not unlimited knowledge. Their comprehension accords with what is God's will for them to know.[1] Nor was it given to the Son to know the time of his return. This is an important Christological statement—it is an example of Jesus' voluntarily limiting his divine attributes. He willingly remains uninformed.

The theological doctrine of the *kenosis* (meaning "emptying"; cf. Phil. 2:7) generally contends that in Jesus' incarnation he voluntarily limited the use of his divine attributes so that he could experience the full human life. While he did not in any sense give up his deity, Jesus voluntarily limited the use of those divine characteristics so that he could experience human life in its entirety (cf. Heb. 4:14–16). It was only at the will of his Father that he could use his divine attributes, if it was the Father's will for him to do so. He acted primarily in his humanity and was empowered by the Spirit (see comments on 4:1–11).

For example, he was not omnipresent in his human manifestation, and on other occasions there was a restriction on his omnipotence (see comments on 13:58; cf. Mark 6:5). Here he does not know the future with regard to his return at the end of history. The independent use of his supernatural knowledge was limited to whether it was the Father's will for him to use it. In his earthly ministry Jesus came to do the will of his Father in heaven. It was not the Father's will for him to know the date of his return during his time on earth. In his human consciousness, Jesus restricted himself to normal human knowledge while retaining omniscience in his divine nature.[2] On other occasions he demonstrates supernatural knowledge of the present and the future (e.g., John 2:4; 4:17–18; 6:70; 11:4, 11; 13:10–11, 38).

This saying of Jesus apparently governs the rest of the discourse and should be the key to interpreting the next section. In the light of the unknown day or hour of his return, he exhorts his disciples to watch and be prepared.

---

1. For an overview, see Erickson, *Christian Theology*, 1:441.

2. An overview of the theological issues can be found in any standard systematic theology, such as Erickson, *Christian Theology*, 769–72; Grudem, *Systematic Theology*, esp. 547–53. Some theologians emphasize that Jesus operated exclusively in his humanity during his stay on the earth and that displays of supernatural activity are really the Spirit's power working through him (cf. Acts 2:22–23; 10:38). Others, such as Erickson and Grudem, emphasize that Jesus operated frequently in his divine nature while on earth.

**Analogy of the days of Noah (24:37–39).** Jesus emphasizes the unexpectedness of his return by making a comparison to the time of Noah. The people in the days of Noah did not heed the warnings of judgment that were given to them. They continued to carry on in the everyday activities of eating and drinking, marrying and giving their children in marriage. Although this was a profligate generation (Gen. 6:11–12), Jesus' point is not that these activities were sinful, but that the people were so wrapped up in everyday activities that they were caught off-guard because they had no concern for righteousness and spiritual realities.

By contrast, Noah and his family went about with preparations for the coming flood, even though they saw no specific signs of its coming and did not know when it would arrive. Jesus' return will catch unawares all who do not heed whatever warnings are given and who are spiritually unprepared (cf. 1 Thess. 5:1–6).

**Some will be taken, some left (24:40–41).** Two other scenes from daily life illustrate the unexpectedness of the coming of the Son of Man: "Two men will be in the field; one will be taken and the other left. Two women will be grinding with a hand mill; one will be taken and the other left." While men are working in the field and women are grinding grain with a hand mill, one is prepared, the other one is not. The mention of two reiterates that preparedness is an either-or proposition (for "hand mill," see comments on 18:6).

The "taking" and "leaving" are intriguing. These expressions may indicate that one is taken away to judgment (like those swept away by the Flood) and the other is left to enjoy the blessing of salvation at the arrival of the Son of Man (as Noah and his family were saved by God's warning),[3] although the verb for "taken" in 24:40–41 is different from the verb for "took them all away" in 24:39. Or vice versa, one is taken away to safety to enjoy the blessing of the arrival of the Son of Man (like Noah and his family in the ark) while the other is left to experience the wrath of the Son of Man (like those who died with the arrival of the Flood).[4]

The latter view has in its favor that it corresponds, in some sense, with the angels who gather the elect at the coming of the Son of Man (24:31) and seems more consistent with the following parables. Also, the verb used here means "take to safety" in 2:13, 14, 20, 21, while the verb "left" in Matthew often has a meaning of "abandon" or "forsake" (e.g., 4:20, 22; 8:22; 19:29; 23:38; 26:56).[5] The point is that the Son of Man gathers his people at his

---

3. E.g., Gundry, *Matthew*, 494; Blomberg, *Matthew*, 366.

4. E.g., Morris, *Matthew*, 614–15; Hagner, *Matthew*, 2:720; Davies and Allison, *Matthew*, 3:383.

5. Davies and Allison, *Matthew*, 3:383.

return to enjoy the full manifestation of the kingdom of God, while those left behind experience his judgment.

### The Parable of the Homeowner and the Thief (24:42–44)

JESUS BEGINS WITH a summarizing conclusion to the preceding paragraph, which also introduces the parables to follow: "Therefore keep watch, because you do not know on what day your Lord will come." "Watch" implies not only to keep looking but also to be prepared. Jesus stresses the deep division between those who are ready and those who are not. Their preparedness will mean either blessing at the coming of the Son of Man or judgment, so they must keep watch and be ready at all times. This is the only time that the expression "your Lord" occurs in Matthew's Gospel and accentuates that Jesus, as the coming Son of Man, is the disciples' Lord (cf. 25:21, 23).

Jesus draws a comparison between his coming and the unexpectedness of a thief's activity, calling his disciples to recognize and know the lesson he is teaching. "But understand this: If the owner of the house had known at what time of night the thief was coming, he would have kept watch and would not have let his house be broken into." This parable stresses that vigilance is necessary if a thief should appear. The term for thief (*kleptes*) designates a common thief who steals for his own benefit rather than an insurrectionist, such as Barabbas.

The responsibility for the safety of each home lay upon the "owner of the house" since the modern conception of a police force was nonexistent. Some protection was provided by military forces for rulers and for the upper classes but not for individuals. If a homeowner knew that a robber was coming, he would do whatever was necessary to be prepared, either staying up all night watching or perhaps enlisting the help of neighbors.[6] The parable here stresses the alertness necessary to thwart a burglar who might attempt to dig through a roof that was covered with reeds and a layer of clay or tiles (cf. Mark 2:4; Luke 5:19). This parable is consistent with what we know of the roofing materials and clay walls of common homes in the first century.

A householder can relax if he knows at what part of the night a thief is going to try to break in. But since he doesn't, he has to keep watch all night long. The same is the case for Jesus' disciples. Since they do not know the hour of his coming, they must watch all through the age because he can come at any time.[7]

Like many parables, one particular aspect of the parable is used as a comparison—here, unexpectedness. Other aspects of the parable have no

---

6. For the idea of "breaking into a house," see comments on 6:19–20.
7. Cf. 1 Thess. 5:1–2; 2 Peter 3:10; Rev. 3:3; 16:15.

comparisons, such as the fact that Jesus is not a thief who has intent to steal (see comments on 24:8). Alert watchfulness is important, but perhaps more important is "preparedness." Appropriate watching must be accompanied with preparedness as disciples ready themselves for the Lord's sudden appearance by making sure of their salvation, by keeping short accounts of their behavior, by continually seeking first the kingdom of God, and so on. The appropriate kinds of preparedness is stressed in the following parables.

## The Parable of Two Kinds of Servants (24:45–51)

THE PARABLE OF the two servants continues the theme of the preceding parable, now focusing on faithfulness as one's responsibility in being prepared for the Lord's return.

**Faithful servant (24:45–47).** The servant (*doulos*) placed in a position of responsibility to oversee and care for other servants in the master's household was often called a "steward" (*oikonomos*), a term used in a similar parable in Luke 12:41–46. This man is the chief servant, head over the master's household affairs and staff and expected to care for the master's personal affairs. The test of his responsibility occurs when the master is absent; will he faithfully carry out his tasks? If he has done so, when the master returns he will be given more responsibility.

**Unfaithful servant (24:48–51).** However, the test of the master's absence will also reveal an unfaithful steward. His wickedness is in noting the master's long absence—"But suppose that servant is wicked and says to himself, 'My master is staying away a long time.'" The long absence of his master allows the servant to abuse his authority, mistreat his fellow servants, and consort drunkenly with bad acquaintances—activities that are characteristic of idolaters, pagans, unbelievers, and those who have turned away from the faith (Ex. 32:6; Isa. 28:7; 56:12; 1 Cor. 10:7; Gal. 5:21). When the master does return, the slave is caught unaware. As a result, he is cut in pieces (cf. the use of this verb in Jer. 34:18). The wicked servant is further described as being placed with "the hypocrites," one of Jesus' favorite expressions for sinners who put on external righteousness that attempts to mask an evil heart (e.g., Matt. 6:1–17; 23:13–29). His place with hypocrites deserves treatment that is proverbial for the eternal condemnation of hell, "where there will be weeping and gnashing of teeth" (24:51; cf. 8:12). The wicked servant is a false, professing disciple.

As with the preceding scenes, such as Noah and the two in the field and the two women grinding, this is an either-or proposition. The good servant reveals his nature by his good actions; the wicked servant reveals his depravity when left to his own devices. The parable reveals the moral nature of both servants, indicating their relationship to the kingdom of God. The personal transformation that accompanies entrance to the kingdom will affect disciples righteously from the heart to their behavior (cf. 5:20; 15:18–20). The master's departure and delay give rise to a test, while his return demands an accounting that reveals the servants for what they were even before the master's departure and delay.[8]

This parable is not talking about rewards or punishment for believers, nor is it advocating "cutting off" believers who have fallen away. It is a contrast between true and false believers and addresses the consequences of those who show by their lives that they are deserving of hell. We must also be careful not to use this parable to suggest that one can earn his or her salvation by watchfulness or preparedness; rather, a person who truly is a disciple of Jesus will watch and be prepared, because it is his or her kingdom nature to do so. The warning for professing or nondisciples is that they should not delay repenting too long, thinking they will have time. Rather, their own death or the return of Jesus will find them to be unrepentant sinners who hypocritically put on a show of kingdom life, but who are spiritually corrupt.

The focus of this parable has been taken to refer primarily to leaders, who are responsible to care for the needy within the church. Others see it referring generally to all believers. The overall context of the discourse favors the latter. The good slave is the true, faithful disciple of Jesus who is responsible and wise in the outworking of his or her Christian life. But leaders can profit from applying this as well to their leadership responsibilities.

What prompts the servant's wickedness is his noticing that his master has been away a long time. The way one thinks about the Lord's return will eventually influence what one says and how one acts. Perhaps the servant thinks that the master will never return or that he can get away with his wickedness before he is caught. This may be a subtle hint here that Jesus' return will be delayed,[9] which will act as a test to the heart of each person.

## The Parable of the Ten Virgins (25:1–13)

THE NEXT PARABLE advances the themes of watchfulness (24:42–44) and faithfulness (24:45–51) to include readiness: "At that time the kingdom of heaven will be like. . . ." Jesus introduces this parable in a way not found elsewhere in the Olivet Discourse, though it is similar to parables introduced in the Parabolic Discourse on the mysteries of the kingdom of heaven (cf. 13:10–17, 24, 31, 44, 45, 47). This indicates that this parable (and the next) points explicitly to conditions during this age, the age in which the kingdom operates in a "mystery" manner.

---

8. See Scott, *Hear Then the Parable,* 211–12.
9. Carson, "Matthew," 510.

This parable specifically teaches readiness in the light of the unknown time of the coming of the Son of Man. The Old Testament portrayed Yahweh as the "husband" of his people Israel (Isa. 54:4–6; 62:4–5; Ezek. 16:7–34; Hos. 2:19), which paves the way for Jesus as the messianic Son of Man to be pictured as a bridegroom (cf. Matt. 9:14–17). The ten virgins are bridesmaids who are not yet married. Following typical Jewish marriage customs[10] (see comments on 1:18), a groom left his parents' home with a contingent of friends to go to the home of his bride, where nuptial ceremonies were carried out. After this, the entire wedding party formed a processional to a wedding banquet, normally at the home of the bridegroom. The wedding feast was often held at night (22:13; 25:6).

The word for lamp (*lampas*) is different from the lamp (*lychnos*; 5:15) in the SM that is set on a lampstand to light a typical Palestinian home. It was a larger dome-shaped container with rags soaked in the oil to light the way while a person was walking outside.[11] These outdoor torches could last for several hours when extra containers of oil were brought for replenishing the lamp, as the wise virgins have done. They are prepared for what may be a long wait.

The long wait causes both the wise and foolish virgins to become drowsy and fall asleep, which is not a note of condemnation but a detail that heightens the drama of the interval. After the long wait the cry rings out in the middle of the night: "Here's the bridegroom! Come out to meet him!" The wise virgins awake and trim their lamps to get the brightest light possible for the procession, but the parable takes a surprising turn when the foolish virgins say to the wise, "Give us some of your oil; our lamps are going out" The wise virgins cannot comply because their own lamps will go out if they share, so they tell the foolish virgins to find their own at a local shop. Although it is probably difficult at such a late hour, they eventually do find oil, because they arrive later (or else they slowly make their way to the banquet in the dark).

While the foolish virgins are off to find oil, the procession with the bridegroom finally arrives. The reason for referring to the virgins as "wise" in all the prior references is now revealed: They are "ready" to go with the bridegroom to the wedding banquet (25:10). Only those who have been adequately prepared are ready to go. The foolish virgins are not, which Jesus accentuates by stating, "And the door was shut."

The foolish virgins finally arrive, but the bridegroom calls out to them as they stand in the night darkness, "I tell you the truth, I don't know you"

---

10. See J. S. Wright and J. A. Thompson, "Marriage," *IBD*, 2:955–56; Victor P. Hamilton, "Marriage (OT and ANE)," *ABD*, 4:559–69; Jeremias, *The Parables of Jesus*, 173–74.

11. For discussion of different types of lamps, see R. E. Nixon, "Lamp, Lampstand, Lantern," *IBD*, 2:871–73.

(25:12), a stark, straightforward statement of rejection of a person who does not have a true relationship with Jesus (7:23). Throughout the Old Testament God is said to "know" those whom he has chosen to be his people (Jer. 1:5; Hos. 13:5; Amos 3:2), a theme reiterated throughout the New Testament to speak of a saving relationship found with God through Jesus Christ (cf. Gal. 4:8–9; 2 Tim. 2:19).

Jesus addresses his disciples directly to drive home the lesson of the parable: "Therefore keep watch, because you do not know the day or the hour." As in the preceding parable, this is another distinction between two types of people—those who are truly disciples of Jesus and those who are not. Disciples of Jesus will be ready for the arrival of the Son of Man. The destiny of those who are not ready awaits outside the shut door. The previous parable (24:50–51) and the following parable (25:29–30) both speak of hell as the destiny for those who do not "watch" correctly by being properly prepared with salvation to accompany the Son of Man when he arrives. Therefore, the "shut door" points to damnation here as well, especially with the ominous comment from the bridegroom: "I tell you the truth, I don't know you."

## The Parable of the Talents (25:14–30)

JESUS CONTINUES HIS parables about the profitable character qualities of those who await his return. Now the preparedness of those who await the coming of the Son of Man is fleshed out in productiveness and industriousness, where faithfulness in service accompanies watchfulness.[12]

**Talents (25:14–18).** Wealthy landowners often entrusted their property and affairs to trustworthy servants (*doulos* again, as in 24:45) when they went away on business or for personal dealings. The landowner is portrayed here as wealthy, for he has liquid disposability of at least eight talents (25:15; for the value of a talent, see comments on 18:24). In terms of today's value, the landowner disperses approximately $1,977,600 to the three servants. Comparisons are difficult to appreciate, however, because such a sum in first-century Palestine would have been far more disproportionate to the average worker than in modern times.

**Faithful servants (25:19–23).** The sums dispersed by the homeowner apparently symbolize personal giftedness or abilities, but only generally: "each according to his ability" (25:15). The first and second servants immediately make effective use of their entrusted amounts, probably setting up some kind of business and making a capital return on the original invest-

---

12. Young, *The Parables*, 89–112. For a similar parable, probably given on a different occasion but with a similar emphasis, see Luke 19:11–27.

ment that equals the original five and two talents (25:16–17). The third servant simply digs a hole, into which he places the master's one talent (25:18).

After a long interval, similar to the expression in the prior two parables, the master returns and settles accounts with them. He exclaims to the first two servants, "Well done, good and faithful servant! You have been faithful with a few things; I will put you in charge of many things. Come and share your master's happiness!" The identical statement of praise to both servants indicates that the point of the parable is not on the total amount earned but on faithful responsibility in living up to one's potential and giftedness. The reward of earnings bestowed may differ, but both servants received the identical joy in the presence of their master.

**Wicked servant (25:24–27).** In contrast to the first two slaves, the third comes to the master with a different accounting of the one talent given to him: He has hidden it in the ground. The master replies, "You wicked, lazy servant!" The wickedness of the third slave primarily stems from his attitude about his master, which in turn has led to laziness and bad stewardship. The way he conceives of him ("you are a hard man, harvesting where you have not sown and gathering where you have not scattered seed") causes him to fear and then to hide away the talent and not seek to advance the master's capital. The servant's misperception of the master has produced alienation, mistrust, fear, and then personal sloth. Had he truly loved his master, he would not have attempted to place the blame on him but would have operated out of love.

The master tells him that he should have at least deposited the talent "with the bankers." "Banker" here most likely refers to money-changers, who charged a fee for their services. Investment houses or banks as we know them were basically nonexistent in ancient Jewish society. For safe-keeping a private person would either bury valuables (see 13:44; cf. Josh. 7:21) or entrust them to a neighbor (Ex. 22:7).

But the blame in the servant is because he was not industrious enough to seek to earn his master interest (*tokos*; cf. Luke 19:23) on the talent. The Old Testament prohibited charging interest from other Jews (Ex. 22:25; Lev. 25:35–37; Deut. 23:19) but not from Gentiles (Deut. 23:20). While contemporary usage distinguishes interest from usury—a higher rate of interest charged for a loan than is allowed by law or common practice—ancient Judaism and later rabbinic practice made no such distinction and consistently avoided all appearance of charging interest from each other.[13]

Jesus is not advocating setting aside the Old Testament law here; rather, he is referring to investing the talent with money-changers, who performed

---

13. For discussion, see "Interest," *DJBP*, 319.

a valuable service of exchanging a variety of forms of currency for those traveling through Palestine from the Diaspora. This is different from the money-changers who were perverting temple practice (see comments on 21:12). Less likely, Jesus may be pointing to the practice of Jews in Palestine charging interest on loans to Gentiles. Or, given the flexibility with which Jesus used comparisons in parables, he may be using a prohibited practice of earning interest to make a point about a good thing (cf. the correspondence between the thief and the Son of Man in 24:43–44).[14]

**Abundance and punishment (25:28–30).** In a surprising twist to the story, the master declares that the talent is to be taken from the wicked servant and given to the one who has ten and who has proven his industriousness. The lesson is summed up in the saying, "For everyone who has will be given more, and he will have an abundance. Whoever does not have, even what he has will be taken from him." This maxim parallels the saying in 13:12, illustrating a similar point about spiritual responsiveness; here it emphasizes that wise and conscientious use of one's God-given abilities is a responsibility that accompanies a right relationship with God.

But the punishment is not simply taking away the talent from the wicked slave, now called "worthless." The master instructs that he should be thrown "outside, into the darkness, where there will be weeping and gnashing of teeth." As in the other parables, the contrast is between those whose eternal destiny is salvation in the presence of the long-expected Son of Man and eternal damnation.[15] The first two servants are true disciples; the third is not. A person's faithfulness is evidence as to whether he or she is truly one of Jesus' own. As the disciples await the return of the Son of Man, they must teach that industriousness of discipleship is a testimony of one's love and trust of Jesus as Lord. But their perseverance should not come from a self-advancing motivation; it should be demonstrated in serving others as Jesus did (20:20–28).

## Judgment at the End (25:31–46)

THIS FINAL SCENE in the Olivet Discourse is unique to Matthew's Gospel. Up to this point, Jesus has addressed two basic issues. In the first part, he gave a running account, generally chronological, of the events that would accompany his return as the Son of Man (24:4–35). In the second part, through sayings and parables, he propounded various lessons on watching, waiting, and being prepared for his second coming (24:36–25:30). In this third part, Jesus gives promises of reward and warnings of judgment that will accompany his

---

14. See Carson, "Matthew," 517.

15. For a scholarly discussion of judgment in Matthew's Gospel, see Sim, *Apocalyptic Eschatology in the Gospel of Matthew*, esp. 130–39.

coming as the glorious Son of Man (25:30–46). Each of the preceding four parables included statements of judgment, but the emphasis was on getting one's life prepared. Now the emphasis is squarely on judgment of those who are excluded and the reward for those who are admitted to the kingdom (25:34).

**Sheep separated from goats (25:31–33).** The scene switches now to the glorious coming of the Son of Man. He is accompanied in his glory with all the angels, and he sits on his throne of glory. Before him all of the nations will be gathered (25:32). The debated expression "the nations" has been interpreted to mean the church, all humanity, or all unbelievers, but within the Matthean context it is most likely intended to mean both Jews and Gentiles who throughout this age are the combined object of the Great Commission (see comments on 24:14; 28:18–20).[16] The nations as entities are not judged but rather the people (NIV) within them: "He will separate the people one from another as a shepherd separates the sheep from the goats."

The shepherd metaphor softens the judgment image but does not diminish the foreboding consequences of separating the sheep from the goats. "Sheep" is a consistent image of the people of God, whether it refers to Israel (9:36; 10:6; 15:24; cf. Ezek. 34) or Jesus' disciples (Matt. 10:16; cf. 26:31 quoting Zech. 13:7; John 10). Goats do not occur often in the New Testament, but in the Old Testament 70 percent of the references to them concern their use as animals for sacrifice, such as the goat offered for sin sacrifice and the one that was the scapegoat on the Day of Atonement (Lev. 16:8–10, 26). In most areas of the world the issue of separating sheep from goats would never arise, since flocks are unlikely to mix. But in the lands surrounding Palestine they often run together, and native breeds can look alike in size, color, and shape.[17]

There seems to be no significant reason why Jesus contrasts sheep with goats, except for the symbolism that will be attached to both in a surprising manner: "He will put the sheep on his right and the goats on his left." The right-hand side is the place of honor (see comments on 20:21). The left-hand side is not usually a place of disfavor, although it does seem to be so here.

**The reward of the sheep (25:34–40).** The King gives the explanation for the separation as he says to those on his right, "Come, you who are blessed by my Father; take your inheritance, the kingdom." The King represents the

---

16. For a detailed history of interpretation at to the identity implied here, see S. W. Gray, *The Least of My Brothers: Matthew 25:31–42—A History of Interpretation* (SBLDS 114; Atlanta: Scholars Press, 1989), although Gray argues that the judgment of the church is described in 24:45–25:30, and judgment of those outside the church in 25:31–46 (358–59).

17. George S. Cansdale, "Goats," *ZPEB*, 2:739–41.

Son of Man sitting on the throne (25:31), bringing to mind Daniel 7:13–14, where the Son of Man receives the kingdom from the Ancient of Days. This is one of the rare times that Jesus refers to himself as King, although the theme is there throughout Matthew's Gospel. Matthew traces Jesus' lineage to King David (1:1–17), Jesus is sought by the Magi as the one born king of the Jews (2:2), he announces the arrival of the kingdom of heaven (4:17), his earthly ministry comes to a climactic point in his triumphal entry to Jerusalem where he fulfills the expectation of Israel's king coming to her (see comments on 21:5), the Sanhedrin accuses him of claiming to be king of the Jews (27:11), and he is mocked as king in his crucifixion (27:29, 37, 42).

The King addresses the sheep on his right as "blessed by my Father." The blessing consists of their inheritance, which is the kingdom they now receive, not because they have earned it through their own efforts but because it is a gift of their relationship with the Father and the Son. God's assured purpose is carried out as the blessing of the inheritance of the kingdom for the sheep is realized.

The transitional "for" in 25:35 introduces the explanation why the sheep receive the inheritance: Kingdom inheritance is the reward for caring for Jesus' physical needs. The king pronounces, "For I was hungry and you gave me something to eat...." The sheep cared for Jesus when he was in need with hunger, thirst, being a stranger, naked, sick, and imprisoned. The precedent is found in those Old Testament admonitions, where God rejects Israel's external displays of religiosity (e.g., fasting) as a sham and declares that true righteousness is displayed in caring for the needy (e.g., Isa. 58:6–10).

But there is a surprised reaction from those who are rewarded: "Lord, when did we see you hungry and feed you...?" The surprise of the "righteous" sheep (cf. 10:41; 13:43, 49; 25:37) comes from their taking literally his words, because they can recall no time when they have done this to the King. Such surprise indicates that these were not intentional meritorious acts to gain access to the kingdom. Rather, these acts of mercy are evidences that the sheep belong to the kingdom, just as the preceding parables pointed out external behavioral evidences of a person who has truly received the gift of salvation and the resulting transformation by the Spirit.

Jesus responds, "I tell you the truth, whatever you did for one of the least of these brothers of mine, you did for me" (25:40). Following on the surprise of the righteous, this statement of Jesus is a central principle of the passage—in caring for the needs of "the least" of these brothers of Jesus, they have served Jesus.

**The least of these brothers of mine (25:40).** Solving the question of the identification of these "brothers" is important. The answer to that question determines what Jesus gives as the basis for one's acceptance into eternal life or departure into eternal punishment (25:46). Five primary solutions have been offered.[18] (1) *All needy persons in humanity.* This view emphasizes that mercy is to be displayed toward all persons.[19] (2) *All Christians.* Others suggest that all Christians are in view, since the most explicit reference to "brothers" in Jesus' usage in Matthew refers to his disciples.[20] (3) *Christian missionaries.* Others suggest that these are Christian missionaries, the treatment of whom determines the fate of all people. Those who receive them receive Jesus; those who reject them reject Jesus—a theme not unlike the reward offered in the Missionary Discourse (10:40–42).[21] (4) *Jewish Christians.* Some conclude Jesus is referring to Jewish Christians, especially focusing on the way that converted Christians treat converted Jews who are missionaries for him during the Great Tribulation.[22] (5) *Tribulation martyrs.* This view suggests that Jesus refers to Christians who were martyred for the faith during the Great Tribulation and who will return with the risen Lord at his second coming.[23]

The consistent way that Jesus refers to his disciples as "brothers" in Matthew's narrative leads to the second view. But the expression "least" points explicitly to *needy* disciples. Needy disciples are often the ones who are excluded from care—attention is often wrongfully diverted to prominent members of the discipleship community. This is in line with the admonition Jesus gave to the disciples arguing about who was the greatest in the kingdom of heaven (18:1). He charged them to become like children, and receiving children in his name is like receiving Jesus himself (18:2–5). This is also in line with the apostle James's rebuke of his church for showing partiality to the rich in the assembly while dishonoring the poor in the church (cf. James 2:1).

Thus, Jesus affirms that believers are to care for one another, but especially the least and insignificant among them. This does not absolve a general mercy that Christians must demonstrate toward all in need. As Morris says, "Everyone in need is to be the object of Christian benevolence."[24] But perhaps the best guiding light is given by the apostle Paul, who stated the principle,

---

18. See Gray, *The Least of My Brothers*; Eugene W. Pond, "Who are 'The Least' of Jesus' Brothers in Matthew 25:40," *BibSac* 159 (October–December 2002): 436–48.

19. This was a minority position for much of church history but has found many recent adherents. For a recent defense, see Davies and Allison, *Matthew*, 3:428–29; C. E. B. Cranfield, "Who are Christ's Brothers," *Metanoia* 4 (1994): 31–39.

20. See 5:47; 12:49–50; 18:15–17; 23:8; 28:10. Those who take this position: Hagner, *Matthew*, 2:744–45; Carson, "Matthew," 519–21.

21. Blomberg, *Matthew*, 378.

22. E.g., Barbieri, "Matthew," 81; Glasscock, *Matthew*, 491–92.

23. E.g., Pond, "Who are 'The Least' of Jesus' Brothers in Matthew 25:40," 443–48.

24. Morris, *Matthew*, 639.

"Therefore, as we have opportunity, let us do good to all people, especially to those who belong to the family of believers" (Gal. 6:10).

But we should reiterate that these good deeds are not the works by which one enters the kingdom; they are the substantiation of the kind of kingdom life that has been produced through the transformation of the heart of his disciples through regeneration. Their works of caring for the needy among them will confirm that they belong to Jesus. Otherwise they are not truly his sheep, because they have not been born again by the Spirit of God.

**The punishment of the goats (25:41−45).** Jesus now addresses those on his left, the "goats," in almost the same wording he used to commend the "sheep" on his right, except that the goats are condemned because they have not demonstrated mercy to Jesus in his need. Eternal fire is the punishment for not caring for Jesus' physical needs (25:41−43). The goats respond similarly to the way that the sheep have (25:44). Jesus responds in the same way as he has to the sheep, except the goats have *not* acted in behalf of "the least." Jesus omits the reference to "of these brothers of mine," but we should assume that he intends this as a shortened reference.

The goats are just as surprised as the sheep, but they are surprised like those in the preceding parables. The five foolish virgins (25:1−13) and the wicked servant who did not invest his talent (25:14−30) were not condemned to eternal punishment for some externally heinous sin but for their failure to do the right thing. So here, "sins of omission" are also worthy of eternal damnation, because they are evidence that a person has not been made righteous by association with the kingdom of God (5:20). Righteous acts spring from a heart sanctified by the Spirit of God while unrighteous acts, even of omission, indicate a heart lacking in the Spirit's work of transformation (cf. 15:19; Titus 3:1−8).

**Eternal punishment and eternal life (25:46).** Jesus concludes the dramatic judgment scene by stating, "Then they will go away to eternal punishment, but the righteous to eternal life" (25:46). Daniel's prophecy of a future time of great tribulation that will come on the earth also leads to a prophecy of eternal life and punishment: "Multitudes who sleep in the dust of the earth will awake: some to everlasting life, others to shame and everlasting contempt. Those who are wise will shine like the brightness of the heavens, and those who lead many to righteousness, like the stars for ever and ever" (Dan. 12:1−3; cf. 2 *Bar.* 51:5−6). Daniel's prophecy echoes here in the final words of Jesus' concluding discourse in Matthew's Gospel.

Those who have responded to Jesus' announcement and have become his disciples have all along been called "sons of the kingdom" (13:38), but now they enter into the full blessing and experience of life in the kingdom. Many understand this judgment scene to be the same as that occurring at the end of this earthly age, just prior to the eternal state (Rev. 20:11–13).[25] Others understand this judgment to take place prior to the inauguration of the earthly millennial kingdom by Jesus, who will rule over those who are blessed to enter that reign with him.[26]

The former view is in harmony with the references to the eternal life or punishment into which the sheep or goats now enter (25:41, 46). Premillennialists who hold this position have to explain how the immediacy of the coming of the Son of Man throughout the discourse gives way to a scene of judgment that occurs a thousand years later. Most do so by suggesting that Jesus has compressed future events. The latter view is more in harmony with the consistent reference to the immediacy of the coming of the Son of Man throughout the discourse, but they must explain the references to entering into "eternal life" at the time of the Millennium—either Jesus is speaking nonchronologically and is compressing future events, or more likely, "eternal" is used here not as an experience of their final state but a confirmation of it before the final experience.[27]

The evidence is scanty either way, but the important point throughout this scene is clear: Judgment will come.[28] In that way this judgment scene provides a dramatic conclusion to the entire discourse and a sequential culmination to the preceding parables. The presence of kingdom life will always produce evidence in the transformed speech, thought, actions, and character of Jesus' followers. The absence of transformation is proof that a person has not accepted the invitation to the kingdom. Reward or penalty is distributed according to the evidence.[29]

As has been the emphasis throughout the Olivet Discourse, and ultimately throughout this Gospel, there are only two types of people. Those who have not followed Jesus are actually against him and will endure separation from him in their eternal punishment. Jesus' disciples are with him and will enjoy with him life that is eternal. This should produce the greatest joy in Jesus' disciples, as we consider our eternal destiny. But the fate of the wicked should also weigh heavily upon us, provoking the same kind of anguish that the apostle Paul experienced as he considered the eternal fate of his fellow Jews who had rejected Jesus (Rom. 9:1–3; 10:1–2).

---

25. Erickson, *Christian Theology*, 1200–1203; Hagner, *Matthew*, 2:742–43; Blomberg, *Matthew*, 376; Morris, *Matthew*, 634–35.

26. E.g., Eugene W. Pond, "The Background and Timing of the Judgment of the Sheep and Goats," *BibSac* 159 (April–June 2002): 201–20; Saucy, *Progressive Dispensationalism*, 130.

27. Pond, "The Background and Timing of the Judgment of the Sheep and Goats," 219–20; Saucy, *Progressive Dispensationalism*, 288 n. 67.

28. See Sim, *Apocalyptic Eschatology in the Gospel of Matthew*, 130–39.

29. Ladd, *Theology of the New Testament*, 206–7.

THIS SERIES OF sayings, parables, and judgment scenes completes Jesus' final discourse in Matthew's Gospel (for a summary of its content, see comments on 24:1–3). Jesus' intent in the present section is not to give a timetable; he focuses on the attitudes and character qualities that guide their discipleship to him for that time when he will no longer be with them physically.

As we discussed in the preceding chapter, the relationship of the return of the Lord in the Olivet Discourse to Paul's discussion of the "rapture" of believers (1 Thess. 4:13–18) is debated. Many expositors suggest that Paul speaks of a separate return of the Lord either prior to or halfway through the Tribulation to rapture believers away from the earth to protect them from God's wrath during the Great Tribulation. Others contend that Paul and Jesus refer to the rapture of believers at the end of the period of tribulation, when Jesus will return to take believers to be with him who have been safely guarded through the Tribulation.[30] The issues are far too complex to resolve here, but for our purposes it is important to keep two things in tension, which appears to be Jesus' primary intention in this discourse.[31]

**Suddenness.** The suddenness of the return of the Son of Man permeates each scene in this section of the Olivet Discourse. This accords with Paul's encouragement to the Thessalonians, when he assures them that Christ's coming has not already occurred (1 Thess. 4:13–18). Paul implies that Jesus' coming could come at any time and catch believers away. The world around them is saying, "Peace and safety," after which comes destruction (5:3). The appearance of the Lord in the parables in the Olivet Discourse is sudden, with no warning. Therefore, since Jesus addresses disciples who will live throughout this age, one crucial feature of our discipleship to him entails awaiting his return, which will arrive with suddenness.

**Preparedness.** The theme of preparedness also permeates the Olivet Discourse. Whether in the context of peace or trouble, all believers throughout this age are guaranteed that we will experience both (cf. 10:24–25). So we must be prepared for the Lord's return regardless of our circumstances. Each of the following parables emphasizes different aspects of that preparedness:

---

30. For a presentation of each view and interaction between adherents, see Gleason L. Archer Jr., Paul D. Feinberg, Douglas J. Moo, and Richard R. Reiter, *The Rapture: Pre-, Mid-, or Post-Tribulational?* (Grand Rapids: Zondervan, 1984).

31. Personally, I hold that a pretribulational rapture best explains several theological issues (e.g., the reestablishment of Israel during the Millennium and the time required for developing a people who would populate the Millennium). But I also believe that taking the discourse in the context of Jesus' instruction to his disciples best highlights principles of discipleship that inform any eschatological position.

responsibility (24:45–51), readiness (25:1–13), productivity (25:14–30), and accountability (25:31–46).

Some people focus so much on Jesus' return in glory at the end of the period of tribulation that they exhibit little concern to be prepared now, thinking they can wait until they see the events of the end begin to unfold and then they will prepare. Others focus so much on the expectation of Jesus' return at any moment that they have little concern for the long haul, thinking that Jesus will return so soon that they don't have to make any plans. Balanced discipleship entails both immediate and long-term readiness. Jesus' sayings in the remaining parables and scene of judgment in the discourse are addressed to his disciples, then and now, who are called to be urgently prepared for a sudden, unexpected return of the Lord, but who must plan for an extended absence and make profitable use of their giftedness in the meantime.

MY WIFE AND I woke up this morning to breaking news of the devastating loss of the space shuttle *Columbia* on its final sixteen minutes of reentry to earth's atmosphere. It was a tragic loss to our space program, but in my view it was an even more agonizing loss of the seven men and women aboard the shuttle. In the first official statement, NASA Administrator Sean O'Keefe confirmed that the shuttle broke up in flames as it reentered the earth's atmosphere and spread debris all over Texas. He described the crew as having performed their mission brilliantly, but then said in a broken voice, "The loss of this valued crew is something we will never get over."

These heartrending events strike home to each of us in dramatic ways to remind us that life is fragile and fleeting. In one brief moment, all of the work and effort and expense of these men and women throughout their lives were gone.

That is the message of the Olivet Discourse in a nutshell. Life as we know it is going to come to an end. All history will come to a climactic finale when Jesus returns. That conclusion may be sooner than we think, so be prepared. I have a life motto that expresses what I believe to be the reflection of this exhortation:

Live as though Jesus is coming back today;
plan as though he is not coming back for a hundred years.

Regardless of your theological view with reference to the return of Jesus, this exhortation is relevant, for life is fragile and fleeting, but we do not know when the end will come. Whether it is at the end of history as we know it with the return of Jesus or at the end of our life as we know it with our own death, we must be prepared. But that does not mean we should withdraw and count moments. Rather, our privilege and charge are to maximize the precious moments of life with which we have been gifted to make a difference for the sake of the kingdom.

In the light of the fact that the time of his return is unknown (24:36), Jesus emphasizes that a sure separation will come for those who are taken and those who are left (24:37—41). It's an either-or proposition. There is no middle ground. Therefore, we should live with the certain expectation that the end is near for each of us, which will affect our daily discipleship to him. At the conclusion of our lives or when he returns in glory and power, we will either be with him or not. Jesus gives four parables and a judgment scene that illustrate why and how his disciples can be assured that they will be approved when Jesus comes again. But these parables and judgment scene teach the obverse as well, that judgment awaits those who are not faithful. On the primary level they indicate who it is that demonstrates true life of the kingdom to receive life eternal. On the secondary level each indicates how discipleship to Jesus can be advanced.

The first parable, the homeowner and the thief (24:43—44), gives the general principle that faithful discipleship to Jesus while awaiting his return is demonstrated in those who *watch by being prepared*. The three following parables demonstrate how: We must be *responsible* (the two kinds of servants; 24:45—51), *ready* (ten virgins; 25:1—13), and *productive* (the talents; 25:14—30). The concluding scene of the judgment of the sheep and the goats (25:31—46) brings a climactic conclusion by announcing that watching and waiting throughout one's life, and throughout history, requires us to be *accountable* to our discipleship.

**Prepared (24:43—44).** The parable of the homeowner and thief sets the stage for how we should live our lives in the expectation that Jesus will return: We are to *watch* diligently. But observing doesn't just mean sitting around waiting to see what will happen next. It means that we will be *prepared* for his arrival at any time or day. For example, my wife's cat Maui watches our home diligently while we are gone. She notices everything that goes on. But she isn't prepared to do anything about it. She runs and hides in the closet if she hears a sound! And some dogs certainly aren't much better. The best kind of watchdog is one that watches and is ready to do something about an intruder.

So it is with us. We must watch, but awaiting the Lord's return must be accompanied with the appropriate kinds of preparedness. On the primary level this means we will nurture a lively expectation of his Parousia.[32] Our entire worldview must be kingdom-oriented, as Jesus has been emphasizing

---

32. Daniel J. Lewis, *3 Crucial Questions about the Last Days* (Grand Rapids: Baker, 1998), 135.

throughout his ministry. Our hope lies in God's fully established kingdom on earth, not in the kingdoms we create.

We wait with all of creation for its full liberation (Rom. 8:18–25), but our waiting and watching mean that we are prepared by responding to the invitation to the kingdom on earth now and experiencing the beginning of regeneration as our own souls are washed and renewed by the Holy Spirit (Titus 3:4–7). As we nurture the blessed hope of Jesus' return daily, the grace of God teaches us to say "No" to ungodliness and worldly passions "and to live self-controlled, upright and godly lives in this present age" (Titus 2:12). When this is our daily, even hourly, focus, we watch and wait for Jesus' return fully equipped to meet him with peace and confidence.

**Responsible (24:45–51).** The parable of the two kinds of servants continues that theme by teaching that a person truly demonstrates that he or she is prepared with kingdom life by *responsible* behavior. A person's faithful responsibility is the external evidence of whether or not a person is truly one of Jesus' own. We must examine ourselves as to whether or not we are true believers, which will be evidenced by the way we think, treat others, and live righteously or unrighteously. The wicked servant revealed an evil heart when he contemplated the long delay of his master's return. He was primarily motivated by the master's presence; when that was removed, his wicked heart produced wicked actions.

A faithful and good heart lives righteously regardless of circumstances. Whether we are with other believers or not, whether we think that we will be caught or not, a pure heart is intent on producing responsible behavior (cf. comments on 5:20; 15:18–19). The apostle John writes, "Dear friends, now we are children of God, and what we will be has not yet been made known. But we know that when he appears, we shall be like him, for we shall see him as he is. Everyone who has this hope in him purifies himself, just as he is pure" (1 John 3:2–3).

Jesus' discipleship community, the church, is the primary instrument by which the reality of the gospel of the kingdom is made known to a watching world. It is our responsibility to make known the gospel by all that we are and say. When we live with the blessed hope of Jesus' soon return, we are motivated to live up to our responsibilities. This means we are ethically responsible for daily purity in the light of the expectation of Jesus' coming.[33] Someone has said well, "Live each day so that you will neither be afraid of tomorrow nor ashamed of yesterday."

We must also take seriously the responsibility as stewards of God's world and resources. Our role as spouse or parent means that we care for others

---

33. Lewis, *3 Crucial Questions about the Last Days*, 135–36.

as God would. Our chosen career path means that we serve dutifully God through our work, whether it is "sacred or secular" (cf. Eph. 6:7–8). In the leadership positions that we undertake, whether in business, school, or church, we serve people by serving Jesus as our Master, and we are ultimately responsible to him for the way we treat those for whom we have responsibility (Eph. 6:9). The more responsibly we carry out the Master's affairs, the more responsibility we are given. Those who put off their duties, thinking that the Master will be delayed, may discover that it is too late to make amends.[34]

**Ready (25:1–13).** The parable of the ten virgins continues the theme of watchful preparation, namely, being prepared for the Lord's coming by our *readiness* to meet him at any moment. At the end of life or at the return of Jesus, it will be too late to get ready. We must be spiritually prepared to meet Jesus now.

I especially see in young people a feeling that they are invincible. They operate as though they believe they will have plenty of time to get their life straightened out later on. But one of the great lessons that leads to maturity is that our life is not our own, and it can be taken away at any moment. When young people reach that point, they recognize that they must get prepared spiritually so that they are ready.

We are ready when our relationships with God and others are what they should be. We are ready when at any moment of our day, whether in the privacy of our home or in the apartment of our girlfriend or in the recesses of our mind, we are not ashamed to have the Lord meet us. We are also ready when we make sure that our children are adequately cared for, when we will not be ashamed at our credit card accounts being made public. We are ready when past grievances have been acquitted.

My wife and I have made a commitment that we don't ever want to say "if only": if only we had taken care of our health more; if only we had spent more time with our kids; if only we had been more disciplined to pay off our debts; if only we had not allowed that relationship quirk to pull us apart. The more we take care of those "if onlys," the more we are prepared to meet Jesus.

The Jewish custom of the bridegroom coming at an unexpected time for his bride added to the anticipation. The lack of preparation by the five foolish virgins is a dramatic representation of the unthinkable. In today's terms, a bride or groom who doesn't plan to be on time for his or her own wedding wouldn't simply be seen as unfortunate, but emotionally deficient to appreciate the importance of the day. As disciples who love and are committed to

---

34. Blomberg, *Parables*, 193.

Jesus, it would similarly be unthinkable that we do not ready ourselves for his coming. The parable points out the personal nature of our relationship to the Lord. Our commitment and desire to see Jesus face to face when he comes for us should encourage us to prepare appropriately.

One of the most important ways of equipping ourselves is to ponder deeply the parable's significance in such a way that we act on its surety. The apostle Paul lived his life in the light of the return of Christ. Donald Hagner states, "Uncertainty concerning the time is in a sense a non-issue; the *fact* of the future return of the Son of Man is what counts."[35] Much of Paul's writings ground ethical behavior not only in our current redeemed state but in its connection to our future life with Christ (cf. Col. 3:4). This is the attitude we should have now, and we should encourage the church to have it also. A suitable attitude of readiness in the church and in our own lives allows our anticipation of eternal things to make more insignificant some of our petty concerns and more manageable some of our bigger concerns.

**Productive (25:14–30).** The parable of the talents also demonstrates that disciples are prepared for the Lord's coming by their intentional *productivity*. The English term "talent" is derived from this parable. In common usage today "talents" often refer to the natural endowments of a person. That is an appropriate usage, but to draw even closer to the intent of the parable, the talents symbolize the giftedness that is bestowed on each person who is graced with kingdom life and with how we use our gifts in service of the kingdom (1 Cor. 12:7).

A combined perspective is important. All that we are—whether naturally endowed or Spirit-bestowed—must be employed in service of the kingdom of God. Not everyone is born with the same talents, and not everyone is endowed with the same gifts of the Spirit, yet each of us can be productive in our own unique ways. All of our service in the kingdom is inherently valuable, whether it is in sacred or secular realms, whether it receives a greater or lesser return. Our responsibility is to plan for the long haul and use our giftedness to advance the kingdom of God.

Unfortunately, one of the unproductive side-effects of the study of prophecy is sensationalistic speculation in preaching and conferences about the end times. Such speculation consumes the attention of people, often paralyzing them with fear of a stereotyped picture of God or else devouring them with detailed conjecture. Others turn away from any kind of productive study of prophecy because of their bad experience with those involved with unproductive speculation. Solid study of prophecy is beneficial because

---

35. Hagner, *Matthew*, 2:716.

it motivates people to godly living, it promotes intentional outreach, and it clarifies sound doctrine.[36]

The explicit problem with the wicked servant is his attitude about his master. This is the way many people deal with God. Their wrong attitude about God (God is mean, God is unconcerned with our fate, etc.) results in an excuse for disobedience to his calling. It can also be applied by Christians who develop wrong attitudes about God. They see God as unloving because of their circumstances, and they then depart from the path of obedience.

But faithfulness is contingent on an accurate view of God. Inaccurate views of God allow us to rationalize our own irresponsibility and unfaithfulness. Thus, it is vitally important to have a correct biblical perception of God's character, his activities, and his goals for us. This is the important role of solid Bible teaching and preaching, for our view of God determines our behavior. The parable reveals that the wickedness of the servant impelled him to pervert the image of his master, which then provided him with an excuse for his personal irresponsibility.

We can see this in people who tragically put off coming to Christ for salvation because they will not come to faith until they can figure out how a supposedly good God can continue to allow suffering. We can also see this in believers who blatantly blame God for their own laziness and irresponsibility. We can also see this in people so caught up in personal grief and tragedy that they cannot see the light of God's love and care. A former student of mine is a pastor who has just lost his wife to a long battle with cancer. He wrestles with trying to understand why God would take away his wife and the mother of his children at a time when she was most needed. He even says that his grief has so consumed him that he cannot read the Bible to see clearly a truthful vision of God.

The parable teaches us that a truthful understanding of God will bring about the productive investment of our lives. That causes me to examine my own ministry to these kinds of people. I realize I must ultimately turn them over to their own accountability to God, but I also realize that I must have as much patience with them as I can until they are called to give that accounting. I must seek to help them to rightly understand God's nature, which will cause them to invest their lives productively in service of the kingdom.

**Accountable (25:31–46).** The scene of the judgment of the sheep and goats brings these parables and the discourse to a dramatic conclusion with the pronouncement that we will all be accountable for what we do in this life

---

36. For an attempt to demonstrate how detailed study of prophecy has historically led to productive outcomes, see Larry D. Pettegrew, "The Rapture Debate at the Niagara Bible Conference," *BibSac* 157 (July–September 2000): 331–47.

while awaiting the return of the King. The powerful twist to the scene is that our service to Jesus is demonstrated best by how we serve the least of Jesus' brothers. The preceding parables also reveal a person's heart—preparedness, responsibility, readiness, productivity—but caring for the most needy among Jesus' disciples is the clinching evidence of kingdom life.

There is a primary responsibility that we must care for those of the household of faith, but also all of God's creatures. There is inherent value in those created in God's image, even those who are living lives separate from God as well as those who are unattractive emotionally, relationally, or even physically. God truly loves the world and desires that none should perish (John 3:16; 2 Peter 3:9). We must have great empathy for all individuals made in his image and understand their eternal nature. This should give us a heart for missions and an intense desire that none would perish eternally.

Humble ministry to the lowliest demonstrates Jesus' own humility in leaving the glories of heaven to bring salvation's story to the weak and the downtrodden, the tax collector and sinner, the sick and dying. We cannot serve these solely out of a motivation of religious obligation, for then we do so out of our own prideful strength. We serve because we have been served, we love because we have been loved, we lift up because we have been lifted up—and we never forget it. Religious duty and public ministry can easily be turned around to the kind of hypocrisy that Jesus consistently condemned—serving out of a desire to receive community and professional commendation (cf. 6:1–17). But a heart that has been truly transformed by the righteousness of the kingdom of God will serve out of humility.

My wife and I had had a somewhat hurtful exchange a while back over this very point. I had just given a chapel message at our seminary on "ambitious servanthood," where I encouraged all of us—faculty, administration, staff, students—to commit ourselves to be ambitious in ministry with the overarching motivation of serving Jesus by serving our people. At home that evening my wife received a phone call from one of our neighbors whose father was having recuperative problems following surgery. That was the fourth evening in a row that my wife spent an hour or more on the phone with a needy neighbor or family member or friend. I felt as if she was being taken advantage of by these people, and so I warned her when she got off the phone. (I probably was also feeling a bit neglected personally.)

In the ensuing exchange the issue of "servanthood" came up, and she gently reminded me of my message at the seminary chapel. In many ways I am paid to be a servant. That's part of the ethos I must develop. But what am I like away from that environment? Is service to the least not only my public mission but also the mission of my heart in private? That is what Jesus is getting at. Our final judgment is not the greatness of our public ministry, but the ministry that flows from the humility of Jesus' own heart for the needy among us.

**Life is fragile and fleeting.** The tragic loss of the space shuttle *Columbia* illustrates that life is fragile and fleeting. This is the message of Jesus' exhortation as he concludes the Olivet Discourse. We must be ready to meet him as our Master and Lord, whether at the end of life or at the end of this age. Yet we are all called to account for what we have done with our lives. *Live as though Jesus is coming back today; plan as though he is not coming back for a hundred years.*

# Matthew 26:1–46

❧

**W**HEN JESUS HAD finished saying all these things, he said to his disciples, ²"As you know, the Passover is two days away—and the Son of Man will be handed over to be crucified."

³Then the chief priests and the elders of the people assembled in the palace of the high priest, whose name was Caiaphas, ⁴and they plotted to arrest Jesus in some sly way and kill him. ⁵"But not during the Feast," they said, "or there may be a riot among the people."

⁶While Jesus was in Bethany in the home of a man known as Simon the Leper, ⁷a woman came to him with an alabaster jar of very expensive perfume, which she poured on his head as he was reclining at the table.

⁸When the disciples saw this, they were indignant. "Why this waste?" they asked. ⁹"This perfume could have been sold at a high price and the money given to the poor."

¹⁰Aware of this, Jesus said to them, "Why are you bothering this woman? She has done a beautiful thing to me. ¹¹The poor you will always have with you, but you will not always have me. ¹²When she poured this perfume on my body, she did it to prepare me for burial. ¹³I tell you the truth, wherever this gospel is preached throughout the world, what she has done will also be told, in memory of her."

¹⁴Then one of the Twelve—the one called Judas Iscariot—went to the chief priests ¹⁵and asked, "What are you willing to give me if I hand him over to you?" So they counted out for him thirty silver coins. ¹⁶From then on Judas watched for an opportunity to hand him over.

¹⁷On the first day of the Feast of Unleavened Bread, the disciples came to Jesus and asked, "Where do you want us to make preparations for you to eat the Passover?"

¹⁸He replied, "Go into the city to a certain man and tell him, 'The Teacher says: My appointed time is near. I am going to celebrate the Passover with my disciples at your house.' "
¹⁹So the disciples did as Jesus had directed them and prepared the Passover.

²⁰When evening came, Jesus was reclining at the table with

the Twelve. ²¹And while they were eating, he said, "I tell you the truth, one of you will betray me."

²²They were very sad and began to say to him one after the other, "Surely not I, Lord?"

²³Jesus replied, "The one who has dipped his hand into the bowl with me will betray me. ²⁴The Son of Man will go just as it is written about him. But woe to that man who betrays the Son of Man! It would be better for him if he had not been born."

²⁵Then Judas, the one who would betray him, said, "Surely not I, Rabbi?"

Jesus answered, "Yes, it is you."

²⁶While they were eating, Jesus took bread, gave thanks and broke it, and gave it to his disciples, saying, "Take and eat; this is my body."

²⁷Then he took the cup, gave thanks and offered it to them, saying, "Drink from it, all of you. ²⁸This is my blood of the covenant, which is poured out for many for the forgiveness of sins. ²⁹I tell you, I will not drink of this fruit of the vine from now on until that day when I drink it anew with you in my Father's kingdom."

³⁰When they had sung a hymn, they went out to the Mount of Olives.

³¹Then Jesus told them, "This very night you will all fall away on account of me, for it is written:

"'I will strike the shepherd,
    and the sheep of the flock will be scattered.'

³²But after I have risen, I will go ahead of you into Galilee."

³³Peter replied, "Even if all fall away on account of you, I never will."

³⁴"I tell you the truth," Jesus answered, "this very night, before the rooster crows, you will disown me three times."

³⁵But Peter declared, "Even if I have to die with you, I will never disown you." And all the other disciples said the same.

³⁶Then Jesus went with his disciples to a place called Gethsemane, and he said to them, "Sit here while I go over there and pray." ³⁷He took Peter and the two sons of Zebedee along with him, and he began to be sorrowful and troubled. ³⁸Then he said to them, "My soul is overwhelmed with sorrow to the point of death. Stay here and keep watch with me."

³⁹Going a little farther, he fell with his face to the ground and prayed, "My Father, if it is possible, may this cup be taken from me. Yet not as I will, but as you will."

⁴⁰Then he returned to his disciples and found them sleeping. "Could you men not keep watch with me for one hour?" he asked Peter. ⁴¹"Watch and pray so that you will not fall into temptation. The spirit is willing, but the body is weak."

⁴²He went away a second time and prayed, "My Father, if it is not possible for this cup to be taken away unless I drink it, may your will be done."

⁴³When he came back, he again found them sleeping, because their eyes were heavy. ⁴⁴So he left them and went away once more and prayed the third time, saying the same thing.

⁴⁵Then he returned to the disciples and said to them, "Are you still sleeping and resting? Look, the hour is near, and the Son of Man is betrayed into the hands of sinners. ⁴⁶Rise, let us go! Here comes my betrayer!"

MATTHEW SIGNALS THE end of Jesus' Olivet Discourse with his regular statement "When Jesus had finished saying all these things..." (26:1; cf. 7:28; 11:1; 13:53; 19:1). The difference between this and the earlier ones is the statement that he "finished saying *all* these things," indicating that Jesus now has finished his five primary discourses to his disciples. Jesus later describes the content of these discourses as "everything I have commanded you" (28:20), which must be taught to disciples throughout the age until his return as his binding words of guidance.

Jesus' destiny with the cross moves inexorably forward. Having finished his Olivet Discourse, he spends that evening again in Bethany, where they spent each evening of Holy Week (cf. 21:1, 17). In just two short days they will go back to Jerusalem for the final hours of Jesus' earthly life and mission. He declares to his disciples dramatically, "As you know, the Passover is two days away—and the Son of Man will be handed over to be crucified" (26:2).

Matthew concludes his Gospel with two long chapters that narrate the events leading up to Jesus' death and a shorter chapter that narrates Jesus' stunning resurrection and final commission to his disciples. We will look at the events of Jesus' death in three sections: (1) the events surrounding the celebration of the Passover and institution of the Lord's Supper, with the fateful movement to Gethsemane (26:1–46); (2) the arrest, trials, and conviction of

Jesus (26:47–27:26); (3) the flogging, crucifixion, death, and burial of Jesus (27:27–66).[1] The length of Matthew's treatment of these events indicates the central place that Jesus' death holds in God's plan of salvation. As Malcolm Muggeridge exclaims, "It was manifestly the most famous death in history. No other death has aroused one-hundredth part of the interest, or been remembered with one-hundredth part of the intensity and concern" as the death of Jesus of Nazareth.[2]

### Jesus' Prediction and the Plot of the Religious Leaders (26:1–5)

THE PASSOVER (26:1–2). The Passover Feast was celebrated annually to commemorate Israel's escape from Egypt (Ex. 12). The month of Passover, the first month of the religious year for the Israelites, was first called Abib (Ex. 13:4) but later changed to Nisan (Est. 3:7). After dark on Nisan 15, the Passover meal was eaten (Ex. 12:2–11), which began the seven-day Feast of Unleavened Bread. Jesus' statement that "the Passover is two days away" (lit. "after two days") points ahead to Thursday evening at sundown, when he and the disciples will celebrate the Passover together, after which he initiates the "Lord's Supper."

This is now the fourth and last time that Jesus predicts his arrest and crucifixion: "The Son of Man will be handed over to be crucified" (cf. 16:21; 17:22–23; 20:17–19). Although this prediction is briefer than the others, Jesus connects his death with the celebration of Passover. Later, Paul recognizes the spiritual significance by referring to Jesus as "our Passover lamb" (1 Cor. 5:7).

The religious leaders plot Jesus' arrest and execution (26:3–4). At the same time that Jesus predicts his crucifixion, "the chief priests and elders of the people" are plotting his arrest. The "chief priests," controlled by the high priest and the wealthy aristocracy of Jerusalem, were dominated by Sad-

---

1. For an evangelical exposition of the meaning of the cross as it is anticipated in the Old Testament, narrated in the Gospels, and explained in the rest of the New Testament, see Derek Tidball, *The Message of the Cross: Wisdom Unsearchable, Love Indestructible* (BST; Downers Grove, Ill.: InterVarsity Press, 2000). Matthew's perspective is explored by Donald Senior, *The Passion of Jesus in the Gospel of Matthew* (Wilmington, Del.: Michael Glazier, 1985). For an extensive scholarly study of the passion activities commencing with Gethsemane, see Raymond E. Brown, *The Death of the Messiah: From Gethsemane to the Grave. A Commentary on the Passion Narratives in the Four Gospels*, 2 vols. (New York: Doubleday, 1994). For one other extensive scholarly bibliography, see David E. Garland, *One Hundred Years of Study on the Passion Narratives* (Macon, Ga.: Mercer Univ. Press, 1989).

2. Malcolm Muggeridge, "The Crucifixion," *Observer* (March 26, 1967); cited in Tidball, *The Message of the Cross*, 117.

ducean influence (see comments on 3:7–10). They are among the most eager in Jerusalem to get rid of the threat to their influence in the temple posed by Jesus and his messianic following, so they plot to arrest him "in some sly way and kill him."[3] They gathered together in the palace of Caiaphas, the current high priest. The "palace" (*aule;* lit., "courtyard") means the private home of the high priest. As the conspiracy against Jesus proceeds in Matthew's narrative, the close cooperation between Caiaphas and the Roman government will be important in accounting for the way in which Jesus is so readily condemned and crucified.

For the first time in Matthew the high priest is identified as "Caiaphas," who is son-in-law of the previous high priest, Annas (who still wielded much influence). Caiaphas was appointed high priest in A.D. 18 by the Roman prefect Valerius Gratus, Pontius Pilate's predecessor.[4] He maintained the position until being deposed in A.D. 36 by Vitellius, the Roman consular legate of Syria.[5] Because the Roman governor appointed and deposed the high priest, the office was essentially a political one, and apparently Caiaphas knew how to manipulate it well. Because of this, the reputation of the office was ruined.[6] The Qumran community was especially critical of the high priestly leadership, whom they called the "Wicked Priest."

**The plot to arrest Jesus (26:5).** The chief priests and elders cannot arrest Jesus openly because of his popularity with the people. They saw the tumultuous welcome Jesus received from the crowds just two days prior at his triumphal entry into Jerusalem (21:8–11). At this time of Passover, with thousands of pilgrims jamming Jerusalem and with nationalistic fervor running high as they celebrate the way that God liberated their ancestors from bondage in Egypt, the people have been stirred by the rumors that Jesus is their expected Messiah. Until the religious leaders can turn that stream of emotion against Jesus, they dare not upset the crowds by moving too soon against him.

Popular uprisings were increasingly common in first-century Palestine, as the people grew weary under the oppression of the Romans and the duplicity of their own religious leaders. These religious leaders may well have remembered the uprising in the temple at the Passover after the death of Herod the Great in 4 B.C. His son Archelaus quickly displayed the same kind of cruelty that marked his father's reign by sending in troops and cavalry, who

---

3. See comments on 26:59, and the helpful overview of the Sanhedrin in Keener, *A Commentary on the Gospel of Matthew* (1999), 614–16.

4. Josephus, *Ant.* 18.2.2 §35.

5. Ibid., 18.4.3 §95.

6. On the high priests, see Flusser, *Jesus,* 195–205; Bruce Chilton, "Annas," *ABD,* 1:257–58; idem, "Caiaphas," *ABD,* 1:803–6.

killed about three thousand pilgrims taking part in the riots.[7] The religious leaders will bide their time until the most propitious, secretive moment to arrest Jesus.

### Jesus Anointed at Bethany (26:6–13)

MATTHEW (AND MARK 14:3–9) recounts the story of Jesus' anointing thematically, placing it in the context of the conspiracy to arrest Jesus, whereas John 12:1–8 narrates the story chronologically, showing that it occurs on the Saturday night before Jesus' triumphal entry. This sort of thematic arrangement is typical of Matthew (see comments on 21:12–17). Placed in this context, it provides a link between the conspiracy of the religious leaders (26:3–5) and the betrayal by Judas (26:14–16). The woman's act of homage stands out conspicuously against the duplicity of Judas and the plotting of the high priest, Caiaphas. The characters at the anointing remain largely unidentified in Matthew's narrative, which places full attention on the anointing by this woman and the reaction of the disciples.[8]

**Mary anoints Jesus (26:7).** On Saturday evening, just after the end of the Sabbath at sunset, Jesus and the disciples attend a dinner at the home of "Simon the Leper" in Bethany. Since Simon is hosting a meal in his own home, he has probably been healed of leprosy by Jesus, for lepers were required to live away from the common population. According to John 12:2, Lazarus and his sisters, Mary and Martha, are there.[9] Lazarus, of course, was a celebrated figure because he had been raised from the dead by Jesus, and Martha and Mary were long-time followers of Jesus (Luke 10:38–42).

During the dinner, a woman (identified in John 12:3 as Mary) approaches Jesus carrying an alabaster jar of very expensive perfume, "which she poured on his head as he was reclining at the table." Unguents of various sorts— whether ointments, oils, liniments, or perfumes—were used much more freely in the ancient world than they are today. Some were for cleansing, others were medicinal, still others were ceremonial (cf., e.g., Ps. 133:2). At a Jewish banquet a host sometimes poured small amounts of oil on a guest's head, which remained on the hair and clothing, enhancing the fragrance at the feast.[10]

---

7. Josephus, *Ant.* 2:111.

8. This anointing is in the home of "Simon the Leper" (26:6), which is a similar, but quite different event than the anointing of Jesus by a woman in the home of Simon the Pharisee, which Luke recounts (Luke 7:36–50).

9. Some have suggested that Simon may have been the father of the brother and sisters, or the husband of Mary or Martha, though nothing in any context supports this hypothesis.

10. Notice Jesus' comment at the other anointing scene: "You did not put oil on my head, but she has poured perfume on my feet" (Luke 7:46).

The perfume Mary uses is pure nard (see Mark 14:3; John 12:3), an oil extracted from the root of the nard plant grown in India.[11] This is not a typical household oil for anointing, but an expensive perfume oil used for a solemn and special act of devotion. By breaking the flask, Mary shows that she is not just pouring a few drops to enhance the aroma of the feast but is performing the highest act of consecration to Jesus, even anointing his feet (cf. John 12:3).

**The disciples' objections (26:8–9).** The perfume costs at least three hundred denarii (Mark 14:5), equivalent to about a year's wages for the average worker (i.e., the equivalent of over $12,000; see comments on 18:28; 20:9). John's Gospel informs us that Judas Iscariot is the one who expresses the feelings of some of the apostles, especially his own, that the perfume could have been sold for money and given to the poor (John 12:4–5). But John likewise exposes Judas's real motives (12:6), since he regularly pilfered money from the moneybox. The other disciples do not know of Judas's thievery, but they also think that this is a waste of precious funding. Poverty was a pervasive problem in Jerusalem and throughout Israel.

**An act of memorial (26:10–13).** But Jesus indicts them all: "Why are you bothering this woman? She has done a beautiful thing to me. The poor you will always have with you, but you will not always have me." Jesus is not relieving the disciples of caring for the poor, for drawing on the law (cf. Deut. 15:11), he recognizes that because there will always be the poor among them, giving to them is a duty of ideal conduct. Note too the last parable of the Olivet Discourse, where Jesus left the disciples with a dramatic scene of reward and punishment related to caring for the needy, which would be their ongoing obligation (Matt. 25:31–46). In other words, Jesus here emphasizes that the woman is performing an act of homage to him that can only be done at this time while he is with them (cf. similar comments about not fasting in 9:14–17). There are special circumstances that affect the disciples' practices while Jesus is still with them.

Jesus goes on to show the even more profound significance of Martha's deed: "When she poured this perfume on my body, she did it to prepare me for burial." It is not impossible that Mary is able to see from the gathering storm clouds of opposition from the religious leaders that Jesus will soon be arrested and executed and so comes here to prepare him for that fate. However, this seems unlikely, for we do not find evidence that anyone really understood his prophecies of the cross and resurrection until after the fact. Rather, Mary's anointing of Jesus is more an act of special tribute and thanksgiving for him for what he has done for her and her family. It also may be an

---

11. Rousseau and Arav, "Ointments, Perfumes," *Jesus and His World*, 216–20.

intended act of worship, as she may be increasingly recognizing his true identity. But whatever her actual motivation, Jesus tells his disciples that what she has performed is an act of homage far more significant than even she knows. She unknowingly has begun the preparations for his burial, which will come sooner than any of them conceives possible.

Mary's act presents an example that will set a right precedent for all ages: "I tell you the truth, wherever this gospel is preached throughout the world, what she has done will also be told, in memory of her." Whatever she consciously understands about Jesus, she is memorializing his death for all generations to come. In the proclamation of the gospel, the true story behind this story will be told that she is performing an act of worship to her Lord in setting him above all other values. Her example should set a high precedent for all subsequent disciples of Jesus.

### Judas Arranges the Betrayal (26:14–16)

MATTHEW NEXT RECOUNTS the dastardly deed of Judas's receiving payment for betraying Jesus. Judas is specified as "one of the Twelve," a fact known to Matthew's readers (cf. 10:1–4), but the designation heightens the culpability of this one who has been privileged to be included in the inner circle of Jesus' closest followers, was designated for leadership in the church to come, and would have exercised authority over the twelve tribes of Israel (19:28). Instead, his privilege gives him opportunity for inconceivable treachery, which will result in staggering condemnation.

The arrangements for the betrayal probably occur on Wednesday of Holy Week. If so, it is the only incident in the Gospels that occurs on this day. Jesus and the other apostles most likely stay in Bethany, perhaps at the home of Lazarus, Mary, and Martha (see comments on 21:17). This often is called "silent Wednesday," since no specific activities of Jesus are recorded of this day of Holy Week.

Judas leaves Bethany and travels the two miles to Jerusalem, where he meets privately with the chief priests to ask what they are willing to pay him to betray Jesus (26:14–15). Matthew is the only Gospel that specifies the agreed-upon amount of thirty pieces of silver (cf. Zech. 11:12). This amount is not only the price of a slave accidentally gored to death by an ox (Ex. 21:32) but is also apparently a way of indicating a paltry amount. This may reflect the insignificance of Jesus in the minds of Judas and the chief priests, though it may have been only a partial payment of the agreed-upon sum. The identity of the coin is not specified, but most likely the amount is the equivalent of four months wages, or about five thousand dollars. Once Judas receives the amount, he probably returns to Bethany to join Jesus and the other disciples and to watch for an opportunity to hand Jesus over to the temple authorities (26:16).

As Judas enters this plot, his spiritual nature is revealed; he is not a true believer (cf. Luke 22:3−4, which tells us that Satan entered him). Many reasons have been suggested as to why Judas does this: avarice and love of money; jealousy of the other disciples; disillusionment at the inevitable outcome of Jesus' ministry; an enthusiastic intention to force Jesus' hand and make him declare himself as Messiah; a bitter spirit that arose when his worldly hopes for a place of prominence in the messianic kingdom were crushed, and this disappointment turned to spite, and spite became hatred. Perhaps all of these have some place in his heart, but most likely he is disappointed in the spiritual nature of Jesus' messiahship and decides to recoup what losses he has suffered in following Jesus for three years. Whatever the reasons, Judas's betrayal stands as history's most infamous act of traitorous treachery.

## The Passover and the Lord's Supper (26:17−30)

ISSUES OF CHRONOLOGY. Matthew now tells us that "on the first day of the Feast of Unleavened Bread, the disciples came to Jesus and asked, 'Where do you want us to make preparations for you to eat the Passover?'" The traditional understanding of the day of the week of the Passover and the celebration of the Lord's Supper, and thereafter the day of the week of Jesus' death, derives from a basic comment from all of the Gospels, namely, that Jesus was crucified on the "day of Preparation." Mark gives an explicit clarification for his readers, "It was Preparation Day (that is, the day before the Sabbath)" (Mark 15:42; cf. Matt. 27:62; Luke 23:54; John 19:14, 31, 42.). This expression points to Friday, the day before the Sabbath, when the Jews prepared everything for the beginning of the Sabbath. When Sabbath began at sundown on Friday, all work ceased. Therefore, Jesus died on Friday afternoon.

However, several passages in John's Gospel suggest that when Jesus was led away to trial and crucifixion, the Passover meal had not yet been eaten by the Jews, which would imply that Jesus' final meal with his disciples was not a Passover meal (cf. John 13:1−2; 13:27−29; 18:28; 19:14, 31). The following points must be reconciled with that perspective. (1) All the Gospels state that Jesus ate the Last Supper the day before his crucifixion (Matt. 26:20; Mark 14:17; Luke 22:14; John 13:2; cf. 1 Cor. 11:23). (2) The Synoptic Gospels (Matt. 26:17; Mark 14:12; Luke 22:7−8) portray the preparations for the Passover as occurring on Thursday afternoon (Nisan 14), with Jesus eating the Passover meal with his disciples after sundown on Thursday evening (now Nisan 15) and then instituting the Last Supper later that evening. Then Jesus was crucified during the next day, Friday (still Nisan 15).

Some insist that either the Synoptics or John is wrong, but if we look deeper, we can find a plausible explanation for the differences. There have been several attempted explanations of the differences between the Synoptics and John,[12] but the two most promising are as follows.

(1) One view suggests that Jesus and the disciples celebrated the Passover according to a solar calendar known from *Jubilees* and possibly used by the Qumran community.[13] In this view, the Synoptic Gospels follow the method of the Galileans and the Pharisees, by whose reckoning the day was measured from sunrise to sunrise. Jesus and his disciples had their Paschal lamb slaughtered in the late afternoon of Thursday, Nisan 14, and ate the Passover with unleavened bread later that evening. John's Gospel, however, follows the method of the Judeans, especially the Sadducees, in reckoning the day from sunset to sunset. These Jews had the Paschal lamb slaughtered in the late afternoon of the Friday Nisan 14 and ate the Passover with the unleavened bread that night, which by then had become Nisan 15. Thus, Jesus had already eaten the Passover meal when his enemies, who had not yet celebrated the Passover, arrested him.[14]

(2) Another view is perhaps stronger. This view suggests that the passages in John that seem to contradict the Synoptics (e.g., John 18:28; 19:14, 31) all point to a use of the expression "Passover" for the weeklong series of events, not just the Passover meal itself.[15] For instance, when John 18:28 says that the Jews did not want to become ceremonially unclean by entering Pilate's palace during Jesus' trial, it was so that they could continue to participate in "Passover Week," not just the meal itself. In other words, Jesus and his disciples ate the Passover meal on Thursday, the beginning of Nisan

---

12. For an overview, see Karl P. Donfried, "Chronology," *ABD*, 1:1015–16. Some suggest that the Last Supper was not a Passover meal but a meal the night before the Passover (John 13:1, 20). However, the Synoptics explicitly state that the Last Supper was a Passover (Matt. 26:2, 17–19; Mark 14:1, 12, 14, 16; Luke 22:1, 7–8, 13, 15). Others suggest that Jesus and his disciples had a private Passover. However, the Passover lamb had to be slaughtered within the temple precincts and the priests would not have allowed the slaughter of the paschal lamb for a private Passover. Still others suggest that the Passover was celebrated on two consecutive days, because it would have been impossible to slay all the Passover lambs on one day, but there is not explicit evidence for such a practice.

13. Annie Jaubert, *The Date of the Last Supper*, trans. Isaac Rafferty (Staten Island, N.Y.: Alba, 1965). So also Morris, *Matthew*, 654.

14. Harold Hoehner, "Chronology," *DJG*, 121; so also Thomas and Gundry, *The NIV Harmony of the Gospels*, 312–13.

15. This view is best presented by Carson, *John*, 455–58; so also Blomberg, *Historical Reliability of the Gospels*, 175–78.

15 and the weeklong feast, at the same time as the rest of those assembled in Jerusalem (cf. Mark 14:12).[16]

**Preparations for the Passover (26:17–19).** Knowing that Jesus has come to Jerusalem to participate with them in the Passover meal, his disciples ask where they should prepare for the celebration (26:17). They are still in Bethany, early in the day on Thursday. Jesus directs them to go into Jerusalem where they will find a specific man, whom they will tell, "The Teacher says: My appointed time is near. I am going to celebrate the Passover with my disciples at your house" (26:18). Finding a man carrying a water jar would not be difficult, since women normally lugged water. Either Jesus has made pre-arrangements for the room with friends in Jerusalem in order to avoid the Jewish authorities, or else these were divine arrangements. Either way, Jesus' statement, "My appointed time is near," recognizes that he is on a divinely ordained timetable (cf. 26:45).

Matthew follows this with the briefest account: "So the disciples did as Jesus had directed them and prepared the Passover."

**The Passover meal and the order of that night's events (26:20).** Matthew narrates briefly the events as Jesus and his disciples gather in Jerusalem to celebrate the Passover. With the other Gospels, we can see a fuller order of events that night.

1. Beginning to eat the Passover meal after evening came (Matt. 26:20)
2. Dissension among the disciples as to who is the greatest (Luke 22:24)
3. Washing the disciples' feet (John 13:1–20)
4. Identifying Judas as the betrayer, after which he leaves (Matt. 26:21–25)
5. Institution of the Lord's Supper (Matt. 26:26–29)
6. Messages and prayers in the Upper Room (John 14:1–17:26)
7. Walk to Gethsemane (Matt. 26:30)
8. Prediction of Peter's denials (Matt. 26:31–35; cf. Luke 22:31–38)[17]
9. Jesus' prayers in Gethsemane (Matt. 26:36–46)
10. Betrayal and arrest in Gethsemane (Matt. 26:47–56)

---

16. For a brief overview of the difficulties and a helpful resolution of the various possibilities of the actual date in the first century, see the article "Problems in Dating the Crucifixion," at the website of the Astronomical Applications Department of the U.S. Naval Observatory: *http://aa.usno.navy.mil/faq/docs/crucifixion.html*. They offer the dates of Jesus' crucifixion as either Friday, April 7, A.D. 30, or Friday, April 3, A.D. 33. See also Doig, *New Testament Chronology*, who contends for the A.D. 30 dating.

17. Some conflate the predictions in Matthew and Luke, while others suggest that Jesus predicted Peter's denials twice; see Thomas and Gundry, NIV *Harmony of the Gospels*, 202, note b.

**The betrayer revealed (26:20–25).** Matthew narrates merely that when evening came, "Jesus was reclining at the table with the Twelve." The parallels tell us that Jesus first celebrates Passover with the Twelve, and as the evening goes on, he initiates the Lord's Supper. The most widespread style of formal dining in the Greco-Roman world was the *triclinium*. This was a dining room in which the guests reclined on a couch that extended around three sides of a room. The host was seated in the center of the U-shaped series of tables, with the most honored guests on either side, their heads reclining toward the tables and their feet toward the wall.[18]

During the Passover, Jesus reveals the betrayer: "I tell you the truth, one of you will betray me." Jesus has anticipated the betrayal and even warned the disciples on their journey to Jerusalem that he will be betrayed (20:18; cf. John 6:71; 12:4), but his prediction of the treacherous act at the meal apparently comes as a surprise to all. Hence, they "are very sad" or distressed. They do not expect a betrayal to come out of their tight-knit group that has experienced so much together for the last three years. Yet the disciples are now fully aware that Jesus has an understanding of events beyond their comprehension. He knows more about them than even they know themselves. So one after another they ask, yet hesitantly declare, "Surely not I, Lord?" This question expects a negative answer, but they do not speak confidently.

Jesus prolongs their dismay as he states, "The one who has dipped his hand into the bowl with me will betray me." Each of those around the room have dipped their bread into bowls that served the group, so this implies no more than one of those at the meal at that time will betray him, but no one knows who. "Judas seems to have covered his tracks pretty well."[19]

Even with the treachery, the betrayal does not thwart God's plans, for Jesus declares: "The Son of Man will go just as it is written about him." Jesus affirms the divine certitude of his death by alluding to what "is written" about him, a reference to the Suffering Servant prophecies (Isa. 42–53).[20] The Old Testament prophecies of a coming Suffering Servant were not widely held up as a primary expectation, not even among Jesus' own followers. But Jesus drives home the truth that the Scriptures have prophesied the coming of a slain Messiah. This points again to the profound interplay of God's sovereign

---

18. For various customs, see Gene Schramm, "Meal Customs (Jewish)," and Dennis E. Smith, "Meal Customs (Greco-Roman)," *ABD*, 4:648–53.

19. Morris, *Matthew*, 656.

20. See Markus Bockmuehl, "A 'Slain Messiah' in 4Q Serekh Milhamah (4Q285)?" *TynBul* 43 (1992): 155–69. Bockmuehl finds little expectation of a slain messiah within first-century Jewish interpretation of Old Testament prophecies and probably none in the Dead Sea Scrolls, but posits it as likely within wider Jewish circles.

control over all human activity with each one's personal responsibility and culpability for one's own decisions.

The divine judgment anticipated on the one who betrays the suffering Son of Man is staggering: "But woe to that man who betrays the Son of Man! It would be better for him if he had not been born." With Judas's death, his existence will continue in a conscious hell. Jesus reiterates the reality of hell for those who reject his invitation to turn away from their own perverted will and find the righteousness of the kingdom of heaven.[21] If Judas had truly accepted the invitation to kingdom life, another person would have betrayed Jesus, because the necessity of the cross was divinely decreed. But Judas has sealed his own eternal destiny by his personal choice, and he is now personally accountable.

Matthew accentuates the contrast between the larger group around the table who address Jesus as "Lord" (26:22) and Judas, who addresses Jesus as "Rabbi" (Teacher). Although "Lord" (*kyrios*) can be used as a formal address (7:21), when directed to Jesus it came to designate discipleship. Significantly, Judas is never recorded to have addressed Jesus as "Lord." This is perhaps a clue to the fact that Jesus knew all along those who did not truly believe in him as their Lord and who would betray him (cf. John 6:60–65).

Matthew then points to the interaction between Jesus and Judas, which apparently was heard by the rest of the Twelve (26:25). Judas, the one who will betray him, says, "Surely not I, Rabbi?'" (26:25). The tone of his reply is disingenuous, deceptively sincere, expecting a negative reply from Jesus. Judas has been carrying out his arrangements for the betrayal in secret, with no thought of anyone knowing about it. But Jesus' knowledge is divinely revealed: "Yes, it is you."

The NIV rendering of this phrase accurately reflects the literal Greek expression: "You yourself have said." This phrase is a way of making an affirmation that places the responsibility back on the one making the inquiry. Rather than masking his insincerity, Judas's own question has indicted him. This same expression recurs in the important dialogues with Caiaphas (26:64) and Pilate (27:11). Jesus' reply confirms the truth that the interrogator is trying to avoid.[22] Although Matthew does not record Judas's response or his exit, he most likely leaves at this point to make final arrangements for the betrayal. His deception is known, but he is satanically driven to accomplish his treachery. John gives a wretchedly tragic comment: "As soon as Judas had taken the

---

21. E.g., 8:12; 11:20–24; 13:42, 49–50; 25:46; cf. John 17:12 where Judas is called "the one headed for destruction" (lit., "the son of destruction").

22. Senior, *Matthew*, 298.

bread, he went out. And it was night" (John 13:30). The time of eternal darkness for Judas's accountability for his decisions looms.

**The institution of the Lord's Supper (26:26–30).** With the traitor gone, Jesus continues the Passover with the rest of the Twelve. He dramatically brings the symbolic significance of this meal to its intended fulfillment as he institutes what becomes known as "the Lord's Supper."

*The bread (26:26).* The "Haggadah of Passover" was the set form in which the Exodus story was told on the first two nights of Passover as part of the ritual Seder (lit., "order").[23] Central to the meal were three foods—unleavened bread, bitter herbs, and the Passover offering (a lamb in temple days)— along with the four (traditional) cups of wine. Jesus uses the bread as a stunning illustration, saying: "Take and eat; this is my body." He sets off the significance of the new observance as he invokes a prayer of blessing from God. God's activity alone makes possible what he is about to illustrate and undertake.

During the meal proper the host blessed the unleavened bread, broke it, and shared it with those around the table. But Jesus gives it a wholly new significance—he identifies himself with the Passover sacrifice. The Old Testament prescribed that the paschal sacrifice should be consumed by a company previously invited (Ex. 12:4), so Jewish practice always focused on the corporate character of the Seder.[24] The corporate nature of the Lord's Supper is also a primary characteristic, pointing ahead to the church that collectively proclaims the Lord's death until he comes again (cf. 1 Cor. 11:23–33).

Jesus' twofold injunction with the explanation ("Take and eat; this is my body") demonstrates that his body will be the fulfillment of the ceremonies surrounding the Passover lamb, as he becomes the sacrificial atonement for the "passing over" of the sins of the people. It is significant that Jesus uses bread, not the paschal lamb, to initiate the commemoration. Because of his death, the killing of a lamb will no longer be necessary. To emphasize the once-for-all nature of his forthcoming sacrifice, Jesus focuses on the bread, which also had redemptive significance within the Seder and could be eaten as a continuing memorial while upholding the cessation of animal sacrifice.[25] The later theological debates about the meaning of "body" and its relation

---

23. Baruch M. Bokser, *The Origins of the Seder: The Passover Rite and Early Rabbinic Judaism* (Berkeley: Univ. of California Press, 1984). The expression "Haggadah of Passover" then came to be used for the entire Seder ritual as well as for the book containing the liturgy and ritual narration of the events of Deut. 26:5–9.

24. For an overview of Second Temple Jewish practices, see "Haggadah of Passover," *DJBP*, 266–67; Robin Routledge, "Passover and Last Supper," *TynBul* 53 (2002): 203–21; Joachim Jeremias, *The Eucharistic Words of Jesus*, trans. Norman Perrin (London: SCM, 1966), 84–88.

25. Routledge, "Passover and Last Supper," 215–16.

to the presence of Jesus in the bread would not have even entered the minds of those hearing Jesus' words. They are having difficulty enough understanding the symbolism. But once the events of the cross transpire, they will, like Paul, recognize that the bread and the cup are profound memorials of the single most important event in history.

*The cup* (26:27–28). Continuing the symbolism, Jesus takes a cup, gives thanks, and asks all of them to join in drinking from it. Of the four cups of wine consumed at a Passover celebration (the cup of benediction, the cup just before the meal, the third cup [of blessing] after the meal, and the cup following the singing of the Hallel), this is most likely the third cup, which Jesus takes and says, "This is my blood of the covenant, which is poured out for many for the forgiveness of sins."

This third cup was often called the cup of redemption, corresponding to God's third promise in Exodus 6:6, "*I will redeem you* with an outstretched arm and with mighty acts of judgment." The death of the Passover lamb and the smearing of its blood opened the way for the redemption of God's people from Egypt, but the shedding of Jesus' blood, which this cup foreshadows, opens the way for the redemption of all humanity to enter into a new covenant relationship with God.[26] With this statement Jesus indicates that he is fulfilling the new covenant promised to the people of Israel (see esp. Jer. 31:31, 34; Ezek. 36:26–27).[27]

Throughout his ministry Jesus based his invitation to the kingdom of God and the attendant forgiveness of sins and promise of regeneration upon the initiation of the new covenant (cf. 5:17–20). The time has come for its inauguration with the cross and the coming of the Spirit at Pentecost. Those who receive Jesus' gracious invitation to partake of his sacrificial death live in the blessing of the new covenant. We experience forgiveness of sins and the beginnings of transformation into the image of Christ that accompanies our regeneration through the Holy Spirit (cf. Titus 3:4–7; 2 Cor. 3:18). On the expression "for many," see comments on 20:28.

*The poignant promise* (26:29). Jesus gives a surprising twist to the occasion as he states, "I tell you, I will not drink of this fruit of the vine from now on until that day when I drink it anew with you in my Father's kingdom." The fourth cup of the Passover was associated with God's promise, "*I will take you as my own people*" (Ex. 6:7). It was poured, and following the conclusion of the antiphonal singing of the second part of the Hallel (Ps. 115–118), drunk by all. It is possible that the hymn mentioned in Matthew 26:30 is the Hallel and that Jesus abstains from the fourth cup as an illustration that he will not

---

26. Ibid., 219.
27. Cf. Clay Hamm, "The Last Supper in Matthew," *BBR* 10 (2000): 53–69.

partake of this cup until his return.[28] However, in later Judaism a dispute arose as to whether a fifth cup was obligatory during the Passover celebration, called the cup of Elijah. This is the cup kept in readiness for the advent of the prophet Elijah, who they believed would come on the Festival of Redemption from Egypt to herald the messianic redemption. Perhaps this practice went back to Jesus' day.[29]

Either way, Jesus' words hold out a poignant promise (that his sacrificial death will bring forgiveness of sins) and a sad indication (that he will have to go away), but also an assurance (that he will return). When he comes again and brings the final establishment of the kingdom on earth, he will bring to fulfillment the time of peace and redemption for which his disciples are waiting and the consolation for which the people of Israel await. Until then, the Lord's Supper is a perpetual reminder of the new and greater exodus by which all who embrace its significance and historical accomplishment find release from sin's bondage and deliverance into everlasting life.[30] The blessings of the kingdom, inaugurated through the finished work of Christ on the cross, are a permanent reminder that he is coming again to bring the final establishment of the kingdom to those who await his fellowship.

The final evening together with the Twelve concludes with Jesus giving his Upper Room Discourse (John 14–17). After this discourse they sing a final hymn—perhaps the Hallel (Ps. 113–118) or else the last great Hallel psalm (Ps. 136), in which the antiphonal refrain, "His love endures forever," recurs throughout the recounting of God's great and good deeds.[31] Or perhaps this is a spontaneous hymn of praise led by Jesus.

### Prediction of the Falling Away and Denial (26:31–35)

AFTER THEY SING together, Jesus goes with the Twelve to the Mount of Olives. They are most likely on their way back to Bethany, where they have spent each evening during Holy Week (cf. 21:17). The two-mile walk to Bethany from Jerusalem takes them over the Mount of Olives, on which is located the Garden of Gethsemane. This garden was a favorite place of prayer for Jesus, as well as a gathering place for people camping during their pilgrimage to the Passover.

Along the way Jesus startles the disciples with another ominous prediction: "This very night you will all fall away on account of me." Earlier Jesus

---

28. Routledge, "Passover and Last Supper," 219–20.

29. See "Haggadah, Passover," *EJR*, 166–67.

30. Eugene H. Merrill, "Remembering: A Central Theme in Biblical Worship," *JETS* 43 (March 2000): 27–36.

31. H. Rusche, "Das letzte gemeinsame Gebet Jesu mit seinen Jungern: Der Psalm 136," *Wissenschaft und Weissheit* 51 (1988): 210–12.

predicted that one of the Twelve would betray him; now he implies that all of them will lack courage. The expression "fall away on account of me" (cf. 11:6; 13:57) indicates that there will come that night an extreme test of their loyalty to him as their Master. They will not cease being his disciples, but they will fail the test of courage to stand up for him. This lacking will later be dealt with as they become the courageous foundation of the church, but their strengthening comes through failure.

Their failure was also prophesied by Zechariah, as Jesus demonstrates: "I will strike the shepherd, and the sheep of the flock will be scattered." The shepherd who is struck by the sword is the one described by the prophet as pierced (Zech. 12:10; cf. Matt. 24:30) and rejected (Zech. 11). But the scene shifts in Zechariah 13:7, as this time Yahweh strikes the shepherd. This shepherd is identified as Yahweh's companion, who is side by side with him as his equal. As this messianic Shepherd is smitten, the sheep are scattered, which in the Zechariah context speaks of the dispersion of the Jews.[32] This quotation demonstrates that even when God's actions are carried out by others, they are a result of his sovereign activity.

Four times Jesus predicted his arrest and crucifixion (16:21; 17:22–23; 20:17–19; 26:2). In the first three he also predicted his resurrection, which he now does for the fourth time: "But after I have risen, I will go ahead of you into Galilee" (cf. the recall of this statement in 28:10, 17). Jesus prophesied judgment for Judas's betrayal (26:24), but the promise to the other disciples is that after they falter, they will be restored in fellowship with him.

But with his usual bravado, Peter steps forward to say, "Even if all fall away on account of you, I never will." Peter has played a prominent role in Matthew's Gospel in both a positive and negative sense (see 14:28–31; 15:15; 16:17–19; 17:24–27; 18:21). He is both an imperfect disciple and a leader in process of development. The difference between growth and failure is whether Peter continues to be receptive to God's will. When he remains open to the things of God, he grows both in his personal discipleship and in his leadership responsibility. When he does not remain receptive to the things of God, he fails in both.

Here Peter fails on both accounts. He does not listen to Jesus' warning and heed its caution, and his false bravado leads the rest of the disciples to join him (26:33). Jesus warns Peter that he will fail even more than the others— "this very night, before the rooster crows, you will disown me three times." Roman military guards were organized around various "watches," which accorded to the natural phenomena of sunrise, midday, sunset, midnight. The crowing of the rooster is proverbial for the arrival of the day. Thus, the

---

32. Kaiser, *The Messiah in the Old Testament*, 226–27.

denial will take place before the end of the fourth watch or at dawn. Peter's bravado prompts him to reassert vehemently his allegiance to Jesus: "Even if I have to die with you, I will never disown you."

The difference between Judas and Peter (and the rest of the disciples) is demonstrated by their behavior *after* their failures. Judas is satanically driven to accomplish his treachery (cf. Luke 22:3–4; John 13:2), because he never was a true believer (John 6:60–65). Peter and the other disciples falter, but their repentance later brings them back to Jesus for restoration. "One may either deny or betray Christ and be forgiven if one genuinely repents. Without repentance (a change of heart followed by right action), both remain equally damning."[33]

### Gethsemane: Jesus' Agonizing Prayers (26:36–46)

GETHSEMANE (26:36). On their way out of Jerusalem, Jesus and his disciples stop at a place called Gethsemane, which John calls a "garden" (John 18:1, 26). This word comes from the Hebrew/Aramaic *gat šemanim,* which most likely means "oil-press." Putting the accounts together suggests that Gethsemane was a garden area among the olive tree groves on the Mount of Olives that had a place for the preparation of olive oil. Jesus and his disciples often frequented the place (John 18:2).

At least four current sites have been suggested as the actual identity, but two primary ones claim scholars' attention.[34] The first site now houses the Church of All Nations, which is adjacent to an olive grove about fifty-five yards square, with olive trees perhaps more than a thousand years old. The second, more likely site is located a few hundred feet north of the traditional garden. This site is a cave in which archaeologists have found evidence of preparing olive oil. Some suggest that a cultivated garden area originally surrounded the cave.

**Watching and praying (26:37–38).** Joan Taylor suggests that the disciples go to the cultivated garden area to sleep in the cave that they frequented on other occasions. Once at Gethsemane, Jesus directs the larger group of disciples to stay in the cave (26:36), but he asks the inner group of three disciples (Peter, James, and John; see comments on 10:2–4) to stay awake with him while he prays. Jesus wants them to share with him this overwhelming time of sorrow and trouble as he faces the cross: "My soul is overwhelmed with sorrow to the point of death. Stay here and keep watch with me."

---

33. Blomberg, *Matthew,* 393.

34. Joan E. Taylor, "The Garden of Gethsemane: NOT the Place of Jesus' Arrest," *BAR* 21.4 (July–August 1995): 26–35, 62. See also Rousseau and Arav, "Gethsemane," *Jesus and His World,* 110–11.

Jesus does not ask them to pray but to watch. As he grievously anticipates his looming death, his overwhelming sorrow reveals a heart broken almost to the point of death itself, because he knows that he will experience his Father's forsakenness (cf. 27:46). This reveals the depth of Jesus' human relationships he feels is necessary to sustain him in his time of greatest need. It may be difficult to grasp that the Son of God had such needs, but to do so gives us a more adequate understanding of his incarnation.

**Jesus' first prayer (26:39).** Jesus goes away from the trio of disciples to be alone, because he must plead with his Father privately, although having his closest followers near provides necessary human support. There alone, "he fell with his face to the ground and prayed." In this posture of abject humility, Jesus lays his life before his Father in utter honesty and trust. Matthew reveals one of the most profound insights into the intimacy between Father and Son. In this time of prayer that lasts an hour (26:40), Jesus probably reiterates various expressions of this central theme, which accounts for the variation among the four Gospel writers.

With harmless urgency and trustfulness, Jesus lays his life in his Father's safe-keeping as he calls out with tender intimacy, "My Father." This continues Matthew's unique insight into the special relationship of Son and Father in this Gospel (cf. 7:21; 10:32–33). Jesus pleads, "If it is possible, may this cup be taken from me. Yet not as I will, but as you will." Jesus is facing a real temptation, the most severe of his life. He started his earthly ministry by being tempted by the devil in the desert (4:1–11), and he was variously tempted by satanic devices at other points in his ministry (e.g., 16:22–23). The significant feature of the earlier temptations was the satanic attempt to deter Jesus from the cross (cf. 4:8–9; 16:21–23). Now, at the moment when he is ready to accomplish his life's mission, the temptation is intensified to its maximum. This is the devil's last-ditch effort to attempt to convince Jesus that the cross is unnecessary.

But Jesus has demonstrated a complete confidence in his Father's sovereign power and perfect will throughout his life, so at this moment of greatest temptation, he turns to his Father for guidance. Jesus has prophesied that he must endure this cup of crucifixion to accomplish redemption of humanity (cf. 20:22–23, 28; 26:27), but Satan still tempts him to believe that it is not absolutely necessary.

Jesus lays the temptation out to his Father, but he does not ask to shirk his destiny. He wants only to obey his Father's will. This is the landmark example of honesty and trustfulness in prayer. The Father will not respond to the petition in the way requested, but it does not reflect any fault in the One requesting. The Father does hear the Son's plea, but it is the Son's obedience to the Father's answer to continue to the cross that brings salvation to humanity (Heb. 5:7–10)

It is not death itself that evokes this plea from Jesus but the kind of death. Jesus faces the most intense suffering imaginable as he endures not simply death, but a divinely sustained human death, in which he suffers punishment for the sins of humanity. His overwhelming sorrow (26:38) comes from the grievous anticipation of separation from his Father that he will experience in his human consciousness as "God made him who had no sin to be sin for us" (2 Cor. 5:21). Although dreading the prospect of pain and death on the cross, the prospect of separation from the Father is a greater horror and a greater sorrow (Matt. 27:46). But doing the will of the Father is Jesus' only motivation because he knows that millions of men and women, before and after his triumph over sin at the cross, will be reconciled to the Father through his death.

**The disciples' first failure (26:40–41).** After intensely wrestling in prayer, Jesus returns to find the trio of disciples sleeping. He addresses Peter as the leader of the disciples. Peter must continue to be receptive to the leading of God if he is to become stronger personally as well as be a future leader in the church. Matthew does not mince words in his appreciation for Peter's leadership role or in his recounting of Peter's failure to provide proper leadership (cf. 14:28–32; 16:16–23). Though addressed to Peter, Jesus also chides the trio (the verbs in 26:41–42 are plural) for not watching with him while he prayed.

Jesus goes on to admonish them, "Watch and pray so that you will not fall into temptation. The spirit is willing, but the body is weak." Jesus called them to watch with him so that they could support his prayer to the Father. They have failed that charge, but he calls them to continue, yet now they must also pray about their own temptation. In the immediate context, the temptation is to succumb to physical sleep at this late hour when they are being asked to watch with Jesus. It points to the temptation to fail in their responsibility to support Jesus in his great hour of need. It may point even more deeply to the temptation that they themselves will face as Jesus is led away to the cross—a temptation to deny Jesus, as he has predicted (26:31–35).

Jesus draws a contrast between their human spirit (not Holy Spirit) and its aspirations and their human nature that is impacted by sin, specifically here their physical humanness. Jesus is not creating a proverbial expression to excuse human weakness but is giving an example of how obedience to God's will is accomplished. Spiritual disciplines of watching and praying enable the spiritual heart to direct all aspects of a person's human nature so that the entire person is obedient to God's will (see comments on 5:20; 15:17–19). Unfortunately, the disciples fail Jesus at his moment of personal need by falling asleep, but as Leon Morris states, "There is a sense in which [Jesus] had to be alone in prayer, for only he could pray the prayer he prayed. But there is also a sense in which he could have been encouraged by the support of his closest followers nearby."[35]

**The second and third prayers and failures (26:42–44).** As Jesus goes away to pray a second and third time, he prays the same thing. However, in the second prayer there is a slight but significant variation: "My Father, if it is not possible for this cup to be taken away unless I drink it, may your will be done." Now there is the conscious recognition that it is not possible for the cup to be taken away and that Jesus must drink its wrathful onslaught. He consciously submits to that destiny in the words, "May your will be done." This is probably what the writer of Hebrews understood when he wrote that Jesus "learned obedience from what he suffered" (Heb. 5:8).

But the disciples have not yet learned this obedience, because again Jesus goes back to find the trio sleeping, "because their eyes were heavy." They have not learned the discipline of spirit over flesh. So Matthew tells us that Jesus leaves them, though Mark states, "They did not know what to say to him" (Mark 14:40). As he goes away to pray again a third time, Jesus prays the same thing. Although there may be some development in Jesus' understanding of the nature of the temptation and the Father's will for him, Matthew allows us to see that even from the start, there is no deficiency in Jesus' prayer. He continues only to seek the Father's will.

**The betrayer arrives (26:45–46).** After the third time of intense prayer, Jesus returns to the trio to find them still sleeping. He chides them for dozing when they could have supported him, and they will also find themselves asleep spiritually when the time for alertness finds them denying their Master. But it is too late to get ready now. He calls out, "Look, the hour is near, and the Son of Man is betrayed into the hands of sinners. Rise, let us go! Here comes my betrayer!" Jesus' instructions to the disciples earlier that day were impelled by the recognition that his "appointed time is near" (26:18), and now the "hour is near." The divine clock ticks inexorably on; the time for Jesus to accomplish his mission of salvation through the cross has arrived.

Jesus has perhaps watched the troop of temple police being led by Judas cross the Kidron Valley coming to the garden with torches. Instead of fleeing, he calls his disciples to meet this challenge head-on. These armed representatives of the temple, in spite of their authority as the chief priests' representatives, are "sinners." The Pharisees accused those who ate with Jesus of being "sinners" because they did not conform to their legal purity prescriptions (9:11), but Jesus calls "sinners" those who oppose God's will,

---

35. Morris, *Matthew*, 668.

even these temple officials.[36] They attempt to thwart God's will as represented in Jesus' ministry, and chief among them is Judas, the betrayer.

CHAPTERS 26–28 FORM the heart of Matthew's story of Jesus Messiah. Jesus is tried, crucified, and buried, but also raised from the dead. He then sends out his disciples on their worldwide commission. Dale Bruner calls these chapters "The Church's Passion," because "the suffering, death, resurrection, and sole universal Lordship of Jesus are what the church has always suffered most for preaching and yet has been most 'passionate' to preach."[37]

The hand of history is evident in these chapters. The earliest preaching of the church was the death, burial, and resurrection of Jesus. This is the *kerygma*, the good news, the preaching of the gospel of the kingdom of God.[38] These stories were told over and over in every location that the early missionaries traveled. Matthew records that historical record in order to move his readers to faith in Jesus Messiah, who offers salvation and discipleship through his cross and resurrection. The themes that began in the first section of his Gospel—especially the inevitability of God's plan of redemption and humanity's responsibility to it—unfold and interweave throughout this final narrative.

**The crucified Messiah.** From the very beginning of this Gospel, which announced the arrival of the son of David, the son of Abraham (1:1), Matthew has carefully detailed Jesus as the Messiah who fulfills Israel's expectations and the nations' hopes. As the spotlight of history focuses on the events of the cross, Matthew draws our attention to Jesus once again as Messiah, but in a tragically ironic way. Jesus is the Messiah, but in a way that baffled his own followers, disappointed the crowds, and enraged the religious leaders. He will be a crucified Messiah. With four strokes of his narrative brush throughout the Passion Narrative, Matthew fills in the details and the colors of his portrait of Jesus as the crucified Messiah. Derek Tidball highlights this purpose of Matthew's historical artistry:

> He wants our attention to be held by who it was that was pinned in such a humiliating and fatal way to a stake on the hill of Golgotha. It is a portrait which in a myriad ways tells us about the real identity of the central figure and so of his mission.[39]

---

36. Cf. Wilkins, "Sinner," *DJG*, 757–60.
37. Bruner, *Matthew*, 2:930.
38. E.g., Acts 2:23–36; 3:13–26; 7:51–53; 10:39–43; 13:26–31; 1 Cor. 15:1–7.
39. Tidball, *The Message of the Cross*, 134.

(1) *Prophesied Deliverer*. As the anticipated Messiah, Jesus fulfills Scripture that prophesied his actions during these final hours that lead him to the cross for the deliverance of his people. It is divinely appointed time (26:18), his hour of reckoning (26:45), prophesied in the Old Testament (26:24). The people of Israel anticipated a deliverer, but Jesus will deliver them in ways that not all expected. He will be stricken (26:31), fulfilling the prophecies of a slain Messiah who brings healing to his people and deliverance from iniquity (Isa. 53:4–12; Zech. 12:9–14). Later rabbis interpreted these verses to mean that they should expect a slain Messiah (*b. Suk. 52a*), but for many this will be a stumbling block.

(2) *Sacrificial Servant*. In fulfilling the prophecies of a crucified Messiah, Jesus will spill his blood as the servant who is the willing sacrifice to bear the sins of humanity. He raises the Passover cup of redemption and declares, "This is my blood of the covenant, which is poured out for many for the forgiveness of sins" (26:28). He is the fulfillment of the symbolism of the Passover lamb as he becomes the Servant of the Lord (Isa. 53:12). The events of the cross are not pleasant. They are bloody, and modern sensibilities want to clean them up to make them more palatable. But to do so minimizes the awfulness of sin and its requisite eternal penalty that makes necessary the excruciating punishment.

(3) *Willing Lord*. Throughout his ministry Jesus exercised control over the forces of nature and the spirit world. That control does not cease as he goes to the cross. He is not a victim of these circumstances but a willing Lord. His anointing by the worshiping woman expressed more than any could comprehend, because he is truly the anointed Davidic Messiah who is David's Lord (22:43). Yet the woman's act unknowingly anoints him for death (26:12). Jesus sovereignly initiates the prophesied new covenant, but through the cup of wrath that he willingly accepts (26:28, 39–44).

(4) *Humble King*. Jesus was worshiped "king of the Jews" at his birth (2:2, 11), and he will be mocked as he is crucified "king of the Jews" (27:29). Both of these settings find Jesus in humble surroundings—the first in a poor Bethlehem home, the second in the humiliation of the powerful Roman Praetorium. But Jesus knows who he is and what he has come to do. He does not have to prove anything to anyone, for he knows he is the king of the Jews (27:11). The humiliation of his incarnation brought the arrival of the kingdom of heaven to those who dared to respond to his invitation (4:17). The humiliation of his crucifixion brings the redemption of humanity to those who dare to respond to his inauguration of the new covenant in his blood (26:28). But the humiliation of his death is also a poignant promise that his kingdom will soon manifest itself with power and glory when he comes again (26:29; cf. 13:41–42; 24:30–31).

**Divine inevitability.** Interwoven throughout the Passion Narrative is the divine inevitability of these events. Matthew emphasizes that there is no doubt that God is in control. Jesus' ministry seems to be spiraling out of control, because the religious leaders are plotting against him, one of the Twelve will betray him, the rest of the Twelve will deny him, and there is no avoiding the cup of wrath. Yet behind the scenes God holds the spiral firmly in control. The events will transpire tragically, but not hopelessly, because divine inevitability controls the outcome. It is seen especially in Jesus' predictions of the events that he prophetically foresees and humanly undertakes.

*(1) Jesus' death.* Jesus predicts the forthcoming crucifixion (26:1−2), which Matthew narrates is being arranged by the plotting of the religious leaders (26:3−5). Jesus predicts his burial, for which the woman prepares him through the anointing (26:12−13). Throughout these scenes Jesus watches the divine clock that slowly ticks off the arrival of his appointed time (26:18) and hour (26:45) of betrayal, arrest, and crucifixion. But the reprehensible betrayal and crucifixion are not foisted on the Son of Man. He knowingly accepts them as part of his mission, since Scripture has given him advance warning of their arrival (26:24). The new covenant was long ago prophesied by the prophets, but as Jesus spends his last earthly night with his disciples before the crucifixion, he demonstrates with the cup that it is only through his blood that the covenant will be inaugurated (26:28). Jesus' death is inevitable, but it is divinely predicted.

*(2) Judas's betrayal.* Likewise, Jesus' arrest is not accidental. He sees the plotting of the religious leaders, knows the duplicity of one of his closest followers, and predicts that those two forces will combine to arrange for his betrayal. Matthew narrates the arrangements for the treachery (26:14−15) that Jesus predicts (26:20). It is not just a wild guess, however. As Jesus raises the issue to all of the disciples, he forces Judas to answer his own duplicitous question (26:25). Jesus knows that the final arrangements have been made and that the betrayer has accomplished the deed (26:45−46). While this act by Judas is inevitable, it is divinely predicted.

*(3) The disciples' denials.* Moreover, Jesus' abandonment by his closest followers is neither a disappointing slip nor a missed appointment. They abandon him because of their own failure to honor his name and value his relationship as their Lord and Messiah. But once again, Jesus predicts the outcome. Not only will all of the disciples fall away from owning their allegiance to him (26:31), but so will the designated leader for the establishment of the church, Peter (26:33−34). At the incident where Jesus pronounced Peter's leadership role (16:17−19), his overbearing impetuosity caused him to succumb to the satanic temptation to attempt to deter Jesus from the cross (16:21−23). Peter may have thought he had overcome that weakness, but the

bravado of his vehemence cannot mask from Jesus the reality of his susceptibility to cowardice. Jesus predicts that Peter will three times over deny him
that very night.

But this is not just some special insight that Jesus employs. Scripture not
only prophesied that God would strike the shepherd (Jesus) to bring about
the redemption of humanity (26:31; cf. Isa. 53:4–6; Zech. 13:7), but also
that his sheep would be scattered. The disciples' denials are inevitable, but
they are divinely predicted.

**Human accountability.** In addition to divine inevitability, however, those
humans who participate are held accountable for what they do. Matthew paid
less attention to specific individuals in his account of Jesus' ministry than do
the other evangelists,[40] but throughout the Passion Narrative he reverses
that tendency and highlights repeatedly identifiable characters. Each scene
highlights a person's accountability to God's will as it is being carried out by
Jesus.

(1) *Caiaphas* (26:1–5). As high priest Caiaphas is responsible to lead the
people in their sacrifices. His privileged position should have prepared him
to anticipate the arrival of a priestly Messiah in the order of Melchizedek (Ps.
110:4; cf. Heb. 5:10; 7:11–17), but his political ambitions and manipulations blind him. He will be held accountable for his failure (cf. Matt. 26:57–
27:1).

(2) *Mary* (26:6–13). The second person is the woman who anointed Jesus,
whom we know to be Mary, the sister of Martha and Lazarus. As a long-time
follower of Jesus, she is responsible to exercise her faith in Jesus, which means
to give to him as much of herself as she knows him to be. The value of the
perfume is representative of her belief in Jesus as her Messiah, who has inaugurated the kingdom of God and raised her brother from the dead. So she
gives all she has to anoint Jesus. Her understanding of his identity and mission is probably not yet complete, but her action is an expression of unqualified faith in what she knows to be true. Her story will be told throughout
this age as an example of properly exercised faith in Jesus.

(3) *Judas* (26:14–16, 20–25). As the treasurer for the apostolic band and one
of the Twelve, Judas Iscariot is responsible not only to carry the gospel message during Jesus' earthly mission but throughout the age (10:1–6, 17–23).
His privileged position would have placed him on one of the twelve thrones
judging the twelve tribes of Israel (19:28). But as the events of this section
unfold, his privileged position increases his responsibility, which leads to
increased susceptibility to temptation—all of which increases his accountability (cf. 26:46–56; 27:1–10).

---

40. Cf. Wilkins, *Discipleship in the Ancient World and Matthew's Gospel*, 169–70.

*(4) Peter (26:31–35, 37–46)*. Like Judas, Peter has been privileged to be with Jesus throughout his earthly ministry. But not only is he one of the Twelve, he was privileged to be with Jesus for the one year of relatively private ministry Jesus had in Judea before his Galilean ministry began (cf. John 1:35–42).[41] He appears with all of the disciples to receive the stinging indictment that he will soon deny Jesus, but when he vehemently declares his allegiance, Jesus singles him out for further culpability in declaring that he will deny him three times. Peter is also privileged to be among the inner three called to be with Jesus in his hour of need in Gethsemane. Yet once again Peter is singled out for failing to stay awake and watch with Jesus. His allegiance to Jesus is as weak as is his flesh.

Peter was honored to be singled out for a special leadership role in the establishment of the church (16:16–19), but with that increased responsibility comes increased accountability. As the events of the evening transpire, Peter slowly abdicates his leadership and denies his relationship to Jesus (26:50–58, 69–75), which leaves him vulnerable to the same judgment that Judas faces. He was tempted before to use his position of responsibility to advance his own arrogant understanding of God's will for Jesus (16:21–23). He failed there, and he will fail again as Jesus needs his support throughout the night. His cowardly example is a warning to leaders and disciples, but his later repentance provides a picture of hope that encourages them as well.

*(5) Jesus*. The final person in these scenes is Jesus. Throughout the narrative the future for Jesus looks increasingly grim. He knows full well that the cross lies ahead, with the unfathomable suffering it will entail. In Gethsemane he is tempted in the same way that all of the others are tempted to abuse their responsibility to God's will for their lives. But Jesus is tempted to the extreme limit available to the satanic forces. What he endures there is unimaginable. But there is only one option for Jesus—his Father's will. Jesus is the prototypical example of one who understands God's will, wrestles with the difficulty of carrying it out, and demonstrates that petitioning God about the inevitability or necessity of his involvement in these events is not inappropriate, but who demonstrates unreserved commitment to obeying God's will.

Thus, as in the first temptations in the desert, Jesus endures temptations unique to his mission, but his obedience stands for all his disciples as the premier example for our own wrestling with temptation (see comments on 4:1–11). Our life mission, like that of Jesus, should consist of saying again and again to the Father, "not as I will, but as you will" (26:39).

---

41. See comments on 4:18–20; 10:1–4.

"In His will is our peace." That well-known saying from the medieval poet Dante enabled him to experience peace while all around him were religious people dominated by a craving for worldly power. Dante Alighieri (1265–1321), the great Italian poet, prose writer, literary theorist, moral philosopher, and political thinker, is best known for his monumental epic, *The Divine Comedy.* He lived at a time when religious and political turmoil tore apart much of the Italian landscape and caused Dante himself to be exiled by Pope Boniface VIII. The plot of *The Divine Comedy* finds a man, generally assumed to be Dante himself, miraculously journeying from Good Friday evening through Easter Sunday to visit the souls in Hell, Purgatory, and Paradise. He has two guides: Virgil, who leads him through the *Inferno* and *Purgatorio,* and Beatrice, who introduces him to *Paradiso.*

These fictional encounters enabled Dante to comment on the religious and political climate of his day. He was profoundly disturbed by the pope's craving for worldly power. There were no spiritual models among the religious leadership of his day that exercised any kind of restraint on human appetites, and the weakness of the empire supplied no law that was sufficient to exercise a physical restraint on the pope's appetite or any other will. The pope's deception had been responsible for Dante's exile and the torching of his home city of Florence, so in the epic Dante foretells these events after the fact as a warning to his countrymen. But Dante also intended to show the means by which he triumphed over his personal disaster, thus making his poem into a true "divine comedy."[42]

Dante's most important contribution to the daily lives of perplexed Christians is found in the cantos of *Paradiso.* He helps them focus on the glories of heaven as a way of navigating the sullied appetites of religious officials dominating political and social life. The *Paradiso* is a profound contemplation of spiritual realities that Dante fictionally experiences as he journeys through Paradise. The souls he encounters hint at the joy and peace of the future kingdom.

The first soul is Piccarda Donati, Dante's relative by marriage, who was unfaithful to her religious vows on earth. He does not recognize her at first because of her new vivid beauty, which he compares to "a pearl upon a milk-white brow." The beauty comes from the glow of "the first fire of love" that she now experiences in the recesses of experiencing God's will. She reveals

---

42. Ricardo J. Quinones, "Dante," *Encyclopædia Britannica* 2003, *Encyclopædia Britannica Premium Service,* www.britannica.com/eb/article?eu=117772.

to Dante her complete joy in the statement, "In His will is our peace; it is the sea into which all things are drawn by Him who created all the works of nature" (*Paradiso* 3:85–87).[43]

"In His will is our peace." This is the compass that Dante finds that will help him navigate the secret appetites of men and women who betray, deceive, deny, and destroy all who stand in their way. It is a reflection of Proverbs 3:5–6: "Trust in the LORD with all your heart and lean not on your own understanding; in all your ways acknowledge him, and he will make your paths straight." This is also one of the most important themes in this section of Matthew's story. In spite of the duplicity, the political maneuvering, and the betrayal of the religious establishment, Matthew would likewise say that "in His will is our peace."

**God is in control.** Perhaps the most important lesson that we can learn from this section of Matthew's Passion Narrative is that God is in control. Despite the downward spiral of events and his disappointment in people around him, Jesus resolutely goes forward. He trusts the Father's will even when everything looks bleak. The sure lesson for us is that we must continue to follow God's known will when we cannot see what is unknown—and the most complete delineation of that will is found in the Scriptures, from which Jesus also learned.

Like the ancient patriarch Job, we may not always have the privilege of knowing the reason or the good that results from particular events in our lives. However, when we rest in God's known will, we will find our peace. God is ultimately in control of all events around us. Human power structures, no matter how powerful they look, are not powerful enough to thwart God's intention to fulfill his ultimate desires and ends. We find today that our suffering is not foreign to God. Jesus' suffering in his humanity enables him to empathize with us directly in the midst of our pain. And in that empathy we can affirm God's love for us. Jesus willingly went to the cross to meet our deepest need of forgiveness of sin, so that we can enter the blessed existence of the kingdom of God. It is there that we enter into the peace of God's will.

How to experience this in our day-to-day activities is one of the chief growing points of our discipleship to Jesus. You may have been laid off work. Your church board and pastor may be experiencing a deepening rift. Your youngest child may have been diagnosed with autism. You may have an erratic neighbor who threatens to sue you over water rights to his farm. You may have an ongoing struggle with your husband in which he inappropriately accuses you of flirting with other men. You may have sustained an

---

43. Quinones, "Dante."

injury that wipes out your chances of getting that potential scholarship to college. All of these can be a threat to the stability of your life.

I have walked with people through each of these scenes. The impact varies from incident to incident, but in each the reaction is to think that life is out of control. Depending on the maturity level and the circumstances of one's life, it may be on the verge. But the lesson from each of the Passion Narrative scenes is that God is there to walk us through anything, if we will only turn to him. That is why the institution of the Lord's Supper is so centrally significant in this passage. It gives us a schematic in which we can evaluate our varied circumstances to draw on Jesus' proven redemptive activity and his ever-present help.

**The Lord's Supper as life's schematic.** The institution of the Lord's Supper gives us a crucial experience of God's will for us, individually and corporately. It is not simply a religious exercise but a schematic for our lives. Many churches celebrate the Lord's Supper at least once a month. It is a special time. One might think that the routine could turn to ritual that robs the celebration of its significance. However, in the symbolism "realities beyond verbal expression are acted out."[44] We will do ourselves much good to explore continually the many dimensions of the Lord's Supper, of which there are at least six.[45]

*(1) Backward.* The Lord's Supper points backward to Jesus' historical accomplishment of salvation as a finished act. It further looks back to the history of salvation that prompted the Passover meal. By looking back, we are prompted to rest in the finished work of salvation on the cross and give thanks as we consider Jesus' body and blood expended for us (26:27–28). As a memorial to his sacrifice, the Lord's Supper is a powerful reminder of the historical bedrock of our faith in his finished work of the cross.

*(2) Forward.* The Lord's Supper looks forward to the time when we will enjoy the consummation of the kingdom of God and enjoy fellowship with Jesus in drinking the cup anew together with him (26:29). We also look forward with confidence to each new day with a conviction that our future is secure with him whether we live or die. But we also look forward with sober recognition that he will come again to reward those who long for his appearance (2 Tim. 4:8) and judge those who eat unworthily (1 Cor. 11:32).

*(3) Inward.* The celebration of communion is also an important time of self-examination, as Paul reminds us. Those who live in blatant sin when approaching the table are guilty of sinning against the body and blood of the Lord (1 Cor. 11:27–28). Communion times can be important occasions of

---

44. Boring, "Matthew," 472.
45. Boring (ibid., 472–73) discusses five of these six.

looking inwardly at one's heart and holding oneself personally accountable before God. The original Lord's Supper is warning enough to us since it comes in the context of betrayal and denial, a sober reminder for us all to take heed lest we too fall.

(4) *Upward.* The Lord's Supper also looks upward as we remember that Jesus' death on the cross and burial in the tomb is not the end of the story. His resurrection is the sure declaration that his death was efficacious. So we look up with conviction and joy in knowing that the Savior lives and is seated at the right hand of the Father. His resurrection is the foundation of our faith that we too have been raised with him, so that we set our minds on things above (Col. 3:1–4).

(5) *Around.* Communion is also a time to emphasize the corporate nature of the Lord's Supper. John's account of the evening's activities includes the well-known story in which Jesus girds himself like a slave and washes his disciples' feet (John 13:3–16), a powerful reminder of the lesson he taught earlier that they are to serve each other (Matt. 20:20–28). The evening will later find Peter boastfully declaring that even if all the others deny Jesus, he will resist to the point of death (26:33–35). That kind of self-deceptive pride is a sure formula for failure. Without community we fail alone. Jesus' disciples need each other to help them stay faithful, and times of communion are powerful opportunities to renew our service to each other in the body.

(6) *Outward.* The corporate nature of communion also points to the outward dimension of the Lord's Supper. As Paul recounts the institution of the meal, he proclaims that as we partake, we "proclaim the Lord's death" until he comes (1 Cor. 11:26). The world is dying without the message of the good news that Jesus has provided salvation from sins through his death on the cross. As we renew our common commitment to that message, we are renewed individually to walk with that risen Savior in a world that waits to hear our personal testimony.

In the regular celebration of the Lord's Supper, we can focus on a different dimension each time for a consistent rehearsal of the depth of this blessed time of communion with our Lord Jesus. Some approach the Lord's Supper by keeping the ritual unvaryingly the same so that people are not distracted and can turn inward in the meditations of remembrance or confession. Others approach the communion service by varying the ritual from service to service so that people focus their meditation in a fresh way on some aspect of the Lord's Supper.[46] Regardless of what we do, the Lord's Supper becomes life's

---

46. See Lloyd John Ogilvie, *The Cup of Wonder: Communion Meditations* (Wheaton: Tyndale, 1976), 10–11.

schematic in understanding God's salvation-historical will for our lives, individually and collectively.

**Jesus, the "Prince of Peace."** The experience of peace in this world of chaos sounds like an imaginary pipe dream. Jesus said that wars and calamities will be the common experience on earth until his return in glory (24:4–8). So where really can we find peace in God's will? Nowhere else than in the finished work of the crucified Messiah.

Matthew has demonstrated that Jesus' life is the fulfillment of the prophecies of Isaiah concerning a messianic deliverer: from birth (1:23; cf. Isa. 7:14), to ministry (Matt. 4:14–16; cf. Isa. 9:1–2), to miracles (Matt. 12:15–21; cf. Isa. 42:1–4). But what about the "peace" that was prophesied to come when the "Prince of Peace" established his kingdom (Isa. 9:6–7)? Many Jews today disregard Jesus as the true Messiah since he did not destroy the enemies of Israel and establish a time of worldwide peace and prosperity. Shalom is integral to the anticipated eschatological time (cf. Ps. 85:8–10; Isa. 55:12), and Ezekiel speaks of the Davidic messianic Shepherd who will make a covenant of peace (shalom) that will usher in a time of blessing and security (Ezek. 34:23–30).

Christians also live in the anticipation of the establishment of the kingdom, when Jesus will return to bring worldwide peace. But Christians also live in the reality of the new covenant peace that Jesus, the Passover lamb (1 Cor. 5:7), brought through his work of the cross. The new covenant brings personal peace as a disciple's alienation from God is solved through the forgiveness of sin (Rom. 5:1; Col. 1:20), but it also brought, and brings, peace between Jew and Gentile as the two became one new person in the church of Jesus Christ (Eph. 2:11–18). The new covenant enables Jesus' disciples to be instruments of peace in this world through their message (Acts 10:36) and their lives (Rom. 12:17–21; 14:19), and it enables them to have personal inward peace regardless of the circumstances of this world (Phil. 4:7). The writer to the Hebrews gives this concluding benediction in Hebrews 13:20–21:

> May the God of peace, who through the blood of the eternal covenant brought back from the dead our Lord Jesus, that great Shepherd of the sheep, equip you with everything good for doing his will, and may he work in us what is pleasing to him, through Jesus Christ, to whom be glory for ever and ever. Amen.

Jesus found peace in the Garden of Gethsemane as he rested in obedience to his Father's will—and that in spite of knowing that his worst battles were yet to come. We likewise will find our life's greatest peace as we rest obediently in God's will for us individually and corporately. "In His will is our peace."

❦

WHILE HE WAS still speaking, Judas, one of the Twelve, arrived. With him was a large crowd armed with swords and clubs, sent from the chief priests and the elders of the people. ⁴⁸Now the betrayer had arranged a signal with them: "The one I kiss is the man; arrest him." ⁴⁹Going at once to Jesus, Judas said, "Greetings, Rabbi!" and kissed him.

⁵⁰Jesus replied, "Friend, do what you came for."

Then the men stepped forward, seized Jesus and arrested him. ⁵¹With that, one of Jesus' companions reached for his sword, drew it out and struck the servant of the high priest, cutting off his ear.

⁵²"Put your sword back in its place," Jesus said to him, "for all who draw the sword will die by the sword. ⁵³Do you think I cannot call on my Father, and he will at once put at my disposal more than twelve legions of angels? ⁵⁴But how then would the Scriptures be fulfilled that say it must happen in this way?"

⁵⁵At that time Jesus said to the crowd, "Am I leading a rebellion, that you have come out with swords and clubs to capture me? Every day I sat in the temple courts teaching, and you did not arrest me. ⁵⁶But this has all taken place that the writings of the prophets might be fulfilled." Then all the disciples deserted him and fled.

⁵⁷Those who had arrested Jesus took him to Caiaphas, the high priest, where the teachers of the law and the elders had assembled. ⁵⁸But Peter followed him at a distance, right up to the courtyard of the high priest. He entered and sat down with the guards to see the outcome.

⁵⁹The chief priests and the whole Sanhedrin were looking for false evidence against Jesus so that they could put him to death. ⁶⁰But they did not find any, though many false witnesses came forward.

Finally two came forward ⁶¹and declared, "This fellow said, 'I am able to destroy the temple of God and rebuild it in three days.'"

⁶²Then the high priest stood up and said to Jesus, "Are you not going to answer? What is this testimony that these men are bringing against you?" ⁶³But Jesus remained silent.

The high priest said to him, "I charge you under oath by the living God: Tell us if you are the Christ, the Son of God."

⁶⁴"Yes, it is as you say," Jesus replied. "But I say to all of you: In the future you will see the Son of Man sitting at the right hand of the Mighty One and coming on the clouds of heaven."

⁶⁵Then the high priest tore his clothes and said, "He has spoken blasphemy! Why do we need any more witnesses? Look, now you have heard the blasphemy. ⁶⁶What do you think?"

"He is worthy of death," they answered.

⁶⁷Then they spit in his face and struck him with their fists. Others slapped him ⁶⁸and said, "Prophesy to us, Christ. Who hit you?"

⁶⁹Now Peter was sitting out in the courtyard, and a servant girl came to him. "You also were with Jesus of Galilee," she said.

⁷⁰But he denied it before them all. "I don't know what you're talking about," he said.

⁷¹Then he went out to the gateway, where another girl saw him and said to the people there, "This fellow was with Jesus of Nazareth."

⁷²He denied it again, with an oath: "I don't know the man!"

⁷³After a little while, those standing there went up to Peter and said, "Surely you are one of them, for your accent gives you away."

⁷⁴Then he began to call down curses on himself and he swore to them, "I don't know the man!"

Immediately a rooster crowed. ⁷⁵Then Peter remembered the word Jesus had spoken: "Before the rooster crows, you will disown me three times." And he went outside and wept bitterly.

²⁷:¹Early in the morning, all the chief priests and the elders of the people came to the decision to put Jesus to death. ²They bound him, led him away and handed him over to Pilate, the governor.

³When Judas, who had betrayed him, saw that Jesus was condemned, he was seized with remorse and returned the thirty silver coins to the chief priests and the elders. ⁴"I have sinned," he said, "for I have betrayed innocent blood."

"What is that to us?" they replied. "That's your responsibility."

⁵So Judas threw the money into the temple and left. Then
he went away and hanged himself.

⁶The chief priests picked up the coins and said, "It is against
the law to put this into the treasury, since it is blood money."
⁷So they decided to use the money to buy the potter's field as a
burial place for foreigners. ⁸That is why it has been called the
Field of Blood to this day. ⁹Then what was spoken by Jeremiah
the prophet was fulfilled: "They took the thirty silver coins, the
price set on him by the people of Israel, ¹⁰and they used them to
buy the potter's field, as the Lord commanded me."

¹¹Meanwhile Jesus stood before the governor, and the governor asked him, "Are you the king of the Jews?"

"Yes, it is as you say," Jesus replied.

¹²When he was accused by the chief priests and the elders,
he gave no answer. ¹³Then Pilate asked him, "Don't you hear
the testimony they are bringing against you?" ¹⁴But Jesus made
no reply, not even to a single charge—to the great amazement
of the governor.

¹⁵Now it was the governor's custom at the Feast to release
a prisoner chosen by the crowd. ¹⁶At that time they had a
notorious prisoner, called Barabbas. ¹⁷So when the crowd had
gathered, Pilate asked them, "Which one do you want me to
release to you: Barabbas, or Jesus who is called Christ?" ¹⁸For
he knew it was out of envy that they had handed Jesus over to
him.

¹⁹While Pilate was sitting on the judge's seat, his wife sent
him this message: "Don't have anything to do with that innocent man, for I have suffered a great deal today in a dream
because of him."

²⁰But the chief priests and the elders persuaded the crowd
to ask for Barabbas and to have Jesus executed.

²¹"Which of the two do you want me to release to you?"
asked the governor.

"Barabbas," they answered.

²²"What shall I do, then, with Jesus who is called Christ?"
Pilate asked.

They all answered, "Crucify him!"

²³"Why? What crime has he committed?" asked Pilate.

But they shouted all the louder, "Crucify him!"

²⁴When Pilate saw that he was getting nowhere, but that
instead an uproar was starting, he took water and washed his

hands in front of the crowd. "I am innocent of this man's blood," he said. "It is your responsibility!"

²⁵All the people answered, "Let his blood be on us and on our children!"

²⁶Then he released Barabbas to them. But he had Jesus flogged, and handed him over to be crucified.

IN THE LAST section of Matthew's Passion Narrative (26:1–46), we looked at the celebration of the Passover and institution of the Lord's Supper, the plotting of the Jewish leaders with Judas to have Jesus arrested, the woman anointing Jesus for his burial, and Jesus' predictions of both Judas's betrayal and the disciples' denying their allegiance to him. That section concluded with the fateful trip to Gethsemane, where Jesus engaged in his agonizing prayers. In this present section we look at his arrest, trials, and conviction. The extended length of Matthew's treatment of these events indicates the central place that Jesus' death holds in God's plan of salvation, which should alert us to the central place it should hold for us in the development of our theology, in the practice of our corporate worship and personal growth in Christ, and in the message we proclaim to a waiting world.

A crucified Messiah was an anomaly to common Jewish expectations, but it became one of the bedrock historical factors in the preaching and teaching in the early church. A crucified Messiah can also seem an anomaly to modern people, Christian and non-Christian alike, who want a more sanitized kind of "good news." But the blood of Jesus' cross is a fact of history that offers the only good news, that the incarnate Son of God willingly endured an ignominious death so that humanity can experience a glorious life that is liberated from sin's death-grip.

## Jesus Is Arrested (26:47–56)

AFTER JESUS' THREE agonizing prayers to his Father in Gethsemane (26:36–44), in which he committed himself to obey his Father's will, he returns to the inner trio of disciples to find them sleeping once again. The larger group of disciples is likely asleep in the cave they frequented before (see comments on 26:36). Jesus declares that the inexorable path to the cross is speeding up because of the arrival of his betrayer (26:45–46).

**Judas and the armed temple troop (26:47).** Judas left Jesus and the others during the Last Supper in the Upper Room to finish making arrangements for the betrayal (cf. John 13:26–30). The garden was a favorite meeting place for Jesus and the disciples (cf. John 18:2), so Judas knows where to find him. He arrives with a large crowd of armed personnel. Matthew highlights the treachery by referring to Judas as "one of the Twelve." This is insider betrayal, an unbelievable exploitation of a trusted relationship.

The most heavily armed of those coming with Judas would be a contingent of Roman soldiers assigned by Pilate for temple security (cf. John 18:3, 12; see comments on Matt. 27:65; 28:11), who were authorized to carry swords (*machairai*), the short double-edged weapon used in hand-to-hand combat (cf. 26:51; Eph. 6:17). Levitical temple police and personal security guards of the chief priests and Sanhedrin carrying clubs also probably make up another large detachment in the arresting crowd. They have been sent by the chief priests and the elders, the ones with whom Judas made arrangements for the betrayal (Matt. 26:14–16); they represent the highest authority of the Jewish people and are endorsed by the Roman governor's own forces.

The common people hoped at Jesus' triumphal entry to Jerusalem that he was the messianic deliverer who would break the yoke of Rome's oppression (cf. 21:8–11), so perhaps the temple authorities send the armed troop with Judas in case he does begin an uprising. This is consistently the misunderstanding of Jesus' mission, reflecting the skewed perspective that comes from a misplaced comprehension of God's purposes. But Judas also leads the armed troop in the dead of night to the secluded garden where they find Jesus away from the crowds of the city, who may otherwise have attempted to resist his arrest.

**Judas's kiss of death (26:48–49).** Men in ancient (and modern) Palestine customarily greeted one another with a kiss to the cheek. Judas has arranged to kiss Jesus as a signal to the troops to identify him for the soldiers (26:48), since they do not know the Galilean pilgrim, and other groups of Passover pilgrims are probably camping on the hills surrounding Jerusalem. This was the customary way of greeting a venerable rabbi and would have seemed to the other disciples as a greeting of peace rather than shameless hypocrisy. In his typical manner, Judas greets Jesus as "Rabbi," not "Lord" (26:49; see comments on 26:25). From this event onward, Judas is forever known in biblical and historical infamy for his betrayal of Jesus.[1]

**An insider betrayal (26:50).** Jesus offered a relationship to Judas, but Judas abused and manipulated it to his own ends. With a touch of sad irony Jesus says, "Friend, do what you came for." The designation "friend" (*hetairos*) is found three times in Matthew. The preceding two times Jesus used it in

---

1. See 10:4; 26:25; 27:3; Mark 8:19; Luke 6:15–16.; John 6:71; 12:4; 13:2; 18:2, 5. See Wilkins, *Following the Master*, 164ff.

parables to address a person who abused a privileged relationship (20:13; 22:12). Here Judas has violated the most privileged relationship with Jesus Messiah.[2] He has scorned and taken advantage of the love and friendship Jesus extended to him.

Jesus' response can be rendered as a question (RSV: "Why are you here?"), but the NIV appropriately renders it as a command, "Do what you came for" (cf. also NRSV), continuing the theme of divine inevitability that permeates the Passion Narrative (cf. John 13:27b). Judas manipulates friends and enemies to advance his goals, but within the deception Jesus maintains control of his own destiny to reconcile friends and enemies to God and to each other.

**A disciple's armed resistance (26:51–54).** At the deceptive signal of a kiss of honor, the dishonorable betrayal is done, and the assembly of armed forces steps forward to arrest Jesus. One of Jesus' disciples, whom John tells us is Simon Peter (John 18:10–11), tries to defend Jesus by taking the sword he is carrying (*machaira*, the same kind as the arresting troops) and striking Malchus, the high priest's servant. But he only grazes him, cutting off his ear (Matt. 26:51). Luke records that Jesus heals the ear (Luke 22:51).

But Jesus tells Peter to put away his sword, "for all who draw the sword will die by the sword" (26:52). The way of the world is to assert its will on others through human power, even violence, and the way of the world is to retaliate against violence with violence. The inevitable consequence of championing violence is often one's own violent end. Jesus is not giving a blanket endorsement of pacifism, which would require broader scriptural support than this one saying.[3] But he does reject the notion that God's will is advanced or should be imposed on others through violent means. A general principle to guide the use of force is that allegiance should be given to the goals of the kingdom of God (cf. 5:38–42). Peter's use of force is not guided by kingdom priorities but by the human desire to retaliate.

Jesus' own life illustrates this principle, as he declares, "Do you think I cannot call on my Father, and he will at once put at my disposal more than twelve legions of angels?" Jesus has already indicated that angels will accompany him when he returns in glory as the Son of Man, who will do his bidding as they gather the elect (24:30–31). This is another picture that coincides with Jesus' status as the sovereign Son of God, at whose disposal are the angelic beings of heaven. A Roman legion had six thousand soldiers, which means that Jesus could have called on 72,000 angels. The number may have symbolic value, but more importantly points to the enormous

---

2. Rengstorf, "ἑταῖρος," *TDNT*, 2:701.
3. France, *Matthew*, 375–76.

resources at Jesus' disposal (cf. also 1 Kings 6:17). Circumstances may indicate that Jesus' mission is thwarted, but events are not out of control.

Jesus has come to carry out God's plan of redemption as prophesied in "the Scriptures" (26:54). Jesus does not point to a particular prophetic passage here but to the Scriptures as a whole that indicate the purpose of his earthly ministry, which "must" (*dei*) lead him to the cross. This is "divine necessity."[4] As was the point in the prayers at Gethsemane, obedience to the Father's will for his life is Jesus' ultimate desire, not pursuing his own will.

**Jesus is no rebel (26:55–56a).** Jesus mocks the contingent that has come out so heavily armed to arrest him, for he has been within their reach in the temple precincts teaching throughout the week. His teaching has been an obvious threat to the authority of the religious establishment. They could not counter that teaching since they had no answer for his divinely authoritative words. Yet they could not arrest him for fear of Jesus' popularity with the crowds, so they come out to arrest him with the only power that they can muster—swords and clubs under the cowardly cover of night. The question in the NIV, "Am I leading a rebellion. . . ?" (26:55), clearly repudiates Jesus of any intention of being a militaristic insurrectionist.

Matthew uses the same word (*lestes*) here that he later uses to describe the two persons between whom Jesus is crucified (27:38; Mark 15:27); it is also the same word that describes Barabbas (John 18:40) as a rebel who resists the Roman occupation.[5] Jesus consistently rejects violence as the method of establishing the kingdom of God. But the temple authorities cover their own rebellion against God's will by accusing Jesus of exactly what he has rejected, and this will be the charge that they lodge against him when they take him to Pilate.

But even their clever manipulations cannot thwart God's purposes. Jesus declares to these representatives of the religious authorities that God has ordained their deception long ago. In "the writings of the prophets," an expression found only here in the New Testament (see esp. Isa. 53; Zech. 12–13), God's spokespersons predicted their wickedness. His plan of redemption through the events of Jesus' crucifixion is divinely foretold, but those who carry out the evil deeds bear their own responsibility. The evil deeds of the religious establishment will accomplish God's plan, but it will be to their ultimate personal and national demise.

**The disciples abandon Jesus (26:56b).** Peter's impetuosity and desire to retaliate with force by wielding the sword make the disciples vulnerable to arrest along with Jesus, so they all run away. Jesus' pronouncement of the

---

4. Hagner, *Matthew*, 2:790.
5. Horsley and Hanson, *Bandits, Prophets, and Messiah*, 48–87.

divine inevitability of these events should have caused the disciples to stand firm in their trust of God's control. He predicted their cowardice (26:31–34), which they rebuffed with false bravado, but Jesus' prophetic word comes to pass. Once again at Jesus' greatest time of personal need for human support, his closest followers desert him. He faces the cross alone.

### The Jewish Trial of Jesus (26:57–68)

AFTER JESUS IS arrested in Gethsemane, he is taken to "Caiaphas, the high priest, where the teachers of the law and the elders had assembled." The Jewish religious authorities have hastily gathered to interrogate Jesus, find him guilty of violating their laws, and then establish a case by which they can accuse him of violating Roman law. The Romans exercised control over all judicial proceedings but allowed some freedom to subjected peoples to try their own legal matters. However, they kept the death penalty under their own jurisdiction and reserved the right to step in on any case and take over the proceedings. The high priest apparently knew well how to frame anyone who was a threat to his power by staying in cahoots with the Roman governor.

Scholars have long noted the irregularities of the Jewish legal proceedings against Jesus according to later Mishnaic procedures (esp. *m. Sanh.* 4–7). Among the anomalies are that it is held at night, it is held in the high priest's home instead of the temple courts, it is on the eve of a festival day, it begins with reasons for conviction instead of reasons for acquittal, the witnesses disagree and are false, and the verdict of conviction is confirmed on the same day instead of waiting until the next day after a night's sleep. However, since the Mishnaic standards were compiled nearly two hundred years later, it is difficult to know exactly what the Sanhedrin's practices were at the time of Jesus' trial. Likewise, a trial controlled by a Sadducean high priest would not likely follow Pharisaic practices, which are those found in the Mishnah.[6]

The anomalies of this trial, therefore, do not invalidate the historicity of the Gospel records; rather, they point to the devious expediency by which the trial is conducted.[7] The unexpected fortuitous betrayal of Jesus by Judas prompts the religious authorities to act quickly to take advantage of the chance to get rid of him while they have opportunity. The Sabbath is approaching, and the Roman authorities apparently support the chief priests' attempts to quiet Jesus before he gains much more of a following. If they can

---

6. For discussion, see Brown, *Death of the Messiah*, 357–63; Carson, "Matthew," 551–53; Garland, "Mark," 291.

7. For a classic, vigorous defense of the historicity of the Gospels' account of Jesus' trials, see Sherwin-White, "The Trial of Christ in the Synoptic Gospels," *Roman Society and Roman Law in the New Testament*, 24–47.

---

convince the Romans that Jesus is a threat to national security, they can discredit him in the eyes of the people with a crucifixion.[8]

Matthew highlights the fraudulence of Jesus' arrest and trial by pointing out that the teachers of the law and the elders have already assembled with the high priest, Caiaphas (26:57; see comments on 26:3). They are waiting to make a quick pronouncement of doom. None of the Gospel writers gives a full account of the judicial process leading to Jesus' death, but the overall pattern that emerges is that the Jewish authorities first try Jesus and convict him of blasphemy. Jesus is taken first before Annas, the former high priest and Caiaphas's father-in-law (John 18:13–24), then before the partially assembled Sanhedrin (26:57–68), and then after dawn before a fully assembled quorum of the Sanhedrin, which pronounces the verdict (27:1–2). Then they take him to Pilate and change the accusation to treason (see comments on 27:11).[9]

**The house of Caiaphas (26:57–58).** After his arrest in Gethsemane, Jesus apparently is taken to the home of the high priest, Caiaphas, which is a palatial mansion. Archaeological findings suggest that a mansion owned by a person of Caiaphas's stature was large enough to house both Annas and Caiaphas along with offices, so that Jesus' double appearance in a short period of time in the early morning hours is entirely within reason.[10]

As Jesus is taken before the Jewish religious authorities, Peter follows along at a distance behind the arresting troop. John's Gospel informs us that Peter is accompanied by another disciple, presumably John himself (cf. John 18:15–16), who has some connection with the high priest. Peter demonstrates a personal courage that compels him to follow Jesus and the arresting delegation to the courtyard of the high priest, where he sits down incognito among the guards. Peter is able to watch as Jesus is shuffled from hearing to hearing.

**False witnesses (26:59–60).** For the first time Matthew notes that "the whole Sanhedrin" is assembled to try Jesus, which means that the necessary constituents are in place. Up until now the focus has been on the "chief priests and the elders of the people" (26:3, 47), probably a smaller, select group of Caiaphas's allies. "Sanhedrin" (*synedrion*) denotes a gathered council, rendered loosely in Judaism to indicate both a local Jewish tribunal (5:22; 10:17) and, as here, the supreme ecclesiastical court of the Jews, which at this

---

8. Hagner, *Matthew*, 2:797.

9. Brown, *Death of the Messiah*, 357–63; Morris, *Matthew*, 678–80.

10. For a recounting of the excavation of a huge palatial mansion in Jerusalem and the possible relationship to the Gospel accounts, see Arthur Rupprecht, "The House of Annas-Caiaphas," *Archaeology in the Biblical World* 1/1 (Spring 1991): 4–17. See also Rousseau and Arav, "Jerusalem, Caiaphas's House," *Jesus and His World*, 136–39.

time meant the assembly of Jewish leaders in Jerusalem. Later, the term became a title for the tractate in the Mishnah dedicated to the organization of the Jewish government and court system.

Although the Sanhedrin had seventy members plus the high priest, cases concerning theft or personal injury could be decided by as few as three members. When a capital case was involved, the sages required that twenty-three members must make up a quorum (*m. Sanh.* 1.1). The composition of the Sanhedrin at the time of Jesus is debated, but it probably was a mixture of the priestly nobility and the aristocratic elders of Jerusalem (i.e., dominated by the Sadducees), but with some elements of Pharisee influence through their legal experts, the "teachers of the law" (26:57).[11]

Instead of presuming innocence until proven guilty, the Sanhedrin tries to find false witnesses who will testify against Jesus that he has violated the law. There is no lack of false witnesses, because many come forward, but their testimony does not stand. Mark states the Sanhedrin is unable to convict Jesus because the witnesses cannot put together consistent testimonies (Mark 14:56). The entire proceedings are a sham, for the Jewish leaders are manipulating the events to get Jesus out of the way as quickly as possible.

**Destroying and rebuilding the temple (26:61–63a).** Finally, out of the pack of false witnesses are two who testify that Jesus made the declaration, "I am able to destroy the temple of God and rebuild it in three days." Their disdainful reference to Jesus as "this fellow" shows that they are not among Jesus' followers, so they have a skewed perspective of his saying. They are apparently referring to a statement made by Jesus during the earliest stages of his ministry, in which Jews demanded from Jesus a "miraculous sign" to justify his actions in cleansing the temple. Jesus replied to them, "Destroy this temple, and I will raise it again in three days" (John 2:19). This saying was difficult enough for Jesus' own followers to understand, but easy to distort by those unsympathetic to its intention.[12] Apparently the saying circulated among Jesus' opponents in a variety of forms wherever stories about Jesus were told.

Matthew does not explain why this charge catches the attention of the high priest when the others have not, but he considers this a serious charge against Jesus, for he stands up and confronts Jesus: "Are you not going to answer? What is this testimony that these men are bringing against you?" (26:62). This may seem innocent enough, but in this charge the high priest apparently views Jesus as exalting himself over the temple of God.

---

11. For a full discussion of the Sanhedrin and its changing nature, see Brown, *Death of the Messiah*, 340–57. Cf. Saldarini, *Pharisees, Scribes, and Sadducees.*

12. John clarified for his readers that Jesus did not mean the physical temple but was prophesying the future resurrection of his body (John 2:21).

Jesus' audacious actions in cleansing the temple earlier in the week most likely still infuriate the high priest. Jesus' actions were a symbolic statement of judgment against the religious leadership of Israel and a declaration of his authority over the purposes of the temple practices.[13] Furthermore, as Jesus healed the blind and the lame in the temple (21:14–16), he displayed his authority to create purity in all those desiring to worship God. It was likely also communicated to the high priest that Jesus had earlier declared that he was greater than the temple (12:6), which would be a blasphemous claim, as it supplanted God's prescriptions through Moses concerning temple practices. Such a charge would be worthy of death (cf. Acts 6:11–14).

**Jesus is silent (26:63a).** Such patently distorted charges cannot be answered, for whatever Jesus might say to defend himself will be further distorted. So he remains silent. But it is "a sovereign silence."[14] Throughout this long night Jesus has spoken of the divine inevitability of these events. The Scriptures have prophesied them, and the Father's will superintends them. The theme of silence is noted at various times during the trials, fulfilling Isaiah 53:7 and placing the responsibility for his death back on his accusers.

**Are you the Christ? (26:63b).** Jesus' silence frustrates the high priest since he cannot get Jesus to incriminate himself on the trumped-up charge from the two witnesses. So he goes to the source and places Jesus under a solemn oath by the living God: "Tell us if you are the Christ, the Son of God." At the heart of the controversies surrounding Jesus is whether he is the Messiah. In the minds of the common people the title *Christ* (Heb. *Messiah*) implies the hope of a deliverer out of the house of David who will liberate them. By leading the questioning this way, Caiaphas is trying to get Jesus to pit himself against the Roman rule, so that Caiaphas can take him to Pilate with charges of insurrection.

"Messiah" and "Son of God" are basically equivalent expressions in this context, emphasizing that the expected Messiah is both the son of David and the Son of God (16:16; cf. 2 Sam. 7:14; Ps. 2:7; 89:26–27). The high priest is not thinking of Messiah in a Trinitarian sense that we know today to be true of Jesus. Rather, Caiaphas draws on the Jewish conception of Messiah as the Davidic king, God's Anointed, who will rule his people forever.[15]

**Jesus as the divine messianic Son of Man (26:64).** Jesus replies dramatically, "Yes, it is as you say." This NIV rendering accurately reflects the Greek

---

13. France, *Matthew*, 300–303; Morris, *Matthew*, 525–26; Davies and Allison, *Matthew*, 3:133–37; Sanders, *Jesus and Judaism*, 61–69.

14. Hagner, *Matthew*, 2:799.

15. For helpful overviews of this concept, see Guthrie, *New Testament Theology*, 301–21; A. R. Millard and D. W. B. Robinson, "Sons (Children) of God," *IBD*, 3:1474–75.

expression, which is literally, "You yourself have said." It is an indirect way of making an affirmation that places the responsibility back on the one making the inquiry. This is the way Jesus replied to Judas's question of whether he was the betrayer (see comments on 26:25; cf. also 27:11). Jesus affirms that he is the Messiah, but it allows him to go beyond Caiaphas's inadequate conception to give a further clarification of the kind of Messiah he is and in what way he is the Son of God. Jesus avoided those kinds of titles in his ministry because of the way that they could be misunderstood. Now is the time for clarification: "But I say to all of you: In the future you will see the Son of Man sitting at the right hand of the Mighty One and coming on the clouds of heaven."

Jesus declares that he is not just a human messianic deliverer; he is the divine Son of Man foretold in Daniel 7:13–14 and the object of the psalmist's reference to the divine figure who sits at the right hand of God (Ps. 110:1–2), cited earlier in his debates with the Pharisees (see comments on Matt. 22:41–46). The very title that Jesus used throughout his ministry to clarify his identity, "Son of Man," now unmistakably clarifies for Caiaphas and the Sanhedrin[16] that the next time they see Jesus, he will come as the everlasting King who will reign forever. He is the Messiah, the Son of God, but in an exalted way they cannot possibly conceive. Jesus is making himself to be equal with God. The Jews did not believe that the Messiah would be divine, but here Jesus confounds them by showing that he sustains a divine relationship to Yahweh.[17]

**The charge of blasphemy (26:65–68).** Caiaphas does not miss Jesus' point. He tears his clothes[18] and says, "He has spoken blasphemy! Why do we need any more witnesses? Look, now you have heard the blasphemy." Blasphemy means to act or, more specifically, to speak contemptuously against God.[19] Leviticus 24:11 tells of the stoning of a man who "blasphemed the Name with a curse" (cf. Dan. 3:29; 2 Macc. 15:22–24). The culpable act of blasphemy in Jesus' case is not speaking against the name of God, but rather his assertion that he has divine status as the Son of Man. He claims for himself prerogatives that belong to God alone.[20]

---

16. The phrase "you will see" is second person plural.

17. For a full discussion of the imagery, see Darrell L. Bock, *Blasphemy and Exaltation in Judaism: The Charge Against Jesus in Mark 14:53–65* (Grand Rapids: Baker, 1998).

18. Note *m. Sanh. 7.5*, that after confirming a charge of blasphemy, "the judges stand up on their feet and rend their garments, and they may not mend them again." Note too how Barnabas and Paul tear their clothes in horror when the people at Lystra try to assign them divine status (Acts 14:14).

19. Cf. "Blaspheme," *DJBP*, 97–98.

20. Brown, *The Death of the Messiah*, 523.

After hearing Jesus' blatant claim to divine status, Caiaphas pronounces that there are enough witnesses to the blasphemy. He turns to the Sanhedrin for their verdict, to which they reply, "He is worthy of death" (26:66). From the standpoint of the Jewish law (Lev. 24:10–23), as interpreted by the rabbis as well (*m. Sanh.* 7.5), Jesus deserves death because he has made himself to be divine. The sad irony is that Jesus is speaking the truth and will be sentenced to death for telling it.

From the standpoint of Roman law, however, blasphemy is not a crime deserving of death. Therefore, they will have to manipulate the charges and focus on Jesus as a common messianic pretender, who is dangerous to Rome as an insurrectionist and is gathering around himself men whom he will lead in an uprising against the military government (cf. 27:1–2, 11).

With what they perceive to be the height of blasphemy, the Sanhedrin officials spit in his face, strike him with their fists (26:67), and mock him almost as in a children's game gone cruelly sour, attempting to humiliate this one who has declared himself to be the divine, all-powerful Son of Man (26:68).[21] Spitting on him shows disdain for his claim to divine status, striking him shows how powerless he is, and slapping and mocking him for not knowing who has hit him attempts to demonstrate that he has no prophetic gift to know the future.[22]

## Peter's Denials of Jesus (26:69–75)

DURING JESUS' INQUISITION at the hands of the Sanhedrin, Peter waits in the inner courtyard. Peter stays here throughout the various phases of the trial, making him increasingly obvious to the various personnel serving there and to others awaiting the end of the trial. His three denials are likely spread out over a lengthy period of time. Compressing them into just a few verses makes their impact on the reader all the more striking.

**First denial—a servant girl (26:69–70).** Peter is first accosted by a servant girl on duty at the entryway (cf. John 18:16) to the courtyard: "You also were with Jesus of Galilee." This is the least threatening of the three confrontations, because it is directed to Peter, not to those around him. She charges that he was "also" with Jesus of Galilee, perhaps including the other disciple with whom Peter initially came to the courtyard (John 18:15–16) or Judas.

Peter has courageously stayed through the early morning hours in that hostile environment. But when his own personal safety is threatened by pub-

---

21. Flusser ("Who Is It That Struck You?" in *Jesus,* 187–94) connects the mockery directly with children's games known then and today, but also with prisoner of war scenes, where Gentiles mock Jewish prisoners.

22. Morris, *Matthew,* 686.

lic exposure of his affiliation with Jesus, Peter's courage deserts him. He does not deny her charge but evades it by denying to all within hearing range that he does not know what the girl is talking about (26:70). Obviously, he misses the chance to declare his allegiance to Jesus.

**Second denial—another girl (26:71–72).** Peter recognizes that the threat to his safety is increasing, for he leaves the warmth of the fires in the openness of the inner courtyard for the cold and shadows of the entryway. But another servant girl confronts him. This confrontation escalates from the previous one because she speaks out loud to the people surrounding them, "This fellow was with Jesus of Nazareth." The designation "Jesus of Nazareth," when used by his followers, was an expression of faith in him as the messianic deliverer (Acts 2:22; 3:6; 10:38). But used by his enemies, it was a title of scorn to deny his messianic identity (see comments on Matt. 2:23). Referring to Peter as "this fellow" may also be contemptuous (cf. 26:61).

This second girl's confrontation escalates from the first, and Peter's denial also escalates. "With an oath" he denies his affiliation with Jesus: "I don't know the man." The oath is not vulgar swearing but the invocation of something sacred (e.g., the name of God) to affirm the truthfulness of one's statement. Jesus warned earlier about invoking these kinds of oaths, since they are often attempts to hide one's deception (cf. 5:33–37). Peter is sinking deeper into personal denial as he denies his allegiance to Jesus. In Caesarea Philippi, Peter had given the most profound declaration of Jesus' identity to that point in his ministry as "the Christ, the Son of the living God" (16:16). Now, however, Jesus is nothing more than "the man" (26:72).

**Third denial—those standing there (26:73–75).** Another period of time elapses (Luke 22:59 says about an hour), which by now may parallel the final stages of Jesus' interrogation by the high priest and the Sanhedrin. Jesus declares openly his divine identity, which will result in the sentence of death. Peter's interrogation likewise intensifies, but with an accompanying intensity of denial of any relationship to Jesus, in order to save his own life.

Some bystanders intentionally come up to Peter with certainty in their identification and accost him by saying, "Surely you are one of them, for your accent gives you away." Jesus' disciples were mostly from Galilee (except Judas), where Jesus had restricted the majority of his ministry. This causes his disciples to stand out among the Judeans in the Jerusalem region. Judeans were contemptuous of the way Galileans pronounced certain words.

This third and final confrontation escalates the threat to Peter, so he intensifies his own denial by calling down curses on himself and swearing, which are most likely a doubling up of emphatic invocations of God's wrath on himself if he is lying. The more likely to others that Peter is lying, the more emphatic become his attempts to dupe the crowd with his deceptive sincerity—a well-known tactic of flagrant liars. His third and final denial takes the same form as the second, "I don't know the man!"

Peter's denial of his Lord was prophesied. He may try to hide his denials even from himself, but the prophesied signal resounds, "Immediately a rooster crowed." Peter then recalls Jesus' prediction: "Before the rooster crows, you will disown me three times." The vehement promise he made to stand up for Jesus is now thrust on him most deeply. He knows how phony he is. "Intent cannot always be judged when a thing is done once. But this is not true of something done thrice: repetition reflects resolution. This is why Peter's multiple denials are so damning."[23]

The brutal poignancy of Peter's self-revelation is stated starkly, "And he went outside and wept bitterly." The bitter weeping is recognition of his nothingness, because he has thrown away all that has given him a new identity as Jesus' disciple. But the weeping is perhaps also the first sign of his repentance. "Peter's example warns us to be ready for testing; but it also summons us to start afresh if we have failed, and to show mercy to those who have already stumbled but wish to return to the way of Christ (compare 18:10–35)."[24] This is the last time Peter is mentioned by name in Matthew's Gospel, but he will surface again among the Eleven (28:16) and becomes the prominent leader in the early church (cf. Acts 1–10).

## Jesus Condemned by the Sanhedrin and Delivered to Pilate (27:1–2)

THE DELIBERATIONS DURING the early morning hours rendered a verdict of death for blasphemy (26:57–68). Now at daybreak on Friday morning, probably a larger number of the Sanhedrin assemble with a quorum so that they can give, during daylight hours, a more formal ratification of the earlier pronouncement to put Jesus to death. According to later Mishnaic criteria, when a capital case was involved, the sages required twenty-three members to make up a quorum (*m. Sanh.* 1.1). However, Matthew has made it clear that the Sanhedrin is not hindered by legal protocol, since they are intent on finding Jesus guilty at any cost.

Since the Jewish religious leaders at this time did not have the liberty under Roman law to perform capital punishment, they bind Jesus and take him to Pilate. Pilate may have been concerned about the commotion surrounding Jesus in the temple and pressures Caiaphas to take care of him in a religious court. When that produces a guilty charge, Jesus is taken to Pilate, who also finds him guilty and has him executed. The working relationship

---

23. Davies and Allison, *Matthew*, 3:549.
24. Keener, *Matthew* (1997), 380.

between the high priest and Roman governor appears to be harmonious for each one's politically motivated ends.

Pilate was the Roman prefect and governor of Judea under Emperor Tiberius. When he first became governor, he attempted to impose Roman superiority throughout Israel. He hung images of the emperor throughout Jerusalem and had coins bearing pagan religious symbols minted. But Pilate was exposed to increasing criticism from the Jews for such acts, which may have encouraged the religious leaders to capitalize on Pilate's vulnerability, leading them to align themselves with him in his attempt to maintain peace. Their demand for a legal death sentence on Jesus, a falsely accused rival to Caesar (27:11–14; John 19:12), would not have been an unwelcome way of putting down a popular uprising.

### Judas's Remorse and Suicide (27:3–10)

JUDAS LAST APPEARED in Matthew's narrative at his betrayal of Jesus in Gethsemane. Presumably Judas accompanied Jesus and the temple troop to Caiaphas's palatial compound, where he remained through the hours of the Jewish trial.

**Judas' remorse (27:3–4).** Only Matthew records Judas's feelings of remorse and his attempt to reject the blood money, although Luke records a parallel account of the suicide in Acts 1:16–19. Matthew shows the magnitude of his "remorse" but appears careful not to suggest that Judas repents of the sin. The word "remorse" (*metamelomai*) is different from the normal word for "repentance" (*metanoeo*). "Repentance" means a change of heart either generally or in respect of a specific sin, whereas "remorse" means to experience feelings of regret. The terms can overlap, because a person who repents and chooses a different pattern of behavior will also often experience regret. However, "remorse" here indicates that Judas's pain of guilt produces an act of restitution but does not produce true repentance (cf. 2 Cor. 7:8–10).

Judas confesses that he sinned by betraying innocent blood (27:4); the enormity of his act of betrayal rests heavily on his conscience.[25] Had he truly repented of his pattern of rebellion, he would have been impelled to seek forgiveness of his sin from God.[26] Instead, he turns to the chief priests and the elders, who are just as guilty of Jesus' blood and who respond, "What is that to us? That's your responsibility" (27:4). Their hearts are even more hardened than Judas's.

Judas tries to return the thirty pieces of silver he received when making arrangements for the betrayal (cf. 26:14–15), but he cannot relieve himself

---

25. Morris, *Matthew*, 694–95.
26. Otto Michel, "μεταμέλομαι, ἀμεταμέλητος," *TDNT*, 4:626.

of the guilt of the sin, even though he throws the "blood money" into the temple (27:5). It is unlikely that he goes into the inner sanctuary, so presumably he gets as near as he can to the restricted area of the priests and throws the coins over a separator.

**Judas's suicide (27:5).** Then Judas "went away and hanged himself." This is the only incident of suicide in the New Testament (cf. 1 Sam. 31:4–5; 2 Sam.17:23; 1 Kings 16:18). Rabbinic Judaism considered suicide morally wrong, a rebellion against God, who gave life and who alone may choose to take it (*b. ʿAbod. Zar.* 18a). The early church also regarded suicide as a kind of murder (murder of oneself) and was therefore prohibited by the sixth commandment.

The discussion in Acts 1:15–25 of Judas's replacement among the apostles includes the comment, "which Judas left to go where he belongs" (1:25; cf. John 6:64). This is ominous language, which suggests that Peter knows Judas's final outcome—being consigned to the place of eternal judgment for which he was responsible. The act of suicide itself is not the focus of condemnation but rather the act of turning away from Jesus and betraying him. He was controlled by the devil himself (Luke 22:3; John 6:71; 13:26–27). He was an unbeliever who chose suicide in order to escape the daily horror of facing his actions, for which he would not repent.

The traditional reconciliation of the accounts of Judas's death by hanging in 27:3–10 and by falling headlong in Acts 1:18–19 is that the priests used the money of Judas to acquire the field, whereupon Judas hanged himself out of remorse (either in this field or elsewhere). Part of the structure on which he was hanging (perhaps the branch of a tree) broke, resulting in his falling headlong on some obstacle (perhaps rocks), when his insides spilled out.[27]

**The religious leaders purchase the potter's field (27:6–10).** After Judas leaves, the chief priests collect the coins and say, "It is against the law to put this into the treasury, since it is blood money" (they based this on the principle found in Deut. 23:18). They are fixated on scrupulous adherence to religious custom but hardhearted about their unscrupulous complicity in the betrayal of Jesus to death. The irony is that they are careful not to defile the temple treasury with blood money, but they are the very ones who earlier schemed to provide the money that shed the blood of an innocent man.

Thus, they decide to "use the money to buy the potter's field as a burial place for foreigners. That is why it has been called the Field of Blood to this day" (27:7–8). "Field of blood" occurs in transliterated Aramaic as *Akeldamach* in Acts 1:19, variantly spelled *Akeldama* or *Acheldama.* Apparently the chief

---

27. E.g., Leen and Kathleen Ritmeyer, "Akeldama: Potter's Field or High Priest's Tomb?" *BAR* 20 (November–December 1994): 22–35, 76–78; esp. 25.

priests find an area previously known to provide materials for making clay pots. They purchase it with the thirty silver coins and make it into a burial ground for travelers to Jerusalem who die prior to returning to their homeland. It came to be called "Field of Blood" since it was associated with violent death (i.e., of Jesus and Judas).[28]

Matthew summarizes his narration of Judas's death and the chief priests' hardhearted business deals with his final fulfillment quotation. "Then what was spoken by Jeremiah the prophet was fulfilled: 'They took the thirty silver coins, the price set on him by the people of Israel, and they used them to buy the potter's field, as the Lord commanded me.'" Note, however, that this quotation is largely from Zechariah 11:11–13.[29] This is similar to the way that Matthew earlier conflated messianic "branch" themes of several prophets (see comments on Matt. 2:23), and the way that Mark conflates quotations from Isaiah and Malachi but only cites Isaiah (Mark 1:2; cf. Isa. 40:3; Mal. 3:1). Jeremiah is the more prominent of the two prophets, especially in Matthew's Gospel, where he is named three times (Matt. 2:17; 16:14; 27:9).

Drawing on a combination of Jeremiah and Zechariah, Matthew demonstrates that the events surrounding Jesus' fateful journey to the cross are not the random tragedies of history but prophesied actions in which God superintends the redemption of humanity. As repulsive and tragic as the betrayal and demise of Judas and the duplicity and hardhearted manipulations of the chief priests are, they have been foreseen by God. The betrayal price figures prominently as a theme of judgment on Israel's leadership.[30] Whether it is in the days of Jeremiah, Zechariah, or Jesus, Israel rejects good leaders and suffers under bad ones, but the bad leaders who refuse to act justly will experience God's justice.

## The Roman Trial of Jesus (27:11–26)

MATTHEW RETURNS TO the center stage of his narrative of Jesus' journey to the cross: "Meanwhile Jesus stood before the governor." The Jewish officialdom has tried Jesus and found him guilty of blasphemy, for which they

---

28. The majority of scholars concede that the location of the original potter's field remains unknown today. See the discussion in Ritmeyer and Ritmeyer, "Akeldama," 22–35, 76–78; also in the same issue, Gideon Avni and Zvi Greenhut, "Akeldama: Resting Place of the Rich and Famous," *BAR* 20 (November–December 1994): 36–46.

29. For extended discussion of the difficulties, see Douglas M. Moo, "Tradition and Old Testament in Matt 27:3–10," in *Gospel Perspectives*, 3:157–75; Knowles, *Jeremiah in Matthew's Gospel*, 15, 52–81.

30. Knowles, *Jeremiah in Matthew's Gospel*, 77–81; L. Nortjé, "Matthew's Motive for the Composition of the Story of Judas's Suicide in Matthew 27:3–10," *Neotestamentica* 28 (1994): 41–51.

sentence him to death. However, without the final authority to impose a death penalty, they must take Jesus to Pilate the Roman governor to have the verdict carried out. The religious charges are not sufficient to impose the death penalty under Roman rule, so they change the charges when they hand him over to Pilate. The high priest knows well how to frame Jesus by collaborating with the Roman governor, but there is veiled double-dealing below the surface of their relationship.

Just as the Jewish trial developed in three phases (see comments on 26:57–68), so the Roman trial also develops in three phases: Jesus first appears before Pilate (27:2, 11–14), then he is sent to Herod Antipas (only in Luke 23:6–12), and finally he appears for a second and last time before Pilate, who condemns him to death (Matt. 27:15–26).

**Jesus before Pilate (27:11–14).** Pilate carried the title "procurator,"[31] which in the Roman imperial administration indicated the financial officer of a province but was also used as the title of the "governor" (*hegemon;* 27:11) of a Roman province of the third class, such as in Judea. A governor was a "legate" with control over the military legions. Pilate also originally carried the title "prefect," a title that designated various high officials or magistrates of differing functions and ranks in ancient Rome and carried administrative, financial, military, and judicial functions. Tiberius had created a hybrid of responsibilities in Judea in Jesus' time, so that Pilate had a combination of duties as prefect and procurator/governor.

The significance of the change of legal venues is evident in Pilate's first question posed to Jesus: "Are you the king of the Jews?" (27:11). This is similar to the question asked by Caiaphas, "Are you the Christ, the Son of God?" (26:63), though Caiaphas had a different emphasis—a charge of blasphemy deserving death under Jewish law but not under Roman. This new charge focuses on treason and insurrection, that Jesus claims to be a rival king to Caesar. Jesus replies in the same indirect manner that he responded to Judas (26:25) and to Caiaphas (26:64), "Yes, it is as you say" (27:11). His answer affirms the question but places the responsibility back on Pilate to discern properly what the question implies.

Jesus affirms that he is the king of the Jews, but it is incumbent on Pilate to get to the heart of what this means. But just as Jesus remained silent when accused by the chief priests and the elders (see comments on 26:63), so Jesus remains silent before Pilate, for the false testimony is brought by the high priest and the Sanhedrin, who will concoct whatever charges they believe will convince Pilate of Jesus' threat to the Roman occupation. As the Messiah of Israel, Jesus is indeed the king of the Jews (cf. 2:1–6), but the Jewish leaders

---

31. Recorded in Tacitus, *Annals* 15.44, where he explains the rise of the term "Christians."

have loaded the charges to make him a rebel and a rival king to Tiberius Caesar.[32]

Jesus has answered Pilate's original question and needs to say nothing more, so he does not respond to the concocted charges, "to the great amazement of the governor." Pilate has certainly heard of Jesus prior to this encounter, but he is not prepared for the sovereign silence that Jesus maintains in the middle of these threatening circumstances. Jesus recognizes the trial is a sham, so he does not grace the charade with a reply. His refusal to speak may bring to mind among Matthew's readers the servant of Isaiah 53:7: "He was oppressed and afflicted, yet he did not open his mouth; he was led like a lamb to the slaughter, and as a sheep before her shearers is silent, so he did not open his mouth."

**The crowd, Barabbas, and Jesus (27:15–18).** Pilate's position as prefect gave him the authority to acquit a prisoner, whether or not already convicted and condemned. In an ingenious way of attempting to enfold the people to his favor, he apparently initiated a custom in earlier years in which he released a prisoner at Passover whom "the crowd" (*ochlos*) favored. The people of Jerusalem have just a few days prior shouted "Hosanna!" at the entry of Jesus to Jerusalem. Perhaps if he offers to release Jesus to them, this will be a way of quelling any social unrest by ingratiating the crowds to himself.[33] There is evidence of widespread customs of prisoner releases at festivals in the ancient world,[34] and the Gospel account of a custom of reprieve of a prisoner at the Passover echoes the practice.

Matthew calls the prisoner Barabbas "notorious," evidently for his reputation as a freedom fighter esteemed by the people. His name does not occur elsewhere in the New Testament outside of the Gospel accounts of Jesus' trial, and there is no extrabiblical account of his activities. But he occurs in all four Gospels as the criminal chosen by the crowd—at the prompting of the religious leaders—for Pilate to release on the feast of the Passover.

The terms used to describe Barabbas (27:16; Mark 15:7; Luke 23:19; John 18:40) closely resemble the characteristics of social banditry that have been examined in recent studies of the social history of first-century Palestine.[35] As a "bandit" (*lestes*), Barabbas may have belonged to one of the rural bands. Social unrest was common, instigated in part by these guerillas. The two criminals between whom Jesus was crucified are also called by this same term (see comments on 27:38). These bandits were popular with the common

---

32. Luke 23:2 expands this into a threefold charge: we have found this man subverting our nation, he opposes payment of taxes to Caesar, and he claims to be Christ, a king.

33. See Flusser, *Jesus*, 164–66.

34. Robert L. Merritt, "Jesus Barabbas and the Paschal Pardon," *JBL* 104 (1985): 53–68.

35. Horsley and Hanson, *Bandits, Prophets, and Messiahs*, 48–87.

people because they preyed on the wealthy establishment of Israel and created havoc for the Roman government (similar to the twelfth-century Robin Hood, who robbed from the rich to give to the poor).

The Roman trial before Pilate would have begun in the quiet of the early morning hours (assuming the Jewish trial ended at daybreak, 27:1). Pilate may have thought he could conduct the trial relatively quickly and dispatch Jesus before the crowds of the city are stirred with the knowledge that the popular Jesus has been arrested. But now they arrive. Pilate sees that this may be his chance to gain more public support, so he asks the crowd, "Which one do you want me to release to you: Barabbas, or Jesus who is called Christ?"

An interesting variant occurs in 27:16–17, where Barabbas is called "Jesus Barabbas." While extant manuscript evidence is weak, Origen implies that most manuscripts in his day (c. A.D. 240) included the full name. Many scholars today accept the full name as original, and suggest that it was probably omitted by later scribes because of the repugnance of having Jesus Christ's name being shared by Barabbas.[36] If this is so, Matthew's text reads more dramatically with two holders of the same name: Which do you want— Jesus the son of Abba, or Jesus the self-styled Messiah?[37]

Matthew gives a subtle commentary on Pilate's motivation for asking the crowds to choose between Barabbas and Jesus: "For he knew it was out of envy that they had handed Jesus over to him." Pilate knows that the high priest and Sanhedrin have not indicted Jesus because they care about the potential threat to Roman rule. Rather, they are envious of Jesus and his popularity with the people (see 7:28–29; 9:8, 31, 33–34; 21:8–16), and they want him out of the way. Moreover, his authoritative ministry threatens their entire way of life. If what he says is true, they must repent and follow Jesus, as John the Baptist warned them to do long ago (3:7–10). But they have hardened their hearts throughout the months and years of Jesus' ministry. Jesus' threat to their religious establishment has come to a climax, so now they know that they must get rid of him.

Pilate is wise to their maneuverings, and he thinks that he has found a way to ingratiate the crowds to himself while subtly putting the Sanhedrin back in their place. The old expression is true: Politics makes strange bedfellows. But it is also true that political plotting can come back to bite the hand that attempts to manipulate the other.[38]

---

36. Metzger, *TCGNT*, 56.

37. W. F. Albright and C. S. Mann, *Matthew* (AB 26; Garden City, N.Y.: Doubleday, 1971), 343–44.

38. See Barnett, *Jesus and the Rise of Early Christianity*, 144–48; Anselm C. Hagedorn and Jerome H. Neyrey, "'It Was Out of Envy That They Handed Jesus Over' (Mark 15.10): The Anatomy of Envy and the Gospel of Mark," *JSNT* 69 (March 1998): 15–56.

**The dream of Pilate's wife (27:19).** Matthew records an intriguing aside about Pilate's wife that occurs while her husband is sitting on the judge's "seat" or tribunal (*bema*, the platform on which a Roman magistrate sat, flanked by counselors, to administer justice). The *bema* was traditionally erected in some public place, as apparently here, because Pilate is able to address the assembled crowd (cf. John 19:13). The location where Pilate adjudicates Jesus' case is debated (options include the Fortress of Antonia, at the northwest corner of the temple; the old Hasmonean royal palace, on the west slope of the Tyropean Valley; and the magnificent palace of Herod the Great, built on the western edge of the Upper City); the best candidate is the third option. Pilate stayed at this palace, which was newer and more opulent than the other places.[39]

Matthew alone records the incident of Pilate's wife attempting to dissuade him because of her dream. Dreams have figured prominently in Matthew (see esp. chs. 1–2), so perhaps this dream is a supernatural one used by God to make clear to Pilate that Jesus is innocent of any crime. Nevertheless, the Romans often took dreams as omens. Since there is no indication that Pilate's wife is either a God-fearer or a disciple of Jesus, this dream may be a natural, though profound premonition. In any case, whether supernatural or natural, her plea to her husband is an exoneration of Jesus for Matthew's readers. But Pilate does not heed his wife's warning.

**The chief priests and elders persuade the crowd (27:20).** The same religious leaders who plotted Jesus' arrest, conspired his betrayal, manipulated his Jewish trial, and bound him to Pilate now arrive at the Roman trial to persuade the crowd to ask for Jesus' crucifixion. Most likely they try to convince them that Jesus is a blaspheming charlatan and not their expected liberator. Throughout Jesus' ministry, the "crowd" (*ochlos* again) has been the object of his offer of salvation and discipleship, but all along it was an either-or matter (see comments on 5:1–2). A person is either with Jesus or against him (12:30); there is no middle ground. If a person responds to his invitation, he or she will come out of the crowd to become Jesus' disciple. But now the religious leaders attempt to persuade the crowd to join them and go against Jesus. They are simply that—a crowd. They have shouted with amazement and enthusiasm at his teaching (7:28–29), miracles (9:7), and triumphal entry to Jerusalem (21:8–16). But when something better is offered, they give up their shallow allegiance.

Matthew does not tell us the means that the chief priests and elders use, but it is not hard to imagine that they persuade the crowds that Barabbas is the kind of freedom fighter who will lead the nation in an uprising to finally throw off

---

39. Josephus, *J.W.* 5.4.4 §177ff.

the yoke of Rome's oppression.[40] They probably recount to the crowds how Jesus has consistently preached peace, mercy, and forgiveness, even of their enemies, which certainly hasn't improved their material lot. The governor has given them only two options, and at this point their hope is directed by the religious authorities to go with a known notorious insurrectionist. They want a kingdom on earth now. So with escalating clamor they demand that Barabbas be released to them and that Jesus be crucified (27:21–22).

**The crowd turns ugly (27:21–23).** The wily Pilate recognizes that the chief priests and the elders have tried to dupe the crowd and take away his maneuvering against them, so he tries to reverse the logic. He asks the crowd, "What shall I do, then, with Jesus who is called Christ?" Pilate understands that Jesus is not the dangerous hero whom the religious leaders are trying to portray. But he also understands that Jesus has claimed the title "Christ" as one who offers spiritual hope. That seems harmless enough to Pilate, so he tries to get the crowd to recall that many of them, even recently, have pinned their hopes on Jesus.

But the crowd is unifying into a mob, and they "all" answer, "Crucify him!" This is the first time that this verb is used in the Passion Narrative, though it will recur six more times as the climactic events move inevitably forward. The crowd is well aware that the alternative fate for the one not chosen to be released will be death on a cross.

As Jesus demonstrated in his parables, when the crowd refuses to allow the message of the gospel to penetrate to their hearts, they become increasingly hardened to his mission and are unable to repent and believe in him (13:10–17). That time has now come. Pilate tries to get them to think rationally about Jesus' innocence by asking why they should want him crucified and to spell out the crime he has committed (27:23). But they are losing any semblance of order and shout louder and louder, "Crucify him!"

**Pilate's charade (27:24).** The crowd is getting into a frenzy that may get out of control and erupt into a riot, something that has happened before during the Passover.[41] Not wanting to bring more suspicion on his shaky rule, Pilate washes his hands with water in front of the crowd and says, "I am innocent of this man's blood. . . . It is your responsibility!" There is abundant background from Jewish as well as Hellenistic sources for the practice of washing one's hands as a way of showing public innocence. This is a virtual admission that Pilate has not found anything in Jesus deserving of the death

---

40. See Michael J. Wilkins, "Barabbas," *ABD*, 1:607.

41. E.g., Archelaus overreacted to an uprising in the temple at Passover after the death of his father Herod the Great in 4 B.C., sending in troops and cavalry who killed about three thousand pilgrims (Josephus, *Ant.* 17.9.3 §§213–18; idem. *J.W.* 2.6.2 §§88–90).

penalty. But his duplicity cannot force the full responsibility of Jesus' death on the crowd or the religious leaders, for he still could have, and should have, released Jesus for lack of any evidence of insurrection and treason.

**Israel's responsibility for Jesus' blood (27:25).** The term "crowd" (*ochlos*) has been the normal word Matthew has used to designate the masses of people who have been witnessing the trial and who have asked for Jesus' crucifixion (27:15, 20, 24). Matthew now switches to a different word, "people" (*laos*), in the expression "all the people answered" (27:25). In doing so, he emphasizes that the crowd and the religious leaders have had their opportunity—now they must bear responsibility for not repenting and for asking for Jesus' death. *Laos* is the word that Matthew normally uses to designate Israel as a nation (e.g., 1:21; 2:6; 4:16; 15:8). Used here, the implications are ominous. The Jewish leaders and the crowds claim responsibility for Jesus' death as they declare boldly, "Let his blood be on us and on our children!"

Blood on a person (or "on the head") was a common idiom to indicate responsibility for someone's death[42]; "on our children" indicates the familial solidarity of generations within Israel (e.g., Gen. 31:16). These people are so convinced that Jesus deserves death that they brashly proclaim their responsibility for his death and extend that responsibility to their descendants. This statement has been called "the darkest and hardest verse in this gospel,"[43] because Matthew puts the responsibility for Jesus' crucifixion directly on the Jewish nation. Pilate tries to escape the blame, but he cannot wash his hands of the matter. By not finding any guilt in him and still ordering Jesus to be executed, Pilate is just as guilty as they are.

But even though they ignorantly crucify their own Messiah, God takes their grievous deed and provides salvation for them and for the world (Acts 3:17–19). In his first public sermon at Pentecost, the apostle Peter indicts the religious leaders, the Jewish crowds, and the Romans for Jesus' death (cf. Acts 2:23, 36). But to those who acknowledge their guilt, he also extends an offer of forgiveness of sins and salvation (2:37–41; cf. 3:19–4:4). Thousands of Jewish people, including many priests, received that offer in the first days after Pentecost (2:41; 4:4; 6:7). In their ignorance they called down responsibility on their children, but this does not in any way excuse any form of anti-Semitism, then or now. Everyone is responsible for his or her own actions, but God's forgiveness awaits any who repent.

**Jesus is flogged and sent for crucifixion (27:26).** This section of the Passion Narrative ends on a heart-breaking note: "Then he released Barabbas to

---

42. E.g., Lev. 20:9; Josh. 2:19; 2 Sam. 1:16; Ezek. 18:13; Acts 5:28; 18:6.

43. Robert H. Smith, "Mt 27:25—The Hardest Verse in Matthew's Gospel," *Currents in Theology and Missiology* 17 (1990): 421.

them. But he had Jesus flogged, and handed him over to be crucified." Flogging was a beating administered with a whip or rod, usually on the person's back. It was a common method of punishing criminals and of preserving discipline. Flogging is endorsed in the Old Testament (Deut. 25:1–3), and later rabbinic tradition gave extensive prescriptions for flogging offenders in the synagogue (cf. Matt. 10:17; 23:34).

But Roman flogging was different from Jewish flogging. The word Matthew uses for flogging (*mastigoo*) in the Jewish synagogue is different from the word used here (*phragelloo*). This is a horrific method of torture. Whereas flogging in the Jewish synagogue was limited to forty lashes (see Deut. 25:3), no such restrictions limited Roman flogging. A condemned man (women were not flogged) was tied to a post and beaten with the cruel *flagellum*, a leather strap interwoven with pieces of bone and metal that cut through the skin, leaving it hanging in sheds.[44] The repeated flaying often exposed the bones and intestines, and in many cases it was fatal. Flogging weakened the accused before crucifixion. With the Sabbath approaching, the Romans flog Jesus nearly to death so he will not be left on the cross after sundown.

THROUGHOUT MOST OF his Gospel, Matthew spotlights Jesus at center stage. Other figures come on and off the stage and share the spotlight momentarily for what they reveal about Jesus. However, in both the introductory and concluding chapters, other figures share much more of the narrative focus. In the opening chapters the spotlight was on the infant Jesus, but his parents Joseph and, to a lesser degree, Mary moved to center stage. The Magi and Herod the Great came in for special focus, as did John the Baptist. Each of these supporting figures had much to say about Jesus' identity and mission, from a positive or negative example.

Likewise, in his narration of the final chapters of Jesus' life, Matthew continues to feature Jesus as the primary figure on the narrative stage, but in the passion scenes other figures come forward for special attention. Caiaphas, the Jewish high priest, and Pilate, the Roman governor, are on either end of the narrative stage. Their politically motivated manipulations result in the execution of Jesus, but their verdicts unknowingly stand for all of history as testimonies to Jesus' true identity as the divine messianic Son of Man and the king of the Jews. Their actions also tell us much about them as individuals

---

44. See Wilkins, "Matthew," 176, for a picture of a flogging instrument with a wooden handle and six leather straps.

who compromised their divinely ordained responsibilities because of their flawed character.

Between Caiaphas and Pilate, Peter the denier and Judas the betrayer flank Jesus even more closely. Their actions tell us much about them as individuals who abandon their divinely initiated calling as Jesus' disciples because they do not draw upon the transformational realities that Jesus made available to them. Their differing responses and their consequences are stark lessons for all of humanity.

**Judas.** The event for which Judas is known in biblical and historical infamy is his betrayal of Jesus.[45] He was under the direction of Satan (Luke 22:3; John 13:2), and his greed, which had prompted him to steal (John 12:4–6), may have motivated him to betray Jesus for the paltry amount of thirty pieces of silver (Matt. 26:14–16). Although Jesus anticipated the betrayal (John 6:71; 12:4), the treacherous act apparently came at the Last Supper as a surprise to all except Jesus (Matt. 26:20–25). Securing a band of soldiers from the chief priests and Pharisees, Judas leads them to where Jesus is alone with the disciples in the Garden of Gethsemane, away from the crowds, and kisses Jesus to identify him for the soldiers (26:47–56).

Judas is a complex individual. Since he was the treasurer for the apostolic band, we may assume that he displayed some positive characteristics recognizable by the others. This office is not usually given to one known to be greedy and irresponsible. It was a respected position and probably indicates the degree of esteem in which the Twelve held him.[46]

However, love of money has contributed to the downfall of more than one person, and Judas appears to have fallen victim to it. According to John, Judas's objection to Mary's anointing of Jesus with costly ointment was not because of his concern for the poor but his greed. During his time as treasurer, he had become a thief, pilfering from the treasury funds (John 12:6). Jesus indicates elsewhere that Judas never believed in him but only appeared to be a believing disciple/apostle (John 6:64, 70–71). "Thus to covetousness there is added the trait of deceit."[47]

This leads to the complexity behind Judas's betrayal of Jesus. Why does Judas betray Jesus, whom he faithfully followed and served? A wide spectrum of possible explanations have been advanced to explain his betrayal (see comments on 26:14–16). But underlying all attempts to understand Judas's motivation is a clear recognition of his spiritual state.

While the predetermined plan of God includes Judas's betrayal, clearly Judas bears spiritual responsibility for his actions. Jesus' call of Judas to be a

---

45. See Wilkins, *Following the Master*, 164–67.
46. Morris, *John*, 578.
47. Ralph P. Martin, "Judas Iscariot," *IBD*, 2:830.

disciple and an apostle was sincere, and all appearances indicated that Judas responded sincerely. Yet, as with others who responded to that call and then turned and walked away, Judas never truly believed (John 6:64). Inwardly he was always a part of the devil's corps (6:70) while on the surface he followed Jesus. It was finally at the end that his true inner nature was revealed as a "son of perdition" (17:12), a tool of Satan (13:2, 27–30). Judas enters into a plot to betray Jesus because Satan has entered him (Luke 22:3). Judas's eternal verdict is solemnly declared in Acts 1:25: "this apostolic ministry, which Judas left to go to where he belongs." Ralph Martin declares vividly:

> Judas was never really Christ's man. He fell from apostleship, but never (so far as we can tell) had a genuine relationship to the Lord Jesus. So he remained "the son of perdition" who was lost because he was never "saved." His highest title for Christ was "Rabbi" (Mt 26:25), never "Lord." He lives on the stage of Scripture as an awful warning to the uncommitted follower of Jesus who is in his company but does not share his spirit (cf. Rom 8:9b); he leaves the Gospel story "a doomed and damned man" because he chose it so, and God confirmed him in that dreadful choice.[48]

Judas's spiritual state is the true underlying motivation for the betrayal; he who is not truly with Jesus is against him. Judas stands as a dreadful example of the outcome for a person whose apostasy stems from spiritual deficiency.

**Peter.** Peter's denials of Jesus are ominously juxtaposed next to Judas's betrayal and suicide. Peter holds a prominent place in Matthew's Gospel up to this point. Matthew narrates five incidents in which Peter figures prominently that are found nowhere else in the Gospels: walking on the water to Jesus in the storm (14:28–31), asking for an explanation of one of Jesus' parables (15:15), confessing Jesus as the Christ, evoking a statement from Jesus about his foundational role in the church (16:17–19), recommending to build shelters on the Mount of Transfiguration (17:24–27), and asking how many times he should forgive a brother (18:21). Now Peter denies three times that he knows Jesus.

Matthew does not whitewash Peter, even though he will become the courageous leader of the church. Instead, he focuses on Peter as an example of the way in which Jesus takes everyday men and women, with all of their strengths and weakness and all of their successes and failures, and transforms them into his kind of disciples. Matthew also focuses on Peter as an example of the way that Jesus takes everyday disciples and transforms them into

---

48. Martin, "Judas Iscariot," 831.

his kind of leaders—leaders who stumble and fall but who, when they learn to fix their eyes of faith firmly on Jesus, are able to lead Jesus' people.

This leads to the complexity of the reasons behind Peter's denials of Jesus. Why does Peter deny Jesus, whom he vowed he would follow even to his own death (26:35)? He is probably in some danger, because he used force against the high priest's servant during Jesus' arrest in Gethsemane (26:51). The accusations against Jesus grow increasingly hostile in the court-yard of Caiaphas's home while Peter waits in the shadows. But none of this is certain to end in his arrest. I suggest that Peter and the other disciples abandon and deny Jesus because of the profound transitional period in which they find themselves. But once they experience the death, resurrec-tion, and ascension of Jesus and the descent of the Spirit at Pentecost, they are forever transformed and become the example of our own potential for transformation.

So why specifically does Peter deny and abandon Jesus? (1) *Peter does not yet clearly understand who Jesus is.*[49] Throughout the time the disciples followed him, they have an increasing understanding of who Jesus is. However, their own preconceptions often get in the way. Because they do not clearly under-stand who Jesus is, they are not able to let him be who he really is in their lives. The Jesus whom they have followed does not seem to offer much to them now. He is led away to a Jewish trial and will be crucified just like other insurrectionists. What can he possibly offer now? All of their hopes are dashed with Jesus' arrest and forthcoming crucifixion. Peter must think that this is the end of the dream, and there is no sense risking anything more for a dream turned nightmare.

It will take the most radical miracle in all of history, the resurrection, to demonstrate to Peter that Jesus is more than he has imagined and that he is now able to bring about the change in his life that he has promised. Know-ing that he serves a risen Lord will give Peter the vision and the courage to give himself unreservedly.

(2) *Peter does not yet believe who he is as Jesus' disciple.* Jesus all along promised transformation to his disciples with the arrival of he kingdom of God. Although they have made a commitment to be his disciples, they do not yet clearly believe that they will be forever changed by God from the inside out. But the danger of the hour causes Peter and the others to lose sight of Jesus' radical new vision of who they are to be as his disciples. So they scat-ter and deny him.

Peter tries desperately to live up to his calling, but he is notorious for his inconsistency, including his denials. But it is this same Peter who later

---

49. See further in Wilkins, *In His Image*, 28–30.

encourages exiled believers to be faithful during their persecution by writing, "For you have been born again, not of perishable seed, but of imperishable, through the living and enduring word of God" (1 Peter 1:23). He now understands clearly that discipleship is an inner work in which God produces resurrection life and that transforms him in such a way that he will courageously confess Jesus for the rest of his days.

(3) *Peter does not yet know what is available to him to live courageously as Jesus' disciple.* Those trembling disciples have looked to Jesus for strength and leadership. Now with him arrested and crucified, they have nowhere to turn. Jesus' promise to send another Counselor must seem like vague wishful thinking (John 14:15–27; 16:5–16). All the disciples flee in Gethsemane, and Peter scurries away from a young girl's questioning. And he will hide when Jesus is led to the cross. Even after they hear of his resurrection, they hide away in fear for their own lives (John 20:19). They do not yet know fully what is available to them to live courageously and victoriously in a hostile world.

But soon they will know. With the coming of the Holy Spirit at Pentecost the ancient promise of the prophet Joel and Jesus' own promise are now a reality (cf. John 14:15–17; Acts 2:16–36). The Holy Spirit is the gift to everyone who calls on the name of Jesus for salvation (Acts 2:38–39), which now provides the boldness to preach and heal, the courage to stand up under persecution, and the power to be transformed in their personal characteristics and values.

(4) *Peter does not yet grasp his calling as Jesus' disciple.* The disciples heard Jesus declare that the kingdom of God was at hand (4:17), but they often turned this around to mean privilege and position for themselves (cf. 18:1; 20:20–28). Peter and the others do not yet understand fully that Jesus has not called them simply for their own comfort and benefit. Peter is called to be an ambassador of the kingdom. He will bring a message of transformation to a lost and dying world. But as Jesus is led away to die for that world, Peter's hopes and vision seem to die with him. Peter and the others do not yet grasp the calling of God on their lives.

But when they encounter their risen Master, they look with a new light upon the cross. Yes, it is a symbol of suffering and pain, but now it also is a symbol of sacrifice and service. Jesus has not come to be served but to serve, and to give his live as a ransom for many (20:28). His purpose in coming to earth is to go to the cross to bear the sins of a lost and hopeless world. Thus, Peter and the other disciples will understand in a new way Jesus' call to deny themselves, take up their cross, and follow him. They also must deny their own will for their lives in exchange for the Father's. In doing so they will actually find real life (cf. 16:24–27).

THE INTRIGUE OF these passion scenes reveals the undoing of those who come on and off of Matthew's narrative stage—Caiaphas, Pilate, the crowds who demand Jesus' blood, and Peter. All fail the responsibility that is their lot in life. Although their actions are motivated by humanly contrived means of achieving success, each ultimately fails. By contrast, one solitary life maintains his divinely ordained course— Jesus. Although his ultimate end seems to be a failure, his perseverance brings about ultimate victory.

As these various figures come in for special focus in Matthew's Passion Narrative, the spotlight reveals character deficiencies that both warn and instruct us. Their contrast to Jesus' faithful confession tells us much about him—which is in the end Matthew's purpose.

**Caiaphas—religious conviction forced by a leader.** During the Jewish trial Jesus declares that he is Daniel's prophesied divine Son of Man, which infuriates the religious leaders and compels them to have him executed. Caiaphas is driven by the conviction of what he believes to be right—Jesus cannot possibly be who he claims to be—so he manipulates the Sanhedrin and the witnesses to get the guilty verdict he wants. Not only is his religious conviction misguided, but his blindness to the truth and his own lack of integrity prevent the nation from receiving the Messiah, the task for which he as high priest is ultimately responsible.

Religious leaders today have responsibility to understand God's message and with it to shepherd God's people for him. Their certainty about biblical truths must be their unwavering passion, but there is always the temptation to believe that their convictions equal the truth itself. On his own, Caiaphas had reason to doubt the claims of Jesus to be Israel's Messiah. Jesus did not conform to his Sadducean party's expectations, which did not believe in a personal messianic deliverer. Since they derived doctrine from the Pentateuch, which did not give them enough evidence of a prophesied Messiah,[50] Caiaphas rejected Jesus' messianic claims. But how tragic that Caiaphas did not have the courage to buck his religious party's trend and look to the entire Old Testament, which would have led to his understanding of Jesus' claims. Instead, he turned to manipulation and falsehood to deny the truth of the broader canon of revelation.

I have recently watched unfold a church situation that illustrates how we can learn from Caiaphas's negative example. The pastor of a local church was convinced of a particular form of church government, which was the

---

50. For further background, see Wilkins, "Matthew," 25.

opposite of the church's constitution. He knew that the church held that form of government when he took the position, but he felt that with his guidance the church would be swayed. The intriguing situation was skewed by the fact that the pastor derived primary support for his ecclesiology and polity from Old Testament models, in particular, Moses. The church, however, based their understanding of church organization and leadership on New Testament models, primarily Paul's Pastoral Letters, which led them to emphasize a plurality of elders in leadership for the church.

The pastor and the elders studied the positions seriously for six months. In the end both sides became more convinced of their own position. With the constitutional position in place, the elders argued to continue with their model. Ultimately, the pastor was asked to resign, and the church was spared an ugly drawn-out fight between the two sides. There was a desire for true dialogue and prayerful examination of the biblical teachings and the needs of the church.

This is a positive example where equally held convictions were aired appropriately and all maintained their integrity. The pastor did not try to manipulate the church to get his way. In fact, the church body and even the rest of the pastoral staff were not informed of the impasse until the very end. I believe that the pastor held misguided convictions, but to his credit he believed that his personal integrity was a higher priority than his convictions on this matter.

These are tough issues. I personally felt that an even better conciliation would have been for the pastor to continue to concede on the issue, as he did when he originally took the position, and submit to the church elders and the church's long-established constitution. But nonetheless, God's work in the church continues.

**Pilate—political conviction compromised by a leader.** Historian Paul Maier in his historical novel of Pilate's life states:

Pilate could never know it—he would have been astonished to know it—but, apparently insignificant ex-prefect that he was, his would eventually be the most familiar name in all of Roman history. For uncounted masses in future ages, who knew little about a Caesar or Augustus or even Nero, would confess in The Creed: "I believe in Jesus Christ ... who ... suffered under Pontius Pilate."[51]

Pilate's infamous act of ordering Jesus' execution was carried out in the political backwaters of first-century Palestine. His actions were conducted in relative obscurity, with no thought that they would have historical and spir-

51. Paul Maier, *Pontius Pilate* (Grand Rapids: Kregel, 1996), 349.

itual consequences for all of humanity for all time. But Pilate is known forever as one whose political machinations perverted his integrity. Yet in spite of his maneuverings, God's will was accomplished. A pagan leader like Pilate does not consciously seek God's will, but the clear statement of Proverbs is that "the king's heart is in the hand of the LORD" (Prov. 21:1). God has established all authorities to exercise justice according to the conscience with which they are born as humans created in God's image (cf. Rom. 13:1–5). Pilate's responsibility as a leader, whether he consciously considered God's will or not, was to maintain integrity that accords with the highest ideals of human nature.

It is impossible to get into Pilate's head to understand all that he experienced and all the options that he considered, but it is obvious that he operated out of a political frame of reference. He was trying to appease too many sides. He was trying to manipulate people and circumstances. In this backwater region of the Roman Empire, he thought that he could get away with maneuverings with his reputation intact and the peace maintained.

By contrast, Jesus' resolve to maintain the "good confession" (1 Tim. 6:13) was expressed with silent witness to what his entire life had expressed. He did not resort to double-dealing or compromise to accomplish his life's ambitions. His silence before Pilate is a booming testimony to his unwavering commitment to God's calling. As the writer to the Hebrews proclaims in Hebrews 12:2–3:

> Let us fix our eyes on Jesus, the author and perfecter of our faith, who for the joy set before him endured the cross, scorning its shame, and sat down at the right hand of the throne of God. Consider him who endured such opposition from sinful men, so that you will not grow weary and lose heart.

It is Jesus' steadfast pattern that contrasts the weakness of Pilate's concession.

They may not be many, and they may not come often, but there are hills that are worth fighting and dying for, even when they may come in the relative obscurity of our own little worlds. We may be far from centers of power and acclaim, but the responsibilities allotted to us have untold consequences. They are a test of our character. Pilate compromised at his life's most important moment, knowing that the sentence of crucifixion he pronounced was on an innocent man. The intriguing feature of the narrative is that God supplied trustworthy advice from his own wife that could have given him the courage to buck his politically motivated intuitions. Instead, he decided to go it alone, and his attempt at political negotiation marks him for all of history as a man of weakness and failure.

When the opportunity presents itself, each of us must contend for what we know to be right and for those for whom we are responsible, regardless of whether we think that the outcome will ever be known by others. A dramatic example is found in the experience of John McCain, U.S. senator from Arizona. He spent seven horrific years in a North Vietnamese prison camp after being shot down over Hanoi while on a bombing run. But early in his captivity he was given an offer that many of us would consider too good to refuse. One year after his capture, an English-speaking North Vietnamese officer, whom the prisoners called The Cat, asked him, "Do you want to go home?" When McCain realized he was hearing a legitimate offer of freedom, the prospect of returning home lifted his emotions like an activated ejection seat. He was given three days to think over the offer.

During that time, the reality of what his decision would mean to his fellow prisoners sank in. Unbeknownst to McCain, his father, an Admiral, had just been promoted to be Commander over all United States forces in the Pacific. The North Vietnamese captors saw an opportunity to offer the younger McCain the chance to go home, which would immeasurably harm the morale of the other prisoners. The captors would mock those left behind. "Your father's not an admiral. You'll never get out of here. Give up now and denounce your country." A positive decision by McCain would have greatly distressed his band of fellow prisoners left behind.

Three days later, McCain shocked The Cat when he declined to the offer. The result was six more brutal years in that prison camp. But God has redeemed those years multiple times over in McCain's life today. He couldn't know that in the obscurity of a North Vietnamese prison camp, one decision would inspire millions of people to maintain their own integrity.

Family counselor John Trent tells of Jim, a senior vice-president on a fast track for the CEO position. When his kids hit high school, he was asked to take a promotion necessitating another move. He sat down and counted the cost, recognizing that he had promised the family that his present position would be a long-term stay. After much thought and prayer, he said no to the promotion. As is often the case, when a person bucks the corporate will, Jim was unceremoniously "downsized." For five months he was unemployed, but he maintained his trust that he had made the best decision. God honored Jim's commitment to his family with an incredible job offer— a position that has kept him close to home, furthering his relationship with his wife and children.

A yes decision to a great offer isn't always in the best interest of those to whom we are closest. Sometimes saying no will gain us better ground. Writing to give advice to men who face similar challenges, Trent offers helpful words to all who may be facing a decision.

1. *Where is your spiritual life today?* If you are not spending time in God's Word or prayer, how can we expect to make a God-honoring decision about a move or transition?

2. *How much more time will be taken away from your family?* Be ruthlessly honest in answering this question. Will your new position require 10, 15, or 50 percent more time away from your family? Ask your spouse what percentage she (or he) would pick.

3. *Is your spouse warning you away from this new opportunity?* If your spouse's "warning lights" are flashing about this change, don't ignore her (or him). God often speaks through our spouses.

4. *Have you broken previous promises about your job?* Did the last move or job come with the promise, "This will just be a short-term thing"? Promises that never materialize can undermine your family's trust in you.[52]

These are sound words of advice. Pilate should have listened to his wife, and he should have listened to his own intuitive read that Jesus was innocent. But his political machinations perverted his integrity. Even pagan leaders are accountable to God for the integrity of their conscience. Our decisions require accountability to God's calling in our lives, regardless of the obscurity or seeming insignificance of its impact.

**People—responsibility claimed does not deserve discrimination.** The crowd that demanded the release of Barabbas turned ominously ugly at Jesus' trial before Pilate. They wanted the kingdom on earth now, and when Jesus did not live up to their expectations, they wanted a freedom fighter with a proven track record for bucking the Roman occupation. They had had enough of Jesus' announcement of the arrival of the kingdom that had not materialized in the way they wanted. So the Jewish leaders and the crowd, as representatives of the people of Israel, demanded Jesus' execution and declared that they would accept responsibility for his death: "Let his blood be on us and on our children!" (27:25).

We noted above that this statement has been called "the darkest and hardest verse in Matthew's Gospel." One of the reasons is because it has been used throughout history as a basis for persecuting Jews. Anti-Semitism is a cancer that has plagued humanity for much of history, and Matthew's narration of the people's statement has been wrongly interpreted to condone, and even promote, anti-Semitism. But Matthew is not invoking a self-curse by the Jews, nor is he making an oblique reference to God's eternal curse on Israel. Matthew records the statement to show how the religious leaders and some of the Jewish people at that time offered to take the blame for Jesus' death. They believed him to be a blasphemer and wanted him executed for it.

---

52. John Trent, "A Father's Heart," *Christian Parenting Today* 13/5 (May–June 2001): 56.

These words reflect the same accusatory statements elsewhere in the narrative, when Jesus placed the blame squarely on the religious leaders for not receiving him as the Messiah of Israel and for their role in turning the people away from him (e.g., 23:13–15). Israel bears responsibility for rejecting her Messiah and has had her functional responsibility as caretakers of the kingdom of God taken away from her in this present age (cf. comments on 21:43). But this certainly does not mean that later Jews should be labeled with racist titles like "Christ-killer," or that Christians should abuse Jews in the name of seeking revenge for God.

The sad and painful tragedy of this verse is that Israel has rejected their Messiah. The apostle Paul weeps for his countrymen because he knows they have suffered the consequences of that rejection—they do not participate in the blessings they would be enjoying had they accepted him (e.g., Rom. 9:1–5; 10:1–4). Israel is at this time experiencing a hardening because they have rejected the Messiah, a hardening that they will continue to experience until the fullness of God's timetable with regard to the Gentiles has come in (Rom. 11:25). But God's love for Israel continues, and he will remain loyal to the covenants he made with the nation. There still awaits a time when Israel will return to the one whom they have rejected and will experience a national awakening (Zech. 12:10–13:1; Matt. 23:39; Rom. 11:26–32).

Those who reject Jesus, whether Jew or Gentile, will suffer the consequences. Today each individual Jew must consider the claims of Jesus and the message that the apostles bring. Only days after the crucifixion, thousands of Jews do repent at Peter's preaching about the Jesus whom they put to death (Acts 2:23, 37–41), and even many of the priests will become believers (Acts 6:7). The responsibility of Christians today is to love the Jewish people as God does, to recognize the special place they enjoy in God's plan for the ages, and to share the gospel with them as we would any other people.[53] No one can support racial bigotry toward Jews by appealing to Matthew's record.[54]

---

53. See John J. Johnson, "A New Testament Understanding of the Jewish Rejection of Jesus: Four Theologians on the Salvation of Israel," *JETS* 43 (June 2000): 229–46.

54. As Jewish scholars themselves note, "Despite the Christian use of Matthew for anti-Semitic attacks, the harsh polemics in the gospel do not attack Jews as a group but the leaders of the Jews (scribes, Pharisees, Sadducees, chief priest, elders) and those people who have been misled into hostility toward Jesus" ("Matthew, Jews in the Gospel of," *DJBP*, 416). For a similar perspective from a broadly Christian perspective, see Anthony Saldarini, "Reading Matthew without Anti-Semitism," *The Gospel of Matthew in Current Study*, ed. David E. Aune (Grand Rapids: Eerdmans, 2001): 166–84; he gives six "concrete rules for preaching and teaching about Judaism and about Jews" that have relevance for practical application (cf. 182–83).

**Peter—personal defeat requires intentional restoration.** During the intimacy of the final night that he spent with the disciples—sharing the Passover and the institution of the Lord's Supper—Jesus ominously predicted that they would all deny him. To Peter's brash declaration that he would never deny him, even to the point of death, Jesus directed an even more ominous prediction of a threefold denial that very night (26:31–35). But preceding Jesus' prophetic statements, Luke records a profound statement of Peter's restoration: "Simon, Simon, Satan has asked to sift you as wheat. But I have prayed for you, Simon, that your faith may not fail. And when you have turned back, strengthen your brothers" (Luke 22:31–32).

Little does Peter know the immensity of Jesus' prediction. It holds out promise for all of us to know that within any temptation is Jesus' sustaining prayer. Furthermore, it holds out to Peter the promise of his recovery and the responsibility he has to strengthen his brothers who will also falter. Owning his responsibility is a key to Peter's repentance, recovery, and transformation.

J. Glyn Owen followed Dr. Martyn Lloyd-Jones as the minister of Westminster Chapel in London, England. Over the course of several years he preached a series of messages about Peter. The special concentration of the series of messages, which was later transcribed into book form, was on the transformation of Simon into Peter—from an eagerly rambunctious fisherman into the rock-solid foundational character of the church. The encouraging nature of this transformation is that it has much to offer us as an example for our own. Owen states:

> I believe that the story of this transformation is one of the great epics of history. It is a remarkable story made all the more remarkable because Simon represents all of us. Impetuous, impulsive, unstable, he is so human and so obviously made of the same stuff as we are that his character symbolizes ours. We all see ourselves in him at some point. For this reason we cannot help but take courage as we see how the Lord teaches and transforms Simon. We learn what the grace of God can do for us, too.[55]

In the Bridging Contexts section we considered several reasons that may explain why Peter and the rest of the disciples denied Jesus. Later, after the resurrection and Pentecost, each of these issues is reversed in their lives. They willingly become courageous leaders in the church, and many of them became martyrs for their allegiance to Jesus as the divine Messiah of Israel. They now know that discipleship is far more than a functional relationship—it entails their ongoing transformation into Jesus' image. They now know what is avail-

---

55. J. Glyn Owen, *From Simon to Peter* (Herts, England: Evangelical Press, 1985), 4.

able through the ministry of the Holy Spirit in their lives to maintain their discipleship to Jesus. And they now know their calling is more than their comfort—they are driven by Jesus' commission to make disciples of all the nations.

From our historical perspective, we have a clearer understanding of all of these issues, which today are essential for the realistic carrying out of our own faithful discipleship to Jesus.[56] But have we willingly given ourselves to the full realization of these issues in our daily lives? That is what responsible discipleship is all about.

Two young Christian women discovered the reality of these issues in a most unexpected way. Dayna Curry and Heather Mercer served as short-term missionaries in Afghanistan during 1998. That trip convinced them that God was calling them to serve among these needy people. In Dayna's words: "I felt as if God told me to go and lay down my life for them."[57] Like Peter's boldness, Dayna's words would be tested.

She went to Afghanistan with Heather, where they served with Shelter Now as relief workers especially among the poor and starving children. They were soon arrested by the ruling Taliban for showing the *Jesus* film to an Afghan family. While imprisoned, the allied forces invaded Afghanistan following the tragedies of the September 11, 2001, terrorist attacks on New York and Washington, D.C. Many innocent people got trapped in the military operations—among them Dayna and Heather. But through events that were followed live by an international audience, the young women and the other missionaries with them were rescued.

Unlike Peter, when it came to their moment of testing, these young women stood firm. They live in the blessed period where they knew Jesus' true identity and his enabling presence, they knew who they were as his disciples, they knew the resources available to them to stand firm in the Spirit, and they knew their calling to bring the good news of Jesus Messiah. In an interview after they returned home, Dayna recalled her earlier bold statement about going to Afghanistan, and she recalled a later reaffirmation of that conviction as she and Heather were in prison, perhaps awaiting their execution. She had prayed, "Lord, if it's the best for me to die and be a martyr so that there will be a breakthrough in Afghanistan, then that's okay." In the face of that prayer, she went on to say, "But I just had a supernatural peace most of the time."[58]

---

56. I have developed these practically in Wilkins, *In His Image*, 27–30.

57. Cited by Bob Paulson and Scott D. Noble, "Captive in Afghanistan," *Decision* 43/7 (July 2002): 8.

58. "Double Jeopardy," interview of former Taliban hostages Dayna Curry and Heather Mercer by Stan Guthrie and Wendy Murray Zoba, *Christianity Today* (July 8, 2002): 26–32, esp. 30.

Dayna and Heather are normal Christians who were abnormally persecuted as well as supernaturally strengthened. The apostle Peter will experience that supernatural strengthening after he repents and returns to his Master. He later writes to other young leaders of the church, much like you and me or Dayna and Heather, who likewise must learn of the abundant provision available to all of Jesus' disciples. His prayer for them is a prayer for all of us.

> Humble yourselves, therefore, under God's mighty hand, that he may lift you up in due time. Cast all your anxiety on him because he cares for you. Be self-controlled and alert. Your enemy the devil prowls around like a roaring lion looking for someone to devour. Resist him, standing firm in the faith, because you know that your brothers throughout the world are undergoing the same kind of sufferings.
>
> And the God of all grace, who called you to his eternal glory in Christ, after you have suffered a little while, will himself restore you and make you strong, firm and steadfast. To him be the power for ever and ever. Amen. (1 Peter 5:6–11)

Peter learned his lesson and stands as a powerful example of one who denied his Lord, but he was courageous enough to allow Jesus to restore him so that in turn he could help to restore others.

# Matthew 27:27–66

T HEN THE GOVERNOR'S soldiers took Jesus into the Praetorium and gathered the whole company of soldiers
around him. ²⁸They stripped him and put a scarlet
robe on him, ²⁹and then twisted together a crown of thorns
and set it on his head. They put a staff in his right hand and
knelt in front of him and mocked him. "Hail, king of the Jews!"
they said. ³⁰They spit on him, and took the staff and struck
him on the head again and again. ³¹After they had mocked
him, they took off the robe and put his own clothes on him.
Then they led him away to crucify him.

³²As they were going out, they met a man from Cyrene,
named Simon, and they forced him to carry the cross. ³³They
came to a place called Golgotha (which means The Place of
the Skull). ³⁴There they offered Jesus wine to drink, mixed
with gall; but after tasting it, he refused to drink it. ³⁵When
they had crucified him, they divided up his clothes by casting
lots. ³⁶And sitting down, they kept watch over him there.
³⁷Above his head they placed the written charge against him:
THIS IS JESUS, THE KING OF THE JEWS. ³⁸Two robbers were crucified with him, one on his right and one on his left. ³⁹Those
who passed by hurled insults at him, shaking their heads ⁴⁰and
saying, "You who are going to destroy the temple and build it
in three days, save yourself! Come down from the cross, if you
are the Son of God!"

⁴¹In the same way the chief priests, the teachers of the law
and the elders mocked him. ⁴²"He saved others," they said,
"but he can't save himself! He's the King of Israel! Let him
come down now from the cross, and we will believe in him.
⁴³He trusts in God. Let God rescue him now if he wants him,
for he said, 'I am the Son of God.' " ⁴⁴In the same way the robbers who were crucified with him also heaped insults on him.

⁴⁵From the sixth hour until the ninth hour darkness came
over all the land. ⁴⁶About the ninth hour Jesus cried out in a
loud voice, "Eloi, Eloi, lama sabachthani?"—which means,
"My God, my God, why have you forsaken me?"

⁴⁷When some of those standing there heard this, they said,
"He's calling Elijah."

⁴⁸Immediately one of them ran and got a sponge. He filled it with wine vinegar, put it on a stick, and offered it to Jesus to drink. ⁴⁹The rest said, "Now leave him alone. Let's see if Elijah comes to save him."

⁵⁰And when Jesus had cried out again in a loud voice, he gave up his spirit.

⁵¹At that moment the curtain of the temple was torn in two from top to bottom. The earth shook and the rocks split. ⁵²The tombs broke open and the bodies of many holy people who had died were raised to life. ⁵³They came out of the tombs, and after Jesus' resurrection they went into the holy city and appeared to many people.

⁵⁴When the centurion and those with him who were guarding Jesus saw the earthquake and all that had happened, they were terrified, and exclaimed, "Surely he was the Son of God!"

⁵⁵Many women were there, watching from a distance. They had followed Jesus from Galilee to care for his needs. ⁵⁶Among them were Mary Magdalene, Mary the mother of James and Joses, and the mother of Zebedee's sons.

⁵⁷As evening approached, there came a rich man from Arimathea, named Joseph, who had himself become a disciple of Jesus. ⁵⁸Going to Pilate, he asked for Jesus' body, and Pilate ordered that it be given to him. ⁵⁹Joseph took the body, wrapped it in a clean linen cloth, ⁶⁰and placed it in his own new tomb that he had cut out of the rock. He rolled a big stone in front of the entrance to the tomb and went away. ⁶¹Mary Magdalene and the other Mary were sitting there opposite the tomb.

⁶²The next day, the one after Preparation Day, the chief priests and the Pharisees went to Pilate. ⁶³"Sir," they said, "we remember that while he was still alive that deceiver said, 'After three days I will rise again.' ⁶⁴So give the order for the tomb to be made secure until the third day. Otherwise, his disciples may come and steal the body and tell the people that he has been raised from the dead. This last deception will be worse than the first."

⁶⁵"Take a guard," Pilate answered. "Go, make the tomb as secure as you know how." ⁶⁶So they went and made the tomb secure by putting a seal on the stone and posting the guard.

IN THIS CRUCIAL section of his Passion Narrative, Matthew takes us to the very heart of his gospel about Jesus Messiah. The crucifixion narrative culminates a critical theme of this Gospel, a theme that marks a central purpose of Jesus' entire earthly mission: Jesus brings salvation from sin. The infancy narrative commenced with the announcement that the soon-to-be-born child would be named Jesus, "because he will save his people from their sins" (1:21). As the narrative unfolds, Jesus makes pronouncements about forgiving sins (9:1–8) and about providing a ransom for many (20:28). At least four times Jesus predicted he would be handed over by the Jewish leaders to be killed at the hands of the Gentiles (16:21; 17:22–23; 20:17–19; 26:2).

For Matthew's readers, those Old Testament passages that spoke so darkly of a suffering Servant who would bring forgiveness of sin are now crystal clear (e.g., Isa. 42:1–4; 52:13–53:12). They point to the crucifixion of their Messiah, who brings true redemption in his sacrifice on the cross. Matthew narrates these events starkly, with little commentary about their meaning. But for his readers the meaning is clear—Jesus is the crucified Messiah, whose death liberates his people through the unimaginable horror of dying for their sins in their place. Somberly, with deepest sorrow, yet with unimaginable joy, we watch our Savior go to the cross.

The full account of the events of the crucifixion leading up to Jesus' death as recorded in the four Gospels is as follows:

1. Arrival at Golgotha (Matt. 27:33)
2. Jesus' rejection of the soldiers' offer of wine mingled with gall (27:34)
3. Division of Jesus' clothes (27:35)
4. Placard over Jesus' head: "THIS IS JESUS, THE KING OF THE JEWS" (27:37)
5. Crucifixion between the two robbers (27:38)
6. The *first cry* from the cross, "Father, forgive them, for they do not know what they are doing" (Luke 23:34)
7. Jesus' being mocked by all passing by (Matt. 27:39–44)
8. Conversation with the robbers (Luke 23:39–43)
9. The *second cry* from the cross, to the robber, "I tell you the truth, today you will be with me in paradise" (Luke 23:43).
10. The *third cry*, to his mother, "Dear woman, here is your son," and to the disciple, "Here is your mother" (John 19:26–27)
11. Darkness overtaking the scene at Golgotha (Matt. 27:45)
12. The *fourth cry*, "My God, my God, why have you forsaken me?" (27:46)
13. The *fifth cry*, "I am thirsty" (John 19:28)

14. The *sixth cry*, "It is finished" (John 19:30)
15. The *seventh cry*, "Father, into your hands I commit my spirit" (Luke 23:46)[1]
16. Jesus' death by giving up his spirit (Matt. 27:50; cf. John 19:30)

## The Soldiers' Flog and Mock Jesus (27:27–31)

AFTER PILATE PRONOUNCES the death verdict (27:26), his soldiers take Jesus to the Praetorium, where he is flogged. The Praetorium was the official residence of the Roman governor, but the term was also used of the camp of the troops who served him. The location of where Pilate stayed while in Jerusalem is debated, though it was probably Herod's palace (see comments on 27:19). Each of the three possible residences had been built to double as a fortress, so a large military contingent was available at Pilate's residence.[2]

In the Praetorium Jesus stands surrounded by Pilate's soldiers. The expression "whole company [*speira*] of soldiers" may indicate a Roman military cohort, from four hundred to six hundred soldiers,[3] which is the tenth part of a legion. But the term was also used of a *maniple* (a third part of a cohort, i.e., from one hundred and twenty to two hundred soldiers[4]). Josephus says that a large contingent of Roman soldiers was permanently quartered at the Fortress of Antonia.[5] The wording "the governor's soldiers" (27:27) may indicate that in addition to the cohort at the Antonia, a smaller *maniple* was housed as Pilate's personal guard at the former palace of Herod the Great.[6] With the latter in view, Jesus is surrounded by a mocking group of at least a hundred to two hundred soldiers.

Jesus has already been flogged (see comments on 27:26). Typical of the treatment given to those about to be crucified, the soldiers strip Jesus of his own clothing and put on him a scarlet robe. Roman soldiers in Jerusalem at the time were known to play a cruel game with condemned prisoners, especially revolutionary brigands. The prisoner was dressed up like a burlesque king and used as a game piece. With each roll of "dice" the prisoner "king" moved around a game board etched in the floor. All for the entertainment

---

1. Of the seven cries of Jesus from the cross, three are recorded by Luke (#1, 2, 7) and three by John (#3, 5, 6). Matthew and Mark record only the fourth saying.

2. Page, *Jesus and the Land*, 147–48; Rousseau and Arav, "Jerusalem, Herod's Palace," 151–52.

3. Similar to a U.S. Army battalion.

4. BDAG. Similar to a U.S. Army company.

5. Josephus, *J.W.* 5.5.8 §244. This would support Antonia being Pilate's residence.

6. For background to the Roman military contingents, see Everett Ferguson, *Backgrounds of Early Christianity*, 2d ed. (Grand Rapids: Eerdmans, 1993), 46–52.

of the troops, they hurled verbal and physical abuse at the mock king.[7] The charges against Jesus makes him fair game for this torturous pastime. The soldiers dress him up and mock him as "the king of the Jews."

A "scarlet robe" worn by one of the Roman soldiers becomes a mock royal robe. Plaited branches with thorns become a mimic crown, perhaps inflicting wounds to his head but certainly becoming a malicious imitation of a Roman emperor's crown. A common wooden "staff" is a nasty hoax for a ruler's scepter. This staff is used to beat Jesus again and again around the head as they spit at him and hurl abuses. Jesus suffered similar cruel treatment in the house of Caiaphas after he was condemned. There the high priest's guards played a brutal game with Jesus in order to ridicule his claim to prophecy (26:68); here the Roman soldiers play an even more brutal game to ridicule his claim to be the messianic king of Israel (27:29).[8]

After the cruel sport, the soldiers put Jesus' own clothes back on him for the fateful walk through the streets of Jerusalem to where they will crucify him outside the city walls.

### The Journey to Golgotha (27:32–34)

CRIMINALS CONDEMNED TO die were customarily required to carry to the scene of crucifixion the heavy wooden crosspiece (*patibulum*), on which they were to be nailed.[9] The crosspiece was then secured to the vertical beam (*palus*), and the entire cross was hoisted into the air with the victim attached to it. The *patibulum* usually weighed thirty to forty pounds and was strapped across the shoulders. Jesus had already been scourged (27:26), bringing him close to death. The scourging and loss of blood had so weakened Jesus that he could hardly walk and carry the *patibulum* because of the tremendous injury to his skin, muscles, and internal organs.

**Simon of Cyrene (27:32).** Leaving the military quarters at Pilate's palace to crucify Jesus, the soldiers recognize that Jesus will not be able to carry the cross to the execution site. Apparently at random they force a man named Simon from the city of Cyrene to carry the cross. Cyrene was a town in North Africa that had a large Jewish population (like Alexandria). Simon is likely a Jew who has made a pilgrimage to Jerusalem for the Passover.[10] Like most pilgrims,

---

7. See Wilkins, "Matthew," 177, for a picture of a Roman era pavement on the Via Dolorosa inscribed with images related to "the king's game." See also Page, *Jesus and the Land*, 149–51.

8. Flusser, *Jesus*, 169.

9. See Plutarch, *Moralia* 554A/B; cf. 554D; *De sera numinis vindicta* (*On the Delays of Divine Vengeance*) 9.

10. The Gospel of Mark makes a passing reference to "a certain man from Cyrene, Simon, the father of Alexander and Rufus" (Mark 15:21), which suggests that Alexander and

Simon probably stayed through to Pentecost. Tradition tells us that this incident of carrying Jesus' cross so impacted Simon that he became a Christian, perhaps through Peter's preaching on Pentecost (cf. Acts 2:41; 4:4).

**Golgotha (27:33).** The soldiers escorting Jesus and Simon arrive at the crucifixion site, which Matthew says is called "Golgotha." The name is a transliteration of the Aramaic word for "skull," which Matthew clarifies by providing a Greek translation, "which means The Place of the Skull." The common designation "Calvary" comes from the Latin word for skull, *calvaria*. The identity and location of the place have been given considerable attention throughout history. No known place in ancient Jerusalem has ever been found that was called Golgotha, but three primary reasons for the name have been proposed: (1) It was a place of execution; (2) it was an area known for having a number of tombs; (3) the site in some way resembled a skull.

The most important clues to the identity and location of Golgotha are as follows. (1) The place must have been outside of Jerusalem, because Roman law (and Jewish law, Lev. 24:14) directed crucifixion to take place outside the city. (2) It must have been a fairly conspicuous spot, probably not far from a city gate and a highway, because the Romans used crucifixion as a deterrent and wanted the gruesome scene to be witnessed by as many people as possible (see comments on 27:39). (3) A garden containing a tomb was nearby. The tomb belonged to Joseph of Arimathea, who later claimed Jesus' body and placed him there (John 19:41–42).

Two primary locations have been proposed. (1) A popular location is "Gordon's Hill" with its accompanying Garden Tomb, named after General Charles George Gordon, a renowned British military hero. During a brief service in Israel (1883), he identified a hill that looked similar to a skull, located north of the northern wall of the Old City of Jerusalem. Underneath the hill is a vast underground cemetery, including one crypt identified as Jesus' burial tomb. However, these tombs were not used in the first century, so it cannot be identified as the newly hewn tomb of Joseph of Arimathea.[11]

(2) The better candidate is the place where "The Church of the Holy

---

Rufus were persons well known to Mark's audience, which is most likely the church at Rome (cf. Ben Witherington III, *The Gospel of Mark: A Socio-Rhetorical Commentary* [Grand Rapids: Eerdmans, 2001], 393–94; for bibliography see Thomas R. Schreiner, *Romans* [BECNT; Grand Rapids: Baker, 1998], 791). Many suggest that Rufus in Mark is the same person named Rufus whom Paul addresses in his greetings to the church at Rome (Rom. 16:13; cf. Alexander in Acts 19:33).

11. For pictures of the Garden Tomb, see Wilkins, "Matthew," 182. For further discussion see Gabriel Barkay, "The Garden Tomb: Was Jesus Buried Here?" *BAR* 12 (March–April 1986): 40–57; John McRay, "Tomb Typology and the Tomb of Jesus," *Archaeology in the Biblical World* 2/2 (Spring 1994): 34–44.

Sepulchre" was built by Emperor Constantine as a memorial to Jesus' crucifixion and burial. It is located in the heart of the Christian quarter of the Old
City, inside the city wall. Three Christian communities—Armenian, Greek,
and Latin—all point to this site, west of the city of Jerusalem, as the place of
both Jesus' crucifixion and his burial. Most scholars agree for several reasons.
(a) During the time of Jesus this location was outside of the city walls. A later
wall built by Herod Agrippa between A.D. 41 and 44 enclosed this site within
the city. (b) The area was likely near a thoroughfare. (c) The site was an
ancient limestone quarry, which had been exhausted of its useable stone by
the first century B.C. At that time the quarry was filled and used as a garden
or orchard, and by the turn of the era contained a large burial ground.[12]

**Wine and gall (27:34).** At the crucifixion site the Roman soldiers offer
Jesus "wine ... mixed with gall." But after Jesus tastes the mixture, he refuses
to drink it. A rabbinic tradition indicates that when a prisoner was led out to
execution, he was given a goblet of wine containing a grain of frankincense
to numb his senses (*b. Sanh.* 43a, citing Prov. 31:6). The practice was done out
of compassion. Some scholars have suggested that since Jesus refuses such
sympathetic attention, we may assume that he wishes to experience the fullness of his atoning sacrifice with undulled senses.[13]

However, those who have brought Jesus to Golgotha are the ones who
offer him the drink, and they are hardly sympathetic. They have already
flogged Jesus and mocked him. More likely the present drink is another
attempt at cruelty by the Roman soldiers. Feigning that they are offering
Jesus a cup of refreshment, the wine has instead been mixed with "gall," a bitter herb that may even be poisonous. When Jesus tastes the bitter drink, he
knows it is not for refreshment but is only another way of torturing him.
The bitterness will only intensify his parched thirst, so he refuses (see Ps.
69:20–21). Like King David before him, Jesus, the Messiah King, also seeks
sympathy but instead finds scorn (cf. also Luke 23:36).[14]

### Jesus Is Crucified (27:35–38)

THE GOSPEL WRITERS do not focus on the details of Jesus' crucifixion. Recent
historical and archaeological studies have helped bring a realistic sense of its

12. For a picture of a chamber inside the Church of the Holy Sepulchre and an artist's
recreation of the levels of the original tomb and Constantine's monuments in relation to later
building, see Wilkins, "Matthew," 184–85. For further discussion, see Dan Bahat, "Does the
Holy Sepulchre Church Mark the Burial of Jesus?" *BAR* 12 (May–June 1986): 26–45; Joan
E. Taylor, "Golgotha: A Reconsideration of the Evidence for the Sites of Jesus' Crucifixion
and Burial," *NTS* 44 (1998): 180–203; Flusser, *Jesus*, 255–57.

13. E.g., Morris, *Matthew*, 715; Keener, *A Commentary on the Gospel of Matthew* (1999), 678.

14. Cf. Carson, "Matthew," 575; Hagner, *Matthew*, 2:834–35.

horrors for us who live so far removed from the practice.[15] Crucifixion was a painful and slow means of execution. Those passing by hurled insults at the crucified one (cf. 27:39). A victim usually died after two or three agonizing days—of thirst, exhaustion, and exposure. The hands were often nailed or tied to the crossbeam, which was then hoisted up and affixed to the upright stake, to which the feet were then nailed. Death was sometimes hastened by breaking the legs, but not in Jesus' case, since he is so weakened by the earlier flogging that he is already near death (cf. John 19:33).

**The guards cast lots and keep watch (27:35–37).** In the first of a series of allusions to Psalm 22,[16] Matthew quotes nearly verbatim the LXX of Psalm 22:18, but without using any sort of fulfillment formula as he does elsewhere. Yet his readers know that as the soldiers divide up his clothing by casting lots, this fulfills Scripture. The lot was cast in the Old Testament to discover God's will on various matters, such as the goat to be sacrificed on the Day of Atonement (Lev. 16). But here the lot is a form of gambling by the Roman guards as they divide up whatever is left of Jesus' clothes, which is probably not much. By so doing they take away his final external dignity and protection from the flies and elements that torture his beaten body.

Once Jesus has been affixed to the cross and hoisted in place, the guards sit down to watch, probably to make sure that none of Jesus' many followers attempt to rescue him. Only Matthew records this detail, which prepares the way for his insights to the later details of the guards' reactions to Jesus' death and resurrection (27:54, 62–66; 28:11–15).

As they watch Jesus die, the soldiers carry out what was probably a regular practice to deter further crimes of the sort that resulted in Jesus' crucifixion. Jesus was falsely accused and convicted of being the seditious messianic King of the Jews (cf. 27:11–14; see comments on 27:1–2). As a deterrent to any Jews thinking of continuing his sedition or causing any other kind of uprising against Rome, the soldiers place a placard above his head with the written charge, "THIS IS JESUS, THE KING OF THE JEWS." Perhaps Jesus wore this placard strung around his neck as he walked to Golgotha. Ironically, however, this is a statement of truth about Jesus. He *is* the king of the Jews, who has been rejected and framed by the very people he came to redeem.

**The two robbers (27:38).** Jesus is not alone at Golgotha. On his right and left are two "robbers" (*lestes*). These are not common thieves but political insurrectionists (cf. comments on Matt. 27:16). This same term occurred

---

15. The most important historical study is Martin Hengel, *Crucifixion in the Ancient World and the Folly of the Message of the Cross* (Philadelphia: Fortress, 1977), 77.

16. See also 27:39, 42–43, 46.

earlier when Jesus chided those who came to arrest him in Gethsemane as though he were a *lestes* (26:55); it also described Barabbas (John 18:40). Pilate apparently was rounding up, arresting, and convicting people who were stirring the crowds to insurrection. Had the people not selected Barabbas over Jesus, Barabbas may have been crucified with these compatriots in revolution. Instead, Jesus, falsely accused of those political crimes, receives a rebel's execution. The two sons of Zebedee had requested the privilege of being seated at Jesus' right and left hand side in his kingdom (20:21); with bitter irony, Matthew records that two rebel criminals form Jesus' right- and left-hand attendants on a cross, not a throne.

### The Mocking of Messiah (27:39–44)

THIS SECTION IS a sad scenario of three groups who hurl insults at Jesus while he is on the cross: the people, the religious leaders who have condemned Jesus, and the two thieves. In the cases of the former two, the issues similarly relate to Jesus' identity as God's Son.

**The people (27:39–40).** "Those who pass by" may include people randomly entering or leaving the city, but also those who have witnessed the trials. They had been convinced by the charges against Jesus, because they "hurled insults at him, shaking their heads." The expression "hurled insults" is literally "blasphemed," indicating that they deride him for his blasphemous claims (see comments on 26:65–66) and for the bogus charge that he would destroy the temple and build it in three days (cf. 26:61). This derision mocks Jesus' claim at supernatural power. If he has such powers, he should be able to save himself.

At the beginning of Jesus' ministry, the devil tempted Jesus in the same way (4:3, 6); now the people throw another cruel temptation at him to escape the cross: "Come down from the cross, if you are the Son of God!" Their taunt says more than they know, but Jesus will continue to pursue the Father's will, as he resolutely affirmed three times in Gethsemane (26:39–44). Matthew's readers will hear in these taunts from the passersby another allusion to Psalm 22: "But I am a worm and not a man, scorned by men and despised by the people. All who see me mock me; they hurl insults, shaking their heads" (Ps. 22:6–7).

**The religious leaders (27:41–43).** The religious leaders who comprise the Sanhedrin—the chief priests, the teachers of the law, and the elders—join in the mocking. Their presence indicates more fully that those who observe the crucifixion are not there simply by happenstance. The highest tiers of Israel's officialdom have followed Jesus out to Golgotha intentionally to hurl their final insults at this one whom they despise for being who he actually is. They throw back at Jesus the claim he made when he was on trial (see comments on 26:64).

Like the people, they taunt him for his claim to supernatural powers. How can he save others and not himself? They have witnessed him heal the sick, rescue the demon-possessed, and even raise people from the dead. Throughout his ministry they have tested him by asking for signs of his true identity (12:38–39). Now they do not address him directly in asking for a sign; rather, with cruel derision they turn to one another joking: "Let him come down now from the cross, and we will believe in him."

Matthew again alludes to Psalm 22 (cf. Matt. 27:35) as the religious leaders mock Jesus' supposed trust in God (Ps. 22:8).[17] If he really is the Son of God, God would not allow him to die on a cross. To them, a crucified Messiah is unthinkable. A final proof to them of his identity would be for God to rescue his Son. But as Jesus earlier declared, the definitive sign of his identity will be his resurrection from the dead, which will also be a sign of God's judgment on these religious leaders (Matt. 12:40–42). Although they taunt him to save himself, Jesus must pursue his life's mission to the very end, because there the Son of God will truly save humanity.

**The robbers (27:44).** The two between whom Jesus is crucified join in the mockery by heaping insults on Jesus. It seems incongruous that the two others being crucified would insult Jesus, but Luke fills in some details. One of them ridicules Jesus for his ineffectual claim to be the Messiah: "Aren't you the Christ? Save yourself and us!" (Luke 23:39). But Luke goes on to recount that the other bandit halts the ridicule and acknowledges the innocence of Jesus. He exhibits a form of repentance that Jesus declares will cause the bandit to be joined with him in paradise (heaven) that very day (23:40–43).

## The Death of Jesus Messiah (27:45–50)

THE TONE OF mockery from the witnesses at Golgotha suddenly turns somber as darkness comes over the land from the sixth hour until the ninth hour (i.e., from 12:00 noon to 3:00 P.M.). This is not a solar eclipse, for the Passover occurred at full moon; rather, this is some unknown act of God. Jesus had already been on the cross for about three hours (Mark 15:25).

**The darkness (27:45).** "Darkness" in both Old and New Testaments is an evocative word. If light symbolizes God, darkness suggests everything that

---

17. The religious leaders apply the words of Psalm 22:8 to Jesus either in a way that they are consciously (Hagner, *Matthew*, 2:839) or unconsciously (Carson, "Matthew," 577; Keener, *A Commentary on the Gospel of Matthew* [1999], 681) aware of the connection. If consciously, they mock Jesus by making a parallel to a known messianic prophecy. If unconsciously, this is like the unconscious prophecy that Caiaphas voiced (John 11:51–52).

is anti-God: the wicked (Prov. 2:13–14; 1 Thess. 5:4–7), judgment (Ex. 10:21; Matt. 25:30), and death (Ps. 88:13). Salvation brings light to those in darkness (Isa. 9:1; Matt. 4:16). The time of God's ultimate judgment, the Day of the Lord, is a day of darkness (Amos 5:18, 20; Joel 2:2; Zeph. 1:15; Matt. 24:29; Rev. 6:12–17). Darkness here displays a limitation on the power of Satan (cf. Luke 22:53), God's displeasure on humanity for crucifying his Son, and God's judgment on the sins of the world.[18]

**Eloi, Eloi, lama sabachthani? (27:46).** At about 3:00 P.M., Jesus' tortured body is nearly lifeless. From out of the darkness surrounding Golgotha, Jesus' voice cries out, " *'Eloi, Eloi, lama sabachthani?'*—which means, 'My God, my God, why have you forsaken me?'" The connection between the darkness and Jesus' cry is close—the darkness is a symbol of its agonizing content.[19] Once again the crucifixion scene recalls the lament of King David in Psalm 22:1. David goes on to recount his vindication (21:21–22), but Jesus' cry does not go that far. Matthew's readers, who know the full story, can think of the entirety of Psalm 22 as a preview of Jesus' vindication by the resurrection. But Matthew focuses on Jesus' abandonment, a theme that pervades the narrative.[20]

Of the seven cries of Jesus from the cross, this is the only one that Matthew and Mark record, the meaning of which is profoundly difficult to grasp fully.[21] Matthew does not interpret its meaning, though this cry does indicate that Jesus' death does not catch him by surprise. Yet this is not the declaration of victory that ultimately comes from Jesus' completion of his atoning sacrifice, which John records (John 19:30). Matthew gives us a singular focus on Jesus' feelings of being abandoned on the cross. He must be separated from the Father in order to bear the sin of his people (Matt. 1:21; 20:28; 26:28). He bears the divine retribution and punishment for sin, as the Father's cup of wrath is poured out on him in divine judgment.

Not only does Jesus bear the load of humanity's sin, but he becomes sin on our behalf (see 2 Cor. 5:21). He became cursed by God for us, "for it is

---

18. Wilkins, "Darkness," *BTDT*, 142–43; Hans Conzelmann, "σκότος, κτλ." *TDNT*, 7:423–45; H.-C. Hahn, "Darkness," *NIDNTT*, 1:420–25.

19. Hendriksen, *Matthew*, 970.

20. E.g., Boring, "Matthew," 492.

21. Hagner says of this cry of Jesus, "This is one of the most impenetrable mysteries of the entire Gospel narrative," and "Perhaps it is best simply to let the words stand as they are—stark in their impenetrability to us mortals" (Hagner, *Matthew*, 2:845–46). Morris points out, "Pious and earnest Christians have always found these words very difficult" (Leon Morris, *The Cross of Christ* [Grand Rapids: Eerdmans, 1988], 67). For a discussion of how Jesus perceived his own death, see Scot McKnight, "Jesus and His Death: Some Recent Scholarship," *CurBS* 9 (2001): 185–228.

written: 'Cursed is everyone who is hung on a tree'" (Gal. 3:13). William Hendriksen comments graphically on the darkness that portends Jesus' cry:

> The darkness meant judgment, the judgment of God upon our sins, his wrath as it were burning itself out in the very heart of Jesus, so that he, as our Substitute, suffered most intense agony, indescribable woe, terrible isolation or forsakenness. Hell came to Calvary that day, and the Savior descended into it and bore its horrors in our stead.[22]

Jesus' abandonment is horrific, but it is not without purpose.

From later theological reflection we understand that Jesus' forsakenness by the Father did not affect their ontological relationship; that is, Jesus was not separated in his essence or substance from the Father as the second Person of the Trinity. Rather, Jesus' divinely sustained humanity consciously experienced the full penalty of death for the sins of humanity. Earlier he told his disciples that his life's mission was to be a "ransom for many" (20:28). Here that fateful prediction is carried out. This lays the foundation for the theological doctrine of the atonement, in which Jesus' sacrifice on the cross is one of "penal substitution" or "vicarious atonement"—Jesus suffers our punishment for our sin. The wages for sin is death (Rom. 6:23), and in Jesus' separation from God he experiences deathly punishment for the sins of humanity.[23]

But even in the depth of Jesus' abandonment to his atoning sacrifice, he still knows that this experience is not one of despair—he still calls his Father "my God, my God." The relational separation while bearing the sins of humanity cannot separate him entirely from God, because his consummate trust in the Father expects that he will not be abandoned forever and because the oneness of their ontology is indissoluble.

**The bystanders think of Elijah (27:47–49).** Jesus' call to God in Aramaic (*eli eli;* 27:46) sounds similar to the Hebrew name for Elijah (*ʾeliyyah*), so the bystanders misunderstand him to be attempting to summon the prophet. At the sound of his cry, someone in the crowd runs to get a sponge, which he fills with vinegar and places on a stick to reach up for Jesus to have a drink. The drink offered is *oxos*, a sour wine used by common people and soldiers as a daily drink with meals. It relieved thirst more effectively than water and, because it was cheaper than regular wine, it was a favorite beverage of the lower ranks of society. Perhaps one of the bystanders (a Roman guard?) is offering an act of kindness and mercy to Jesus. Or perhaps this person is

---

22. Hendriksen, *Matthew*, 970.

23. For full discussion of the doctrine of the atonement, see Erickson, *Christian Theology*, 802–23; Grudem, *Systematic Theology*, 570–86.

continuing the earlier mockery (see comments on 27:34); nothing indicates that the mockery of the crowds has ceased.

If this person is attempting to give a sympathetic drink to Jesus, the crowd wants none of it. Or if he is continuing the mockery by giving Jesus bitter gall, the bystanders don't want anything to interfere with their cruel entertainment. They instruct him to stop giving Jesus the drink so that they can see if Elijah will come to rescue him.[24] The majority in the crowd are toying with Jesus for their own curiosity or amusement. But unbeknownst to them, God observes their cruelty and will indeed rescue his Son from death by raising him after the redemptive work of the cross is accomplished. Such profound love for those who are so cruel is unfathomable.

**Jesus gives up his spirit (27:50).** Jesus knows that his suffering is nearing its completion. He cries out again in a loud voice. Neither Matthew nor Mark gives the content of Jesus' final cry, but the implication is that this is one final agonizing experience of separation from the Father as he bears humanity's sin-punishment. Then "he gave up his spirit" (cf. "breathed his last" in Mark 15:37). This is a shorthand representation for the experience of death, though none of the Gospel writers describes Jesus death by simply saying, "He died"—a clue that they view his death as singularly unique.

In fact, Matthew shows that to the very end Jesus maintains volitional control over his destiny. He approaches his death willingly (cf. John 10:17–18). This points to what John's Gospel makes explicit, that Jesus comes to the recognition that he has paid in full the debt for sin; with a shout of victory Jesus cries out, "It is finished" (John 19:30). John uses a single word *tetelestai* to record this triumph, a phrase used often in this sense on ancient Greek receipts, "Paid in full." The redemption that Jesus came to achieve was accomplished once for all.

## Testimonies to Jesus' Death (27:51–54)

MATTHEW IMMEDIATELY RECORDS several events that follow upon the death of Jesus, all of which give significant historical and theological testimony to explain the impact of Jesus' death.

**Testimony from the temple (27:51).** The first testimony comes from the temple, where at the moment of Jesus' death, "the curtain of the temple was torn in two from top to bottom." The word for curtain (*katapetasma*) is used in the LXX both of the curtain between the Holy Place and the Most Holy Place (e.g., Ex. 26:31–35; 27:21; 30:6; 2 Chron. 3:14) and of the curtain over the entrance to the Holy Place (e.g., Ex. 27:37; Num. 3:26). The for-

---

24. See Hans W. Heidland, "ὄξος," *TDNT*, 5:288–89.

mer is more likely here (cf. Heb. 6:19; 9:3; 10:20). The curtain was an elaborately woven fabric of seventy-two twisted plaits of twenty-four threads each, and the veil was sixty feet high and thirty feet wide.[25]

It would take a significant rift to tear this imposing veil, so the incident gives momentous testimony to the meaning of Jesus' death on the cross. This tearing of the curtain that separated the Holy of Holies from the rest of the temple signifies the removal of the separation between God and the people and is a further sign of God's judgment on Israel's temple activity (cf. 21:12–22). The sixty-foot-high curtain was split from top to bottom, which is a sign that God himself abolished the separation from the Holy of Holies, signifying that the new and living way is now open for all people to enter into his presence through the sacrifice of Jesus on the cross (Heb. 10:20; Eph. 2:11–22). Since only the priestly aristocracy would have known about the tearing of the veil, when only a few weeks later a number of priests became believers (Acts 6:7), they would have informed the Christian community of this event.[26]

Matthew's consistent emphasis on "fulfillment" here reaches its pinnacle. Jesus fulfilled all righteousness as he undertook his earthly ministry (3:15–17), he fulfilled the Law and the Prophets as he authoritatively pronounced its intended meaning (5:17–48), and in his ministry one greater than the temple arrived (12:6). The tearing of the temple curtain testifies that Jesus' sacrifice on the cross has fulfilled the hopes expressed in Israel's years of temple sacrifice. Jesus is the great high priest, whose sacrifice is the permanent satisfaction of God's wrath on humanity's sin (Heb. 4:14–5:10). Jesus is the permanently accessible new temple in whom all who turn to him are reconciled to the Father.

**Testimony from the dead (27:51b–53).** The second testimony is a complex of earthquakes, splitting rocks, and raised bodies. Matthew says first that "the earth shook and the rocks split." This language implies that this is a significant earthly reaction to the divine events on the cross. Because of the geological characteristics of Palestine, which sits on a major seismic rift, an earthquake would not be an unusual event, but coupled with rocks splitting to open tombs, this is another significant testimony to the meaning of Jesus' crucifixion. Another earthquake will soon testify to a further significant divine event—Jesus' resurrection (cf. 28:2).

Matthew then records an incident found in none of the other Gospels: "The tombs broke open and the bodies of many holy people who had died were raised to life. They came out of the tombs, and after Jesus' resurrection

---

25. See *m. Šeqal.* 8.5; Josephus gives a detailed description of the curtain in *J.W.* 5.5.4 §§212–13.

26. Cf. Keener, *A Commentary on the Gospel of Matthew* (1999), 687.

they went into the holy city and appeared to many people." While earthquakes can damage tombs, since they were carved out of stone, raising of bodies can only be attributed to God's direct action, which implies that he is behind the earthquake.

Matthew's unique record of these events emphasizes the victory over death that Jesus' sacrifice on the cross accomplishes. Those who are raised are described literally as those "who had fallen asleep" (27:52; NIV "had died"), a common New Testament idiom for a person who has died but whose eternal destiny is secure (e.g., 1 Cor. 11:30; 15:18, 20; 1 Thess. 4:13–15). As with the preceding miraculous testimonies, the supernatural raising of the bodies of these holy ones and their appearances in Jerusalem is striking testimony to Jesus' accomplished work on the cross and thereafter his resurrection.

The expression "holy people" probably refers to pious Old Testament figures—heroes and martyrs from Israel's history selected to bear miraculous testimony to these events.[27] We may think of the way in which Moses and Elijah were selected to appear with Jesus on the Mount of Transfiguration (17:1–8). But in this case it is a resurrection of the bodies of such holy people. This allows the reader to see that even with the acted judgment of Jesus on Israel's leadership and their condemnation in chapters 23–24, Israel does remain in God's plans.[28]

The NIV placement in 27:53 of a comma after the phrase "they came out of the tombs" along with the insertion of the conjunction "and" may imply that the bodies were raised at the time of the earthquake and then later appeared in Jerusalem. It would seem strange to have raised bodies remaining in a tomb for days until they make their appearance. However, the Greek text has no punctuation, and the conjunction "and" is not in the text. A better explanation is to place a period after the phrase "the tombs broke open" and to begin a new sentence with the next phrase. As such it then reads, "And the bodies of many holy people who had died were raised to life. Coming out of the tombs after Jesus' resurrection, they went into the holy city and appeared to many people."[29] With this rendering, Matthew indicates the following sequence: (1) The tombs are opened by earthquakes at Jesus' crucifixion; (2) Jesus is raised three days later; (3) the bodies of these holy ones are then raised, and they enter the city and appear to many.

In this way the miraculously opened tombs at the time of Jesus' death are a prolepsis of the resurrection of Jesus, and the bodies of the holy people fol-

---

27. Davies and Allison, *Matthew*, 3:633.

28. See Blomberg, *Matthew*, 421.

29. Cf. John W. Wenham, "When Were the Saints Raised?" *JTS* 32 (1981): 150–52; Carson, "Matthew," 581–82; Blomberg, *Matthew*, 421.

low in a mere three days. Their appearance to people in Jerusalem is a witness to the efficaciousness of Jesus' work on the cross and the declaration of his victory over death in his, and their, resurrection. This anticipates Paul's teaching on Jesus being the firstfruits of the dead (1 Cor. 15:20–23).

Some brand this incident as legend or, at best, only theological narrative (i.e., theology set forth as history). However, there is little within any of the events surrounding Jesus' crucifixion (the darkness at the crucifixion, the temple curtain being torn from top to bottom, an earthquake that opens tombs, and the resurrection of Old Testament saints) that makes sense on the normal historical level. These are all unique events that uniformly testify to God's unique acts in human history—Jesus' vicarious death on the cross and his vindicated resurrection from the death. These are extraordinary, supernatural testimonies that confirm "that Jesus is who he had claimed to be and that his ministry stands vindicated before the nation."[30]

Recalling the imagery of Ezekiel, who prophesied that the Sovereign Lord would open graves and resurrect people to life in the valley of dry bones (Ezek. 37:11–14), Matthew lets this event stand unadorned because its meaning is clear. Derek Tidball relates, "The raising of these holy ones is a foretaste of the resurrection to which all believers can look forward. Through the death of Jesus a new day has arrived, a day when death has been defeated by death, and resurrection to life eternal has been made possible."[31] Matthew does not answer all the questions we would like answered about these miraculous events, but in narrating them he presents a unified testimony to the supernatural confirmation of Jesus' identity and mission.

**Testimony from Gentiles (27:54).** The third testimony following the death of Jesus is that of the centurion and the guards at the crucifixion scene. The centurion, an officer in charge of one hundred soldiers (see comments on 8:5), has probably been in attendance since Jesus' Roman trial and subsequent flogging and mocking by the soldiers. He has probably witnessed many crucifixions, but the cataclysmic events of the earthquake and opened tombs, plus the manner of Jesus' death, combine to evoke the statement, "Surely he was the Son of God!"

Opinions vary as to what the centurion and those with him mean by this exclamation. (*1*) *A pagan reaction.* Some suggest that this is a pagan reaction to the dramatic events unfolding, but it does not indicate true faith. They suggest that the expression can best be rendered, "Truly this was a son of a god." The centurion and those with him view Jesus merely as a typical Greco-Roman

---

30. Darrell L. Bock, *Jesus According to Scripture: Restoring the Portrait from the Gospels* (Grand Rapids: Baker, 2002), 391.

31. Tidball, *The Message of the Cross*, 133.

"divine-man" figure, a great human hero deified upon death. However, the centurion and his men are more likely commenting on the current Jewish charges against Jesus, not associating this with far-removed Greco-Roman deities.

(2) *A response of fear.* Others suggest that the soldiers' statement is an acknowledgment of guilt and defeat in the face of the divine. They are greatly "terrified," an expression that implies dread. These soldiers are the same ones who brutalized and executed Jesus, and they are wicked characters right through the Passion Narrative. "The terror and subsequent cry of defeat on the part of the evil soldiers prefigures the attitude of the wicked on the day of reckoning as they learn of the horrible fate in store for them."[32] However, the positive way in which this confession is reported leads Matthew's readers to understand that the centurion and his men are not simply terrified but are recognizing that Jesus is indeed ("surely" or "truly") the Son of God.

(3) *A beginning confession of faith.* The most satisfactory understanding of this statement is that as little as these men may have understood, it is a true step of faith. The centurion is gaining an insight into Jesus' true identity. The charge of blasphemy from the Sanhedrin was in part lodged against Jesus' claim to be the Son of God, to which Jesus responded with an affirmative (26:63–64). The centurion is certain to know the various charges against Jesus, because the military chain of command necessitates that he know about potential uprisings to rescue the convicted Jesus. As he watches the events unfold, he and his men are overwhelmed by the realization that the identification is truthful. Jesus is innocent of the contrived charges (cf. Luke 23:47), which then leads to the logical conclusion that he is truly who he claimed to be—*the* Son of God, who sustains a divine relationship to the Ancient of Days as the Son of Man.[33]

However much the centurion and his men understand these words, Matthew's point is clear. He emphasizes for his readers that the reaction of the centurion and his men ("they were terrified") is exactly the same as that experienced by the disciples at the Transfiguration (17:6), and their confession is nearly identical to the conclusion drawn by the disciples at the calming of the sea (14:33). Therefore, the evaluative point of view of these Roman guards agrees with that of God the Father (3:17; 17:5) and Peter (16:16), a confession that is now given publicly.[34]

---

32. David C. Sim, "The 'Confession' of the Soldiers in Matthew 27:54," *Heythrop Journal* 34 (1993): 401–24. Cf. Whitney T. Shiner, "The Ambiguous Pronouncement of the Centurion and the Shrouding of Meaning in Mark," *JSNT* 78 (2000): 3–22.

33. For a technical discussion of Colwell's Rule and Apollonius' Corollary (to Apollonius' Rule), which point in the direction of the construction being rendered "the Son of God," see Wallace, *Greek Grammar*, 256–70.

34. Kingsbury, *Matthew As Story*, 90.

Matthew has given increasing emphasis to Jesus as the Son of God since the Jewish trial evinced charges of blasphemy (26:63–65). The centurion's evocation is in dramatic distinction from the religious leaders and the bystanders at the cross, who mocked Jesus for his claim to be the Son of God (27:40–43). It is a striking picture for Matthew's readers. The cataclysmic events recorded here testify to Jesus' true identity, and the centurion and his men make a step of faith to acknowledge the truth of that testimony.

### The Women Followers of Jesus (27:55–56)

MATTHEW NOW NARRATES a peaceful, yet melancholy scene of the women who have faithfully watched these events unfold. All of the Gospel writers mention a group of women who followed and served Jesus in Galilee, accompanied him to Jerusalem, and witnessed the events of the final week, including the crucifixion and the resurrection.[35] Matthew's description of them at the crucifixion and burial scene prepares for their significant role in the resurrection scenes.

(1) "Many women were there, watching from a distance." In the crucifixion passages of the Gospels, at least six women are identified, though Matthew and Mark indicate that an even larger group of unnamed women watched the crucifixion. John's Gospel indicates that at least during some of the time, Jesus' mother and three other women and one of his disciples were near enough to the cross so that Jesus could speak to them and give directions for his mother's care (John 19:26). But for most of the time they stand off in the distance, possibly because there is still danger of being accosted by the Roman guards if it is known that they are associated with Jesus.[36] Nevertheless, their courage and commitment to Jesus keep them from running off.

(2) These women "followed Jesus from Galilee." The expressions used to describe these women concur with the evidence elsewhere that they are Jesus' disciples.[37] The verb "follow" can be used in simply a spatial sense (e.g., 4:25; 9:19). But the context indicates the metaphorical sense of "follow" here—accompanying Jesus as his disciples. A "disciple" is the one who has counted the cost, made a commitment of faith, and then "followed" Jesus.[38]

---

35. Cf. Mark 15:40–41; 16:1; Luke 23:49, 55–56; 24:1, 10–11; John 19:25–27; 20:1–18.

36. Cf. Keener, *A Commentary on the Gospel of Matthew* (1999), 691–94.

37. See esp. Jane Kopas, "Jesus and Women in Matthew," *TT* 47 (1990), 20; G. Osborne, "Women in Jesus' Ministry," *WTJ* 51 (1989): 275; Witherington, *Women in the Ministry of Jesus*, 122–23.

38. Jack Kingsbury suggests that two factors—cost and commitment—is the key to understanding whether "following Jesus" should be taken literally or metaphorically in Matthew (Kingsbury, "The Verb AKOLOUTHEIN [To Follow]," 58).

---

As the women followed Jesus, they cared for his needs (Matt. 27:55; Luke 8:1–3; Mark 15:41), called him Lord (John 20:2, 13, 18), and worshiped him after the resurrection (Matt. 28:9). These descriptions not only designate the women to be disciples but also describe them as *exemplary* disciples of Jesus. They are displaying a commitment to Jesus that the Twelve themselves should have displayed.

(3) These women "cared for his needs." While they were not involved in actual proclamation, it is unwarranted to imply that the term "care" or "serve" (*diakoneo*) indicates that these women simply cooked and cleaned for Jesus and the Twelve.[39] *Diakoneo* means much more than simply "waiting on tables." This verb encapsulates Jesus' entire redemptive purpose for coming to earth (20:28; Mark 10:45) and will characterize both the mission of the apostles (1 Cor. 4:1) and the calling of the disciples in the early church (cf. Luke 22:24–27; Gal. 5:13). Perhaps we can say that, besides providing financial support for the missionary outreach, the women joined the Twelve as Jesus' companions and as witnesses of his ministry.[40]

(4) Matthew names three of these women, who appear to be the most prominent among them. "Mary Magdalene" is a well-known person, though not previously named in this Gospel. "Magdalene" implies that she was from Magdala, a town and region on the western shore of the Sea of Galilee, about three miles north of Tiberias (see 15:39). Luke 8:2 mentions that she is a woman "from whom seven demons had come out." Mary Magdalene figures prominently here at the crucifixion scene and even more so in the resurrection scenes (esp. John 20). Being listed first suggests that she is likely a leader among the women.

"Mary the mother of James and Joses" is perhaps the woman listed third in John's account of the crucifixion, identified as Mary the wife of Clopas. Nothing more is known of this Mary, although her prominent listing in second spot implies that she is a woman of some significance within the discipleship band.

"The mother of Zebedee's sons" is likely Salome, the one listed second in John 19:25 as Jesus' "mother's sister," or Jesus' aunt on his mother's side (see comments on Matt. 20:20)[41] This perhaps clarifies why Jesus places his

---

39. E.g., Witherington, *Women in the Ministry of Jesus*, 118; Hengel, "Maria Magdalena und die Frauen als Zeugen," *Abraham unser Vater*, ed. Otto Betz and Martin Hengel (Leiden: Brill, 1963), 247–48. A critique against the assumption that the women only provided domestic help for the traveling ministry team is given by David C. Sim, "The Women Followers of Jesus: The Implications of Luke 8:1–3," *Heythrop Journal* 30 (1989): 51–62. Sim does not speculate what their exact role is, beyond providing some economic support.

40. E.g., Joel Green, *The Gospel of Luke* (NICNT; Grand Rapids: Eerdmans, 1963), 317.

41. Cf. Beasley-Murray, *John*, 348–49; Carson, *John*, 616.

mother in the care of the beloved disciple, the apostle John, Jesus' cousin (John 19:26–27).

One of the most important perspectives on the women is that God used them as witnesses not only to the central redemptive act of history, Jesus' death on the cross and the sealing of the tomb (cf. 27:60–61), but also as witnesses to his resurrection from the dead. Since the women are present for Jesus' death and his burial by Joseph of Arimathea (cf. 27:55–56, 61), they can verify that Jesus is truly dead, not just unconscious. God is bestowing a special honor on them. They are exemplary of true discipleship to Jesus, and because of their faithfulness and courage, they are given the special honor of being witnesses to these profound events.

## The Burial of Jesus Messiah (27:57–61)

THE SKY HAD darkened until 3:00 P.M. on Friday afternoon (27:45), the "Preparation Day" for the Sabbath (cf. 27:62; Mark 15:42; Luke 23:54; John 19:42), after which Jesus died. Jewish custom dictated that the bodies should be taken down before evening, especially before the Sabbath, which began at sundown on Friday (approximately 6:00 P.M.).

**Joseph of Arimathea (27:57).** Matthew now narrates the remarkable arrival of a man named Joseph who claims the body of the crucified Messiah. Joseph, one of the most common names for Jewish men, was from Arimathea. The location is in doubt, identified by some as Ramathaim, the birthplace of Samuel (1 Sam. 1:1, 19), in the hill country of Ephraim, about twenty miles northwest of Jerusalem, which Luke describes as the "Judean town of Arimathea" (Luke 23:51). Some suggest that it is otherwise known as Rathamein (1 Macc. 11:34) or Ramathain.[42] The portrait painted of him in the Gospels is historically plausible.[43]

No adequate explanation accounts for his coming forward at this point except, as Matthew writes, he "had himself become a disciple[44] of Jesus." We are not told when or how he had come to faith. Although Joseph is called a disciple, he is not one of the Twelve, but like the women is among the wider circle of Jesus' adherents.[45]

---

42. Josephus, *Ant.* 13.127.

43. For a refutation of recent attempts to discredit the historicity of Joseph of Arimathea, see Gerald O'Collins and Daniel Kendall, "Did Joseph of Arimathea Exist," *Bib* 75 (1994): 235–41.

44. Matthew uses the verb "become a disciple" three times (cf. 13:52; 28:19).

45. Cf. Przybylski, *Righteousness in Matthew and His World of Thought.* The expression "adherents to Jesus" expresses the central meaning of the relationship in typical first-century usage; cf. Wilkins, *The Concept of Disciple in Matthew's Gospel,* 41–42, 124–25.

Joseph is a fellow member of the Sanhedrin with Nicodemus, both of whom appear as exemplary Jews anticipating the arrival of the kingdom of God (Mark 15:43; Luke 23:50–51; John 3:1–15; 19:38–42). These two are examples of persons who apparently did not follow Jesus around in his earthly ministry, but who were still considered his disciples, even while continuing to serve within the religious establishment of Israel.[46] Although it is dangerous for them to reveal their attachment to Jesus at this time, when their help is needed, they step forward to show their true colors. Luke 23:50 tells us that Joseph did not consent to the actions of the Sanhedrin against Jesus. He not only likely stirred the ire of the other members of the Sanhedrin, but he now is walking into the den of the Roman executioners. To be associated with one condemned for treason is a dangerous matter, even though Pilate equivocated.[47]

**Joseph requests Jesus' body from Pilate (27:58).** Joseph's high standing within the Jewish community allows him access to Pilate, to whom he goes to request the body of Jesus so that he can give it a proper burial. Pilate releases Jesus' body to him immediately. Pilate attempted futilely to wash his hands of responsibility for Jesus' execution and perhaps sees in Joseph's request an opportunity to relieve himself of any responsibility for Jesus' burial.

Because Joseph is rich (only Matthew records this detail), he had the resources to purchase a newly hewn tomb, which becomes the fulfillment of the proper burial place for Jesus (Isa. 53:9).[48] His courage in asking for the body and his service to Jesus are exemplary of what a disciple should do. Joseph is a fitting foil for the disciples who have forsaken Jesus (26:56).[49] As a member of the Sanhedrin, it would not have been easy for him to follow Jesus, but when all the disciples flee, he comes forward to give Jesus a proper burial.

Joseph's action in initiating the burial of Jesus is both an act of obedience to Jewish law and an act of devotion to the One who is his Master. Not only is the Sabbath approaching, but Deuteronomy 21:22–23 instructs that a person hanged on a tree should be buried the same day so that the land should not be defiled, for that person is under God's curse.

**Joseph prepares Jesus' body for burial (27:59).** Joseph begins preparing Jesus' body for burial by placing it in a clean linen cloth or "shroud" (RSV; 27:59). John's Gospel fills in some other details, such as another secret dis-

---

46. Michael J. Wilkins, "Named and Unnamed Disciples in Matthew: A Literary/ Theological Study," *SBLSP* 30 (Atlanta: Scholars Press, 1991), 418–39.

47. Cf. Keener, *Matthew* (1999), 691–94.

48. Cf. W. Boyd Barrick, 'The Rich Man from Arimathea (Matt 27:57–60) and 1QIsaᵃ," *JBL* 96 (1977): 235–39.

49. Gundry, *Matthew*, 580; Kingsbury, *Matthew As Story*, 27.

ciple, Nicodemus, unveiling himself at this critical moment to aid Joseph (John 19:39–40; cf. 3:1–21). Together they prepare Jesus' body.

The Jews did not practice cremation or full embalming of corpses, but the body was prepared for burial by washing it, dressing it in special garments, and packing it in the linen cloth with fragrant spices. Along with stifling the smell of the body decaying, myrrh and other aromatics represented the preservation of the body, which to the Jewish mind was the prerequisite of resurrection. Joseph of Arimathea and Nicodemus perform acts even more significant than they themselves understand.[50]

**Joseph's new tomb is Jesus' burial place (27:60).** After the body is wrapped in the linen cloth, Joseph places it in his own new tomb cut out of the rock. During this era burial was generally in cave-like tombs. The tomb was a rectangular underground chamber cut into rock, sometimes in an abandoned quarry. It was accessed through a low entry vault, closed with a stone that could be rolled back and forth, mostly to protect the body from wild animals that fed on carcasses. The dead were laid out on benches cut parallel into the rock or placed in perpendicular burial slots or recesses cut into the sides of the tomb. The body remained in its niche until the flesh decayed (from one to three years), whereupon the bones were collected and placed in ossuaries (small, carved stone, bone-box receptacles).

After Jesus' body is laid in the tomb, Joseph rolls a large stone in front of the entrance. He and Nicodemus return to the city. Although part of the preparation for burial has been accomplished at this point, because the Sabbath is approaching, they cannot work with the dead and thus must return after the Sabbath to complete the preparations.

**The women's sad vigil (27:61).** Matthew tells us that at least two of the women who witnessed Jesus' crucifixion—Mary Magdalene and the "other Mary" (cf. Mark 15:47)—sit opposite the tomb and witness the sad and lonely ceremony. These faithful women still stay with Jesus even in death. It is even possible that these women (and perhaps others) who have followed Jesus from Galilee and who have been close to Jesus and his family worked together with Joseph and Nicodemus to prepare Jesus' body for burial.[51]

## The Guard at the Tomb (27:62–66)

MATTHEW ALONE RECOUNTS an incident that occurs on the day "after Preparation Day," that is, the Sabbath. While some doubt the historicity of this

---

50. See Kjeld Nielsen, "Incense," *ABD*, 3:404–9; Victor H. Matthews, "Perfumes and Spices," *ABD*, 5:226–28; Joel Green, "Burial of Jesus," *DJG*, 88–92.

51. Cf. John Wenham, *Easter Enigma: Are the Resurrection Accounts in Conflict?* 2d ed. (Grand Rapids: Baker, 1992), 60–67.

event,[52] Matthew is writing for a Jewish-Christian audience, who would have heard the charges circulating among the Jews that the disciples had stolen Jesus' body (28:11–15). Therefore, Matthew addresses a situation of pressing concern to his readers.[53]

**Wanting to keep a dead man dead (27:62–63).** Not satisfied with Jesus' execution and burial, the chief priests and the Pharisees go to Pilate to make certain that the dead man does not rouse more support even after his death. Despite the Sabbath and the other celebrations associated with the Passover, the Jewish officials obtain an audience with Pilate because of the threat of Jesus' followers. As long as they do not travel more than a Sabbath Day's journey or enter the residence of the governor (cf. John 18:28), they will not be defiling the Sabbath.[54]

This is the first time that the Pharisees surface in the narrative since Jesus' woes against them (ch. 23), though they participated in the larger Sanhedrin's rulings. Now they come to the front with an accusatory remembrance. On at least one occasion Jesus specifically predicted to the Pharisees that he would rise in three days (12:40). They have not forgotten. What they understood by Jesus' declaration is unknown, but they assume Jesus' followers will come to their senses and gain courage to continue the movement by perpetuating Jesus' deception. So they approach Pilate, likely back in the Praetorium, and address him with deference: "Sir [*kyrie*] . . . we remember that while he was still alive that deceiver said, 'After three days I will rise again.'"

It is interesting that not even the disciples recall this prediction, probably because of their personal fear and grief. But these religious leaders are savvy. They have witnessed Jesus' miraculous powers, and they want to make certain that whatever power is behind Jesus is not liberated. The cataclysmic events at the crucifixion, with the fearsome darkness, the tearing of the temple curtain, and the earthquakes portend ominous powers. The Jewish religious leaders sense that things may get out of control, so they enlist Pilate's aid in keeping the tomb secure.

**A deceptive attempt to prevent deception (27:64).** The religious leaders have no authority to post guards on a criminal executed by the Roman authorities, so they request Pilate to send a contingent of guards. If the people and Jesus' disciples are stirring, the guard must be secured immediately

---

52. E.g., Brown, *Death of the Messiah*, 2:1310–13; Davies and Allison, *Matthew*, 3:652–53.

53. Cf. Keener, *A Commentary on the Gospel of Matthew* (1999), 696–97; Carson, "Matthew," 585.

54. Ex. 16:29 set a standard for travel on the Sabbath, admonishing people not to go out so that they could observe the Sabbath rest. The rabbis allowed a total distance of two thousand cubits for travel on the Sabbath—approximately three thousand feet or a little over half a mile.

until the third day is past. They offer as an explanation that Jesus' disciples are liable to attempt to perpetuate a grand hoax about Jesus' resurrection.

Little do they know the truth of what they themselves attempt to deceive. The religious leaders allege that Jesus' first deception was his claim to be the Messiah, and his second deception is his claim that he will be raised from the dead. If this kind of rumor gets spread, they know it will be far more difficult to squelch the stories about Jesus' claims. But Matthew makes it clear that the real deceivers are the religious leaders, who actually deceive themselves.

**Pilate orders a guard placed at the tomb (27:65–66).** Pilate concurs with the potential threat to the peace in Jerusalem if a hoax about Jesus' resurrection were perpetuated by the disciples after stealing the body, so he orders a guard to be placed. The same guard of the Roman military assigned to the temple security (see comments on 26:47) are now available to the Jewish officials to make the tomb secure. The expression rendered as a charge, "Take a guard," may be a statement, "You have a guard" (NASB, NRSV), indicating that they are authorized now to use the troops for this security assignment. Note how these guards later go to the temple authorities to report Jesus' resurrection rather than to Pilate himself (28:11).

After a family placed the body of one of its members in a burial recess in the tomb, a stone was placed over the entrance and was often sealed with clay.[55] However, the "seal" here seems to be more of an official security device, so it was more likely an apparatus such as a cord attached to both the stone that blocked the entrance and to the rock face of the tomb, with wax imprinted with the Roman seal anchoring both ends so that any tampering could be detected (cf. Dan. 6:17). The military contingent standing guard acts as the final security seal. While the religious leaders and Pilate have gone to extreme lengths to prevent a hoax about Jesus' resurrection, they provide another witness to the factuality of the empty tomb and the resurrection of Jesus, to their own judgment.

*Bridging Contexts*

THROUGHOUT HIS GOSPEL, Matthew has drawn our attention to the way in which Jesus is the fulfillment of the hopes and dreams of the people of Israel. Jesus is the fulfillment of the great Davidic and Abrahamic covenants (1:1), of Old Testament prophecies (1:22–24; 2:5–6, 15, 17–18, 23, etc.), righteousness (3:15), and the Law (5:17). He inaugurates a new era with the arrival of the kingdom of God (4:17), which is a

---

55. See citation of examples in "Burial Sites," *DJBP*, 104.

mystery reality that is visible only to those with eyes and ears of faith (13:10–17). With Jesus' arrival there is a change in ages.

At the center of this change stands the cross. Sin and death are swallowed up in its pain and love. So Matthew gives us a bold view of the passion of the cross, which culminates Jesus' purpose for coming to his people. But Matthew also wants us to know that the cross changes people. It has defeated death, brought us into the loving hands of a wrathful God, and initiated a new life for those who dare to follow its example. Coupled with the victory declaration in the resurrection, the cross marks the transition to a new world that Jesus has inaugurated through his blood. "In his coming a new age has dawned; nothing will ever be quite the same again."[56]

Matthew slows the pace of his narrative as he nears his conclusion so that we can ponder fully the immense events of Jesus' crucifixion. In a threefold movement he recounts the horrific nature of Jesus' suffering (27:27–44), but then points beyond the agony to its meaning (27:45–53) and results (27:54–66). Therein lies Matthew's, and our, understanding of the cross as the consummate symbol of this age.

**Jesus' suffering (27:27–44).** We watched Jesus' life from infancy as he was born in the middle of a harsh, cruel world dominated by Herod the Great (2:1–23). Even as a baby Jesus was caught up in the battle for this world, and the warfare never let up. Whether in confrontation with Satan in his temptations (4:1–11), in the relentless onslaught of nature's furies in the storm (8:23–27), the harassment of demoniacs (8:28–34), or the opposition of Israel's leaders (12:22–45), Jesus continually battled powerful forces in his mission to establish the kingdom of God.

As he nears the final scene of battle—the cross—his suffering increases exponentially. Horror by horror the Savior suffers. The soldiers' flog and mock him unmercifully until he is near death (27:27–31). The journey to Golgotha is a painful, relentless march toward the final showdown with sin and death (27:32–34). At the final destination, which Matthew ominously renders "the Place of the Skull," Jesus is nailed to a cross like a common revolutionary criminal. (27:35–38). The soldiers place a placard above his head that sadly and ironically bears a true charge: THIS IS JESUS, THE KING OF THE JEWS (27:37). Jesus is persistently mocked by the crowds, who have gathered to watch his death. Common passersby revile him for supposedly being the Son of God (27:39–40), the religious leaders mock him as the supposed Savior of Israel, King, and Son of God (27:41–43), and the insurrectionists crucified with Jesus insult him for not being the same kind of courageous revolutionaries that they were (27:44).

---

56. France, *Matthew*, 38.

Matthew's painful narration causes us also to pause and ponder Jesus' suffering. This is the same Jesus who rebuffed Peter's attempt to rescue him with a sword by pointing to twelve legions of angels who stood ready at his beckoning if he so desired (26:50–53). Jesus' suffering is no accident of history, nor is it a masochistic attempt to assert his life's meaning. His torment is the wall of pain that he must breach to enter into the realm of his life's mission.

Suffering is a well-known reality of life this side of heaven, a reality that all of us must learn to master or at least learn how not to have it master us. But Jesus' suffering uniquely shows us a whole new dimension of our own, in which he had earlier tried to instruct the sons of Zebedee and the rest of the disciples (20:20–28). Our suffering must have a higher purpose than just our own advancement. Jesus suffered not for what he got out of it, but for what we did, and that brings us humbly to consider our own pain. Does every creak and strain cause us to focus on furthering our life's purpose in establishing the reality of the kingdom of God in the lives of others, or does it cause us to bewail life's misfortunes?

I have not suffered anywhere near what Jesus has, but when I ponder his purposeful march to the cross and the tribulation of everyday saints around me who have purposely taken up their life's cross to follow him, I am impelled to humble myself to accept whatever suffering comes my way to advance Jesus' purposes in my life. The powerful preacher of nineteenth-century London, Charles Spurgeon, said of the impact that Jesus' suffering on the cross will have on us:

> If you are not humbled in the presence of Jesus, you do not know Him. You were so lost that nothing could save you but the sacrifice of God's only begotten Son. As Jesus stooped for you, bow in humility at His feet. A realization of Christ's amazing love has a greater tendency to humble us than even a consciousness of our own guilt. Pride cannot live beneath the cross. Let us sit there and learn our lesson. Then let us rise and carry it into practice.[57]

**The meaning of Jesus' suffering (25:45–53).** Nowhere does Jesus give a full exposition of the meaning of the suffering of the cross that he predicted awaited him in Jerusalem. That full theological explanation awaits the rest of the New Testament authors, especially the apostle Paul. But throughout his life Jesus gave hints of the cross's meaning, and then in the cataclysmic events surrounding the crucifixion the meaning of the cross is illustrated.

---

57. Charles H. Spurgeon, "The Lesson of the Cross," *Evening by Evening* (Springdale: Whitaker House, 1984), 157; cited in Calvin Miller, ed., *The Book of Jesus*, rev. ed. (New York: Simon & Schuster, 1998), 368–69.

*Allusions to the cross's meaning in Jesus' ministry.* Right from the beginning of Matthew's Gospel, we read that Jesus would realize the people's hopes of salvation. His name "Jesus" indicated that he would save his people from their sins (1:21), and as his life unfolded it was clear that he would save them in a unique and costly manner. His authority to forgive sins (9:6) pitted him against the authority of the religious system, as did other events in his life. He predicted his future suffering on the cross (16:21; 17:22–23; 20:17–19; 26:2), which contains allusions to the cross's meaning—he was a threat to both Israel's religious establishment and the Roman military and political machine.

Jesus' way of manifesting power was not in serving self but in serving others, which he cited as becoming a "ransom for many" (20:28), a theme that has inherently ominous connotations. Because he suffered at the hands of wicked men (21:38–41), his death hints at his own righteousness. As he promised a new era of kingdom life on the earth, he did so by signaling the end of the functional role of Israel and the beginning of a new nation of his own fruit-bearing disciples, which would come to fruition even as he was rejected and killed (21:42–44).

*Illustrations of the cross's meaning in events at Jesus' death.* All of these allusions to the meaning of the cross as foretold in Jesus' ministry are graphically illustrated in this chapter.

1. The darkness (27:45). The darkness that came over the land at the crucifixion scene displays a limitation on the power of Satan (cf. Luke 22:53), God's displeasure on humanity for crucifying his Son, and, most importantly God's judgment on evil.

2. Jesus' cry on the cross (27:46). Jesus' experiences and his painful cries on the cross result from his human suffering. But throughout church history these cries of Jesus from the cross have been understood to bear witness to much more profound experiences. None of his cries is more powerful than "My God, my God, why have you forsaken me?" (27:45–46). Jesus' divinely sustained humanity consciously experienced the full penalty of death for the sins of humanity. As later theologians reflected on Jesus' utterance from the cross, they recognized that at the infinitely significant moment of his death, he suffered humanity's punishment for sin, namely, death (Rom. 6:23), and in Jesus' separation from God he experienced deathly punishment for the sins of all. This lays the foundation for the theological doctrine of atonement in which Jesus' sacrifice on the cross is one of "penal substitution" or "vicarious atonement."

3. Jesus gives up the spirit (27:50). As Jesus calls out again with a great cry from the cross, this is one final agonizing experience of separa-

tion from the Father as he bears humanity's punishment. Then "he gave up his spirit." This is the final voluntary demonstration of his divine dignity, in which he gives the irrevocable expenditure of his life for the sins of his people.

4. The temple curtain is torn (27:51). The tearing of the temple curtain from top to bottom testifies to God's activity of removing the separation between himself and his people through Jesus' death. No longer is the high priest alone allowed access to the Most Holy Place to commune with God. No longer are any high priestly sacrifices necessary (Heb. 10:10–22). All who are cleansed from sin by the blood of Jesus are a holy priesthood to God (1 Peter 2:5) and live in his presence constantly through his indwelling in our hearts and the ever-present comfort of God's Spirit (Eph. 2:11–22; 3:16–17).

5. Holy people are raised and testify (27:51b–53). The earthquake and unsealing of tombs that occurs at Jesus' death are signals of grand events to follow in three days—Jesus will be raised to life, as will many Old Testament saints. These latter will appear to people in Jerusalem as a witness to the efficaciousness of Jesus' work on the cross and the declaration of his victory over death in his, and their, resurrection. These raised holy people are a powerful testimony to Jesus' work and identity and of the reality of the future, final resurrection. Because of Jesus' and the holy people's resurrection, victorious life over death is a reality.

*Theological reflections on the cross's meaning.* The Gospels are often referred to as theology enacted, whereas the New Testament letters are theology explained. In the Gospels we find God acting in history in the person of his Son, Jesus Messiah, to accomplish salvation for his people. In the letters we find the church leaders reflecting back on and giving inspired, theological explanation of what God did in history. Theologian Wayne Grudem summarizes the atoning work of Jesus' life and death by first citing four needs of sinful humanity:

1. We deserve to *die* as the penalty for sin.
2. We deserve to *bear God's wrath* against sin.
3. We are *separated* from God by our sins.
4. We are in *bondage to sin* and to the kingdom of Satan.

These four needs are met by Jesus' death in the following ways:

1. Jesus died as a *sacrifice* for us to pay the penalty of death that we deserved because of our sin (Heb. 9:26).
2. Jesus died as a *propitiation* for our sins to remove us from the wrath of God (1 John 4:10).

3. Jesus experienced death and separation from God to overcome our separation from God. He provided *reconciliation* for us to be brought back into fellowship with God (2 Cor. 5:18–19).

4. Through Jesus' death, we experience *redemption* from bondage to sin and Satan so that we now live in newness of life in the Spirit in the kingdom of the beloved Son (Matt. 20:28; cf. Rom. 6:11, 14; Col. 1:13; Heb. 2:15; 1 John 5:19).[58]

As much as the suffering of Jesus on the cross baffles our limited understanding, serious reflection yields powerful insights into this which is God's central act of mercy on humankind. The *meaning* of Jesus' suffering on the cross is essential for our understanding of the good news of the kingdom of God. The *results* of Jesus' suffering likewise are worthy of contemplation.

**The results of Jesus' suffering: Boundaryless discipleship (27:54–66).** The results of Jesus' suffering on the cross are inextricably linked with the meaning of his suffering—his sacrifice for sin, his propitiation of the wrath of God on sin, his reconciliation of sinners to fellowship with God, and his redemption of lost sinners from sin's grip. But here specifically we look at three sets of people who illustrate the results of Jesus' suffering in their lives and point to a central tenet of the life of the kingdom of God in this age—*boundaryless discipleship to Jesus*. What this teaches us, in the words of the old proverb, is that "the ground is level at the foot of the cross." We find a oneness and an equality at the cross that transcends national, cultural, ethnic, gender-based, social, and political boundaries. These "individuals who do not reject Jesus stand out: the Roman centurion confesses Jesus as Son of God (27:54), women who watch the crucifixion are named (27:55), and Joseph of Arimathea provides Jesus with a tomb (27:57ff.)."[59]

*Gentiles and powerful* (27:54). The Roman centurion and his men are Gentiles. They represent the most powerful military and political machine of that time, and one of the most significant of all human history. The centurion is responsible for carrying out the orders of Pilate, who represents the might of the Roman Empire. This centurion is likely the one who supervised Jesus' flogging, who allowed the guards to ridicule Jesus, who ordered the nails to be driven into Jesus' body, who watched with amusement as his guards taunted Jesus with the sour drink, who heard Jesus' own people mock and taunt him, and who had probably watched with some anxiousness for the uprising that might occur.

---

58. Grudem, *Systematic Theology*, 580–81. See here Grudem's important caveat on using the "ransom" analogy.

59. Howell, *Matthew's Inclusive Story*, 158.

But the centurion and his men watch Jesus die and hear his eerie cry to God about his forsakenness. As they watch the supernatural darkening of the sky, the temple curtain torn in two, the earth shaken, and the tombs opened, they are struck with the realization that Jesus just may be who he said he was. And in awe they pronounce, "Surely he was the Son of God!" (27:54). The cataclysmic events surrounding the crucifixion testify to Jesus' true identity, and the centurion and his men make a step of faith to acknowledge the truth of that testimony.

As a result of this acclamation from Gentiles, the way is now open in principle to go and make disciples of all nations (28:19).[60] Matthew has hinted at the salvation of Gentiles from the very first verse of his Gospel as he recalled Jesus fulfilling the Abrahamic covenant (1:1). A Roman centurion early in Jesus' ministry had expressed faith in Jesus' ability to heal his servant (8:5–13), and now another centurion steps forward to give a profound declaration of faith in Jesus' true identity. This pagan centurion has humbly taken a step toward following Jesus.

*Women and the marginalized (27:55–56, 61).* Women and the marginalized are among Jesus' closest disciples. Women and men were originally created by God as equal and as complementary coworkers in ruling God's creation for him (Gen. 1:26–28). But in some circles within Judaism, because of misinterpretation of Scripture and cultural bias, women lost their dignity, value, and worth. Josephus stated, "The woman, says the Law, is in all things inferior to the man,"[61] apparently interpreting Genesis 3:16 to indicate that women are not only under the authority of men but also have a lower personal status. One of the most widely cited rabbinic prayers reflects an attitude prevalent at least among some of the rabbis: "Praised be God that he has not created me a gentile! Praised be God that he has not created me a woman! Praised be God that he has not created me an ignoramus!"[62]

One direct result of Jesus' ministry was the restoration and affirmation of women that God intended from the beginning of creation, as is demonstrated in the following ways:

- Women were equally worthy of Jesus' saving activity (John 4:1–42).
- Women were called to be Jesus' disciples (Matt. 12:48–50).
- Women received instruction and nurture as Jesus' disciples (Luke 10:38–42).
- Women were part of his ministry team (Luke 8:1–3).

---

60. See Kingsbury, *Matthew As Story*, 90.

61. Josephus, *Against Apion* 2:201.

62. *t. Ber.* 7:18.

- Because of their courageous presence at the cross and the empty tomb, women were designated as the first to testify to the reality of Jesus' resurrection (Matt. 28:10; Mark 16:7; John 20:17).

For women to be disciples of a great master was certainly an unusual circumstance in Palestine of the first century. Yet here we find another instance of the unique form of discipleship Jesus instituted. While women were not part of the Twelve, several of these women traveled with Jesus and had a significant part in his earthly ministry. Jesus restored and reaffirmed to women their dignity and worth as persons fully equal to men as humans created in the image of God. He also preserved the male-female distinction of humans, so that they were restored and affirmed in the different roles that God had intended from the beginning. Jesus restored to women the status of being coworkers with men in God's plan for working out his will on earth.[63]

*Wealthy and religious (27:57–60, 62–66).* The wealthy and religious stand together before the crucified Jesus Messiah. The rich man from Arimathea named Joseph requests the body of Jesus to give it proper burial. His courage in asking for the body and his service to Jesus are exemplary of what a disciple should do. As Jesus' disciple, he is a fitting foil for the disciples who forsook Jesus. An earlier rich man had walked sadly away when he realized that Jesus must be his sole Master and that any other "god" of his life must yield to him (19:16–22). It is harder for a rich man to be saved than it is for a camel to go through the eye of a needle, but as Jesus declared then, all things are possible with God (19:23–26). And so we see here that God enabled Joseph to yield to Jesus as Master, to become his disciple, and to be saved.

This is a remarkable disciple of Jesus. He bucked the religious establishment, put his life on the line, and gave over his own family tomb to his Master. What a striking contrast to the religious leaders who recalled that Jesus had given them the "sign of Jonah" (12:40) and then joined forces with Pilate to see to it that a guard secured the tomb (27:62–66)! Their aim was to prevent Jesus' disciples, now among them Joseph, from stealing his body and proclaiming a resurrection (27:64). Accordingly, the Jewish leaders continued their active opposition against Jesus even after he died. But the example of Joseph is outspoken testimony that even the wealthy and religious are welcome to the cross and to discipleship with Jesus.

---

63. This material is developed more fully in Wilkins, "Women in the Teaching and Example of Jesus," *Women and Men in Ministry*, 91–112.

SITTING IN THE little Rose of Sharon Chapel on our campus is always a moving experience for me. The tiny chapel is a quiet, peaceful place to share my heart with our Savior. It is a prayer chapel. No preaching or teaching is scheduled there. It is a place where one can find solace amidst the scurry of a university campus in the overwhelming activity of southern California.

The chapel stands for much more, however. An empty cross starkly adorns the wall. It is a powerful testimony to young Sharon Lynn Menshew. She was a nursing major preparing for medical missions. She met her future husband, Robert, while she was working part time at his family restaurant while attending school. They started dating, but before long she was diagnosed with cancer. This was a young couple who were in love, and even though the future looked grim, they married anyway. Not long after, Sharon died. As Bob continued to attend school, he sought answers from God about Sharon's death. He could find no quiet place to pray, so God led him to raise the funds to build a little chapel on our campus in his beloved young wife's name.

The Rose of Sharon is a poignantly peaceful little chapel with an empty cross as a joyous reminder of their hope, but also as a reminder of their dreams of a life in missions. Even though young Sharon lost her life on this earth far too quickly, she is alive today because her Savior lives. The empty cross of Golgotha points ahead to an empty tomb and trumpets the call to sacrificial service.

What comes to mind when you hear the word "cross"? For some of us it may only indicate a piece of jewelry. For others it brings to mind the difficulties in life that we are required to bear. For others it produces an emotional reaction as we think of Jesus hanging between two thieves. But for Jesus, the word "cross" is the symbol that best expresses his *heart*. In this powerful final scene of the Passion Narrative, Matthew calls us to recognize that the cross represents Jesus' entire earthly ministry and allows us an intimate look into the heart that he has for this world; it also symbolizes God's work in our lives.

**The outrageous cross commands our contemplation.** A slain Messiah is difficult to fathom intellectually, but it is perhaps even more difficult to encounter spiritually, relationally, and emotionally. Matthew slows the pace of his narrative so that we are forced to ponder the cross. Hear this challenge about the cross from Lloyd John Ogilvie:

> Feel it if you will. Let it happen to you if you dare.
> Take the most precious friend of your life. The person with whom you've known joy and fun and sorrow. With whom you share the deep bonds of caring. Place him upon the cross and watch him writhe in pain.

The nails driven into those beloved hands are driven into our hands. The muscles excruciatingly stretched are our muscles. The terrible burning of his tongue and mouth is in our tongue and mouth. We feel it all as if we were there ourselves because the most precious person in all the world is there on our behalf.

Feel it. Experience it if you will.[64]

Pastor Ogilvie was elected the sixty-first chaplain of the United States Senate in 1995. As a pastor for many years and as an evangelical leader, he understands the centrality of the cross for life and ministry. I believe that we need to take his challenge seriously—and regularly—and attempt to enter into the experience of the cross. It is vitally important for the accurate development of our theology and just as important for our own personal transformation.

In many of our evangelical churches and chapels, the empty cross that adorns our walls is an intentional declaration that Jesus is no longer on the cross but has accomplished his sacrifice once-for-all. Our emphasis is on the empty tomb, not the cross—and rightly so, for the empty tomb is a permanent reminder that Jesus' work on the cross has effectively cancelled the penalty for our sins. As Paul declares, "And if Christ has not been raised, your faith is futile; you are still in your sins" (1 Cor. 15:17).

But we must not hurry so quickly to the empty tomb that we don't fully ponder the inclusive events of the cross. Paul gives prominent place to the empty tomb, but in the same letter just mentioned, he begins by stating, "I resolved to know nothing while I was with you except Jesus Christ and him crucified" (1 Cor. 2:2). To catch the full significance of what Paul expresses, we can render the word translated "and" in the last clause in an explanatory manner as "even" or "that is": "I resolved to know nothing while I was with you except Jesus Christ—that is, Jesus Christ crucified." Paul's purpose in writing to the Corinthians is to lay out for them the truth about Jesus Christ—which is wrapped up in the fact and meaning of his crucifixion.[65]

The profound depth of Jesus' crucifixion tempts us to minimize its horror, so that we hear in his cry from the cross just another human who suffers death. But we must not minimize the outrageousness of the cross, because it is there that the God-man suffered a death that was unique—bearing the load of sin for humanity and experiencing ultimate separation from God, while retaining in his consciousness a painful intimacy with his Father.

---

64. Lloyd John Ogilvie, *The Cup of Wonder: Communion Meditations* (Wheaton: Tyndale, 1976), 75.

65. Cf. W. Harold Mare, "1 Corinthians," *EBC*, 10:198; Fee, *1 Corinthians*, 92; William F. Orr, *1 Corinthians* (AB 32; Garden City, N.Y.: Doubleday, 1976), 162–63.

In our desire to get to the empty tomb of chapter 28, we must not rush past these final verses of chapter 27. We must reflect on them meaningfully, because here we see Jesus' heart for us, and we also see ourselves more clearly. But we must ponder rightly. In Martin Luther's call to meditate on the cross, he gives this warning: "Some do so falsely in that they merely rail against Judas and the Jews. Some carry crucifixes to protect themselves from water, fire, and sword, and turn the suffering of Christ into an amulet against suffering. Some weep and that is the end of it."[66] Luther exhorts us to sincerely evaluate the cross so that we do not trivialize it nor brush by it too fast lest we miss its deepest significance. He goes on to say:

> The true contemplation is that in which the heart is crushed and the conscience smitten. You must be overwhelmed by the frightful wrath of God who so hated sin that he spared not his only-begotten Son....
>
> If, then, Christ is so firmly planted in your heart, and if you are become an enemy to sin out of love and not fear, then henceforth, the suffering of Christ, which began as a sacrament, may continue lifelong as an example. When tribulation and trouble assail you, think how slight these are compared to the thorns and the nails of Christ. If thwarted, remember how he was bound and dragged. If pride besets you, see how the Lord was mocked and with robbers despised. If unchastity incites your flesh, recall how his flesh was scourged, pierced, and smitten. If hate, envy, and vengeance tempt you, think how Christ for you and all his enemies interceded with tears, though he might rather have avenged himself. If you are afflicted and cannot have your way, take heart and say, "Why should I not suffer when my Lord sweat blood for very anguish?"
>
> Astounding it is that the cross of Christ has so fallen into forgetfulness, for is it not forgetfulness of the cross when no one wishes to suffer but rather to enjoy himself and evade the cross?[67]

As we ponder the cross, Luther (and the New Testament authors) tells us that we will find in its shadows an example for our own lives—not in some kind of mindless self-abasement but in a lifelong conforming of our lives to the example of Jesus, who saw in the cross his life's mission of giving his life so that others could live. This is called by some "cruciformity"—that is, the salvation experience of dying and rising with Christ that embarks us on a lifelong sanctification experience of being conformed to his image and encountering a

---

66. Martin Luther, *Luther's Meditations on the Gospels* (Philadelphia: Westminster, 1962), 135.
67. Ibid, 135–36.

kingdom life that is expressed in faith, love, power, and hope.[68] The cross commands our continual contemplation as we open ourselves to God's transforming and conforming power.

**The empty cross creates our peace.** As I write these words in spring 2003, the allied invasion of Iraq and the assault on Baghdad is underway. Young men and women in the military face death for the first time in a unique manner. Seeing violent death up close changes young men and women—permanently. During their training they thought of death and considered their own. They probably joked about their bravery and stiffly rejected thoughts of fear. Many hopefully knelt in prayer before they entered into their first battle. But none of their bravado or even their prayers could fully immunize them against the harsh reality of their first combat experience.

Columnist Gordon Dillow was traveling with the Marines of Alpha Company of the 1st Battalion, Marine Regimental Combat Team 5. These young Marines engaged one of the first battles of the war at Pumping Station No. 2 in the al-Rumeilah oil fields and suffered one of the first U.S. casualties of the war—2nd Lieutenant Therrel "Shane" Childers, age 30, of Harrison, Mississippi. In his first column after the start of the war, journalist Dillow reflected on the change that came over these young Marines after their first battle and their first encounter with violent death. He writes, "After the firefight, some of the Marines were exhilarated by their first combat experience. Others had to admit to themselves that when the shooting and killing started, they were more bothered by it than they'd thought they'd be." He wrote of one young Marine:

> "It wasn't like I thought it'd be," said Cpl. Martin Vera, 27, of Long Beach [California], who had re-enlisted in the Marines after the Sept. 11 attacks because he thought that now, finally, he would get a chance to see some action. "It wasn't like the movies and stuff. After 9–11 it was like, yeah, I wanted to come back for this. But it bothered me, shooting at those guys. I had to do it; it's my job. But it bothered me. A lot."

Dillow concluded his column with these reflections:

> Despite the blood they've seen so far, the young Marines of the 1/5 haven't turned hard yet—or at least not any harder than young Marine grunts already are. They still look fresh-faced and eager and generally unafraid. They will do what they have to do.
>
> But their first firefight has changed them.
>
> Somehow, they aren't quite as young as they were yesterday.[69]

---

68. E.g., Michael J. Gorman, *Cruciformity: Paul's Narrative Spirituality of the Cross* (Grand Rapids: Eerdmans, 2001), 369.

69. Gordon Dillow, "Battle Transforms Fresh-Faced Troops," *Orange County Register* (March 23, 2003), News: 1, 21.

Dillow rightly observes that seeing death up close changes people. You and I aren't any different. In much of Western culture we have isolated ourselves from death. We send sick people to hospitals, where they die away from view. We send old people to retirement or nursing homes, where in isolation from normal life they die—often alone. Death is an uncomfortable, if not fearful, part of life that many try to avoid and push as far away as possible.

But death is a real part of life. An important dimension of our discipleship to Jesus is to learn how to handle it. That is at least one lesson we can learn by looking at the empty cross of Jesus. He has conquered sin and death. The empty cross means not to focus on our own death but to look to the resurrection beyond. To meditate on an empty cross should bring us the greatest expectation of our own destiny. In so doing it will become one of our most important messages to the world around us.

Although I was not a Christian when I fought in Vietnam, and I was quite outspoken in my disdain for Christians, I was impacted profoundly by a young man in my platoon who was a devout Christian. I don't remember his name now—over thirty years later—but I remember his life. He was a tall, well-built former football player, who had short-cropped bright red hair and a face full of freckles. He had the most peaceful demeanor of anyone I had ever known—peace in the middle of the horror of war. In combat we lived with our fear of death held in check, otherwise it would paralyze us. But fear was never far away.

I once jokingly quizzed "Red" about his peacefulness, asking him if maybe he was doing drugs. But he replied only to say with his usual calm that he did experience fear, but that he knew what would happen to him if, and when, he died. He would be in the safe hands of Jesus, who gave him peace no matter what happened to him. "Red" was wounded one day, not seriously, but enough to be sent back to the States. After that battle, he was loaded onto a helicopter to be sent to the rear. He looked at me with the same peaceful expression and said, "Sergeant Mike, think about what I've said."

I never forgot. Years later when I became a Christian, I came to understand what he had experienced, and I now recognize that my own discipleship to Jesus involves how I look at death and the way I witness to my own peace as I think about what is beyond.

But facing death isn't just for those involved in the combat of war. It is what everyone faces in the combat of everyday life. One of the most profound testimonies of our discipleship is how we face death. Howard Hendricks, a beloved professor at Dallas Theological Seminary, recently wrote a series of articles that include his own reflections on his aging and approach to the latter years of his career and life. In one of the articles he made a critical observation.

Perhaps the most important task of an elderly Christian is to teach the world how a believer dies. If God does not bring an unexpected ending to our lives, then, like Zechariah the priest and the apostles Paul and John, we are on stage before a younger generation acting out the process of leaving this life.[70]

Western culture idolizes the young, the beautiful, the strong, and the virulent. At times that same idolization creeps into the church. But if we wisely face our own mortality and appropriately emphasize our eternal destiny, we will give much more prominent place to the elderly saints among us who have so much knowledge, experience, and wisdom to pass on to the succeeding generations. Part of that is how to die well.

My wife's parents lived with us during their later years while my mother-in-law, Marge, suffered increasing deterioration from multiple sclerosis. Quite suddenly during the Thanksgiving season one year, with all of the family gathered at home for the holiday, she was rushed to the hospital with lung failure. We didn't think that it would be a long stay, but on the third day her attending nurse called to have us all get to the hospital as quickly as possible—Marge was failing. We spent the morning in her room sharing last thoughts and expressions of love, and tears. As she slowly began to fade, we all gathered around her bed. She looked at me at the foot of her hospital bed and asked me to read a passage of Scripture. I remembered that one of her favorite passages was Philippians 4:6–7, which I read out loud. We all passed the Bible around and read passages that we knew she loved and that we all needed to hear right then. We all prayed together, and then as her breathing became increasingly more labored, she looked calmly around the bed. One by one she looked each family member in the eyes and waved the fingers on her frail little hand. Her eyes went to each of her children, grandchildren, and then finally to her beloved husband of over sixty years, and she waved goodbye. Then she closed her eyes, and before too long was gone.

None of us will ever forget that moment. Marge was the matriarch of the family. She was a strong, willful, stubborn, yet incredibly loving Norwegian—a true Viking-type! And her love for her Savior was at the center of her life. She was an unwavering disciple of Jesus. In those final moments of her life, she left an indelible mark on all of us. She died well, full of the peace of God. As her eyes went around her bed, she was passing on the charge to each family member to live—and to die—well with the Savior.

Marge would want me to share her favorite passage: "Do not be anxious about anything, but in everything, by prayer and petition, with thanks-

---

70. Howard Hendricks, "Me, Myself, and My Tomorrows," *BibSac* 157 (July–September 2000): 268.

giving, present your requests to God. And the peace of God, which transcends all understanding, will guard your hearts and your minds in Christ Jesus" (Phil. 4:6–7). Jesus' empty cross is a call to each of us to expand our vision of this life and courageously face life, and death, with the peace that passes understanding.

**The wondrous cross demands our all.** In Gerd Theissen's fictional account of the events surrounding the death and crucifixion of Jesus, *The Shadow of the Galilean*, he includes an imagined letter written by Barabbas to the main character of the story, Andreas, after the death of Jesus. Although Barabbas's conclusions do not lead him to embrace the ministry program of Jesus, he does have an intuition regarding the substitutionary nature of Jesus' death for him and what it requires of him in return. He says in his letter:

> I'm writing above all to thank you. I've heard how much you did for me. I barely escaped death. The price was high. Another died in my place. Two of my friends were crucified with him. Since then I've been asking myself: Why the other? Why Jesus? Why not me?
>
> I know that Jesus is close to your heart. You defended his gentle way of rebellion and rejected my way of resisting. Now I'm indissolubly bound up with him. I keep thinking what that means for me.
>
> If he has died in my place, then I am obliged to live for him. . . .[71]

Our response ought to be similar. A contemplation of the wondrous cross of Jesus should cause us to take serious pause and ask *Why?* Why would Jesus do this for me? It should leave us with a sense of gratitude as we determine it is simply a result of his love for us. But it should also leave us with a sense in which we are "indissolubly bound up with him" if we accept his payment in place of our own, resulting in our obligation to live for him. We are bound up with him in such a way that when God sees us, he sees Jesus and the sacrifice he made for us, allowing us to be justified in his sight; we no longer need to take the penalty for our own sins. As a result, we are now free to live for him, to become who we were intended to be before sin had its devastating effect upon the world. Lord John Acton, the brilliant nineteenth-century historian, defined a free culture as one that is free to do the right thing, free to become virtuous, but not free to do whatever one so desires.[72]

In this sense, we should see the freedom that Christ bought for us such that we are obligated now to follow his call in our lives. He declared,

---

71. Gerd Theissen, *The Shadow of the Galilean: The Quest of the Historical Jesus in Narrative Form*, trans. John Bowden (Minneapolis: Fortress, 1987), 177.

72. Lord John Emerich Edward Dalberg Acton, *The History of Freedom*, "Introduction," by James C. Holland (Grand Rapids: Acton Institute, 1993).

"If you hold to my teaching, you are really my disciples. Then you will know the truth, and the truth will set you free" (John 8:31–32). Yet it is an obligation that brings peace and fulfillment as we learn to "be holy, as God is holy."

Consider the little-known figures around the cross. Their diversity is remarkable, but the confession of their lips and life is uniformly exemplary for us. The Roman centurion and his men brave harsh reprisals for taking their first step of faith by vocalizing aloud their recognition that Jesus surely was the Son of God (27:54). The wealthy Jewish religious leaders Joseph of Arimathea and Nicodemus risk alienation from their colleagues and punishment from the Roman occupying forces by stepping forward to claim Jesus' body as his faithful disciples (27:57–60). And the women, Jesus' ever-devoted servants and followers, risk social and religious ostracism as well as legal punishment for associating with a convicted criminal and never straying far from the cross or the tomb (27:55–56, 61).

These three groups set historical precedents for our own discipleship. We may not ever accomplish great feats in the eyes of the world, but when we are gripped by the profound truths that Jesus accomplished on the cross, we too will be energized by the Spirit of God to be men and women whose service to our Master is a courageous witness that the gospel of the kingdom has triumphed. Their example is a striking reflection of the challenge that Jesus laid down at a crucial turning point of his earthly ministry:

> If anyone would come after me, he must deny himself and take up his cross and follow me. For whoever wants to save his life will lose it, but whoever loses his life for me will find it. What good will it be for a man if he gains the whole world, yet forfeits his soul? Or what can a man give in exchange for his soul? (16:24–26)

Isaac Watts, the prolific hymn writer, understood these truths. He composed the powerful words of one of his most famous hymns, "When I Survey the Wondrous Cross," with Jesus' words from this passage clearly in view.[73] As Watts focuses our attention on the cross, he shows us the implications for our own lives as we learn consistently to deny ourselves, take up our cross, and follow Jesus. Look especially at the personal humility that Watts understands comes from seeing clearly Jesus' sacrifice on the cross for us and Watts's own response of sacrificial surrender of his life to Jesus in return.

---

73. Watts's personal life was a model of consistent faithfulness as a minister of the gospel from 1674 to 1748. He not only carried out a significant ministry of preaching and writing, but wrote over 460 hymns.

When I survey the wondrous cross
On which the Prince of glory died,
My richest gain I count but loss,
And pour contempt on all my pride.

Forbid it, Lord, that I should boast,
Save in the death of Christ my God!
All the vain things that charm me most,
I sacrifice them to His blood.

See from His head, His hands, His feet,
Sorrow and love flow mingled down!
Did e'er such love and sorrow meet,
Or thorns compose so rich a crown?

His dying crimson, like a robe,
Spreads o'er His body on the tree;
Then I am dead to all the globe,
And all the globe is dead to me.

Were the whole realm of nature mine,
That were a present far too small:
Love so amazing, so divine,
Demands my soul, my life, my all.

Watts demonstrates in his own life the powerful meaning of a person fully surrendered to the will of God. You and I may not write hymns as beautiful as these. I can't even read music! But in our own way, we can look at his hymnic example and draw encouragement for our own commitment to God's will. And for those of us in leadership, we must do the hard work of translating this into the plain language of our people, to help them to live this out consistently in their daily lives. Jesus' amazing, divine, sacrificial love for us demands our soul, our life, our all, whether we are hotel housekeepers or hotel owners, school children or school teachers, ex-cons or police officers. That is the only proper response of a life that surveys the wondrous cross.

# Matthew 28:1–20

٭

**A**FTER THE SABBATH, at dawn on the first day of the
week, Mary Magdalene and the other Mary went to
look at the tomb.

²There was a violent earthquake, for an angel of the Lord
came down from heaven and, going to the tomb, rolled back
the stone and sat on it. ³His appearance was like lightning,
and his clothes were white as snow. ⁴The guards were so
afraid of him that they shook and became like dead men.

⁵The angel said to the women, "Do not be afraid, for I
know that you are looking for Jesus, who was crucified. ⁶He is
not here; he has risen, just as he said. Come and see the place
where he lay. ⁷Then go quickly and tell his disciples: 'He has
risen from the dead and is going ahead of you into Galilee.
There you will see him.' Now I have told you."

⁸So the women hurried away from the tomb, afraid yet filled
with joy, and ran to tell his disciples. ⁹Suddenly Jesus met them.
"Greetings," he said. They came to him, clasped his feet and worshiped him. ¹⁰Then Jesus said to them, "Do not be afraid. Go and
tell my brothers to go to Galilee; there they will see me."

¹¹While the women were on their way, some of the guards
went into the city and reported to the chief priests everything
that had happened. ¹²When the chief priests had met with the
elders and devised a plan, they gave the soldiers a large sum of
money, ¹³telling them, "You are to say, 'His disciples came during
the night and stole him away while we were asleep.' ¹⁴If this report
gets to the governor, we will satisfy him and keep you out of trouble." ¹⁵So the soldiers took the money and did as they were
instructed. And this story has been widely circulated among the
Jews to this very day.

¹⁶Then the eleven disciples went to Galilee, to the mountain
where Jesus had told them to go. ¹⁷When they saw him, they worshiped him; but some doubted. ¹⁸Then Jesus came to them and
said, "All authority in heaven and on earth has been given to me.
¹⁹Therefore go and make disciples of all nations, baptizing them
in the name of the Father and of the Son and of the Holy Spirit,
²⁰and teaching them to obey everything I have commanded you.
And surely I am with you always, to the very end of the age."

THE *PAX ROMANA*, the famed "peace of Rome," was a surface condition imposed by Caesar Augustus and the Roman military might, but it did not bring freedom to all her subjects. Just below the surface swirled tides of discontent and insurrection. Matthew opens his Gospel by declaring that in one of the remote regions of the empire, where a variety of disturbances repeatedly surfaced, the hoped-for freedom finally arrived in a most unexpected way. A rival to Augustus was born in Bethlehem. But this rival did not appear with fanfare, nor would he challenge directly the military and political might of Rome. The revolution was brought by Jesus, the long-awaited Messiah of Israel, who fulfilled the covenantal promises of an anticipated Davidic king and the covenantal promises of Abrahamic blessings through Israel to all the nations of the earth (1:1). But throughout his life's mission Jesus disappointed many of his own people, because his was a revolution of the heart, not a revolution of swords or chariots.

Jesus resolutely set about bringing the kingdom of God to earth in his own way, with his own anticipated conquest of the ultimate enemy, Satan and his forces. But that conquest once again did not come in the way that many within Israel expected. It came through Jesus' execution. In the longest extended narrative of this Gospel, Matthew tells the stunning tale of Jesus Messiah's final betrayal, denials, arrest, trials, and crucifixion (chs. 26–27). That narrative ends on such a somber note that readers might assume that all Jesus came to accomplish was lost. But in one of the shortest narratives in his Gospel, Matthew gives an equally stunning account of Jesus Messiah's resurrection from the dead (ch. 28).

The brevity of the resurrection account is almost anticlimactic. But like the brevity of the announcement of Jesus' conception, the resurrection was a well-accepted historical fact for Matthew's readers, so there was no need for extensive narrative. The resurrection declares that Jesus is who he said he was, that what he came to accomplish at the cross was efficacious, and that he now lives to be the faithful Companion, Master, and Lord of all who respond to his Great Commission. That is what brings the ultimate peace, the forgiveness of sins that reconciles humans to God and humans to humans, a revolution that the Roman Empire could never crush. The new age of real peace, *pax Dei*, the "peace of God" that transcends all understanding (Phil. 4:7), has begun for all who dare to become Jesus' disciples.

Matthew's concluding chapter climaxes the amazing story of Jesus Messiah. He was conceived in a miraculous manner as the Savior of his people. He lived a sensational life in the Spirit's power, announcing the arrival of the kingdom of heaven. But he was tragically betrayed by his own people and crucified by the Roman government. Would that be the end of the story? Indeed not! Jesus Messiah is found missing from his grave, just as he predicted. The angel announces the resurrection, his women followers are the first to witness both the empty tomb and the risen Jesus, the authorities try to concoct a tale to counteract the miracle, and all of his followers now have a commission to invite people to enter into a relationship with the risen Jesus as his disciples.

As the astonishing verification of his divine identity as Son of God (Rom. 1:4) and of the efficaciousness of his atoning work on the cross, Jesus' resurrection figures prominently in all four Gospels. While we cannot resolve all of the differences between the resurrection accounts, their variations strengthen the truth that these Gospel writers are independent witnesses and are not attempting to reproduce a concocted deception.[1] "The proposal that Jesus was bodily raised from the dead possesses unrivalled power to explain the historical data at the heart of early Christianity."[2] Indeed, the variations add to the historical plausibility of this most momentous event of history.[3]

Three elements are common to all four Gospels: the empty tomb, the announcement of the resurrection to the women, and the meeting of the disciples with the risen Jesus.[4] A further plausible synchronization of the events surrounding Jesus' resurrection and appearances found in four Gospel versions and in Paul's account in 1 Corinthians 15:1—11 is as follows:[5]

---

1. Cf. Morris, *Matthew*, 733; Hagner, *Matthew*, 2:868.

2. N. T. Wright, *The Resurrection of the Son of God*, vol. 3 of *Christian Origins and the Question of God* (Minneapolis: Fortress, 2003), 718.

3. The literature on the resurrection is massive, but the following will give the reader a start. For the most thorough study of the historical and exegetical issues, see Wright, *The Resurrection of the Son of God;* see also Richard N. Longenecker, *Life in the Face of Death: The Resurrection Message of the New Testament* (Grand Rapids: Eerdmans, 1998). The historical reliability of the resurrection narratives is set forth by Blomberg, *The Historical Reliability of the Gospels*, 100–110; William Lane Craig, "Did Jesus Rise from the Dead?" in *Jesus Under Fire*, 142–76; and at a more scholarly level, William Lane Craig, *Assessing the New Testament Evidence for the Historicity of the Resurrection of Jesus* (Lewiston, N.Y.: Edwin Mellen, 1989). On a popular, apologetic level are Gary R. Habermas, *The Resurrection of Jesus: An Apologetic* (Grand Rapids: Baker, 1980) and George Eldon Ladd, *I Believe in the Resurrection of Jesus* (Grand Rapids: Eerdmans, 1975). The theological distinctives of each Gospel are explored by Grant R. Osborne, *The Resurrection Narratives: A Redactional Study* (Grand Rapids: Baker, 1984). For a discussion of the philosophical issues, see Stephen T. Davis, *Risen Indeed: Making Sense of the Resurrection* (Grand Rapids: Eerdmans, 1993); at a more scholarly level, Peter Carnley, *The Structure of Resurrection Belief* (Oxford: Clarendon, 1987). For devotional meditations, see James Montgomery Boice, *The Christ of the Empty Tomb* (Chicago: Moody Press, 1985).

4. Morris, *Matthew*, 733; Hagner, *Matthew*, 2:868.

5. This reconstruction is suggested by John Wenham, *Easter Enigma*, 139 and passim. For a similar reconstruction see Craig L. Blomberg, *Jesus and the Gospels: An Introduction and Survey* (Nashville: Broadman & Holman, 1997), 354–55.

1. A group of women come to the tomb near dawn, with Mary Magdalene possibly arriving first (Matt. 28:1; Mark 16:1–3; Luke 24:1; John 20:1).
2. Mary and the other women are met by two young men who actually are angels, one of whom announces Jesus' resurrection (Matt. 28:2–7; Mark 16:4–7; Luke 24:2–7).
3. The women leave the garden with a mixture of fear and joy, at first unwilling to say anything but then resolving to report to the Twelve (Matt. 28:8; Mark 16:8). Mary Magdalene may have dashed on ahead, telling Peter and John before the other women arrive (John 20:2).
4. Peter and John run to the tomb and discover it to be empty (Luke 24:12; John 20:3–5).
5. Mary also returns to the tomb and sees the angels. Jesus then appears to Mary, although at first she supposes him to be a gardener (John 20:11–18).
6. Jesus meets the remaining women and confirms their commission to tell the disciples, with the reminder of his promise of meeting them in Galilee; the women obey (Matt. 28:9–10; Luke 24:8–11).
7. During the afternoon Jesus appears to Peter individually, in or near Jerusalem on the Sunday afternoon of the resurrection day (Luke 24:34; 1 Cor. 15:5).
8. Later in the day Jesus appears to Cleopas and his unnamed companion on the road to Emmaus. They return to Jerusalem to tell the Eleven (Luke 24:13–35; cf. Mark 16:12–13).
9. While Cleopas and his friend are in the Upper Room with the disciples (without Thomas) behind locked doors, Jesus appears to them (Luke 24:36–43; John 20:19–25).
10. Sunday evening a week later Jesus appears to the Eleven at the same place in Jerusalem, with Thomas now present (John 20:26–29; 1 Cor. 15:5; cf. Mark 16:14).
11. Perhaps three days later Jesus appears to seven of the disciples beside the Sea of Galilee (John 21:1–14).
12. Jesus appears to the apostles as well as about five hundred believers in the hills of Galilee (1 Cor. 15:6). Further appearances take place over a forty-day period (Luke 24:44–47; Acts 1:3; 1 Cor. 15:6).
13. Probably during this time in Galilee, Jesus appears to James, his half-brother (1 Cor. 15:7).
14. Jesus gives his climactic Great Commission to the Eleven (and others?) on a mountain in Galilee, commanding them to make disciples throughout the world (Matt. 28:16–20; cf. Mark 16:15–18).

15. Back in the Jerusalem area, Jesus gives parting instructions to the disciples to await the coming Holy Spirit. He ascends into heaven near Bethany on the Mount of Olives, outside of Jerusalem (Luke 24:44–53; Acts 1:4–12; cf. Mark 16:19–20).

## The Women Disciples of Jesus Discover an Empty Tomb (28:1–4)

MATTHEW LEFT OFF the crucifixion narrative with Joseph of Arimathea wrapping the body of Jesus in burial cloths and placing him in Joseph's own tomb. At least two of the women disciples of Jesus, Mary Magdalene and the other Mary, watched these beginnings of the preparations of the body for burial. Perhaps these women, along with others who had followed Jesus from Galilee, worked together with Joseph and Nicodemus to prepare the corpse for burial.[6]

Mark 16:1 tells us that at the conclusion of the Sabbath, the women disciples went to purchase materials for anointing Jesus' body. Sabbath restrictions limited the women's travel and ability to purchase all of the necessary materials. They apparently began before the Sabbath to gather what burial elements they had available (cf. Luke 23:56), and after sundown, the women were able purchase the remaining materials when the shops reopened.

**After the Sabbath, at dawn (28:1).** Matthew begins his narrative of the resurrection scenes by recounting how certain women come to the tomb "after the Sabbath."[7] Jesus repeatedly said he would be raised "on the third day" (16:21; 17:23; 20:19). Keeping in mind that the Old Testament regularly reckoned a part of a day as a whole day,[8] we understand that Jesus was in the tomb for a part of three days. Dying at approximately 3:00 P.M. on Friday, he was placed in the tomb before sundown (day one). He remained in the tomb all day Saturday (day two) and from sundown Saturday until his resurrection on Sunday morning (day three). Thus, he was raised on the third day, as he prophesied (see comments on 12:40; 26:16).

Most of the same women who courageously witnessed Jesus' gruesome crucifixion and burial plan to visit the tomb in order to assist the family in finalizing the body for burial. Jewish custom permitted both men and women to prepare corpses, with women allowed to attend to corpses of either gen-

---

6. See comments on 27:57–61; cf. Wenham, *Easter Enigma*, 60–67.

7. This is the root of the later practice of Christians gathering on Sunday morning to worship the risen Jesus (e.g., 1 Cor. 16:2); cf. Carson, "Matthew," 587; Davies and Allison, *Matthew*, 3:663; France, *Matthew*, 406; Hagner, *Matthew*, 2:868–69; Keener, *A Commentary on the Gospel of Matthew* (1999), 700; Morris, *Matthew*, 734 n. 3.

8. Cf. Gen. 42:17–18; 1 Sam. 30:12–13; 1 Kings 20:29; 2 Chron. 10:5, 12; Est. 4:16; 5:1.

der but men not allowed to attend to women's corpses.[9] The women go to the place where Jesus was laid prior to the Sabbath (see comments on 27:60–66). Mary Magdalene takes a prominent role here again, but accompanying her is "the other Mary," the mother of James and Joses (cf. 27:56). While Mark and Luke cite other women as well (see comments on 27:55–56), Matthew focuses only on Mary Magdalene and this other Mary.

**An earthquake, an angel, and a rolling stone (28:2–4).** Another earthquake (see comments on 27:51) now rocks the Jerusalem area, apparently before sunrise. While not uncommon in this region, this second earthquake surrounds the supreme supernatural event, the resurrection of Jesus. A. T. Roberston quotes Cornelius à Lapide as saying, "The earth, which trembled with sorrow at the Death of Christ as it were leaped for joy at His Resurrection."[10]

The conjunction "for" (*gar*) that begins the phrase "for an angel of the Lord came down from heaven" (28:2) suggests that the earthquake accompanies the appearance of the angel or is the means used by the angel to roll the stone away, or perhaps the angel's moving the stone causes the earthquake.[11] The miraculous conception, birth, and infancy of Jesus were superintended by an angel of the Lord (1:20–21; 2:13, 19), so it is not surprising that an angel of the Lord now superintends the resurrection, thereby framing Matthew's story of the divine message God gives to his people in the person of his Son, Jesus Christ. As in the infancy narrative, this angel is one of God's privileged messengers, perhaps Gabriel, who seems to have a special role in announcements (see Luke 1:11–20, 26–38).[12]

Entrances to burial tombs were sealed in a variety of ways; this one was sealed by a cylindrical stone that rolled up a trough, which was wedged open while a body was being attended inside the chamber. Matthew alone relates that as the angel of the Lord rolls away the stone, he sits on it. The stone that was sealed by the guards to assure that the body of Jesus would remain in the crypt now becomes the seat of triumph for the angel. The stone is rolled away, not to let the risen Jesus out but to let the women in to witness the fact of the empty tomb.

The dramatic appearance of the angel is "like lightning, and his clothes were white as snow." The brilliance of the angel of the Lord is often associated with descriptions of lightning (cf. Rev. 4:5; 16:17–18), as is Jesus' own

---

9. Keener, *A Commentary on the Gospel of Matthew* (1999), 700. See also the comments on 27:59–61.

10. Robertson, "Matthew," *Word Pictures in the New Testament*, 1:240–41.

11. See Wright, *The Resurrection of the Son of God*, 636.

12. See Hurtado, *One God, One Lord*, 71–92; Carol A. Newsom, "Gabriel," *ABD*, 2:863; Carol A. Newsom and Duane F. Watson, "Angel," *ABD*, 1:248–55.

return (24:27). The white clothing symbolizes angelic, brilliant purity. The women have come to the tomb with the fear that someone might steal the body; now they find the stone rolled away and an angel seated inside. Quickly they discover that something very different is occurring: Jesus has been raised and is alive again.

The appearance of a fiery angel often terrified people (Judg. 13:19–20; 4 *Ezra* 10:25–27). When the guards see the angel, they are so afraid that they shake and become "like dead men." "Shake" is the same verb as used for the earthquake at the crucifixion (*seio*, 27:51). Their becoming "like dead men" is the same expression used of John's reaction to his vision of the ascended Jesus in Revelation 1:17. Perhaps they faint from the shock of the angelic visitation, but Donald Hagner points to the inescapable irony: "The ones assigned to guard the dead themselves appear dead while the dead one has been made alive."[13] These guards are battle-hardened veterans, used to facing fearful situations. But nothing has prepared them for this encounter. After the angel speaks to the women, the guards hurriedly go into the city to report to the chief priests.

### The Angel Announces the Resurrection of Jesus (28:5–6)

THE ANGEL CALMS **the women (28:5).** For the first time the angel speaks to the women: "Do not be afraid, for I know that you are looking for Jesus, who was crucified." Luke includes a second angel, but Matthew and Mark focus only on the one who speaks for both.[14] The angel of the Lord told Joseph not to fear at the events surrounding Jesus' conception and birth (1:20), which is the same message needed at the events surrounding Jesus' resurrection. No prior experience could adequately prepare humans to handle emotionally the supernatural events of the incarnation and resurrection. These women have come for Jesus in whom they placed their hopes of messianic deliverance, but who is now merely the One "who was crucified."

The perfect participial phrase "who was crucified" is used substantivally in apposition to Jesus. We can render this "Jesus, the Crucified One." The perfect tense generally indicates an ongoing result as a result of the completion of past action. Here and elsewhere in the New Testament, Jesus remains the Crucified One (cf. 1 Cor. 1:23; 2:2; Gal. 3:1). Matthew has demonstrated the power of the cross, and he does not negate that. Here, however, there may also be a sense of irony in the appellation. The women are seeking Jesus as

---

13. Hagner, *Matthew*, 2:869.

14. This is the reverse of the earlier Matthean practice, such as when Matthew reports two demoniacs while Mark and Luke focus only on one (cf. Matt. 8:28; Mark 5:1–20; Luke 8:26–39).

the one who was crucified, but he is no longer in that state. He is not there as the Crucified One.

**The angel announces Jesus' resurrection (28:6).** The angel goes on to announce the reason for the empty grave: "He is not here; he has risen, just as he said. Come and see the place where he lay." While other stories will be concocted to try to cover up the truth (cf. 28:11–15), God's word of revelation through the angel tells the real story—Jesus has indeed been raised from the dead. Judaism hoped for the bodily resurrection of all people; now Jesus is the dramatic firstfruits of that expectation (cf. 1 Cor. 15:20, 23). These events are not unfolding haphazardly. The angel bears testimony to the fulfillment of Jesus' prophecies of his death and resurrection (16:21; 17:23; 20:19), which forcefully verify Jesus' words about his mission and identity.

The agent of the passive voice "was raised" (not "has risen" as in NIV) is not expressed, but this is a clear use of the "divine passive," where agency is left unexpressed since it is obvious from the context that God the Father is the One who raised Jesus from the dead.[15] He has made the final affirmation and declaration of the Son's identity and ministry by raising Jesus (cf. Rom. 1:1–3), completing a theme of approval in his baptism and transfiguration.[16]

To complete the verification of the resurrection, the angel invites the women to enter the tomb to see the place where Jesus was laid just a few short days earlier. Jesus was not just raised spiritually; he was resurrected physically; his body was no longer in the tomb.

## The Angel's Instructions to the Women Disciples (28:7)

THE ANGEL THEN instructs the women to go immediately and tell Jesus' disciples about this remarkable news and tell them that they will see him in Galilee. The expression "his disciples" probably refers to the Eleven. They will go to Galilee to spend concentrated time with their resurrected Lord, who will clarify his role in salvation history in relationship to the arrival and nature of the kingdom of God and so prepare them for their leadership role in the church (cf. Luke 24:44–47; Acts 1:3).

**Women witnesses.** One of the most important perspectives on the women here is that God uses them as witnesses not only to the central redemptive act of history, Jesus' death on the cross, but also to his resurrection. Since the women were present for Jesus' death on the cross and his burial by Joseph of Arimathea (cf. 27:55–56, 61), they can verify that he was truly dead, not just unconscious. Several of them witnessed the sealing of the tomb (27:60–61;

---

15. Cf. Wallace, *Greek Grammar*, 437–38.
16. See 3:16–17; 17:5; cf. Blomberg, *Matthew*, 427.

Mark 15:46–47; Luke 23:55), and they are the first witnesses of the empty tomb and the resurrected Jesus (Matt. 28:1–6; Mark 16:1–6; Luke 24:1–8; John 20:1–16). They are designated by both the angel and Jesus to carry their witness to the other disciples as the first to testify of the reality of the resurrection (Matt. 28:10; Mark 16:7; John 20:17).

**Galilee.** Galilee was the location of Jesus' boyhood, but even more importantly the central location of his earthly ministry (cf. 4:12). Now Galilee continues as a central place of his ascended ministry. This fulfills Jesus' own prophecy that after he was raised, he would go before them to Galilee (26:32). Jesus will appear to his disciples over the course of about a week in Jerusalem until they can fully comprehend the fact of his resurrection (cf. Luke 24:11; John 20:24–25). Then they go to Galilee, where he appears to them over the course of about thirty days (cf. Matt. 28:16; John 21; Acts 1:3).

## The Risen Jesus Appears to the Women Disciples (28:8–10)

THE WOMEN RUN **to tell the disciples (28:8).** The women heed the urgent directive from the angel to go quickly to tell the disciples of Jesus' resurrection. They came to the tomb expecting to find the death of their hopes, but now everything is turned upside down, and even their wildest dreams pale beside the astonishing message that Jesus has been raised. Their reaction is one of "fear," but yet of "great joy." The empty tomb, the appearance and message of the angel, and the urgency of informing the disciples produce fear. Moreover, the uncertainty of the future also produces fear of the unknown. These women disciples probably only have a faint awareness of all that this means, but they have followed Jesus long enough to know where it has gotten him—rejection from his own people and death. Their own lives will never be the same.

Yet there is great joy. Something deep within them is beginning to recognize that all they hoped for in Jesus is actually beginning to come true. These women know just enough of what the future now may hold, for the prediction of Jesus' resurrection has been fulfilled. Jesus is alive. Their future now includes the risen Jesus, the long-anticipated and now fully realized Messiah of Israel and Savior of the world.

**The risen Jesus appears to the women, who worship him (28:9).** As the women go, the risen Jesus meets them to confirm the reality of their hopes. He "suddenly" appears and gives an ordinary greeting, one they must have heard him utter on many occasions but which now prompts them to fall at his feet to "worship" him. The presence of the risen Jesus turns their fear into worship. By mentioning that they "clasped his feet," Matthew subtly emphasizes that this is no mere spiritual vision but a physical resurrection.

The reality of Jesus' resurrection tells the women something about him that evokes their profound adoration. The word for "worship" (*proskyneo*) in Matthew can either indicate kneeling before an esteemed religious figure (e.g., 8:2) or, when linked with the action of grasping of feet, worship. By allowing this act of worship here and in 28:17, something which neither angels (Rev. 22:8–9) nor apostles allow of themselves (Acts 10:25–26; 14:11–15), Jesus accepts the acknowledgment of his deity. Only God is to be worshiped (cf. Matt. 4:9–10; 14:33; Rev. 22:9), and these women now prostrate themselves before the Risen One, who is rightly to be accorded that honor.

**The risen Jesus commissions the women as the first witnesses of the resurrection (28:10).** The women are probably still afraid because of the extraordinary events they have just encountered, and the appearance of Jesus escalates their apprehension. Events are unfolding at a pace that outstrips their ability to maintain their grip. So Jesus calms their fear by repeating the same word of comfort from the angel ("Do not be afraid"), but he also repeats a charge from the angel: "Go and tell my brothers to go to Galilee; there they will see me." Jesus switches from "disciples" to "my brothers." This may simply be a stylistic variation to refer to the Eleven, or it may indicate the larger group of disciples, who also will witness the risen Jesus (e.g., 1 Cor. 15:6). The latter may explain the reaction of "some" who doubt (see comments on 28:17).[17]

In 12:49–50, Jesus' disciples are called his "brother, and sister, and mother," indicating not only their relationship to him but also to each other. They are now brothers and sisters of one family of faith. There are still functional differences within the family of faith, especially with reference to positions of leadership (e.g., 16:16–19; 1 Tim. 3:1–15; 5:17–20; Heb. 13:17; 1 Peter 5:1–5). But emphasis is placed on the equality of all brothers and sisters in Christ. All who believe on Jesus as the Risen Savior are his disciples, his brothers and sisters.

Many scholars consider God's choice of these women as the first witnesses of Jesus' resurrection to be one of the bedrock truths of the resurrection narratives and the historicity of the resurrection itself.[18] It is unlikely that any Jew would have created such a story as fiction. (1) There was disagreement among some of the rabbis as to the acceptability of a woman giving testimony in a court of law. Some rabbis did not accept women as valid witnesses, for they were said to be liars by nature.[19] However, this seems to be a minority opinion,

---

17. See Carson, "Matthew," 589–60; Hagner (*Matthew*, 2:874) doubts the wider association.

18. E.g., Grant R. Osborne, "Women in Jesus' Ministry," *WTJ* 51 (1989): 270.

19. E.g., Rabbi Akiba in *m. Yeb.* 16:7. See also *m. Šeb.* 4:1; Josephus, *Ant.* 4:219.

for a number of others did allow women to give testimony.[20] But because of that disagreement, it would seem unlikely that a Jew would fictionalize a woman's testimony in the case of Jesus' resurrection.

(2) The cowardly picture painted of the men hiding away in Jerusalem while the women boldly carry out their responsibilities to prepare Jesus' body for burial would certainly offend the sensibilities of Jewish readers and doubtless would not have been recorded unless it were true.

(3) The listing of the names of the women weighs against being fiction, because these women were known in early Christian fellowship and would not have easily been associated with a false account.[21]

**They will see Jesus in Galilee (28:10).** Matthew does not specify where in Galilee Jesus intends to meet with the disciples, but he later records that the Eleven go "to the mountain where Jesus had told them to go" (28:16). Insofar as they have spent so much time together, they would know the spot to rendezvous. They will soon be so taken with the reality of the resurrection that they will know that the risen Jesus is able to find them wherever they may be.

Jesus' intention in directing these women to call for his brothers to meet him in Galilee marks an important salvation-historical turning point. Since they are the first witnesses to the resurrection, this suggests that they should be regarded as equal in value to men and be restored as coworkers with men in the community of faith, a role they had been assigned from creation (Gen. 1:26–28). The mention of "my brothers" likewise reiterates that all Jesus' disciples are equal in value within the family of faith. Moreover, the return to Galilee harks back to the region of "Galilee of the Gentiles" (cf. 4:15–16), thus preparing the way for Jesus' commission to make disciples of all nations (28:16–20). The historical precedence of going to Israel (10:5–6; 15:24) has been fulfilled. Now the family of faith includes all who are Jesus' disciples, from every gender, every ethnicity, and every religion.

## The Conspiracy to Deny the Truth of Jesus' Resurrection (28:11–15)

JESUS' WOMEN FOLLOWERS immediately obey their risen Master by hurrying to tell the miraculous story of the resurrection, but Jesus' enemies scurry to put an end to the history-altering events of the empty tomb. This incident

---

20. See Witherington, *Women in the Ministry of Jesus*, 9–10, for a discussion of the mixed rabbinic attitudes toward women's ability to give witness.

21. For discussion of the broader issues, see Craig, "Did Jesus Rise From the Dead?" 151–55.

about the conspiracy to deny the truth of Jesus' resurrection continues the earlier incident in the crucifixion narrative when the chief priests and Pharisees go to Pilate to request a guard be placed at the tomb (see 27:62–66).

Matthew is the only Gospel writer who recounts these incidents, which has led some to doubt their historicity because of their obvious apologetic nature.[22] However, if no rumor had ever been circulating, it is difficult to imagine why Christians would make up such a story and put this idea into other people's minds. And if the tomb were not empty, the religious leaders would have pointed to the evidence of a body.[23] Rather, Matthew is writing for a Jewish-Christian audience who have presumably heard about the charges circulating among the Jews that Jesus' body was stolen by his disciples, while the audiences of the other evangelists may not have been aware of such charges. Therefore, rather than being a late legend created by the Christian community, in this story Matthew addresses a situation that is of uniquely pressing concern to his readers.[24] As N. T. Wright comments:

> The point is that this sort of story could only have any point at all in a community where the empty tomb was an absolute and unquestioned datum. Had there been varieties of Christianity that knew nothing of such a thing—in other words, if Bultmann was right to say that the empty tomb was itself a late apologetic fiction—the rise both of stories of body-snatching and of counter-stories to explain why such accusations were untrue is simply incredible.[25]

Therefore, behind the story as Matthew tells it seems to lie a tradition-history of Jewish and Christian polemic, a developing pattern of assertion and counter-assertion like the following:

Christian: "The Lord is risen!"
Jew:      "No, his disciples stole away his body."

---

22. E.g., Beare, *The Gospel According to Matthew*, 543; George Wesley Buchanan, *The Gospel of Matthew* (The Mellen Biblical Commentary; Lewiston, N.Y.: Mellen Biblical Press, 1996), 2:1022–23; Hare, *Matthew*, 326–27.

23. There is a far-fetched recent theory that the body had only been placed in a shallow grave, barely covered by dirt, and then scavenging dogs ate the corpse (John Dominic Crossan, *Who Killed Jesus* [San Francisco: HarperCollins, 1995], 187–88). But this does not accord with the respect with which the Jews treated all bodies and with the grudging respect that the Romans accorded Jewish bodies because of their desire to keep the peace (see Wright, *The Resurrection of the Son of God*, 638).

24. For a defense of the historicity of the events see William Lane Craig, "The Guard at the Tomb," *NTS* 30 (1984): 273–81; Wright, *The Resurrection of the Son of God*, 638–40; Keener, *A Commentary on the Gospel of Matthew* (1999), 713–15.

25. Wright, *The Resurrection of the Son of God*, 638–39.

Christian: "The guard at the tomb would have prevented any such
theft."

Jew:       "No, his disciples stole away his body while the guard slept."

Christian: "The chief priests bribed the guard to say this."[26]

**The guards report to the chief priests (28:11).** While some of the
guard apparently stay at the tomb since they have not been officially relieved
of guard duty, others go into the city to report to the chief priests.[27] With
such a serious breach of their responsibility to maintain the integrity of the
sealed tomb, the guards need to inform their superior officers. These are
Roman military personnel assigned by Pilate to the temple authorities for
security, which is why they report to them and not to Pilate (see comments
on 26:48; 27:65). Their report presumably includes what transpired up to
the point when they fainted away—the earthquake, the stone being rolled
back, the appearance of the brilliance of the angel, and the empty tomb.
They apparently did not see the risen Jesus, only the results of his resurrection. But they know that they have failed their orders to secure the burial scene, because the tomb is empty.

**The chief priests conspire with the elders (28:12).** As soon as the chief
priests hear the guards' report, they gather together with the elders for an
immediate attempt at damage control. They must account for the empty
tomb. Once again the religious leadership conspires to rid themselves of
Jesus' ministry (cf. 16:21; 21:23; 26:3–4). As in the earlier scene where the
chief priests and Pharisees laid aside their theological and political antago-
nisms to collaborate in securing the tomb (27:62), the religious leaders again
conspire together because of the threat to their religious and political power
base if the truth of Jesus' resurrection gets out. If Jesus were known to be
raised, as he predicted, it would be a validation of his messianic claims, and
the people will turn to him—which thousands do at Pentecost and thereafter
(Acts 2:41; 4:4; 6:1, 7).

Why do these Jewish religious leaders try to prevent the verification of
Jesus' messianic identity? We need to remember that they truly believe that
Jesus' ministry is satanically empowered (12:22–32), and they undoubtedly
think that they are doing the right thing in preventing what they believe to
be another satanically empowered event to deceive the people. Overall,
however, the Jewish leaders are themselves sadly deceived. Yet, the wonderful good news is that God can break through any hard heart, if one truly

---

26. Craig, "The Guard at the Tomb," 273; citing also Paul Rohrbach, *Die Berichte über die
Auferstehung Jesu Christi* (Berlin: Georg Reimer, 1898), 79.

27. This implies that the tomb was outside the city walls; for significance, see comments on 27:33, 60.

repents, as is demonstrated in the earliest days of the church when even priests became obedient disciples of Jesus (e.g., Acts 6:7).

Even as the chief priests and the elders bribed Judas to betray Jesus (26:3–4, 15), so now they bribe the guards to concoct a story. One might wonder how these deliberations became known to the Christian community until we recall that some of Jesus' own followers, such as Nicodemus and Joseph of Arimathea (see comments on 27:55–61), were privy to the highest echelons of the Jerusalem religious elite.

**The concocted story (28:13).** The specific plan that the chief priests and elders devise is to have the guards say, "His disciples came during the night and stole him away while we were asleep." This is an extremely dubious story. It is unlikely that all of the guards would have been asleep on guard duty, because the penalty for falling asleep while on duty could be execution (cf. Acts 12:19). Further, would not rolling the stone away have awakened at least some of them? And if they were asleep, how do they know the disciples have stolen the body? Besides, the disciples did not have sufficient courage to attend the crucifixion and even denied Jesus. Would they have mounted up a plot to steal his body from a well-guarded tomb?

Why then do the religious leaders concoct such a dubious story? And why do the guards agree to be implicated for negligence of duty? As noted above, the religious leaders are desperate and want to hide what really happened. The guards are likewise in a predicament. If they accept the plan of the Jewish religious leaders, they are putting themselves in jeopardy with their Roman superiors for falling asleep. But at the same time, they are already in jeopardy because they have allowed the security of the tomb to be breached. They cannot deny the tomb is empty, and who would believe them about some angelic being? Additionally, they failed to put up a fight. Either way, therefore, they face possible execution for dereliction of guard duty. Thus, with the backing of the Jewish religious leaders, they at least have a chance to escape punishment, and the religious leaders see in their proposal a crafty way of accounting for the empty tomb.

**The Jewish leaders' ruse (28:14–15).** The religious leaders must thus keep the guards out of trouble with Pilate. So they tell the guards, "If this report gets to the governor, we will satisfy him and keep you out of trouble." There has been a devious collaboration between the religious leaders and Pilate already, in which both sides have attempted to use the other for their own purposes (see comments on 27:1–2, 21–25). It would do Pilate no good to have rumors circulating that Jesus has been raised from the dead, so the Jewish leaders are confident that they can maintain a collaboration with Pilate to hide the truth of the empty tomb and at the same time cast the disciples in a negative light for trying to perpetuate a deception of Jesus' resurrection.

Military personnel are trained to do as ordered without asking questions of their superiors. These soldiers know well enough the truth of the empty tomb, but they do not know the significance of the threat to the religious establishment or the religious significance of the empty tomb. If both Jewish and Roman superiors are agreed, there is no threat to the guards from either of them, if they simply take the bribe and keep quiet. So they accept it and carry out the Jewish leaders' ruse.

Matthew writes upwards of thirty years after these events, and yet he states, "And this story has been widely circulated among the Jews to this very day." This Matthean aside indicates an active attempt by the Jewish leaders to counteract the increasingly widespread declaration that Jesus was raised from the dead in vindication of his claim to be Messiah. Nearly a century later the rumor was still being spread among the Jews, as is evident in the writings of Justin Martyr.[28] The truth is often harder for a person to believe than a lie, and many then, and even now, fall for this conspiracy to avoid the radical truth of Jesus' resurrection.

## Jesus' Great Commission (28:16–20)

THERE ARE VARIATIONS on the theme of commissioning in the other Gospels and Acts (cf. Luke 24:44–49; John 21:15–23; Acts 1:8), but this concluding paragraph is unique to Matthew's Gospel and bears his unique emphases. Themes that have characterized this gospel are here culminated and united:[29]

1. Jesus' unique authority as the divine Son of God demands the worship of his followers (e.g., chs. 1–2; 3:17; 4:1–11; 14:33).
2. Jesus' form of discipleship transcends ethnic, gender, and religious boundaries to form a new community of faith called the church (e.g., 12:46–50; 16:18–19;18:17–18).
3. Jesus' final move, from particularism in fulfilling the covenantal promises to Israel, to universal salvation offered to all the nations, is proclaimed in preaching of the gospel of the kingdom of God (e.g., 1:1; 10:5–6; 15:21–28).
4. Jesus' call to inside-out righteousness is experienced through obedience to his teachings as the fulfillment of God's will for his people (e.g., 5:20–48; 15:1–20).
5. Jesus' promises of his eternal presence with his disciples is fulfilled because he is Immanuel, "God with us" (e.g., 1:23).

---

28. See his *Dialogue with Trypho* 108.2.

29. Cf. Blomberg, *Matthew*, 429; Hagner, *Matthew*, 2:881–83; Keener, *A Commentary on the Gospel of Matthew* (1999), 715–21.

---

The brevity of the final narrative in comparison to the length of the rest of the Gospel accentuates, by understatement, the radical importance of these events. It starkly highlights the miraculous resurrection of Jesus as the cause of the empty tomb, and then just as starkly emphasizes the universal authority of the risen Jesus as the One who begins the alteration of human history with the universal invitation to personal discipleship and transformation through the preaching of the gospel of the kingdom of God. The five short verses that comprise this Great Commission passage are among the most important to establish the ongoing agenda of the church throughout the ages. That sentiment is caught by the early church father Chrysostom:

> Observe the excellence of those who were sent out into the whole world. Others who were called found ways of excusing themselves. But these did not beg off.... With Jesus' resurrection his own proper glory is again restored, following his humiliation. Jesus reminded his disciples of the consummation of all things, so that they would not look at the present dangers only but also at the good things to come that last forever. He promised to be not only with these disciples but also with all who would subsequently believe after them.... So let us not fear and shudder. Let us repent while there is opportunity. Let us arise out of our sins. We can by grace, if we are willing.[30]

This is also our clarion call to hear and obey Jesus' final words in this magnificent Gospel according to Matthew.

**The risen Jesus appears to his disciples in Galilee (28:16–17).** Matthew cites only Jesus' resurrection appearances to the women on resurrection morning in Jerusalem (28:9–10) and then his appearance in Galilee to (at least) the eleven disciples. Approximately ten days after the resurrection, the eleven disciples arrive in Galilee to meet with Jesus as he and the angel instructed them (28:7, 10). Thus "Galilee of the Gentiles," an expression laden implicitly with importance at the beginning of Matthew's narrative of Jesus' ministry (4:15–16), comes to explicit fulfillment as the gospel will go to all the nations (28:19).[31]

For the first time those who had been designated as the Twelve (cf. 10:1–2) are called "the eleven disciples." The designation "eleven" has poignant significance. Judas has betrayed Jesus and hanged himself (27:3–5), so he is excluded. But although Peter denied his Lord and hid away at the moment of

---

30. Chrysostom, "The Gospel of Matthew, Homily 90.2," cited in Simonetti, *Matthew 14–28,* 1b:314.

31. Cf. Paul Hertig, *Matthew's Narrative Use of Galilee in the Multicultural and Missiological Journeys of Jesus* (Mellen Biblical Press Series 46; Lewiston: Edwin Mellen, 1998), 82–127.

testing, he is still numbered among the disciples (Luke 24:9–12, 33–34) and is restored to a position of leadership among them (cf. Acts 1:15–26; 2:14–39).

As the eleven disciples proceed to Galilee, the region where they spent the most time with Jesus, they go to the mountain where Jesus told them to go. Mount Tabor is the traditional site associated with this appearance, but for the same reasons as it was most likely not the site of the Transfiguration (cf. 17:1–8), it is most likely not the scene of this resurrection appearance. Rather, Jesus arranges to meet with the disciples at some spot known to them in the many hills surrounding the Sea of Galilee, which has never been specifically identified.

For the first time in Matthew's narrative, the disciples encounter the risen Jesus, and appropriately their response is to "worship" him. All along Jesus has been leading them to understand his true identity as the Son of God, a fact in his earthly ministry that was difficult for them to comprehend. But now that he has been raised, which is the declaration that he is indeed God's Son, and they have received at least two to three appearances from the risen Jesus prior to this in Jerusalem, they are prepared to give him the homage that is due him.

But then Matthew strikes a jarring, although remarkably believable, note when he comments further that "some [*hoi de*] doubted."[32] Since Matthew mentions only the eleven disciples, is he saying that some of them doubted? How many are "some"? This appears inconsistent with the previous phrase, where the eleven worship Jesus. Commentators are divided on how best to understand what Matthew intends here.

(1) Many scholars contend that Matthew means that some of the Eleven doubt (taking *hoi de* in a partitive sense).[33] The cause for their doubt may be that Jesus is and is not the same as prior to the resurrection. While some among the Eleven have a fuller understanding, others are still puzzled, perhaps even fearful, of all of these events. Doubt takes over, hindering them from giving over their full confidence to the One whom they understand Jesus to be.

(2) Other commentators take the *hoi de* as a pronoun meaning "they,"[34] which implies that all of the Eleven doubt.[35] In this view, the verb *distazo*

---

32. Wright refers to this statement as having "the strongest mark of authenticity in this paragraph" (*The Resurrection of the Son of God*, 643). This ambiguous comment would not have occurred to someone telling the story as a pure fiction.

33. Cf. Wright, *The Resurrection of the Son of God*, 644; Davies and Allison, *Matthew*, 3:681–82; P. W. van der Horst, "Once More: The Translation of οἱ δέ in Matthew 28.17," *JSNT* 27 (1986): 105–9; McNeile, *St. Matthew*, 434.

34. For discussion of the article as a personal pronoun, see Wallace, *Greek Grammar*, 211–13.

35. Hagner, *Matthew*, 2:884, points to the following examples, although he grants some of them are ambiguous: 2:5; 4:20, 22; 14:17, 33; 15:34; 16:7, 14; 20:5, 31; 21:25; 22:19; 26:15; 26:67; 27:4, 21, 23; 28:15.

---

should not be rendered as "doubted" in the sense of unbelief or disbelief, for which other terms are used,[36] but rather more like "were uncertain." *Distazo* can indicate uncertainty or hesitancy about a particular course of action.[37] In other words, with all that has transpired, the disciples are not sure what to do. Too much has happened too fast for them to understand fully what is going on.[38]

Either of these views accords with the disciples' actions at Jesus' transfiguration (17:5–8), where at the voice of the Father the disciples had a mixture of worship and fear until Jesus appeared to them with a touch and word of admonition and commission.

(3) But other scholars suggest that *hoi de* points to others not among the eleven disciples. They argue that if "worship" (*proskyneo*) is intended in its most complete sense, then its separation from "some" indicates two separate groups. Carson notes that "doubt about who Jesus is or about the reality of his resurrection does not seem appropriate for true worship."[39] The most likely identity of these others is the unexpected use of "brothers" in 28:10, distinct from "disciples" in 28:7. When Jesus instructed the women disciples to tell his "brothers" to go to Galilee, where they will see him, this likely indicates the wider group of disciples beyond the Eleven. The Eleven will be privileged to see Jesus in Jerusalem, but the broader band of disciples who have not yet encountered the risen Jesus will see him at the gathering in Galilee.

This latter view seems more in line with the broader resurrection appearances of Jesus. The eleven disciples, who have received at least two or three appearances from the risen Jesus in Jerusalem prior to this appearance (Luke 24:36–49; John 20:19–28), are prepared to worship him. However, those disciples in Judea and Galilee who have not yet seen the risen Jesus (i.e., "brothers" in Matt. 28:10) doubt, much like Thomas (John 20:24–29), until Jesus appeared to them bodily. It is difficult to grasp how those who question Jesus here could be those very eleven who have witnessed the dramatic removal of Thomas's doubt.[40]

This reminiscence stresses the historicity of Jesus' resurrection, which is not met by gullible enthusiasm but by logical hesitancy until people are convinced by the facts. Were not all the dead to be raised together? What does it mean that Jesus Messiah alone is raised? These are the kinds of questions that many Jews have until they personally see Jesus raised bodily. If this last view

---

36. E.g., 17:17 *apistos* ("unbelievers") or Luke 24:38 *dialogismoi* ("doubts").
37. BDAG, 252.
38. Hagner, *Matthew*, 2:884.
39. Carson, "Matthew," 593.
40. See also Morris, *Matthew*, 745.

is correct, this passage may well be an allusion to the group of more than five hundred persons to whom Jesus appeared (see 1 Cor. 15:6). This would further correspond with Jesus' directive to the disciples to meet him in the mountainous area (28:16), a place where he had often met with large groups of people (e.g., 5:1; 15:29–30). Once the doubt of these people is removed by seeing Jesus, they too will fall down in humble worship of the risen Son of God.

**The risen Jesus gives his Great Commission to the disciples (28:18–20).** As Matthew comes to the final three verses of his Gospel, he encapsulates the primary thrust of the whole book. Otto Michel perhaps overstates the significance of these verses, but he catches their importance to Matthew's purpose for writing his Gospel:

> It is sufficient to say that the whole Gospel was written under this theological premise of Matt 28:18–20 (cf. 28:19 with 10:5ff.; 15:24; v. 20 with 1:23; also the return to baptism, cf. 3:1). In a way the conclusion goes back to the start and teaches us to understand the whole Gospel, the story of Jesus, "from behind". *Matt 28:18–20 is the key to the understanding of the whole book* [his emphasis].[41]

Hagner likewise states that these verses are "the hallmark of the gospel of Matthew. For these words, perhaps more than any others, distill the outlook and various emphases of the gospel."[42] In this famous "Great Commission," Jesus declares that his disciples are to make more of what he has made of them. In that sense, the Commission encapsulates Jesus' purpose for coming to earth, and its placement at the conclusion of this Gospel indicates Matthew's overall purpose for writing.[43] Jesus has come to inaugurate the kingdom of God on earth by bringing men and women into a saving relationship with himself, which heretofore is called "discipleship to Jesus."

*All authority in heaven and on earth*. In the mixed state of worship, hesitation, bewilderment, and astonishment found among the broader group of disciples, Jesus comes close to them and addresses them to bring strength and calm. He was and is and always will be their Master, whose presence and words are what bring meaning and guidance to their daily lives. His first words are an essential foundation for the disciples' personal security, but also for the commission to follow. The all-inclusiveness of the Great Commission for the present age is indicated by the repetition of the adjective *pas* ("all"): "all authority,"

---

41. Otto Michel, "The Conclusion of Matthew's Gospel: A Contribution to the History of the Easter Message," *The Interpretation of Matthew*, ed. Graham N. Stanton, 2d ed. (Edinburgh: T. & T. Clark, 1995), 45.

42. Hagner, *Matthew*, 2:881.

43. For discussion, see Doyle, "Matthew's Intention As Discerned by His Structure," 34–54; David R. Bauer, *The Structure of Matthew's Gospel* (Sheffield: Almond Press, 1988).

---

"all nations," "all things" (NIV "everything"), "all the days" (NIV "always"). Several points flow from Jesus' declaration of his all-inclusive authority.

(1) Jesus now possesses all authority. In his earthly ministry Jesus declared his authority as the Son of Man to forgive sin (9:6) and to reveal the Father (11:27). Now as the risen Messiah he clearly alludes to his fulfillment of Daniel's prophecy of the Son of Man who has been given all authority, glory, and power, who is rightly worshiped by all nations, and whose dominion and kingdom last forever (Dan. 7:13–14). Jesus can make this claim only if he is fully God, because the entire universe is contained in the authority delegated to him.[44] During his earthly ministry he had absolute authority, but his exercise of it was restricted to his incarnate consciousness. In his risen state he exercises his absolute supremacy throughout all heaven and earth.

(2) This authority, as emphasized by the (divine) passive voice, "has been given" to him by the Father. The Son of God is the mediatorial King through whom all of God's authority is mediated. The resurrected Jesus appears before the disciples to initiate a new order of existence that anticipates his future glorious exaltation and enthronement at God's right hand (Luke 24:51; Acts 1:9; Phil. 2:9–11).

(3) As the One with all authority, Jesus rules the plan of establishing God's kingdom throughout the earth. The particularism of the gospel message restricted to Israel during his earthly mission is fulfilled and lifted, as he now authoritatively directs his disciples to a universal mission.[45] A. T. Robertson states:

> It is the sublimist of all spectacles to see the Risen Christ without money or army or state charging this band of five hundred men and women with world conquest and bringing them to believe it possible and to undertake it with serious passion and power. Pentecost is still to come, but dynamic faith rules on this mountain in Galilee.[46]

*The structure of the Great Commission.* The Great Commission contains one primary, central command, the imperative "make disciples," with three subordinate participles, "go," baptizing," and "teaching." The imperative explains the central thrust of the commission while the participles describe aspects of the process. These subordinate participles take on imperatival force because of the imperative main verb and so characterize the ongoing mandatory process of discipleship to Jesus.[47]

---

44. Cf. Blomberg, *Matthew*, 431.

45. Cf. Carson, "Matthew," 595; Hagner, *Matthew*, 2:886.

46. Robertson, "Matthew," 244–45.

47. For the way in which participles attendant to an imperative accrue imperatival force, see Wallace, *Greek Grammar*, 640–45; also Carson, "Matthew," 597; Hagner, *Matthew*, 2:886–87.

Jesus' Great Commission implies more than securing salvation as his disciple. Implied in the imperative "make disciples" is both the call to and the process of becoming a disciple.[48] Jesus spent a great deal of time guiding and instructing the disciples in their growth. He now sends them out to do the same. The process will not be exactly the same as what Jesus did, for the circumstances after Pentecost change the process. However, the process will be similar in many ways. As a person responds to the invitation to come out of the nations to start life as a disciple, she or he begins the life of discipleship through baptism and obedience to Jesus' teaching.[49]

*Make disciples.* Even as the Son of Man exercises dominion over all nations in Daniel's prophecy (Dan. 7:13–14), so Jesus demonstrates his messianic authority to call people of all the nations to be his disciples. Jesus committed his earthly ministry to "making disciples" within Israel (cf. John 4:1), and he commissions his disciples to "make disciples" among the nations.

This is the third time in Matthew's Gospel that he uses the verb *matheteuo* ("to make disciples"; cf. 13:52; 27:57). In the first two uses, *matheteuo* has a passive flavor: "has become a disciple, has been made a disciple." Here the verb takes on a distinctively transitive sense, "make a disciple," in which the focus is on calling individuals to absolute commitment to the person of Jesus as one's sole Master and Lord.[50] This command finds remarkable verbal fulfillment in the fourth and final occurrence of this verb in the New Testament as the early Christians proclaim the message of Jesus and "make disciples" (Acts 14:21; NIV "won ... disciples"). The injunction of the Great Commission is given both to the Eleven and to the broader circle of disciples.

To become a disciple was a common phenomenon in the ancient world, but throughout his ministry Jesus developed a unique form of discipleship for those who followed him. He broke through a variety of barriers—gender, ethnic, religious, social, economic, and so on—by calling all peoples into a personal discipleship relationship with himself. Being a disciple of Jesus was primarily not an academic endeavor like the Pharisees (e.g., 22:16), nor even commitment to a great prophet like John the Baptist (e.g., 9:14). A disciple of Jesus comes to him and him alone for eternal life and will always be only a disciple of Jesus (cf. 19:16, 25–30; 23:8–12; John 6:66–71). The expression is virtually synonymous with the title "Christian."

---

48. Osborne, *The Resurrection Narratives*, 91; cf. the note in Moisés Silva, "New Lexical Semitisms?" *ZNTW* 69 (1978): 256 n. 9.

49. For a discussion of the similarities to, yet distinct differences of, discipleship after Pentecost, see Wilkins, *Following the Master*, chs. 13–16.

50. See comments on 13:52 and 27:57; also Davies and Allison, *Matthew*, 3:684; Hagner, *Matthew*, 1:401–2; Morris, *Matthew*, 746; Przybylski, *Righteousness in Matthew*, 109–10; Wilkins, *Discipleship in the Ancient World and Matthew's Gospel*, 160–63.

*All the nations.* The object of making disciples is "all the nations." People of every nation are to receive the opportunity to become Jesus' disciples. When we read the Commission here in the light of Luke's Gospel, that "repentance and forgiveness of sins ... be preached in his name to all nations, beginning at Jerusalem" (Luke 24:47), we understand that Jesus' ministry in Israel was the beginning point of a universal offer of salvation to all the peoples of the earth.[51]

Some suggest that "all the nations" means only "Gentiles," not "Jews," since Matthew normally refers to Gentiles by this title.[52] Many often appeal to this view because of Jesus' harsh statements about the rejection of the Jewish nation (e.g., 21:43). Most scholars, however, recognize that Jesus' overall intention is to include Jews in his commission, and Matthew intends his readers to understand their inclusion.[53] The Jewish leaders of Jesus' day experienced punishment for their failed leadership and for their culpable role in conspiring to bring Jesus to the Romans for execution (see comments on 27:25). However, God continues to love the whole world, for whom Christ died, which includes Jews (cf. John 3:16; Rom. 5:8).

The rest of the New Testament clearly presents the evangelism of Jews as part of missionary strategy (e.g., Acts 2:22; 13:38–39; Rom. 1:16; Eph. 2:11–16). Although Israel has been rejected for the present time as the instrument and witness of the outworking of the kingdom of God, individual Jews are still invited to participate in the salvation brought by Jesus.[54] Matthew uses the full expression "all nations" in settings that most naturally include all peoples, including Jews (cf. 24:9, 14; 25:32). Most important, Matthew here returns to the universal theme of 1:1, where the blessings promised to Abraham, and through him to all people on earth (Gen. 12:3), are now being fulfilled in Jesus the Messiah. Matthew's theme of universal salvation through Jesus (e.g., 1:1; 2:1–12; 4:15–16; 8:5–13; 10:18; 13:38; 24:14) thus climaxes this Gospel in the command to "make disciples of all the nations."[55]*Therefore*

---

51. See Wilkins, *Following the Master*, 188–89.

52. E.g., Stephen Hre Kio, "Understanding and Translating 'Nations' in Mt 28:19," *BT* 41 (1990), 230–39; Douglas R. A. Hare, *The Theme of Jewish Persecution of Christians in the Gospel According to St. Matthew* (Cambridge: Cambridge Univ. Press, 1967).

53. E.g., see Davies and Allison, *Matthew,* 3:684; Keener, *A Commentary on the Gospel of Matthew* (1999), 719–20; Charles H. H. Scobie, "Israel and the Nations: An Essay in Biblical Theology," *TynBul* 43 (1992): 283–305; esp. 297–98.

54. Likewise, this does not abolish the promises made to Israel nationally. We contended earlier that there remains a future role for Israel (cf. Matt. 21:42–43, see comments; Rom. 11:25–33).

55. Alfred Plummer, *An Exegetical Commentary on the Gospel According to St. Matthew* (Grand Rapids: Baker, 1982), 430.

*go.* The first participle that modifies the command to make disciples is "go." Because Jesus now exercises universal authority, "therefore" his disciples must go out and engage in the universal mission to make disciples of all nations. And because of that authority, they have the utmost confidence that he is sovereignly in control of all universal forces.

The disciples had been focused on assisting Jesus in establishing the kingdom on earth, but now that he is crucified and raised, they do not know what they should be doing. According to Acts 1:6, they are still expecting Jesus to restore the kingdom to Israel, even after the resurrection. So Jesus now gives them their marching orders for the present age. The entire earth is to be their mission field "as a testimony to all nations, and then the end will come" (24:14).

To obey Jesus' commission may require some to leave homeland and go to other parts of the world, but the imperatival nature of the entire commission requires all believers to be involved in it. The completion of the commission is not simply evangelism. Rather, it means calling unbelievers to be converted and embark on the process of being transformed into the image of Jesus in lifelong discipleship.[56]

*Baptizing them in the name of the Father and of the Son and of the Holy Spirit.* Even as one is called from among the nations to begin life as a disciple, one must in turn follow the Lord through baptism and through obedience to Jesus' teaching. As a person responds to the invitation to believe in Jesus, she or he is regenerated to start life as a disciple. The participle "baptizing" describes the activity by which a new disciple identifies with Jesus and his community, and the participle "teaching" introduces the activities by which the new disciple grows in discipleship.[57]

Purity washings were common among the various sects in Israel, either for entrance to the temple or for daily rituals. Proselyte baptism increasingly indicated conversion from paganism to Judaism. At first Jesus and John the Baptist carried out baptism side by side, marking the arrival of the kingdom of God (cf. John 3:22–4:3). But with the initiation of the new covenant through Jesus' death and resurrection and the arrival of the Spirit, Jesus' form of baptism is unique. It is the symbol of conversion, indicating a union and new identity with Jesus Messiah who has died and been raised to new life (cf. Rom. 6:1–4).

In the act of baptism, the new disciple identifies with Jesus and his community of faith and gives public declaration that she or he has become a life-

---

56. E.g., Blomberg, *Matthew*, 431; Keener, *A Commentary on the Gospel of Matthew* (1999), 718–19.

57. Richard DeRidder, *Discipling the Nations* (Grand Rapids: Baker, 1975), 190. For discussion of the meaning of baptism as "adherence," see William B. Badke, "Was Jesus a Disciple of John?" *EvQ* 62 (1990): 195–204.

long adherent to Jesus. The earliest converts on Pentecost in Jerusalem would quite likely have undertaken baptism in the public *mikveh* baths surrounding the temple, a powerful, public testimony of their newfound commitment to Jesus Messiah (cf. Acts 2:41).[58]

The uniqueness of Jesus' form of baptism is emphasized in that new disciples are to be baptized "in the name of the Father and of the Son and of the Holy Spirit" (28:19). The use of "name" is common in Scripture for God's power and authority.[59] Jews were not baptized in the name of a person. Baptism in the "name" (note the singular) of the Father, Son, and Holy Spirit associates the three as personal distinctions, an early indication of the Trinitarian Godhead and an overt proclamation of Jesus' deity.

This is the clearest Trinitarian language in the Gospels and is often accused of being a later theological "formula" inserted by Matthew, because it is purported to be too theologically developed to have been used by Jesus at this stage. However, this is not the earliest such Trinitarian expression in the New Testament (cf. Gal. 4:4–7; 1 Cor. 12:4–6; 2 Cor. 13:14), and even in Jesus' earlier ministry and teaching we catch beginning hints of the plurality of the nature of the Godhead (e.g., Matt. 3:17; 11:27; 12:28).

We have noted regularly how difficult it was for Jesus' followers to move from strict theological monotheism to recognize the plurality of the Godhead in the person of Jesus in relation to his heavenly Father. Now in his risen state, however, the cognitive dissonance is so profound that the shock has enabled a more complete paradigm shift to occur. This alone explains the ability of the strictly monotheistic Pharisee Paul, after being confronted by the risen Lord Jesus, to grasp the plurality in the nature of the Godhead. As God's Messiah, now revealed to be divine, Jesus wields all authority given him by the Father, and the mode by which that authority is exercised is through the Spirit.

Jesus' commission regarding baptism is also congruent with what we find in the rest of the New Testament.[60] In the book of Acts baptism is normally "in" the name of Jesus (e.g., Acts 2:38; 8:16; 10:48; 19:3–5) and in Paul's writings "in" Christ (e.g., Rom. 6:3; Gal. 3:27).[61] The risen Jesus is at the heart of the Christian life and the tangible picture of the living God. He is not so much giving a formula as he is emphasizing a theological truth symbolized with baptism. Baptism is a ceremony of entry into the family of God,

---

58. Cf. Clinton E. Arnold, "Acts," *ZIIBBC*, 2:236.

59. E.g., *onoma* in LXX (Ex. 3:13–15; Prov. 18:10; cf. *Jub.* 36:7).

60. Cf. Davies and Allison, *Matthew*, 3:685. For the use of *eis* with *onoma* in the sense of "in" employed here, not meaning *into*, see 18:20; cf. 10:41–42.

61. Various prepositions are used, such as *epi*, *eis*, and *en*, but without significant differences in nuance.

the family of the new covenant, so what one does in the name of Jesus one does in the name of the Father, Son, and Holy Spirit. Paul explicitly links baptism to what the living God has accomplished in Jesus' resurrection.[62] Baptism marks the profound truth that with the new covenant, all new disciples are brought into a new existence that is fundamentally determined by God.

*Teaching them to obey everything I have commanded you.* The final participial phrase in Jesus' Great Commission, "teaching," indicates the process by which disciples of Jesus are continually transformed through discipleship and the discipling process. *Discipleship* is the process by which a disciple (Christian) is transformed, while *discipling* is the involvement of one disciple helping another to grow in his or her discipleship.

The basic elements of this final participial phrase are packed with significance. (1) The pronoun "them" indicates that everyone who has become a disciple of Jesus is to be involved in the process of discipleship. Access to education by an esteemed rabbi was normally reserved for privileged men in rabbinic Judaism. Some rabbis denied young girls even the basics of Torah instruction. But Jesus once again breaks down all barriers to indicate that all of his disciples—women and men, Gentile and Jew, poor or rich—must be taught to obey everything he has commanded. This means that everyone who has heard the gospel message and has responded by believing on Jesus for eternal life is a disciple/Christian/believer, all of which are virtually synonymous terms (cf. Acts 2:44; 4:32; 5:14; 6:1, 7; 11:26; 26:28).

Today many incorrectly use the title "disciple" to refer to a person who is more committed than other Christians or to those involved in special "discipleship programs." But we can see from Jesus' commission that all Christians are disciples. It is just that some are obedient disciples, while others are not. That leads us to the next elements of this participial phrase.

(2) The activity of discipleship is involved with "teaching." New disciples are to be taught the rudimentary elements of the Christian life, while more advanced teaching is given to mature disciples as they advance in the Christian life. But the emphasis is not simply on acquiring knowledge; the distinguishing feature is always that disciples are to obey or conform their lives to the teaching. Obedience was the hallmark of Jesus' disciples (see 12:49–50).[63]

(3) All disciples, new and mature, are to be taught to "obey everything that I [Jesus] have commanded [*entellomai*]," so that they increasingly become like

---

62. Cf. Wright, *The Resurrection of the Son of God*, 644–45.

63. This term is also important as a theme of discipleship in John's Gospel (e.g., John 14:15, 23–24). See Melvyn R. Hillmer, "They Believed in Him: The Johannine Tradition," in *Patterns of Discipleship in the New Testament*, ed. R. N. Longnecker (Grand Rapids: Eerdmans, 1996), 92.

him (cf. 10:24–25; Rom. 8:29; 2 Cor. 3:18). Does *entellomai* imply only specific "commands" Jesus gave (as in the Old Testament understanding of "giving the law"), or does it include Jesus' entire verbal ministry? This verb in Matthew and in the New Testament generally can refer to a general commission (Matt. 4:6; Mark 11:6; 13:34; Heb. 11:22), the commands of God from the Old Testament (Matt. 4:6 with Luke 4:10; Heb. 9:20), and the command of Moses (Matt. 19:7; Mark 10:3; John 8:5). Its most distinctive use is found in the present context, where it has a more all-inclusive sense. Jesus is not pointing to particular commands but rather to the full explication in his life and ministry for disciples.[64] All that Jesus communicated by word of mouth is included in his commands, whether they are teachings, proverbs, blessings, parables or prophecies.

But we should go even further to suggest that all of Jesus' *life* is included in *entellomai*. This verb unifies Jesus' words and deeds and therefore recalls the entire Gospel of Matthew.[65] Jesus' life, whether in word or in deed, fulfills God's will in the Old Testament, and as his disciples teach other disciples to obey his commands, their lives will reflect the transforming will of God in their own every word and deed.[66]

The verb *entellomai* and the noun *entole* have a summarizing effect in other contexts as well, especially when love is considered a summarizing of God's will, of the Law and the Prophets (Matt. 22:34–40). Love summarizes all that Jesus said and did (cf. John 13:34–35). Thus, in the expression "teaching them to obey all I have commanded you," the content of "commanded" is the complete expression of all that Jesus said and did. For the purposes of the context of the Great Commission, we can say that the content is Matthew's Gospel itself. All disciples, new and mature, are to look at Jesus' authoritative life and words in this Gospel—indeed, throughout Scripture— and they must be taught to obey it, follow it, and practice it in their own lives.

In the five discourses and the alternating narratives of Jesus' life that are recorded in his Gospel, Matthew has prepared a convenient compendium of

---

64. Gottlob Schrenk, "ἐντέλλομαι, ἐντολή," *TDNT*, 2:545: "In this context the word ἐντέλλεσθαι simply expresses the unconditional obligation to obedience which, grounded christologically, is the obedience of faith."

65. Davies and Allison, *Matthew*, 3:686: "But more than verbal revelation is involved, for such revelation cannot be separated from Jesus' life, which is itself a command. ἐνετειλάμην accordingly unifies word and deed and so recalls the entire book: everything is in view. The earthly ministry as a whole is an imperative."

66. Carson, "Matthew," 599: "Jesus' words, like the words of Scripture, are more enduring than heaven and earth (24:35); and the peculiar expression "everything I have commanded you" is . . . reminiscent of the authority of Yahweh (Exod 29:35; Deut 1:3, 41; 7:11; 12:11, 14)."

the material that Jesus initially gave his first disciples. Matthew's Gospel became a handbook on discipleship in the early church for next generations of disciples of Jesus. H. N. Ridderbos says succinctly, "The apostles had to teach people to obey all that Jesus commanded them during His ministry on earth. Their listeners had to be brought under His commandments so that they could show by their lives that they really belong to Him. That is the final purpose of the preaching of the gospel."[67] What Jesus did in making disciples of his first followers, succeeding generations of the church will do in the making of new disciples of Jesus.

In other words, in the Great Commission it would be inappropriate for Jesus to state, "teaching them to obey everything I *taught* you." He did more than teach. He gave a new authoritative basis for life as a disciple in this age. We are to "obey all Jesus *commanded* or *authoritatively revealed as binding upon our lives as God's will for us,*" especially as Matthew has structured it in the Gospel generally, and in the five discourses specifically.

*And surely I am with you always, to the very end of the age.* Jesus' entrance to history is encapsulated in the name Immanuel, "God with us" (1:23), and his abiding presence with his disciples is evident in his concluding assurance, "I am with you always." A true Israelite would proclaim only God to be eternal and omnipresent, so here Matthew records a concluding claim by Jesus to his deity. Thus, Jesus concludes the commission with the crucial element of discipleship: the presence of the Master. Both those who obey the commission and those who respond are comforted by the awareness that the risen Jesus will continue to fashion all his disciples.

- Jesus is present as his disciples go throughout the nations with the gospel of the kingdom of God, inviting all to become his disciples.
- Jesus is present as new disciples are baptized and are taught to obey all that he has commanded.
- Jesus is present as maturing disciples go through all the stages of their lives.
- Jesus is present as the church sojourns through this age awaiting his return.
- Jesus is always present for his disciples to follow as their Master.

We worship and follow a risen Master, who is with us constantly. All he commanded in word and deed as necessary for our growth as his disciples is included in the Scriptures, but his real presence comforts our individual needs and sustains us through all of our days, whether in our weakness, sorrow,

---

67. H. N. Ridderbos, *Matthew*, trans. Ray Togtman (Bible Student's Commentary's; Grand Rapids: Zondervan, 1987), 555–56.

joy, power, or pain. To the "very end of the age" or until the completion of God's plans for this age, Jesus promises to be the sustaining presence that assures us that history is not out of control, that the kingdom of God has indeed been inaugurated, that he is a very present help in times of trouble, and that the work he accomplished on the cross is continually available through his risen and ascended ministry.

This wonderful promise of Jesus' continual presence invites us as readers into the story. This should not evoke fear or a guilty conscience; rather, it should spur all his disciples on to proclaim the good news of the presence of the kingdom of God in our lives. We are the ongoing chapter of this story, walking receptacles of the presence of the risen Jesus and living demonstrations of the power of the kingdom of God.[68] May we be faithful and obedient disciples of Jesus as we walk in the closest intimacy with him and proclaim this good news that he is with us to the very end of the age.

FOR THREE LONG hours a great darkness came over the land as Jesus hung upon the cross (27:45). From the perspective of Jesus' disciples who had hidden away, the darkness must have seemed like a cruel joke. Death seemed to have won. Matthew had narrated the beginning of Jesus' ministry in Galilee with a bright promise (4:15–17):

> Land of Zebulun and land of Naphtali,
> > the way to the sea, along the Jordan,
> > Galilee of the Gentiles—
> the people living in darkness
> > have seen a great light;
> > on those living in the land of the shadow of death
> > a light has dawned.

But as Jesus hung upon the cross for those three long hours, the bright light went out. The shadow of death claimed the land—not just in Galilee of the Gentiles, but throughout the earth. The bright hope of salvation that Jesus announced seemed to be extinguished.

But the light wasn't extinguished. At the dawn of the new week, the bright light of the sun, the brilliant light of the angel, and the glorious light of the risen Savior greeted the world. And the blessed women disciples can only draw near, hold tight to Jesus' feet, and worship him. That is all of the answer they need. The risen Jesus dispels all darkness, all fear of death, all of the

---

68. Green, *Matthew*, 322–23.

wearisome burden of sin, pain, and sorrow. Because he lives, they can face tomorrow.

For twenty chapters Matthew recounted the most wonderful life ever conceived and lived on the face of this earthly planet—thirty-some wonderful years narrated in twenty mind-boggling chapters. Then Matthew slows the pace for seven long chapters to walk with Jesus, almost ponderously, through all of the events of Passion Week, including his crucifixion and burial. Then in one brief chapter, the second shortest in his Gospel, Matthew recounts simply, but elegantly, the resurrection of Jesus Messiah. Twenty short verses declare the really good news that humanity needs to hear: Jesus is alive, it is not a hoax, and he is triumphing over history.

The light of the gospel of the kingdom of heaven was not extinguished with Jesus' death. His resurrection has overcome the darkness, and the light of his life lived through his disciples is going throughout the world. This is the message Matthew presents in his final chapter. We might wish more details of the final days that the risen Jesus spends with his disciples before his ascension, but Matthew gives us what we need to hear—death is vanquished. Richard Longenecker states, "Death is a stark and haunting reality that is very much a part of the personal story of us all."[69] That was a dark reality that stung the hopes of Jesus' followers and seemed to overcome them. But now Matthew dispels the darkness and reignites hope with the only truth that is needed: "Do not be afraid, for I know that you are looking for Jesus, who was crucified. He is not here; he has risen, just as he said" (28:5–6).

It is vital to grasp the truth of the resurrection as well as Matthew's perspective in giving it to us. The work of the cross culminates Jesus' atoning purpose for his incarnate life and ministry on this earth. That is why Matthew slowed the pace of his narrative. However, the fast-paced resurrection story is the simple but profound confirmation that Jesus' death on the cross succeeded in carrying out his life's work. Once we grasp that truth, we recognize that Matthew need say no more. Indeed, the rest of the New Testament and our lives are the rest of the story. Because Jesus lives, *we* can face tomorrow. As victorious as was Jesus' own resurrection, we too have been raised with him in newness of life. The apostle Paul understood this truth deeply:

> Don't you know that all of us who were baptized into Christ Jesus were baptized into his death? We were therefore buried with him through baptism into death in order that, just as Christ was raised from the dead through the glory of the Father, we too may live a new life. (Rom. 6:3–4)

---

69. Longenecker, "Introduction," *Life in the Face of Death*, 1.

The resurrection is the confirmation that the darkness of death has been conquered and that Jesus offers the beginning of new life for all who dare to follow him. That theme is unfolded in Matthew's concluding narrative in several brief themes.

(1) **The resurrection of Jesus fulfills the deepest hopes of humanity.** The expectation of a resurrection of the righteous to new life and the wicked to punishment is well attested in the Old Testament (Isa. 26:19; Dan. 12:2) and Second Temple Jewish literature (e.g., 2 Macc. 7; *1 En.* 102; *2 Bar.* 49–51). Resurrection in rabbinic Judaism refers to the concept of all the dead being brought back to life by God on the Day of Judgment, giving eternal life to the righteous and consigning the wicked to Gehenna. But the resurrection of Jesus Messiah has even more far-reaching implications. Jesus is declared with power to be the Son of God (Rom. 1:2–6), through whom all peoples now gain access to salvation through his sacrifice on the cross. And with his resurrection, this new age of the gospel of salvation is inaugurated with the sending of the Spirit of God at Pentecost. In his life, death, and resurrection, Jesus is the exemplar of those who will be regenerated and transformed into his image (Rom. 6:1–11; 8:29; 1 Cor. 15; 2 Cor. 3:18).

(2) **Jesus the Crucified One lives as the Risen One.** The angel's message to the women disciples is designed to dispel the darkness that the pall of death held over them. They witnessed firsthand Jesus' death on the cross and his body being carried away and placed in a tomb. They probably fear retribution for seeking their executed leader. They have come to prepare the body of him whom they had hoped was the Coming One to whom John the Baptist pointed but who is now merely Jesus, the Crucified One. As they approach the tomb in the murkiness of dawn, an earthquake rocks the area, the stone is discovered rolled away, fearsome Roman guards lie like dead men on the ground, and a brilliant angelic figure appears to them.

This angelic figure says to them, "Do not be afraid, for I know that you are looking for Jesus, who was crucified." This angel then dispels the fears of the women and of Jesus' followers for all of history with these words: "He is not here; he has risen, just as he said. Come and see the place where he lay." The resurrection of Jesus—bodily, physically—is held out as the only hope against uncertainty.

It's important to see the relationship of the resurrection and crucifixion. According to Paul, Jesus as the Crucified One was the center of his message to the Corinthians (see 1 Cor. 2:2). Matthew has demonstrated the powerful significance of the cross, and he does not negate that fact. Although the angel announces that Jesus has been raised, this does not mean that he was uncrucified. Rather, Jesus is no longer in that crucified state. He is now the Risen One. Without the resurrection, we who believe in Jesus are to be pitied and are hopeless, for the crucifixion in and of itself was not efficacious (see 1 Cor. 15:17–19). The Crucified One is victorious because he is the Risen One, and we are no longer in our sins because Jesus is both crucified and risen.

**(3) Jesus' resurrection restores men and women to equality of discipleship.** The crucifixion and resurrection accounts tell us a number of things about God's purposes for women in the life and ministry of Jesus. Throughout his ministry Jesus restored men and women to a place of equality denied many women in first-century Israel (see comments on 12:46–50; 27:55–56). In Jesus' commissioning of the women as the first witnesses to his resurrection, we have one of the bedrock truths of these narratives (see comments on 28:10).

Several attendant points are important to note. (a) God is bestowing a special honor on these women. They are exemplary of true discipleship to Jesus, and because of their faithfulness and courage, they are given the special honor of being first witnesses to the empty tomb and the postresurrection appearances of Jesus. (b) Women are restored in Jesus' community of faith to their original status as equal with men because both were created in God's image (Gen. 1:26–28). (c) Women are validated as worthy of the most privileged service in the community of faith, bearing witness to the reality of the risen Lord Jesus.

**(4) Jesus' resurrection outlives hoaxes.** Matthew wants his readers to know that from the very beginning there were attempts to cover the truth of Jesus' resurrection. No one could deny the stark reality of an empty tomb. Therefore, those who had the most to lose were forced to come up with a story to account for it.

To the chief priests, Jesus' resurrection went against their Sadducean theology, which denied the resurrection (22:23). That theology forced them to deny anything that went contrary to it, so they denied accounts of Jesus' bodily resurrection. It also threatened their personal security. If it really was true that Jesus was the Messiah, the people would turn on them for having him executed. And it threatened their position of authority as religious leaders. They did not know how to account for what Jesus did, so they, like the Pharisees in Galilee, had to say that Jesus did what he did because Satan empowered him. The only other alternative was to acknowledge that Jesus operated in God's power; but their hardened heart prevented them from repenting.

The guards also had much to lose. All they knew for sure was that the tomb was empty. They had stories of an earthquake, the stone being rolled back, and some bright, shiny creature confronting them, but after that they had no recollection. They became like dead men, which implies that they either fainted dead away or were so gripped with terror and shock that it incapacitated them. Either way, they had committed a serious dereliction of duty and were facing possible execution for failing to secure an enemy site while in occupied territory. Their desperation forced them to cooperate with the Jewish leaders' ruse.

The desperation of both the religious leaders and the guards resulted in a pathetic rumor that lasted until Matthew's day and beyond. Had Matthew simply invented the story to try to perpetuate a mythic resurrection, all the religious leaders needed to produce was Jesus' body. And they surely would have wanted to, because the widespread belief in Jesus' resurrection was causing turmoil in Jewish circles throughout Palestine and the broader Mediterranean world. But the empty tomb continued to stare blankly in the face of these Jewish leaders, who could only hope that some were foolish enough to prefer their pathetic rumor over the history-altering truth of Jesus' resurrection.

(5) **The risen Master continues to disciple his disciples through Matthew's manual on discipleship.** Jesus' thundering Great Commission, which in its unique emphases graces the conclusion to Matthew's Gospel, is outward, inward, and upward looking.

*Outward looking.* The Great Commission obviously looks outward because of its impelling missionary thrust to make disciples of all nations. The world out there is lost and dying without a Savior. Jesus' final Great Commission makes sure that we do not become ingrown, complacent, or callous. We must look outward and bring the good news of the gospel of the kingdom of heaven to people of all nations. Matthew's Gospel is a powerful recounting of how Jesus Messiah entered history with the purpose of redeeming lost humanity. His life mission to the world becomes our example as we go out with his passionate love for lost people.

*Inward looking.* The Great Commission also looks inward because it speaks to the ongoing transformation of those who have become disciples of Jesus. Individual disciples consider their own personal discipleship transformation as they are united in baptism to Jesus and to his community of faith and as they yield their obedience to all that Jesus commanded. Only this obedience will produce transformation into the likeness of Jesus.

But this cannot be accomplished alone. More mature disciples must teach other disciples how to obey all that Jesus commanded. The community of disciples looks within itself to provide concrete examples, compassionate encouragement, and structured and informal teaching of Jesus' life and words, in the process of teaching other disciples how to obey all that Jesus commanded. The other Gospels, and indeed all of Scripture, is a ready resource. But Matthew's Gospel is an essential manual of discipleship because its very structure of alternating narrative and discourse lays before disciples the most extensive collection of Jesus' commands in word and deed to be found anywhere in the New Testament

*Upward looking.* The Great Commission also looks upward because disciples are to have only the risen and ascended Jesus as Master, Teacher, and Lord. No other master can ever supplant Jesus, and we must never consider ourselves to be master of any other disciples. That is one of the radical departures of Jesus' form of discipleship from other forms in the ancient world (cf. comments on 23:8–10). What makes this possible is that Jesus promises to be with us always, to the very end of the age (28:20). Matthew's Gospel assures us that as we walk with Jesus through this world and this age, he continually provides for us the example of life, the guidance of his words, and the supply of his power to transform continually our lives from the inside out until he comes again in power and glory to fully establish his kingdom on earth.

IN THE DAYS prior to electronic communication or twenty-four-hour news reporting, news of great occasions had to be passed on primarily by word of mouth. In nineteenth-century England, the people were anxiously awaiting news of the outcome of the strategic battle of Waterloo, where the British forces under General Wellington faced off against the French forces under Napoleon. A signalman was placed on top of Winchester Cathedral with instructions to keep an outlook on the sea. When he received a message, he was to pass it on to another man on a hill. That man was to pass it on to another, and on and on. In that way, the news of the outcome of the battle was to be relayed finally to London and then all across Britain.

At long last a ship was sighted through the fog, which on that day lay thick on the channel. The signalman on board sent the first word—*Wellington.* The next word was *defeated.* Then the fog closed in, and the ship could no longer be seen. "Wellington defeated!" The tragic message was sent across England, and a great gloom descended over the countryside. After a few hours the fog lifted, and the signal came again—*Wellington defeated the enemy!* Now the full message went racing across the countryside again, but this time the nation rejoiced!

James Montgomery Boice recounts that story and then makes the striking parallel that when Jesus died his cruel death on the cross, his followers plunged into the most profound sorrow. Jesus had apparently experienced a tragic defeat, and the hopes of his followers died with him. But after three days the fog lifted, and the full message came through: "Jesus has risen; Jesus defeated the enemy!"[70]

---

70. Cited in Boice, *The Christ of the Empty Tomb,* 79–80.

Looking just at the crucifixion, Jesus' followers didn't get the full message of Jesus' mission. They had to look beyond to the resurrection. We do not get the full message of Jesus unless we get the total picture. We can become so familiar with the story of Jesus that we don't experience the staggering impact that the crucifixion, and then resurrection, had on his first followers. Sometimes we need to look through others' eyes.

When our daughters were young, I began a habit of reading to them before they went to bed, talking over the reading, and then praying with them before they went to sleep. I was still a relatively new Christian then, and as I explored a variety of types of reading, a whole world opened up as I looked at stories through their eyes.

Someone suggested that I read to them *The Chronicles of Narnia* by C. S. Lewis. I had been profoundly influenced by Professor Lewis's apologetic books as I had come to faith just a few years prior, but I hadn't read any of his fictional stories. So we thought it sounded good and began reading the entire set. While reading the first volume, *The Lion, the Witch, and the Wardrobe*, we were profoundly struck with sorrow when the great lion, Aslan, was sacrificed. His immense mane was shaved off, he was bound with cords, and there upon the Table of Stone a wicked knife was plunged into the great lion to appease the Deep Magic caused by the actions of the foolish, selfish, little boy, Edmund.

Our hearts were heavy that night, our little daughters and me, as we talked and prayed. They were only eight and four years old then, but I could tell that our little girls were profoundly impacted by the story, as tears streamed down their faces for dear Aslan.

The following evening as we read the next chapter, it was one of the most stirring times we ever shared. As the little girls in the story, Lucy and Susan, went looking to see the fate of Aslan, the great lion appeared to them, alive again. The three of us were beside ourselves. I read the words of the story but had a big lump in my throat, and we were all close to tears of joy. And as the little girls in the story romped around the hilltop with Aslan, my little girls were leaping around their bedroom with joy! And what a talk we had that night. About death, about life, about Jesus dying for us and coming back alive to set us free and romp around life with us.

That was a beautiful experience that we have never forgotten, now nearly twenty years later. It was perhaps an even more beautiful experience for me as I looked through my little daughters' innocent eyes at Jesus' death and resurrection. A sort of fog lifted from my own eyes, so that Jesus' death and resurrection were as real as my own daughters' eventual death and resurrection. They have not yet experienced death, but they will, and it is only in clinging to the truth of the resurrection that the sting will be taken away. Our older daughter had already professed Jesus as her Savior at that point, but just a couple of weeks after that our younger daughter asked if she could ask Jesus into her heart, as her sister and Mommy and Daddy had. And now because Jesus lives, we all can face tomorrow with the utmost confidence.

Although brief, Matthew's account of Jesus' resurrection and postresurrection appearance to the disciples in Galilee yields some immensely significant points for us to ponder.

(1) **Resurrection perspective on life.** Matthew teaches us how vitally important it is to maintain a resurrection perspective on life. The empty tomb is a demonstrable fact of history to which the angel pointed. The women were probably just as frightened as the guards, but as they listened to the angel and focused on the empty tomb, their world was turned upside down. They still did not totally get it, mixed with fear and joy as they were, but as they encountered the risen Jesus, it all started falling into place. They now saw who Jesus really was, and they fell down to worship him. Their lives would never be the same, because their Master is not just another religious leader or authority but is the God of the universe. That is likewise the reaction of the Eleven who worshiped Jesus when he appeared to them in Galilee. Those who hadn't encountered the risen Jesus doubted, but those who had, worshiped (28:16—17).

Our lives will be like theirs if we maintain a resurrection perspective. To stay fixed on the historical evidence for Jesus' empty tomb will open us to encounter him on a personal level, in which he is not just a religious figure but our God. As we have seen all along in our study of this Gospel, Matthew wants us to know that Christianity is a historically based faith in which we find the credible evidence that God has entered history in the person of Jesus Messiah. Between the crucifixion and resurrection, it must have seemed to the disciples as if things were coming to a tragic close. However, the reality is that their discipleship to Jesus was being prepared to be infused with a new reality. Likewise with us, the reality of our discipleship experience is grounded and gets its starting off point from Jesus' resurrection.

As we learn to view life through the empty tomb, it puts everything else into perspective. Our career takes on an eternal perspective, so that we can put our priorities of time and finances and success in line with God's will for our lives. Likewise, our marriage becomes a shared life with a fellow disciple of Jesus as we support each other to fulfill God's calling for us individually and as a couple. Similarly, whether it is the illness of our parents, the death of our child, or our own sudden battle with cancer, the empty tomb puts all our sorrow into perspective when we know that because Jesus lives, we can face tomorrow and plan for an eternity.

The women disciples running away to tell the others about the empty tomb suddenly feel as if their world is turned upside down. They will never be the same. But their experience of fear and joy should instruct us. Jesus, like the great lion Aslan, cannot be tamed. Later in the story, Mr. Beaver warned the children, "One day you'll see Aslan and another you won't. He doesn't like being tied down—and of course he has other countries to attend to. It's quite all right. He'll often drop in. Only you mustn't press him. He's wild, you know. Not like a *tame* lion."[71]

We cannot tame Jesus. He is our Lord and God and Master. Whenever or wherever he drops in on our consciousness, we must be ready to worship him, whether at school or the market or the gym or the beach. We really don't know our future, but he does. And all he asks is that we be prepared for whatever he calls us to be and to do. Even if he disrupts our comfort zone, he will be there to create a new safe space within his loving arms. Then joy erupts from the depths of our being as we live focused on a risen Savior.

(2) **Resurrection power for life.** The resurrection and the following commissioning scene in Matthew exude ultimate power. Jesus, who was seen as "unable to save himself," is now the recipient of a power that raised him from the dead. His resurrection is accompanied by an earthquake, an angel, and a huge stone removed from the tomb entrance. But those flexings of divine muscle pale next to the resurrection itself. And the might of the Roman army as represented in the guards quakes and falls when confronted with these events. At the commissioning scene, Jewish monotheistic purists fall down and worship the risen Jesus, who then declares that all authority on heaven and earth has been given him. There is no higher authority, and he has the power to back it up.

In fact, there is no power like this known to humans. Think of the power of an eight-cylinder truck or an immense construction crane. Think of the power that is behind lighting a city the size of New York. Think of the massive power of a hydrogen bomb that can eliminate a city that size. We have much power as humans to do good, and much to do evil. But with all that power, we do not have the power to raise someone from the dead. It took the power of the Godhead to raise Jesus, and that is but a portion of his power as he exercises "all authority in heaven and on earth."

Now that the risen Jesus indwells each of his disciples, that is the kind of power available to us to live the kind of discipleship to which he calls us. A wonderful passage in Paul's letter to the Ephesians lays this out for us. In Ephesians 1:18–21 the apostle prays:

> I pray also that the eyes of your heart may be enlightened in order that you may know the hope to which he has called you, the riches of his

71. C. S. Lewis, *The Lion, the Witch and the Wardrobe* (New York: Religious Book Club, 1973), 1:149.

glorious inheritance in the saints, and his incomparably great power for us who believe. That power is like the working of his mighty strength, which he exerted in Christ when he raised him from the dead and seated him at his right hand in the heavenly realms, far above all rule and authority, power and dominion.

Notice the power that Paul prays will be ours for our daily lives. That is the power that is available to us to live out our discipleship to Jesus.

So when we live with a resurrection perspective, we must focus our lives so that we can tap into resurrection power. We will then have the power to accomplish anything to which Jesus calls us—controlling our temper, overcoming addictions, remaining faithful to our commitments, maintaining patience with a parent demonstrating increasing dementia. Whatever in life comes our way, discipleship to the risen Jesus includes the power to accomplish it.

This power inherent in Jesus' resurrection gives us great boldness as we go about doing what Jesus asks of us. As great as Jesus' public ministry was before his death, it was his resurrection that became the bedrock of the apostolic message. In the early church the central message is summarized: "The apostles were teaching the people and proclaiming in Jesus the resurrection of the dead" (Acts 4:33). Paul's message focused on "the good news about Jesus and the resurrection" (17:18), which was the basis for his theology (1 Cor. 15:14–19). Peter Kreeft and Ronald Tacelli argue that the resurrection is foundational to every message and every life:

> The existential consequences of the resurrection are incomparable. It is the concrete, factual, empirical proof that: life has hope and meaning; "love is stronger than death"; goodness and power are ultimate allies, not enemies; life wins in the end; God has touched us right here where we are and has defeated our last enemy; we are not cosmic orphans, as our modern secular worldview would make us. And these existential consequences of the resurrection can be seen by comparing the disciples before and after. Before they ran away, denied their Master and huddled behind locked doors in fear and confusion. After, they were transformed from scared rabbits into confident saints, world-changing missionaries, courageous martyrs and joy-filled touring ambassadors for Christ.
>
> The greatest importance of the resurrection is not in the past—"Christ rose"—but in the present—"Christ is risen." The angel at the tomb asked the women, "Why do you seek the living among the dead?" (Lk 24:5). The same question could be asked today to mere historians and scholars. If only we did not keep Christ mummified in a casket labeled "history" or "apologetics," he would set our lives and

world afire as powerfully as he did two millennia ago; and our new pagan empire would sit up, take notice, rub its eyes, wonder and convert a second time. That is the existential import of the resurrection.[72]

Maintaining a resurrection perspective on life has the same potential to light *our* lives on fire with resurrection power. If we grant the benefits and inherent power in the resurrection, what have we to lose? Death no longer has its sting; it can no longer keep us down, as it was unable to keep Jesus down. This gives us great boldness as we go about taking the message of the gospel to the world and committing our lives to Jesus' kingdom program.

(3) **Resurrection persuasion against lies.** The eighteenth-century author Daniel Defoe, often considered to be the founder of the modern novel, wrote the classic tales *Robinson Crusoe* (1719) and *Moll Flanders* (1722). He also wrote a witty satirical poem, *The True Born Englishman* (1701), in which he said:

> Wherever God erects a house of prayer,
> The Devil always builds a chapel there;
> And 'twill be found, upon examination,
> The latter has the largest congregation.[73]

Sometimes good news sounds too good to be true. It often is, but the devil often tries to take the really good news and turn it into a hoax—and the hoax becomes more believable to the hard-hearted than the truth. The religious leaders had the opportunity to know the truth that would have transformed their lives, as it did to those priests who became obedient disciples of Jesus after Pentecost (Acts 6:7). But their hard-heartedness against God's message caused them to reject the truth and to try to substitute Satan's scam (28:11–15).

The resurrection of Jesus will always have its dissenters. The life of discipleship is one of opposition, and we must anticipate rejection by those who are of the same mindset as the religious leaders. Matthew notes that the trumped-up story of Jesus' body being stolen "has been widely circulated among the Jews to this very day" (28:15). Doubt in Jesus' resurrection is a given reality in this world because of the hardened nature of people's hearts. We should see this as both an encouragement in the midst of the doubts of others as well as an encouragement to defend the reality of the resurrection. The apostle Peter writes, "Always be prepared to give an answer to everyone who asks you to give the reason for the hope that you have" (1 Peter 3:15).

---

72. Peter Kreeft and Ronald K. Tacelli, *Handbook of Christian Apologetics* (Downers Grove, Ill: InterVarsity Press, 1994), 177.

73. Daniel Defoe, *The True Born Englishman* (1701), pt. 1, 1.1.; cited in "Defoe, Daniel, " *Encyclopædia Britannica* (2003).

People still use the "stolen body" hypothesis to try to discredit Christianity, and we cannot become slack in our defense of the gospel and endorsement of the Christian worldview in a culture that brings Jesus' resurrection into question. As we saw earlier, much of the hardness of heart of the religious leaders had to do with their preconceived notions of what it is to be in right relationship with God. Today, the preconceived notions that prevent individuals from accepting the reality of Jesus' death and resurrection include the naturalistic worldview, which insists these types of miraculous occurrences are impossible; hence, there must be some sort of naturalistic explanation. The reasons may be different, but individuals with hard hearts will always find reasons to reject God's revelation to us, and our tactics must adjust to address these objections.

(4) **Resurrection purpose for life.** The conclusion of any book, letter, or treatise usually contains an explicit statement or summary of the author's purpose for writing; Matthew is no exception. In his concluding verses, he gives us a resounding statement of the significance of Jesus' resurrection for his followers. F. Dale Bruner states:

> Has anything like the resurrection of Jesus Christ happened on our planet? Christians do not believe so. Precisely because it is *the event* par excellence, it follows almost naturally that the great responsibility of those who know this event is, of course, Mission. The resurrection does not happen for its own sake, and Matthew's gospel does not end, therefore, with the resurrection; it ends with the Great Commission of world-wide mission.[74]

Because Jesus lives, we have an impelling purpose for our lives. Whether or not we are professional missionaries traveling the world, all of us have a central calling to make disciples of all the nations, and Matthew's Gospel shows us how.

This book is intended, at least in part, as a resource tool to help Jesus' disciples in their task of making and developing other disciples. It can be called "a manual on discipleship." Matthew points to Jesus as the supreme Lord and Teacher and emphasizes that his life and teaching produced in his disciples obedience to and understanding of the truth of God's revelation. That same obedience and understanding will continue to be the hallmark of disciples, and his Gospel is readily usable for this purpose.

As in the ministry of Jesus, we are to call people to repent and believe in the gospel of the kingdom. That is how they become disciples. Then we are to enfold them into the family of faith as they are baptized, publicly declar-

---

74. Bruner, *Matthew*, 2:1072.

ing their allegiance to Jesus and identifying with the community of disciples. It is perhaps in carrying out the directive of the final participle that we have failed the most: "teaching them to obey everything I have commanded you." Do we have a personal strategy for carrying this out? Because most of us personally and most of our ministries lack such a strategy, many have called this the *Great Omission* of the Great Commission.

But here is where we can learn from history and heed Matthew's purpose for writing. For much of church history the Gospel of Matthew was used as one of the primary catechetical tools for teaching disciples how to obey all that Jesus commanded.[75] With its alternating sections of narrative and discourse, it gives one of the most complete pictures of Jesus' actions and words. In other words, Matthew has collected the entire life ministry of Jesus so that it can be passed on to succeeding generations of the church. Since discipleship is basically equivalent to the teaching on spiritual formation that we find in Scripture, Matthew has provided us an invaluable tool for our growth in the Christian life and in a full-orbed obedience to Christ.

The five major discourses are directed toward the development of disciples and are intended as instruction in, and clarification of, what it meant to be Jesus' unique kind of disciple. But also we see that there is a progression in the discourses that addresses the fullness of the disciple's life. The basic thrust of each discourse points to that kind of intentional well-roundedness, as we can see briefly in a summary of each discourse and the kind of disciple that will result from each.

The *Sermon on the Mount* develops *kingdom-life disciples* (chs. 5–7). Jesus expounds the reality of a radical, everyday discipleship lived in the presence and power of the kingdom of God within the everyday world. As his disciples, we should be a living demonstration of the reality of the kind of life that is available to everyone.

The *Mission Mandate* develops *mission-driven disciples* (ch. 10). Jesus commissions all his disciples to go out to share and live the gospel of the kingdom of God to an alien and often hostile world.

The *Parabolic Disclosure* develops *clandestine-kingdom disciples* (ch. 13). Through his parables Jesus tests the hearts of the crowd to reveal whether the message of the kingdom has taken root and is producing fruit. He also reveals to his disciples what it means for them to live as kingdom subjects in a world that has not yet experienced the fully consummated kingdom of God.

The *Community Prescription* develops *community-based disciples* (ch. 18). Jesus shows how kingdom life is to be expressed through the church he will establish on earth. Discipleship is to be expressed through a church characterized

---

75. Guthrie, *New Testament Introduction*, 21.

by humility, responsibility, purity, accountability, discipline, forgiveness, reconciliation, and restoration.

The *Olivet Discourse* develops *expectant-sojourner disciples* (chs. 24–25). Jesus looks down the long corridor of time and prophesies to his disciples of his return, the end of the age, and the establishment of his messianic throne. He describes how his disciples are to live each day in this age of the already–not yet consummation of the kingdom of God, in expectant preparation for his return with power.

With an intentional strategy to develop this kind of disciple, Matthew's Gospel becomes a God-given guideline for intentional development. I once heard someone say that the church is filled with "undiscipled disciples." In other words, although we may be committed to missions to the extent that we are *going* to the world and participating in *evangelism*, which produces disciples, and in *baptism*, which enfolds disciples, we have not fulfilled Jesus' purposes until we are likewise committed to carrying out the rest of the Great Commission—teaching disciples to obey all that Jesus commanded. That is the purpose behind Matthew's Gospel, and it is the purpose of the resurrected Jesus in calling us to carry out fully his Great Commission.

The final saying of Jesus in this Gospel is what gives us the greatest assurance that we can carry out his purpose in our lives, because he promises unconditionally: "Surely I am with you always, to the very end of the age" (28:20). Our discipleship to the risen Jesus continues to be our greatest source of comfort, power, and security. As Matthew has demonstrated over and over, the arrival of Jesus began the greatest revolution that history has ever known. It begins in the heart, where Jesus enters and begins the transformation. But then it extends to every area of our lives, so that our physical, emotional, thought, and relational lives are impacted by the power of the kingdom of heaven. I pray that as we conclude the study of this magnificent Gospel, our lives have been revolutionized as well.

# Scripture Index

**Genesis**

| | |
|---|---|
| 1:2 | 77, 142 |
| 1:26−29 | 675 |
| 1:26−28 | 703, 921, 942, 962 |
| 1:26−27 | 242, 722 |
| 2:2 | 453 |
| 2:4 | 55 |
| 2:18 | 655 |
| 2:24 | 246, 643 |
| 3 | 136, 450 |
| 3:1−7 | 168 |
| 3:1 | 392 |
| 3:16 | 921 |
| 4:8−11 | 757 |
| 4:15 | 450 |
| 4:17−18 | 57 |
| 4:24 | 453, 622 |
| 5:1−32 | 58 |
| 5:1 | 55 |
| 5:3−32 | 57 |
| 6:9 | 255 |
| 6:11−12 | 801 |
| 8:10 | 142 |
| 9:3 | 242 |
| 9:6 | 242 |
| 9:9−17 | 247 |
| 10:1−32 | 57 |
| 12:1−3 | 29, 56, 150, 342 |
| 12:2−3 | 389 |
| 12:3 | 540, 953 |
| 13:2 | 302, 650 |
| 14:18−20 | 701 |
| 15:1−9 | 150 |
| 17:1 | 255 |
| 18 | 76 |
| 18:4 | 534 |
| 18:16−19:29 | 420 |
| 19:2 | 534 |
| 21:17 | 76 |
| 21:21 | 73 |

| | |
|---|---|
| 21:28 | 453 |
| 22:2 | 143 |
| 22:5 | 370 |
| 22:15−18 | 76 |
| 22:18 | 29, 56, 342, 389 |
| 23:53 | 74 |
| 24:16 | 79 |
| 24:26−27 | 518 |
| 24:43 | 79 |
| 24:59 | 73 |
| 24:60 | 74 |
| 26:12 | 475 |
| 27:1 | 294 |
| 28:12 | 76 |
| 29:27 | 74 |
| 31:16 | 877 |
| 34:3 | 79 |
| 34:4 | 79 |
| 34:12 | 73 |
| 35:19 | 113 |
| 37:5−11 | 76 |
| 37:34 | 133 |
| 38 | 60 |
| 38:6 | 73 |
| 38:27−30 | 59 |
| 39:9 | 244 |
| 42:17−18 | 451, 936 |
| 42:33−36 | 302 |
| 43:11−15 | 100 |
| 45:7 | 302 |
| 45:22 | 717 |
| 46:8−27 | 57 |
| 48:7 | 113 |
| 48:14 | 646 |
| 48:16 | 616 |
| 48:18 | 294 |
| 49:8−12 | 59 |
| 49:10 | 59, 117, 703 |
| 49:12 | 686 |
| 50:5 | 349 |
| 50:20 | 155 |

**Exodus**

| | |
|---|---|
| 2:8 | 79 |
| 3:2−6 | 76 |
| 3:6 | 724 |
| 3:13−15 | 955 |
| 3:14 | 516 |
| 3:15 | 393, 775 |
| 4:6−7 | 443 |
| 4:31 | 370 |
| 6:3 | 393, 775 |
| 6:6−8 | 423 |
| 6:6 | 837 |
| 6:7 | 837 |
| 9:16 | 393, 775 |
| 10:21 | 186, 902 |
| 11:4 | 328 |
| 12 | 826 |
| 12:1−4 | 375 |
| 12:2−11 | 826 |
| 12:4 | 836 |
| 12:5 | 255 |
| 12:8, 15−20 | 483, 556 |
| 13:4 | 826 |
| 13:9, 13, 16 | 747 |
| 13:21−22 | 592 |
| 14:19 | 96 |
| 15:18 | 704 |
| 16 | 278 |
| 16:4 | 279 |
| 16:29 | 914 |
| 19−20 | 191 |
| 19 | 130 |
| 19:4 | 757 |
| 19:6 | 235 |
| 19:16 | 592 |
| 20:1−17 | 648 |
| 20:2−8 | 230 |
| 20:3−7 | 276 |
| 20:7 | 132, 247, 393, 775 |
| 20:8−10 | 438 |
| 20:10 | 453 |

| | | | | | |
|---|---|---|---|---|---|
| 20:12 | 349, 748 | 11:9–12 | 489 | 27:30 | 230 |
| 20:13 | 241, 242 | 11:20–23 | 133 | **Numbers** | |
| 20:14 | 244, 261 | 11:23, 41 | 753 | | |
| 20:17 | 244, 261, 296 | 12:6 | 691 | 1:7 | 59 |
| 20:18 | 592 | 13–14 | 340 | 3:26 | 904 |
| 21 | 260 | 13:2 | 340 | 5:2–4 | 340 |
| 21:23–25 | 248 | 13:45–46 | 340 | 6:1–21 | 116 |
| 21:32 | 830 | 14:1–32 | 340 | 11:17, 25 | 157 |
| 22:2 | 242 | 14:7 | 101 | 11:26, 29 | 157 |
| 22:7 | 807 | 15:14 | 691 | 12:6 | 76 |
| 22:25 | 807 | 15:25–30 | 371 | 14:24 | 157 |
| 22:26–27 | 250 | 15:29 | 691 | 15:30–31 | 448 |
| 23:1–3 | 262 | 16 | 899 | 15:37–42 | 371, 747 |
| 23:4–5 | 252 | 16:8–10 | 809 | 15:40 | 747 |
| 23:20 | 96 | 16:11–19 | 228 | 18:21, 24 | 753 |
| 24:13 | 56 | 16:26 | 809 | 19:11, 14 | 353 |
| 24:15 | 591 | 16:29–34 | 281 | 19:16 | 353, 754 |
| 24:18 | 156 | 16:29, 31 | 368 | 23:21 | 704 |
| 25:9 | 592 | 17:11 | 622 | 24:2, 18 | 157 |
| 26:31–35 | 904 | 18:16 | 512 | 24:15–17 | 702 |
| 27:21 | 904 | 19:12 | 247 | 24:17 | 95, 375, 773 |
| 27:37 | 904 | 19:16 | 262 | 27:18 | 646 |
| 28:41 | 26, 558 | 19:18 | 249, 252, 315, | 28:9–10 | 440 |
| 29:35–42 | 375 | | 648, 725 | 30:2 | 247 |
| 29:35 | 957 | 19:34 | 725 | 34:11 | 176 |
| 30:6 | 904 | 20:9 | 877 | 35:31 | 242 |
| 30:9 | 101 | 20:10 | 74, 244 | | |
| 30:11–16 | 598, 691 | 20:21 | 512 | **Deuteronomy** | |
| 30:18–21 | 534 | 21:2 | 349 | 1:3, 41 | 957 |
| 30:23 | 101 | 21:3 | 79 | 3:17 | 176 |
| 30:34–38 | 101 | 21:18–19 | 692 | 4:33 | 592 |
| 31:14 | 443 | 23:15 | 255 | 5:5 | 592 |
| 32:6 | 803 | 23:26–32 | 281 | 5:7–21 | 648 |
| 33:20 | 209 | 23:27 | 368 | 5:7–11 | 276 |
| 34:5–7 | 592 | 23:30 | 255 | 5:16 | 349, 748 |
| 34:6–7 | 622 | 23:32 | 368 | 5:17 | 241, 244 |
| 34:8 | 518 | 23:37 | 281 | 5:21 | 24, 296 |
| 34:29–35 | 592 | 23:42 | 592 | 5:22 | 564 |
| 34:40 | 592 | 24:5–9 | 440 | 5:23–27 | 592 |
| 35:2 | 443 | 24:10–23 | 355, 866 | 5:28–29 | 701 |
| 40:34–35 | 592 | 24:11 | 865 | 6:4–5 | 315 |
| 40:36–38 | 592 | 24:14 | 897 | 6:4 | 89 |
| **Leviticus** | | 24:18–20 | 248 | 6:5 | 725 |
| | | 25:2–8 | 453 | 6:6 | 315 |
| 2:1 | 101 | 25:35–37 | 807 | 6:8 | 747 |
| 5:7 | 691 | 26:12 | 83 | 6:13 | 159, 161 |
| 11:4 | 753 | 26:13 | 423 | 6:14 | 89 |
| 11:7 | 352 | 27:30–33 | 753 | 7:2 | 252 |

| | | | |
|---|---|---|---|
| 7:11 | 957 | 24:19–22 | 439 |
| 8:2–3 | 156 | 25:1–3 | 619, 878 |
| 8:2 | 158 | 25:3 | 878 |
| 8:3 | 158 | 25:5–10 | 723 |
| 8:16 | 279 | 26:5–9 | 836 |
| 9:25 | 156 | 26:10 | 370 |
| 11:18 | 747 | 28 | 271 |
| 12:3–5 | 276 | 28:1–14 | 650 |
| 12:5–19 | 753 | 30:7 | 252 |
| 12:11, 14 | 276, 957 | 32:1 | 757 |
| 13:1–18 | 324 | 32:6 | 275, 749 |
| 13:1, 2 | 76 | 33:5 | 704 |
| 13:6–11 | 393 | 33:8–11 | 702 |
| 14:1–2 | 539 | 33:9–10 | 397 |
| 14:1 | 21, 275, 749 | 34:6 | 591 |
| 14:8 | 352 | | |
| 14:22 | 230 | **Joshua** | |
| 15:7–11 | 251 | 1:6–9 | 102 |
| 15:11 | 272, 828 | 2 | 60 |
| 17:6 | 353 | 2:1–21 | 60 |
| 18:13 | 254, 255 | 2:19 | 877 |
| 18:15–22 | 592 | 5 | 671 |
| 18:15–19 | 228 | 7:21 | 807 |
| 18:15–18 | 557, 689, | 10:13 | 255 |
| | 701, 702 | 12:3 | 176 |
| 18:18–19 | 701 | 13:27 | 176 |
| 18:18 | 591 | 19:10, 15 | 92 |
| 18:21–22 | 324 | 23:6–11 | 102 |
| 19:5 | 242 | 23:18 | 870 |
| 19:15–21 | 248 | | |
| 19:15–18 | 618 | **Judges** | |
| 19:15 | 353, 618 | 1:8 | 716 |
| 19:20–21 | 248 | 3:10 | 77 |
| 21:18–21 | 612 | 5:10 | 687 |
| 21:22–23 | 912 | 6:11–24 | 76 |
| 22:12 | 371, 747 | 6:36–40 | 160 |
| 22:13–21 | 74 | 13:5 | 116 |
| 22:22 | 244 | 13:7 | 116 |
| 22:23–24 | 74, 244 | 13:19–20 | 938 |
| 23:3 | 60, 67, 564 | 16:17 | 116 |
| 23:19 | 807 | | |
| 23:20 | 807 | **Ruth** | |
| 23:21–23 | 247 | 1:4 | 60 |
| 23:21 | 246 | 2–4 | 73 |
| 23:24–25 | 439 | 2:1 | 60 |
| 24:1–4 | 644 | 2:2–3 | 439 |
| 24:1 | 246, 642 | 2:6 | 60 |
| 24:12 | 250 | 2:12 | 757 |
| | | 3 | 60 |

| | | | |
|---|---|---|---|
| 4:12–22 | 57 | | |
| 4:17, 21 | 59 | | |
| | | | |
| **1 Samuel** | | | |
| 1:1, 19 | 911 | | |
| 8:7 | 83 | | |
| 9:7–8 | 100 | | |
| 10:2 | 113 | | |
| 16–17 | 59 | | |
| 16:14–23 | 446 | | |
| 17:25–37 | 668 | | |
| 17:43 | 310, 539 | | |
| 17:50–54 | 102 | | |
| 21:1–7 | 439 | | |
| 22:9–23 | 439, 440 | | |
| 24:8 | 518 | | |
| 24:9 | 370 | | |
| 25:32 | 518 | | |
| 25:41 | 534 | | |
| 30:12–13 | 451, 936 | | |
| 31:4–5 | 870 | | |
| | | | |
| **2 Samuel** | | | |
| 1:14 | 26, 558 | | |
| 1:16 | 26, 558, 877 | | |
| 3:31 | 133 | | |
| 5:2 | 98, 121 | | |
| 5:14 | 58 | | |
| 7:8–17 | 20, 162 | | |
| 7:11–17 | 79 | | |
| 7:11–16 | 26, 56, 133, 378, 559, 701 | | |
| 7:12–16 | 58, 372 | | |
| 7:12–14 | 117, 727 | | |
| 7:14 | 27, 559, 864 | | |
| 7:16 | 703 | | |
| 8:11–15 | 102 | | |
| 11:1–27 | 61 | | |
| 12:9 | 242 | | |
| 14:4 | 688 | | |
| 16:9 | 310 | | |
| 17:23 | 870 | | |
| 22:16 | 351 | | |
| 22:24–27 | 255 | | |
| | | | |
| **1 Kings** | | | |
| 1:15–21 | 667 | | |
| 1:16, 23 | 370 | | |
| 1:33 | 687 | | |

| | | | | | |
|---|---|---|---|---|---|
| 2:19 | 668 | 23:10 | 243 | **Nehemiah** | |
| 4:1 | 623 | 23:31–24:20 | 61 | 5:4–8 | 623 |
| 6:17 | 860 | 24:6, 8 | 62 | 7:7 | 56 |
| 8:10–13 | 592 | 24:8–9 | 62 | 9:1 | 133, 281 |
| 9:7–8 | 758 | 24:12, 15 | 62 | 13:9 | 101 |
| 10:1–29 | 298, 452 | 24:18–25:7 | 62 | | |
| 10:1–2 | 100 | 25:27 | 62 | **Esther** | |
| 14:21–31 | 61 | | | 2:13 | 101 |
| 15:1–7 | 61 | **1 Chronicles** | | 3:7 | 826 |
| 15:10–11 | 61 | 1–9 | 57 | 4:1–3 | 420 |
| 16:18 | 870 | 1:34 | 57, 59 | 4:16 | 281, 451, 936 |
| 17:2–3 | 130 | 1:39 | 60 | 5:1 | 451, 936 |
| 17:17–24 | 162, 370 | 2:1–15 | 57 | 6:8–9 | 717 |
| 17:22 | 558 | 2:3–4 | 60 | | |
| 18:4 | 697 | 2:4 | 60 | **Job** | |
| 18:26 | 274 | 2:5 | 59 | 1–2 | 155 |
| 19:1–18 | 413 | 2:11–12 | 59 | 1:6–12 | 155 |
| 19:3–18 | 130 | 2:12 | 59 | 4:19 | 293 |
| 19:8–16 | 591 | 2:16, 18 | 60 | 14:1 | 415 |
| 19:8 | 156 | 2:24, 26, 29 | 60 | 15:8 | 476 |
| 20:29 | 451, 936 | 2:48–49 | 60 | 15:14 | 415 |
| 21:9–14 | 355 | 3:1–24 | 57 | 20:8 | 516 |
| 21:19 | 242 | 3:9 | 60 | 22:28 | 186 |
| 21:23 | 328 | 3:10–14 | 61 | 25:4 | 415 |
| 22:41–44 | 61 | 3:17 | 62 | 30:1 | 540 |
| | | 17:23–27 | 133 | 31:24–25 | 296 |
| **2 Kings** | | 21:1 | 155 | 33:15–17 | 76 |
| 1:8 | 133 | 29:11–12 | 704 | 33:29, 30 | 622 |
| 2:11–12 | 591 | 29:11 | 280 | 38:7 | 96 |
| 2:12 | 749 | | | 38:17 | 565 |
| 4:1–7 | 162 | **2 Chronicles** | | 42:10–15 | 302 |
| 4:32–37 | 370 | 3:14 | 904 | | |
| 4:34–35 | 558 | 7:14 | 355 | **Psalms** | |
| 6:21 | 749 | 9:1–28 | 298 | 1 | 205 |
| 6:26 | 688 | 10:5, 12 | 451, 936 | 1:1 | 205 |
| 6:30 | 133 | 20:1–4 | 281 | 2 | 144 |
| 8:16–19 | 61 | 20:7 | 302 | 2:2 | 559 |
| 8:25–26 | 61 | 24:20–22 | 757 | 2:6 | 703 |
| 9:13 | 687 | 36:9 | 61, 62 | 2:7 | 142, 143, 559, |
| 12:1–3 | 61 | 36:10 | 62 | | 592, 864 |
| 12:9–11 | 100 | | | 2:12 | 205 |
| 14:1–4 | 61 | **Ezra** | | 4:5 | 252 |
| 14:21–22 | 61 | 2:21 | 112 | 5:4 | 252 |
| 15:29 | 173 | 3:2 | 62 | 5:7 | 370 |
| 16:3 | 243 | 5:2 | 62 | 7:12 | 397 |
| 19:15 | 704 | 7:1–5 | 58 | 8:2 | 693 |
| 20:8–11 | 554 | 7:9 | 94 | 8:3–8 | 297, 703 |
| 21:6 | 243 | 8:21–23 | 281 | 8:5 | 27, 348 |

| | | | | | |
|---|---|---|---|---|---|
| 9:13 | 565 | 55:17 | 273 | 112:1–3 | 650 |
| 16:5 | 668 | 58:5 | 392 | 113–118 | 688, 838 |
| 16:11 | 668 | 59:14–15 | 310, 540 | 115–118 | 837 |
| 17:8 | 757 | 63:1 | 208 | 116:13 | 668 |
| 18:15 | 352 | 65:7 | 352 | 118:19–29 | 688 |
| 21:21–22 | 902 | 68:25 | 79 | 118:22 | 698 |
| 22 | 899, 900, 901, 902 | 69:8 | 118 | 118:25–26 | 698 |
| 22:1 | 902 | 69:20–21 | 118, 898 | 118:25 | 688 |
| 22:6–8 | 118 | 72:10–11 | 100 | 118:26 | 137, 412, 758 |
| 22:6–7 | 900 | 72:11 | 94 | 119:10–11, 20 | 208 |
| 22:8 | 901 | 73:1 | 209 | 119:136 | 206 |
| 22:16–17 | 311 | 78 | 111 | 119:176 | 616 |
| 22:16 | 310, 539 | 78:2, 9 | 484 | 126:1–2 | 675 |
| 22:18 | 899 | 80:13 | 311 | 127:3–5 | 612 |
| 23 | 375, 616 | 81 | 111 | 128:3–4 | 612 |
| 24:3–6 | 209 | 85:8–10 | 853 | 129:6 | 298 |
| 25:6–7 | 208 | 88:13 | 186, 902 | 130:7–8 | 85 |
| 25:14 | 476 | 89:4 | 727 | 130:8 | 77 |
| 26:4–5 | 252 | 89:9 | 352 | 132:11–12 | 58 |
| 27:1 | 186 | 89:19–29 | 58 | 132:17 | 117 |
| 28:3 | 210 | 89:26–27 | 864 | 133:2 | 828 |
| 29:10 | 704 | 89:27 | 559 | 136 | 838 |
| 34:6 | 217 | 89:35–37 | 58 | 139:12 | 186 |
| 34:7 | 616 | 91:4 | 757 | 139:13–14 | 612 |
| 35:13 | 281 | 91:11–12 | 159 | 139:21–22 | 252, 295 |
| 37:2 | 298 | 91:11 | 616 | | |
| 37:4 | 169 | 95 | 677 | **Proverbs** | |
| 37:9, 11 | 207 | 99:1–4 | 704 | 2:13–14 | 186, 902 |
| 37:21 | 251 | 102:4, 11 | 298 | 3:5–6 | 850 |
| 40:8 | 277 | 103:3 | 355 | 3:32 | 476 |
| 40:17 | 205 | 103:13 | 275, 749 | 4:23 | 408 |
| 42:1–2 | 208 | 103:19 | 704 | 5:15–23 | 245 |
| 45:7 | 252 | 104:6–7 | 352 | 6:1–11 | 251 |
| 45:8 | 101 | 104:7 | 352 | 6:6 | 302 |
| 45:14–15 | 74 | 104:10–16 | 297 | 7:17 | 101 |
| 46:10 | 316, 319 | 105–6 | 111 | 8 | 419 |
| 48:1–2 | 684 | 105:15 | 26, 558 | 10:23 | 243 |
| 49 | 296 | 105:23–45 | 102 | 14:21 | 208 |
| 49:16–20 | 302 | 106:9 | 352 | 18:10 | 955 |
| 51 | 232 | 107:18 | 565 | 18:22 | 655 |
| 51:2 | 232 | 107:20 | 342 | 19:14 | 73 |
| 51:4 | 244 | 107:23–32 | 352 | 19:17 | 304 |
| 51:5 | 612 | 110 | 703, 732 | 20:9 | 209 |
| 51:7 | 232 | 110:1–7 | 58 | 20:22 | 248 |
| 51:10 | 209, 232 | 110:1–2 | 865 | 21:1 | 885 |
| 51:12 | 284 | 110:1 | 668, 727 | 22:11 | 209 |
| 51:14–17 | 235 | 110:4 | 701, 847 | 24:29 | 248 |
| 51:16–17 | 232, 441 | 110:5 | 668 | 26:11 | 310, 539 |

| | | | | | |
|---|---|---|---|---|---|
| 27:1 | 300 | 11:10–12 | 783 | 42–53 | 834 |
| 30:19 | 79 | 11:10 | 727 | 42 | 144 |
| 30:25 | 302 | 13:8 | 773 | 42:1–7 | 378 |
| 31:6 | 898 | 13:10 | 783 | 42:1–4 | 142, 143, 444, |
| 31:10–31 | 302 | 13:21 | 453 | | 853, 894 |
| | | 14:12–15 | 420 | 42:1 | 142, 143, 592 |
| **Ecclesiastes** | | 14:12–14 | 161 | 42:6 | 215 |
| 2:1–11 | 296 | 14:12–13 | 96 | 42:7 | 372 |
| 3:8 | 210 | 14:13 | 432 | 42:14 | 773 |
| 5:3 | 76 | 14:25 | 423 | 43:10–13 | 516 |
| 9:7–8 | 282 | 17:11 | 376 | 43:15 | 704 |
| | | 18:3 | 783, 784 | 44:1–3, 21 | 444 |
| **Song of Solomon** | | 21:3 | 773 | 45:4 | 444, 780 |
| 3:6 | 101 | 23:1–17 | 420 | 49:3 | 444 |
| 4:6, 14 | 101 | 24:23 | 704 | 49:5–7 | 444 |
| | | 25:6–9 | 342 | 49:6 | 215 |
| **Isaiah** | | 25:8–9 | 355 | 49:7 | 118 |
| 2:2–5 | 215 | 26–29 | 559 | 49:11 | 597 |
| 2:2–4 | 80 | 26:3 | 210 | 50:2 | 352 |
| 2:2–3 | 704 | 26:17–19 | 773 | 50:9 | 293 |
| 3:16 | 328 | 26:18–19 | 413 | 51:8 | 293 |
| 4:1–6 | 592 | 26:19 | 722, 961 | 51:17 | 668 |
| 4:2 | 117 | 27:13 | 784 | 52–53 | 121 |
| 5:1–7 | 697 | 28:7 | 516, 803 | 52:7 | 210, 704 |
| 5:3–12 | 716 | 29:18–19 | 413 | 52:13–53:12 | 126, 345, |
| 5:8–22 | 751 | 29:18 | 372, 413 | | 346, 894 |
| 5:24–25 | 716 | 30:18 | 205 | 53 | 143, 346, 670, 860 |
| 5:24 | 716 | 31:20–21 | 427 | 53:2 | 117, 118, 345 |
| 6:5 | 704 | 33:22 | 704 | 53:4–12 | 845 |
| 6:9–10 | 478 | 34:4 | 783 | 53:4–6 | 847 |
| 7:6 | 79 | 34:14 | 453 | 53:4–5 | 375 |
| 7:14–17 | 80 | 35:1–10 | 378 | 53:4 | 345, 346, 413 |
| 7:14 | 79, 81, 118, | 35:4–6 | 414 | 53:6–8 | 539 |
| | 121, 853 | 35:5 | 372, 413 | 53:6 | 616, 670 |
| 8:4, 8 | 79 | 35:6 | 413 | 53:7 | 864, 873 |
| 8:13–15 | 699 | 38:7–8 | 554 | 53:8 | 368 |
| 9:1–6 | 184 | 38:10 | 565 | 53:9 | 912 |
| 9:1–2 | 81, 173 | 40–52 | 444 | 53:11 | 140 |
| 9:1 | 902 | 40 | 559 | 53:12 | 845 |
| 9:2–7 | 80 | 40:1 | 206 | 54:4–6 | 805 |
| 9:6–7 | 210, 853 | 40:2 | 625 | 54:10 | 597 |
| 9:6 | 81 | 40:3 | 132, 871 | 55:12 | 853 |
| 9:7 | 81 | 40:4 | 597 | 56:3–8 | 342 |
| 11:1–16 | 80 | 40:6–8 | 298 | 56:7 | 228 |
| 11:1–5 | 117, 121 | 40:10–11 | 375 | 56:10 | 540 |
| 11:1 | 110, 116, 117, | 40:49 | 597 | 56:12 | 803 |
| | 118, 126, 727 | 41:8–10 | 444 | 58:3 | 281 |
| 11:2 | 142 | 41:8 | 302 | 58:6–10 | 810 |
| 11:6 | 323 | | | | |

| | | | | | |
|---|---|---|---|---|---|
| 60:5–6, 11 | 100 | 24:1 | 61 | 34:23–31 | 94, 446 |
| 60:21 | 117, 118 | 25:1–11 | 303 | 34:23–30 | 853 |
| 61:1–3 | 206 | 25:15–29 | 668 | 34:27 | 423 |
| 61:1–2 | 414 | 25:22 | 420 | 36:25–27 | 234 |
| 61:1 | 142, 217, 413 | 27:3–7 | 420 | 36:26–32 | 198 |
| 62:4–5 | 805 | 30:7–10 | 773 | 36:26–27 | 149, 545, 837 |
| 62:5 | 368 | 30:8 | 423 | 36:26 | 266 |
| 62:11 | 228 | 31:9 | 275, 749 | 37:9 | 785 |
| 64:1 | 141 | 31:15 | 110, 113, 121 | 37:11–14 | 907 |
| 64:10–11 | 758 | 31:16–17 | 113 | 37:24–28 | 83, 446 |
| 65:6–7 | 271 | 31:31–35 | 114 | 37:24 | 375 |
| 65:25 | 323 | 31:31–34 | 113, 234, 426 | 39:11–15 | 353 |
| 66:3 | 311 | 31:31 | 837 | | |
| 66:6 | 271 | 31:33 | 545 | **Daniel** | |
| 66:7–11 | 773 | 31:34 | 837 | 2:18–19 | 476 |
| 66:20 | 100 | 33:15 | 117 | 2:19 | 76 |
| | | 40:1–2 | 113 | 2:34–35, 44–45 | 700 |
| **Jeremiah** | | 46:18 | 704 | 3:29 | 865 |
| 1:5 | 326, 806 | 50:6 | 616 | 4:9–27 | 483 |
| 2:6 | 111 | 51:27 | 784 | 6:10 | 273 |
| 2:20 | 423 | 52:31 | 62 | 6:17 | 915 |
| 2:21 | 664, 696 | 52:34 | 62 | 7:1–28 | 76 |
| 3:4 | 275, 749 | | | 7:13–14 | 27, 347, |
| 3:6–10 | 380 | **Lamentations** | | | 602, 728, |
| 4:4 | 150 | 5:5 | 423 | | 784, 865, |
| 4:21 | 784 | | | | 951, 952 |
| 5:5 | 423 | **Ezekiel** | | 7:13 | 27, 348, 783 |
| 6:1 | 784 | 1:1 | 141 | 7:14 | 727 |
| 6:13–15 | 322 | 2:1, 3, 6, 8 | 27, 347 | 8:8 | 785 |
| 6:16 | 424 | 4:6 | 156 | 8:10 | 96 |
| 6:26 | 133 | 6:9 | 245 | 8:13 | 778 |
| 7:22–25 | 111 | 13:1–23 | 322 | 8:15–26 | 76 |
| 7:31–32 | 243 | 16:7–34 | 805 | 8:17 | 27, 347 |
| 8:10–12 | 322 | 16:32 | 244 | 9 | 789 |
| 12:1 | 293 | 16:48 | 420 | 9:20–27 | 76 |
| 13:17 | 616 | 17:22–24 | 483 | 9:25–27 | 779 |
| 17:9 | 209, 545 | 18:7 | 250 | 9:26 | 118 |
| 19 | 691 | 18:13 | 877 | 9:27 | 777, 778, 779, 789 |
| 19:1–13 | 243 | 18:31 | 545 | 10:3 | 281 |
| 20:1–2 | 697 | 20:1–20 | 111 | 10:13 | 76, 616 |
| 21–22 | 380 | 22:27–29 | 322 | 11:4 | 785 |
| 22:23 | 773 | 26:2–9 | 420 | 11:31 | 778, 790 |
| 22:24, 28 | 61 | 28:2, 11–19 | 161 | 12 | 789 |
| 23 | 139 | 29:21 | 117 | 12:1–3 | 812 |
| 23:1–4 | 616 | 31:2–18 | 483 | 12:2 | 558, 722, 961 |
| 23:5 | 117, 121, 727 | 32:7 | 783 | 12:11 | 778, 789 |
| 23:30 | 62 | 34 | 809 | 12:12 | 205 |
| 23:32 | 76 | 34:1–30 | 616 | | |

### Hosea

| | |
|---|---|
| 1:10 | 210 |
| 2:19–20 | 368 |
| 2:19 | 805 |
| 4:13 | 244 |
| 4:14 | 244 |
| 6:6 | 441 |
| 7:11 | 392 |
| 9:10 | 693 |
| 10:1 | 664, 696 |
| 11:1–2 | 111 |
| 11:1 | 110, 121, 275, 539, 749 |
| 13:5 | 326, 806 |
| 13:13 | 773 |

### Joel

| | |
|---|---|
| 1:8 | 79 |
| 1:15 | 378 |
| 2:1 | 378 |
| 2:2 | 902 |
| 2:11 | 378 |
| 2:28–29 | 138, 147, 149 |
| 2:31 | 378, 783 |
| 3:4–8 | 420 |
| 3:13 | 376 |
| 3:14–21 | 378 |
| 3:15 | 783 |

### Amos

| | |
|---|---|
| 1:3 | 622 |
| 2:6 | 622 |
| 2:8 | 250 |
| 3:2 | 326, 806 |
| 3:7 | 476 |
| 5:18, 20 | 902 |
| 8:9 | 783 |

### Jonah

| | |
|---|---|
| 1:16 | 352 |
| 3:1–5 | 451, 555 |
| 3:5–8 | 420 |

### Micah

| | |
|---|---|
| 2:15 | 113 |
| 4:1–2 | 704 |
| 4:9–10 | 773 |
| 5:2 | 98, 121 |
| 6:1–4 | 111 |
| 6:8 | 209, 230 |

### Nahum

| | |
|---|---|
| 1:4 | 352 |

### Habakkuk

| | |
|---|---|
| 2:6–20 | 751 |
| 3:2–6, 16 | 592 |

### Zephaniah

| | |
|---|---|
| 1:15 | 902 |
| 3:1–4 | 322 |
| 3:10 | 100 |
| 3:15 | 704 |

### Haggai

| | |
|---|---|
| 2:7–8 | 100 |

### Zechariah

| | |
|---|---|
| 1:1 | 757 |
| 1:8–17 | 76 |
| 3:1–12 | 155 |
| 3:8 | 117 |
| 3:10 | 693 |
| 6:12 | 117 |
| 8:3 | 328 |
| 8:19 | 281 |
| 9:2–4 | 420 |
| 9:9–13 | 686 |
| 9:9 | 228, 412, 686, 688 |
| 10:3 | 616 |
| 11 | 839 |
| 11:11–13 | 871 |
| 11:12 | 830 |
| 12–13 | 860 |
| 12:9–14 | 845 |
| 12:10–13:1 | 888 |
| 12:10–14 | 579 |
| 12:10 | 784, 839 |
| 13:7 | 616, 809, 839, 847 |
| 14:3–21 | 686 |
| 14:9 | 704 |

### Malachi

| | |
|---|---|
| 2:16 | 246, 643 |
| 3:1 | 133, 415, 417, 427, 871 |
| 3:11 | 293 |
| 4:4–6 | 591 |
| 4:4 | 693 |
| 4:5–6 | 133, 417, 427, 591, 593 |
| 4:5 | 417, 557 |
| 4:6 | 134 |

### Matthew

| | |
|---|---|
| 1:1–4:16 | 174 |
| 1–4 | 183, 330 |
| 1–2 | 55, 119, 120, 140, 875, 946 |
| 1:1–17 | 29, 83, 147, 810 |
| 1:1–16 | 25 |
| 1:1–14 | 703 |
| 1:1–2 | 93 |
| 1:1 | 25, 26, 29, 72, 76, 77, 84, 111, 183, 184, 342, 372, 412, 538, 540, 688, 844, 915, 921, 933, 946, 953 |
| 1:3 | 74, 703 |
| 1:5 | 74 |
| 1:6 | 74, 77, 94 |
| 1:13 | 703 |
| 1:16–18 | 26 |
| 1:16 | 74, 77, 412 |
| 1:17 | 412, 705 |
| 1:18–2:23 | 55 |
| 1:18–25 | 25, 63, 64, 68, 104, 147, 184, 645 |
| 1:18 | 55, 393, 412 |
| 1:20–24 | 784 |
| 1:20–23 | 27 |
| 1:20–21 | 937 |
| 1:20 | 96, 101, 100, 142, 143, 393, 727, 938 |
| 1:21–23 | 26, 141, 559 |
| 1:21 | 26, 146, 173, 206, 345, 356, 372, 877, 894, 902, 918 |
| 1:22–24 | 915 |
| 1:22–23 | 29, 121, 173, 228, 234 |
| 1:22 | 444, 484, 490 |
| 1:23 | 35, 64, 113, 143, 209, 345, 853, 946, 950, 958 |
| 1:24–25 | 92, 455 |
| 1:24 | 621 |
| 1:25 | 63, 92, 345 |

| | | |
|---|---|---|
| 2 | 147, 183, 511 | |
| 2:1–23 | 60, 916 | |
| 2:1–12 | 953 | |
| 2:1–6 | 25, 872 | |
| 2:1–2 | 178 | |
| 2:2–6 | 705 | |
| 2:2 | 60, 146, 161, 191, 228, 810, 845 | |
| 2:3–4 | 135 | |
| 2:3 | 115, 688, 757 | |
| 2:4–5 | 29 | |
| 2:4 | 347, 412 | |
| 2:5–6 | 78, 173, 234, 915 | |
| 2:5 | 78, 490, 948 | |
| 2:6 | 77, 113, 121, 877 | |
| 2:7 | 112, 774 | |
| 2:9 | 703 | |
| 2:11 | 178, 845 | |
| 2:12–23 | 784 | |
| 2:12 | 76, 110, 172 | |
| 2:13 | 76, 96, 101, 102, 172, 574, 801, 937 | |
| 2:14 | 102, 172, 443, 801 | |
| 2:15 | 25, 26, 29, 78, 143, 173, 228, 234, 345, 444, 484, 559 | |
| 2:16–20 | 98 | |
| 2:16 | 93 | |
| 2:17–18 | 78, 173, 228, 234, 915 | |
| 2:17 | 29, 78, 558, 703, 871 | |
| 2:19 | 76, 96, 101, 937 | |
| 2:20 | 99, 801 | |
| 2:21 | 99, 801 | |
| 2:22–23 | 102 | |
| 2:22 | 76, 96, 101, 172, 443, | |
| 2:23 | 73, 78, 143, 173, 228, 234, 345, 445, 490, 508, 867, 871, 915 | |
| 3–4 | 456 | |
| 3:1–14 | 413 | |
| 3:1–11 | 418 | |
| 3:1–6 | 234, 414 | |
| 3:1–3 | 591, 594 | |
| 3:1 | 154, 703, 950 | |

| | | |
|---|---|---|
| 3:2 | 174, 195, 390, 447, 482, 501, 648, 650 | |
| 3:5 | 231, 414, 450, 534, 537, 554, 574, 722, 755, 756 | |
| 3:7–12 | 227, 343 | |
| 3:7–10 | 695, 827, 874 | |
| 3:8 | 323, 450 | |
| 3:9 | 77 | |
| 3:11–17 | 695 | |
| 3:11 | 412, 486, 393 | |
| 3:12 | 615 | |
| 3:13 | 159 | |
| 3:13–17 | 154, 164, 175 | |
| 3:15–17 | 905 | |
| 3:15 | 111, 207, 231, 490, 591 | |
| 3:16–4:1 | 198 | |
| 3:16–17 | 77, 939 | |
| 3:16 | 393 | |
| 3:17 | 25, 26, 27, 72, 89, 111, 158, 216, 275, 353, 396, 421, 444, 559, 592, 697, 728, 908, 946, 955 | |
| 3:22–23 | 178 | |
| 4 | 183 | |
| 4:1–11 | 86, 279, 350, 459, 571, 690, 800, 841, 847, 916, 946 | |
| 4:1–4 | 313 | |
| 4:1–3 | 178 | |
| 4:1–2 | 281, 513 | |
| 4:1 | 142, 393, 554 | |
| 4:2–10 | 421 | |
| 4:2 | 26, 559 | |
| 4:3 | 27, 353, 728, 900 | |
| 4:4 | 278, 591 | |
| 4:5 | 97, 486, 559, 774 | |
| 4:6 | 27, 76, 353, 728, 900, 957 | |
| 4:8–9 | 841 | |
| 4:8 | 191, 486 | |
| 4:9–10 | 941 | |
| 4:11 | 76, 784 | |
| 4:12–18 | 102 | |
| 4:12–17 | 25, 26, 77, 538 | |
| 4:12 | 412, 443, 641, 940 | |

| | | |
|---|---|---|
| 4:13–17 | 411 | |
| 4:13 | 341, 420, 509 | |
| 4:14–5:10 | 703 | |
| 4:14–17 | 490 | |
| 4:14–16 | 78, 228, 853 | |
| 4:14 | 78, 345 | |
| 4:15–17 | 959 | |
| 4:15–16 | 215, 942, 947, 953 | |
| 4:16 | 77, 186, 473, 703, 877, 902 | |
| 4:17–16:20 | 174 | |
| 4:17 | 131, 132, 146, 159, 190, 195, 227, 234, 353, 354, 384, 390, 482, 501, 538, 569, 648, 650, 774, 810, 845, 882, 915 | |
| 4:18–22 | 84, 90, 192, 350, 365, 384, 385, 388, 489, 521, 600, 651 | |
| 4:18–20 | 847 | |
| 4:18 | 31, 561 | |
| 4:19–20 | 667 | |
| 4:19 | 422, 504 | |
| 4:20 | 344, 948 | |
| 4:20 | 350, 372, 801 | |
| 4:22–25 | 190 | |
| 4:22 | 350, 372, 801, 948 | |
| 4:23–25 | 191, 193, 339, 340, 355, 356, 501 | |
| 4:23 | 123, 146, 374, 385, 420, 480, 776 | |
| 4:24–25 | 443 | |
| 4:24 | 183, 325, 342, 355 | |
| 4:25 | 192, 372, 385, 909 | |
| 5–7 | 32, 181, 190, 200, 330, 339, 357, 374, 384, 385, 399, 412, 425, 427, 456, 476, 491, 759, 770, 788, 971 | |
| 5:1–2 | 33, 179, 181, 211, 321, 326, 328, 404, 454, 472, 586, 626, 875 | |
| 5:1 | 950 | |

| | | | | |
|---|---|---|---|---|
| 5:2–16 | 706 | | 398, 422, 424, 433, | 6 | 198 |
| 5:3–20 | 482 | | 445, 472, 489, 491, | 6:1–18 | 33, 151, 198, |
| 5:3–16 | 502, 626 | | 503, 534, 536, 545, | | 228, 241, 292, 307, |
| 5:3–11 | 560 | | 578, 626, 699, 706, | | 308, 322, 422, 424, |
| 5:3–10 | 257, 613 | | 717, 735, 751, 754, | | 535, 536, 545, 626, |
| 5:3 | 191, 257, 324, 413, | | 755, 793, 804, 812, | | 720, 751 |
| | 414, 560, 814 | | 817, 842 | 6:1–17 | 803, 821 |
| 5:4 | 258 | 5:21–48 | 193, 228, 231 | 6:1–4 | 649 |
| 5:5 | 258, 424 | | 235, 236, 283, | 6:1–3 | 488 |
| 5:6 | 140, 231, 258, 299 | | 328, 502, 545 | 6:1–2 | 310, 326, 494 |
| 5:7 | 258, 308, 316 | 5:21–47 | 425, 491 | 6:1 | 140, 215, 299, |
| 5:8 | 258, 294, 544 | 5:21 | 236 | | 318, 494, 746 |
| 5:9 | 258 | 5:22 | 120, 486, 615, | 6:2–4 | 251 |
| 5:10–12 | 398 | | 752, 862 | 6:2 | 309, 726, 751 |
| 5:10 | 140, 191, 258, | 5:23 | 753 | 6:4 | 675 |
| | 287, 299, 324 | 5:25–32 | 316 | 6:5 | 309 |
| 5:11–12 | 480 | 5:26 | 396 | 6:6 | 675 |
| 5:11 | 393, 775 | 5:27–30 | 614, 645 | 6:9–11 | 22 |
| 5:12 | 271, 398 | 5:27–28 | 644 | 6:9 | 420, 749 |
| 5:13–16 | 257, 277, 504 | 5:27 | 236 | 6:10 | 191, 325, 455, |
| 5:13 | 194 | 5:28 | 294, 545 | | 487, 620 |
| 5:14–16 | 189, 524 | 5:29–30 | 309, 615 | 6:11 | 300, 583, 664, 673 |
| 5:14–15 | 473 | 5:29 | 201, 510 | 6:12 | 308, 316 |
| 5:14 | 194 | 5:31–32 | 643 | 6:13 | 193, 248 |
| 5:16–20 | 725 | 5:32 | 644 | 6:14–16 | 486 |
| 5:16 | 27, 275, 287, | 5:33–37 | 229, 867 | 6:16–18 | 368 |
| | 318, 494 | 5:34–37 | 752, 753 | 6:16 | 309 |
| 5:17–48 | 29, 307, 355, | 5:34 | 201 | 6:18 | 675 |
| | 424, 441, 538, 905 | 5:37 | 280 | 6:19–34 | 270 |
| 5:17–47 | 438 | 5:38–42 | 737, 859 | 6:19–24 | 481 |
| 5:17–20 | 77, 78, 111, | 5:38 | 236 | 6:19–21 | 202 |
| | 192, 198, 219, | 5:39–40 | 201 | 6:19–20 | 802 |
| | 315, 441, 490, | 5:39 | 280 | 6:20 | 100 |
| | 726, 739, 837 | 5:40 | 308, 687 | 6:21–24 | 649 |
| 5:17–19 | 599 | 5:43–48 | 726 | 6:22–23 | 473 |
| 5:17 | 32, 140, 240, 313, | 5:43–47 | 284, 316, 319, | 6:23 | 665 |
| | 325, 369, 417, 491, | | 463, 653, 775 | 6:24 | 730 |
| | 545, 591, 592, | 5:43 | 295 | 6:25–34 | 318, 480 |
| | 725, 915 | 5:44 | 462 | 6:25–33 | 673 |
| 5:18 | 787 | 5:45 | 275 | 6:26 | 275 |
| 5:19 | 191 | 5:46 | 364 | 6:30 | 351 |
| 5:20–48 | 219, 946 | 5:47 | 811 | 6:31–33 | 201 |
| 5:20 | 32, 33, 140, 191, | 5:48–6:18 | 368 | 6:31 | 583 |
| | 175, 191, 193, 195, | 5:48 | 32, 196, 198, 199, | 6:32–33 | 583 |
| | 197, 198, 208, 218, | | 270, 275, 284, 285, | 6:33 | 140, 169, 191, |
| | 219, 241, 270, 292, | | 292, 299, 319, 425, | | 275, 730 |
| | 299, 321, 322, 326, | | 491, 659 | 6:34 | 278 |
| | 328, 346, 356, 369, | 6:1–7:12 | 307 | 7–10 | 703 |

| | | | | | |
|---|---|---|---|---|---|
| 7 | 198 | 8:5 | 324, 354, 551 | 9:8 | 192, 385, 874 |
| 7:1–12 | 270, 494 | 8:8 | 369, 591 | 9:9–17 | 339 |
| 7:1–5 | 323 | 8:10–12 | 551 | 9:9 | 193, 384, 388, |
| 7:6 | 323, 324, 354, | 8:10 | 705 | | 420, 521, 599 |
| | 488, 521, 539 | 8:11–12 | 705 | 9:10–13 | 88 |
| 7:11 | 275, 377, 538 | 8:11 | 77 | 9:10–11 | 717 |
| 7:12 | 228, 725 | 8:12 | 486, 624, 717, | 9:11 | 446, 457, 599, |
| 7:13–27 | 222, 313 | | 803, 835 | | 720, 843 |
| 7:13–14 | 219, 418, | 8:14–17 | 567 | 9:12–13 | 717 |
| | 502, 776 | 8:14–15 | 177, 188 | 9:13 | 379, 441 |
| 7:15–23 | 310, 398 | 8:14 | 31, 439, 472, 485, | 9:14–17 | 412, 418, |
| 7:15–20 | 450, 480, 481 | | 537, 611, 641 | | 805, 829 |
| 7:16–20 | 310 | 8:15 | 372, 373 | 9:14–15 | 154, 281 |
| 7:20 | 257 | 8:16 | 325, 385 | 9:14 | 412, 952 |
| 7:21–23 | 191 | 8:17 | 78, 368, 375, | 9:16, 17 | 473 |
| 7:21 | 26, 28, 396, 422, | | 385, 446, 577 | 9:18–35 | 339 |
| | 455, 516, 559, 616, | 8:18–22 | 27, 363 | 9:18 | 161 |
| | 835, 841 | 8:18 | 30, 192 | 9:19 | 909 |
| 7:22–23 | 28 | 8:19 | 98, 180, 328, 441, | 9:20–22 | 519 |
| 7:22 | 799 | | 534, 570, 745 | 9:20 | 518, 747 |
| 7:23 | 806 | 8:20 | 28, 118, 325, 485, | 9:23–26 | 116, 390 |
| 7:24–27 | 473 | | 593, 670, 784 | 9:24 | 446 |
| 7:24 | 328 | 8:21–22 | 398, 455, 544 | 9:27–32 | 413 |
| 7:25 | 257 | 8:21 | 28, 31, 192, | 9:27–31 | 446, 671 |
| 7:28–29 | 33, 192, 193, | | 193, 516 | 9:27 | 56, 538, 727 |
| | 197, 228, 328, | 8:22 | 801 | 9:28–34 | 354 |
| | 347, 355, 356, | 8:23–9:8 | 370 | 9:28 | 28, 324, 340 |
| | 374, 626, 874, 875 | 8:23–27 | 516, 916 | 9:30 | 341, 396, 568, 593 |
| 7:28 | 32, 339, 352, | 8:24 | 176, 516 | 9:31 | 874 |
| | 369, 412, 508, | 8:25 | 28, 324, 516 | 9:32–33 | 596 |
| | 652, 724, 825 | 8:26 | 298, 517 | 9:33–34 | 874 |
| 7:29 | 231, 357 | 8:27 | 530 | 9:33 | 541 |
| 8–9 | 181, 330, 339, 357, | 8:28–34 | 510, 916 | 9:34 | 395, 457 |
| | 369, 374, 375, 384, | 8:28–32 | 385 | 9:35–38 | 192, 501, 705 |
| | 385, 412, 413, 425, | 8:28 | 374, 418, 938 | 9:35–36 | 356 |
| | 456, 693 | 8:29 | 385, 559 | 9:35 | 146, 181, 191, 385, |
| 8:1–9:8 | 363 | 9 | 34, 234, 376, 690 | | 420, 44, 480, 776 |
| 8 | 376, 690 | 9:1–12 | 754 | 9:36–10:4 | 339 |
| 8:1–17 | 363, 370 | 9:1–8 | 279, 443, 894 | 9:36 | 87, 389, 391, 422, |
| 8:1–4 | 413 | 9:1–7 | 442 | | 445, 551, 746, 809 |
| 8:2–4 | 370 | 9:1 | 173, 420 | 9:38 | 28, 325, 384, 686 |
| 8:2 | 28, 161, 324, 941 | 9:2–7 | 370 | 10–12 | 523 |
| 8:3 | 325 | 9:2 | 375 | 10 | 32, 200, 412, 425, |
| 8:4–13 | 567 | 9:3–4 | 370, 411 | | 457, 476, 491, 759, |
| 8:4 | 373, 396, 568, | 9:3 | 374, 442, 457, 446 | | 770, 774, 788, 971 |
| | 593, 776 | 9:6 | 28, 85, 348, 385, | 10:1–15 | 376 |
| 8:5–13 | 67, 70, 540, | | 557, 918, 951 | 10:1–7 | 411 |
| | 921, 953 | 9:7 | 875 | 10:1–6 | 515, 564, 847 |

10:1–4        178, 368,
              829, 847
10:1–2        193, 947
10:1   182, 191, 357, 325
10:2–4        193, 840
10:2   31, 521, 537, 561
10:3          23, 365
10:4          858
10:5–23       375
10:5–15       502
10:5–7   172, 175, 178,
              776
10:5–6   29, 538, 705,
              942, 946
10:5     131, 146, 950
10:6   56, 87, 144, 809
10:7–8        325
10:7     132, 482, 357
10:8          413
10:11–15      310
10:12         253
10:16–42      502
10:16–25 480, 672, 756
10:16–24      774
10:16–23      376, 411,
              772, 777
10:16 464, 473, 809, 952
10:17–23      847
10:17–21      32, 491
10:17 181, 619, 862, 878
10:18    523, 776, 953
10:19–20   32, 491, 776
10:19         296, 799
10:20         77
10:21         523
10:22–23      794
10:22         776
10:23 28, 348, 557, 577,
       579, 706, 776, 777
10:24–42      193
10:24–25  32, 126, 199,
       211, 255, 284, 447,
       491, 523, 814, 957
10:24    32, 491, 686
10:25–39      952
10:25    295, 461, 490
10:27         189
10:28–33      32, 491

10:28         464, 624
10:32, 33     26, 32,
              325, 422, 491,
              559, 841, 728
10:34–39      32, 295,
              455, 491, 523,
              544, 652, 748
10:37–39      350
10:40–42  32, 491, 614
              811
10:40–41      697
10:40         728
10:41–42      955
10:41         755, 810
11–12         412, 472
11:1–6   457, 462, 465
11:1     32, 328, 384,
              508, 652, 825
11:2–19       134
11:2–6   104, 175, 372,
       492, 511, 554, 671
11:2–5        372
11:3          137
11:4–6        182
11:4–5        138
11:4          591
11:5     206, 207, 217
11:6   207, 510, 560, 839
11:7–24       457
11:7–10       591
11:8          133
11:10         78
11:11–15      482
11:11         130, 612
11:13         228, 229
11:14         594
11:15         476
11:16–19  116, 118, 473
11:19         348, 557
11:20–24  138, 149, 391,
       411, 447, 452, 462,
              538, 751, 835
11:20         173, 686
11:21         615
11:23         354
11:25–30  86, 38, 441
11:25–27      26, 559
11:25         487, 686

11:27  27, 275, 325, 456,
       460, 472, 616, 697,
       718, 728, 951, 955
11:28–30 206, 438, 442,
              445, 673, 746
11:28–29      458
11:28         30
11:29         28, 207
11:30         332
12        34, 425, 472
12:1–45       411
12:1–14       355, 534
12:1–8        208, 236
12:1–7        534
12:1–2        642
12:2          595
12:3–5        236
12:6   600, 692, 864, 905
12:8     28, 295, 348, 557
12:9–14   236, 553, 555
12:9          181
12:15–21  102, 104, 853
12:15         721
12:16    154, 341, 373,
              568, 593
12:17–21   78, 143, 345
12:17         83
12:18–21      142
12:18  77, 142, 393, 776
12:21         298
12:22–45      916
12:22–37      553
12:22–32   33, 104, 192,
       227, 373, 540,
              611, 944
12:22–23  104, 504, 192
12:22         374, 555
12:23         26, 56, 727
12:24–32      626
12:24    374, 418, 509,
              555, 705, 395
12:27         395
12:25–32      706
12:27–29      473
12:28    77, 132, 339,
              353, 393, 955
12:30–32  496, 521, 696
12:30 295 477, 484, 875

| | | | | | |
|---|---|---|---|---|---|
| 12:31–32 | 478, 510 | 13:19 | 248 | 14:1–14 | 412 |
| 12:32 | 28, 574, 348 | 13:21 | 774 | 14:1–13 | 553 |
| 12:33–37 | 480, 481, 625 | 13:22 | 658 | 14:1–12 | 115, 171 |
| 12:34–35 | 545 | 13:23 | 625 | 14:1–2 | 538 |
| 12:34 | 135, 756 | 13:24–50 | 794 | 14:1 | 114 |
| 12:38–42 | 554 | 13:24–30 | 735 | 14:2 | 558 |
| 12:38–39 | 706, 901 | 13:24 623, 664, 715, 804 | | 14:4 | 439 |
| 12:38 | 570, 599, 720 | 13:29 | 537 | 14:6–11 | 557 |
| 12:39 | 418 | 13:30 | 376, 804 | 14:12–14 | 102 |
| 12:40–42 | 901 | 13:31–33 | 33 | 14:13–21 | 191, 418, |
| 12:40–41 | 555 | 13:31 | 623, 664, 715 | | 541, 553 |
| 12:40 | 28, 348, 570, | 13:33 | 556, 664 | 14:13–14 | 192 |
| | 914, 922, 936 | 13:34–36 | 193 | 14:13 154, 191, 443, 538 | |
| 12:41–42 | 418 | 13:35 | 78 | 14:14 | 374 |
| 12:43–45 | 473 | 13:37–43 | 557 | 14:15–21 | 546, 583 |
| 12:43 | 385, 418 | 13:37 | 28, 348 | 14:17 | 948 |
| 12:45 | 418 | 13:38 | 248, 812, 953 | 14:19 | 274, 289, 351 |
| 12:46–50 | 33, 119, 193, | 13:39 | 76, 154, 155, | 14:22–36 | 553 |
| | 242, 254, 509, | | 376, 784 | 14:27–31 | 546 |
| | 544, 578, 618, | 13:41–43 | 33 | 14:28–32 | 842 |
| | 626, 946, 962 | 13:41–42 | 845 | 14:28–31 | 31, 537, 558, |
| 12:47 | 82 | 13:41 76, 348, 71, 784 | | | 591, 839, 880 |
| 12:48–50 | 70, 253, 564, | 13:42 537, 624, 717, 835 | | 14:28 | 28, 31, 324, 388 |
| | 566, 600, 749, | 13:43 | 398, 810 | 14:30 | 28, 31, 324 |
| | 811, 921, 941, 956 | 13:44 | 623, 664, 715, | 14:31 | 298, 597 |
| 12:50 | 26, 277, 325, | | 804, 807 | 14:32–33 | 546 |
| | 422, 472, 559, 616 | 13:44–46 | 33 | 14:33 | 27, 28, 85, 154, |
| 13 | 25, 32, 200, 759, | 13:45–46 | 311 | | 161, 324, 353, 421, |
| | 771, 788, 971 | 13:45 | 623, 664, 715, 804 | | 561, 595, 728, 908, |
| 13:1–17 | 454 | 13:47 | 623, 664, 804 | | 942, 946, 948 |
| 13:1–3 | 514 | 13:49–50 | 33, 624, 835 | 14:34 | 538 |
| 13:1–2 | 33, 192, 626 | 13:49 | 76, 398, 784, 810 | 14:36 | 747 |
| 13:2–3 | 192 | 13:50 | 717 | 15 | 34 |
| 13:4 | 439 | 13:51–52 | 33 | 15:1–20 | 233, 519, 553, |
| 13:8 | 625 | 13:51 | 537, 595 | | 611, 754, 946 |
| 13:10–23 | 545 | 13:52 100, 715, 911, 952 | | 15:1–19 | 209 |
| 13:10–17 | 33, 193, 510, | 13:53–58 397, 538, 553 | | 15:1–9 | 328, 350, 380, |
| | 513, 519, 537, 554, | 13:53 | 32, 328, 412, | | 746, 752 |
| | 556, 595, 626, 641, | | 652, 825 | 15:1 | 347, 554, 595, |
| | 706, 804, 876, 916 | 13:54–58 | 455 | | 642, 754 |
| 13:10–16 | 421 | 13:54 | 181, 724 | 15:3–9 | 455 |
| 13:10 | 645 | 13:55–58 | 119 | 15:3–6 | 278 |
| 13:11 | 27, 561 | 13:55–56 | 455 | 15:4 | 748 |
| 13:12 | 808 | 13:55 82, 119, 309, 327 | | 15:6–9 | 219 |
| 13:14–15 | 78, 449 | 13:57 | 839 | 15:7–8 | 118 |
| 13:16 | 560, 561 | 13:58 | 328, 540, 597, | 15:8–19 | 817 |
| 13:17 | 398, 755 | | 724, 800 | 15:8 | 877 |
| 13:18–23 | 33 | 14–17 | 529, 611 | 15:10–20 | 754 |

| | | | | | |
|---|---|---|---|---|---|
| 15:12 | 645 | 16:16–19 | 31, 525, | 17:10–13 | 417 |
| 15:13 | 26, 559 | | 847, 941 | 17:10 | 231 |
| 15:14 | 752 | 16:16–17 | 598, 601, | 17:12–13 | 557 |
| 15:15 | 31, 388, 521, 525, | | 602, 670 | 17:12 | 28, 348, 574 |
| | 558, 591, 839, 880 | 16:17–20 | 178 | 17:14–21 | 182 |
| 15:16–20 | 219, 232 | 16:17–19 | 31, 388, 521, | 17:14–20 | 354 |
| 15:16 | 489 | | 591, 839, 846, 880 | 17:14–15 | 31, 192 |
| 15:17–19 | 842 | 16:17 | 204, 325, 422, | 17:15 | 28, 324, 340 |
| 15:18–20 | 754, 804 | | 591, 616 | 17:17 | 351, 418, 949 |
| 15:18–19 | 294 | 16:18–19 | 426, 485, 501, | 17:18 | 446 |
| 15:19 | 245, 615, 812 | | 599, 620, 946 | 17:20–21 | 694 |
| 15:20 | 950 | 16:18 | 25, 30, 77, 120, | 17:20 | 298, 343, 351, |
| 15:21–34 | 411 | | 611, 618, 620 | | 483, 517 |
| 15:21–31 | 553 | 16:19 | 620 | 17:22–23 | 443, 508, |
| 15:21–28 | 102, 389, 946 | 16:20 | 341, 373, 444, 593 | | 569, 611, 666, 670, |
| 15:21 | 172 | 16:21–28:20 | 174 | | 826, 839, 894, 918 |
| 15:22 | 26, 28, 56, | 16:21–28 | 508 | 17:22 | 28, 171, 348, |
| | 324, 340, 727 | 16:21–27 | 160 | | 556, 574 |
| 15:24 | 29, 56, 144, | 16:21–23 | 104, 841, | 17:23 | 451, 698, 936, 939 |
| | 175, 400, 697, | | 846, 847 | 17:24–27 | 31, 521, 526, |
| | 705, 809, 942, 950 | 16:21 | 174, 443, 451, | | 558, 611, 623, 664, |
| 15:25 | 161 | | 611, 666, 670, 698, | | 691, 720, 839, 880 |
| 15:28 | 343, 705 | | 826, 839, 894, 918, | 17:24 | 31, 525, 556, 720 |
| 15:29–30 | 950 | | 936, 939, 944 | 18 | 32, 33, 200, 476, |
| 15:29 | 192 | 16:22–23 | 525, 841 | | 492, 508, 642, 652, |
| 15:30–31 | 373, 413, 446 | 16:22 | 31 | | 671, 672, 759, 771, |
| 15:32–38 | 191, 583 | 16:23 | 154, 160 | | 788, 971 |
| 15:32 | 176, 374 | 16:24–27 | 882 | 18:1–5 | 418, 421, |
| 15:34 | 948 | 16:24–26 | 398, 930 | | 646, 650 |
| 15:36 | 274, 289 | 16:24 | 169 | 18:1–4 | 426, 649 |
| 15:37–40 | 22 | 16:25 | 28, 324 | 18:1 | 399, 654, 669, |
| 15:39 | 554, 910 | 16:27–28 | 28, 348 | | 750, 811, 882 |
| 16:1–12 | 611 | 16:27 | 76, 450, 783, 784 | 18:2–5 | 399, 811 |
| 16:1–4 | 135 | 17 | 34 | 18:3–4 | 717 |
| 16:1 | 156, 647, 719 | 17:1–8 | 508, 574, | 18:6–9 | 654 |
| 16:4 | 418 | | 906, 948 | 18:6 | 801 |
| 16:5–12 | 135 | 17:1 | 31, 191, 525, 585 | 18:7 | 571, 794 |
| 16:6 | 310 | 17:2 | 388 | 18:8–9 | 245 |
| 16:7 | 27, 948 | 17:4 | 28, 31, 324, 525 | 18:8 | 721 |
| 16:8 | 298 | 17:5–8 | 949 | 18:9 | 243 |
| 16:12 | 310, 595 | 17:5 | 25, 27, 89, 111, | 18:10–35 | 868 |
| 16:13 | 28, 348, 590 | | 143, 353, 421, | 18:10–14 | 658 |
| 16:14 | 689, 871, 948 | | 444, 697, 908, 939 | 18:10 | 76, 325, 422 |
| 16:15–19 | 508 | 17:6 | 908 | 18:12–20 | 794 |
| 16:16 | 27, 179, 353, 421, | 17:9–13 | 134 | 18:14 | 455 |
| | 518, 525, 591, 728, | 17:9–12 | 557 | 18:15–17 | 811 |
| | 864, 867, 908 | 17:9 | 28, 341, 348, | 18:16–18 | 567 |
| 16:16–23 | 842 | | 373, 444, 568 | 18:17–18 | 310, 946 |

| | | | | | |
|---|---|---|---|---|---|
| 18:17 | 25 | 20 | 611, 654 | 21–28 | 709 |
| 18:18–20 | 561 | 20:1–28 | 284 | 21–23 | 789 |
| 18:18 | 521, 564, 565, | 20:1–16 | 284, 490, | 21 | 715, 744 |
| | 567, 568, 580 | | 652, 659, 696 | 21:1–11 | 769 |
| 18:19 | 325, 422 | 20:1–15 | 345, 642, 651 | 21:1 | 799, 825 |
| 18:20 | 654, 671, 955 | 20:1–11 | 684 | 21:2 | 600 |
| 18:21–35 | 279, 280 | 20:1–6 | 473 | 21:3 | 28, 295, 325 |
| 18:21–22 | 243 | 20:5 | 948 | 21:4–5 | 78 |
| 18:21 | 28, 31, 324, 388, | 20:8 | 270, 295, 686, 829 | 21:4 | 412 |
| | 526, 558, 591, 839, | 20:9 | 829 | 21:5 | 207, 228, 810 |
| | 880 | 20:13 | 717, 859 | 21:8–16 | 874, 875 |
| 18:23–35 | 578 | 20:16 | 659 | 21:8–11 | 827, 858 |
| 18:23 | 664 | 20:17–22 | 574 | 21:9 | 26, 56, 137, |
| 18:24–28 | 664 | 20:17–19 | 443, 508, | | 727, 758 |
| 18:24 | 806 | | 569, 784, 826, | 21:10 | 757 |
| 18:25 | 295 | | 839, 894, 918 | 21:11 | 116, 228 |
| 18:27 | 374 | 20:17 | 384 | 21:12–22 | 905 |
| 18:28 | 829 | 20:18–19 | 346 | 21:12–17 | 260, 769, 828 |
| 18:33 | 209 | 20:18 | 28, 348, 557, | 21:12–13 | 356 |
| 18:34 | 243, 260 | | 698, 833 | 21:12 | 808 |
| 19–20 | 653, 671 | 20:19 | 451, 936, 939 | 21:13 | 228 |
| 19 | 34, 262, 654 | 20:20–28 | 104, 426, | 21:14–16 | 864 |
| 19:1 | 32, 328, 412, 508, | | 578, 612, 642, | 21:14–15 | 373, 446 |
| | 556, 611, 666, 825 | | 808, 882, 917 | 21:15 | 26, 56, 347, 356, |
| 19:3–12 | 246 | 20:20–21 | 654 | | 570, 669, 727 |
| 19:3 | 439, 719 | 20:20 | 161, 910 | 21:17 | 770, 825, 829, 838 |
| 19:7 | 957 | 20:21 | 750, 809, 900 | 21:18–22 | 785 |
| 19:12 | 245 | 20:22–23 | 841 | 21:19 | 600 |
| 19:16–22 | 296, 488, | 20:22 | 574 | 22:21–26 | 58 |
| | 664, 922 | 20:23 | 26, 325, 422, | 21:21–22 | 597 |
| 19:16 | 599, 720 | | 559, 616 | 21:21 | 641 |
| 19:19 | 667 | 20:24 | 692 | 21:23–22:46 | 769 |
| 19:21 | 205 | 20:25–28 | 627 | 21:23–46 | 421 |
| 19:23–30 | 664 | 20:25 | 357 | 21:23 | 357, 715, 719, |
| 19:23–26 | 922 | 20:26–27 | 464, 749 | | 728, 744, 944 |
| 19:23–24 | 132 | 20:28 | 28, 77, 87, 341, | 21:24–27 | 715 |
| 19:23 | 156 | | 346, 348, 557, 569, | 21:24 | 357 |
| 19:24 | 214, 447 | | 607, 718, 750, 784, | 21:25 | 948 |
| 19:25 | 328, 724 | | 837, 841, 882, 894, | 21:27 | 357 |
| 19:27 | 31, 177, 344, | | 902, 903, 910, 918, | 21:28–22:14 | 744 |
| | 665, 672 | | 920 | 21:28–46 | 664, 715 |
| 19:28 | 28, 308, 348, | 20:29–34 | 642 | 21:28–32 | 473, 718, 728 |
| | 385, 515, 557, 573, | 20:29 | 611, 684 | 21:28 | 716 |
| | 667, 669, 706, 783, | 20:30–31 | 26, 56, 727 | 21:31–32 | 140 |
| | 829, 847 | 20:30 | 28, 324, 340 | 21:31 | 325, 447, 455 |
| 19:29 | 666, 801 | 20:31 | 28, 324, 340, 948 | 21:32 | 140 |
| 19:30 | 664, 665 | 20:33 | 28, 324, 340 | 21:33–46 | 718, 728 |
| 20–22 | 34 | 20:34 | 374 | 21:33–43 | 490 |

| | | | | | |
|---|---|---|---|---|---|
| 21:33 | 490, 716 | 23–24 | 906 | 24:6 | 393, 574, 953 |
| 21:38–41 | 918 | 23 | 34, 380, 728, 914 | 24:9–13 | 392 |
| 21:41 | 718 | 23:1–36 | 684, 694, | 24:11–12 | 322 |
| 21:42–44 | 918 | | 719, 769 | 24:13 | 393 |
| 21:42–43 | 953 | 23:1–12 | 180 | 24:14 | 146, 181, 480, |
| 21:42 | 563 | 23:2 | 192 | | 809, 953, 954 |
| 21:43–46 | 343 | 23:4 | 98, 422, 424 | 24:15–28 | 672 |
| 21:43 | 57, 447, 550, | 23:5–7 | 424 | 24:15 | 78 |
| | 577, 718, 750, | 23:5 | 371 | 24:22 | 718 |
| | 758, 888, 953 | 23:7–10 | 347 | 24:24 | 322, 718 |
| 21:44 | 29 | 23:8–12 | 673, 952 | 24:27 | 28, 348, 557, 938 |
| 21:45 | 719, 734 | 23:8–10 | 964 | 24:29–31 | 175 |
| 22 | 744 | 23:8 | 811 | 24:29 | 450, 902 |
| 22:1–14 | 74, 421 | 23:13–29 | 803 | 24:30–31 | 573, 845, 859 |
| 22:1–13 | 60 | 23:13–15 | 233, 888 | 24:30 | 28, 348, 557, |
| 22:7 | 260 | 23:13 | 347, 420, 566 | | 602, 839 |
| 22:10 | 30 | 23:14 | 751 | 24:31 | 76, 486, 718 |
| 22:11–13 | 369 | 23:16–22 | 247, 537 | 24:32–35 | 799 |
| 22:12 | 859 | 23:17 | 260 | 24:34 | 418 |
| 22:13 | 343, 805 | 23:23 | 230, 725 | 24:35 | 957 |
| 22:14 | 22 | 23:25–28 | 421 | 24:36–25:46 | 790 |
| 22:15–22:46 | 694 | 23:25–26 | 219 | 24:36–42 | 414 |
| 22:15–46 | 744 | 23:27–28 | 232 | 24:36 | 76, 421, 559 |
| 22:15–26 | 690 | 23:27 | 219 | 24:37 | 28, 348, 557 |
| 22:16 | 368, 599, 952 | 23:29 | 398 | 24:39 | 28, 348, 557 |
| 22:17 | 599 | 23:32 | 309 | 24:42–44 | 295 |
| 22:19 | 948 | 23:33–34 | 392 | 24:42 | 28, 325, 559 |
| 22:23–33 | 556 | 23:33 | 135, 450 | 24:43 | 490 |
| 22:23 | 962 | 23:34 | 181, 211, 398, | 24:44 | 28, 348, 557 |
| 22:24 | 599 | | 697, 771, 878 | 24:46 | 560 |
| 22:30 | 76 | 23:35–36 | 272 | 24:51 | 624, 717 |
| 22:31 | 78 | 23:36–38 | 770 | 25:1–13 | 772 |
| 22:33 | 328 | 23:36 | 418 | 25:12–13 | 368 |
| 22:34–40 | 775, 957 | 23:37–39 | 577, 579, | 25:13 | 326 |
| 22:34–35 | 156 | | 706, 782 | 25:14–30 | 202, 302, 772 |
| 22:36–40 | 252, 648 | 23:38 | 28, 325, 801 | 25:15 | 623 |
| 22:36 | 599, 697 | 23:39 | 137, 784, 888 | 25:21, 23 | 169 |
| 22:37–40 | 315, 545 | 24–25 | 32, 33, 200, 476, | 25:25 | 487 |
| 22:37 | 169, 258, 296 | | 477, 492, 684, 700, | 25:26, 30 | 717 |
| 22:38–39 | 236 | | 744, 758, 759, 788, | 25:30 | 186, 902 |
| 22:40 | 228 | | 799, 971 | 25:31–46 | 398, 772, |
| 22:41–46 | 865 | 24:1–25:46 | 709 | | 783, 829 |
| 22:42 | 26, 56 | 24:1–28 | 24 | 25:31–34 | 160 |
| 22:43–45 | 28, 325 | 24:1–3 | 716, 814 | 25:31–26 | 60 |
| 22:43 | 845 | 24:3–4 | 192 | 25:31 | 28, 76, 348, |
| 22:44 | 295 | 24:3 | 191, 486 | | 557, 573, 784 |
| 22:45 | 26, 56 | 24:4–31 | 799 | 25:32 | 298, 953 |
| 22:46 | 903 | 24:4–8 | 853 | 25:33–46 | 668 |

| | |
|---|---|
| 25:34 | 26, 325, 422, 616 |
| 25:35 | 207 |
| 25:37 | 28, 325, 398 |
| 25:41 | 76, 154 |
| 25:42 | 615 |
| 25:44 | 28, 325 |
| 25:46 | 398, 648, 835 |
| 26–28 | 844 |
| 26–27 | 684, 933 |
| 26:1–46 | 857 |
| 26:1–2 | 104 |
| 26:1 | 32, 328, 412, 652 |
| 26:2 | 28, 348, 557, 569, 666, 894, 918 |
| 26:3–5 | 690 |
| 26:3–4 | 944, 945 |
| 26:3 | 570, 694, 862 |
| 26:4 | 443 |
| 26:6–13 | 685, 709 |
| 26:8 | 669 |
| 26:10 | 721 |
| 26:11 | 205 |
| 26:14–16 | 576, 710, 879 |
| 26:14–15 | 869 |
| 26:14 | 384 |
| 26:15 | * 943, 948 |
| 26:16 | 936 |
| 26:17–19 | 710 |
| 26:17 | 641 |
| 26:18 | 749 |
| 26:20–35 | 710 |
| 26:20–25 | 879 |
| 26:20 | 384 |
| 26:21–25 | 575, 598 |
| 26:22 | 28, 324, 649 |
| 26:24–25 | 473 |
| 26:24 | 28, 348, 557, 615 |
| 26:25 | 858, 865, 872, 880 |
| 26:26–29 | 198, 208, 426, 545, 700 |
| 26:26 | 747 |
| 26:27–28 | 345, 346, 549 |
| 26:28 | 279, 341, 345, 902 |
| 26:31–35 | 668, 889 |
| 26:31–34 | 861 |
| 26:31 | 78, 809 |
| 26:32 | 940 |

| | |
|---|---|
| 26:33–41 | 526 |
| 26:33 | 31 |
| 26:35 | 388, 881 |
| 26:36–46 | 160, 513, 710 |
| 26:36–44 | 857 |
| 26:36 | 857 |
| 26:37 | 31, 388, 526, 649 |
| 26:39–44 | 900 |
| 26:39–42 | 111, 620 |
| 26:39 | 25, 26, 143, 154, 277, 325, 421, 422, 616, 668 |
| 26:40–41 | 526 |
| 26:40 | 31, 388 |
| 26:41 | 279 |
| 26:42 | 25, 26, 86, 143, 154, 277, 325, 422, 455, 456, 460, 472, 616 |
| 26:44 | 274 |
| 26:45–46 | 857 |
| 26:45 | 28, 348, 367, 557 |
| 26:46–56 | 847 |
| 26:47–27:26 | 826 |
| 26:47–56 | 710, 833 |
| 26:47–50 | 575, 598 |
| 26:47 | 694, 915 |
| 26:48 | 944 |
| 26:49 | 180 |
| 26:50–58 | 847 |
| 26:50–53 | 917 |
| 26:50 | 717 |
| 26:52 | 397 |
| 26:53 | 26, 76, 159, 325, 422, 559, 616, 784 |
| 26:55 | 192, 900 |
| 26:56 | 78, 801, 912 |
| 26:57–27:1 | 847 |
| 26:57–75 | 710 |
| 26:57–68 | 729 |
| 26:57 | 95, 98 |
| 26:58 | 31, 526 |
| 26:61 | 690, 900 |
| 26:63–65 | 909 |
| 26:63–64 | 26, 263, 908 |
| 26:63 | 421 |
| 26:64 | 28, 348, 450, 557, 783, 835, 901 |

| | |
|---|---|
| 26:65–66 | 900 |
| 26:67 | 948 |
| 26:68 | 896 |
| 26:69–75 | 31, 526, 576, 847 |
| 26:71 | 116, 119 |
| 27 | 925 |
| 27:1–10 | 847 |
| 27:1–2 | 443, 710, 899, 945 |
| 27:1 | 695 |
| 27:2–14 | 710 |
| 27:3–5 | 598, 947 |
| 27:4 | 948 |
| 27:5–10 | 102 |
| 27:5 | 172 |
| 27:6 | 439 |
| 27:8 | 25 |
| 27:9–10 | 78 |
| 27:9 | 78, 558 |
| 27:11–14 | 703, 899 |
| 27:11 | 60, 810, 835, 845 |
| 27:12 | 345 |
| 27:15–26 | 710 |
| 27:15–25 | 193 |
| 27:15–16 | 175 |
| 27:16 | 899 |
| 27:17–25 | 462 |
| 27:19 | 76, 895 |
| 27:20–25 | 448, 724 |
| 27:20 | 98, 492, 700, 757 |
| 27:21–25 | 945 |
| 27:21 | 948 |
| 27:22 | 689 |
| 27:23 | 948 |
| 27:24–25 | 173 |
| 27:25 | 77, 98, 757, 953 |
| 27:26 | 571, 895 |
| 27:27–66 | 710, 826 |
| 27:29 | 60, 703, 810, 845, 896 |
| 27:32 | 250 |
| 27:33 | 944 |
| 27:35 | 250, 571 |
| 27:37 | 60, 810 |
| 27:38 | 345, 860 |
| 27:42 | 60, 810 |

| | | | |
|---|---|---|---|
| 27:43 | 421 | 28:19 | 26, 29, 57, 77, | 5:26 | 371 |
| 27:45 | 959 | | 147, 199, 275, 298, | 5:29–30 | 371 |
| 27:46 | 85, 120, 841 | | 400, 456, 550, 559, | 5:37–40 | 388 |
| 27:51 | 692, 937, 938 | | 777, 783, 911, 921 | 5:41 | 120 |
| 27:53 | 97 | 28:20 | 20, 32, 35, 81, | 6:1–6 | 509 |
| 27:54 | 85, 353, 421 | | 84, 190, 199, | 6:3 | 510 |
| 27:55–61 | 945 | | 256, 283, 328, 394, | 6:5 | 800 |
| 27:55–56 | 666, 667, 688, | | 399, 491, 548, 621, | 6:7 | 384, 387 |
| | 937, 939, 962 | | 653, 749, 770, 776 | 6:30 | 412 |
| 27:55 | 193, 542 | | | 6:32–44 | 514 |
| 27:56 | 193, 667, 937 | **Mark** | | 6:51–52 | 518 |
| 27:57–61 | 404, 755, 936 | 1:1 | 55, 65, 184 | 6:52 | 595 |
| 27:57–60 | 187, 733 | 1:2 | 871 | 6:56 | 747 |
| 27:57 | 193, 302, 651, | 1:4 | 137 | 7:3–4 | 543 |
| | 658, 952 | 1:9–11 | 139 | 7:5–8 | 231 |
| 27:60–66 | 937 | 1:10 | 141 | 7:11 | 535 |
| 27:60–61 | 939 | 1:18 | 709 | 7:18 | 537 |
| 27:60 | 944 | 1:20 | 177 | 7:31 | 541 |
| 27:61 | 193, 939 | 1:21–31 | 344 | 7:32–37 | 413 |
| 27:62–66 | 943 | 1:21–28 | 345 | 8:2 | 176 |
| 27:62 | 831, 944 | 1:21 | 438 | 8:10 | 542 |
| 27:65 | 858, 944 | 1:24 | 116 | 8:19 | 858 |
| 28 | 684, 925 | 1:29 | 439 | 8:21 | 595 |
| 28:1–20 | 570 | 1:35 | 191, 513 | 8:29 | 26, 27, 388 |
| 28:1–8 | 193, 710 | 1:41 | 87 | 8:34 | 586 |
| 28:2–5 | 784 | 2:1–12 | 355 | 8:37 | 573 |
| 28:2 | 76, 905 | 2:4 | 802 | 9:1 | 575 |
| 28:5 | 76 | 2:6–12 | 162 | 9:2–10 | 575, 590 |
| 28:9–20 | 710 | 2:7 | 355 | 9:5 | 180, 388 |
| 28:9 | 85, 910 | 2:14 | 23, 24, 365 | 9:9–13 | 23 |
| 28:10 | 811, 839, 922 | 2:18 | 368 | 9:9 | 23 |
| 28:11–15 | 20, 899, 914 | 2:23–3:6 | 438 | 9:10–11 | 24 |
| 28:11 | 858, 915 | 3:6 | 719 | 9:10 | 595 |
| 28:16–20 | 28, 401, | 3:7–8 | 444 | 9:14 | 590, 595 |
| | 502, 777 | 3:13–19 | 384 | 9:27 | 26 |
| 28:16 | 191, 868 | 3:16–19 | 386, 387 | 9:32 | 595 |
| 28:17 | 161, 839 | 3:18 | 24, 366 | 10:3 | 957 |
| 28:18–20 | 29, 67, 178, | 3:21 | 397, 454, 509 | 10:17–22 | 647 |
| | 357, 385, 392, | 4:10 | 384 | 10:17 | 647 |
| | 394, 500, 404, | 4:11–12 | 493 | 10:24–25 | 132 |
| | 411, 422, 426,: | 4:12 | 477, 478 | 10:28 | 388 |
| | 578, 626, 699, | 4:37 | 176, 351 | 10:35–36 | 667 |
| | 706, 717, 735, | 4:38 | 351 | 10:45 | 464, 910 |
| | 788, 809 | 5:1–20 | 353, 938 | 10:46 | 671 |
| 28:18 | 144, 172, 173, | 5:13 | 354 | 10:47 | 116 |
| | 357, 749 | 5:18–19 | 354 | 11–16 | 709 |
| 28:19–20 | 234, 389, 456, | 5:22 | 370 | 11:1–10 | 709 |
| | 490, 759 | 5:23 | 370 | 11:6 | 957 |

| | | | | | |
|---|---|---|---|---|---|
| 11:11 | 689, 709 | 15:37 | 904 | 2:34–35 | 87 |
| 11:12–14 | 689, 693, 709 | 15:40–41 | 909 | 2:39–50 | 120 |
| 11:15–17 | 709 | 15:40 | 667 | 2:39 | 73, 92 |
| 11:17 | 691 | 15:41 | 910 | 2:41–51 | 119 |
| 11:19 | 693, 709 | 15:42 | 831, 911 | 2:49 | 569 |
| 11:20–26 | 693 | 15:43 | 912 | 2:52 | 87, 298 |
| 11:20–21 | 709 | 15:46–47 | 940 | 3:1 | 114 |
| 11:25 | 243 | 15:47 | 913 | 3:3 | 137 |
| 11:27–12:44 | 709 | 16:1–8 | 710 | 3:21–22 | 139 |
| 12:13 | 719, 730 | 16:1–6 | 940 | 3:23–38 | 58, 82 |
| 12:18 | 730 | 16:1–3 | 935 | 3:23 | 119, 130 |
| 12:34 | 725, 732, 733 | 16:1 | 667, 909, 936 | 3:28–38 | 57 |
| 13:1–37 | 709 | 16:4–7 | 935 | 3:31–32 | 58, 60 |
| 13:1 | 770 | 16:7 | 922, 940 | 3:32 | 58 |
| 13:3 | 388 | 16:8 | 184, 935 | 3:38 | 58 |
| 13:9–13 | 392 | 16:12–13 | 935 | 4:1–13 | 690 |
| 13:14–20 | 771, 777 | 16:14 | 935 | 4:1–2 | 281 |
| 13:14 | 778 | 16:15–18 | 935 | 4:3–12 | 159 |
| 13:34 | 957 | 16:19–20 | 936 | 4:5–6 | 161 |
| 14:1 | 832 | | | 4:10 | 957 |
| 14:3 | 829 | **Luke** | | 4:16–31 | 172 |
| 14:5 | 829 | 1:1–4 | 65 | 4:16–30 | 181, 508, 509 |
| 14:3–9 | 828 | 1:5–25 | 130 | 4:16–20 | 120 |
| 14:10–11 | 710 | 1:6 | 75 | 4:31–39 | 344 |
| 14:12–16 | 710 | 1:11–20 | 76, 937 | 4:34 | 116 |
| 14:12 | 831, 832, 833 | 1:17 | 417, 594 | 4:40 | 345 |
| 14:14, 16 | 832 | 1:26–56 | 87 | 5:1–3 | 472 |
| 14:17–26 | 710 | 1:26–38 | 76, 937 | 5:1 | 176 |
| 14:17 | 831 | 1:26 | 76 | 5:2 | 176 |
| 14:32–42 | 710 | 1:28 | 81 | 5:16 | 513 |
| 14:36 | 120 | 1:31 | 82 | 5:17–26 | 355 |
| 14:40 | 843 | 1:32 | 82 | 5:19 | 802 |
| 14:43–52 | 710 | 1:35 | 82, 86 | 5:21 | 355 |
| 14:53–65 | 710 | 1:36 | 74, 130 | 5:27 | 23, 365 |
| 14:53 | 98, 695 | 1:38 | 82 | 5:29–30 | 24, 366 |
| 14:56 | 863 | 1:39–80 | 130 | 5:33 | 368 |
| 14:58 | 690 | 1:56 | 74 | 6:1–11 | 438 |
| 14:67 | 119 | 1:78 | 95 | 6:6 | 442 |
| 15:1 | 171, 710 | 1:80 | 130 | 6:12 | 274, 513 |
| 15:2–5 | 710 | 2:1–7 | 92 | 6:13 | 349 |
| 15:6–15 | 710 | 2:4–5 | 73 | 6:13–16 | 386, 387 |
| 15:7 | 873 | 2:6–7 | 82 | 6:15–16 | 858 |
| 15:16–39 | 710 | 2:9 | 76 | 6:17–49 | 193 |
| 15:21 | 250, 896 | 2:11 | 228 | 6:17–19 | 193 |
| 15:23 | 101 | 2:17 | 99 | 6:17 | 349 |
| 15:25 | 901 | 2:19 | 87 | 6:22 | 211 |
| 15:27 | 860 | 2:27 | 99 | 6:24–26 | 193, 218 |
| 15:34 | 120 | 2:29 | 92 | 6:26 | 211 |

| | | | | | | |
|---|---|---|---|---|---|---|
| 6:31 | 313 | 14:25–33 | 651, 652 | 22:53 | 902, 918 | |
| 6:35 | 251 | 14:25–26 | 350 | 22:59 | 867 | |
| 6:47–49 | 326 | 14:26 | 295, 544 | 23:1 | 114 | |
| 7:1–10 | 341 | 14:34–35 | 194 | 23:2 | 873 | |
| 7:13 | 87 | 15:3–7 | 617 | 23:6–12 | 114, 115, 511, | |
| 7:36–50 | 367, 828 | 16:1–13 | 675 | | 710, 872 | |
| 7:43 | 308 | 16:8 | 186, 343 | 23:19 | 873 | |
| 7:46 | 828 | 16:16 | 181 | 23:33 | 176 | |
| 8:1–3 | 666, 910, 921 | 17:37 | 781 | 23:34 | 266, 464, 894 | |
| 8:1 | 384 | 18:1–8 | 274 | 23:36 | 898 | |
| 8:2 | 542, 910 | 18:12 | 281 | 23:39–43 | 894 | |
| 8:3 | 665 | 18:18 | 647 | 23:39 | 901 | |
| 8:22 | 176 | 18:23 | 647 | 23:40–43 | 901 | |
| 8:23 | 176, 351 | 18:24–25 | 131 | 23:43 | 894 | |
| 8:26–39 | 353, 938 | 18:35 | 671 | 23:46 | 895 | |
| 8:38–39 | 354, 404 | 18:37 | 116 | 23:47 | 908 | |
| 8:41 | 370 | 19–24 | 709 | 23:49 | 909 | |
| 8:42 | 370 | 19:1–10 | 24, 365 | 23:50–51 | 733, 912 | |
| 8:43 | 371 | 19:2–10 | 302 | 23:50 | 912 | |
| 8:44–45 | 371 | 19:3 | 298 | 23:51 | 911 | |
| 8:44 | 747 | 19:8 | 364 | 23:54 | 831, 911 | |
| 9:1 | 384 | 19:9–10 | 651 | 23:55–56 | 909 | |
| 9:10–17 | 514 | 19:11–27 | 806 | 23:55 | 940 | |
| 9:10 | 412 | 19:23 | 807 | 23:56 | 936 | |
| 9:28–36 | 575, 590 | 19:37 | 688 | 24:1–12 | 710 | |
| 9:28 | 590 | 19:39 | 688 | 24:1–8 | 940 | |
| 9:51–55 | 406 | 19:41 | 464 | 24:1 | 909, 935 | |
| 10:3 | 391 | 19:42–44 | 689 | 24:2–7 | 935 | |
| 10:5 | 391 | 19:47–48 | 356 | 24:5 | 968 | |
| 10:18 | 155 | 20:27 | 730 | 24:7 | 27, 348 | |
| 10:30–35 | 685 | 21:3 | 676 | 24:8–11 | 935 | |
| 10:38–42 | 693, 828, | 21:20–24 | 771, 777, | 24:9–12 | 948 | |
| | 921 | | 782 | 24:10–11 | 909 | |
| 10:41 | 296 | 21:20 | 771 | 24:11 | 940 | |
| 11:1–4 | 193 | 21:28 | 787 | 24:12 | 935 | |
| 11:1 | 368 | 22:1 | 832 | 24:13–53 | 710 | |
| 11:2–4 | 280 | 22:3–4 | 831, 840 | 24:13–35 | 935 | |
| 11:3 | 278 | 22:3 | 870, 879, 880 | 24:33–34 | 948 | |
| 11:4 | 278 | 22:7–8 | 831, 832 | 24:34 | 564, 935 | |
| 11:29 | 555 | 22:13 | 832 | 24:36–49 | 949 | |
| 11:33 | 194 | 22:14 | 831 | 24:36–43 | 935 | |
| 11:44 | 754 | 22:15 | 832 | 24:38 | 949 | |
| 11:45–46 | 98 | 22:24–27 | 910 | 24:44–53 | 936 | |
| 12:3 | 189 | 22:24 | 833 | 24:44–49 | 946 | |
| 12:28 | 298 | 22:31–38 | 833 | 24:44–47 | 935, 939 | |
| 12:41–46 | 803 | 22:31–32 | 889 | 24:44 | 228 | |
| 13:34 | 277 | 22:44 | 165 | 24:47 | 953 | |
| 14:15–24 | 715 | 22:51 | 859 | 24:51 | 951 | |

**John**

| | | | | | |
|---|---|---|---|---|---|
| 1:1 | 65 | 3:23 | 141 | 9:2–3 | 355 |
| 1:4–14 | 215 | 3:28 | 560 | 9:5 | 215 |
| 1:4 | 186 | 3:31–36 | 138, 414 | 9:35 | 392 |
| 1:7–13 | 216 | 3:36 | 175 | 10 | 809 |
| 1:11–13 | 70 | 4:1–42 | 921 | 10:7–18 | 616 |
| 1:14, 18 | 591 | 4:1–3 | 135 | 10:10 | 433 |
| 1:18 | 702 | 4:1 | 952 | 10:11 | 98 |
| 1:19–27 | 594 | 4:13–15 | 208 | 10:14–18 | 463 |
| 1:19 | 695 | 4:17–18 | 800 | 10:17–18 | 904 |
| 1:21 | 417 | 4:25–26, 29 | 560 | 10:39–43 | 844 |
| 1:26–4:3 | 171 | 4:34 | 86, 169, 277 | 11:1–44 | 693 |
| 1:26–27 | 695 | 4:36 | 666 | 11:1 | 685 |
| 1:29–34 | 139 | 4:52 | 345 | 11:4, 11 | 800 |
| 1:29 | 379 | 5 | 510 | 11:16 | 211 |
| 1:31 | 130 | 5:22 | 308 | 11:17–18 | 685 |
| 1:32–34 | 142 | 5:25–35 | 138, 414 | 11:18 | 685 |
| 1:33 | 130 | 5:30 | 86 | 11:45–53 | 686 |
| 1:35–42 | 178, 412, 848 | 6:1–15 | 514 | 11:51–52 | 901 |
| 1:38 | 180 | 6:1 | 176 | 11:55 | 754 |
| 1:41 | 179, 187, 560 | 6:14–15 | 515 | 12–21 | 709 |
| 1:42 | 120, 561 | 6:14 | 557, 689, 702 | 12:1–10 | 685 |
| 1:43–51 | 405 | 6:18 | 176, 351 | 12:1–8 | 685, 828 |
| 1:44 | 344 | 6:35 | 208 | 12:1–3 | 688 |
| 1:45–46 | 118 | 6:38 | 86 | 12:1 | 709 |
| 1:49 | 180 | 6:60–66 | 310, 349, 613 | 12:2–8 | 709 |
| 2:1–10 | 509 | 6:60–65 | 310, 840 | 12:2 | 828 |
| 2:2 | 187 | 6:64 | 870, 879, 880 | 12:3 | 828, 829 |
| 2:4 | 800 | 6:66–71 | 952 | 12:4–6 | 389, 879 |
| 2:11 | 179, 187 | 6:66–68 | 179 | 12:4–5 | 829 |
| 2:13–17 | 689 | 6:67 | 384 | 12:4 | 834, 858, 879 |
| 2:19 | 690, 863 | 6:68 | 388 | 12:6 | 829, 879 |
| 2:20 | 770 | 6:70–71 | 879 | 12:7 | 758 |
| 2:21 | 863 | 6:70 | 384, 800 | 12:9–11 | 686 |
| 2:23–36 | 844 | 6:71 | 389, 834, 858, | 12:12–18 | 709 |
| 3:1–21 | 913 | | 870, 879 | 12:12 | 688 |
| 3:1–15 | 912 | 7:3–5 | 397 | 12:13 | 687 |
| 3:1–9 | 544 | 7:5 | 454, 509 | 12:17–19 | 686 |
| 3:1–7 | 255 | 7:40 | 557, 689, 702 | 12:23 | 27, 348 |
| 3:2 | 180 | 7:42 | 98 | 12:31 | 161 |
| 3:3 | 651 | 7:50–51 | 544 | 12:36 | 186 |
| 3:3–7 | 149 | 7:52 | 557, 689 | 12:38–39 | 78 |
| 3:13–26 | 844 | 7:51–53 | 844 | 12:46 | 215 |
| 3:16 | 108, 265, 463, | 8:5 | 957 | 13–17 | 710 |
| | 821, 953 | 8:12 | 186, 215 | 13–16 | 549 |
| 3:19 | 186 | 8:16 | 308 | 13:1–20 | 833 |
| 3:22–4:3 | 412, 954 | 8:31–32 | 169, 238, | 13:1–10 | 534 |
| 3:22–24 | 135 | | 607, 930 | 13:1–2 | 831 |
| | | 8:31–31 | 237 | 13:1 | 265, 832 |

| | | | | | |
|---|---|---|---|---|---|
| 13:2 | 831, 840, 858, | 18:5 | 116, 858 | 20:19–25 | 935 |
| | 879, 880 | 18:7 | 116 | 20:19 | 882 |
| 13:3–16 | 852 | 18:10–11 | 859 | 20:22–23 | 567, 568, |
| 13:10–11 | 800 | 18:12 | 858 | | 578, 620 |
| 13:16 | 386 | 18:13–24 | 710, 862 | 20:23 | 521, 568, 580 |
| 13:18 | 78 | 18:15–16 | 862, 866 | 20:24–29 | 949 |
| 13:20 | 832 | 18:16 | 866 | 20:24–25 | 940 |
| 13:26–31 | 844 | 18:19–23 | 690 | 20:25 | 23 |
| 13:26–30 | 858 | 18:26 | 840 | 20:28 | 23, 324 |
| 13:26–27 | 870 | 18:28 | 754, 831, 832, 914 | 20:30–31 | 35 |
| 13:27–30 | 880 | 18:31 | 443 | 21 | 564, 940 |
| 13:27–29 | 831 | 18:40 | 860, 873, 900 | 21:1–14 | 935 |
| 13:27 | 575, 859 | 19:12 | 869 | 21:1 | 176 |
| 13:30 | 836 | 19:13 | 875 | 21:15–23 | 946 |
| 13:34–45 | 238 | 19:14 | 831, 832 | 21:15–19 | 521 |
| 13:34–35 | 237, 254, | 19:19 | 116 | 21:16 | 98 |
| | 586, 957 | 19:20 | 120 | | |
| 13:38 | 800 | 19:23–24 | 250 | **Acts** | |
| 14–17 | 838 | 19:24 | 78 | 1–10 | 868 |
| 14:1–17:26 | 833 | 19:25–27 | 909 | 1:3 | 935, 939, 940 |
| 14:6 | 603 | 19:25 | 910 | 1:4–12 | 936 |
| 14:15–27 | 882 | 19:26–27 | 894, 911 | 1:4 | 788 |
| 14:15–17 | 882 | 19:26 | 909 | 1:6 | 954 |
| 14:15 | 956 | 19:28 | 78, 894 | 1:8 | 388, 946 |
| 14:23–24 | 956 | 19:30 | 895, 902, 904 | 1:9 | 95 |
| 14:30 | 161 | 19:31 | 831, 832 | 1:13 | 368, 386, 387 |
| 15:6 | 136 | 19:33 | 899 | 1:15–26 | 564, 948 |
| 15:7–8 | 237, 238 | 19:35 | 667 | 1:15–25 | 870 |
| 15:7 | 586 | 19:36–37 | 78 | 1:16–19 | 869 |
| 15:12 | 586 | 19:37 | 784 | 1:18–19 | 870 |
| 15:13 | 87 | 19:38–42 | 404, 733, 912 | 1:19 | 870 |
| 15:16 | 699, 735 | 19:38–39 | 544 | 1:25 | 870, 880 |
| 15:18–25 | 211 | 19:39–40 | 913 | 2 | 147, 566, 579 |
| 15:21 | 393, 775 | 19:39 | 101, 733 | 2:14–39 | 948 |
| 16:5–16 | 882 | 19:41–42 | 897 | 2:14 | 388, 564 |
| 16:8 | 222, 449 | 19:42 | 831, 911 | 2:16–36 | 882 |
| 16:11 | 161, 175 | 20–21 | 710 | 2:22–36 | 555 |
| 16:13, 14 | 764 | 20 | 910 | 2:22–23 | 164, 800 |
| 16:33 | 329 | 20:1–18 | 909 | 2:22 | 116, 119, 163, |
| 17 | 86, 289 | 20:1–16 | 940 | | 867, 953 |
| 17:1 | 514 | 20:1 | 935 | 2:23–36 | 701 |
| 17:5 | 591 | 20:2 | 910, 935 | 2:23 | 877, 888 |
| 17:11–17 | 467 | 20:3–5 | 935 | 2:29 | 755 |
| 17:12 | 835, 880 | 20:11–18 | 935 | 2:31 | 566 |
| 17:15–19 | 503 | 20:13 | 910 | 2:33–35 | 733 |
| 18:1 | 840 | 20:17 | 922, 940 | 2:34–36 | 733 |
| 18:2 | 840, 858 | 20:18 | 910 | 2:36 | 877 |
| 18:3 | 858 | 20:19–28 | 949 | 2:37–41 | 877, 888 |

| | | | | |
|---|---|---|---|---|
| 2:37–38 | 564 | 8:16 | 955 | 15:13–21 | 565 |
| 2:38–39 | 882 | 8:27 | 645 | 15:13 | 509 |
| 2:38 | 568, 955 | 9:9 | 281 | 16 | 564 |
| 2:41 | 877, 897, 944, 955 | 9:10 | 456 | 16:1 | 456 |
| 2:42 | 289 | 9:17–19 | 373 | 16:19–34 | 393 |
| 2:44 | 956 | 9:36–43 | 404 | 17:1–9 | 393 |
| 3:1–10 | 162 | 9:36–42 | 162 | 17:18 | 968 |
| 3:2 | 273 | 9:36 | 272, 456 | 18:2 | 20 |
| 3:4 | 564 | 10 | 389, 566, 579 | 18:6 | 877 |
| 3:6 | 116, 119, 564, 867 | 10:2 | 272 | 18:12–17 | 393 |
| 3:12 | 564 | 10:9–11:18 | 564 | 19:1–7 | 512 |
| 3:13–26 | 701 | 10:9–16 | 756 | 19:3–5 | 955 |
| 3:17–22 | 557 | 10:11 | 141 | 19:4 | 137 |
| 3:17–19 | 877 | 10:25–26 | 941 | 19:13–16 | 335 |
| 3:19–4:4 | 877 | 10:28 | 342 | 19:33 | 897 |
| 3:22 | 228, 689, 702 | 10:34 | 388 | 19:34 | 274 |
| 4:1–22 | 393 | 10:36 | 686, 853 | 20:28–30 | 334 |
| 4:1–3 | 733 | 10:37–38 | 444 | 20:29 | 323 |
| 4:4 | 877, 897, 944 | 10:38–39 | 163 | 20:35 | 676 |
| 4:8 | 564 | 10:38 | 119, 164, 800, 867 | 21:18 | 509 |
| 4:10 | 116 | 10:39–43 | 701 | 21:27–23:11 | 393 |
| 4:19 | 722 | 10:44–48 | 444 | 22:8 | 116 |
| 4:23–30 | 289 | 10:48 | 955 | 22:22–29 | 264 |
| 4:32 | 956 | 11:1–4 | 389 | 22:29 | 251 |
| 4:33 | 968 | 11:12 | 439 | 23:6–10 | 556 |
| 5:3 | 568 | 11:15 | 389 | 23:7–8 | 135 |
| 5:14 | 456, 956 | 11:19–26 | 25 | 23:8 | 723 |
| 5:17 | 393 | 11:26 | 956 | 23:12 | 290 |
| 5:28 | 877 | 11:27–30 | 304 | 23:24–26:32 | 393 |
| 5:29 | 264, 722, 737 | 12:1–17 | 509 | 24:5 | 116, 119, 124 |
| 6:1–7 | 456 | 12:1–4 | 393 | 24:17 | 272 |
| 6:1 | 944, 956 | 12:2 | 668 | 25:11–12 | 264 |
| 6:2 | 384, 386 | 12:19 | 945 | 26:9 | 116 |
| 6:7 | 733, 877, 888, 905, | 13:1–3 | 25 | 26:20 | 137 |
| | 944, 945, 956 | 13:6, 8 | 93 | 26:28 | 124, 956 |
| 6:11–14 | 864 | 13:13 | 22 | 27:9, 33 | 290 |
| 6:14 | 116, 690 | 13:24 | 137 | 28:8 | 345 |
| 6:17–18 | 733 | 13:26–31 | 701 | 28:17–31 | 393 |
| 7:12 | 393 | 13:38–39 | 953 | | |
| 7:37 | 557, 689, 702 | 13:51 | 391 | **Romans** | |
| 7:51–53 | 701 | 14:4 | 386 | 1:1–3 | 939 |
| 7:54–60 | 756 | 14:5 | 393 | 1:1 | 669 |
| 7:56 | 27, 141, 348 | 14:11–15 | 100, 941 | 1:2–6 | 961 |
| 8 | 566, 579 | 14:14 | 386, 865 | 1:3–4 | 163 |
| 8:3 | 456 | 14:21 | 952 | 1:3 | 593 |
| 8:14–25 | 564 | 14:23 | 290 | 1:13 | 481, 503 |
| 8:14–17 | 406 | 15:9 | 266 | 1:16 | 389, 953 |
| 8:14 | 388 | 15:10 | 423 | 2:9–10 | 389 |

| | | | | | |
|---|---|---|---|---|---|
| 3–4 | 195 | 12:17–21 | 853 | 9:14 | 390 |
| 3:9–18 | 607 | 12:17–19 | 264 | 9:22 | 600 |
| 3:21–31 | 717 | 12:19–21 | 250 | 9:24 | 631 |
| 3:21–26 | 572 | 12:19–20 | 264 | 9:25 | 631 |
| 3:21 | 228 | 12:20–21 | 264 | 10:4 | 563 |
| 4:1–25 | 398, 478 | 13:1–7 | 263, 264, | 10:7 | 803 |
| 4:22–25 | 717 | | 721, 730, 737 | 10:13 | 155, 165, 167 |
| 4:25 | 171 | 13:1–5 | 260, 885 | 11:2 | 544 |
| 5:1 | 853 | 13:13–14 | 660 | 11:23–33 | 836 |
| 5:8 | 106, 251, 265, | 14:13–23 | 600, 608 | 11:23 | 171, 831 |
| | 463, 953 | 14:19 | 853 | 11:26 | 852 |
| 5:10 | 265 | 15:7–13 | 577, 579, 706 | 11:27–28 | 851 |
| 5:12–14 | 313 | 15:8–9 | 539 | 11:30 | 372, 906 |
| 5:18–21 | 236 | 15:19 | 777 | 11:32 | 851 |
| 6:1–14 | 607, 712 | 15:25–27 | 304 | 12 | 481 |
| 6:1–11 | 961 | 16:1 | 669 | 12:1–31 | 503 |
| 6:1–4 | 954 | 16:7 | 386 | 12:4–6 | 955 |
| 6:3–4 | 960 | 16:13 | 897 | 12:7 | 819 |
| 6:3 | 955 | 16:19 | 392 | 13:12 | 766 |
| 6:11, 14 | 920 | | | 14:20 | 255 |
| 6:23 | 903, 918 | **1 Corinthians** | | 14:21 | 228 |
| 7:7–13 | 261 | 1:23 | 938 | 14:22 | 450 |
| 7:7–12 | 649 | 1:24, 30 | 419 | 15 | 961 |
| 7:7 | 235 | 2:2 | 924, 938, 961 | 15:1–11 | 934 |
| 7:12 | 233 | 2:7 | 419 | 15:1–7 | 701, 844 |
| 8:1 | 319 | 2:8 | 419 | 15:1 | 544 |
| 8:9–11 | 169 | 3:8 | 666 | 15:5 | 935 |
| 8:9 | 288, 880 | 3:10–11 | 327 | 15:6 | 935, 941, 950 |
| 8:18–25 | 277 | 3:11 | 563 | 15:7 | 386, 509, 935 |
| 8:22–23 | 773 | 3:12–15 | 293 | 15:8–10 | 386 |
| 8:29 | 86, 199, 255, | 3:18 | 255 | 15:12–34 | 710 |
| | 957, 961 | 4:1 | 910 | 15:14–19 | 968 |
| 8:32 | 171 | 5:5 | 310 | 15:17–19 | 962 |
| 9–11 | 784 | 5:7 | 826, 853 | 15:17 | 924 |
| 9:1–5 | 888 | 5:9–13 | 237 | 15:18 | 906 |
| 9:1–3 | 813 | 6:12–20 | 237 | 15:20–23 | 372, 907 |
| 10:1–4 | 888 | 7:5 | 74 | 15:20 | 906, 939 |
| 10:1–2 | 813 | 7:7–9 | 645 | 15:23 | 939 |
| 11:7 | 780 | 7:12–16 | 657 | 15:25–28 | 733 |
| 11:25–33 | 579, 699, 953 | 7:27 | 658 | 15:51–55 | 372 |
| 11:25–32 | 577, 706 | 7:32 | 296 | 15:51–52 | 784 |
| 11:25 | 888 | 7:39–40 | 658 | 16:22 | 277 |
| 11:26–32 | 888 | 8:1 | 764 | | |
| 12:1–2 | 237, 586 | 8:13–9:1 | 600, 608 | **2 Corinthians** | |
| 12:1 | 675 | 8:13 | 600 | 1:3–7 | 207 |
| 12:2 | 590 | 9:1–5 | 386 | 1:6 | 322 |
| 12:3 | 257 | 9:3–14 | 304 | 1:15–24 | 248 |
| 12:15 | 206 | 9:12 | 600, 608 | 1:18 | 248, 263 |
| | | | | 3:6 | 669 |

| | | | | | |
|---|---|---|---|---|---|
| 3:16 | 586 | 6:1–5 | 310 | 2:5 | 586 |
| 3:18 | 86, 126, 152, | 6:5 | 424 | 2:6–7 | 591 |
| | 199, 268, 284, 465, | 6:7–10 | 304 | 2:6 | 86 |
| | 590, 837, 957, 961 | 6:10 | 812 | 2:7 | 800 |
| 4:4 | 161 | | | 2:9–11 | 951 |
| 4:8 | 322 | **Ephesians** | | 2:15 | 189, 215 |
| 5:17–21 | 86 | 1:11 | 277 | 2:20 | 296 |
| 5:17 | 573, 651 | 1:18–21 | 967 | 2:25 | 386 |
| 5:18–19 | 920 | 1:18–20 | 738 | 3:4–6 | 235 |
| 5:21 | 842, 902 | 1:18 | 207 | 3:6 | 648 |
| 6:14 | 186 | 1:22 | 733 | 3:7–9 | 573 |
| 7:8–10 | 869 | 2:1–10 | 208 | 3:8 | 235 |
| 8:1–15 | 304 | 2:1–2 | 161 | 3:12 | 164 |
| 8:23 | 386 | 2:2 | 155 | 4:6–7 | 928, 929 |
| 10–13 | 760 | 2:8–9 | 233, 666 | 4:6 | 278, 297 |
| 9:5 | 289 | 2:11–22 | 905, 919 | 4:7 | 853, 933 |
| 9:7 | 676 | 2:11–18 | 853 | 4:14–19 | 304 |
| 11:11–15 | 323 | 2:11–17 | 210 | | |
| 12:14 | 302 | 2:11–16 | 953 | **Colossians** | |
| 12:20 | 466 | 2:19–22 | 386 | 1:5–10 | 699, 735 |
| 13:14 | 955 | 2:19 | 565 | 1:10 | 323, 481, 503 |
| | | 2:20 | 565, 579 | 1:12–13 | 186 |
| **Galatians** | | 3:7 | 669 | 1:12 | 207 |
| 1:8 | 233 | 3:14–21 | 289 | 1:13 | 920 |
| 1:10 | 669 | 3:16–17 | 919 | 1:15–20 | 86, 255 |
| 1:13–16 | 544 | 3:17 | 703 | 1:20 | 210, 853 |
| 1:17 | 386 | 4:13 | 255 | 1:23 | 669 |
| 1:19 | 386, 509 | 4:26 | 260 | 2:3 | 100 |
| 1:20 | 248, 263 | 4:27 | 504 | 2:8 | 481, 544 |
| 2:9 | 386, 509 | 4:28 | 304 | 2:11–14 | 572 |
| 2:19–20 | 572 | 5:8 | 186, 189, 215 | 3:1–4 | 852 |
| 3 | 195 | 5:18 | 738 | 3:4 | 819 |
| 3:1 | 938 | 5:19 | 675 | 3:5 | 296 |
| 3:13 | 903 | 5:20 | 675 | 4:12 | 669 |
| 3:24 | 235 | 5:21–33 | 656 | 4:14 | 22 |
| 3:27 | 955 | 5:25 | 107 | | |
| 4:2 | 665 | 6:7–8 | 818 | **1 Thessalonians** | |
| 4:4–7 | 955 | 6:9 | 818 | 1:1 | 386 |
| 4:6–7 | 694 | 6:10–20 | 402 | 2:6 | 386 |
| 4:8–9 | 326, 806 | 6:10–18 | 168, 169 | 3:10 | 251 |
| 5:1 | 423 | 6:12 | 631 | 4:13–18 | 372, 793, 814 |
| 5:13–26 | 694 | 6:14 | 408 | 4:13 | 206 |
| 5:13 | 910 | 6:17 | 858 | 4:16 | 784 |
| 5:16–24 | 323 | 6:21 | 669 | 5:1–6 | 801 |
| 5:16–23 | 503 | | | 5:1–2 | 802 |
| 5:21–24 | 699, 735 | **Philippians** | | 5:4–7 | 186, 902 |
| 5:21 | 803 | 1:11 | 323 | 5:5 | 186 |
| 5:22–23 | 223, 481 | 2:5–7 | 602 | 5:15 | 250 |

5:18 675
4:11–12 304
4:13–15 906

**2 Thessalonians**
2:1–12 777
2:3–4 778
2:10 481
2:15 544
3:6 544
3:10 264, 319
3:6–15 278, 304
3:6–13 188
3:9–12 201, 335

**1 Timothy**
2:1–7 737
2:18 402
3:1–15 941
3:2, 12 261
4:7–8 285
4:8 631
5–6 278
5:3–7 304
5:8 188, 210, 304
5:17–20 941
5:17–18 304
5:18 390
5:19–22 636
6:9 481
6:10 296
6:13 858
6:15 228

**2 Timothy**
2:19 326, 806
3:12 126, 211, 393, 407, 775
3:15–16 229
3:16 233
4:8 851

**Titus**
1:6 261
2:12 817
3:1–8 812
3:1–2 90, 737
3:3–7 288

3:3 90
3:4–7 149, 198, 267, 549, 817, 837
3:4–6 90
3:5–6 666
3:5 651

**Hebrews**
1:6 162
1:13 733
1:14 616
2:6 27, 348
2:15 920
2:17–18 156, 228
2:18 165
3:1 386
4:12 546
4:14–5:10 905
4:14–16 152, 157, 228, 800
4:15–16 86, 165
4:15 86
5:1–10 228
5:7–10 236, 841
5:8 842
5:10 847
5:14 255
6:1 255
6:16–18 263
6:19 905
6:20 733
7:11–17 847
7:24–25 228, 703
7:26–28 600
9:3 905
9:11–10:13 236
9:11–14 228, 229
9:15 207
9:20 957
9:26 919
10:10–22 919
10:13 733
10:20 905
10:24–25 223, 237
10:37 137
11:11 298
11:17 155
11:22 957
11:37 133

12:2–3 885
13:17 941
13:20–21 853
13:20 98

**James**
1:1 670
1:10 298
1:11 475
1:12–13 279
1:13–15 167
1:13 155, 165
2:1 399, 811
2:23 302
3:1 760, 767
3:9–12 323
4:6 424
4:7 162, 168, 453
4:12 308
4:13–15 300
4:15 302
5:12 248

**1 Peter**
1:3 651
1:6–9 527
1:7 279
1:22–2:3 220
1:23 882
1:24–25 298
2:4–8 563
2:5 919
2:9–10 625
2:9 186, 699
2:13–17 721, 730
2:20–25 251
2:20 211
2:21 86, 126, 166
2:23–34 265
3:14 211
3:15 969
4:10 677
4:12–17 408
4:13–14 211, 393, 775
4:14–15 211
4:16 124, 125
5:1–5 941
5:2–4 616
5:2 98
5:4 98

| | | | | | |
|---|---|---|---|---|---|
| 5:5 | 424 | 4:21 | 549 | 8:10, 11 | 96 |
| 5:6–11 | 891 | 5:13–15 | 587 | 8:13 | 751, 781 |
| 5:8–9 | 168 | 5:13 | 735 | 9:1 | 96 |
| 5:9 | 162 | 5:14–15 | 607 | 9:12 | 751 |
| | | 5:19 | 920 | 11:3 | 594 |
| **2 Peter** | | | | 11:14 | 751 |
| 1:1 | 670 | **3 John** | | 12:6 | 779 |
| 1:10 | 734 | 5–8 | 390 | 12:7, 8 | 76 |
| 1:16–18 | 575, 591 | 6 | 404 | 12:12 | 751 |
| 1:16 | 601 | 8 | 404 | 13:1–2 | 161 |
| 1:19 | 95 | | | 13:11–18 | 777, 778 |
| 2:1–3 | 323 | **Jude** | | 13:13–14 | 335 |
| 2:3 | 296 | 1 | 670 | 14:14–20 | 376 |
| 2:13 | 481 | 6 | 353 | 14:14 | 27, 348 |
| 2:17–22 | 323 | | | 16:15 | 802 |
| 2:22 | 311, 354 | **Revelation** | | 16:17–18 | 937 |
| 3:7 | 321 | 1:1 | 670 | 17:8 | 321 |
| 3:9 | 253, 821 | 1:7 | 784 | 17:14 | 228 |
| 3:10 | 787, 802 | 1:9 | 668 | 18:10, 16, 19 | 751 |
| | | 1:13 | 27, 348 | 19:5–8 | 718, 734 |
| **1 John** | | 1:16 | 96, 591 | 19:10 | 100 |
| 2:15–16 | 168 | 1:17 | 938 | 19:11–16 | 785 |
| 2:18–27 | 775 | 1:20 | 96, 616 | 19:16 | 228 |
| 2:22 | 775 | 2:1 | 96 | 20 | 155 |
| 3:2–3 | 817 | 2:28 | 95 | 20:1–10 | 277 |
| 3:2 | 268 | 3:1 | 96 | 20:6 | 652 |
| 3:9 | 481 | 3:3 | 802 | 20:10 | 353 |
| 3:11–16 | 464 | 3:20 | 312 | 20:11–13 | 813 |
| 3:15 | 242 | 3:21 | 652 | 21:1 | 787 |
| 4:1–6 | 775 | 4:5 | 937 | 21:13 | 95 |
| 4:1–3 | 323 | 4:7 | 781 | 21:14 | 386, 565 |
| 4:1 | 310 | 4:10–11 | 673 | 22:4 | 209 |
| 4:2–3 | 775 | 6:12–17 | 902 | 22:8–9 | 941 |
| 4:4 | 453 | 7–19 | 780 | 22:9 | 941 |
| 4:7–21 | 284, 464 | 7:1–8 | 577, 579, 706 | 22:16 | 95 |
| 4:10 | 919 | 7:3–8 | 780 | 22:20 | 277 |
| 4:12–21 | 266 | 7:4–8 | 784 | | |
| 4:16 | 254 | 7:9–12 | 781 | | |
| 4:19 | 676 | 7:17 | 98, 616 | | |

# Subject Index

abomination that causes desolation, 777–79

accountability, 633–36, 820–21

acts of righteousness/spiritual disciplines, 270–71, 285–90

adultery, 74, 75, 244–45

angels, 75–76, 96, 615–16, 937–38

anger, 242–44, 260

anti-Semitism, 877, 887–88

antitheses, the, 240

apostles, 193, 386

Archelaus, 114, 115

authority of Jesus, 357–58, 950–51; over nature, 351–52; over the spirit world, 352–54, over sin, 354–56

balance in a Christian's life, 317–19, 428, 494–95, 583–84, 815

baptism, Jesus' form of, 954–56

baptism, John's, 134–35, 137

barriers broken down by Jesus, 340–45, 358, 920–22, 952

Beatitudes, the, 204–5, 216–26, 257–58

Bethlehem, 92, 93, 98, 99, 112–13

betrothal, 73–74

blasphemy, 865–66

blasphemy against the Holy Spirit, 449

Branch of David, 117–18, 119, 124

Caesar Augustus, 54, 92, 97, 114

capital punishment, 260

chief priests, 98, 570, 694, 826–27, 944–45

Christian era, 123–24

Christian, the name, 124–26

community of faith, the church, 30, 33, 564–66, 578–79, 621, 626–29, 655, 672, 817, 946

Community Prescription, 33, 200, 492, 611, 626, 630, 634, 652–53, 654, 971–72

compassion, 88, 374, 380–81

covenants, covenantal promises, 56, 58, 63, 70

cross, the, 896, 916, 917–20, 923–26, 929–31

crowds, the, 30–31, 182–83, 185, 192–93, 197–98, 328–29, 346, 356, 422, 448, 454, 477–78, 484–85, 492–93, 515, 731–32, 875–77

crucifixion, 571, 899

darkness, 901–3, 918

devil, Satan, 154, 155, 156, 162, 280

Dionysius Exiguus, 123–24

discernment, 310–11, 334

disciples, discipleship, 21, 30, 32–34, 35, 84, 87, 179–80, 192, 193, 197, 199–202, 214–16, 225–26, 237, 256–57, 315, 329, 364, 395–402, 424–25, 427–28, 456, 459, 490, 581–87, 613–15, 882, 889–90, 930–31, 941, 952–54, 956–59, 963–64, 971–72

disciples, false, 324–26, 334–35

discipleship and religious traditions, 368–69

discipline, church, 617–21, 628, 635–36

discipling, 956–59, 972

divorce, 75, 246–47, 262, 642–45, 654, 656–58

dreams, 76, 101, 875

ekklesia, 30, 611

Elijah, 417, 593–94

elitism, 287

end of the age, 771–77

Eschatological Forecast, 200

eternal life, 648

faith, 104, 517, 522, 527, 540, 546, 551, 596–98, 605–7

faithfulness of God, 66–67, 68
fasting, 154, 280–82, 289–90, 368
Father in heaven, 215–16, 275–76
fire of hell, 243
forgiveness, 279, 280, 622–25, 628–29, 636–39
fulfillment formula, 78, 120–21
fulfillment: of all righteousness, 139–40, 905; of the law, 227–29, 233, 241, 592; of Old Testament Scripture, 55, 56–57, 66, 110–12, 113–14, 120–22, 228–30, 346, 458, 915

Galilee, 172, 180, 184, 186, 940, 942, 947
Gentile ancestors of Jesus, 67–68
Gentiles, 172, 342–43, 540, 541, 706, 920–21
giving sacrificially, 105, 107–8
giving to the needy, 271–73, 288–89
gold, 101
Golden Rule, the, 313–14, 315–16, 725–26
Golgotha, 897–98
gospel of the kingdom, 146, 180–81, 776
gratitude, 284, 306, 666, 672–73, 674–75
Great Commission, 29, 32, 950–59, 963–64
great tribulation, the, 777–82
greatness in the kingdom of heaven, 612–13, 626–27, 673

heart, centrality of, 544–45, 549–50, 754
heart, hardness of, 478, 479–80, 493–94, 495–97, 510, 519, 549–50, 653–54
Herod, 93, 96–99, 101–2, 103, 104, 110, 112, 114, 123
Herod Antipas, 114–15, 171–72, 511–12, 519–20, 719–20
Herod Philip, 114
Herodians, 719–20, 730
Holy Spirit, 77, 89–90, 149, 150, 154, 164–65, 222–23, 882
Holy Week, 700–701, 707–12

humility, 151–52, 614, 626, 632–33
hypocrites, hypocrisy, 272, 273, 288, 309–10, 674, 746, 751, 754

incense, 101
inspiration of Scripture, 229–30
Israel, 577, 579, 693–94, 698–99, 704–6, 716, 718, 757–58, 877, 888, 906, 953

Jerusalem, 97–98
Jesus and his Father, 421–22, 426, 559, 841–42, 903
Jesus as prophet, priest, and king, 701–4
Jesus, the name, 25, 56, 77, 81
Jesus, titles of: Immanuel, 35, 80, 81, 83, 84, 141; King of the Jews, 60, 94, 96, 98, 106, 810, 845; Lord, 28, 324–25, 686, 845; Messiah/Christ, 20–21, 25–26, 56, 69, 98, 558, 560, 864; the Nazarene, 118–19, 124; Prince of Peace, 853; Servant/Suffering Servant, 28, 143, 345–46, 444–45, 834, 845; son of Abraham, 29, 55, 56, 63, 66; son of David, 26–27, 29, 55, 56, 63, 66, 372–73, 446, 864; Son of God, 26–27, 143, 146–47, 157, 353, 518, 529, 559–60, 864; Son of Man, 27–28, 347–49, 356, 557–58, 865
Jewish religious leaders, 30, 34, 97–98, 104, 106, 135–36, 138–39, 150–51, 192, 198, 327, 328, 488, 569–70, 694–97, 700, 751, 944–46
John the Baptist, 104, 115, 116, 130–35, 171–72, 412–19, 425–26, 510–12, 695–96; and Elijah, 417, 593–94
Joseph, 74–77, 81–82, 87–89, 110, 119, 126–28
Joseph of Arimathea, 911–13, 922
Judas, 879–80
judging others, 308–10
judgment, 148–49, 489, 699–700, 794–95, 812–13, 816

Kingdom-Life Proclamation/Discourse, 32, 200
kingdom of God, 33, 34, 132, 447, 578–79, 721

kingdom of heaven, 25, 33, 77, 132–33, 135–36, 148–50, 174–75, 191, 206, 216, 217–18, 223, 276–77, 299, 482–84, 485–89, 498–99, 501–5, 578–79, 721
kingship, 60

Law and the Prophets, 228, 235–36, 313
law of retaliation (*lex talionis*), 248–51, 263–64
leaders and leadership, 759–60, 762–67
legalism, 88, 241, 286, 422, 545
leprosy, 340
light of the world, 214–16, 224
Lord's Supper, 836–38, 851–53
love, law of love, 236, 265–67, 463, 726, 739

Magi, 93–102, 103, 106
marriage: faithfulness in, 261–62; sanctity of, 655–58
mercy, merciful, 208–9, 636–39
mission of disciples, 395–402, 403–405
Mission Mandate, 32, 200, 491, 971
motives, 270–74, 283–85, 288–90, 659, 666, 672, 674
mourning, 206–7
murder, 241–42
myrrh, 101

Nazareth, 92, 115–20
Nazareth Decree, 20

oaths, 247–48, 262–63, 752–53, 760
obedience, 81–82, 88, 187, 234, 258, 456, 460–61, 548, 605, 848
Old Testament Scripture and the Christian, 235–36, 256
Olivet Discourse, 33–34, 200, 492, 770–72, 788–91, 972

parables, 473–74, 476–79, 499–501
Parabolic Disclosure/Discourse, 32–33, 200, 472–74, 492, 971
*pax Romana*, 54, 933
perfection, 254–55, 267–78

persecution and suffering, 210–11, 401–2, 406–8, 461–62, 774–75, 917
Peter, 516–17, 521, 525–27, 560–68, 570–71, 579–80, 581, 585, 591–92, 839–40, 842, 848, 866–68, 880–82, 889–91
Pharisees and teachers of the law, 98, 135–36, 138, 150–51, 198, 208, 218, 219, 231, 241, 270, 346–47, 355–56, 367–68, 374, 377, 422, 443, 450, 457–60, 490, 534–36, 537, 556–57, 570, 726–28, 732–33, 744–45, 752–57, 758–60; disciples of, 719, 729–30
poor in spirit, 205–6, 217
*porneia*, 644–45, 654, 657
prayer, 273–74, 289, 312
prophets, true and false, 322–26, 334
pure in heart, 209

reconciliation, 243, 260, 628, 658
redemption, 86, 112, 904
repentance, 131, 133, 134, 136–37, 138, 232
resurrection, 961–63, 966–70
rewards, 270–71, 283, 284–85, 651–52, 659, 672, 675
righteousness, 75, 77, 88, 140, 207–8, 219, 230–33, 234–35

Sabbath, the, 438–43
Sadducees, 135–36, 138, 150–51, 556–57, 722–24, 730–31, 733, 734–35
Satan, *see* devil
salt of the earth, 212–14, 224
salvation, 28–29, 67, 68, 70, 77, 85, 661, 894
second coming of Jesus, 799–800, 801–3, 814–17
Sermon on the Mount, 32, 190–202, 491, 971
servanthood, 669–70, 672, 673, 678–80, 750, 821–22
sign, 554–55
Simon of Cyrene, 896–97
sin, 278–79, 360, 375, 376–77
singleness/celibacy, 645, 658

sovereignty, divine, 103, 104, 846–47, 860; and human responsibility, 477–78, 834–35, 847–48, 860

Spirit-led life, 164–65

spiritual warfare, 377, 385, 459

Star of Bethlehem, 94, 95–96, 99, 102, 103

substitutionary atonement, 670, 903, 918

table fellowship, 366

tax collectors, 364–67

teachers of the law, see *Pharisees and teachers of the law*

temple tax, 598–600

temptation, tempt, 155–56, 158, 161–62, 165–69, 279

temptation of Jesus, 157–62, 848

test, testing, 155–56, 279

tradition of the elders, 534–36, 542–44, 732, 740

Transfiguration, the, 589–93, 601–3

Trinity, the, 955–56

Twelve, the, 193, 384–89, 402, 405–6, 579–80, 651–52, 667, 706, 830, 947–48

unpardonable sin, 449–50

virgin birth, 63–64, 77, 79–80, 82–83, 85–86

wealth and materialism, 292–93, 296, 301–2, 303–4, 481, 649–51, 658–59

wine and gall, 898

wisdom, 419

women, 60, 67, 456, 911, 921–22, 939–40, 941–42, 962

Word of God, supremacy of, 542–44, 547–49

worship, 530, 941

worry, 296–300, 301–2, 304–6

yoke, 423–25, 428, 433–34

# Praise for the NIV Application Commentary Series

This series promises to become an indispensable tool for every pastor and teacher who seeks to make the Bible's timeless message speak to this generation."

—Billy Graham

"The NIV Application Commentary series shares the same goal that has been the passion of my own ministry—communicating God's Word to a contemporary audience so that they feel the full impact of its message."

—Bill Hybels, Willow Creek Community Church

"The NIV Application Commentary is an outstanding resource for pastors and anyone else who is serious about developing 'doers of the Word.'"

—Rick Warren, Pastor, Saddleback Community Church

"The NIV Application Commentary series doesn't fool around: It gets right down to business, bringing this ancient and powerful Word of God into the present so that it can be heard and delivered with all the freshness of a new day, with all the immediacy of a friend's embrace."

—Eugene H. Peterson, Regent College

""If you want to avoid hanging applicational elephants from interpretive threads, then The NIV Application Commentary is for you! This series excels at both original meaning and contemporary signficance. I support it 100 percent."

—Howard G. Hendricks, Dallas Theological Seminary

"The NIV Application Commentary series dares to go where few scholars have gone before—into the real world of biblical application faced by pastors and teachers every day. This is everything a good commentary series should be."

—Leith Anderson, Pastor, Wooddale Church

"This is THE pulpit commentary for the 21st century."

—George K. Brushaber, President, Bethel College & Seminary

"Here, at last, is a commentary that makes the proper circuit from the biblical world to main street. The NIV Application Commentary is a magnificent gift to the church."

—Dr. R. Kent Hughes, Pastor, College Church, Wheaton, IL

"The NIV Application Commentary series will be a great help for readers who want to understand what the Bible means, how it applies, and what they should do in response."

—Stuart Briscoe, Pastor, Elmbrook Church

"The NIV Application Commentary series promises to be of very great service to all who preach and teach the Word of God."

—J. I. Packer, Regent College

"The NIV Application Commentary meets the urgent need for an exhaustive and authoritative commentary based on the New International Version. This series will soon be found in libraries and studies throughout the evangelical community."

—Dr. James Kennedy, Ph.D., Senior Minister,
Coral Ridge Presbyterian Church

*Look for the* NIV Application Commentary *at your local Christian bookstore*

ZONDERVAN™

GRAND RAPIDS, MICHIGAN 49530 USA

WWW.ZONDERVAN.COM

*Bring ancient truth to modern life with the*

# NIV Application Commentary *series*

Covering both the Old and New Testaments, the **NIV Application Commentary** series is a staple reference for pastors seeking to bring the Bible's timeless message into a modern context. It explains not only what the Bible means but also how that meaning impacts the lives of believers today.

### Matthew
*Matthew* helps readers learn how the message of Matthew's gospel can have the same powerful impact today that it did when the author first wrote it.

Michael J. Wilkins                      ISBN: 0-310-49310-2

### Mark
Learn how the challenging gospel of Mark can leave recipients with the same powerful questions and answers it did when it was written.

David E. Garland                        ISBN: 0-310-49350-1

### Luke
Focus on the most important application of all: "the person of Jesus and the nature of God's work through him to deliver humanity."

Darrell L. Bock                         ISBN: 0-310-49330-7

### John
Learn both halves of the interpretive task. Gary M. Burge shows readers how to bring the ancient message of John into a modern context. He also explains not only what the book of John meant to its original readers but also how it can speak powerfully today.

Gary M. Burge                           ISBN: 0-310-49750-7

### Acts
Study the first portraits of the church in action around the world with someone whose ministry mirrors many of the events in Acts. Biblical scholar and worldwide evangelist Ajith Fernando applies the story of the church's early development to the global mission of believers today.

Ajith Fernando                          ISBN: 0-310-49410-9

## Romans

Paul's letter to the Romans remains one of the most important expressions of Christian truth ever written. Douglas Moo comments on the text and then explores issues in Paul's culture and in ours that help us understand the ultimate meaning of each paragraph.

Douglas J. Moo                                    ISBN: 0-310-49400-1

## 1 Corinthians

Is your church struggling with the problem of divisiveness and fragmentation? See the solution Paul gave the Corinthian Christians over 2,000 years ago. It still works today!

Craig Blomberg                                    ISBN: 0-310-48490-1

## 2 Corinthians

Often recognized as the most difficult of Paul's letters to understand, 2 Corinthians can have the same powerful impact today that it did when it was first written.

Scott J. Hafemann                                 ISBN: 0-310-49420-6

## Galatians

A pastor's message is true not because of his preaching or people-management skills, but because of Christ. Learn how to apply Paul's example of visionary church leadership to your own congregation.

Scot McKnight                                     ISBN: 0-310-48470-1

## Ephesians

Explore what the author calls "a surprisingly comprehensive statement about God and his work, about Christ and the gospel, about life with God's Spirit, and about the right way to live."

Klyne Snodgrass                                   ISBN: 0-310-49340-4

## Philippians

The best lesson Philippians provides is how to encourage people who actually are doing quite well. Learn why not all the New Testament letters are reactions to theological crises.

Frank Thielman                    ISBN: 0-310-49340-4

## Colossians/Philemon

The temptation to trust in the wrong things has always been strong. Use this commentary to learn the importance of trusting only in Jesus, God's Son, in whom all the fullness of God lives. No message is more important for our post-modern culture.

David E. Garland                    ISBN: 0-310-48480-4

## 1&2 Thessalonians

Paul's letters to the Thessalonians say as much to us today about Christ's return and our resurrection as they did in the early church. This volume skillfully reveals Paul's answers to these questions and how they address the needs of contemporary Christians.

Michael W. Holmes                    ISBN: 0-310-49380-3

## 1&2 Timothy, Titus

Reveals the context and meanings of Paul's letters to two leaders in the early Christian Church and explores their present-day implications to help you to accurately apply the principles they contain to contemporary issues.

Walter L. Liefeld                    ISBN: 0-310-50110-5

## Hebrews

The message of Hebrews can be summed up in a single phrase: "God speaks effectively to us through Jesus." Unpack the theological meaning of those seven words and learn why the gospel still demands a hearing today.

George H. Guthrie                    ISBN: 0-310-49390-0

### James

Give your church the best antidote for a culture of people who say they believe one thing but act in ways that either ignore or contradict their belief. More than just saying, "Practice what you preach," James gives solid reasons why faith and action must coexist.

David P. Nystrom                    ISBN: 0-310-49360-9

### 1 Peter

The issue of the church's relationship to the state hits the news media in some form nearly every day. Learn how Peter answered the question for Christians surviving under Roman rule and how it applies similarly to believers living amid the secular institutions of the modern world.

Scot McKnight                    ISBN: 0-310-49290-4

### 2 Peter, Jude

Introduce your modern audience to letters they may not be familiar with and show why they'll want to get to know them.

Douglas J. Moo                    ISBN: 0-310-20104-7

### Letters of John

Like the community in John's time, which faced disputes over erroneous "secret knowledge," today's church needs discernment in affirming new ideas supported by Scripture and weeding out harmful notions. This volume will help you show today's Christians how to use John's example.

Gary M. Burge                    ISBN: 0-310-486420-3

### Revelation

Craig Keener offers a "new" approach to the book of Revelation by focusing on the "old." He stresses the need for believers to prepare for the possibility of suffering for the sake of Jesus.

Craig S. Keener                    ISBN: 0-310-23192-2